WALL

LONDON WALL

MOORGATE

THROGMORTON ST.

OLD BROAD STREET

LOTHBURY

BARTHOLOMEW LANE

CAPEL COURT

18

1

THREADNEEDLE STREET

BISHOPSGATE

3

16

CORNHILL

LEADENHALL STREET

10

POULTRY

STREET

12

LOMBARD STREET

KING WILLIAM STREET

ST SWITHIN'S LANE

15

GRACECHURCH STREET

FENCHURCH

STREET

14

MINCING LANE

MARK LANE

7

HOUNDSDITCH

MINORIES

CANNON STREET

EASTCHEAP

5

STREET

LONDON BRIDGE

13

LOWER THAMES STREET

4

19

River Thames

11

TOOLEY STREET

TOWER BRIDGE

Broad Street Station

Liverpool Street Station

Barings

A CLUB NO MORE

King Labour: The British Working Class, 1850–1914
The Secretary of State
The Chancellor of the Exchequer
Bobby Abel, Professional Batsman
Archie's Last Stand: MCC in New Zealand, 1922–23
The Financial Times: A Centenary History
WG's Birthday Party
Cazenove & Co: A History
The City of London, Volume I: A World of Its Own, 1815–1890
The City of London, Volume II: Golden Years, 1890–1914
LIFFE: A Market and its Makers
Phillips & Drew: Professionals in the City (with W. J. Reader)
The City of London, Volume III: Illusions of Gold, 1914–1945

THE CITY OF LONDON

Volume IV

A Club No More
1945–2000

DAVID KYNASTON

CHATTO & WINDUS
LONDON

Published by Chatto & Windus 2001

2 4 6 8 10 9 7 5 3 1

First published in Great Britain in 2001 by
Chatto & Windus
Random House, 20 Vauxhall Bridge Road,
London SW1V 2SA

Random House Australia (Pty) Limited
20 Alfred Street, Milsons Point, Sydney,
New South Wales 2061, Australia

Random House New Zealand Limited
18 Poland Road, Glenfield,
Auckland 10, New Zealand

Random House (Pty) Limited
Endulini, 5A Jubilee Road, Parktown 2193, South Africa

The Random House Group Limited Reg. No. 954009
www.randomhouse.co.uk

A CIP catalogue record for this book
is available from the British Library

ISBN 0 7011 6949 4

Papers used by Random House are natural,
recyclable products made from wood grown in sustainable forests;
the manufacturing processes conform to the environmental
regulations of the country of origin

Typeset by SX Composing DTP, Rayleigh, Essex
Printed and bound in Great Britain by
Mackays of Chatham Ltd.

This book is dedicated to the memory of Arthur Kynaston (1925–1999)

A Club No More completes a quartet of books about the City of London during the nineteenth and twentieth centuries. Its overarching theme is how the City, seemingly almost dead and buried at the end of the Second World War, managed from the late 1950s to re-internationalise itself and eventually return to something like its pre-1914 power and prosperity as an international financial centre. The celebrated 'Big Bang' of October 1986 accelerated that process, but much had already happened during the preceding quarter of a century. In that sense, the 1960s and 1970s lie at the heart of this book – decades when the British economy appeared at times to be in terminal decline, but the City began to chart an increasingly autonomous trajectory. That paradox was seldom appreciated even in the City itself, where the fortunes of the stock market faithfully mirrored the fluctuating domestic mood, but in retrospect is obvious.

Each book has had a central figure: Nathan Rothschild in *A World of Its Own*, Ernest Cassel in *Golden Years*, Montagu Norman in *Illusions of Gold*. Here it is Siegmund Warburg, the gifted, deservedly legendary merchant banker who for more than thirty years built a bank in his own image. He was one of the pioneers of the Eurobond market and did more than anyone to destroy the insular, complacent assumptions of the City establishment. Warburgs itself enjoyed from the 1960s an astonishingly high reputation, and during the City revolution of the 1980s it emerged as the national 'flagship' investment bank. Yet by 1995 it had, in humiliating circumstances, lost its independence. Other merchant banks – traditionally the City's crème de la crème – suffered a similar fate, and at the end of the twentieth century the City was no longer 'British' in either ownership or character. We should not necessarily mourn the fact; but it would be wrong not to ponder the implications.

The modern City is in many ways a cruel, heartless place, and its occupants work such cripplingly long hours that inevitably they lack much of the roundedness of earlier generations. The chances of it producing another George Grote, or John Lubbock, or indeed a Siegmund Warburg, seem remote. But during the summer of 1996, while researching the history of the financial futures market LIFFE, I was reminded that each age yields its epiphanies. Each lunchtime at 'The Pit Stop' almost all the traders in their coloured jackets were doing one of three things – playing cards, reading the *Sun* or simply slumping at the table, head down. One day, on the far side of the room, I spotted a trader reading a book. I crept round, looked over his shoulder and saw that it was *A Short History of the World* by H.G. Wells. It was a moment that would have surely gladdened that autodidact's heart.

Contents

PART ONE

1945–59

COLBY   Excuse me, but I must remind you:
You have that meeting in the City
Tomorrow morning. You asked me to prepare
Some figures for you. I've got them here.

SIR CLAUDE   Much depends on my wife. Be patient with her, Colby.
– Oh yes, that meeting. We must run through the figures.

T.S. Eliot, *The Confidential Clerk* (1954)

CHAPTER ONE

Moving Among Ghosts

Few imagined in 1945 how long it would take to eradicate the physical scars of war. It was not until the mid-1950s, as building controls were gradually relaxed, that derelict bombsites gave way to the pioneer constructions of a new City. Pending the arrival of an experiment in high-rise living, the Barbican was virtually a wild heath, littered with the remnants of a commercial civilisation. Rose Macaulay portrayed this magical, fugitive moment in her novel *The World My Wilderness*. The two central characters encounter Mavis, one of the heath's motley inhabitants:

> The girl was from Bankside, and had worked as a messenger in the city until her place of business had gone up in flames. She knew the ruins intimately, calling them and the anonymous alleys that ran between them by their old names, peopling them with industrious business men, chattering, tea-bibulous typists, messengers and clerks: she moved among ghosts, herself solid, cheerful and unconcerned . . .
> 'I am very, very fond of ruins, ruins I love to scan,' Mavis hummed. She pointed across the wilderness towards the bastion. 'That's Mr Monty's room up there, that was. Mr Monty always had his joke. He'd look in at the warehouse – that was our warehouse, that pit with the pink flowers and nettles all over it – pretty, isn't it? Mr Monty'd look in and speak to old Mr Dukes, he was the head clerk, and he'd have his joke with him, except on a Monday morning, and then it was look out for squalls. Poor Mr Dukes, he was ever so upset when it all went; for weeks he'd go wandering about the ruins, seeing if he could save anything, but of course he couldn't, what the fire left the rescue men grabbed as quick as you could say knife' . . .
> They climbed out through the window, and made their way about the ruined, jungled waste, walking along broken lines of wall, diving into the cellars and caves of the underground city, where opulent merchants had once stored their wine, where gaily tiled rooms opened into one another and burrowed under great eaves of overhanging earth, where fosses and ditches ran, bright with marigolds and choked with thistles, through one-time halls of commerce, and yellow ragwort waved its gaudy banners over the ruin of defeated business men.[1]

*

At the end of the war the City of London was devastated, and not just physically. In almost every respect the outlook seemed dark:

2

internationally the dollar reigned supreme; almost one-third of overseas investments had been liquidated; export trade was in shreds; the domestic industrial base was ravaged; and debts, largely to the United States, the Dominions and the colonies, were enormous. In sum, it is generally reckoned that Britain had lost about a quarter of its pre-war national wealth.

Not surprisingly, given that daunting legacy, it took a long time for anything like a vibrant atmosphere to return to the post-war City. The sense of lassitude prevailing at 20 Fenchurch Street, home of Kleinworts, was typical of many other overmanned offices. With each department having formed its own coffee syndicates, the nearby Lyons and ABC coffee houses were full of idle clerks and typists, 'all drinking coffee at 4d a cup and smoking like chimneys'; while one assistant manager recalled this as a period dominated by the chore of 'locking the safes'. What work there was on hand tended to be hamstrung by a panoply of wartime controls that had not yet been relaxed. 'Business today,' a manager of Hambros lamented in 1949, 'does not only mean selling or buying – that may often be the easiest part – nor financing, but the most intricate and time-wasting labour is in complying with all the various regulations here and abroad.' Capital market restrictions (under the auspices of the Capital Issues Committee), continuing exchange controls, world trade still in a battered state – it was hardly a propitious environment in which to operate. Moreover, perhaps because of the Labour government's instinctive dislike of futures trading, with its unpalatable speculative connotations, it took an extraordinarily long time for most of the City's commodity markets to reopen. Rubber in 1946 and tin in 1949 were exceptions, but others remained firmly shut until the new decade. Also in mothballs until the 1950s were the gold and foreign exchange markets; and two principals in the market, Geoffrey Astley and Vi Pearce of Astley & Pearce, went so far as to leave the City entirely for six years, forming a Surrey-based company specialising in industrial clothing. Very slowly, however, the City began to revive. Some of this revival took an international form – marine insurance at Lloyd's, for example, or ship-chartering at the Baltic Exchange – but mainly it related to the British economy. The inter-war shift in the Stock Exchange, away from the international and towards the domestic, now became even more palpable (in terms of both government and industrial securities), while the trend in the money market was similar. The inexorably increasing British component of the London Trust Co's investments, measured by book cost, was symptomatic: 45 per cent in 1933, 54 per cent in 1939, 64 per cent in 1945 and 76 per cent by 1951.[2] For better or worse, the City was now locked – for the time being, at least – into the fortunes of the British economy.

The international role would eventually return, but the sharp decline of the *commercial* City was irreversible.[3] On the eve of war, 26 per cent of the City's floor-space had been occupied by warehouses; ten years later, in 1949, the comparable figure was only 18 per cent. This was largely the result of bombing, but London did not help its cause when it failed to prevent the National Dock Labour Scheme in 1947, which over time would mean that the Port of London virtually priced itself out of existence.[4] Yet among these and other factors, most important was the loss of human capital entailed by the war, above all the amalgam of specialist knowledge and an intricate international network of connections. By the 1950s, when some semblance of normality had returned, almost all of that human capital (much of it foreign in character) had been eroded, and a more insular City had painful lessons to relearn. Some it was able to, but many had gone beyond recall. It was an appealing but misleading fact that the original adventures of Thomas the Tank Engine and friends were published in the City from 1945 by Edmund Ward of Bishopsgate; for the post-war City would become predominantly financial, not commercial, in composition, purpose and outlook – the reality at last corresponding to the popular image.

This narrowing of the City's base was perhaps regretted, but the prevailing post-war assumption was that as long as sterling could somehow be enabled to survive as a world currency, albeit subordinate to the dollar, then the City would not be entirely reduced to a parochial financial centre. Over twenty and more years the strength of sterling – and, behind it, the sterling area – was equated, automatically and unquestioningly, with the strength of the City. It was an understandable assumption, but in the event an almost wholly fallacious one.[5] Instead, as the final third of the century would conclusively demonstrate, what really mattered to the City's well-being were two other, quite different matters: the degree to which it would escape from state control; and the extent to which it would be open to talent from outside. Of course, any such outsiders would inevitably have to wrestle with the entrenched City culture – a culture appreciably more conservative, inward-looking and 'clubby' than forty or fifty years earlier. Nowhere epitomised that culture more than the merchant banking sector. Yet within months of the war ending, two merchant bankers were poised to shake up the City.

One, Kenneth Keith, brought to bear ruthless, aggressive determination rather than financial creativity or cerebral qualities. His vehicle was the issuing house Philip Hill (not yet a member of the Accepting Houses Committee and, in that sense, not yet a pukka merchant bank), whose eponymous founder – a *bête noire* of Montagu Norman – had died in 1944. The reassuring figure of Hubert Meredith was left in charge, and Keith joined the firm in April 1946. Before the war, as an ambitious young accountant at Peat Marwick, he had done some work for it; and during the war, as a P.O.W., he had struck up a close friendship with Brian Mountain, the heir apparent at the insurance company Eagle Star, which had a significant stake in Philip Hill.[6] During the early post-war years, while Keith won his spurs in corporate finance, Philip Hill was still based in the West End, but was even more active in promoting new issues than it had been in the 1930s. Keith had gentlemanly attributes – educated at Rugby, an imposing physical presence, a good war record with the Welsh Guards – but felt no excessive veneration for playing by the gentlemanly rules.

The other merchant banker – just as resolute, but not so obviously a bruiser – was Siegmund Warburg.[7] In 1980, thirty-four years after establishing S.G. Warburg & Co as the successor to the New Trading Co, he gave his first full-length interview, to the American magazine *Institutional Investor*:

What qualities do you look for in someone you hire?

I think the most important thing is the courage and the common sense of a fellow. Experience is for me completely secondary. As a rule, those with whom I am close in my firm are people with whom I can also talk about books, about music, about human beings, human problems.

What about someone who says he has been so involved in business that he hasn't had time for these other things?

I wouldn't be too favourably impressed. And if a fellow would come to me and say his only interest is athletics, I wouldn't think he would stand a chance.

One of your stranger hiring procedures is that everyone considered for responsible positions must go through handwriting analysis. Why do you insist on that?

I was always very interested in graphology. I read lots of books about it and I knew some very important graphologists. I believe that graphology is a very important element in psychological analysis.

Does everyone you hire for a responsible position have to submit to this?

I think the word 'submit' is not the proper term. Nobody has ever refused me.

Another Warburgs practice that people have gossiped about over the years is your custom of having two sittings at lunch in order to squeeze more clients in. Do you encourage your colleagues to schedule two different luncheons for the same day?

Isn't this question of yours rather irrelevant?

No, it isn't. So many people have taken interest in this that I feel you should answer it.

Well, since you insist, I will say that I don't approve of this idea of someone having two luncheons in one day. This all started when my wonderful colleague and friend, Eric Korner, was very active – and there were so many people he wanted to have lunch with in a week that he had

Mr X at 12.30 and Mr Y at 1.30. That happened perhaps five times a year.

It was an act of enormous audacity to start a new merchant bank in London, as you did, from scratch. Did people say you were crazy, that you wouldn't make it?

Every one of my personal friends thought it was right, even people who were not close personal friends but who were close acquaintances. Only some members of my more distant family thought it was wrong.

Did you always think you could mould the firm into an important merchant bank?

I didn't think in terms of an important merchant bank. It may sound a little bit conceited, but I thought it could be something good *sui generis*. I felt that I brought something to England which was a little bit different because I was a damn foreigner, a German Jew. I like to be a nonconformist, and I thought I could contribute something quite different from the others.

Didn't it help that many other merchant banks were a bit sleepy in the post-war period?

Absolutely. I don't have such a terribly high opinion of myself, but wasn't it Lloyd George who said that the last war was won because the enemy made so many mistakes?[8]

At 82 King William Street, where S.G. Warburg & Co opened for business in January 1946, Warburg drew much support during the early months and years from the 'Uncles', the firm's other three founding fathers: the ultra-realist Henry Grunfeld (above all responsible for persuading Warburg to change the bank's name), the more dynamic Eric Korner and the meticulous Ernest Thalmann. From the start the pace of work was intense, the frequency of double-lunches greater than Warburg would later concede and, in the field of industrial finance, the firm found itself pushing at an almost open door. Warburg had some friends in high places – including at Rothschilds – but he had little or no instinctive affinity with the City establishment as a whole. 'Most of the important people in the City', he privately reflected, 'are so anxious to avoid any unpleasantness that they will knowingly make blunders, with the sole aim of sparing themselves any conflict.' Was the prevailing, somewhat malevolent atmosphere of gossip and rumours, he speculated, 'a way of compensating for some sexual deficiency in those people'? Warburg, working incredibly long hours (by the standards of the day), travelling all over the world in order to forge contacts and always trying to take the long, disinterested view on behalf of his clients, was not inclined to be charitable either outside or inside his office. 'He knew neither pity nor even compassion,' a French colleague recalled:

One lapse and one immediately saw his face close. If the fault was judged serious, it closed for ever. Average transgressions entailed a period of penitence lasting from three days to three months. For others, he was pitiless, an attitude of permanent suspicion on his part would drive the wrongdoer to resignation within a few weeks or a few months.[9]

Life at Warburgs was not, in short, the world of gentlemanly capitalism to which the City had become accustomed.

Hardly surprisingly, neither Keith nor Warburg was top of the popularity stakes. There was no such antagonism, or even any misgivings, about another 'outsider', Arthur Trinder of Union Discount. The son of a sergeant major, he had joined the firm as a sixteen-year-old in July 1918, had acquired by the 1930s the reputation of being a brilliant dealer in the money market and in 1947 succeeded 'Gus' Ellen as manager of Union Discount. Universally known in the market as 'Trin', and blessed with 'a long pocket and strong nerves', he is vividly evoked by his biographers as 'a small, tubby man with a tremendous presence and black boot-button eyes which he fixed on a person' and which 'gleamed for a moment before he delivered some pithy comment'. The rhythm of his working day was distinctive: he would rarely arrive at 39 Cornhill before eleven, when he would breakfast – a smoked salmon sandwich and the first drink of the day; in the evening, after the market had closed, he would stay at Union Discount and entertain his many City friends over drinks in the Green Room. All the time one 'Trinderism' after another would pour forth: 'Honesty is the best policy; we've tried both.' And: 'I've got one rule in life. I never lend money to people with swimming pools.' And, after seeing the film *The Lost Weekend*: 'I didn't think he drank all that much.' Trinder's capacity to absorb alcohol was unrivalled, even in the hard-drinking discount market, his memory was phenomenal (based on assiduous scrutiny over the years of the company's 100,000 or so information cards) and he was, as he always said, 'wedded to Union Discount'. Somewhere in the background there was married life in a house on Wimbledon Common, but few in the City knew much about it. The historians of Union Discount add, however, that Trinder 'had a hatred of being on his own and when, having gone to bed he eventually composed himself for sleep, he would usually read well into the night'.[10]

CHAPTER TWO

Red Ties Not Worn

'We hardly know what the future of Houses like ours will be under the present administration,' Evelyn Baring confided to an American banker in November 1945. 'Nationalisation is the order of the day . . . Perhaps our turn will come. Anyway there seems little incentive to private enterprise.' And he added, more in hope than in expectation, 'I think we all feel that what is wanted today is a National Government under the leadership of a man such as Churchill.' Midland Bank's recently knighted Clarence Sadd relished being the exception – 'I find great pleasure in daily praising our Government to my Director colleagues & others in the City to their undisguised surprise, even consternation,' he wrote that same month to a fellow-sympathiser, the equally recently ennobled William Piercy of the newly established Industrial and Commercial Finance Corporation (ICFC); but in the City at large, certainly among those at a senior level, precious few during these perturbing months after the landslide election dared to come out as Labour supporters. Sir Charles Lidbury of the Westminster Bank was as uncompromising as ever in his end-of-year assessment to an American correspondent:

> A call for hard work is not a popular slogan these days but the only way we shall get out of this mess is by hard work. It is of course not easy for a Labour Government to preach these elementary facts of life to an electorate who voted them to power in the expectation of a rosy future with everything nationalised and everybody tied down by rules, regulations and statutory orders.

The elderly Ernest Muriel, who had come from India after the war to be the Hongkong and Shanghai Bank's London manager, agreed in spades. 'We are now under a government which is quite frank in its purpose of governing for part of the nation and not the whole,' he privately asserted in February 1946. 'I believe it is useless to try and beat the Socialists at their own game. Pink can never beat red, but blue may.' For the bullion broker Sir Henry d'Avigdor-Goldsmid, whom the diarist James Lees-Milne visited later in the year at his palatial house in Kent, the situation was too far gone for half-measures: 'He is astringent, disputatious, political. They are spending a fortune of capital on the house

8

and horses. Harry's attitude is that the country has gone to the dogs and he may as well spend whatever capital he pleases.'[1]

Of course, there were perfectly rational grounds for being opposed to the Labour government – not only higher personal taxation, but the nationalisation programme that at a stroke wiped out significant areas of popular investment – but in many cases the City's attitude went beyond reason. When the young Colin Knock, straight from school, attended an interview at the jobbers Prior & Williams, he made the mistake of wearing a red tie. 'Does that have any political implications?' he was asked by the partner. None at all, he replied, and thereby got the position of office boy. At the stockbrokers Chase Henderson & Tennant, the known Labour sympathiser Nicholas Davenport felt compelled to leave, his relations with his partners having become 'too unpleasant to tolerate'. At Panmure Gordon the senior partner, Richard Hart-Davis, insisted that the Prime Minister was Chinese and invariably referred to him as A.T. Lee.[2]

The City's paranoia was, as ever, overdone. 'The City in the middle of a socialist state is as anomalous as would be the Pope in Moscow' may have been Attlee's purported view, but in practice the City escaped remarkably unscathed from its first experience of Labour in office with an overall majority. Why? To a variety of impersonal explanations – including an obstinate adherence to physical controls as the best way of planning the economy, a Keynesian belief that the state did not need to command *all* the commanding heights, and a view of industry that favoured industrial rather than financial solutions – one should surely add the personal element. Chancellor of the Exchequer for almost the first two and half years of the Attlee administration was Hugh Dalton, a robust and in some ways attractive figure whose approach to the City was fatally undermined by a mixture of ignorance and emotional immaturity, the latter sometimes taking the form of an almost ludicrous overconfidence. Relishing Lloyd George's term for the City Establishment, the 'flapping penguins', he enjoyed a little teasing – beginning in October 1945 with his first appearance at the Lord Mayor's annual Mansion House dinner:

> Once upon a time, nearly three hundred years ago, the City of London was a stronghold of Radicalism, an outpost of the Left. There is a picture in the Palace of Westminster, showing the famous Five Members who, in loyalty to Parliament, had defied King Charles I, leaving the Water Steps in a rowboat. They were rowed downstream, to take refuge with the Roundheads of the City, where the King's men could not find them. Since then the City seems to have moved a few paces to the Right . . .

Unfortunately, despite being the author of an often-reprinted textbook on *Principles of Public Finance*, and a long-time friend of Davenport, Dalton's grasp of the City was sketchy. 'Stop talking details, Nicholas! Stick to principles,' he would boom whenever Davenport tried to explain its workings; and by the time he became Chancellor he still did not understand the functions of the government broker, let alone the difference between brokers and jobbers.[3] Moreover, in a larger sense, neither Dalton nor his colleagues seriously questioned the national desirability of a strong sterling area, an assumption that inevitably demanded that sterling be a powerful (or anyway, as powerful as possible) world currency, whatever the domestic deflationary consequences.[4] Ernest Bevin, that old critic of the City going back to Macmillan Committee days and earlier, was now Foreign Secretary; and he would have been the last to countenance a policy that might jeopardise Britain's assured place at the top table. One way and another, the City was safe in their hands.

*

Nevertheless, these were not easy years for either party in the relationship: politicians were at the mercy of economic forces beyond their control, while the City had to adjust to an unprecedentedly marginalised peacetime existence. The negotiations in the autumn of 1945 leading to a huge American loan – the defining economic event of the Labour government – revealed a shared powerlessness.[5] Lord Keynes led the British delegation in Washington, and the basic deal that he reluctantly accepted was a $3.75bn loan in return for multilateral trading arrangements, early convertibility of sterling and an interpretation of the Bretton Woods agreement that gave the whip hand to the Americans. There was no one present from the Bank of England at the key decision-making meeting in London on 23 August, prior to the delegation sailing; and when, in mid-October, the Deputy Governor, Cameron Cobbold, pushed hard for the recall of Keynes, the Governor, Lord Catto, failed to support him. 'Clearly he does not want any general settlement on the lines contemplated with the Americans,' one of Keynes's colleagues, James Meade, noted of Cobbold's attitude. 'He would like us to snap our fingers at the Americans . . . He is a clever ass.' Keynes was also unimpressed. 'Some fig leaves which may pass muster with old ladies in London wilt in a harsher climate,' he dismissively cabled the Treasury in early November about Treasury/Bank concerns over the sterling area.[6]

Eventually, despite what Meade described as further 'hysterics' on the part of those two august institutions, as the telegrams continued to wing in from Washington, London – above all the Cabinet – could do little more than accept Keynes's deal. 'The consequences of present refusal of American aid would be more grievous than the possibility of subsequent failure to live up to its conditions,' the *Financial Times* (which had recently merged with the *Financial News*) conceded in December, explicitly supporting Dalton's similar line in the Commons. Most Conservatives abstained in the key vote, and the general mood in both the

City and Westminster was troubled. Some weeks later Keynes privately explained these misgivings: 'England is sticky with self-pity and not prepared to accept peacefully and wisely the fact that her position and her resources are *not* what they once were.' As unreconciled as anyone was Montagu Norman (by now Lord Norman). 'He is entirely opposed to Bretton Woods and the whole of the Washington Loan ramp,' Leo Amery recorded after a conversation with him in March 1946. 'In his curiously ingenious way he said that he did not understand the economics of the matter but that he had a strong hunch that we were being done down and resented it.'[7] A month later Keynes, with whom Norman had had such charged dealings and non-dealings over the years, was dead.

Norman was even unhappier about what had been happening, almost simultaneously, to the love of his life: the Bank of England.[8] The commitment to nationalise the Bank was an integral part of Labour's election manifesto, and within days of the change of government Catto emphasised to Dalton his hope that 'the method giving the least possible disturbance to the existing set-up would be chosen'. At this delicate stage the Bank, itself well prepared for the coming negotiations, received invaluable support from the Treasury, where Sir Wilfrid Eady argued in early August that 'there is everything to be said for viewing the Bank as a public corporation, subject to control on policy but not to interference in the running of the machine', on the grounds that 'the more the permitted independence on inessentials the easier will it be for the Bank to maintain its intimate relations with other parts of the financial system and with City interests'. As for Dalton himself, he saw few insuperable problems. 'Today,' he noted on 17 August, 'I have had a most successful talk with Catto who is taking everything very well and said that he would like to go on as Governor under the new regime. He is a splendid little asset.'[9]

Over the next six and a half months the process unfolded with remarkably little trouble. The bill to nationalise the Bank (praised by Dalton as 'a streamlined socialist statute, containing the minimum of legal rigmarole') worked its passage through Parliament during the winter, amidst only muted discussion and public controversy; and on 1 March 1946 the Old Lady, now almost 252 years old, passed into public ownership. Two days earlier, on 27 February, the 'Last Supper' took place there: native oysters, clear turtle soup, lamb cutlets and fruit salad with ice cream were washed down by 'Old Trinity House' Madeira, Steinberg 1935 hock, and Cognac 1884 brandy. 'I am deeply appreciative,' Catto told those present, 'of the manner in which all members of the Court stood solidly behind me in this crisis in the Bank's history':

A break in our ranks would have enormously increased the difficulties! The policy we adopted has proved its worth and gradually everyone is coming to realise that although the essential principle of Public ownership had to be conceded, on all other matters, particularly those questions concerning the future of the Bank and its management and the protection of the Staff, we put up a fight behind the scenes and obtained every point we considered essential to the well being of this great and ancient institution.

Catto coupled the toast – 'Long live the Bank of England' – with the name of his predecessor, who 'has given all the best years of his life in living up to that Toast'.[10]

Catto was justifiably proud that, despite holding lowish cards, he had won for himself and the Bank a signal tactical triumph. Later in 1946 he even privately boasted of 'how he had succeeded in keeping things surprisingly unchanged in daily practice, how he had held to a refusal to disclose secret reserves to the government, how he had got compensation for stock-holders which left their income unaffected, how the "halo" of mystery and power was an asset which he had preserved . . .' Catto might also have added that, on the key question of the issuing of directives to the clearing banks, the Treasury would in effect be permitted to do so only via the Bank of England and not autonomously. Most of the City seems to have agreed that Catto had done the very best he could in that particular situation – 'so far as status – apart from ownership – is concerned, the Bank's unique and responsible position is maintained,' the *FT* asserted as early as October 1945 – but Norman refused to be mollified. He insisted that Catto should somehow have prevented the Labour government from going ahead with the legislation, and when asked a few weeks after nationalisation whether the Bank was still the same place, he replied mournfully, 'They try to pretend it is the same place.'[11]

In truth, if Norman had overseen the Bank's public image more effectively during the inter-war years – and had not allowed the false impression that he, not government, was ultimately responsible for monetary policy – there would have been far less political momentum for nationalisation, an act viewed by Dalton and his colleagues as essentially symbolic. In the climate of 1945 it is by no means impossible that the Conservatives would have nationalised the Bank, if they had been elected. Nevertheless, even if he did intend to do no more than formalise the Bank's *de facto* public character, Dalton clearly lost most of the tricks to Catto. Dalton was underprepared for the technicalities involved, but Cobbold, looking back some thirty years later, was more inclined to stress the human element:

> He [Dalton] met his match, partly because when Catto had really made up his mind about something he stuck to his guns, but more particularly for the curious reason that Dalton was frightened of him. I thought at the time, and nothing has since happened to change my view, that this was because

Dalton had a guilt-conscience about his upbringing as a Canon of Windsor's son, Eton etc, whilst Catto started work on an office stall in Scotland. Though he was apt to be offensive and overbearing to people of his own background and to 'establishment' officials, Dalton seemed to feel that his attacks on privilege, etc, would not stand up to a public row with Catto.

'My relations with Mr Dalton were most delicate, but very cordial,' Catto himself recalled, and if one reckons that the emphasis is to be placed on the first adjective, there may be an important psychological truth to Cobbold's explanation.[12]

Inevitably nationalisation *did* make a difference. 'The prestige of the Bank is not what it was,' Arthur Villiers of Barings informed an American correspondent in January 1947. 'Various Directors have been appointed for their political views. Some of the Directors are excellent and others just average. To be a Director of the Bank in former times was a considerable honour; today that is not the case.' The larger point, however, is that nationalisation failed to make enough of a difference: there was no vision of how a central bank should function in the new era of a more planned economy; no convincing model of the ideal triangular relationship between government, central bank and commercial banks; and no insistence that the Bank shed its highly damaging culture of secrecy and the deliberate cultivation of mystique. There was an obligation on the Bank to start publishing an annual report, but when the first one appeared in 1947, the *Banker* was scathing: 'On the finances of the Bank itself, nothing whatever is revealed ... On the Bank's internal activities, the only glimpses behind the curtain reveal facts which are mainly of formal significance.' This instinctive unwillingness on the Bank's part to accept the burdens of public accountability, to complement public responsibility, both reflected and exacerbated its reluctance to stake the intellectual high ground. 'My "economics" are simple and old-fashioned,' a future Deputy Governor, Humphrey Mynors, perhaps ingenuously confessed to Eady in 1948. 'I do not move easily in the post-Keynesian terminology, although I believe it is largely only restating the old truths.'[13] Norman's distaste for the dismal science had permeated the Bank, and in some sense it remained Norman's Bank for a full generation after his enforced retirement.[14] Dalton, whatever his personal animosity towards the traditional City élite, may have believed in 1945 that the fact of nationalisation was in itself enough to serve the New Jerusalem's purposes – but, if so, this was a serious error of judgement.

Dalton's lack of ambition in relation to the nationalisation of the Bank of England may be partly explained by the hopes he had invested in not only the newly formed ICFC, but also the proposed National Investment Board (NIB), which according to Labour's election manifesto would 'determine social priorities and promote better timing in private investment'.[15] In the event, the NIB completely failed to get off the ground, and in its place was established an almost wholly lame-duck, purely advisory National Investment Council, which achieved very little. As for ICFC, that object of first Norman's and then Catto's midwifery, it expended much of its energy in countering City opposition.[16] The attitude of the clearers remained broadly recalcitrant – Sadd in his letters to Piercy enthusiastically onside, Barclays helpful in a low-key practical way, and most of the others (led by Lidbury) wishing the infant dead – while Sir Edward de Stein lasted barely a year on the board before resigning on the grounds that ICFC was trespassing on territory that belonged to the merchant banks. As with the clearers, the attitude of the merchant banks was not uniformly hostile, but in spring 1947 there was a short, sharp squall when ICFC agreed to underwrite an issue (for Viscose Developments) at well under the usual City rate. There was also a protest from the issuing houses over an issue that was seen as lying outside ICFC's permitted scope. ICFC's top two, Piercy and John Kinross, were forging an effective alliance – one the front man, employing a highly developed mixture of cunning and aggression, the other the technician and investment specialist – but its long-term future was still highly doubtful.

The body that (more or less unavailingly) protested to ICFC was the recently formed Issuing Houses Association (IHA). Its prime instigator was Olaf Hambro, who in July 1945 had, in the company of Colonel Bertram Abel Smith of M. Samuel, outlined to Catto 'their dislike of the issuing business done by some Stock Exchange firms'. He had expressed the hope that the formation of an association 'might produce a definition of an Issuing House which would tend to keep Stock Exchange firms out of the business'. Catto in turn had 'expressed some sympathy with their ideas on this subject'.[17] The inaugural meeting was held in November 1945 at Shell House in Bishopsgate; Abel Smith was elected Chairman; and within a few months membership was up to some four dozen issuing houses, including Philip Hill and Warburgs, as well as all the leading merchant banks.

The IHA could never hope to be as select a body as the Accepting Houses Committee, but standards were standards, and during the winter of 1945–6 the big question was what to do about Arthur Whitehead and his very active, but barely reputable Whitehead Industrial Trust of 177 Regent Street.[18] 'Constantly on the wriggle' was how Basil Catterns at the Bank had privately described Whiteheads towards the end of the war, while in December 1945 the Chairman of the Stock Exchange told Abel Smith that 'some of their prospectuses, which give profits but not the dividends which have been paid, are not liked'. Nevertheless, the Stock Exchange view was that, in Abel Smith's words, 'you cannot ignore them' and that 'if they were not brought into our fold, they would have a grievance and might be most difficult'. Accordingly, Abel Smith told his committee, the Chairman 'would like us to issue them an invitation as he hopes that if they belong to our organisation we may be able to have a wholesome influence over them'. On the back of this advice, the IHA duly issued an invitation – only to have it brusquely rejected by Whitehead, on the grounds that it came from 'a self-appointed body'. Eventually, in mid-January 1946 Abel Smith and his deputy (Lionel Fraser of Helbert Wagg) had two meetings with Whitehead in his flat in Grosvenor House, where he was recovering from an operation. 'They had found him not unreasonable,' they reported back, and in due course Whitehead Industrial Trust joined the IHA. Whitehead himself was soon back in harness, and in 1947 the number of issues (twenty-four) done by his organisation was more than those done by Barings, Hambros, Lazards, Rothschilds and Schroders put together.

Whitehead always struggled to attain respectability in the eyes of the City, but at least he was not regarded as personally offensive, or not unduly so. The same did not apply to the unfortunate Ernest Strangman. 'He is continually collecting cigarette ends from the tins at the inside doors of the House, rummaging the waste paper baskets for newspapers or anything he may desire, picking up cigarette ends at two local railway stations,' Ernest Cunningham of Francis Egerton & Co complained to the Stock Exchange Council (as the old Stock Exchange Committee was now called) in February 1946. 'Should he be re-elected a member of the Stock Exchange?' Cunningham, and those on whose behalf he was writing, had no doubts: 'We do not consider he is one who upholds the dignity of a Member. And finally, he is dirty, his clothes disgusting and he smells horribly.' Duly informed that there had been an objection to his re-election, Strangman promised to be 'more discreet'. Consideration was postponed until 25 March (the start of the new Stock Exchange year), and during the interim the Council received further communications from both Strangman – formally promising 'as regard to my appearance' to 'endeavour to improve it with other clothes' – and Cunningham:

> This man is *still* picking up Cigarette ends from the S/E bins, also Warnford Court. The height of filth was when after washing himself in the Members' washing room, he blew his nose on the towel. I personally have not seen this, but it is fairly general talk.
> He brought a parcel into the Lobby last week and put it in his usual place. It was knocked over and scattered a collection of pieces of rolls and bread crusts. Surely this is not a Member we others have to tolerate. I personally am very nervous of using the Members' washing room for fear I contact something this man has used.

Perhaps reluctantly, the Council voted 19–3 to re-elect him. Strangman's reprieve, however, was only brief, for a year later there was a 15–6 vote against re-electing him. 'It will cause me very great trouble and inconvenience and I have a good many commitments still to complete,' Strangman complained, but his inglorious Stock Exchange career was over.[19]

The club that had thrown him out was generally trying, in the new post-war order, to smarten up its act. Early in 1946 a Memorandum of Guidance drawn up by the Stock Exchange Council had the effect, by insisting on a more orderly market, of removing most of the criticised elements of the placing method for new issues. Even so, there was still something of a public scandal that summer involving the marketing by the brokers Keith, Bayley & Rigg of St Helena Gold Mines shares. Under grilling from the Council, the firm's senior partner, Colonel R.S. Rogers, 'agreed that the public, in order to obtain an interest in these shares, had to pay a premium to Keith, Bayley & Rigg and their friends of £2 a share'; 'asked whether he realised that wherever the blame lay the St Helena incident had brought grave discredit to the Stock Exchange, Mr Rogers said no one regretted it more than he did'. Rogers was suspended for two years, and six jobbers who had also made very handsome profits out of the operation received lesser punishments. The long-established broking firm J. & A. Scrimgeour complained to the Council that Keith, Bayley & Rigg as a whole should have been penalised, not just one partner: 'The times are difficult and the difficulties will not be alleviated by timid measures, neither can we expect the prestige of the Stock Exchange to be enhanced until full measures for the protection of the public, and members generally, are adopted.'[20]

Not surprisingly the Stock Exchange trod very carefully later that year as, under the guidance of the Bank of England, it negotiated with the Treasury to restore fortnightly accounts, but only on a cash basis, without any speculation-inducing contangos (that is, carrying over purchases from one account to another) or options. The public image now mattered as never before, and the Council commissioned from Wilfred King of the *Banker* a book about the Stock Exchange and its positive role in the nation's economic life. This was published in 1947, with chapter titles like 'Mobilising the Nation's Savings', 'The Importance of a Free Market' and 'Protecting the Investor'; but the eminent financial journalist Oscar Hobson argued in his review that there was still scope for future 'advances', especially in introducing a professional qualification, with examinations.[21] His point was no less compelling for having been made by Montague Newton to the Royal Commission on the Stock Exchange some seventy years previously.

In the markets themselves, the Stock Exchange for a time actually benefited – to its surprise – from Dalton's chancellorship, in particular his passionate espousal of cheap money.[22] Declaring that the occupant of his office 'must be on the side of the active producer as against the passive *rentier*', and quoting with approval Keynes's famous phrase about how ever-falling interest rates would lead to 'the euthanasia of the rentier', Dalton sought strenuously to place credit on a 2½ per cent footing. April 1946 saw a new 'tap' issue in the form of 2½ per cent savings bonds: this went reasonably well, though Dalton later claimed that he could have got better terms, but for flawed advice from Cobbold at the Bank. At this point investor sentiment to the further cheapening of money, following the economic successes of cheap money policy since the early 1930s, was by and large favourable. 'We are in the middle of a Stock Exchange boom,' Villiers of Barings noted fairly soon after the new issue was announced. 'One Member of Parliament even suggested in the House that a statue should be put up to Dalton in Throgmorton Street as he has been the principal factor in bringing it about.'[23]

With plaudits, sincere or otherwise, ringing in his ears from all sides, Dalton decided by the autumn of 1946 to go for broke and convert 3 per cent Local Loans into a 2½ irredeemable Treasury stock. For this, he received only luke-warm support from the Bank, but firmer backing from the Treasury. Within hours of the announcement, on 16 October, Dalton was addressing the City's assembled bankers at the Mansion House. It was a speech that lacked nothing in bounce, as the Chancellor repudiated recent suggestions that his cheap money policy had been made possible only by large-scale intervention in the market, explicitly compared his newly announced move to Goschen's historic conversion operation in 1888, and generally called on the City to continue to show all its time-honoured 'skill and experience' on behalf of the national economic cause.[24] There was, the market rapidly decided, only one possible name for the new 2½ stock: 'Daltons'.

Immediate City response was mixed, but the financial press made an almost unanimous dead set. According to the *Economist*, it was asking investors 'to give a complete hostage to the policy of ultra-cheap money for a generation', while the *FT* even started to quarrel with the cheap money policy as a whole, calling it 'a powerful discouragement to thrift'. However, the most compelling attack came from King in the *Banker*, as he appraised 'The Modern Goschen'. Amidst much technical refutation, he argued that this latter-day statesman was asking investors to assume not only 'that Governments for a generation and more to come will always rely, and rely successfully, upon physical control to maintain equilibrium whenever demand for capital outruns supply', but also 'that the Governments of the future will never return to the classical policies that were abandoned in 1932, but, through good times and bad, will ever eschew the interest rate as an instrument of economic control'. The strong instinct of Dalton and his colleagues, King implicitly maintained, might be to consign traditional monetary policy to the dark ages of Norman, but there was no guarantee how long that instinct would continue to prevail. In short, 'The fate of gilt-edged investors now turns absolutely on the whim of the Chancellor, on the scale and direction of his operations.'[25] The attack hit home, and by the end of the year it was clear that, despite heavy government propaganda, 'Daltons' would be at best only a very qualified success.

The new stock, following the end of the tap, was floated in January 1947 – just as a memorable winter was about to take grip, leading to the fuel crisis and an *annus horribilis* for the Labour government. 'We had power cuts and we had no heat and we were put into rooms that you would not put a dog into today,' a new recruit to the solicitors Coward Chance recalled more than forty years later; and in February, in the depths of the big freeze, that firm's partners sanctioned the purchase of sixteen Aladdin lamps 'from an itinerant vendor of ex-Government stores at a cost of about £50'. At another firm of solicitors, Slaughter and May, clerks clustered round the library table, where they toiled by the light of a single candle, while secretaries stuffed typewriter covers with crumpled newspaper pages to try to get some circulation back to their feet. Even 8 Bishopsgate suffered. 'Life here is quite impossible,' Evelyn Baring reported to Al Gordon of Kidder Peabody in mid-February, 'and really no-one would have believed it if they had read it in a novel. From 9 to 12 and 2 to 4 we work in the dim glow of candlelight or nightlight.' A colleague, Arthur Villiers, looked at the broader aspect of the fuel crisis: 'The immediate effect is to put thousands of fellows out on the street at a peculiarly unpleasant time for them, because the weather is very cold and most of their homes are very badly off for fuel. To some extent, it is their own fault for having deserted Churchill even before the war ended – a most ungrateful thing to have done. Even in this wicked world, ingratitude seldom pays . . .' By early March the big freeze had still not relented, and at about that time Hobson ran into Norman on the steps of the Athenaeum. The journalist made some remark about the difficulties of the economic situation and the possibility of stricter rationing of food. 'Yes,' Norman replied, 'I think grub will be short.'[26]

As the government's honeymoon period ended, so Clarence Sadd found himself in an increasingly exposed position in Midland Bank's head office at Poultry. On 14 January 1947 his inaugural address as President of the Institute of Bankers gave a predictably favourable spin to Dalton's cheap money policy; and just over a fortnight later, on the 29th, it was undoubtedly Sadd who was responsible for penning the annual statement attributed to his Chairman, Lord Linlithgow, carefully eschewing any criticism of government policies. Next day, by contrast, National

Provincial's Chairman, Captain Eric Smith, castigated cheap money as an unfair tax on the rentier: 'It carries in its train considerable hardship to those who live on the income from savings and the products of commendable thrift. It reacts unfavourably on life assurance and the benefits to be derived from pension funds. It discourages those with an incentive to save and encourages prodigality . . .' It was not only Linlithgow, a former Viceroy of India, but also a prominent member of his board, the former Colonial Secretary William Ormsby-Gore, now Lord Harlech, who privately agreed. That spring, not inappropriately on 1 May, Harlech wrote to Linlithgow ('Dear Hopie') in a state of white heat, having 'just received at the expense of the Midland Bank with the personal compliments of your vice-Chairman [Sadd]' a copy of a recent speech by Sir Stafford Cripps, President of the Board of Trade:

> I make to you my emphatic protest against such circulation of his speeches and clear instructions given that I decline to receive in future copies of his or his typical colleague that swine Dalton's speeches. In the interests of their political and personal ambition & venom against the interests of the Empire, commerce, industry & all fair play these two enemies of all we stand for at the Midland Bank are the two worst elements in this bloody government & I seek your protection against such missives from Sir Clarence Sadd.[27]

The situation at the top of Midland was becoming inherently unsustainable.

Also close to destruction was Dalton's cheap money policy, which by April 1947, with 'Daltons' at a discount, was under renewed, unforgiving attack in the press. 'Twilight of Cheaper Money?' asked the *Banker* hopefully, declaring that 'the magician's wand has lost its cunning' and that 'in future he must use the weapons of ordinary mortals'; while the *FT* laid particular stress on cheap money's inflationary implications and Dalton's unwillingness 'to take major effective action against them'. By this time, however, Dalton's particular *bête noire* was the *Economist*, under Geoffrey Crowther's editorship, which was pitiless in its campaign against his conduct of monetary policy. Lees-Milne was present at a luncheon in July attended by Dalton. 'He is affable, bombastic and diabolically clever . . . he thumped the table when speaking about the editor of the *Economist*, saying: "He persistently misrepresents all my endeavours and I damned well won't be interfered with. He will get nothing out of me . . ."' Confidence was now rapidly waning in Dalton's policy – in the Treasury and in the Bank, as well as in the City at large – and it was clear that 3 per cent, not 2½ per cent, represented a realistic floor for cheap money. Dalton would later blame the City (and its helpmate the financial press) for having sabotaged his policy, while at the Bank of England the effect was merely to intensify already well-entrenched suspicions about academics and intellectuals getting involved in the practical niceties of market matters.[28] So much turned, in retrospect, on October 1946 and the creation of 'Daltons': the product of a finance minister in the throes of hubris and an uncertain, newly nationalised central bank unable to restrain him.

One hardy favourite, meanwhile, had resurfaced to perplex City minds: the German Standstill debts, amounting after the war to some £40m (including interest) that British bankers now hoped to recover.[29] The Accepting Houses Committee made some initial moves during 1946–7, but for some time received no help from either the clearers or the government. 'It is quite clear that no money can come out of a dismembered and disrupted Germany for years,' Lidbury declared in June 1946, a year before he retired; while not only did Dalton take the line that the money was irretrievably lost, but Bevin publicly described the original Standstill agreement of 1931 as 'the foundation on which Hitler built up his war potential'. Dalton had already been equally dismissive about the prospects of those hoping to see the resumption of service of the Japanese government loans dating back to 1899. 'If there is anything to be screwed out of the Japanese,' he elegantly stated in the Commons in February 1946, 'there is a long list of stronger claimants than the pre-war owners of Japanese bonds.' There was anyway, at this time, a significant amount of anti-Japanese feeling in the City, and it was perhaps predictable that when in June 1947 a consortium (involving Schroders, Barings and the Hongkong and Shanghai Bank) approached Catto about a possible Anglo-American loan to the Bank of Japan, he was unable to offer meaningful assistance, on the grounds that (as he privately noted) it was better 'to play the matter long until we can all see a bit clearer about Japan'. Ultimately, however, the City would have to try to restore itself as an international financial centre; and even in these dark days there was an encouraging portent in the formation later in 1947 of the Foreign Banks' Association, actively encouraged by the Bank of England and with founder-members including Banque Belge, Bank of China, Comptoir National d'Escompte de Paris, Crédit Lyonnais and Swiss Bank Corporation.[30]

In the meantime, however, the principal focus was domestic, typified in 1947 by seven merchant banks coming together to make a huge £15m offer for sale of Steel Company of Wales debenture stock. Designed, in the words of the prospectus, 'to enable an old established British industry again to make an important contribution to the country's export trade', this was an important initiative, symbolically as well as in substance. It would not have been possible without some delicate mediation by Catto after one of the main bankers involved, Lord Kindersley of Lazards, had gone too far too fast without consulting other potential members of the consortium. Early on 23 April the Governor telephoned Sir Edward Peacock at Barings:

> I said, all right, let us have a meeting in my room at 11.30 this morning. He said he would attend and bring one of his partners with him. I then telephoned to Lord Bicester but he had not arrived, but Mr R.H. Vivian Smith said he was sure Lord Bicester would be glad to attend the meeting. He suggested that as some of the other Houses that were coming would be bringing a second partner with them, perhaps his father would bring him. I also telephoned to Mr Anthony de Rothschild and asked him if he would attend, and he stated he would be glad to do so. (Barings, Morgan Grenfell & Co and Rothschilds being, in particular, the three houses who felt objection to co-operating in the business in the form put forward by Lord Kindersley.) I then telephoned to Lord Kindersley and told him I was ready for a meeting and that Barings, Morgan Grenfell and Rothschilds were each sending representatives. I told him Sir E. Peacock was bringing a partner with him and so was Lord Bicester. Lord Kindersley asked if I would mind if he brought his partner, Mr Horsfall, and I replied that I would welcome that. Later, I telephoned to Lord Kindersley and suggested that perhaps he might feel it helpful to get a partner or two partners from Helbert Wagg. He thanked me and said that would be most helpful and he would arrange it.

Arranged in such classic fashion, the meeting could hardly fail to be a success, and there were some suitably conciliatory words from Kindersley. Hambros and Schroders later joined the consortium, though in the event the issue proved something of a flop when it was made in July, with the threat of nationalisation of the steel industry rattling already nervous markets. Later that same month Barings, Glyn Mills and Cazenove's were all closely involved in a rather smaller issue: the offer for sale of 200,000 shares of Bertram Mills Circus. The circus itself was a sell-out at Olympia for the next two winter seasons, and there was a splendid list of assets, but market conditions were deteriorating so rapidly that the sub-underwriters were left with almost half the offering. It was the first and last circus venture with which Cazenove's (for one) was involved. Or as Hubert Meredith, from his vantage-point at Philip Hill, is said to have asked pointedly: 'What security is a sea-lion?'[31]

The panic in the markets that so severely affected both issues was almost entirely caused by the unfortunate but inescapable fact of sterling becoming fully convertible from 15 July 1947.[32] 'Today,' the *FT* observed on the 15th itself, 'the curtain rises on the second act in the drama of the Bartered Bride, or Sold for Gold. The first act opened when a reluctant Britain signed the Anglo-American Loan Agreement in Washington, nineteen months ago.' The editorial ended: 'If the dollar blizzard descends, then indeed we shall see a case of *sauve qui peut*.' The blizzard did descend, with an appalling drain of dollars almost immediately, and by the second week of August the suspension of convertibility was being urgently considered. 'The Government are in these matters, as in all others, worried, nervy, and incapable of reaching decisions,' the Bank of England's 'Ruby' Holland-Martin (approaching the end of his executive directorship) noted. With the dollar blizzard showing no signs of abating, suspension was announced on the 20th, by Dalton on the wireless. 'It is in fact a default,' commented the *FT*. 'Such a misjudgment of the situation and such precipitate abandonment of the position taken up so recently cannot fail to bring the gravest discredit upon this Government of self-styled planners.' Villiers of Barings, writing to a Boston correspondent on the day of suspension, agreed entirely that the Labour government was 'grossly incompetent', but felt that the blame should be shared: 'The experts tried to make a plan which was obviously premature and in addition the mess we are in is in a great measure due to the fact that we got so heavily into debt during the war years. It is exasperating to think that we are supposed to owe £400,000,000 to the Egyptians, one of the feeblest races in the world.'[33]

Given the American determination in 1945 to impose early convertibility as part of the loan agreement, and the parlous balance-of-payments situation that Britain still found itself in by 1947, it had been an inevitable humiliation. The Bank of England may, for once, have been guilty of not issuing the government with enough dire warnings in advance, but suspension would still have happened, even had it been more accurately prophesied. The effect of the crisis was to delay permanent convertibility of sterling by a full decade, during which London inevitably operated as a domestic, rather than international, financial centre. Less than a fortnight after suspension, one observer with a uniquely privileged sense of the City's history called it right, at least in the short term. 'I fear that the various ancient businesses of London have practically come to an end, or continue perhaps as shadows,' Norman wrote at the start of September to an American banker.[34] Economic and financial internationalism seemed dead, New York and not London ruled the roost, and Norman would die in February 1950 believing that in the central aims of his life he had failed.

In its September retrospect on the convertibility crisis, the *Banker* was struck by the City's mood swings: irrational bullishness in the earlier part of the year, followed by near-panic, with the FT 30-Share Index losing 10 per cent in just over a week in late July. Overall, 'the stock markets never grasped the implications of convertibility and are now more than ever bewildered by its abandonment'. Shortly after suspension, the journalist Sydney Moseley ran into 'a young stockbroker', who 'declared to me that the country was "doomed"'. It is tempting to imagine that this pessimistic young man was Kenneth Fox, a half-commission man on the Stock Exchange who by 1947 was attached to the brokers Vivian, Gray & Co.

Since the start of the previous year his main client had been a wealthy film producer called George King, whom Fox had known before the war and who allowed him considerable discretion in handling his investments. From an early stage those investments – in reality, speculations – had fared poorly, but Fox had managed to keep King in the dark while he tried to redress the situation. At the end of June King demanded to know his position, but Fox was able to fob him off. Then, towards the end of July and with the convertibility crisis under way, King went to the Continent for six weeks. 'Shortly after,' Fox later confessed to the Stock Exchange Council, 'the first major slump in share values took place. It was in this movement that the losses were nearly doubled in a very short time. I knew, then, that the position was hopeless and beyond recovery.' King returned at the start of September. 'I was literally frightened out of my mind. For months I had thought of nothing else, and now I was incapable of thinking straight at all.' Fox gave false figures to King, but when the film producer revealed that he had sent the figures to his accountants, Fox decided to come clean. His firm brought the matter to the Council's attention. 'I realise that I have done a rotten thing,' confessed Fox later that autumn in a time-honoured phrase, 'totally unworthy of a member of the Stock Exchange, and that I must expect to suffer the consequences of my action.' There followed the usual two pleas for clemency: the absence of any intention of dishonesty or personal gain; and the wife and two children (aged ten and seven) who needed supporting. Soon after making those pleas Fox received an offer of employment outside the City, and he resigned from the Stock Exchange before the Council could mete out its punishment.[35]

Dalton too, for less discreditable reasons, was changing his station in life. Going into the Commons on 12 November to deliver his budget, he absent-mindedly leaked a secret to the *Star*'s lobby correspondent and the following day was compelled to resign. During the speech itself he had turned to his proposed fiscal changes with the remark that 'it is past four o'clock and the Stock Exchange will soon be shut'. To which a Tory MP gleefully cried out: 'It closes at three o'clock.' City reaction to the resignation was summed up by Villiers a week later: 'He was an unpopular figure and there were not many regrets, although I think he got a little sympathy because he made a clean breast of his stupidity and no one made a penny through his indiscretion.'[36] Dalton, in relation to the City, had lost the important battles, and somehow it was a suitably bathetic end.

*

The new Chancellor was Stafford Cripps, whom the City instinctively found preferable to his hectoring predecessor. Nevertheless, the general tone in early 1948 of the annual round of bank chairmen's speeches was still dissatisfied, with extensive criticism of government policies. The exception was again Midland's Linlithgow. 'It is because we are seeing our problems more clearly,' he blandly asserted in his statement, 'and showing ourselves readier to take the measure of them, that we can look back upon an eventful year with considered satisfaction, and forward to the promise of better times in years that lie ahead.' Linlithgow, the *Banker* commented tartly, 'evidently prefers to smooth away all the sharper edges of controversy'. It added that, unlike his fellow-chairmen, 'Lord Linlithgow, it seems, prefers that investment should be regulated by physical controls and by its counterpart of capital issues control'. Of course, Linlithgow had again allowed himself to be the mouthpiece for Sadd's views – views with which he strongly disagreed – and now at last there was the inevitable reckoning, probably precipitated by an internal matter at the bank. That spring saw Sadd's enforced retirement, under the disguise of sick leave. Four years later, in 1952, Cobbold quizzed Linlithgow's successor, Harlech, about Midland's unhealthy-looking balance sheet. 'The real trouble was that they were much too long,' Cobbold noted of their discussion, 'and at the Midland Bank Sadd is unanimously judged the villain of the piece.' Such was the view of Harlech's general managers, and for all Sadd's popularity with the lower-ranking staff at Midland, it was a dispiriting way to be remembered for someone who, in the first flush of triumph after the 1945 election, had described Labour as 'the party of Freedom, the direct heir of Magna Charta' and himself, almost as gloriously, as 'an untamed Radical all my life'.[37]

It was a further irony that at the time of Sadd's fall in 1948, the City as a whole was probably feeling less threatened by Attlee's government than at any time since its formation. Physical controls over the economy were easing, the Marshall Plan was about to swing into action and 'the carrot-crunching Cripps' (as Brendan Bracken liked to call him) was a not wholly unpopular figure. He tacitly accepted that 3 per cent rather than 2½ per cent constituted 'cheap money', had a perceptibly more relaxed attitude than Dalton's towards the gilt-edged and discount markets and in April produced a budget that won broad praise from the *Banker,* above all for its deflationary implications. Put another way, as Dalton's biographer has ruefully pointed out, Cripps was far more willing than his predecessor to follow City advice, and his reward was to have epithets such as 'courageous' attached to his policies. Villiers, in his end-of-1948 report to a Boston correspondent, reflected the general approbation: 'As far as England is concerned, there has been a considerable improvement in many directions and undoubtedly the policy of Stafford Cripps has been an immense improvement on that of Dalton.' Nevertheless, there were dissenters, among them the Hongkong and Shanghai's Ernest Muriel. By May 1948 he was contemplating retirement to South Africa – 'a country,' he informed a no-doubt sympathetic correspondent in Cape Town, 'which has many attractions as against Britain, where we are hedged around with so many restrictions and frustrations and where the retired rentier has to pay penal taxation, and, in the Socialist mentality, is looked upon as a cross between a drone and a criminal'.[38] Many in the City would have silently – or not so silently – concurred, and at best it was only a temporary, uneasy rapprochement between Labour and the square mile.

ICFC remained a touchstone of the City's tolerance, or otherwise, towards the 1945 settlement. When Linlithgow became Chairman of the Committee of London Clearing Bankers (CLCB) at almost exactly the same time that he was at last rid of Sadd, he began a series of skirmishes with the Labour-sympathising Piercy.[39] The Corporation was already in some difficulty over the extent of its bad debts, and Linlithgow now demanded that it give its shareholders fuller disclosure of information not only about customers that were failing, but also about its own operations. Piercy and Kinross dug in their heels, and in August the clearers were in effect told by Catto to lay off ICFC. The next rumblings came, the following winter, from the Issuing Houses Association, after a complaint from Lazards had more or less accused ICFC of entering the new issue market in a competitive way. Piercy disclaimed any such intentions, and in a progress report that he sent to Cripps in early 1949 claimed that, as far as 'relations with the City generally' were concerned, 'we are sniped at from time to time, but by deliberate policy we are gradually becoming a part of the general symbiosis of the City'. Piercy was less sanguine about ICFC's shareholders, the clearing banks: 'Too many Chairmen and General Managers are still of Sir Charles Lidbury's (reputed) opinion that "the damn thing's not wanted". The stage has still to be reached where a preponderance of bankers see in ICFC a public service or a collateral help to their business.' The year of 1949 was, as it turned out, the one in which ICFC started to come good on the actual business side – in his memo to Cripps, Piercy referred to how 'the famed Macmillan Gap has merged into a wider area of dearth of capital' – but that did not prevent further 'sniping', including some from the IHA that summer about ICFC's advertising. Again, however, Piercy's critics received no encouragement from the Bank.[40] Although never a personal favourite in Threadneedle Street, he was chairman of an institution that was coming to represent for the City what the Welfare State was for the Conservative Party: in both cases, however reluctantly and not without refuseniks, an inescapable post-war reality.

Inflation would be another great post-war fact of life, invariably raising the question of how to control it, and it could be argued that the original modern monetarist was the Labour minister Douglas Jay.[41] As Economic Secretary, he argued forcibly from late 1947 in favour of reducing the money supply, partly through keeping a tight rein on the advances made by clearing banks. During the first half of 1948 the Bank of England made little more than non-committal noises, while the volume of bank advances and deposits steadily grew. Robert Hall, who since the previous year had been running the government's Economic Section (and keeping an invaluable diary), was in a scathing mood by September:

> There is quite a hunt going on against the Bank over the increase in deposits . . . The Bank tends to the early 19th century heresy that *because* prices are rising therefore more money is needed. It is astonishing to find this view held in 1948. But the whole relationship is astonishing, especially after the nationalisation of the Bank by Dalton. If ever there was anything done for show, not for effect, this is it.

In early November, with press criticism of the failure of the government's credit policy becoming increasingly sharp, Hall met Mynors to discuss the latest figures from the clearing banks. He was underwhelmed: 'It is hard not to get the impression that the Bank, and the banks generally, do not think at all about credit control as economists do, and indeed that they don't quite understand what it is all about.' Whatever the truth of that charge, Mynors at the Bank was unapologetic about his disinclination to buy the monetarist nostrums. 'To suppose that anything can be achieved by pegging the volume of money in circulation is like Canute telling the waves to stand still, *unless* the indirect effects of such an instruction are to reduce investment and/or increase saving to the appropriate extent and in the appropriate quarters,' he wrote soon afterwards to Eady at the Treasury and to Hall.[42]

The political temper was starting to rise, and in late November the first meeting was held, under Jay's chairmanship and involving Bank as well as Treasury representatives, of a Working Party on Bank Deposits and Advances. Its recommendation, pushed strongly by Hall, was for a ceiling on bank advances – a recommendation far from the taste of the Bank. 'The more I think about it,' Cobbold wrote to the ailing Catto on 8 December, 'the less do I like any idea of trying to limit advances by asking the banks to keep down to certain figures. If it is necessary from the angle of credit policy to try to keep advances down, I still believe that the only satisfactory way is the old-fashioned one of making borrowing more expensive.' That 'old-fashioned' approach was of course, in Labour's eyes, fatally tarnished by its association with Norman and inter-war monetary policy; but Catto on his sickbed was not deterred from writing to Cripps in the strongest terms shortly afterwards. It was with 'the utmost alarm' that he viewed the suggestion for 'a ceiling for deposits and advances', being 'not practical' and likely to 'land us in a mess of violent deflation'. And, in distinctly intemperate language, he declared that 'it is an entire fallacy to suppose that pressure from the Bank of England on the banks could rectify inflationary pressure which comes from overgearing the country's economy'.[43] No doubt Catto genuinely believed the macro-economic truth of that argument, but almost certainly what he and Cobbold were at least as concerned about was the threat posed by the quantitative 'ceiling' approach, not only to the working of the banking system, but also to the Bank's own powers of moral suasion over that system – powers that relied heavily on discretion and judgement rather than directives and figures.

By Christmas a compromise had been reached, and it largely ceded to Catto's standpoint. During 1949 the growth in the money supply was checked, not really thanks to the Bank, and the controversy over credit policy temporarily abated. But as Jay's working party faded into obscurity, unmourned by the Bank, the reality was that there had been no fundamental tightening up of the mechanism of bank credit, and in somewhat bitter retrospective mood Hall noted in September 1949 that 'we have been defeated by the direct cowardice or else disingenuousness of Cobbold, whose people have on several occasions agreed to do something and then gone back on it'.[44] Government, the Bank and the banks: the triangular saga was only just beginning.

Cobbold himself, after four years as a particularly strong Deputy Governor, had succeeded Catto in March 1949. It was hardly a shock appointment, but there had been other possibilities. Correctly anticipating that Catto would not want to go on beyond the age of seventy, Dalton had made a firm recommendation to Cripps in favour of Piercy, shortly after resigning the chancellorship: 'He has a wide range of practical experience, having been a stockbroker as well as an industrialist, and he has made a considerable success of ICFC since its formation.' Dalton conceded, however, that Piercy had never been a banker, and added that 'among bankers the best man would be Sir Clarence Sadd, who combines practical experience with a broadminded political approach'. The latter possibility soon receded, but during much of 1948 Piercy (according to Kinross) was confident that the job was in the bag. It seems, however, that Sir Edward Bridges at the Treasury persuaded Cripps that such an obviously Labour nominee, so soon after nationalisation, would send all the wrong signals to the City about the Bank's operational autonomy. Cripps then went to the other extreme by sounding out John Hanbury-Williams, Chairman of Courtaulds and a director of the Bank since 1936. Hanbury-Williams took the offer seriously, discussed it with colleagues at the Bank, but then turned it down. By September 1948 Cobbold's candidature was unstoppable – though Dalton did warn Cripps that he was 'reactionary' and that 'we should be landed with him for 10 years'. To this Cripps responded, erroneously as it turned out, that

Cobbold 'wouldn't want to go on for more than 5 years' and would then succumb to the lure of his country house at Knebworth.[45] It is unclear whether George Bolton, four years older than Cobbold and made an executive director in 1948, was ever seriously considered. Since the early 1930s his high-level experience had matched Cobbold's, and he undoubtedly possessed far more vision. He would have been the bolder, perhaps better choice, though the Bank itself would have had mixed feelings. In Bolton's own mind, it was a major disappointment to be passed over.

In July 1949, four months after the revolution in the chairs (Dallas Bernard replaced Cobbold as Deputy Governor), Hall chewed the cud with Sir Edwin Plowden of the Treasury: 'P. denigrated the Bank and Cobbold, and apparently S.C. [Cripps] agreed that Cobbold was no good and said (a) he had only appointed him because he could not get anyone else, (b) he had turned out far worse than had been expected.'[46] Cameron ('Kim' to friends and colleagues) Fromanteel Cobbold was forty-five years old, the son of a lieutenant-colonel, and after Eton had left Oxford before taking his finals, on the grounds of boredom.[47] His first City mentor was the underwriting genius Cuthbert Heath; he then joined a firm of international accountants, making his name in the late 1920s by investigating why the British Italian Banking Corporation had failed; in 1930 he married Lady Hermione Bulwer-Lytton; and in 1933, on Norman's invitation, he joined the Bank. Over the rest of the decade he worked mainly on the overseas side, and Bolton recalled him as not only 'a staunch traditionalist' who 'faced the future as a complete and unrepentant pragmatist, determined to salvage as much of the past as he could', but as someone who 'brought balance into the Bank's external relations, preached the importance of improving relations with Paris, and also liked the Italians whom he regarded as a race of lovable children'.[48] His office was next to Norman's, with a connecting door, and from the time Cobbold became an executive director in 1938 he was generally seen as Norman's anointed.

Even then, middle-aged before his time, he possessed an innate presence, solidity and authority; while Governor, he allegedly played the part even while shaving in his pyjama trousers. The pen-picture by Fforde, the historian of Cobbold's Bank, perhaps best captures his style:

> He was a careful listener and a thoughtful reader. But he was not a lengthy debater. His meetings were inclined to be short and to the point. He was determined to maintain the authority of the Governor as the Chairman and Chief Executive of the Bank. He was certainly a commanding personality and was to exercise command in an almost military fashion for over twelve years. He was, however, sensitive to any questioning of the decisions that he was not slow to take but in which he may not always have

had complete self-confidence. Once he had firmly declared a point of view he had as often as not announced his decision, or at least the general shape of it. Persuading him to change his mind was not impossible but was not a task to be taken lightly.

Shortly after becoming Governor, Cobbold noted a talk he had had with Linlithgow about the quarterly meetings with the clearing bankers: 'I have a feeling that they are sometimes a little bare and I had in mind, without trying to launch a Debating Society, to say a word or two occasionally about things of particular interest at the time.'[49] The disclaimer was quintessential Cobbold, and goes a long way towards explaining why thoroughbred economists like Hall found him so exasperating. An empiricist to his fingertips, Cobbold's ultimate strength was that he had a sense of proportion and slept well at night. Few in the post-war City – still a profoundly non-intellectual place – would have wished for a different sort of Governor.

There were other, less momentous changes at the Bank on 1 March 1949. Leaving the Court were two less than popular left-wing directors, Robin Brook and George Wansbrough, both of whom had been appointed three years earlier at the time of nationalisation. From 1946 there was also on the Court a 'statutory' trade unionist, beginning with George Gibson. He, however, blotted his copybook and had to step down in late 1948, his berth going in March 1949 to Sir George Chester of the Boot and Shoe Operatives. Chester, unfortunately, died barely seven weeks later, and it took a while to find someone else. Altogether more resonant, in City terms, was the appointment of Michael Babington Smith, Deputy Chairman of Glyn Mills, to the Court in March 1949. He thereby became the first clearing banker – albeit not from one of the Big Five – to be a Bank of England director at the same time.[50] Little fuss, however, was made – itself a reflection of how, since the fundamental changes initiated between the wars, power in the Bank rested almost wholly with the full-timers. For all Cobbold's instinctive division of those permanently around him into gentlemen and players, he expected both classes to put in the hours.[51]

As it happened, Cobbold's accession coincided with the Bank agreeing to support the Stock Exchange's campaign to persuade the Treasury to permit a modified resumption of contangos, thereby allowing bargains to be carried over from one fortnightly account to the next. The background was sharply dwindling confidence in the Stock Exchange's future as a prosperous and liquid market. The daily average of bargains marked was only 6,179 during the second half of 1948, barely half what it had been during the first half of 1947. The young Patrick Sergeant, working for Mullens, the Government brokers, as an unauthorised clerk (a blue button), decided that the Stock Exchange had no future and went into financial journalism instead. In March 1949, in a 'Memorandum on Contangoes' sent to the Treasury via the Bank, the Stock Exchange made its pitch, in effect arguing that the provision of continuation facilities, from one fortnightly account to another, was indispensable to the functioning of 'a ready market place in which the public may exchange cash for securities and securities for cash'. The crux was the jobbing system, for so long 'a unique feature' of the London stock market:

> Its function is to render a service of great value both to buyers and sellers, by taking up the time lag which usually occurs between their appearance. For this purpose it is requisite to the jobbing system that financial accommodation in the shape of both stock and cash should be easily available. Such a condition only exists today in the gilt-edged market, which, for that reason, is still, even under prevailing conditions, a live and free market where the public needs can be satisfied . . .

Accordingly, 'it is now desired to re-introduce contangoes simply and solely in the interest of reviving and maintaining the freest and most efficient market possible'. The argument, however, ignored the extent to which an unnecessarily restrictive approach by the Stock Exchange authorities during recent years had encouraged the bypassing of the market, particularly by merchant banks and discount houses. Cobbold had a quiet word with Eady, who intimated that the Treasury was willing to bow to the Bank's wishes over 'a piece of Stock Exchange mechanics', with the proviso that the Bank was 'happy that an eye can be kept on any possible speculative dangers'.[52] Contangoes were duly re-introduced in May 1949, but as yet option dealing – following a clear negative steer from the Bank – remained outlawed.

Earlier that spring a special issue of the *Banker* had examined the problems facing the Stock Exchange. Much of the emphasis was on important technical matters – the reduction of settlement costs, the sharing of commissions, the thorny area of jobbers' capital – but there was also considerable stress on how the Stock Exchange must continue to build on its gradual inter-war evolution from more or less a private club into something resembling a national institution, with all the attendant responsibilities. Such an attitude was like a red rag to one leading broker, Graham Greenwell. 'Can there be a Free Market?' he asked in the following issue. Not unless, he claimed, the institution returned to its sturdy, laissez-faire roots. Asserting that government control was 'deaf to merchanting and to the free flowering of the human spirit of enterprise', arguing that a change of government would make little difference and predicting that unless the Stock Exchange ceased to be 'a national institution' it would 'find itself a department of the Public Trustee Office', he then went full tilt at what he saw as the corporatist fallacy:

Assuming that in the coming struggle, which may extend over many years, between the socialist-communist-Christian state and the Liberal free economy, the latter resumes its march of progress, interrupted so rudely by reactionary forces in 1914, the Stock Exchange will survive and prosper. But if it becomes an ally, as it looks like doing, of all the forces – whether labelled Conservative or Labour – which are at present triumphantly suppressing every vestige of individual liberty in human affairs under the resounding catchwords of prestige, national honour, full employment and dollar shortage, it will be the architect of its own ruin. The Stock Exchange must be a free market, and its Council must hold the ring in which its members, by daily struggles, permit the market to function of its own volition. The Council must guard its members from the public, not the reverse – for that is a work of supererogation they are not called upon to perform. They must support free trade in securities, and permit and improve every device for such trading, whether contangoes, options or dealings for the Account. They are not – any more than the Law Courts – a court of morals, and will stultify themselves if they try to become one.

Or, as another broker, Charles Branch, put it back in the 1870s, 'the Stock Exchange is a channel, not a filter' and 'it argues no fault in the construction of an aqueduct that the water it conveys is often dirty'.[53]

Over the next decade, and indeed beyond, Greenwell and like-minded members would continue to resist the completion of the Stock Exchange's journey away from being a private club; even the Council itself was not wholly enthusiastic. In April 1949 it considered a BBC request asking the Chairman to participate in a radio debate about the Exchange's future. Such a debate, the producer made clear, would include someone 'who will advocate for more or less complete elimination of the Stock Exchange as a virtually useless relic of private enterprise'. The Council voted not to participate. That summer, however, John Braithwaite, of the brokers Foster & Braithwaite, succeeded as Chairman and, although in his mid-sixties, turned the position into a full-time job. In polar opposition to Greenwell, he was determined that the Stock Exchange should attain the stature of a nationally accepted institution, beyond the scope of party political controversy. An admirable aim perhaps, but would it be compatible with Greenwell's free and vibrant market? Shortly before Braithwaite became Chairman, the brokers Henry Ansbacher & Co, very active in industrial finance, decided to evade the Stock Exchange's restrictions by leaving the institution altogether and operating from outside as a merchant bank. The firm's key figure was the naturalised George Ansley, just the sort of person whom a dynamic market should have kept on board.[54]

Ansbachers' defection was also a response to the larger drift of new issue business away from stockbrokers and towards the other issuing houses, in particular the merchant banks.[55] As the capital requirements of individual

British companies became ever greater, and their financial problems ever more complex, merchant banks at last systematically spotted the gap in the market and became the kingpins of domestic industrial finance. Accordingly, between 1946 and 1956 members of the Accepting Houses Committee were responsible for handling almost three-fifths of all the capital issues made by public companies. Almost certainly the 1948 Companies Act accelerated the process, for the stockbrokers lacked the resources to cope with the vastly enlarged, infinitely more demanding prospectuses, and the massive accompanying documentation, that the new legislation required. There was also the costly matter of employing teams of lawyers, accountants, and so on. Moreover, as issues became larger as well as more complex, most stockbroking firms lacked the capacity to make the necessary in-depth assessments of companies. Faced by all these considerations, as well as by the downbeat mood in the Stock Exchange, most company brokers from the late 1940s allowed merchant banks to resume their historic role as issuing houses (though now domestic) in the face of little serious competition. A few, such as Kit Hoare, felt strong enough to stand up to the merchant banks and, as far as they could, do issues without them, but most did not.

The ranks of those who tucked in behind the merchant banks' slipstream in an important but ultimately subordinate role – mainly in relation to pricing and underwriting – included Cazenove's, such a dominant issuing force in the 1930s. That stockbroking firm did, however, enjoy one last hurrah in August 1949. Lord Hambleden, the proprietor of W.H. Smith, had died the previous year, estate duty of up to £10m was payable and the only way out seemed to be an issue of ordinary shares. Smiths' financial advisers were Barings, but Sir Edward Reid and Evelyn Baring visited Cobbold at the start of the month to express their uncertainty about 'the wisdom or practicability of making an issue of Ordinary Shares at the present time'. Cobbold was inclined to share their doubts. The company therefore turned to Cazenove's, whose coming man, Antony Hornby, was the son of St John Hornby who had made Smiths into a great force. Something of a playboy before the war, but now more serious, he took up the challenge:

> The underwriting went well and the issue was a great success and the family got their money. I was exhausted and proud. No business would ever frighten me now. It was a terrific baptism. It did the firm's reputation and mine a great deal of good and I got letters and congratulations from all sides. Moreover we made about £40,000, the largest sum we'd ever made on an issue . . . It almost might have been preordained by fate.

Was there any embarrassment at 8 Bishopsgate? At the start of September Peacock told Cobbold that 'he was delighted that Smiths had been able to get the money but he was glad that Barings had not done it as he does not feel certain about the future prospects of the Stock'.[56]

The nervousness of Barings – and Cobbold – owed much to the shadow of devaluation that was hanging over the London market by the summer of 1949.[57] $4.03 to the pound, the rate agreed at the outbreak of the war, was looking ever less sustainable, not least as Britain's threadbare reserves began to suffer serious losses. At the Bank there was an instinctive, deep-seated concern that the politicians would choose devaluation as the soft option in preference to tougher choices more directly affecting the domestic economy, and thus the British electorate. Sir Otto Niemeyer, as usual, took a harder line than anybody. 'Jiggling about with devaluation of Dollar exchange will not help us,' asserted his stiffening note to Cobbold on 21 June, with an ominous reference to 'the damage it would ultimately do to us as a financial centre'; and he insisted that 'devaluation should certainly not be presented as an *alternative* to real measures to reduce costs'. Two days later Cobbold took precisely this line to the Treasury: any action 'in the monetary field' must be 'secondary and supplementary to a cut in Government expenditure', and 'unless it were preceded by such appropriate action, a change in the rate would not be effective and might prove gravely damaging to the future of sterling both as a domestic and as an international currency'.[58]

Over the next six weeks Cobbold's tune barely changed. To read his note of a conversation with Cripps on 5 July is to sense, in its Bankspeak, a certain timelessness, with echoes of 1931 and pre-echoes of sterling crises ahead:

> ... I went on to express concern about the present shape of his memorandum to the Cabinet. I reiterated the view that the main thing necessary to restore confidence was evidence of action about Government expenditure, and that devaluation was not a positive policy but rather a recognition of disagreeable facts ...
>
> Finally, I said once again that I thought financial opinion both here and overseas very much on edge and that, if they got the impression that things were not being taken in hand, there might be quick uncomfortable developments. Whilst I recognised the political difficulties, which were no concern of mine, I hoped that the Chancellor would do everything possible to show that HMG were taking a firm grip on the internal situation and were not merely relying on help from outside and the support to be derived from eventual devaluation.[59]

There was seemingly an umbilical relationship between cuts in government expenditure and the 'confidence' of sterling's holders, but Cobbold always resolutely refused to identify where those cuts should fall. The 'political difficulties', after all, were 'no concern' of his.

Nevertheless, he had keen political antennae, and although reiterating to Attlee in early August that 'devaluation by itself cannot be a remedy for the present difficulties', Cobbold was careful to add that 'it is no part of our submission that the present rate should be maintained at all costs by what may be termed a classic deflationary policy'. Not surprisingly, the ghosts of 1931 loomed large in the minds of Labour ministers that summer. 'Montagu Norman walks again,' Dalton (back in the Cabinet) exclaimed in his diary. At the end of July Attlee complained that he was, in Dalton's words, 'being served up from the Treasury and the Bank arguments which he thinks are fallacious on evil effects of our public expenditure'. As a result, during the three-month crisis, the government made a determined, broadly successful attempt to marginalise the Bank. Ministers may also have been influenced by the strong anti-Bank views of their economic adviser, Robert Hall. 'They have been against doing anything on exchange or interest rates and have been as negative as possible while all the time keeping a hedge out,' he noted in early July. ' "These measures won't help". "We may be forced to devalue". "We must consider interest rates" and so on. It is absolutely intolerable that there should not be a clear line on these things from the people who have the primary responsibility.'[60] Two allowances should be made: that Hall's own preferred option, that of floating the pound, was given short shrift by the Bank; and that he generally dealt with the Bank at a level below Cobbold, who does seem to have had a perfectly consistent line, though it was not one with which Hall agreed.

Ultimately, the government saw no alternative to devaluation, and Cobbold reluctantly concurred, while achieving little movement in terms of expenditure cuts. That failure, however, hardly surprised him, and indeed he anticipated it by insisting that if there was to be a devaluation, it should involve a change in parity that was sizeable and, hopefully, once and for all. On this the government eventually yielded, with Cripps and Bevin deciding, in Washington on 12 September, on $2.80. The City watched and waited, with the rumour mill active, but one veteran of the 1931 drama was having a deserved sabbatical from financial crises. 'Peacock is particularly well,' Villiers wrote that same day to a Los Angeles banker, 'and was relating at luncheon how he defeated some expert on the golf links yesterday.' Almost a week later, on the evening of Sunday the 18th, just before Cripps's broadcast to the nation, Cobbold spoke solemnly to an informal meeting of the Court. After observing that devaluation on its own could never be a solution, but rather a recognition of a state of affairs, and noting that government had 'felt unable to take more drastic action in their policy in other economic fields', he continued, 'The one essential thing – and this I repeat and underline – is that devaluation can be done once but can and must not even be in question a second time unless there have been major events such as a world war in the intervening period.'[61]

A momentous pronouncement, and the City was indeed in a shocked state next day, though as much because of the size of the devaluation as because of the fact itself. Even so, as gold shares boomed and equities improved in a busy street market (with the Stock Exchange itself closed for the day), the *FT* felt compelled to warn its readers on the Tuesday that 'until it becomes clear where this shot in the dark is leading us, official enthusiasm over the virtues of devaluation is a case of counting chickens before they are hatched'. A week later, as Parliament prepared to debate devaluation, the same paper outlined what it – and, by silent implication, the City – believed the underlying issue to be:

> What, in sober fact, can be done if the Government persists in the illusion that current levels of national expenditure are in no way responsible for the domestic inflation which has priced our goods out of certain critical overseas markets and forced a drastic currency devaluation? Unless this illusion can be dispelled, any improvement in our competitive position in the world economy must surely be transient. Another expedient will have been exhausted and we shall stagger on to another crisis . . .
>
> No one is suggesting that the apparatus of the Welfare State should be dismantled, nor is there any necessity for such action even at this critical juncture in our affairs. But there are many who believe that unless the apparatus is operated with much greater restraint and with a proper regard for our straitened circumstances, the foundations of the Welfare State will inevitably crumble and decay.

Aneurin Bevan, speaking in the Commons, naturally preferred to look elsewhere: 'We have asked the miners, the steel men and the railway men not to imitate the obscene plundering that went on on the Monday in Throgmorton Street.'[62]

*

'Came to the City for the first time in years,' Sydney Moseley wrote in his diary a week and a half after devaluation. 'What bitterness there is against the Labour Government!' The financial press continued to give that government a hard time. 'Building on Sand' was the title of the *Banker*'s editorial on devaluation, while in November it was scathing about the accompanying cuts in government expenditure of £280m: 'There has been no change of heart, no reconsideration of the characteristic policies which keep the economy gripped in the vice of excessive expenditure and correspondingly oppressive taxation, no weakening of the hold on merely party principles . . .' During much of the autumn there was also a sharp – at times even bitter – division of opinion between government and City over monetary policy and bank credit. Jay found Cobbold increasingly 'truculent', he told Dalton in October, and the following month Cripps wrote a letter to Cobbold, in effect accusing him of lacking resolve vis-à-vis the clearing banks when it came to determining 'the total volume of money' – a letter that the Treasury, after informally showing it to Cobbold, persuaded Cripps not to send.[63]

A few weeks later, on 15 December, Dalton ran into Sir Vaughan Berry, the former Union Discount man who had been co-founder in 1932 of the Labour-supporting XYZ Club. Berry reported a 'venomous' feeling in the City against the Labour government, and Dalton paraphrased what Berry had told him: 'He was abused violently for twenty minutes by a bank manager in a City shoe shop, where they were both trying to buy shoes. This man said, "Why do you come to the City? You have no friends here now. You went over to the other side." Berry hears that at the Bank of England "Labour is out" and the Board is just an Old Etonian Club.' Perhaps it was this encounter that prompted Dalton, in a speech at Devizes two days later, to lay into the City with singular ferocity. He argued that its conduct during the devaluation crisis had been both speculative and unpatriotic, referring darkly to 'very disgraceful goings-on on the Stock Exchange – deliberate attempts to talk down the national credit, making money out of rumours derogatory to the credit of this country'; and he warned that it might be necessary to take measures ensuring that 'vested interests' in the City were 'prevented from doing damage to the welfare of the country as a whole'.[64]

If, as is likely, this was little more than mischief-making on Dalton's part, he would have been gratified by the results. Meeting on the afternoon of the 19th, the Stock Exchange Council listened to a statement from a fired-up Braithwaite:

> The Chairman's Room felt that some action must be taken . . . He had called upon the Governor of the Bank that morning and had urged upon him strongly that the City ought not to let its case go by default, and that any action taken should be taken on behalf of the City as a whole rather than by sectional interests.
>
> The Chairman felt that his representations had not been unfavourably received . . .

The new Chairman perhaps overestimated his influence with the new Governor. Braithwaite had indeed been to see him in an attempt to mobilise the City, Cobbold's notes confirmed, but 'Linlithgow agrees generally with me that we should be wise to go pretty slow'. Even so, Cobbold did agree to call a meeting in the New Year of the City's main institutions and interest groups; and to them, on 6 January 1950, he took the line that it was best 'to regard these attacks as electioneering tactics and take the view that the City had more to lose than to gain by getting itself involved in argument on this question and would be wiser to go on quietly with its business'. He then asked for the meeting's views. Braithwaite wanted a deputation to Attlee, 'in order to lay the true facts before him', and in general 'laid stress on the importance of such personal contacts'. Linlithgow agreed, remarking that 'on reflection, he had come to the conclusion that some action should be taken'. And, although the Chairman of Lloyd's and the Deputy Chairman of the Committee of London Clearing Bankers lined up behind Cobbold, 'the consensus of opinion seemed generally to favour exploration of the possibilities of action'. It was agreed that the representatives would continue to discuss the matter themselves, and another meeting was called for the 11th. By then, however, the situation had fundamentally changed, for Attlee had called an election, for 23 February. Accordingly, on 11 January Cobbold categorically said that the City must wait for the formation of a new government before it sent a deputation. There was no dissent from the view that the City must not allow itself to be dragged into party politics, though Braithwaite reserved his right to repudiate any specific attacks made on the Stock Exchange during the election campaign. Herbert Morrison, speaking at Portsmouth five days before polling, duly obliged, charging the Stock Exchange with the crimes of 'irresponsibility and flippancy', and Braithwaite issued a suitably portentous public defence.[65]

For all Cobbold's preference for keeping out of the fray, there was no doubt where the City's political sympathies lay in February 1950. 'Which Way To-Day?' the *FT* asked. The answer was clear: 'One road leads towards increasing State control, increasing rigidity and a lower standard of living ... The other road leads to change, expansion, freedom and independence.' Among those voting to go down the latter road was Siegmund Warburg, in politics as in other things more independent-minded than most. The Tories lost, but only narrowly, and Villiers of Barings declared the election result 'really not at all unsatisfactory from a Right Wing point of view'. In this new, less threatening climate, the mooted City deputation to Attlee faded from the picture, with Cobbold and Linlithgow both agreeing that 'it was better to let things lie for the time being'.[66]

Anyway, as Braithwaite well knew, petitions to Downing Street were no answer to the Stock Exchange's underlying problems. Early in February the Council had received an important communication from a group of thirty younger members who had become 'increasingly alarmed at the future of the House'. The suggestions made by these Young Turks were many and various: a quarterly policy report by the Council to the members; publication of 'a technical journal' to discuss policy matters, and so on; the establishment of a public relations department; the review of the traditional ban on members advertising; the demand that no inexperienced members be admitted (though with no mention as such of exams); and the setting up by the Council of 'a special "Planning Committee" empowered to engage as much outside professional help as may be required', for 'only by the establishment of such an additional body can the Stock Exchange hope to keep pace with the present march of events and meet the problems with which it will be faced'. A challenging agenda, and it took the Council almost the rest of February to formulate its response – which was to state that it already had 'some of the matters' in hand and to ask 'that the Press should not be informed of their activities'.[67] With that, apparently, the memorialists were satisfied, as they waited to see what reforms the Council had in mind.

Precious few, as it turned out: that spring a compensation fund, protecting clients against members' malpractice, came into existence, but it had already been planned; and in May approval was given to the construction of a public gallery, almost three-quarters of a century after it had been recommended by the Royal Commission. On the public-relations front, no full-time official was appointed, but the Stock Exchange did decide to employ the advertising agency J. Walter Thompson in an advisory capacity at £5,000 a year. Crucially, however, no significant move was made towards putting the Stock Exchange on a more professional basis, in terms of either its membership or its management. Moreover, in the critical area of pulling the market out of its post-war doldrums and thereby attracting fresh talent and resources, Braithwaite was profoundly unwilling to alienate the goodwill of the government and the Bank. His memorandum in October 1950 on the revived question of restoring option dealings was symptomatic. He pointed out that although 'the Stock Exchange is not under statutory control of any kind', over the past thirty or forty years, as it had become increasingly 'a national institution', a system had developed whereby 'we keep the Bank informed of changes that we contemplate that would make any impact on public policy, and we receive their advice upon such changes, which is given usually after contact with the Treasury, and sometimes after the matter has gone to the Chancellor himself'. He went on:

> It is very strongly our opinion in the Chairman's Room, and I am sure it will be the opinion of the Council, that this informal control, if it is operated reasonably, as it has been hitherto, is infinitely to be preferred to formal or statutory controls. Models for statutory control are ready to the hand of anyone who wants to use them, both in New York and in Johannesburg. It should be a first matter of policy with us to avoid having such a control imposed upon us here.

In that light, Braithwaite counselled caution about a precipitate return to pre-war options. Not only were the authorities 'very much pre-occupied with the fear of increased inflation', but there was a new Chancellor (Hugh Gaitskell) not wanting 'to put a foot wrong'; in all, 'if we were to insist on pressing it now, we should probably get an adverse answer, which would make a later approach very much more difficult'. The following year did see a well-supported move among the members for a return to options, but with no backing from the Council it ran into the ground.[68]

Nothing, though, was more symptomatic of the Stock Exchange's malaise than the Council's negative attitude towards Julius Strauss. A very able German who as a young man had come to England in 1933 and joined Vickers da Costa, rapidly becoming manager of its foreign department, he was an integral part of Strauss, Turnbull & Co on its formation in 1938. His application for naturalisation was interrupted by the war, during which he served in the Intelligence Corps, and in 1946 he was eventually naturalised. In August 1950 the Council voted unanimously against admitting him to membership, apparently on the grounds that he had not been naturalised for long enough.[69] In other words, the Stock Exchange may have been bold enough, during the following year's Festival of Britain, to open the House to public scrutiny on Saturdays in July between ten and noon, but *au fond* it had become a deeply conservative, increasingly bureaucratic institution to which the winds of change outside as well as inside the City almost invariably represented a threat, rather than an opportunity.

Few, if any, of these strictures applied to Philip Hill, which was about to become an integral part of the City landscape. Still based in the West End, off St James's Street, it was starting to be widely recognised as a dynamic force in new issue finance, with Kenneth Keith to the fore. From early 1950 it became the aim, an internal memo recorded, 'to acquire some existing company or institution of good reputation in the City, which could be used as a means both for widening the basis of the company's business and also providing a means of entry into the City'. Significantly, the paper conceded that the alternative strategy – of Philip Hill 'setting up on its own in the City' – would not achieve its 'major objective' of taking its place 'amongst the leading financial institutions in London'. Why not? Presumably a mixture of inadequate resources and City prejudice, though unfortunately the paper did not elaborate.

So, Plan A it had to be, and that spring an approach was successfully made to Higginson & Co. That house had had a disastrous run in the late 1940s (a profit of only £656 in the year ending June 1949), but its City credentials were impeccable, helped by having such gentlemanly partners as Rudolph Edgar Francis de Trafford of Buttersteep House, Buttersteep Rise, Ascot, Berks; Pierre Joseph Augustin Lackland of The Mere, Merstham, Wilts; and Christopher Evelyn Blunt of Wilton House, Hungerford, Berks. 'Eventual aim combined firm' was the note made at Philip Hill of a conversation with de Trafford in March 1950; though in June, when Philip Hill's acquisition of Higginsons was announced, it was made clear that the two businesses would, for the time being at least, 'retain their separate identities'. Fairly soon it became obvious that it would be more efficient to operate from one building in the City, while as a Philip Hill memo put it in July 1951, a further advantage of amalgamation was that 'it should facilitate the acceptance of the Philip Hill name as a City house'. That October – shortly before the public announcement that, from the start of 1952, Philip Hill, Higginson & Co would be a single operating entity from its new City offices at 34 Moorgate – Lieutenant-Colonel the Hon George Akers-Douglas of Higginsons went to the Bank to explain matters to Cobbold. 'De Trafford will become Chairman,' noted Cobbold, 'and Higginsons are satisfied that the management will effectively remain in their hands . . . They are hoping that in due course it will become possible for them to come back into the acceptance business . . .' Cobbold responded cautiously, telling Akers-Douglas that 'if they were thinking of coming back into the acceptance business they would of course have to make some changes in the sort of policy on issue business previously followed by Philip Hill & Partners'. To which, Akers-Douglas 'agreed and mentioned that the one or two difficult situations into which P.H. had got themselves were now cleared up'.[70] It was, in short, only a muted blessing – but, for the purposes of Keith and his partners, adequate.

Cobbold's misgivings about Philip Hill were probably mild in comparison to his feelings about Denys Lowson, the unit-trust whizz-kid of the 1930s. In the mid-1940s, however, Lowson's career had almost foundered because of a murky affair involving the Texas Land & Mortgage Co, and it was only by a narrow squeak that the Lowson Group was admitted in 1945 to the Unit Trust Central Council. 'While he quite understood the general dislike of Lowson which the Board of Trade themselves shared,' Marker of the Board of Trade told Basil Catterns of the Bank of England, 'he himself was rather in favour of getting Lowson into the new Association if possible, rather than leaving him out, in view of the heavy representation of his Group in relation to the rest.' Four years later, in April 1949, Sir Robert Pearson, a former Chairman of the Stock Exchange, had a private word with Cobbold about this controversial figure, whom he described as 'a bit of a thruster'. Cobbold's reaction was judicious: 'I did not know anything concrete against Lowson and I thought that he was probably mellowing a bit, having by now "thrust" a good way. He was certainly active but I should personally still share Pearson's view about sitting on a Board with him.' That summer Cobbold was asked by the Lord Mayor to make discreet enquiries about how the City would view Lowson becoming the next Lord Mayor. Cobbold's response was 'that, in my judgement, informed inner circles in the City would regard the proposed appointment as highly damaging to the prestige of the Mansion House'.[71]

It proved only a short reprieve, for though Lowson agreed to stand down as a candidate for the 1949 election, he felt no such compunction a year later – and, in Cobbold's diary for 1950, there is no record of official disquiet. During the weeks immediately before the election of a new Lord Mayor on 29 October by 600 Liverymen, the *City Press* was full of praise and puff for Mr Alderman Denys Colquhoun Flowerdew Lowson, MA. He was just back from grouse shooting in Scotland, where he had been looking after his farming interests in Perthshire and Aberdeenshire; he was a member of the Royal Company of Archers; he stood at six feet four inches; he was pictured with his 'tall, beautiful and talented' aristocratic wife in their home at Brantridge Park, Balcombe in Sussex; and in all, he was a 'giant, vigorous personality whose crowded, successful career has followed no stereotyped course'. During his actual year of office, marked by the Festival of Britain, Lowson entertained three European queens and reputedly spent £20,000 out of his own pocket. A young man working for one of his companies was Edward du Cann (later to leave his employment in disgust), who recalled how during that golden year his chief 'never refused an invitation and the office buzzed with stories of his eating two dinners on several evenings'. Indeed, 'once, it was whispered, he ate three'. However, as the *City Press* had prophesied on the eve of these Falstaffian twelve months, 'one feels that he will inevitably remain ambitious'.[72]

ICFC's Lord Piercy, despite being denied the City's top job, also remained ambitious. During the latter part of 1950 he was engaged in one of his periodical guerrilla campaigns against his shareholders, the clearing banks, over the question of a further extension of his organisation's borrowing powers. Cobbold, at the start of 1951, had a classically gubernatorial, 'off-the-record word' with Linlithgow:

> I told him that I was satisfied that there was a clear moral obligation for the Banks to go up to £45 million. I was prepared to support B. of B. [Lord Balfour of Burleigh, Chairman of Lloyds] in any talk he might wish to have with Piercy to discourage Piercy from treading on other people's ground. I was also prepared to warn Piercy that the pit was not bottomless. I said that I had it in mind to have a word with B. of B. on these lines next week and then let things simmer whilst I was away. This would suit Linlithgow.

Balfour of Burleigh had succeeded Linlithgow as Chairman of the CLCB, and at their next meeting the clearers agreed to accept a moral obligation up to £45m, although Linlithgow insisted they should 'stand firm on that figure'.[73]

If anything, however, relations continued to deteriorate. Later in January 1951, John Kinross was asked to lunch by W.G. Edington, Chief General Manager of Midland. 'His purpose,' Kinross recalled, 'was to ask if I would be prepared to take over the Chairmanship of ICFC from Piercy, who was, he said, neither liked or trusted by himself and his colleagues.' That covert initiative came to nothing, but only a few weeks later Bernard at the Bank had Balfour of Burleigh sounding off to him: 'Balfour had taken note of a published interview with Piercy recently at which the latter said that in due course the ICFC will be bigger than the Banks. Balfour thought Piercy was aiming high and to get into the position of providing a great deal of the equity capital required.' Bernard added that his visitor 'did not err in the direction of being too complimentary'. The fullest exposition of the clearers' animosity came later that year, when Kinross lunched at National Provincial and was given an earful by its Chairman, Lord Selborne. He complained that ICFC was doing business outside the terms of the Macmillan gap, was taking on substantial sub-underwriting commitments, was 'touting for business' and was in general trying to supersede existing financial institutions, whereas its original rationale had been to function in situations where the support of those institutions was not 'readily or easily available'. Kinross replied by saying that if ICFC confined itself solely to discarded business, then 'it could only be a matter of time before we should have to close down and the Banks would lose their money'.[74]

In his diary note of their meeting, Kinross added that 'Selborne seemed to me to be a courteous and sincere man though perhaps with only limited imagination' – and, arguably, that was the fundamental problem.[75] ICFC, an organisation that was semi-missionary as well as semi-business, represented a disconcerting challenge to conventional ways of thinking – or not thinking – about industrial finance. Added to which, Piercy (quite apart from his latter-day socialist inclinations) had precisely the sort of agile, high-powered, not entirely scrupulous mind that was anathema to stolid clearing bankers. It was, from the national point of view, an extraordinarily unhelpful relationship, and if the fault lay largely with the clearers, it was a pity that Piercy was not a more straightforward operator.

All this time the vexed matter of sterling and its future was never far from more thoughtful minds. Significantly, the European Payments Union eventually came to fruition in 1950, with little thanks to the Bank of England, whose attitude during the protracted negotiations was almost uniformly suspicious and negative.[76] 'The special position of sterling has virtually disappeared,' Bolton complained in June 1950 about the emerging European dispensation; while in the apt words of Fforde, looking back on the late 1940s when the negotiations began, 'it no doubt required a considerable effort of mental adjustment in London, the centre of the sterling world, to accept that the tune should at this time be called by a minor power like Belgium'. In the City, as in British politics at large, there was an almost automatic assumption during these post-war years that questions of Empire and sterling area had a higher importance and priority than those of Europe. Typically, one of the few who questioned that assumption was Siegmund Warburg. 'After the Second World War,' he recalled some thirty years later, 'I said to everyone – I even put it in writing – that we have become a debtor nation instead of a creditor nation, and a reserve currency status doesn't make sense for a debtor country. It's a very expensive luxury for us to have.' Had the Bank of England appreciated that viewpoint? 'No, the Governor of the Bank of England at the time didn't like this statement at all, it was against the general view.'[77]

Against this background – the assumption that sterling and the sterling area represented Britain's financial ticket to the world's top table – the City met the outbreak of the Korean War in summer 1950. The Labour government's response until January 1951 was hugely to increase the country's rearmament programme, a policy whose economic wisdom the City never seems to have challenged, to judge by the compliant tone of the *FT*. Not only were there very adverse affects on domestic investment and consumption, but international confidence in sterling began yet again to erode. During the first nine months of 1951 various ideas flew around the Bank and elsewhere – of further revaluing the sterling-dollar exchange rate, of floating the pound – but for the moment the general preference, on the whole shared by a politically enfeebled government, was to avoid drastic action.[78]

Hugh Gaitskell had become Chancellor in October 1950, and during his year in that office, under the economic shadow of the Korean War, he came under considerable pressure from the Bank to strengthen sterling and check inflation by sanctioning an increase – albeit modest – in Bank rate.[79] This pressure came in two main phases, with the first occurring around the turn of the year. 'I stressed,' Cobbold noted, after his meeting with Gaitskell on 2 January 1951, 'that the Bank would be taking great responsibilities in not raising Bank Rate (which was still the warning signal best understood by the financial and commercial community) at a time when they felt a dangerous situation was threatening.' In this, as in earlier meetings, Gaitskell gave no ground, and on the 17th formally wrote to Cobbold rejecting such a rise: 'Our discussions showed . . . that the main – indeed almost the only – argument for the change in Bank Rate was the psychological effect . . . In this you may be right; but I cannot feel sure myself how lasting this effect could be.' Instead, Gaitskell pushed – as Cripps had done in the late 1940s – for a greater degree of co-operation within the banking system in restricting the increase in advances. 'We shall take further opportunities of reminding them of the importance which we attach to this policy,' ran Cobbold's bland, minimalist reply two days later. For the moment that sufficed, but over the past few weeks Gaitskell (the arch-Wykehamist among post-war politicians) had been ever less impressed by the men from the east. 'I must say,' he wrote about

Cobbold in his diary on 10 January, 'that I have a very poor opinion not only of him – he is simply not a very intelligent man – but of also most of the people in the Bank. Whether they are right or not in matters of judgment, they are singularly bad at putting their case, and judging by experience they are usually wrong in their conclusions.'[80]

By late May 1951 the Bank was preparing to return to the attack, and Mynors wrote a memo on how to make an effective case for 'Dearer Money'. There were, he believed, two basic difficulties: first, 'the sentimental (in a sincere sense) argument that "dear money" is associated with unemployment'; and, second, 'the political argument that "dearer money" is a confession of the failure of the planned economy'. In general, he added in a sentence symptomatic of the Bank's deep distaste for anything that smacked of theoretical abstractions, 'we are dealing with people of no experience who see things on a fanciful plane and will not accept a judgment based on experience without seeing what it looks like on that plane'. But however it was put to him, Gaitskell declined over the next few weeks to accept the case for dearer money. 'The B/E still want to put up the Bank Rate,' Hall noted on 27 June, 'but the C. has refused and wants them to get the banks to go in for selective credit restriction.' On 3 July, in a meeting at which the atmosphere was palpably uncomfortable, Cobbold tried again. As usual Gaitskell refused, whereupon (in Cobbold's words):

> I replied that on the political side he must be the judge and I was not disposed to argue. On merits it was a question of judgment. I had a definite view which was in disagreement with his. His arguments might be right politically and I was not competent to argue the case on economic doctrine but I was pretty certain that from a financial and practical angle I was right.
>
> We agreed therefore to differ and let the matter stand as it is until the Autumn.

At this point Gaitskell said 'that he was nevertheless anxious to see some more tightening up of credit', that indeed he 'would like to have a talk to the Clearing Bank Chairmen some time', and Cobbold agreed to arrange this for late September.[81]

This was, potentially, a highly charged development, not least in terms of the Bank's own authority within the City. Almost immediately after Gaitskell had made that request, Cobbold set down his thoughts:

> I think we may be approaching another period of difficulty in relations between City and Whitehall. I believe in the voluntary system by which our banking arrangements are run and I believe that once we get into direct Government interference in the credit system we run into very deep waters. The DG [Deputy Governor] and I have fought for maintenance of the voluntary system and shall continue to fight for it because we believe it to be in national interest. But this means that we must be in a position to put our

hand on our heart and say that the voluntary credit restriction can be effective even when it makes shoes pinch and in spite of difficulties of competition between banks and of relations with customers.

On the same page as that undated memo there was a scribbled addendum by Cobbold, dated 5 July:

> I spoke to Clearing Banks Committee on above lines, with the last part firmed up a bit. DG present.
>
> They said that main inflationary influence lay outside their control (i.e. Govt.) but assured me of their co-operation & promised to have another go at it.

It was, from Cobbold's point of view, a reassuring acceptance by the clearers of the Bank's role as the indispensable intermediary. Moreover, because of the political situation, Gaitskell never had his meeting with the clearers, and the danger passed. As for the larger question of monetary policy, in particular what Fforde neatly calls 'direct credit control v. the interest-rate weapon', that had ended in an attritional, unrewarding stalemate.[82]

Lack of harmony in the policy-making sphere reflected the continuing gulf between Labour and the City. The latter's gut instincts were by now finding expression in the person of Harold Wincott, who had made his journalistic reputation as 'Candidus' in the *Investors Chronicle*, before beginning a Tuesday column in the *FT* in July 1950. 'Rediscovering Capitalism' could not have been a more appropriate title for the first column; over the years the single strongest theme in his writings – attracting a devoted following – was the virtue, moral as well as economic, of popular, free-market capitalism. He was also an old-fashioned, sound-money man, and had little truck with the more paternalist Tories. 'If a British electorate wants the Santa Claus State,' he declared in December 1950, 'it will vote Socialist, anyway, because it knows instinctively the Socialists will always beat the Tories at that game. The Conservatives' forte, trite enough though the observation is, is conserving. The Great British Public could do with some conserving – of the purchasing power of its money – right now.' Sometimes Wincott's anti-socialist rhetoric went over the top, as it did in a column about Gaitskell in August 1951 headed 'Herr Finanzminister'. The occasion for the attack was a recent speech by Gaitskell supporting a policy of dividend limitation – a speech that had, Dalton publicly observed with his usual tact, 'thrown the Stock Exchange into complete disorder and that is always good fun'. There followed the by now customary rebuke from Braithwaite, while Lionel Fraser of Helbert Wagg wrote to *The Times* calling for the City to become much more systematic about persuading public opinion of its value to the country. 'I pleaded, I made speeches all over the country to chambers of commerce and other small societies and groups,' he remembered. 'But nothing of a concrete nature emerged. The City did not see the point of co-operation for such a purpose. There was practically no response. Perhaps they were right, perhaps it was a tribute to an independent, competitive spirit.'[83]

The City, anyway, rightly suspected that the sands of time were running out for Labour. Within a few weeks of Dalton's final provocation, a general election was called for 25 October. 'The market reation,' noted the stockbrokers Read, Hurst-Brown & Co, 'was one of immediate relief at the prospect of the end of the Socialist discrimination against the investor and the still-birth of dividend limitation.' Three days before polling day, while the Stock Exchange Council was failing to come to a decision over the momentous question of whether the waiters should revert to the pre-war practice of wearing top hats, the Bank of England's Chief Cashier, Kenneth Peppiatt, wrote to 'Gus' Ellen, formerly of Union Discount, asking him to call at the Bank on the 24th. 'Perhaps I should add that I do not wish the fact you are coming to see me to be known to your old friends at the UD!' With the imminent prospect of a Conservative government, Cobbold had every hope of something like a return to what he regarded as proper monetary policy, and Ellen's guidance was required in relation to the very rusty mechanism for Bank-rate changes. On the night of the 25th and the day after, the *FT* sponsored a large election results board near the Royal Exchange, and crowds of City workers thronged the street to cheer Churchill home.[84] The six-year nightmare was over.

CHAPTER THREE

20 m.p.h.

The stockbrokers S.C. Maguire & Son, despatching the regular *Monthly Financial Report* shortly after the Conservative return to power, took an unashamedly global perspective. 'Considerable importance should be attached to the psychological result of the Socialist defeat,' they proclaimed, 'to the substantial recovery of confidence in Britain which will spread all over the world, and to the lifting of frustration and defeatism at home. We shall regain confidence in ourselves and we shall be welcomed back to play what part we can in world leadership.' Nevertheless, it would not all be plain sailing, for 'ever since 1940 we have been out on a spending spree' and consequently 'seldom has any new administration inherited so appalling a legacy'. The new Chancellor was 'Rab' Butler – to the disappointment of the City, which had hoped for its own man, the more right-wing Oliver Lyttelton – and on his desk he found an ominous scare letter from Cobbold, written three days before the election and calling for urgent expenditure cuts, as well as a tougher monetary and credit policy. However, he was careful to delineate the lines of responsibility and thus of blame:

> Assessment of the political practicability or expediency of particular lines of policy is no part of the Bank's function. The Bank consider it their duty to set out for submission to His Majesty's Government, on the formation of a new Administration, the very serious view which they take of the situation and the general lines of action which, without regard to political considerations, they judge necessary to protect the currency.[1]

As usual, the Bank and the City saw the protection of sterling as the government's highest duty; as usual, the government had to gauge the broader picture. Cobbold's battle through the 1950s would be to keep a succession of Tory Prime Ministers and finance ministers on-message.

Things began well enough, with Butler fully accepting the need to break with Labour and resurrect Bank rate as an integral part of peacetime economic policy-making.[2] On 7 November 1951 the rate rose, from 2 to 2½ per cent, and the City expressed little disquiet. By February 1952, with the balance-of-payments as well as the sterling position seemingly deteriorating quite quickly, Cobbold was pushing hard for a more substantial rise, to 4 per cent. Again, on 11 March, Butler obliged. 'This sharp rise,' he recalled, 'was announced in the Budget – an unusual course which left the country, and the foreigner, in no doubt that I was prepared to make a thoroughgoing use of monetary as well as fiscal policy in controlling the economy.' The next day Cobbold sent him a perhaps unduly sanguine assessment of the City's reaction: 'Budget in general very well taken and decisions welcomed by Banks and Stock Exchange in spite of immediate discomforts from Bank Rate. A lot of sore heads and a good deal of uncertainty about prices.' The sorest heads belonged to the discount market, where back in November the Bank of England's broker (or Special Buyer), Lawrence Seccombe, had persuaded it to play its part in the so-called 'forced funding' operation. This had involved the take-up, under considerable moral pressure, of a mass of newly issued serial funding bonds; unfortunately the sharp rise four months later led directly to substantial capital losses for all holders, including Seccombe's own firm. In terms of economic policy as a whole, there was no vast City enthusiasm for the dawning age of a 'Butskellite' consensus. 'The City is in low spirits at the moment,' John Phillimore of Barings informed a Washington correspondent in May. 'The bright hopes that we had entertained about our Conservative Government have now largely evaporated. They do not seem to have the courage of their convictions.'[3]

It is doubtful whether Phillimore was one of the relatively few in the City in the know about 'Robot' – a highly secret, potentially momentous episode, which for many years would be only whispered about, often inaccurately.[4] It was a plan that took its memorable name from the three officials Sir Leslie **Ro**wan (Treasury), Sir George **Bol**ton (Bank of England), '**Ot**to' Clarke (Treasury) most closely associated with its formulation during the winter of 1951–2. In essence 'Operation Robot' involved simultaneously making sterling convertible and floating the pound. Bolton, in his key memo of 16 February, made his pitch in typically bold terms, arguing that a fundamental choice existed 'between allowing sterling to become a domestic currency involving the collapse of the international sterling system and the sterling area, or accepting convertibility of non-resident sterling, thus retaining sterling as an international currency'. Given that choice, he proposed that 'the present policy of partial convertibility and partial inconvertibility should be replaced forthwith by a policy of comprehensive convertibility of all sterling in international use through the machinery of the exchange markets'.[5] He did not, however, discuss the domestic implications (inevitably deflationary) of such a policy.

Nevertheless, it seemed briefly that Robot had the political legs. 'C of E sold, PM interested and great hopes favourable decision,' Bolton buoyantly noted on the 20th, after hearing Cobbold's report on his dinner the previous evening with Churchill and Butler. Soon afterwards, on the 22nd, Churchill received a Bank deputation, headed by Cobbold, formally advocating the plan. According to Donald MacDougall, economic adviser to Lord Cherwell, the Paymaster General, Churchill subsequently 'reported that they were a fine, patriotic body of men, anxious to do what was right for the country'. Cherwell himself – who was in effect Churchill's personal economic adviser and had a distinctly low regard for the Bank – now took the lead in opposing Robot. 'The view of the Bank,' he wrote disparagingly to Butler on the 25th, 'is that there is now such a drain on the reserves that they cannot be held on present policies, and that measures of the kind now proposed are inevitable. I have seen no evidence for this.' Three days later, with Butler pushing as hard as his temperament allowed in favour of Robot, there took place the decisive discussion between Churchill, his Chancellor and Sir Anthony Eden, his Foreign Secretary. After an hour Cobbold joined them, and (he noted fairly soon afterwards) 'it was plain that nervousness was developing'. At this stage that nervousness seems to have come less from Churchill – who, despite memories of 1925, 'felt in his bones' (in Butler's words) 'that it was right to free the pound' – but rather from Eden. Many years later Cobbold reflected that the crux had been his 'intervention to the effect that Robot would mess up what he had been doing in Europe', which swung Churchill away from the plan. The next day Cobbold talked matters over with Butler, and they decided to try again after the budget. By now Bolton was thoroughly gloomy. 'Cabinet ... completely divided,' he noted on the 29th. 'Eden principal opposition. Looks as though failure.'[6]

Cherwell, for one, did not see the danger as being over. On 18 March, a week after the budget, he sent Churchill a brilliantly crafted remonstrance:

> I have been rather anxious about your remark last week that you looked forward to the day when we could 'free the pound' which the Cabinet decided against a fortnight ago ...
>
> Our fundamental problem is that the Sterling Area is spending more than it is earning. We have to put that right by exporting more and importing less. No monetary tricks can overcome this hard fact. Indeed I remain convinced that the Bank's plan would make our problem much more difficult, and might well have disastrous effects on the next few months.
>
> It is at first sight an attractive idea to go back to the good old days before 1914 when the pound was convertible and strong and we never had dollar crises. No doubt the bankers honestly believe that, if only the pound could be left to market forces, with the Bank of England free to intervene when necessary by varying the Bank Rate at their discretion, all would be well. The country's economy, they think, would be taken out of the hands of politicians and planners and handed over to financiers and bankers who alone understand these things ...

Cherwell argued that the consequences, however, were likely to be 'an 8%

Bank Rate, 2 million unemployed and a 3/- loaf'. He then wound up with a peroration that played on Churchill's most sensitive spot:

> Sterling, I repeat, cannot be made strong by financial manipulation. It is the real things that count – more steel mills in Britain, more ship loads of British manufactures crossing the Atlantic, more Australian farmers growing wheat and meat for England, more cotton plantations in the Colonies. That is the way to make sterling strong. It is a hard way and it will take time. But it is the only way. I trust we shall not allow ourselves to be persuaded that there is a painless, magical way – by leaving it all to the Bank of England.

It was an important shifting of the agenda, and Cobbold implicitly acknowledged as much in a memo to the Treasury shortly afterwards, when from his broadly pro-Robot stance he asserted that 'we are moving towards losing control of the value of our currency, which would involve hunger, mass unemployment, break-up of the existing sterling system and loss of the economic strength on which our political position must be founded'.[7] Arguably a more politically adept central bank – especially a nationalised central bank – would have protected those flanks rather earlier.

Robot came round for the final time during the early part of the summer. Although accepting that 'overseas confidence in sterling is better than pre-Budget', Cobbold insisted to Butler on 6 May that 'the crust is thin'. Above all, he called for political clarity:

> At the moment no definite decision has been taken between convertibility as a real and early objective (which must mean a tight credit policy internationally as well as domestically) and the opposite objective of building up areas of 'soft' trade on a structure of credit and inconvertibility. Arguments can be adduced for either horse, but no argument can favour riding both horses at the same time or alternating between one and the other.

He wrote again the following month, but by the end of June, following an unambiguous Cabinet negative, Robot was dead. 'The episode has been very unpleasant,' noted Hall (an influential opponent of the plan) at the start of July. 'The Bank has done its best to cause a run on sterling by telling everyone that we would be ruined unless we did Robot.'[8]

Perhaps it was a plan doomed not to happen. There was about it an element of a panic reaction, to an extent based on misleading figures, for in fact the trend in sterling reserves was reasonably well under control. Moreover, the plan's assumption that moving to a floating rate would automatically benefit sterling as a reserve currency was in itself questionable. Ultimately, its advocates failed to build a consensus around the plan, with divisions in government, the Treasury and even the Bank (where Maurice Allen, the economic adviser, was opposed). In Cabinet, a significant dissenter was that rising force, Harold Macmillan, who in June circulated a paper attacking Robot as nothing less than an old-fashioned 'Bankers' Ramp'.[9]

Did the burial of Robot matter? Butler came to believe that fundamentally it did, arguing that 'the absence of a floating exchange rate robbed successive Chancellors of an external regulator for the balance of payments corresponding to the internal regulator provided principally by Bank rate'. Samuel Brittan, perhaps the most perceptive commentator on post-war British monetary policy, has agreed, speculating in the early 1990s that 'a floating and convertible pound in the 1950s might have brought forward by two or three decades the dash for economic freedom without the need for the passions of the Thatcher era'. In any case, although Robot itself may have been declared dead and buried in June 1952, it left a significant shaping legacy for the rest of that decade, as it became clear by the end of the summer that the government was committed to achieving the convertibility of sterling in the medium term, even if not immediately. This would be achieved through what became known as 'the Collective Approach', involving American help and European co-operation. The failure of Robot reflected the political impossibility of attempting to turn the clock back to a pre-Keynesian paradise; equally, the lack of significant opposition to the *goal* of achieving full sterling convertibility, and thus underpinning sterling as a reserve currency, indicated the limits of Keynesianism. Macmillan may have tried to persuade himself that national and international priorities were compatible, and indeed interdependent – 'Our economic survival in the next year or two will largely depend upon world confidence in sterling,' he privately reflected in the course of 1952 – but even for that instinctively Keynesian prestidigitator the reality would prove uncomfortably different.[10]

*

In the day-to-day world, away from high policy, the City gradually returned to something approximating normality. Even under Labour, early in 1951, the cocoa and tea markets had reopened, while that December the new Conservative government reopened the foreign exchange market. By the end of 1953 most of the remaining commodity markets had reopened, followed in March 1954 by the gold market. On the Stock Exchange the mood of confidence became such that, despite continuing restrictions on new issues, the FT 30-Share Index rose from 103 in June 1952 to 224 by July 1955. Overall, the City's contribution to Britain's invisible earnings almost tripled between 1946 and 1956, up from £49m to £145m.[11] A success story, of a phoenix rising from the ashes, was in the making.

Nevertheless, the City was only *starting* to recover as an international financial centre.[12] Exchange control was still in place; sterling was less than robust and prone to sudden collapses of international confidence; and London's historical role as an exporter of capital barely functioned. There were other troubling trends. The City's post-war recovery as a trading centre was at best patchy and temporary; the futures markets in commodities were starting to be outstripped by international rivals, especially the markets in New York and Chicago; foreign exchange dealing, pending the full convertibility of sterling, stagnated for most of the decade; and insurance, always a key sector in terms of the City's earnings, was in relative decline internationally.[13] Nor was the City of the 1950s, if looked at more anthropologically, permeated by that 'independent, competitive spirit' that Lionel Fraser fondly imagined as he sought to defend its reputation before the bar of public opinion. Instead, it was still on the whole run by elderly men of 'Establishment' background, along very conservative, clubbish and only intermittently competitive lines. There was the odd sign of change, but the pace was even more sluggish than in British society at large.

Take the merchant banks and a couple of richly suggestive snippets. In 1951, when Frank Perkins, a Peterborough-based manufacturer of diesel engines, had to decide between Barings and Morgan Grenfell as his issuing house, he chose Barings on the no doubt sensible grounds that it had fewer peers as directors. And four years later, in December 1955, Lord Ashburton of Barings informed Mynors at the Bank that Howard Millis would be retiring at the end of the year, and that 'the sort of work he has been doing will fall largely to Carnwath, who is young but very highly thought of'.[14] A necessary reassurance, for Andrew Carnwath had recently celebrated his forty-sixth birthday.

In most merchant banks, certainly the more traditional ones, the convention remained for the senior partner (or chairman) to stay at the helm for as long as humanly possible. Lord Kindersley of Lazards was in his eighties by the time he retired in 1953, to be succeeded by his oldest surviving son; at Morgan Grenfell, Lord Bicester stayed firmly *in situ* until his death at the age of eighty-nine. Family control remained the norm, even though most merchant banks had by now become limited companies. In a world of increased personal taxation and death duties, this was not always easy. Rothschilds, so troubled during the war, continued to have a difficult time financially for several years afterwards, while at the start of 1952 Cobbold received an anxious visit from W.E. and W.A. Brandt of the City's fourth-oldest merchant bank, Wm Brandt's, Sons & Co: 'They have concluded pretty definitely against amalgamation as they do not want to risk losing the name and the family control.' They needed, however, to raise £0.25m from 'an institutional lender', and Cobbold's advice was 'to put themselves in the hands of somebody like Sir Edward

Peacock rather than go round looking for it themselves'. That veteran Canadian may have been outstaying his welcome at Barings, from where he would eventually retire in 1954; but for Cobbold, with many other things on his mind, Peacock was a valuable aid in helping to smooth out problems among the merchant bankers. 'He was doing some umpiring,' the Governor noted after a visit from Peacock in June 1952, 'in some trouble between Helmut Schroder and Henry Tiarks, both on the settlement of past affairs and on the future management of J. Henry Schroder.' Nothing epitomised more the clubbish, undemanding way in which the leading merchant banks did most of their everyday business than the system that emerged in the 1950s for the syndication of credits for leading British companies, as David Forsyth of Schroders recalled:

> The routine was that you went to the head of the Discount Office at the Bank of England and said 'we have been commissioned to form a credit syndicate and we are thinking of asking so-and-so to join us'. In effect you were saying 'do you approve and have you any other names you'd like to chip in?' Once or twice the Bank of England said 'Oh, do ask so-and-so to come in, they don't seem to have had much business for some time'. Then a partner picked up his bowler hat and went round to see the other firm and said 'would you be kind enough to help us out with this syndicate?' There was never any great discussion . . . It took less than five minutes and to get there you'd walked half-way across the City. Bowler hats and all . . .[15]

There were, nonetheless, some merchant bankers with a bit of zip off the pitch, not only at Warburgs and Philip Hill. To mention but three, Mark Turner at Bensons was a particularly able corporate financier, Alan Russell at Helbert Wagg anticipated the rise of the pension funds and pioneered the tailoring of investment management to their needs, and 'Boy' Hart of Ansbachers was ahead of the game in various ways, including documentary credit business. Nor should one assess individual merchant banks too monolithically. Shortly after the 1948 Companies Act came into force, compelling the publication of consolidated accounts and thus making it possible to discover what companies were actually earning, the stockbroker Gerald Ashfield and his senior partner Ralph Vickers went round to Morgan Grenfell in order to point out that some companies were on earnings yields that made them very cheap securities. They talked first to Bicester (his tie as ever worn through a wedding ring), but got precisely nowhere, before encountering a more positive response from Morgan Grenfell's main investment man, Willie Hill-Wood. Yet overall, despite exceptions, there prevailed in the merchant banking parlours a pervasive atmosphere of stagnation, complacency and even indolence. 'One of the dominant attitudes in the City is tolerance towards mediocrity,' Siegmund Warburg noted bitterly in 1956, and he was right. Or as another outsider, an American banker who in the 1950s served a

London apprenticeship at Morgan Grenfell, remembered wryly rather than affectionately: 'By Thursday afternoon at four, one of the senior partners would come across to the juniors and say, "Why are we all still here? It's almost the weekend." '[16]

The work ethic was more pronounced at the clearing banks, but there was little excitement in the air.[17] 'It was like driving a powerful car at twenty miles an hour,' Oliver Franks recalled about his eight years as Chairman of Lloyds Bank. 'The banks were anaesthetised – it was a kind of dream life.' It was a life little to the taste of this distinguished former academic, civil servant and diplomat, who had been on the board for only a year before he assumed the chairmanship in 1954. Soon afterwards he remarked that his task at Lloyds was like 'dragging a sleeping elephant to its feet with your own two hands' – a task that proved too much for Franks.[18] Nor were there many signs of life from Midland, which was in tangible decline for most of the decade after Sadd's unhappy departure.[19] Harlech, who succeeded Linlithgow as Chairman in 1952, was a weak leader; the board was elderly, with communications between board and management ineffective; and the instincts of the dominant post-Sadd manager, W.G. Edington, were deeply conservative. Yet arguably they could hardly have been otherwise, granted not only the inhibiting macro-economic and monetary environment during much of this period (characterised by balance-of-payments crises, 'stop-go' economic policies, and almost permanent credit restriction), but also the informal cartel arrangements under which British commercial banking operated. The prevailing economic and monetary climate, the wishes of the Bank of England and a natural desire for a quiet life all contributed to the banks' willingness to go along with such a cartel. Typical was the attitude of A.H. Ensor, Joint Chief General Manager of Lloyds Bank, who in 1953 stressed to his managers that there should be no thought of attempting to establish 'conditions of intensive competition' by cutting interest or commission rates – competition which, he was adamant, would be inimical not just to the banks, but also to the public.[20] It was hardly a valid case, especially in the light of empirical investigation of the banks' extraordinarily rigid and conservative lending policies, which indicates that there was a significant bias against small and medium-sized firms, the very sector upon which British economic growth mainly depended. The contrast with post-war Germany – with its proactive banking system and powerful *Mittelstand* – was sharp and lamentable.

At least London's discount market could not suffer from international comparisons, for that particular mechanism and way of life were unique to the City. To an extent, but only to an extent, the revival of monetary policy under the Tories did see some vitality return to the money market after its long period in the doldrums. In November 1951, shortly after

Butler's first Bank-rate rise, Peppiatt of the Bank saw Trinder 'for a long and *completely* off the record talk about the new arrangement'. He was able subsequently to assure Cobbold that 'the Banks may be more difficult to educate than the Discount Market, but I feel confident that Trinder, once he knows the form, will succeed in putting life into the Market'. Cobbold himself was about to see Trinder, and Peppiatt wanted him to make it clear that the discount market 'would be very unwise, if only in their own interests, to allow the rates to become rigid again', and 'that any fixed arrangement for selling Bills to the Clearing Banks would also be undesirable'.[21]

For the rest of the 1950s there was a new edge to the discount market, nicely caught by Richard Sayers soon afterwards in his history of Gilletts:

> It became very important indeed to secure understandings with the Clearing Banks about how much money they would allow to run on at steady rates. It became essential to tap every possible source of day-to-day money. It became important to be highly sensitive in anticipating the development of shortage or glut of funds in the market. The element of routine quickly declined and the scope for true business enterprise – the nice balance between adventure and caution – as quickly broadened. A firm that was always being caught and forced to borrow on penal terms at the Bank of England would soon feel a hole opening in its pocket; equally, a firm always so cautious that it never had to go to the Bank would have missed many opportunities for a quick turn or the cementation of good relations with a rewarding customer . . .

There were those, however, who doubted what larger purpose the discount market served. From the perspective of the late 1960s, W.M. Scammell in his authoritative study of the market was scathing about the costive, over-protected discount houses of the 1950s, declaring that they were in the ignominious 'position of ageing retainers in a somewhat decrepid household, for whom work is being found because no-one wishes brutally to dispense with their services'.[22] Against that, it was arguable that, in an era prior to inter-bank lending becoming the norm, the discount houses did provide an essential element of liquidity and lubrication in the financial system, being in effect the only place from which banks could get short-term money.[23]

Either way, the discount market of the 1950s remained in essence a hard-drinking, old-fashioned, congenial gentlemen's club, although tolerant of other ranks if they were good company. Union Discount had the greatest clout of the dozen or so houses that comprised the London Discount Market Association (LDMA), but perhaps the most prestige was attached to Smith, St Aubyn & Co. Its Chairman was Duncan Mackinnon, a keen race-goer whose broker Angus was Chairman of Brown Shipley; its assorted Smiths (including Oliver Martin Smith,

Major Dennis Smith and Jeremy Smith) provided further personal links with the merchant banks; and it had, reputedly, the best lunch room in the City.[24] Unfortunately, it and the other houses were caught napping – presumably after a long lunch – by the rise of the so-called 'parallel' money markets, beginning in 1955 with the local authority loans market.[25] The differences between these markets and the traditional discount market were stark: telephonic dealing, as opposed to business being done on the basis of personal visits; loans made on an unsecured basis; and no kindly supervision from the Bank of England, ultimate lender of last resort to the discount houses. Such business was not, in short, their thing.

The willingness of the discount market, and above all of Trinder, to fall in with the sometimes inconvenient requirements of monetary policy was an integral part of the Bank's authority over the City.[26] 'He was a "Market Man" in the full sense of the word' was the tribute to Trinder paid by Hilton Clarke, principal of the Discount Office from 1953. 'That was his great contribution to us in the Bank; he carried out the responsibilities that had been assumed by the Discount market of making a market in short-dated securities, which we wanted.' Or as Trinder himself, with a classic Trinderism, congenially observed when the Bank rate changed: 'Well, Clarke, we shall have to have a *penser* and a *regarder*.' Without such personal interaction it would not have been possible, for better or worse, for Cobbold to inform Butler in September 1953 that the commercial bill rate was currently being 'held purely by "moral suasion"'. As for Clarke himself, his obituary captured some of the salient qualities of a Bank of England man through and through:

> As principal, Clarke was in effect the eyes and ears of the Governor of the day. In his disciplinary role, which he executed with wisdom and good humour, he was the personification of 'the Governor's eyebrows'. Clarke's breadth of acquaintance and his ability to gather City intelligence were legendary. A master of the calculated indiscretion, he would appear to let slip confidential snippets while extracting information from his unwitting interlocutors.
>
> Tall, dapper and resplendent in his silk hat, Clarke controlled the discount market by the force of his presence. His firmness was never resented. When a young bill broker asked for the customary seven-day loan to cover a cash shortage, Clarke replied that the Bank would make the loan for nine days at a punitive rate. When the supplicant protested, Clarke cut him short: 'And it'll be eleven days in a moment'.[27]

The Discount Office was sometimes called 'the window in the windowless wall'; and from his vantage-point there, directly responsible for the creditworthiness of the City's most sensitive markets and houses, including the accepting houses, Clarke was on just the right wavelength –

firm, humorous, decidedly non-cerebral.

But of course, the City's main man through the 1950s was the more straitlaced Cobbold. Throughout his governorship he tended to divide the world into two types of people: decent chaps and those beyond the pale. Early in 1955 he was told by Bracken that John Colville, Churchill's Private Secretary, was 'flirting' with the idea of going into Philip Hill:

> I said that from the City point of view I was in favour of Philip Hill being 'respectabilized' and I should be quite glad to see somebody like Colville there. I was bound to say that if I were advising my own brother I would still raise an eyebrow and, as Lord Bracken knows, there are people in Philip Hill who are not generally liked. I did not see why he could not give Colville an idea of the position on these lines and let him make up his own mind.

Another banker who gave Cobbold problems was Walter Salomon, Chairman of Rea Brothers, who during much of the decade badgered him to endorse its membership of the Accepting Houses Committee and to recommend that it become a Treasury-authorised foreign exchange dealer. On one such occasion, in 1956, Cobbold told him that although 'their standing in the City had definitely improved', the Bank could not yet oblige, but that Salomon should come back in a year's time with his next balance sheet. 'I admitted,' Cobbold added in his note of the conversation, 'that in forming these judgments the Bank, like other Banks, and in accordance with general City tradition, were somewhat conservative and somewhat cautious, though I would by no means admit that we were over-conservative or hide-bound.'[28]

Ultimately, like British rule in India, it was a system of control that relied on consent. Occasionally there were signs of restiveness or even a local rebellion. In November 1951, a fortnight after the Bank-rate increase, Balfour of Burleigh on behalf of the clearers as a whole complained to the Bank, via the Treasury, that Cobbold had been 'pushing some of them around a bit', in the sense of encouraging the banks to raise their rates before they had all digested the recent increase. Then, the following June, Midland incurred Cobbold's displeasure by refusing to participate in a bankers' syndicate to raise £5m additional capital for the beleaguered Yorkshire Penny Bank. And soon afterwards Hugh Kindersley, wearing his hat as Managing Director of Lazards rather than as a director of the Bank, complained bitterly to the Bank's Harry Siepmann about the way in which 'the eternal delays' in the system of exchange control were frustrating the efforts of accepting houses like his own to arrange 'lines of extended credit' for British exporters. 'Inevitably,' he added, 'faith in the Bank as the leader and parent of the City becomes progressively shaken'; as a result, 'the reputation of the Bank is at stake'. These were telling criticisms, and over the next few years the Bank did start streamlining the irksome process of exchange control. Significantly, all three episodes occurred early in Cobbold's governorship, as he was establishing an authority that by the mid-1950s would become almost unquestioned. When in 1955 S.W.P. Perry-Aldworth became the Hongkong and Shanghai's senior London manager, almost his first move was to call on the Governor. 'Now, I'm at your personal disposal any time,' Cobbold told him. 'If there's a crisis, come and see me personally, don't hesitate. And if you possibly can, come see me before the crisis, not after the crisis has started.'[29]

Overall, the relationship between the Bank and the bankers may not have been one of equals – Anthony Tuke, Chairman of Barclays, would compare it to 'the type of co-operation which exists between a headmaster and his prefects', namely 'a bit one-sided' – but there is no doubt that both parties were essentially content.[30] At one level it was underpinned by the hierarchical, even public-school code of that era; at another, it allowed the banks access to government via the Bank with an ease and speed denied to most interest groups; and for the nationalised Bank, its combined role of sole spokesman for, and *de facto* regulator of, the City did much to fortify its potentially endangered authority. All in all, then, it was a snug set-up: insular, personalised and profoundly resistant to change.

CHAPTER FOUR

All the Burdens

The slow re-internationalisation of the City continued. Three Japanese banks returned to London in the summer of 1952, including the Yokohama Specie Bank, now reconstituted as the Bank of Tokyo. A particular friend was Schroders, which did however politely decline when the Bank of Tokyo's Yosuki Ono (father of Yoko) asked to see its balance sheet. Instead, Helmut Schroder asked Ono to lunch at his country house, Dell Park near Windsor. 'I have seen Schroder orchids – no need to see balance sheet,' Ono told his host after a tour of the gardens. Not everyone in the City was as welcoming. An internal Westminster Bank note of September 1952 recorded L.J. Williams, Chief General Manager of National Provincial, being 'very strong in his feeling' that the clearing banks 'should have nothing to do with Japanese paper at all at the present time'; that, indeed, 'in his view the Japs have come in much too quickly'.[1]

Nor was the attitude towards Germany invariably one of sweetness and light. The dominant banker there was Hermann Abs, trying hard from the late 1940s to get the Standstill and other debts settled, so that West Germany could return as a full member of the international financial community.[2] 'There is no doubt about his ability,' Cobbold observed in 1950 of Abs, 'but I always used to think him, to say the least, a bit quick off the mark.' Eventually, after a marathon conference at Lancaster House, agreement was reached in August 1952, giving West Germany's external creditors 4 per cent interest for thirteen years in addition to the repayment of principal. It was an important achievement, owing much to Sir Edward Reid and Ernest Kleinwort, but failed to persuade Cobbold to imitate Norman's strong pro-German tendencies. 'I had a tedious dinner at the German Embassy with Erhard,' he noted in February 1956. 'The only practical point discussed was East–West trade, on which I made suitable noises.'[3]

A more pressing concern for the Governor than either the German economic miracle or the changing economic map of Europe was the execution and efficacy of domestic monetary policy. 'Can Monetary Policy Carry the Load?' the *Banker* asked in May 1952, after the second Bank rate change only five months into Butler's chancellorship. Although acknowledging that 'the bankers themselves have been rediscovering, generally with some surprise, the strength of the weapons entrusted to them', the article concluded that ultimately all depended on 'the degree of the Government's courage' – about which the early signs were 'not propitious'. Cobbold himself, constantly nagging Butler to reduce his expenditure and borrowing programme, was probably under few illusions that monetary policy alone was sufficient. 'I stressed the danger of thinking that monetary policy could do more than it can,' he noted in July 1953 after one of his quarterly briefings to the clearing bankers. 'The main problems remain those of Government expenditure, taxation and the tendency for wage increases.'[4] Nevertheless, monetary policy *was* a significant weapon, and in September 1953 Cobbold and Butler were in agreement that it would be safe to reduce Bank rate from 4 per cent to 3½ per cent. It was the first Bank rate change since the war to be announced in the traditional way, with a notice being posted in the front hall of the Bank of England at precisely the same time that the Government broker – Derrick Mullens at this time – arrived on the floor of the Stock Exchange, climbed on to the customary bench, took off his top hat and bawled out the new rate to the assembled gilt-edged market.[5]

It was an appropriate ritual for what was still in some ways an amateurishly conducted monetary and indeed economic policy. In his approach to monetary matters Cobbold was determined to squeeze out the Treasury, certainly below the very top level, while the Treasury for its part was similarly exclusive when it came to macro-economic questions. 'I think we are at present too close to Whitehall,' Mynors (who was about to become Deputy Governor) privately warned in February 1954 – a fear shared by Cobbold, who was determined both to enhance the Bank of England's status in the City and to resist the politicisation of monetary policy. It was a high-risk strategy, for it depended entirely on the monetary policy itself working, the chances of which hinged on a whole range of factors, many beyond the control of the Bank or, indeed, the City. 'Undoubtedly during the last two years,' Villiers of Barings reflected to an American banker near the end of 1953, 'there has been a great improvement in the general position in England and much more confidence, particularly by foreigners, in the soundness of our economy.' However, he went on, 'Naturally the increased wages and the consequent rise in the cost of living will cause difficulties which seem inevitable in a so-called Welfare State.'[7] Cobbold would have nodded, perhaps reflecting that the world had once been simpler.

For Cobbold, as for the City at large, an important aspect of the Conservative Party's return to power was its commitment to denationalise the recently nationalised steel industry.[8] Mindful, however, that there would be nothing to stop a future Labour government renationalising steel, the task of selling off the industry to British investors was not the

City's dream ticket. 'Barings and Morgans feel that this is all difficult and intensely political,' Cobbold noted in November 1951, following a visit from Peacock exactly a week after the election. 'They have come to the conclusion that they would find it difficult to handle an issue and they feel that it would have to be left on the Bank of England's doorstep. I made doubtful noises.' At this stage the game was pass the parcel, and although soon afterwards a working party was established under the Bank's chairmanship, Cobbold warned Butler shortly before Christmas that the whole operation was likely to prove extremely problematic and that 'it would be a mistake to think in terms of bringing undue pressure on underwriters or investors to take up more than they considered justifiable on general business grounds'.[9]

During 1952 the Bank obdurately resisted the idea of sponsoring the issues, until at last in April 1953, with the bill denationalising steel about to receive the Royal Assent, the City was compelled to get its act together, under Cobbold's firm, not entirely unsympathetic leadership. The crucial meeting was held at the Bank on the 9th, attended by representatives of Helbert Wagg and Bensons, as well as the familiar big six of Morgans, Barings, Rothschilds, Schroders, Hambros and Lazards. All agreed to participate in an issuing consortium, headed by Morgan Grenfell as the major 'steel house', but David Colville of Rothschilds forcibly expressed his firm's unhappiness about the wider process:

> This whole matter is far too political. Nationalisation was a spiteful act, carried through without a mandate, and denationalization is being effected to redeem a party pledge. The City is much best kept out of politics.
>
> What the Bank of England is in fact doing is to use its influence in the City, acting as the nationalised agent of a Government controlled by a political party, to obtain the support of private enterprise to help implement the election promises of that party. In effect, private enterprise is being suborned by a nationalised institution for political ends and the Bank is, moreover, seeking to throw the whole political onus and possible loss on the City, without taking either risk or responsibility.[10]

This was a remarkably frank attack on the recently nationalised Bank, and implicitly on Cobbold himself. Predictably, in the instinctively hierarchical City of the time, it received little support. Moreover, not only was there broad support for the fundamental principle of denationalisation, whatever its financial uncertainties, but most of the merchant banks present were keen to position themselves for subsequent new issue business relating to the steel industry.

The next six months were taken up with the all-important preliminaries, with the attitude of the institutions (above all the insurance companies and investment trusts) throughout seen as critical to the chances of the operation's success. Cobbold talked to various key figures,

such as Carlyle Gifford of the Scottish investment trusts, while Sir George
Erskine of Morgans tried to keep the Prudential fully posted and, as much
as possible, on side. United Steel was chosen as the first issue, with the
prospectus to be published on 26 October, and reasonably generous
terms, including for an allotment brokerage, were agreed. 'It is felt,'
Erskine had privately commented as early as May, 'that if we are going to
get the banks and brokers generally to take their coats off and have the
considerable work of dealing with applications in the form of
Government securities, they will have to be adequately recompensed for
their work.' The price was set at 25s a share (politically too low, thought
the Treasury; dangerously high, thought the bankers, but in fact more
than adequately discounted); the institutions played the game, sub-
scribing in strength ahead of the public flotation; and the issue as a whole
was oversubscribed three times. 'It has all been most satisfactory, but I do
not think that any of us quite anticipated the success we have met with,'
Bicester wrote to Cobbold in mid-November, with the City awash with
mutual congratulations.[11]

Unfortunately, especially for the many small investors, United Steel
shares soon went to a discount, largely through a shortage of buying orders
from the institutions, still nervous about possible renationalisation.
Moreover, 'the Pru', Cobbold was told on 20 November, 'are talking
about cutting their participation in future steel underwriting arrangements'. Early in 1954, although the Bank of England acted as a long stop
in the underwriting, the Lancashire Steel Corporation's offer engendered
a disappointing response. A pause for reflection ensued. 'We spoke about
Steel,' Cobbold noted in late February after seeing Butler, 'and agreed that
it should be left to simmer for a bit and that there was nothing to be
gained by rushing any fences.' Two months later, in discussion with
Erskine, Cobbold agreed to 'have a word with the Chairman of the Pru';
and in June, helped by a bull market, the successful issue of Stewarts &
Lloyds marked the turning-point in the steel denationalisation programme. When an offer was made early in 1955 of ten million ordinary
shares of Colville's, as many as 150,000 applications were received for a
total of 130 million shares.[12] This completed the sale of six of the biggest
newly privatised steel companies; in all, although Erskine's invention of a
system of irrevocable applications by underwriters had been immensely
helpful, it had been a triumph for the old-style City, dominated by the
élite merchant banks and led from the front by a Bank of England
Governor possessing considerable force of personality.

Almost concurrent with the selling of steel was the rise of the 'takeover'
(the term itself coming into general usage in 1953) and the City's rather
muddled response to this disturbing phenomenon.[13] The disclosure
aspects of the 1948 Companies Act, enabling would-be corporate

predators to make more accurate financial estimates, reduced dividend pay-outs to shareholders as a result of increased company taxation since the war, and the natural appeal to shareholders of tax-free capital gains – these, among other factors, fuelled the coming of the takeover bid. Its most proficient exponent during the 1950s was that pragmatic, hard-bitten outsider Charles Clore. A biographer's phrases are striking. He possessed an 'utterly ruthless honesty'; his will had 'the force of granite'; a pair of 'cobalt eyes made people cringe'; and 'he expected the worst of people and was rarely surprised'. An entirely self-made man (the son of Russian Jewish immigrants), he was in his late forties by 1953 and had made most of his money in property. At this stage he had relatively few friends in the City, apart from Philip Hill and the stockbrokers Sebags. The City, however, was compelled to take notice of him that January and February, as he made a contested bid for J. Sears & Co, parent company of Freeman, Hardy & Willis. Investment Registry (based in the West End) acted for him; and amidst much press attention and the despatch of rival circulars to shareholders, Clore's offer proved too good to refuse. The valedictory words of the departing Sears chairman were eloquent: 'We never thought anything like this would happen to us.'[14]

Undoubtedly the City at large was shocked by this turn of events, but 'Why Not Trust The Shareholders?' was typically the title of Wincott's *FT* column on the matter. 'From what I know of Mr Clore,' he asserted, 'he's the last man to make an extravagant bid. Our Mr Clore is a firm believer in the lore of nicely calculated less or more, and there's no more of the more from Mr Clore than is absolutely necessary to achieve his purpose – which is as it should be.' In other words, 'natural forces always do win out in the end', a theme dear to Wincott's heart. The Bank of England instinctively disagreed, and in March 1953 drew up an internal 'Memorandum on Real and Fictitious Share Bids', arguing that 'this kind of manoeuvre may mean the break-up of businesses which are making an important contribution to the country's needs'.[15]

A few weeks later Cobbold received a visit from Rex Benson:

> They were flirting with the idea of taking Mr Clore, as he put it, under their wing. He [i.e. Clore] seems to want to be looked after by some reputable House. He [i.e. Benson] had made a lot of enquiries and could find out nothing improper in Mr Clore's financial history.
>
> I said that we knew nothing against Mr Clore on grounds of improper conduct. Bensons must decide but I would put two things to him strongly. If they thought of going ahead with this, they must make very clear arrangements with Mr Clore and have it definitely understood that he does not do any business of which they do not approve. Secondly, they must go in with their eyes wide open that they are taking risks of damage to their credit and standing generally . . .

Benson, whose sense of City proprieties ran deep, needed no further hint and dropped the idea. Clore himself by now had the taste of blood, and soon some of the City's most venerable dovecotes were fluttering. In June, Cobbold had another visitor:

> Lord Bicester came in to say that he was very agitated about further manoeuvres by Mr Clore and wondered whether I could not suggest to the Insurance Companies that they should not lend him money. I said that I thought this would be extremely difficult. I started by being reluctant to interfere with other people's business. Although I had no love for Mr Clore's activities, I found it very difficult to draw a line between what was moral and what was immoral in this field and I certainly had no evidence of any misbehaviour by Mr Clore. Finally I thought that if I talked to people, the nice people would play and lose the business which would be taken by the nasty people . . .

'Nice people' and 'nasty people': it was one way of looking at the world. Cobbold's final visitor in this illuminating sequence was even more distinguished, even more elderly. Peacock, he noted in October, 'is unhappy about Mr Clore and similar activities which seem to be spreading but he agrees with me in not seeing what on earth can be done about it'.[16]

Peacock presumably had in mind the developing battle for the Savoy group of hotels, which included Claridges and the Berkeley, as well as the Savoy itself. During the autumn of 1953 it became clear that the property developer Harold Samuel, in informal liaison with Clore, was in the process of acquiring a substantial holding in the company, whose shares rose sharply. The City's links with the Savoy were long and intimate, strengthening its natural inclination to support the party under siege. Churchill also valued that hotel's hospitality, and in mid-November he asked his Economic Secretary to the Treasury, Reginald Maudling, to prepare a note about takeover bids. Maudling duly sounded out Cobbold, who told him that 'any remedy would cause more trouble than the disease', and government policy remained one of reluctant non-interference.[17]

Accordingly, the Savoy was left to save itself. It did so in two ways: first, by devising a controversial scheme which in effect meant that even if Samuel acquired the majority of Savoy shares, he would still find it well-nigh impossible to alter the existing use of the Berkeley and turn it, as he intended, into an office block; and, second, by buying a huge number of Savoy shares, with the major part of the purchase being financed by Barclays. Masterminding the Savoy's operation, and much helped by his friendship with Cazenove's, was the hotel's utterly determined Chairman and Managing Director, Hugh Wontner. He was in constant touch with ministers, and even tried to give the impression to Anthony Tuke of

Barclays that his bank providing the finance to enable the buy-back of
Samuel's shares 'ought [in Cobbold's sceptical words] to be treated as a
matter of high State policy'. Tuke himself called on Cobbold four days
before Christmas. 'Barclays are anxious to help their old customers and
they think that the Savoy are on the side of the angels in this controversy,'
Cobbold noted, adding however that he had told Tuke to 'bear in mind'
that 'there was quite likely to be a good deal of publicity about all this and
that even if his customers were on the side of the angels they seemed to
have put a foot wrong here or there'. Early in the New Year, he saw the
Chairman of Barclays again:

> Mr Tuke told me privately that they had fixed up the Savoy business. The
> Savoy people had managed to collect some quite good guarantees but it had
> still meant Barclays taking the shares at 40/- instead of the 30/- they had
> originally contemplated. They were a bit reluctant but felt they had no
> alternative.

Cobbold's note at the foot of his memo was Normanesque: 'I am telling
HMT 1st sentence only'.[18]

Despite some consternation about the 'poison pill' aspect of the scheme
to thwart Samuel (who consoled himself with a massive killing from
selling his recently acquired shares), few in the City were unhappy with
the outcome. 'The dominant feeling after last month's dramatic
dénouement of the tussle for control of the Savoy group of hotels seems
to have been one of relief – relief that some highly tricky issues were not,
after all, pushed to ultimate conclusions,' was how Harold Cowen
summarised the prevailing mood in the January 1954 issue of the *Banker*.
Significantly, when a few weeks earlier Cobbold requested the British
Insurance Association and the American banks, as well as the clearing
banks and merchant banks, 'to use special caution in respect of any
invitations coming before them which appear to be connected with these
take-over operations', on the grounds that 'in some at least there would
seem to be a considerable speculative element', the only dissent quickly
gave way to compliance.[19]

However, it was not a problem that was likely to go away, and Clore in
particular (who had himself sold out at a high price to Samuel) remained
an object of deep mistrust, allied to a certain condescension. Later in 1954,
when Clore tried to get involved in the selling off of the South Durham
Steel & Iron Company, he was in effect vetoed by Cobbold, who took a
strong view that 'any deal with Clore' would 'upset the applecart in the
City'. The agreed tactic that autumn was to stall 'Mr C.', and Clore's
accountant was told that Sir John Morison, Chairman of the Iron and
Steel Holding and Realisation Agency, was 'prepared to treat with Mr C.,
but in his own time'. Upon this, it was reported back to Mynors at the

Bank that 'Mr C. is so pleased that he is not out of court on his reputation that he has sent the Accountant back to ask whether there is any other small Steel Works which his highly efficient young team of engineers [Bentley Engineering] could pull round.'[20] In this elaborate game, it was unlikely that the cobalt eyes would blink first.

On another controversial part of the City/industry workface, ICFC continued to be dogged by tensions with its shareholders. 'Whether the Banks like it or not,' argued one of Westminster's joint General Managers in January 1954, 'they have been almost out-manoeuvred by Piercy (he appearing to have the ear of the Governor) . . . The Banks have missed the opportunity of disciplining Piercy and establishing once and for all how far the Banks were committed before indicating a "limit" of £45 millions . . .' Three months later, Westminster's chairman, Lord Aldenham, an 'old' City figure with his roots in the family merchant bank Antony Gibbs, succeeded Tuke as Chairman of the Committee of London Clearing Bankers and initiated two years of acrimonious relations between himself and Piercy – to a point where they were hardly on speaking terms. ICFC celebrated its tenth anniversary in 1955, but Aldenham personally made sure that no clearing bankers were present at the festivities.[21]

It was an attitude, combining personal pique and deep conservatism, which surfaced that same year when Sir George Erskine – by some distance the most dynamic figure at Morgan Grenfell – gave a presidential address to the Institute of Bankers that seemingly challenged the most fundamental tenets of British deposit banking. Mynors at the Bank of England recorded Midland's Edington, due to move the vote of thanks, calling on him in early May:

> The Address proves to be a highly provocative essay on the shortage of industrial capital in the future. It suggests that the Clearing Banks should invest in industrial equities, foster industrial investment finance, and assist their customers in making investments in industry. Edington is furious. He will consult Lord Aldenham privately, and thinks he must make a slashing attack on Erskine if he cannot evade the duty of speaking.

Mynors managed to calm down his visitor, and though Erskine did duly deliver his bold proposals ('*Banque d'Affaires for Britain?*' was the title of the *Banker*'s report of his address), they fell on almost uniformly deaf ears.[22]

Significantly, one of the supporting contexts offered by Erskine for seeking to improve the mechanism behind the supply of risk capital to British industry was that, as the City in due course returned to its traditional role of meeting the needs of overseas borrowers, so the domestic supply might run short. Indeed, the City had already taken a long step towards a return to the world stage with the reopening on

22 March 1954 of the London gold market. Such a step, Butler assured Churchill a week before the event, would 'help to strengthen sterling as an international currency and London as an international financial centre'. To which Churchill scribbled a one-word comment, 'good'.[23]

The decision had already caused some heart-searching at the Bank, leading to an uncomfortable quarter of an hour for Anthony de Rothschild and his nephew Edmund:

> The governor told them that it was proposed to re-open a Gold Market, but that this did not entail convertibility and all that. In the first place, it was proposed to re-open the Market on the old lines, but he could give no assurance that this would be welcome to the other members, nor that the relations between Rothschilds and the Bank would remain exactly as before. At this stage he wished to know whether Rothschilds thought they could undertake what was necessary: and to tell them that if a Market on the old lines did not prove satisfactory, he must feel free to promote some other arrangement.
>
> Mr [Anthony] de Rothschild said that their physical facilities were still in existence, and he thought they could do it.

In the event, Rothschilds did remain a pivotal part of the London gold market, in which at this stage anyone could sell, although in order to buy it was necessary to have an American, Canadian or registered sterling account.[24] Sterling itself, despite Cobbold's cautious disclaimer, was inching laboriously towards convertibility, achieved early in 1955, though only on a *de facto* rather than on a *de jure* basis.[25] It was a factor that gave an extra twist to what would be a traumatic year for British economic policy and City/government relations.

*

'Market Boom Goes On' was the *Banker*'s headline back in May 1954, with the paper warning that 'the optimists in the markets would do well to remember that, at these speeds and these altitudes, the stresses are apt to be both severe and unforeseen'. Four months later Cobbold had 'a gossip' with Braithwaite of the Stock Exchange. 'I asked whether he was concerned about speculative positions. He agrees that there are signs of rather more speculation than he would like but he cannot put his finger on any danger spots and is keeping his fingers crossed.' The forces were gathering for a pre-election boom, and some weeks later Cobbold told Butler that he was 'a little bothered' about the 'atmosphere of complacency which showed signs of developing'. He went on, 'I was all for an optimistic view but was nervous about ideas which seemed to be gaining ground that increasing prosperity is certain and that there is no reason why anybody should work too hard or be content with their present reward.' The less moralistic *FT*, however, was sanguine, declaring on New

Year's Day that 'with the monetary weapon available to check inflation', Butler in his budget (due as usual in the spring) would be able to concentrate on reductions in taxation, in the long run 'the best incentives to higher production and increased productivity'.[26] Expansion without tears, boom without bust, go without stop: the tantalising chimera of post-war British economic life was making the first of what would become regular appearances. With monetary policy charged at the start of 1955 with turning that chimera into reality, Cobbold found himself in an unenviable position.[27]

A couple of Bank rate rises took some of the immediate heat out of the situation, but on the same day as the second rise, 24 February, the Governor warned Butler that other, non-monetary measures were needed – in order, it did not need to be spelled out, to protect sterling, keep control over inflation and avert a balance-of-payments crisis. Yet could more be done in Cobbold's own patch? Robert Hall, the government's economic adviser, certainly thought so, arguing forcibly in early March that credit policy needed to be tightened and, pregnantly, that 'if a central bank has not got adequate powers to control the other banks, it undoubtedly ought to have such powers'. Hall's memo was for the Chancellor, and Butler informed Cobbold at the start of April that 'some of his Treasury advisers were critical of the Clearing Banks and doubtful whether credit policy was working through quickly enough'. The two met again soon afterwards, when Butler 'again referred to the Treasury's anxieties about credit policy but added that he was not bothered himself'.[28] Bank advances might have been rising twice as fast as in 1954, but Butler had no desire to trespass in Cobbold's domain.

He had, anyway, a politically very sensitive budget on his mind. On 15 April the new Prime Minister, Eden, announced the date of the general election (26 May), and four days later Butler proceeded to cut the standard rate of income tax by sixpence, while publicly pinning his faith on 'the resources of a flexible monetary policy' in order to counterbalance this fiscal generosity. Cobbold's unease can only have deepened, especially in the light of his conversation the previous day with Lord Aldenham and David Robarts of the clearing bankers. The banks, they complained to him, were 'finding great difficulty in practice in selecting what sort of advance they ought to restrict', to which Cobbold responded by saying that although he 'recognised the difficulties', he had 'heard a good deal of gossip round the place that there was little or no change in the attitude of the banks towards lending', and he 'thought this ought to be put right'. Next day Peppiatt glossed Cobbold's note of that exchange: 'If they want HMG (present and future) to run their business, this is the way to go about it. The banks should read the signals themselves and act accordingly.' Hall laid the blame elsewhere. 'The Bank of England haven't been as co-operative on monetary policy as they might have been,' he wrote in his diary on budget day. 'They have never been too keen on being tough with the Banks. Now the Governor tells the Chancellor that he *is* being tough with them, but Oliver Franks (now Chairman of Lloyds) tells me that this is not so. . .' Hall added ominously that 'altogether we are working up to some sort of *éclaircissement* with the Governor, but whether the Chancellor will support us I don't know – he has always felt that the Governor is in the saddle and that it is a very serious thing to disagree with him.'[29]

Conscious of the imminent election and anxious not to see a change of government, the City's response to Butler's give-away budget was broadly to cross its fingers and hope. 'The Chancellor was right to take his risks on the side of expansion,' the *FT* stated categorically; and while it did not deny Gaitskell's charge that it had been an inflationary budget, it argued that 'as Mr Butler has been prepared to use the Bank Rate, there was no need for him to rely on the budget as the sole disinflationary influence he can exert'. For Cobbold, with a huge responsibility having been placed on monetary policy, these were anxious times. Not long after the budget he was asked by representatives of the LDMA 'if he would express an opinion as to how much longer the present acute uncertainty that was worrying all sections of the City was likely to be maintained'. In reply, he was 'forthright . . . to the effect that the methods employed at the moment, of which the money rate was only one, had to be given time to work', though he added hopefully that the objective of tightening credit by means of restricting bank advances 'now seemed to be beginning to work'. At the election itself, with the stockbrokers Read, Hurst-Brown & Co warning that in the event of a Labour victory 'the rentier could safely expect treatment which would make Dr Dalton's efforts look like those of a clumsy amateur', the Conservatives – to the City's general relief – increased their majority.[30] Butler's budget had achieved its political task.

The City's post-election reckoning came soon, in the face of renewed inflationary and balance-of-payments pressures during the summer. 'Advances have gone on rising,' Hall complained on 18 July, 'and I feel very unhappy about our mechanism for controlling the supply of money.' By then it was clear that something was going to have to be done rapidly to tighten that mechanism; and some hectic, ill-tempered July days were later recalled by Hall. They began with the Treasury and Hall himself managing to persuade the Bank of England to let them talk to two representatives (Robarts of National Provincial and Ronald Thornton of Barclays) of the clearing banks, though with Mynors and Allen present in order to keep a watching brief on behalf of the Bank:

> It became clear almost at once that the banks thought they were doing all that was expected but that they could do more if we 'did not mind

bankruptcies or unemployment'. In fact the Bank of England had not conveyed to them that the Government was serious in trying to use monetary tightness as an anti-inflationary measure ... H.B. [Sir Herbert Brittain of the Treasury] drafted a letter for the Chancellor to send to the Governor asking the banks to get their advances down by 10% before Christmas, and to maintain a liquidity ratio of at least 32%. Naturally as soon as the Governor heard of this he protested, said it was quite unnecessary, and he would speak to the banks. They wanted (as they had told us) the Government to *say* that it wanted a squeeze so that they could refer their disgruntled customers to Government policy. The result of all this was the Chancellor's statement on July 26th ...[31]

The round of credit measures that Butler now introduced not only marked the beginning of the end of his chancellorship but also triggered a significant challenge to the Bank of England's authority.

Hall himself set the ball rolling on the 28th, when he sent Butler a memo arguing that the failure in the course of the year to apply with any degree of effectiveness a restrictive credit policy had shown '*either* that the Bank of England did not understand that the policy was meant to be serious *or* that they failed to tell us that it would not work properly'. The next day Brittain saw Cobbold and suggested further meetings between the Treasury and the clearing banks. 'The Governor was very definitely hostile to this idea,' Brittain noted. 'He said that he must be the channel for dealing with the Clearing Banks, and that we must accept his assurance that the Banks fully intended to give effect to the Chancellor's request.' Furthermore, Cobbold was hostile to the notion of supplying the Treasury with more frequent information about bank deposits and advances. Over the following week he stuck resolutely to his fundamental standpoint – that it was he, not Whitehall, who dealt with the clearing banks – and even took the attack to the enemy, emphasising to the Treasury 'the widespread feeling in the City that, whilst the credit squeeze has had considerable effect, and will now have more, on private enterprise, little has been done to cut back public spending where the "credit squeeze" cannot bite'. The Bank did, however, have to give some ground. In August the practice began of the Bank providing each week a report on the general money-market position, especially the Bank's own operations in it, with the Chief Cashier (Leslie O'Brien) coming to the Treasury each Monday to discuss it. Nonetheless, as Brittain noted, the purpose of these weekly discussions was 'for our education only', and 'we should not appear to question or criticise the Bank's management of the market'.[32]

As the credit squeeze took hold over the next few months, an important sub-plot was the fate of Piercy's ICFC. Its new business virtually dried up, in what Kinross would remember as a period of 'unprecedented' difficulty, and by 28 October Piercy was warning Cobbold that he feared the clearing banks were on the verge of taking a decision that 'would have the effect of putting ICFC out of business'. Cobbold promised to 'try to keep the position somewhat open' and saw Aldenham on 1 November, ahead of the clearers' meeting. The Governor, according to Aldenham's account, 'said very politely and apologetically that he had some impression that we were using the credit squeeze to "rat" on our obligations to ICFC'; to which Aldenham replied that 'I should much like to "rat" on them, but that I knew that we must not do so'. Full-scale ratting was indeed out of the question, once Cobbold had raised his eyebrows, though ICFC got only half of the £2m that it had been seeking in order to tide it over the next few months. 'The trouble with Piercy,' Peppiatt of the Bank noted on the 4th, 'is that he is apt to overstate his case.'[33]

By this time, the inadequacy of Butler's reliance on monetary policy alone had been exposed by the emergency budget that, following severe pressure on sterling, he delivered in late October. Cuts in government expenditure did not, however, take the spotlight off the monetary aspect, and on being told by the Treasury in early November that ministers were 'critical' of the way in which the credit squeeze was being implemented by the clearing banks, Cobbold responded strongly that 'in the last few months they had done much more than anybody else to fight inflation'. Nor did he believe that the emergency package was enough, telling Butler on 10 November that he 'continued to feel doubts whether it was possible to run a defence programme and a social programme of the present size at the same time, without keeping the economy overloaded'.[34] Increasingly, East End was telling West End how to run its affairs, and vice-versa: an unhappy situation. The Treasury more or less believed that it and Butler had been the victims of a tacit conspiracy between the Bank and the banks not to implement credit policy with sufficient stringency, while the City despaired about what it saw as government profligacy.

Soon afterwards Cobbold jotted down his private, end-of-year thoughts. After praising the banks for having met their July obligations ('considerable performance against continuing boom atmosphere nationally and internationally'), he surveyed in characteristic tones the larger field of play:

> *Change of bowling* most necessary. Public fed up with hearing about credit squeeze and does not believe it will stop inflation unless forcible attacks made in other directions, notably public expenditure generally and nationalised industries development plans. Further moves in credit field alone unlikely to achieve objectives and likely to discredit policy.
>
> Perhaps worth considering appeal to big industry to go slow in 1956 on development (supported by continued firm credit policy) provided HMG prepared to give firm lead at public and nationalised end, i.e. keep the off-

spinner on at one end, but put on a fast bowler at other end with new ball. Must get more directly at the critical points.

Unfortunately, there was a new captain. Macmillan, who succeeded Butler as Chancellor shortly before Christmas, had watched with interest as the events of 1955 unfolded – in particular, the tax-cutting budget of April and the ensuing widely believed accusation that it had been designed solely for electoral purposes. 'I do not think it really was that,' Macmillan reflected after becoming Chancellor. Rather, 'it was due to ignorance, lack of proper statistical information, bad Treasury advice, a weak Governor of the Bank, & resistance of the Clearing Bankers'.[35] Put another way, quite apart from what he might or might not do with the new cherry, he was not convinced that the off-spinner could be relied upon to give it enough tweak.

*

'Besought him not to make a lot of speeches or talks to journalists & to drop veiled threats of "tightening the credit squeeze",' Cobbold recorded on 6 January 1956 after one of his first talks with the new Chancellor. 'Can he not invent a new catchword & stop talking about "inflation" which nobody understands?' The suspicion between these two Old Etonians was mutual. 'I find the Governor of the Bank rather hard to pin down to any definite decisions,' Macmillan noted some days later. 'It is essential that the "credit squeeze" sh[d] be operated with ever increasing effect during the next few weeks.' On the 19th Macmillan gave a dinner party that had a certain whiff of corporatism about it. Guests included Cobbold, Franks and Tommy Brand of Lazards, while also present (and taking mental notes) was Hall:

> After dinner the Chancellor asked for a discussion of where we were and what we ought to do. The Governor said that the credit squeeze was going on but time was short and the reserves low. He felt sure that a reduction in Government expenditure and investment was essential. O.S.F. [Franks] made quite an oration on the lines that urgent action was needed, this must be Government expenditure and investment, the banks would do their share and he hoped the Governor would be making this clear . . .

During the discussion, Hall added, Franks was 'the dominant figure', whereas Cobbold was 'rather on the defensive' and Brand 'did not say much'.[36]

Over the next week or two there was a somewhat disgruntled tone to the annual round of bank chairmen's speeches. Robarts of National Provincial called the credit squeeze that had been introduced the previous July 'artificial and arbitrary', Tuke of Barclays dubbed it a 'retrograde and regrettable step', and almost all wanted direct restraint ended as soon as possible. Moreover, both Tuke and Harlech strongly criticised the existing policy – or at least the way the policy was implemented – of full employment, while Robarts (in the summarising words of the *Banker*) 'feels that the effectiveness of the money weapon will always be limited because it is never likely now to be pushed to the point of causing unemployment, and yet he wants to reduce the general level of demand'.[37] It was a circle that was proving increasingly hard to square: the Bank of England and the banking system wanted to stick as far as possible to a voluntary system of credit control; such a system was at best only semi-effective; and naturally the Bank and the bankers were looking to shift the blame elsewhere.

Hall's exasperation, even outrage, continued to know few bounds, especially after lunching on 7 February with the eminent retired civil servant Sir Edmund Hall-Patch. 'He told me that the Bank of England are claiming that the Treasury refused all last year to do the things they recommended in monetary policy. They did just the same after devaluation. It is difficult to get used to people in such circles who tell downright lies about official secrets.' Soon afterwards, with sterling in trouble, Bank rate was raised to 5½ per cent, but only after Macmillan had agreed to Cobbold's demand that there also had to be a package (announced the following day) of expenditure and investment cuts. 'Having been, I am afraid, something of a critic in the last few months of the insufficient (in my view) support at the Whitehall end of monetary measures at this end,' Governor wrote to Chancellor on the 16th, 'I have thought it proper to let it be known among my colleagues and a few "intimates" in the City that (taking a general view and without going into details) I regard HMG's present proposals as measuring fully up to what the City could reasonably expect. I hope that Whitehall and City may now work this through as a joint endeavour.' Not quite an intimate, but an important conduit, was Maurice Green, assistant editor of *The Times* and a former editor of the *Financial News*. 'The Bank Court would have been unwilling to take further monetary action in isolation,' Cobbold wrote categorically enough to him the following day.[38]

The new Chancellor, with his expansionary instincts, must have been feeling distinctly boxed in, though he consoled himself later in the month by recording that it was 'a great advance' to have established a series of 'formal meetings between the Bank & Treasury officials'. Moreover, looked at specifically from a City point of view, Cobbold's temporary ascendancy over a new Chancellor could not disguise the long-term damage that the fiasco of 1955 had done to the reputation of the Bank of England and the banking system as a whole. Taking the risk of being blackballed by his fellow-chairmen, who presumably did not know about it, Franks of Lloyds spoke illuminatingly to the XYZ Club on the last day of February. 'He has evidently come down strongly in favour of using the liquidity ratio much more definitely and openly,' Gaitskell noted. 'He thinks the American system is better and does not agree with all the mystique and secrecy which surrounds the Bank of England . . .'[39]

Macmillan himself, some three weeks later, sought to regain the initiative:

> I am wondering [he wrote to Cobbold] whether you could not help me, not merely by what you are doing but by getting the full benefit of everyone knowing what you are doing. For it is not only what we are, but what we seem to be, that matters . . .
>
> The question of liquidity ratio seems to be worth considering again from this point of view. I know at present you rely on the banks carrying out your general wishes. But is there not a lot to be said for this system being more regularised? For instance, could I announce in the Budget that the liquidity ratio was now to be imposed by the Bank of England on the banks? This might offend the chairmen and managers of the Clearing Banks. But I don't think it would necessarily do so if you could explain to them that this was a public gesture which had a real value . . .

Macmillan added that 'we must not neglect any weapons, however distasteful or contrary to our traditions'. In his reply the Governor gave no ground. After arguing that the banks were already being squeezed as severely as possible, and that it was the expenditure side of things that really needed the Chancellor's attention, Cobbold upped the stakes by strongly defending the banking system:

> There has been no major banking failure or moratorium in living memory, no Government has had in this country to rescue the banks from unliquid commitments, the banks have survived two great wars and immense economic changes without loss to anybody and they have provided enormous help to the Government of the day in war and peace . . .
>
> Our banking system is incomparably better co-ordinated, more responsible and more willing (some critics would say too willing) to listen to official advice and requests than any other banking system in the world. Far from being senile and out of date, the system has been constantly adapted to meet changing conditions . . .

As an example, he cited 'the recent contraction of bank lending in the face of boom conditions'. Again, the Governor carried the immediate day, with Hall recording regretfully in early April that 'the Chancellor very nearly screwed himself up to prescribing liquidity ratios but the Governor has been much against it'. And, scathing as usual, he went on: 'All the Governor does is to explain away the actions of the Banks and say that nothing but reduced Government expenditure will help the situation.'[40]

Relations between the two men continued to be strained. 'The Governor is putting a fast one over me, I fear,' Macmillan noted in early

May after a further discussion on the vexed issue of liquidity ratios. 'Anyway, I want to know more before I commit myself.' That question was temporarily settled by late June, when a joint Treasury/Bank working party ruled out the concept, unless in an emergency, of a prescribed liquidity ratio. Instead, it would be business (since July 1955) as usual, with the banks being asked to go on with the squeeze. Macmillan accepted this verdict, but informed Cobbold on 4 July of the price for his assent. 'I want to *see & talk* to the Clearing Bankers myself,' Macmillan wrote in his diary later that day. 'Mr Governor does not like this, as he regards himself as the right person to deal with the Clearing Banks. We compromised. He will see them, & tell them my wishes this week. I will see them later on in the month . . .' The encounter duly took place on the 24th. 'At 4 p.m. 17 Bankers came to the Treasury,' Macmillan recorded. 'This is without precedent, I am told. I made them a speech & then there was quite a good discussion. Some of them asked some good questions; others were puerile. It took just over an hour & the communiqué was agreed.' This was a moment of some satisfaction for Macmillan, after a difficult half-year at the Treasury, but he would hardly have been surprised by Cobbold's diary entry of the previous day: 'I had a talk with Mr Robarts [who had succeeded Aldenham as Chairman of the CLCB] and Sir Oliver Franks about tactics at the Bankers' Meeting with the Chancellor.'[41]

Within days of that meeting, however, all such matters were put into a state of suspended animation by President Nasser's nationalisation of the Suez Canal Company.[42] 'The Prime Minister has defined his policy as one of firmness,' the *FT* observed with approval on the 28th, and over the succeeding weeks and months the broad consensus in the City seems to have been that if necessary the West would have to use force against Nasser. Inevitably the crisis involved the City in some tricky moments, and Macmillan regaled the Cabinet with one as early as 3 August:

> I had to report a very unpleasant visit wh. I had had from the Deputy Chairman & General Manager of the Westminster Bank at 10.30 that morning. They were in doubt as to whether they could pay out to the Suez Canal Company (the legitimate one) moneys in their a/c. I asked 'why not?' Because, they said, it was possible that a court w^d hold that Nasser's action was justified & that the money now belonged to the new nationalised authority. I was so angry with this that I turned in fury on them & called them harsh names. They went away saddened; but they promised to do what seemed obviously right & take a chance. They actually had the impertinence to ask for an 'indemnity' from the Treasury. I said that I w^d much rather issue a decree to nationalise the Westminster Bank. I told this story with particular glee to the Cabinet, because PM [Eden] used to be a director of the Westminster Bank. But I was only shocked by their behaviour. Poor Mr Stirling (the Deputy Chairman) was ashamed; but the Manager (whose name I forget) was brazen.

Equally inevitably, markets suffered – though not spectacularly so, and in the Stock Exchange the intense volatility in the oil market was more than made up for by the huge turnover. 'I remember never looking up from my book booking bargains from ten o'clock through till two o'clock,' Brian Peppiatt recalled about his time as a blue button with Akroyd & Smithers, which had recently merged with the major oil jobbers Blackwell. 'There was no question of going to the loo or having a cigarette or anything, you were just absolutely glued there, but it was an immensely exciting time.' Military action began at the very end of October – 'No Time for Delay' was the title of the *FT*'s leader on 1 November, calling in vain for a spirit of national unity behind the military intervention – but ended after only a week, as a result of intense financial as well as political pressure on Britain from the United States. As early as the 1st the discount market was told by Cobbold that 'the pressure on Sterling was considerable and that he didn't wish it to continue in this way for 365 days in the year'.[43]

Suez marked, with brutal clarity, the end of Britain as a world power. It also cost Britain, between 30 October and 8 December, $450m of reserves. A week later, on the 15th, the *FT* asked two crucial long-term questions about sterling and its role: 'The first is whether the extent of Britain's banking commitments through sterling is not excessive in comparison to the country's real economic power and resources. The second is whether British economic policy is not now too much influenced by attempts to calculate the reactions of foreign exchange dealers to British policy.' Yet in Cobbold's eyes – as in the City's generally – there could be no thought of answering either question in the affirmative. 'The feeling of the markets both here and abroad is quite clear,' he unequivocally told Macmillan five days later:

> They do not anticipate early devaluation. But they have been shocked by the weakness exposed by recent developments and they have their eyes firmly fixed on what they regard as three question marks; our willingness to live within our means, our overseas commitments and our productive capacity (or will to work). Unless these questions are answered to their satisfaction, the underlying pressures will remain against us and will become stronger.

And, having identified the holding of the currency with the maintenance of 'our way of life', Cobbold ended his letter by asserting that 'we are, I believe, at a cross-road, where the whole future of sterling, and everything which that implies, depends on the decisions of the next few months'.[44]

Macmillan, as requested, showed the letter to Eden, who responded shortly after Christmas. After acknowledging that during the crisis Britain had been at the mercy of an international loss of confidence in sterling, and conceding the problems of going any further with either the credit squeeze or public expenditure cuts, Eden threw out an idea perhaps more in hope than in expectation:

> We should ask the Governor whether there is any means of reducing our vulnerability to the 'confidence factor'. This inevitably springs from our position as bankers for the sterling area. As such we no doubt derive benefits. But do these offset the damage our reserves suffer when sterling is under pressure? The gains we painfully win from improved trading returns vanish almost overnight. Is there any way of meeting this?
> Why must sterling continue always to bear all of these burdens?

Macmillan's reply on New Year's Eve was wonderfully laconic:

> There is no way of avoiding the dangers to sterling which come from being bankers to the sterling area. We have inherited an old family business which used to be very profitable and sound. The trouble is that the liabilities are four times the assets. In the old days a business of this kind, like Coutt's or Cox's Bank, would have been sold to one of the big five. The trouble is I do not know who is to buy the sterling area banking system . . . So we must either carry on the business with all its risks, or wind it up and pay 5s in the £.[45]

Macmillan may have seen the sterling area as an inescapable deadweight – but at least, unlike almost everyone in the City, he did see it *as* a deadweight. There, one of the few notable exceptions was, typically, Sir George Bolton, who by the end of the Suez crisis was starting to believe that sterling's days as a major international currency were numbered and that the City of London would have to reinvent itself for a post-sterling future.[46] Early in 1957 he left the Bank of England, after a quarter of a century, and became Chairman of the Bank of London and South America (BOLSA). Bolton's perception was probably shared by Siegmund Warburg, but in almost all other minds the City's fortunes remained inextricably entwined with those of sterling and the sterling area.

CHAPTER FIVE

Too Much Ballyhoo

To the City's satisfaction (according to Cobbold), it was Macmillan, not Butler, who succeeded Eden as Prime Minister on 10 January 1957. The move had a significant City repercussion, for one of Macmillan's Cabinet appointments was the Earl of Perth (formerly Lord Strathallan) of Schroders. It proved a crystallising moment for that bank, which had been having problems at the highest level. Five years earlier Cobbold had noted serious friction between Helmut Schroder and Henry Tiarks. Matters remained unresolved in May 1955, when Cobbold saw Schroder: 'The internal personal position is still not quite happy and Mr Schroder went over the whole ground again with me. He is sticking to his view that Perth must run the business in his absence but H.T. is still very unhappy.'[1] Schroder's instincts were sound – almost certainly Perth had done more than either Tiarks or himself to rebuild the business since the war – and there is no doubt that his surprise call to the political colours left the partnership (as it still was, though the firm was about to be incorporated) in something of a hole.

The saviour was a man without a drop of City blood in his veins. Born in Nottingham in 1915, the son of a well-off local provision merchant, Gordon Richardson read law at Cambridge before becoming a successful London counsel specialising in company law. In 1955 he decided to try his luck in the City, going to ICFC. Such was his immediate impact there that by the following year Piercy, in conversation with Cobbold, was identifying Richardson as a possible successor. That, however, did not materialise – partly because of the septuagenarian's unwillingness to step down, and partly for reasons recorded later in 1956 by Mynors after a conversation with 'Ruby' Holland-Martin. Richardson, it had transpired, 'is not happy to end his days with ICFC', apparently on the grounds that 'it is not the kind of business nor does he in general meet the sort of people which he hoped for when he left the Bar'. Accordingly, 'E.H-M. asked me to bear in mind that he would be on the transfer list ...' It was much to Helmut Schroder's credit that, at this difficult and important moment in his family firm's history, he decided to recruit at a very senior level someone of Richardson's background. 'There was something very agreeable about Schroders,' Richardson himself recalled. 'I talked to the people and they were very nice, and of course it was after the German debt settlement so the agonies, so to speak, were over. The situation offered a tremendous challenge.'[2] In other words, a berth at Schroders offered a potential passport to the innermost circles of the City in a way that even being the Chairman of ICFC never could.

The contrast between Schroders and Rothschilds, which had been going through a not dissimilar crisis, was illuminating. Rothschilds' troubles began in June 1955, when the senior partner, Anthony de Rothschild, had a severe stroke. 'I took the opportunity of saying to Lord Ashburton,' Cobbold recorded some weeks later, 'that I hoped Barings (who are their oldest friends) would hold Rothschilds' hand a bit during this awkward time. He said they were conscious of the difficulty and would certainly do their best.' During the autumn it became clear that Anthony would never return to work. The problem was that the only other partner, his nephew Edmund, had plenty of energy but was not regarded in the City as a heavyweight. Over the past few years he had been much involved with the British Newfoundland Corporation (BRINCO), which would ultimately lead to a massive hydroelectric project at the Churchill Falls; but reports filtering back to the Bank of England were less than complimentary about his role, not least when Sir John Woods of English Electric described him to Mynors in October 1956 as 'a headache' and 'a pain in the neck to the local management'. Edmund de Rothschild himself recognised some of his limitations, but it was still an awkward position in which the bank found itself, as ever obstinately refusing to bring in partners from outside the family. Granted that deep-seated obstinacy, Cobbold and Peacock agreed in November 1956 that 'there was for the moment nothing to be done', though fortunately 'it seemed that the younger Rothschilds were shaping gratifyingly well'.[3] No doubt they were, but Schroders had the right of it in their respective attitudes to new blood.

A merger was one way out of a shortage of capital and/or talent. At the start of 1955 not only was the ailing Japhets taken over by Charterhouse, but the hungry Philip Hill, Higginson & Co (of which Kenneth Keith had been Managing Director since 1951) acquired British Shareholders Trust. It was a route that one elderly, struggling accepting house preferred not to go down. 'They want to carry on business and maintain the name,' Cobbold noted on 4 January, following a visit from Reginald and Bobby Seligman in the wake of the capital-diminishing deaths of Sir Charles Seligman and Louis Fleischmann. 'They would like to get somebody else in . . . I said that I was glad to hear that the family wanted to go on.' By the end of 1956 Seligmans was still independent, but Cobbold's private information was that 'there was a row going on within the Seligman family' and that 'one of them is accusing others of various malpractices including a dishonest balance sheet'.[4] Accordingly, early in 1957, a member of the Accepting Houses Committee was up for sale, and Warburgs quickly clinched a bargain for £45,000, with the merged firm to be called on its letterhead 'S.G. Warburg & Company (incorporating Seligman Brothers)'. It was Siegmund Warburg's ticket to the City's inner circle – the Accepting Houses Committee – and as he reflected the day after signing the agreement, 'An opportunity never presents itself twice, and that settles everything.' This ruthlessness had been presaged in miniature only a few weeks earlier, when Warburg had blatantly defied convention by poaching Sam Hamburger, one of the brains of Bensons' new issue department, with no warning at all, even though Rex Benson had been one of his earliest supporters in the City.[5] Not surprisingly, Warburg became the object of more admiration than friendship, more mistrust than admiration.

About this time, reputedly, people in the City began to snicker at Warburgs as upstart 'bond-washers'. Bond-washing itself had been a familiar practice between the wars – more or less tacitly tolerated by the authorities – and was now back in prominence. Essentially, it was a lucrative manoeuvre that involved selling stocks full of dividend from high taxpayers to those who wanted their dividends gross, and then buying the stocks back for those taxpayers when they were ex-dividend. Unsurprisingly, the prospect of an untaxed capital gain was attractive to institutions as well as individuals. By 1956 the Inland Revenue was expressing its unhappiness, and in August that year the Government broker, Derrick Mullens, issued a circular to the gilt-edged market calling on bond-washing in short gilts to stop. The leading jobbers in that market solemnly initialled the memo, but simply turned their attention to bond-washing in long gilts. Over the winter it became clear to the Stock Exchange Council not only that bond-washing had become the easiest way to make money in Capel Court, but that the phenomenon had the potential to turn into a major, heavily publicised scandal. A special committee was established in April 1957 to re-examine the whole question.

One of the first to give evidence was Dick Wilkins of Wedd, Jefferson & Co, one of the dominant jobbers of his generation. 'He agreed that it should be stopped, particularly when dividends were manufactured. He could not offer a solution to the problem . . . He suggested that an appeal should be made to those carrying on this kind of business . . .' Another prominent jobber, Jack Jarrett of Francis & Praed, was more forthcoming. Arguing that 'it was extremely difficult to decide where legitimate business stopped and the other business started', he stated that he was 'quite positive that in this kind of business there was nothing pre-arranged and that a chance was taken on the market'. By early May Mynors at the Bank was being told by Mullens that it was becoming ever more evident that 'bond-washing is much more widely spread and its possibilities realised by a much wider section of the public than anybody had expected'. To which paraphrase Mynors footnoted: '"Common talk in all the bars in Switzerland", as Mullens put it'. The eventual upshot of the committee's report was an August circular from the Council calling on members to bring this business to an end. Braithwaite also addressed in person representatives of the gilt-edged market. 'Bond-washing operations,' he declared, 'have become a scandal; note of them is being taken in Parliament, and they are beyond all question detrimental to the interests of the Stock Exchange.' The operations themselves he called 'nothing less than fraud upon the Inland Revenue', and he warned of harsh penalties.[6] Solemn words, but this was a money-spinner not yet quite ready for the history books.

Bond-washing was not the only subject of formal inquiry during 1957. 'I mentioned ideas floating around about a new Monetary Committee,' Cobbold noted after calling on Sir Roger Makins, Permanent Secretary to the Treasury, at the end of January. 'I said that, whilst we had opposed the idea strongly a year ago when we thought it premature, I personally saw some advantage in the near future. I promised to think about names.' Over the next two months there took shape – with the blessing of Peter Thorneycroft, Macmillan's successor as Chancellor – what became the Radcliffe Committee on the Working of the Monetary System, the belated response to that system's embarrassing failure in 1955 to deliver the credit squeeze on which Butler's tax-cutting pre-election budget had been predicated.[7] A fairly staid, eminently respectable array of Bank-vetted names was assembled, while mid-May saw a perceptible narrowing of options and a closing of ranks.

The process began on the 13th when Cobbold sent Lord Radcliffe, an eminent lawyer, a memo entitled 'Some Thoughts at Random' on the forthcoming committee:

> I think you will find that working relations between the Bank of England and the Banking System are pretty good. The Banks dislike 'directives' and are getting tired of the credit squeeze – but, even so, relations are close and harmonious. The only place I expect you to hear contrary views is among some banking economists who feel that they are inadequately consulted . . .
>
> Many people (and some members of your Committee) will press for more information from the 'Authorities'. I have been moving a bit along the line of making a few policy speeches and there may be some more to be done here and there. But we ought not to go too fast or too far. And Heaven protect us from a monthly 'Federal Reserve Bulletin', a duplication of Government Economic services, and a continuous spate of unreliable statistics and prophecies . . .

Faced by the prospect of outside scrutiny – and probably criticism –

Cobbold was also in fruitful correspondence with Makins. 'Each of us will keep in touch with the other's thinking while we prepare our positions,' the latter assured the Governor, adding that 'as our work proceeds, I am sure that we shall feel the need for your advice, and when such occasions arise I hope we may ask for it'. To which Cobbold replied, 'We are, I think, in full agreement and I foresee no difficulty in practice.' As final preparations were made over the next few weeks, Hall watched the process deepen. 'R. Makins has a Committee to co-ordinate Treasury thinking, on which O'Brien of the Bank sits,' he noted in late June; and, more generally, he added that 'the Banks are turning out rather undistinguished papers at a rapid rate'.[8]

An early witness was of course Cobbold himself, and in one of his appearances in July he stressed in a prepared statement that the Bank 'regard it as absolutely vital in the national interest that the Bank should keep entirely out of political issues'. He elaborated:

> There is a long history in all this. We are bound to take account of the history in the 1930s of the public view of monetary action. I think I should convey my meaning not improperly if I used the words 'bankers' ramp' about which we heard a good deal at those times. Since then we have had the nationalisation of the Bank. The present Court have, I think, seen it as one of their prime objectives to create conditions and so to manage their affairs that the Bank could and would settle down as a national institution, accepted as such by the country as a whole, but retaining sufficient independence of thought to do its job properly.

Later in the same statement, with a rare flash of passion, Cobbold remarked that 'it would quite certainly make Bank relations with Government intolerable if discussion and argument were conducted by the Bank and the Treasury in public instead of between themselves'. Similarly, in answer to Radcliffe's question as to whether he equated his position 'with that of a leading Civil Servant', he replied indignantly, 'Not at all. I am a servant of the Bank Court.'[9]

Giving public evidence, even to what was a broadly well-disposed inquiry, was far from this particular central banker's dream scenario. 'I have seen O. Franks [a member of the Radcliffe Committee] several times,' Hall recorded at the end of July. 'He says that the inability of the Governor to talk coherently is going to be a great barrier.'[10] There was an unmistakable echo of Norman's struggles in front of the Macmillan Committee a quarter of a century earlier.

*

At about the time of Cobbold's second tranche of evidence, a City branch of Midland asked the stockbrokers Pember & Boyle for advice about 'the advantages and disadvantages of investing in good industrials'. The reply on 30 July was that although the long-term outlook was largely positive (with an approving nod being given to the recent 'substantial increase in the equity shareholdings of institutional investors – pension funds, insurance companies and the like – who can afford to take a long term view'), the more immediate outlook was far less favourable. In addition to 'our present economic difficulties', 'support for the Government has undoubtedly suffered a setback over its inability to find some way to check the world-wide inflationary trend and the next election, whenever that may come, could therefore reflect the disappointment of the electors in returning a Left Wing Government'. Such a government, Pember & Boyle warned, would be likely to lead to 'a policy of further nationalisation', as well as 'the imposition of price controls, restriction of share dividends and a general return to the conditions of a closed economy'.[11]

Within a fortnight, compounding what Bank and Treasury (as well as the City as a whole) felt to be a grim domestic inflationary outlook, sterling reserves were starting to tumble fast. On 22 August, as he was about to go on holiday to Sardinia, Cobbold despatched a warning shot to Thorneycroft: 'We have a difficult time ahead. The Germans are going to behave like Germans – it looks like a new boomlet internally – and round the corner there are some hints of some drying-up of international liquidity – which all indicates that we should be ready to take any necessary steps in the autumn . . .' An accompanying memo to the Treasury wanted Thorneycroft to toughen his expenditure stance, so that there was no need for a huge Bank rate rise to protect sterling, granted that 'in the monetary field we have come to the end of what can be done by talking to the banks about advances'. Two days later Macmillan had a long talk with Thorneycroft, especially about the weakness of sterling. 'We *must* be bold; caution is no good,' he privately noted afterwards. 'All our political future depends on whether we can combine prosperity with stability.'[12] One of the classic episodes of post-war British history – political and social, as well as financial – was about to unfold.[13]

While the politicians deliberated, and the Governor relaxed, Mynors was left on the bridge. To two absent Bank directors, Michael Babington Smith and 'Tony' Keswick, he wrote almost identical handwritten letters on 3 September, putting them in the picture. After noting that the August exchange figures 'will shock most people', he went on:

> Our friends in the West End are now I think alive to the fact that the world expects not only the D-mark to go up but the £ to come down. They are considering what action could be taken in short order to convince the world that we will master our chronic inflation: but nothing is yet decided. A part of the picture might well be a swingeing rise in the Bank Rate, intended not to last for long.

To a third absent director, the trade unionist Sir Alfred Roberts, Mynors gave a deliberately more domestic spin: 'We may be in for a real exchange tussle . . . I remain convinced that our prosperity and standard of living will suffer a mortal blow if the pound goes again, even though it is not easy to put this across as it is not apparent in everyday life.' Nor indeed was it – and not only in 1957, as sterling's defenders tried over the years, often in vain, to explain to an instinctively deferential but still somewhat bemused larger public exactly why sacrifices always had to be made to protect the pound. In 1957 itself one of the absent directors, Keswick, replied on the 5th from Glenkiln, Shawhead, Dumfries, saying that he was due to 'go South' on the 14th, but that if necessary he was happy to return beforehand. And he gave his telephone number: Lochfoot 280.[14]

Over the next week and a bit, pending Cobbold's return on Saturday the 14th, much of Mynors's energies were devoted to resisting Thorneycroft's urge to impose, if necessary through a formal directive from the Bank of England, a 5 per cent reduction in bank advances. Such would have been Mynors's instinctive attitude anyway, even had he not been told by Robarts on the 5th that the clearers 'would be willing to maintain their existing restrictive attitude to advances, but they could not commit themselves to any particular level'. Mynors, Robarts and Franks were all at the Treasury on the 9th to see Thorneycroft, who told them that he intended to make a statement, with a view to restoring foreign confidence in sterling, before he went to Washington on the 20th. The clearers talked tough, with Robarts saying that 'a specific limit to the total of advances' would be not only 'unwise' but also 'unworkable'; while Franks, seeking to shift the blame, was positively aggressive, asserting that 'in the past the Government had gone back on any measures that produced unemployment' and that 'he thought it unlikely that they would behave differently this time'. To that Thorneycroft riposted that 'politically an increase in unemployment was preferable to the fall of the pound', adding that 'the main object must be to limit the supply of money, but he did not rule out dearer money as a supporting measure'. In conclusion, he stated that 'his present intention was still to announce a limit on the supply of money by the banks as well as by the Government' and that he would 'like the opportunity to discuss the matter further with all the members of the Committee of Clearing Bankers'.[15]

Before that meeting was held, on the 11th, Mynors rose to what was probably the biggest challenge of his ten-year deputy-governorship. He did so by writing to Thorneycroft on the 10th to assert that it was very desirable that the voluntary approach to bank credit be continued and that, under the 1946 Bank of England Act, it would require fresh powers to enable government to impose a formal limit on bank advances without doing it via the Bank of England. Moreover, quite apart from the urgency of the situation, 'to take fresh powers . . . would raise the gravest questions of the relations between the government and the banking system'. The following afternoon the clearers, plus Mynors, attended a meeting in Thorneycroft's room. 'The Chancellor opened by saying that the pound could not be defended unless inflation was more tightly gripped' and that, to do this, the government must 'hold the level of investment in the public sector', while 'in the private sector he looked for a limit on bank advances'. Thorneycroft reiterated that there must be a public statement by the 20th and that devaluation was not an option. To this, Robarts and Franks insisted that their views two days earlier – 'that a limit on the level of bank advances was neither appropriate nor workable' – had been endorsed by the CLCB as a whole. At this delicate point Thorneycroft waved a big stick in preference to pressing the nuclear button. He said that his statement would call on the banks not to increase their level of advances over the next twelve months; that on his return from America he would closely monitor the situation; and that, 'if the results were not adequate, the Government would be obliged to consider and discuss with the banks what statutory provision Parliament might be asked to make in order to bring about the required results'. There is some evidence that, prior to this semi-climbdown, he had considered dismissing Cobbold, but had found that the 1946 Act also prevented him from doing that.[16]

Cobbold himself, once back from holiday, fully backed up Mynors and the clearers, telling Thorneycroft on the 15th that 'I do not believe that bank advances are the source from which present inflationary pressures are coming', and expressing the hope that in the forthcoming statement 'no threat would be included of further legislation' – in other words, in relation to the banking system, which according to him 'could easily be read abroad as a threat of nationalisation – with a most damaging effect on confidence in sterling'. Next day Cobbold sent Thorneycroft a draft of the relevant sentence (from the imminent statement) with which the clearing bankers would be happy: 'I have asked the Bankers to continue their co-operation in restricting advances and to use their best endeavours to ensure that the average level of Bank advances during the next twelve months should not exceed the average level for the last twelve months'.[17] The City's united front had worked, and there was to be – at least in public – no hint of criticism of the banking system.

Limited action on advances meant, ineluctably, a significant (at the very least) increase in Bank rate. Mynors had intimated to the Court on the 12th that a big increase was likely. Next day one of the Bank's directors, the Birmingham industrialist Laurence Cadbury, wrote to him opposing this policy, on the grounds not only that it would lead to further unnatural swings in the British economy (essentially the stop-go argument), but also that it was the wage/price spiral that was primarily responsible for inflation. 'As I see it,' Mynors replied to Cadbury on the 14th, 'the one thing that would have a real effect on the wage/price spiral would be a novel conviction that the Govt were prepared to throw 99 per cent employment overboard if necessary in order to maintain the value of the currency. It certainly cannot be done by the Rate alone.' As for the stop-go argument, he contended that 'we should be able to bring the Rate down gradually before long without too much of a green light, because the underlying climate would have changed'.[18] In a sense, as Cobbold rapidly appreciated on his return, a major hike in Bank rate was all that was left – granted that on the one hand there would be no significant reduction in bank advances and that on the other Thorneycroft lacked the clout, even if he had the will, to impose on Macmillan substantial expenditure cuts.

Cobbold now wanted the rate to rise from 5 to 7 per cent – an increase double that of Thorneycroft's preference – and a memo sent to the Chancellor on the morning of the 17th summarised his reasons for such a large jump:

> It would give a jolt, show that the exchange position is serious (which will anyhow become painfully evident at end-month) but that the Bank propose to fight for the pound by determined use of their weapons.
> A rise of this sort would have a considerable effect on borrowers, and is likely to cause deferment of spending plans. It would, in our view, be at this stage the most effective contribution on the monetary side to restriction of spending in the private sector – much more effective than any pressures or directives on the banks . . .
> It would strengthen our arguing position with the Germans in international forum, and remove accusation that it is we and not the Germans who ought to change policy.
> Technically it would put London rates more where they should be in comparison with other centres and with the relative strength and weakness of currencies . . .
> If no firm Bank Rate has been taken by the time September exchange figures come out, overseas opinion and perhaps domestic opinion would judge that we were not prepared to act firmly and would have increasing doubts of our determination to hold the value of the pound.
> The objections are the obvious ones of cost to budget and interest on sterling balances – but the main objectives are now so important that these should not be overriding . . .

Whether deliberately or not, Cobbold was silent on the question of whether another 'obvious objection' to a 2 per cent rise in interest rates was that it might do serious damage to British industry. The Cabinet met that afternoon. 'The Bank want to raise Bank rate by 2 per cent – a thing practically without precedent,' Macmillan noted in his diary. 'After much argument, this was left for me & Chancellor to settle. The Cabinet lasted from 3–7. Then a little dinner, then Governor etc at 9 p.m. I argued &

questioned the experts to 11 p.m., & said I w^d sleep on it.'[19] He did, but the priorities and parameters imposed by the primacy of sterling did not miraculously vanish: 7 per cent it would be.

The change was announced by Thorneycroft to the Commons on the morning of Thursday the 19th, as part of his statement, and by the Government broker almost simultaneously on the floor of the Stock Exchange. Once the news got about, big queues quickly formed for the Stock Exchange gallery, and that day there were more than a thousand visitors, the most since soon after it had opened in November 1953. Those actually on the floor would not forget the moment of the announcement. 'Absolutely dead silence,' recalled David LeRoy-Lewis. 'Everybody was stunned.' Graham Ferguson of Wedd Jefferson was another young jobber present when the rise was posted: 'I remember Dick Wilkins' face when it went up, because we lost more money in two minutes than we'd ever thought possible . . . There was absolute shock-horror and then absolute hectic dealing everywhere.' More generally, the press reaction to the bombshell was neatly summed up by Macmillan in his diary. 'So well was the secret kept,' he observed on the 20th, 'that the Press seemed dazed.'[20]

Of course, quite apart from the jobbers who had failed to read the signals, it was hardly welcome news to most people. The *FT* for one was still sufficiently in command of its faculties to argue that not only was it possible that foreign opinion might see this dramatic hike in Bank rate (now the highest rate since the early 1920s) as 'an unfavourable indication of the seriousness of the British difficulties', but that 'as an economic policy for the future' these were measures that 'do not take us very far', in that 'apart from exchange speculation the weakness of the British economy rises largely from the constant pressure of trade union demands'. Even so, fairly soon a consensus seems to have emerged that this was a necessary dose of strong, anti-inflationary medicine. 'We have great hopes that this rise in Bank Rate may have a restraining influence on the amount of money borrowed from the banks, with the resultant strengthening of our reserves' was how Evelyn Baring put it on 1 October to an American correspondent. And, just over a month after the hike, Cobbold was pointing out to the Treasury that 'some of his colleagues got rather hot when the Chancellor spoke about the 7 per cent Bank Rate as if it was entirely his idea'.[21]

There was another, completely unexpected dimension to the rise. 'I'm spending far too much of my time on this damned leak business,' Cobbold expostulated to a colleague about a week after Thorneycroft's announcement. So indeed he was, for within days – even hours – of the rise taking effect, rumours began to spread, in the City and elsewhere, that powerful figures had had advance warning of that rise – and, furthermore, had taken advantage to sell heavily in the gilt-edged market. On 24

September the Shadow Chancellor, Harold Wilson, formally drew the government's attention to 'the very disquieting reports in a number of responsible newspapers and City circles about a premature leakage of information' and demanded an inquiry. Cobbold was vexed but unimpressed, telling the government the next day that 'so far as Bank Rate is concerned, I have never known an important move where I have seen less signs of rumour or expectation beforehand'. He did not deny that 'there were one or two vague references to Bank Rate in the morning papers of Thursday', but insisted that 'nobody took them seriously'. On the basis of his findings, as well as Braithwaite's at the Stock Exchange, the government refused Wilson's demand. During October the opposition pressed again – and yet again was denied. Makins of the Treasury told Cobbold on the 18th that Thorneycroft was 'a bit concerned about rumours that Stock Exchange people were dissatisfied', to which Cobbold responded that a certain amount of criticism was 'probably inevitable on such a sharp Bank Rate change'. He added that the larger jobbers were 'sore at losing a lot of money', felt that 'they ought to have been tipped off that something was coming' and altogether 'had been outsmarted by some of the brokers'. It was an exchange that prompted Thorneycroft to note sardonically that 'the main complaint in the City appeared to be not that there had been a leakage of information but that there had not'.[22]

In the end Macmillan gave way, not least because he found himself coming under pressure to do so from the Conservative Party's Deputy Chairman, Oliver Poole, who was also a senior figure at Lazards. Rumours were increasingly implicating him, and he believed his honour to be at stake. 'The appointment of a Tribunal of Enquiry into the alleged Bank Rate Leak, after all this time, is a fearful nuisance, to put it no higher,' Mynors wrote on 18 November to one of the Bank's directors. 'Although interest in the subject has always been political rather than at our end of Town, we shall doubtless have to go through all the motions of explaining how the Rate is in fact changed, what honest fellows we all are, etc, etc.' The Bank's two part-time directors under enemy fire were Tony Keswick and Hugh Kindersley (son of the first Lord Kindersley, who had died in 1954), and the next day Cobbold noted that 'Lord Kindersley called to ask for my help in reconstructing some time-table of his meetings with me during the Bank Rate discussions'. The City's nervousness was tangible. On the 26th, six days before the start of the Tribunal under Lord Justice Parker, Hall ran into Bolton: 'He said that his lawyer had told him he mustn't mention Bank Rate (not the leak – but at all!) till after the inquiry. And that the City had been advised to hold *no* communication with any member of the Labour Party except by letter approved by legal advisers . . .' The next day Hall was told by a Treasury source that 'no firms were buying gilt-edged', on the grounds that 'their books might be inspected and why should they put down any more transactions'.[23]

Proceedings began at Church House, Westminster, with an opening statement by the Attorney-General, Sir Reginald Manningham-Buller. He quoted various market comments by the press on 20 September, including Francis Whitmore in the *Daily Telegraph*: 'There was strong criticism in the City among gilt-edged dealers and in the discount market of some leakage of information of the forthcoming Government measures the day before. In both quarters, heavy selling of gilt-edged stocks was reported late on Wednesday.' One of the crossest jobbing firms was Wedd & Owen, whose circular of four days later he also quoted: 'We have for many years past been prepared to continue to deal after the close of the House. This facility had occasionally been abused, but never to the extent that it was on the night of Wednesday, 18th September last.'

Various press and Stock Exchange witnesses gave evidence, the latter especially in the context of Mathesons having on that Wednesday sold over £1m of gilts. It was now that the letter was disclosed that Keswick of Mathesons – but also a director of the Bank of England – had sent on 16 September to Jardine Matheson in Hong Kong:

> I have just returned from Scotland where we had a wonderful time, record shooting and good fun all round. But I returned to a very depressed City. I believe the trade figures are dreadful, and one hears on all sides ugly rumours about devaluation.
>
> John [Keswick's brother, then on holiday in Scotland] tells me you were asking for a cable about our views on devaluation, and especially about the merits of selling Gilts. This is not easy, and whatever view one takes, one is apt to be wrong. I shall telegraph you today. Personally I do not believe that the Chancellor dare devalue and, therefore, he will resort to all measures before so doing. Speculative pressure against sterling is very severe indeed. It seems a heads-I-win-tails-you-lose bet for the sellers of sterling Short, and I do not see how they can be stopped.
>
> What measures the Government will take to check inflation which is rampant, and to protect the pound, I do not know. I am certain, however, that the credit squeeze will go on, and it looks to me as if money will get tighter.
>
> Consequently, it must be right policy to keep as liquid as possible.

Probably just after writing and despatching this letter, Keswick drafted a cable – anticipating tighter money and recommending that gilts be sold – but delayed sending it. He then went to have lunch at the Bank, where he was told by Mynors that a 'swingeing' rise in Bank rate was possible, but that nothing was yet decided. Keswick did not return to his office that afternoon, going instead to his dentist and hairdresser. Shortly after noon the following day, the 17th, the cable was sent, and some hours later the timely selling of gilts took place.

Tony Keswick himself faced a tough cross-examination on 6 December from Manningham-Buller, who made much of Mynors's letter to Keswick in early September, while he was still on the Scottish moors:

> You would agree, would you not, that it would be very wrong if you were told as a Director of the Bank of England that there was likely to be an increase in the Bank rate, or that an increase was under consideration, for you to communicate or hint at that to anyone with whom you were associated in business? – I would consider it wrong.
> Very wrong? – Very wrong.
> Your position was a difficult one, was it not? – Yes, it is.
> You had an obligation to give honest advice to Jardine, Matheson & Co? – Yes, I did.
> And you had a duty not to disclose anything directly or indirectly in relation to the Bank rate? – Yes, I did.
> Which duty did you regard as the most important? – I regard them equally important.

Soon afterwards the question came up of the discussion between Keswick and his brother on Saturday the 14th about the situation concerning the 'squeeze' and so on. 'It is difficult for me,' Keswick observed in a memorable phrase that would be much cited, 'to remember the exact timing of conversation on a grouse moor.' Of more immediate moment, however, were the implications of Keswick's visit to the Bank on Tuesday the 16th:

> Did you not as a result of that lunch regard it as a possibility that the Bank rate would be raised on the Thursday? – It must have gone through my head that it was possible that Thursday or the following Thursday.
> And the more serious the situation, the more likelihood for immediate action rather than deferred action? – I think that depended entirely on the politicians at that time. That is what would be my guess.
> Whether or not it depended on politicians, would you not agree that the more serious the situation, the greater the need for prompt action? – One should say yes.
> And as the situation was obviously regarded as very serious, did you really not consider that there was a serious possibility of the Bank rate being raised on the Thursday? – Actually I did not. I think in my folly I did not. I thought there would have been quite different measures. . .

It was, at the last, an answer that hardly tallied with three key words in the cable to Hong Kong: 'anticipate tighter money'.

Attention during the Tribunal's second week focused mainly on Lazards, which had sold £1.5m gilt-edged on the 17th and 18th. Poole and Kindersley (the latter lunching at Pruniers each day during the ordeal) both played their cards more skilfully. A sub-plot of Kindersley's evidence was the £30m Vickers issue that Lazards had been helping Morgan Grenfell to get underwritten in the days immediately before the rise. He related how, on the 16th, he had unsuccessfully tried to persuade Cobbold to agree to pull the Vickers issue; and how, on the morning of the 18th, he had found himself in a car next to Cobbold's on the Embankment, had joined the Governor's car and told him that he would support a Bank rate rise, even if the Vickers issue could not be postponed. One answer nicely evoked the close relationship between Lazards and Morgan Grenfell: 'I do not think Lord Bicester [the second Lord Bicester, son of Vivian Hugh Smith] would find it in the least surprising that I should come to him and say to him: "Look here, Rufie, is it too late to stop this business or not?" '[24]

At the start of the third week Cobbold himself spent three uncomfortable hours in the witness box. 'I did not think he did too well' was Hall's predictable comment. 'He seems to have told the PM a little less than the full story about the deals by firms with members on the Court – and as Ministers do not like him much anyway, this won't help.' Bolton, another witness, gave a more generous assessment of the Governor's evidence: 'Voice bad but sincerity obvious.' Two days later it was the turn of Trinder of Union Discount:

> My Company is the largest day-to-day trader in London. I run a big book, and the Bank rate is more or less the thing that I stand or fall by . . . If I am wrong I certainly lose a lot of money, and if I am really wrong I could become insolvent or my Company could, but fortunately that has not happened. So a 2 per cent rise in Bank rate when it turned up on the Thursday was a bad blow for me. I did not think the Bank rate would go to 7; I thought the Bank rate could rise. . .

After insisting that he did not know, then or later, of any leakage, Trinder was asked by Lord Justice Parker why, if he thought the Bank rate would probably rise on the famous Thursday, he had sold only £1.5m more than he had bought in the immediate preceding period:

> We are the biggest dealers. I cannot always do what I want to. I make the market. If the Union Discount suddenly appears to sell £5,000,000 or £10,000,000 worth of stock, generally I cannot deal, because nobody is buying from me. So you have to sit reasonably quiet and hope for the best at certain times.[25]

By Christmas the Tribunal had finished taking evidence, and soon afterwards Hall heard that 'the City is in a rage against Ministers over the Bank Rate Inquiry, because they think the Attorney-General attacked the Governor and the Court and let off the politicians'. Hall himself reflected that this was in part 'due to a feeling of guilt as they (the City end) did come out of the inquiry rather badly', adding that 'even' Lionel Robbins had said to him that 'the position of the Bank would never be the same again'. There was no doubt about the City's rage. 'I thought the Attorney General went out of his way to be offensive about the Governor in his big winding up speech,' Kindersley wrote to Bolton. 'If he was the next gun to me tomorrow I would certanly use my cartridges in a different direction to the pheasants!!!' Kindersley was less inclined to reflect on the fact that it was now known that the three major concerns he chaired – Lazards, Royal Exchange Assurance and the British Match Co – had between them sold almost £2.5m of gilts in the day and a half before the Bank rate announcement.[26]

Meanwhile, as those concerned waited for the Tribunal's findings, there was what Macmillan blithely and immortally called a 'little local difficulty'. Four days before the end of 1957 Cobbold wrote gravely to Thorneycroft: 'I am bound to express the view that if HM Government accept estimates of the order which you mentioned to me this morning, it will be seen at home and abroad to be in flat contradiction with your statement of 19th September'. And he warned that, despite 'a distinct improvement in atmosphere and small increase in the reserves' since 19 September, 'there is no prospect that any weakening of policy . . . would escape immediate notice and strong criticism'.[27] Thus fortified, Thorneycroft fought a bitter battle over the next ten days with most of the rest of the government to reduce the amount by which the draft estimates for public expenditure for 1958–9 showed an increase over the previous year. He managed to whittle down that increase from £153m to £50m, but could get no further; and ultimately, on 6 January 1958, he and the other two Treasury ministers (including Enoch Powell) resigned.

That same day, having been told by Thorneycroft that it was not over the actual sums that he was resigning but rather the principle of restraining public expenditure, Cobbold wrote to Macmillan:

> I should always feel chary about resignations over comparatively small figures, but, feeling as he does on the question of principle, I myself think he is right . . . I am very sorry, because I felt that with P.T.'s courage and with you behind him at No. 10, we were on an improving wicket from the currency's point of view. And I still feel – perhaps I am prejudiced! – that the success or failure of the next two years depends more on the currency than on anything else.

The next day the *FT* was inclined to argue that Thorneycroft had made a mountain out of a molehill – and looked forward to an economic policy under his successor, Derick Heathcoat Amory, 'somewhat more expansionist, but inside the limits set by confidence in the pound'. However *The Times* squarely blamed Macmillan for not having supported his 'courageous' Chancellor. The following Tuesday in the *FT* Harold Wincott was equally unequivocal, declaring his wholehearted support for Thorneycroft's recent refutation of 'the Keynesian doctrine' that 'internal policies take precedence over the external value of the currency'. He added that he was happy, like Thorneycroft, to be considered 'a hard-faced, hard money man', before concluding in characteristically vernacular-cum-portentous tones:

> In the ultimate resort, if Mr Amory is not to be as expendable as Mr Thorneycroft was, it is the attitude of mind in the Conservative Party which has got to change. For over six years now, that attitude has been the 'Dear-Mother-I-am-going-to-save-7s. 6d.-but-not-this-week' attitude. It still is. But the supply of weeks is running out.[28]

In due course Thorneycroft's resignation, and this sort of endorsement, would attain an almost mythic status as an early (perhaps the earliest) marker of Thatcherism, the start of the turning of the tide against the post-war settlement and accompanying priorities of the managed economy.[29] Yet at the time Wincott was perhaps a little ahead of his natural constituency. 'I would like to see the Government cutting every penny off expenditure,' a leading broker reported to Rab Butler, charged with gauging reaction in the City. 'But if it is a matter of political judgement I would prefer to trust Macmillan rather than Thorneycroft.'[30] So if the socialists could be kept out, then a certain loss of free-market purity was an acceptable price to pay. It was a trade-off that, for almost another twenty years, would continue to govern City assumptions.

While the Thorneycroft drama was being played out, the specific government worry about the Bank Rate Tribunal's imminent report was that, if it criticised the Bank of England at all sharply, Cobbold might feel compelled to resign. This anxiety, however, proved groundless. 'I have just read the Report of the Parker Tribunal,' Makins informed Heathcoat Amory on 10 January. 'It could scarcely be more satisfactory from the point of view of the government, the Bank of England and the City. Everybody connected with the Government and Bank of England is completely exonerated.' Formally published on 21 January, the report indeed concluded that 'there is no justification for allegations that information about the raising of the Bank Rate was improperly disclosed to any person'; as for those who were in receipt of advance warning of the rise, 'in every case the information disclosed was treated by the recipient as confidential and . . . no use of such information was made for the purpose of private gain'.[31]

The City's relief was heartfelt. Next day Cobbold sent a message to all the staff, noting the complete exoneration of the Bank and referring to how the previous few months had been 'a very worrying time for all of us'. With the honour of the City vindicated, the solicitors Linklaters & Paines decided to charge its clients expenses only – but received in return an oil painting (of Sir Sam Brown, senior partner of Linklaters) from Lazards and a valuable clock from Mathesons, the latter gift being inscribed with a slightly wry phrase about 'an act of unusual kindness in the City of

London'. Keswick himself, like Kindersley and Poole, survived unscathed as a major City figure. In later years he took a mischievous delight in purchasing Henry Moore sculptures for his Dumfriesshire glens. The only thing that worried him, he liked to say, was the prospect of art critics upsetting the grouse.[32]

Yet not even a whitewash came cost-free. The press response to the report was somewhat critical, while Labour – probably at the insistence of Nye Bevan – successfully demanded a two-day debate, which was fixed for 3 and 4 February. 'It must be a source of relief to the whole country that the high reputation which the Bank of England, and the City of London as a whole, have enjoyed for so long – [HON MEMBERS: "Oh."] – has been vindicated' was how Butler got the ball rolling in front of a crowded House of Commons. Then came Wilson, who, while accepting the Tribunal's findings about the innocence of Keswick and Kindersley, strongly attacked the Bank of England and its Court:

> We cannot defend a system where, for instance, merchant bankers are treated as the gentlemen and the clearing bankers as the players using the professionals' gate out of the pavilion. Indeed, the joint stock bankers with their greater contact with trade and industry, have more to contribute to the Bank of England than have the merchant bankers, not only at home but also overseas.

There followed a disparaging reference to Mynors's letter to 'the part-time director on his grouse moor', before an attack on the Bank, 'supposed to be a nationalised industry', for behaving 'like a sovereign State' and conducting its relations with the Treasury 'with too much out-dated stiffness and protocol'. Nor, in terms of 'the essentially amateurish way in which vital decisions affecting our whole economic well-being are taken', did Wilson spare the City more generally:

> I do not know what view the man in the street will take of the stockbrokers and jobbers who gave evidence. One thing he may decide to do is to go elsewhere for advice in future. We had, for instance, the gentleman who reads the City columns to see what the investor is likely to do next, while the City editor whom he reads goes to the jobbers and the brokers to see what he should write. Hardly one of those who gave evidence gave a thought to the possibility of an increase in Bank Rate that week. They were all hedging against devaluation. Yet hardly any of them thought of getting into gold shares. It is very remarkable . . .

Jo Grimond, leader of the Liberals, was altogether less critical, as he pleaded against imposing 'too rigid a form' on the City: 'A great deal of business is done on the nod without all the paraphernalia of memoranda, conferences, contracts, and so forth. That is wholly to our advantage. We have here an institution that works on trust . . .'

The next day, Tuesday the 4th, Labour's Patrick Gordon Walker launched a memorable broadside against Kindersley's attempt to get the rise postponed because of the problems of underwriting the Vickers issue:

> What's striking about this is that Lord Kindersley was absolutely unconscious of any conflict of interest whatever. He absolutely identified what was good for the City, to avoid indigestion in the City, with what was good for the national interest, although he himself had come to the conclusion that it was essential in the nation's interests to raise the Bank Rate. He was going on the automatic assumption that what was good for the City was good for Britain . . .

A still more effective attack came from Harold Lever, who was in the process of establishing his reputation as Labour's expert on monetary matters:

> The policies of the Bank of England directorate have meant that our dollars have been diddled away into the hands of every second-rate currency dealer on the Continent. Every commodity shunter has outwitted them. Every dealer in American stocks and shares appears to have been able to get hold of our dollars. Yet all the time the charades of the Bank are religiously maintained. Simple, honest, patriotic and highly talented people have, with great social discipline, continued their efforts to put the country on its feet again, and all the time their efforts have been frustrated because, at one stroke, these blind doctrinaires have poured out the wealth which our people have laboured so hard, so patriotically and with such discipline to produce.

At this point Jennie Lee called out, 'Let them answer that one'.[33] No one did, perhaps because the inherent conflict between the Bank's and indeed the City's national and international priorities was as yet so rarely articulated.

Two days later the Munich air disaster cast a long shadow over everything, but by the end of the week Labour's Dick Crossman was reflecting that the debate had gone 'a good deal better than I had feared'. He especially praised Wilson for his 'sheer guts in battling his way through the entrenched hatred he had engendered among the Tories' and noted that, for all the absence of an actual leak, 'the workings of the City as revealed by the Report are more fantastic, cumbersome, priggish, hypocritical than even I believed'. Soon afterwards Hall too praised Wilson for having 'stuck to his guns', however much this made him the City's *bête noire*; and he added that 'the Government story is that the Governor misled the PM' – in other words through his reticence – in the immediate aftermath of the first wave of rumours, about the fact that 'members of the Bank Court's firms had done some of the selling of gilt-edged'. What no one could deny, whatever their particular slant, was that the whole episode, going back to September, had been a hugely upsetting experience for the City.

It was the first time that its inner circle had found itself subjected to public gaze and even mockery. Moreover, the very fact of the Tribunal's evidence, and the way it was publicised, now made the City – as never before – a sociological phenomenon. Within a year there would appear in the journal *Manchester School* a pioneering analysis, employing heavy use of those proceedings, of 'The Social Background and Connections of "Top Decision Makers"', in effect the dry-run for Anthony Sampson's *Anatomy of Britain.*[34] Things would never quite be the same again.

*

As early as 17 February 1958 Cobbold used the occasion of an Overseas Bankers' Club dinner at Guildhall to acknowledge that times were changing. In his speech, having emphasised that 'today merchant bankers do not dominate the Court, as they used to', and that the Bank's relations with the clearers were intimate, he went on to make what would become a celebrated assertion: 'The Bank of England must be a bank and not a study group. The prime requirement must be operational competence. But I most emphatically reject any accusation either that the Bank is influenced solely by City and Banking interests or that it is hidebound by tradition.' There followed robust denials of two increasingly common charges – that the Bank was 'bereft of professional economic thinking' and that it was unnecessarily secretive – before the Governor reached for the predictable metaphor: 'The Old Lady is no dowager clinging to dowdy fashions. She may be a bit reticent about it, but she keeps her wardrobe up to date – albeit with a touch of old style befitting her years.' Less than three months later Cobbold was sitting in his room at the Bank being grilled by Robin Day for a programme in the ITN series *Tell the People*. Cobbold's preparatory notes for the interview made it clear that he wanted to concentrate on what the Bank of England actually did, but there was one striking passage:

> We are trying all the time to increase our direct contact with business around the country as well as just in London . . . I think that we, and the City as a whole, have more to do in this field – we are certainly trying to break down such barriers as there are between the City and the business life of the country . . .

In terms of the Bank's mechanics, the Parker Tribunal had pointed out – not surprisingly, given the evidence – that part-time directors did sometimes find themselves possessing foreknowledge that potentially put them in 'a difficult and embarrassing position'. The Bank, however, was reluctant to abandon the traditional process of all directors being allowed to debate in advance proposed Bank rate changes. Accordingly, the matter was referred to the Radcliffe Committee, which in due course reported in favour of changing the procedure. Finally, late in 1959, the tradition of prior consultation with the Court came to an end. In Fforde's apposite words, 'the old arrangements, perhaps typical of the inner City of Norman's time and further back, had been judged out of date'.[35]

Radcliffe itself chuntered on through the whole of 1958. Trinder batted as early as 23 January, with two other representatives of the LDMA. Much of the evidence was dauntingly technical, but one exchange gave a nice sense of Trinder the market man:

> Do you know what people mean when they say that the Government broker has been edging the price up? – No, I do not think I do. You can always sell better on a rising market than you can on a falling market; that is correct. It sounds odd, but it is so. When he edges the price up he sells so many at one price and then another so many millions at a higher price, or something like that. In this sort of market, as it has been the last month or so, he gets his own way . . .

Next day it was the turn of the clearers, for whom Robarts was adamant that the existing system of all contacts between the clearing banks and the Treasury being mediated through the Bank of England was 'the best possible'. Radcliffe wanted to be sure:

> Is it that, with all your other duties and responsibilities it would be difficult for you to get much advantage from increased contact with the Treasury? – I would say so. I personally should think that the more and closer the contacts we have with the Bank of England the better. That is very important indeed; and we do have them; I am quite satisfied with that. Having arrived at that position, I do not think we want to go and discuss very much the same problems with the Treasury.[36]

Inevitably, as the real world changed, the inquiry came to seem less relevant. 'Our Radcliffe Committee goes on and on,' the Bank of England's economic adviser, Maurice Allen, complained in August to Eddie Bernstein of the IMF, 'and I should give it at least another year before they report.' Some weeks later Mynors was also complaining, this time about the Committee's apparent lack of direction. That autumn it heard a distinguished voice from the past, Lord Brand. With some glee he told a story about Cunliffe's sublime ignorance in 1919 (in order to demonstrate his point that the City had since become a far more knowledgeable place), defended the 1946 Bank/Treasury constitutional settlement ('I think it works all right') and disputed the fashionable nostrum that it was time for clearing banks to be represented on the Court ('I regard the "big five" as very powerful, big men whom the Bank of England has to keep in order; perhaps it is better they should face one another rather than mingle'). One of the Committee's members, the economist Alec Cairncross, cast a more critical eye on the clearers who actually gave evidence. 'Chesterfield [Westminster] was anxious to be conciliatory,' he noted in his 'Radcliffe' diary in early October, 'but he sat between two thugs in Wood [Midland] and Thornton [Barclays], the latter wearing an almost undisguised sneer whenever it appeared that we might be asking for additional statistics.'[37]

Shortly before Christmas the Committee heard from 'Butskellism' incarnate. Gaitskell appeared on the morning of 18 December, Butler in the afternoon. The main thrust of the Labour leader's evidence was that there was an urgent need to improve the frequency and depth of contact between Treasury and Bank. He also wanted the Treasury (including the finance minister himself) to enjoy direct access to the leading clearing bankers. Neither proposition was exactly welcome to Cobbold, who must have known that if Labour were to win the next election (likely to be held during 1959) he would almost certainly be swiftly replaced by Franks. Butler, as ever, was altogether more emollient, indeed feline:

> I think that there are things the Bank can do that the Treasury cannot, and things the Treasury can do that the Bank cannot. The Bank is more instinctively intuitive, and the Treasury is more instinctively deliberative – at least, so it seems to me – and so the two partners rather supplement each other. The management of the day-to-day market, which is the fundamental job of the Bank, apart from their agency functions in relation to the debt, the note issue and so forth, is a different sphere than the more deliberative long-term policy aspect of the Treasury . . .

There was no hint that the Bank of England's failure three years earlier to deliver him the monetary conditions it had apparently promised had gone a long way towards costing him the premiership. Or, as Cairncross acutely put it, 'He took pains to defend the Bank and seemed to want to tell us that everything was all right *now*. No question at all that *he* would tell a different story in private.'[38]

*

The fateful month, September 1957, saw not only the imposition of a 7 per cent Bank rate, but also the temporary forbidding of London banks using sterling to finance third-party trade. Dollar deposits had already been mounting up in Paris and London – in part reflecting the Cold War reluctance of Soviet and East European banks to trust their dollars to New York – and it was these dollars that some of London's banks, with the encouragement of the Bank of England, now sought to use in order to keep intact their trade finance business. Such, in a nutshell, were the 1957–8 origins of what would become known as the Eurodollar market.[39]

One of its pioneers was Bolton, who early on spotted the potential of Eurodollars: partly to enable him to transform BOLSA from a regional (South American) bank to an international bank, as he would later put it;

and partly because he believed, or at least was starting to believe, that Eurodollars might give the City an international future in a world after sterling. It was not an inevitable outcome. In terms of the financing of trade between foreign countries, 'the natural solution' – the evergreen Paul Einzig, one of the earliest chroniclers of the Eurodollar market, commented in 1964 – 'would have been for New York banks to seize upon the opportunity to take London's place'. However, 'generally speaking, American banks were kept too fully occupied with expanding domestic credit requirements to be too keen on increasing their foreign commitments suddenly and substantially'; 'nor were any of the continental financial centres', including most notably Paris, 'ready or able to step into the breach to anything like the full extent required'. In short, 'There was a distinct gap in the international financial machinery. In the circumstances the appearance of the Euro-dollar system was well-timed and providential.' One should not exaggerate the immediate impact. The Eurodollar system in 1957–8 was still in its infancy, operating essentially as an inter-bank deposit market; while in the apt subsequent words of one merchant banker, 'You would have drawn a fair number of glazed looks in the City if you mentioned Eurodollars in those days'.[40] Even so, what was happening was a crucial pointer – arguably, *the* crucial pointer – to the City's future.

In a more familiar market, the Stock Exchange, things were booming during most of 1958. The Thorneycroft clampdown may have taken its toll (the FT 30-Share Index lost almost nine points on 19 September 1957), but from March it was one-way traffic, with the index bursting through its 1955 high of 223.9 by the end of the year. Cheaper money helped, as did a better-than-expected American economic backdrop, prevailing financial liberalisation and an increasing belief that Macmillan was, against the earlier odds, on course for re-election. Antony Hornby, senior partner of Cazenove's, reflected the 'never had it so good' mood when he wrote to a retired colleague in November:

> We have been doing a terrific business the last month or two; I think a bigger turnover than we have ever had. I expect the market has gone up too much, it generally does in these sort of times, but it is astonishing the new buyers for Ordinary Shares who turn up almost every day in the shape of Charities, Labour Controlled County Councils and God knows what . . .[41]

This sustained bull market did indeed set the seal on the so-called 'cult of the equity' that had been developing during the 1950s.[42] The single figure most commonly associated with implementing it was George Ross Goobey, who became the first investment manager of Imperial Tobacco's pension fund in 1947. Soon afterwards he put his Bristol-based fund into the shares of a long string of smaller companies, attracting much publicity, which in turn helped to make the cult self-fulfilling. By 1955 some two-thirds of British company securities were being issued in the form of ordinary shares, not debt; and as the price of Consols headed ever southwards, traditional principles of investment, based on the assumption that money would hold its value, were stood on their head.

The rush into equities was by no means headlong. Even a notably progressive stockbroking firm like Phillips & Drew was distinctly cautious as, in successive editions of its brochure on *Pension Fund Investment*, it advised what percentage of a fund might legitimately be devoted to equities: 10 per cent by 1949, 20 per cent by 1952 and 35 per cent by the end of 1956. Soon afterwards, at a meeting of actuaries to discuss investment policy, Ross Goobey still felt the need to argue forcibly that the advantages of ordinary shares far outweighed any of the pitfalls that more cautious voices were pointing to:

> Let us take take-over bids, for instance. We are getting them almost weekly these days. When somebody makes a take-over bid of 150 for 2½ Consols I shall change my view and think there might be something in gilts after all. I would like also to put this point of view to those people who are fearful of dividend limitation. We have had dividend limitation in gilts for the last 200 years.

The City's conservatism was hardly out of character. Take the experience of the young Edward du Cann, as he toured the square mile in search of backers for a new unit trust management company, based on the idea of – in an increasingly affluent society – popularising share ownership:

> All without exception gave the same discouraging two-part response. The first part was a flat statement that the idea was very unlikely to succeed. No one I spoke to had the least confidence in it. The second part of the response was in effect the *coup de grâce*: 'If this is such a good idea, Mr du Cann, pray tell us, why has no one else thought of it before?' All those I saw, merchant bankers, investment trust managers, entrepreneurs, the representatives of the UK's leading financial institutions, thirty or so in all, were plain sceptical; some were disdainful; a few were rude; all told me that my optimism was misplaced, if not foolish . . . My carefully typed prospectus grew increasingly dog-eared with repeated handling . . .

Unicorn Unit Trust, involving a life-assurance element, was nevertheless launched in October 1957; and despite strong criticism from actuaries it became a huge success, begetting many imitators, not least the very merchant and clearing banks that had poured scorn on the idea.[43]

Another Tory MP trying hard to convert the idea of a share-owning democracy from rhetoric into reality was Sir Alec Spearman, senior partner of the stockbrokers Grieveson Grant. Specifically he wanted the high-street clearing banks to sell share units over the counter; but in October 1957 the chief executive officers of the clearers made clear their opposition to this. A year later Midland's Chairman, Lord Monckton, considered an internal memo on 'Trust Units':

> A degree of pressure is undoubtedly mounting to persuade Banks to undertake to sell Trust Units over their counters.
>
> In common with the other Banks, we have given much thought to the matter. There is sympathy with the idea of extending the investment habit over a wide field but it is felt that there are both points of principle and practical difficulties which warrant the Banks adopting a very cautious attitude to the whole subject.

One of the problems was the implied approval of the trust units being sold; another was that the sale of such units was 'not in the direct line of a Bank's business'.[44] In practice, over the next twenty years, the decline of the individual investor would be as steep as the rise of the institutional investor was irresistible. The trend would mean, among other things, that the City seemed an irrelevance in the day-to-day lives of most people.

In 1958 the financial liberalisation that was helping to fuel the bull market took various forms. One was the return of option dealing on the Stock Exchange, banned since 1939. It was an outcome that, hitherto, Braithwaite had managed to prevent – telling the Council in May 1953, for example, that a return to options would fortify 'the "casino" legend' surrounding the Stock Exchange, and inflict damage on 'the major policy of defending the Stock Exchange against the attempt that is sure to be made sooner or later to bring it under Government control'. In May 1958, shortly before a mass meeting of members, he told the Governor that (in Cobbold's words) 'the agitation stems from only two or three people, and that any more general support is merely due to vague sentimental feelings that this is something the Stock Exchange used to be free to do, and they ought to get rid of any shackles on their freedom'. Cobbold himself reiterated to Braithwaite the Bank's opposition: 'We should feel (not forgetting the Parker Tribunal) that, just at a time when the Stock Exchange are engaged in telling the public that they are not a gambling den but an essential service to British industry and public authorities, they would be most unwise to hand this particular weapon to their critics.' But later that month, the day after the meeting, Braithwaite was compelled to inform Cobbold that the Council would not be able to resist 'the overwhelming vote' in favour of restoring option-dealing facilities. 'He had considered resignation as he still takes a strong view against,' noted Cobbold. 'He has, however, decided it would serve no useful purpose.' However, when option dealings did restart in October, a new rule meant that a member could deal in options only with another member – a rule that, according to a letter of complaint within days from Leon Bros and five other firms, represented a 'crippling restriction'.[45] Braithwaite had, in his final year as Chairman, salvaged something.

The options story mirrored the larger problem for the authorities in 1958: how to maintain an adequate measure of control while permitting financial liberalisation. By the spring it was clear that the days were numbered for the credit restrictions that had been put in place in July 1955, in effect a self-denying ordinance on the part of the banks. With memories of that year still fresh, as well as of the subsequent sterling crisis of 1957, the Bank of England pinned its hopes on a scheme known as 'special deposits', a form of ratio control by which it could seek to dampen demand for credit by calling for cash deposits from the banks.[46] In late June, with Heathcoat Amory intending shortly to announce the easing of credit restrictions, Cobbold made his pitch to the clearing bankers at an informal meeting held at the Bank. Ahead of it, he prepared some revealing notes:

> I wanted to have this talk without officials and records – talk freely. Main argument largely a political one – not in any sense party political – but banking politics in relation to Government.
> Absolutely satisfied that if we run into another crisis, for whatever reason, or in any way get to a position where clamping down is necessary, a Government of either main party would insist on the introduction of some new instrument rather than rely entirely on informal co-operation. Been through this for 10 years – 6 Chancellors of 2 parties – held this up to now in way I think has worked best and in line with traditional arrangements. Several of you over period seen these relations strained . . . Since last Sept I have been convinced end of that story – very near a blow-up then. Always tempting to a Government when in trouble about inflation to beat the banking system over the head rather than take disagreeable action in their own field. Seen it threatened again and again over 10 years and it would certainly happen next time.

Therefore, Cobbold intended to argue, if the banking system took the initiative over special deposits (something that he knew Macmillan was keenly in favour of), this would help to pre-empt future legislation 'putting banks under more direct control and some "hand in the till" machinery'.[47] He duly made these points, the bankers reluctantly agreed to play ball and the following week, on 3 July, the Chancellor lifted the restrictions on bank lending.

An immediate aspect of the new, more liberal dispensation was Cobbold's decision to allow the clearing banks to buy into hire-purchase concerns, a very profitable, barely regulated part of the financial services sector. For several years he had been resisting this, but in April he was told by Heathcoat Amory that the government had no immediate plans to introduce regulatory legislation. Accordingly Cobbold told him that he was 'toying with the idea of getting closer to the Finance Houses on an informal basis and seeing what could be done, though this would still leave a great deal to be covered by legislation'. His way of getting close would be through the clearers; and once he fired the starting gun, the effect was undeniably dramatic in terms of the reshaping of British hire purchase, which itself was due to have existing controls removed in the autumn. By the end of July, following some hectic activity, four major clearing banks had acquired stakes in hire-purchase companies. 'I was away on holiday in Wales at the time,' a prominent clearer recalled, 'and came back to find the whole bloody lot in hire purchase. They went into it like the herd of Gadarene swine.' Yet despite the buying panic – prompting Mynors to complain that the press was indulging in 'much too much ballyhoo' on the subject – it was all done with a certain air of holding a handkerchief over the nose. 'It is not ourselves engaged in the selling of hire purchase any more than we sell groceries,' Tuke of Barclays announced after his bank had taken a 25 per cent stake in United Dominions Trust, apparently disreputable a quarter of a century after being blessed by Norman. Still, as Tuke himself had deathlessly observed earlier in the year: 'It is extraordinary what you can get on hire purchase these days'.[48]

Midland (jointly with its subsidiary the Clydesdale Bank) acquired a Birmingham-based hire-purchase business, Forward Trust. For Midland watchers, it was a sign that the somnolent giant was at last starting to flex its competitive muscles. The cautious Edington had retired as Chief General Manager in 1956, while from July 1957 there was a new Chairman in place of Harlech, the very able and much-liked barrister-turned-politician Walter Monckton.[49] After five months in the job he was telling Mynors that 'the Board contains too many old men, and there are too many absentees'; that 'he is gradually changing Harlech's habit of reading through the agenda at meetings without comment'; that 'he has formed a high opinion of his top management, and it is a good team'; and that previously sticky relations with the other clearing banks were improving, so that 'he feels he can now go and consult Tuke and be treated like a brother'.[50] In September 1958, just two months after Heathcoat Amory's announcement, the revitalised Midland showed an impressive turn of speed, as it pioneered (in terms of high-street banks) what it called 'personal loans'. And a few days later this was followed by the introduction of a 'personal cheque account' service. With a full-time PR man appointed for the first time, Midland was leading the way in looking outwards.

'You certainly put the cat among the banking pigeons,' Macmillan wrote to Monckton after the introduction of personal loans. He did not exaggerate. On 16 October, ahead of his Mansion House speech that evening, Cobbold informed Franks that he would be publicly welcoming the resumption by the banks of more competitive services, but added that he did not intend to suggest 'an indiscriminate "free for all"'. The next day Franks replied, 'I agree that competition between the Banks cannot be unrestricted. At the same time Banks have lost a great deal of ground over the last 25 or 30 years by not adapting themselves to changing social patterns. Also I think some response must be made to the engaging initiatives of the Midland.' The cat was indeed among the pigeons, as the other banks hastily rediscovered the joys of competition. 'There is a good deal of soreness around,' Cobbold updated Heathcoat Amory later in October concerning recent banking developments, explaining that 'some people think the Midland bounced the others a bit quick and there was a major row inside Barclays about whether or not to do personal loans'. Broad-mindedly, Cobbold added his own view about the banks that 'the more they can attract the new highly paid classes to open bank accounts the better'.[51]

Even before the lifting of the credit squeeze, the London capital market was far from inactive. In December 1957 the £41m British Petroleum debenture issue, done jointly by Morgan Grenfell, Schroders and Flemings, represented the largest amount of capital that the City had yet raised for a single company. The main broker involved was Hoare's, still under the 'terribly jealous and omnivorous' Kit Hoare, in the subsequent phrase of Antony Hornby of Cazenove's, who was deliberately excluded by Hoare from the issue. Two months later Hornby had his revenge, managing to keep Hoare's out of a £40m Shell rights issue.[52] In July 1958 the rules relating to the Capital Issues Committee were relaxed, and on the back of a bull market it was full steam ahead for a hectic period of corporate finance, involving both new issues and takeover bids.

Things were also looking up, at last, for Piercy's still somewhat strapped ICFC. Aldenham had stepped down in April 1956 as chairman of the clearing bankers, being replaced for the next four years by the far more reasonable Robarts of National Provincial. By 1958 the latter realised that it was time to end the piecemeal approach, which had served all parties so poorly since ICFC's establishment in 1945, and in July Piercy was able to report to Cobbold that 'he had had a satisfactory talk with Mr Robarts who shares his view that the financing of ICFC should be put on a more permanent basis'. Four months later Piercy remained optimistic about the progress he was making with the bankers. 'What has thawed them I cannot imagine,' he reported to Kinross, 'except that two decent men like Robarts and Franks feel as bad as we do about this cat-and-mouse business which really – without any touch of animus – one can impute above all to Aldenham's peculiar character. However, if we can get this done right, it may mean open water for us.' The new deal was duly reached early in 1959, giving ICFC capital-raising independence from its shareholders.[53] At last, twenty-eight years after the identification of the 'Macmillan gap', it could start to do its job properly.

There was one final part to the liberalising jigsaw: the full convertibility of sterling.[54] This was achieved, simultaneously with the French and West German currencies, on 29 December 1958. Congratulations poured in to Threadneedle Street at this hugely important moment, both symbolically and substantively, in the City's determination to reassert itself as an international financial centre. There were few notes of public dissent. Even so, earlier in 1958 a 'Penguin Special' had been published that would become very influential in starting to reshape left-of-centre economic thinking. This was *British Economic Policy Since the War*, written by Andrew Shonfield, formerly of the *FT* and now economics editor of the *Observer*. An astringent intellectual, with a Central European background, Shonfield argued strongly that – especially in the light of the financial crisis of September 1957 – the policy-making priority given to the strength of sterling and the sterling area imposed an unacceptable burden on British industry and economic growth generally. Lucidly outlining the strain on the balance of payments caused by Britain's obligations to the rest of the sterling area, and noting that 'the suggestion that the strain is worth bearing, because the sterling system somehow brings us "a great deal in the way of wealth", is a standard traditional view', Shonfield argued that in fact at least two-thirds of the City's total estimated £125m of foreign exchange earnings would remain intact, even if sterling was not a major international reserve currency. He did not deny, however, that 'what would inevitably suffer is the City's banking and acceptance business'. In all, it was an analysis not calculated to endear Shonfield (who during the war had served in the British Army as a gunner and intelligence officer) to the authorities. In May 1958 an internal note by Mynors, shortly after the book's publication, referred caustically to 'the output associated with names like Kaldor, A.C.L. Day and Andrew Shönfeld'.[55] Either one played the game or one did not, and in that crucial respect Shonfield was found wanting.

Someone who did play the game, and for one day was made an honorary chap, was the British film starlet Sabrina. On 29 April, at the invitation of a veteran member, Major Max Karo, she visited the Stock Exchange, with Karo escorting her to the public gallery. There was a big cheer from the floor when she was spotted, and Sabrina spent most of her twenty minutes blowing kisses from above. Asked by the press if she was going to buy any shares, she replied, 'I must think about it with all those wonderful men here!' It was a year of less jollity for Trinder, compelled at the age of fifty-seven to retire at the end of summer 1958 from Union Discount, under the company's forty-year rule. His final stretch had been clouded by discord with his board, which had presciently but vainly tried to persuade him to reduce his large holding of gilts, prior to their taking a tumble. Trinder was also, in the careful words of Union Discount's historians, 'further criticised for not preparing his junior management team'. Indeed, 'some of his staff had not found Trinder an easy man to work for'. After his retirement he refused all directorships, hardly showed his face in the City, and died suddenly at the London Clinic in July 1959.[56]

Not long after Trinder left Cornhill, another controversial, less endearing figure began to ease out from the financial world. This was Arthur Whitehead, whose West End issuing house, Whitehead Industrial Trust, had managed to survive various squalls over the previous decade. Several times the IHA had its attention drawn to one or another of his dubious practices, but felt unable to take action. Now, in September 1958 at the age of sixty-five, Whitehead found himself on trial at the Old Bailey accused of having the previous year pushed shares of Tati Goldfields and Sage Oil solely in order to benefit himself – pushing that had included the printing of 120,000 copies of a booklet involving dishonest concealment of material facts. Others involved in the share-pushing (including a financial journalist) were found guilty and sent to prison, but Whitehead himself was discharged on the grounds of lack of evidence. Some weeks later a brief item appeared in the press to the effect that he was resigning from Whitehead Industrial Trust and leaving shortly for Canada.[57] Since its formation in 1936, Whitehead's issuing house had marketed more than 400 million shares in British manufacturing and trading companies. No doubt some good concerns had benefited, but over the years he had consistently used the City as his vehicle for pushing shares that were far from worth the money. It was – back to Hatry, back to Bottomley, back to 'Baron' Grant – an old, old story.

CHAPTER SIX

Monkey Business

For Siegmund Warburg and his bank there remained, even as a member of the Accepting Houses Committee, no primrose path into the City's inner circle. Nevertheless, Warburg did now have an entrée to the Governor's room, and in October 1957 he told Cobbold that in his view Abs had more authority in high financial matters 'than anybody else in Germany', adding that 'if constructive ideas could be put to Mr Abs, with the emphasis on Anglo-German co-operation, he might get them through'. Cobbold, however, showed no enthusiasm for employing Warburg as a go-between: 'I said I fully agreed about Mr Abs' capacity and influence. I thought however that ideas would have to be clarified a bit before this suggestion could be pursued.' The following March Cobbold had another visitor: 'Mr Reginald Seligman came in to tell me that he was resigning from Warburgs as it does not fit and he thinks he has been ill-treated.' That was eloquent enough, but some six weeks later a note from Maurice Parsons (on the international side at the Bank) to Cobbold was even more so:

> Mr Grunfeld of S.G. Warburg & Co Ltd came to see me to say that they had read in the newspaper the report that HMG might be considering a borrowing operation in New York. He had received a telephone call from Mr Warburg, who is at present in New York, instructing him to call at the Bank and say that the services of Kuhn, Loeb & Co [in which Warburg was a partner] would be available if needed in connection with an operation of this kind. I said that I also had read the report in the newspaper and thanked him very much for the offer which we would note. I reminded him that HMG still had close links with J.P.M. [J.P. Morgan] & Co.[1]

This was, in fine, the delicate sound of the bum's rush.

Warburg's historic moment was, however, at hand.[2] 'In some businesses,' Charles Clore told *Fortune* magazine in September 1957, 'the profits earned show that existing assets are not being employed in the fullest capacity. I maintain that neither this country nor any business can afford to have its resources remain stagnant.'[3] By the following year – with a bull market, easier money and the clearing banks showing the way in their acquisition of hire-purchase houses – the conditions were right for a sustained wave of takeover bids. One company ripe for the plucking was

British Aluminium (BA). It had never properly recovered from the war and was badly short of financial and smelting capacity. Its management in 1958 could hardly have been in more traditional hands: Managing Director was Geoffrey Cunliffe, son of a former Governor of the Bank of England, and Chairman was Lord Portal of Hungerford, Chief of Air Staff during the war and now President of MCC. The BA board realised it needed outside help, and from the early summer was in negotiation with the giant Aluminium Company of America (ALCOA) about some form of partnership. These discussions were soon given added urgency as it became clear that the aggressive, expansionist Reynolds Metals of Virginia wanted to acquire BA and in particular the plant in Quebec that it had recently started to build. Reynolds's financial advisers were Warburgs, which insisted that if the bid was to succeed it would have to be made in conjunction with a British firm. The ally chosen was a Midlands-based engineering group, Tube Investments (TI), in large part the creation of the self-made Sir Ivan Stedeford. TI in turn took advice from Helbert Wagg (headed by the equally self-made Lionel Fraser) and Schroders. Together, Reynolds and TI quietly built up a 10 per cent stake in BA by the early autumn.

On 25 November, shortly before skirmishings turned to open warfare, Stedeford came at short notice to see Mynors at the Bank. 'I think his main purpose,' Mynors told Makins at the Treasury, 'was to ensure that the Bank had his side of the story correctly, as the only direct contact on his behalf had been through Mr Grunfeld of Warburgs, who might have been misunderstood.'[4] Three days later, flanked by his advisers (the pre-eminently respectable Lazards and Hambros), Portal announced that BA had signed a contract by which ALCOA would subscribe to one-third (as yet unissued) of the company's capital at a price of 60s per share. The recently made Reynolds-TI offer, equivalent to 78s per share, was therefore deemed irrelevant. The price differential was such that it was a palpably unconvincing standpoint. Nor did it help BA's cause that ALCOA, unlike Reynolds, had as yet no clear international strategy, and that whereas Reynolds was prepared to supply the firepower (floating a new stock issue in the States in order to raise the cash), ALCOA was not.

'A great row is developing about the future of the British Aluminium Company,' Macmillan noted in his diary on 2 December, adding that his Chancellor, Heathcoat Amory, owned shares in the company and accordingly was going to leave it to him to take the lead for the government. By this time it was also known that the largest single British shareholder in *both* BA and TI was the Church Commissioners, a fact described by Mynors as 'the only comic relief' in the situation. As the Treasury became involved – in due course deciding that BA shareholders must be allowed to consider the Reynolds-TI offer, which was open until

9 January – an impatient Warburg attempted to short-circuit the process. On the 2nd he telephoned the Bank 'with a suggestion that the head of an independent City House like Barings should be consulted to express a view on the ethics of the present position as he would not expect officials in Whitehall to be able to judge on these aspects'. He was, however, politely told that 'the Bank would be able to reflect City opinion on this matter'. Next day Mynors (in the continuing absence of Cobbold) reported to the Treasury that 'City opinion dislikes the Alcoa proposal which they think has been very badly handled by the BAC Board'. Over the next week or two Warburg – who had been advised by his friend Bolton to 'either fight or get out' – continued to force the pace. He telephoned the Bank again on 9 December. 'They have decided,' the Bank's note of the conversation ran, 'against requisitioning a meeting of shareholders as being an unnecessary complication. They are aiming at getting a straight 51 per cent of the shares by means of the offer and Mr Warburg seems confident that he will get at least this majority because he reckons that he will get the support of the Institutional investors.'[5]

The BA board was by now very much on the back foot, so much so that on the 16th there appeared in the press the first-ever major 'defensive' advertisement against a hostile bid, a tactic that would in time become an art form. A photograph of aluminium ingots at the company's Falkirk Rolling Mills accompanied the text, which emphasised ALCOA's resources and the nationalist theme: 'British Aluminium is not "selling out to the Americans". It is going into partnership with them.' Even when Portal tried to attack, it served him ill. Thus when he rashly accused Reynolds-TI of seeking to acquire 'a powerful empire for the price of a small kingdom', many were baffled as to why in that case ALCOA should have been let in (as the *Economist* later put it) 'for the price of a minor principality'. And when he suddenly announced that, if the ALCOA deal went through, the BA board would increase its 1958 dividend from 12 to 17½ per cent, *The Times* wondered about the economic logic and remarked that such a move 'invites the criticism that the increase is solely the result of Tube Investments' intervention'.[6]

What were BA's City advisers doing to help the beleaguered company? Ten days before Christmas, Mynors was put in the picture by the Government broker about one aspect of the emerging line-up of forces:

> Mr Arthur Anderson (Rowe & Pitman) and Mr Antony Hornby (Cazenoves) would like it to be known here that they are Brokers to both BA and TI. They are therefore taking a neutral position and are not even sounding out institutions on what they intend to do . . .
> I guess that behind this lies the fact that the names of various Merchant Bankers appear on one side or another in the contest but that the Brokers appear to have been left somewhat in the cold.

Soon afterwards Anderson and Hornby called on Mynors, to whom they confirmed that 'they were not consulted by either side in the formative stages of the dispute' and that 'in the circumstances they decided that their only course was to remain completely neutral'. They added, however, that 'they were resisting some pressure that they should now appear to commend one side or the other'.[7]

They were indeed being put under 'some pressure' during what were highly charged pre-Christmas days, as Hornby subsequently related to an absent partner:

> Arthur and I were summoned to a meeting by Lazards and Hambros, at which practically all their partners were present, and we were told that in their view 'he that was not for them was against them', that they could not accept neutrality and that they must have brokers working for them, and naturally very badly wanted us. We reiterated at this meeting that they had done their best to lose us by not consulting us, because I didn't see why we should be put in the position of being 'naughty boys'. We said that we must have a little time to make up our minds, but we very soon found that our sympathies were, and had been all along, with British Aluminium, whose citadel was being stormed, and decided that we must go and tell Lionel [Fraser] that we must resign from being brokers to Tubes. This naturally was a sad thing to have to do . . .

Hornby added that although both Fraser of Helbert Wagg and Jock Backhouse of Schroders felt 'sore' that Cazenove's and Rowe & Pitman had not made up their minds earlier, 'this was a situation without precedent and what I have learned from it is that neutrality is untenable in this sort of affair, and Englishmen are not neutral by nature, and one simply cannot sit on a fence'.[8]

Nor were Hambros and Lazards bent merely on coercing the brokers into line. On the 22nd, Sir Charles Hambro and Lord Kindersley called on Cobbold:

> They went over the history of developments whilst I was away, stressing their view that HMG's attitude, whatever its intention, was having the practical effect of favouring Tube Investments at the expense of British Aluminium Board. They also stressed that Warburgs had behaved extremely badly, although they had no complaint against Helbert Wagg and Schroders who had only come at a late stage as Tube Investments' bankers and advisers.
>
> They also told me that they and others are now organising a powerful City group, which will come out shortly with a firm recommendation in favour of the Board's proposals, and with a syndicate ready to acquire a sufficient number of shares which, together with shares they know to be firmly held, would block the Tube Investments' proposal.

Cobbold himself, whatever his instinctive affinity for Hambros and

Lazards and his equally instinctive distaste for Warburgs, was determined that the Bank should remain scrupulously neutral and above the fray. There matters rested over Christmas, though on the 27th Macmillan found himself shooting at Arundel in the company of, among others, Portal. BA's Chairman said 'a few discreet words' to the Prime Minister, but according to Macmillan he understood that the government could not publicly show its hand until the shareholders had made up their minds.[9]

With rumours and counter-rumours flying around the City and the press paying considerable attention to the story, the Aluminium War (as it would become known) entered its decisive phase on New Year's Eve, a Wednesday. 'BAC/Reynolds/Tube Drama crescendo' ran Bolton's diary entry. 'S.W. continually on telephone.' Cobbold spent much of the day speaking to Kindersley and Hambro, who had duly formed a City consortium to defend BA from the unwanted attentions of Reynolds and TI. Describing it as 'a ridiculous situation, damaging to the City as a whole and to everybody concerned', Cobbold told the two merchant bankers that it was his intention to arrange a truce between the parties. In principle they were not unwilling; and on being prompted by Cobbold to talk to Stedeford, they found that he too was apparently amenable. For his part, he noted afterwards, Cobbold promised that 'whilst I could not prevent Reynolds or anybody else giving orders to Warburgs to buy shares, if TI could stop Reynolds I was prepared to see Warburgs and discourage them from any monkey business'. The word from the Treasury was also encouraging, with Makins phoning Cobbold to say that ministers 'would be pleased to see a truce'. All the Governor's efforts, however, came to naught, for 'Lord Kindersley and Sir Charles Hambro telephoned at 5.30 to say that it had not proved possible to persuade the lawyers [presumably for TI] that the TI offer could be withdrawn' and that 'they therefore felt it necessary to go ahead with the banking group's offer', which 'will therefore appear in the Press tomorrow morning'.[10] It was a guarantee, Cobbold perhaps wearily reflected, that 1959 would start with a bang.

On the Thursday morning, in a circular published in all the leading papers, the great City consortium at last came out. Fourteen august houses, headed by Hambros and Lazards but also including Morgan Grenfell, Brown Shipley, Samuel Montagu and Robert Fleming (though excluding Barings and Rothschilds), publicly affirmed to BA's shareholders their support for the ALCOA solution and made a partial bid, worth up to £7m, for BA shares at 82s each, four shillings more than the Reynolds-TI offer. Why did these famous names put themselves out on such a limb? Almost certainly it was not the result of dispassionate analysis of the industrial problems facing BA, though in fact there was a perfectly good industrial case to be made for that board's preference. Nor probably was it on nationalist grounds – despite some propaganda points in the circular – for most good judges realised that, whatever the outcome, BA would effectively find itself under American control. Nor did it simply come down to a snobbish dislike of the outsiders or parvenus on the other side, above all Warburg. Hostile takeover bids were still a relative rarity, and undoubtedly there was a strong natural disposition to support the party being attacked. Hornby's dislike of BA's 'citadel' being 'stormed' was wholly genuine, and for all the widespread criticism of BA's clumsy handling of the situation, many others would have fully shared that feeling. Ultimately, on the part of the City establishment, it was an emotional reaction in an unfamiliar, disturbing situation, reflecting an entrenched belief that, within its citadel, the board knew best. Not only Warburg, however, begged to differ; also on New Year's Day an interview appeared in the *Evening Standard* with Fraser, who condemned the consortium's action as 'unprogressive' and declared that 'the whole thing smacks of fear'.[11] So it did, and it was already apparent that the battle for BA was shaping up to be a hugely symbolic, epochal episode.

On 1 January itself the key document – indicating conclusively the destiny of the battle – was written by Makins, after Cobbold had called at the Treasury at 2.30 p.m. to give the latest news:

> Talks between TI and Hambros and Lazards went on until late yesterday evening. As a result Sir Ivan Stedeford on behalf of TI agreed not to buy any more shares. But the American Reynolds Group are buying like fury and Sir Ivan Stedeford cannot control them. Nor does the Governor feel that he can intervene to prevent the share buying activities of an American company. Meanwhile the British Consortium of Merchant Banks are holding off. They do not want to bid the shares up.

Put another way, one team and half of the other team were playing the game, but the remaining half-team was not. 'Counselled full show of compromise but no weakness' was Bolton's note of his advice that day to Warburg – presumably with the emphasis on 'show'. Cobbold may have promised to warn off Warburgs from any 'monkey business', but for whatever reason he had seemingly failed to do so. To Makins, the Governor 'added that he did not quite know what the next move was'. A baffled Cobbold returned to the Bank, twice ringing the Treasury in the late afternoon to report that 'the City Group' and TI were in 'very friendly discussions', but that the problem was how to stop Reynolds buying. At the end of another difficult day he sent an identical note to Portal, Stedeford and Kindersley, as well as to the Treasury:

> The City group and TI have continued friendly discussions but cannot see a basis of solution, because of the Alcoa-Reynolds situation.
> There seems no prospect of bringing both Alcoa and Reynolds in on terms acceptable to all parties. BA would not and probably could not drop

Alcoa out of the picture. TI are not prepared to drop Reynolds out of the picture.

Accordingly, Cobbold's note ended, the City group and TI had agreed that there was no further point in continuing talks.[12]

Friday the 2nd was another hectic day, with much of the inside story revealed by Cobbold's carefully written note for the record:

> Sir Roger Makins gave me the state of play at lunchtime. The Prime Minister proposes to take no decision before Monday. It is realised that by this time the TI/Reynolds group will have acquired a large holding by market purchases, which would make any pro Alcoa action by HMG (if they should decide in that direction) more difficult. They had seen both Stedeford and the bankers' group this morning and had cross-questioned them about assurances on British control. The more convincing assurances seemed to be forthcoming from the TI group . . .
>
> Mr Warburg came in. He said that he understood I had seen Sir Ivan Stedeford and he did not therefore wish to develop their side of the case. He wanted, however, to say that if at any time I wished to hear his side of the story, he would be glad to give it to me, as he understood there was a lot of criticism of him in the City. I said that this was undoubtedly the case, but I did not wish to get into the details . . .

Undoubtedly the government's tacit support of the hostile bid was crucial. Its prime concern, understandably, was the future of the British aluminium industry, and on 3 January the Economic Secretary to the Treasury sent a memo to Macmillan stating that, by this criterion, the Reynolds/TI bid was preferable 'on grounds of national interest . . . mainly because legal control would remain in British hands'. A month earlier BA's Managing Director had expostulated to Heathcoat Amory that TI 'knew nothing about the aluminium business and the decisions would all lie with the Reynolds Company', but clearly Geoffrey Cunliffe lacked the bullying persuasiveness of his father.[13]

Warburg's tactics were now relatively simple: not only to ensure that Reynolds/TI increased their offer (which they did, to 85s, on the 4th), but also to continue to orchestrate massive buying on the open market of BA shares, thus ensuring that their price became and stayed well above the consortium's offer. It was a strategy that depended on the willingness of the shareholders to sell and the reluctance of the consortium to mount a counter-operation in the market. Both these optimistic assumptions proved correct. Importantly, Warburg had the press on his side, especially the Beaverbrook papers. On the 2nd, the day after running its interview with Fraser, the *Evening Standard* had a picture of the 'battling' Stedeford and made much of '"our own" Tube Investments'; while in the *Daily Express*, the City editor Frederick Ellis offered unequivocal advice on the 5th: 'Take the 85s from Sir Ivan or through the markets.' *The Times* concurred, as also on the 5th did the magisterial 'Lex' (Arthur Winspear) in the *FT*: 'Few may now see the advantage of accepting the offer put forward last week by a syndicate of brokers and others.' Some of the smaller sellers may have had a misguided patriotic motive, and some of the institutional sellers may have been antagonised by the consortium's rather overbearing tone, but in essence the spur was the same time-honoured one for all concerned: an eye to the main chance. Making an estimated £0.5m from selling at this propitious moment were the Church Commissioners, though the *Church Times* was unable to persuade their spokesman to divulge details.[14] What is less explicable is why – after peace discussions under Cobbold's auspices had broken down by the end of the 1st – the consortium, with its considerable resources, did not mount a serious buying operation on its own account. Perhaps Hambros, Lazards and their allies were unduly influenced by the government's refusal to back the ALCOA solution; perhaps ALCOA's own semi-reluctance in comparison to Reynolds was a further factor; and perhaps the informal steer from Cobbold was that a pitched battle in the market could only further damage the City's reputation.

'It would be a grave political error to interfere now,' Macmillan privately reiterated on the 5th. 'Let the rival forces fight it out . . . It's the only safe course. But it is *not* a pleasant one, for I fear that a great deal of ill-feeling has resulted from the Tube Investment/Reynolds methods & a lot of our friends in the City are upset.' Next day the war was over, as Reynolds/TI achieved majority control of BA even before the postal response to its formal offer was completed. Lunching at Vickers on the 7th, Macmillan chatted to Morgan Grenfell's Lord Bicester and was 'relieved to find' that Bicester 'thought we had done quite right in letting the contestants for British Aluminium fight it out between themselves'.[15]

This presumably was a source of comfort when on the 12th *The Times* published an extraordinary letter by Olaf Hambro, declaring that the wishes of the City had been violated and roundly criticising the financial editors. This view received little sympathy from Harold Wincott in the *FT*. He expressed astonishment at the initial remoteness shown by the BA board towards 'the man-in-the-street shareholder', who, 'given half a chance, would express his displeasure with his directors as surely as passengers on London Transport express theirs when they similarly feel they are being pushed around without being told the reason why'. Warburg considered making a public reply to Hambro, before being dissuaded by Cobbold, but the leading jobber Esmond Durlacher did enter the lists, referring in *The Times* to 'a body of men who also work in the City, men of good common sense, of good standing and probity', for whom the consortium, however impressive, had not spoken. A rising Labour politician, Anthony Crosland, argued in the same paper that during the episode the City had failed to attach enough importance to the larger economic consequences. As for the houses that had formed the unsuccessful consortium, 'Their outlook appears about as contemporary as the architectural style in which the City is now being rebuilt; both make one shudder.'[16]

Almost twenty years later Cobbold would wryly refer to the Aluminium War as 'a troublesome little trouble'. Indeed, it had, among other things, delineated as never before the limits of the Governor's papal power. It would have needed a Norman to keep Warburg in check – and perhaps not even Norman could have done so. In the immediate aftermath feelings against the German outsider continued to run high. 'I will never speak to that fellow again,' Kindersley was heard to say, and over the years it would become part of City folklore how, in a chance encounter in the street between the two men, probably on New Year's Day, he had put the question directly to Warburg, 'Are you buying shares?' and had been given the economical answer, 'No'. There was, however, one notable reconciliation. Warburg himself, in his 1980 interview, told the story:

> You know, Olaf Hambro was a great man and a very good friend of mine. I had a sort of relationship with him like a relationship with a grandfather. About three months after the British Aluminium war, a mutual friend came to see me and said, 'Olaf feels so sad that this old friendship between him and you doesn't exist any more.' I said this is nonsense. His people had behaved strangely but I have nothing against him. And this friend said, 'Oh, then would you be prepared to see him again?' I said, 'I would be delighted. In fact, I'm perfectly prepared to ring up Olaf Hambro and go to see him in his office.' So I went around to see the great Mr Olaf Hambro in his office.
> **What happened when you got there?**
> Have you ever been in Hambros? To get to his room you had to go through the big partners' room. So I came in from one side, and he came in from the other. And when we finally met in the middle of the room, he took his big arm around my shoulders – he was very tall, about three heads taller than I – and he said, 'Siegmund, haven't we been *awful fools?*'
> **So that was the turning point in your acceptance in the City?**
> Yes. From about that time onward, we started gradually to be recognised as members of the British establishment. . .[17]

Whether the recommendation to Reynolds that it acquire BA was ultimately such good advice was another matter, but unquestionably the Aluminium War established Warburg's reputation as a master financier.

It also came to be regarded as a watershed in the history of the City. Not only was it a severe blow to the prestige of the City establishment that the consortium symbolised, but it was as if the whole atmosphere now changed, becoming altogether more competitive. 'A decisive blow had been dealt to the unhurried, "gentlemanly" style of business,' was the retrospective view of Edmund de Rothschild, adding that 'for better or worse, the City never seemed to me to be quite the same again'. The two-class theme was one that Macmillan had picked up on even during the war. 'It's becoming rather a "Gentlemen v. Players" affair,' he reflected the day after the consortium had shown its hand.[18] It was, in almost every sense, an appropriate analogy. None can have felt it as acutely as the hapless Lord Portal, whose MCC tourists (under the captaincy of the leading amateur, Peter May) were in the middle of undergoing a 4–0 thrashing at the hands of a particularly uncompromising Australian side. Perhaps the ultimate lesson of the Aluminium War was that, for a man who so despised flannelled fools, Siegmund Warburg could chuck with the best.

PART TWO

Old City, New City

Snow falls in the buffet of Aldersgate station
  Toiling and doomed from Moorgate Street puffs the train,
For us of the steam and the gas-light, the lost generation,
  The new white cliffs of the City are built in vain.

John Betjeman, from 'Monody on the
Death of Aldersgate Street Station' (1958)

CHAPTER SEVEN

Ped-way to Heaven

It was 1950, and in those days there was a train at thirty-two minutes after eight on weekday mornings, travelling all the way from Wimbledon to Holborn Viaduct, carrying up to the front line yet another force of office workers . . . The train had its regulars, usually in the same place every day. In one carriage there would be four men, always in exactly the same seats in their sober business suits, and they would spread a cloth over their knees for a daily game of whist, which I suppose they played all the way to the City. If you had to get out on their side, they would frown and sigh and raise their eyes to heaven as they lifted their improvised card-table to let you pass . . .

The irritant was the future broadcaster Paul Vaughan, starting his working life at a pharmaceutical firm near Loughborough Junction. A year later, in October 1951, Derrick Penley-Edwards left a life in the theatre and, in his early thirties, faced his first day working for an insurance broker:

I caught an early morning train up to London Bridge, where I had to join the throng crossing the bridge on my way to Fenchurch Street. All the men were wearing hats, mainly bowlers, trilbies and some Anthony Edens, and carrying umbrellas. My hat was a trilby, which didn't suit me and because of my small head blew off at the slightest hint of a breeze, but I soon learnt that a hat was de rigueur in the City and decided that I would also get a bowler. After all, I wore a bowler as an eight-year-old prep school boy so why shouldn't I wear one now? That throng crossing London Bridge was just as thick as any crowd going to a football match on a Saturday afternoon and I was totally bewildered. My goodness, do they all do this every morning? I asked myself. How ghastly!

The choice of headgear was spot-on. Not long afterwards an ambitious young man called Peter Walker, on finishing his National Service, secured a berth at another Lloyd's broker, Griffiths Tate. 'You will be joining the American Department on 1 May,' the letter of appointment informed him:

Your salary will be £300 per annum, your hours of work will be 8.45 a.m. to 5.30 p.m. Monday to Friday and 8.45 to 12 noon on Saturday. You will have two weeks holiday a year.
You will wear a bowler hat to and from the office.[1]

*

In 1958, thirty years after leaving the Royal Exchange for Leadenhall
Street, Lloyd's moved no distance at all to a more spacious – and,
mercifully, air-conditioned – new building in Lime Street. It was an
entirely rational step, but most of their underwriters and brokers muttered
about the unnecessary bother and expense, dubbing their new home
'Drysdale's Folly', after the Chairman, Sir Matthew Drysdale. 'Lloyd's,
handling one-fifth of British insurance business – one-third if life
insurance is excluded – is potent, clever, honest, successful and can safely
be described as unique,' Paul Ferris observed two years later in his
pioneering survey (not least for its incisiveness) of the City. He did,
however, record without comment the remarks of a young underwriting
member who was convinced that, in international terms, the pre-war
glory days had gone for ever:

> There are a lot of people who think they're living in that era. In fact both
> the Germans and the Swiss are fast trying to muscle in. The Americans are
> retaining more and more of their own good business, but they're not as yet
> trying to take business from other countries. I think it's a good thing it
> should be ventilated. Some of the underwriters live in a dream world and
> don't realise what's happening. It would be a bloody good thing if they were
> woken up.

Some eyes were perhaps opened, for in his *Anatomy of Britain*, published
in 1962, Anthony Sampson noted how 'with the growing insurance
centres in New York, Paris or Frankfurt, many underwriters doubt if they
can maintain their proportion of international business, particularly
marine insurance'.[2]

Historically there was no doubt who bossed the show. 'They treated
Names like dirt,' Leonard Toomey recalled about the 'old-time underwriters' whom he got to know during and after the war. 'Arrogant to a
degree . . . They were the masters of Lloyd's.' Only in one, most literal
sense was it not a fairly cushy life – 'underwriters and their all-male staffs
sit in traditional, unalterable discomfort on narrow wooden pews' was
how Ferris described their working position in the Room, adding that
'sometimes there is a car cushion or a pneumatic pad', but 'usually not
even that'. A possible consolation was that their counterparts in the Stock
Exchange, the jobbers, had to stand all day. Julius Neave, who spent a year
on secondment to the biggest brokers at Lloyd's, Willis Faber & Dumas,
remembered being impressed by the system he encountered:

> The underwriters were much more specialised than they are now, to the
> point that certain risks were led by certain underwriters and everybody knew
> who they would be. If it was a tanker you would go to one underwriter. If it
> was a passenger liner you would go to another. But any rate everybody knew

who was going to be the best person to lead. Because once you've got a lead as a broker then the others would follow . . . If you've got the right lead people would say, 'Oh well, if old Joe has written it must be all right, then put down my line'.

The brokers had their specialists, too. 'This old man Dennis knew the depth of every harbour in the world without looking it up in a book,' Neave recalled about the 'pretty ancient' character at Willis Faber running the firm's underwriting agencies. 'He knew intimately the conditions everywhere. And it will surprise you to hear he'd once left this country when he wanted to take his daughter on a day trip to Boulogne. And that was the only time he'd ever left these shores.'[3]

By the early 1960s, however, two important trends were starting to become apparent. Colin Forbes of the brokers Price Forbes touched on both in the course of his annual updates about Lloyd's to the Bank of England. 'The principal domestic event in the past year,' recorded Mynors in October 1962, 'has been the flotation as public companies of several firms of brokers. This he attributes mainly to the Estate Duty problem.' It was the first decisive step on the road to Lloyd's brokers becoming extremely rich and very diversified concerns – a development that, among other things, would fundamentally alter the balance of power at Lloyd's. The other trend was towards larger, less independent syndicates. 'He regrets the continuing tendency for the smaller syndicates to be absorbed into larger units,' Mynors had already noted of Forbes the year before, adding that although 'inevitable because the cost of doing a £15,000 item of business is virtually the same as that of doing a £150,000 item . . . it tends to make business rather slower to get through and not so easy to see the right man'.[4]

What they did not seem to discuss at all was the way in which, since the late 1940s, the underwriting syndicates, sometimes comprising many dozens of Names (most of whom never set foot in Lloyd's), were increasingly owned neither independently nor by the big underwriters, but by the brokers. In both the selling and buying of such syndicates, tax reasons provided the dominant motive. Unfortunately, changing the ownership of the syndicates did nothing to improve the quality of the agents responsible for their organisation. Sir Peter Miller, arguably one of the better chairmen of Lloyd's in the traumatic late-century years that lay ahead, was scathing in retrospect:

The getting in of Names, you put your duds in in the old days [i.e. 1950s and 1960s], because it was the Old Boy network. It was an honour to be asked to join Lloyd's, you knew you were very likely to make money; yes, there was the occasional syndicate that didn't, but basically, it was a jolly good thing to join. You longed to join Lloyd's, any syndicate, it didn't matter which, and you didn't know whether it was good, bad, or indifferent

. . . you couldn't tell because there were no published results. So everybody wanted to get in Lloyd's if they possibly had enough money. So, your members' agent didn't have to show a high level of expertise whatsoever . . .

'And,' Miller added to his interviewer in 1989, 'have we paid for that.'[5]

Of course, the insurance market at Lloyd's was only one of the many internationally oriented services provided by the City as it gradually emerged from the grip of the severe controls that had followed the war. At the end of the 1950s Ferris was particularly struck by the robust and cosmopolitan foreign exchange market, comprising 'the foreign exchange departments of about 120 banks, dealing sometimes direct with one another and with banks throughout the world, sometimes through one of eight or nine firms of brokers'. Invariably in these departments the key items of equipment were 'telephones, teleprinters and calculating machines'. As often as not the most important dealers, whether at British banks or the London branches of foreign banks, were of continental origin, impressing Ferris with their rather sparkier approach to life and work:

> It may be the choice of an unusual dish at lunch, and the napkin tucked high in a soft collar. Some of the older dealers look jolly where the City man would look distant. The suit may be lighter, the tie brighter. You hear direct rudeness now and then, which is rare between Englishmen in the City (oblique rudeness is another matter). 'I treat my dealers like dirt when they're new,' said one head dealer of foreign extraction. 'I'm not going to miss my lunch for one of them, I'm not going to be messed about by their mistakes. "Do that again," I tell them, "and you're *out*." What I won't put up with is mental laziness. I can honestly say that I'm ruder to my staff than anyone's been to them since their prep school' . . .[6]

Since its modern origins as a fairly wild telephone market in the immediate wake of the First World War, the foreign exchange market never had been – and never would be – a place for the Bertie Woosters of the City.

Traditionally no sector was more internationalist in business-getting outlook than the merchant banks, a strength emphasised in July 1958 by the financial journalist William Clarke in *The City's Invisible Earnings* (subtitled 'How London's financial skill serves the world and brings profit to Britain', and written explicitly to counteract the unfavourable publicity engendered by the Bank rate leak). He was at pains to emphasise that tradition's continuing post-war vitality. Lazards, he pointed out, 'has formed a consortium to supply French wool importers with a revolving credit'; Samuel Montagu 'was prominent for a time organising sales of "premium" gold on the world's free markets and has now established a new bank in Zurich'; Brown Shipley 'has developed what is now the main market in foreign bank notes in the City'; and Hambros and Kleinworts 'are running merchant companies which have developed new export trade to the dollar area'. He could also have highlighted Schroders, whose international activities during the 1950s included the provision of sterling reimbursement credits to local banks in South America, investment in Argentinian real estate, a close relationship with Chilean and Bolivian concerns, the resumption from 1954 of sterling credit provision to German clients and productive ties with leading Japanese commercial banks. 'Who holds the balance of the World?' Byron had once famously asked. The answer may no longer have been 'Jew Rothschild and his fellow, Christian Baring', nor the rest of the Accepting Houses Committee, but the 'Merchant Banks of Olde England' (in Ferris's mischievous chapter title) still punched around the world a little above their weight.[7]

Accepting itself (in effect the provision of trade credit) remained a core activity. By the mid-1950s the volume of world trade was growing rapidly, and the total acceptances outstanding of all the accepting houses jumped sharply from £95m in December 1956 to £131m in September 1957. Over the next few years, with money clearly to be made from financing the trade boom (at home as well as abroad), the London accepting market started to become distinctly more competitive, to the discomfort of some of the traditional accepting houses. The credit department at Barings, in its annual report at the end of 1960, commented on a recent acceptance credit arranged by Morgan Grenfell, in which Barings was participating:

> An interesting feature of the AEI [Associated Electrical Industries] syndicate was the appearance among the participants of Morgan Guaranty Trust. The interest lay, not so much in the old connection with J.P. Morgan & Co [which had taken over Guaranty Trust in 1959] being the obvious reason for the participation, as in the nature of the acceptor – the London Office of an overseas bank. Almost on the same day as the arrangement of that credit, a member of the Discount Market expressed to us the opinion that Bank of America must nowadays be among the biggest acceptors in London. Many other branches of overseas banks appear also to be going in for acceptance business . . .

Even so, despite competition from this quarter and from the clearing banks, the business of the accepting houses continued to increase – to the point, in the case of Barings itself, where by September 1961 its volume of acceptances outstanding was up to £11.8m, the house's highest total since March 1920. Without doubt, however, the leading acceptor in the early 1960s was Hambros, with acceptances outstanding of some £40m by spring 1963. 'Another House conveyed to us a rumour,' noted the manager of Barings' credit department that year, 'that the Bank of England might have commented to Hambros on the extent of their acceptances, and that Hambros had decided that they would prefer not to have to restrict their own customers, and would accordingly reduce their participations in syndicate credits arranged by other Houses.' What united the accepting houses, even if it meant losing market share to their undercutting competitors, was a determination – assiduously fostered by Sir Edward Reid of Barings, Chairman of the Accepting Houses Committee for twenty years until 1966 – to hold the line at 1¼ per cent per annum, established in the early 1950s as the 'prime' commission rate for all home credits. When Schroders controversially broke ranks in early 1964, organising a £10m credit to the British Sugar Corporation at well below that rate, the end-of-year comment of Reid's man at 8 Bishopsgate was that 'it smacked a little too blatantly of competition to attract business from the banks'; he added with some satisfaction that 'the Bank of England subsequently expressed, to Schroders, disapproval of the elastic commission arrangement'. Inelasticity remained the order of the day for at least another eight years.[8]

The finance of trade may have been a profitable activity, but the commercial City as a whole continued, broadly speaking, to decline during the post-war years.[9] As usual, the floor-space figures tell the story: by 1968 warehouses occupied only 13 per cent of the City's utilised space, half of the area they had occupied on the eve of war, whereas in the same period the space occupied by offices had increased from 45 to 62 per cent. The human figures are even more striking: whereas in 1911 more than 95,000 of those working in the City owed their employment directly or indirectly to the commodity markets, by the mid-1960s the comparable total was fewer than 44,000. An outsize shell was still proudly displayed outside the Bishopsgate offices of M. Samuel & Co, but the larger reality was that the City's character was becoming ever more financial.[10]

Nevertheless, as all observers agreed, the commercial sector still mattered, not least because it gave the City a helpful degree of diversification during bear markets. In 1958 – by which time all of the commodity markets had at last been reopened – Clarke estimated that those markets and the merchant houses generated between them an annual turnover of roughly £1,000m, contributing some £25–30m to the UK's invisible earnings. For most commodity markets, however, the post-war economic environment was far from easy. Governments around the world reluctant to relinquish control over key commodities, increasingly large producing and consumer units, vertical integration in some trades – all these factors could lead to 'thinner' turnover in some of the main markets, making them (in Clarke's words by the mid-1960s) 'far more vulnerable to temporary shifts in supply or demand'. Moreover, even though the Labour Party had gradually lost its visceral hostility to the concept of dealing in futures, Clarke noted then that the mainly foreign users of the commodity markets had not been their most 'natural defenders' and that 'their administration has not been as purposeful as that in other parts of the City'. Furthermore, west of Gracechurch Street, few knew much about the various open outcry markets in the City's East End. Almost certainly ignorance was mixed with condescension – with perhaps just a twist of anxiety, especially after 1955 when a pepper-cum-shellac swindle on Mathesons cost that august Lombard Street house about £0.25m.[11]

The grain market was typical of the post-war problems. Whereas before the war the floor of the Baltic Exchange had rightly boasted of being 'the World's Grain Exchange', the subsequent rise of giant milling combines like Spillers and Ranks meant a sharp diminution in the number of grain brokers operating there. As a result the Baltic became more or less a shipping market pure and simple. Or take wool. 'Is The Wool Exchange Doomed?' asked the *City Press* in July 1959, noting that by now only about one-tenth of the world's wool was sold in London, with most being allocated through the wool sales in Australia and other producing countries. Symbolically the Wool Exchange in Coleman Street, home to wool sales since 1875, was demolished not long afterwards; and through-out the 1960s it was the greasy wool contract in the Sydney market that made most of the global running in futures trading. Another stagnant 'terminal' market (to use the preferred London word for futures), until finally starting to pick up from the mid-1960s, was in cocoa; meanwhile the plight of the shellac market (a commodity traditionally used for 78 rpm records, but increasingly being superseded by plastic) was nicely caught by one broker, Hale & Son, in its review of 1963:

> This has been another disappointing year. . . Imports of Lac and Seelac into the UK to date have averaged the same quantities as last year, reflecting an even demand, but, unfortunately, showing no increase in consumption. With the continuation of Controlled Selling Prices in Calcutta, resulting in a non-fluctuating market, it is obvious that there is little of interest to report . . . Forward trading on the Terminal Market has been stultified by the control of Calcutta prices, and no transactions have been recorded.

A commodity of far greater historical resonance in the City was rubber, with a few veterans still alive to recall the great rubber boom of 1910; but here again, the trend was one of decline, as the markets in the East became more dominant and the London market subsided into a domestic role. Several well-known firms traditionally specialising in rubber sank into oblivion, or were taken over; and when in 1955 the exceptionally energetic and astute commodity trader Harry Kissin gained control of Lewis & Peat, after a bitter power struggle with Ted Peat, he began rapidly to expand into a diverse range of other commodities, and into such varied fields as food production and distribution, chemicals and pharma-ceuticals, and insurance. Ultimately, in 1972, he would merge Lewis & Peat with Guinness Mahon, a member of the Accepting Houses

Committee.[12]

The two last commodity markets to be reopened were the futures markets in sugar and coffee, in January 1957 and July 1958 respectively. Both were based in Plantation House in Mincing Lane and both, as it happened, bucked the generally gloomy trend. In 1960 the United Sugar Terminal Market Association introduced a particularly successful contract for raw cane sugar, and very soon the London sugar market was pulling well ahead of its rival market in New York, which was handicapped by the deteriorating US/Cuba situation. As for the market run by the Coffee Terminal Market Association of London, the contract that did the trick was for Uganda unwashed, native-grown Robusta coffee, with not far short of 100,000 contracts (each representing five long tons for future delivery) being traded during 1965 alone. Another market that prospered on the whole – despite the often unwelcome attention given by various foreign governments to the production, distribution and exchange of copper, tin, lead and zinc – was the London Metal Exchange (LME), with its celebrated if mysterious 'ring' trading and staccato bursts of dealing. Its success in maintaining its position as the world's leading barometer for price determination, and in enabling both producers and users to hedge their risks, owed much to the clear-sighted guidance of Philip Smith, the third generation of his family in metal trading (Bassett Smith & Co) and chairman of the LME's management committee from 1954, the year after the exchange had reopened. A comparable figure, in a less important but equally taxing arena, was Arthur Frayling, from the late 1940s the key figure on the fur trade side at the Hudson's Bay Company's warehouse and auction room in Garlick Hill. He had joined the famous company (still British-owned, still controlled from London) as a boy and, according to his obituary:

> It was Arthur Frayling's self-imposed mission to maintain and expand London's position as the international fur centre despite all the temptations the producers had to sell in their own countries . . . He had to persuade foreign governments and co-operative associations to consign their fur crops each year to London and then, by reliable sorting, cataloguing, and market forecasting, to induce buyers to venture far from home to bid for them. Often this involved 100,000 miles of travel in a year but somehow he gained and held the confidence of both seller and buyer . . .[13]

Frayling's achievement in the consolidation and growth of this international market for fur skins, in a country where little fur was produced and not much more consumed, was quintessential City as entrepôt: a classic, continuing function, albeit rarely or never in the headlines.

Yet so often in the commercial sector it was an uphill struggle. The correspondence of Tribble, Pearson & Co, East India merchants since 1896, sheds some revealing light on these larger difficulties. Based at

Leadenhall House, 101 Leadenhall Street, and with the portentous Geo W. Church firmly in charge, the firm plugged away through the 1950s with diminishing rewards. In February 1953 Church half-opened his heart to Messrs J.K. Doss & Group Industries of 211 Old China Bazaar Street, Calcutta:

> As you are doubtless aware, the format of business with India has considerably changed during the past 13 years, and many lines previously shipped in large quantities have ceased due to the growth of industrialisation in your Country, or curtailed on account of existing economic conditions, or restricted under present Import Licensing regulations and quotas. We have therefore been compelled to exploit many other avenues, both as regards imports to and exports from India, and although this has entailed a great deal more work which has not yet been rewarded, on the whole we are not dis-satisfied with the results to date.

Perhaps; but what Church almost invariably saw as the forces of ignorance on the subcontinent made his life no easier. 'Import Licences [i.e. in India] seem to be more plentiful,' he grudgingly conceded in March 1954 to the son of a Calcutta merchant with whom he was on good terms, 'but values constantly dwindle, and new Firms continue to come into existence with increasing regularity. Generally speaking the majority have little idea of business or of the goods for which they have been granted Licences!' Church seems to have been a well-meaning man, but often, as in a dismissive letter in October 1955 to the Madras branch of Messrs Capco Limited, his tone could descend to one of bullying paternalism:

> You will, of course, appreciate that in these days of keen competition there is not any margin left from which we can afford to grant you any return commission, let alone 3% or 5% as suggested by you, and we can only suggest that you place your orders with any of our competitors who are quoting £9. 12. 6. per ton and can also give you 3% or 5% return commission, but at this point we may state without fear of contradiction that your efforts will be unsuccessful.

The product in question was Gibbs's Brand English Powdered Whiting, a speciality of Tribble's.

Occasionally there was a frank confession. 'Despite local competition we are still shipping regularly to all markets in your Country, although we must admit that the tonnages are very small in comparison with those of some 10 and 20 years ago,' Church wrote in January 1957 to a Calcutta firm. By this time India had been independent for almost ten years, and in February 1958 he let himself go when corresponding with Messrs Devidayal Private Ltd, Bombay-based exporters of manganese and iron ore:

> Even despite the financial assistance that the Government of India is to

receive the fact remains that your Country is already vastly overspent, and steadily increasing their present indebtedness by further purchases of machinery and materials in furtherance of the second five year Plan, also with State controlled organisations superseding Private enterprise at your side, exports of Indian ores, produce and merchandise are steadily declining mainly due to more competitive offers being received from other sources of supply, also failures to complete and despatch existing contracts in the time originally agreed upon . . .

When three months later a complaint reached Tribble's from the merchant Sudhangshu Bimal Chowdhury, of Chittagong in East Pakistan – 'I painfully inform you that in my last consignment of 88 Cwt of Lump Chalk imported from you . . . I received less than half the quantity due to my bad luck' – Church was predictably adamant in his denial of any blame:

> Any damage sustained occurred either in transit (which is unlikely) or on discharge at Chittagong where the stevedores and dock labourers are prone to use hooks in dealing with cargo packed in sacks and paper bags . . . We can assure you that every care is taken at this end to ensure that all our shipments in such packings are delivered to the Docks and stowed on board in perfect sound condition . . .[14]

Yet for all his pride in the City's mercantile traditions and standards, and for all his stern words of admonition to those elsewhere, Church himself was about to sound the retreat. Shortly before the end of 1959, Tribble, Pearson & Co left its offices in Leadenhall House and began to operate, on a reduced scale, from Church's own home at 'Dragonstail', 114 Creighton Avenue, East Finchley. The winds of change were blowing, the British Empire was being wound down, and London was no longer the world's commercial centre.

*

Church left behind an environment that was also starting to change fundamentally. 'After the Great Fire, Charles II called for "a much more beautiful City than is at this time consumed". After 280 years the City has a magnificent new opportunity for comprehensive rebuilding . . .'[15] This clarion call by *The Times*, made in August 1945 as one-third of the City lay in ruins, would have found few dissenters either then or over the next two decades. The problem, however, was how best to execute such a noble vision.

During the immediate post-war period the City Corporation's consultants for the rebuilding programme were the architect Charles Holden and the town planner William Holford. Their first report, published in 1946, fully accepted the need for a road system capable of carrying twice the existing traffic, but sought to balance the criteria of utility and beauty:

'What is now picturesque should be retained, wherever possible, no matter to what period it may belong nor how various its component elements may be; it should be swept away only to make room for a redevelopment which has equal architectural value as well as being more convenient. The City cannot afford mediocre architecture.' Indeed, if one now reads that report, together with the following year's final report and the consultants' subsequent accompanying commentary in their historically well-informed *The City of London: A Record of Destruction and Survival* (1951), one is struck by the moderation of both the tone and the proposals. 'It would not be wise,' Holden and Holford declared, 'to adopt a new aesthetic and a new scale for building for the City of London until the old one has been definitely lost or outmoded; and at the present time the opinion of the authors of the plan is that the seventeenth-century scale should be preserved and that St Paul's Cathedral – the noblest in the City – should remain architecturally, as in other ways, its chief building.' Nevertheless, the latent prescription for wholesale, high-rise change was there, couched though it was in those high-minded terms so typical of the prevailing post-war climate of planning and reconstruction. Thus:

> It is not the directors, or chief officials, on the first or on the top floors of large buildings who have to be thought of, so much as the bulk of City workers – clerks, typists, warehousemen and others – who require daylight for as long as it is obtainable every day ... The effects of planning for adequate daylight will call for an architectural revolution in the City. It will mean the abandonment of small internal courts and their replacement by buildings which have the bulk of their accommodation towards the centre of the site and then step down in stages to street level.

Developers must therefore be encouraged 'to place the mass of floors in a building in the centre of the site rather than along its frontage to a street'; this meant that 'offices will be quieter and better lighted and streets will not be such canyons of noise and petrol fumes'. In general, for all their warnings, Holden and Holford were sanguine enough about the prospect of change and the new: 'The City is tremendously absorptive.'[16]

Given the government's understandable preference to accord a higher priority to public housing and factory regeneration than to offices, when it came to allocating building licences in the era of rationing, the reconstruction of the City remained largely on hold until the mid-1950s. As the volume of business steadily picked up, especially with the first post-war bull market under the Tories, there were inevitably some problems. Explaining that its present lease in Throgmorton Street was shortly to expire, and that it was having difficulty in finding alternative office accommodation within reasonable distance of the Stock Exchange, the stockbrokers Vickers da Costa managed to persuade the Stock Exchange Council in 1955 to let the firm move as far away from the market as the first floor of Regis House in King William Street. 'The shortage of suitable accommodation is so acute that we really have no alternative,' stated its irrefutable plea. One young newcomer to the City at about this time was the future novelist Leslie Thomas, working as a sub-editor at the Cannon Street offices of the Exchange Telegraph Co, the rather moribund international news agency:

> I used to spend my lunch hours walking around the City of London, much of which was still scarred with wartime bomb-sites, looking for stories. I found a family of wild cats living among the shut-off ruins and then realised that there were whole tribes of the fierce and skinny animals hunting the wide spaces in the centre of London . . .
>
> The fencing-off of large areas of the City, which had been cleared of rubble but still remained void, resulted in colonies of wild flowers appearing, foxgloves, dog roses and honeysuckle . . . Countryside birds appeared; there were rumours of foxes. Owls nested . . .

There was nothing wild about Lombard Street, where for a few more years yet, until the coming at last of tarmac, the road was still paved in rubber (and very stickily so when it rained), so that the metal wheels of passing traffic did not disturb the bankers and bill brokers inside their ancient offices.[17]

Elsewhere in the City's financial core there was a reassuringly, seemingly timeless quality to the daily rituals. Canteen provision for staff may have been increasing (though it was by no means the rule), but for those above the salt there was usually a leisurely lunch out to look forward to – whether at the City Club or the Gresham, or such restaurants clustered round the Stock Exchange as Birch's, Moores, Slaters and the celebrated Long Room of 'The Throg' in Throgmorton Avenue. 'You'd have a plate of Cornish oysters, a slab of stilton and a bottle of Guinness – and a jolly good lunch it was,' the stockbroker Tony Sheppard recalled in the brisk 1980s about the 'five-bob' menu (perhaps more austere than some) that he used to enjoy at another popular haunt, Gow's. Everywhere, in equally time-honoured London fashion, there was smog and smut, until the Clean Air Act of 1956 took effect; and almost everyone did their bit by smoking, generally untipped and often like the proverbial chimney. Smoking was restricted in the Stock Exchange itself, but by the steps going up to the Throgmorton Street entrance there were long trays for cigarette ends. Loitering beggars would evade the Stock Exchange waiter, put their hands into the tray, take out a still-smouldering bundle of these ends and start rolling their own. It was cheaper than going to Jn. Brumfit, the City's main chain of tobacconists.[18]

By the mid-1950s the first wave of post-war office buildings was starting to go up. Holden and Holford had exhorted quality; now it was largely down to the developers and their architects. However, one developer,

Rudolph Palumbo (father of Peter), had got off the mark as early as 1948, erecting his monolithic, six-storey, crudely conceived St Swithin's House in Walbrook. Five years later, in 1953, the designs were revealed for two major new buildings: the large premises commissioned by the Bank of England to site its Accountant's Department, more or less opposite St Paul's on what would become known as New Change, a new road running from Cheapside down to Queen Victoria Street; and the fourteen-storey Bucklersbury House, the construction of which would lead to the dramatic excavation of a complete Roman shrine, the Temple of Mithras. Professor Anthony Blunt of the Courtauld Institute led the attack on the Bank's unimaginative, backward-looking effort, while pressure from the London County Council compelled the intended Portland stone of Bucklersbury House to be replaced by what was in effect the City's first glass box. Even so, it failed to win many plaudits. 'This mass of building,' the feisty architectural critic Ian Nairn wrote about Bucklersbury House in 1964, some six years after its completion, 'has a lot of storeys, a lot of windows, freedom from pointlessly applied period detail, freedom from obvious gracelessness, freedom from aesthetic megalomania. It has no virtues and no vices; it is the null point of architecture . . .' Very different, but built almost simultaneously by W.H. Rogers for the City of London Real Property Co, was the pioneering – and, for better or worse, trend-setting – Fountain House in Fenchurch Street. In essence it was a twelve-storey tower on a low horizontal podium (the podium in this case being a branch of Midland Bank), and took its inspiration from the recent Lever House building in New York. Crucially, it was curtain-walled, in the sense that its external walls were hung curtain-style from the concrete floors; and, not least for reasons of cheapness, this swiftly became the norm in the City's dawning generation of high-rise towers. In 1956 the *Architects' Journal* nominated the development company's chairman as one of its 'Men of the Year', for having had the courage to break with what it called the City's 'jelly mould tradition'.[19]

A key moment in the triumph of the modernists came soon afterwards, in 1957, when Dr Nikolaus Pevsner published, as part of his series *The Buildings of England*, his survey of the City of London. His individual judgements lacked nothing in certainty. The 'vast pile' being erected in New Change for the Bank of England was 'shockingly lifeless and reactionary'; the new head office being perpetrated by the same unfortunate architect, Victor Heal, at the corner of Queen Street and Queen Victoria Street for BOLSA was merely 'lifeless and reactionary'. More generally, Pevsner complained that 'to this very day the City has hardly a major building which is in the style of the C20', and accused it of still being in thrall to the assumptions of the two most favoured inter-war architects, Lutyens and Baker. 'It is a style of timidity, of playing safe, of introducing just enough of the C20 to avoid being ridiculous and keeping just enough of giant columns and the other paraphernalia of Empire to stake the claim of remaining a great nation. In the end no one is satisfied . . .' What was the alternative? Pevsner laid down his far from ignoble mission statement:

> The essential qualities of the City are closeness, variety, and intricacy, and the ever-recurring contrasts of tall and low, of large and small, of wide and narrow, of straight and crooked, the closes and retreats and odd leafy corners. All this a modern plan can keep – not preserve, but recreate, and combine with the amenities of C20 planning such as good lighting and safe walking. By interwoven traffic roads and pedestrian paths, by making use of the changes of level which the City affords, and by many more such means a new City could arise as fascinating as the old and yet not, functionally speaking, obsolete as the old City was . . .

However, he warned, 'the lack of architectural enterprise which is so alarming makes one doubt if sufficient enterprise will be shown by the City'. Pevsner's test-case was the not yet begun Barbican development, where the City Corporation hoped to reverse a century-and-a-half trend by encouraging those who worked in the City also to live there. The existing plans for the Barbican area would, asserted Pevsner with complete confidence, 'give us the rhythm of road and precinct, of low and high, and the punctuation by towers (the C20 substitute for Wren's steeples) which visually the City needs – and not only visually, but to satisfy all the senses of those who spend most of their lives in the City.'[20]

The pivotal year, in retrospect, was 1959. Among other things, it saw the passing of the Rights of Light Act (1959), immediately introducing what one historian has described as 'an orgy of new building . . . to prevent rights of light arising twenty years after the destruction of the original buildings in 1940'. Indeed, as early as January the City's own weekly paper, the *City Press*, looked ahead optimistically to progress on several key fronts: final permission from Common Council for both the Barbican scheme and the development (along lines planned by Holford) of the Paternoster precinct to the north of St Paul's, with the latter 'expected to become one day the modern shopping centre of London'; just to the south of the Barbican, 'another big occasion soon will be the opening of the first section of the 62 feet wide carriageways of Route 11 between Aldersgate and the London Wall-Moorgate junction'; the construction of new buildings alongside Route 11, including an eighteen-storey block by Moorfields, as well as Common Council's imminent decision 'on the scheme to build overhead footpaths around and across this part of Route 11'; and the widening of Cheapside that would be necessitated by large new blocks there.

By March one reader, George Russell, could bear no more: 'Let us have the redevelopment by all means. Replace square foot for square foot only and let us have the resulting space for grass and trees. Confine all bombed and bomb damaged sites not yet started to be for private accommodation only. Throw all plans, including that for St Paul's area, into the waste paper basket and start again.' Sadly, no vigorous debate ensued. Instead, the paper's headline not long afterwards was 'Grisly Games on Route 11', with a story about how the road's contractors had found themselves disturbing some 200 skulls and other bones buried beneath the old Barber-Surgeons' Hall; how these bones had been piled up in a pit, with a wooden cover built for it; and how children had got in at weekends and used the skulls for games of Cowboys and Indians. On 7 July the intrepid Duchess of Kent opened the first section of the new route, to be called London Wall. 'Route 11 Puts Accent on Beauty' was how the *City Press* billed the event. Four months later, on 11 November, Common Council approved both the Barbican scheme and the principle of high-level walkways over and alongside Route 11. During a keen debate, one member, Mr Deputy Alfred Teuten, 'said opposition to elevated walkways was based on prejudice' and that 'once people were up on the walkways there was no need for them to come down at all – until they wanted to go home'. C. Ernest Link agreed: 'Young girls could be seen dashing across the traffic in Cheapside – it was a wonder they were not killed. The future would bless the Court if they approved elevated walkways.' Or as B.G. Arthur, Chairman of the Improvements and Town Planning Committee, summed up: 'The fundamental purpose of the scheme was the protection of the public, the saving of human life, the removal of traffic congestion.' The village paper gave the story perhaps its best headline yet: 'City Prepares for the 21st Century'.[21]

By 1964 a carefully planned (by the City Corporation) sequence of five tower blocks had been erected, three just to the north of the stretch of Route 11 and two just to the south.[22] The first, completed in 1960 at the corner of Moorfields, was Moor House (developer: Charles Clore). 'Impressive chiefly because of its height [225 feet], otherwise anonymous in design,' was Pevsner's unenthusiastic assessment soon afterwards in the second edition of his survey. Within two years it was followed, a little to the west, by the fairly similar St Alphage House. The third tower, again further to the west on the north side, was Lee House, ready for occupation in October 1962 and named after Jackie Kennedy's sister, Princess Lee Radziwill, whose husband was on the board of one of its developers. Nairn two years later reckoned it the best by some way of the five eighteen-storey, curtain-wall, steel-and-glass blocks, praising its 'roof treatment and the colour of the spandrel panels'. The fourth and fifth towers, on the south side, were Royex House and City Tower, the former (co-developer: Harry Hyams) the work of Richard Seifert, who by the mid-1960s was becoming known as 'the king of the developers' architects', partly for his ability to locate regulatory loopholes.[23] Lee House may have been the pick of the five 'matchboxes', but when it was demolished after only twenty-five years (to make way for Alban Gate), few tears were shed on aesthetic grounds. The other four blocks still stand, in an ever shabbier, unloved state.

Intrinsic to the planning was the concept of elevated walkways – or, as they were often called, 'ped-ways'.[24] Within a few years of the Corporation's approval of them in principle in 1959, detailed plans existed for a dense network of more than thirty miles of these walkways, mainly at first-floor level. When in July 1965 the Corporation gave its permission to the Stock Exchange to go ahead with rebuilding on its existing site, this was subject to 'the requirement to provide high-level pedestrian ways as part of the system planned by the Corporation for the northern part of the City'. Given the powerful endorsement of the City engineer, the thinking behind this proposed network of walkways was brutally simple: to keep pedestrians off the streets, thereby leaving cars and lorries as unimpeded as possible. Or as Rachel Hartley put it more gently in 1967 (in her book *No Mean City*, published in association with the Corporation), once this 'web of pedestrian ways' had been completed over the next ten years, 'the pedestrian will be able to cross the City without ever having to compete with the traffic'.[25] In the end, barely one-tenth of this network became a reality, mainly in the Barbican and London Wall area; but the plan's impact on the scale of the City's streets and buildings was catastrophic, premised as it was on the assumption that the demands of traffic circulation enjoyed an unquestionable priority. There had already been a considerable amount of street widening in the late 1950s, and in every sense the pace accelerated during the following decade.

The most high-profile victim among buildings unfortunate enough to be in the wrong place was the Coal Exchange, created by J.B. Bunning in the late 1840s and standing on the corner of Lower Thames Street (on its way to becoming a racetrack) and St Mary-at-Hill. In 1956 John Betjeman called it 'the most beautiful Exchange', describing its 'great domed interior' as 'one of the very best in the City, impressive, vast and exquisitely detailed'. Pevsner, by contrast, found the iron detail 'immensely elaborate and crushingly tasteless'. The Coal Exchange was soon under serious threat, and in November 1960 Betjeman succeeded in convening a meeting between representatives of the City Corporation, the London County Council (LCC) and the recently formed Victorian Society. At that meeting the blunt message from the LCC was that it would not accept any second-best traffic scheme in the interests of preserving a Victorian building. Nor ultimately was the Corporation any more sympathetic, deciding in March 1962 to invite tenders for demolition, in the context of the road-widening scheme due to reach the site in two years' time. The debate in the Court of Common Council took place the day after the matter had been raised in the House of Lords, and members were keen to assert the City's independence of thought:

> Mr Chester Barratt said he regarded the building as an interesting but extremely dated edifice which was lacking in aesthetic appeal. They had to take into account the site's commercial value . . .
>
> Mr D.G. Mills, chairman of the Streets Committee, described the Coal Exchange as a dingy, brown building, which was devoid of artistic merit . . .
>
> Mr E.F. Wilkins wondered why there should be this sudden rush of interest to save what was a very ordinary Victorian building . . .

Demolition was completed in November 1962, not long after the Lord Mayor had opened a multi-storey car park (or 'Zidpark') in Upper Thames Street. At this nadir of public esteem for things Victorian (the Euston Arch would go the next year), it was thin consolation that a photographic record existed of the Coal Exchange prior to demolition, with the City Corporation having generously spent £200 on cleaning it first.[26]

Within months of the Coal Exchange coming down, construction was under way of Europe's tallest residential building, the 412-foot tower blocks of the Barbican development. Pevsner remained bullish about the scheme: 'With its consistent pedestrian overpasses and terraces, and its variety of tower blocks, lower slabs, and small buildings, it promises to be of high aesthetic value and London's most advanced concept of central area development.' The brutalist influence of Le Corbusier was tangible – and, arguably, for once beneficial. The Barbican embraced schools and an arts centre, as well as residential housing, and although taste is inherently subjective, the notably positive verdict three decades later from Pevsner's successor, Simon Bradley, compels respect:

> Though the asymmetrical planning and absence of one all-commanding viewpoint recalls the picturesque ambience of some post-war New Towns, that adjective inadequately describes the experience of perambulating these huge spaces. The aesthetic is rather that of the Sublime. It is apparent in the stunning height of the tower blocks seen from below and in the tremendous unbroken length of several lower blocks, no less than in the thrillingly vertiginous crossing of the lake on a gangway slung between the tall columns of the cross-slab. From here one can overlook the rushing water of the cascades as if from a bridge across some mountain gorge . . .[27]

From the wildness of Rose Macaulay's heath people to the wildness of 'man-made Sublime' in one huge, unfaltering leap – the City Corporation and its visionary architects (Chamberlin, Powell & Bon) deserve, on this occasion at least, the praise.

There would be few bouquets for another much-publicised development, Holford's drear and bleak Paternoster Square precinct to the north of St Paul's, before the war the site of a thriving, warren-like book trade. In March 1964, some three years before the development's eventual completion, a sharp squall suddenly arose when the Dean of St Paul's, Dr Matthews, called for work to be halted on the eight-storey office block, Juxon House, that was an integral part of Holford's plan but obscured the view from Ludgate Hill of the west front of the cathedral. 'I still hope something might be done,' the Dean told the press. 'After all, what is put up now is going to last for centuries.' With the relevant minister, Sir Keith Joseph, declining to interfere (even after Ivo Pakenham in the *Daily Telegraph* had denounced the block as 'this shameless and vulgar national scandal'), a protest meeting was held on the steps of St Paul's one Wednesday lunchtime. Undeterred by *The Times* condemning 'An Uninformed Campaign', it was quite well attended, though speakers struggled to be heard above the noise from the building site.[28] The plan, however, went ahead.

Elsewhere in the City there was a rash of new buildings. A classic in terms of *Zeitgeist* was a new branch (1963–9) of Westminster (by the time of completion, National Westminster) Bank. It eloquently demonstrated, in Bradley's words, 'what the traffic-obsessed 1960s had in mind for the future of Lombard Street: plain and rectilinear in stone, seven storeys high, set far back for street widening', with a 'long porte-cochère . . . to facilitate drive-in banking'. However, the dominant architectural phenomenon of the decade was, without doubt, the tower. A handful stood out. Drapers' Gardens (1962–5), off Throgmorton Avenue, saw Seifert making his first major impact in the heart of the City. Built for the developer Harry Hyams (who managed to let it to National Provincial Bank at what was then a staggering over £5 a square foot), it was twenty-eight storeys high and, with its convex back and front, had an elegance denied to the box-like towers alongside London Wall. The same, unfortunately, was not true of Britannic House (1964–7) in Ropemaker Street, built as BP's headquarters and for some years the City's tallest building, at thirty-five storeys and 395 feet. 'The architecture is again anonymous rather than personal,' commented the now somewhat disenchanted Pevsner in 1973. Happily, he was cheered up by 'the outstanding newcomers to City architecture' – namely, the ten-storey P&O tower and the twenty-eight-storey Commercial Union Tower (both 1963–9) located in the large piazza by St Mary Axe, formerly the site of Shell's head office.[29] Their spirit, it almost goes without saying, was uncompromisingly modernist.

Also uncompromising, but without the distinction, was the new Stock Exchange (1964–72, tower completed 1969). It came out at twenty-four storeys and 320 feet, but had not always been intended that way. 'Architecturally, the City authorities will prefer a comparatively low and compact development,' a Stock Exchange Council memo noted in August 1961. 'It is considered that a high tower would be somewhat undesirable in relation to the Bank of England.' Over the next year or so those constraints seem to have been removed, and in December 1962 another internal memo outlined the architect's plans: 'The external appearance is not yet finally decided but will certainly not be of the curtain-wall, plastic-panel type of construction but will probably be of re-inforced, polished concrete designed on the tower so as to give a ribbed surface allowing for changing patterns of light movement'. What was eventually built was a rather brutalist, seven-sided tower – and it may well be that few on the Council, let alone member firms, knew exactly what they were letting themselves in for.[30] If so, there was an analogy with the inter-war rebuilding of the Bank of England, over which the Stock Exchange *would* in due course tower.

Did this rapidly changing workscape presage the end of the City's individuality, its time-honoured identity as a highly concentrated mass of people and activities that, in sum, constituted a 'village', undeniably different in feel and appearance from the rest of London – indeed the rest of the country? 'The restaurants are crowded with rows of pale-faced, black-coated men,' Anthony Sampson wrote in 1962. 'Since the war tens of thousands of girls have strayed into the City, to work on the adding machines, typewriters and files, and their stiletto heels and jaunty walk contrasts with the solid lope of City men; but they are kept well apart, and have giggling lunches at the tea-shops while the men have beer and steaks.' Small, telling signs of the City's distinctiveness persisted through the 1960s. It was still possible, even if one was not Governor, to have a traditional haircut at Geoffrey's (proprietor: Lionel Lee), the barbers tucked in on the Cornhill side of the Royal Exchange; to consume oysters or grilled fish, washed down by Black Velvet out of pewter tankards, at Sweetings in Queen Victoria Street; or even, though only for a few more years, to toddle along to Birch's in Angel Court and sample 'Jelly (Invalids) – Wines – Liqueurs – Iced Punch – Soups', as promised outside by gold lettering on frosted glass. *Offbeat in the City of London* was the alluring title of Geoffrey Fletcher's 1968 booklet. He recommended, among sundry pleasures, 'three magnificent late Victorian experiences' in the Leadenhall Market area, though 'for men only': a haircut and shampoo at the Baltic Salon, boasting an interior 'pure 1910, with white painted Lincrusta wallpapers, an art nouveau frieze, mirrors, mahogany and marble'; a comfortable, club-like lunch at the Court Tearooms, 'with tile-topped tables, mirrors under bell-shaped electric light shades and a cornice decorated with William de Morgan type blue and white plates above all'; and afternoon tea, with sponge cake or swiss roll, amidst mahogany and stained glass, at the Leadenhall Tea and Billiard Saloon, while 'listening to the click of billiard balls'. This third treat was down two flights of stairs, by the side of the shortly-to-be-concreted graveyard of Wren's St Dionis Backchurch (demolished 1878) – a secret, subterranean world.[31]

Two years earlier, in 1966, Penguin had published *Nairn's London*, a wonderfully readable, idiosyncratic guide by the intense, melancholic, far from reactionary Ian Nairn. In a compelling paragraph he tried to encapsulate his complex feelings about the City and its probable fate:

> Still as insular as if it were walled and gated. But, like all of Central London, you feel that the character is shrinking away from a whole city-pattern into isolated attractions which will eventually become as phoney as the Tower. Meanwhile, there is a noble coherence between City plan and City people – though it is hideously distended, with three or four times as many workers as it ought to have, abandoned in the evening and excruciating at lunch-time. . .But the old City places, where bombs, misplaced traditional or misguided modern architecture has not got at them, are memorable: narrow, dark-coloured, so that the occasional widening for a street or a City churchyard is something that you remember. The true City gent has a genuine sobriety and discretion to match, best seen around the Stock Exchange, which dovetails perfectly with the ribald slang of messenger-boys or Billingsgate porters. But it is all slowly being flushed out by the alien tide that flows in across London Bridge at 8.55 a.m. every Monday to Friday; and, much more viciously, by the false idea that the upper crust of the City has of itself. Clean the buildings, bleach the Wren woodwork, pile on the civic banquets, but for God's sake don't actually *live* there. Perhaps the new Barbican will alter things, but I doubt it: the change has gone too deep. And when the last City pub goes gay, and the last honest café or hairdresser has been leased away into smartness, then the heart will have gone out of London . . .[32]

*

The City's working population was some 339,000 in 1951 (compared with half a million on the eve of war), rising to 390,000 by 1961. All but one or two per cent of these were commuters, Nairn's 'alien tide'. The various British Railways termini took much of the brunt. Figures privately released in April 1962 by the Ministry of Transport (Staggering of Hours Committee) revealed 8.45–9.00 as the peak quarter of an hour of morning arrivals each weekday at Cannon Street (Southern Region), with 7,062 passengers, of whom 1,664 had been forced to stand on their journey. Perhaps reflecting Essex man's traditionally lowly status in the City, the worst quarter of an hour at Liverpool Street (Eastern Region) was a little later, 9.00–9.15, with 8,459 clerks, typists and others gratefully leaving their trains, a gratitude especially felt by the 4,729 who had been unable to sit down. In the evening the peak quarter of an hour was 5.30–5.45, when from Liverpool Street almost as many as in the morning had to stand. 'Here those extraordinary, cramped and uncomfortable Great Eastern carriages are drawn out above the East End housetops to wide acres of Essex suburb, two-storey houses, flat recreation grounds, strange chapels of strange sects, the well-trodden commons on the fringes of Epping Forest,' Betjeman wrote fondly in 1949.[33] The 40,000 or so who commuted each day from those points east and north-east would have agreed about two adjectives anyway.

From the stations they dispersed to a myriad network of offices, shops and other places of work. Take Kent House, in Telegraph Street off Moorgate.[34] E.W. Payne & Co, insurance brokers, and the Western Assurance Co occupied the ground floor in 1957; Paroma Ltd, paper exporters, B. Hansford & Co, stockbrokers, and the Association of Investment Trusts were on the first floor; the second floor seems to have been untenanted; the floor above was the sole domain of the leading gilt jobbers Francis & Praed; Agar, Cross & Co, South American merchants, jostled on the fourth floor alongside Brooke Industries Ltd, ceiling-fan manufacturers, and Nielson & Maxwell Ltd, export merchants; the fifth floor had a touch of class with Jackson, Pixley & Co, chartered accountants, and the Standing Council of the Baronetage; while the sixth and seventh floors were occupied respectively by (again) E.W. Payne & Co and the medium-sized stockbrokers Norris Oakley. Learning his craft in the latter was the senior partner's son, Paul Smallwood. Unfortunately, a couple of years later he managed to mislay the proceeds of most of a BICC rights issue on his way to the bank; and knowing that his reputation at Norris Oakley would forever be that of a prize booby, he went elsewhere, to pursue a distinguished career in institutional equities.

In almost all these thousands of City offices the work remained essentially manual for ten or fifteen years after the war. Dundas Hamilton, another son of a senior partner, started out in 1946 at Carroll & Co, a small stockbroking firm at 5 Copthall Buildings:

> The general office consisted of a girl who worked with a comptometer (a sort of machine where you got your fingers in a certain formation and banged away at the keys), a man who kept the books, an office boy and a girl typist. We all sat in the outer office. There were gas fires, the lift went by hydraulics and not electricity, so when you got in you pulled a string and when you got to wherever you wanted to stop you had to grab the string and try and make sure the bottom of the lift hit the right point for opening the doors.
>
> I wanted to revolutionise the office because it appalled me that they had handwritten ledgers. It seemed to me absolute nonsense to rewrite the whole thing in longhand, so I photographed the sheets but nobody particularly wanted them. The older partners thought my photography system too modern. I wanted to have envelopes with windows in them and that wasn't considered to be the kind of business we had – we had the kind of clients

that expected sealed white envelopes.

At Wallace Brothers, the well-known East India merchants, Jack Spall was a young 'gofer' soon after the war: 'There was a big pile of used envelopes and a big pile of sticky labels and I'd wipe them with a sponge and stick them on, that was my job. Eventually I was allowed to touch the stamp book – there were no franking machines, of course – and to enter things in it, like "To Messrs Smith & Jones – 2d".' Another of his jobs was 'taking letters to the directors' room for signature and standing there with one of those rocker blotters. That's when I thought I should like to be a director of a company because they had a very nice time – came in after lunch on Monday, went off to the country on Friday afternoons . . .'[35]

Little changed during the greater part of the 1950s, and the words of the historian of the National Mutual Life Assurance Society (based at 39 King Street) were broadly applicable to many other firms:

> If someone who had worked in the head office in 1900 had been able to return in 1955, he would have recognised, apart from pension schemes, all that was going on. He would have found the policy registers, still bound in half-calf, still being written up by hand. He would have found himself, together with many others, working out each member's bonus by an individual calculation and after all had been checked, writing the answers with pen and ink on notices to be sent to the members. He would have understood the make-up of all departments.

Adding machines and mechanical calculators were starting to become more common, but the older, time-honoured skills persisted – and, to a large extent, still prevailed. One clerk has recalled how he used to balance his firm's daybook: 'You cast straight down with mental arithmetic. Pounds, shillings, pence. You became very good.' Perhaps nowhere were practices as antiquated as at many of the Stock Exchange's member firms. At Cazenove's a wet copying machine remained in place as late as 1955, while in general it was not until eight years later, with the passing of the Stock Transfer Act (by which it was no longer compulsory to have a buyer's name on the ticket recording a bargain), that the cumbersome, time-consuming system of settlement could begin to move on to a more automated basis. The book-keeping side was also thoroughly manual, as Les Turtle, in the back office at the major jobbing firm of Durlachers, remembered without undue fondness:

> Always on the first night after the end of the account – the Monday – we would be very late, 9, 10, 11 o'clock at night, trying to reconcile the three sets of books. The rough sheets, in theory, were very important because these were actually kept daily. They were your actual jobbing positions in theory. In practice they were often quite wrong. And of course the other problem was that by the time you'd actually valued them out and cast them up in the

individual sheets to actually get to whatever the dealing position was, it would be about midday before the dealer knew his dealing position of the day before.[36]

It was, in short, a far from satisfactory method of keeping tabs; but – then and later – if there was one aspect of City life that partners and directors rarely or ever felt impelled to take an interest in, it was the problems of their own back offices.

This indifference stemmed in large part (but not wholly) from the deeply entrenched tradition by which the office manager or departmental manager was more or less left alone as a despot – and often a very capricious despot – in his own sphere. Salary, bonus and promotion structures tended to be sketchy or non-existent, being essentially a matter of grace and favour, and few managers possessed the sort of progressive mind that welcomed the latest office technology. Instead, most were martinets of the old school, determined that things should be run along exactly the same disciplinarian, hierarchical lines that they had themselves found on coming into the City some twenty, thirty or forty years earlier. At National Mutual for instance, where Hugh Recknell was Chief Officer from 1932 to 1956, 'his style of management was autocratic and rigidly professional', while 'his elegance of dress, dignified bearing and authoritative voice made his presence a commanding one'. In many offices in the 1950s it was still 'Mr this' and 'Mr that', with no ready assumption of first-name terms. 'You may call me Ernest,' Thalmann of Warburgs announced towards the end of the decade to a recent recruit, Peter Spira, and the proverbial pin was heard to drop when the young man eventually mustered up the courage to do so. As for sartorial standards, Dundas Hamilton's stockbroking experience was probably typical, at least outside the even more formal, top-hatted discount and gilt markets. As well as the regulation bowler hat and rolled umbrella, 'I came to work in a short black jacket and striped trousers, and we all wore white shirts and stiff white collars. We also had a ban on the soft shirt or the coloured shirt, and if I'd worn a striped shirt and a soft collar people in my office would have said to me, "Why haven't you got out of your pyjamas yet?" '[37]

However dressed, it was usually counter-productive for a member of staff to ask for a pay rise, not least because if one threatened to leave and had one's bluff called, the prevailing culture of job immobility was such that this was usually a black mark in the eyes of other potential employers. Far better, it seemed to most, to know one's place, stay put and limit rebellion to using (even misusing) the partners' lavatory after those noble presences had gone home early for the day. The sense of lingering resentment is understandable. 'The partners for the most part were not particularly agreeable,' Spira recalled about his four years at the accountants Cooper Brothers & Co before going to Warburgs in 1957. 'They were the sort of people who were charming to clients or potential clients but treated us lower orders like the minions that we were.'[38]

Yet as often as not there was another side to this coin: an intimate, family-like working environment, knit together by seemingly inalienable ties of mutual trust and loyalty. Most firms were still small enough for that roseate ambience to be possible, if far from inevitable. Only seventy to eighty people worked at Seligmans in the early 1950s; the numbers were similar at James Capel in 1957; while at Gilletts, the total turning up each day at 52 Cornhill was a mere twenty-two in 1951 and only eight more by 1960. Examples of paternalism in action included Mullens, the Government brokers – among the first City partnerships 'to offer its staff housing loans, bridging loans, and private health insurance', as well as having 'the reputation of never sacking anyone'. Similarly the merchant bank Bensons, especially up to 1958 when it was still based at Gresham House in Old Broad Street, could hardly have been more close-knit. Nearly everyone (seventy or so) worked on one large floor; even the most senior figures were readily approachable, with their doors rarely closed; venison, pheasants and grouse littered the long corridors during the shooting season, enabling the staff to take home their free brace; and at 'Piccadilly Circus', the firm's acknowledged hub, Floss Lincoln, who had been there since 1927, combined the roles of telephonist, receptionist and one-woman collective memory, complete with a rogues' gallery of photographs of almost everyone there. The camaraderie was at its most intense (and profitable), according to the historian of Bensons, when there was a new issue on and 'everyone downed tools to help':

> The secretaries remember the panic when they used to work late and were allowed to buy some shares. The managing directors' secretaries had a communicating door with the dealing room. One of the dealers used to open the door and say 'Girls, do you want to buy some Rank rights?' and they would ask, 'Do we?' And he would reply 'Yes, you do', so they would buy them. Then a few days later he would open the door with the question, 'Do you want to sell your Rank rights, girls?' 'Do we?' 'Yes, you do!' And sure enough they would have gone from 7d to 1s 6d . . .

There was also, at such paternalist outfits, the occasional memorable evening treat. In March 1949 the partners of Barings decided to resurrect an old tradition, as Evelyn Baring explained in a letter of invitation to Sir Everard Meynell, a trustee of the staff pension fund:

> Before the war Alfred Mildmay was in the habit of entertaining the male members of our Staff to dinner once a year at 28 Portman Square. This dinner was very much appreciated, and I think all the chaps liked going into a private house and seeing the beautiful pictures, china etc. Now unfortunately none of us have houses where we can entertain in this fashion,

but we wanted to start the dinner again and so we have invited all the male members of the staff to a party at the Canning Club [in Hamilton Place, off Piccadilly], on Wednesday, 20th April, at 7 p.m. for 7.30 . . . After dinner, at I suppose 9 o'clock, we shall have some form of magician to keep the chaps amused, the idea being that the whole party should be over by 10 p.m.

The first-choice entertainer was Giovanni the Pick Pocket, whom Mildmay remembered from the pre-war dinners; but he was no longer in the country, so Barings settled for Ernest Sewell (Magician). On the night, ninety-five were present, including such 8 Bishopsgate eminences as Baring and Mildmay themselves, Lord Ashburton, Sir Edward Peacock, Sir Edward Reid, Arthur Villiers and Viscount Errington (a future Governor of the Bank of England). A late addition was a film show at 9.15, an enticing triple bill consisting of 'The Grand National 1949', 'Barn Yard Romeo' and 'Crazy News Reel'. As a result, the programme ran a little behind schedule, and Sewell's performance had to be cut short. Neither Peacock nor Reid was heard to grumble.[39]

The City of these years was still an intensely *personal* place. Recruitment relied far more on word-of-mouth recommendation than formal qualifications, thereby doing much to ensure the pervasive inculcation, from one generation to another, of tacitly agreed values and assumptions. There was little in the way of either systematic graduate recruitment or internal training of recruits. When Murray Lawrence began as an underwriter at Lloyd's, the head of his syndicate contented himself with checking that the youth had a desk; ensuring that he had introduced himself to the others in the office; and leaving with the words, 'Good luck, well good luck my boy, get on with it, and do what you can.' For many who poured into the City each day there was in effect a trade-off: relatively poor pay (and often prospects) on the one hand; a relative absence of pressure (and the threat of redundancy) on the other. 'They were very poor payers,' Michael Abram, a future successful entrepreneur, would recall of Anglo-African Shipping Co, a confirming house. 'The only reason I could exist was that I was living at home. I started off on £4 a week and ended up on £10. They could not pay me any more because a senior buyer, who had been with them since before the war, was on £12 a week.' As for the other half of that compact, another reminiscence evokes something of the flavour of an altogether less stressful era. 'Quite often Roy Tylie and I used to take the boat from Tower Pier down to Greenwich at lunchtime, with some sandwiches and a bottle of beer, and go down to Greenwich and come back, that would take an hour and a half, two hours,' conveys how it was for Peter Miller in the mid-1950s, beginning a career in marine insurance. 'It wasn't that we were lazy or having an exotic lunch, there wasn't the business around . . .'[40]

Towards the end of the 1950s a 'beardless youth' called David Kinsella spent a year or so with the discount house Smith, St Aubyn & Co. The firm itself, and the milieu at large, made a lasting impression. His fragment of memoirs evokes a world that, slowly but surely, was about to vanish:

> Smith St Aubyn was at the eastern end of Cornhill, opposite Websters shirt shop and minutes from Leadenhall Market, Lloyd's in Lime Street and the Baltic Exchange in St Mary Axe. The side entrance was in White Lion Court, which carried the huge SSA nameplate in brass. Several Smiths were directors, together with two of the Ness family, Archie Kidston (son of 'Bentley Boy' Glen), Jeremy Lowndes (Lowndes Square family) and Duncan Mackinnon, chairman. In all some thirty souls worked at Smiths in the friendly atmosphere of a village-type City.
>
> It was usually a 9 to 5 day, although Warburgs were sometimes referred to as the 'night club' because of late hours. Each morning the directors of the discount companies, perfectly turned out and wearing black silk top hats, would visit the banks and discuss loans. Meanwhile in their offices, public school clerks would record events in hide-bound ledgers, make calls via a dolls-eye switchboard, and parcel up bills in readiness as security for loan cheques. The physical business of moving the cheques and bills around the City was done by an army of liveried messengers (Smith St Aubyn had six). Again top hats were worn, although bank messengers usually donned bowlers. But uniforms tailored in dark blue or black, often with striped trousers, were no match for tails: grey (Lloyds Bank), green (Royal Exchange Assurance), pink (Bank of England), black (often Coutts), blue with red trim (Lloyd's insurance). Wallets in a large inside pocket held the bills, a long round often meaning that several thousands in value would be carried at a time.
>
> The chief area of operations was small and seldom beyond Finsbury Circus in the north, the Thames in the south, Fenchurch Street Station in the east, and St Paul's in the west. But here could be found scores of banks keen to do business . . .

Each interior had its distinctive ambience. Martins Bank in Lombard Street was 'famous for its display of flintlock pistols', Barings in Bishopsgate had 'huge lead water tanks', the Smiths branch of the National Provincial featured 'the Smith family roll of honour'. 'Other banks were noted for their furniture polish or disinfectant smells and rosewater sprays in summertime. Blazing open fires in winter, the cool of Lazards marble in August. Several, such as Rothschilds, were baronial and impressive.' Street life also fired Kinsella's imagination:

> Cornhill in particular was quite posh in those days. Along the side of the Royal Exchange were several stylish shops offering sporting gear, shirts, cigars, collectable books, etc. Memorable was a magnificent silver shop [Searle & Co] with all manner of engraved and crested items. Boys on delivery bikes from Leadenhall Market would cycle around with stilton, smoked salmon on boards, crates of wine, all manner of meats, game and

shell-fish for the dining rooms. A late session would see the delivery of quality sandwiches from Ullmans in Cullum Street. Parcels would also arrive from the big stores, shirt shops, shoe shops, tailors and gunsmiths, for in the City 40 years ago a gentleman would *not* be seen carrying a parcel. Even swimming togs were carried beneath a bowler hat, to and from the RAC pool.

Office equipment and fittings were basic but of good quality. All the chairs and desks and cabinets were of wood, the larger desks often leather-topped with drawers on either side. Several rulers were of the round, black-wood type, and all calculating machines were mechanical, simple in capacity and often of the hand-crank kind. Pens and ink prevailed, my first Biro being seen at the HQ of the Midland Bank. All our cheques were finally collected from the banks and hand-cancelled as a security measure. All ledgers were large, bound in leather, well made and heavy. At the end of the day all bills and day books of account were put in the basement safe. Office fun and games were not unduly suppressed and ranged from a wrestling match in the safe to a senior's desk and chair finding their way to the pavement in Cornhill . . .[41]

*

The signs of change – from 'old' City to 'new' City – were already apparent by the late 1950s. When Bensons reluctantly moved in 1958 from the Gresham House rabbit-warren into Aldermanbury House in what would be called Aldermanbury Square, its new home was still surrounded by the debris of war and was reputedly the City's first new building on a bomb site. The office was spread over several floors; at least one secretary found that 'the difference between Old Broad Street and there was ghastly because there were concrete stairs and things like that'; and by all accounts it proved impossible to re-establish the old, treasured sense of *Gemütlichkeit*. This move to part of the London Wall scheme also pushed Bensons away from the traditional core. The same applied two years later when Durlachers moved to the newly built Austral House, a low block set back from the corner of Coleman Street and London Wall. 'We managed to take two floors, one above the other, so it was all open plan,' Richard Durlacher recalled. 'It was about ten minutes away from the Bank of England, ten minutes away from the Stock Exchange. People told us we were mad because nobody thought that anybody could operate that vast distance.' By March 1963, when Phillips & Drew took possession of the fourth to seventh floors of Lee House, further along London Wall, there was less sense of eccentricity about the decision – indeed, to a self-consciously progressive firm like Phillips & Drew, it seemed like a brave new world that it was now entering. 'We thought our new premises were marvellous,' Martin Gibbs, who was on the research side, remembered:

The outside walls were largely glass and the interior designers had been asked to produce an open-plan system in most areas, using a minimum number of partitions, so that we had beautifully light rooms to work in. All the furniture was new, including our desks [metal rather than wood, despite the personal preference of the senior partner], and had been carefully colour-coordinated with the carpets. The whole effect make a striking contrast to the grubby dinginess of Pinners Hall. I remember Peter Swan [an ebullient Australian partner] enthusiastically exclaiming, 'We *must* keep it like this!'

The semi-beloved financial village was still largely intact, but there now gleamed in the distance various outlying suburbs, causing far more onerous duties to the City's messenger class. At Phillips & Drew there was a keen debate (eventually decided in the affirmative) about hiring a Humber Hawk to ferry the more old-fashioned partners to and from the City Club.[42] Far greater dispersion lay ahead, but already the traditional intimacy could never be quite the same again.

Yet despite all the new office blocks going up on old bomb sites, the City's daytime population fell from 390,000 in 1961 to 361,000 five years later. There were two main reasons. First, a long-term trend was under way of relocating back offices. 'The experiment of moving part of their routine office work to Croydon has paid handsomely,' Mynors at the Bank recorded as early as 1957 in relation to the insurance brokers Price Forbes. 'A better type of staff (a good many married women) working in more comfortable conditions . . .' The second reason was mechanisation, which at last, between the late 1950s and mid-1960s, made a quantum leap forward in the City at large, above all through the introduction of mechanised accounting. The British Tabulating Co was among those who developed punch-card accounting systems for City firms, including by 1957 the Hollerith system for Stock Exchange firms, and soon they were becoming almost commonplace. In 1960 even the traditionally rather ponderous organisation responsible for settling the City's futures markets, the London Produce Clearing House (now owned by United Dominions Trust), installed punch cards. Some firms persisted with the manual preparation and balancing of accounts for as long as they could – the solicitors Slaughter and May did not feel the need for punch cards until as late as 1965 – but mechanised accounting had such obvious advantages that its spread was irresistible.[43]

In other areas of office technology 1960 seems to have been the key year. In the course of those twelve months Linklaters & Paines acquired its first Rank Xerox photocopier and first telex machine, the latter especially important for the way it quickened international communication; another legal firm, Ashursts, had by then four electric typewriters; and the discount house Allen, Harvey & Ross installed closed-circuit television in its Cornhill offices. That same year Durlachers marked its move to Austral

House by inaugurating a much-publicised, diamond-shaped dealing room, equipped with as many as forty or fifty telephone handsets (probably more than any other dealing room in the City) and used each day before and after the six hours or so of dealings on the Stock Exchange floor. So the march of progress continued, not least in those towers by London Wall. Summer 1964, for example, saw the arrival at Phillips & Drew of a round-the-clock telephone-answering service. 'If, at the end of this announcement, you dictate a message,' part of the announcement snappily explained to those ringing NATional 4444 outside normal business hours, 'it will be recorded and, as soon as the office opens, it will be transcribed and passed to the partner concerned.' Two years later the same firm decided that it needed more calculators and that 'there was a very good case for the electronic type both from the noise point of view and speed of operation'.[44]

But of course it was the almost ubiquitous coming of the computer – that fabled monster in the eyes of many – that most powerfully denoted the accelerating pace of change. Durlachers was, as it had been with punch cards, ahead of most of the pack:

> We became involved [Les Turtle recalls] in the very early stages of computers in 1959. Esmond Durlacher met Anthony Salmon who was the head of Leo Computers at the time. It was a cocktail party I believe . . . Leo II was a vast valve machine and was a very unreliable machine, because of the valve probably, so we had a lot of trouble with it. Anyway, we developed an accounting system to go on to that machine to take the place of our punch card system. Most of it was ready by about 1963. I think it was 1965 when we actually went 'live' on it, against my recommendation because one thing that it proved to be was totally unreliable, and our debits invariably wouldn't equal credits because somewhere along the line the way the machine worked it would drop binary bits which changed values. The manager of the firm made the decision to go live and we scrapped our punch card system, which was getting old by then. And we never balanced again for another two years – well, we balanced sometimes with a great struggle, but it was very difficult . . .

At Phillips & Drew, equally go-ahead despite certain conservative elements, there were also frustrations. An IBM 1440, employing a system specially designed for a stockbroker's office, was ordered in autumn 1963 for delivery in early 1965. The eventual cost was about £100,000. By March 1966 it was running for an average of more than twelve hours each day, sometimes deep into the night, and the firm's comptroller was authorised 'to make suitable arrangements over amenities, with particular regard to refreshments and a music programme, whether by radio or Muzak'. Even so, not everyone was happy, and a year later a partner noted after taking soundings that the computer 'had not been properly sold to the staff, as they see many people in the General Office still working overtime and the broad difficulties of a computer are not properly appreciated'.[45] For so long essentially Luddite in its working practice, it was hardly likely that the City was going to give an enthusiastic welcome to the dawning of the age of HAL.

A lot else changed in the 1960s. Partly through natural growth, partly through taking over smaller companies, the size of most leading firms significantly increased. James Capel, for instance, had a staff of about 180 by 1964, more than twice that of seven years earlier. The result, inevitably, was a greater sense of anonymity in office life, a loosening of the old personal ties. 'It was no longer practicable for new entrants to be conducted round the office and introduced to everybody,' Ronald Palin noted regretfully in the 1970s about his latter years at Rothschilds. 'Increasingly one saw faces about to which one could not put a name . . .' Equally inevitably, the employee's traditional sense of loyalty to his firm – that indispensable, reciprocal part of the paternalist package – began to be eroded. Peter Swan of Phillips & Drew, from his vantage-point as head of equity selling to the investment institutions, reflected illuminatingly in November 1963 on the new culture, and in particular on what he and some of his partners saw as 'the lack of enthusiasm of many of the staff':

> The causes of this, I think, arise from our recent expansion both in income and staff [almost 200, and rising rapidly]. In the old days a man's efforts were more noticeable than today. An order then worth £50 is now more like £5 or £10 percentage-wise in the total day's take. In the old days we all knew if we dealt for A.R.D. Thomson, did a large gilt-edged switch, or did a large equity order. We all knew who did the security analysis. With our size, we seem to be moving towards a civil service approach . . .
>
> With one or two exceptions, they do not seem concerned at how the rest of the firm works and, although reasonably good at arriving, go promptly at 5.30 p.m. Apart from reading the usual papers, I should not think they do any homework.

Fuelling this more instrumental approach towards work, and job mobility, was the increasing competition for capable staff. By 1968 (when the annual New Earnings Survey began) the average gross salary, excluding bonuses, for a full-time non-manual male in the City was £1,966 a year, significantly above the £1,648 for Britain as a whole.[46]

The culture was altering in other ways. Godfrey D'Arcy Biss (known to his intimates as 'Bun') was the portly, splendidly old-fashioned senior partner of Ashursts throughout the 1960s; but when in 1963 he tried to persuade his new partners to acquire bowler hats, they simply refused to do so. It was the decade in which not only the bowler ceased to be the unquestioned norm, but also the black jacket and striped trousers; it became possible to appear on the floor of the Stock Exchange in a soft collar and/or striped shirt without being made to feel a freak. There were even sightings of women in trousers, though if permitted this was usually only in tandem with a matching jacket. First-name usage became much more widespread, and it was no longer possible to assume an unthinking deference on the part of those born below the salt. 'In order to abolish the opprobrious word "Clerk",' Mynors at the Bank of England noted in January 1964 with evident lack of enthusiasm, 'the Court have decided that the Classed Staff shall be known from the 1st March next as Firsts, Seconds and Thirds.'[47] The unblushingly hierarchical structure remained, but it was a timely concession.

One can, nevertheless, exaggerate: the basic, undeniable fact was that the City during this decade changed rather less than British society at large. In an era when size tended to be equated with virtue, the majority of City firms were still quite small (in 1967, for example, only thirty-six people worked at Gilletts); and there lingered in many offices the discipline of the quill, while a surprising amount of work continued to be done manually. At the Bank of England an internal directive from the Governor on 12 September 1963 (just as the Beatles were about to top the charts with 'She Loves You') announced unequivocally that the better type of old-style paternalism was still alive and kicking:

> I am afraid that many people's holidays and week-ends have been spoilt by the wretched weather we have had so far this year. If we do get any sunshine during the remaining weeks of the summer, I hope that the Heads of Department will do their best to enable the staff to take advantage of it, subject of course to requirements of the work. With this proviso, I would like people to get away as early as possible and perhaps even be allowed to have the odd afternoon off, where this can be managed.

Sartorial standards, moreover, were far from being *wholly* relaxed. When the young David Walker was seconded from the Treasury to the Bank in 1966, in order to learn about the foreign exchange market, he was firmly advised by the Deputy Chief Cashier to wear a white collar (preferably stiff) while he was in the City.[48]

Both sartorially and otherwise, the case of Cazenove's is instructive. For most of the decade fewer than 200 people worked at 12 Tokenhouse Yard (once the home of Huths) just to the north of the Bank, allowing it to remain – as its senior partner, Sir Antony Hornby, was determined that it should – an organisation of manageable size. The prevailing approach to everyday conduct was essentially male, conservative and propounded from the top. Several partners took an interest in the welfare of the staff, keeping the firm a fairly tight-knit community; but the enforcer was the disciplinarian General Manager, Cyril Jolly, a stickler for smart appearance. By the end of the decade all partners still wore bowlers, almost all men still wore stiff collars and no female member of staff dared to wear either trousers or too provocatively short a skirt. Overall, it was probably a happy enough ship – quite unlike the London office of the Hongkong and Shanghai Bank. Philip Stubbs, who as a young man in the 1930s had been in the London office before going East and had had a run-in with the authorities because of his penchant for bringing in a shooting stick to sit on when tired of standing, returned to London in 1966 as Manager. He found Gracechurch Street a poorly run, demoralised outfit, with each morning wasted by a queue of departmental managers waiting to get a decision from the more senior manager, and typified by the unseemly sight of men in their mid-fifties having to sign the attendance book.[49] In other words, a 1960s' update of *Psmith in the City* (1910) would not have been too difficult to write for that bank's most distinguished alumnus, P.G. Wodehouse.

One way in which the post-war City *did* mirror British society was in the continuing virtual absence of women from positions of any seniority. The male secretary may have vanished, and many of the punch-card and computer operators may have been women, but the notion of a female partner in a merchant bank, a female bill broker, a female member of the Stock Exchange or a female director of the Bank of England remained inconceivable. Mary Murry, a playwright in her spare time, worked for many years for one of the Big Five banks as a shorthand-typist-translator. Her 1961 essay, ' "The Final Stroke of Nine" ', provides a rare insight:

> Our most revered curio was a genuine candlestick telephone, still in use, and with it I noticed a curious reluctance among the women in the office to answer it. They would even let the telephone go on and on ringing when none of the men happened to be in. And when I, the newcomer among them, at last unhooked the receiver, I was warned that about five or six years before another new typist had done the same, but at the mere sound of her voice the receiver at the other end had been peremptorily replaced, and later in the day the Principal had been sent for by one of the Powers That Be, who thundered at him, outraged: 'I rang through to your department – and a *woman* answered!' . . .
>
> Even today woman is tolerated in the City only as a handmaiden. However agreeably disguised, with a deep-pile carpeted sanctum of her own, a secretary's secretary, and even her own telephone, only the menial positions are readily open to her, and she will find it prudent to conform, or seem to conform, to one or other of moneygetting man's alternating pair of images of her – the nurse-aunt figure, patient, ministering, devoted, impeccably dowdy, and sure as the Rock: or the 'little woman', equally at home at the Master's feet ('Oh, Mr Minories, what a marvellous idea! I'd never have thought of that myself' – the idea that she had put forward only that morning and had had turned down as quite unworkable); or saucily perched upon his knee ('Oh, Mr Minories, just suppose anyone was to come in!') . . .
>
> Even the City shops reflect moneygetting man's two women. Sedately

and legitimately in her lunch hour, the one may be measured in the ladies' annexe of an old-established gentlemen's tailor for a faultless costume in orthodox City suiting, with two skirts to the jacket and extended credit terms (two references, one of which should be a banker). Or in her coffee break the other may skip illicitly down the backstairs into one of the myriad of cupboard-like *boutiques* which have sprung up wherever there is space enough to hold a saleslady, her customer and a showcase, and take her choice of gossamer nylons that ladder at a breath, of mock-Eliot camisoles in *broderie anglaise* threaded through with cerise nylon ribbons, and – no, not stays – not stays, but rather the last word in transatlantic bras she has seen advertised all the way up the Bank escalators, fitted with the latest built-in, floating-action devices. But when a real woman in the City (as most of us are, however much the men oblige us to dissemble) has any real shopping to do, she takes the Central Line westward on a Thursday night . . .[50]

*

Half a million or so men and women worked in the City at one time or another during the twenty years after the war; yet we know dismayingly little about what it *really* felt like to be one of that sea of faces emerging each morning from Bank underground station. The psychological experiences and observations of a quartet of individuals – none of them well known, even in the City – may, taken together, stand proxy for a deeper set of truths that anyway go beyond the resources of language.

J.D.W. Raimbach, the first of the four, spent a quarter of a century at the still systematically overmanned Old Lady. He went there soon after the war, on a year's probation and with other ex-servicemen:

> We discovered that mid-morning coffee breaks were frowned upon, if not forbidden. There was a strict dress code. Non-conforming was slow death. It dawned upon us that we had entered a time warp in which lingered the vestiges of the British Empire. A number of my colleagues had held high-ranking commands; most of us had at some time been very seriously frightened (sometimes by our own side) and it became hard for us to adapt to this fusty, outmoded regime.
>
> Some sought solace in drink. I remember the uproar when an inebriated clerk ('Adequately Refreshed' was the Bank euphemism) was helped to the washroom, his arms draped around his supporting colleagues' shoulders and his feet trailing along the wooden floor. I discovered a clerk who daily descended to the sub-vaults. He sat at his desk on which rested a ledger so huge that two hands were needed to turn the pages. This ledger contained hundreds of long-closed accounts which needed cancelling. His daily task was to roll a long cylindrical ebony ruler down the page, line by line, striking through each entry with pen and ink. I believe that he had been an infantry officer, who had seen much action. He rarely spoke . . .
>
> Living with the Hump [the term for the post-war bulge in the age profile of Bank staff] meant concentrated competition for promotions. We had the regular pantomime called 'Black Thursday' aka 'The Feast of the Passover'.

The Court of Directors assembled on (I think) the first Thursday in the month, when promotions, if any, would be announced. This was a sure trigger for the disenchanted to repair to the bar and drown their sorrows, or go sick, or break down in tears . . .

By my fortieth birthday, in 1963, I had arrived at the dizzy heights of 1st Class Clerk, with a princely salary of £1,000 pa. About that time a man with a clipboard and stop-watch started haunting the corridors of New Change. One day he sat alongside me, and asked me a number of penetrating questions about what I thought I was doing. Something was in the air . . . and, in the fullness of time, I was offered an early pension.

Raimbach left the Bank of England in 1972, at the age of forty-nine, and trained to become a teacher. Three years later he duly started teaching. 'By then,' as he notes at the end of his memoir with a good-natured exclamation mark, 'the Hump had disappeared!'[51]

Michael Burns offers a rather less benign perspective. A grammar-school boy from the suburbs, he went in 1956 to the stockbrokers Ross-Munro, Duff & Co and was there for a few eye-opening years:

Teddy Miles [one of the four partners] was inevitably rude and bad-tempered. He literally threw the contract pad back at you if there was a mistake. I was told I had to accept this because the stump that was left after his leg had been blown off in the war gave him constant pain. I can still hear, and sense the fear, as the clicking and thumping sound of his false leg approached my desk. Miles was also a snob of the most objectionable kind. I once played cricket for the Stock Exchange at the Hurlingham Club. When Miles, who was a Hurlingham member, saw me in the bar having an after-match drink with the other players, he ordered the steward to make me drink outside the members' bar.

RMD's most flamboyant partner was Henry Duff. A slim, slightly round-shouldered man with a generous, Jimmy Edwards style moustache who was always dressed in the formal City wear of black jacket and waistcoat and striped trousers. He lived in Winchester and never arrived in the office before 10 a.m. and left soon after 3.30 p.m. Duff was no intellectual. The only items he carried to and from work were his bowler hat and umbrella and his box of stiff collars, laundered and delivered weekly to the office by *Collars of Wembley*. He was at his most entertaining in the afternoons when he was recovering from his frequent alcoholic lunches. During this recuperation period before he left for his unsteady walk to 'The Drain', he never needed much encouragement to start reminiscing about his days as a prisoner-of-war.

My period at RMD coincided with a prolonged boom in the stock market, and consequently the firm was constantly taking on extra staff. One advert placed in *The Times* during this period read: 'City stockbrokers require person to train as a blue button – Etonian preferred'. The long-running boom meant that after I finished in the dealing room each afternoon I was required to go into the general office to help with the enormous amount of clerical work that was generated. No extra money was paid for these overtime hours. Instead there was a promise of a golden handout in the form of a Christmas bonus. During these interminable evenings it was my task to enter the day's bargains into the enormous red, leather-bound loose-leaf 'Bought' and 'Sold' ledgers. At the time of the fortnightly balance we all had to add and check long lines of figures, and not until both ledgers were balanced to the last farthing, was anybody allowed home. On some occasions it was past ten o'clock before I made my weary way down a deserted Moorgate.

Jack Gregory, the clerk responsible for the 'Bought' ledger, in what little spare time he had, played the alto saxophone around the clubs and pubs of Brighton. He introduced me to jazz and on occasions I went with him to the Dome at Brighton to hear such bands as the Count Basie Orchestra and the Gerry Mulligan Quartet. Gregory's wife died in her early thirties, an event he never recovered from, dying himself a few years later. One evening, soon after he returned to work after his wife's death, in his despair he opened the window next to his desk and sent the bought ledger crashing down into the well of the building.

One of the consequences of this boom period in the Stock Exchange was the constant flow of new issues. Bundles of copies of the *Financial Times* were bought and application forms for new shares were filled in with the names of every member of RMD's staff. The market was so buoyant at this time that within hours of the new stock opening on the market there was a profit to be made. Needless to say the quick killing from the sale of shares in ICI or British Petroleum issued in the name of Michael Burns did not make the humble clerk any richer. We all meekly signed over the proceeds to our honourable employers.

As a reward for our loyal service, the partners laid on a lunch-time Christmas party for the staff. Glasses and bottles were collected from the Red Lion next door and on the last lunchtime before the holiday, the office staff and the partners came together to uncomfortably sip our light ales, nibble ham sandwiches and stare out at the frost-covered girders that had been growing up on the building-site opposite. This structure, which was normally populated by sure-footed Irish navvies, was deserted, that is until we saw Henry Duff, a gin and tonic in one hand, tightrope walking across a six-inch girder, fifty feet above the ground. One of the inebriated Guinness-drinking navvies was persuaded out of the pub to climb up and lead our swaying partner down to earth. Duff then invited all the building workers, whose skills he had been admiring over the months, to join us at the office party.

Christmas was also the time when RMD's staff were informed as to what their annual bonus was to be. I was staggered to be told that, after months of relentless overtime and at a time when the firm had been making record profits, I was to be awarded the princely sum of £50. £50 in crisp, white, five-pound notes was what, every Friday afternoon, the office manager handed Henry Duff for his weekend's expenses.

Firsthand experiences of such inequalities gained the Labour Party a supporter . . .[52]

His view of society thus formed, Burns soon left the City and became a television cameraman and then an independent film-maker.

Stanley McCombie, in complete contrast, not only lasted the course but had no regrets about doing so. Known to everyone as 'Mac', he spent forty-four years in the service of the merchant bank Antony Gibbs & Sons before retiring in 1958. Later that year, in October, the firm celebrated its 150th anniversary with a cocktail party at the Grocers' Hall for family, partners, staff and pensioners. In mid-September an invitation was naturally sent to 'Aberdeen', 51 Wallwood Road, Leytonstone, E11, but the letter of acceptance from 'Mac' to 'Mr Antony' struck a less than joyous note:

> I caught a chill working in the garden early in August, and it turned to my old foe – Dermatitis, again. For some weeks I have been a most uncomfortable little man, & today it seems to have flared up again. Being summer I was able to keep about, and even went on a Scottish tour at the end of August, but it was not a success so far as I was concerned. So far I don't consider my retiring to be an unqualified success, and my wife is threatening to send me back to the Office as a washout so far as home is concerned . . . I miss you very much, but am sure all goes on as usual without me.

Two days later, supplying some names of other former members of staff to ask to the party, poor 'Mac' was in an even lower state: 'In addition to my itch, I am now plagued with boils, & an acute attack of depression (surely the work of the Devil) . . . Please don't write & sympathise with me, I'll climb out of the dark hole soon.'[53] Those forty-four years had been his whole life, the source of his identity, and the firm meant as much to him as it did to 'Mr Antony' – perhaps even more.

Did McCombie ever feel the different sort of itch experienced by Maurice Holdstock, resident versifier of Midland Bank's staff magazine? 'Come, fly with me' was the seemingly insurgent call to his readers in the summer of 1963:

> High on the seventh floor of 60 Gracechurch Street is the place of my
>   employment,
> And on this summer day it gives me only a modicum of enjoyment.
> The only prospect that pleases as I gaze through the wide windows is the
>   horizon of distant hills beyond the Thames' cranes and the City's spires,
> And I come to the conclusion that they who say they love their work and
>   find pleasure in being tied to desks or harnessed to lathes when the sun is
>   a-shining to welcome the day, heigh-ho, are lires,
> Because right now there's nothing less I feel like doing than work;
> Nothing less I want to be than a clork . . .
> I too know a bank whereon the wild thyme blows –
> Not a bank with highly polished counters and similar cashier, I don't mean
>   one of thows.
> My bank is a private bank that never clowses,

All hung about with shady branches above a limpid pool suitable for the dabbling of towses.

There would I watch dragonflies and frogs on water-lily leaves, and fishes flashing among bullrushes like unto those associated with Mowses.

'Tis there I could discard my old complexes and shake off my neurowses,

And write immortal verses and deathless prowses

Instead of surveying the City, as it were silently on a peak in E.C.3, and considering how my life is spent in Overseas

Composing mundane missives to the Moroccans and penning polite epistles to the Porgugeas . . .[54]

CHAPTER EIGHT

Not Very Reliable Signposts

Shortly before Christmas 1948 it was Sir Edward Peacock's task to inform the mother of a young Baring that her son, about to get married, had no long-term future at 8 Bishopsgate:

> We are all devoted to him, staff and partners alike, and his leaving here will cause real sorrow. Therefore it has been with great reluctance that I have reached the conclusion, with which the other partners agree, that he is not suited to the rather stolid life of a banker. He has a charming personality, gets on well with everyone and loves meeting people. I'm sure that he would be unhappy in the dull routine of office business which would be his lot for some years at least. Business has changed radically and even the seniors are more and more involved in legal problems which take the pleasure out of their work . . .
>
> The firm of Gerald Hodgson & Co is our oldest Stock Exchange connection, the partners are young, keen, very nice men and they would be glad to take him and to guarantee him a minimum salary of £1,000 a year until he becomes a partner. We would try to see to it that having one of the family would be good for them.
>
> His gift for friendship and getting on with people should prove of great value on the Stock Exchange and I should expect him to do well there.

Those occupying the City's most eminent parlours showed no inclination to overrate the qualities of the inhabitants of Capel Court. 'Philip Darwin is the son of a near neighbour of mine,' Maurice Parsons observed to a Bank of England colleague in 1965, 'and, although a member of the Stock Exchange, nevertheless quite a bright fellow.' Peter Spira, looking back on his time as a merchant banker from the late 1950s, could hardly have been more explicit about what remained the traditional pecking order until the 1980s: 'Bankers used to despise stockbrokers. When I was at Warburgs, the idea of ever calling on a stockbroker was absolute anathema . . . Jobbers – you didn't even know jobbers.' But if those at the top of the City tended to regard the Stock Exchange as a regrettable necessity, the rest of the world was inclined to be almost completely indifferent. In 1952 a survey found that 96 per cent of the British population was 'apathetic' to Stock Exchange affairs; and although eight years later this came down to 80 per cent, it still reflected an institution marginalised from national life.

If there was a public attitude towards the Stock Exchange, it mingled mild distaste with a residual sense of boredom. 'Few people want to spend the whole evening laughing heartily at someone else's capers,' the Bloomsbury diarist Frances Partridge noted in 1961 about a disagreeable dinner-party companion, adding that 'it was like a night out with stockbrokers'. At the other end of the decade an early Monty Python sketch was called 'The Dull Life of a City Stockbroker'.[1] The Stock Exchange, in fine, was not a happening place.

*

No one in the 1950s or 1960s ever denied that the rhythms of the stock market remained the City's daily, indispensable pulse; equally, no one during these years ever praised the Stock Exchange Council as a streamlined, fast-moving body capable of taking imaginative, far-reaching decisions.[2] Filled on the whole by elderly, safety-first men, whom their partners were happy enough to see booted upstairs, it was a body that, if it could prevaricate, tended to do so. Typical of this institutional conservatism was its persistent refusal to overcome jobbers' inhibitions and publish (even retrospectively) relevant statistics about the volumes of business being done in the market. It was not until 1964 that, at last, monthly turnover totals began to be published. And in another area, the scandal of non-voting shares, the London Stock Exchange did nothing to initiate or encourage reform, despite the notable efforts of its counterpart in Birmingham to tackle the problem. Instead, under the leadership of Sir John Braithwaite almost throughout the 1950s, the Council concentrated on good relations with the Bank of England (and thus the government), the cultivation of an intense respectability and a carefully measured public-relations campaign to enhance the institution's standing. A boisterous clubbishness endured on the market floor, but it was a symptomatic moment when in September 1952 'the Council decided that the notice referring to the throwing of paper balls and other missiles should no longer be exhibited in the House'.[3]

Indeed, the question of non-nuclear missiles was brought sharply into focus early the following year when, after much delay, the necessary building licences were granted for the construction of a visitors' gallery. The news prompted a last-minute flurry of letters to the Council, including one from the brokers Francis, How & Lowndes of 5 Copthall Court:

> We cannot think that the interests of the Stock Exchange will be advanced if we allow the public to see the rather school-boyish activities of certain dealers in the matter of throwing paper balls, flying paper aeroplanes and darts, and occasional ragging. Nor can we think our interests will be served by the spectacle of members draped in undignified attitudes on the benches more or less asleep.

These things could and would be used against us politically. In addition, we think some members would have a hard task explaining to their wives what a really hard day in the City means if their spouses were allowed to go into the gallery and see for themselves.

Eventually, after a hostile petition signed by 188 members and six firms, the Council saw no alternative but to hold a members' referendum. Voting cards were sent out in March, with a memo explaining that the Council supported the proposal as part of its campaign over the last few years 'to make the Stock Exchange better known, in order to establish its position as a national Institution, to remove misconceptions about it, and to attract more business'. The result was clear-cut: 2,274 members voted in favour of the gallery; 541 were against; and there were twenty-three spoiled papers.[4] The visitors' gallery opened on 16 November 1953, a magnet over the years for amateur sociologists and anthropologists.

In July 1958 (the year after a resident public-relations officer had been appointed) the filming took place of *My Word is My Bond*, to be shown in the small cinema that formed part of the gallery. Robin Bailey played Mr Johnson the Stockbroker, showing round a young married couple (also played by actors) who were keen to invest, but just before the cameras started rolling his suit was judged to be 'a little too dashing'; 'accordingly a messenger was urgently dispatched to a well-known firm of theatrical costumiers who quickly supplied the prescribed dress, namely a black double-breasted coat and striped trousers'. Complete control was exercised over that inevitably rather bland and stilted production, but it was potentially a different matter five years later when the BBC asked to film in the Stock Exchange for a forthcoming series on City institutions. Fred Althaus, of the Council's Public Relations Committee, noted with alarm that the script was to be co-written by Andrew Shonfield and Paul Ferris, the latter 'the author of a satirical book on "The City"', a felony compounded by the fact that 'more recently he wrote the script and spoke the commentary for a somewhat satirical programme on the City for ATV'. Permission, however, was granted, on the basis that the BBC agreed to submit a rough script, and that a Stock Exchange representative would be able 'to act as a censor' about what was filmed in the House and what was not.[5]

The Chairman of the Stock Exchange during the first half of the 1960s was Lord Ritchie of Dundee, 'a handsome, rather theatrical-looking stockbroker with a monocle and pearl tie-pin', whom Anthony Sampson interviewed for his *Anatomy of Britain*. ' "We're trying to dispel the Victorian idea that the Stock Exchange is something mysterious, doing fiddles on the side," he said: "we're showing that it's a straightforward job, and part of the nation's business. But we've avoided advertising like 'you want the best shares, we've got them'".' Before the Second World War the

Stock Exchange had banned members from advertising, mainly in order
to enforce quality control, in practice between authorised brokers on the
one hand and outside brokers on the other. By now, however, the old
bucket shops had been legislated out of existence, and unsurprisingly there
were those who wanted the ban on advertising to be lifted. 'Now that HM
is reduced to public advertisements to induce young men to take
commissions in her fighting services it can scarcely be considered any
longer to be vulgar practice' was how one stockbroker, Vernon Laurie of
Heseltine Powell, tried to persuade the Council in February 1963.
Towards the end of 1967 the Council specifically canvassed the views of
member firms:

> *Argenti & Christopherson:* Paid advertising would presumably lead to
> some form of competitive bidding for business which we would regard
> as both undignified and liable to lead to abuse.
> *Carlebach, Scott, Young & Co:* I do not think that Stockbrokers should
> do what Accountants, Solicitors and Doctors do *not* do, i.e. advertise.
> It seems to me that such a step would be a lowering of our status as
> professional men.
> *Cazenove & Co:* The ability to insert paid advertisements will surely put
> firms under competitive pressure to do so from their friends and
> acquaintances in the advertising world.
> *Foster & Braithwaite* [where the octogenarian Sir John Braithwaite was
> now senior partner]: Paid advertising might well provide an
> opportunity to those here who wish to see the Stock Exchange brought
> under Government control.

Some firms, unavailingly, took a contrary line: but the truth was that,
quite apart from advertisers' unfortunate social and cultural connotations,
most large firms were doing well enough not to need to advertise, while
most small firms were afraid of the cost and the competition that might
ensue if advertising were permitted. Moreover, given the seemingly
unassailable fixed commission structure that still prevailed – making the
Stock Exchange one of post-war Britain's most sheltered business
environments – ambitious, retail-minded stockbrokers, even if they
existed, could only dream about advertising on the basis of price.[6]
The market itself was heavily domestic in orientation during these
twenty years or so after the war. Between them, the British government
and British industrial securities comprised by 1960 over two-thirds of the
entire market, as measured by market value. Any number of factors
inhibited a return to the old-style, pre-1914 – even pre-1931 – international
orientation. These included the continuing fact of exchange control, the
existence of the so-called 'dollar premium' (adding up to one-fifth in the
cost of dealing in non-sterling securities) and the Stock Exchange's innate

hostility to encouraging arbitrage dealings; but the most important factor was the complacent insularity of the whole investment community. 'Recommendations invariably need to be in writing,' a member of one stockbroking firm's struggling foreign department complained in 1963. 'For most clients there is little familiarity with foreign stocks. For this reason, it is very exceptional to be able to "punt" a stock to the department's clients by telephone.' As for dealing on behalf of foreign clients, an estimate in 1967 reckoned that rather less than one-sixth of London's stockbrokers made this a regular part of their business.[7] By this time there was no shortage of opportunities in international business, but few firms were inclined to make the effort to take them.

The membership remained as parochial as the stock and shares in which it dealt. Occasionally the Council made an exception, and admitted a foreign-born person into the elect, but even that usually took a long time. Julius Strauss, for example, continued to plug away after his rebuff in 1950, eventually becoming an unauthorised clerk in April 1959 and a member more than five years later. Nor was nationality the only bar, as shown by the case of Phillips & Drew's Denis Weaver, a trained actuary who during the 1950s effectively founded investment analysis in Britain.[8] Unfortunately he was also a Quaker who had registered as a conscientious objector during the war, and after it, despite several applications, the Stock Exchange refused to make him a member. That remained the position until 1960, when a colleague of Weaver's, the well-connected Hon Peter Vanneck (a future Lord Mayor), kindly agreed to 'roll the pitch' with the Council, which at last relented. By then Weaver was in his fifties, and his chance of becoming senior partner had disappeared for good.

For women, of course, there could be no exemption, belated or otherwise. Yet in the winter of 1966–7 it did seem that this inviolable assumption might be successfully challenged, after Miss Muriel H. Bailey, a registered clerk with the brokers Jas Flower & Sons, made a peculiarly persuasive case for becoming a member in order to take her place in the firm's partnership. She outlined her personal history:

> I started in the City in 1925 as a Shorthand typist with the firm of Chandler & Co (the Senior Partner, Mr Lionel M Walter, being a friend of my Father's). About 1934 I joined Jas Flower & Sons. When the war broke out there were so few of us left that the firm managed to get me exempted from the Forces, and in consequence I became responsible for the running of the office. Towards the end of the war I started to build up a personal business and over the period of years have been very successful, and can say with no hesitation that all my clients, both male and female, have the utmost confidence in me . . .

Bailey promised, if she became a member, 'never to enter the "House" as

I fully understand that the presence of a woman on the "floor" would be an embarrassment to Members, and that is far from my wish'. On this restricted basis (in other words, no access to the floor), the Council was willing to support her candidature, but first needed to get the principle accepted by at least three-quarters of the membership, in order to amend the deed of settlement. A ballot in April 1967 produced a small but inadequate majority in favour of women members; a further ballot in May 1968, that most revolutionary of months, saw 663 members voting in favour and an unyielding 1,366 against.[9]

Not surprisingly, this society of white Anglo-Saxon males reacted sluggishly to the two major, closely related developments in post-war investment: the cult of the equity and the rise of the institutional investor.[10] From the late 1940s Ross Goobey in Bristol and Lewis Whyte in London had been pushing the merits of investment (especially institutional investment) in equities, including as a hedge against inflation; but such was the stock market's innate reluctance to see the conventional wisdom about the superior safety of gilts overturned that it was not until August 1959 that the so-called 'reverse yield gap' was created, by which gilts offered a higher yield than equities. A few months later end-of-decade market reviews demonstrated that whereas gilts had fallen by about one-third, the value of equities had trebled. If those figures were eloquent enough, the triumph of the ordinary share was sealed in 1961 when that year's Trustee Investments Act for the first time enabled trustees with restricted powers, including many local authorities, to put up to half of their funds into equities. This gave institutional investment a considerable fillip, and by 1963 personal holdings (as measured by market value) had declined to 51 per cent of the total equity market, well down on the 61.8 per cent as recently as 1957.[11] The individual investor, in other words, still had the numerical edge, but the trend was clear.

Among the institutional investors – or, as they were increasingly called for short, the 'institutions' – the insurance companies were still dominant, owning a 9 per cent share of the total equity market in 1963, compared to 3.2 per cent for the investment trusts and 2.9 per cent for the pension funds. 'The one-and-a-half millions a day that come from the insurance companies, demanding to be invested, has influenced the market much as the arrival of the SS *Caronia* in an African port,' Sampson noted in his *Anatomy*. 'When the insurance companies buy, they buy in tens of thousands, and they hardly ever sell: by favouring some kinds of shares, they can push the price up steeply, so that the whole market turns around. But the insurance companies, like rich men, are fussy, and demand much more information and service than individual investors.' One of the most demanding of these investment kings was Legal & General's Louis Ginsburg, a man of powerful intellect who in January 1964, on behalf of the Investors Protection Committee of the British Insurance Association, met the Stock Exchange's Lord Ritchie to put the case for commission on gilt deals over £0.25m to be reduced by 50 per cent. The Stock Exchange account of that meeting was revealing of attitudes:

> He stressed, at first very strongly, on the question of the increased expenses of Brokers (and I think everybody considered it was rather impertinent!) that the Statistical Department of Brokers' dealings in gilt-edged was far too large and expensive for mainly two reasons: firstly that the insurance institutions had their own statistical departments and, secondly, that the supply of information to insurance institutions was almost identical whether given by Broker A or Broker B, could not the departments be pooled etc. It was pointed out to Mr Ginsburg that there were other clients than insurance companies and from then on he rather piped down on this particular point.[12]

The client, in the eyes of the old Stock Exchange, rarely knew best – and ultimately, in the case of the institutions, revenge would be sweet.

As for the increasingly beleaguered individual investors, there was on the Stock Exchange's part a profound reluctance to make the leap into American-style retail broking. Back in 1953 the Council had responded with polite indifference to a scheme put forward by John Kinross of ICFC to encourage the small shareholder; a decade later, in his letter to the Council about advertising, Laurie of Heseltine Powell noted not only that 'last year we spent a considerable sum of money on corporate advertisements to enlighten the Public but not to attract business,' but also that friends on the Council had told him 'that the institutional brokers thereon do not wish for more small investment business and are afraid that any major increase would lead to serious congestion of the existing broker machinery'.[13] Over the years the Stock Exchange authorities would continue to mouth platitudes about the merits of popular capitalism, but in practice there was seldom the will-power to do anything fundamental in bringing it about.

What was the quality of the advice and execution on offer to these clients, whether individual or institutional? In 1955 the Council appointed a committee under Althaus's chairmanship to examine the requirements for membership. Its report, submitted in October, firmly came down against the establishment of an Institute of the Stock Exchange, which would arrange exams and grant diplomas:

> Stockbroking, being, at best, an inexact science, differs in its require-ments from the learned professions. Whereas, for example, a profound knowledge of the law and of case law is essential to legal practice, and may best be established through sitting for the examinations of a central body, successful stockbroking calls for other qualities. They are, in the main, judgement, experience, a sense of timing and a 'nose'. A man may be born

with, or acquire, the first. Time and his elders will provide him with the second. Even if teachers could be found it is doubtful whether the last two qualities could be learnt.

The report added that this committee had 'endeavoured and failed to discover grounds for supposing that the present Members of the House are insufficiently qualified in the carrying out of their business'. Faced by this self-evident truth, the Council voted 27–0 to adopt the report. This proved, however, only a stay of execution, and by the mid-1960s the Council had accepted, albeit reluctantly, that for the sake of the Stock Exchange's image there would have to be exams for prospective brokers before they became members. There was little cheering in the ranks. 'The object of introducing exams is presumably to try and raise the standard of stockbroking, but is this going to be the result?' the broking firm Galloway & Pearson asked in a letter to the Council in June 1966. 'If there are to be exams they must be of the very highest standard and the result will probably be that the "boffins" and the back room boys will be able to pass ... whereas those with common sense, honesty and a "nose", for these are the essentials for a stockbroker, will probably fail.' Hugh Vanderfelt, senior partner of Vanderfelt & Co, was similarly worried: 'I am quite sure that we should have some examination, but if we make it too tough, then we are certain to end up with a lot of long-haired bespectacled youths or young men who may, on paper, know all the answers, but who won't I am quite certain, make good stockbrokers.'[14] In the event, the exams that were introduced soon afterwards were not too ferocious, and plenty of non-boffins still became stockbrokers.

The need for a more qualified membership was one of the central demands put forward by Jock Hunter of Messels and Hugh Merriman of Akroyd & Smithers in a major reforming memorandum submitted to the Council in May 1957 following their consultation with some forty firms. The memo's underlying argument was that 'the future prosperity of both Broker and Jobber depends on improving the efficiency of the House and cultivating the confidence and familiarity of all potential investors'. To achieve this, they wanted two other important changes: 'the day-to-day running of the Exchange should be in the hands of a paid General Manager'; and there should be constructed 'a trading floor with modern communications', since 'to see queues of Brokers and Jobbers standing outside telephone booths waiting to make calls seems inconceivable in the middle of the 20th Century'. The first of these two wishes got nowhere. 'Their thoughts are moving in the direction of a more professional management of the Exchange on New York lines,' Mynors at the Bank was told by the Government broker in February 1958 about the latest thinking of Hunter, Merriman and their supporters, mainly among the

younger members; but when Cobbold saw Arthur Anderson of Rowe &
Pitman, to get the latest on Stock Exchange matters, and asked him
'whether he thought there was any strong move towards a salaried
Managing Director', Anderson replied that 'he thought not'. On the
question of a new floor, however, linking members to their offices far
more efficiently, there was relatively speedy movement. Negotiations to
buy adjoining properties on Threadneedle Street were under way by the
start of the 1960s, and the decision to build a new Stock Exchange on the
site of the Victorian building was taken and announced in 1961. By the
end of 1962 plans had been drawn up for a new floor of 25,000 square feet,
'slightly larger than the present floor, but without the many
encumbrances and obstacles'. Although there were various planning
delays and obstacles, by September 1965 the Council was able to announce
to members that rebuilding was definitely going ahead.[15]

*

'You're never going to survive,' Frank Douglas, senior partner of the
largish brokers Fielding, Son & Macleod, told Dundas Hamilton in 1951
on hearing that the latter was with his father's tiny broking firm, Carroll
& Co. 'The tendency is for the big firms to get the business. You really
ought to be thinking of joining us.' Hamilton reluctantly saw Douglas's
point and joined his firm, which merged in 1958 with another broking
firm, Newson-Smith & Co, to become Fielding, Newson-Smith. Even
so, many small broking outfits still remained in existence, and by the end
of the decade the average number of partners per firm was only six. It was
not until the first half of the 1960s that merger activity began to quicken,
under pressures that included the growing complexities of taxation, the
increasing importance of the institutional investor, and more onerous
auditing and capital requirements, given formal effect by the Council
from 1962. James Capel & Co, for instance, absorbed Gordon L. Jacobs
& Co in 1961, Nathan & Rosselli in 1965 and Clayton, Byng & Paget in
1967. By then – when, crucially, the legal limit of twenty on the size of a
partnership was removed – the number of broking firms was down to
209, well under half of the 465 or so firms that had been operating shortly
before the war. Nevertheless, there was still an average of barely eight
partners per firm, and one young jobber, Geoffrey Green, who joined
Bisgood Bishop in the Industrial market in 1963, was a sceptical observer:

> Quite a lot of brokers, how shall I put it, didn't earn their money. They
> didn't have to have the skill or the instincts that the jobbers had to compete
> to survive . . . Their business seemed to come to them by way of connections
> etc, they didn't necessarily earn it; as long as they had the business coming
> in they had their commission, they had their income. Traditionally they had
> dealt for firms, for families or private individuals, obviously for years and

years and years, and it was regular business for them. . .

Green added, as he reminisced in 1990, that 'this was all to change'.[16]

So it was, but meanwhile the forces of tradition and continuity were as deep-rooted as they were in most parts of the City. At Foster & Braithwaite, founded in 1825 with roots deep in the Quaker network, the partnership was not opened up to those who did not happen to be a descendant of Isaac Braithwaite of Kendal until the late 1960s. The ruling family was almost as deeply entrenched at de Zoete & Gorton, where Miles de Zoete (fifth-generation and a fast-scoring batsman at Eton) presided amidst a distinctly autocratic atmosphere. Another firm that valued continuity was Sheppards & Co, whose senior partner in the late 1950s, Christopher Barclay, once saw a new partner on his first day and simply told him, 'In Sheppards the partners always wear a hat in the House'. Brokers in general tended to be less flamboyant than jobbers, but a larger-than-life exception was Dundas Hamilton's senior partner during most of these post-war years:

> Frank Douglas was enormous, very generous, always showering people with presents. He was a man of great contrasts. He was a most awful snob. He was in the Royal Lodge of Masons and he hob-nobbed with earls and princes and peers yet he also had some extraordinarily unattractive moneyed friends. Everything about him was huge. He got his parachute-dropping badge after the age of forty, when he was about seventeen stone. He had both a Rolls and a Bentley and he always had a loader with three guns instead of two. He hated personal conflicts; if anybody had to be sacked, he wouldn't do it and always sent me to tell the chap . . .

Rather more understated in its social aspirations was the well-liked, medium-sized broking firm of Read, Hurst-Brown & Co. Its partners during the 1950s included Derek Moore-Brabazon (son of the well-known aviator-cum-politician), Edward Bromley-Davenport and a former Lord Mayor, Sir Edmund Stockdale. It was a partnership noted for its golfing prowess, and in February 1959 two partners shared a round at the Berkshire Golf Club with Oxford University's current captain, John Littlewood. By the eighteenth hole he had been recruited to the firm.[17] It was the City in classic, old-style action – yet for all this less-than-meritocratic form of recruitment, Littlewood possessed considerable intelligence and would become a distinguished investment analyst. It helped to be able to handle a niblick, but brains were now also starting to play a part.

At any one time a handful of firms (including of course the Government brokers Mullens) were renowned as gilt-edged brokers, almost entirely on behalf of banks, insurance companies and other institutions. Gilts was a market in which it certainly paid to have breeding as well as brains, and probably the leading broking firm during the 1950s was the very gentlemanly Pember & Boyle. 'I stumbled into my life in the City in the way in which I suppose a number of people did,' George Nissen would remember. In 1951:

> I thought I might become a solicitor, but on my twenty-first birthday my mother took me to Claridges and across the room was the noble figure of Fred Althaus, wearing as always a red carnation in his buttonhole. He knew me because I was at school [Eton] with his son, Nigel. He came across and discovered it was my birthday and gave me a white fiver and said, 'If ever you think of coming into the City, you should come to Pember & Boyle. It's not like other firms. Just think about it.'

Nissen followed Althaus's advice two years later, on coming down from Cambridge, and found a largely congenial world. 'Our premises were excellent – the office was in Princes Street, right beside the Bank of England. We used to walk through the Bank to get to the Stock Exchange, which was not actually permitted.' There was, complete with butler and under-butler, an additional bonus in the shape of one of the best lunch-rooms in the City: 'There was a lot of talk about sport, about national news, about politics, who was doing what in the City. We very often had MPs to lunch to talk about general affairs. John Betjeman came once, everyone said he was delightful and what a mess he looked and that his cuffs were undone. . .'[18]

Grieveson, Grant & Co was another powerful, well-connected force in gilts, but towards the end of the 1950s the intolerably dictatorial approach of its senior partner, Roger Watson, provoked a mass desertion. Such migrations were rare indeed in the old City, but three partners simultaneously left and joined Greenwells, where the ambitious Philip ('Pip') Greenwell, son of the iconoclastic, fiercely reactionary Graham, was keen to build up – almost from scratch – a broking operation in both short and long gilts. The trio comprised Jack Tremlett, Charles Noble (in another life, Commodore of the *President*) and Piers St Aubyn (a younger son of Baron St Levan). They specialised in dealing in shorts with the discount market; and they brought with them Charles Frappell, who during the 1960s, with the help of his protégé Gordon Pepper, would turn Greenwells into the dominant broking firm in longer-dated government stocks.

Whether specialising in gilts or equities, in private or institutional clients, in the new issue market or the secondary market, any stockbroking firm depended hugely on the quality and character of its senior partner. Jock Hunter was both a notably progressive force on the Council and, for sixteen years from 1955, senior partner of Messels. The firm had slumbered between the wars, but under Hunter's rather strong if slightly dour leadership the firm prospered and built up a good corporate business. 'The poor man's John Knox' he was sometimes called, because of his propensity to see things in terms purely of black and white, and perhaps also because he kept his small change in a pocket purse; but he was broad-minded enough to have the firm's economic commentary written by the left-leaning journalist Nicholas Davenport, who later praised Hunter's 'great integrity and decisive judgements'. The City's other, equally admired 'Jock' was Sir John Gilmour, senior partner of Joseph Sebag & Co from 1950. The son of a Lord Provost of Edinburgh, Gilmour developed considerable knowledge of industrial securities and turned Sebags into one of the three or four leading corporate brokers, helped by Kenneth Keith's sense of gratitude after Gilmour had persuaded Hubert Meredith to step out of Keith's way at Philip Hill. Gilmour's obituary in *The Times* evoked a figure shaped in the very finest City mould:

> His advice was much sought; he could sum up the essentials of a matter in a few words and give the answer in even fewer. His direct attitude to a problem was backed by hard work. Before he went to a meeting he liked to feel he knew the meat of the matter before the dish was served. In this task he was assisted enormously by his ability to read the most complicated documents, to put his finger on the essentials and pick out the flaws in any arguments in a short space of time. At a meeting people came to him, he did not seem to go to them, and in his very solidity they found strength.[19]

The rapid decline of Sebags after Gilmour's retirement as senior partner in 1964 would suggest that these were more than merely conventional phrases.

No senior partner, though, had a stronger presence than Kit Hoare of Hoare & Co. With his unforgettable bushy eyebrows, he could still, twenty years after his death in 1973 at the age of ninety-one, evoke strong feelings from three different people who had known him:

> Kit Hoare was a splendid pirate. If you said 'Kit' everybody knew you meant Kit Hoare, he was the only one. He was a very good, tough stockbroker. He made a lot of money and he loved the City. He was also a terrific snob and a fair-sized name dropper with an eye to the main chance. He was always on the coat-tails of anybody who had been successful, but rather disregarding how they had got their success. He would have boarded any ship . . .
> Kit Hoare was a lovely man and a bit of a rascal. He had free access to Kleinworts. I used to find him walking up and down the passages. The idea of a broker being able to gain unrestricted access to a merchant bank's Corporate Finance Department is ridiculous by today's standards – of course, he wasn't allowed to do this, he used to claim he'd lost his way! . . .
> Kit was still wandering around the office at the age of eighty-eight, making a nuisance of himself. We had to employ a chauffeur to carry him around and parcel him off in the afternoons to somewhere else. There's a terrible portrait of him in the room where I work even today, so I can't

forget what he looked like . . .

For all his highly developed 'feel for the market', as the phrase went, ultimately his reputation rested on his force of personality. 'He prided himself,' noted an obituary, 'on never carrying even a slip of paper and nothing pleased him better than to be able to underwrite a new issue in his firm's name alone, everything being agreed in the first instance just by word of mouth – the City's bond.'[20]

Hoare's firm was not mentioned in 1965 when *Queen* magazine nominated which two stockbroking firms were socially 'in' and which two 'out'. Instead, Sebags and Rowe & Pitman got the favourable nod; Mullens and Cazenove's the thumbs down. At Rowe & Pitman, which like both Hoare's and Sebags was active in corporate (or, as it was called at the time, company) broking, the senior partner since 1951 had been Arthur Anderson. His background was that familiar combination, Eton and Trinity College, Cambridge; he adhered rigidly to the unwritten rule that no shop was to be talked in the partners' dining room; and he would end a meal with the crisp announcement, 'Now I must go and tighten my stays.' Under his auspices Rowe & Pitman continued to recruit partners as much as possible from either the families of existing partners or recommendations of the two main merchant banks to which it was beholden, Hambros and Morgan Grenfell. There were, not surprisingly, some business lightweights among its numbers. Wilfred de Knoop, a Morgan Grenfell protégé landed on the firm in 1947, was principally valued (according to the firm's historian) 'for his intimate knowledge of the *Guide Michelin*', and each Friday 'would despatch a messenger to Twinings to buy freshly roasted coffee for his weekend in the country'; while Hilary Bray, a partner until the early 1960s, was 'a charming, old-world figure who, for all his proficiency at golf and knowledge about birds and wild flowers, was not temperamentally suited to stockbroking' – indeed, so unsuited that 'he would speak disparagingly of "grubbing in the money-pile" '. By contrast, Bill Mackworth-Young and Peter Wilmot-Sitwell (partners from 1953 and 1960 respectively) were both, despite the double barrels, intelligent, ambitious and unfrightened of change. Yet perhaps the more representative Rowe & Pitman figure was Julian Martin Smith, a partner from 1949 on the say-so of his uncle, Olaf Hambro, and in due course the effective successor to Anderson. An obituary gives something of the flavour:

> This large, genial and immensely capable man never sought publicity. The MC won on the ridge at Hamman Lif in 1943 and his long service as senior partner with Rowe & Pitman and on many other boards in the City of London remain as evidence of his courage and of his legendary financial judgement, but what his friends will never forget was the enormous fun it

always was to be with him whether in the Army, the City or on the golf course at Brancaster . . .

Like another gentle giant, the one in Oscar Wilde's story, Smith's 'conversation was limited', but it was worth listening to. This was not always easy as it emerged filtered through a heavy moustache and a much-chewed pipe-stem. 'I can't take a man who uses sex-appeal to make points at a board meeting,' was one of his more pungent comments on a colleague in the City.[21]

It was largely birth that had got him where he was, but it was more than birth that kept him there.

That same duality permeated Cazenove's, *the* leading broker in the primary, capital-raising market. 'The big firms have become regarded as intelligence service for the City, at the centre of the telephone network of mmms and wells and meaningful grunts,' Sampson noted in 1962. ' "Better ask Cazenove's", a banker will mumble, and the answer will come back with the authority of the market-place.'[22] This firm had become a major force between the wars, and during the post-war period it consolidated its position, partly through the continuing excellence of its connections, but perhaps even more through its sheer Anglo-Saxon reliability – the fact that, if it said it would do something, it did it. Certainly it was far from a thrusting meritocracy. Cedric Barnett and Geoffrey Akroyd were both the sons of former partners. Barnett, an austere, dignified figure in charge of gilts, had technical ability but lacked force. 'I suppose he's taken his top hat for a walk round the market,' another partner remarked one afternoon when his absence from the office was noted. When not perambulating, Barnett was responsible for coining the three aphorisms that between them were emblematic of the whole, post-war gentlemanly City: namely, 'shoes have laces', 'motor cars are black' and, most tellingly of all, 'jelly is not officer food'. As for the red-faced, good-natured Akroyd (almost a complete nonentity in business terms), his most celebrated *bon mot* was the avuncular advice he gave to one newcomer to the firm, 'You'll find the Savoy a jolly nice little place for lunch, and nice and handy because you can get there on a number 11 bus'.

Of course, there was another, quite different side to Cazenove's. For one thing, it became from the 1950s the unwritten rule that a partner could bring in only one son, and that that son had to run 110 yards to everyone else's 100 in order to prove himself; for another, it was becoming possible in this period for the occasional self-made person to emerge as a major figure in the firm, perhaps epitomised by the unassuming Ernest Bedford, a supremely persuasive as well as conscientious placer of shares with the institutions. Beneath the gentlemanly façade lay a toughness and professional edge – an edge that owed much to Peter Kemp-Welch, whose progress had been blocked at Foster & Braithwaite before coming to Cazenove's immediately after the war. Convivial, and with a quick, humorous mind, he took stock of the situation and in August 1948, while nominally on holiday in Scotland, prescribed what he saw as the necessary medicine. His memo noted various current failings on the part of the firm, including the fact that 'we don't produce many "ideas" or up to date offers, other than our own issues'; remarked that 'we have always rather prided ourselves on being enthusiastic amateurs'; and concluded bluntly enough that 'one doesn't want to take business too seriously but there is bound to be a grave risk of losing efficiency by not taking it seriously enough: the trouble is that if we don't take it seriously enough someone else will!'

Kemp-Welch's memo was for the eyes of Antony Hornby, the firm's commanding presence for a quarter of a century after the war. That autumn, on the basis of Kemp-Welch's analysis, Hornby persuaded the partnership as a whole of the need to adopt a more systematic, serious-minded approach. In the notes for his speech at the decisive meeting, there was, after his nod to the inter-war achievements of Claud Serocold, Charles Micklem and Jimmy Palmer-Tomkinson, a particularly telling passage:

> Anyway we have now got Cazenove's as it is and it is something to be very proud of. I'm afraid there is little money incentive in business today – one is only allowed to get away with so much and no more. But obviously we in this firm would never be content to let our retainable income influence our efforts. Our incentive for the present at any rate must be our pride in keeping Cazenove's at the top.

Later, Hornby reiterated Kemp-Welch's point about attitude: 'One doesn't want to make a burden of business but I do think there's a risk of not taking it seriously enough.' There was, in short, a fine balance to be struck. 'Amateurism' was clearly no longer enough; but nor, equally, was 'professionalism' alone the solution for the future, at least as far as Cazenove's was concerned. Hornby himself, born in 1904, was a Wykehamist, an increasingly renowned art collector, arrogant but unstuffy, occasionally hot-tempered, a convinced non-egalitarian, and the embodiment of his own, oft-quoted dictum that 'merchant bankers don't want long faces'. In 1960, with the firm doing especially well, he listed with typical self-confidence what he perceived to be some of the reasons:

> Reliability. Secrets are safe. We do not make use of confidential information for our own ends.
> We all work hard and full time. We know our job and most of the answers!

We are known not to be gamblers in private or business life.

We are not unduly mercenary. Obviously one wants to make money, but we are not greedy. The amount of money to be made out of a business is not the reason for doing it.

We are a happy firm at all levels and enjoy our business life and show it. We are serious but not too desperately serious.

The firm is run as a benevolent autocracy, but is at the same time essentially democratic.

And, undeterred by that apparent contradiction, Hornby added that in the future 'we must be careful to have in the partnership people who fit and who think the same way as us, and whom we are really fond of'.[23]

Neither Rowe & Pitman nor Cazenove's was remotely near the forefront of the revolution that was gradually unfolding in investment analysis. Although a statistical department was inaugurated at Rowe & Pitman in 1954, such was the instinctive opposition to it on the part of Anderson as senior partner that it was a long time before 'Stats' was permitted to change its name to the research department. Instead, the firm continued to rely largely on the traditional, personal approach, as each morning the appropriate partners continued to make their ritual visits to the parlours and boardrooms of the respective institutions to which they were most intimately connected: Lazards and the Charterhouse Group, as well as Hambros and Morgan Grenfell. There, armed with the latest prices and a few morsels of gossip and, on a good day, market-sensitive information, they would expect to be given a reasonable slab of business to execute. Through deeply entrenched habits and instinct the priorities were similar at Cazenove's. In 1961, in another of his inimitable memos, Hornby put down on paper his investment philosophy. While not denying that 'the analyst's role is necessary and important', he contended not only that most of their reports were 'too lengthy for us to have time to read them,' but that even a concise piece of analysis was inadequate without being 'cross-fertilised by the sea of experience' and having added to it 'a good pinch of flair or hunch'. There was, he insisted, 'more to it than figures, past profits, and projection of future profits', and 'it is an enormous help to know the personalities involved, to become intimate with the flavour of a business'. How well did this method – essentially a cast of mind – work on behalf of the partners and their clients? Pretty well presumably, although one client had rueful memories of being allowed to walk up the main staircase at 12 Tokenhouse Yard:

I was taken – as if I was being anointed with class and quality – to Cazenove's in 1964. They looked at me as if I was an idiot and they were geniuses, and proceeded to buy for me a lot of shares that were a disaster. I lost about £40,000, which was a lot of money in 1964. I was about twenty-eight at the time and so, when I first met Cazenove people I was tremendously impressed – here were these very posh people in suits. I'd been recommended to see them by a peer of the realm and I felt as though I was being let in Valhalla . . .

The young wannabe was the film director Michael Winner, who may or may not have been consoled by Hornby's timeless investment apophthegms: 'Don't worry; don't be impatient; don't press; don't panic; don't fidget. Enjoy the whole fascinating affair.'[24]

The atmosphere was rather less relaxed at Phillips & Drew. There, the self-made actuary Sidney Perry – a small, uncharismatic man with gold-rimmed glasses, looking more like a local bank manager than a City notable – was senior partner through most of the 1950s, turning the firm into an explicitly meritocratic, non-nepotistic organisation. Stockbroking, he believed (and, largely successfully, trained those under him to believe), should become a genuine profession in its own right, run along scientific lines. He was also convinced, in his own prediction of 1949, that 'the future lies with the big firm doing an institutional business'. During the ensuing decade Phillips & Drew was so professional in its approach that it was able to attract considerable business from insurance companies and pension funds, of both industrial companies and local authorities – at the very time that pension funds themselves were beginning to see enormous growth. A key factor from the mid-1950s was the firm's pioneering of investment analysis, a development that owed everything to Perry's protégé, Denis Weaver. By the end of 1958 his team had completed analyses of forty-two different companies (for carefully selected distribution), and in 1960 he and a colleague submitted an impressively technical paper to the Institute of Actuaries on 'The Assessment of Industrial Ordinary Shares'. It began, though, with an apposite quotation from the Iron Duke: 'All the business of war, and indeed all the business of life, is to endeavour to find out what you don't know by what you do; that's what I called "guessing what was at the other side of the hill".' Weaver himself, barred by his Quaker beliefs from more orthodox progress, had found his true niche; and it was a far from idle boast when he observed in 1961, six years after the establishment of the Society of Investment Analysts, that 'nowadays when any report on any investment topic is mentioned it is generally assumed that Phillips & Drew wrote it'. At the start of the 1960s the research capability at Phillips & Drew was far ahead of almost all its stockbroking rivals – indeed, most firms still barely knew the meaning of the term 'investment analysis'. Perry, the founding father, had retired in 1959, but the alluring prospect beckoned of an ever-higher reputation automatically accompanied by massively increased profits.

It did not *quite* work out that way. Partly this was because some other firms caught up and became equally proficient in investment analysis;

partly it was because of significant – and telling – strains within Phillips & Drew itself. Critically, the firm's so-called 'equity table', selling equities to the institutions, was unable through the 1960s, despite the firm's extraordinarily high reputation for research, to achieve a greater market share than, at best, 2 per cent. Inevitably there was a tendency to blame the analysts for being too remote and academic in their approach. 'Like a lot of ballet dancers, very touchy about this and that,' thought Peter Swan, in charge of equities. In another part of the firm, dealing for private clients, the robustly old-fashioned Jos Drew did not even pretend to have any time for the men of science. 'One tip is worth a million analyst's hours' was one of his favourite maxims; 'bullshit always baffles brains' another. Put another way, for all the firm's continuing overall progress, there was still far from complete endorsement of the Perry/Weaver approach to stockbroking. 'Flair' and 'no egg heads' were two of the criteria explicitly laid down by Swan in terms of deciding who should be selected for the aggressive, extrovert equity table, and certainly neither Perry nor Weaver would much have enjoyed sitting there.

The crux of the matter was that the City was not yet ready for new-style, cerebral stockbroking – it was still perfectly possible to make a good living on the familiar basis of whom, rather than what, one knew. On at least one occasion the partners of Phillips & Drew admitted as much. In 1965 a committee of the three leading partners (including Weaver) noted that 'more could be done in meeting clients and in use of outside societies', conceded that this could mean 'long, tedious and wasted evenings' and concluded that 'this may be hard graft but it is essential if we are not to turn to recruiting blue-blooded, well-connected Old Etonians'.[25] Moreover, if personal connection was not Phillips & Drew's forte, nor was that other indispensable component of the traditional City: namely, inside information. In an era pre-dating its illegality, and with the Stock Exchange making only fairly ineffectual attempts to stop it (usually after the horse had long bolted), how prevalent was insider dealing?[26] Decisive evidence is sparse, but there are some pointers. 'You had to get your information as and where you could,' Dundas Hamilton would recall of the late 1940s and early 1950s. The drill was to 'know chairmen and other people who mattered in a company. They'd tell you what was happening, and if you judged it good, you'd put your clients into the shares.' Nor was the use of inside information solely for clients, to judge by Nissen's recollections of Pember & Boyle in the mid-1950s:

> Speculation and making money was the name of the game . . . The idea of dealing PA [i.e. personal account, on behalf of oneself] was totally accepted and there was very little control over what you did for yourself . . . Nobody thought that it was a disgraceful thing if you got a tip from somebody who really knew something about what was going on in a

company; there was nothing disgraceful about helping yourself to a few shares if you possibly could.

The official line was that the coming of investment analysis later in the 1950s, fuelled by the institutions' demand for greater professionalism, dramatically changed these practices. 'The days of the third-hand "tip", offered over a glass of sherry, are happily long past,' the member-journalist Donald Cobbett optimistically declared in 1957. The truth was surely different. The jobber Geoffrey Green recalled insider trading as 'a fact of life' in the Stock Exchange of the 1960s; and when the young Christopher Heath joined the stockbroking firm of George Henderson & Co near the end of the decade, he encountered a world in which PA trading was still the norm. Perhaps Peter Spira of Warburgs put it best. 'Insider dealing was a regular occurrence,' he observed. 'The reason why people had their investment affairs managed by merchant bankers and stockbrokers was precisely because they had better information.'[27]

These and related matters were all too rarely discussed in public, but Harold Wincott in the *FT* in September 1966 did touch on them in two illuminating Tuesday articles. The context was a recent attack by A. C. Rayner and Ian Little on the ability of the Stock Exchange to assess corporate performance with a view to profitable investment in the future; and Wincott conceded that the investment world had been all too susceptible to herd-like fashions, that indeed 'the post-war years have been littered with booms which went wrong in, for example, atomic energy, hire purchase, insurance, industrial holding companies and so on'. In other words, and with infinite regret on Wincott's part, 'on the whole I think we must accept that the London Stock Exchange hasn't erected very reliable signposts over an extended period'. Why? The main reason, according to Wincott, was not the shortcomings of the Stock Exchange itself, but rather that 'for as long as I can remember, it has been a tradition in the British company world to tell the investment community as little as possible as seldom as possible'. Examples that he gave included the refusal of diversified companies to account by division, the adverse effects of non-voting shares, 'the frequent lack of up-to-date valuations of fixed assets', and 'the distortions in share values which can be caused by "insider dealings"'. In consequence, despite the beneficial effects of the 1948 Companies Act, the stock market during the previous quarter of a century 'has too often been a sort of Blind Man's Buff, which may be good fun but is not calculated to make for an efficient and well run economy'.[28] Wincott could not quite bring himself to blame the City as such, but from someone as committed as he was to free-market capitalism, it was little short of a devastating indictment.

Whatever the sadness about the passing of other aspects of the old City, there can be few regrets in this area. Ross-Munro, Duff & Co was one stockbroking firm among many that would not last the course, and Michael Burns's recollections of it at the tail-end of the 1950s represent part of a largely submerged literature about an almost entirely submerged reality:

> Most of RMD's clients were advised to have a spread of shares – government stock; blue chips; foreign bonds; and a small proportion of high-risk shares that just might take off. Recommendations to buy and sell shares were made with the minimum of amount of analysis. Neither of the two people in the firm responsible for portfolio management had any formal economic qualifications. They leant very heavily on the financial press for their information and large files of cuttings from all the newspapers, from the *Financial Times* to the *Sunday Express*, were dutifully kept . . .
>
> The firm relied for a good deal of their income on a small number of clients. By far their biggest client was H.T. Morris who was a millionaire living in Cheshire. Regular suggestions were made to adjust his portfolio throughout the years. Despite the flimsy research that justified these recommendations he would almost always accept the advice. Occasionally a tip would come in from one of the dealers, or from a partner after a long lunch with some of his cronies. Likely clients were then called to see if they fancied a flutter . . .
>
> Several years later, when my days as a stockbrokers' clerk were but a distant memory, I read a novel called *Bargains at Special Prices* [by the young Alan Clark, the future politician]. The fictitious stockbrokers, partnered by a bunch of spivvy crooks, featured in this book could have been modelled on Ross-Munro, Duff & Co. It was only after having read this book that I realised how much insider dealing, corruption and sharp practice I had been surrounded by during my days under the dome in South Place . . .[29]

*

The jobber – everyone agreed – was a different animal from the broker: more instinctive, more extrovert, less articulate, often wealthier. Jobbers had long been recognised as the indispensable nerve-centre of the Stock Exchange, but that was far from making them socially desirable in the world at large or, indeed, much of the City. 'I would have said jobbers were considered the lowest of the low,' Jimmy Priestley recalled of the 1930s, when he joined Wedd Jefferson in the gilt-edged market, and attitudes changed only slowly after the war. This is not to say either that there were no Etonians or Wykehamists among the jobbing fraternity, or that the post-war years saw a plethora of East End barrow boys coming into the jobbing system and making a fortune. Nevertheless, most jobbing firms tended to be less hierarchical than their broking counterparts; while to do well as a jobber usually demanded rather more mental agility. 'That's all a jobber was, just a bookie,' Priestley added self-deprecatingly.[30] Perhaps, but the art of fixing the odds was not given to everyone.

Without doubt the single most dominant figure in the post-war jobbing system was 'The Emperor' – Esmond Durlacher, senior partner of Durlachers for some thirty years from 1936. A trim, slightly austere, always immaculately turned-out man, he combined to a remarkable extent connection and intelligence. His connections were partly with the world at large (through his marriage to the daughter of the Earl of Clonmell, his sporting activities in several fields, his charitable work) and partly through his intimate knowledge of the investment requirements of leading institutions. Jobbers were supposed not to have direct dealings with the public; but although Durlacher obeyed the letter of the rule, by always being careful to book bargains through a handful of favoured brokers, the spirit of it he simply ignored, being powerful enough to get away with it. Years later the firm's Tommy Anderson was asked to explain its success: 'What used to happen – I don't think I'm giving away trade secrets – was the senior partner, more often than not, used to come in in the morning with orders in his pockets . . . Mr Esmond Durlacher had very good contacts outside. And I believe this is where a lot of it came from. So that was beneficial to the firm, and to the staff . . .' Harley Drayton was one satisfied client, especially when he wanted to build up a big holding in brewery shares, while it became the stuff of City legend how Jack Butterworth, investment manager from the 1940s of BP's pension fund, would meet partners from Durlachers for mid-morning drinks in the Angel Court Club to settle the day's business.[31]

As for Esmond Durlacher's intelligence, he put into practice his pioneering belief that the way forward for a firm of any ambition was to be able to job in as wide a range of markets as possible. This in effect meant a policy of acquisition, and between 1953 and 1965 the original firm of F. & N. Durlacher (traditionally specialising in breweries) merged with or absorbed no fewer than eight partnerships. These included Deacon Godson (textiles and woollens) in 1953, Bone Oldham Mordaunt & Seal (industrials, with Sir Nigel Mordaunt presiding as 'The Baronet') in 1960, and Kitchin Baker Shaw (steel, chemicals and stores, among other sectors) in 1965, by which time the firm's style was Durlacher Oldham Mordaunt Godson.

At any one time at least four or five dozen other firms were operating in the industrial and related markets. At Kitchins, an apparently mighty outfit until 1965, the senior partner after the war had been George Tozer. 'A mountain of a man with a personality to match' was how one broker assessed him. 'I think he enjoyed determining share prices somewhat more than making a profit. Before going to lunch at the City Club, which was quite a prolonged affair, he would hand his jobbing book to an assistant and name perhaps a dozen shares saying that their present prices were to be maintained until he returned from lunch.' A more far-sighted senior partner was Lewis Powell of C.D. Pinchin & Co, who was always happy to talk to his son Val about the day's work: 'Sometimes he'd rub his hands and say, "Yes, today was a real jam and cream day" and one got an idea that he had had a very good one; whereas you'd ask him another day and he'd say, "No, no good, you'll have to have water tonight". And one got a flavour that it was very volatile . . .' The traditional specialities of Pinchins were electricals and engineering, but Powell was similar to Durlacher in seeing the need to expand through acquisition; off his own bat he also initiated a trend by starting a fixed-interest department at Pinchins. Another firm with a future in the industrial market, in its case mainly the motor-car and engineering segments, was Bisgood Bishop. In the mid-1950s it had a young recruit in the person of Brian Winterflood, who had left the stockbrokers Greener Dreyfus on the basis that, for someone like himself, with no particular social connections, there was a better future in jobbing than in broking:

> I was with a man called Howard Taylor, who was the second partner. He was a tyrant. He was a most awful man. He had no patience, he was foul-mouthed, he was more interested in the races every day and he spent his lunch-hour in one of the telephone boxes on to his bookie. He would come back from lunch where I would be looking after the book, and if he'd had a good day, he wasn't too bad, in other words if he'd won on the horses; if he'd had a bad day, or been to the club and somebody had upset him, he'd come back and he would sit on the bench and he'd look through all the jobbing book pages, and he'd look at whatever we were dealing in, let's say it was Elswick Hopper, he'd look at the bargains and say, 'Fucking hell'. All he kept grunting was 'fucking this' and 'fucking that'. And I remember on one particular occasion I'd done such a fantastic bargain; I can't tell you, we'd made a lot of money on this bargain and I was waiting for him to get to this bargain and he was 'fucking this' and 'fucking that' and all nasty, and he got up to it and I thought this is going to be really my day. And he didn't grunt, he didn't do anything, he went past it. I couldn't contain myself. I said, 'Excuse me sir, but did you see so and so?' He said, 'It only pays for the bad ones'. I thought, 'I really can't go on. I'll go bonkers in the end'. And then finally there was a change round and I was taken off his book and was put on Jimmy Bisgood's. And it was like, I can't tell you, it was like going from Hell to Heaven . . .[32]

A gruelling apprenticeship, but Winterflood had found his métier and would become in time the jobber's jobber.

One firm, merciless in its prices, was increasingly acknowledged as the Stock Exchange's ultimate traders. This was Smith Brothers, a Jewish family firm established in the 1920s. Geoffrey Lederman, who joined in 1951, aptly reflected on its progress during his first twenty or so years: 'There's no doubt that in my early days we didn't see the cream of the business of perhaps the very blue-blooded firms. We had to fight our way up very much on merit and our prices had to be more competitive, larger in size . . . The firm wasn't flush with a great deal of capital so we had to turn over our stock very, very quickly . . .' The firm's not entirely friendly nickname on the floor of the House was 'Smudge Brothers', because of its habit of writing prices in pencil so that they were easier to change as the market moved. No one moved the prices faster than the firm's number two in the 1950s, Sydney King, a major presence in the booming Stores market. A member since 1931, he had 'a sort of slightly notorious reputation in the Stock Exchange', Lederman would concede, adding that he was 'a ruthless type of jobber' who 'had no compunction in calling prices up or down to try and sort his book out if he thought it was necessary'. Hardly a popular figure, King was known in the market as the 'The Spiv'; indeed, he once told the broker Denzil Sebag-Montefiore that 'he could not get a good night's sleep unless he had an open position'. Pride, in King's case, came before the fall. The story is told by Tony Lewis, who was starting to emerge by the late 1950s as a rising force at Smiths:

> Sydney King made the other partners' lives impossible; I was just a junior, but he was an impossible man, bombastic and domineering and a bully, but he was a good jobber. He had an argument with the partners. We had moved office to Drapers Gardens, and King's wife happened to be an interior decorator, and he persuaded the other partners that it must be a good thing to let his wife plan the decorations of the new office, which they agreed to. And the bill came in and it was worked out that she had actually charged us about £7,000 for the light bulbs – it was ludicrous. There was a whole argument and row about taking us to the cleaners, because it was his wife. But he eventually said, 'I'm going on my own, I'm leaving you boys, I'm going on my own'. And he started [in 1959] the firm of S. C. King & Co. There was a whole kerfuffle in the firm, and Sidney Davis said to me, 'Well, there's nobody else, you'll have to go and take over the store book that he's been running', which upset Sydney King, because he thought that when he left the firm, he was going to take his store book with him. He stood where he had been standing all the time. And I moved over that next morning and stood two feet away from him. He said, 'You can piss off for a start'. I said, 'I'm very sorry, I'm running the Smith Brothers store book.' The whole business went upstairs to the Council, because you can't stand two feet away from a competitor, obviously. And there was a big enquiry in the Council the same morning. We both went up there for arbitration. And the Council came down and said, 'Mr King, you'll have to go and stand over there'. Which made for a lot of bad blood between myself and Sydney King . . . A lot of the brokers took my side, they thought that he was out of order, and I got a lot of business. And I built a good business there in the store book. Sydney King, in due course, went bust . . .

That was a decade or so after he had left Smiths, and King was taken on by a much larger firm to help it run its store book. But there was still time for a final run-in with the uncompromising Lewis:

> Gussies [Great Universal Stores] announced a set of disappointing results. I don't think I had much of a position, but a broker came up to me and gave me quite a substantial selling order in them; and to my great surprise, King, who was a definite enemy by that time of mine, started to bid for them openly on the market, which was very unusual in the equity market. And I stuffed him. Every time he opened his mouth I stuffed him, and he then carried on bidding, so eventually he bid for stock without mentioning a quantity of price, so I said, 'I'll sell you 10,000'. And he said, 'I'll buy a thousand', and sat down. And that absolutely went round the House. Because Gussies fell out of bed. They collapsed the next morning and he got in trouble with the firm, and eventually they sacked him . . .

The Spiv, according to Lewis, had been 'just a bit too big for his boots'.[33]

The other main area where Smith Brothers operated was the market in South African gold mines (still also known as the Kaffir market). As a market it was very volatile, very professional and distinctly unscrupulous, with George Lazarus of Lazarus Brothers the dominant figure in the immediate post-war period. Lewis is again the guide:

> He was as crooked as hell – he eventually went bust. He was a funny man, he made a lot of money out of the devaluation in 1949 and he made a mistake of printing in the paper that Mr George Lazarus had made a million, or something, trading in gold out in the street. And his house got burgled the next day and he lost a priceless collection of jade – I always remember that. He was a well-known jade collector, he was very funny. These things appeared funny to me at the time. You've got to be a market man to understand the ludicrous humour that used to go on. There was the old story about George Lazarus. He used to have quite a big following in the Stock Exchange in those days, and he used to have his circle of friends who he'd put into things if he thought they were right. I always remember one guy went up to him and he put him into something or other – Grootvlei or something, some rubbish stock – and nothing happened in these Grootvlei things, and in the middle of the morning the guy walked up to him and said, 'You know those Grootvlei you put me into this morning?' and George says, 'Yes'. 'What's happening to them?' George said, 'You haven't still got them have you?' It was only two hours later . . .

Lewis's firm would eventually become the undisputed kings of the gold market, while Lazarus himself on his death in 1997 was principally remembered as a notable collector of Dutch paintings and modern rare books and manuscripts (especially by D. H. Lawrence), as well as imperial jade – a fate unlikely to befall the partners of Smudge Brothers.[34]

It was all rather different in the world of Consols and other British government securities. 'The gilt-edged market was always its own rather peculiar little place,' Jeremy Wormell (the leading authority on it) has observed. 'It was always said that Akroyd, one of the big jobbers, were gentlemen, whereas Wedd, the other big jobbers, were always said to be Harrovians.' In fact, although the larger point probably held, the dominant force at Wedd Jefferson through much of the 1950s and 1960s had been educated at Uppingham. This was the larger-than-life Dick Wilkins, son of a senior partner of the firm and second only to Esmond Durlacher as the outstanding jobber of his generation – indeed, rivalled by none in terms of charisma and general outsize properties. He was a huge man (owning three wardrobes, as his weight fluctuated between sixteen and twenty-two stones), with a penchant for driving his own racing cars, until one Sunday morning he needed his butler's help to be extracted from a diminutive Porsche competition car that he had been exercising. In 1967 a typically meticulous Phillips & Drew internal memo characterised his lifestyle in a few pithy sentences: 'A jovial bachelor. Has a suite at the Savoy. Owns racehorses. Houses in Cornwall and Hertfordshire. A personal friend of the Queen Mother. Has owned a powered speed-boat which did well at a recent *Daily Express* powered race. Likes a party.' In later years, long after his retirement from Wedds in 1979, he would loom large in the Stock Exchange collective memory:

> Dick was a tremendous personality within the Stock Exchange: a person who was tremendously mischievous, loved creating trouble, but mischievously and never with any real spite or venom. But on the other hand he was a super person for taking your troubles to, providing that you remembered to make him promise to keep your troubles to himself and not tell anybody about it . . .
>
> Dick Wilkins was the sort of person who could talk anybody into anything. You could have a fiendish row with him and swear you were never going to speak to him again and the next morning he'd say 'Good morning' and you'd suddenly realise you were the only person in the world he cared about and you forgave him anything. He had the most monumental personality. And he was a remarkably generous man – but he wasn't clever. He just had an absolute instinct for people and how to use them to his best advantage . . .
>
> He was always pulling people's legs and joking. He and George Read of Pember & Boyle had a very close relationship and did a great deal of business together. They used to go to the Savoy and have these drinking sessions in the evening. Dick always believed that if he got George sufficiently drunk, he would find out the secrets of all the business he was doing. They drank a huge amount of kümmel and brandy and whisky and a decent amount of champagne . . .

For all the bonhomie, Wilkins could also – like so many of the City grandees of his generation – be pitiless. When he took a particular dislike to the dealing partner of Messels, he simply informed the senior partner of that broking firm that he would no longer deal with it unless that dealer was sacked; the unfortunate offender duly walked the plank. He was senior partner at Wedds from 1955, and under him the firm became the undisputed number one in the gilt-edged market. Over the years he worked closely with Jimmy Priestley, who described the secret of the firm's success:

> I think I was a fairly good technician. I was the one who said what prices we will make. I was the one who said I think the market's going to go better or it's going to go easier, I was the person who basically decided the policy for the day. And if I wanted to find something out, what the Government broker was likely to do or something, I just said to Dick, 'Can you find out?' and he'd be jolly good at that. I'm not saying he did anything he shouldn't do, but he just had a way with everybody. He was wonderful at avoiding making a price. Normally, people would go to several people to make a price, but Dick Wilkins would say, 'Well, what do you want to do?'

And, Priestley added, 'they would tell him, which made it very much easier . . .'[35]

During most of these years Wedds had only one serious rival in gilts: Akroyd & Smithers, under the impressive leadership of Hugh Merriman. He was a disciplinarian who also understood human nature; he had a deep understanding of the market; he was close to the Bank, Mullens and the discount houses; he was linked with Jock Hunter in trying to turn the Stock Exchange into a more progressive institution; and, perhaps above all, he pursued a systematic policy of bringing on younger talent, notably Brian Peppiatt as the 'flair' dealer and David LeRoy-Lewis as the 'boffin'. The contrast was stark between Akroyds and Francis & Praed, which declined from being the top gilts jobber immediately after the war to barely number three by the 1960s. Angus Ashton went there in 1955, in his mid-twenties, and found a 'geriatric' organisation in which everyone was at least twenty years older than him. The partnership was almost entirely interrelated, several of the partners were approaching retirement and since the war there had been little or no policy of recruitment. Then came the twin disasters of 1957: restrictions on bond-washing (on which Francis & Praed was over-reliant), followed by Thorneycroft's Bank rate hike on which the firm came a cropper. Just over two years later, in January 1960, Francis & Praed's senior partner, Jack Jarrett, called on Cobbold to discuss the firm's future. He explained that most of the capital in it belonged to two septuagenarians and expressed his wish to get in 'two young men with money'; to which Cobbold said that he would have a word with Mullens. At this point, according to the Governor's notes, 'Mr Jarrett tried to introduce one or two other subjects but I stopped him.' Unfortunately the 1960s saw no great infusion of either capital or talent, while from 1966 the senior partner was Humphrey Mackworth-Praed, a delightful, gentle man whom Ashton thought should have been an Oxford don rather than a City jobber. He was a passionate, extremely knowledgeable naturalist, and in the early 1970s he left to become a full-time conservation officer for the National Trust, by which time the family firm was virtually on its knees.[36]

In whichever market, a considerable number of small-time, often elderly jobbers continued operating on the floor of the House for a surprisingly long time. 'When I first dealt,' remembered Peter Stotesbury, who became a broker in the mid-1950s, 'there were many, many jobbers and most of them didn't have price boards up or anything and you had to find your own way around. It was very much a club. People were very helpful, if you respected age. They seemed to work until they dropped in those days.' A glance at the membership book for 1955 reveals a fair sprinkling of one-partner firms, including J. C. Connell of 2 Copthall Buildings and Coppen & Robson of 5 Copthall Court, not to mention Christopher Edwards, for whom no office or phone number was given, while his home address was apparently the National Liberal Club, Whitehall Place, SW1. When Norman Whetnall became the *Daily Telegraph*'s stockmarket correspondent four years later, he was struck by the fact that there remained quite a number of one- or two-man firms, especially in the gold market:

> They would have a tiny little pitch against the wall tucked away somewhere where you could always go and say, 'Good morning, how are you today? What are so and so's shares?' He being a small man, he might well be prepared to give you a slightly different price from somebody else, if you were a small dealer. Those people used to live on small investment business and the brokers knew them for what they were and dealt accordingly. And also there was the friendliness of the situation and people used to say, 'We'll give so and so a turn this morning because he was very good last time and he hasn't had much business. He'll be standing there all day doing nothing, let's help him out' . . .[37]

There were also many small to medium-sized jobbing firms, and recollections of three of them evoke the way of life of a distinctive, if more or less doomed, species.

Stephen Raven was seventeen when he joined the family firm of Stocken & Concanon in 1955. Competing with about a dozen other jobbers in American and Canadian securities, it was a typical niche firm, employing only about five or six in the back office, with a partnership that was about par for the course:

> Our senior partner, Colonel Concanon, lovely old boy, member of the Stock Exchange Council, was reputed to be the best-dressed man in the City of London in his time, but was getting on. He looked about 120 to me, he may only have been in his seventies. One of the jobs the junior blue button had was to ensure that the Colonel's white spats were changed at lunchtime – there was a great box of white spats in the Colonel's roll-top desk. The

Colonel always lunched at the Gresham Club. And because the poor old chap was half blind and shuffled a bit with a stick, he really needed someone to help bring him back from the club, and then change his spats . . . The second partner was a Major Love, who was certainly in his sixties when I arrived. Then we had somebody called Harold Moore, who was an eccentric old bugger but everyone loved him, hopeless jobber but attracted people because he was such a nice person: he would have been at that time probably in his fifties. He would deal with people and shout out, 'Boy, did you get that bargain?' And then there was my father, who would have been in his late forties, and then Harold Moore's son, Pat Moore, who was very much younger. . . We used to have Colonel Concanon's son in the firm, but he drank himself to death just about the time I joined. Wasn't suited to the business – a brilliant engineer apparently and the poor chap hated being in the firm. His father should never have brought him in. The one place you'd be guaranteed to find him at half-past eleven was the bar across the road with a very large gin and tonic on the counter waiting for him . . .

There was also a mixed bunch of partners at C. D. Clark, jobbing in various food, rubber and industrial securities, as Brian Carpenter found on arrival in 1957:

John Clark was an incredibly nice man and probably shouldn't have been a jobber. His interests were very broad. He was more of an intellectual man than a business man, it's reasonable to say. His brother Alan Clark had had a very unfortunate history in that he was in the Guards Regiment in the War and was pushed into the landing at Salerno and they had a hell of a battle there. Then they were given leave and he went to Rome, and the next thing he knew he woke up in a hospital in Liverpool. He eventually came into the firm in about '48. He could hardly move and was always on callipers and sticks and things, and you had to help him round the place; a very irascible man, very, very difficult bloke; generous, but he didn't suffer fools gladly and he didn't suffer quite a lot of other people gladly either. Then there was a fellow called Harold Ellis, who was the brother of the Ellis [Frederick Ellis] who wrote the financial columns for the *Daily Express* at the time. There was Beasley, Jim Beasley, who was a bit of joke really and had medical problems and died quite young. He suddenly flaked out. And there was Sir Charles Frederick, who was Alan Clark's major in the Guards and came in on the old boy network as it were, who again should not have been a jobber, he wasn't made for it . . .

A rather more focused outfit, staying a deliberately small, family firm, was S. Jenkins & Son, specialising from 1960 in leisure shares, such as greyhound stadiums and amusement parks. The 'Son' was Tony Jenkins, who would recall the trading attitude of his father, Sidney, as being never to borrow money, never to borrow stock and always to be able to sleep at night. 'Well, I won't overtrade,' his father would say, 'I'm going to survive.' Sidney Jenkins's origins were humble; he was never tempted to move the firm out of its homely offices on the third floor in Warnford

Court; and he delayed for as long as possible the introduction of computers, fearful that something could get wiped out and there would be no written record of the previous fortnight's trading.[38] His policy was conservative to a fault, but the firm survived.

For many small and medium-sized jobbers, the post-war years were a time of considerable strain, which did not always end with the apparently merciful release of being taken over by larger jobbing firms. Moreover, both within and without the Stock Exchange Council, the viability of the jobbing system came under scrutiny as never before. Harold Wincott argued in January 1952 that the high rates of taxation that had prevailed since 1939 made it almost impossible for jobbers any longer to accumulate capital, through saving from earnings; and he warned that the jobbing machinery as a whole was 'slowly but inevitably being strangled for want of capital . . . without which it cannot function'. Should outside capital be employed in jobbing partnerships, somewhat along the lines of syndicates at Lloyd's? Wincott was unsure, but wanted the Council at least to investigate the issue. A few months later there was a further, this time private, straw in the wind, when Anthony Tuke of Barclays remarked to Cobbold that 'there were too many small Firms on the Stock Exchange' and even expressed 'some doubt whether in modern conditions the jobber machinery was really necessary or satisfactory'.[39]

The following winter the Council belatedly appointed a committee 'to examine matters affecting Jobbers'. At an early stage an important memo was read from L. C. Denza, himself a jobber with Paul E. Shaw & Co. His diagnosis agreed with Wincott's, and he noted that 'a careful analysis of the number of Firms actively engaged in jobbing and running a book on a sufficient scale to help to constitute a market has recently been computed at hardly more than 60', adding that 'it will hardly be disputed that this number is barely sufficient for present-day requirements, if the present system is to continue'. Helpfully, Denza spelled it out: 'When markets are difficult and particularly when they are falling, dealings in many Securities frequently becomes virtually impossible, in other than small amounts. This discourages many clients from placing large orders, and must increase the tendency for business in big amounts to be transacted outside the House.' In particular, he was concerned about the gloomy future for the younger jobbers, of whom there was already a distinct shortage. In practice, with junior partners finding it very difficult for fiscal reasons to save money, 'the Death or Retirement of a Senior Partner ipso facto frequently curtails a Firm's business activities'. Calling for infusions of outside capital, Denza concluded resonantly: 'It is better to have PG's in one's House than no House at all'. This was not, however, a proposition to which the authorities instinctively warmed – 'such a change would be of a very revolutionary nature', the committee's report flatly stated – and though one or two discreet enquiries were apparently made 'of selected bodies and institutions', the question of paying guests was soon put to one side.[40]

The respite was only temporary, for in October 1955 a major, anonymous article by a member in the *Stock Exchange Journal* focused lucidly on the problems afflicting the jobbing system, in the context of the number of jobbing firms having declined over the past eight years from 237 to 134. Again the crux was capital, in that the post-war growth of institutional business had in turn led to the growing size of the average bargain, which meant that the jobbing system required greater capital resources if it was 'to perform its traditional function of ironing out market movements caused by changes of sentiment'. He then discussed the issue of bringing in outside capital from insurance companies, merchant banks, investment trusts, and so on, 'all of whom are interested in the existence of a market in securities'. His answer helps to explain why it would be over thirty years before the Big Bang occurred: 'London may eventually have to take some such steps, but there is little doubt that most Members, with their genius for improvisation, would prefer to control their own affairs for as long as they can, and manage their own business within the framework of the existing Rules, rather than adopt new methods which might in the long run threaten their independence'.[41]

Eventually, a special committee in early 1957 specifically considered the question of outside capital, with a view to checking the palpable decline in the jobbing system, by now down to 123 firms. The most striking contribution came from Douglas Eton of the jobbers Murton & Adams. He argued that outside capital was *not* the answer, since if the business was a good risk, then money should be forthcoming from a jobber's banker; anyway, 'jobbers need large amounts of capital in temporary "bursts" rather than large permanent capital'. Moreover:

> Judged entirely from the view-point of an outside user of the Stock Exchange, the Jobbing structure appears to be either fragile, trivial and obstructionist or openly usurious.
> It is only the Members of the Stock Exchange themselves who pay lip service, of varying quality and content, to the barely organised chaos which struggles to maintain itself as the only entirely Free Enterprise market left.

Accordingly, 'the natural cure' was 'the formation of a small number of large jobbing units operating "take-it or leave-it" price systems'. In time the committee produced an inconclusive report, with its members split on the question of outside capital. One jobber who had no doubts about what needed to be done was Esmond Durlacher. 'He thought that more and more business would go to the big jobber and that the system would not work properly until this happened,' he told another committee in July

1958. 'The small jobber offered no service that the big jobber did not give. He did not agree that the market would be finished if there were only big jobbers; there would still be competition . . .' By that autumn the number of jobbing firms was down to 108, and barely one-fifth of members were now jobbers.[42]

The crux of the matter was that – partly because of the increasing importance of institutional clients, partly because of the growing use of the telephone – 'a fundamental change in the transaction of Stock Exchange business has taken place due to the considerable number of deals which are negotiated by Brokers between non-members and which only reach the Jobber on put-through terms'. Such was the Stock Exchange's own admission in November 1958, strictly for private consumption. The big jobbers (such as Durlachers) had the resources to deal direct with these non-members; the small ones did not. Was the answer, in order to keep the jobbing system within the Stock Exchange family, perhaps for the brokers to buy into many of these jobbers? Early in the 1960s an *ad hoc* committee set up by the Council recommended that before any outside capital be brought into the jobbing system, broking firms should be given first refusal at providing it. This recommendation, however, was rejected: the concept of single capacity remained, as it would for the next two decades, the great sacred cow. Meanwhile, the jobbing system was contracting ever more rapidly – from 100 firms in June 1960 to a mere fifty-nine five years later. 'In my mind,' Eton wrote to the Council in July 1962, somewhat changing his tune from his earlier pronouncement, 'there is absolutely no doubt that, in ten years at the current rate, there will be about twenty Jobbing Firms left'; and he urged that henceforth any proposed merger between firms dealing in the same stocks should require the Council's approval. Another member, P. F. S. Moore, writing a year later to the Council, was even more apocalyptic. After comparing the existing jobbing system to 'a 1926 vintage Rolls Royce, supreme in outward appearance, with no wheels,' he went on:

> With all due respects to the planners of the new Stock Exchange, it does appear as if the floor trading area is a little on the huge side for the number of men who will be available to stand on it within the next decade . . . We will drift down an unknown course in ever-increasing uneasiness with the rich waxing richer, and casualties amongst the not so wealthy increasing with attendant hardships. . . I visualise the new Stock Exchange in ten to twenty years' time as a small cathedral of city life, with a galaxy of bishops, few in number, surrounded by an admiring group of archdeacons, a little more in number, and a few deacons; but no congregation, and they all sing harmonious hymns in praise of each other . . .

Two years later, in September 1965, welcoming the recent establishment of a committee of jobbers (but under the chairmanship of the broker Jock Hunter) to try to see what could be done, Wincott added his own prediction about the jobbing system: 'Maybe, left to itself, it will coalesce into a mere handful of firms which might get referred to the Restrictive Practices Court . . .' Maybe, but Wincott for one, mindful of how these jobbers had 'done fine work, vital to the nation, in the past', hoped not.[43]

Hunter's committee mainly comprised representatives of the leading jobbing firms, and perhaps predictably its report in January 1966 failed to come up with anything very exciting. It did favour price-maintenance agreements, which on a wholly informal basis had become increasingly common in recent years; but a few months later a strong broadside from that most competitive of firms, Smith Brothers, arguing that 'fixed price margins are a restrictive practice', ensured that henceforth all such agreements had to be notified to the Council. That September a report commissioned from the accountants Spicer & Pegler revealed that during the previous five years only a handful of jobbing firms had been managing to make net profits. 'After a year's thought and the advice and discussion of many of the best jobbing brains,' Hunter wondered aloud to fellow-members of the Council, 'I think that the answer lies simply in brokers and others remembering that if they conspire to take all the profit from jobbing they will not have left what is perhaps the most efficient market in the world.' However, Bisgood Bishop was unwilling to trust to such good intentions on the part of the broking capacity. Instead it contended, in a forceful memo soon afterwards, that outside capital was the only answer: 'In order to attract it Jobbing partnerships will have to be large and widely spread through the markets, a pattern which should be conducive to relatively stable profits. This will necessitate mergers . . . We believe that the "Free for all" days have gone for ever . . .'[44] The price of such a solution, Bisgoods did not need to say, would be to turn the Stock Exchange into a club no more – and that, for the time being, was a price too high to pay.

A human price was already being paid for the rapid contraction of the jobbing system. A man with a high sense of honour and distinguished military record, as well as chairman of the Stock Exchange Arts Society, 'Boddy' Shaw was senior partner of his family jobbing firm. The story seems to have been kept from the wider public, but Donald Cobbett told it twenty years later:

> P.E. Shaw was one of the many firms to be embraced by bigger brethren, who took into their fold the substance of the victim's connections, had ample capacity to handle the added business, and promptly shed the then surplus, over-staffed offices of the acquired. So, as a market friend of mine cynically put it, what the Japs failed to do, the changing post-war pattern of the Stock Exchange succeeded. A thorough gentleman of infinite sensibility

and charm, he was so conscious-stricken by the ruthless dismissal of old, cherished employees, and anxious as well for the financial well-being of his sisters, that on Tuesday, 21st September 1965, in his Barbican flat, he tragically took his own life.

If that was tragedy, there could also be farce. When John Clark, senior partner of C. D. Clark, decided one fine day in September 1966 to wind up the firm, there and then, one of its dealers, the self-made Keith Knowles, was away on holiday. What happened became the stuff of Stock Exchange legend. 'He came back,' Winterflood relates, 'and the day he came back he walked in – just to his usual pitch – and they weren't there. They had actually gone bust and they'd never told him. Poor old Keith, literally he didn't know – he came back to the Stock Exchange and they said, "Well, they're bust, mate, they've gone."' Winterflood adds that the story of 'the guy who went on holiday, never to return, literally finished his career on the Stock Exchange'; but Knowles did in due course become a very successful gilt dealer at Union Discount.[45]

His firm was not the only one to go under that autumn. Esmond Durlacher, Dick Wilkins and Sydney King were all in their very different ways major jobbing figures, but no one on the floor of the post-war Stock Exchange quite matched Percy Duke – a member since 1919, senior partner of P. A. Duke & Co, and residing at The Island, Walton-on-the-Hill, Surrey. Winterflood remembered this intimidating figure with respect rather than affection: 'Percy Duke was really the old school. He always dressed in clerical trousers and wing collar. He was a very tall man and had a lot of bearing and he would never speak to blue buttons, and I'm not sure that he really spoke to junior dealers, but certainly you almost had to get permission to speak to him . . .' Duke's firm, operating mainly in industrials, was small, despite Duke's overbearing manner on the floor (and propensity, in the pre-Christmas charades, for dressing up as a schoolmaster). Val Powell remembered him as someone who reacted to pressure by becoming an out-and-out bully:

> He used to take great pleasure in knocking into a blue button and pretending that he [i.e. the blue button] had been running or had barged him. His business basically was going downhill, so the further it went downhill the more sticky and difficult he became. And one day – it was at the time of the rebuilding of the Stock Exchange – he knocked into what he took to be a young blue button and gave him a most terrific rocket for running. The chap said, 'I don't know what you're talking about, guv. I come from Trollope & Colls, the builders.' So the laugh was on him . . .

The variant story has a man accidentally standing on one of Duke's shining shoes and moving smartly away, prompting the irate jobber to close his book, run after the offender and interrogate him. 'Young man, you've trodden on my foot. I want the name of your senior partner. What's your firm?' This time the reply was the equally blithe, 'I'm with the GPO, mate!' In any event, Duke's firm ceased trading on 28 October 1966. Duke himself gave up his membership of the Stock Exchange, but his three partners managed to find berths with Pinchin Ferguson Clark, where the young Powell was due to become a partner about a fortnight later. The demise of P. A. Duke & Co, and the humiliation suffered by its senior partner (who lost his entire capital), made a profound impression. It was, Powell reflected, 'a very sad commentary on just how somebody could put on an air and a grace in the Exchange and his real life was crumbling away behind him'. He concluded from the episode – and did not subsequently change his mind – that 'fear and greed' were what drove human beings.[46]

*

Philip Larkin, though not known as an habitué of the square mile, tended to agree. 'I am sorry to hear life has had you by the balls,' he wrote to a friend in 1950. 'It is a grim business, & I do sympathise: it is also a business that appears differently to every man. To me it appears like the floor of some huge Stock Exchange full of men quarrelling & fighting & shouting & fucking & drinking & making plans and scheming to carry them out, experiencing desires & contriving to gratify them, and in general acting & being acted upon . . .'[47]

Few of those who actually spent any time on the floor of the old House, before its demolition began in 1966, ever forgot the experience. A clutch of reminiscences, from a quarter of a century later, evoke something of its uniqueness – attractive or rebarbative according to taste:

> I didn't think that I could possibly stand it, because the noise and the people, as a Guards officer at Dunkirk so wittily said, appalled me. It was like being at a cocktail party without any drinks. But within a week I discovered the people were delightful and the noise I didn't even notice. It was like a rugger club, it was all boys together . . .
>
> You still had that wonderful atmosphere where you had a laugh and a joke; a situation where they played the fool when there wasn't much business; the old idea of buying a box of chocolates outside, eating the chocolates, then placing the box on the market floor with water in it, until some idiot came along and kicked it, which always happened. And the idiot would of course get a soaked foot . . .
>
> I think it was the way of letting off steam. There was always the throwing of paper balls and that sort of thing, particularly at guys that were wearing top hats; and another joke was putting torn-up newspaper – little bits of newspaper – in a chap's umbrella, put down his umbrella and then as he started to walk out, up went the umbrella, so of course the shower of paper came down . . .

Standing next to me was a fellow called Gerry Barber, and he looked like a parrot, and that was often a source of amusement. Chap named Nicky Nichols – Tom Nichols with Hadow – would imitate a parrot and rather take the mickey, which he used to get terribly annoyed about. There was a chap called Lightfoot, and he had a habit when he was called of waving his handkerchief from his top pocket. The waiter would repeat 'Lightfoot', and then all of a sudden four or five hundred people would take their handkerchiefs out and they would all be waving them. There was 'Punch' Davis, who was with Vickers da Costa. He looked like Mr Punch. He got permission for one of the Gurkhas – the last Gurkha to win a VC – to come into the market, and he walked right the way round the floor and was clapped the whole way round. I remember when the King died there was a junior there, who wasn't wearing a black tie, and he got really told off over this. 'How dare you come into the market, don't you realise?' The Queen's birthday, the King's birthday, the Stock Exchange Choir always formed up in the gilt market and always sang the National Anthem and the whole market joined in . . .

The particular thing that impressed me more than anything was this old man who would occasionally come into the gilt market and the whole House would sing 'Jerusalem'. It was a most magnificent sound. I mean it brought tears to your eyes. It was unbelievable, and I don't think I've ever been impressed with anything more than that . . .[48]

Some markets were more boisterous than others, while the introduction of the visitors' gallery in 1953 occasionally made members think twice about doing something outrageous; but under the world's third-biggest dome there remained a real continuity between the Stock Exchange during its Victorian heyday and that now inhabited by the not-so-new Elizabethans.

During breaks from the singing, home for most jobbers was their particular pitch on the floor. Some of these pitches were permanent (often erected alongside one of the many pillars or walls), while others comprised a more temporary, circular seat and stand in the middle of the floor itself, but all were made of wood – well-carved, beautifully polished oak. On these stands would be pinned sheets of white paper, with the printed names of the stocks in which the particular jobber dealt and the latest prices scribbled alongside the names. When full up, the page was simply torn off and another page started. Inevitably there was, as Tony Jenkins recalled, a strong territorial imperative concerning these pitches:

In fact, father's pitch was the same pitch he was on in the thirties. This was something that was treasured and protected at all times . . . Your dealing pitch could be a small board on the wall, perhaps 24 inches by 12, and somewhere to stand probably four feet away from there, and that was your pitch. Then if you knew a firm was closing down and they were friendly towards you, they would, as we did, move pitches, but we only moved about four feet to the right. We knew the firm was shutting down, and as they literally took their board off the wall, ours went on theirs. There was no application for a pitch, and no charges for pitches. I remember saying to father one day, 'Do you realise we must have the cheapest shop in the City of London?' He said, 'What do you mean?' Our combined fees in those days were £125, and I said, '£125. That's all we pay for this pitch. We've got rates, the rent's paid, we've got electric lighting, heating and a captive audience.' Of course when the Stock Exchange was rebuilt they started making a charge for it. But I suppose that is why there were so many small firms. The overheads were peanuts really. It was different days . . .

Durlachers, at the other end of the jobbing spectrum, had several pitches under its command, including one that went by the name of 'Treasure Island'. There, according to another market veteran, there was always a price to be found in up to 500 diverse stocks that could not be readily classified, 'and you would always find people clustered around trying to deal inside and usually getting some sort of service and satisfaction because it was a fun place – that's why it was called 'Treasure Island'.[49]

Whether deployed on behalf of a big or a small firm, what qualities were actually required to be a successful jobber?[50] 'I think you've got to be totally flexible at all times,' Brian Peppiatt reckoned, 'because the skill of a jobber is to admit when you're wrong at a very, very early stage indeed. They always say in Stock Exchange terms, "the first cut is the best cut".' Peppiatt, by general consent one of the most gifted jobbers of his generation, also believed that 'you had to interpret the press, and interpret world events, and interpret economic happenings, just that much quicker than anyone else because the facts were all there'. But for another Wykehamist, the somewhat younger Val Powell, it was that sort of rapid reaction, based inevitably on instinct as much as ratiocination, that he found hard to master. 'Intellectually one felt on a different level,' he recalled about coming to his father's firm in the 1960s. 'I found the humour and the give and take of the market something which I couldn't get on with. So many people took commercial decisions by the seat of their pants rather than by any sort of judgemental process. And essentially that is the essence of the jobber. You couldn't ask him why he did a deal, he just did a deal because it felt right . . .' Michael Sargent, who likewise started jobbing in the 1960s, did not disagree with the adage of his father (also a jobber), that 'all you need to be a successful jobber is a pleasing personality and a bit of common sense', though he added that it was also necessary to have 'a good gut for the market'; while according to Graham Ferguson, who started jobbing for Wedds in the 1950s, 'the good jobber was the one who looked less clever than he was'. Over the years a considerable mystique built up around the jobbers and their arcane craft, but not everyone bought into it. 'Did you feel a jobber was a very different kind of person to a broker?' one experienced figure on the market floor was asked:

Oh yes.

Could you elaborate?

Yes, in my view a jobber is just a spiv. He's a complete trader, doesn't really worry about the fundamentals of anything – gets up in the morning, comes in, obviously inherits or has yesterday's position perhaps or maybe was lucky and went home level, turns over a bit of stock, hopes to make a turn on it, and as soon as five o'clock comes goes home and forgets about it. It's day-by-day stuff. There's no long-term goal or plan. It's just there for the moment . . .[51]

Such was the less than enchanted view of John Brooks, who dealt for many years for Kit Hoare's broking firm. Most other brokers would have agreed – indeed, in their different ways, both brokers and jobbers were distinctly (albeit usually silently) inclined to regard each other as unfortunate necessities.

With the senior partners of broking firms increasingly office-based, dealing partners like Brooks were becoming important figures on the floor, even if that prestige was not always reflected within the firm. 'There was always a way into the partnership at Pember & Boyle through the dealing side,' George Nissen recollected. 'The senior dealer much of the time I was a partner was an extraordinary and very difficult man who was not much liked. He wasn't on anybody's visiting lists, certainly not on the partners', and he wouldn't have made any effort to cultivate the other partners socially. But he made quite a lot of money. He probably regarded us as rather pathetic amateurs . . .' He and other senior dealers could be tough, forbidding operators. 'He was a very, very shrewd cookie and pretty well as near the knuckle as you could do' was how Jimmy Bisgood recalled Geoffrey Perkins of Grieveson Grant. None exuded greater presence than 'The Rook', Charles Purnell of Cazenove's. 'He had quite enormous sort of beetling eyebrows,' Bisgood remembered, did 'all the enormous business' in equities, and 'one had to swallow hard when you were going to take him on'. Purnell took pride in usually dealing only in big orders, dispensing them with regal magnanimity, and was punctilious in his insistence on business being conducted in the right and proper manner; but he had been born on the wrong side of the tracks, and it was not until 1956 – more than twenty years after he had started to emerge as an accomplished dealer in the industrial market – that Cazenove's made him a partner. On the floor, backed by his firm's clout, he could (in the words of one of his successors) 'virtually walk up to a jobber and tell him what he wanted to do and the jobber had to do it', but at 12 Tokenhouse Yard the pecking order was rather different.[52]

Everyone knew 'The Rook', but jobbers were not always certain about the identity of the person with whom they were dealing. The problem was (as Gerald Lederman recalled about his youthful days at Smith Brothers) an inviolable aspect of market etiquette:

If a broker came up to your pitch to deal and you weren't quite sure which firm he was with, you were not allowed to ask him. The theory was that, as he left the pitch and went walking round the Stock Exchange, the blue button (such as myself) had to follow him round, and when he went to speak to a chap a few yards away you went up to that fellow and said, 'Excuse me, Sir, could you tell me who that gentleman was with?' And he would. I managed to get hold of a chap once who came on the pitch, dealt with us, and we weren't sure who he was with, so I had to go and follow him and he went round the Stock Exchange, just staring at boards, didn't speak to a soul, then walked out of the place and started to walk down to Bank tube station, by which time I thought, well, I'd better abandon this one . . .

This unauthorised clerk perhaps lacked persistence, for one favourite Stock Exchange anecdote told of the jobber's blue button who was compelled to tail a broker all the way to the latter's home in Pirbright, where the blue button at last got the crucial name from a station porter.

Eventually, in 1959, it was decided that when dealing all members must wear a badge to identify themselves. 'In the days of the rubber boom, the Kaffir boom, the oil boom and various industrial booms, jobbers had managed to survive in the past without labelling their customers' was the predictable, but unavailing, protest of Graham Greenwell. Meanwhile some twenty broking firms signed a petition complaining that it 'would entail the constant putting on and removal of Badges, as obviously it would not add to the dignity of the Stock Exchange as a whole were Members to be seen walking round the City wearing whatever form of Badge is finally decided upon'. Brokers, being far more numerous, had little difficulty in identifying the members of the other capacity; rather, their problem – keenly felt by younger brokers – was knowing which jobber to deal with. 'You had to try and persuade your seniors to tell you which jobbers dealt in which shares,' Nissen remembered of his early days at Pember & Boyle. 'It didn't help the competitive process at all. It was a sort of convention – "I made it to the top and I did it through my own efforts and there's no reason why I should give you a leg up" – a slight tradition of that.' Help, however, was already at hand by the early 1950s, with the annual publication by a member (L.M.S.N. Connolly) of the *Industrial Jobbers Index*, listing jobbers and the stocks in which they specialised. This invaluable guide rapidly acquired a characteristic sobriquet: 'The Squirts Guide'.[53]

Meanwhile, in this closed, almost hermetically sealed market, 'My word is my bond' remained a day-to-day reality, as well as the stuff of promotional films. All contracts continued to be made by word of mouth throughout the 1950s and 1960s, with confirmation on paper awaiting the next morning. What is harder to be sure about is how far this pervading atmosphere of trust extended to an unwritten code of *fair* as well as accurate dealing. Undoubtedly there were some grave matters of market etiquette that it was behoven to observe. Brokers were ill advised, for example, to indulge in the superficially attractive policy of 'picking up' jobbers – in other words, either buying shares from one jobber and selling to another or (the lesser crime) going to a jobber who was quoting the wrong price. Geoffrey Green, jobbing for Bisgoods in the 1960s, described another aspect of dealing manners:

> If a broker had asked you to 'come inside', which was to make a narrower price than you had originally quoted – if he'd asked you for a 'way', as it was known – then he would have to deal with you. I recall a rather senior gentleman having asked me the way, I then opened my way which didn't suit him, and he tried to walk away to go and deal or improve with another firm, which he was not supposed to do. I stopped him, by saying 'Excuse me, sir, would you mind holding on a minute?', called in a more senior person on the book and, having explained the situation, he then obviously had to deal with us. Otherwise he would lose a bit of reputation and standing . . .

Inevitably in some cases a close personal relationship developed between a broker and a jobber. George Birks, for instance, dealing for Phillips & Drew, got very close to Herbert Wilson and his son Nigel, of the gilt-edged jobbers Wilson & Watford, an almost notoriously upright and Christian firm that ranked just behind Francis & Praed in that market. 'There's no doubt about it,' Tony Jenkins remarked in general, 'certain brokers favoured certain jobbers so they saw most of their trade. It might have been a common denominator between the two traders – they collected stamps, or both belonged to the same tennis club – but there was this complete trust . . . It was all down to personalities at the end of the day really. The ones that you didn't get on with, you didn't trade with or tried to avoid trading with . . .'[54]

In an era before most brokers had begun to plug into the joys of investment analysis, the ambivalent, ultimately symbiotic broker-jobber relationship was perhaps epitomised by the whole question of market intelligence. 'For many years we produced a market slip on most of the companies in which we dealt,' Jimmy Bisgood recalled. 'Just factual – giving details of capital, past record, sometimes details from the last AGM, etc.' He added, however, that 'smaller brokers would often ask for recommendations as to share purchases'. It was also the same, according to Stephen Raven, at Stocken & Concanon:

> Brokers very much wanted the advice of jobbers in those days. The broker had an idea that he wanted to look at a particular Canadian oil company, shall we say, but he didn't know much about it. And it wasn't easy to find out about stocks. We had the ability to find out more about these companies from the Canadian broker that we used as a correspondent, and passed that

information on to the brokers. So you got a fairly good feel for the dozen or so companies that you were specialising in, and you knew roughly when the movements were going to take place in price, there would be peaks and troughs . . .

That may have been the case, but on the trading floor few jobbers were renowned either for their analytical skill or for their deep knowledge of the intrinsic worth of securities. A notable exception was David Blackwell, whose grasp of the oil industry and its 'chartist' implications was legendary, but Richard Durlacher subsequently regarded the information peddled out to brokers by his own firm as being based on 'very primitive research'. Brian Winterflood of Bisgoods was frankness itself:

> I always felt that you should be able to run any book . . . In very crude terms, I've always said that stocks and shares, so far as the market maker is concerned, they're apples and pears . . . It wasn't for us to say what a company was worth. We were merely reflecting supply and demand – a bit like a bookie. If all the weight's on one horse, then you lay it off on something else. And so that's the science of it . . .

Inevitably, brokers suspected jobbers of talking their own book – yet, to a remarkable extent, that does not seem to have deterred them from asking jobbers for their opinions. Geoffrey Green, one of Winterflood's partners, saw the incongruity of the situation:

> The funny thing was that it was a bit like being a car salesman. If the chap came along and said, 'What do you think of Plessey shares?', although you gave a factual account about 'Well, they had some good results last month', or 'they're expecting some good results next month', or whatever you would know factually about them, if you were a Bull of them, obviously you would try to sell them. You would talk him into buying them. Whereas if you were perhaps a Bear of them, and it didn't suit your book to sell them, you would try and put him off. The same as if you go along to a showroom and you want to buy a certain type of car but they haven't got any to sell, they'll obviously try to sell you something else, or try and tell you, you don't really want to buy that one anyway. So they were asking us an opinion on the Company where we obviously had a vested interest as to how we worded it or how we put it. So I think it was the skill of giving them some facts and dressing it up with a bit of fiction . . .[55]

The simple truth was probably that most brokers were too lazy or too ignorant to spend hours scouring annual reports, balance-sheets, and so on. A word with an apparently well-disposed jobber was so much quicker and, usually, so much more congenial.

The dealing itself was the nub of the relationship. Often it was straightforward enough; at other times it involved shadow-boxing; at yet other times something resembling guerrilla warfare. George Birks viewed matters from the perspective of a particularly clear-minded broker:

I always felt that if you asked a jobber a price you might well hear something you didn't want to hear and it was far more important, in my book, to know what the situation of jobbers' books was in the market, both as a whole and in individual stocks. And you gleaned this by experience and being trusted by them. If you got an order, very often the way to do it was to say, 'I'll give you so much for such and such a stock', and forget what they were calling them. Because if you were a buyer and they wanted to sell stock, okay they couldn't put the price up against you because they were your way; if on the other hand you were a buyer and they were short of stock, well then, that is a different situation entirely and you have to be careful and you have to obviously ask for the price and pin them down on what they were calling the stock. But if you were doing what they wanted to do – that is, buying stock when they wanted to sell it – then there was much more scope for stating what your price was . . .

It is impossible to know, in general, whether the broker or the jobber was more likely to emerge smelling of roses. For Stephen Raven, much depended on knowing the enemy:

You had to have a feel for the type of broker that you were dealing with; you had to have a feel for his credit rating; you had to have a feel whether he might be a buyer or a seller. You had to have a feel for the type of client that he had, because if he had some pretty sharp information coming from clients who maybe knew more of the story of the company than anyone else knew – which today would probably be totally illegal and be classed as insider trading; in those days it was all part of the game – if he knew somebody might be taken over in the next hour or two, he'd come and try and buy as many shares as he could. Well, once bitten twice shy . . .

Partially masked by the mainly good-humoured banter, and amidst the general hubbub of the market floor, most brokers and jobbers watched each other pretty closely. 'I found out always when one had to be especially careful, you'd see him rubbing his finger and thumb,' Jimmy Bisgood remembered about Geoffrey Perkins of Grievesons. 'Unfortunately, after a couple of years, somebody told him about it, which was a great pity.'[56]

In this visible marketplace – where one could see what one's rivals were doing, or at least have a fairly shrewd idea – what were relations like *between* the jobbers? The accounts we have suggest a fairly spiky atmosphere (certainly outside the gentlemanly gilt market), if not quite fear and loathing. Tactical use of their boards, supposedly giving the latest prices, was a key element. 'Did you ever have any way of knowing what the other jobbers were quoting?' Geoffrey Moy (whose family firm jobbed in the rubber market) was asked:

No, you didn't. There was no way of telling at all, unless you looked at their boards. Those days the art of a good jobber was to completely hide what he'd done and give the other jobbers the impression that instead of actually having bought the shares, he'd actually sold them. This was supposed to be very clever. Well, it is actually, because under these circumstances the price wouldn't change radically and you wouldn't be in a position where you might lose a lot of money having sold 100,000 shares.

Well, how would you conceal what you were doing if you were putting your prices on the board?

You might change the price, but it needn't necessarily be correct. Say, for example, you sold some shares at £1, a lot of shares; well, in order to be clever you would mark the shares down to 19s 9d or something like that, you see. So that the other jobbers would think you'd probably bought the shares. So this was all part of the skilful back and forth play in the art of jobbing . . .

'Spoofing' was the term usually given to this use of the boards, but there were plenty of other ways of doing down the opposition. Terrence Ahern, operating in the open outcry Kaffir market, described some of them:

Sometimes you would go in there looking very miserable when the market had had a bit of a rise and you'd take a chance, you'd go and bid openly for it. You'd only bid openly because you hoped someone would bid a bit more. When they bid a bit more, bang straight away. You'd sell them. And you never had a query in your bargains. There were all those skills that one could use, so it was sometimes very difficult to know what your opposition was up to. If you didn't know you were cautious. Another thing was a thing called 'spoiling'. Well, supposing you found out that one of your competitors was a buyer of stock and had an order there to buy stock. You had no business and then you deliberately bid over his price just to stop him doing his business. That was known as spoiling. That was quite common. There was a lot of lip-reading done. So someone would come round to me and say, 'What are Randfontein?' A lot of argy bargy – '4½–7½'. Let's say he bought quite a few, which was in those days a tenner. So you'd say, 'all right, sell 10,000 to you at 7 pence ha'penny.' They'd wait [i.e. the other jobbers] until he'd gone, they would see you book the bargain so they'd know you've dealt, and then they'd bid 7 pence ha'penny for it deliberately to spoil.

So that meant that there was a lot of bad feeling or hostility between jobbers?

No, no, it was only when these people spoilt one another, then it would soon be forgotten: 'So and so spoilt me', and then you watch out for him.

What were relations between jobbers like generally?

Basically very friendly.

Did you see each other outside of the House?

Not a lot really, no, not a lot. Saw enough of one another all day long.

There may have been another reason for this lack of socialising, if Jenkins's firm was typical in its practice of instantly dismissing anyone found guilty of disclosing any trade that had gone on within it. 'If a jobber's taking on a chap in half a million shares,' Jenkins himself observed, 'he doesn't really want to tell the world about it, because if you've got enemies in the market, they'll ruin your book. That wasn't unusual . . .' Eventually, he added, the problems confronting the jobbing system pushed the jobbers closer together – but, even then, the habits of secrecy and mutual suspicion ran deep.[57]

*

'The greedy basis of the Stock Exchange may seem sordid and deplorable, compared to the ideals of public service or the dedication of teachers,' Anthony Sampson wrote in the early 1960s. 'After spending two months talking to people in the City, I felt oppressed and dispirited by its narrowness and bleakness, the quasi-sexual fascination with money concealed behind large layers of humbug, and the sheer boredom of it.'[58] His critique tells an important truth; yet almost four decades later, with the City and its securities industry wholly transformed, and virtually unrecognisable from the world that Sampson described, it is permissible to feel some nostalgia for the old Stock Exchange, a place where real human beings encountered each other and experienced the meaning of trust and fear, of hope and greed. Those primary emotions have far from gone away, but there is no longer a frame in which to set – and make sense of – them. 'Are Friends Electric?' was one of the many questions never asked by the fortunate inhabitants of Capel Court.

CHAPTER NINE

Part of the Training

In spring 1952 the Chairman of the Central Electricity Authority was at a Bank of England meeting, with Cobbold in the chair, to hammer out the fine detail of a forthcoming Treasury-backed loan:

> We had a protracted discussion – the longest (according to an attendant) that he had ever known in his many years at the Bank – but I remained unconvinced that the terms were satisfactory. I was finally asked, 'Don't you think we are competent to advise you?' I retorted, 'Competent, most certainly. But not infallible.' And I went on to say that I thought our next step would be to take independent advice. There was astonishment at this. Not only would it be irregular to do this, but the proposed terms of the loan might leak out. The discussion was adjourned from the Friday afternoon until the Monday. On that morning, we were informed that the terms had been somewhat improved.

Lord Citrine, in an earlier life a tough-minded trade unionist, was not the only unimpressed observer of the City in action. 'It was almost impossible to transact any business without having a prior relationship,' George Soros would recall about his frustrating experiences as a young man in the 1950s. 'That was the main reason why I left London. Because I was not well connected in London, my chances were much better in New York.' Presumably the future manipulator of nations and their currencies had yet to score one of the City's most coveted invitations, lunch at New Court; but when, near the end of the decade, the government's economic adviser, Sir Robert Hall, received that privilege, the fact that 'one cannot help feeling a bit romantic' about Rothschilds and its past did not deter him from giving a fairly cool account of the experience:

> The present man, Sir [in fact Mr] Edmund, showed me all the family pictures and some of the documents, e.g. a letter from No 10 in 1815 asking Rothschild's to collect gold wherever they could on the Continent up to £600,000 to pay the Commissary General in France. But I did not think Sir Edmund has inherited much of his family's flair unless he was concealing it very carefully. All the talk at lunch was on a highly trivial level, mostly contributed by an aged diplomat called Sir R. Leeper who used to be Argentine Ambassador and is now with de Beer's and whom I rather liked. But our host had nothing to say either on finance or on literature. He had

looked everyone up in *Who's Who* beforehand as I suppose most intelligent people do, but got them somewhat wrong all the same, e.g. he said I was the chief statistician, no doubt a genuine inability to see any difference, but if I had cared, not very wise . . .

It was also by invitation only that one could lunch at the City's oldest club – the Gresham, tucked away in Abchurch Lane. Members had personalised napkin rings, the lunches were long and splendid (no office papers allowed on the premises) and the smoking room was available for drinking port through the afternoon. The staff of three dozen or so included billiard markers, a lift attendant on each of the four floors – and, in the 1960s, a waitress called Ruth Valentine. 'While the rest of London was letting it all hang out, the (male, of course) great and powerful seemed mainly to be having tantrums and refusing to eat their nice veal-ham-and-egg pie until I'd found their very own napkin ring' was how the place first struck her. 'My second lesson in political reality came when I went round with an order pad. "My usual," said one bald gentleman with glasses, annoyed to be asked. I explained that it was my first day and I hadn't yet learned what his usual might be. This was even worse. "I am Lord C——n," he said. "Find out." '[1]

*

To be one of the City's élite was, almost all observers agreed, to be a member of an enviable club. But what exactly were that club's code, assumptions and general *Weltanschauung*? The *FT*'s economics correspondent, George Cyriax, attempted an answer, in a post-Profumo article in *Punch* in August 1963, nicely entitled 'Integrity Is Not Enough'. First he deftly sketched the City's 'emotional impact' – 'Silk top hats. Sleek limousines. The bee-like activity of clerks on the floor of the Stock Exchange. Solid, imposing banks, sporting the occasional window box of discreet hydrangeas. Above all, the heavy, heady scent of money . . .' – and was emphatic that 'the City, at least on the surface, is a thoroughly honest place', that is, in the sense of word-is-my-bond and general business integrity. There were, however, less attractive aspects, not least its blinkered ideology:

> The City has a purer brand of right-wing politics than any other group I have ever come across. Public school upbringing – often into the firm of family or friends – daily journeys to and from commuterland with a lot of like-minded people – a handsome farm and four-day week if you are one of the élite – little competition on the basis of ability – there is little here to challenge or broaden the political view. It is an atmosphere in which not merely decent right-wing opinions, but cranky right-wing extremism, can flourish. Unlike the run-of-the-mill businessman who has to deal with him, in other words, City men can honestly believe that the shop steward wears horns.

After remarking how well financially the City was accustomed to doing for itself out of its activities, Cyriax then analysed 'the City personality':

> Bearing in mind all along that the City, like anywhere else, encompasses a huge spread of outlooks, it still seems to be true that the predominant ethic – commercial honesty, political naïveté, the assumption that one is entitled to do very well – is heavily influenced by the public school. Everyone important has been there, and this common background is a vital part in preserving the City's standards. But I think a deeper clue to the City's personality is given by thinking of what the City does. Buying and selling for profit at the end of telephone, acting as a middleman for financial transactions, estimating whether a pest in Ghana is going to put the price of cocoa up before a large crop in Brazil puts it down, taking a position against the Argentine peso, keeping your ear to the ground in City pubs or even fighting off a take-over bid are not experiences leading to a breadth of human sympathy. Dealing constantly with money can, and does, give one an alert sense of power; it makes a few of the best all-rounders there are. But, combined with a fairly protected upbringing, it tends to be a narrowing way of life and has the result of leaving many City men – and I say this at the risk of being called pompous myself – with a personality that verges on the immature.

Turning specifically to ethics, Cyriax did not deny that over the years there had been relatively few major financial scandals. Rather, he believed the problem was 'the City's somewhat uncritical belief in the value of its services' – a lack of self-criticism that could all too easily shade into the characteristic English vice of hypocrisy. 'Take as a concrete example what happens before there is a merger that is going to enhance substantially the price of a share,' he argued. 'In this situation, the jobbers like to be given the word, so they can lengthen their books in the share in question and so meet the anticipated demand; their argument, deeply believed, is that this is necessary to preserve an orderly market. Looked at another way, of course, it makes them money . . .' Finally, Cyriax ventured into waters rarely if ever braved by his own paper:

> The City, unlike many foreign centres of wealth, does not have a sex life of its own. The strip clubs in London are in the West End; the symbols of the City are much more the Rolls-Royce, the Old School tie, the bowler hat and the commuter train. Wealthy City men have their *pied-à-terre*; my own impression – it can clearly be no more than that – is that they seldom contain mistresses. The male world of the City, in fact, is not particularly concerned about sex in any form, with the single proviso that if the form is an unusual one, it must not be made public. If it is – as it was in the case of a businessman whose very successful enterprise was found recently to contain a string of brothels – then credit dries up. 'One does not want to finance a man as foolish as that,' said a banker to me on that occasion.

'I have always felt,' Cyriax concluded, 'that this remark, a combination of realism and stuffiness, of high moral tone and thin moral content, is typical of attitudes in that last home of the business gentleman, the City.'[2]

There was no doubt about which gentleman set the tone during the 1950s. 'During my time in the City,' the merchant banker Michael Verey recalled, 'those who hadn't been to Eton were striving for Eton standards, and the Eton ethos dominated from Kim Cobbold, Governor of the Bank of England, downwards. Good Etonian standards means a total trust – if you say you'll do something, you'll do it. On the whole, dealing with Etonians in the City, you had a sense of confidence that they would behave impeccably.' Through endless meetings, and through the reports he received from the Bank's trusted ears and eyes, Cobbold (like his mentor Montagu Norman before him) kept the closest possible tabs on the City as a whole – and, crucially, was always available to offer a view about the appropriateness of a course of action or choice of person. In February 1958, for instance, David Colville of Rothschilds asked if there would be any objection to him going on the board of Bowmakers, a finance house increasingly active in hire purchase. Cobbold said he would prefer not, but it was up to Colville; and he added, in his note of the meeting, 'I should certainly have felt strongly about this if one of the Rothschild family considered going on'. Lord Longford, Chairman for eight years from 1955 of the National Bank of Ireland (one of the eleven London clearing banks), regularly attended Cobbold's quarterly lunches of the bank chairmen. 'He was in my eyes curiously reluctant, though far from intellectually unable, to tell the bank chairmen what he wanted done,' Longford wrote shortly after leaving the City. 'It was part of his whole philosophy that only in the last resort does the Governor impose his views on the various techniques open to him.' That was almost as true of the Governor's senior subordinates as it was of the Governor himself, but occasionally things had to be spelled out. In the late 1940s the youngish Kenneth Cork (who had recently become senior partner of the accountants W. H. Cork, Gully & Co, specialising in insolvency work) badly needed to establish the whereabouts of a Mr Price, in order to locate his assets:

> I knew the Bank of England would have his address, so I wrote to them saying please could I have it. I received a very pompous letter back, saying the Bank of England didn't disclose such information.
> I wrote back saying that unless they gave me, an officer of the Court, the information I needed I would have the Governor of the Bank of England up for private examination for refusing to co-operate with an officer of the Court. There was a deafening silence.
> Later, I received a telephone call from a senior partner of Freshfields (lawyers for the Bank of England), who were enormously influential in the City, asking if I would go and see him. Duly flattered at being called up by an important person on some great matter, I went along. I was ushered up to his elegant office, he greeted me in a friendly way, and gave me coffee,

and then we went on to discuss hunting, shooting and fishing (which I knew nothing about) and sailing, which I did. Then he said: 'You know, your father was a difficult man, too. I hear that you are trying to have the Governor of the Bank of England up for private examination in front of the bankruptcy court. I don't think that's a very good idea.' I replied with the dignity of youth that I was entitled to do so. He smiled. 'I think we can arrive at a solution. Shortly, I will be called out of the office. On my desk you will find an address. If you are ungentlemanly enough to read it, you will obtain the information you want. In the City, we don't call the Governor of the Bank of England up in front of the Court, and it won't help your career very much.'[3]

It was a story that Cork, a future Lord Mayor, enjoyed telling in his anecdotage – not least because when he did find Mr Price, someone had already tipped his quarry off.

Ultimately the City obeyed the Bank of England because its leaders had been inculcated in the virtues of a hierarchical society and it barely occurred to them not to do so. Before the loosening-up of the 1960s, strong echoes remained of Shonfield's exasperated retrospective description of Norman as 'the apotheosis of the English cult of the administrator as artist-leader – a kind of *Künstlerführerprinzip* which sees the only satisfactory means of communication in the action itself'. The Bank itself generally continued to keep a low profile and, Norman-style, tried to justify its actions only when there was strictly no alternative. This in turn encouraged the City in its deeply held belief that the Bank always knew more than it was letting on. On neither side of the relationship was there much self-reflection, but in 1962, apparently in the context of an internal course being devised on central banking, the Bank's Maurice Allen and Humphrey Mynors, economic adviser and Deputy Governor respectively, assembled a list of propositions circumspectly called 'Opinions Attributed to Central Bankers'. Ten of the best were eloquently indicative of how the world seemed from the Threadneedle Street fortress:

A central banker needs a sense of smell. Analysis is only theorising but may be encouraged when it confuses critics.
No civil servant understands markets.
Politicians do not sufficiently explain the facts of life to the electorate.
Central bankers should always do what they say and never say what they do.
Taxes are too high.
Bankers are people who do, in the main, what you wish. The rest are fringe institutions. They do not exist.
Wave the big stick if you like, but never use it; it may break in your hand. Better still, try wagging your finger.
In banking, the essence of solidity is liquidity.
Never spit into the wind.
Always lean against the wind.[4]

The pragmatism of the final two propositions was important. The Bank's rectitude, high-mindedness and even arrogance were all, in the eyes of the City, admirable qualities; but refusing to face up to facts – even awkward facts – would almost instantly have lost the respect of the practical City man. That still, of course, left plenty of scope for prejudice, which was perfectly acceptable if it was the right sort of prejudice.

Everyone who mattered knew almost everyone else who did. 'Tommy' Gore Browne, who joined Mullens in 1948 and became Government broker a quarter of a century later, was (an obituary noted) 'known for his encyclopedic knowledge of City people and the intricacies of City relationships'. Such knowledge – knowing with whom one could safely and quickly do business – underpinned the single most important element, outside as well as inside the Stock Exchange, that made the City such a formidable machine: trust. An investor's confidence in his stockbroker, a broker's in his jobber, a shipowner's in his insurance at Lloyd's, and a trader's in a bill of exchange on London – all came down to trust. 'In London I have on occasion signed an underwriting agreement for £2,000,000 or even larger amounts without any more than verbal agreements noted on a piece of paper, for most of the issue,' the financier Edward Beddington-Behrens (founder of the issuing house Ocean Trust) proudly remarked in his 1963 memoirs. 'In this small circle we all know and trust each other and every man's word is his bond. Whilst this standard remains, the City will always hold its own.' Taking it on trust . . . Pat (later Lord) Limerick was an aspiring young accountant when he joined Kleinworts in 1958 and soon discovered how the T-word worked in practice:

> I used to go with the General Manager along to the Bank of England, to see the Head of the Discount Office, and he'd say, 'How's business?' and we'd say, 'Well, quite good. We've added a few new good accounts, and the size of the balance sheet has expanded.' And so we talked a little about the balance sheet and liquidity and so on. They were fairly ritual questions. He'd say, 'How about trading? What sort of year?' And we'd say, 'Well, perhaps it was a little better than last year.' And that was really the sum total of the information that he got. Underlying this informal relationship was the unwritten but vital expectation that we would tell the Bank immediately of the first sign of trouble . . .

It was Hilton Clarke putting the questions, and his own recollections of the annual process were more laconic: 'You had to learn how to look at a balance sheet and in that respect you either got a lot of help or no help at all from the merchant bankers themselves.'[5]

Reputation – slow to gain, quick to lose – was integral to the reposing of trust. In April 1952 Cobbold received a visit from Sir Edward Peacock of Barings to discuss 'the Barings-Morgan venture in Canada for which permission has just been granted'. However, there was a hitch: 'Morgans are anxious to go in under their own joint names. Barings do not like the use of their name outside this country. I expressed a good deal of sympathy with this view.' Morgan Grenfell in due course came round, for a few months later Peacock was able to reassure Cobbold that 'it is not intended to use the Baring or Morgan name, at least for the moment'. By this time probably the most influential figure at Barings, at least in terms of upholding its reputation, was Lord Ashburton, who as Alec Baring had come to 8 Bishopsgate in 1923 and whose great-great-grandfather had led the firm for much of the early nineteenth century. Ashburton himself was never formally senior partner, but on important matters there was no partner more consulted. 'My father had always had a tremendous reputation for sound judgement,' his son, Sir John Baring, would observe years later, 'though he was never immensely involved in the sense that he was never immensely keen about the work of the City. But he had an extremely good judgement – and because he was not tremendously keen was very good at saying no to doubtful things which people might get enthused about.' Another Baring, Peter, expressed even better this eternal (post-1890, pre-1995) family characteristic on Ashburton's death in 1991: 'His approach to the firm's work was highly individualistic, being rooted in an acute sense of quality. He was disinterested to a degree that, when faced with anything less than first-rate, he could quite readily become uninterested.'[6]

Another utterly trustworthy, almost equally old-fashioned firm that liked to say 'no' was Cazenove's – 'Cazenove's should be hard to get and not available to all-comers,' would be one of Hornby's parting *dicta* in 1970 – while at Kleinworts, perhaps mindful of its over-commitment to German trade finance in the 1920s, the emphasis was on not allowing avarice to distort judgement. 'Your best investment is your backside,' Ernest Kleinwort was wont to tell his son Kenneth. 'Buy something and sit on it.' And: 'Never be greedy. Never try and buy at the bottom and sell at the top. Always let somebody else have the final ten per cent. In the long run, that'll pay you and you can let the greedy wolves cream off the top of the milk.'[7] Annual profits at merchant banks were still just as likely (certainly in the 1950s) to be six as seven figures, while running expenses remained relatively modest, and the wonderful world of systematic, Monday-to-Friday proprietary trading – as opposed to taking quietly lucrative advantage of inside information, as and when opportunities arose – would have been beyond the ken of these City elders.

So much depended on personal judgement – often nuanced, occasionally inscrutable. When Cobbold was asked by Catto in January 1947 to comment on the Chief Cashier's suggestions about how to implement a policy of giving Bank staff more outside training, he replied,

'I should have a slight preference for starting with a rather more neutral Accepting House and certainly not with Kleinworts, although I agree that they might well offer the best training in credit work.' What precisely was the charge behind that word 'neutral'? It was less than two years since the end of the war, and Kleinworts of course had strong German connections, but in general, if not quite a Barings or a Rothschilds, it was hardly a Philip Hill or a Singer & Friedlander. Six years later, as Governor, Cobbold received a visit from a Colonel Buxton. 'Rea Brothers were looking for a Chairman who would give them a bit of a lift,' he noted, 'and Colonel Buxton was anxious that he should be somebody who could perform watch-dog functions. Sir Cyril Jones had been mentioned. I thought he would be good for the watch-dog function but not much for the other side.' Towards the end of his governorship, in July 1960, Cobbold gave his views to the Treasury about who should (or rather, should not) succeed Lord Cromer as economic minister in Washington: 'He would not trust the judgment of Sir Mark Turner . . . Mr Charles Villiers was agreeable and sensible, and his wife would be an asset, but he was perhaps a bit lightweight for this job.'[8] Turner had been an ebullient corporate financier at Bensons since the 1930s, while Villiers was a rising force at Helbert Wagg during the 1950s, but neither was quite right, with apparently no supporting evidence required.

It was all about picking the right people – definitely an art rather than a science – and by the early 1960s there were few more renowned people-pickers than Jocelyn Hambro, who after a distinguished war (in which he had lost a leg) had joined the family bank. 'If he decides somebody really isn't quite up to it, he's made his mind up,' a friend recalled about Hambro in his prime. 'He might not appear to know someone very well; he was very quick to notice details about them; he either thought highly of them or he didn't, but he was never neutral about people, but you would never guess that when they were talking to him. He would treat people exactly the same.' The family lawyer described the behaviour at meetings of this quintessential Hambro: 'He would ask one question. If you answered that question correctly, he was quite happy to let you get on with it. If you didn't, then you knew you'd lost . . .'[9] The Victorian precept may have been that 'Servants talk about People: Gentlefolk discuss Things'; but in the City it was the clerks and their managers who shuffled the paper round and looked after the nuts and bolts, the partners who concentrated on the all-important human dynamics and, especially if blessed with the right family name, liked to think of themselves as 'generalists'.

Behind the outer reserve that tended to characterise the City's top men, it was a highly intimate, personal world. 'If I want to talk to the representatives of the British banks or indeed of the whole financial community,' Cobbold famously observed in 1957, 'we can usually get together in one room in about half-an-hour.' The two men whom he most relied upon in maintaining the Bank's City relations were Hilton Clarke and Sir Kenneth Peppiatt, and both relied heavily on exercising the personal touch. 'I always reckoned you were idling if you were sitting at your desk in the Bank, I loved putting on my top hat and going round and dropping in on the banks and having a chat,' Clarke recalled. 'The managers and partners were not always that busy. It was lovely just to sit there and have a glass of sherry and talk about what was going on in the world outside . . .' Humour mattered – one of the City's gravest charges against Siegmund Warburg was his reputed lack of that commodity – and Edmund de Rothschild was one of many who used it to leaven the daily routine. 'One of our regular callers,' he remembered about New Court days, 'was a bill broker named Toby [Dick?] Jessel, who wore a monocle and had the knack of reading upside-down. One day I left among the papers on my desk a note with the words "Mr Toby Jessel is an Old Ass" – and when he read it his monocle fell out, bouncing on the end of its cord.' City humour tended to be of the practical, non-cerebral variety, as when Tom Harvey of Mullens negotiated for the Prudential a huge exchange of stock valued at more than £30m in 1958. The historian of Mullens tells the story:

> To celebrate this event, the partners commissioned an engraved goblet from the distinguished artist Laurence Whistler. It was to be presented to the Prudential directors by the Mullens partners at a luncheon at Moorgate. At the end of a convivial meal, Tom Harvey left the room to fetch the goblet for the formal presentation. Then the partners and guests sitting at the table heard from outside the room the crash of breaking glass . . . Tom Harvey walked into a room whose occupants were reduced to horrified silence: the Mullens faces turned to the door were white. But in Tom Harvey's hands was the Whistler goblet, unharmed. Passing the pantry, he had seen a tray of used glasses; three he reckoned, dropped on to the tiled floor, would make about the right sound . . .[10]

The ensuing laughter must have been, for the rather staid men from the Pru, a liberating moment.

Within individual firms, even if they had formally become limited companies, the partnership culture was almost as strong as ever. Rather like the Governor of the Bank of England towards the City, the senior partner set the tone, in effect laying down what was permissible and what was not; while as Hugh Peppiatt observed about becoming a partner at Freshfields in 1960, it was virtually 'a one-way option', in that 'it would never have been in our minds to suggest a partner should go because he was somewhat weaker than the others'. The partners of a merchant bank or stockbroking firm based themselves for much of the day at their desks (often shared) in the partners' room (almost invariably oak-panelled): there they discussed the day's concerns, listened to each other's phone conversations and generally knew what was going on. The artist Simon Elwes painted in the mid-1950s two delightful conversation pieces of these rooms, first at Morgan Grenfell and then at Cazenove's, the latter painting nicknamed by staff 'A Study in Still Life' because of the seniority of the eight sitters. One partner, Geoffrey Akroyd, complained that his face was too red, but Elwes was adamant, 'I paint as I see'. He did, however, place a bright-red *Directory of Directors* on Akroyd's desk, which helped to take one's eye off his face.

The partnership at Cazenove's was one of the most cohesive in the City, and something of its flavour comes through in the 'Betting Book' which was kept in the partners' room for recording wagers on really important matters. 'Mr Frank Holt wagers £1 that the South Africans will win one Test Match of the next series played in England. This wager was made with Mr R. A. Hornby. 16th June 1953.' And: 'A.H. lays J.R.H. £6 to £1 that Northamptonshire will not win the County Cricket Championship of 1959.' Hornby recorded on the opposite page that 'Johnny [Henderson] gave up the sponge and paid up like a man on Aug 17th'. Occasionally there were wagers on financial matters or forthcoming general elections, but the book's most celebrated motif concerned cherry stones. 'After a somewhat unusual helping of cherries taken by one of the lunchers,' it recorded in July 1960, 'a market developed in the number of stones. Prices made were 35–40 by E.R.B. and 32–35 by H.I. J.R.H. bought at 35 and was paid. The price made up at 41.' At the bottom of the page was an addendum, dated 15 September: 'On further consideration, the luncher concerned remarked that it was a *slightly* bigger helping than usual!' The cherry-lover was Philip Cazenove (who, when spelling out the name 'Cazenove' over the telephone, would say 'v for veterinary surgeon'), and in May 1963 there was a subsequent entry in the book: 'Subsequent to his retirement, P. de L.C. joined us at lunch, cherries being again available: after a liberal helping a market developed in stones, opening price 40–45. No business. 42–47 was then quoted. J.R.H. bid 45 at which price C.R.P. [Purnell] sold the stock; the m/u price was 54. This did not take account of any stones which may have been swallowed.'[11]

Neither rhetorical nor emotional extravagance was encouraged in the partners' rooms and board rooms. A trio of 1990s' obituaries give suggestive snippets. Montagu Norman's nephew, Mark Norman of Lazards, was 'a man of deep integrity and feeling, which he disguised by a hearty manner'. Peter Samuel of M. Samuel & Co was, for all his 'shrewd judgement', a 'modest, kindly man who was sometimes disconcertingly silent in meetings if he felt he had nothing vital to say'. And, as Chairman of British & Commonwealth Shipping and a bastion of the City's shipping community, Sir Nicholas (later Lord) Cayzer was 'a tall, commanding figure and a stickler for punctuality and routine'. Each of these three was a capable businessman, none was remotely an intellectual – nor would have wanted to be. In Evelyn Baring's despatch to New York in October 1949 – 'You will surely be expecting some intelligent (!) comments from me on the results of devaluation and the effect it may have on our business and political prospects' – the self-deprecating parenthesis said much. The incorrigibly analytical Sir Oliver Franks found it hard to make much impact on the City as Chairman of Lloyds Bank between 1954 and 1962, while when towards the end of the 1960s Churchill's last Private Secretary, Anthony Montague Browne, began to work for the discount house Gerrard & Reid, he was forcibly struck by City people's 'sheer lack of intellectual horse-power or any general historical or political knowledge'. Independence of outlook was rarely welcomed. 'He spoke his mind and was disinclined to back off from an argument, irrespective of the protagonist's seniority,' the obituarist of Sir Charles Pickthorn (who joined Schroders in 1959) noted, adding that 'such qualities did not make for easy success in the City'. The City may have rubbed along perfectly adequately without egg-heads, but its lack of imagination was depressing. A small but symptomatic instance was the cause of understandable discontent in January 1957:

> You know just how I am placed. I have every reason to be grateful to Hambros for bread and butter; but not for the bread of life. They have not known, or cared to find out, how to make the best use of me, and, inevitably, I have been rusting. Yet I am pretty sure that my capacities, such as they are, remain relatively unimpaired; I have time and energy to spare; my health gives me less trouble than might be expected at my age; and my material necessities and obligations still require that I should keep going . . .[12]

The very able Harry Siepmann (writing here to a former colleague) had retired three years earlier as an executive director of the Bank of England, and this was a sad end to a notable career.

The ultimate disloyalty to the club (or school or tribe) was political incorrectness. The classic case in the post-war City was Lord Longford. He was hardly the City's type of person anyway, and the National Bank of Ireland (head office in Old Broad Street) was obviously not one of the 'inner' banks, but what really stuck in the gullet was his unrepentant allegiance to the Labour Party. 'You could work for years in the City as a director and lunch out every day, without meeting a recognisable Socialist,' he would note soon afterwards, adding that Franks (educated at Bristol Grammar School) had been regarded by the City as a socialist, though he was in fact a Liberal. Accordingly, 'Conservative ex-Ministers, whether it is they or their Party who disappear from office, and whether their departure is voluntary or involuntary, are soon bedded out with lucrative full-time or part-time appointments in the City.' Indeed, 'if a case arose where this didn't happen it would be thought that something was seriously wrong'. Longford himself tried hard to bridge the gap – even, prior to the Bank Rate Tribunal debate in 1958, acting as an intermediary between Cobbold and Gaitskell – but to little avail. He was even, he recalled, blackballed 'for a famous City club', and he quoted the reasons of one member: 'I love Frank, but I'm not going to have him coming in here and getting all the advantages of the City when he and his lot want to smash it all up'.[13]

Longford, for all his Etonian credentials, might also have struggled to gain admission to 'the best club in Europe': Lloyd's of London. Membership remained pretty enviable at the end of the 1950s, an insider telling Paul Ferris that 'there is no business in my experience where such an agreeable income can be earned in such agreeable surroundings with a minimum of output'. Lunch in 'The Captain's Room', the permanent exhibition of Lord Nelson's relics, the red-and-black liveried attendants serving the Committee, the traditional lines along which business in 'The Room' continued to be done – all these things, and many others, contributed to the old-world atmosphere and reinforced the unique cachet. Joseph Wechsberg, writing in the *Sunday Times* in 1963, was utterly smitten: 'To work for Lloyd's is a passion rather than a profession. Young men grow up in the very special atmosphere of The Room, learning the traditions, unwritten rules, Lloyd's esprit de corps and code of decency. They like the sense of freedom, the relaxed schoolboy atmosphere, the anonymity . . .' Ferris found less horseplay than at the Stock Exchange ('not until late in the afternoon, when smoking is allowed and work is dying down, is there much sign of leg-tripping and paper-slinging'), but the retrospective evidence of one member, Terence Higgins, was that 'it was not unknown for either a broker or an underwriter in the box to drop a stinkbomb somewhere and cause a disturbance', while 'if anybody made a noise – a loud guffaw or dropped a pile of books – everyone in the underwriting boxes would pick up their pen and hammer away rat-tat-tat-rat on their metal lampshades'. This introverted world did not suit everyone. The future gossip columnist Nigel Dempster drifted into Lloyd's in his late teens, working for a broker, but he soon left – on the grounds that 'it was just like boarding-school where I had been from the age of six'.[14]

If there was one man who, in hindsight, would come to symbolise the old Lloyd's of these seemingly untroubled years, it was Peter Green.[15] The family firm was Janson, Green & Son, where his father was a leading marine underwriter; he was educated at Harrow and Oxford; an energetic yachtsman, he was one of the founders in 1957 of the Admiral's Cup; and by the 1960s he was becoming one of the market's heavyweight presences.

Brusqueness characterised his attitude towards brokers, while towards prospective underwriting members a certain rough charm was disguised by his habit of asking them to write a blank cheque and then, having pocketed it, flatly announcing: 'That's the risk you are now undertaking as a Name at Lloyd's.' Like the market itself, he was by his lights essentially honest; but also like the market, there was a lack of self-criticism, an arrogance, that would prove well-nigh fatal.

There was a strong public image of Lloyd's – mighty, unimpeachable, A1 – but relatively few outside the City, probably even after the Radcliffe Report, were even aware of the existence of the discount market, arguably the quintessence of the City code in action. At the very heart of its being, and seemingly oblivious to the invention of the telephone, was the ritual morning visit by a few dozen bill brokers to the main banks, whether merchant, clearing or overseas. In fact, the real business *was* largely done by phone, later in the day, but the morning visit was crucial in establishing what cash and bills were available to the market. In 1960 Ferris memorably described the 'top-hatters' on their morning round:

> They can be seen queuing at a bank, four or five in a row on a hard bench, striped trousers tugged up to show uniformly dark socks, polished pointed shoes neatly side by side on the cold tiled floor. Time passes. A *Times* is exchanged for a *Telegraph*. There is an absence of documents, a bland assurance that events are being coped with – as indeed they are, since between them the discount houses are smoothing out the surpluses and shortages of the banking system . . .
>
> When his turn comes the bill broker steps into the office of whatever official the bank employs to deal with the market, says 'Good morning', pulls up a chair and begins to talk about cricket or last night's television. This is hearsay: it would be unthinkable to let an outsider accompany a bill broker on his rounds . . . But all the versions agree: sport, weather, a little politics are usually touched upon, and there may be some innocuous banter, before either reaches the naked word 'money'. The official who looks at his watch and sticks grimly to business will be the exception; he will also be unpopular. Ideally the relationship between the two is of equals who show an equal amount of respect. If anything the bill broker is inclined to be more deferential. He lives by the goodwill of the banks. He's the one who does the asking and even though he may not receive the compliment in return, he's likely to call the bank official 'Sir' at some point in the conversation, probably the beginning. 'Sir', of course, has two meanings in Britain. To many it smacks of servility, but to the middle-class Englishman who has been to a public school it is a recognition signal, flown on a hundred occasions. It means: 'I am an Englishman. I hope you are too. Let us get together. You are probably as good as me. I am definitely as good as you' . . .

Whatever the formalities later in the day, involving cheques and bundles of bills as well as telephone calls, everything was predicated on the personal touch. 'All we do is deal by word of mouth: our word is our bond and speed is the key,' Fred Arnold (Trinder's successor as Manager of Union Discount) declared with some pride on returning from a business trip to the States during which he had been unfavourably struck by the American insistence on putting everything in writing. And, he added to disbelieving colleagues, 'Do you know, in some of the New York banks they have phones in the loos! That's too much, we're not having that here!'[16]

In all parts of the City, not least in the discount market, it was advisable (certainly up to the 1970s) to have a head for the hard stuff. Lord Hampden would recall in 1988 the distinctive experience thirty years earlier of being a trainee at Lazards, still at 11 Old Broad Street. One of the bank's most formidable managers, Mr Vanstone, invited the young 'orchid' on the alcoholic equivalent of an Outward Bound course:

> We started promptly at noon at the Long Bar at Slaters, opposite the old Stock Exchange, with half a pint of draught Guinness. This order was repeated before moving sharply up Adam's Passage (passing Lord Exeter's AAA 1 registered Rolls-Royce and Mr Lionel Fraser's more modest chauffeur-driven Wolseley outside Helbert Wagg) to Pimm's Red House in Bishopsgate where we had two large 'gin and Its'. After a modest lunch (Mr Vanstone thought food interrupted the more enjoyable part of the lunch hour), I was asked whether I would like coffee or a glass of port, couched in such terms that I knew what answer was wanted. We retired to a dive in Old Broad Street called El Capataz where we downed large glasses of vintage port. I staggered, totally out of control, into Lazards' august Banking Hall to be met by the ever vigilant but ever tolerant staff manager, who took one look at me and said, 'Part of the training, I suppose.'[17]

*

How, apart from such initiation rites, did one join this club? Often it was a case of waiting for the call. 'Mr Keswick [W.J. ('Tony') Keswick of subsequent Bank rate 'leak' fame] came in for a word about Hudson's Bay Board,' Cobbold noted in January 1956. 'Alanbrooke may drop out and he wants another "top hat" Director ... He also wants one or two City Directors for Alliance [the insurance company] in 35–50 age group.' Yet sometimes it paid to be more proactive. 'He has got a directorship in one of Colonel Lancaster's companies (Bestwood) and another in the Guardian Assurance,' Monckton memoed in February 1958 about Enoch Powell, not long after that politician's resignation from the Macmillan government. 'Has turned down industrial offers. He would like to get something in the City ...' Powell had been Financial Secretary to the Treasury – sufficient qualification for a City directorship. Many had no meritocratic qualification at all for enjoying the City's rewards. 'His son was a partner later in the firm,' Sir Peter Daniell of Mullens would tell an interviewer in 1990 about Sir Kenneth Peppiatt of the Bank of England.

'That sounds a slightly incestuous relationship?' the interviewer tentatively probed. 'Well, he loved the firm,' Daniell replied. 'He wanted his son to be a stockbroker. So he asked Derrick [Mullens] I suppose whether he would take Robin his elder son. And he said yes. And he eventually became a partner.' The interviewer continued to press: 'That's a very cosy relationship. Isn't that sort of relationship rather frowned on nowadays?' Daniell's unambiguous response spoke for a whole way of life in the old City: 'Could well be and damned stupid I think. Doesn't do any harm at all.'[18]

In practice, and to its discomfort, the City was under sociological scrutiny, albeit intermittent, from the late 1950s onwards, beginning in January 1959 when Tom Lupton and C. Shirley Wilson published their pioneering analysis of 'The Social Background and Connections of "Top Decision Makers"', taking the recent Parker Tribunal evidence as a starting point. Their City sample comprised the directors of the Bank of England, the 'Big Five' clearing banks, fourteen merchant banks or discount houses and eight leading insurance companies – in all, 422 leading City figures. The available data was incomplete, but at least 199 had been to Eton, Winchester, Harrow, Rugby, Charterhouse or Marlborough. Only two were known to have attended a state elementary school. Less than half had been to university, almost invariably Oxford or Cambridge. As for London clubs, the most popular were Brooks's (57), White's (51), Carlton (48), MCC (34) and Athenaeum (28). Lupton and Wilson also traced many kinship connections, both within the City and between leading City figures and eminent politicians and civil servants. Lord Kindersley, for example, a Bank of England director and a prominent Tribunal witness, was part of an influential web. 'His brother married a niece of the 2nd Earl of Iveagh, father-in-law of the Rt Hon Alan Lennox-Boyd, MP, Minister of State for Colonial Affairs. The Earl of Iveagh is father-in-law to a sister of another Conservative Minister, the Rt Hon John Hare, MP, whose wife is sister to Viscount Cowdray.' Cowdray in turn controlled the Pearson group of companies, which had a controlling stake not only in Lazards but also (from 1957) in the *Financial Times*. Inevitably, within the sample, there was a huge number of multiple directorships. All in all, it showed a comfortably entrenched ruling class, and despite its publication in a fairly obscure academic journal it received considerable publicity. So much so that four months later, at the City of London Society's annual luncheon at the Mansion House, that body's self-made Chairman, Harley Drayton, was compelled to declare, boldly if unconvincingly, that 'if a young man has talent, integrity and courage, not only is there nothing to stop him going to the top, he will almost be kicked there'.[19]

The tide of opinion, however, was running the other way. That same year a notably intelligent stockbroker (and former journalist), Victor Sandelson, contributed 'The Confidence Trick' to Hugh Thomas's collection of essays on *The Establishment*. In it he stressed the numerical smallness of the City élite and invoked the memorable words of Richard Fry of the *Manchester Guardian*, about 'men 10 feet tall, who are the heads of the big merchant banks and who have the ear of the Governor of the Bank of England before anyone else'; argued that this élite 'are not so much members of the Establishment because they have succeeded in the City', but that 'they have succeeded in the City because they are members of the Establishment'; and stated as an undeniable truth that although the occasional outsider might acquire wealth in the City, his chances in the main City institutions were slender 'unless he is backed by respectable inherited wealth and a suitable education'. Sandelson's main concern was with the ten-footers – the inner élite, on easy terms with the Governor of the Bank of England – but Anthony Sampson in his 1962 inspection of the City was struck by how school and family background were just as important, perhaps even more important, to the standard six-footers:

> The City remains the unchallenged bastion of the minor public schools, and within the square mile you hear more talk about men's schools, background, and above all their families, than anywhere else except perhaps in the Guards. The waves of the meritocracy, of examination wallahs and managerial revolutions which have swept through the civil service and industrial corporations, have hardly rippled the City. The 'Old Boy Net' which has become a sheepish or satirical phrase in other areas, remains a venerable concept . . .

Martin Gordon was in his mid-twenties when in 1963, after Harrow, Oxford and two years in the Army, he applied for a job at various merchant banks. Every interview, to his exasperation, included a question about which school he had been to – until at last he went to Warburgs, where there was no such question. Presumably none of these interviews took place on a Friday, because that was the day, as decreed by City tradition, when one wore one's old school tie.[20]

The face had to fit. Take the top-hatted discount market, where in 1958 the firm of Cater, Brightwen & Co (Cater, Ryder & Co from 1960) managed five *Who's Who* entries from its nine-strong directorate. The Chairman, Sir John Musker, led the way:

> Kt. cr. 1952; Banker; Chairman, Cater, Brightwen & Co., Bankers since 1935; Hon. Treasurer London Municipal Society since 1936; b. 25 Jan, 1906; o.s. of late Capt. Harold Musker, JP, Snarehill Hall, Thetford, Norfolk; m. 1932, Elizabeth, d. of Capt. Loeffler, 51 Grosvenor Sq. W1; two d.; m. 1955, Mrs Rosemary Pugh, d. of late Maj.-Gen. Merton Beckwith-Smith. Educ.: privately; St. John's College, Cambridge (BA). Member LCC for City of London, 1944-49. Lieut., RNVR, 1940. Address: Shadwell Park, Thetford,

Norfolk. T.: Thetford 3527; Suffolk House, 117 Park Lane, W1. Clubs: White's, Royal Yacht Squadron, Jockey Club Rooms (Newmarket).

The four who were not asked to contribute an entry included Hugh Colville – the person who, as in effect manager, made the firm tick. He had originally come as a junior clerk and then worked his way up; he was always there, Monday to Saturday, unlike the twice-a-week directors; the directors called each other by their first names, but he was always 'Colville'; and he obdurately refused to wear a top hat, instead sticking to a battered old black Homburg. There was a similar division of labour in the other dozen or so discount houses, and their character remained deeply gentlemanly well into the 1960s and indeed beyond, perhaps typified by the two long-standing directorship qualifications at Smith St Aubyn: *not* to have been to Harrow and an ability to carve ham. The young Robert Fellowes, for example, would have had no compunction about joining Allen Harvey & Ross in 1963. His father was the land agent at Sandringham, while he himself had, after Eton, taken a short-term commission in the Scots Guards; and at 45 Cornhill he became a director, leaving in 1977 to become the Queen's Assistant Private Secretary. Fellowes had played a couple of times for Norfolk, but the best-known cricketer in the discount market was J.J. Warr, the Cambridge University, Middlesex and even England fast bowler. A big man (who once won the Binney medal for apprehending a villain in one of the narrow alleys off Cornhill) and a superb raconteur, he was one of the managers of Union Discount who in due course became a director. His Test record was in fact modest, but at least he had played at the highest level, and the discount market was the sort of place where there was huge kudos attached to such an achievement.[21]

The old-established merchant banks were more explicitly dynastic. The most extreme example was Wm Brandt's Sons & Co, which in 1959 had five directors: R.E. Brandt, W.E. Brandt, H.A. Brandt, W.A. Brandt and J.M. Brandt. Similarly there was – as there had been for well over a century – only one ruling family at Hambros. Olaf, Charles and Jack Hambro were all powerful forces in the post-war firm, and indeed in the City (Jack Hambro being at one time a director of twenty-four companies, including five investment trusts), while from the 1960s it was the conscious policy of Olaf's son Jocelyn to maintain what he liked to call 'enlightened nepotism'. The reality lying behind the first word was the fact that partners' sons made it beyond the trainee stage only if they were given the nod by the departmental managers for whom they had worked; the reality behind the second was the pinning-up in the dealing room of a large genealogical chart, for young non-Hambros to study, with unmarried and eligible female Hambros underlined in red. At Lazards the ruling family figure was the second Lord Kindersley, whom Sampson found 'a tall, confident banker with a military moustache', possessing 'the quiet, superior manner of hereditary bankers'.

The genes, however, did not always guarantee either aptitute or application. 'He and his labrador would be picked up in the Rolls by the chauffeur and driven from Grosvenor Crescent to the beginning of the park, precisely 300 yards, where he would get out and walk the dog to Admiralty Arch where the car would pick him up again and take him to the City, and the labrador home,' David Montagu recalled about his father, the third Baron Swaythling, senior partner of Samuel Montagu & Co on strictly hereditary grounds. 'I thought he must be a great banker to have to go off to the office every day. In point of fact, what he used to do when he got there was his herd books or answer letters from the English Guernsey Cattle Society.'[22]

Gradually and grudgingly, however, some of the oldest houses began to open their doors, the classic cases being Rothschilds and Morgan Grenfell. David Colville had been an 'assistant' to the partners at New Court since 1946, after being recruited from Lloyds Bank, and was renowned for his investment expertise. On 30 June 1960, the same day that the retirement of Anthony de Rothschild was announced (five years after his stroke had removed him from action and created a serious hole at the centre of the bank), Colville was made a partner – the first person outside the family to receive that honour. He was followed in October 1961 by Michael Bucks, thirty-seven years after coming to Rothschilds. 'There's not enough talent to go round,' Colville openly admitted on the occasion of this second break with precedent. 'To attract the right people, it's useful to point out that it's possible for partners to come from outside the Rothschild family.' Even so, the family itself remained firmly in control, and everyone knew that the bank's fortunes would depend heavily on how the new generation of Rothschilds (specifically, Evelyn and Jacob) shaped up. If Rothschilds was hardly a byword for dynamism, neither was Morgan Grenfell, where Vivian Hugh Smith's son, 'Rufie', succeeded to his father's chairmanship in 1956, as well as to his title of Lord Bicester of Tusmore. 'Rufie is not very bright, but everyone likes to do business with him' was the line uniformly given to Diana Mallory as she prepared an article in 1961 for *Queen* on 'The Merchant Bankers'. And, off her own bat, she had some fun:

> At sixty-three, he must be the perfect merchant banking specimen of the old variety. His recreation is shooting. All his life he has played a straight bat, kept his shoulder to the wheel and his eyes peeled for what the other feller's going to do. In every way he is utterly conventional. Eton, Sandhurst, the 17th Lancers, and married to Dorothea, daughter of the 3rd Lord Northbourne. Brooks's and the Cavalry Club, of course . . .

It was under his genial chairmanship that at last in 1961, with the promotion to the board of the very capable Kenneth Barrington of the new issue department, 'a player became a gentleman'.[23] In Great Winchester Street as in St Swithin's Lane, this represented a tacit recognition that even the most comfortable houses could no longer afford wholly to ignore how the world outside was changing.

The clearing banks, notwithstanding their provincial, non-establishment origins, were hardly more progressive. In March 1950 Cobbold discussed with Lord Balfour of Burleigh, Chairman of Lloyds, the bank's future chairmanship. Balfour, noted the Governor, 'thinks that [Sir Jeremy] Raisman would make a good successor to himself, though he has slight qualms (which I fully share) about the wisdom of this appointment in the best interests of Lloyds'. Accordingly, the two men agreed that 'to carry on as No 2' was 'what Raisman really wants'. Not long afterwards Balfour reported to Cobbold that his board had 'now decided to leave the question of succession to him in the Chair entirely open', but that 'they have, however, made it clear that, if he were run over by a bus, Raisman would succeed'. Three years later the question of the succession was raised again, and this time Raisman let it be known that he would prefer not to be considered. What was the problem? He was outstanding intellectually, had had a very successful career in the Indian civil service and had been Vice-Chairman of Lloyds since 1947. His age perhaps told against him (though sixty-one was hardly ancient in the City of the 1950s), but the crux seems to have been that (to quote the tactful words of one historian of the bank) Raisman 'sensed some anti-Semitic feeling still lurked in parts of the City'. His face, in other words, did not quite fit, in an era (lasting to the 1960s) when the non-Etonian chairman of one of the 'Big Five' was the exception, not the rule. Lupton and Wilson found that Eton provided just under 30 per cent of their boards, while Sandelson was struck by the 'array of military talent' in those five boardrooms – an array 'which might have justifiably terrified Britain's enemies in the field, but must surely have the opposite effect on the acute men of Zurich'. Apart from these military philosophers, and the inevitable sprinkling of the great and the good, also on the boards of the clearing banks were some who were essentially private bankers rather than joint-stock men. They were typified, in Longford's eyes, by Tony Acton, one of the National Bank of Ireland's English directors and for many years a managing partner at Lazards. 'He has had many advantages beyond that of the average or typical man,' Longford wrote in 1964. 'He was a leading figure and excellent athlete at Eton; is indubitably wealthy; is fond of beautiful objects, and can afford to acquire them. He is the husband of a charming and popular wife. In short, the beau idéal of the successful old Etonian in the City, an inside member of the club if ever there was one . . .'[24] At all the clearing banks there was an unambiguous divide between the directors and the managers. Most of the directors worked to an undemanding gentlemanly routine, but an exception was Barclays, where there was a strong culture of selecting its leaders from the bank's traditional ruling families and expecting them to put in the hours. The atmosphere was far from grimly Stakhanovite – Sampson described Anthony Tuke, Chairman for eleven years from 1951, as 'an amiable and witty Wykehamist, with a bushy grey moustache and a habit of quoting Greek or nursery rhymes in his annual reports' – but something of the Quaker virtues still lingered, and indeed Tuke himself was known as 'The Iron Tuke' on account of his attacks on the laxness of government economic policy.[25]

Nevertheless, the City élite *was* broadening, not least through its absorption of lawyers and accountants – those indispensable 'service professionals', as Paul Thompson has called them. The trend had already started to become apparent between the wars, but quickened from the 1950s, in part a reflection of the new complexity of company finance following the 1948 Companies Act. Gordon Richardson was an accomplished barrister before going to ICFC and then Schroders, while Philip Shelbourne was a matchless figure at the Revenue Bar before moving to New Court in 1962 to become the third non-family partner in Rothschilds. As for accountants, Sampson in 1962 listed the four dominant firms (Peat Marwick Mitchell, Price Waterhouse, Deloitte Plender Griffiths and Cooper Brothers), declared that 'in the City their incantatory names have acquired a respectability equal to Barings' and added that 'the arrival of their senior partners, in bowlers and black coats, far from suggesting calamity, brings calm and confidence'. Sampson, though, perhaps underestimated the residual hostility towards the profession. When Francis Holford joined the metal brokers Rudolf Wolff in 1967, as a trained accountant, he soon became aware that he and his ilk were looked on as 'parasites', with the result that 'for the first six months I wasn't allowed to see the books or the accounts'. Without argument, the leading City accountant by the 1960s was Henry Benson of Coopers. He was a largely self-made man, born in 1909 and educated in South Africa, and advanced through sheer ability, integrity and unbending resolve. 'While I was at Coopers it was my life, and practically everything else was subordinated to it,' he recalled in old age. 'The dedication was, for practical purposes, complete.' More specifically:

> The big client-getting job began after the war. Getting clients is the most extraordinary feature of one's life. The first thing is, you've got to get known. I used to look in my diary every week and if I had a free lunch date then I would see whom I could ask for lunch. I wanted either to get something from him or to tell him something. As soon as people realised

you will give service, they pass it on to their friends and it quickly gets round the City. It's an astonishing thing and it grows of itself . . .

Significantly, one obituarist noted, 'it was his enormous concentration, clarity and logical thought that impressed rather than any brilliance of ideas'.[26] He was on the City's wavelength, and he would not have achieved as much as he did if it had been otherwise.

Another group becoming in some sense part of the City élite, and owing everything to financial muscle, were the leading figures in the key investment institutions. The decisive episode – a microcosm of the larger shift from individual buccaneers to grey institutional giants – occurred on 1 August 1956, at the Extraordinary General Meeting of the Birmingham Small Arms Co, held in the ballroom at Grosvenor House. The company's recently ousted Chairman and Managing Director, Sir Bernard Docker, was attempting to achieve reinstatement, despite well-substantiated accusations of misuse of BSA funds. Insisting that he had 'never paid a single bob for my wife's clothes' (Lady Docker was famous for her furs and jewels), he stated that if the Prudential, the largest shareholder in the company, had been seeking an independent investigation into BSA, he would regard this as 'a slight impertinence'. The room was filled with Docker's supporters, and after he sat down not only were 'succeeding speakers critical of the part played by the Prudential', but 'when a representative of that company went to the microphone there was uproar'. Eventually he managed, quietly but firmly, to introduce himself – 'My name is Leslie Brown, and I represent the Prudential Assurance Company' – but the report in *The Times* suggested that he continued to be given a far from easy ride:

> When he began to say that last January his company had begun to receive reports and criticism from various sources, there were cries of 'What sources?' 'In our view,' the speaker went on, 'the reports merited investigation. It is our clear policy in the Prudential not to interfere in the management of industrial companies in which we invest.' (A shout of 'Thank God for that!') 'In this case where there were no other large individual shareholders whom we might consult we came to the conclusion we had a duty to all the shareholders as well as to ourselves, to take some action.'

Docker lost the eventual vote by a wide margin, and Brown's short, effective speech entered City lore. Six years later, by which time the power of the institutions was starting to become even more apparent, Sampson tellingly described Brown, a Fellow of the Institute of Actuaries and 'sometimes talked of as the most powerful man in the City':

> He is stocky, quietly-spoken, with a neat bristly moustache and twinkling eyes, who talks in a frank, humorous way about the problems of his job. He

worked his way through the Pru after leaving grammar school in Croydon and taking his actuarial course. He is not part of the 'old boy net' of the City: he does not drive in a Rolls, or shoot grouse, and there is no mention of him in *Who's Who*. He is sometimes seen at stockbrokers' lunches or financiers' banquets, but he prefers to stay in Holborn and wait for people to come to see him. In the Stock Exchange, his name is a legend: for a new issue can depend on the raising or falling of his eyebrows . . .

There were of course other important figures in the investment institutions, but no institution came close to rivalling the Pru's market clout. Having a billion pounds to invest, the old City was reluctantly forced to accept, spoke for itself.[27]

Some outsiders slipped easily into the City establishment, or at the least found a ready enough acceptance. Alexander Ross, for example, was the son of a small-town New Zealand timber contractor and became the world's youngest governor of a central bank, before in the mid-1950s being head-hunted by Gibson Jarvie, founder of United Dominions Trust (UDT) and father of British hire purchase. Ross was in his late forties when he came to the City and immediately proved an outstanding success, becoming in due course chairman of UDT and expanding its business. Helped no doubt by being a well-built six feet two inches (he had rowed in the Empire games), he would be remembered as 'a natural leader to whom people often turned for a decision'. Another foreigner, K.C. Wu, became in his own way a City legend. He had joined the Bank of China as a fifteen-year-old, and from 1944 was the courteous, patient, infinitely resourceful head of its London office. The communist revolution of 1949 was inevitably a hiccup, but Wu ensured that it disrupted his bank's overseas trade and foreign exchange business as little as possible. Over the years he became a symbol of continuity, while the natives came and went, and on the occasion of the Bank of England's tercentenary conference in 1994 the former Governor chairing the opening session announced, 'Ah, K.C. is here. Now we can start.'

The aptly named Roy Merrett had travelled rather less far. 'Mr Merrett is a successful and well-regarded underwriter at Lloyd's and has at his desk for training the son of the chairman of Lloyd's,' an internal memo to the Midland Chairman early in 1956 explained why he was due to propose the vote of thanks at Midland's annual meeting. 'He began his career as a clerk without influence and has built up a large business by his own efforts . . . Mr Merrett lives at Purley . . . He is keenly interested in current affairs . . .' Merrett was also commended for his 'generally progressive outlook', so he was probably not one of those outsiders who came to the City and, while flourishing there, fell in love with the place and its traditions. Such an outsider was Godfrey Chandler, who as a sixteen-year-old arrived at Cazenove's in 1941 having achieved the highest mark for the whole of

England in the commercial mathematics examination set by the London Chamber of Commerce. The tight-knit, paternalist atmosphere at Tokenhouse Yard at once reminded him of the Cheeryble brothers from *Nicholas Nickleby*, and over the next four and a half decades he rose to become the *éminence grise* of the firm, indeed its very soul and conscience.

Finally, among self-made men receiving more or less unequivocal acceptance, there was the outstanding figure of Lionel Fraser. Some found him rather pompous, and because of his father's background as butler to Gordon Selfridge he got the unkind nickname of 'the butler', but his ability was beyond dispute. In addition to being Chairman of the Issuing Houses Association and the dominant force for many years at Helbert Wagg, he had a clutch of important directorships, outside as well as inside the City. But for all his manifest intelligence, he did not question the City's deepest values and assumptions, and in 1963 his rather bland memoirs were characteristically entitled *All to the Good.*[28]

The borderline between establishment and non-establishment could be a shifting one, not always easy to define, and during these years there were four stand-out City heavyweights who at one time or another found themselves on different sides of that divide: Louis Franck, Siegmund Warburg, Kenneth Keith and Harley Drayton. Franck was a quick-witted Belgian who came to dominate Samuel Montagu and, specialising in arbitrage, made a huge amount of money in the gold and currency markets. 'Henry,' he once companionably remarked to Henry Benson after inspecting his own portfolio of investments, 'I'm living on the income of the income of the income.' Franck acquired a CBE and represented Samuel Montagu on the Accepting Houses Committee, but for all his prowess he does not seem to have been quite 'one of us', and in the end there would be a huge, acrimonious bust-up at Samuel Montagu with the youngish David Montagu.[29] As for Warburg, despite his astute use of the well-connected Billy Straker-Smith, one of the very few old Etonians at Warburgs, to smooth his path with the City establishment, the acceptance that he achieved even after the momentous Aluminium War was both partial and grudging. 'Warburgs have proved themselves to be the most successful Merchant Banking House to have been formed since the war,' Evelyn Baring conceded to an American correspondent in 1961. He even added that Warburg himself now counted as 'a good friend of ours'. Nevertheless, the fact remained, Baring went on, that 'in our old-fashioned way we should not want to appear on a prospectus with them'.[30]

There remained something of the incorrigible outsider, too, about Keith, for all his best efforts. 'His marriage to a daughter of Lord Stonehaven was dissolved three years ago,' a magazine profile noted in 1961. 'He has since taken up shooting and farming and become a member of four decent clubs, including White's. Keith is tough and capable and immaculately tailored.' Sampson interviewed him at about the same time and found 'a tough, casual, feet-on-the-desk banker, with swept-back grey hair and a brisk way of talking'. Cobbold, meanwhile, continued to raise at least half an eyebrow. 'He asked my advice about Philip Hill,' he noted in April 1960 about a visitor who was moving his business base from South Africa to London and had been offered a position there. 'I said that I saw nothing against it, but just wondered whether he and Keith would easily get on together.' Keith's achievement was undoubted – he had built up Philip Hill into a major force, partly through his deliberate recruitment of qualified men, especially lawyers and accountants – but he would never, perhaps not to his deepest dismay, be everyone's cup of tea.[31]

It is a shame that table plans do not talk. On 18 June 1962, in the Chairman's private room at Midland's head office in Poultry, Monckton hosted a small luncheon party: Charles Clore and the property developer Jack Cotton were on either side of him; two senior managers were across the table; and the remaining seat was occupied by H.C. Drayton. The 'Drayton Group' itself was based in 117 Old Broad Street, which Sampson had recently visited to interview Harley Drayton, 'a big, bucolic man with a red face, white hair brushed back, a monocle dangling over his pin-stripe suit, and tall, laced boots'. It was a generally favourable sketch that Sampson produced, stressing in particular the way in which Drayton had defied conventional City opinion in the mid-1950s by backing commercial television and, after early losses, making a great deal of money out of it. He also allowed Drayton, puffing at a cigar as he looked out of the window from his old leather chair, to ramble on:

> The twenty-fifth chapter of Ecclesiasticus is the only economic system which ever worked. It tells you how to run a sinking fund, how to manage a business, how to make an issue . . . My job is the picking of high executives. You have to make yourself available when they're in a hole. Otherwise I don't interfere. Sometimes I just give them a bit of advice like, 'Boys, be careful, copper's going up' . . . Most of the City has the idea that you must conform. What stops most people in the City is snobbery. You don't have to worry about being popular. You have to take risks and stick your neck out. If you're an artist, nobody worries if you're a failure: but in the City it's regarded as a crime almost against the Holy Ghost to make a mistake . . . You have to have a burning belief in what you're doing, and sell it to people who will back you. I'm still prepared to see people in my bath at eight in the morning, and I'm ready to do a deal at midnight . . . The City by and large lost its position after the first world war and still more after the last war – but most people didn't tumble to it. Between the wars, big money was still in the hands of merchant banks – Lazards, Rothschilds, Barings, Morgans – each with one, two or three million. But with inflation, and the rise of the new financial institutions, one or two millions became chicken feed . . .

Drayton was also, Sampson noted, 'proud of having the Earl of Airlie's son as one of his protégés' – the Hon Angus Ogilvy had joined the group in 1952, eleven years before his marriage to Princess Alexandra.

There was, however, a murkier side to the picture, accurately reflected by Drayton's failure to feature in an honours list. Writing a quarter of a century after Drayton's death, the financial journalist Barry Riley provided the most lucid summary of how Drayton ran his affairs very much along the old-style lines of the City's investment trust groups:

> They specialised in interlocking shareholdings, so that central control could be exercised over a large empire. In certain respects the Drayton Group was almost like a Japanese *keiretsu*, with a string of industrial satellites including Rediffusion, BET, BICC, United Newspapers and to some extent Eagle Star. In the Japanese style, there was a strong whiff of exploitation and market-rigging. Some 17 investment trusts were controlled by the same clique of directors, and supported various group companies. It became the practice for the trusts to have annual rights issues even though they stood at discounts of 30 to 40 per cent to their underlying assets. This stream of issues damaged outside investors, but enabled the interlocking shareholdings to be strengthened as the trusts underwrote each others' unwanted rights . . . At the centre of the Drayton Group was a kind of mini-merchant bank called Securities Agency which did the deals; it handled not only the big new issues and mergers, but even the routine share transactions of all the trusts, creaming off a slice of commission in the process. One of its articles of association stipulated that half the profits, after payment of a fixed dividend, should go to the directors, who of course comprised the élite of the group . . .

From the late 1950s Drayton's methods were being publicly criticised, especially by Harold Wincott; and during the weeks immediately preceding his death in April 1966 the 117 Old Broad Street Group (as it was still called during his lifetime) was under fire for having allowed two of its trusts, Second Premier and Garda, to be used, in Riley's words, 'as the highly-geared vehicles for lucrative share options for group executives'.

Yet the surprise is that after his death he should have been memorialised in the *Dictionary of National Biography* by none other than Sir Antony Hornby of Cazenove's, an epitome of the City establishment. The tone was warm (with no fewer than three mentions of Drayton's 'courage' in financial matters), while Hornby argued that the absence of any official recognition of his achievements was 'perhaps on account of his unwillingness to compromise and conform', adding that 'had he been a better public speaker he might have been more widely known'. Of accusations of malpractice, however, there was not a word.[32] Perhaps, though, there is no great mystery. Drayton was, in his bluff way, an attractive figure; he was a notably generous host (Hornby paid particular tribute to the quality of his claret); he brought much valuable business to

Hornby's firm; and, most importantly, the two men were as one in their deeply felt conviction that the complexities of finance were no business of the prying eyes of the fourth estate.

If one was not a ruddy-faced Suffolk landowner, it could be a long, hard and not necessarily availing struggle to achieve an adequate degree of acceptance and thus respectability. The classic case, notwithstanding the claims of Warburg and others, was arguably Walter Salomon. His troubles began in December 1945 when he submitted an application for his firm (Walter H. Salomon of 59a London Wall) to become a member of the newly established Issuing Houses Association. One of his three references was National Provincial, but the IHA chairman, having made enquiries to that bank, could reach only one conclusion about Salomon's application: 'Definitely *no*'. Salomon continued to press, and early in 1948 an internal IHA note summed up the case against him:

> Mr Randell of Bank of England says he is a very pushing individual – German Jew – who established himself here in 1938. They don't know a lot about him, but think it would do no harm to let him cool his heels a bit more. They wouldn't be sorry if he wasn't accepted for membership.
>
> They don't consider him a bank and if he did accept bills they wouldn't be rediscountable. He knows all about foreign exchange business but they 'haven't caught him out yet'.
>
> He is related by marriage to Ernest Binden of New Trading Co. His office is full of foreigners.

That was damning enough, but just for confirmation two directors of Brown Shipley were sounded out soon afterwards: 'They said he was a very pushing man – a go-getter but very shrewd. A German Jew. Everything they had done with him had been perfectly satisfactory.' This final sentence gave food for thought, so the IHA went back to the Bank of England, to elicit the views of A.C. Bull at the discount office. The Bank's man did not disappoint:

> He doesn't like the way he [i.e. Salomon] sets out to consider himself a banker merely because he has a clearing number and has got himself in the *Bankers' Almanac*. . . His very varied activities are against him rather than for him . . . Mr Bull quoted the old saying, 'I do not like you Dr Fell, the reason why I cannot tell' . . .

Salomon's application was duly turned down, but two years later his firm, by now based at 13 Copthall Court, merged with – and effectively took over – the more or less moribund merchant bankers Rea Brothers. The Bank of England continued to take the line that Salomon and his firm 'do not entirely conform to the usual City standard', even though it was 'difficult to pin down any real reason' for its dislike; at the same time it accepted the awkward position in which the IHA found itself, and later that year Rea Brothers did become members.

During the rest of the decade Salomon became an increasingly prominent City figure, as well as persuading the Hon Gerald Legge (the future Earl of Dartmouth and husband of the flamboyant Raine) to become a director of Rea Brothers. Yet even as late as 1963 he was a far from contented visitor to the Old Lady:

> He launched into a long justification [Maurice Parsons recorded] as to why his firm should have an account with the Bank of England. It was along the lines that one might have expected, namely, that it was a mistake on our part to confine ourselves to the limits set by recognised associations such as the Accepting Houses Committee. He made some play with the word 'growth' and implied that by our present formula we were tending to discriminate against the most active and adaptable elements in the City, amongst which he classed himself as an outstanding factor. I asked him why he was so anxious to have an account here. Was there any reason why the lack of it should be regarded as hampering his business? He replied that while he would have no intention whatever if he had an account here of advertising the fact, it still remained that, by some mysterious means, the fact that he had no account at the moment did become known and could be regarded as reflecting on the status of the firm.

The syntax was shaky, but the sentiments – on both sides – were unmistakable. What was so wrong with Salomon? His antecedents were unfortunately German and Jewish, and admittedly he had a tendency to criticise in his strongly guttural voice such hallowed institutions as the Stock Exchange, but was that really all? Perhaps not, for Riley would dub Salomon a 'rather sinister' figure, whose 'group of trusts centred on the tiny merchant bank Rea Brothers' and whose 'financial tangle has still to be fully unravelled in the 1990s'. Yet whatever the truth of that charge, it is also worth quoting another retrospective judgement on him: 'A fierce fighter in many causes, he deserves immortality for writing "Human" on an official form, somewhere abroad, that asked to what race he belonged.'[33] This latter judgement is all the more striking for coming from John Fforde, the post-war Bank of England's official historian and a long-time employee at that very institution which so disparaged Salomon.

Another Jew, the king of mail order, also found the going hard. In March 1961 the Bank of England's Mynors politely summoned Isaac Wolfson, following press reports that Wolfson was buying the Anglo-Portuguese Bank:

> His intention [Mynors noted] is that this bank should continue for at least two years in every respect exactly as it is. He has bought it for the benefit of his son, Leonard G. Wolfson, now aged 33. Great Universal Stores has now become an institution. One has to hire people to do the business, to check their budgets, but otherwise it is too large to make possible keen

personal and family interest. He wants his son to be a great man, perhaps a politician. He should be in the City. He should be a banker. . . Mr Wolfson seems to see in the Anglo-Portuguese Bank primarily a means of satisfying these paternal ambitions . . .

We also had a long but one-sided talk on Meissen china, old masters, Great Universal Stores, the Wolfson Foundation, Israel and hire-purchase finance.

In June there was another visit from the great man, but this time, though Wolfson 'still envisages his son as a great banker', he did have to admit that it was 'disappointing that he goes to the Test Match [Australia was playing England at Lord's] while his father starts work in the office at 7.10 a.m.' There was a nice end to Mynors's memo: 'I resisted his request that I should telephone for a Minicab into which he could be seen stepping from the front door of the Bank of England. This led to an interesting disquisition on the economics of Minicabs.'[34] Presumably there never would have been a Wolfson dynasty in the City, but certainly there was no encouragement from the keeper of the keys.

Yet in the end, questions of establishment and non-establishment can deceive: for, as in any occupational sphere, what mattered to most people in the City was doing a reasonable job of work and earning an adequate reward. Anthony Foord, for instance, was a wartime Squadron Leader and peacetime solicitor who during the 1950s very successfully ran the money-brokers Long, Till and Colvin. By the early 1960s he was in a position to ease out of the City and concentrate on good works, as a county councillor and leading figure in the Suffolk Preservation Society. Victor Wood had also been in the war, but as a Sergeant, in which capacity he met one of the partners of Wedd Jefferson and was recruited into that jobbing firm after the war. Quite without any City background, 'Woody' was so naturally able that he became in due course the acknowledged doyen of the short-dated end of the gilt-edged market. 'He was a great man for saying, "Last half million here, come and get it quickly. 64th cheaper off",' Sir Nigel Althaus of Pember & Boyle recalled. If Wood was one of the pioneer working-class traders – eventually such a distinctive City phenomenon – then Ron Adams was another, epitomising the characteristics that the East End brought to the financial and commercial markets. He became a floor member of the London Metal Exchange in 1958, replacing a retired Colonel, and soon became renowned for what one press profile called 'his speed of response, biting sarcasm, and colourful language'. Or, in the measured words of a more staid figure on the LME, 'he could talk you into a paper bag and out again'. There was also, in a class of his own, Ephraim Margulies, eventual Chairman of the S&W Berisford commodity trading empire. 'He was the very caricature of the émigré, self-made businessman,' a financial journalist who had met him noted after his death in 1997. 'Asked what his business philosophy was, he said in his thick eastern European accent: "We buy a little, we sell a little, and with God's help we make a little." I haven't made this up, I kid you not. He really did say it. He was also as bent as a nine bob note . . .'[35]

None of these four would probably have disagreed about the bottom line: that the City, for all its possibilities of congenial company, was ultimately about making money. Some were disenchanted, most rubbed along, but the very roundest pegs were those for whom the making of money was their prime motivation in life. One such, a self-made underwriter, was Leonard Toomey:

> By the late sixties and early seventies I had a very large income relatively speaking. I could tell you to the penny about my earnings because I've noted everything down since I've started work. In 1947 when I came out of the army and went back into the firm, as a married man, I earned £478 gross. Ten years later I had an income of about £16,000. . . I've always saved. When I earned a pound a week, I'd save half a crown. There's a lot of people who are very land-rich in Lloyd's but have no money; they haven't always got the cash, as I have. I could realise all my assets, other than my house, today because I've only got to lift the phone and get hold of my stockbroker and sell everything . . . The only other interests I've had apart from Lloyd's is the stock markets. My wife and I both saved our money and I'd buy a share. I used to sit in bed reading balance sheets; it's not been very pleasant for my wife. Except that she's quite wealthy now . . .[36]

*

'Luncheon at the Baltic Exchange,' the Prime Minister noted in July 1962 soon after a famous by-election. 'I made a little speech to some 1,000 or more brokers & clerks. I had a markedly enthusiastic reception from an assembly of typical "Orpingtonians".' Harold Macmillan's laconic diary entry was a reminder that for every City man owning a house in the country, there were many – even at a quite senior level – who week-on-week seldom ventured beyond the suburbs and their daily City routine. For example, the Stock Exchange's Chairman through most of the 1950s, Sir John Braithwaite, was in every sense at home in Hampstead Garden Suburb; while 'the father of the Stock Exchange' (and of the cricket writer E.W. Swanton) was for many years Treasurer of Forest Hill Cricket Club in leafy but undeniably suburban south London. In general, at partnership level within the Stock Exchange, it all rather depended on the sort of firm. At the meritocratic Phillips & Drew, for instance, the top five on the list in spring 1955 were Sidney Perry of 16 Courteney Gate, Kingsway, Hove, Sussex; Neville Williams of 54 Cheniston Gardens, Kensington, W8; Bill May of Sunridge, 34 Mount Pleasant, Cockfosters, East Barnet, Herts; Lionel Potter of 87 Blacketts Wood Drive, Chorley Wood, Herts; and Jonathan Rashleigh of 23b Stanhope Gardens, South

Kensington, SW7. None of these addresses was exactly Brixton or Balham, but nevertheless there was a distinct contrast with the five counterparts at Cazenove's: Antony Hornby of 12 Radnell Place, W2; Geoffrey Akroyd of 9 Lowndes Court, Lowndes Square, SW1; Frank Follett Holt of Riffhams, Danbury, Essex; Peter Kemp-Welch of Morleys, Great Hallingbury, Bishop's Stortford, Herts; and Philip Cazenove of Cottesbrooke Cottage, Northampton. A few years later Paul Ferris observed that the public expectation of 'Stock Market Men' was that they were comfortably off rather than spectacularly so and that they lived 'in the stockbroker belt, not less than ten and not more than forty miles from Charing Cross, preferably to the west or south of London'. The reality, he added, more or less chimed with the stereotype.[37]

Still, even in high-tax, post-war Britain there remained some decent-sized country piles belonging to City men. Somerhill (now housing no fewer than three schools) was a huge, sprawling Jacobean house near Tonbridge that was owned by the well-connected Jewish bullion broker Sir Henry d'Avigdor-Goldsmid, who for motives more of duty than pleasure acted as High Sheriff of Kent and Master of Foxhounds to the Eridge Hunt; and Sezincote in Gloucestershire was Cyril Kleinwort's eighteenth-century house, famous for a bedroom described in 1960 by the journalist Drusilla Beyfus:

> The shattering impact of the decor conspires to bring out the Nabob in whoever occupies it. The whole room glows in flamboyant easternised colours, in Chinese yellow and peacock blue, in gold and turquoise. The gigantic four-poster is considered to be one of the great beds of the century. It took nearly three years to complete, hundreds of yards of material were needed for the drapery, and the interior decorator had to stand on a ladder for three days whilst he stitched a canopy into one piece . . .

Gardens also mattered. Sir David Bowes Lyon, younger brother of the Queen Mother and a partner for many years in the merchant bank Edward de Stein & Co, was remembered on his death in 1961 more than anything for his wonderful garden at Walden Bury in Hertfordshire: 'It was laid out in the style of Le Notre and the superb avenue of beeches was planted by Sir David's own hands. It is a delightful combination of the formal and informal.' His other principal recreation was shooting – a pastime shared by merchant bankers as utterly different as Rex Benson and Kenneth Keith. Other favoured activities inevitably included hunting and fishing – 'Alec,' Evelyn Baring reported to an American banker in February 1955 about the movements of Lord Ashburton, 'is up on the Tweed, enduring the most terrible weather but having absolutely first-class fishing' – while the prominent Lloyd's underwriter Kenneth Butt was far from alone in being an active and successful bloodstock breeder. Butt's City career had almost foundered back in the 1930s, when as a young insurance broker he had done business for his father, after his father had had budget secrets confided in him; it was principally through the flourishing 200-acre Brook Stud, near Newmarket, that the family name reacquired some respectability.[38]

City men rarely write their memoirs, but *A Gilt-Edged Life* is the attractively honest title of the amiable, thoroughly unpretentious memoirs of Edmund de Rothschild. Never a City heavyweight, though not entirely a negligible force, he devoted much of his post-war energies to sorting out the magnificent but badly overgrown azalea gardens at Exbury near Hampshire that he had inherited from his father, eventually opening them to the public in 1955. During the week he stayed in London, while weekends were spent with his wife and children at Inchmery House, overlooking the Solent near Exbury House. His memoirs unself-consciously evoke a happy, middlebrow way of life:

> During summer weekends we all used to play tennis and croquet, and make the most of the swimming pool Elizabeth [his wife Elizabeth Lentner, who came from a family of prosperous Austrian Jews] built for us at Inchmery. In the evenings I would show films, usually concluding with an early, silent Mickey Mouse cartoon which my father used to show me . . . We would also play a lot of games, especially word games, such as Bali and Scrabble, which Elizabeth used to enjoy, as well as mah-jongg and card games – bezique, bridge, Slippery Anne (or Hearts) and misère . . .[39]

It is a pleasing description, consistent with the almost entire absence in de Rothschild's book of the arts, literature and ideas or any sense of the changes in British life and society – or, indeed, almost any reflection on the City itself.

Jocelyn Hambro, though similarly born into the merchant banking purple and similarly no intellectual, was a more major – certainly more motivated – City figure. During the 1960s and beyond he was largely responsible for keeping Hambros more attuned to changing times than most of the other merchant banks. Yet to read his biography, Andrew St George's *JOH*, is to be struck by how his lifestyle was not so different from that of a nineteenth-century Hambro.[40] For a quarter of a century from 1946 he lived at Coopersale House near Epping in Essex, a handsome property (eventually acquired by Rupert Murdoch) from which the City was easily commutable. The house itself overlooked a four-acre lake; there was a working farm of 125 acres, in which Hambro took an active interest; and with gardens (including a huge kitchen garden), orchard and woods, it was indeed 'the perfect place to bring up the boys'. Life at Coopersale was run along strictly regimented lines (involving the services of a butler, housemaid, cook and kitchen maid, nanny, nursemaid and three gardeners); each Sunday afternoon, following the ritual of clearing the woods, there was a grand bonfire; and as many weekends as possible featured rough or more formal shooting. Racing was another passionate interest of Hambro's, while he was also a keen golfer. As for his cultural tastes, he much preferred John Buchan to Jane Austen, and Fats Waller (especially 'My Very Good Friend the Milkman') to Beethoven.

Was the younger generation any different? Probably not, to judge by *Queen's* feature in February 1960 on 'The Twenty Most Eligible Men'. The City men in that enviable category included Viscount Chelsea (a tall twenty-two-year-old whose favoured haunts were Château de l'Horizon, Gstaad and Perth Races) and Edmund's cousin, Evelyn de Rothschild, whose impeccably old-fashioned credentials nevertheless permitted one humorous nod to the *Zeitgeist*: '28, very tall, dark banker. Has an estate in Bedfordshire. Flat in London. Jensen, Fiat, horses. Haunts: Hotel Lotti, El Morocco, Mirabelle, and Cowdray Park. Interests: Breeding, hunting and riding horses, polo, farming, gardening and ice-cream.' If life in the end comes down to getting and spending – as Wordsworth, in a sour moment, had it – then the City's upper and upper-middle crust remained the masters of both these needful activities. Jobbers were especially renowned for living for the day, and in April 1967 a Phillips & Drew memo gave brief lifestyle notes on some of the partners of Durlachers:

> *Esmond Durlacher.* Keen fisherman. Has lease (2 months in each year for the next five years) of 'Goldeneye' which was Ian Fleming's house in Jamaica.
> *Jack Durlacher.* Is a cousin of Esmond. Owns racing cars and his latest appears in the new film 'Grand Prix'. Skis every winter.
> *Ronnie Clarke.* Defined as a 'member of the Chelsea set'. Interested in fast cars. Went to Stowe.
> *Basil Sharp.* Naval background. Interested in improving his property in Hampshire. Has a flat in the West End. One son going into the Navy.
> *Richard Durlacher.* Son of Esmond. Married two years ago to daughter of senior partner of R. Raphael & Sons which was one of the weddings of the season. Plays squash.
> *David Johnstone.* First-class golfer and collected a blue at Cambridge for it. Went to Marlborough. Young and gay. Married.[41]

The summer of love was just around the corner, but these were lives – predicated on prosperity, on action rather than reflection, on an unwavering sense of social and cultural identity – familiar among City men at almost any time in the previous century and a half.

*

Paul Ferris, researching his study of the City, spent a day (probably in the summer of 1959) in and around the Stock Exchange, including some time in the visitors' gallery:

> It was a hot afternoon, and some of the brokers had replaced the jackets

of their dark suits with light linen coats. At one end of the gallery a girl was painting the scene in oils on a small canvas. A dark, elegant young man of about twenty was standing by her, pointing out people he knew down below – he seemed to be cousin or brother or nephew to half the Stock Exchange. His suit was near-black; his shirt had narrow blue and white stripes, and his collar was white and glassy. 'I think chaps without their jackets look scruffy,' he said at one point – I had taken my jacket off and was carrying it over my arm, and the interesting thing, I thought, was that when he turned a moment later and caught my eye, I was the one who blushed. He was so beautifully self-assured – no wonder, if you hate the City, you really do hate it hard . . .

It is a marvellous and, in its way, timeless vignette of City haughtiness – yet arguably the post-war City that Ferris so skilfully anthropologised was in a period of *decline* in terms of its prestige and general status. 'Before the Second World War,' the historian Hugh Thomas noted in 1959, 'the City was probably more powerful than industry, but the relationship has now been altered in industry's favour, due to the decline of British world-wide commercial eminence.' Moreover, whatever their relative standings, both City and industry shared an inability to attract young talent. Instead, 'the really bright people all went into the Foreign Office or the Treasury,' as the future Stock Exchange Chairman Sir Nicholas Goodison self-deprecatingly noted in the context of the late 1950s, when he joined his family stockbroking firm, H.E. Goodison & Co. More bluntly (but perhaps less typically), a non-City man, the educationalist Harry Ree, recalled being told at his public school, Shrewsbury, that 'only shits go into the City'.[42] Either way, the underlying fact was that those with something positive to offer were not, on the whole, making a beeline for the square mile.

The City, with its traditional secrecy and instinctive dislike of explaining (let alone justifying) its activities, hardly helped itself. In 1952 as the official, bicentenary history of Glyn Mills was approaching completion, the Bank of England was told that that bank was 'in two minds whether to make it a private issue or for sale to the public'. The problem with the latter course, apparently, was that 'the history would be reviewed in the press and might give an opportunity to evil-minded persons to make it the occasion for an onslaught on the iniquities of the Banker'. Roger Fulford's history *was* publicly published, though with only a briefish, uncontentious epilogue devoted to the twentieth century. Almost two decades later Edmund de Rothschild was asked about the desirability of an authorised history of Rothschilds, in order to blow away the persistent myths attached to that house. 'It wouldn't do to have an arc light or a microscope,' was his seemingly definitive reply. The prevailing attitude was simple: the less said, the better. The practice of underwriting at Lloyd's, right through the post-war years up to the end of the 1970s and perhaps even beyond, exemplified the cult of secrecy. 'It was to a large extent,' one experienced underwriter, Stephen Burnhope, reflected, 'a state of affairs perpetuated by the practitioners, guarding the secrets of their craft as zealously as any member of the Magic Circle protects that mysterious interaction of white bunny rabbits and top hats.' The market's outside investors, the Names, were kept almost completely in the dark, and even if they sought guidance, there was little insight to be gained from the specialist press. In the City generally, few firms or institutions saw it as either a duty or in their own self-interest to shed light on what they were doing. The upshot, inevitably, was a high degree of public ignorance. 'Even when we allow for the fact that much of the criticism of the place is emotional, made by people who really don't want to learn the facts, it is still true that the City of London remains a mystery to the great majority of British people,' Harold Wincott mildly, but firmly, pointed out in 1958.[43] In one sense, of course, the City benefited from its deliberate and (in its own terms) successful cultivation of a mystique: life is much simpler, and more comfortable, if one's actions – and the basis for those actions – are not questioned. On the other hand, there was a clear danger of being exposed to ill-directed but potentially lethal attacks, should the political climate change. There was no entirely satisfactory solution.

Two fiascos for the City Establishment in quick succession – first the damaging revelations made to the Bank Rate Tribunal, then the Aluminium War – decisively tipped the balance towards the beginning of a greater openness, even if this was mediated by the burgeoning public relations industry. For a generation of City leaders accustomed to the mores of silence, it was not an easy process. On 6 May 1958 (after the Tribunal, but before the War) Cobbold held a small dinner party at the Bank for the purpose of what he described to Monckton as 'a gossip' about 'public relations and all that'. Those present were Cobbold and Mynors of the Bank; the clearing bankers Monckton, Franks and Robarts; Reid of the Accepting Houses Committee; Ritchie of the Stock Exchange; Sir Walter Barrie of Lloyd's; Charles Trustam of the British Insurance Association; and Richard D. Hyde of the Baltic Exchange. Unfortunately, though the menu survives (turtle soup, roast saddle of lamb with new potatoes and French beans, soufflé femina), there is no record of the discussion. However, it is clear that a small committee was formed, comprising Barrie, Ritchie, Franks and Trustam, with these four eminences meeting exactly a month later at Lloyd's under Barrie's chairmanship. At the outset of their discussion, Barrie emphasised that 'any suggestion of promoting publicity was anathema to Lloyd's', though he did concede that 'in regard to the question of luncheon entertainment at Lloyd's, some thought had already been given to the possibility of widening the scope so as to include those who did not necessarily "think the same way as we do", e.g. leaders of Trades Unions, Labour Members of Parliament, etc'. The most incisive questions were asked by Trustam: 'Was the desire to do something to increase the size of our business, or to defend the business we have? Was there not a danger that any steps which were taken could lead to prejudice and possible adverse political implications?' However, he went on:

> If it were true that there was a feeling abroad that a vicious group existed in the City Square Mile, which impression could be exploded, then perhaps something should be done. Mr Trustam felt, however, that whilst a film would be useful to achieve the desired end, lectures would not suffice. Even with a film, however, it was no use wallowing in history; perhaps just a little history, but then, as far as Insurance was concerned, concentrate on the construction of a building, showing the viewer the need for insurance from many angles . . .

A consensus emerged, during the general discussion, over two questions:

> Appearances on television were not helpful. It seemed to be the policy of the 'interviewer' to put questions which of necessity forced one on the defensive, and it was not a good thing to appear always on the defensive before the public . . .
> If more people were to be entertained to lunch, that should not be restricted to our own circles. One's friends were probably converted, but one's opponents – political or otherwise – needed to be cultivated. On the other hand, however, such people might agree with one over the luncheon table, but it was another thing to get them to say in public what they found it easy to say at lunch . . .

It was all, in short, very difficult; and though later that year the City Public Relations Committee held its first formal meeting, chaired again by Barrie at Lloyd's, little was achieved either then or subsequently, and after March 1960 the Committee apparently petered out.[44]

Press relations – for so long distant and spasmodic, with an undeniably condescending attitude on the part of the City's grandees – were almost as problematic. The official body that sought to ensure favourable treatment was the Banking Information Service, based at 10 Lombard Street with Sir Cecil Ellerton of Barclays as a key figure by the late 1950s. Periodically it organised press luncheons, usually at the Reform Club, where in June 1959 Monckton and two other bankers were invited to meet Maurice Green of *The Times*, John Appleby of the *Daily Telegraph*, Gordon Tether of the *FT*, Sir Oscar Hobson of the *News Chronicle*, Harold Wincott of the *Investors Chronicle*, Fred Hirsch of the *Economist* and George Schwartz of the *Sunday Times*. 'I was most grateful for the way in which you warded off the blows which I should not have been able to deal with,' Monckton wrote to Ellerton afterwards. Ellerton's reply spoke volumes:

> Please do come again. We do not always have the same bunch of journalists. There are between ten and twenty whom we invite and we never have more than ten at a time and there are usually three or four on what I would call 'our side'. They are always quite pleasant and I never have much trouble. Sometimes some awkward questions are asked and when they are I let them go past for four byes. They are not a bad lot of fellows and most of them I have known for very many years. They all have their funny little ways; some are just Journalists, others are Economists and occasionally they are incomprehensible![45]

It was a sanguine enough assessment, but over the next decade, especially in the context of the City's increasingly high-profile role in contested takeovers, it would no longer be possible to rely quite so blithely on letting the extras mount up.

Undoubtedly, there was by the late 1950s a growing perception that the City had become remote from the British mainstream. Sandelson, a rare critical voice from within, put it best:

> The City establishment, if not fanatically and openly Conservative, is certainly conservative by instinct and training to an extent that cuts it off from the life of the nation in a much more deep-rooted way than political bias alone could ensure. Its public school standards of conduct; its upperclass standard of life, its sports and its formality; even its assumption that the City is of vital importance to the economic well-being of the country and that free markets are inevitably the best markets, mean that it lives in a world, physically and mentally, apart from the world of the vast majority of the population. This, when the City is undoubtedly economically very powerful indeed, is certainly dangerous. There is nothing to parallel the situation (with the possible exception of Russia) in any other advanced industrial country . . .[46]

Would the City reconnect with the rest of the country? And, if it did so, would it be on the City's terms? The next forty years would see these two questions resolved – in both cases, eventually, in the affirmative, but only through the creation of a very different City itself.

PART THREE

1959–70

They did not pretend, at Blowdon & Debly's, to be 'heavy' brokers. To be concerned, that is to say, with 'yield', and 'earnings cover', and 'dividend record' over the years. Capital appreciation was what was wanted and the sooner the better. They observed, naturally, the City convention that 'speculation' was as unmentionable a word as 'cancer' in an old folk's home, but they talked often of 'avoiding stagnation', 'watching trends', 'making your money work for you', and so on.

Alan Clark, *Bargains at Special Prices* (1960)

CHAPTER TEN

Fingers in the Honey

With sterling convertible from the end of 1958, though with exchange controls still in place, the City could at last begin – in theory anyway – to search more systematically for its pre-1914 internationalist roots. An encouraging staging-post occurred on 20 March 1959 when the Bank of England, anxious to ensure that the London bullion market was no longer at a disadvantage compared with Zurich, quietly removed the long-standing ban on forward dealings in gold. There was also the continuing growth of dollar deposits in London – usually for one month and either converted into sterling by the London bank and lent to local authorities, hire-purchase finance houses, and suchlike, or simply relent as dollars, often to Canadian banks. Moreover, there were deposits in other foreign currencies, and in July 1959 the *Economist* reckoned that at any one time outstanding foreign currency deposits amounted to about $500m, 'of which the major part would be dollars borrowed and relent by London banks'. This market did not yet have a name, but it soon would. At least one pillar of the City, however, was far from ready to lift its gaze to wider shores. 'An increasing number of securities which are dealt in on the London Stock Exchange are also being traded on overseas Stock Exchanges,' the broker Julius Strauss – who else? – had warned the Council just a few weeks earlier.[1] Eventually, of course, the Stock Exchange would accept that it could no longer remain a ring-fenced British market predominantly feeding off the British economy, but it would take twenty years and more for a full state of enlightenment to be attained. Granted the continuing existence of minimum commissions, assorted restrictive practices and a generally comfortable way of life, there was for most members simply no compelling incentive to shape up to the challenges of internationalism. Even so, for the City at large (including in time even the Stock Exchange), the triumph of Warburgs in the Aluminium War at the beginning of 1959 had unequivocally pointed the way to a more bracing future. Appropriately, it was in the immediate wake of that episode, with all its attendant press publicity, that a Cambridge undergraduate, John Nott, approached the firm and managed to secure a berth there. His father, who ran a small commodities business in the City, would have much preferred his son to take up an impending offer from

Glyn Mills – indeed, was horrified at the prospect of his going to Warburgs – but Nott's instincts concerning where the more interesting future lay were entirely sound.

*

Some time before the expiry (at the end of February 1959) of his second five-year term as Governor of the Bank of England, Kim Cobbold and the government had agreed that he should stay on until after the Radcliffe Committee on the workings of the monetary system had submitted its report, expected that year. A general election was also on the horizon, and the conventional wisdom in informed circles was that, if the Conservatives won, the next Governor would be Lord Harcourt of Morgan Grenfell; if things went the other way, Gaitskell would get Oliver Franks into Threadneedle Street as soon as he decently could. The economist Alec Cairncross watched Cobbold and his deputy giving another tranche of evidence, written as well as oral, to Radcliffe on 15 January:

> The Governor talked far more sensibly than his paper ... George Woodcock [the trade union representative on the Committee] asked one particularly sharp question that implied a resemblance between the Bank of England and the House of Lords pre-1911. The Governor obviously disliked a couple of long questions that I put at the end and fell back on his usual stonewalling tactic – put that to the Treasury. Mynors said nothing but nodded agreement once or twice when appealed to by the Governor.

Cobbold was determined throughout the Radcliffe process not to forfeit the Bank's operational independence, and the following week he emphasised, in a bilateral communication to Radcliffe himself, not only that 'the Bank, to do its job properly, must be a "market" animal and not an "administrative" animal as a Government Department must be', but also that there were two 'even more fundamental reasons for favouring a degree of Central Bank independence'. These were the desirability of a 'free and intimate interplay of ideas and criticism between Treasury and Bank'; and the Bank's role in helping to prevent the 'democratic government' of the day from being 'pushed in directions which will tend to prejudice confidence in paper money, thereby risking inflation, exchange crises and all the social troubles to which they give rise'.[2]

Soon afterwards Radcliffe's team spent a Thursday lunchtime discussing Cobbold's evidence, with Cairncross observing that the Governor seemed to him 'still to dream of taking monetary policy out of the political arena, and to want to exercise more influence on economic policy than was altogether wise'. For this proposition the Scottish terrier received short shrift: 'Radcliffe thought I was "inhuman" and R.S.S. [Richard Sayers] also disagreed, saying that Cobbold saw how things were going but didn't want to go there fast.' Next day various clearing bankers gave evidence. 'They were at times very blimpish,' Cairncross thought. 'Robarts [David Robarts, Chairman of National Provincial] got away at the start with a wrong answer . . . On statistics, they saw no point in telling the public anything, least of all their profits. Robarts ended up by casting doubt on the wisdom of including in the oral evidence a hint from Chesterfield [Arthur Chesterfield, Westminster Bank's very capable General Manager] that some of the banks had made losses in the early fifties.' In February the Committee tried to prise some statistics out of the overseas banks and accepting houses. 'We had an enormous array of bankers,' Cairncross noted about one session, 'all looking a bit glum and puzzled but relieved to find that we weren't asking for as much as they had supposed.' Cairncross added in his invaluable Radcliffe diary that when a representative had called at Barings in search of statistics, Sir Edward Reid had 'lamented the disappearance of the secrecy of the City' and 'taken care not to show any of the records of the firm'.[3] The final day of evidence took place at the end of April, and there ensued a summer of waiting for the report, which was written mainly by Sayers.

The other summer uncertainty was political: would it, as the City strongly hoped, be a hat-trick of Conservative election wins? In early 1959 Macmillan saw a familiar obstacle to his hopes. 'Just as Montagu Norman was obsessed by the gold standard,' he privately reflected in February, 'so Cobbold is obsessed by "funding". So he is selling securities when he ought to be buying – at least that is what I feel . . .' To Midland's Monckton, a bank Chairman with especially keen political antennae, Macmillan held out the beguiling scenario that if only ministers were allowed to pursue a Keynesian stimulus to consumption, then 'the Conservative party will be re-elected, prosperity will be secured, the Bank of England will be preserved, and funding in 1960 will be easier than ever before'. Monckton, fortified by his own economic advisers, agreed; and over the next few weeks the upshot was that although Cobbold successfully resisted the wishes of the Chancellor, Heathcoat Amory, to reduce Bank rate, this was effectively at the price of allowing by default a distinctly reflationary budget. 'It is now necessary to raise consumption not only to expand the use of available resources and to raise the level of employment, but also to encourage confidence and investment,' the *FT* declared on budget morning, 7 April; and a few hours later, with a little help from his Prime Minister, Heathcoat Amory obliged, cutting income tax by ninepence and overall releasing into the economy some £5bn in present-day values. The City celebrated, even if Cobbold did not, and throughout the summer the FT 30-Share Index almost daily hit new all-time highs. Few now saw equities as inherently risky, and on 27 August equities for the first time yielded less than gilts – the famous 'reverse yield gap', an almost permanent feature of the market ever since. 'Through at

Last' was the *FT*'s front-page headline on the morning of the 28th, marking a notable moment in the City's collective consciousness.[4]

There was little, meanwhile, that Cobbold felt able to do. In late May he 'warned' Heathcoat Amory that 'if Conservatives were returned in an autumn Election, it might be necessary to pull in the reins rather sharply'; in mid-June he and the Chancellor 'agreed, generally speaking, that it still looked right not to put on any brakes before the summer but to watch closely in September and October'; and towards the end of July, after Heathcoat Amory had perhaps disingenuously told the Governor that he was 'a little concerned that things may be going too fast', Cobbold replied that the Bank's 'view was still to keep a close eye on them and have a serious look in the early Autumn'. A few days later, on 29 July, the two men went to see Macmillan. They reiterated their apparently shared view about taking no action yet to check expansion, while in terms of when such action might be taken, this would no longer be 'early autumn' but the rather more reassuring 'autumn'. Cobbold added that 'in the event of an autumn Election and a Conservative victory some boom conditions might develop rather quickly'.[5] Cobbold perhaps guessed that at this particular juncture it was not a warning likely to cause Macmillan or even Heathcoat Amory to lose much sleep.

There was another aspect to this memorably hot summer. On 25 May, barely four months after the government had changed for ever the market in corporate control by siding with the aggressor during the Aluminium War, Sears Holdings made what was, nevertheless, widely seen as an audacious move.[6] '£20m Bid For Watneys: Mr Clore In Field Again' ran the headline in *The Times* about that restless man's first takeover bid for more than two years. In the City the sense of shock was palpable, for there had never before been a bid by a non-brewer for a brewer, while the reaction of Simon Combe, Old Etonian and fifth-generation Chairman of Watneys, was eloquent. 'Preposterous,' he snapped to a young financial reporter, William Davis, who had broken the news to him on the telephone. 'Utterly absurd. Who is this Mr Clore?' Watneys rejected the bid, and within hours the shares had jumped from 51s 3d to 70s. Over the next few weeks Clore was demonised by the brewing industry, and to some extent by the press, and eventually on 19 June, after a peace initiative by Lionel Fraser of Helbert Wagg, agreed to withdraw his bid. From his head office at the Stag Brewery in Pimlico, which Clore had wanted for redevelopment, Combe was suitably grateful when he wrote a few days later to Lord Ashburton at 8 Bishopsgate: 'All along I have felt that you all, particularly Giles [Wally Giles], have treated this whole affair as if Barings were being attacked as much as Watneys.'[7]

There were other contested takeovers, fuelled by easy credit and the stock market boom, but the Watneys situation received the most publicity.[8] 'We had a talk about take-over bids,' Cobbold noted as early as 29 May, after calling on the Chancellor that day. 'He feels, as I do, that it may not be a bad thing in some instances, but that it is damaging to the general idea of prudent and conservative management of companies and might, in a few cases, be excessively embarrassing.' During June the Labour opposition picked up the ball and ran with it hard, one MP (Sydney Irving) even comparing takeovers to 'economic gang warfare'. In the Commons debate at the end of the month Heathcoat Amory was clearly bested by the Shadow Chancellor, prompting an alarmed comment from Harold Wincott in the *FT*: 'The average person . . . is so offended by the trappings of some bids and mergers that he tends to be sickened by the whole process. Get hold of a copy of *Hansard* for June 29 and read Harold Wilson's speech. It contains just about the only issues on which the Socialists could win an election these days.' Cobbold was by now seriously concerned, describing 'the public relations aspect' of takeover bids as 'deplorable', and during July he had two meetings with chairmen of the main City bodies. Despite some scepticism about the enforcement of any rules, there emerged a consensus that 'a code of conduct would be of value', and the inevitable working party (under the auspices of the IHA) was set up. On 18 August Cobbold was visited by the Chairman of Barclays: 'Mr Tuke came in to say that he was in stronger sympathy about my anxieties on take-over bids than some of his colleagues in the Clearing Banks seemed to be. I suggested that he should poke up Mr Robarts and Mr Chesterfield.'[9] The general election had not yet been called, but Cobbold had been around long enough to spot a hot potato.

Of less political moment, there was a takeover within the City itself. Philip Hill, Higginson had become in the course of the 1950s, under Keith's aggressive leadership, an increasingly significant force, its assets and profits more than quadrupling; it was a mark of how far the firm had come when Cobbold at the end of May told the discount market that from 1 June the Bank of England would take acceptances drawn on Philip Hill 'in a parcel of prime bank bills at the fine rate'. Soon afterwards, at the next meeting of the Accepting Houses Committee, Sir Edward Reid in the chair 'referred to the conversation that he had had with all the members regarding the election of Messrs Philip Hill, Higginson & Co Ltd to membership of the Committee and outlined the position'. There followed a unanimous vote for that not entirely popular firm's election, and Reid tactfully added 'that he understood that their representative on the Committee would be Mr Rudolph de Trafford'. Almost certainly the Bank had exercised a degree of moral suasion. Barely a month later, on 24 July, Cobbold noted a brief exchange: 'Mr Leo d'Erlanger called and asked if the proposed arrangement with Philip Hill Higginson had my blessing. I said "Yes".' Erlangers was a good name (which had not always been the case), but though it had a banking department, it was by now doing little business and mainly lived off bond-washing and dividend-stripping. Philip Hill perhaps paid over the odds (£2.5m), but the merger further cemented the firm's reputation as, in the *Economist*'s words, 'one of the most thrustful of City houses'; it now had ambitions to expand beyond the new issue field (though still with relatively few large corporate clients) in which it had largely made its name. Philip Hill, Higginson, Erlangers was the new, rather ponderous name, and soon the *City Press* featured a full-page advertorial headed 'Moorgate Home for Great Firm of Merchant Bankers', including a photograph of Keith himself. The merger also fired a starting gun, for on 12 August, less than a week after the announcement, David Robertson of Kleinworts – struggling to add a successful corporate finance arm to that house's traditional strength in banking – informed his fellow-partners that he had 'come to the conclusion that we must take another careful look at the possibilities open to us for a merger'. He drew up a shortlist, and potential marriage partners included Flemings, Helbert Wagg and Bensons.[10]

August 1959, however, was above all the month of the Radcliffe Report, publicly available from the 19th, but released a fortnight or so earlier to key figures. 'I have had a private copy of Radcliffe,' Cobbold informed one of his directors on the 6th. 'In general the background is not too bad but there are a few very tiresome suggestions . . . As a whole I do not find the document very constructive – but it is unanimous, which is important.'[11] From a specifically City-cum-Bank standpoint, there were perhaps six main aspects: a broadly clean bill of health for both the clearing banks and the discount market, with no great objection being raised to their anti-competitive elements; the recommendation, in the light of the events of 1957, that the Bank's part-time directors be excluded from Bank rate discussions; the further recommendation that Bank rate changes be made at the explicit directive of the Chancellor of the day; the assertions that economic policy needed to be integrated, that monetary policy alone was not enough and should not be allowed to pursue autonomous objectives, and that within monetary policy interest rate changes were a more effective weapon than attempts to control the money supply; a call to the Bank to provide more statistics and information generally; and, finally, the recommendation that a Standing Committee on monetary policy be set up, to include representatives from the Bank, the Treasury and the Board of Trade, with the chair to be taken by the Economic Secretary to the Treasury.[12]

However, before the world at large was allowed to make up its mind about the report, there occurred an intriguing passage of play, as the spinners got to work. The inside story was given by Robert Hall, the government's economic adviser:

It seemed clear when we read it that the recommendations about the Bank of England would be the ones to get the headlines as these clearly reduced the Bank's importance and especially that of the part-time directors. The Governor did not like this at all and took it (as he should have done) as an expression of some lack of confidence.

We all felt that it would be a pity if too much was made of this and O. Franks came to see me in Oxford on August 7th – he and Bill Harcourt [both men had signed the report] were getting slightly cold feet. We agreed that he should write to the Governor to urge him to use the time between when the Press got the Report (August 17th) and publication (August 19th) to let it be known that he welcomed the Report and took these particular recommendations as being logical developments of current practice rather than anything very revolutionary. I was to urge the same thing from my end and also to use any influence I had with the newspapers to get them to take the same line. All this was duly done and the Governor replied rather ungraciously to Oliver but at the same time accepted the view, and Makins and Armstrong [both of the Treasury] urged the same thing on him and he said he would . . . Anyway the upshot of it all – or perhaps it had nothing to do with it – was that the reception played down the bits about the Bank a great deal and it all went off as smoothly as possible. In fact if anything it has been overdone. However Roger Makins accepts that there will have to be some sort of Bank/Treasury Committee and he says that the Governor accepts this also . . .

'As smoothly as possible', perhaps, but Cobbold's institution did not entirely escape censure as soon as the report was published, with the *Economist* for example noting that 'the Bank comes in for a fair dose of criticism . . . and most of it is well deserved'. As for Cobbold's willingness or otherwise to accept the report's recommendations, he did not have any great problems with either the part-time directors or the statistical/PR aspect, but he did unequivocally tell Makins on 17 August that he was unhappy 'that the full responsibility for Bank Rate decisions should be transferred to the Chancellor' and that 'a Standing Committee should be appointed in Whitehall to which all decisions on monetary policy should be referred by the Chancellor for advice'. He insisted that 'Bank Rate is an integral part of the Central Bank's own business' and, while not disputing the fact of the Chancellor's 'over-riding decision', maintained that 'to place on the Chancellor direct responsibility for what is essentially a market and operational decision would blur the real responsibilities'.[13]

It did not dismay Cobbold that over the next few weeks the report received at best a fairly tepid response in the press, typified by Sir Oscar Hobson's complaint in the September issue of the *Banker* that 'after losing itself in a maze of subtleties and obscurities on the fundamentals of monetary control it fails to give any clear guidance to those who have to conduct that control in practice'. Hobson was also critical of the notion of a standing joint committee, not least one in which the Bank's representatives would be outnumbered six to four; as for the notion that the Chancellor's decisions on Bank rate should be issued in the form of a directive to the Bank, Hobson asked, 'Why gratuitously go out of your way to impede its operations [i.e. in the financial markets] by taking steps calculated to lower its prestige and the respect in which it is held by men of finance throughout the world?'[14] There was by early autumn, in the monetary as in the political field, still everything to play for.

On 8 September the election was called for exactly one month later, and on the 18th the *Investment Letter* that the stockbroking firm Read, Hurst-Brown & Co sent to its clients looked ahead with reasonable confidence to a Conservative win, noting that 'public opinion polls at the moment point to a third successive victory, which would be unprecedented in modern times'. If Labour won, the letter went on, not only would the road haulage and steel industries be nationalised, but the lesson of the Attlee government was that 'the Left Wing can only be kept quiet by some form of attack on the rentier class', with a capital gains tax 'a certainty', even if dividend limitation was less likely. Accordingly, 'those who expect a Socialist victory should sell equities and either await events or reinvest in high grade American, Canadian or Australian shares'. Cobbold for one did not discount the possibility, and a week later he was impelled to reassure the discount market that he 'felt very strongly that the Socialists if elected would be bound to support Sterling up to the hilt and to do nothing that would endanger the Country's gold stock'. At about this time, as chance had it, a minor City scandal suddenly blew up – the 'Jasper Affair', involving takeover malpractice and the misuse of building society funds. The working party was still working, and Cobbold in a note on the 28th referred with some exasperation to 'the song and dance about "take-over bids" in the past few days and the statement by both political parties of their intention to review the Companies Act in this connection'. Still, on the back of 'you've never had it so good' euphoria, the election campaign was going Macmillan's way, the markets were bullish and Cobbold may only have been going through the motions when a week before polling day the discount market's representatives were warned by the Governor that 'in the event of a Labour Government being returned to power he hoped that we would do nothing violent with the rates'; or as Cobbold apparently added, 'don't put your heads on the block'.[15]

On 8 October itself the *FT* surprised no one by strongly endorsing the Conservatives, on the grounds that they were 'more firmly wedded to a policy of ensuring that the pace of economic growth is fully compatible with a sound currency, strong reserves, and stable prices'. That evening, after an official dinner at the Skinners' Hall, Cobbold and his wife, Lady Hermione, went to the *Daily Telegraph* reception at the Savoy, for the election results. It soon became clear that the Conservatives had been returned with an increased majority, and a fellow-guest, Lady Cynthia Gladwyn, recorded Cobbold's intriguing, unexpected remark that 'on the whole a Labour victory might have been better for the country in the long run'.[16]

*

Back in August the Stock Exchange Council had decided to close the visitors' gallery the day after the general election, but then a few weeks later changed its mind. Some Council members must have regretted this on the memorable morning of Friday, 9 October. Paul Ferris described the scene:

> At 9.30 brokers and jobbers were milling round the doors of the Exchange; coats were torn as they surged in, and presently a queue formed from Throgmorton Street leading to the public gallery as word went round that the floor of the House had to be seen to be believed. Brokers crowded jobbers, forcing them on to seats, where they stood, sweating and happy, as orders to sell at a profit and buy for a bigger one flooded in. Steel shares, freed from the fear that the steel industry might be renationalised if Labour won, had £60,000,000 added to their value within an hour. It was pandemonium, and if you had your fingers in the honey it was lovely . . .

That first hour was indeed remarkable, and at 10.19 the Extel tape stated that 'veteran members with up to forty years' experience on the floor are prepared to admit that the scenes witnessed this morning exceed anything they had ever seen before'. The market as a whole, especially the steel sector, remained frantic until the middle of the following week, and even when things quietened down somewhat, prices continued to press ahead, with the FT 30-Share Index bursting through 300 on the 30th. A week or so earlier the discount market had asked Cobbold 'whether he thought the Stock Exchange boom in the gilt-edged market and other markets was growing too fast and becoming dangerous'. Happily, 'the Governor said no he did not think so – there was considerable pent up funds available waiting the result of the election and this was now being reflected in the prices quoted'. Was it the end of – if not history – then at least ideology? The next quarterly missive from Read, Hurst-Brown, dated 18 December, seemed to sanction this blessed thought, arguing that there were 'good grounds for the belief that the Labour Party has little chance of being returned to power unless it is prepared to jettison many of its doctrinaire beliefs, especially nationalisation'. If such were indeed the case, the circular added seductively, 'the investor can obviously face the future with more confidence than at any time since the War'.[17]

There were two other main bits of unfinished business. On 15 October the Bank of England approved the working party's draft version of 'Notes on Amalgamations of British Businesses', and the next day Cobbold received a private visit from Ted Leather. His purpose, noted Cobbold, was 'to say that he and the other two or three Conservative MPs with an active City connection are keen to push along the idea of City institutions tightening up their rules and procedures without necessarily waiting for new legislation'. The Governor made suitably polite noises, but did point out: first, that 'if you are going to have a Free Market you can never prevent foolish people from being fleeced'; and second, that 'there is no advantage in the City suddenly appearing in a brand-new white sheet'. Undeniably, though, the subject of regulation was in the air – perhaps especially as the stock market boomed – and a few days later Robert Collin and William Rees-Mogg, both of the *FT*, called at the Bank, though not at gubernatorial level, and reported that 'there are some people in the City who feel that the Council of the Stock Exchange will never be able to exercise adequate protection of the small investor and that what is needed is something on the lines of the SEC [Securities and Exchange Commission] in the United States'. The dreaded example of the SEC would become over the years the great stick, and it was a significant moment on the alternative, self-regulatory road when on the last day of October the eight-page pamphlet called 'Notes on Amalgamations of British Businesses' was published, costing sixpence. It did not, from a latter-day point of view, go very far. The guiding principle concerning takeovers – though that emotive word was deliberately eschewed – was that 'there should be no interference with the free market in shares and securities'; and in general it came forward with notably little that was specific about the protection of shareholder rights. Nevertheless, the *FT* called the pamphlet 'encouraging and valuable', while other press response was broadly favourable, and for the moment it seemed that enough had been done.[18]

The other unfinished matter concerned the Radcliffe recommendations. One aspect caused few problems, with the Bank of England within weeks setting up a Central Banking Information Department for the collection and publication of statistics, from December 1960 in the *Bank of England Quarterly Bulletin*. Economists were recruited to run this new department, though significantly the word 'research' was kept out of its name, on the grounds that the connotations were too American. As for Radcliffe's recommendation of a new Bank/Treasury/Board of Trade joint body, Heathcoat Amory on 20 October informed a no doubt equally relieved Cobbold and Makins that 'he accepted fullest co-ordination of economic and monetary policy and was reviewing internal machinery to this end, but did not propose to set up a new organisation'. He added that he would 'square' the President of the Board of Trade 'on the abandonment of the idea of a Standing Committee before speaking to the Prime Minister'. Why this retreat from the notion of a special monetary committee? In the same meeting Heathcoat Amory referred to 'the general coolness towards the Report'; while Hall reflected some weeks later that 'it is very sad for the members of the Committee that the Report has been taken so badly by Central Bankers and right-wing Tories everywhere', though he did concede that 'it is partly their own fault for putting what they had to say about liquidity in a form which implied that money did not matter'. There was also a retreat, though a more partial one, on Bank rate decisions. The non-executive directors were indeed to be eased out of the decision-making process, but though it was now to be made explicit that the last word rested with the Chancellor, it was also made clear that proposals about the Bank rate would continue to emanate from the Bank. On 27 November – the day after Heathcoat Amory's formal statement to the Commons about the government's response to Radcliffe, followed by a fairly lacklustre debate – Cobbold wrote to central bankers around the world telling them that, overall, 'we here feel that this is a satisfactory outcome, which makes virtually no change in the reality of existing normal practices'.[19]

For the past two years Bank and Treasury had, in their anxiety to minimise change and maintain autonomous empires, formed a solid, united front, and it was appropriate that Makins was given a dinner in his honour at the Bank a week before Christmas. Hall was an observant guest:

> As the Governor made clear in his speech, it was a sort of demonstration of appreciation for all the help Roger gave them in the troubled weeks of the Bank Rate Tribunal and of Radcliffe. Almost the whole Court were there. . . We were received by swarms of tall footmen in their plush livery and had sherry in the ante-room and dinner in the Court Room, which was comfortably filled but with plenty of room. One large table with a white cloth and a good deal of silver, nearly all bought by the Bank because it was around 1694. They do not have the custom of getting presents from retiring members. A very good but not elaborate dinner which reminded me of Sitwell's description when he was the Guards Officer on duty. All the servants have learned one's name for the occasion and whisper in a friendly manner when they offer you anything. In fact it was rather like dining in one's own College.
>
> The Governor made a little speech about how much their safe survival owed to Roger, and he replied pleasantly. I sat between the Governor and Cadbury [a non-executive director] – the former much more talkative than I had ever known before and making slightly malicious sketches of his colleagues. Afterwards we stayed at table and the hosts moved around – I talked to Bicester and Babington Smith. About 9.45 the Governor began to edge us out and it must have been all over about 10. And it was really extremely well done and most enjoyable . . .

Bank/Treasury relations were, at a personal level, better than they had been for years; in short, it had all worked out rather well. Or, as the credit department at Barings was putting it rather nicely at about this time, in its end-of-year report: 'The Radcliffe Report, on the whole, gave the City its blessing. At least that seemed to be the interpretation the City wanted to place on it.'[20]

Yet, in at least three significant ways, the report and the way it was implemented meant that the City was leaving the 1950s in a weaker state than need have been the case.[21] First, it was a chance missed – just at the time of financial liberalisation and the emergence of new money markets – to shake up the domestic banking system, after some forty years of semi-cartelised ossification. Some specific improvements resulted (for instance, in the areas of servicing agriculture and small businesses), but the larger structure stayed in place. Second, Radcliffe's conclusions that 'money' was not measurable, that interest rates alone were not sufficient to control the domestic economy and that monetary policy objectives were ultimately political had the total effect, within the domestic sphere, of confirming and indeed underpinning the Bank's subordination to the Treasury. And third, more broadly, the Bank's passionate, entirely understandable wish that its day-to-day independence be upheld would mean that in practice it continued to be marginal to the ever-growing Whitehall machine, with the result that whatever influence it did wield depended to an unhealthy degree on the political clout (or otherwise) of the Governor of the day. The age of corporatism was about to dawn, with the Bank of England – and thus the City – largely missing from its ranks.

CHAPTER ELEVEN
Italian Motorways

Speaking at the bankers' dinner at Mansion House on 12 November 1959, barely a month after an historic electoral triumph, achieved almost wholly on the back of a boom economy and rising material prosperity, Heathcoat Amory was naturally disinclined to emphasise any looming clouds on the horizon. 'I had a word with the Chancellor,' Cobbold recorded next day. 'He wondered whether he might have been a little bit complacent last night. I reassured him.' The post-electoral brakes, however, were always going to have to be applied sooner rather than later, and three weeks into 1960 saw the Bank rate being nudged up from 4 to 5 per cent. In a more leisurely age, Macmillan was away in Africa during the early part of the year, on his 'wind of change' tour, while Cobbold was due to leave London on 18 February for a trip to Australasia that would take the best part of a month; but on the 17th the two men were briefly in the country at the same time and, with Heathcoat Amory present, they discussed the coming budget and related matters. Cobbold made his usual point, long pre-dating Radcliffe, that monetary policy alone was not enough – 'stressing' that he 'thought nothing of the argument that, though you could monkey about with credit policy and Bank Rate, you could not make taxation changes in one year and reverse them in another year' – but Macmillan as ever saw before him the deflationary ghosts of Bank governors past. 'An hour with the Chancellor of the Exchequer and the Governor of the Bank,' he noted. 'They do each other harm – for there is a sudden mood of despondency and alarm. We are spending too much. We are too rich. Wages are going up. Imports are going up. Unemployment is falling. We are in for another inflationary boom. I said "What about Savings?" This rather took them aback . . .'[1]

That was on the fiscal side, while on the monetary side the Bank also lost, having to accept the Radcliffe-recommended scheme of so-called special deposits, surrendered to the Bank by the clearing banks in order to restrict credit at large. Cobbold told Heathcoat Amory that although the clearers 'obviously disliked any form of restriction', they 'were now conditioned to the idea of implementing the Special Deposits Scheme'. Significantly, he added that he 'thought that they would wear the absence of restrictions on other financial institutions for a while, though it would be a continuing sore which would get progressively worse if not coped with'. The first call for special deposits was made in late April. It was not, for those most intimately involved, a happy development: the clearing banks now felt that the playing field was starting to become uneven, while (as Cobbold had long feared) any move towards quantitative controls inevitably started to erode the traditionally strong, almost unquestioning support that the banks gave to the Bank itself in the area of monetary policy. Samuel Brittan recalled disparagingly a few years later that the Bank at this juncture had 'proved very troublesome' and 'put up a last-ditch emotional stand in favour of "voluntary cooperation" with the joint stock banks', before eventually being compelled 'to restrict their credit forcibly by means of Special Deposits'.[2] Yet this dismay was more than an emotional spasm, for over the years practical bankers had appreciated the benefits of being left alone to make their own dispositions.

'The exuberance engendered by the result of the Election is now very much a thing of the past,' Read, Hurst-Brown observed to its clients towards the end of May, and indeed during the whole of 1960 the stock market did little more than drift in a rather distracted way. By early June, with the balance of payments position continuing to deteriorate, it was obvious that there were going to be further credit restrictions. 'What do we do about the widening Trade Gap?' an unhappy, perplexed Macmillan asked in his diary on the 17th. 'The Bank of England (through Cobbold) speaks with a still, small and uncertain voice.' On the 23rd Bank rate was increased by a further point and a second tranche of special deposits was removed from the clearers. Later that Thursday afternoon the discount market's representatives sought elucidation from the Governor at their regular weekly meeting. 'There is no crisis,' they noted afterwards with relief. 'Asked whether he [Cobbold] had not fired two barrels at once, he said that it was no bad idea to discharge an extra round at the retiring enemy.' That was a comfortable enough exchange, couched in readily intelligible language, but the impression given of the Bank being at the centre of the economic battlefield was somewhat misleading, to judge from the visit that William Clarke, City editor of *The Times*, had paid an hour or two earlier to Cobbold's deputy, Mynors. 'He asked me point-blank whether the Chancellor would be making any complementary announcement in the House about public expenditure,' Mynors recorded the next day. 'I told him that I had not heard of any such thing. Shortly afterwards we both learned of the Chancellor's statement about expenditure in 1961/2. I have apologised to Clarke.'[3]

Press response to the package was far from ecstatic – 'each time expansion has started it has been chopped off in its prime,' the *FT* observed dolefully about the post-war history of the British economy – but Cobbold, defending the policy to Al Hayes (President of the Federal

Reserve Bank of New York), insisted that the charge that the authorities were 'acting too quickly and too heavily at a time when the boom may be starting to fade' was one for which he could 'see little evidence'. Nevertheless, writing that same day, the 24th, to Sir Frank Lee (Makins's successor at the Treasury), his tone was sternness itself:

> I must warn you and the Chancellor that you should not rely on the present Special Deposits scheme as a permanent arrangement unless you take control over Finance Houses [largely responsible for hire-purchase finance] . . . I think it very unlikely that, unless something is done about 'other financial institutions', the Banks would accept a third dose without public protest. Indeed I, and the Court, would find it very difficult to ask them to.

Whatever the methods, for the time being that was enough 'stop'. When a few weeks later, near the end of July, the discount market saw Cobbold and expressed its wish that there would be no further rise in Bank rate, he replied, 'We don't want our holidays upset, do we?' – but whether in an ironic or sympathetic tone of voice it is impossible to know. Presciently enough, Cobbold added that 'he thought the world's danger spot was Cuba'.[4]

That was on the 22nd, a few days before Heathcoat Amory voluntarily stepped down as Chancellor, privately warning Macmillan that whoever succeeded him would before long have to accept the necessity of either an incomes policy or a permanently higher level of unemployment. There was another, more City aspect to Heathcoat Amory's swansong. Hall told the story:

> We had rather an interesting last day. The July figures for bank advances showed a very large rise even allowing for seasonal corrections and I was particularly annoyed because the Governor, at the meeting with Ministers on June 21st, had claimed that the June figures showed that he had the banks under control, and very nearly wrecked the operation for this piece of personal vanity, belied by the statistics of the Bank itself. So we had a meeting yesterday morning [27 July] and in the afternoon persuaded the Chancellor as almost his last act to write to the Governor expressing alarm at the figures and pointing out that the banks could not expect any help from the Government if they got into difficulties with their liquidity ratio in January and February of next year.
>
> I rather imprudently said it was a good time to send such a letter as the Chancellor would not be here to take it back again if the Governor brought it, as he had done once before when I got Stafford [Cripps] to send a letter asking if the Bank of England considered themselves responsible for the level of bank deposits! The Chancellor, a gentleman to the end, thereupon sent it by special messenger to give the Governor a chance to bring it, though he said he would refuse to let it be returned. Fortunately the Governor was taken up with the première of a film about the Bank of

England and he did not read the letter till after 6. He then rang up Frank [Lee] to protest and said it was an intemperate letter and that he did not accept a lot of the implications . . .

Cobbold had indeed been watching the flickering screen. *The Bank of England* was a thirty-four-minute, officially commissioned colour film, and he had recently congratulated its maker, Ian Dalrymple, 'on the way in which you have managed to convey the spirit of The Old Lady of Threadneedle Street, embodying as it does respect for tradition combined with flexibility of outlook'.[5]

The new Chancellor (the seventh of Cobbold's governorship) was Selwyn Lloyd, and within a few days he was reading a memorable missive from Macmillan:

> One of the things which has been my experience in my year at the Treasury, and would I think be confirmed by both your predecessor and my successor, is the very unsatisfactory relations between the Treasury, the Bank, and what is roughly called the City, especially the Clearing Banks. Relations between the Bank and the Treasury were quite strained in my time. They are now better, especially at the lower levels. Nevertheless the Governor at that time refused to attend meetings and treated the Chancellor as one power might treat another. He is perhaps a minor power but an independent one. I did get him to attend a meeting or two, but he did not like it.
>
> Secondly, I think the Bank is not organised on a basis to deal with some of the problems of today which go beyond central banking in its narrow form. Somehow it has got to have leadership. Whether we agree with Montagu Norman's policies or not he did at least lead, and he led not only the Bank but the City, who were frightened of him.
>
> Finally, the City, especially the Clearing Banks, seem to me to be out of touch with modern conditions. It is all very well for them to say that it is their job to make money for their shareholders and that they won't co-operate with the Treasury on something which may cause them losses or may reduce their profits. If capitalist society as a whole were still to take that view we should be very near the crash. It is because, broadly speaking, the owners of property have not taken that view, have accommodated themselves to changing conditions, and have begun to regard themselves not merely as trustees for their beneficiaries but for the whole nation, that we are in such a politically healthy position today.
>
> I do not feel that the City with its narrow life shares in this attitude.

Macmillan then delivered a rallying call to his new man:

> It should be possible for the Chancellor of the Exchequer, the Governor and the leading members of the City to work together as a team. If the Chancellor says that he wants the base of credit restricted, he ought to be able to have a meeting with them, tell them what he wants, and rely on them to carry it out, or *vice versa*. At present it is all kept as a sort of mystery, very much on an 'old boy' basis. This is all very well, but it needs some new look at it all.

I send you this because it is particularly germane to the problem as to who is to be the new Governor of the Bank. Cobbold is meant to be retiring on January 1, and should at all costs be held to this decision.[6]

So soon after Radcliffe, the cry for 'some new look at it all' concerning monetary policy had a certain poignant eloquence.

Cobbold himself recalled long after his retirement that the succession question was 'mainly handled' by Macmillan and himself. It was, one way and another, a fairly troublesome process. For a long time the two more or less equal front-runners had been Oliver Franks and Lord Harcourt, until in December 1959 the Court of the Bank of England, perhaps taking its cue from the outcome of the general election, decided to recommend Harcourt as Cobbold's successor. A great-grandson of J.S. Morgan, Bill Harcourt had spent most of his working life at Morgan Grenfell, but he was more than just a merchant banker, having in the mid-1950s spent three years at Washington as the UK's economic minister. This nomination, however, was soon in trouble, for by January 1960 Lee (just arrived at the Treasury) was telling Hall that he had managed to persuade Heathcoat Amory that Harcourt was not the best-qualified person for the job and that Franks should be seriously considered. In that Franks was a brilliant administrator, who had been British Ambassador in Washington before going to Lloyds Bank as Chairman, this was a reasonable point of view. Nevertheless, over the next six months little or no progress was made; and when Lloyd succeeded Heathcoat Amory on 27 July he was, Hall noted, 'aggrieved' that the matter had not yet been settled. On 19 September, presumably endorsed by Macmillan, Lloyd offered the position to Franks. 'He [Franks] . . . was obviously extremely pleased,' Hall recorded the next day after a conversation between them, following Franks's meeting with Lloyd. 'He was anxious to know what the salary was (nobody knows) and how long the hours were but otherwise was only concerned to be sure that he was being asked as the Chancellor's candidate, not as one of a short list.' Hall added that 'Frank Lee was determined to get Oliver and now he has succeeded'; as for the likely attitude in the East End, he reckoned sanguinely that 'the Governor won't like it and the Deputy perhaps will be a bit prickly but in nine months' time everyone will be saying what a good thing it is and the relations between the Treasury and the Bank will be transformed'.

It all seemed settled – certainly the Treasury thought it was – yet a month later, on 19 October, Hall was reporting that Franks was unable to make up his mind whether or not to accept the governorship. Why not? The clue perhaps lay in Hall's same diary entry, which stated that 'Cobbold got Hanbury Williams, [Sir Charles] Hambro and Basil Sanderson to see (a) Amory, (b) Selwyn Lloyd, (c) the PM himself this week, to say they did not want Oliver and would like either Harcourt *or*

Cromer *or* Mynors better.' All three of Cobbold's messengers were long-standing non-executive Bank of England directors, and it is hard to imagine that Franks remained oblivious to the dissent that was brewing. He was obliged definitively to make up his mind by the 25th, and on that day he told Lloyd that he would not accept the governorship. 'It is a frightful blow,' Hall reflected on the 28th, after Franks had refused to change his position. Within a couple of years, as Provost of Worcester College, Oxford, he would be forever lost to the City. Why had Cobbold done it? Partly because he did not want to hand over the Bank to someone whom he regarded as a civil servant, not a City man; partly because he believed that the next Governor must be someone more willing than the fastidious Franks to open up, at least to a degree, to the press and even to television; and perhaps above all because he mistrusted the powerful, ultra-analytical intelligence that Franks so manifestly commanded. 'Alien to petty stratagems' and 'formidably objective, a classicist in every sense', in the telling phrases of an obituarist, the one-time Professor of Moral Philosophy perhaps had a lucky escape.

That left Lord Harcourt or Lord Cromer or the commoner deputy. 'Cromer seems the most probable candidate now,' Hall also observed on 28 October, 'though I would have preferred Harcourt. The Chancellor does not want him and neither does Frank [Lee].' A few days later he referred to how Cobbold and the Court had been 'plugging' Cromer 'ever since they knew they could not have Harcourt'; indeed Cromer, having been summoned to London by Lloyd, was offered the job on the 31st. 'I saw Cromer in the afternoon,' noted Hall next day, 'and as I expected he was worrying about whether he could do it. I told him I felt sure that he could. He is seeing Cobbold today to find out what sort of a job it is . . .' Cromer then flew back to Washington (where he had been British economic minister since the previous year), consulted his wife Esmé and quickly signified his acceptance. The public announcement was made on 10 November that he would succeed Cobbold the following July.[7]

How had he managed to come through so late in the day and claim the crown? In part the answer lay in one fact: he was a Baring. Back in April 1947, when the young Rowley Errington was about to spend an apprentice year in New York, Arthur Villiers at 8 Bishopsgate sent a letter of introduction to a New York banker: 'He is the son of Lord Cromer and his grandfather was the Cromer who was in Egypt. Errington was a Colonel in the Guards during the war and did very well on the administrative side after D-Day. He married the daughter of the present Rothermere. . .' He became a partner at Barings in 1948 and five years later succeeded as third Earl of Cromer. The *FT*'s 'Observer', writing the day after the announcement, detected 'almost an air of inevitability' about Cromer's rise to the governorship:

Although he hardly had time to make his mark in the City, his economic despatches from Washington have marked him indisputably for higher things. And with membership of the right clubs (Brooks's and the Beefsteak), descended from a family which has combined business acumen and great wealth with pro-consular tradition, and married into one of the great 20th century newspaper dynasties his qualifications must have appeared irresistible to the Prime Minister. Even his age has a magic quality about it: 43 – the Kennedy vintage.

In fact Cromer was even more Kennedyesque, being only forty-two. Other instant press reaction was generally warm (*The Times* being an exception), while from New Court Leo de Rothschild wrote to Evelyn Baring that 'we were all very thrilled to hear of Rowley's appointment, and to feel that the Merchant Banking Community should be so well represented by the honour'. Baring himself had been less thrilled, apparently telling Macmillan, 'all right, we'll let Lord Cromer go, but after you've finished with him we can give no assurance that we will take him back'. It was in its way a bold stroke, and there was some justice in the *Banker*'s optimistic assessment that Cromer was 'no seasoned banker in whom the "City view" has already hardened', but rather 'a young man still building his career'. Although not denying Cromer's thoroughly establishment background, it professed itself unconcerned: 'The taunt that this appointment proves again the power of the "old boy network" was obvious enough; it is too obvious to merit serious consideration.'[8]

Far away from these manoeuvrings, the climate of opinion about how best to manage the British economy was starting to change. In November 1960 what Brittan would call 'the Brighton Revolution' took place – the celebrated conference of the Federation of British Industries (FBI) that addressed 'The Next Five Years' and publicly called for a more planned, French-style approach. The driving force behind this conversion was the chairman of the FBI's Economic Policy Committee, Hugh Weeks, whose main base was at ICFC, right on the City/industry interface. A few weeks later, on 5 January 1961, *The Times* published a letter from the merchant banker (and by now grand old man of the City) Lionel Fraser, explicitly endorsing this dirigiste initiative: 'Ought we not to formulate a five-year Plan? . . . Some long-term thinking and action must be embarked upon . . . There is not the slightest doubt in my opinion that the vast majority of the people would rise magnificently to concrete, far-reaching, long-term proposals.' In the subsequent correspondence on the letters page, Norman's old henchman on the industrial reconstruction front, Ernest Skinner, was aghast ('One shudders to think of the areas of judgement, political expedient, and bureaucratic authority that might be cemented into such a plan'). And Weeks from ICFC's Drapers Gardens offices noted that 'unfortunately the word "plan", though acceptable in the business sense, is suspect in a national sense because of the implications of rigidity, centralised control and political colour', before going on defiantly, 'Should there not be for the country, as for any large business, a long-term programme, modified according to changing circumstances, in the light of which short-term decisions are made?'[9]

Fraser's personal initiative, motivated principally by a desire to banish the frustrations of the stop-go cycle, may well have had some influence on official thinking, but almost certainly was received fairly dimly in the City at large. 'I hear you are joining the Communists!' was how an old friend greeted him at luncheon soon afterwards. The Bank, for its part, preferred to stick to familiar terrain, as Cobbold marked the new year by sending Macmillan and Lloyd some thoughts on the darkening economic situation. Insisting that 'the root causes lie much more in the politico-social than in the monetary field', he argued that Britain, unlike West Germany, had since the war 'been far more concerned with the spectre of unemployment than with the spectre of inflation'. More investment, less consumption, was the key; and as far as the incoming US administration was concerned, he wanted the British government to stress to it that 'confidence in the continuing stability of sterling and the dollar is a linch-pin of the free world economy', and that 'short of some major upset, we could not now move to a more flexible rate system without causing far more troubles than we cured – the moment for this passed in the early 1950s'. Macmillan passed on Cobbold's memo to a mandarin, whose eventual comment said much about Whitehall attitudes to the Bank: 'I found the paper, perhaps inevitably, unimaginative and indecisive. This is the sort of analysis which any uninformed person could make from reading the newspapers . . .'

Cobbold's last few months were far from easy. The troubles began in March, as an unexpected re-evaluation of the Deutschmark led to a sudden surge of pressure on Britain's gold and foreign exchange reserves. The man in day-to-day charge of defending these reserves was the Bank's Roy Bridge, subsequently described by his US counterpart, Charles Coombs, as 'a small, dapper man with a thin, grizzled moustache, intelligent grey eyes, and the air of an experienced old cat quietly appraising an unwary mouse'. The two men had first met a few months previously, when Bridge 'spontaneously welcomed me as a comrade in arms, facing the common enemy of misguided government policy and consequent speculation in the exchange markets'. In March 1961 the immediate outcome of sterling's exposed situation was the 'Basle credits', with Cobbold and Bridge to the fore on Britain's behalf during the monthly meeting of the Bank for International Settlement. Bilateral credits were negotiated, to run through to July and totalling $1,000m, credits that Coombs would describe as 'a major breakthrough in post-war international finance', in that 'at one stroke, European central bank cooperation had not only saved sterling but also had protected the dollar against heavy gold drains'.[10]

The credits, though, did nothing to help Britain's poor balance-of-payments position, and when Lloyd in mid-April produced a budget that pleased his chief by being only barely disinflationary, the reaction in the markets was far from friendly. Shares had boomed in the year's first quarter, but by early summer the mood was all the other way, exacerbated by industrial strife on the home front. 'Sterling is again coming under heavy pressure,' Cobbold wearily observed on 6 June, as he noted 'first the recurrent market rumour about early sterling devaluation' and 'secondly an anxiety in informed circles about whether there is something fundamentally wrong in the UK which makes it impossible to avoid recurrent crises in spite of a reasonably tough record in fiscal and monetary policy'. What should be done? Cobbold, due to meet Lloyd that afternoon, sang for practically the last time his old song: 'I believe that any action in the monetary field, either by raising Bank Rate or tightening credit, would not deal with the realities of the problem and would be regarded as again attempting to do by monetary action what should mainly be done in other fields.' Accordingly, he wanted 'an urgent review of future Government expenditure and the possibilities of a statement being made in July'. The next day he was able to inform Bill Martin, Chairman of the Federal Reserve Board, that he had been talking with ministers and was 'hopeful that in the course of July they will take some further decisions'. As for those pernicious devaluation rumours, he reiterated, as one guardian of sound currency to another, 'we are determined to hold the present position and are most anxious not to give public opinion the slightest excuse for detecting any weakness in that determination'. That was sincere enough, but perhaps more candid was his admission soon afterwards to the discount market that he was 'confident that the short-term situation could be handled but was worried about the long term'.[11]

Gathering sterling crisis or no, June 1961 had a valedictory atmosphere, as the second-longest of all Bank of England governorships drew to an end. 'It has all been great fun,' Cobbold wrote appreciatively to Louis Franck on the 22nd, thanking him for his farewell present, 'and I have indeed been fortunate in the quality and personality of so many people in the City with whom I have worked over these difficult years.' Over the years he had grown into his office and, through strength of personality as much as anything else, had become perhaps the ultimate 'Mr Governor' of the twentieth-century Bank. An unusually critical perspective, among City men anyway, was that of Sir George Bolton, who might have become Governor himself back in 1949. A year or so after Cobbold had retired, he submitted to *The Times* a notably trenchant draft obituary:

> Cobbold was a man of violent contrasts and many puzzling contradictions. He inspired loyalty rather than affection among the immediate circle of his friends in the City and among his colleagues in the Bank, but as a public figure he appeared remote and cold. He could be ruthless too, and was never quite at ease with financial journalists. He enjoyed the respect of Civil Servants and the City and, to some extent, industry, but was never able or willing to develop an atmosphere of personal warmth and therefore failed to get the best out of his relations with his contemporaries . . .
>
> His general method of organising the Bank was 'divide and rule', and in consequence while very competent experts were available, the Bank as an organisation did not acquire a corporate body of monetary policy and theory, and tended to develop the pragmatic approach to all problems.[12]

Cobbold's successor, who took over on 1 July, was the youngest governor since the eighteenth century. In an admiring profile, soon after the handover, the *Tatler* remarked that Cromer had, like Cobbold before him, 'a love of the country', living at Frenchstreet Farm, a Tudor house in Westerham, Kent, complete with a Jersey herd. 'Lord Cromer,' the society magazine gushed optimistically, 'has come to the Bank of England at a time when the City as a whole is explaining itself more fully than ever to an interested and curious public. This is something he will do superbly. He has Prince Philip's gift of speaking crisply to the point with an economy of words and a neat sense of humour.' Those who actually worked for Cromer would come to have mixed feelings about his stewardship: to some he was an accessible figure who brought a welcome, indeed novel, degree of verve and imagination to the job; to others he seemed self-important and, in an unacceptably patrician way, lacking in sympathy for life's toilers in the ranks. A well-meaning letter that he sent in March 1964 to Andrew Carnwath at Barings gives a flavour of the man. 'My dear Andy,' he wrote:

> I had a letter out of the blue the other day from a Mr [Arthur] Wareham, who is established as a Public Relations Consultant, asking for an introduction to you as he understood that Barings might be interested in employing a Public Relations Consultant. I know Mr Wareham quite well. He was for some time Editor of the *Daily Mail,* when that paper was going through one of its more sober but unfortunately less lucrative phases. If, indeed, you are looking for a Public Relations Consultant, I think that the very qualities which were less valuable to the *Daily Mail* might be of more value to you. He is a thoroughly decent little man and I have no hesitation in passing on the introduction. Needless to say, I have no idea whether you have the slightest interest in such services.

Overall, the Bank under Cromer did become rather less rigidly hier-archical than it had been during the Cobbold years; even so, Court proceedings were still distinctly formal, with little free discussion and directors having to stand up when they spoke.[13] More generally, with the country at large poised to undergo a social revolution, it was at best a moot point whether George Rowland Stanley Baring, third Earl of Cromer, was quite the right man to be the increasingly spotlit public face of the City of London.

In July 1961 Cromer began as he meant to go on, with a strongly worded nine-page letter to Selwyn Lloyd, sent on the 7th. Starting with the assertion that 'sterling is under extreme pressure and the threat of imminent devaluation is only being held in abeyance by massive short-term support enlisted from other Central Banks', and contending that notwithstanding this temporary respite, the underlying circumstances were 'more serious in many ways than the previous all too frequent post-war sterling contretemps', he called for a comprehensive statement by the end of the month. His opening volley did not lack for a high moral line: 'Wage and salary increases unrelated to increased productivity, sometimes even pre-empted on the conjecture of it, have perpetrated a fraud on other sections of the people, with less bargaining power or more public spirit; and the final bill has been paid from the reserves, which are now running out.' Nor was it just a case of wages and salaries: 'I suggest we cannot afford either the restrictive practices on the part of labour, and the high degree of complacency on the part of some employers.' As for public expenditure, that subject on which his predecessor had spilt so much ink, Cromer flatly stated as if it were a truism that there was too much 'non-productive investment', although he did not deny that there was 'much expenditure in the social fields that is highly desirable in itself'. Significantly, he expressed the hope that a defence policy would start to be fashioned that was no longer 'a heritage from the great days of our Imperial past', but was related to contemporary needs. One unfortunate fact, however, could not be gainsaid, and that was that Britain was a parliamentary democracy. Montagu Norman for one would have sympathised with Cromer's final sentence: 'If public opinion is to be effectively enlisted in support of the Government policies a great deal of education will need to be done to overcome the considerable ignorance and misunderstanding which prevails at the present time'.[14]

The next two and a half weeks saw fairly intense negotiations about the detailed shape of the package. Lloyd's biographer would deny that the Chancellor had been guilty during this process of 'deferring' to Cromer, though he did concede Lloyd's 'sense of social diffidence in Cromer's presence'. Alec Cairncross (who had succeeded Hall as the government's economic adviser) was an observer-cum-participant at one meeting, where Cromer was 'obviously a little taken aback' by Lloyd's unalarmist draft preamble. Cromer's own diary recorded him keeping up the pressure over government expenditure, while at lunch at Chequers on Sunday the 23rd he was, according to Macmillan, shown the text of the Chancellor's statement and expressed himself 'anxious to alter Hire Purchase terms back to the stiffest on record' – Macmillan correctly, if cynically, adding that 'this is, of course, to make the monetary measures less unattractive to the Clearing Banks'.[15]

The package itself, announced on the 25th, included various personal credit and government expenditure restrictions, a hefty rise in Bank rate from 5 to 7 per cent and a call for a 'pay pause'. Taken as a whole, the *FT* called them 'the toughest economic restraints since the austerity period of Sir Stafford Cripps', but argued with some justice that it was a response that was both belated and exaggerated, granted that demand had not in fact been bursting its seams in recent months. By contrast, coming from a quite different angle of attack, *The Times* wondered whether 'the cautious and shrewd Swiss banker' would see enough in Lloyd's measures 'to convince him that at last the British economy is going to stand on its feet'. Cromer, of course, was sympathetic to this critique, and indeed would have preferred a still tougher package. By early September, summarising to Lloyd the impact so far of the measures, he observed gratefully enough that sterling was no longer under pressure, but that he could discern no great flow of funds to London, despite the Bank rate hike. The 'fundamental reason' for this, he went on, was 'unquestionably still lack of confidence in our taking measures to increase our competitiveness'.[16] Over the next few years he would tend to dart about in terms of what precisely those measures should be, but concerning the basic fact of Britain's uncompetitiveness he never wavered.

Was corporatism the answer? Clarke for *The Times* reported that in the immediate wake of Lloyd's announcement the City was 'highly sceptical' about most of 'the measures impinging on the economy's longer term problems, ranging from wages policy and the planning of the economy in general to the cutting down of overseas commitments'. As for the Chancellor's exhortations against needless dividend increases, and his proposal to introduce the following spring a capital gains tax, 'sceptical' was not the word for it.[17] The next day, the 26th, Lloyd made his detailed proposals about setting up a body that, representing government and both sides of industry, would examine the country's economic prospects for several years ahead and plan accordingly. Thus was born the National Economic Development Council (NEDC), or 'Neddy'. Lionel Fraser may have been pleased, but to most City men it was not quite what they expected from a Conservative government.

*

'Few people would be surprised if other mergers follow,' the *Economist* had observed in August 1959 after the announcement of the tie-up between Philip Hill and Erlangers. 'At a time when some of the traditional business of merchant bankers is being done by the clearing banks with their long-term advances, and other business is being hit by the discount houses, quoting fine rates direct to certain finance houses and industrial companies, merchant bankers find important advantages in bigger groupings and a stronger capital base'.[18] There was also a growing mood, in the City as elsewhere, in favour of bigger units: size seemed to smack of modernity, and following the various traumas of recent years – above all the Bank rate leak – accusations of being out of date could no longer be laughed off quite so easily. In the course of 1960 no fewer than three merchant bank mergers were announced, providing one of the best examples of a 'buying panic' in the City before the unrivalled follies of the mid-1980s.

The first name in play was de Steins, the finance and issuing house, where its elderly, childless founder, Sir Edward de Stein, was looking to make a profitable exit. He left the detailed negotiations to his partners Mark Norman and Sir David Bowes Lyon, who told Cobbold in September 1959 that they had had two offers, one from a house they did not name but was 'undoubted first-class', and another from Samuel Montagu. 'They wondered what I would think about the latter,' recorded Cobbold. 'I said that they were very active, progressive and successful and we had nothing against their performance since 1939. If I were going in with them I should personally want to know more than I do about the strength of the organisation below Louis Franck. I should also want to be sure that I was in a position to know exactly what was going on all the time.' Perhaps that was not encouraging enough, for soon Lazards (presumably the unnamed house) emerged as front runner for the hand of de Stein. The second Lord Kindersley was still senior partner there, and in November he told Cobbold about the proposed union and asked for his opinion on a suggestion – from de Stein himself? – to change the name to Lazard, de Stein & Co. Cobbold's response was classical: 'I raised an eyebrow.' Soon afterwards de Stein informed Cobbold that the negotiations with Lazards were at 'an advanced stage', and the Governor gave his blessing. The formal announcement was made in February 1960. The *FT* called it 'A Marriage in the City'; the combined operation would shortly come under the Old Broad Street roof of Lazards, and the name of de Stein was relegated to parentheses.[19] Lazards itself was still fairly sleepy, but at least this was a sign that it intended to remain in the game.

The other two mergers saw bigger fish being swallowed up.[20] Helbert Wagg had had a good run, mainly but not solely as an issuing house, since leaving the Stock Exchange in 1912, in latter years under the skilful, largely benevolent guidance of Lionel Fraser. By the end of the 1950s, however, he was looking to retire and could see no obvious successor. At Schroders meanwhile the rising force, Gordon Richardson, had no thoughts of retirement, but discerned the potential of uniting Helbert Wagg's expertise in industrial finance with the more traditional banking strength of Schroders. One or two conversations, initiated by Richardson, ensued, but nothing was settled. Matters moved sharply into higher gear in March 1960. Helmut Schroder told Cobbold on the 22nd that 'after a lot of discussion' he and his partners were proposing to make Richardson Deputy Chairman, with a view to succeeding Schroder himself in due course. 'I thought this a sensible decision,' Cobbold noted. Fraser, on holiday in Antibes, was already in the know, and the next day he sent his senior colleagues at Helbert Wagg a memo about the implications of Richardson's 'terrific and surprising, but I think farsighted' appointment:

> It set me thinking about a tie-up with them . . . I feel we have much to offer one another – they are all delightful, if not great, people, and would be pleasant partners in every way, well-behaved and all that. At first sight, there would seem to be vast scope to develop in Europe – it would make us straightaway a force in international banking, both merchant and investment.
>
> They think somewhat like us. I mean they are not grabbing, acquisitive people. They have a sense of service, to use a ripe old cliché, and could be relied upon to play the game . . .

Negotiations took place over the next six weeks or so (producing an eventual purchase price of Waggs of a little under £3m), with the main dissenter there being the independent-minded Michael Verey. 'I didn't regard there as being the slightest necessity for us to merge with anybody and I was dead against it,' he later unsentimentally reflected, though he added that 'once it had been decided I got down to it and did my best for it'. There still remained the question of the Governor's consent, which Richardson sought to obtain early in May. After sleeping on the matter for a night, Cobbold's measured words were a masterpiece of Bankspeak: 'Our attitude towards a tie-up between Schroders and Helbert Wagg would be one of benevolent neutrality, by which I meant that we should raise no objection, nor indeed have any reservations, but it would not have been a suggestion that we should have put forward ourselves, feeling that it was an ambitious project which would involve a lot of difficult assimilation.' The announcement was made on the 19th ('The marriage is a very natural one,' thought the *FT*), staff reaction in both camps was exaggeratedly fearful and within two years the merger was fully effective, though Schroder Wagg did not come under one roof, at 120 Cheapside, until 1965.[21]

Richardson was Chairman from May 1962, and over the rest of the decade he proceeded to turn Schroders (in the words of a client and close observer of City matters, Charles Gordon) into 'one of the smoothest, best-operated merchant banks in the City', with the general tenor being 'overall expansion, little publicity, less fanfare, superb results'. Another keen-eyed practitioner, John Kinross of ICFC, crisply described Richardson's qualities: 'First-class brain, moral courage, persistence, strong personality, a very shrewd man, a very nice man, but he could be hard as nails'; while Richardson himself, befitting an essentially self-made man, had little time for the Etonian aspect of the City and enjoyed saying things like 'I look at Morgan Grenfell's clients today and say they will be ours tomorrow.' Striving consciously for excellence (with a particular focus from 1966 on attracting qualified recruits), and developing a wide range of contacts with leading people in politics and industry, he was increasingly seen as the City's coming man, just the right sort of meritocrat. 'Richardson is a highly professional banker, ruthless but fair, opposed to nepotism, and his directorships range from the Royal Ballet to Lloyds Bank,' Sampson admiringly noted in 1965.[22] If there was a downside to his leadership of Schroders, it was his lawyer's unwillingness to reach a decision that was not on the basis of full information and equally full deliberation; but at least this meant that a high proportion of his decisions were right.

If Schroder Wagg was the marriage of an accepting house and an issuing house, so too was Kleinwort Benson, though this was more a union of equals. The Chairman of Bensons from March 1959 was Phil Macpherson, a shrewd Scot who had come up on the investment side and had, perhaps surprisingly, been chosen in preference to the more flamboyant new issue specialist, Mark Turner. On his appointment Macpherson told Cobbold that Bensons was 'more liquid at the moment than he ever remembers', with immediate prospects looking good. Not surprisingly, then, the initial push towards a merger came entirely from Kleinworts, where several years of increasing dissatisfaction about its inadequate corporate finance arm had been crystallised first by the Aluminium War (when it was a humiliatingly long time before anyone troubled to court its support) and then by the enlargement of Philip Hill through the Erlangers deal. Bensons was at first one of a short list of three, but with Helbert Wagg more or less bespoke and Flemings unwilling, that short list quickly narrowed to Bensons alone. During autumn 1959 preliminary discussions took place before and after board meetings at Commercial Union, where both Cyril Kleinwort and Turner were directors. Turner was keen (arguing that the only plausible long-term growth route for Bensons was merger with an accepting house and thereby becoming a proper merchant bank), and by the following spring detailed negotiations were under way.

They were not easy – as much as anything because of Kleinworts' insistence that its name must come first, on the grounds that even in a merged enterprise banking would still be *the* core activity – but Turner just about managed to keep the Benson crew on side, partly through his apparent certainty (ultimately misplaced) that it would not invariably be a Kleinwort person who took the top job. In September 1960 the word to Cobbold was that 'it looks like a nearly 50/50 arrangement with assets just above £10 million on either side', which, thought Cobbold, 'sounded a sensible arrangement'. The announcement was made two months later, provoking such gratifying headlines as 'Strength through Size' and 'Merchant Bankers à la Mode', while the *Daily Telegraph* thought that this new, well-capitalised group would 'rank as one of the largest and best diversified' in the City. Writing that same day to Lee at the Treasury, Cobbold was broadly reassuring: 'It is a good arrangement – the business of the two firms is complementary and the merger will strengthen both. The personalities are not quite easy, but they have thought it out carefully (after initial blessing from me) and are satisfied that it will work.' The merger took effect in March 1961, though it would be a full eight years before the two firms physically came together at the rebuilt 20 Fenchurch Street, cruelly tagged 'the leaning tower of Fenchurch Street' during the endless delays and structural problems before it was ready.[23]

At the three most prestigious merchant banks there were varying signs of life. Some capable 'players' were starting to arrive at Morgan Grenfell – one of them, an accomplished, aggressive corporate financier called Guy Weston, created waves by uttering the word 'cunt' in the partners' room – but the 'gentlemen' remained firmly in control as far as the foreseeable future was concerned. In particular, Morgans was struggling to retain its traditionally strong position in industrial finance, as takeovers and mergers became more fiercely competitive after the Aluminium War watershed. Indeed, in the 1960s one City editor (Ansell Egerton) reputedly kept a headline in standing type, 'FIRST WIN FOR MORGAN GRENFELL', on the grounds that some day it might be needed.[24] There was rather more movement at Rothschilds, where the 'Battle of Long Acre' – the humiliating failure early in 1961 to prevent Odhams Press being taken over by Cecil King's Daily Mirror Group (advised by Warburgs and Helbert Wagg) – caused something of a seismic shock.[25] Over the next few years the rapidly emerging driving force was Jacob Rothschild, still in his twenties when he became a partner in April 1963. 'Like his father [the third Lord Rothschild], he doesn't care to hunt, race, play polo or go fishing,' a profile of him had noted in 1960, not long after Jacob's arrival at New Court. 'Unlike him, he prefers history to science. He took a First at Oxford, is joining his cousins in the family firm, and plans later to write a history of the merchant banks.' A symbolic break with the past occurred in October 1962, when the firm moved to temporary premises (City Gate House in Finsbury Square) so that New Court could be rebuilt. Edmund de Rothschild naturally found the disappearance of Baron Lionel's New Court 'extremely sad', and it was hard to be very thrilled by the modern six-storey building to which Rothschilds returned in July 1965, although in a changing world it was consistent with Jacob's assertion that 'we must try to make ourselves as much a bank of brains as of money'.[26]

At 8 Bishopsgate, where Norman Shaw's elegant, intimate building still stood, the equivalent generation of the Baring family could only look with some envy at the freedom of manoeuvre of Jacob and his cousin Evelyn. Sir Edward Peacock had retired back in 1954, but under the ultra-conservative leadership of first Evelyn Baring and then Sir Edward Reid his shadow – what some irreverent, youthful spirits called 'The Dead Hand' – persisted, taking the form of a largely negative approach to new business and the carving out of defensive fiefdoms. The proprieties continued to matter. 'You must remember that Brazil is a Rothschild country,' the young Nicholas Baring was warned as he set off for South America. The business ticked over, and undoubtedly there were some first-rate operators (such as the astute Wally Giles in new issues), but overall the house was not yet facing up to the new challenges.

This was true notwithstanding the dramatic events of the winter of 1961–2.[27] Shortly before Christmas it was leaked to the press that ICI had made a £180m offer for Courtaulds – the biggest bid yet in British corporate history, prompting the *FT* to wonder 'whether such a merger does not create a group too large to be in the national interest'. Courtaulds quickly lined up Barings in defence (believing that the bank's unimpeachable reputation would be an asset), while ICI looked to Morgan Grenfell and Flemings, and Cromer's initial contribution was limited to telling the protagonists, 'We don't want too much jawing' – in other words, warning against a repeat of the damagingly high-profile Aluminium War. Cromer (for all his natural sympathies with the defence) was also conscious of the government's view, which was that an ICI victory (although probably undesirable) was inevitable, and that therefore it did not intend to intervene. Soon the still-novel cut and thrust of a hostile bid was in full swing – including the bid being raised and various defence stratagems being deployed, amidst advertising and counter-advertising, accusation and counter-accusation – while the large institutional shareholders weighed up their options. A key factor, as in the aluminium saga, was the Church Commissioners, whose Sir Malcolm Trustram Eve wrote to Sir John Hanbury-Williams of Courtaulds on 20 February requesting more information for the shareholders about the range of possible alternative solutions and their implications, and suggesting that this information might best be elucidated if the ICI offer were temporarily withdrawn and talks took place between the two companies under an independent chairman. Hanbury-Williams passed on this tempting idea to Cromer, whose inclination was to try to implement it. However, he was dissuaded by Selwyn Lloyd after the President of the Board of Trade (Frederick Erroll) had joined their meeting and, in Cromer's words, 'argued vehemently that as the Government had declined to intervene it would be highly embarrassing if I were to do so now of my own volition'.

By early March the tide was anyway turning in favour of Courtaulds (helped by the backing of the 'Lex' column in the *FT*), and ICI was compelled to announce on the 12th the failure of its bid. This was a particularly damaging blow to its ambitious Chairman, Paul Chambers, but few tears were shed. He, for his part, largely blamed the City. 'When I invited Chambers to come and see me,' Cromer told Mynors later in March, 'he at first demurred but, as you may imagine, toed the line in the end. I could not but help thinking of the Bateman drawing of the guardsman who dropped it.' The mood at Barings, where Andrew Carnwath had led the defence, was bittersweet; Evelyn Baring, gloriously unconcerned with fee income, told a cousin, 'I only hope we shall not again be involved in such an operation which was entirely unnecessary, cost a great deal of money, and gave a great deal of work.' Yet it is debatable how vital a role Barings played in the successful defence of Courtaulds. At the time, in his three-part account in the *Observer*, Roy Jenkins argued not only that the adroit scheme for a bonus issue that Courtaulds came up with was essentially 'the product of Arthur Knight's brain' (a reference to the company's Finance Director), but also that it had been a battle more lost by ICI than won by Courtaulds, especially through ICI's mistaken decision in late February to make its offer unconditional. Jenkins did not discuss the responsibility of Morgan Grenfell and Flemings for that fatal decision. Moreover, if anyone *had* positively won the battle for Courtaulds, that person was, by general agreement, the company's up-and-coming Frank Kearton, who in later years would recall Barings as 'the most reticent bank of the day' and add that 'the aggression had to come from us'.[28] Indeed, one could argue that it would have been a blessing in disguise to Barings if the outcome had gone the other way, as that might well have shaken up the firm in much the same way as the Odhams episode had done Rothschilds the previous year.

Most of the merchant banks were by now public companies, and in November 1961, even before the ICI/Courtaulds battle, one of them, M. Samuel, unrestrainedly advertised its services in the *FT* as 'Financial Advisers', declaring that 'we have under one roof [Shell House at 55 Bishopsgate] experts on all aspects of company finance, who can be called upon at short notice to advise on a wide variety of problems'. Mergers and acquisitions, whether friendly or unfriendly, were proliferating in the early 1960s, and they included the restructuring of much of the British insurance and brewery industries, as well as mergers between J. & P. Coats and Paton & Baldwins, City and Central Investments and City Centre Properties, and Rio Tinto and Consolidated Zinc. The temptation for the merchant banks, of course, was to stress how valuable to the nation their role was in this process. 'Apart from the direct raising of capital for industry, we have played an increasing part in advising on negotiations and in providing technical assistance in amalgamations of companies,' Ernest Kleinwort told his shareholders as he reviewed Kleinwort Benson's business during 1962. 'Such amalgamations are a natural consequence of the need to build larger units in industry which are better able to carry rising overheads and, even more important, the heavy cost of research and development that will be necessary if the country is to remain abreast of competition, particularly in overseas markets.' Beneath the guff, however, there was (*pace* Evelyn Baring) a serious money-making purpose, as the merchant banks in these years moved heavily into corporate finance as a way of generating significant profits on a far less capital-intensive basis than wholesale banking. Certainly there had been a previous involvement – going back to the late 1940s and, more patchily, even earlier – but this drive was something rather different, in effect an occupying of much of the terrain traditionally occupied by stockbrokers, accountants and lawyers. 'I was discussing a problem with my then senior partner and there landed on his desk the third proof of a take-over document from a firm of merchant bankers,' David Caruth of Linklaters recalled. 'He was justifiably furious because it was the first time he had been informed of the matter in question. "How times have changed," he said.'[29] It was in many ways a confidence trick – at least if one accepts that in a takeover bid a lawyer may be needed for transactional reasons, an accountant to check the figures and a broker to advise on the market, but that a merchant banker is no more than a highly paid orchestrator (arguably a self-appointed orchestrator) of these activities.

The self-promotion at Warburgs was rather more subtle. When the firm moved at Easter 1961 to new premises, at 30 Gresham Street, Warburg refused, as he had done in King William Street, to allow a nameplate by the entrance. He continued, moreover, to decline to give interviews, but in the years after the Aluminium War did little or nothing to discourage the press from according a cult status to the firm and its founder. It was not a cult to which the Bank of England yet subscribed. In November 1962, following a trip to Germany and France, Warburg called at his own request on Cromer and suggested that, if the Bank were to hold a higher proportion of its reserves in dollars, this would be well received on the Continent. Cromer's note of their meeting adequately conveys the tone of his response: 'I thanked Mr Warburg for his opinion but told him that our position as holders of a key currency placed upon us rather exceptional responsibilities and we were unlikely to depart lightly from our present practices.' Warburg was unabashed, and the following spring he was gratified to be asked by the government for his advice concerning the Treasury's dollar portfolio. Cromer, furious when he heard, fired off a complaint to the Treasury: 'Warburgs enjoy a high reputation for ingenuity but they do not have at their command the degree of experience in international government finance that is at the disposal of some other Houses . . .'[30] Nor perhaps did they, but there was much to be said – and there was an increasing acceptance that there was much to be said – for 'ingenuity'.

*

Few observers during either Cobbold's or Cromer's governorship would have been inclined to describe the Bank of England as a progressive, outward-looking institution. There was a symptomatic encounter in November 1960 when Mynors hosted a visit to the Bank by two US Congressmen, 'a somewhat brash pair of young men with a keen interest in the Federal Reserve's operations'. Naturally, he showed them the Court Room. 'They asked me whether at meetings of the Court we were surrounded with charts as at meetings of the Federal Reserve Board. In reply I pointed to the wind vane and for the first time they did not quite know what to say.'[31] Yet over the next three years the Bank played an indispensable role in a process that went a long way towards re-establishing London as a major international financial centre. Others outside the Bank took the key initiatives, but the guardian of London's interests seldom let them down. It was, in its way, a remarkable story, still imperfectly understood.

Most of the City's (and indeed some of the Bank's) instincts ran the other way. Sterling may have become convertible in December 1958, but exchange controls were still almost as much in place as they had been since 1939; a British resident or institution wishing to invest abroad had to pay a so-called 'dollar premium', which was often substantial; and there was an obvious commercial logic to the decision of the merchant banks to concentrate increasingly on UK corporate finance. As for the London Stock Exchange, it was by now an institution almost wholly geared to the domestic economy, and its lack of serious interest in international business was typified by the restrictions that it imposed in the early 1960s on the arbitrage activities of jobbers. A few brokers, though, did have the energy and imagination to look successfully overseas, notably Strauss Turnbull under the tough-minded Julius Strauss, and Vickers da Costa, where Ralph Vickers, senior partner from 1961, ignored City prejudices and got heavily (and very profitably) involved in Japanese securities. His recurring nightmare, he would say in later years, was that he found himself living in Japan with his money invested in England. There was also in the early 1960s, partly in the context of Britain's possible entry into the Common Market, a greater enthusiasm for investing in Europe, exemplified by M. Samuel's pioneering New European and General Investment Trust. Towards the Common Market itself the City was broadly, if not on the whole passionately, in favour. Harley Drayton was Honorary Treasurer of the United Kingdom Council of the European Movement, which in November 1961 held a bankers' conference in the Fishmongers' Hall at which Kenneth Keith 'discussed the great contribution which the City of London could make to the Common Market'. Even so, Mynors noted the following summer that there was 'a suggestion in one or two quarters that people in the City were not entirely of one mind about the Common Market'; and in his *Anatomy* of the same year, Sampson supported his thesis that bankers were pretty blinkered creatures by observing that 'on the issue of the Common Market, where one might expect bankers to lobby strongly, their influence was small'.[32]

If there was a truly visionary figure in the City in the early 1960s it was surely Sir George Bolton, once of the Bank of England, but now Chairman of the Bank of London and South America (BOLSA).[33] In December 1960 he sent, without Cobbold's knowledge, a bold paper to Macmillan in which he inveighed against exchange controls, not just in Britain but in Western Europe as a whole:

> The existence for twenty years of such a policy has produced a political and national feeling in Europe that capital should be used primarily in the country of origin, and that it should be jealously hoarded and not made available to the foreigner. While this was a wartime and an immediate post-war necessity, it now makes no sense whatever, and conflicts with the interests of the United Kingdom . . .

Accordingly, Bolton called – in typically sweeping terms – for the comprehensive mobilisation of western European finance. Or, as he put it a few weeks later to a City audience, at the annual banquet of the Overseas Bankers' Club, 'the real cause' of 'the world-wide hunger for capital' was 'the persistence of exchange controls, the restriction over the movements of people and the consequent granulation of Europe's capital and human resources into isolated jealous particles'.[34] Capital had not flowed freely round the world since 1914; but Bolton well knew that if it once more began to do so, then London – with its entrepôt expertise and traditions – would be the spectacular beneficiary.

Before the Eurobond market, however, there was the Eurodollar market, and Bolton's BOLSA was at the end of the 1950s one of the London banks already pushing hard for dollar deposits.[35] It was purely a telephone market, and over the years old-timers in Fleet Street would enjoy instructing novice photographers to call at the Bank of England and obtain a picture of a Eurodollar. An early public sighting of the term itself occurred in *The Times* on 24 October 1960. In a piece entitled 'London – Centre of the Euro-Dollar Market', Clarke described 'the so-called Euro-dollar market' as 'a market where dollar deposits earned and owned by foreigners can be left and still earn a higher rate of interest than is available in New York'; and he emphasised recent German and Swiss moves to restrict such deposits entering their own financial centres. The following month a parliamentary question asked whether London would similarly seek to discourage Eurodollar deposits, to which the government reply was that such a policy would damage London's international financial standing and that anyway the inflow of dollars benefited the central reserves. Some months later, in April 1961, Maurice Parsons of the Bank noted how, during recent conversations in Basle, Coombs of the Fed had 'made it clear that American thinking had swung around from an attitude of relative indifference to one of some hostility', and that they were 'now inclined to think that this market constitutes a danger to stability'. After some internal discussion, however, the Bank refused to be moved from its policy of benign neglect. 'There is no doubt that the restrictive effect of the American Regulation Q [which since 1957 had made it unattractive to leave one-month deposits in the US] has been the main factor in stimulating the growth of the Euro-dollar market,' Parsons noted a few days later. 'If this market serves a useful purpose – as appears to be the case – it would not be in the interests of international trade that it should be suppressed.' The Treasury still knew very little about this offshore market – that summer it felt compelled to ask for the Bank's assistance to enable it to achieve 'further understanding' of this 'phenomenon' – and almost certainly the Bank's role was crucial in stilling any government doubts about the possibly damaging 'hot money' effects. According to the financial journalist Gordon Tether in June 1961, it was a market deploying 'considerably more than the $1,000 millions that is a fairly generally accepted estimate of its size', and he tried to show how this huge pool of international credit centred upon London was utilised for many purposes, but above all for the financing of trade.[36]

Why London rather than, say, Paris or Frankfurt or Zurich? It was not just because of the more liberal attitude of the London authorities, important though that was; there were also, in the admiring words earlier in 1961 of a leading French financial commentator, Paul Turot, London's 'excellent technical organisation' and its 'abundance of specialised personnel'. In terms of who was making the running in this rapidly expanding market, Tether thought that 'top names' included 'such widely differing types of institution as the Bank of London and South America, Schroders, the Société Générale, the Australia and New Zealand Bank,

Kleinwort Benson, and Brown Shipley – the last two institutions claiming to be the originators of the market in its present form'. Back in the mid-to-late 1950s the British clearing banks had been to the fore, but the requirement that 8 per cent of all their deposits, in any currency, had to be held at the Bank of England blunted their competitive capacity in bidding for funds. Accordingly, by 1960 their Eurodollar market share (that is, of dollar and foreign currency deposits held by non-residents with UK banks) was down to less than 10 per cent, whereas American banks, British overseas banks and accepting houses were running respectively at about 35, 20 and 16 per cent.[37] There were still not many American banks in London, but the trend was clear.

Bolton had two key allies in his ambition to make London the unrivalled international financial capital of Europe. One featured in his diary in February 1960: '3.30. Warburg: Criticisms B of E: Ex. Control frozen attitudes'. The other was Cromer, Governor of the Bank from 1961 and largely responsible for temporarily relaxing its attitude towards exchange control. A passage from his initial remonstrance to Selwyn Lloyd set the tone and, indeed, explicitly opened up the whole question of how international or otherwise the City's orientation should be:

> The restraint on the foreign exchange earning power of the City by the continuation through all these years of the Exchange Control mechanism has been insidious and by no means insignificant and that has played its part in diminishing the contribution which the City makes to the 'invisibles' element in the balance of payments. Our failure to mobilise more effectively this earning capacity in foreign exchange has resulted in much unique expertise in the fields of international finance being diverted to studying Take-Over Bids, supervising the investment of pension funds and other activities, none of which contribute one iota to our exchange earnings. The attitude of mind which looks to Exchange Control as a rampart to be manned when attack threatens is dangerous in undermining the will to create conditions where such controls are no longer necessary . . .

Cromer, in his vision of where the City's destiny lay, got it half right: that ultimately it would be an international future, in a world without exchange controls. What he did not appreciate, and perhaps neither Bolton nor Warburg *wholly* did as well, was that it would be a future independent of whether or not sterling was a strong, reserve currency. Ironically, within weeks of the new Governor setting out his vision, Lloyd's sterling-induced July 1961 measures saw UK exchange controls being not relaxed but intensified, with restrictions imposed on direct investment in countries outside the sterling area. Cromer kept his counsel, but Bolton was furious, telling Lloyd later that summer that international opinion at large saw this intensification as nothing less than 'a confession of weakness'. The Chancellor's eventual reply sounded a suitably regretful note: 'This is, frankly, a policy forced on us by the very difficult situation which we face in the balance of payments. I do not pretend that I like the policy, or that I want to keep it for longer than is necessary . . .'[38]

The following year showed that it was not only ministers who were risk-averse. After some exchange control relaxations had been announced in May 1962 (notably that residents could make greater use of so-called 'switch dollars' in running their portfolios of foreign currency investments) – though this was far from enough to satisfy Cromer – the Treasury's H.A. Copeman warned two months later against buying too slavishly into the Governor's line about exchange control matters generally: 'I feel that individual proposals tend to be put to us by the Bank of England with a general presupposition that we must go for the maximum degree of freedom and that this is necessary to maintain London's place in Europe . . . I think we should be clear about the internal implications of this.' One of the Treasury seniors, Sir Denis Rickett, was equally cautious in his approach in October, commenting that 'we do not want too much capital investment overseas and too little in modernisation and expansion at home'. Lloyd's recent successor at No 11, Reginald Maudling, agreed. 'You mentioned to me the general question of invisible earnings,' he wrote to Macmillan in November. 'The City could probably increase its earnings if we allowed people to lend more freely to foreigners. But this would mean large capital payments across the exchanges for a small immediate return and I don't think we can afford that yet.'[39] Granted sterling's continuing vulnerability, granted the continuing assumption (promulgated by no one more than Cromer) that the fixed parity must be defended, and granted that the next election would be determined by the immediate state of the British economy rather than by the prospect of the long-term City contribution to the nation's invisibles, it is tempting to argue that Cromer was simply backing the wrong horse. Nevertheless, it *was* the horse that eventually won.

Starting with the Eurodollar market – where among the merchant banks the main operator was probably Hambros, whose non-sterling deposits had reached the equivalent of £28m by March 1962, compared to £9m a year before. Nevertheless, in the annual statement that he issued in May to the bank's shareholders, Sir Charles Hambro (who had succeeded Olaf Hambro the previous year) expressed his belief that Eurodollars were likely to be 'a temporary phenomenon' in the European economy; and the *FT* commented that Hambro was probably wearing his hat as a Bank of England director when in the same statement he 'referred to the bidding-up of rates for foreign deposits by local authorities and hire-purchase firms and suggested that it would be better for the economy if rates were kept at a level which did not attract this hot money'. Sir Charles remained anxious about this market, as did others at the Bank, and in November he had a word with the Deputy Governor specifically about Eurodollars. 'Hambros are one of the biggest people in the business,' Mynors noted, 'and he is getting quite alarmed at the way it is growing . . . He wondered whether we here had any general guidance to give on the extent to which business in Euro-dollars should be allowed to expand, e.g. in its relationship to the acceptance business done by several of the people concerned. I said we would think about this . . .' Over the next couple of months the Bank did just that, and in late January 1963 its economist, Maurice Allen, submitted a memo on 'London as a trader in non-sterling currencies':

> The Euro-dollar, Euro-sterling business already conducted represents a very important activity. It is unsafe to regard this business as founded on sand and likely to crumble if US deposit rates rise or if credit becomes easily available in all European centres. The business rests also on a new 'efficiency' of the market; holders of funds and borrowers of funds are managing to get together with fewer intermediaries – and so fewer charges – than before. Discoveries of this kind are not easily forgotten.

It was an illuminating analysis of what was increasingly becoming an inter-bank, wholesale market; and though Allen warned of the potential threat to sterling's status as an international currency, the notion that the Eurodollar market had come to stay was now unambiguously accepted – and welcomed – by the Bank, as shown next day by the important letter (endorsed by Cromer) that Mynors wrote to Hambro:

> It is natural enough that London banks – and merchant banks in particular – with their expertise and international connections should not only have become involved but also have sought to participate actively in this business. It is par excellence an example of the kind of business which London ought to be able to do both well and profitably. That is why we, at the Bank, have never seen any reason to place any obstacles in the way of London taking its full and increasing share. If we were to stop the business here, it would move to other centres with a consequent loss of earnings for London.

Sir Charles took on board this message, and by the end of March his bank's non-sterling deposits were up to the equivalent of £37m, representing over one-fifth of the balance sheet.[40]

On the same day (Tuesday, 29 January 1963) as Mynors's cardinal letter to Hambro, General de Gaulle said '*Non*' to Britain's application to join the Common Market. The City's reaction was broadly one of patriotic dismay, and at Westminster Bank the foreign exchange dealers insisted for a time on speaking in English to their counterparts in Paris. 'Asked why they were not using French as usual,' *The Times* reported, 'they replied that they were Anglo-Saxon and English was their natural language. The irritated Frenchman had to search for a colleague to interpret.' There was no censure from above. 'I'm jolly glad the Westminster stuck up for the old country,' the bank's Chairman, Duncan ('Golly') Stirling, told his board. It is difficult to know to what extent the General's *démarche* altered Cromer's thinking. A few days before the bombshell Cairncross had reflected disapprovingly that 'Cromer still thinks of a great liberalisation of the capital market, whether we are in EEC or not, as an important step forward'; anyway, the fact was that over the next few months Cromer decided to make one more big push on the question of exchange controls.[41]

At the end of April, as the Governor prepared to write a set-piece letter to the Treasury, Parsons indicated to him what he saw as the real political truth of the matter:

> The fact is that there is now a wide measure of agreement between the Bank and the Treasury regarding the ineffectiveness and irrelevance of exchange control as regards current problems. However, we have discovered by long and bitter experience that Tory Chancellors have no particular convictions on this major policy question except that they should be spared any embarrassments in the House of Commons. What they are afraid of is that, having abandoned exchange control (and they still have a sneaking affection for it), they will then run into difficulty with the reserves at some future date and have to put some kind of restraint on the economy. At this point it will be stated by the Opposition that the restraint would have been unnecessary but for the fact that exchange control had been abandoned . . .

Cromer's own letter, to the Permanent Secretary at the Treasury, Sir William Armstrong, began memorably:

> I start from the basic belief that exchange control is an infringement on the rights of the citizen, either individually or collectively, to dispose of his own property as he sees fit either in his wisdom or whim. Except in a totalitarian state this infringement of freedom is only tolerable as long as the safety of the state in the widest sense is in jeopardy. I well recall the contempt mixed with pity in this country when exchange control was imposed by Hitler in peace-time in the 'thirties in Germany . . .

Cromer then argued not only that exchange control was very limited in its effectiveness – in that 'the unscrupulous, I suspect, have little difficulty in achieving their ends whereas those who are punctilious in such affairs may well be turned down' – but that, with the passing of 'the era of so-called dollar shortage', any safety-of-the-state arguments were no longer valid. As for the dangers of 'outward investment by the resident', always invoked by defenders of exchange control, Cromer was scathing:

> Why should the residents of this country be suspected by authority to be so anxious to invest embarrassingly large funds abroad? As far as the individual is concerned, unless he is frightened into doing so by hostile Government policy, the individual tends to be insular and patriotic in employment of his savings and capital. If there were ever to be an outflow

of funds of what might be described as a refugee nature it would be unwise to regard exchange control as much more than a façade and a deterrent. My personal experience as a merchant banker leaves me in no doubt that the mass of the investing public have no great enthusiasm in investing in unfamiliar territories beyond our shores.

After being similarly dismissive about the reputed evils of outward direct investment, Cromer concluded (in words drafted by Parsons) that the continuing existence of exchange control 'proclaims to the world at large a sense of our weakness while providing the British Government of the day with a wholly unjustified feeling that in it they have a defence against the consequences of misfortune or mismanagement'.[42]

The 'fact is that Governor wants to get to position where there is no control on foreign investment,' an alarmed Cairncross correctly noted on 1 May, and two days later Cromer, Armstrong and others gathered in the Chancellor's room at the Treasury. The record of what should have been a fascinating meeting was entitled 'Inward and Outward Investment', but unfortunately it appears, for whatever reason, to have been a rather flat, even perfunctory discussion. Maudling's position was summarised in three sentences, with virtually no further elaboration:

> The Chancellor commented that the UK was bound by international obligations to give freedom for current payments but forced by the facts of its economic situation to control capital movements . . .
> The Chancellor said that it was necessary to consider the whole problem from a practical standpoint. There could be no question of abandoning control of direct investment and the only question was how to determine the total that could be approved and the method of approval.

Undeterred, over the next few weeks Cromer came up with an ingenious plan, in effect using the dollar portfolio to buttress the reserves and thereby provide a cushion for greater freedom of capital movement. However, writing to Maudling at the end of May, he unwisely conceded that 'there may be an initial strain in the first year', granted that it would take several years to liquidate the Treasury dollar portfolio for foreign exchange. The crunch for this plan, and Cromer's larger hopes of achieving something not far short of virtual abolition of exchange controls, arrived in July. Unfortunately for the Governor, and contradicting Parsons's optimistic analysis, the Treasury view was almost unanimously hostile. Most tellingly, Armstrong reflected that not the least of his reasons for being unable to recommend Cromer's proposals was that 'those who think that we are not expanding as fast as we might would say that if we have sufficient resources to be able to devote them to overseas investment, we ought rather to use them for a further reduction to unemployment at home'. It was, in short, a classic either/or nostrum, and a year or so before a general election it would have taken a brave politician to challenge what was still an almost axiomatic assumption. Cromer did persist that autumn with a rather less ambitious campaign – prompting Armstrong to observe in November that 'the basic issue here, as the Chancellor is aware, is whether given the prospect for the balance of payments in 1964 we should be taking any moves now to relax exchange control' – but he surely knew that he was not going to succeed. 'Bank must be very disappointed that so little of what they propose gets through' was how Cairncross put it at the start of 1964, as with some relief he looked back on the previous year.[43]

In fact, unbeknown to most in the City and virtually ignored by policy-makers outside, 1963 had been the most important year since 1914 in the history of London as an international financial centre.[44] The origins of what would come to be known as the Eurobond market lay partly in the existence of the huge floating pool of stateless Eurodollars, with much of that pool residing in London, but arguably even more in the peculiarities of the New York foreign dollar bond market.[45] Between 1945 and the early 1960s – the era of the almighty dollar – that market raised some $6.5bn, largely for governments and state-owned bodies in different parts of the world. Yet such was the insularity of the American investment community that increasingly the secondary market for these issues resided not in the US, but in Europe. It was, from a European perspective, an illogical, even exasperating situation. In the immortal, retrospective words of Julius Strauss, whose stockbroking firm Strauss Turnbull specialised in placing foreign dollar bond issues, 'the American houses got all the cream but did none of the work'. Strauss himself was later credited with coining the term 'Eurobond', but if there was one figure who appreciated more than anyone that the 'cream' lay in arranging the underwriting, and that there was no reason why European syndicates should not sell foreign dollar bond issues to what was anyway largely a European clientele, that figure was surely Siegmund Warburg. Through his close connection with the New York investment bank Kuhn Loeb, and in particular that firm's Gert Whitman, he had learned much about the European marketing of foreign dollar bond issues; by the early 1960s he was conscious that the freedom of the New York foreign dollar bond market was under threat from the worsening US balance-of-payments position; and by early 1962 he was busy negotiating a London-based dollar loan for the European Coal and Steel Community (ECSC), which had previously looked to New York to arrange its issues.[46] In the event that ECSC issue failed to get much beyond square one (possibly because Warburg decided against treading on the toes of Kuhn Loeb and company, possibly because ECSC decided it did not need the money), but what it did do was point Warburg, his firm and the City of London in the most fruitful of future directions.

Warburg and Bolton were pretty close over the years, and that summer it was Bolton who made significant progress on a rather broader front. 'I spoke to you last week,' he reminded Cromer on 6 June, 'about a certain exchange of ideas that is currently taking place regarding the opening of the London market to a wide variety of borrowers for loans denominated in foreign currencies.' He added that 'conversations, so far, have been kept within the very small group of representatives of Barings, Samuel Montagu, Warburgs and ourselves [i.e. BOLSA], but we would not wish to proceed more actively unless the ideas have the general blessing of the authorities'. An enclosed note put forward the arguments in favour of the proposals; some weeks later, on 11 July, Bolton updated Cromer, telling him that 'Charles Hambro has been brought into the group', having 'expressed a wish that Hambros Bank should be associated with this kind of transaction if they are permitted'. As for the plans themselves 'for helping to restore London's function as a capital market and for finding some alternative to the greatly weakened New York market', Bolton mentioned various possibilities. These included Belgium looking for a $50m loan, a group of Austrian public utilities seeking to raise $50m, and Hambros and Warburgs examining the possibility of placing 'in Europe' a $15–20m loan for the Kingdom of Norway, which Kuhn Loeb had been forced to back out of because of deteriorating conditions in the New York market. Almost a fortnight later Cromer at last replied, noting various practical difficulties (such as those relating to bearer and stamp duty) that would need to be overcome, but emphasising that 'we are sympathetic to this proposal and will give it what practical support we can'.[47] It was, for Bolton, Warburg and a few others, enough.

That autumn both Warburg and Bolton were in the States, where they each learned important things – Warburg from friends at the World Bank that around $3bn was in circulation outside the US and thus potentially available for the purpose of long-term loans; Bolton from contacts on Wall Street that American banks were under pressure 'to cease giving financial loans to foreign customers', in the context of continuing pressure on the US balance of payments and the dollar. 'The Administration have no legal powers to prevent non-residents borrowing dollars, either short or long-term, and if methods of persuasion fail I would not exclude legislation,' Bolton added in his memo on his return. 'In any event, I now regard the restoration and revival of the London Market machinery to enable issues of foreign loans to be made as a matter of immediate importance to the Western World . . . The only centre that can help New York is London, as we are all uncomfortably aware of the isolation and inefficiency of the European capital markets . . .'[48]

By the end of 1962 it was neck and neck as to who would arrange London's first foreign currency loan. One of Warburg's many European banking friends was Guido Carli, Governor of the Banca d'Italia, and it emerged that Finsider, the steel-making subsidiary of IRI (the Italian state industrial holding company), urgently needed funds. However, the word from Whitman (whom Kuhn Loeb had generously seconded to Warburgs in order to lend his considerable expertise in the foreign dollar bond market) was that an issue explicitly in the name of Finsider would be critically hobbled by the fact that its statute did not allow it to pay interest on bond coupons without deducting Italian coupon tax. Consequently Finsider arranged, at a price, that the apparent beneficiaries should be Autostrade, the Italian toll-motorway company whose statute did allow it to pay coupons gross. Autostrade was also an IRI subsidiary, and on 14 January 1963 an agreement was formally reached between IRI and Warburgs.[49] There was still much to be done, however, before the issue could become a reality, and meanwhile Samuel Montagu was busy seeking to raise $30m for the Belgian government. It was almost certainly with this in mind that on the 30th, barely a fortnight after the Autostrade signing, Dudley Allen at the Bank of England put various other central banks in the picture:

> You may be interested to know that market interests here are trying to arrange a loan operation in London of a new kind. It is not completely certain that the operation will be mounted but the approval of the authorities has been given . . .
>
> The operation concerned would be the issue in London by an overseas country of a loan denominated in a non-sterling currency and for subscription in non-sterling currencies. The object of such an operation, as you would guess, would be to pick up some of the funds in the Euro-dollar market. Further, we have always been keen, as you know, to see London's expertise used to the maximum. We would not expect a loan of this kind to affect the sterling balance of payments position in any way, nor will it have, in our opinion, any perceptible effect on the prospects of sterling Commonwealth borrowers borrowing sterling on the London market.

Allen was right to sound a cautious note, for by 11 February the Bank was letting it be known that the proposed Belgian loan had fallen through.[50] The news was probably a spur rather than a deterrent to Warburgs, which moved into top gear with the Autostrade issue over the next few months. Ian Fraser, who had been with the firm since 1956 after some years at Reuters, has provided the authoritative inside account:

> Whitman, who by now had joined as a director, was in charge of marketing our bonds and it was my responsibility to engineer their construction. Peter Spira made up the team and was an invaluable member of it. It took Peter and me six months to hack our way through the obstacles . . . Those we had to deal with were designed to stop UK residents from lending abroad, buying foreign bonds and, above all, from investing in bearer securities, which the taxman and the Exchange Control could not

trace. For instance, there was a British stamp duty of 4 per cent on the capital value of all bearer bonds issued in Britain; so we decided to issue them on Schiphol Airport in Holland, in which country there was no such impost. The British Inland Revenue would insist on deducting 42½ per cent income tax from all coupons cashed whether by UK residents or by foreigners; so we arranged for the coupons to be cashed in Luxembourg and in several other places abroad. Most of the banks in the syndicate which Whitman was putting together would not underwrite unless we put in place a listing on a major stock exchange, such as London. After a lot of hard work we persuaded Throgmorton Street to admit our bonds to the official list even though they could not be 'delivered' (in settlement of a transaction) in Britain but only in Brussels or Luxembourg. Then we had major difficulties with the central banks of France, Holland, Sweden, Denmark and of course Britain, about the exchange control consequences of allowing the bonds to be underwritten, purchased, sold, the coupons cashed and ultimately the bonds redeemed all in a foreign currency – US dollars.

Finally, we could not find any printing firm to do the security printing of the bonds to a standard required by the rules (written in the 1920s) of the London Stock Exchange, until at the last moment De La Rue, the playing card printers, came forward and said they had two aged Czech engravers whom they would bring out of retirement who could do it for us. Spira and I had to run round the whole of Western Europe to get everybody in line. It was hard work but it was worth it . . .

The records of Warburgs remain closed, unfortunately, but there is enough contemporary documentation to suggest that, in the eyes of Warburgs and its close associates, all this painstaking work was justified because of the possibility that this pioneering issue might lead to something big. 'Our main purpose in introducing this and similar issues to the London Stock Exchange is to attract business to London on an international scale' was how Eric Korner of Warburgs put it when applying at the end of the April to the London Stock Exchange for an official quotation; in his supporting letter, Jock Hunter of Messels (co-brokers, with Strauss Turnbull, to the issue) typically summed up matters in a nutshell:

> The situation is really that there has developed since the War a considerable business in New York of issuing foreign dollar bonds which are not taken up by the Americans but in general are bought by Europeans. It is hoped that this business can be captured from the Americans and brought to London and that issues can be made in dollars in London by European borrowers and it is expected that the purchasers of these bonds will be largely in Europe.

Korner and Hunter were successful in their request to the Stock Exchange Committee that the minimum commission on such foreign dollar bonds be reduced from ¾ to ½ per cent, though that was still double the rate obtaining in the New York foreign dollar bond market. Hunter's letter

1 *Queen Victoria Street, 1945: rose-bay willowherb, ragwort and groundsel*

2 ABOVE
Throgmorton Street,
19 September 1949:
the day after devalu-
ation, with the Stock
Exchange closed
3 RIGHT *Cameron*
(Kim) Cobbold

4 Above A. W. Trinder (on left)
5 Right Hilton Clarke: *outside the*
Bank of England, 1967

6 ABOVE *Stock Exchange waiter: taking a message for a member, 1947*
7 RIGHT *Messengers leaving the Bank of England after a Bank rate change, 1955*

8 *Stock Exchange floor, 1958*

Partners' Christmas Dinner: Schroders, 1956
9 ABOVE *Alec Cairns, Edward (Tommy) Tucker, Lord Perth, Helmut Schroder*
10 BELOW *Jonathan Backhouse, Alexander Abel Smith, Henry Tiarks, Alec Cairns*

11 *Painting by Simon Elwes of the partners' room at Cazenove's, 1957: Geoffrey Akroyd, Derek Schreiber, Peter Kemp-Welch, Antony Hornby, Philip Cazenove, Ernest Bedford, Frank Holt, Albert Martin*

12 *Exodus at 5.30 over London Bridge, 1957*

made it clear, though, that he did not expect an active market to develop in these bonds on the London Stock Exchange, and he was absolutely right.[51]

Yet in a sense Warburg and the others were pipped at the post – for in mid-May Samuel Montagu *did* manage to arrange a placing for the Belgian government of $20m in 5 per cent bonds. *The Times* saw the importance of this development: 'As the first non-sterling foreign loan to be organised by the City since the war, it signals the resurgence of London as an international capital market.' And the paper added that 'the use of "Euro-dollars" for subscriptions to this placing marks a major step forward towards the use of non-resident dollar deposits for medium-term financing'. The *Banker* agreed that it was 'the City's first foreign currency loan since the war', with the issue being purchased at par by a consortium of banks (including Schroders and Kleinwort Benson) 'out of their substantial holdings of Euro-dollars'. It also noted that 'no market will be created' in these bonds; and that is why over the years this Belgian loan has not generally been regarded as representing the start of the Eurobond market.[52] There was, in other words, no retail element. That, however, was about to come.

'UK Shares In $ Loan To Finance Italian Motorways' was the *FT*'s not entirely accurate headline on 2 July 1963, the day after Warburgs and the rest of the underwriting syndicate had gathered in London to sign the underwriting agreement with Autostrade. It was to be a $15m loan, with a 5½ per cent coupon for the fifteen-year bonds. The syndicate itself comprised Warburgs, Banque de Bruxelles, Deutsche Bank and Rotterdamsche Bank; while at the press conference Fraser (representing Warburgs, as Warburg himself kept a low profile) told *The Times* that 'he hoped the issue would mark a step forward in the process of reestablishing the position which the London capital market held before the war'. He added that 'he expected between 10 and 15 per cent of the issue to be taken up in London, but he doubted whether much of this would be placed in the United Kingdom because of the 10 per cent premium on the investment dollar'.[53]

Two of the firms now responsible for finding an ultimate home for these Autostrade bonds were Strauss Turnbull and White Weld. 'I remember it so well because Julius Strauss came into the office,' one of the up-and-coming dealers at the London brokers recalled. ' "Ross", he said, "I have good news and bad news. The good news is that we are to be brokers to a new issue. The bad news is that it's your job to trade it." For me, it was just one more issue to trade, sandwiched in with all the other things we were doing – arbitraging oil shares between London and New York, gold shares between South Africa and London.'[54] As it happened, the Eurobond market would be the making of Stanley Ross, turning a bus conductor's son into a market legend. Ross looked largely to Strauss Turnbull's continental connections to trade the Autostrade issue in the secondary market, and that was even more the case – indeed, almost wholly the case – as far as White Weld was concerned.[55] A few years earlier this New York firm, which already had offices in Paris and London, had opened an office in Zurich, where under Robert Genillard it was well plugged into the Swiss market for foreign dollar bonds. White Weld had a large international clientele, had traditionally specialised in international bonds and its involvement in the Eurobond market was merely a logical development.

Fraser's account suggests that the Bank of England was not notably helpful in the overcoming of the various Autostrade hurdles, and it has even been claimed, perhaps implausibly, that 'one particularly hostile authority' was Cromer himself. The Governor no doubt had one eye on the American reaction, and on 8 July he wrote tactfully to Al Hayes at the Fed about the two recent dollar issues in London:

> It would seem to me that operations of this character, in so far as they provide useful employment of existing externally held dollars, are, if anything, a stabilising factor in the Euro-dollar market. If, on the other hand, they were to attract new funds from the United States, then clearly this would be something which would only aggravate your own position. My feeling, therefore, is that we should watch these operations carefully, and providing one can accept the assurances of the sponsors [to whom Cromer had recently talked] that the funds are being found from externally held dollar resources, then we should do nothing to discourage. I think it unlikely that the volume of this type of operation will grow to any very great extent . . .

Cromer may or may not have been sincere in his limited expectations about 'the volume of this type of operation', but only ten days later the Eurobond market's defining moment occurred, as President Kennedy sought to protect the US balance of payments by announcing the Interest Equalisation Tax (IET), which crucially involved a 15 per cent tax on the purchase by Americans of foreign securities from foreigners. The story goes that, as the news came through, the Chairman of Morgan Guaranty in New York, Henry Alexander, at once gathered together some senior colleagues and uttered a trenchant forecast – 'This is a day that you will remember forever. It will change the face of American banking and force all the business off to London. It will take years to get rid of this legislation.' However, to read the *Wall Street Journal* of the days immediately after the 18th is to be struck by the sheer absence of discussion about the possible damage that the IET was liable to inflict on New York as an international financial centre. Indeed, the New York bond markets reacted almost bullishly, with one dealer declaring that 'if enacted, this tax would keep more money in this country and some of it would find its way into US Treasury and other bonds'. Nor was Hayes of the Fed unduly concerned when on the 22nd he discussed with Cromer on the phone the question of the dollar bond issues in the London market: 'I told him that, in general, we agreed with his view that we could afford to stand aside and observe developments, especially as to the source of the dollars used to take up these issues.' Hayes did add, though, that because of the tax-evasion aspect that might ensue from the IET, he would not want 'a sudden burgeoning' of such issues; and Cromer, according to Hayes's account, said that he 'fully understood' this attitude.[56]

In London generally there was a mixed reaction to the news from Washington. Kennedy's proposals, Nicholas Baring informed a Wall Street banker, had 'burst as something of a bombshell here in London'; *The Times*'s City editor noted that the probable 'isolation of the American capital market' would provide for London 'an opportunity for a great expansion of its *entrepôt* capital issue business, particularly in dollar loans'; and there was a disappointingly inconsequential entry in Bolton's diary: 'Kennedy. Tax on foreign investments. Great confusion.' Nor had the penny completely dropped by mid-August, with Mynors observing to a foreign correspondent, in the context of the Canadian government hoping to raise a substantial dollar loan in London, that 'the impact of the Kennedy announcement about the interest equalisation tax has been to put a marked damper on the enthusiasm of European investors for this kind of issue'. According to Mynors, this was attributable to 'the uncertainty in people's minds as to both the content of the proposed legislation and the likelihood of its becoming law'.[57] In due course it did become law, and as is the way of these things soon appeared to be a blindingly obvious turning-point.

As far as the new London market itself was concerned, the key fact was that the Bank of England remained firmly, if a tad unenthusiastically, onside. This became clear later in August following a visit from Morgan Grenfell's Harcourt to Mynors (with Cromer away). Mynors's memo on the 22nd was revealing:

Warburgs have recently made a dollar loan in London on behalf of Autostrade. Competition in the merchant banking field is now very keen and it is being said that such established names as Baring, Lazard, Morgan, are out of date, which they do not appreciate. Hope & Co [of Amsterdam] have now invited Morgan Grenfell to join with them (and possibly Morgan et Cie and the Deutsche Bank) in making a dollar issue in London on behalf of the City of Oslo. Morgan Grenfell have said that, with the switch dollar premium at 7+ per cent, they could not undertake to find a single subscriber in the UK. Hope & Co replied that the loan must have a market somewhere, that London is the obvious place and that they hope that Morgan Grenfell will come in with them on this ground even though they can find no money . . .

It does not really make sense to Lord Harcourt that a Norwegian City should borrow dollars through a Dutch bank with a market in London, but these things are happening and he thinks they should go along unless the Authorities object. If they do object, they must definitely stop this kind of thing. If they say, on an old boy basis, that they would rather it did not happen, it will be done but by everybody except the best people.

I promised Lord Harcourt a reply *urgently* on the view of the Authorities, as he must reply to Hope & Co.

The next day, Parsons's memo to the Governors was decisive:

The answer to Lord Harcourt's enquiry about the attitude of the authorities to the suggested City of Oslo dollar issue in London is that we do not put any obstacle in the way of such issues on the basis that London is thereby conducting a brokerage business, which on the whole we are inclined to favour. Admittedly, we in the Bank would much prefer to see this kind of business done in sterling but unfortunately that is only possible in the case of a limited number of countries . . .

A month later Jacob Rothschild rang the Bank to check that it had no problem over Rothschilds floating dollar-denominated foreign bond issues in London. The Bank, he was told soon afterwards, had no problem. Almost a century and a half after Nathan Rothschild's drive to centre the international capital market on London, possibilities were afoot by November 1963 in what Mynors was tentatively calling 'the Euro-Capital Market'.[58]

The successful emergence of this new London market in foreign dollar bonds was not, though, the whole story. There had also, more or less simultaneously, been a noteworthy sterling aspect – an aspect that Cromer was highly conscious of when, back in June 1962, he told the Treasury that he 'proposed to pursue every possible method of improving the London capital market as the leading market for Europe'. By early 1963 the main candidate for the honour of receiving a sterling loan was the Japanese government; and in April Cromer was able to persuade the British government that a £5m refunding loan would not irremediably damage the UK economy, emphasising Japan's historical ties with the City and its creditworthiness.[59] This was the cue for Japan's traditional 'London Group' of bankers to reform (Barings, Westminster and the Hongkong and Shanghai, joined on this occasion by Morgan Grenfell, Rothschilds and Schroders), organising what *The Times* greeted in early August as 'the first true foreign loan raising operation in the City since the war', in that 'previous foreign government loans in London have been for members of the sterling area and especially Commonwealth or former Commonwealth countries'. Yet although this particular issue was almost thirty times oversubscribed, there was some truth in Parsons's regretful observation later that month that sterling issues were only likely to be possible in the case of 'a limited number of countries'. Maudling may have been disingenuous therefore, when in his Mansion House speech in October he looked forward confidently to the reopening of the London international capital market. Certainly the *FT*'s Tether was sceptical: 'I realise that the efforts being made to liberalise the London capital market could encourage money to flow into the UK as well as out of it. But in a capital-hungry world it is far from certain that we won't be left with a substantial gap to bridge.'[60] Of course, what no one yet conceived – probably not even Bolton – was the extent to which dollar loans issued in London would be capable of feeding that hunger.

The City, in truth, was poised to become at least as much a dollar as a sterling City, as the events of 1963–4 in the Eurodollar market graphically showed. 'Our enquiries lead us to believe that the bulk of this business through London is on a bank-to-bank basis; in other words, there is a reputable and responsible intermediary,' Cromer reassured the Treasury in June 1963. Over the next few months, however, runs on banks in Switzerland and Germany, apparently caused by prominent clients (such as the two Stinnes groups) being deep in the Eurodollar market, prompted widespread anxiety about the stability – or otherwise – of Eurodollar deposits. Hermann Abs of Deutsche Bank was particularly concerned, and on 9 November, writing from the British Embassy in Bonn, Frank Roberts reported how that most illustrious of post-war German bankers had recently 'read me a long warning about the Eurodollar Market, which was under no central bank of control and in which quite small firms were handling enormous sums of money', with Abs advising that 'we should all be very careful indeed about this Market'. Soon afterwards Abs spoke publicly in London along the same lines, provoking on the 19th an important article from Tether in the *FT* entitled 'How Serious is the Danger of a "Euro-Dollar Explosion"?' This influential journalist (with a particular following in Washington) did not deny that 'for some considerable time' his Lombard column had been trying to show that 'the growth of international short-term money traffic through the Euro-dollar market' (traffic that he estimated was now running at $4,000m) was 'far from being the unmixed blessing for the world at large that banking institutions engaged in promoting it have been accustomed to represent it to be'. However, Tether argued emphatically that what he called 'the recent fashion of portraying this phenomenon as a gigantic financial powder-barrel that could be sparked off at any moment should lenders begin to experience difficulty in getting their money back' ignored the will-power of the financial authorities of the lending as well as the borrowing countries to contain any such threat. And, he concluded confidently, 'in this day and age there are ready means available for dealing with such situations'.[61]

Not everyone at the Bank of England accepted this analysis. 'I am filled with foreboding,' George Preston, an inveterate pessimist on this subject, reflected on 4 December, finding echoes of pre-1931 in the present situation; but importantly that pragmatic operator Roy Bridge (by now an adviser to the Governors) was altogether more sanguine in a memo the next day. The recent problems, he thought, 'may well have shown an amber light and caused a number of banks here and elsewhere to review the way they were doing their business', and Tether-style he added that 'the international framework of monetary co-operation which we now have can, I believe, deal with misplaced lack of confidence in currencies'. The Bank of England, consequently, held the line and continued not to interfere in the Eurodollar market – in marked contrast to the Banque de France, which that same month instructed French banks to curtail substantially their Eurodollar business. The proof lay in the pudding, as the total of foreign currency (mainly Eurodollar) balances held with London banks by overseas residents increased by the equivalent of £214m during the first half of 1964, having understandably declined in the last quarter of 1963. Bridge himself explained his thinking more fully in March 1964 to the Chief Economist of Bankers Trust in New York:

> The so-called Euro-dollar market is nothing other than a natural international money market. My point of analysis is that while domestic money markets are subject to the supervision of the monetary authorities and indeed to the banking laws of the countries concerned, there is not in existence any comparable international monetary authority to supervise and, where necessary, regulate the international money market nor, if there were, is it immediately evident by what means it could or would exercise its control.

Nevertheless, having made this attractively honest admission, Bridge was not unduly worried: 'There may indeed be some unsound banking here and there. Too much lending long against short borrowings. But this is where the experience and the judgment of the international banker should come in . . .'[62]

The Eurodollar market's younger *alter ego*, the Eurobond market, also prospered during 1964. January saw two major dollar loans in London, one a $10m loan arranged by Hambros for the Norges Kommunalbank to finance hydroelectric schemes in Norway, the other an $18m loan for the Austrian government organised by Warburgs in conjunction with Hambros, Rothschilds and Credit Anstalt. The latter loan was particularly significant, for it was originally going to be made the previous summer on the New York foreign dollar bond market, but was prevented by the proposed IET; then it was going to be a London sterling issue in the autumn, but was prevented by a sudden break in the gilt-edged market; and so ultimately it was a dollar loan issued in London. The *Banker* did sound a somewhat sour note about these Eurodollar loans, speculating that 'the process of subscription must presumably involve several intermediaries borrowing short to lend long'; but by April any such criticism was stilled as it reported a further flurry of dollar issues in London in recent weeks, in particular four big loans 'arranged by international consortia through London'. Two were headed by Hambros ($12.5m for K. Itoh, a Japanese trading company, and $12m for the Copenhagen Telephone Co), one by Hambros and Warburgs ($12m for the Danish Mortgage Bank) and one by Lazards ($10m for Tyssefaldene, the Norwegian hydroelectric company). Altogether, the *Banker* calculated, a total of some $200m worth of foreign currency loans had been placed in London since May 1963. By the end of the year the best estimate for 1964 itself was that a total of forty-four foreign dollar issues had been made in Europe, mainly in London, raising the equivalent of $681m.[63]

Behind those figures lay two particularly interesting developments. One was the refusal of the Bank of England to bow to US pressure about the automatic involvement of American banks in these issues. 'I think each case probably has to be judged on its own merits,' Cromer politely insisted to Hayes in March. The already acknowledged leader of the Eurobond market would doubtless have been unhappy not to have had that degree of support from the Bank, for Parsons noted later that month that he 'shared Mr Warburg's views about the inappropriateness of having an American firm as leader of a London syndicate'; though Warburg did also explain that he was 'not averse from taking in an American underwriter, on occasions, when Warburgs were heading a syndicate'. In April there was a new initiative from the US Treasury, which led Cromer to tell the IHA that the Bank had made it clear to the American authorities 'that in a London issue the leader of the syndicate must, in our view, be a London house and that the London practice does not correspond to that of the New York market in the manner in which underwriters are listed on the prospectus'. The other development in this fledgling market was anticipated by Warburg when he called on Cromer on the last day of 1963. 'He felt,' his host noted, 'that there was a limit to the volume of loans which could usefully be floated by London Houses in dollar terms and that it was, in his opinion, only a matter of time after the American interest equalisation tax lapsed before such business would revert to New York. He felt that there might well be scope for issues to be made with a sterling/deutschemark option as the interest rates in Germany and the UK were not too far apart . . .' Events in 1964 did not bear out Warburg's pessimistic scenario for the future of dollar loans in London, but after the Bank had given its go-ahead in March to issues with a sterling/

Deutschmark option he still went ahead. 'In at the beginning with Autostrade, S.G. Warburg and Co is again in pioneering mood,' the *FT* commented on 12 October about its £5m issue with a DM option for the City of Turin; and it noted how 'it is felt that in present conditions – with the US starting to come back as a capital market despite the interest equalisation tax – the psychological appeal of European currency for European borrowers will help to preserve London's position'. Even so, the fact remained that 'for UK investors, unfortunately, the dollar premium still stands'. The issue, nevertheless, was a success, and two days later Cromer saw Henry Grunfeld of Warburgs and gave him his 'compliments'.[64]

By the mid-1960s, in the context of the growth of the Eurodollar market and the coming of the Eurobond market, the City was a rather different place from what it had been even in the late 1950s – though large pockets of it, such as Lloyd's and the Stock Exchange, remained fundamentally unchanged. In particular, although the great rush would come in the second half of the decade, American banks were starting to arrive in numbers.[65] The main lure, naturally, was the Euromarkets, although there was also a 'push' factor in the form of stifling US banking legislation, which made the more ambitious banks look hard for opportunities abroad. There was also by now a Japanese dimension, as the four big Tokyo securities houses (Daiwa, Nomura, Yamaichi and Nikko) all became established presences on the back of no fewer than eleven Eurobond issues for Japanese concerns between December 1963 and April 1964. It was the American challenge, however, that loomed far larger in the collective mind of British banks – not surprisingly, granted the ever more dominant position of American banks in the Eurodollar market – and among the clearers the most innovative response came from Midland. In 1963 it came together with three continental banks to set up the European Advisory Committee, a venture designed to provide large-scale international financing for specific projects; the following year, in alliance with Toronto Dominion Bank, Standard Bank and Commercial Bank of Australia, it set up Midland and International Banks, based at 36 Throgmorton Street and the first of what became known as the consortium banks, whose main purpose was to use the Eurodollar market for medium-term lending. Midland's 'Grand Design' (as the bank's directors liked to call it) contrasted notably with the refusal of Barclays to participate in an ambitious consortium being projected by Samuel Montagu, of a merchant bank, an insurance company and a big commercial bank that between them would offer a comprehensive range of services to British and European companies.[66]

This process of internationalising the City was something that the Bank of England under Cromer's governorship thoroughly welcomed, and it was keen that the relatively flexible legal and tax framework for foreign banks in London should in no way be jeopardised. What was potentially a rather different matter was the issue of sizeable foreign stakes in British firms. The Bank did not object to First National City Bank of New York acquiring a one-sixth stake in M. Samuel, publicly announced in February 1963; but when, a few weeks later, Continental Illinois told Parsons that it was thinking of likewise taking a stake in a London merchant bank, he intimated that it was 'a slightly delicate question' and that, while there was 'no formal barrier', nevertheless 'if a foreign bank were to attempt to acquire a majority holding it would confront us with some difficult problems'. If that was one sighter of the City's future, namely the whole question of ownership, so too was Jack Spall's experience in 1961 when, after fourteen years with the old-established East India merchants Wallace Brothers, he joined the ranks of the 'thundering herd' – the American brokerage house Merrill Lynch:

> It was a complete culture shock. Its offices were just by Fenchurch Station and it was a whole new ball game to me. People earned a lot of money, there was a sudden display of wealth, which I was unused to. I wanted some of it, in the normal way. The offices were grotty. Rain used to come through the roof, they tried to tart it up a bit but it was unsatisfactory. Most of the dealers were Americans and because it was the early days of Merrill Lynch in London, there was a good spirit of camaraderie . . . It wasn't paternalistic in the way that Wallace Brothers was, but we actually got paid money and that was the difference. One of my colleagues was a woman, who was absolutely spot-on and one thought, 'God, I'll never be as good as she is'. I probably thought, 'My God, if I can't do better than a woman, then . . .'[67]

Americans *and* women: the harbingers of the late twentieth-century City were already present.

*

Yet for the City in the early 1960s there were rather more pressing domestic matters. Above all, could a Conservative government manage to break out of the stop-go cycle and deliver growth in such a way as not to jeopardise sterling? And, irrespective of whether it succeeded in that, could the Conservatives win a fourth consecutive term and thus continue to avert the socialist threat? There were, admittedly, a few local difficulties between the City and the Tories during these years, but that remained the larger, shared goal.

For all concerned, an increasingly important element in the equation was the role of organised labour. The trade unions did not take kindly to the wage restraints proposed in Selwyn Lloyd's July 1961 package, prompting the retired Ernest Skinner to sound off to Mynors that November about the latest economic and industrial troubles. 'As a matter of fact,' the Deputy Governor replied, 'we have had very little to say in the matter of the pay pause; although we have been pressing for anti-inflationary action, our target tends to be government expenditure rather than the *TUC*.' As for the unions themselves, the specific target of Skinner's wrath, Mynors did concede that their management was 'old-fashioned, to say the least', but he tried to strike a more balanced view: 'Is none of the blame attributable to management on the other side of the table? Have they not conceded on occasion without getting any rede-ployment as a quo pro quid, knowing that they can always offload the cost on to the home market?' More generally, even though Bank rate gradually came down, Lloyd's squeeze continued through the winter of 1961–2. It seemed to do little good, especially in the field of exports, and the London discount market's representatives thought in January that 'Lord Cromer appeared to be somewhat depressed'; though when a few weeks later one of them observed that 'the trade figures were rather depressing', Cromer did not disagree but said, 'Don't be too despondent; Germany, Italy and others have their problems'.[68]

It was that spring that Mynors and Maurice Allen produced their inimitable maxims for central bankers, and those that concerned economic policy were a salutary reminder of how little, in a supposedly Keynesian age, the Bank's verities had shifted since the time of Montagu Norman:

> All expenditure is inflationary, but government expenditure most of all.
> A foreign exchange rate is sacred, to be touched only when all other corrective measures are seen to have failed.
> Stability in the value of money helps economic growth.
> Confidence in a currency is the first requisite for its stability; weakened confidence can be restored only by policies of a Gladstonian kind.
> Other countries do not owe us a living.

Sterling first, in other words, remained the unquestioned priority – and strikingly, despite his frustrations over continuing deflation, increasing unemployment and rising political unpopularity, Harold Macmillan did not dissent. 'Supreme task is to keep the pound strong abroad and at home,' he briefed his Cabinet on 16 May. 'If we fail *abroad* devaluation will follow causing grave damage. Cost of imports will increase; it would be a breach of faith with our creditors, and would unloose financial disturbances all around the world.' Nevertheless, the D-word was starting to be furtively muttered, to judge by Mynors's note after calling on Lloyd on the 25th: 'He is conscious of two splinter movements among his own colleagues, one or two prepared to contemplate a change in the exchange rate, if need be, while one self-professed expert [presumably Enoch Powell] continues to advocate a floating rate.' Next month Cromer delivered his considered opinion to Lee at the Treasury:

Unilateral devaluation of sterling, which would certainly jeopardise the sterling area (and it should be remembered that sterling liabilities are roughly in the ratio of 4 to 1 of reserves) would not at the present time lead to immediate devaluation either by the Europeans or the Americans. It would certainly initiate a period of the utmost uncertainty which in the course of time and with the generation of the maximum of odium would lead to such devaluations. But it has to be remembered that the people of the United States as a whole, quite apart from the Administration, would regard us as having brought this disaster, for so they would regard it, on them . . .[69]

Devaluation, then, remained a non-starter as a route to growth; Lloyd was apparently unable to conceive – certainly to countenance – any realistic alternatives; and, not helped by his lack of communication skills, he met his political death on 13 July, as Macmillan indulged in 'The Night of the Long Knives'. The new Chancellor was Reginald Maudling, a younger, more ambitious politician not necessarily willing to go to the stake for sterling.

The City did not greatly mourn Lloyd's passing, especially as he had been responsible for implementing the iniquitous policy of taxing short-term capital gains. The tax was originally proposed as part of the July 1961 package, and that autumn it moved up the political agenda as a sweetener for the unions. The Stock Exchange, above all its Chairman Lord Ritchie of Dundee, was outraged. He and his two deputies called on Lloyd in early December, claiming that the tax would do 'grave damage' to the market and that although 'no free market can exist without there being a certain element of speculation', nevertheless 'the backbone of the business and the basis of the need for the market is the hard core of investment business, both small and large'. Lloyd, however, informed Macmillan that he did not find their arguments, either in person or on paper, 'very convincing'. Later that month Cromer had a go, writing to Lloyd in a personal capacity:

I deplore, as much as you do, the spivish sort of society which has been created in this country as the result of the excessively high rate of income and surtax. It is because of this excessively high personal taxation that such a high premium has been put on two scourges of this age, speculation and abuse of the expense account. What you are now suggesting will merely aggravate further without removing the cause which stimulates recourse to this form of defence against Government oppression. What is even worse is that you are creating a precedent that future Governments will quote when they extend your measures to all capital gains, as they inevitably will. I would question whether you realise the degree of disillusionment and bitterness that during the long years of Conservative rule no real move has been made to reward effort and discourage mere opportunism. Successive Conservative

Governments have built up a vested interest in continued inflation by these means . . .

Cromer too got nowhere, so the following spring, three weeks before the date that had been set for what would be Lloyd's final budget, Ritchie tried again, this time in public. 'I believe that the City has very nearly reached the end of its tether and that its loyalty and willingness to co-operate have almost reached breaking point,' he told a crowded conference being held under the auspices of the Wider Share Ownership Council; and, he added, 'We do feel that the subject of investment, the subject of freedom of markets, the subject of the importance of the stock market to the country, to industry, and to us – all is constantly bedeviled by the Government.' Ritchie's remarks, Clarke in *The Times* noted, struck a wider chord: 'There can be little doubt that many in the City are by now bitterly disappointed at the Government's record in economic affairs. Most of all, it is a lack of leadership that is being felt.'[70] In April, to no one's surprise, Lloyd formally introduced the new tax.

That summer Cromer managed to dissuade Ritchie from sending a protest letter to *The Times*, while in December Ritchie himself was on the receiving end of a petition, as more than 300 Stock Exchange members lamented that 'we can look for hindrance, not help from the present government and it appears more than likely that they will be replaced by another which will be no more concerned than they for fostering markets'. It was a sign of the times that, soon afterwards, City names were conspicuous by their absence from the New Year's Honours List for 1963. 'With the exception of the years when the Labour Party was in office, relations between the Government and the City have seldom if ever been as bad as they are today,' the *Sunday Telegraph*'s City editor, Nigel Lawson, reflected in the immediate aftermath of this deliberate snub. Noting that Macmillan 'has never liked the City', and referring back to Stockton-on-Tees in the 1930s, Lawson observed that 'once again we have unemployment in the North-East – at the same time as the Governor of the Bank of England is urging a return to near pre-war freedom for the London capital market'. The City, he added, was also under attack because of the argument that all the country's economic troubles ('stagnation, balance of payments, crises, the lot') were 'due to the fact that we have always had to put sterling first and growth a bad second, to the fact that we have tried to carry on an international banking business whose responsibilities are more than we can bear'. To counter this argument, Lawson cited the examples of Zurich and Amsterdam in order to make the prescient as well as perceptive point that 'it is, in fact, perfectly possible to be a financial centre without any reserve currency obligations'.[71]

Another, rather older financial journalist, Richard Fry, raised the political stakes with a piece in the *Guardian* headed 'City's Feud With Government'. He stressed that the lack of the customary knighthood for the retiring Government broker (Derrick Mullens) had been 'deeply felt in the City as an open and deliberate gesture of hostility'; and, after stating that 'the Prime Minister is generally believed to be wholly in favour of the anti-City legislation', he claimed that City contributions to Conservative Party funds 'have already been drastically reduced'. Macmillan's response was to cede on the symbol ('about Mullens – I have asked Bligh to see that he is put into the List next June,' he told Maudling the day after Fry's article), but to hold firm on the substance. The Chancellor agreed and sought to console his chief: 'I do not believe that the picture drawn in the article is accurate, at any rate so far as the more sensible people in the City are concerned, particularly the banks and the insurance companies. There is a certain amount of grumbling on the Stock Exchange, for which I feel very little sympathy.' As for Fry, Maudling could only reflect that he was 'normally rather more responsible'.[72]

All this mirrored a larger City frustration by the early 1960s that its influence over the government of the day was slipping.[73] Certainly it did not contribute significantly to, nor indeed was sympathetic to, the new planning mechanism in the form of 'Neddy'. The tone that Mynors adopted in October 1962 in his response to that body's first report was symptomatic:

> When I was a student of political economy, plastic kits were not yet on sale, so model-building is an unfamiliar exercise. On a first reading, this report strikes me as a leading example of the kind of economic thinking which has accompanied our arrival in the present doldrums – the competent handling of economic aggregates such as 'investment' or 'consumption', with the most formative influences, such as the better deployment of existing resources or the movement of prices, ignored or assumed unchanged.

Three months later there was an almost forlorn sense of the Bank being out of the corporatist loop, as Cromer sought a personal favour from John Hare, the Minister of Labour:

> It has reached my ears that you are shortly having a cocktail party for employers and the TUC. With considerable temerity I am writing to ask you whether it might be possible for me to receive an invitation. The reason for this rather odd request is that, in the normal course of events, I have virtually no opportunity of meeting the TUC members and on this occasion I have a particular reason for wanting to contrive a meeting with one or two individuals.
> Please forgive such forward behaviour on my part . . .

Cromer clearly saw informal social functions as the key to doing something about the problem, for soon afterwards he initiated what he hoped would become a series of dinner-parties-with-topics to be hosted by himself at the Governor's flat. Their purpose was to get closer not to the unions but to the Treasury, and in his letters of invitation to three Treasury guests and six City people Cromer referred to the desirability of trying 'to increase the flow and interchange of ideas between the City and Whitehall'. Ernest Kleinwort, Kenneth Keith and Sir George Bolton were among those invited to bat for the City on 1 May 1963, and Cromer flagged in advance the rather ponderously worded topic for discussion: 'From the point of view of contribution which could be made to the UK balance of payments, what are the potentialities of developing what might be described as merchant-adventuring business?'[74]

Over the next year or so, as the prospect of a Labour government increased, some wondered whether something more fundamental needed to be done in order to improve the City's formal links with the wider opinion-forming and policy-making world. 'Sir Edward Reid thought the City ought to speak with one voice,' Monckton at the Midland noted in October 1963 after a visit from the Chairman of the Accepting Houses Committee. 'There ought to be some body able to give a concrete view to the whole lot. I said, and Sir Archibald Forbes [who would succeed Monckton in 1964] who was present agreed, that I was against it. I thought those of us who trusted each other should get together occasionally but not as a body.' In January 1964 at the IHA's annual meeting, Walter Salomon took much the same line as Reid, but likewise got nowhere. 'Authority is more likely to accept a City view when expressed by a number of bodies acting independently than it would be if only one representation were made to it,' remained the IHA's adamant view.[75] There was also the strong, if unspoken, assumption that the Bank of England would hardly welcome the emergence of a single body that might easily turn into a permanent rival to itself. Things would have to get a lot worse before the City as a whole stopped looking to the Old Lady to try to do the necessary on its behalf.

Already, though, the Bank's relative impotence had been demonstrated by its inability to restrain Maudling from his reckless 'dash for growth'. Perhaps his Prime Minister during the formative stage of that dash thought he had Cromer on his side. 'In reality, although "sound", Lord C. has a nose,' Macmillan told himself in June 1962, even while Lloyd was still Chancellor, after a long talk with the Governor. 'He is not a Baring for nothing – a long business and financial tradition. He realises that the new danger to the world is not world inflation but competitive deflation.' Perhaps, but what ensued between September 1962 and April 1963, by which point the next election was a maximum of eighteen months away, went far beyond anything that Cromer would willingly have countenanced. The dash was mainly fiscal, with a particular emphasis on cutting purchase tax, and culminated in a boldly tax-cutting budget. 'The theme of this Budget is expansion; expansion without inflation, expansion that can be sustained,' Maudling declared; but, as it had been since the previous autumn when Maudling had begun the process, the stock market was unconvinced and the FT 30-Share Index barely nudged above 300.[76]

Yet the fact remains that although Maudling's stewardship would subsequently become a byword for political opportunism, most economic commentators were prepared to give him the benefit of the doubt, particularly in the context of the general acceptance of Neddy's 4 per cent growth target for the economy. One of those commentators was Samuel Brittan in the *Observer*. 'It was the appallingly bad case put up by the advocates of sound money in the Bank and elsewhere which made me believe in growthmanship, i.e. using rapid demand expansion to stimulate industry into more vigorous performance,' he remembered many years later about the 1960s. 'The demonstration that the end result would be inflation without more growth or jobs came from Friedman, while the Bank was mainly preoccupied with the immorality of letting down sterling balance holders.' No doubt Brittan, for understandable reasons, exaggerated his point – 'there are people in the Bank as intellectually high-powered as almost anyone in the Treasury,' he himself had written in 1964 – yet the ethos behind Cobbold's dictum that 'the Bank is not a study group' would take a long time to banish entirely. Cromer himself, moreover, was no economist, and had strongly free-market instincts that were inimical to advocates of dirigiste growth. The spirit of the times was firmly on the side of planned expansion, typified by the *FT*'s impassioned declaration in January 1963 that 'the best thing the Government could do for the country's future as well as for its own would be to go all out for a faster rate of economic growth' – something that could only be achieved through 'knowing precisely what one wants and dealing ruthlessly (as ruthlessly as the French planners, perhaps) with all the mental and physical obstacles which stand in the way', even if this meant 'hurting established ideas and vested interests'.[77] Arguably the quality of the Bank's economic thinking and advice was immaterial in the face of such a powerful *Zeitgeist*, fuelled as it was by mounting exasperation with Britain's economic decline, entrenched establishment and a cult of muddling through.

Nevertheless, Brittan was surely correct that the Bank lost significant credibility through its overinsistent emphasis on not betraying the international holders of sterling. 'He is, of course, obsessed with the idea that the international obligations of sterling act as a direct restraint on economic growth and is therefore somewhat impatient of the argument that external considerations have to be taken into account,' Parsons warned Cromer in September 1962 after a conversation with the new Chancellor. 'I have been trying to persuade him, and incidentally some of his officials, that no country can ignore the external implications of domestic policy, but he is not altogether convinced.' Shortly before Christmas, Parsons reported to Cromer that Maudling was still privately fantasising about 'freeing the UK economy from the inhibitions of reserve currency status', a prospect that Parsons could hardly contemplate. Maudling, though, did not go public with his aspiration, and in his April 1963 budget speech he made an unequivocal declaration: 'I absolutely reject the proposition that a vigorous economy and a strong position for sterling are incompatible.'[78] Perhaps by this time, he and his Prime Minister may have reflected, a Conservative administration had shed enough of the burdens of Empire; as for the City, certainly outside the Eurodollar market, it remained axiomatic (and virtually undebated) that sterling's strength and its own strength were umbilically connected.

The lights remained green during autumn 1963, as belatedly the stock market decided that 'a vigorous economy' had its advantages. There was one awkward moment in early October when it seemed that, against the wishes of both Bank and Treasury, the clearing banks might insist on increasing their overdraft rates by a ½ per cent. 'This is *very* serious,' Macmillan (in his last days as Prime Minister) noted. 'Why not *nationalise* the Clearing Banks?' The next day he heard, via Monckton, that in this move 'the leading spirit' among the clearers was John Thomson of Barclays, prompting Macmillan to muse, 'I suppose we c^d send Thomson to the Tower, if necessary.' In the end it required Cromer to warn Thomson 'extremely forcefully' that 'the Government would take an extremely serious view if the banks persisted in going ahead with their proposals'; reluctantly Thomson backed off, remarking to Mynors that he would have to 'take his orders'. There was a brief coda in December when the banks revived their scheme, this time with qualified support from Cromer, and Maudling told the Governor that he would not stand in their way, but that he had 'heard nothing to convince him' and that altogether the clearing banks were 'too much marble and monopoly'. The Maudling boom, meanwhile, was in full swing. 'The car was now going downhill fairly rapidly' was how Mynors characteristically expressed it at the end of October to the discount market, adding that 'before long the brakes may be rather difficult to apply'. Maudling himself, arguably to his credit, acknowledged as much. 'He was rather amused,' Cairncross recorded three weeks later after a conversation with the Chancellor, 'at way everything shaping for a splendid bit of expansion next spring followed by election and then efforts by Callaghan and Co to cope with exchange crisis. Said nobody would believe we hadn't planned it.'[79]

Maudling's private view that Labour would win was widely shared, and the City during the winter of 1963–4 made its dispositions and looked gloomily ahead. The Stock Exchange, particularly anxious not to be vulnerable in what was expected to be a bitter election, spent £35,000 on what its Public Relations Committee described as 'an extensive campaign [mainly corporate advertising in the popular press] to emphasise that the Stock Exchange is essential to the running of the nation and that it provides a good service both to the direct and indirect investor'. At the Bank, Cromer recruited a young, Labour-sympathising economist, Christopher (Kit) McMahon. 'As to his political views,' the Governor told a correspondent in January 1964, 'he mentioned them to me and I feel in no way perturbed. He has such a good objective mind and this is what counts most.' At Cromer's old shop, 8 Bishopsgate, Nicholas Baring told a Wall Street banker that, with a Labour government expected by the end of the year, 'it seems a fair assumption that Wilson himself will prove to be, if anything, rather more left-wing than he has appeared in the initial stages of his campaign'.[80]

Harold Wilson's relations with the City had been mutually bad since the Bank rate leak of 1957; and now in February 1964, in the context of poor trade figures for February, he convinced himself that dirty work was afoot at the crossroads concerning the country's true external situation, in particular the state of the sterling reserves. Accompanied by his Shadow Chancellor, James Callaghan, he had a top-secret meeting on the 26th with Maudling and the new Prime Minister, Sir Alec Douglas-Home. 'H.W. made allegations that Bank of England was "cooking the books",' Cairncross recorded. 'Offered to keep quiet but only if Tories didn't publicly accuse Labour of endangering sterling.' A deal was done along those lines, though the ministers also insisted that the allegations were 'unfounded' and that Wilson 'must not attack the rise in Bank Rate and rock the boat'. During spring and into the summer the Tories began gradually to whittle away Labour's opinion-poll lead, but the expectation remained of a Labour victory in what was now certain to be an autumn election. What would be the attitude of a Labour government to sterling? Responding in July to a Treasury paper on 'The Next Five Years', Cromer insisted that, whichever party won, the Bank of England's fundamental priority would remain unchanged: 'Let us be quite clear that the international standing and use of sterling is an inherent and essential part of our external economic relationships, and not merely some out-dated slogan exclusive to "The City" . . .'[81]

Before the election the Stock Exchange had some fire-fighting of its own to do. July saw not only the much-publicised hammering of a stockbroking firm (R.H. Bristowe & Co, whose Commander Bristowe had been a wartime hero), but the even more publicised collapse of John Bloom's Rolls Razor company. It had had a complicated history, including a wholesale reconstruction after the suspension of its shares early in 1960. Then in May 1962, under new management and specialising in the manufacture of washing machines, it had returned to the market with an offer for sale sponsored by Kleinwort Benson. 'Their record of profit growth and of bad debts are most encouraging, and the management is still relatively young,' the *FT* had commented enthusiastically, and the issue was a success. Bloom himself, a charismatic figure, would eventually plead guilty to fraud; and in July 1964 the collapse, quite apart from inflicting some significant (if temporary) damage on Kleinwort Benson's reputation, also seemed to reflect badly on the Stock Exchange. Certainly it heightened fears that an incoming Labour government might be tempted to introduce an American-style Securities and Exchange Commission, and late in August the Stock Exchange surprised its critics by introducing rules on company disclosure that went well beyond existing legal requirements. 'The London Stock Exchange is acting completely out of character,' Charles Anderson (recently retired as editor of *Investors Chronicle*) sardonically observed, granted that 'in managing its own internal affairs it has a long way to go before it draws abreast of latter-day realities'.[82]

'The stock market was more volatile in the course of this election campaign than in any other since the war,' John Littlewood (then an analyst with a stockbroking firm) has aptly recalled of the feverish month leading up to polling day on 15 October 1964. 'Fear and greed exchanged places from day to day. . .' Was this fear irrational? Littlewood, reflecting on the fact that memories of the Attlee government were 'still fresh in the minds of many people', argued not:

> It is conventional thinking today [1998] that no government could impose controls on the movement of capital as long as London remains at the heart of one of the three financial trading centres that make up the 24-hour global market. The sophistication of technology and communications would not allow it. In 1964, world markets simply did not exist in this way and there were genuine reasons to fear that a Labour government could easily erect barriers to contain and control financial assets within a highly effective ringed fence.[83]

The City fully shared the anxieties of investors at large, but for just over the first fortnight of the campaign there was some market optimism that the Tories might yet snatch a famous victory. 'Buyers Hopeful Of Tory Election Victory Send Steels, Insurances, Properties Well Ahead' was the *FT*'s stock-market report headline on 2 October, after the Index had reached its highest point of the year, 377.8. The mood had been fuelled by a series of opinion polls showing little to choose between the parties, but then on Sunday the 4th a Gallup Poll gave a 4½ per cent lead to Labour. Over the following week the Index lost 20.7 points, equivalent to a 5.5 per cent fall, and thereafter market confidence never really recovered.

For Cromer the most unsettling moment came on the 1st, after the *FT* had reported Wilson declaring in a speech at Norwich that the latest gold and currency reserve figures, due to be issued on the afternoon of the 2nd, were going to 'dominate this Election'. This prompted Cromer to telephone the Prime Minister's office and let it be known that he was 'worried at the possibility of the adjustment of the September figures to take account of Central Bank support becoming a factor in the political situation', in that (the office further noted) 'the extent to which the September figures had been cooked would be clear in due course from the Bank of England Bulletin and the Federal Reserve Bank Review and he might be accused of conniving at a political manoeuvre'. Cromer accepted that 'it was out of the question to think of publishing the true figure but said that the compromise that he had in mind was disclosing it privately to the Leader of the Opposition'. The matter was left to Maudling, who told Cromer later that day that he must not even think of volunteering 'the true figure' to Wilson, and Cromer reluctantly complied.[84] The next day the published figures showed a politically containable fall of £16m.

A week later the discount market's representatives saw Cromer, who naturally did not allude to the matter. Instead, 'a lot was said, very little of it of any importance,' they noted. 'The Governor said he thought the outlook was very difficult to assess and not very convincing.' Cromer spent election night itself at a series of parties – at *The Times*, the *Telegraph* and, hedging his bets, the *Daily Mirror* – as it gradually became clear that Labour was going to win, but not by much. 'If Labour wins, there will be no question of industry or the City of London refusing to co-operate,' the City's conscience, Harold Wincott, had written the previous week. 'A Labour Prime Minister will be welcomed and applauded at Guildhall, and Mr Callaghan at the bankers' dinner at the Mansion House.'[85]

CHAPTER TWELVE

The Facts of Life

'The stock exchange was seesawing but no profound losses were reported so far,' ran the Fed's report on a phone conversation with the Bank of England at 8.10 a.m. (New York time) on Friday, 16 October 1964. 'Preston [of the Bank] was of the opinion that with the close vote in view the Labor Party could not do much very fast and that no sweeping changes might be expected.' Two hours later, in another phone conversation across the Atlantic, the Bank's Roy Bridge told the Fed that 'he saw no basis for the Labor Party to re-nationalize the steel industry since the vote was so close'. At this point Bridge was anticipating an overall Labour majority of just two, though in the event it was double that. Next day the new government's three top ministers – Harold Wilson as Prime Minister, James Callaghan as Chancellor of the Exchequer and George Brown in charge of the newly created Department of Economic Affairs – made the cardinal decision that, despite the grave balance-of-payments situation (with the deficit being estimated at around £800m), there should be no question of even considering devaluation as a serious possibility. 'This decision was to put the Government in a straitjacket for the next three years,' Barbara Castle justly observed two decades later, yet more in sorrow than in anger, for it would have been a huge surprise if Wilson had jumped the other way. He had, after all, been a member of the government that had devalued in 1949; he had no wish for Labour to be known as the party of devaluation; and, as he had told the House of Commons in July 1961, a second post-war British devaluation 'would be regarded all over the world as an acknowledgement of defeat, a recognition that we were not on a springboard but on a slide'. It was a view with which the Bank of England, imbued with a deep sense of responsibility to the holders of sterling, fully concurred. Nor was rational discussion of the subject encouraged, to put it mildly. 'It was rather an emotional place then,' Kit McMahon drily recalled of his recent arrival at the Bank, 'and merely to mention devaluation was like saying a four-letter word in church.' Indeed, so potent was the identification of the strength of sterling with the strength of Britain that much the same applied in the wider, opinion-forming world – to the extent that among financial journalists there increasingly applied what was known as 'the self-denying ordinance': a tacit agreement not to discuss the potential merits of devaluation as a policy option. Devaluation may or may not have been the right thing to do in October 1964 (though from July 1966 it surely was); either way, it was hardly a propitious atmosphere in which to formulate policy.[1]

*

No doubt encouraged by the non-devaluation, the City for a few weeks did not give Labour the bumpy ride that many had anticipated. 'He saw nothing to worry the Market,' the discount market men noted on seeing Cromer a week after polling day. 'The Government was not anti-City, at present anyhow . . . The Governor admitted that sterling was supported last Friday but not on a big scale. Sterling was not under pressure this week and he would call it buoyant.' Also on the 22nd Cromer was similarly reassuring to Bill Martin of the Fed, telling him that there was 'entire seriousness' in Labour's 'intent to deal with our balance of payments problems and to strengthen the position of the pound'. Characteristically he added: 'It is bound to take a little while for the new administration to shake down and familiarise itself with the workings of the machine. But these things usually sort themselves out. There are some rather queer academic figures in the periphery but my hope is that they will be found some nice quiet backrooms to work in.' Soon afterwards the government announced a 15 per cent temporary import surcharge, a move welcomed by the stock market as a serious attempt to deal with the huge, now publicly revealed balance-of-payments deficit. At the same time, however, an accompanying White Paper insisted that 'the Government reject any policy based on a return to stop-go economics' – a repudiation of the notion that deflation was the only alternative to devaluation – and the result was to put the pound under some pressure. Nor, from a City perspective, was the situation helped by the Foreign Secretary, Patrick Gordon Walker, saying in Washington on the 27th that Britain would not be raising Bank rate in the near future as a way of dealing with its balance-of-payments problems. Cromer at once protested to Callaghan, 'You will, I know, appreciate that it makes it impossible for me to fulfil my responsibilities as the essential link between the Government and the financial markets if the subject of Bank Rate is to be discussed by Ministers outside their proper sphere.' Even so, the Chancellor and his colleagues were still just about getting the benefit of the doubt. 'The new Government has been more orthodox than some people expected and so the City is somewhat relieved,' Arthur Villiers (who had retired from Barings ten years previously but still had many contacts) wrote to a correspondent in Australia on the 28th. 'The PM is now dressing better and does not look quite such an untidy figure on TV!'[2]

Presumably Wilson maintained his sartorial improvement on Tuesday, 3 November, the occasion of the Queen's Speech, in which the necessary words were inserted to try to boost 'confidence' in the world's foreign exchange markets – 'At home my Government's first concern will be to maintain the strength of sterling.' But the City was more struck by the government's commitment, despite its small majority, to implementing its full programme, including the renationalisation of steel. That evening, at the annual Mansion House bankers' dinner, Callaghan tried to clear up the question of the relationship between the Labour government and the City:

> A lot of ill-informed comment has been written and spoken about this, so let me make it quite clear that we recognise your contribution to the national economy, and we recognise that you need to earn your living; it is not our job to make it more difficult for you to do so. But you in your turn will recognise that your interests must be harmonised with the needs of the nation as a whole. If you have criticisms to make of our actions come and tell us. We shall listen to what you have to say with an open mind and see if we can meet your difficulties. If we cannot do so it will not be because of prejudice against you. I have no doubt that in the City of London and in the wider world of business of which it is a part we shall find many allies in our objective of creating a modern and efficient economy. We invite your co-operation in this joint effort to create a fairer, a more productive and more progressive society.

Cromer's speech at the same dinner hardly represented coming halfway to meet the new administration. 'I am convinced that the future prosperity of this country at home and its power in the world abroad depends above all on the strength of the pound,' he stated gravely, 'and the strength of the pound depends today, as it always has, on wise and prudent husbandry of our resources so that they may grow and fructify.' On the very day that the government had announced its intention to abolish prescription charges and increase pensions, he took the trouble to spell out what he meant by such husbandry: 'We must reduce expenditure in this country which distracts resources from contributing to the top priority of closing the payments gap.'[3] It did not need a genius to compare the two standpoints and see the discrepancy; and Cromer's remarks amounted, from a Labour point of view, to something not far short of a declaration of war. Yet perhaps he had played his hand too publicly and too early.[4]

On the 11th, Callaghan presented an emergency budget to try to tackle the deteriorating economic situation. Taken as a whole it was deflationary, and indeed the initial stock market response was positive, as a relieved 'Lex' noted that 'none of the feared frightfulness was in evidence'. By Friday the 13th, however, that relief had been replaced in the equity market by a mood that Kenneth Fleet in the *Sunday Telegraph* described as 'something approaching despair', as brokers and institutional investors began to contemplate the corporation tax and amplified capital gains tax that Callaghan was pledged to introduce the following spring. In his budget statement he had not divulged either the rates or the mechanics of these new taxes, and over the next few weeks it was largely fear of the unknown that ate into the soul of the investing class. As for the foreign exchanges, they took against the budget more or less from the start. Sterling had a bad day on the 12th, and Tether explained in the *FT* that, in the eyes of international opinion, 'the toughness Mr Callaghan has shown is not generally considered there to be of the type that the situation demands'; he added that 'not surprisingly, there has been a tendency to argue that it is hardly appropriate at a time when the country's economy is badly out of gear to indulge in the wholesale raising of social service benefits'. Tether also contended that the government had exacerbated its own problems by harping so much on the dreadful legacy of its predecessor. The pound fared even worse on the 13th, and that day Cromer wrote to Callaghan asking him to raise Bank rate from 5 to 6 per cent:

> The market, in the sense that I use the word in this letter, embraces all throughout the world and at home who are using sterling in their normal international commercial trading transactions; this is much wider than a small group of professional speculators who by and large can be countered by Central Bank co-operation. The great danger arises from the aggregation of many thousands of independent and bona fide commercial decisions to hasten normal sales of sterling . . . Confidence, therefore, plays a very large part and I get the impression that there is increasing anxiety about the future stability of the currency, however unjustified this may be. Over the weeks that lie ahead there is real danger of increasing pressure on sterling . . .

A Bank rate rise, Cromer believed, would 'mitigate the danger of a further serious fall in confidence'.[5] Still less than a month into the lifetime of the new, growth-minded government, it was the traditional banker's red-light panacea.

Monday the 16th featured first the announcement that Maudling had been appointed as a full-time executive director of Kleinwort Benson and then the Lord Mayor's banquet at Guildhall. 'It was a scene of splendid pageantry,' one youthful minister, Anthony Wedgwood Benn, observed. 'Everyone is expected to wear a white tie but I went in a black one. The only other person in a black tie was George Brown . . .' Wilson expressed his unshakeable determination to keep the pound 'riding high' and explicitly rejected the view that 'we, in Britain, should turn our back on the sterling area, cultivate our own garden, and repudiate our obligations to other Commonwealth countries'. Unimpeachable sentiments expressed, and junketings over, the guests began to depart, but not without a hint of the hosts' real feelings. 'As we left dinner,' Benn noted, 'some City bigwig shouted, "Why aren't you properly dressed?" I didn't hear him but he caught Caroline [Benn's wife] by the arm and repeated it to her. She was extremely angry.'[6]

Over the next two days equities failed to recover, sterling came under renewed pressure and foreign exchange reserves continued to drain away. The markets not unreasonably interpreted Wilson's speech as a signal that the Bank rate would rise on Thursday in order to defend the pound, and Wednesday evening was the unavoidable time of decision. Soon after six o'clock Cromer was in Downing Street, expressing his doubts to Wilson as to whether the $1,500m that the British government hoped to borrow from the US government 'could be mustered'. There was no meeting of minds: 'The Prime Minister said that he assumed that the reasons for the present difficulties were the deflationary prejudices of the more orthodox central banks together with some political manoeuvring. Mr Governor said that it was certainly the case that the proposed increase in old-age pensions was regarded by some people as inflationary in character . . . but he did not believe that there was any political motivation in the attitudes of European central bankers.' Cromer reiterated his advice that an immediate 1 per cent increase in Bank rate 'would stop the outflow'. Wilson was non-committal, and later that evening he and Brown succeeded in overruling Callaghan, who was willing to cede to Cromer's wishes. The markets next day were predictably disappointed, while Wilson and Brown publicly upped the political stakes – Brown by famously lambasting currency speculators as the 'gnomes of Zurich', Wilson by declaring that 'if anyone here or abroad doubts our resolve and acts in consequence, let him be ready to pay the price for his lack of confidence in Great Britain'.[7]

In the short term at least it did them no good, for Friday the 20th was a terrible day in the markets, with only substantial support from the Bank of England enabling the pound to stay above its lowest permissible level of $2.78¼. As ever during sterling crises of the 1960s, the chain-smoking Roy Bridge led the Bank's rearguard action in the foreign exchange markets. The Fed's Charlie Coombs, often in London, would write admiringly of his opposite number in action:

> In adversity, Bridge never bluffed or complained but acknowledged with devastating candour just why the markets were losing confidence in sterling. . . In his office, I could watch the true professional, alert to all the technical and psychological forces of the market, as he took decisions whether to hold a certain rate level at possibly heavy cost or to retreat and risk even heavier losses. Those were not easy judgements, but they were made decisively and courageously as Bridge paced the floor between crackling telephone calls and snarling commentaries on whatever had brought matters to such a pretty pass . . .

George Bolton had known as a young man what it was to take the heat in the foreign exchange market, and that Friday he noted caustically in his diary, '£ under immense pressure. Roly trying to educate Wilson & Co about life.' The educator himself spent part of the day writing in the strongest possible terms to Callaghan:

> The situation of sterling is deteriorating disturbingly quickly . . . I must emphasise once again to you, Mr Chancellor, that I do not consider that by borrowing alone can we get through this present phase of strain on sterling no matter how much we borrow . . . The facts speak for themselves that the Budget has not created the degree of confidence necessary to sustain sterling. . . In my opinion, unilateral devaluation of sterling, even due to force majeure, could easily precipitate a world financial crisis for which this country would be held responsible and which could have far-reaching consequences both political and economic . . .

Less apocalyptically, Cromer repeated his call for an early Bank rate rise, possibly to 7 per cent.[8]

For two or three days the government had been hoping for direct help from the US government, in order to keep British interest rates down, but by Saturday the 21st it was clear that President Johnson was not going to oblige. That afternoon ministers agreed to raise Bank rate on Monday morning from 5 to 7 per cent. Such a 'decisive increase', the record of the meeting noted, 'should clear away rumours of impending devaluation'. Moreover, as Wilson tried to reassure some of his key ministers towards the end of a long Saturday at Chequers, 'the fact that a Labour government was prepared to use the monetary weapon in appropriate circumstances should provide convincing evidence that they had no ideological prejudices on this point; and this should itself help to assure international opinion'. The next day Richard Crossman, perhaps the most intellectual member of the Cabinet, but with zero knowledge of the City, discussed the outlook with his old friend Nicholas Davenport, the sympathetically disposed veteran financial commentator and City man. 'Nicholas's theme was a simple one,' Crossman recorded. 'The City, he said, have lost confidence. After all, Callaghan threatens the City daily with the corporation tax and the capital gains tax, and the City feel they don't know what to fear; then they lose confidence. "You're heading," said Nicholas, "straight for devaluation."' Later that day, mulling it over, Crossman reckoned that 'we were in the kind of classical financial crisis socialist governments must expect when they achieve power and find the till empty'.[9] On Monday the Bank rate announcement caused relatively little surprise, but no one knew whether it would be enough to restore that most precious if mercurial of commodities: confidence.

The markets on Tuesday gave their answer in the negative; and after some eight or nine hours of heavy selling of sterling and desperate attempts by Bridge to prop up the currency, Cromer and his deputy (Leslie O'Brien, who had succeeded Mynors earlier in the year) met Callaghan at the Treasury at 5.30 p.m. Cromer reported a loss of $211m on the day and was asked by the Chancellor what in the Bank's view needed to be done to re-establish confidence on the part of the holders of sterling. It was a temptingly open goal, and he made six specific suggestions:

(a) credit squeeze;
(b) demonstrable action on incomes policy, in particular in relation to restrictive practices on both sides of industry;
(c) the fixing of a date for the beginning of a reduction in the level of the import charges;
(d) the naming of a specific figure in the reduction which the Government would bring about in public expenditure;
(e) the deferment of what foreign opinion would regard as some of the more doctrinal elements in the Government's legislative programme;
(f) the provision of more specific information about the Government's intentions on corporation tax and capital gains tax.

After outlining this ambitious wish list, Cromer was gracious enough to acknowledge that 'it was the Government's misfortune to assume office at an awkward moment in the cycle'. Callaghan then asked Cromer for his views on devaluation. 'To this Mr Governor replied that in his view devaluation was so desperately serious a measure that no Government could contemplate it as a calculated act. If it were now resorted to in preference to restraint at home, it would be regarded internationally as an act of extreme irresponsibility.' Callaghan said that he would pass on Cromer's views to other ministers, and the central bankers departed.[10]

Later that evening – almost certainly after learning from the Fed that the American view now was that currency speculators were threatening not only sterling, but the international financial system as a whole – they were back in the West End, this time for a 10.30 meeting at 10 Downing Street with both Wilson and Callaghan. The occasion soon turned into a memorable confrontation between two very different men. After Callaghan had emphasised that 'it would be wrong to think in terms of deliberate action anywhere to sabotage the United Kingdom economy or the policies of its Government', and had argued that 'the main need was to re-establish confidence in sterling by measures of some kind and to call on central bank assistance which could be put in the shop window', there came the nub:

> Commenting on the suggestion that there might be difficulty in getting central bank assistance the *Prime Minister* said that if central banks and their governors were going to impose a situation in which a democratically elected government was unable to carry out its election programme then he would have no alternative but to go to the country. He would expect to win

overwhelmingly on that xenophobic issue and would then be free to do anything he liked – devaluation included. *Mr Governor* said that the rest of the world did not believe that the policies so far put into effect were sufficient to put the economy straight and this was the real issue.

A little later in the meeting Wilson observed that 'he was coming to the conclusion that an acceptable alternative to devaluation, in both political and economic terms, might be to let the rate float', but this elicited no response from Cromer. Finally:

> It was agreed that no firm decision should be taken until the following day but it might then be desirable to operate on forward sterling and to approach the Germans and other Europeans as well as the United States and Canada for short-term assistance. The *Prime Minister* said that if these measures failed there would be no alternative but to consider seeking a mandate for devaluation. *Mr Governor* replied that to go to the country on that issue would mean putting Party before country.

Faced by the threat (serious or otherwise) of a 'bankers' ramp' election, Cromer had blinked first. It would be his task to send round the begging bowl to the world's central bankers *without* a binding promise from the British government to adopt the policies that he believed to be necessary. According to Wilson's own, retrospective account, Cromer did say that he was 'doubtful whether this could be done unless he was able to convey to them news of major changes of policy'; but Wilson was adamant that he would not 'sacrifice the constitutional rights of a newly-elected Government'.[11] With the ghosts of 1931 almost palpably in the air, it had been a significant moment in British political history.

'Numerous telephone calls made re-negotiations of package deal for $3,000 million, announced at 7 p.m. today.' The Governor's diary entry for Wednesday, 25 November was admirably concise; while as Alec Cairncross (still the government's economic adviser) nicely put it at the end of this day of the $3bn loan, 'it was the old firm that did its stuff', in that 'the Governor delivered the goods, and but for him the Government would have been in a sad way with devaluation inevitable'. Wilson also struck a wry note in his memoirs, recalling the moment when late on Wednesday afternoon he received a message that Cromer had successfully raised the money: 'He had done a magnificent job. Heaven knows what he said about any possible intentions on the international telephone as he explained the alternatives. I did not enquire.' There was, indeed, a somewhat delicate point of honour involved, for the Bank of England's name was very much on this massive loan from eleven other central banks and the Bank for International Settlements. Later that week Cairncross attended the Whitehall Dining Club for mandarins and others, where he found that 'the most interesting contribution came from Maurice Parsons who made it clear that he and others at the Bank had had to make up their minds whether they could invite support from other Central Banks with a clear conscience', granted that 'they were in effect pledging the good behaviour of the Government'.[12] It was no wonder that Wilson had decided not to ask too many questions.

The heat was temporarily off sterling, but the prevailing mood in the City remained far from relaxed. 'If last Wednesday's operations are to be likened to Dunkirk,' Cromer wrote to Callaghan on 1 December in a not unfriendly tone, 'the victory still has to be won.' He added that 'the new Government has been given mercilessly little time to assess the situation and devise means of meeting it'. A week later Cairncross dined with two highly respected bankers, Richardson of Schroders and Eric Faulkner of Glyn Mills, and discovered that 'the City has no confidence that Ministers understand the gravity of the situation'. Soon afterwards, the Bank of England's resident economist, Maurice Allen, sent a paper to the Treasury on 'Consequences of Devaluation', predictably concluding that they would be grave and far-reaching, while doing nothing to cure 'the basic troubles at home'. The paper was shown to Callaghan, and Cromer wanted it to be passed on to Wilson, but Armstrong at the Treasury declined to do so, on the not entirely convincing grounds that 'it would not tell him anything that he did not already know, and his resolution on this topic needed no bolstering'.[13]

The run-up to Christmas again saw the City's nerves thoroughly taut, and on Monday the 21st Cromer despatched a formal warning to Wilson: 'This last week has evidenced in business and financial circles at home the most serious lack of confidence that I recall. Rumours and exaggerations have been rife at home and abroad, creating a most dangerous atmosphere . . . It would take very little to trigger off a movement against sterling beyond our power to arrest. We are close to the brink of the abyss . . .' Cromer then called for action, along the usual belt-tightening lines, and ended, 'I am, Mr Prime Minister, at your disposal to wait upon you at all times.' Next day, while Downing Street pondered, Cromer spoke on the telephone to Al Hayes at the Fed. The American asked (according to the Fed's account) 'why the Bank of England had not seen fit to give the government a public "pat on the back" in connection with some of their recent actions to defend the pound'. To which Cromer replied that there was 'a high degree of solidarity between the Bank and the government' and that 'the Bank habitually is loath to make statements of any kind'. On Wednesday afternoon Cromer was at No 10, but this time he and Wilson tacitly agreed to forgo the fireworks of four weeks earlier. He 'was not a deflationist at heart or in desire,' the Governor insisted, 'but was driven to the conclusion that something more had to be done.' For his part Wilson refused to be defeatist, and Cromer agreed that on the foreign exchanges 'there was every hope that there would be a somewhat different atmosphere in January'. They also agreed, as a fairly inconsequential discussion approached its end, that the end-of-month reserves figures should be adjusted to show a loss of only £8m, whereas the real loss was £115m.[14]

There may have been more than seasonal goodwill behind this thaw, for both men were probably conscious of the intensifying public criticism of the City/government relationship. That had reached a public nadir when Wincott on 15 December devoted his weekly *FT* column to an 'Open Letter to the Chancellor', in which he asserted that the proposed capital gains tax and corporation tax represented a 'fiscal putsch' on the part of one of the government's main economic advisers, Nicholas Kaldor, and that 'there really hasn't been anything like it since Hitler wrote "Mein Kampf"'. Callaghan protested strongly, but a flood of letters to the paper, including ones from Esmond Durlacher and Walter Salomon, backed Wincott. The episode was the cue for two normally Conservative-supporting financial journalists to give the City a dressing-down. Urging both sides to call a halt in their war, the *Sunday Telegraph's* Kenneth Fleet described the City as succumbing to a state of 'hysterical semi-paralysis' and liable soon to find itself accused of being 'incapable of operating unless conditions are tailored to its own liking as they were for a decade under Conservative Governments'. Across at the *Sunday Times*, William Rees-Mogg argued that the City had 'already allowed itself to drift too far away from the rest of national life', as a result of which 'the great majority of Englishmen underrate the City's value as a national asset . . . and suspect it far too much'. He also took the line that after a week of 'mostly ill-informed' rumours and 'mostly ill-conceived' fears, it was time for the City to grow up and take a more realistic view of what he believed to be an essentially conservative administration. 'As for devaluation,' he added with typical confidence, 'that will not happen.'[15]

Did the City really behave as badly as its critics claimed? Looking back in June 1965, in the context of another controversy, the *Economist* certainly thought so, claiming that 'anybody who went to the City at this time [i.e. autumn 1964] was apt to be met with the retailing of venomous personal slanders against every cabinet minister under the sun, and to be disturbed by the spectacle of men in charge of millions of pounds of investable funds who solemnly propounded that the policy of this rather conservative Labour Government was motivated by a deep-laid international communist plot'. The magazine added that Cromer should have tried harder in his 'public utterances', however much he disagreed with government policy, to check 'this neurosis in the City'. Perhaps he should have, yet it would be hard to exaggerate the extent of Cromer's own visceral dislike for what he saw as Labour's objectives. Much the same applied, though in an infinitely less patrician way, to his deputy. A passage from O'Brien's memoirs, written in the late 1970s, conveys well enough the assumptions of central bankers through the ages:

> Harold Wilson and his closest colleagues were perfectly well aware of their vulnerability to a run on the exchanges. They had discussed the subject widely at home and abroad in the months before the election and had sought to be reassuring. Yet what did they do five minutes after taking office against this unpromising background? They obstinately increased social benefits and fought hard against a very necessary increase in Bank Rate. So that when at last the rate was raised, most of the psychological advantage of doing so had been lost. Over the years senior Labour ministers, those so to speak who occupy the front-line trenches, have been brought reluctantly to accept and act on the economic facts of life, postponing to another day the socialist paradise for which they yearn. Not so their supporters, or indeed some of their ministerial colleagues. The clamour for the adoption of potentially disastrous policies goes on behind them all the time and this combined with their own reluctant rectitude does little to engender worldwide confidence in their government.[16]

In short, one does not have to accept claims about a conspiracy of international financiers in order to assert that the sterling crisis of autumn 1964 was the result not just of deep-seated British economic problems, but of a collision between two rather different ways of looking at the world.

'There is nothing surprising, certainly nothing sinister, in the reactions of the international exchange markets,' the *Banker* quite reasonably observed that December. 'When they looked to the City for reassurance they found a stock market demoralised ... simply by the shocking confusion caused by the uncertainties of the coming capital gains and corporation taxes, and by the feeling that even in this difficult economic situation the Government put social purposes as first priority.'[17] What the *Banker* did not point out, though, was that in this competing choice of priorities the government's had been endorsed by an electorate, whereas the assumptions shared by the City and the holders of sterling were simply those that suited themselves best (though they may also have believed in them). It was in its way an honest conflict, ultimately decided by the electorate in 1979 and thereafter in favour of the market rather than more 'social' objectives. But it was ignorance, prejudice and even demonisation, on both sides, that made the City/Labour relationship so unfortunate for so long. With so much accumulated wealth and privilege at its disposal, the strangely cloistered square mile should have known better.

*

For Callaghan the opening phase of his chancellorship had been person-ally traumatic, but by early 1965 his morale had recovered. It was a pity, nevertheless, that he was having to learn on the job. 'One field of experience was not included among my advisers [in the form of pre-election economic seminars at Nuffield College, Oxford], namely a first-hand knowledge of how the City of London works; its strengths and its weaknesses,' he regretfully recalled. 'Like most if not all chancellors, I did not learn the ways of the City until I had held the post for some time, and consequently made mistakes.' The Government broker by the mid-1960s was Peter Daniell, and he remembers Callaghan (by now in office) ringing him up one day, saying that he 'didn't understand in the least what the Government Broker did' and coming to lunch. At least he *was* willing to learn, unlike Dalton when faced by a perhaps even more unfriendly City some twenty years earlier. However, not all his colleagues took kindly to Callaghan's willingness to build bridges. 'When he became Chancellor and constantly referred to "Rowlie", I thought he was talking about a relative or a close friend,' George Wigg typically remarked, adding that Cromer became Callaghan's 'economic and political *alter ego*'; while George Brown went through a period when he could not bear even to hear the Governor's name mentioned. The sense of frustration was understandable. 'Every action we took had to be considered against a background of the confidence factor, particularly against our assessment of what the speculators might do,' Wilson recollected about the inhibiting quality of the sterling situation during his government's first three years. He, Callaghan and Brown very rarely allowed other ministers even to discuss the sterling problem, but occasionally there was a wishful attempt to burst out of the chains. Barbara Castle recorded one such moment in January 1965:

> I suddenly exploded by saying we were trying to do too much at once. We were trying to put all the country's finances right at a moment when we were engaged on fundamental realignments in economic and social policy. 'The Tories have got on all right without financial rectitude for fifteen years,' I declared, at which Harold buried his head in his hands in silent laughter while Wedgie Benn recoiled in horror . . .[18]

Was the Postmaster-General horrified by the prospect of abandoning 'financial rectitude'? Or by the naïvety of the wish? Either way, apparently he had yet to identify the City as one of the enemies of socialism.

Soon afterwards, on 9 February, Cromer informed Callaghan that the central bankers at Basle had agreed to renew Britain's credit facilities for a further three months, but only with 'very grave misgivings'. Their deep doubt, he went on, 'only serves to confirm the advice that I have already tendered to you that the future of sterling depends upon your Budget in early April'. Within a week Cromer was going public with this advice, addressing a bankers' dinner in Edinburgh. There, after the obligatory reference to how 'the respite of last November in itself no more guarantees our future than Dunkirk presaged swift victory in 1940', he contended that it was necessary to start following the example of some of the countries from whom Britain was now borrowing so heavily. These countries were, he declared, 'pursuing fiscal and monetary policies which are disagreeable to their citizens, because these countries and their citizens prefer to try to maintain the purchasing power of their money – they prefer this to the alternative of ever-rising prices – and although success in these aims may vary, they accept that the effort is worthwhile although it leads to deferment of the level of public services they would like to have'.[19]

Cromer's speech received spectacular press coverage and aroused predictable fury. 'Isn't it time that the Governor of the Bank of England was told that any advice he tenders to the Government should come in a regular form?' Brown at once wrote to Callaghan. 'I find his speeches tedious, inappropriate and designed to create the maximum embarrassment for Ministers!' Crossman, writing to Wilson, accused the Governor, for the second time since October, of 'playing politics in a way that no one who runs a nationalised institution should do'. He wanted the Prime Minister to give the Cabinet 'an assurance that this one-man May Committee will be shut up'. The outcome was merely a private rebuke from the Chancellor to an impenitent Governor, though Nigel Lawson's assessment in the *FT* was that the unelected central banker had exceeded his remit – while not denying that 'the Earl of Cromer is an urbane, charming, civilised and above all honourable man' and that his views were shared by the Bank's Court, by foreign bankers and 'many others'. Shortly afterwards, at an informal dinner at No 10 to discuss the economy, Cromer was introduced to Tommy Balogh (like Nicky Kaldor, a Hungarian economist now advising the Labour government). 'PM joined us,' noted Cairncross, 'and we had quite a lively evening; with much chaffing of the Governor (none of the "Cromer must go" stuff) . . .' The reference was to the series of late-evening meetings at No 10 (and sometimes at Chequers) that Wilson had initiated during the winter to enable ministers and officials to enjoy free discussion without papers or a rigid agenda. According to Cairncross, a somewhat disapproving participant, 'the Bank of England are rigorously excluded so that rude comments about the Governor can be freely made'.[20]

By March the build-up to Callaghan's first regular, full-scale budget was intense. 'I found a fair amount of gloom about our situation and not a very high expectation that we would rise to the occasion sufficiently in the Budget,' Cromer, just back from Basle, wrote on the 9th to John Stevens, until recently an executive director at the Bank and now economic minister in Washington. 'I am naturally keeping up the pressure on the west end but what the outcome will be is quite impossible to predict.' The next day, almost certainly using his trusty dictaphone, Cromer wrote to Callaghan himself. 'If confidence were not to be restored by the Budget,' he warned, 'I must make it quite clear that I could see little prospect of a further international rescue operation to support sterling. I fear that foreign opinion would regretfully conclude that it was no use any further trying to save us from the consequences of our own policies.' The crux, he insisted, was reducing public expenditure, though he also counselled 'against any measures either in the Exchange Control field or in the nature of discriminatory taxation, which could be interpreted as moving in the direction of a siege economy'. Yet arguably Cromer's certainty about what would, or would not, inspire foreign confidence was more apparent than real. 'He agreed that all eyes were on the Budget,' the discount market's men noted a fortnight later after seeing the Governor, 'but he did not really know what the European bankers would consider reasonable. "Your guess is as good as mine" he said.'[21]

At least the discount men treated him respectfully, unlike the First Secretary of State and Minister for Economic Affairs. 'G. Brown was there and about 40 others,' Cairncross recorded about a memorable dinner at the Italian Embassy. 'He ragged Cromer unmercifully at the table and passed messages to Lady C. comparing her with Mata Hari . . . Cromer was very annoyed (as who would not) . . .' The budget was by now barely a week away and on the last day of March the Governor sent Callaghan a final blast:

> The acute lack of confidence in sterling, currently widespread through all the financial and commercial markets of the world, is based predominantly on fear – much more than hope of speculative gain – fear that money in sterling terms will lose part of its purchasing power . . . Uncertainty of no matter what cause, intervention by Government to put the market operator at a disadvantage, any action by authority which threatens the free exercise of market forces and the threat of tax changes which may disturb basically accepted relationships, each and all will undermine market confidence at this time . . .

Though Cromer accepted that, however undesirable, the new capital gains tax was going to happen, he also entered a plea to defer corporation tax, as being bad for confidence, even if it was right in principle. Furthermore, he asked Callaghan to abandon his intention of introducing a 25 per cent surrender requirement on the proceeds of all sales of foreign currency securities. With that off his chest, Cromer could only sit and wait, telling Stevens next day that as far as any further international action to support sterling was concerned, 'I find it difficult to see what operations could be set up of a meaningful size if the Budget is not well received.'[22]

The corporation tax and the surrender requirement had not disappeared when all was revealed on 6 April; but there were significant public expenditure cuts, and two days later the discount men found the Governor 'cheerful and relaxed', saying that he 'considered the Budget was good for the pound and by and large he thought many of the measures to be aimed in the right direction'. He also, they noted, 'gave the appearance of having had a considerable say and to have been listened to'. But if Cromer was relatively relaxed, that was far from the case with the stock market, which was dismayed by the details of the new capital gains and corporation taxes. The budget was, one City gentleman standing in Throgmorton Street told the television cameras soon after Callaghan had sat down, 'a most disgusting attack on anyone who wants to make his way in the world. It's Marxism: they want a communist state. Personally, I shall fight like hell on the beaches, and on the streets and in the farms we will fight them.' Even an intelligent stockbroker like Jock Hunter regarded the budget as 'an attack on the capitalist system', as he told the Stock Exchange Council some weeks later; though when the Stock Exchange tried to enlist the support of the clearing banks and accepting houses to make a combined protest to government, it did not succeed.[23]

Further ill feeling was generated in June when, in a speech at the Lancashire miners' gala at Leigh, Brown referred to a 'sinister conspiracy' in parts of the press and the City. An immediate riposte came from Harley Drayton, addressing shareholders of United Newspapers. 'I have never known a Government elected to power who started off with greater goodwill from the whole of the newspaper world and from the City,' he unblinkingly declared, adding that 'the big houses in the City' had tried 'to help this Government' since its election and that 'any change in atmosphere' was the government's fault. The spat helped no one, and a few weeks later Wilson told Cecil King (the newspaper magnate, by now a non-executive director of the Bank of England and gossipy, sometimes malicious, not always trustworthy diarist) that 'he recognized that the Corporation Tax was a mistake, and was now going to try and soothe the City'. The soothing began two days later, on 14 July, as Wilson attended a dinner party at the Bank and met some three dozen prominent City men. 'The guests enjoyed the opportunity of meeting the Prime Minister on this basis,' Cromer wrote afterwards to the principal Private Secretary at No 10, 'and were clearly interested in what he had to say whilst, understandably, not in full agreement.' The evening may not have been everyone's idea of a night out, but Cromer far preferred it to a meeting in Guildhall between senior ministers and an invited City audience – a proposal scotched by Wilson himself, on the Governor's advice, after being put to the Lord Mayor by a recently elected Labour MP, one Robert Maxwell.[24]

The immediate backdrop to Brown's smear, and the ensuing semi-rapprochement between government and City, was several weeks of the most serious pressure on sterling so far in 1965. The problems involved in holding the $2.80 rate once again loomed large, and on 26 July a manifestly angry Cromer scribbled in red biro on a recent Kaldor paper that argued for floating the pound. To that economist's blithe assertion that 'international opinion would gradually accustom itself to the change of relativities', the Governor could not even trust himself to words, simply scribbling '?!' As for the view that, in the event of devaluation, the holders of sterling 'would not *expect* to be compensated', Cromer asked rhetorically, 'Could it be that they trusted us?' And in response to Kaldor's confident prediction that, in the event of competitive exchange devaluations, 'so long as our currency is weaker than those of our main competitors, we are bound to be on the winning side and not on the losing side', Cromer thunderously asked, 'By constantly defrauding those who hold sterling?' In sum, as he wrote on the front of the document, 'It is because Britain has followed policies diametrically opposite to the philosophy of this paper that £ became universally respected. I feel ashamed to read such a paper on HM Treasury stationery'. Within twenty-four hours measures were agreed and announced, involving public investment cuts and still tighter exchange controls, which on the face of it made clear to the world the government's unremitting determination not to devalue. The foreign exchange markets, however, were unconvinced. 'A gloomy session at the Bank,' King noted on 5 August. 'There has been a run on gold and a run on sterling, and the reserves are in sight of exhaustion. It is not thought that any further deflationary gestures would produce any effect. The Governor thinks the only card left to play is a wage and price freeze. This might impress foreign opinion; nothing else would.'[25] For someone whose larger economic instincts were wholly free-market, this remedy was a measure of how the defence of the sterling parity transcended everything in his psyche.

That evening Cromer was at No 10, where the exchanges began ritualistically enough. Cromer gave the figures (showing that the reserves had lost £146m since Callaghan's statement on the 27th); Wilson observed that 'the exchange market seemed to be in the grip of an acute attack of nerves'; and Cromer stated that for other central banks to continue to support sterling, the government would need to make a confidence-imparting statement. By this the Governor meant an immediate wages and prices freeze, in return for an undertaking about international support for sterling – to which Wilson, raising the temperature, riposted that 'we must be allowed to play the hand our own way and to follow the normal democratic processes for securing endorsement of the Government's policies', starting with an appeal to the TUC in early September for voluntary restraint. 'It should be clearly understood,' Wilson continued in more or less a rerun of his November 1964 tactics, 'that if the Government were required to abandon normal methods of consultation and to take arbitrary unilateral action of a kind which no other democratic Government had ever taken, they might be forced to consider that it would be wiser to devalue sterling, to let the rate float and to appeal to the Country.' To this Cromer replied with some dignity that 'he would deplore this alternative course of action' and that 'in particular, to let the rate float would cause the maximum dislocation of the world monetary system'.[26] The meeting ended with a brilliant Wilsonian ploy – graciously insisting that Cromer should not cancel his planned holiday in the south of France – and, just a month later, the TUC's adoption of government proposals to give statutory powers to the Prices and Incomes Board enabled the Bank of England, the Fed and other central banks to mount a joint buying operation and win a rare famous victory against sterling's speculators.[27]

A few days later George Brown at the Department of Economic Affairs produced its long-awaited, much-vaunted National Plan. Britain's annual growth target was to be an ambitious 3.8 per cent, amounting over the six years 1964–70 to total growth of some 25 per cent. 'George Brown's presence ensured that the plan would be launched with the maximum of bravura and panache,' Callaghan's biographer, Kenneth Morgan, has justly observed. 'Sterling would be rescued by socialism. But most economists viewed it with considerable doubts . . .' The City had doubts in spades. On 6 August Cromer had sent to the Treasury the Bank's response to a draft of the Plan:

> The general difficulty is that a five-year plan, however well devised, must be setting out an expansionist, long-run approach to our problems. When this has also to be combined with a relative expansion of services provided by the State, the final picture must look strange when it is set alongside the immediate reality that only speedy, visible progress towards restoring our external position will halt the resumed loss of confidence in sterling.

Moreover, if the Plan was to be published, Cromer had unavailingly wanted 'a strong foreword' to be added, 'declaring that the overwhelming priority is given to prompt restoration of our external position' – expressed in such a way 'that leaves no doubt that while describing our ambitions we still mean to put first things first'. The *Banker*'s view was fairly typical of the City's jaundiced reaction. 'The fundamental flaw of the Brown "Plan" is that it confuses what ought (however arguably) to be done with what can be done and what will be done,' it asserted in October, before making an unexpected reference to television satire. 'To join a topical idiom with a Victorian one, we have here not so much a programme, more a pipedream or reverie. In short, a brown study.'[28]

During the winter of 1965–6, sterling was relatively stable, the mood of the stock market was neither bullish nor bearish, and the City was starting to get used to a Labour government. On 25 November the discount market's chairman 'called on Lord Cromer who said it was quiet compared with a year ago to which our Chairman replied "thanks to you Sir!"'. It was less quiet in the corporate sector, and Rowe & Pitman's monthly assessment perceptively noted in December how 'bids and rumours of bids abound in current markets, drawing attention from deteriorating company and economic news'. The next month saw the unveiling of a government-sponsored institution, the Industrial Reorganisation Corporation (IRC), which was capitalised at £150m and whose explicit purpose was 'to provide rationalisation schemes which could yield substantial benefits to the national economy'. The *FT* was unimpressed: 'If ministers are really anxious to work with the City and with industry, their aim should be to supplement the working of the market, not to subvert it'. But Labour had long been unconvinced of the ability of the City's corporate financiers to take a wide view of how the main industrial sectors needed restructuring for modernisation; the Bank was unwilling to go to the stake for disgruntled merchant bankers and gave the IRC its qualified blessing; and anyway the new organisation was soon dominated precisely by merchant bankers. The IRC, in other words, may have had the funds to give loans or acquire equity stakes, but the City remained the prime source of contacts and expertise. By early 1966 there was a growing City suspicion that Labour would soon look to another election to increase its slender majority. Writing in February to a correspondent in Buenos Aires, John Phillimore of Barings caught the mood: 'Here, it rains every day, the economy of the country continues to deteriorate and it looks as if we may shortly have another Socialist Government with a larger majority. In fact Argentina looks quite attractive by comparison.'[29]

For Cromer, by contrast, 8 Bishopsgate seemed an ever-more attractive haven, as he became an increasingly isolated figure during the final year of his five-year term. By late 1965 there was widespread press speculation that his contract would not be renewed, though on 5 December Cairncross thought it 'unlikely' that Cromer would be 'keen to leave while the future of the pound is in the balance'. The next day Cecil King talked with Wilson about the Bank. 'I said I was impressed by Cromer and if that was the sort of man he wanted, he would not do better. He said, "In fact there is no better Cromer than Cromer?"' There was a touching demonstration of loyalty from one quarter the following week: 'As there was so much being written in the papers and being said in the City about the possible names being put forward for the next Governor of the Bank of England, Mr [Charles] Dawkins told the Governor that as far as the Discount Market was concerned, it would be more than pleased if Lord Cromer would offer his services as Governor for another period.' The assiduous King, meanwhile, continued to sound out and (if possible) influence opinion. 'Warburg came to see me last night to talk about the Bank governorship,' he noted on 21 December. 'He thinks, under all the circumstances, Cromer should probably remain; failing him, then O'Brien with Parsons as deputy. I asked about George Bolton, but Warburg thinks he is too volatile.' On the 23rd he chatted again with Wilson. King's line remained that it would be best to stick with Cromer, 'instead of launching out into the unknown', but Wilson was apparently non-committal.

It is possible that Cromer had already let Callaghan know that he would not wish to be considered for a second term, but it is more likely that he intimated this fairly early in the new year. Either way, he must have known that a Labour government would not welcome the prospect of another five years of his particular style of governorship. There were by this time two main front-runners to succeed him. H.C. 'Nugget' Coombs was a Keynesian-minded Australian central banker, well regarded by Wilson and backed by the *Economist*; John Stevens in Washington, and formerly of the Bank, was the Court's favoured candidate. When approached, however, Coombs decided against leaving Australia, and no real momentum built up behind Stevens. Instead, one day in March 1966, King strode into the Deputy Governor's room and told a startled O'Brien that he was now the favourite for the job, though not without adding, credibly or otherwise, 'They offered it to me, but I did not want it'.[30] There the matter rested, until it became clear who would be the government of the day when Cromer's term expired at the end of June.

There is no evidence, despite some kites being flown in the press, that Wilson and Callaghan ever seriously considered the claims of Siegmund Warburg.[31] Since October 1964 that mercurial figure had emerged as Wilson's unofficial financial adviser, suggesting to him in May 1965 for instance that (in the words of Wilson's note) 'we should take advantage of the present goodwill in the United States to Britain, particularly at Government level, to come to an arrangement under which the resources of either central bank come to the help of the other on the basis that an attack on one is an attack on the other'. On the same occasion Warburg also told Wilson that, in the context of Callaghan's recent tightening of exchange control, 'he stood alone in the City in not supporting the clamour about overseas investment in which he regards the Government as basically right'. Warburg was anxious, nevertheless, not to be seen by the City, and especially by the Bank (which he sometimes called his 'Father Confessor'), as a renegade; and twice in this period he sent letters to *The Times* strongly making the case against devaluation. Almost certainly he wrote them himself, but it was significant that both letters were also signed by Jack Hambro, a trusted member of the City establishment until his death while shooting on Cobbold's estate at Knebworth in December 1965. 'To advocate devaluation seems to us an example of the kind of sickness which seeks to elevate defeatism to the status of constructive thinking,' the first letter stated in a show of moral indignation that apparently took a leaf out of Cromer's book. The Governor, however, continued to take a dim view of Warburg, as was made clear in March 1966 when he submitted his annual recommendations for the Birthday Honours: 'I understand that there is a possibility that Mr Siegmund Warburg may be considered in this connection . . . Whilst Mr Warburg is of course a highly respected banker, he has not in my opinion made any outstanding contribution to the common weal of the City that calls for public recognition.' Damningly Cromer added that 'he has, of course, been very successful in his own affairs'.[32] Warburg did receive a knighthood that summer, but Cromer's files do not suggest that he sent a letter of congratulations.

By this time Labour was well on the way, it was widely believed, to becoming the natural party of government. 'Investors,' Rowe & Pitman's *Market Report* had noted at the beginning of the election campaign in March 1966, 'may dislike [Capital] Gains Tax and other features of this Government's policy, but they recognise in that policy a pronounced inflationary bias which has, if anything, strengthened their belief in the merits of equities.' Cromer, though, did make a valiant effort to upset the apple-cart. On 9 March, just over three weeks before polling day, he attempted to persuade Callaghan that Bank rate be raised from 6 to 7 per cent in order to protect sterling. Late that Wednesday evening at 10 Downing Street came the final round of the Wilson/Cromer bout. Cromer tried to explain why sterling was being sold; Wilson countered that a Bank-rate increase would bring sterling into the election; and Cromer responded by saying that such a move would be seen 'as a symbol of responsible Government'. Wilson, after accusing the Bank of 'deliberate interference with politics', then went on:

> Since the Government were going to win the election anyhow, they would thereafter have to take steps to ensure that a situation of this kind could never arise again. *Mr Governor* asked how this would help sterling. The *Prime Minister* replied that, just as the Bank had to try to cope with irrational people in the money market, so he had to try to cope with irrational people in politics. The plain fact of the matter was that the Government's will must prevail and that, if the Government clashed with the Court, the latter would have to be overruled. *Mr Governor* observed that in that event this country could never again command any international credit.

After being accused of 'an attack on democracy', Cromer asked if he should resign rather than go against his conscience – to which Wilson smartly replied 'that if the Governor resigned, the pound would be a casualty'. At this point, making a rare intervention from the sidelines,

Callaghan remarked that 'leaving aside political [i.e. immediate electoral] considerations, he would feel happier with a rise in Bank rate than without one'. Finally, Cromer astonishingly asserted that the Bank 'had a clear statutory responsibility to act independently as well as to advise'. Faced with this claim, Wilson simply replied that if it tried to do so in the present situation, 'the history of the Bank of England which had begun with Governor Houblon would end with Governor Cromer', that 'the Bank of England would have destroyed itself by throwing itself into the Election' and that 'the City would be totally discredited and in the process it would emerge clearly who had been selling sterling for political reasons'.[33] The meeting broke up half an hour after midnight, with the question of the rise still unresolved and the heart of a 271-year-old institution perhaps missing a beat.

Next morning the movement came from the East End, with Cromer (in King's words) 'advising us that to string along with the Government would do sterling less harm than defying them'. In a Cabinet discussion at about the same time there was little support for Callaghan's view that, with a heavy run on sterling, there was a sound economic case for raising Bank rate. Brown wondered if this was 'deliberate political sabotage' and added that 'he personally would not trust the Governor one inch'; Wilson not only said that 'he didn't altogether absolve the Governor', but added that 'there were too many Tory directors in the City' and that 'the run on sterling last June and August was a planned campaign'. Accordingly, Bank rate stayed where it was, and in the event there was little serious pressure on the pound during the rest of the campaign. Cromer had, Cairncross noted on the 15th, 'overplayed his hand', not least 'by suggesting adverse market reactions where none had shown themselves'. The City's unreconstructed old guard still had some electoral fight left in it – ' "Britain's Clever Little Man" ' was the title of a bitter attack by Wincott on Wilson and the dishonest, degenerate society he represented – but the general mood was one of resigned expectation, with the stock market fully discounting a handsome Labour win.[34] On election night itself, with Labour heading for just short of a three-figure overall majority, Wilson told a television interviewer that the Tories might understand finance, but Labour understood industry. It seemed at the time the more fruitful, as well as more attractive, priority.

One of the re-elected government's first jobs was to decide who should succeed Cromer. According to King's diary, Parsons and Stevens as well as O'Brien were still in the frame, while there was press talk about the highly regarded Sir Eric Roll coming over from the Department of Economic Affairs. In the end it was O'Brien, who in Callaghan's admiring retrospective words 'had entered the Bank of England on the bottom rung without the advantage of family or school' and was 'modest, quiet, considerate of the views of others but firm in his own beliefs', as well as 'technically proficient'. O'Brien was surely correct in judging that his meritocratic background appealed to Callaghan and Wilson, as did the fact that he was not part of the City establishment in the same way as Cromer. O'Brien also had an opinion about the way in which the new dispensation was decided and communicated:

> The Chancellor, James Callaghan, asked me to go down to see him [probably on 21 April], when he offered me the job, telling me that Maurice Parsons, then in the USA, was being appointed Deputy Governor. I accepted my own fate without hesitation, but reflected on the dictatorial style of Labour politicians. There was no hint that the Court had been consulted, which they should have been. Nor were my views sought about the choice of my deputy. Jim did not mean to be discourteous or unkind; like so many of his colleagues he was deaf to the niceties in such matters. The 'we are the masters now' syndrome lived on . . .

The public announcement was made the following week, and according to the *Daily Telegraph* there was 'widespread and openly expressed satisfaction' in the City that the rumours about Roll coming from the DEA had proved unfounded. O'Brien would be the first Governor to have come up through the ranks, but he was manifestly such a competent, straightforward central banker that the prospect did not alarm the City grandees. 'Good plain cook: won't argue about the menu' was reputedly Lord Harcourt's reaction. Cairncross also anticipated an end to Cromer-style controversy – 'Obviously Leslie won't take a public stand with the same backing as Cromer could and can hardly be a public figure in the same way,' he noted – and justifiably there was an expectation that the new Governor would shift the Bank's centre of gravity westwards, especially given his long-standing friendship with Armstrong at the Treasury. Yet any assumption that O'Brien would be the government's 'yes man' underestimated both the man himself and the reliance that the City still placed on the Bank as its principal means of leverage with the government.[35]

The last budget during Cromer's governorship was on 3 May – a mildly deflationary budget notable for its ill-conceived Selective Employment Tax (SET), explicitly designed to penalise service industries, including of course the financial services industry. Cromer was soon publicly stressing the City's contribution (estimated by the Bank at £200m net) to Britain's invisible earnings; while the *Banker* described SET as, in the City's eyes, 'puritan in tone, neo-Marxist in economic intent' and introducing into British economic policy 'a wholly false antithesis between "productive" and "non-productive" activities'. What really began to undermine confidence in sterling, though, was not fiscal engineering but the economically damaging seamen's strike between mid-May and early July. Foreign exchange losses began to mount during June, prompting Cromer on the 15th to send his final warning to Callaghan: 'I have no doubt that if devaluation of sterling were to come about serious antagonism would be generated world wide against this country for jeopardising the international payments system through failing to pursue domestic policies of a type acknowledged universally by individual countries and the international institutions as appropriate to a situation which has been clear for all to see.'[36]

Cromer's last day in office was Thursday the 30th, and King after the weekly Court had 'a long talk' with the Bank's chief economist:

> Allen says (1) the latest [trade] figures coming up are worse than ever and (2) that our reserve figures are faked, thanks to the co-operation of the Americans – a very powerful weapon they hold over our heads. I asked what should be done. He said in default of some large increase of productivity, of which there is no sign or likelihood, the Government should (1) run down its overseas commitments much faster than it is doing, (2) enforce a wage freeze, (3) introduce control of imports. A wage freeze by itself just now would not be enough, as it would not operate quickly enough, and we have, at most, eighteen months. I said I saw no chance of this Government eating its words to the required degree . . .

That evening the Bank held a farewell reception for Cromer, which Wilson attended. To King's wife the Prime Minister 'looked a broken man – bigger, warmer and nicer, but he now knows he can't do it'.[37] The retiring Governor, though, was far from unbroken, as he looked forward to returning to Barings and the more congenial world of private banking.

July 1966 proved a memorable début for his successor.[38] On the 8th, shortly before leaving for Basle, O'Brien called on Wilson to tell him that continuing attacks on sterling and exchange losses were once more threatening the parity of the pound. The situation had not improved by Tuesday the 12th, when O'Brien sent a six-page letter to Callaghan on 'our general situation'. Although his tone was less hectoring and censorious than Cromer's, he argued strongly that unless the right measures were taken quickly, 'a collapse of the sterling parity – which is increasingly widely and cynically being forecast on all sides – will be inevitable'. The right measures, he believed, included major cuts in overseas expenditure and the reducing of domestic demand, even if this raised the level of unemployment. However, as he opportunistically noted, 'a long period of very low unemployment has not produced the hoped-for breakthrough on productivity and restrictive work practices'. O'Brien also suggested a total wages freeze for a year or eighteen months in order to help bring about those 'major changes in attitude' without which, according to him, it would be impossible for the UK to 'secure a reasonable and sustained external balance'. In sum: 'Certainly exhortation is now a debased currency. But a total temporary wage freeze (it would have to be total – harsh, crude and unfair though that would be) represents a way – somewhat dangerous perhaps – in which real leadership might arouse the country.' O'Brien had already suggested a Bank rate increase, and on Thursday the 14th this duly took place (up from 6 to 7 per cent); at the same time it was announced by Callaghan that there would soon be further measures to restore overseas confidence in sterling. 'This is *the* last chance,' declared the *FT* next morning, insisting that the government 'either takes steps itself to avoid devaluation, or the rest of the world will make up its mind for it'.[39]

The sustained attacks on sterling on Friday the 15th accelerated Labour's agonised decision-making process about whether the avoidance of devaluation should remain the supreme goal, if its inevitable consequence was drastic deflation so soon after an election won on the premise of planned economic growth. Stressing practicalities rather than morality, O'Brien wrote Callaghan a strong anti-devaluation letter, prior to an early evening meeting with him and Wilson at No 10. The Governor began the discussion with a summary:

> A critical situation had been reached by the losses of sterling suffered yesterday and today – £24 and £58 million respectively. There was a general selling all over the world. In his view, if the run continued, as at present, it could easily amount to liabilities of £1,000 millions in forwards, by the end of next week. The Governor said that he knew the Prime Minister was in a determined mood to maintain parity and he wished to assure the Prime Minister of his full support to that end. In his view confidence in sterling could only be restored if strong action were taken quickly.

Wilson was indeed determined not to devalue, still convinced that to do so would leave Labour fatally holed in terms of its reputation for economic management, and he and Callaghan explained to O'Brien their plans for a deflationary, confidence-inspiring package. 'It would be quite wrong to produce a package which was regarded overseas as being half-baked,' the Governor insisted after listening to them. Finally Wilson (presumably with a view to securing ammunition for the Cabinet battle that lay ahead) asked O'Brien for his view on devaluation. The official minute suggests that the Governor reiterated his opposition in surprisingly eloquent terms:

> If the British Government were to devalue, it would be regarded by overseas countries as a device by a Socialist Government to avoid having to face the real decisions which were essential if our payments were to be brought into balance. This view he restated on three occasions, and he used a graphic phrase, namely that devaluation would be regarded as the Socialist Government's 'recipe' for dealing with a situation which in fact demanded unpleasant internal measures. On the other hand, if a Socialist Government could maintain the parity of the £ in spite of the present pressures by

introducing tough measures, it would once and for all demonstrate worldwide its determination to solve the problems without recourse to devaluation. From this he believed the Government would gain enormous benefit.

Wilson would later pay tribute to how, during the July 1966 crisis, O'Brien's 'calm and reasoned advice made a deep impression on my colleagues and myself'; and at this critical moment in the Labour Party's history, three and a half months after it had won a commanding majority for the first time since 1945, O'Brien's apparently not unsympathetic stance may have been decisive in stiffening ministerial resolve to place the needs of sterling above those of economic expansion.[40]

Some twenty-four hours later, returning from the Governor's annual cricket match at the Bank's sports ground at Roehampton, O'Brien called, at George Brown's request, at Brown's official flat in Carlton House Terrace. By now Brown knew that only devaluation could save his cherished National Plan, and O'Brien remembered how 'after being harangued for some long time by George pacing round the room in his shirt sleeves we were joined by William Armstrong'. However, 'neither of us would budge and George eventually gave up'. Following Wilson's return from an unfortunately timed visit to Moscow, there was a five-hour Cabinet meeting on Tuesday the 19th, at which the six in favour of devaluation were outvoted by the seventeen against. Next day Wilson announced a heavily deflationary package. It went down well enough in the City, and the sterling crisis eased, though at their weekly meeting that Thursday the discount market's representatives expressed some disappointment to O'Brien. 'It was difficult to think what more could have been done except perhaps a bigger cut in Government expenditure,' O'Brien replied, and he went on, 'Although, in his position, he could not express political views, the action taken was the result of nearly two years of boss shots and now that they have hit the target, nobody believes it. Labour have a built-in disadvantage. This is not fair but is one of the facts of life.'[41] So indeed it was.

*

On 10 September 1966 the ex-Governor sent his partners at Barings some thoughts on the firm's future given the current context:

> Wilson is beset with the idea that he (identifying himself as the personification of the Labour Party) is surrounded by enemies intent on sabotaging the will of the People... Market forces indicating lack of confidence in his government are, in his eyes, manifestations of hostile activity by those who want to bring him (and the Labour Government) into disrepute ... The City is likely to face a period during which its functions are liable to be impaired both at home (credit squeeze, baffling and

discriminatory taxation, activities of IRC, prices and incomes policy, bank profits, politically influenced Companies Act, Monopoly Commission, etc, etc) and internationally (Exchange Controls in many forms, limitations on exchange dealing, exoticisms of Switch $ Market, etc, etc) . . .

To round off his gloomy overview, Cromer also referred to how 'the Sterling Area concept' was currently being destroyed 'with no more than crocodile tears from the IMF'. Seven weeks later, after a lengthy visit to the US, George Bolton offered an altogether more upbeat assessment:

I have found increasing desire among banks, stockbroking and investment houses to open up in London. It is now regarded as the only international banking centre and, with the growing restrictions in the United States associated with the heavy defence expenditure, they believe the only way to maintain their business and protect the interests of their major customers who have subsidiaries abroad is to conduct their international operations from a London address. There appears to be a universal respect for the capacity and efficiency of London, and this feeling does not appear to have been affected by anxieties about Sterling and the future of British industry . . .

Did the bear or the bull have the right of it about the City's future? 'No gin today/the gin has gone away/we're drinking halves of beer/that's the truth, I fear,' members of the Stock Exchange sang that autumn (in their version of the current hit by Herman and his anchorites) as in the afternoon they tumbled out of bars like Slaters in Throgmorton Street.[42] As so often, though, the stock market's animal spirits meant that it was missing the big picture.

Cromer's claim that the policy of the Labour government was undermining London as an international financial centre was not, of course, entirely baseless. In particular, the rule introduced in Callaghan's April 1965 budget that 25 per cent of the proceeds of all sales of foreign currency securities had to be sold in the official exchange market (as opposed to the more attractive dollar premium market) inevitably had a deterrent effect on overseas investment as far as UK institutional investors were concerned. There were other measures too in 1965–6 discouraging British investment overseas, and by early 1966 Cromer was publicly berating a situation in which 'we, the British, sporting though we may be, should want to give our foreign competitors in overseas ventures a start of some 18%, as is the current effect of existing measures'. A few months later, shortly before leaving the Bank, he protested strongly to Armstrong at the Treasury about 'the ill effects on management of investments inherent in the surrender requirements on switching foreign currency investments', claiming that this was not only affecting 'our international financial position', but also 'seriously undermining London as the international market for dealing in foreign currency securities'. Yet to read the 1967 edition of *The City in the World Economy* by William Clarke is to be struck by his seemingly relaxed approach towards the whole question of exchange controls and suchlike.[43] Almost certainly it was starting to be realised that flourishing new markets, operating outside the remit of exchange control, were doing a huge amount to revitalise London as an international centre; and that, anyway, many of the City's big operators were well able to circumvent the controls, or at least to live with them.

By contrast, competitors were shooting themselves in the foot with far deadlier bullets. In the US the deeply negative impact of Regulation Q and the Interest Equalisation Tax was compounded in 1965 by first the Voluntary Foreign Credit Restraint Program, limiting the credit that US domestic banks could provide overseas, and then the Foreign Direct Investment Program, making it difficult for ambitious US corporations to raise money at home to finance expansion abroad. The West German authorities were similarly myopic in 1965, introducing a 25 per cent coupon tax on the interest payments from fixed-interest securities owned by non-residents, a severe and long-lasting blow to Frankfurt's prospects as a centre for Eurocurrency trading. Overall the figures at the end of 1965 were eloquent enough: London had 98 individual foreign banks (excluding Commonwealth banks), well ahead of New York (63), Paris (48) and Zurich (17).[44] Halfway through a decade characterised by capital hunger, monetary instability and increasing amounts of footloose money, as the Bretton Woods system prepared to enter its death throes, the City of London with its fortuitous time zone, critical mass of skills and generally benign environment found itself uniquely well placed – although relatively few yet appreciated the fact, or its significance.

The flourishing state of the so-called 'parallel' money markets (that is, parallel to the traditional money or discount market) epitomised this broad trend.[45] The biggest of the four main parallel markets was the Eurodollar market, which continued to grow and where the London-based American banks were utterly dominant by 1965. By the end of that year American banks in London held overseas deposits to the equivalent of £1,010m, a total almost double that of the merchant banks. These American banks were borrowing heavily in Eurodollars, in order to repatriate them to the US, where their principal customers were the large corporations and multinationals anxious not to be stunted by the latest American credit restraint measures. London's second parallel money market was a wholesale banking market, namely the inter-bank market in Eurodollar and sterling deposits, under way in both currencies by 1964. 'The main dealers, operating as principals, are the merchant banks, foreign banks in London and British banks operating abroad, and include some banks that are subsidiaries of, or associated with, clearing banks,' the *Midland Bank Review* noted in August 1966, adding perhaps wistfully that 'the clearing banks themselves do not take part in the inter-bank market'. Here the deposits (i.e. loans) were unsecured and inter-bank brokers traded with an agility often deriving from a foreign exchange market background, so it was hardly natural territory for the stolid British joint-stock banker. The third market was the local authority loans market, which from 1964 included a market in one-year ('yearling') negotiable bonds after a pioneering issue arranged by Warburgs for Manchester Corporation. Finally, a successful market emerged in negotiable certificates of deposit (CDs), originally pioneered in New York. London's first CD, issued in May 1966, was dollar-denominated, the first negotiable instrument to have been issued under English law since 1896. Its architect was a brilliant young American banker – Michael von Clemm at the London office of First National City Bank of New York (Citibank) – and the London dollar CD proved to be an extraordinarily effective way of simplifying dollar financing for non-dollar banks. Another American bank with an increasingly strong presence, White Weld, did much to develop a secondary market in dollar CDs, and though some other American banks (such as the Bank of America) were surprisingly conservative in their reaction, it was an instrument that had come to stay.[46]

The Eurobond market (primarily in dollar-denominated issues, though with a significant sprinkling of DM issues) was likewise becoming entrenched. New issues amounted to the equivalent of $1,016m in 1965, $1,077m in 1966 and $1,916m in 1967. The great majority of issues were arranged in London, though still almost entirely distributed abroad, and it was from their New Court vantage-point that Jacob Rothschild and Rodney Leach took stock in April 1967:

> The spectrum of maturities and types of offering have broadened, so that borrowers and investors can select short, medium or long-term debt, convertibles, or debt with warrants attached to purchase equity. The scope for private placements has been enlarged and some further institutional sources of funds have become available. The syndication of Euro-dollar finance has made possible large bridging loans, improving the ability of borrowers to accommodate the raising of long-term funds to market conditions and cash requirements. All this rapid evolution has caught the imagination of bankers, whose efforts in proselytising investors and mastering new techniques have not only expanded and matured the Eurobond market itself but have also spilled over into domestic markets, where some international methods are being tested for the first time.

New Court's own finest hour occurred in March 1966 when Rothschilds managed to beat off competition from Morgan Stanley and win the mandate to lead manage the $27.5m issue for Transalpine Finance Holdings, thereby providing the first tranche of funding for a pipeline between Trieste and Ingolstadt. Warburgs took an important place in the Rothschild group, and according to Fraser only ceded lead position after Jacob Rothschild had made 'an emotional appeal' to Warburg. 'Uncle Siegmund yielded, without argument, and explained afterwards to his rather shocked colleagues that he had decided to do so partly because he owed a personal debt of gratitude to Rothschilds who had helped him start up in London after he left Germany, partly because he thought there was a danger of our becoming "too arrogant"'.[47] Transalpine put Rothschilds firmly on the Eurobond map: it was the market's first non-guaranteed loan, in defiance of the Swiss banks that were so important generally in the distribution process.

By this time an increasing number of Eurobond issues were for big US corporations – in 1965 alone, for example, these included IBM, Gulf, Du Pont and Amoco. Indeed, by the following spring Warburg himself was complaining to Parsons at the Bank that the European capital markets were suffering from 'acute indigestion', because of 'the way in which the US corporations have plunged into these markets', and he hoped that central banks would encourage a more orderly approach. There was also, from a specifically City perspective, another problem. 'It should not pass unnoticed,' Cromer noted in his September 1966 reflections, 'that the New York Investment Bankers are becoming more and more reluctant to include London Houses in Euro-dollar issues because the London market with a high switch $ premium takes so little stock . . .' Moreover, when in due course the Eurobond market's league table for 1966 appeared, it revealed the following ranking (by issues initiated and managed): White Weld ($141m), Deutsche Bank ($106m), Kuhn Loeb ($94m), S.G. Warburg ($92m), First Boston Corp and Morgan Stanley ($85m each), and N.M. Rothschild ($72m). Only two British houses, in other words, were among the top seven issuers. In a sense this was hardly surprising. After all, apart from Cromer's point about the lack of British investment appetite for these issues, almost half the borrowing was being done by American companies; and, as Rothschild and Leach pointed out, US investment banks were already organised for distribution via institutional salesmen and syndicates, whereas in London merchant banks 'the selling function hardly exists in an offer for sale and is principally left to brokers in a placing'.[48] Just as in the Eurodollar market earlier in the 1960s, the merchant banks seemed all too likely to drop back behind the Americans after making the early running.

Perhaps, though, it did not matter, granted that the Eurobond market itself was now predominantly located in London. Moreover, irrespective of nationality, the Eurobond market community in these early years had a distinct and very attractive character: intimate but cosmopolitan, co-operative (for instance between Warburgs and White Weld) as much as competitive, intellectually creative and thoroughly can-do in spirit. 'Withholding tax, exchange control, the difficulty of getting judgements and foreign currencies, sovereign immunity, the stock exchange regulations and problems about negotiability were all major problems,' Nicholas Wilson of the solicitors Slaughter and May recalled of this pioneering phase. 'They all seemed insuperable at times, but nevertheless the driving force of people at Warburgs, White Weld and other issuing houses was such that solutions *had* to be found, and they were found.' English law, moreover, was trusted, London and New York had a common language, and the issues had a fixed commission structure (unbreachable for many years) that appealed greatly to the Swiss banks.[49] All in all, it was a new and hugely stimulating market that did indeed, as Rothschild and Leach justly remarked, catch the imagination of bankers.

In the City of the mid to late 1960s, however, nothing quite caught the imagination like a juicy takeover battle, with its attendant glamour and prospective fat fees. Rules tended to be bent, and the City's guidelines (admittedly somewhat more forthright after a revised version of the *Notes on Amalgamations* appeared in 1963) still left a lot of room for manoeuvre.[50] An improving stock market from late 1966 stimulated take-over and merger activity, leading to three episodes that, as the financial journalist Richard Spiegelberg nicely put it, 'finally damaged the delicate fabric of the Queensberry Rules beyond repair'. These were the con-troversial Philips/Thorn struggle for Pye; a stock market 'slogging match' involving Courtaulds, with the wholesaling business of Wilkinson & Riddell as the prize; and the battle for Metal Industries fought between Thorn Electrical Industries and Aberdare Holdings. Barings naturally still represented Courtaulds, and towards the end of the second episode O'Brien told Cromer that he was becoming 'disturbed' about 'the reputation which Courtaulds were earning for themselves in the City', to which Cromer could only reply that Kearton had been keeping 'in the dark' not only Barings but also Knight, his finance director. It was the third episode, though, that earned the most publicity, with Kleinwort Benson (acting for Metal Industries) being much criticised for its apparent disregard for shareholders' rights. Almost immediately afterwards, at a City dinner on 18 July 1967, Wilson called on the City to promulgate 'formal and clear ground rules' about takeover battles and to see that those rules were carried out. O'Brien read the runes, at once getting the IHA to reconvene its working party on the subject, as well as telling its Chairman, Michael Bucks, that the Bank was now in favour of 'a standing advisory committee' in order to implement the takeover code and, if necessary, 'hold the ring'. When Bucks demurred, O'Brien told him frankly that 'if the City were not capable of putting their own house in order it would be open to me to advise HMG that there was no alternative but to introduce a securities and exchange commission on the American model'.[51] Bucks and his colleagues took the point, and soon the regulation (or, rather, non-regulation) of takeover battles would never be quite the same again.

Meanwhile in autumn 1967 a takeover battle took place that, according to the *Economist*, showed that the City had 'grown up'. It explained: 'The investment analysts and professional managers are now in charge. The consequence of their new pre-eminence is that this time both sides have had to show that their arguments made sense in terms of long-term industrial economics as well as short-term cash.'[52] The four key people behind GEC's takeover of Associated Electrical Industries (AEI), a decisive moment in the rationalisation of the British heavy electrical industry, were Sir Frank Kearton and Ronald Grierson (Chairman and Managing Director respectively of the Industrial Reorganisation Corporation, the latter having been seconded from Warburgs), the merchant banker Kenneth Keith, and – above all – Arnold Weinstock of GEC itself. As it happened, Grierson, an inveterately restless figure, was by this time on the verge of leaving the IRC, having told O'Brien in the summer that 'almost daily the Government offended him in one way or another and he was not sure how much longer he could hang on'.

When the bid was launched in late September, Hill Samuel (a fairly recent merger itself) acted for GEC and Barings for AEI (that company, under threat, apparently no longer having faith in its usual merchant bank, Morgan Grenfell, in part because of its close connections with GEC). Over the next few weeks Carnwath of Barings spent much time at AEI's head office at Grosvenor Place, and early on 'the question of Hill Samuel's request for envelopes was discussed and it was decided that only a list [i.e. of AEI's shareholders] should be produced'. In the wider world there was already quite a cult about Weinstock, who was seen simultaneously as a progressive force and a cost-cutter; but although under Keith's vigorous guidance parts of the City warmed to him during the bid, other elements indulged in what one observer described as 'a sharp burst of antisemitic feeling'. Lord Chandos, a former City man (as Oliver Lyttleton) and former Chairman of AEI, was among those not in the fan club. 'If the rationalisation of industry under a Socialist Government is going to depend upon the market-price of a stock exchange deal,' he wrote to Cromer on 25 October in something like a white heat, 'and the whole future depends upon the action of a hatchet-minded operator, then the Government is going to have a pretty uncomfortable afternoon – and more – in both Houses of Parliament. H.W. is quite adroit enough to see these political pitfalls.' With its increasing 'big is beautiful' philosophy, however, the government clearly favoured GEC – and if it had any doubts, these would presumably have been stilled by the sight of Cromer in AEI's corner. Eventually, on 8 November, it was announced that

GEC's £160m bid had carried the day; and Barings never got its £75,000 fee from the victors, with GEC claiming that Hill Samuel had only wished to be paid if GEC won.[53] Taken in the round, the episode lacked the reverberations of the Aluminium War, but in both City and industrial terms it was undoubtedly another defeat for the establishment.

Chandos may have been contemptuous of the fate of a great, if under-performing, company resting on 'a stock exchange deal', but on the floor of the Stock Exchange itself there were few such qualms. At the time of GEC's bid Val Powell was a young jobber in the industrial market:

> I was not allowed on the electrical book at the time, and I do remember that coming up on the screen and there was a hushed silence, unbelievable that this mega-merger could have taken place, and an absolute pandemonium around the jobbers' pitches as people piled in to see what was happening, what the price was and a tremendous turnover developed in the shares thereafter . . .

For five years from 1967, with the old House having been pulled down amidst emotional scenes, jobbers and others were operating in the rather cramped, low-ceilinged, so-called 'temporary market', while the new concrete-and-glass Stock Exchange was being built on the site of the old one. The Chairman who oversaw this complex operation was Martin Wilkinson, and under his guidance the Stock Exchange became more ambitious in the regulatory field, including in 1966 a final and effective blitz against bond-washing, admittedly partly under pressure from the Inland Revenue. There is also some evidence that the principle established in 1967 of forming a permanent body to police a more extensive Takeover Code owed at least as much to Stock Exchange as to Bank thinking. Yet if that was progress, there was an ominous straw in the wind in July 1967 as the Monopolies Commission made a preliminary enquiry to the Stock Exchange about three particular practices perhaps not in the public interest: restrictions on admission; prohibition of members engaging in outside activities; and minimum commissions.[54] An unimpressed outsider was John Nott of Warburgs, who three years earlier had run into Stock Exchange obstinacy and conservatism in the process of creating yearling bonds.

There was also the sorry story of how the Stock Exchange was unwilling to encourage the creation of a strong secondary market in Eurobonds. In October 1964 it turned down Rowe & Pitman's request to allow foreign currency issues to be dealt in 'at discretion', and ten months later that broking firm (in effect speaking on behalf of Hambros) tried again. It argued that such issues were 'of great importance to the position of London as an international capital market' but that 'the present Stock Exchange rules actually inhibit the growth of such a market [i.e. in these bonds] in London'. Rowe & Pitman identified two specific problems: first, rule 88, which required 15 per cent of an issue to be offered to the market, was a futile ritual and caused significant delay; and second, the unfortunate fact that brokers were not allowed to charge discretionary commission in these bonds, granted that in overseas centres 'commission rates are almost all lower than ours'. Rowe & Pitman's appeal concluded by emphasising that it was not the firm's wish 'to try to deprive the jobbers of their existing business in these bonds'.

The Council set up a special committee under George Loveday's chairmanship and during autumn 1965 heard evidence from several members. They included Rowe & Pitman's Julian Martin Smith and the Hon James Ogilvy, who amplified their arguments:

> Commission 'at discretion' would assist in increasing turnover thus enabling the Jobbers to quote narrower prices. They as issuing Broker would prefer to deal in the market if possible . . . They would hope to compete successfully with White, Weld & Co if permitted to charge ¼ per cent or less . . . They felt certain the removal of the present restrictions in relation to this exceptional business would tend to increase turnover and thus benefit the London market as a whole . . .

Similarly, Jock Hunter observed that 'at present the Stock Exchange could not compete with the outside Houses, especially White, Weld & Co', and that 'the trouble was lack of turnover in "after markets"'. So too Edgar Astaire of the brokers Astaire & Co, who said that his firm 'found it embarrassing not to be able to complete business in the market'; who claimed that 'the Merchant Banks like to use Brokers', but that 'on the basis of ½% commission plus the Jobber's turn business was impracticable'; and who, like the others, 'felt steps should be taken which would allow the London Broker to become more competitive with the outside Houses such as White, Weld & Co'. Another broker, Alfred Caplin of R. Layton & Co, elaborated on this far from satisfactory state of affairs:

> The manner in which business in Foreign currency loans was being conducted made it impossible for him to deal in the market. He said it was a non-resident market and mainly professional. The placing Brokers and the Merchant Banks knew where the bonds had been placed . . . Allowing for commission, the prices Mr Caplin could quote to clients looked so futile that he preferred not quoting at all. White Weld & Co had extensive connections overseas and bid on a net basis. Thus it was quite impossible for Jobbers to compete unless they were prepared to make a book. At present they were completely uncommercial. Mr Caplin said that he saw no remedy until the investment premium and the necessity for a seller to remit 25% of proceeds had disappeared. Until resident clients became interested London was at the mercy of trends abroad.

The committee's report, just before Christmas, was predictable: while recommending a commission reduction, it was adamant that any change to rule 88 – although enabling brokers to run books more easily in these stocks – 'would be contrary to all existing rules affecting brokers and jobbers and in the Committee's view is unacceptable'. In other words, the encouragement of an esoteric, minority market, in which the bonds were initially placed almost entirely overseas, was seen as far from sufficient cause to erode the citadel that was single capacity. Even so, for all this institutional conservatism, there was still much truth in the retrospective view of Julius Strauss (whose Strauss Turnbull remained one of the very few firms of brokers to maintain a serious interest in Eurobond trading) that the London jobbers 'were simply not very interested'. In 1968 it would be estimated that each day London was trading some $15m in Eurobonds, but that only 1 per cent of that business was channelled through the Stock Exchange.[55] It was a lamentable failure, reflecting not only unavoidable difficulties but also, deep down, an attitude problem born of insularity and complacency.

The jobbing system meanwhile continued to contract, largely through mergers. In 1960 there had been over a hundred jobbing firms; in 1964 there were still over sixty; by the end of the decade there would barely be thirty. Broking firms, for the most part, preferred to keep their distance; though in accordance with the increasingly fashionable nostrum that size equalled strength, Sheppards did merge in May 1967 with Chase, Henderson & Tennant to become Sheppards & Chase. Among corporate brokers, judged by the number of new issues in 1965 with which they were associated, Cazenove's led the way (176), followed by Sebags (109), Scrimgeours (63, mostly local authorities), Rowe & Pitman (61), Rowe Swann & Co (50), Panmure Gordon (48) and Hoare's (42), this last firm a temporarily declining force as Kit Hoare palpably aged but stubbornly remained in harness. For Sebags, in terms of business *and* reputation, this point represented the apogee, for Jock Gilmour had just retired and the firm would suffer badly from the lack of a strong, descriminating senior partner and a cohesive partnership.[56]

More generally, a large quantity of mediocre dross was still attached to the Stock Exchange and its immediate environs. When Jonathan Aitken in 1967 went in search of *The Young Meteors* of thrusting, meritocratic New Britain, he found few anywhere near Capel Court. One of his interviewees, a twenty-six-year-old Old Etonian now ensconced in the family stockbroking firm, was definitely a non-meteor:

> Do I work hard? Well, frankly no. I get down to the office after the rush hour – about 10.15 – and I leave just before it, about 4 o'clock. Some keen chaps arrive before it and leave after it, but it doesn't really do them much good. Occasionally, if I've been out at a thrash and got harry pissers I don't

get in till about half eleven. That is a bit idle, but you know it's astonishing the business you can do indirectly by being seen at the right places, like deb dances and so on. I once sat next to a man I'd never seen before in my life at a dinner party before a dance, and we got talking when the girls had gone out, and to cut a long story short, we're now managing his whole portfolio . . .

Aitken, though, also talked to a grammar-school educated twenty-eight-year-old stockbroker with an economics degree. 'I'm frustrated all the time because I could get far more business if only the City wasn't hidebound by these elaborate family connections, which give the family firms all the contacts,' he confessed. 'I've got no chips on my shoulder about it, yet I'm quite certain that if I had gone to Eton, which seems to provide about half the people in the City, I'd do far more business through social contacts.' However, though appalled by the overall quality of the people working in the City ('The investment managers for insurance firms are often ludicrously bad, and as a result they can't see through bad stockbrokers who work by virtual guesswork'), he did see hope for the future in the fact that 'while the old firms continue with their private clients and their new issue business, the more go-ahead firms like ours are concentrating on investment analysis', which 'brings in work from fund managers of unit trusts who are young professional people like ourselves, and who above all respect efficiency'. In sum, this broker (at Phillips & Drew?) concluded, 'that's the way the City ought to be moving, but today the old school tie still reigns triumphant'. It did indeed, but the inexorable rise of the institutional investor, hastened in the mid-1960s by the existence of a Labour government that seriously undermined private client confidence, at last meant that that undisputed sway was under threat.[57]

The merchant banking sector enjoyed an altogether more positive image than the Stock Exchange. At a lunch at No 10 in June 1965, with Cairncross attending, Balogh 'made the usual extravagant attack on the City as Tory to a man', but perhaps to his surprise 'the PM didn't endorse this sort of talk and said that the Merchant Banks were becoming more professional than 20/30 years ago'. Ian Fraser's recollections are apt: 'Merchant bankers were supposed to be the answer to every economic problem. The "profession" – if ever it was one – had an extraordinary aura surrounding it. It became the first career choice of graduates leaving their universities.' Benn may have found Grierson 'a rather flabby City type', but Wilson and other Labour colleagues had no compunction about recruiting him to run the IRC. Moreover, when Grierson decided to leave and Kearton, as Chairman, wanted an industrialist to replace him, O'Brien successfully insisted on another merchant banker, Charles

Villiers of Schroders. The merchant banks also began to open up more to the press, for the most part rather skilfully. In February 1967 the *New York Times*'s admiring profile of Richardson of Schroders (recently made a Bank of England director) even itemised his routine on weekday mornings: at eight o'clock a breakfast at his Chelsea home of one egg, toast and coffee; at nine o'clock leaving for his office in a chauffeur-driven car, complete with a reading lamp.[58]

If Richardson and like-minded merchant bankers were committed to the cause of British industrial modernisation, involving the creation of ever-bigger economic units, did that mean that the merchant banks were willing to follow the same route? Would there ever be another wave of mergers to rival that of the late 1950s and early 1960s? Confronted in June 1965 by a paper from one of his economists, John Fforde, that talked sanguinely of 'the emergence of larger and more homogenous merchant banks', Rowley Cromer preferred to stress the blessings of diversity:

> Apart from prestige and standing which is vital to all of them, it is initiative, ingenuity and the readiness to adapt themselves to contemporary situations which provide a common denominator. It is certainly not a question of size . . . The mergers and acquisitions which have taken place for one reason or another (and as far as I am aware on no occasion was rationalisation a reason) give me no cause to believe that size in itself is an asset . . . The quest for rationalisation proposed in the paper is doubtless based on the growth in deposits in recent years of the merchant banks; a growth in deposits largely brought about by the rigidity of the clearing banks. Sooner or later the clearing banks must, in my belief, shake off their self-imposed shackles, in which case the merchant banks will revert to living on their banking wits . . .

That was one perspective, inevitably a rather lofty one. Writing soon afterwards in the *Banker*, David Montagu of Samuel Montagu & Co argued that although significant recent strides had been made in new fields of activity (such as foreign dollar loans, providing finance to industry through factoring, managing newly formed investment and unit trusts, and attracting substantial foreign and domestic deposits), the merchant banks faced a novel, fundamental problem of 'ensuring that industrial or commercial firms have made available to them advice and service in every aspect of their operations' while yet 'attempting to provide a personal relationship that stems from the tradition of family banks'. How was that to be achieved? Montagu could only refer rather vaguely to 'the ability of the merchant bank to forge links with other institutions without necessarily losing its identity'. To another, older merchant banker, the answer to an uncertain future in an era of increasingly large economic units apparently lay in the creation of a race of financial supermen. 'We need people who must be personalities in the fullest sense of the word;

mature in spirit and character, combining caution, a sense of tradition and sober judgement with a sense of progress and things to come and where the qualities of reliability and discretion have become second nature,' Walter Salomon told the shareholders of Rea Brothers in April 1967. 'In my submission, these qualities are essential if private banking is to survive in an age of computers and fonctionnaires.'[59]

If there was a race of financial supermen in the City of the mid-1960s, most observers felt that it resided at 30 Gresham Street, the so-called 'Night Club in the City', where desks were occupied by nine in the morning and often after seven in the evening.[60] In the traditional City, these were unheard-of hours. 'When I came out of the office in the evening,' Martin Gordon (who joined Warburgs in 1963) recalls, 'the only other people I would ever see would be Japanese bankers.' At that time the firm numbered about 150 people; and for the rest of his life Warburg would set his face, not entirely successfully, against size for its own sake. It was well-nigh unprecedented for an accepting house to be located west of the Bank of England, and 30 Gresham Street (tel: Metropolitan 7545) was an ugly, functional, modern mauve building located directly opposite one of Wren's most beautiful churches, Old Jewry. The austerity outside was matched inside, with the visitor being greeted by 'an entrance hall with plain counter, male attendants and lifts that seemed to have been designed for cargo, not passengers'. Lunches were famously abstemious (for many years beer, cider or mineral water was the only choice of drink with the meal), while a pronounced work ethic pervaded the whole atmosphere. Ascot, the Lord's Test and Wimbledon were still important points in the City calendar, but 'it was frowned upon in Warburgs if we took the day off for such occasions,' Peter Stormonth Darling has written. 'Holidays were permitted, with some reluctance, and on condition that you left a telephone number where you could be reached. All business travel had to be at weekends whenever feasible, so as not to miss any working time.' The cult of the all-round, preferably sporting amateur, still a potent force elsewhere in the City, was entirely absent; and one of Stormonth Darling's more iconoclastic colleagues, Andrew Smithers, would enjoy smuggling in cricketing metaphors at meetings where Warburg was present, though the great man never let on until afterwards that he did not understand what a googly was. Otherwise, internal communication was of the essence, with Warburg and the other founding 'uncles' deliberately encouraging an open-door, partnership approach. Ian Fraser recalls how every meeting had to be recorded by a memorandum. 'Copies of all letters, both in and out, were circulated to all the directors and many of the senior managers. The inner circle of directors were expected to arrive by eight o'clock so that they could read all the incoming mail, all the outgoing mail and the office memoranda of the previous day.

The entire management met every morning at 9.15 a.m. to discuss the day's business ...' Then at the end of the long day, 'as we left we were given a cyclostyled twelve-page summary of all the day's letters and memoranda, just in case we had missed something'.[61]

Was it, overall, a happy place? Certainly, for most of the younger generation, working at Warburgs in the 1960s was memorable and usually formative, but not everyone relished the ultra-competitive atmosphere. At any one time one was either 'in' or 'out', and for those who dropped out of favour (not always for purely explicable reasons) there was sometimes no way back. For others it was a hugely enriching experience, combining hard and purposeful work, intellectual stimulation and a sense of being in an élite team getting new business and trying to do it in new, high-quality ways. 'Warburgs was indeed an acquired taste,' Stormonth Darling remarks in his memoir of the firm, 'but it is easy to see why some very able people acquired it.[62]

One of them, Fraser, leaves no doubt in his account as to who, in a day-to-day, hands-on sense, really ran the business. He depicts Warburg as 'the South German romantic who was inspired by an unrelenting determination to restore the standing of his family at the forefront of international banking', but who 'was weak as a technician' and 'never understood the implications of balance-sheet consolidation and therefore could not read a modern British or American set of accounts'. Indeed, 'he did not understand the terms "debenture" or "floating charge" and many times I heard him giving a false definition of English financial terms to clients'. By his side, however, was Henry Grunfeld, 'the North German machine-man who never saw or made a joke but was in many ways the personification of the Prussian *Generalstäbler*, the General Staff officer' – or, put more prosaically, 'a terrific professional who knew the material inside-out'. Peter Spira says of Grunfeld that his was 'the finely honed brain, the incisive negotiator, with a unique skill in simplifying the complicated'.[63]

The business itself, for all the firm's steeply climbing reputation, was far from the biggest among the City's merchant banks: Warburg had no wish to build up the banking side and challenge firms like Hambros or Kleinworts on their own terrain. Instead, he wanted Warburgs to stand or fall by its deeds in company finance and in the world's capital markets, especially those of London and the rest of Europe. Indeed, one of his fundamental principles was never to let corporate financiers get their hands on capital – on the grounds that it would make them lazy, using money instead of their brains. In practice, it proved quite a struggle for the firm's corporate finance arm to land big British companies. Significantly, two were Grand Metropolitan Hotels and Thomson Newspapers, both run by outsiders; but eventually by the end of the 1960s the achievements of Warburgs in the Eurobond market began to translate into a string of major UK corporate clients, the most prestigious being ICI. Revealingly, however, Warburg had limited enthusiasm for the activities of the investment department. 'When he telephoned me, he would ritually ask, "How's the market?"', Stormonth Darling recalls, 'but he paid not the slightest attention to my answer other than to see whether I knew. If I told him it was up when it was down, he was in no position to correct me, nor did he care.'

Warburg had always taken a dim view of the intelligence of stock exchanges, not least the London Stock Exchange, and in their herd-like tendencies he could find none of the subtlety that rendered business life vital. By contrast, he worked ceaselessly to foster his firm's international connections. 'In putting deals together,' an obituary would perceptively note about his thinking, 'the handicap of small size could be overcome by using banking syndicates, the growth of which in London Warburgs was to pioneer.' Yet it was not all plain sailing, and at the end of 1964 he ended his firm's formal connection with Kuhn Loeb, largely as a result of personality disagreements.[64] Warburg may have tried instead to form an alliance with Lehman Brothers, far more go-ahead anyway than Kuhn Loeb, but it came to nothing. Back in the nineteenth century the Achilles heel of Rothschilds had been the absence of an effective American bridgehead; but for the moment such a deficiency would not matter to Warburgs, so long as capability and ambition remained in alignment.

Warburg himself, with his deeply pessimistic streak, always tried his utmost to ensure that they did. For all his protestations about taking a back-seat role (in 1967 he was sixty-five), he could not let go. On Christmas Day 1964, just after noon, the telephone rang at Stormonth Darling's home:

I do hope I'm not disturbing you.
Oh no, Mr Warburg, not at all.
Well, it's about your note dated 22 December on the American stock market. Do you have a copy in front of you?
Er, no, I'm afraid my copy is in the office.
Well, let me remind you of your second sentence in the fifth paragraph. . . I think there should be a comma after the word 'development' . . .

The message, Stormonth Darling observes, was clear. 'He was the boss, and you didn't easily forget it.' Warburg was entirely serious in his insistence that work must come first in an ambitious banker's priorities; family and home life second. When some years later, after his first marriage had collapsed, partly owing to pressures of work, Spira told Warburg that he was remarrying and that he intended to reorder his priorities, the great man 'indulgently (and metaphorically) patted me on the head and said "There, there, we all say that but of course we do not really mean it"'. The positive side to all this was that during these years Warburg pursued a systematic search for young talent and was an unstinting mentor to those prepared to listen. 'Above all,' Stormonth Darling reflects, 'Siegmund liked to be thought of as a teacher':

> We were taught the essential virtue of self-criticism, and the necessity of carrying out our activities with a measured rhythm or tempo. Good manners, consideration of other employees at more junior levels and prompt attention to outstanding matters were requirements of our daily life, while arrogance, self-promotion, sloppiness, bad writing style and bureaucratic behaviour were abhorrent to Siegmund and were to be avoided at all costs . . .

Sometimes, though, the teacher himself did not live up to his admirable precepts. Above all, there were the infamous rages – some simulated, others not – which by the mid to late 1960s were becoming increasingly frequent. Once, inspecting the office in New York that Warburgs occupied after the end of his Kuhn Loeb partnership, he took out his ire on the office manager, a young American woman. Her crime was the untidiness of her desk:

> Siegmund . . . flew into a terrific rage, shouting at the unfortunate woman at the top of his voice, with occasional lapses into German. 'We are a banking house, not a butcher shop!', he screamed. After what seemed an age to the rest of us [including Stormonth Darling], witnessing the incident with rather cowardly vicarious sympathy, the office manager, still seated at her desk, pulled out a Salem filter-tipped cigarette, tapped it, lit it casually, blew out a long trail of blue smoke, looked him in the eye and said, 'Gee, Mr Warburg, you gotta be insecure.'

Consciously or not it was a deadly riposte, temporarily knocking the wind out of Warburg's sails, and it told an important truth. That insecurity was, of course, in large part the source of his ceaseless drive. 'A man of vision, courage, wisdom and boundless energy,' Spira wrote after Warburg's death. 'He was innovative and cultured, yet ruthless and vicious, a wonderful friend to many and a dangerous enemy to a few. Siegmund was mercurial, highly emotional, often irrational, hypnotic and impulsive, provocative and conciliatory, prudish yet fascinated by the erotic. In sum, a character of multiple contrasts – and a German Jewish refugee to boot.'[65] It was no wonder that, in the rather grey post-war City of London, he was such a compelling, divisive and myth-laden figure.

One other merchant bank, on the basis of hard work, merit and aggression, was making a sustained, less-than-welcome challenge to the established order. The creation of Hill Samuel in 1965 was, on the face of it, perfectly rational: Kenneth Keith at Philip Hill had none of Warburg's qualms about size and was mindful that, even after the absorption of

Higginsons and Erlangers, there was still a certain weakness on the banking side; while at M. Samuel there was not only a shortage of younger Samuels, but a disappointing lack of progress in the area of corporate finance.[66] During the negotiations – conducted mainly between Keith and M. Samuel's rather younger Lord Melchett, grandson of the founder of ICI – there was a serious possibility that the new entity might be called Samuel Hill. However, Philip Hill's parent company was Philip Hill Investment Trust, and the prospect of that publicly quoted investment trust being renamed Samuel Hill Investment Trust had unattractive acronymic possibilities. '50–50 Integration Intended' was the headline in *The Times* on the merger's announcement in January 1965, but at Sebags, brokers to each, there was scepticism from the start. 'The two banks' general attitude to business was so very different,' Denzil Sebag-Montefiore recalled, and even that assessment was an underestimate.[67] The prevailing attitude at Philip Hill was that of taking no prisoners, whereas at M. Samuel the ethos was still gentlemanly, paternalistic and rather unambitious. Lord Bearsted (descended from Marcus Samuel) would be Chairman of the new bank, while Keith was to be Deputy Chairman as well as Chief Executive, and by autumn 1965 the two firms were brought physically together at 100 Wood Street, a seven-storey factory-type building until recently owned by Crosse & Blackwell. It was very much the Philip Hill choice, leaving the M. Samuel camp not best pleased.

It was not a happy first winter for Hill Samuel. First there was the episode in which, acting for Clore in his bid for Selfridge's, it increased the offer without the institutional underwriters of the bid being consulted. This led to considerable City criticism, as did the bank's subsequent involvement in a takeover bid for Showerings, the Babycham firm, only three months after it had acted for Showerings in their unsuccessful takeover bid for Harveys, the Bristol wine merchants. But if the Samuel directors now found themselves on a steep learning curve, another source of conflict concerned whether future as well as present day-to-day control was to rest in the hands of Keith or Melchett. 'Personalities – Hill Samuel' was the terse, pregnant subject of Cromer's conversation with Bearsted in March 1966; and in the course of the summer Melchett decided to leave in order to run the British steel industry (about to be renationalised).[68]

As events unfolded, however, the problem for Keith was that one of the bank's significant shareholders, First National City Bank of New York (which had taken a stake in M. Samuel four years earlier), was far from satisfied by the situation. First National's Stillman Rockefeller subsequently, in September, explained to O'Brien his bank's feelings:

> They thought [O'Brien noted] that Samuels' were their kind of people.

They had been somewhat surprised with the link-up with Philip Hill and very displeased with the new attitude which followed that. As Mr Rockefeller put it, this was not the girl we married. Clearly this dissatisfaction centred on Mr Keith who, Mr Rockefeller said, thought more about his own interests than those of his customers.

By then, though, the main drama was over. In brief, First National threatened during July to withdraw precipitately and publicly its representative from the Hill Samuel board, a prospect that (in his leisure moments during the concurrent sterling crisis) alarmed O'Brien. Consequently the Bank knocked Philip Hill, Samuel and First National heads together in order to insist that an independent chairman be appointed, in succession to Bearsted, to hold the ring. After Franks had wisely declined the offer, that thankless task was assigned to Lord Sherfield, the former Sir Roger Makins of the Treasury. Keith reluctantly consented to the plan, though not without telling O'Brien that he 'did not think that any good would come of Lord Sherfield getting mixed up in the day-to-day business'. O'Brien played a difficult hand skilfully, one day assuring First National that Sherfield would be 'a working chairman', the next reassuring Sherfield that a weekly commitment of 'two full days and possibly two mornings as well' would be 'adequate'. The announcement of Sherfield's appointment was made in August, and two months later he became Chairman. By then, presumably unconvinced that Keith was a stoppable force, First National had anyway decided to sell its stake, though in a sufficiently discreet, gradual way as no longer to alarm O'Brien.

'Sherfield said that all is peace now at Hill, Samuel and their next job is to get on with building up the business,' the Governor noted the following January after a visit from the new Chairman. 'Keith is a much-chastened man; indeed, too chastened because at present he seems to have lost confidence in himself and is doing little work. Sherfield is sending him off on a holiday to America and hopes that he will get back into the swim on return.' It was a striking, if perhaps implausible, portrait of a punctured Mr Toad. Later that year, in September 1967, there was no sign of lack of self-confidence when Keith gave an interview to the *FT*. 'It's all dead and buried now,' he insisted. 'The troublesome elements have gone and I'm still here.' He also denied the charge of being a 'fiery' merchant banker: 'Say I'm just a herd driver who won't sit on his bottom waiting for someone to feed him – but not fiery.' There had indeed been a mass migration of the disaffected, many going to the small merchant bank Wallace Brothers (nicknamed the Samuel refugee camp), and in the end only two of the old Samuel directors decided to stick it out in Wood Street.[69] Keith was now right at his peak as a merchant banker, and by the late 1960s Hill Samuel was firing on almost all cylinders. Aggressive pitching for new corporate finance business was actively encouraged, the prevailing atmosphere was bright, hard-working and informal, and ambitious young barons with a notable City future included Christopher Castleman, Jonathan Agnew and Graham Walsh. Hill Samuel was not, however, a serious player in the burgeoning Euromarkets, and Keith himself later conceded that it did not understand them, did not have the right people and that the one or two foreigners they hired proved a disappointment. Ultimately this would be a serious weakness, for it tied the bank's fortunes too much to those of the British economy and the more domestic, stagnant, stock-market oriented part of the City.

Much the same applied to most of the other merchant banks, especially in relation to the Eurobond market, where their ignorance and mistrust were compounded by the increasingly competitive environment. The main exceptions were Warburgs, Rothschilds and, to a lesser extent, Hambros. Even so, there were a few encouraging signs of life among the old guard. At Morgan Grenfell, for example, Sir John Stevens joined as a Managing Director in October 1967, basically to help Harcourt modernise the bank and provide some necessary strategic thinking. Two years earlier, at Lazards, the reins passed to Oliver (now Lord) Poole, who tried to shake up the place ('Too many Etonians at Lazards, we should have more Scotchmen and more Jews,' he once observed); he had the gift of lifting people's morale and his 'strength as an individual' was, in an obituarist's words, 'his commanding presence and great powers of persuasion'. Elsewhere, Jocelyn Hambro was a determined, resourceful and expansion-minded Chairman at Hambros from December 1965, launching the successful Hambro Abbey Trust in early 1967 with Abbey Life's dynamic Mark Weinberg; while at Rothschilds, with the help of the high-calibre Philip Shelbourne and Rodney Leach, Jacob Rothschild continued the process of recovery from the long dog days.[70] It remained, sadly, a rather different story at Barings, where Cromer now found it difficult to establish a role for himself, amidst what was becoming the hurly-burly of the corporate finance world. In particular, in an era of declining client loyalty, he tended to treat corporate clients with the patrician style that had so infuriated Labour politicians. He also made the mistake of filling the board with too many 'yes-men', a source of great friction with the departmental managers who were actually doing the business. Typified by his insistence on having a Rolls-Royce and a chauffeur, which was not at all the bank's style, his return to business did much to retard Barings at a time when most of its rivals were on the move.

Diversification was very much the aim of those more nimble banks, essentially in response to the increased competition not only between themselves but from foreign as well as clearing banks. The foreign banks were particularly effective in the Eurodollar market and in biting into the merchant banks' share of their traditional bread-and-butter business:

accepting. Here the personal influence of Sir Edward Reid of Barings, even after his chairmanship of the Accepting Houses Committee ended in 1966, meant that they stuck to the cartel commission rate of 1¼ per cent throughout the 1960s, despite being increasingly undercut by foreign competition. Were the merchant banks, traditionally undercapitalised but most of them now quoted, vulnerable to takeover? At a press conference in May 1965 Jack Hambro acknowledged that a clearing bank had made an approach to Hambros, but added that, in the *FT*'s words, 'exactly what was intended was never made clear and Hambros was not enthusiastic at the suggestion'. Soon afterwards Westminster Bank's 'Golly' Stirling asked Cromer whether one of the big clearing banks taking an interest of, say, 39 per cent in an accepting house (he probably had Brown Shipley in mind) would be 'tolerable', to which Cromer replied that a '20 per cent interest was the outside that would be tolerable'. There matters remained for two years, though in November 1966 it was announced that Rothschilds and National Provincial were coming together to form a new subsidiary, designed mainly to attract and then relend Eurodollars, to be called National Provincial and Rothschild (London). David Robarts, Chairman of National Provincial, had close links with New Court, but no one imagined that this presaged the beginning of the end of the independence of Rothschilds. What it did show, though, was that if a merchant bank like Rothschilds was to make the most of its opportunities in the rapidly growing Eurocurrency markets, then from one source or another it would probably need access to greater capital. The idea was also that the new subsidiary would make a speciality out of industrial lending overseas, and here again it would need financial resources at its back. At about the same time there was a possibility (not for the first time) of some tie-up between Barings and Glyn Mills, largely to co-operate in the distribution of new issues, but this came to nothing. Barings, as Cromer informed Eric Faulkner of Glyn's, remained 'unbuyable'.[71]

In fact, history was about to be made. David Montagu, the rising force at Samuel Montagu, had become increasingly convinced that his own merchant bank needed more capital and access to a new client base – a conviction that in due course led to Midland's Chief General Manager, Howard Thackstone, having 'a confidential and completely "off-record" chat' with O'Brien in December 1966:

> I explained [Thackstone noted] that S.M. & Co had made a tentative approach with the suggestion that our two organisations should seek a way of entering into some form of association. We were already marching a bit side by side in connection with an embryonic European development connected with our 'Club' and we might soon be at a point where we should have to take up a position.
>
> My main purpose in asking him to see me was to enquire whether he felt

disposed to indicate how he would regard such a move. He did not hesitate to say that he would not look with favour on total acquisition or even a substantial investment but if we had in mind a joint venture alliance for special purposes he would have nothing to say.

So far as the name itself was concerned, although they might be thought by some to be out of a drawer just short of the top he would expect them to prove suitable and capable companions.

The next month four senior Midland managers (including Thackstone) and three Samuel Montagu people (including David Montagu) met for a rather cagey discussion about potential complementary areas of business. After David Montagu had mentioned a possible 'participation' by Midland in Samuel Montagu, there was an early, unmistakable sign of the cultural chasm between the two very different traditions and mentalities:

> We [Midland] on our side indicated that it should possibly be more than a 'token' participation but mentioned our view that the 'authorities' might have their own views on the extent of such a participation of ours in a Merchant Bank. Our impression was that the 'authorities' might well like to set some limit on the extent of our holding. They did not seem to regard this too seriously which perhaps is rather indicative of a Merchant Bank's attitude to such matters.

Over the next few months most of the joint attention was focused on Samuel Montagu joining Midland and the other three members of its European 'Club' to form the Banque Européenne de Crédit à Moyen Term, to be based in Brussels and make medium-term Eurodollar loans for large-scale industrial projects. However, Midland's Chairman, Sir Archibald Forbes, told his board in July 1967 that he had recently received a formal approach by Samuel Montagu, wanting Midland to take a substantial interest. Some of the directors and senior managers may have harboured doubts, but Forbes himself was convinced of the advantages of such a move, and partly under his sway the board agreed.

Two months later, on 19 September, negotiations were concluded for the acquisition by Midland of a 33⅓ per cent interest in Montagu Trust, Samuel Montagu's holding company. By lunchtime that day signs from the Stock Exchange of 'inspired buying' (in Thackstone's subsequent phrase) made it clear that the deal had been leaked, and it was decided to go public that afternoon. Soon after lunch O'Brien was shown the draft press announcement. His mood (as recorded in his own note) was instantly thunderous:

> Although I recall that Mr Thackstone some while ago did mention to me on a personal basis and in vague terms the possibility of some link-up with the Midland Bank and Montagu's, this was the first I had heard of any specific proposal.

Mr Louis Franck [still Chairman of the Montagu holding company] called on me at 3 p.m. to explain the position. I expressed great indignation that the proposal had not been submitted to me in time for me to express my views on it. I told him that I was much disturbed at the Midland Bank taking so large a participation in the Montagu Trust, which meant in effect a large participation in Samuel Montagu's . . . He told a long story of how he had been pressed to sell to foreign interests and how he had resisted this pressure. I said that this was beside the point: my complaint was that both sides had neglected to consult me. I took exception to being faced with a fait accompli.

Later, Sir Archibald Forbes came with his apologies. I made it clear to him that a vague reference by his general manager was not my idea of consultation. This announcement might well precipitate other similar ventures by clearing banks and I should have small grounds for impeding them once the Midland had gone ahead. He rang up Thackstone from my room, seeking to get the percentage reduced from 33⅓% to 25%, which I said I would much prefer. It was clearly too late for this since the press were already in Thackstone's room. Forbes talked about the possibility of making an amending announcement later on with a smaller percentage but I set little store by this.

My extreme displeasure was made evident to all concerned.[72]

It was, in truth, a doubly historic moment: not only was it the first time that a major clearing bank had taken a stake in a merchant bank, but it also indicated that, in a changing City, the Bank of England's authority was neither as extensive nor as automatic as had generally been assumed since the Norman era. Not surprisingly, there was some unease when the announcement was made. 'I've always thought that merchant banking and clearing banking were different businesses,' one anonymous senior merchant banker protested to the press, justifying his decision to reduce his bank's activities with Midland. David Montagu, by contrast, was delighted, confidently proclaiming his belief that the hour had arrived for what he called the 'financial department store' concept of banking, with everything under one roof. A few weeks later Charles Hambro quizzed O'Brien about the implications. The Governor, after revealing in con-fidence that he had not been consulted, explicitly stated that 'although the Midland/Montagu deal had created a precedent as far as British banks are concerned, he would not be prepared to accept that a foreign bank should acquire a shareholding of more than 10/15% in a London merchant bank'.[73] *That*, at least, was a firm line in the shifting sands.

Another portent of the ultimate dissolution of 'the guild system' was the encroachment by at least two clearing banks into new-issue finance. Press reports in September 1965 of the IHA's displeasure at Westminster Bank's apparent intention to start sponsoring some industrial issues prompted a fairly agitated discussion at the IHA itself. Ken Barrington of Morgan Grenfell 'expressed the view that the whole matter was most unfortunate' and that 'it should be played down to the maximum extent' in 'the hope that it would be allowed to die a natural death'. To this proposition there was apparent concurrence, while David Montagu 'thought that the Association should not adopt a "Suez" attitude in the matter by suggesting publicly that Clearing Banks would carry out Capital operations in any worse manner or find it more difficult to do so than Issuing Houses would'. Nevertheless, the meeting did not end without 'reference' being 'made to the Press comment that Issuing Houses appear to be afraid of competition'. Confronted by this canard, 'it was the unanimous opinion of the meeting that this was not so, the main contention being that it would be a very bad thing for the financial world for the two roles in banking to be mixed up'. The specific threat, if it was indeed one, petered out, in that over the next year or two Westminster made only a few issues, without conspicuous success or impact. However, a smaller clearing bank, Glyn Mills, did recruit from the Samuel side at Hill Samuel a youngish merchant banker called Christopher Arnander, who after some eighteen months in Lombard Street, and a lot of hard slog selling the idea to the branches of Glyn Mills' parent, the Royal Bank of Scotland, enabled it in October 1967 to sponsor an offer for sale of over a million shares in Beatson Clark, a Rotherham-based glass manufacturer. 'The issue will undoubtedly go well,' the *Economist* correctly predicted, 'and it is nice to welcome what is virtually a new merchant bank.' Arnander himself, however, was understandably anxious not to upset the merchant banks, especially those who banked with Glyn Mills, and therefore covered himself by telling the *FT* that 'if we lost their good-will we would lose our ability to place loans through them'.[74] The guild system, in short, was still essentially intact – though, in this respect as in others, it was starting to erode at the edges.

In general, the clearing banks received their usual poor press during the 1960s. 'Banking is the worst managed of our major industries,' Kenneth Fleet declared in the *Sunday Telegraph* in 1964, accusing most of the bank chairmen of lacking 'either the character or the will, or it may be the knowledge and experience, to take the big decisions'. Accordingly, 'the banks have won for themselves the unenviable distinction of always following, never leading – and of always following each other in sheep-like fashion'. Certainly British commercial banking remained a depressingly stuffy, rigidly hierarchical, class-ridden milieu, with a poor record for graduate recruitment and an even worse one for graduate retention. When Cairncross lunched at Westminster Bank in 1966, its recently retired Chief General Manager, Arthur Chesterfield, 'expressed himself strongly on Boards that were ignorant of their own bank and its affairs', adding that he 'believed that the Bank of England did a lot of harm in preventing contact between Treasury and clearing banks'. In later years Chesterfield would express the greatest bitterness about the condescending way in which he had been treated by Westminster's directors, always the most pukka of the clearing bank boards. Even at Barclays, which Fleet broadly exempted from his damning critique and where the directors were traditionally practising bankers rather than an almost random collection of the great and the good, the two-class system was still in full swing. To give one small but symptomatic example, the members of the founding families, who still provided most of the banks' directors, did not blink about calling each other by their first names but the general managers by their surnames. This is not to say that there was no new thinking during this decade. 'Mr Thomson said that, having been badly scared by the Westminster Bank's recent acquisition of a stake in The Diners' Club, Barclays Bank were announcing this evening their comprehensive credit card scheme,' O'Brien noted unenthusiastically on 10 January 1966 about the imminent advent of the Barclaycard, while the following year Reg Varney ceremoniously opened Britain's first cashpoint. Nevertheless, the deeply conservative underlying spirit of what was still a more or less cartelised banking system was nicely encapsulated in March 1966, when Midland's Thackstone, in a meeting with the discount market, stated flatly that 'he regarded the efficiency of the London Monetary machine as depending on specialised efficiency in different fields of finance and no poaching'.[75]

Arguably, though, there were two significant mitigating considerations in defence of these bankers.[76] First, there was the prevailing monetary context, which in effect meant that throughout most of the decade they were operating with one hand tied behind their backs. Whether in the form of a voluntarily enforced liquidity ratio, the special deposit scheme, one official 'ceiling' for lending after another or Bank rate changes designed to affect the appetite for loans, the banks were seldom free from some form of lending restraint. Increasingly, moreover, these quantitative restrictions on bank advances were applied by government (O'Brien recalled) 'at very short notice and in a rather peremptory fashion which upset them a good deal'. Inevitably this tendency impaired relations between the banks and the Bank, which they felt was not doing enough to protect them against politicians too cowardly to make the cuts in public expenditure that were the real alternative to always turning off the monetary tap. And, granted that they could not lend freely, they felt there was little point in competing aggressively for deposits, which in practice meant that the cartel on lending rates stayed in place. The second mitigating consideration suggested, though, that this intellectually undemanding arrangement was approaching the end of its long life. This was that the larger playing field on which the clearing banks were operating was fundamentally uneven, in the sense that, both formally and informally, credit restrictions did not apply with anything like the same rigour to either the foreign banks or the new, UK-based so-called 'secondary banks' – both of which were now flourishing in the rapidly expanding wholesale money markets. Losing market share, and increasingly unable to compete effectively with the newcomers, the Big Five knew – or at least, the more progressive there did – that they would soon have to join the fray and compete hard for deposits and lending business.

There were other ways in which the clearing banks were now coming under more pressure than at any time since the war. Particularly grievous from their point of view was the increasing head of steam from government and public opinion in favour of no longer permitting them statutory exemption from publishing full profits and reserves.[77] In August 1966 a quartet of chairmen dined at the Bank to discuss the subject with O'Brien, Armstrong and Cairncross. The bankers' tactic, after Armstrong had observed that compulsory disclosure was almost certain in the new Companies Act, was to ask a barrage of questions. 'In whose interest was disclosure desirable – shareholders, depositors, borrowers, the public? Was it suggested that in the past 50 years or so the banks had fallen down in serving any of these?' And: 'Is it sensible to insist on this step – which could not be reversed – at a time when every part of the economy and credit in general is tightly stretched, and closely watched by foreigners?' And again: 'Banks depend on their credit, and this would not be served by their showing too great a fluctuation in their results.' Cairncross listened quietly. 'Archie Forbes was the most categorical, John Thomson the most incisive but, like Stirling, understanding. The Governor kept fairly quiet but pressed the bankers nevertheless to consider disclosure.' The bankers continued to plug away during the closing months of 1966. In October, at another chairmen's dinner at the Bank, they insisted that disclosure would make British banks vulnerable to 'foreign competition' by 'pointing at our lack of stability'; would 'deprive us of the chance to rebuild reserves after bad years'; would 'leave the judgement of what were adequate reserves to the public', whereas 'in fact only banking experience could judge this properly'; would 'incline the banks to a much more cautious lending policy, since mistakes could not be written off so easily'; and in all, they concluded, 'these considerations carried the risk, especially under a combination of several crises, of a financial calamity and a threat to sterling'. There was a final throw, not long before Christmas, as the chairmen met Callaghan and again put forward their arguments. 'The Chancellor asked whether, if the Merchant Banks were left exempt, the Clearing Banks could get over this difficulty by arranging mergers with Merchant Banks,' Stirling recorded of this non-meeting of minds. 'We said that this was too hypothetical a question to answer directly.'[78]

By this time, there was another, broader threat to the clearing banks, in the shape of the inquiry by Aubrey Jones's Prices and Incomes Board into their dividends, charges and services. 'From a casual glance they look to me to be not unexpectedly naïve,' O'Brien commented after a look at Jones's early notes on the subject, 'and I think we probably have a not very easy task of instruction and persuasion on our hands.' O'Brien continued to monitor the situation closely, and in April 1967 told Jones to his face that the first draft of his report not only 'contained a great many downright assertions, without any fully-reasoned argumentation behind them', but also made the error of straying into questions of monetary policy. On its publication the following month the report earned the crispest of private condemnations from Thomson: 'Lots of comments. No original solutions.' He was doubtless unhappy that it was surprisingly wide-ranging, as among other things it called for more competition between the banks, greater diversification in their role as lenders, full disclosure of profits and reserves, and economies of scale in the branch networks. The report's actual title was *Bank Charges*, and on that subject it asserted, in a less than wildly enthusiastic tone, that 'it does not seem that the actual level of charges could be described as unreasonable'. Disclosure, though, was clearly a pill that was going to have to be swallowed (by the clearing banks, if not the merchant banks), not least because it was a cause for which the Governor was unwilling to fight; indeed, O'Brien frankly told Armstrong some months later that the government's policy on the matter was 'very defensible'.[79] For the clearers, of course, it was a betrayal by their traditional protector.

There was one other sense in which the old, seemingly immutable order of things was on the way out. Since shortly after the First World War there had been no question of any of the Big Five merging with each other, but in 1962 the surrounding ice did begin to break when National Provincial acquired District Bank. That implicitly brought into play Martins Bank, whose head office was still in Liverpool and on whose branch network both Lloyds and Barclays were soon casting avaricious eyes. Cromer told Thomson of Barclays in December 1965 that he had no objection to Barclays having an informal arrangement with Martins that the latter would tell Barclays if it was up for sale; but in March 1967 O'Brien was less encouraging, observing to Thomson that he 'doubted whether the authorities would look at all kindly on Martins Bank being taken over by the biggest of the clearing banks'. He added, 'While some contraction in the number of independent groups among the clearers might be tolerated, the formation of one excessively large group might not be. To that extent he seemed to me to be at a disadvantage vis-à-vis, for example, the Westminster.' This may not have been what Thomson wanted to hear, but the phrase about 'some contraction' reflected significant movement in the Bank's thinking, two months ahead of the famous paragraph 154 in Jones's report, which stated that the Bank of England and the Treasury had 'made it plain to us that they would not obstruct some further amalgamation if the banks were willing to contemplate such a development'. O'Brien was particularly concerned about the competitive threat from large foreign banks, and in June 1967 he told Thomson that he would not now stand in the way of Barclays making an approach to Martins. Lloyds for its part continued to make warm noises in the direction of Liverpool; Martins during the autumn finally decided that it was time to take the money; and on 14 November O'Brien saw Henry Benson of Coopers, instructing that supreme accountant to organise the sale and observing that 'if one of the bigger banks took Martins it would create a very large British bank which could match up to the American giants, and this advantage to London would offset the disadvantage of having one bank much larger than the others'.[80] It was, after all, the dawn of the age of the national champion.

In their much smaller-scale way, London's discount houses similarly found it difficult to be sure how to respond to the new money markets.[81] 'In 1960 the resources employed by the discount market were considerably larger than any of the other markets,' E.R. Shaw would note in his authoritative study, *The London Money Market*. 'By 1965, however, the position had changed dramatically as the traditional market was pushed into third place behind the expanding local authority and Eurodollar sectors.' Why did the discount houses miss the boat? 'The reasons were in part emotional,' Hamish McRae argued in 1970. 'The brash money brokers seemed distasteful to a section of the City most noted for its delight in the niceties of banking tradition.' But he went on, 'More fundamentally, there was sheer disbelief that the local authority market could grow to the extent that it did. When the interbank market emerged at the beginning of the 1960s, there was similar disbelief that banks would be prepared to lend to each other unsecured.' Even during the second half of the decade, as the discount market managed to retrieve a fair amount of lost ground, the innate suspicions and conservatism far from disappeared. Several of the discount houses went only part of the way in broadening their businesses, and when in about 1966 the financial journalist Christopher Fildes was incautious enough to suggest to the Bank of England's Hilton Clarke that London would soon see dealings in dollar bills of exchange, he received the magisterial rebuke, 'Young man, I'll trouble you to remember that this institution has a branded product of its own.'[82]

The main way in which the more enterprising of the dozen members of the London Discount Market Association managed to get a slice of the action in the parallel money markets was through acquiring broking subsidiaries, with the Bank's blessing. The process began in the winter of 1965–6 when Clive Discount Co bought a controlling interest in Guy Butler, inter-bank sterling money brokers. At an early stage of this pioneering deal, the LDMA debated (without Clive) its proprieties, and 'with the exception of Cater Ryder, Gerrard & Reid and Gilletts, members felt . . . that Clive should be told that they should withdraw their intention of securing a controlling interest'.[83] The deal, however, went ahead, and in the course of 1966 it was followed by Gerrards diversifying into the inter-bank money market by acquiring an interest in the brokers P. Murray-Jones. In 1967 Caters bought the foreign exchange and currency deposit brokers M.W. Marshall, while Jessel Toynbee took a 40 per cent stake in Charles Fulton, which broked in most of the new markets. Soon afterwards, after some dithering, the largest discount house, Union, reached an agreement with a money broker called Bernard Roberts, which led to a subsidiary under the name of Roberts Union starting business in May 1968. Finally, in 1969, Jessels and Charles Fulton decided to back a new broking firm in the local authority market, Packshaw and Associates, whose Robin Packshaw had previously been at the local authority brokers Long Till and Colvin.

No one could match the peerless Trinder, but by this time there were two particularly interesting figures in the money market world. One was the buccaneering, aggressive, go-for-volume Kenneth Whitaker, a gentleman who was not quite a gentleman and under whose strong leadership Gerrards rose with astonishing swiftness from being the minnow of the market to a position where it was able, in 1969, to take over the National Discount Co, after that venerable, once-so-prestigious concern had got its gilt book badly wrong. 'The Black Pearl', as he was known, would continue his merry way at Gerrard & National, where every day there was champagne, caviare and other delicacies for fortunate luncheon guests.[84] The other figure, younger and more cerebral, was John Barkshire, joint Managing Director from 1963 of Cater Ryder, itself the result of a merger three years earlier. His background could hardly have been more City establishment, his father having been Private Secretary to Kim Cobbold and then Secretary to the Committee of London Clearing Bankers; Barkshire himself, always impeccably turned out, had since 1955 given Territorial Army service in the Honourable Artillery Company. Yet from the mid-1960s he became one of the City's rare Anglo-Saxon visionaries, partly through his friendship with David Spilman of M.W. Marshall. Together they came to the conclusion that, in Barkshire's subsequent words, 'there was going to be a convergence of the firms making up the money markets in the years ahead, and that we would begin to see money market houses emerging which would be likely to encompass the activities of the discount market, the Eurodollar market, and the various sterling inter-bank markets'. Their vision was cemented in about 1964 when Barkshire spent a few months at Salomons in New York, where he saw dealing rooms that spanned several markets, and over the next year or two he and Spilman nagged away at their respective seniors. Eventually they gave in and the 1967 deal took place between Caters and Marshalls, in Barkshire's words 'putting a foreign exchange money broker together with our newly formed sterling broker and creating a total broking entity'. There were, he added, some rumblings at the time, along the lines of 'breaking up the City club', but this did not worry Caters' Chairman, Johnny Musker, who 'had had his knuckles rapped by the Bank of England for being the first discount house not to hold any Government securities' and who 'adored being written about, whether it was complimentary or critical'.[85] For Barkshire it was the start of twenty often controversial years at the cutting-edge.

If Barkshire rode the waves of controversy as a City insider, it was the opposite for another of the decade's emerging figures, the far more high-profile Jim Slater, whose very name still evokes a particular era.[86] His pre-City years showed that he already had something special about him. Slater was born in 1929 and brought up in Wembley; his father owned a small building-cum-decorating business; after going to the local grammar school, Preston Manor County, Slater qualified as a chartered accountant; and by 1963, seven years after going into the motor industry, he had become right-hand man to Donald Stokes at Leyland and seemed next in line to succeed him. For some time he had taken an active interest in the stock market and now persuaded Nigel Lawson, City editor of the *Sunday Telegraph*, that he should write a monthly share-tipping column. Making his début on 3 March 1963, 'Capitalist' set out his stall: 'My object is not to try and crystal-gaze into the future, but rather to spot anomalies on the basis of existing information before the market does. For the market is not perfect: if it were there would be no point in buying one share rather than another.' His stated aim was capital gain rather than income, with no sentimental attachment to the shares that he selected: 'If by any chance there is any adverse trend, such as a poor interim dividend or statement, I would recommend selling immediately.' Within three months 'Capitalist' was boasting a 30 per cent profit, way above the market's overall rise, but he warned his readers, 'The important thing is not to chase the shares the Monday following my article. If you wait for two or three days you should normally be able to pick them up at no more than 5 p.c. above my own price.' Slater had promised Lawson that he would not exploit the column for personal gain; but according to his resourceful biographer, Charles Raw, he pulled in at least £25,000 in less than two years.[87]

Although they already knew each other, it was probably during the winter of 1963–4 that Slater became friendly with Peter Walker, who –

having done well out of insurance, property and unit trusts – was now, as a Tory MP, focusing on his political career. Slater rang Walker, wanting to talk to him urgently. 'He had, by investing, built up some capital of his own, he told me, and probably had £100,000 of his own resources he could call upon,' Walker recalled over a quarter of a century later of their seminal conversation. 'He felt there were opportunities in investing in badly managed businesses, pulling up their management and doing well in the process.' Should he therefore leave Leyland? 'I did say that if he decided to go off on his own, I would give him any help I could. I was ready to put in capital if he wanted more investment and to introduce him to the many friends I had in the City . . . A few days later he phoned to say he had decided to go it alone and would appreciate my help.' So was conceived and soon afterwards born Slater Walker. In summer 1964 they hatched plans for the Slater Walker Industrial Group (SWIG). According to Raw, this was intended to become 'the instrument through which Slater Walker implemented its new policy of using large shareholdings to influence the management of industrial companies to adopt Slater's gospel of efficiency', and 'the receptacle into which investors were to be invited to pour large amounts of cash'.[88]

On the last day of October, a fortnight after Labour had come to power in a positive frame of mind towards conglomerates and industrial restructuring, a small story in the *FT* revealed that Slater was intending 'to form an industrial group'. One of its components would be Production Mouldings (mainly a manufacturer of foam rubber), which Slater had acquired control of even before leaving Leyland; and during the closing months of 1964 an inexplicably sharp rise in its share price led to the Stock Exchange's quotations committee considering suspension. The committee's chairman was Jock Hunter ('a very pleasant and able stockbroker,' Slater subsequently wrote), and the explanations from Slater himself and his stockbroking advisers, Sebags, proved adequate to avert the threat. It was fortunate they did, for at around this time Slater was also busy getting his financial backers lined up for SWIG, to be capitalised at £2.5m. Three of them were particularly notable: Lazards; Schroders, which involved Richardson quizzing Slater; and Harley Drayton, after Slater had been introduced to Angus Ogilvy and found that 'we had similar views on investment and were on very much the same wavelength from the start'.[89]

Slater Walker's new group was announced on 3 February 1965, with a circular to shareholders declaring that SWIG would acquire 'substantial stakes' in companies that the directors considered capable of 'considerable development'. *The Times* observed without comment that its formation meant that there were now six sides to Slater Walker's activities, 'ranging from property owning and investment management to industrial development'. The other three 'sides' were an investment trust, trading in securities and management services. 'With benefit of hindsight,' Raw wrote, 'it is easy to see just how open to abuse Slater's elegant structure was':

> The larger part of his company's profit was to be derived from investment advice to clients whose combined resources represented a significant sum of money in stock market terms, especially in relation to the size of many of the companies selected for investment. Simultaneously, another corporate limb was to find companies deemed to be in need of management help and to press that help upon them by acquiring effectively controlling shareholdings – yet, on its chairman's own admission, he was not interested in 'long term' investment. Add to this combination a plethora of share dealing companies and a stated interest in 'special situations', and it is not hard to see the danger that existed.

All in all, Raw concludes with some elegance himself, it was a 'combination of functions' that 'would have tried the most punctilious of men'.[90]

Four days later, on 7 February, the 'Capitalist' column appeared for the last time, in the process revealing the author's identity, and that spring the first of many admiring press profiles appeared. Successful investment, James (as he was still known) Slater told Cass Robertson of the *Sunday Express*, depended crucially on 'the will power to cut your losses and run your profits', whereas 'the natural inclination of many people is to do precisely the opposite'. Slater also emphasised the importance of what he called 'method and gearing', by which he meant on the one hand 'picking out shares with good records and high earnings yields', on the other (in Robertson's words) 'obtaining as much credit as possible from banks and brokers to give full scope to your method'. The article concluded by asking whether Slater would turn out to be 'one of those bright young men who flash, comet-like, across the City scene for a few years then burn themselves out very quickly'. Robertson, however, answered in the negative. 'He is quietly impressive, sensible and well-balanced. He admits readily he has made many mistakes already. But he is the type who is not likely to make the same slip twice.'[91]

As yet, Slater stayed based in the West End, not the City, though his investment department did move there in 1966. Always there were many balls in the air, but Raw's version (by far the most detailed) is that during 1965–6 there were two defining strands to Slater Walker's multifarious activities. One was the systematic use of clients' money in order to acquire control of companies; the other, having acquired that control, was to make a quick buck by stripping the company of its supposedly underutilised assets. 'By 1966 Slater's avowed policy of taking over sleepy companies, ripping out (and selling off) the loss-making sectors to build up a profitable core, had become received wisdom among Conservative radicals,' the property developer Nigel Broackes recalled in his 1979 memoirs, before adding regretfully that 'somewhere along the line, industrial rationalisation turned into pass-the-parcel'. 'Alluring dance of the asset strippers' was the heading of an *Observer* article in January 1967 by the paper's City editor, John Davis. ' "I have at least five situations on the boil," says Jim Slater, today's leading exponent of buying assets on the cheap and chairman of Slater, Walker Securities,' it started. 'Last year Slater cleared close on a cool £1 million profit on two deals alone . . .' Davis ended with another pearl from 'the man with the golden touch': 'The problem is not finding the asset situations, but being able to negotiate out of them on a reasonable profit.'[92]

It was during 1967, against the background of a bull market and the start of the merger boom, that Slater Walker really took off, together with Slater's own reputation as a self-made man uniquely in tune with the financial and industrial *Zeitgeist* of big-is-best, industrial efficiency and general go-go. Most of Slater Walker's money was probably being made through opportunistic share dealings, but in the financial and business press he would soon be acquiring something akin to heroic status. 'One per cent of £3 million is worth a day or two of Mr Slater's time' was the title of a *Sunday Times* piece in August 1967, with the sub-heading 'John Mattison talks to the trendiest man in takeovers'. With his group now valued by the stock market at around £10m, Slater was in expansive mood as he discussed the shortcomings of British management: 'A business should be run like an investment portfolio – cut your losses and let your profits run – in other words concentrate your efforts on the profit-makers rather than loss-makers. A lot of British boards seem to do the opposite . . .' Mattison noted there were 'still a number of doubters in the City who feel that Slater is a young man heading for a big fall', but Slater himself denied vigorously that Slater Walker was overstretching itself: 'We get assets first and then profits. We always have a solid base to work from.' As for accusations that Slater Walker was building up a ragbag of interests, he was adamant that 'the only thing that fits in the group as far as I'm concerned is one I can make money out of'. Inevitably, Slater was identified as one of the young meteors. 'We're rather a new breed of merchant bank,' he told Jonathan Aitken (who himself subsequently joined Slater Walker). 'We have no traditional business coming our way obviously, so we have to go out and get it, and we compete with new methods and perhaps a slightly more aggressive attitude than longer-established bankers.' As for the future, Slater remarked that he would only be happy when 'we've built up one of the leading merchant banks'.[93]

Such thrust, such ambition: it was a million miles away from the comfortable, entrenched world of Lloyd's, where according to Aitken such was the strength of 'the follow-my-leader unthinking tradition' that recently several underwriters had 'actually stamped, in all seriousness, an insurance form for "Baa Baa Black Sheep" because one of the leading syndicates had stamped the form as a joke to see who would follow them'. Yet by this time, unbeknown to Aitken and indeed almost all the underwriters and brokers at this City bastion, fundamental and fateful change was in the offing. The unwitting catalyst was Hurricane Betsy, which in September 1965 had done huge damage to the offshore oil industry in the Gulf of Mexico and was directly responsible for the two worst years at Lloyd's in anyone's peacetime memory. Names (whose numbers had grown from fewer than 2,000 before the war to more than 6,000 by 1966) had the disconcerting experience of writing out cheques rather than receiving them, and predictably some decided to put their money elsewhere.[94] Consequently by 1967 the 'capacity' of the market was starting to diminish, at the very time when, as in banking, the American insurance industry was looking to compete hard in London. Could the club still do the business? At Lloyd's, as elsewhere in the City, that was no longer an idle question.

*

On Wednesday, 3 August 1966 – a fortnight after the emergency measures to save the pound, a week before Brown's departure from the Department of Economic Affairs signalled the end of the National Plan, four days after Bobby Moore lifted the Jules Rimet trophy – Wilson and Callaghan gave a dinner party for O'Brien, Parsons and sixteen other bankers. They included John Thomson of Barclays, Lord Bearsted of Hill Samuel, Lord Poole of Lazards, Cyril Kleinwort of Kleinworts, Jocelyn Hambro of Hambros, Sir George Bolton of BOLSA, Louis Franck of Samuel Montagu, Henry Grunfeld of Warburgs, Eric Faulkner of Glyn Mills, Harald Peake of Lloyds and Duncan Stirling of Westminster. They assembled in the Cabinet Room at 7 p.m. for a pre-dinner discussion. After an opening statement from Callaghan, in which he ruled out devaluation as a solution, O'Brien noted how 'disappointing' 'market reaction' to the measures had been, even though they had been warmly welcomed by all central bankers. The floor was then thrown open to the wisdom of some very experienced City men:

> The explanation was to be found in a general malaise throughout the country stemming perhaps from the loss of an empire and the lack of any idea to replace it . . . Bankers, and indeed commerce in general, felt that Government was against them and that the recent tax reforms militated against their activities and discouraged their expertise. The cure was to be found in a rebuilding of national confidence . . . Part of the trouble of the British economy was the publicity which newspapers gave to unfavourable

economic factors, and their reluctance to draw attention to favourable ones. Many of the papers were still seeming after three years to be taking part in a General Election and their constant attacks on public figures did a good deal to lower overseas confidence ... Productivity in British factories was extremely low. The General Motors Corporation which installed the same machinery in its plants throughout the world found that productivity in their British factories was lower than anywhere else in the world. This was attributable to over-full employment and the truculence of labour ...

On management, nothing; on investment, nothing. After dinner, 'a number of criticisms of Government policy were put to the Prime Minister'. They included the predictable arguments that 'the situation called for a cut in Government expenditure on the Social Services, particularly by the restoration of prescription charges', and that 'it would inspire confidence if the legislative programme were curtailed'. At the end of the evening 'there was general agreement that there was no case for devaluation and more than one speaker pointed out the difference between now and in 1949: then the £ was clearly over-valued; today there was no evidence of that'. Wilson concurred, saying that in terms of the competitiveness of exports 'he would be quite ready to see the rate go up to even $3.20'. The following evening he and Callaghan briefed the press. According to King (one of whose editors was there), Wilson took the 'highly misleading' line that the bankers 'were unanimous in thinking the measures taken were adequate', while Callaghan's version of recent events was that 'the whole thing was a wicked French plot to bring down the dollar by bringing down the pound first and making France the financial capital of the world'. King himself dismissed as 'unlikely' this conspiracy theory, though in fact de Gaulle was by this time making a systematic attempt to develop Paris as Europe's leading financial centre.[95]

It was not all that long before, almost to its own surprise, the City's mood started to lighten. 'The groundwork for a major bull market, some day, is quietly being laid,' declared Rowe & Pitman's November *Market Report*, probably more optimistic than most. 'The redundancies in industry will ultimately lead to a more efficient and profitable use of labour; the pound is stronger, the balance of payments improving, interest rates falling; there have been hints of measures to stop the decline in investment, signs of a possible recovery in the Conservatives' electoral fortunes and of an impatience with the increasingly bureaucratic trend of some Government thinking; news from the North Sea is good.' From the stock market's listening post, most of that mood music continued to play harmoniously – above all the balance of payments figures, on an improving trend throughout the winter – and by late 1966 the beginnings of a bull market were indeed apparent, given a kick by a welcome rash of takeover activity. O'Brien continued to be fairly gloomy ('he harped on the rising tide of Government expenditure,' King noted in December), but the City was already taking heart from Wilson's announcement in November that Britain was to try again to enter the European Economic Community – an announcement that, under pressure from the Bank, included a commitment that the pound would not be devalued in order for Britain to do so. Although the City was almost certainly less keen than the CBI on British membership of what was still usually called the Common Market, overall there was a feeling that Europe offered Britain a perhaps promising new economic direction. By April 1967 even O'Brien was more optimistic, praising Callaghan's budget to the discount market. Wilson formally announced on 2 May his government's intention to apply for full membership, but the next day, writing from 8 Bishopsgate to a Wall Street correspondent, Peter Baring sounded a sour if realistic note: 'Here, we have the great non-event of our second application to the Common Market. More important is the question of whether Wilson will really follow the Treasury line of maintaining a higher level of unemployment than has hitherto been deemed acceptable. Most people seem to be betting against it.'[96]

Over the next month or so things went rapidly wrong for the government in three distinct ways: the trade figures deteriorated sharply; the General intimated that another '*Non*' was in the offing; and the Six-Day War, along with the closure of the Suez Canal, led to a flight into the dollar. 'The press openly discusses devaluation and some of the papers are strongly pressing for it,' Cairncross noted on 21 May, and over the summer debate continued about the once unmentionable topic. As far as one can tell, the City's attitude was far from uniform. On the stock market, although sentimental allegiance to the defence of the pound remained almost undimmed, there was a growing feeling that the price of its defence had become too high, certainly if it meant another round of heavy deflation. 'We are now looking for a significant interruption to the nine-months old rise in equity prices,' Rowe & Pitman gloomily commented at the start of August, a few days after Callaghan had publicly reaffirmed the government's determination not to devalue. 'A dismal winter seems in prospect: first hopes of recovery dashed, unemployment high.' At the Bank of England there were perhaps three schools of thought: those who, on moral grounds as much as anything, remained implacably opposed; those who thought that the time had come to devalue before being forced to do so; and the middle group, which preferred to hold to the parity as long as possible. The Governor himself oscillated between the ditchers and the hedgers. 'O'Brien drew me aside after Court to talk about the political situation,' King recorded on 3 August. 'He is acutely unhappy, living from day to day ... He is afraid that the idea of devaluation has gathered so much momentum that it may prove irresistible.'[97]

In their bones, O'Brien and his colleagues must have known that the government's political will to defend the parity was crumbling. O'Brien soon afterwards stressed to Callaghan 'the present extremely delicate state of the exchange markets' and warned the government against even considering reflationary policies because of its fears of high levels of unemployment during the coming winter; but within weeks, on 29 August, ministers defied all such advice and relaxed the hire-purchase restrictions virtually across the board. 'In a quarter when foreign exchange losses were at a rate not far short of the highest in the previous three years,' Cairncross later remarked, 'the government was nonchalantly waving on the speculators.' At the time O'Brien undoubtedly agreed. 'I think he has given up hope of maintaining the exchange value of the pound,' King noted after 'a long talk' with him on the 31st. 'He thinks under pressure ministers are thinking more of full employment and less of our financial position. O'Brien seemed to be already adapting himself to the new situation – a mild devaluation of 10 per cent or so might give our economy a shot in the arm without inviting retaliation.'[98]

That autumn, as Labour entered its fourth year in government with the pound still hanging on at $2.80, London's almost wholly domestic-oriented equity market was buoyant – partly against the backdrop of the GEC/AEI battle, partly because of the expectation that devaluation would come sooner rather than later and thereby stimulate the economy in a relatively painfree way. Things naturally looked rather different from O'Brien's vantage-point. 'People must be punch-drunk,' he sardonically remarked to the discount market on 14 September, after the exchanges had reacted surprisingly calmly to the latest bad trade figures, but over the next few weeks a series of blows put sterling on an irreversible one-way ride towards devaluation. On 18 September a dock strike began in London, Liverpool and other ports; then in mid-October the EEC published a report questioning sterling's long-term future as a reserve currency, the monthly trade figures were even worse than expected, and a Bank-rate rise of ½ a per cent was less than the foreign exchange markets had anticipated. Armstrong at the Treasury told Cairncross on the 13th that the question of devaluation now 'rested with Leslie, whose tactics were to exhaust all possible lines of assistance before throwing in his hand'.[99]

By late October, with a £500m deficit being forecast for both 1967 and 1968, sterling was being sold so heavily that O'Brien seems to have conceded to Armstrong that at last he saw devaluation as inevitable. However, when he saw Wilson on 1 November, he said that he was still unable to recommend devaluation. Instead, the decisive intervention came from Cairncross, who next day sent Callaghan a memo arguing that realistically there was no alternative. The Chancellor saw Cairncross on the morning of the 3rd and reluctantly agreed. Shortly before seeing Wilson (who did not demur) on Saturday the 4th, Callaghan met O'Brien:

> After three years of incessant borrowing and ever-rising debt Jim Callaghan felt he had come to the end of the road and I agreed with him. He said that unless we could mobilise support for sterling of a medium-term character, say three to five years as a minimum, we must accept the inevitable conclusions. I had to advise that I saw no hope of such medium-term support, although I was prepared to put the question to my central banking colleagues. Meanwhile we must prepare for devaluation. A move so large that it provoked many other countries to follow would clearly serve little useful purpose. My soundings suggested that we could devalue by 15% without being followed.[100]

It would be a smoothly organised move, in that for a couple of years a highly secret Bank/Treasury group had been preparing the detailed, complicated mechanics that would be required in a devaluation. The group's code-name of FU accurately reflected official feelings about the contingency.

Public life's rituals, meanwhile, continued as Parliament debated the Queen's Speech. Cromer, speaking in the House of Lords, took the opportunity to declare that 'during the last three years the business world has become progressively more confused and disillusioned', adding that the latest crop of policies was 'inadequate and largely irrelevant to the needs of the nation at present'. Also on the 7th, the Shadow Chancellor, Iain Macleod, attacked in the Commons a recent speech by O'Brien in which the Governor had said that Britain needed to have 'a somewhat larger margin' of 'unused manpower and resources'. In reply, Callaghan seemed to endorse O'Brien's views by referring to the need for 'a somewhat larger margin of unemployment than we used to have' – a unanimity that led to left-wing attacks on himself as well as the Bank and O'Brien. Over the following weekend O'Brien was at Basle, where his fellow central bankers accepted the principle of a 15 per cent devaluation by Britain without any retaliatory devaluation by themselves. On the morning of Monday the 13th, before returning, he rang Callaghan to ask if the government would accept as an alternative to devaluation (in Callaghan's subsequent account) 'a smaller loan of say $2 billions from the IMF, with milder conditions than those initially proposed by the United States'. This, O'Brien said, would 'stop the rot', at least temporarily; but Callaghan now preferred to keep his room for manoeuvre, including if need be devaluation, and anyway reckoned that $2bn was not enough. Early that evening, having returned from Basle, O'Brien went with Callaghan to see Wilson, who did not dissent from the Chancellor's course of action. The trio then went off to the Lord Mayor's Banquet at

Guildhall, where according to Callaghan 'no one could have told from the Prime Minister's demeanour that anything was amiss', before the two politicians returned to Downing Street. There, at 11.15 p.m., they (as Callaghan put it in his note for the record) '*decided finally*'.[101] The pound was to be devalued to $2.40, probably over the coming weekend.

The October trade figures on Tuesday the 14th were startlingly bad (at £107m, comfortably the largest monthly deficit yet recorded), and Callaghan was left in no doubt by the Treasury that there must be a significant package of measures if the proposed new rate was going to stick. That evening, at what his biographer calls 'a ferocious Cabinet meeting', Callaghan told his colleagues that sterling would be devalued on Saturday the 18th and insisted that there must also be major expenditure cuts. Wednesday was quiet, but Thursday and Friday were both days to remember. Thursday began with the Cabinet formally deciding in favour of devaluation, while almost at the same time O'Brien was, according to King, being 'more forthcoming than is usually the case' as he put the Court broadly in the picture:

> Money had been pouring out since May. Though the effect of the bad trade figures on Tuesday had not been quite as bad as it might have been, we had got to the end of our present resources. We could make one last borrowing from the IMF, but if that went, we should be quite helpless. O'Brien plainly implied that we should have to devalue on Saturday and use these final resources for controlling the situation post-devaluation ... He thought the sterling area countries would follow us and they hoped the non-sterling ones would not ... When this exposition was over, Alf Robens [Lord Robens, in charge of the National Coal Board and, like King, a recently elected, Labour-sympathising, very non-executive director of the Bank] passed me a paper: 'Glad to see you can still smile, 1931' ...

Later that day, in the Commons, Callaghan found himself put horribly on the spot. In what would swiftly earn the reputation of being the most expensive Parliamentary question ever asked, a Labour backbencher, Robert Sheldon, asked him whether press reports about a possible $1000m loan from abroad were true. Faced by an impossible situation – in which the answer 'yes' would have been a lie, but any other answer a tacit admission of imminent devaluation – Callaghan said that he had nothing to add to previous statements.[102]

The final event was a late-evening meeting at No 11, where Cairncross with some admiration watched O'Brien as he 'expressed disappointment with size of package', which 'made Chancellor indignant and he flatly refused to think of going back to Cabinet'. Later in the discussion, when Callaghan said that further cuts in expenditure (that is, beyond the £500m in cuts and tax increases already agreed) could wait until the next budget, 'Leslie was unimpressed by all this and stood his ground'. The next morning, in a long letter to Callaghan, he formally set out the case for a more severe package of measures. On this eve of an historic moment, it included one particularly striking, even magnanimous passage:

> For three years the Government has worked strenuously and courageously to avoid a devaluation and repeatedly expressed their determination to maintain the parity. Now at last, and mainly because of circumstances beyond our control, defeat has come. There is no disguising that or the many dangerous consequences that may flow; but now that it has come, we must seize the opportunities that it offers, to make clear that the Government was right when it said so often that devaluation was no soft option and to call for real sacrifices, to impose measures that would really mean something and thereby ensure that within a year or two our whole position was transformed.[103]

How sincere was O'Brien in largely exonerating Callaghan and his colleagues? Perhaps not entirely, but these were emotional days.

While O'Brien penned his phrases, the implications of Sheldon's question were being played out in the foreign exchange market, where the almost certain knowledge of imminent devaluation gave the speculators an irresistibly easy killing. That Friday David Bodner at the Fed recorded his telephone conversations with the Bank of England:

> *6.55 a.m. (New York time).* Robson said that they were holding the rate at 2.7824 with heavy selling going on all day. He said they had been supporting the forwards to a small extent but had been backing away as the pressure built up. He said that so far they had lost something close to $300 million.
>
> *8.45 a.m.* Sangster said the money was still going out with the spot total now $600 million and forwards $100 million.
>
> *8.55 a.m.* Bridge said that gold was now up another $7 million, bringing a total for the day to $43 million. He said that a great deal of sterling was being sold that he was sure people did not have.
>
> *10.25 a.m.* Sangster said the total was now $800 million spot and $47 million on gold.

The Bank spent well over a billion dollars defending the rate, for the last time, on this long bad Friday. 'The pound was under siege in the world's foreign exchange markets yesterday,' the patriotic front-page report in *The Times* began next day. 'In London, the Bank of England battled courageously, non-stop, in an attempt to beat off the biggest selling wave ever seen.'[104]

Devaluation was announced by the Treasury at 9.30 p.m. on Saturday the 18th. At six o'clock the following evening Wilson made his ill-fated 'pound in your pocket' broadcast. Bolton's diary entry was to the point: 'PM Television – half truths & lies'. On Monday afternoon, addressing a packed Commons, a suitably sombre Callaghan expressed the hope that devaluation would confer 'a lasting and substantial improvement' in

Britain's balance of payments and gave details of the accompanying package of measures, essentially those from which he had refused to budge during the meeting with O'Brien on Thursday evening. That day, however, eyes were also on the City, even though all the main markets were closed. Throgmorton Street, the man from *The Times* found, 'had the atmosphere of a black carnival, with market men – jobbers, brokers and clerks – crowding the pavements and formed in clusters alive with conversation'. One of the busiest places was the bar opposite the Stock Exchange's doors, Slaters, where 'a flushed and weary barmaid' looked at her heaving mass of customers and told the reporter, 'It's been like this since opening. It's worse than Christmas.' Even though there was no possibility of business, few City men felt able to stay away, not even Sir Robert Adeane, the 'entrepreneurial investor with an aristocratic style' (in Stormonth Darling's phrase) now running the Drayton group. 'Bloody devaluation,' he complained afterwards, 'I had to miss a whole day's shooting.'[105]

Nevertheless, even for those who believed it was overdue, the actual event of devaluation was a traumatic moment in the City psyche. The sense of humiliation was compounded by the knowledge that neither Australia nor South Africa had decided to devalue, which in effect signalled the end of the sterling area. The tendency, inevitably, was to put all the blame on the government. Devaluation, Cromer told the House of Lords on the Tuesday afterwards, 'need never have occurred if determination to put the integrity of the country, surely the first responsibility of Government, had been given credence by appropriate policies as well as fine words'. He cited, as examples of 'party political dogma', the corporation tax, the selective employment tax and the capital gains tax 'with its all-embracing stranglehold'. Accordingly, 'we have a hard task ahead to recreate confidence and obliterate our past indulgences . . .'. Like many in the City, he did not question that devaluation would be a seriously damaging blow to London's position as an international financial centre. Few, though, perhaps felt the ignominy so much as the Bank of England's Maurice Parsons, who almost up to the announcement itself had been in a state of virtual denial. Writing shortly afterwards to an American correspondent, his tone was calm enough, but behind every conventional phrase lay heartfelt remorse:

> We here were acutely embarrassed by the failure to achieve the objective of maintaining the sterling parity and now our whole emphasis is on gaining a favourable balance of payments as a consequence of taking realistic measures in the domestic economy. However, we are only too aware of the fact that our failure caused embarrassment for other people and in this respect we are deeply regretful. I only hope that we shall now be able to regain people's confidence by acting in a realistic manner.

It was just over eighteen years since, on a Sunday evening in September

1949, Cobbold had told the Court that 'devaluation can be done once but can and must not even be in question a second time unless there have been major events such as a world war in the intervening period'.[106]

CHAPTER THIRTEEN

A Certain Cut and Thrust

'He had met the new Chancellor and was quite impressed by him,' the discount market was told by O'Brien in mid-December 1967. 'He did not think that he would put politics before the necessary measures but he did not expect any announcement to be made before Christmas. He could only hope that before the end of January some of the Sacred Cows might have contracted Foot and Mouth.' The new, post-devaluation occupant at No 11 was Roy Jenkins, who was already uncomfortably aware that the markets regarded the measures that had accompanied devaluation as far from adequate. But sterling spent the closing weeks of the year under renewed pressure; and four days before Christmas, King learned from O'Brien and Allen at the Bank that 'they do not think another devaluation in 1968 is inevitable, but they think it is odds on'. By the New Year the prevailing tone there was positively apocalyptic, with Parsons telling King on the 4th that 'the present crisis is as grave as that of 1940 – with no Winston Churchill waiting to take over'. A fortnight later Jenkins announced an additional £700m spending cuts, but soon O'Brien confessed to the discount market that the measures had 'disappointed' him. The Governor, his listeners thought, 'appeared very depressed'. In the City, as elsewhere, the expectation quickly developed that Jenkins's first budget, due on 19 March, would (as Allen told King) 'either break the pound or give us a breathing space'. With less than two weeks to go, O'Brien confidently predicted to the discount market that 'there would be no flabby Budget' and that 'the Chancellor's intentions were good and an incomes policy was expected'. The reserves, though, continued to haemorrhage (having lost over £1,000m since the previous October), and on Wednesday the 13th King found both O'Brien and his deputy extremely pessimistic. 'They say they are living from day to day – last Friday was disastrously bad and, as the Governor said, pushed us even nearer the brink . . . O'Brien and Parsons both say we may get by if the Budget is tough enough. . .'[1]

Next day the Queen Mother paid an official visit to the Bank. She may have spotted a certain tension in the air. 'Everyone at the Bank gloomier than they were even yesterday,' King noted. 'It appears that the rush for gold is quite out of hand.' During that week the London gold pool that the Bank of England had been operating since 1961 on behalf of most western governments came under intolerable strain from speculators convinced that the dollar was no longer strong enough to hold gold's price at $35 an ounce. The once almighty dollar had long been vulnerable because of the worsening US balance of payments, and now the Tet offensive in Vietnam made nonsense of the pledge given by Bill Martin of the Fed that the $35 price would be defended 'to the last ingot'. During this tumultuous week so much gold had to be flown from Fort Knox to London that the floor of the Bank of England's weighing room finally collapsed. Martin realised by the Thursday that the game was up, asked O'Brien to close the London gold market the next day and summoned an emergency meeting of central bankers and others for the weekend. Late on Thursday evening O'Brien went to No 10 to recommend the American request to Wilson and Jenkins. 'If we were to do as the Americans asked,' he told them, 'we would stem our own currency outflow except in the New York market. Our available funds might or might not suffice for that market, they would almost certainly not suffice to maintain the parity of the £ in London through Friday. The choice was between closure and letting the rate go . . .'[2] He got his way, and in the small hours Friday was proclaimed a Bank Holiday, with London's stock and foreign exchange markets to be shut, as well as the gold market.

That weekend in Washington, with O'Brien present, a two-tier system for gold was agreed, in effect creating an artificial distinction between official and private transactions. The Americans were adamant that the London gold market must remain closed for the time being, and in agreeing to this O'Brien seemingly overrode the advice of Roy Bridge, who was convinced that such a move would result in South Africa diverting its sales elsewhere. The London gold market eventually reopened on 1 April, and some months later Louis Franck called on O'Brien to tell him that London had 'lost the gold market to Switzerland' and that the fortnight of closure had been directly responsible. Zurich, henceforth, would be the main centre for physical gold, and typically Franck added that he was 'proposing to develop the gold market activities of his Swiss subsidiary in order to keep his foot in the door'.[3] It was – seemingly – the end of almost three centuries of London dominance in the world of gold.

'I am certainly breathing a little more freely than I expected when I saw you last week,' O'Brien, back from Washington, wrote on Tuesday, 19 March to Cobbold (now Lord Chamberlain). It was budget day, and Jenkins recalled how in the run-up he had had 'two or three talks' with the Governor, who had been 'modestly reticent about advocating specific courses, although he expressed a general preference for a big Budget (that is, a lot of additional taxation) and for indirect as opposed to direct taxation'. Jenkins added that he had found O'Brien 'a useful sounding board for how badly any Special Charge (or non-recurring mini capital levy) would be received in the City'. The budget itself was grimly austere (removing over £900m from the economy in a full financial year), made a virtue out of the battle to right the balance of payments and was warmly welcomed by the *FT* as 'designed to hold back consumer expenditure hard without weakening the incentive to earn more profit and income through greater efficiency'. O'Brien, who enjoyed a positive working relationship with Jenkins, agreed. 'The Budget was a good effort and better than he expected it to be,' he told the discount market, 'and he felt like showing his approval by lowering Bank Rate, although the public sector was still taking too much of our money.' Half a point was indeed clipped off Bank rate on the 21st, from 8 to 7½ per cent, and Cairncross noted with some amusement that 'the comic side' of this cut was that 'the Governor regarded it from the start as a vote of confidence *by the Bank* in the Budget as if – to quote Denis [i.e. Sir Denis Rickett of the Treasury] – the Bank was quite independent of HMG and itself decided what to do with Bank rate'.[4] On the face of it this was the old story of separate empires, as if Radcliffe had never happened, but in truth the O'Brien governorship did involve a perceptible strengthening at all levels of the Bank/Treasury relationship, helping to diminish (if not banish) the Bank's relative marginalisation of the Cromer years.

For King, a frankly political appointment to the Court and whose presence first Cromer and then O'Brien had always resented, the end was approaching of his regular visits to Threadneedle Street. During April he started to become convinced that there was a conspiracy afoot to conceal the true gravity of the financial situation facing the country. 'He showed me some of the secret figures,' he noted on the 14th after a recent conversation with Allen. 'They were clearly disastrous.' Yet, he added, the fact was that the 'spending spree' continues and 'the Stock Exchange index goes on up and up'. On the 24th he quoted O'Brien ('We are just holding on – afraid almost to breathe unless we bring something down on us'), and on 1 May he recorded without comment that 'we are to announce an increase in our reserves of £21 million in April', even though 'the real figure is a loss of £80 million'. Just over a week later, on the 9th, King tendered his resignation as a director and the following day an outspoken front-page article entitled 'Enough Is Enough' appeared under his name in the *Daily Mirror*. Claiming that the government had lost all credibility, he declared, 'We are now threatened with the greatest financial crisis in our history. It is not to be removed by lies about our reserves, but only by a fresh start under a fresh leader.' The clear implication was that the Bank of England was complicit in these lies, and no one there mourned his passing. 'He never took the trouble to find out or try to understand what the functions of a central bank were,' O'Brien recalled. 'His scorn for everyone was lofty and unending . . . Not by a long chalk one of Winchester's most attractive products.'[5]

To O'Brien's alarm, Wilson's first choice to replace King was Kearton, while Jenkins toyed with Warburg, but in the end it was Sir Eric Roll, who after leaving the Department of Economic Affairs had gone to Warburgs. The conspiratorial aspect aside, King's attack almost certainly struck a sympathetic chord in the City, where Wilson's reputation, never high, was now probably at its all-time nadir. A few weeks later, at a press conference announcing the latest Hambros results, Jocelyn Hambro even went so far as to declare that he was the worst Prime Minister since Lord North – an assertion that prompted a left-wing backbencher, Frank Allaun, to ask a parliamentary question, in the context of the current prices and incomes policy, about the salary that that particular merchant banker enjoyed as Chairman of Hambros. The reply was that the matter was being investigated, prompting Wilson two days later to send a memo to the relevant minister to the effect that both he and the Chancellor were concerned about 'the need to avoid undue provocation in the City'.[6] The subject, perhaps to Hambro's disappointment, was quietly dropped.

For the financial authorities, the spring and early summer of 1968 remained a time of acute anxiety, shadowed always by the fear of another ignominious devaluation. In the City's inner councils, black humour became the order of the day, as on 23 May, when O'Brien 'pointed out' to the discount market 'that Members of the Foreign Exchange Brokers Fraternity were now meeting in Spain where he hoped they would remain indefinitely!' That same day, however, there was a serious blow to the Bank's relations with the clearing banks when, abruptly and quite without warning, it told them that the lending 'ceiling' agreed the previous November was now to be toughened, in that although it would be lifted to 104 per cent of the total November 1967 lending to the private sector, that figure would henceforth include lending for exports. 'Presumably,' the most recent historian of Lloyds Bank has written with justifiable scorn, 'the bureaucrats believed that advances could be turned on and off like a tap.' The bankers were furious, with Midland's Forbes, for example, remarking to his fellow-chairmen on the 24th that 'it was not possible to run a commercial banking business under these conditions'. Three days later he and Robarts went to see O'Brien, who apparently conceded that 'the measures were introduced without real thought and at a moment's notice'. A meeting with Jenkins (though with O'Brien present) was arranged for the 30th, and the day before Robarts wrote to Forbes: 'It has been pointed out to me, and there is in my opinion something in the point, that we in the City may be constituting ourselves as a very convenient target for abuse by the Government to deflect attention from the mess the country is in, but I think we must chance this as we really cannot sit down and say nothing about the atrocious way in which the Credit Squeeze is being conducted.' The two men made their protest to the Chancellor – 'complete lack of prior consultation . . . dissatisfaction that the whole of the impact of the new measures would again fall on the private sector . . . the Banks had been remarkably successful in keeping down lending . . . could not see the necessity for this "panic action" . . .' – and Jenkins apologised at least for the lack of consultation, saying that it would not happen again.[7]

A week or so later Cairncross lunched with Ansell Egerton, a merchant banker who had been an economist and a financial journalist, and was told that the City felt 'disenchanted' with O'Brien because he 'didn't stand up for their interests'. It was not a new feeling, Egerton added, but undoubtedly had been 'inflamed' by the recent credit squeeze. For what it was worth, Cairncross also noted that 'Egerton said it was accepted that the next Governor would have to come from outside the Bank and that John Stevens would be high in the running'. O'Brien himself, the unfortunate pig-in-the-middle, was uncomfortably aware that damage had been done, to judge by the discount market's weekly conversation with him at the end of May. 'David Jessel and [Michael] Allsopp saw the Governor, who was gloomy. Jessel told him that the Market was punch-drunk by the new credit restrictions and the way they had been brought in. The Governor replied that he regretted the way this had happened but he had to try to cut down imports further.'[8]

Another way in which the old order was crumbling was signalled in July 1968 by the Basle Agreement, which in effect involved the world's central banks giving the UK a $2bn credit to enable her in turn to give exchange rate guarantees to all the official sterling holders and thereby run down in as orderly a fashion as possible the sterling area, whose belated demise had been made inevitable by devaluation.[9] The hope at the Bank was that sterling would remain an important reserve asset in the world's monetary system, but that was the larger truth. The problem was how to persuade the individual countries in the area not to get out of sterling in a needlessly precipitate or drastic way, and that summer much of the attention was focused on the attitude of Australia, whose example, it was generally believed, was likely to influence other countries. On the evening of 29 August, a Thursday, Wilson and Jenkins agreed over the telephone that O'Brien should be sent out there: his objective would be to 'impress on the Australians how important the current negotiations were, how serious the implications would be for them if they failed, and to what extent the Australians would be blamed if it became known that they had stood in the way of an agreement'. O'Brien, travelling under a false name and smuggled on board a Qantas flight via the freight loading room at London

Airport, reached Canberra on Sunday morning (local time), 1 September. Negotiations with the Australian Prime Minister, John Gorton, went surprisingly well, despite previous intimations that Australia was unlikely to continue to hold much sterling, and O'Brien was back in London by Wednesday afternoon with his mission more or less successfully accomplished and the press none the wiser.[10] Other countries indeed followed the Australian example, and that autumn the Basle Agreement began to come into effect.

The experienced financial journalist Paul Bareau, writing in October's *Banker*, offered a salutary perspective:

> Seen from the angle of Britain the new arrangements offer short-term relief in that they will considerably decrease the volatility of the sterling balances. Judged in a longer-term perspective they give no cause for exuberant enthusiasm. The welcoming hurrahs at this 'relief from the stranglehold of sterling's international role' intoned by such organs of public opinion as *The Guardian* and, in more muted but still unmistakable terms, by *The Times*, are arrant stuff and nonsense. The retreat of sterling from its international role may, in the prevailing circumstances, have been inevitable, but it must be regarded as a defeat and disaster none the less . . .
>
> For overseas sterling area countries these new arrangements have self-evident and important implications. The sterling system is gradually going the road of the political Commonwealth of which it was the financial counterpart. When the immobilization or blocking arrangements come to an end [scheduled for the early 1970s], sterling balances will only flow back if there is a major improvement of credibility in the Government and confidence in sterling. Fortunately, the know-how, resilience and adaptability of the international banking and merchanting system of this country remains so far unaffected by the tribulations of sterling . . .[11]

O'Brien would not have disagreed. He may have taken legitimate pride in both the plan and the operation of details, but whatever the relative weight of the competing arguments about the impact of sterling as a reserve currency on the management of the domestic economy, he must have known by this time that the fortunes of sterling and the City were no longer indivisible.

On the domestic front, it was not until autumn 1969 that it at last became almost unequivocally clear that the hard fiscal and monetary pounding since devaluation had succeeded in producing the right sort of trade figures, which in turn made it possible to start repaying the mountainous short-term debt. As late as August that year Parsons at the Bank thought that the country was still 'drifting to a major catastrophe', while two months later Allen held that the favourable balance-of-payments figures being hailed by the Labour government were 'faked'. In general, however, even before the turn-round in the balance of payments, the Chancellor's financial rectitude and orthodoxy made him a favourite in the square mile, echoing previous canonisations of Philip Snowden and Stafford Cripps. 'Kenneth Keith agreed with Roy Jenkins,' Benn noted in his diary in December 1968, after a whole-day meeting of Neddy at Chequers, at which Jenkins had insisted that sacrifices needed to be made in order to restore the trade position, with the Minister of Technology adding sourly that 'of course the City always does agree with Roy'. There were plenty of others to the left of Jenkins who were also unhappy about the government's apparent plight of being in a financial straitjacket not of its own choosing; and after some remarks uttered in St Paul's, O'Brien came under personal attack at a conference of the Scottish TUC. Replying to his Govan assailant, he complained of being misreported:

> What I actually said, in response to persistent and aggressive questioning – I was not making a speech as so many seemed to think – was that the total elimination of unemployment was not possible in a free economy like ours, given our balance of payments difficulties and the present limitations on our means of controlling factors such as mobility, training and the introduction and acceptance of efficiency methods.
>
> I beg you not to assume that it follows from this that I am ignorant of the human problems involved or insensitive to them. Even one man who seeks work and cannot find it is a reproach, and I am as concerned as anyone to contribute towards the management of the economy in such a way that it can provide a stable basis for the fullest possible employment.[12]

It was a mercy, O'Brien may or may not have reflected, that governors were not yet obliged to travel to outlying parts of the Isles in order to defend the Bank's corner.

During these 'two years of hard slog', in Jenkins's well-publicised phrase, the clearing banks became ever more aggrieved. In November 1968, on the eve of yet another tightening of credit in order to dampen down consumer demand, O'Brien expressed his anxiety to the Treasury that 'the co-operation of the banks on which we have relied so heavily for so long is sorely strained and might break if we try to impose a further restraint on their lending'. Indeed, 'it might be that the banks would simply go through the ceiling and face us with the dilemma of having our policies flouted or being forced to take direct action'. Jenkins and the Treasury, however, were adamant that the clearers must continue to do their bit, and later that month it was decreed that by the following March they must have reduced their loans to the private sector to 98 per cent (i.e. down 6 per cent) of the November 1967 total. O'Brien had no alternative but to be the enforcer, and in the second week of 1969 he warned Thomson of Barclays that if the banks 'showed any signs of failing to move towards the targets which we had set for them we should have to take resolute and possibly very unwelcome action'. On 27 January, with Parsons and Jasper Hollom present on behalf of the Bank, the bank chairmen met in a grumbling mood about the continuing credit restrictions. After stressing the balance-of-payments situation and the confidence factor, Parsons tried to take the heat out of the meeting by conceding that, however unfairly, 'many people in this country regarded the Bank of England as mainly an agent for pressure by foreigners to put restraint on the economy'. Stirling, however, merely expressed irritation at the banks getting all the blame:

> What steps had the Government taken? We had been told in the Budget that there would be two years of 'hard slog', and then industry took a week's holiday at Christmas. If industry played their part as well as the Banks were doing, the situation might be easier, and it would also be helpful if the Government would stop making optimistic speeches, which were just a soporific . . .[13]

Two months later it was O'Brien's turn to insist on the need to hit the 98 per cent target – and to listen to the bankers' grievances. 'Success in restricting credit still depended quite largely upon the co-operation of banks' customers,' Forbes, Thomson, Stirling and Faulkner stressed. 'This was increasingly difficult to secure. Branch managers complained that their task was not made easier by signs of visibly lavish public expenditure and by what appeared to be inflationary wage settlements.' As a result, 'managers were tending to lose heart and the public image of the banks was getting worse and worse'. The four just men were also disturbed by the approaching completion of a joint Treasury/Bank review: 'Regarding possible abandonment of the "cartel" arrangements, it was felt that a steep rise in lending rates would undoubtedly follow. Was it desirable to increase the financing costs of high priority activities, including the cost of export finance?' Finally, though without going into much detail, 'the banks were increasingly perturbed at the loss of new-style business to outside competitors'. For the moment, at the government's insistence, the cartel arrangements stayed in place; but following a sharp increase in advances, the banks were punished in June when the Bank of England, ignoring protests that 'the target figure was totally unrealistic', reduced the rate of interest paid to them on special deposits. So the irritable dance continued into the autumn, with a delegation of clearing bankers appealing to Jenkins in September to 'revise the target to a more realistic figure', but the Chancellor once more finding himself 'not able to agree to this'.[14] It was not, in the unwonted competitive milieu in which the big clearing banks were now operating, a sustainable policy.

Nevertheless, even if they were starting to be less than satisfied about the Bank of England's ability or will-power to defend their interests, the clearing banks in the late 1960s had little or no truck with the idea of a

specifically 'City Neddy', which was being promulgated both by the TUC
and by Neddy's Director General, Fred Catherwood. On Neddy itself,
located at Millbank Tower, the City's representative was still Kenneth
Keith, who in May 1968 told O'Brien that the idea 'appeared to have some
steam behind it' and that 'it would be more likely to be pursued if he
showed strong opposition to it'. The idea of a City Neddy was for obvious
reasons anathema to O'Brien, but although he agreed with Keith's tactical
approach, he may have wondered whether that ambitious merchant
banker had aspirations to head an alternative, non-Bank City power-base.
Some months later, in October, O'Brien gave lunch to the TUC's General
Secretary, George Woodcock, and sought to justify his position:

> A little Neddy for the City, assuming one could be set up, might start
> with the best of intentions but it seemed to me before long it was almost
> bound to encroach on my preserves. I should naturally resist this very
> strongly. Moreover I had consulted the main City employers and had found
> them uniformly opposed to the idea. Mr Woodcock said that he was not
> quite sure how far my responsibilities extended but he felt there was no need
> for a Neddy to encroach on them. Such a committee would be concerned
> with the use of labour and labour-saving devices such as computers. I
> remarked that this might quickly lead them to propose changes in City
> institutions, e.g. the discount market. He took note of my objections and
> we left the matter there.

The next day, when Keith came in and continued to take his previous line,
O'Brien seems to have tried a little moral suasion: 'I did not demur from
this but made it plain that I hoped the idea would die.' Keith, not for the
first or last time in his career, was reluctant to take the hint, and less than
three weeks later O'Brien had another visitor:

> Lord Sherfield [chairman of Hill Samuel] came in to talk about the City
> Neddy.
> It quickly became clear that he was being pushed from behind by
> Kenneth Keith. The burden of his message was that the City was all at sixes
> and sevens on this subject and ought I not to give them a lead.
> I said that I felt that I had spent a good deal of effort in doing so. The
> only difference between me and Kenneth Keith was that my lead was against
> the idea while his appeared to be for it. I explained the background to my
> thinking.

Over the next year or so the notion did not entirely die (as late as July 1969
O'Brien was having to tell Catherwood that he 'continued to have little
enthusiasm for the whole idea of a City Neddy'), but the Governor was
fortified by the genuine antipathy of the Accepting Houses Committee as
well as the clearing banks.[15] As for Keith, a man anyway with other fish to
fry, he seems to have stopped pressing. For better or worse, the City would
have to face the challenges of the 1970s with no coherent overall voice of

its own, other than that of a central banker appointed by government.

*

The year 1968 would come to mean different things to different people, but for many in the City the dominant image was of a raging bull market, peaking on 19 September when the FT 30-Share Index reached 521.9, but staying strong for the rest of the year. Fiscal policy may have been on the tough side, and interest rates uncomfortably high, but equities boomed on the back of devaluation (the inflationary aspect of which was still viewed as positively good for equities), large company profits and intense speculative activity, often taking the form of takeovers. 'This was the era of Mr Jim Slater and many like him who realised that the acceptability of highly rated paper (price-earnings ratios of 30 and 40 were common) made possible the takeover of asset-rich companies which had failed to join in the share price race,' Barry Riley would explain to *FT* readers a generation later. The paper's then editor, Sir Gordon Newton (knighted in the same list as Warburg), recalled a rare moment, probably from 1968, when Prime Minister and square mile were at one:

> One evening I received a message asking me to call in at Number 10 on my way home, which I did. It had been a good day on the Stock Exchange and our 30-share index had reached a new high, so when Wilson asked me how the City was feeling, I mentioned this to him. He was delighted. He poured two small glasses of brandy and we drank a toast to the FT Index. He said that this was probably the first time that the prime minister and the editor of the *Financial Times* had drunk a toast to the FT Index in the cabinet room at Number 10. I replied that it certainly had never happened before and would almost certainly never happen again. He agreed . . .[16]

On the back of the bull market and the merger boom, the merchant banks were cleaning up probably more than at any time since 1914. 'He and his like are making a great deal of money,' King noted in early September after lunching with Keith at Hill Samuel. 'If they were doing badly we should hear much more of the critical times in which we live. He said his profits last year were 40 per cent up on the previous year and this year are 40 per cent up on last.' Two days later the diarist had a surprisingly 'hilarious' lunch with Richardson of Schroders. 'Gordon was perfectly clear that the last year had been a disastrous one for the country while large numbers of people had made a lot of money. He agreed that the Government had had a relatively easy time in spite of its failure, just because so many important people were making so much money.' There was as yet no widespread criticism of the City's relationship with British industry – that critique would come through much more powerfully in the 1970s – but already there were some rumblings, at this stage mainly from industry itself rather than from the Left. 'They think up deals and egg you on, so they can make a fat profit,' Viyella's Joe Hyman frankly told the financial journalist William Davis about what he saw as the main motive behind the merchant banks' enthusiasm for bids and mergers. Davis added significantly in his study, *Merger Mania*, describing the late 1960s, 'other industrialists, led into making acquisitions which they later regretted, have expressed similar views in private'.[17]

Nevertheless, far from all the mergers were finance-driven. Indeed, one of the most important – the creation of British Leyland, through the union of British Motor Corporation and Leyland announced in January 1968 – owed much to the personal wishes of Wilson. The role of the IRC was crucial in implementing it, and the more traditional City institutions fell fairly passively into line. On the other hand, it is doubtful if Wilson would have been so enthusiastic had he not been swayed by emphatic assurances from Warburg that Donald Stokes was a brilliant executive capable of forging British Leyland into an unbeatable national champion in the worldwide motor industry.[18] At the IRC itself, Grierson's successor as Managing Director was Charles Villiers of Schroders – not the first choice but strongly recommended by Richardson to O'Brien.[19] A genuinely public-spirited man, and a self-professed 'Tory radical', Villiers was far more sympathetic than most in the City to the Labour government's dream of modernising and rationalising British industry. Earlier in his stewardship, in spring 1968, the IRC was involved in a controversial episode in the scientific-instrument sector, as it used its government-backed resources to ensure the preferred outcome of a battle for control of Cambridge Instrument. There was outcry in the City at this blatant subversion of the market mechanism, including a protest from Wincott in the *FT*, but Villiers was unrepentant.[20] Soon afterwards the IRC made another decisive, not uncontentious intervention when it backed GEC rather than Plessey as the more appropriate company to take over English Electric.[21] Then, during the first half of 1969, there was the so-called 'Great Ball Bearing Affair', which in effect saw the IRC, confronted by the prospect of that esoteric industry passing into foreign control, decide instead to roll three British firms into one, Ransome Hoffman Pollard.[22] All of which left the City uneasy: pleased for obvious, fee-receiving reasons by the rash of merger activity over which the IRC presided, instinctively unhappy that competing takeover bids were not always being decided on a level playing field; and unconvinced that the IRC was uniquely able to discern where 'the national interest' lay in industrial matters. Almost certainly there was some sympathy for Sir Keith Joseph's view, on behalf of the Tory opposition, that the IRC was 'arbitrary and often superficial', and that 'special pleadings, with all their risks and evils, lead to judgements thought to be objective but really subjective'.[23] There was always the possibility, in other words, that a national champion might fail to fly and turn into a lame duck.

Did Jim Slater see himself as a one-man, unsentimental IRC? 'The financial predator acted as a catalyst in stimulating fear within the fat and lazy managements, thereby making them more active,' he later wrote in justification of Slater Walker's at times frenzied pursuit of the takeover trail. 'In a sense, fear of the predator was an essential discipline for many boards, as without it they would have tended to rest upon the laurels of their predecessors.' In 1968 – despite Slater's absence for almost the first three months because of jaundice – Slater Walker made nine major acquisitions. 'At 10 o'clock every morning a chauffeur-driven car pulls up outside an office in Hartford Street, Mayfair,' Arthur Sandles wrote in the *FT* in May, soon after Slater Walker had bid for Crittal Hope, Britain's largest manufacturer of metal window frames. 'From it steps a tall slim 39-year-old. Jim Slater has a boyish face and an approachable, but not extrovert, personality.' Sandles called Slater, now worth over £2m, 'the high-wire man of commerce', in that 'no one really wants him to fall but there is always the possibility that he might'. Slater Walker by this time lay at 121 in the league table of British companies in share capitalisation terms, and Sandles asked 'the darling of the market' why he simply did not take his winnings and stop. 'Why? I don't know why. I just want to make this a big and successful international company.'[24] No one, then or later, would deny Slater's brilliance as a bidder (rarely employing a merchant bank, whenever possible using stock not cash, exploiting existing takeover rules to their utmost before they were changed), but it was almost equally undeniable that his industrial approach was flawed – that he was too attracted to the arithmetic of individual situations and did not sufficiently stand back, examine sectors of British industry and see which of them overall had growth prospects.

Early in September, after it had been announced that Slater Walker was bidding for Drages, Sir Isaac Wolfson's master company, a perceptive financial journalist, Christopher Gwinner, argued that Slater Walker had become 'the prime British example of a new type of investment animal, the conglomerate, which seeks to tackle in a rather different way the objectives of the old-style industrial holding company'. This new style, involving a 'stronger and more financially orientated' central management, was explicitly along the lines of US conglomerates. According to Gwinner, such a conglomerate 'must be able to subordinate all industrial considerations to its financial aims' and therefore 'must concentrate on the weight of return of its assets, shuffling these shares in a portfolio if results prove unsatisfactory'. In short, 'its main criteria must be the growth in earnings per share and not the solid industrial base'. Slater Walker was, noted Gwinner, virtually the only British 'pure exponent of the approach', and it was 'no wonder that Mr Slater has described his own operations as capitalising on the skills of both management consultancy and merchant banking'. In fact, what Gwinner called the 'surprise bid' for Drages, successfully accomplished that autumn, was to mark a turning-point in Slater Walker's history. That acquisition brought into the group a bank, Ralli Brothers (Bankers), and with it the potential to become something like an investment bank. Slater Walker was 'almost making money out of air', its tame brokers, Sebags, reputedly said at about this time, as Slater Walker's share price rocketed in the course of the year from 21s 7d to 70s 0d and its shareholders increased from 6,000 to 40,000.[25] Even if Slater's industrial strategy had been more systematically thought out, the temptation was obvious to shift the primary focus from making things to, purely (relatively speaking) and simply (relatively speaking), making money.

For Slater and other professionals in the takeover game there was in operation from March 1968 not only a revised, tougher City Code on Takeovers and Mergers, but also, to supervise that code, a panel chaired by the former Deputy Governor, Sir Humphrey Mynors. 'It is generally accepted,' the new Code's preamble noted, 'that the choice before the City in the conduct of Take-overs and Mergers is either a system of voluntary self-discipline based on the Code and administered by the City's own representatives or regulation by law enforced by officials appointed by Government. The City Working Party [chaired by Michael Bucks of Rothschilds] is firmly of the opinion that the voluntary system is more practicable and more effective.' That was indeed the choice, but the chances of self-regulation continuing to avert the threat of an American-style SEC were hardly increased by the fact that the panel was given virtually no powers with which to enforce the new Code. Nor was Mynors himself, for all his qualities, the most credible figure as City enforcer. Even so, it was not all that long before Bucks, as Chairman of the IHA, was able to report to his executive committee that all the IHA's members bar one 'had undertaken to observe and abide by the City Code' – with the dissenting member, despite a lot of persuasion by Bucks, being willing to give only 'a verbal confirmation that the Code would be observed'. That was in June, the same month that a keenly contested takeover battle for International Paints saw the panel handing out a censure to the victors, Courtaulds, for having breached the Code by not providing adequate information in time to the shareholders of the defending company. On the 25th, the day after the panel had informed the press of its action, Kearton stormed in to see O'Brien:

> Sir Frank was very angry [O'Brien recorded]. He said this notice had been issued without Courtaulds being given an opportunity of answering the criticisms . . . He said that Courtaulds' statement of 29th May had been put out on the advice of Hill Samuel who had specifically deterred them from prior consultation with the Panel . . .

Sir Frank continued with a long diatribe about the iniquities of City institutions and market manipulators, referring in particularly disparaging terms to Mr Ross Goobey [Imperial Tobacco's legendary investment manager] ... He was convinced that he was dealing with crooks and evidently felt that he could not be expected to do so on the basis of Queensberry Rules, such as are enshrined in the Code. I told him that the Code and the Panel had my full support ... I had some sympathy with his complaint that the Panel had acted without warning.

If it had ever had one, the panel's honeymoon was already over, and exactly a month later O'Brien understandably remarked to the discount market that 'he considered it important to have men with business experience on such a panel rather than professors'.[26] But by this time, thanks to events elsewhere, the International Paints episode seemed like ancient history.

The 'Gallaher affair', as it became known, was probably the most acrimonious City episode, certainly in the field of takeovers, since the Aluminium War almost ten years earlier.[27] Gallaher, the Ulster-based tobacco company, had been receiving the unwelcome attentions of the American giant, Philip Morris, which at the end of June put in a partial bid, of twenty-five shillings a share for 50 per cent of the shares. The Gallaher board rejected the bid and there soon appeared another, more welcome contender in the form of American Tobacco. With Imperial Tobacco having earlier that summer sold (through Flemings, Morgan Grenfell and Cazenove's) its controlling interest in Gallaher, the company had become a takeover target. That sale also meant that American Tobacco's merchant bank and brokers, conveniently Morgan Grenfell and Cazenove's, had a pretty shrewd idea which investing institutions were now looking to sell large quantities of Gallaher shares at a profit. The upshot was that Morgan Grenfell instructed Cazenove's to go into the market early on Tuesday, 16 July, following the announcement of a rival partial bid by American Tobacco at thirty-five shillings a share (from the point of view of the investing institutions, satisfactorily well above the twenty shillings a share they had paid in May) and make what later terminology would call a 'dawn raid'. More precisely, according to a Morgan Grenfell memorandum dated the 17th, Sir Antony Hornby of Cazenove's was 'instructed that, as this was a competitive situation, American Tobacco would be willing to buy all stock offered in the market provided that such purchases were at or below the offer price of 35s'.[28] The raiders knew from the start that this operation might land them in trouble. 'If I'm going to be in the shit,' Hornby remarked to Tim Collins, in charge on the Morgan Grenfell side, as he left 23 Great Winchester Street on the eve of battle, 'there's no one I'd rather be in the shit with than you.'

The Morgan Grenfell memo relates what happened on the 16th:

> Sir Antony Hornby's best guess was that if everything went very well for us we might acquire 5 million shares during the day. In a little under two hours trading, enormous numbers of shares were offered to Cazenove. In the last half hour of buying stock, the total rose from just over 4 million to what we believe to be about 10 million and by the time the transactions had all been sorted out and checked it was found that the total was in fact about 12 million.
>
> This exceptional volume of offerings must probably be attributed to the fact that following the recent Offer for Sale of 26 million Gallaher shares, a large amount of stock was still in underwriters' hands who saw a chance of an unexpected profit within a very few weeks.[29]

This analysis of how in effect American Tobacco won the day was undoubtedly correct. The recent sale of Gallaher shares, formerly held by Imperial, had not been absorbed and was in the hands of various institutions, more than one-third being with Flemings. These institutions, well known to Cazenove's, were willing sellers, and from a stockbroking point of view it was a phenomenal operation, netting the firm £0.25m commission for one morning's work – an astonishing amount for those days and the source of understandable envy.

The storm broke almost at once. The *FT*'s Gwinner, speaking on BBC Radio 4 on the 17th, put the controversy in a nutshell: 'The brokers of American Tobacco entered the market early on Tuesday morning and bought about 12 million shares. And the complaint is that this was done in a way which really was in favour of big institutional shareholders and gave the small people no chance to get rid of their shares at that price.' Among those complaining was Warburg, whose firm had been acting for Philip Morris and who went to see O'Brien that day. 'He was sharply critical,' the Governor noted, 'of the action of Cazenove's in going into the market for a brief period to acquire Gallaher shares on behalf of American Tobacco, and doing so by approaching the large institutions who they knew were big holders. As a result, in his opinion the generality of Gallaher shareholders had not been given an equal opportunity of disposing of their shares at the price Cazenove's were offering.' O'Brien did not comment, but merely told Warburg that he 'understood the matter was being considered by the Takeover Panel'. Meanwhile, over at 12 Tokenhouse Yard, Hornby was drafting a memorandum of defence. Its tone was unyielding and thoroughly old-school: 'Nobody has suffered. Some have, but maybe only temporarily, done better . . . If one's hands are entirely tied a complete stop is put to doing any business at all . . . Equality amongst investors is an illusion. We are often disappointed in missing a line of shares in the market. Someone has bought them first. He made up his mind quicker or had a better broker. This is not unfair . . .'[30]

The following day, Thursday the 18th, the Takeover Panel delivered its verdict. It declared that Morgan Grenfell and Cazenove's had broken the Takeover Code, in particular the article declaring that all shareholders in a company being bid for should receive equal treatment. The response of the two firms was to deny vigorously that they had breached the Code, stressing that its rule 29 accepted that it was undesirable to fetter the market and making much of the fact that Barrington of Morgan Grenfell had received Panel approval on the 15th for the proposed course of action. The joint statement could not have ended more brusquely: 'No press enquiries will be answered by either Morgan Grenfell or Cazenove.' That evening Hornby told Tom Mangold of BBC Television that he was most offended by the Panel's judgement and that it had given a misguided verdict. 'There's a certain cut and thrust in the market that is the essence of City dealing,' he explained. 'If you're going to wait for the amateurs then business will stop.' Elsewhere in town the City's leaders were assembled at the Whitehall Dining Club. 'Bill Harcourt was wild because he had just been impugned by the Panel for infringing the Code,' noted Cairncross (seated between Cromer and Richardson). 'The trouble probably was that they offered such a good price that they looked like getting too many shares and stopped buying before the smaller holders had time to offer. He did get a chance to state his case to the Panel but found the verdict in four lines paid no regard to what he claimed. Leslie O'B came over to speak to him, looking a bit glum. I asked if Bill wanted a Securities and Exchange Commission and of course he said No.'[31]

Harcourt and Hornby woke up next day to almost unanimously hostile press reaction, epitomised by the remarks of the financial editor of *The Times*:

> The future of the Takeover Panel hangs in the balance. If Morgan Grenfell and Cazenove's, two of the most eminent firms in their particular spheres, are to break the Code and publicly not to accept the Panel's unanimous ruling, there must be a strong reaction either from the Panel or from the bodies which constitute the Panel. If there is no further sanction against these two firms, the case against a Securities and Exchange Commission will no longer be arguable.

For Harcourt in particular it was a day of high agitation. In the morning he called on O'Brien to explain why he had felt obliged to rebut the Panel's verdict:

> He said that in his opinion this flat statement [i.e. by the panel] contained the implication that Morgan's and Cazenove's had acted in bad faith. This was a reflection on his honour which he could not leave unanswered. If the Panel had phrased their statement in more tactful terms, implying that there could be two views as to the meaning of the Code and that while Morgan's and Cazenove's held one view, they held another, he would not have felt the

need to reply, at least so flatly. He said that he fully supported the Code and the Panel and had no desire to flout either.

I said that I thought it might be useful if he were to let it be known publicly that he had seen me and assured me that Morgan's had acted in good faith on their reading of the Code, and that I had accepted his assurance. He could then go on to say that he had no desire to flout either the Code or the Panel, but was indeed, on the contrary, a strong supporter of both. He said he would think about this and let me know.

Unfortunately for Harcourt's equanimity, there appeared in the *Evening News* later that Friday a piece by its City editor, David Malbert, that was like a red rag to a bull. The headline was provocative enough – ' "Bad boys" of City wait . . . and hope' – and part of the article ran:

> This is one of the sharpest conflicts involving City 'blue bloods' that has been seen for many years.
>
> Ultimate sanctions could be taken against the offending firms by suspending Cazenove partners from dealing on the Stock Exchange for a period and by expelling or suspending Morgan Grenfell from the powerful Issuing Houses Association.

Inevitably, and probably within a few minutes of seeing the paper, Harcourt 'rang up in great indignation' and demanded that O'Brien make 'an immediate statement' refuting the article. Harcourt added that if he himself were now to make a statement along the lines that O'Brien had suggested in the morning, 'it would appear to be a complete climb down' and 'he was not prepared to do this'. O'Brien, however, declined to commit himself. 'I subsequently saw Mr Wilkinson [Chairman of the Stock Exchange] and brought him up to date,' the Governor recorded. 'I said that I was not prepared to make a statement and he concurred. I so informed Lord Harcourt, who was very disappointed.'[32] No longer, in other words, could the City's grandees automatically look to the Bank for protection against the outrages of the fourth estate.

'The City must act to control its members,' a leading article in *The Times* declared on Saturday, while next day the *Sunday Telegraph* specifically called for Hornby's suspension from the Stock Exchange, a suggestion that naturally made him furious. On Monday the 22nd the Stock Exchange Council considered a letter from a member firm, George M. Hill & Co. It paraphrased various unflattering stories going round the market, such as that Cazenove's had 'left the jobbers holding stock which they had in effect bid for'; declared that Cazenove's, 'whose reputation and name have always been second to none in our eyes, should be given the opportunity to refute or justify them'; and added that if such methods were upheld by the Council, 'we may as well throw the book on "etiquette of dealing" out of the window'. The Council responded by appointing a special committee to investigate the various stories.[33]

Attention moved back to the Panel, which over the next few days conducted informal discussions with the aggrieved parties. By now O'Brien was seriously worried about the larger implications, and he confided in the Treasury's Sir Douglas Allen:

> The Governor said that he was very much opposed to the idea of rushing in an SEC before the Panel had been able to demonstrate its effectiveness. He would not wish Sir Humphrey Mynors called in to the Board of Trade for something of this kind to be worked out between them. Allen said that Part [Sir Antony Part, Permanent Secretary at the Board of Trade] had told him that the President of the Board of Trade [Anthony Crosland] had been asking for information on the subject but that his general line was to play the question quietly. Allen had said to Part that he thought it would be quite damaging and wrong for the early life of the Panel to be switched over to an entirely new concept. However, there is an element in the Board of Trade that takes it for granted that something like the United States system is bound to come into operation here sometime in the future. The Governor said that Morgans are in this regard in a horrible position and they are not likely to repeat their performance. Others will clearly have been influenced in the right direction by what has taken place.

The next day, the 25th, there was a further announcement from the Panel, which accepted that the two firms had 'acted in good faith in their belief that such dealings were within the letter and spirit of the Code'. Technically the issue turned on whether or not the Panel accepted market purchases in a partial bid situation: this the Panel did not believe it had acquiesced in, but it accepted that there had been a genuine misunderstanding. Any imputations against the integrity of the two firms were withdrawn.[34]

O'Brien assured the Treasury that 'the announcement by the Panel represented a climb down by Morgan's and Cazenove's', and 'he assumed that Cazenove's would probably be censured by the Stock Exchange', but in the world outside the Panel's latest pronouncement received a generally dusty response. 'An unhappy compromise', the financial editor of *The Times* called it, though accepting that Morgan Grenfell and Cazenove's 'are right when they say that the rules about market buying in partial bids were not clear'. The *FT* continued to maintain a studied neutrality, but at the weekend the *Sunday Telegraph* was again positively savage, on the one hand laying into the City authorities ('the whole thing has been mucked up in a particularly ludicrous fashion'), on the other hand dwelling on the hostility being expressed by much of the City towards Cazenove's ('so aloof, so successful'). In sum, the paper declared, 'the days when Morgans spoke only to Cazenove's and Cazenove's spoke only to God' were at last 'clearly at an end'.[35]

Over the next fortnight the Stock Exchange Council considered the report of the investigating committee, read and listened to submissions from Cazenove's, and deliberated. 'We feel sure,' Cazenove's declared at one point, 'that the Council will not allow themselves to be influenced by Press comment, much of which would have amounted to contempt of Court if this had been a case for trial in the Courts.' On 13 August the Council publicly delivered its judgement. It contained two key sentences: 'There was no evidence to suggest that Messrs Cazenove & Co knew or should have known at the time in the confused and competitive conditions of the contested bid situation that they were in danger of breaching the City Code by their actions . . . There was no evidence to suggest that their decisions were taken otherwise than in good faith.' Tacked on to this acquittal on the fundamental point, the Council did censure the firm for a technical infringement concerning the way it 'put through' the market those Gallaher shares bought from its own clients. Almost certainly this censure was in the nature of a placebo by the Council to its outside critics. Nevertheless, Hornby was jubilant at what he saw as a victory and, in his statement following the judgement, was as unrepentant as ever: 'We still feel we did not breach the Code as it is. We may have breached the Code as they wish they had written it.'[36]

The press remained highly critical, with 'Lex' of the *FT* at last coming down from the fence and describing the Council's pronouncement as 'pitiful but predictable'. O'Brien privately agreed, remarking to the Treasury on the 14th that he had been 'very disappointed at the Stock Exchange Council's decision'. The next day, still hoping to save the system of City self-regulation, the Governor published a letter to the Chairman of the IHA in which he supported the recent decisions of the Panel and declared that 'action in breach of the Code is not justifiable in any circumstances'. Once again, this was too much for Hornby, who told the *Evening News* on the 16th: 'I still say that I resent the rebuke by the Panel. There was no chance of discussion – no chance to put our case. The first announcement was bald and unkind and led to our being pilloried by the Press for eight days.' And he added, in words that perhaps only he could have used, on the need for the Panel to have a stronger secretariat: 'All new things have teething troubles. When I buy a new Rolls-Royce it tends to go wrong at the beginning when it is being run in.'[37] It was at this point that two of his partners took him to one side and convinced him that he was doing more harm than good by these continuing outbursts, especially in the aftermath of victory. There still lay ahead a formal censure for Morgan Grenfell from the IHA, but the high drama of the Gallaher affair was over.

In an overall piece on the episode, Kenneth Fleet argued in the *Daily Telegraph* that, after five months of the Takeover Panel, the City's attempt at self-policing in takeover bids had no long-term future and that 'ultimately it must be replaced with statutory rules interpreted and administered with statutory authority'. He also argued that the City would 'swallow its professional dislike of government interference and decide that the certainty and protection of the law outweigh the law's disadvantages'. It was an argument, though, that underestimated the City's deep, almost atavistic attachment to being left alone to run its affairs, quite apart from O'Brien's determination not to ditch his personal creation so early in its life. As for the culprits who had been given lbw and then refused to walk, Fleet was unable to condone the behaviour of Harcourt and Hornby, 'which rang with High City arrogance we thought had died with Hambros and the British Aluminium affair a decade ago'.[38] Certainly there were many in the City who, while feeling no great love for the Takeover Panel, felt that the two men had badly overreacted. Nevertheless, even if their behaviour was unattractive, the bottom line was that they had ruthlessly defended their client's interests and, in the end, won the day. In the increasingly high-profile world of corporate finance, the stakes would inevitably continue to get ever-higher, and there could no longer even be a vestigial assumption that gentlemen would behave in a gentlemanly fashion. Would even a beefed-up Takeover Panel be capable of resisting this larger trend?

The Takeover Panel Mark I was still in place as an entertaining battle unfolded during the closing months of 1968 for control of the *News of the World*.[39] The first bidder for that venerable rag was Robert Maxwell, part of whose initial capital for his book-marketing business in the early 1950s had come through a loan from Hambros, his secretary having known Sir Charles Hambro during the war. Hambro, however, was persuaded in 1953 by his colleagues, especially Harry Sporborg, not to lend any more – a fortunate decision, in that Maxwell's outfit, Simpkin Marshall, collapsed the following year. Maxwell bounced back, and in July 1964 the merchant bank that floated Pergamon Press on his behalf was 'Boy' Hart's Ansbachers. Maxwell would have preferred Warburgs, but an unfortunate lunch there had resulted in an internal memo from Warburg to the effect that Maxwell was a Jew who pretended not to be a Jew, who exploited Jews and who must on no account be a client of the bank's.[40] In October 1968, when he launched his £27m bid, Maxwell's main financial advisers were Robert Clark of Hill Samuel and Michael Richardson of the brokers Panmure Gordon, while the Carr family that had a major interest in the paper was advised by Hambros and in particular Sporborg, for whom the battle presumably had a special relish. Unfortunately for Maxwell, Clark had been one of the four wise men who had drawn up the latest Code on takeovers, which meant that he was operating with one hand tied behind his back. Sporborg, by contrast, had no such inhibitions, and he drove a horse and cart through the Code by using some £0.75m of Hambros money to go into the market and buy every voting share that he could.

Mynors's panel did little more than stand aside and watch.

By late October there was a further element in play, the ambitious Australian newspaper proprietor, Rupert Murdoch, who reached an agreement with the gullible Sir William Carr that together they would stave off the Maxwell threat. Murdoch's merchant bank was Morgan Grenfell, now rather relishing its new role as buccaneers in the takeover game, but it is likely that Sporborg played a key role in getting Murdoch into place. The Carr/Murdoch deal was a further blow to the panel's threadbare authority – given that it completely ignored the principle that shareholders were supposed to approve anything done to prevent a bid from succeeding – and Maxwell could only pin his hopes on an Extraordinary General Meeting, to be held on 2 January 1969 at the Connaught Rooms near Covent Garden. Predictably Carr and Murdoch won the count, and when asked about the City's conduct, Maxwell remarked to a journalist, 'I'm on the side of the angels; it's amazing.' It might, however, be only a temporary halo, for during the battle he had discovered, in the words long afterwards of Rodney Leach, 'the attractions of an artificially supported price for his company's stock'. He could therefore add this ploy to his 'methods of deception' developed over the years – methods that included 'changes of year-ends, backdated agreements, imaginary goodwill, trading between public and private companies, inflated stock valuations, returnable "sales", bogus profit forecasts, furtive disposals of shares, and so on'.[41] Almost without fail, though, Cap'n Bob would be able to find someone in the City willing to turn a blind eye to these peccadilloes.

There was plenty of other takeover interest that winter of 1968–9. One episode that attracted particular interest was an audacious £95m bid for the old, large and prestigious City of London Real Property Co (CLRP) – a bid made by the upstart property and construction company Trafalgar House, whose youthful dynamo, Nigel Broackes, had recently had the nerve to take over Trollope & Colls. In the event, neither Trafalgar nor the second bidder, Metropolitan Estates, won CLRP; instead that considerable prize went to Sir Harold Samuel's Land Securities, for £161m.[42] More or less concurrently two major mergers were announced, but ultimately failed to happen: between Allied Breweries and Unilever, and between the Rank Organisation and the printers de la Rue.[43] In the former case the government, to the City's disappointment, took fright, perhaps conscious that the public mood was turning against giant conglomerates; in the latter, neither the City as a whole nor the investment institutions in particular were much impressed by the proposed merger's industrial logic.

There was also, in February 1969, Lonrho's bid for the well-known Liverpool-based trading company, John Holt. It was eight years since

'Tiny' Rowland had effectively acquired control of Lonrho, a process in which (according to his biographer) he had been much helped by his gambit of promising 'part of the action' to Angus Ogilvy, who would represent the Drayton Group on the Lonrho board. Rowland himself was entirely lacking in a City background, but two years later, in July 1963, managed to secure a meeting at the Bank of England with Maurice Parsons. He told Parsons that he had been asked by Dr Hastings Banda to advise on how to set up a central bank in Nyasaland and whether Lonrho 'would take on the initial management of the bank'. This information elicited a predictably cool response from Parsons, who told Rowland that 'the request was a nonsensical one' and that 'it would certainly make no more sense if Dr Banda were to request me to give him advice on how to start and run a copper mine'. It was in about 1966 that Rowland, unlike Maxwell, persuaded Warburgs to be his merchant bankers. There he had a particular friend in Ian Fraser, who found him 'full of good ideas'. However, when Rowland in February 1969 acted unilaterally in his pursuit of John Holt – privately buying, without telling Warburgs (let alone John Holt's other shareholders) the 20 per cent stake in Holts owned by Oliver Jessel's go-getting Jessel Securities – he found himself on the verge of being dumped by 30 Gresham Street. 'You've got to stop this man,' Grunfeld warned Ogilvy. 'If you don't, we'll all be in court.' Rowland, summoned the next morning to Grunfeld's office and told that Warburgs had managed to get the deal with Jessels nullified, expressed suitable remorse, and the way was clear for a more conventional, successful bid. Grunfeld and his colleagues were apparently willing to believe that Rowland, used to African-style takeovers, simply did not know that in London it was now mandatory for every shareholder to be treated equally.[44]

O'Brien, meanwhile, had spent a fair part of the winter in a fruitless search for a successor to Mynors. 'I told him that someone in the City would have to make a real sacrifice if the Panel was to be strengthened,' he noted in November after an attempt to put pressure on Hill Samuel's Keith to release Clark. 'It was no use expecting me to produce the rabbit out of the hat unless they provided the rabbit. He [i.e. Keith] was obviously extremely reluctant to fall in with my proposal. . .' Other candidates also fell by the wayside, and at one point O'Brien even suggested to Mynors and Michael Verey of Schroders that the Stock Exchange's Quotations Committee should adopt the work of the Takeover Panel. 'They were not at all enthusiastic,' O'Brien perhaps regretfully noted. 'Michael Verey, in particular, felt that some members of the Committee were very moderate performers, not at all likely to grasp the intricate issues involved with the necessary speed.' Eventually it all fell into place for the Governor, as he successfully adopted the twin-track strategy of appointing a part-time Chairman and full-time Director-General. The Chairman was to be the formidable and well-known lawyer Lord Shawcross, who had become almost a professional non-executive director, including of Morgan Guaranty. His Director-General was to be Rowland's champion, Ian Fraser, who had become increasingly dissatisfied with life at Warburgs and, with backing from the Prudential, was even in the middle of trying to organise a management buy-out by him and other youngish disgruntled elements there. It may never have happened anyway, but his decision to accept O'Brien's offer – with a salary higher than the Governor's own – made certain that the Old Guard remained in charge in Gresham Street.[45]

Both Fraser and Shawcross were insistent that the Code should at last be given 'teeth', a view with which O'Brien entirely concurred, and late in February there was an illuminating exchange between the Governor and one of the three leading merchant bankers of the day:

> Mr Gordon Richardson telephoned the Governor to say that he was alarmed at the rumours which were flying round the City about sanctions in support of the Panel on Take-overs. He personally viewed these developments with apprehension, and felt that there would be several people in the City who, while supporting the operations of the Panel, would object in principle to the quasi-legal status of the sanctions proposed. The Governor replied that he understood this feeling, but that the only people he had been able to find to run the Panel were insistent that the Panel be given teeth. The alternative was a SEC. Mr Richardson accepted the Governor's position, but said that some might prefer a SEC to such arrangements.

The clearing bankers were also concerned about what sanctions should be at the Panel's disposal, and soon afterwards Shawcross explained his thinking to Forbes. He argued that, like most professional associations or trade unions, it should be possible to impose penalties without appeal to the courts being possible, and he drew a memorable analogy: 'I am myself at risk every day from expulsion from White's without any sort of judicial remedy provided of course that the principles of natural justice are observed.' He added more generally about the Panel that 'the whole thing does depend upon the City preferring a voluntary system to what seems to me the disagreeable alternative of a SEC which, if imposed by a socialist government, would certainly involve bureaucratic administering procedures with no appeal to the Courts'. If it had been considering rebellion against the new dispensation, the City now changed its mind and by spring 1969 the Takeover Panel Mark II was ready for action, originally based in the Bank of England, but soon to move its much enlarged secretariat to the twentieth floor of the Stock Exchange. It remained unclear, however, what form in practice the much-vaunted 'sanctions' would take. 'Teeth at last – but how will they bite?' a headline in *The*

Times rather aptly asked.[46] Still, the concept of 'natural justice' would go a long way to ensure that the lucrative takeover game continued to be played out and enforced by merchant bankers without undue interference from the legal profession.

The new regime was helped by the general bearishness of the market during 1969, but its first big challenge still came sooner than it would have wished.[47] In mid-June it was announced that the US conglomerate Leasco, run by the aggressive Saul Steinberg, had bid £25m for Maxwell's Pergamon. Trembling in Maxwell's corner this time was Flemings, where Richard Fleming was making an ill-advised attempt to expand what was traditionally an investment business into the more dangerous realm of corporate finance. Even before the announcement he had become dissatisfied with Pergamon's accounts, in particular the question of the size of its profits, and had threatened to withdraw Flemings' services; if anything, that dissatisfaction increased during the weeks after the announcement. Leasco's merchant bank was Rothschilds, where Jacob Rothschild never had any doubts that Maxwell was a crook, and which in conjunction with the accountants Touche Ross scrutinised as closely as they could Pergamon's books – a task given added urgency by the news that the famed *Sunday Times* 'Insight' team was raking fruitfully into Maxwell's past. Maxwell, professing the deepest indignation about these investigations, at one point summoned Rodney Leach of Rothschilds to his home at Headington Hall, hoping to find out how much Rothschilds had discovered. 'I agreed to the visit,' Leach recalled, 'on one condition, that telephone calls would be put through to the house at specified times, and if I did not reply the caller would summon the police. Maxwell showed not a flicker of offence or surprise.' Finally, in mid-August, it was announced that Leasco was withdrawing its bid, with Rothschilds claiming that Pergamon's stated profits for the past three years had been artificially inflated. Flemings resigned from the Maxwell camp on Sunday the 24th, the same day that a series of revelations appeared in the *Sunday Times*, and during the first half of the following week Maxwell appeared before the Takeover Panel, which was still operating in an outlying office of the Bank of England. After impatiently listening to Fraser explain that Leasco had been justified in pulling the plug, he proceeded to hold the stage, speaking for a total of some nineteen hours during two-and-a-half days. 'The sessions continued until the early hours of the morning and when we dispersed for a few hours' sleep Maxwell's voice was still booming in our ears,' remembered Fraser, who in an earlier life, soon after the war, had encountered Maxwell as a master-smuggler, travelling between Eastern Europe and West Germany in a huge salmon-pink Chrysler with Czech export plates. Eventually, the panel called for a full inquiry by the Board of Trade – a move that in the fullness of time led to a DTI report, published in 1971, which famously stated that Maxwell 'is not in our opinion a person who can be relied upon to exercise proper stewardship of a publicly quoted company'.

There remained the question of who should run Pergamon, as Leasco had acquired a 38 per cent stake prior to withdrawing its bid. An Extraordinary General Meeting of Pergamon's shareholders was called for 10 October, at which the institutions, marshalled by Schroders, implemented the Rothschild strategy of sacking Maxwell as Chairman and replacing him with an old City faithful, Sir Henry d'Avigdor-Goldsmid. The meeting itself was a stormy affair, with Maxwell indulging in a torrent of abuse against Rothschilds, but for the moment he had few cards to play, apart from invective. As for the panel, despite some criticism of its subsequently weak treatment of Flemings (over the potential, and perhaps actual, conflict of interest between investment manager and company adviser), it had come through the episode relatively unscathed, had been praised by Slater for having 'uplifted the standards of the City by several hundred per cent' and had taken a long step on the way to becoming a City fixture.[48] It always helps, Shawcross and Fraser may have reflected, to have an old-fashioned, melodramatic villain of the piece.

*

There was also merger activity and would-be activity close to home.[49] The trigger was the eventual sale of Martins Bank, at last under way by late 1967. The most likely purchasers were Lloyds and Barclays, especially once National Provincial had looked at the figures and concluded it would be too expensive an acquisition. That decision was reached by the second week of 1968, and a few days later, on 17 January, National Provincial's David Robarts suggested to his counterpart at Westminster, Duncan 'Golly' Stirling, that their two similar-sized banks should come together, thereby creating a bank that would be too big to be taken over by anyone else. Early on the 19th Stirling received a visit from John Thomson of Barclays, who suggested a Barclays/Westminster merger; but in the course of the day it became clear that the general preference at 41 Lothbury was to go with National Provincial, which – unlike a fusion with the appreciably bigger Barclays – would be a marriage of equals. Four days later, after telling Robarts and Stirling that he 'looked with favour on their idea', O'Brien discussed the proposal with the Treasury's Sir William Armstrong. His 'initial reaction was favourable' and he promised to 'do everything he can to clear the matter ministerially'. He was as good as his word, and Roy Jenkins told O'Brien on Thursday the 25th that 'he would not raise any objection'. The two banks publicly announced their intentions at a press conference late on Friday afternoon, after the Stock Exchange had closed and after Stirling had informed the other chairmen of the clearing banks – an announcement that apparently made them 'astonished and thoughtful'. Press reaction was generally positive, although the *FT* did report that, among other banks, the reaction was 'mainly surprise tinged with scepticism as to the likelihood of the move obtaining any useful results'.[50] Thus, without reference to the Monopolies Commission and with remarkably little fuss, the National Westminster Bank was created, though it would not begin operating as such until 1970. There had been talk of such a merger at regular intervals since the war, but it had only recently become practical politics. Inevitably some bankers at once asked themselves the obvious question: if the Big Five could, after half a century, so suddenly become the Big Four, might the new, more tolerant climate yet allow a Big Three?

Midland's Archie Forbes set the ball rolling on the 29th by calling on Harald Peake at Lloyds and suggesting some sort of link. This initiative received a dusty response, and two days later Peake called on Thomson and, in the context of their two banks being the only bidders for Martins, threw into the air the idea of a grand Lloyds/Barclays/Martins combine. The two men vigorously pursued the idea over the next week, though with varying degrees of enthusiasm from their respective senior managers, and with the help of O'Brien it had reached the stage by 5 February where Jenkins was explaining to Wilson that Barclays, already in negotiations with Martins, was now wanting 'to merge with and take over Lloyds as well'; if allowed this would give the new group control of some 48 per cent of joint-stock banking. The two politicians agreed that a reference must be made to the Monopolies Commission. The proposed merger was announced three days later and, according to the *FT*'s Gwinner, 'astonished the City'. Reaction was mixed. *The Times* welcomed the potential creation of 'a giant to meet the American challenge' and argued that there were 'tremendous advantages to be won in the international arena by being big', whereas the *Banker* took the line that the new combine 'would create a top-heavy banking structure without helping to remove the restrictions that have distorted bank competition in Britain hitherto'. What critics at the time suspected, but could not know, was that on both sides the motives were predominantly defensive, above all in relation to the perceived threat posed by Midland. Indeed, one of the more able and ambitious managers at Barclays, John Quinton, subsequently asserted that it was only *after* the intention was announced, with the Monopolies Commission requiring evidence, that Barclays tried 'to work out why they wanted to merge'.[51]

The Monopolies Commission considered a range of opinions over the next few months, including of course those from O'Brien. Economies of scale, the greater potential for modernisation, less over-banking, an enhanced size and therefore presence in international banking: he cogently put forward the positive arguments, but was unable to deny either that the creation of three large banks might well lead in time to a duopoly (that is, if NatWest took over Midland in order to combat the Barclays/Lloyds giant) or, still more damagingly, that (in the words of the eventual report) 'a duopoly situation would make nationalisation of the banking system easier to achieve and would bring that possibility nearer'. This latter admission occurred under questioning, but the Governor would hardly have been honest to have said otherwise. The Treasury also expressed concern about the possible duopolistic implications; as for Barclays and Lloyds themselves, their positive arguments were, in essence, little different from those put forward by O'Brien. Towards the end of the process it became clear to the Commission that Thomson and Peake were still keen, but that the senior management of Lloyds in particular was not. One of the Commission's members was the left-leaning Oxford economist Roger Opie, who at the beginning of July told Cairncross that 'the banks concerned made a very bad impression and the Governor had to retract at various points'. Soon afterwards it emerged that Opie and his colleagues had voted, by a majority of six to four, against a merger between Barclays and Lloyds, though without prejudice to either of those banks taking over Martins. The majority view was that the marginal benefits to the public interest resulting from a Barclays/Lloyds merger would be far outweighed by the damage, not least in terms of reducing the sources of finance for medium-sized and small businesses. The report was particularly scathing about the way in which 'the bankers, when questioned by us, made no satisfactory suggestions for measuring their own efficiency let alone for comparing it with that of their rivals'.[52] Coming so soon after the Aubrey Jones criticisms of the service provided by the banking system, this was another blow to an already dented public image.

A six-to-four majority fell short of the minimum two-thirds required, and so, as O'Brien informed the discount market on 11 July, 'the Bank merger was now in the lap of the Government'. By then he had already told Jenkins that although he 'remained on balance in favour of the merger', nevertheless he 'would not feel it necessary to go to the stake about it'. Soon afterwards the outbreak of the Gallaher affair proved a source of much distraction, though on the 17th the rather belated publication of the report did result in a joint Barclays/Lloyds/Martins press conference, held that afternoon at 54 Lombard Street. Most of the talking was done by Thomson, who stressed 'the international aspect' of the proposed merger. Via a network spread throughout the world he envisaged making 'a real contribution towards this country's standing', and he added, 'We welcome the American banks coming to London, but we also welcome the prospect of taking them on.' The next morning he, Peake and Sir Cuthbert Clegg of Martins went to see Jenkins and

Crosland, with O'Brien present. 'No new points were made,' Jenkins recorded, 'and we [i.e. he and Crosland] were still left with the conviction that a decision for or against the merger depends essentially on a judgement as to whether the economies and other advantages are likely to outweigh the damage to the public interest resulting from a reduction in the source of finance for important classes of borrower.' Thomson, a realist, was not sanguine – 'got a good hearing but did not come back optimistic', he privately noted after the meeting – and over the next few days he seems to have made some threatening noises to O'Brien about the possibility that Barclays might try to ignore any block on the merger, noises that stopped once it was made clear to him that any such unilateral action might well result in legislation removing important privileges from the banks.[53]

By the 22nd the key ministers had made up their minds, with Jenkins telling Wilson that he and Crosland agreed with the majority view of the Monopolies Commission. Three days later Crosland announced to the Commons the government's negative decision, and the next day Thomson (taking little comfort in the prospect of Barclays acquiring Martins) sent his mutual commiserations to Peake:

> There is a bit of a 'depression' here as we had so much looked forward to our two Banks working together.
> It was a deplorable decision and even if it had been correct it was arrived at by the wrong means. I am particularly sorry for the Governor, even if it might be said that he partly brought it down on his own head.

O'Brien himself, though, would have few regrets. 'Looking back over the years,' he wrote in retirement, 'I am sure the Monopolies Commission were right to call a halt to bank amalgamations at the point they did.'[54] Most of the City, with no instinctive love for the clearers, would have agreed at the time.

Some months later, in December 1968, the *Banker* noted that 'the vexed question of Lloyds' chairmanship' had finally been resolved, with the announcement that Eric Faulkner was going to leave Glyn Mills in order to take over Lloyds the following March. 'Vexed' was arguably an understatement, in that back in March 1967 the same journal had stated that Peake was to step down from the chairmanship in 1968 and be succeeded by Sir Reginald Verdon-Smith, a director of Lloyds since 1951. That succession, however, had been prevented by a public attack on Verdon-Smith by Anthony Wedgwood Benn, and so Peake stayed in rather ineffectual harness while another candidate was found. In fact, unlike either Peake or Verdon-Smith, Faulkner was a real banker; and when O'Brien told him in December 1968 that he thought Lloyds 'was in need of a shake up', the Chairman-designate 'entirely agreed about this', adding that he intended to become an executive chairman. It was not before time that Lloyds, after many rather stagnant years, prepared to start on the long road to recovery, in that in September 1969 the clearing banks at last succumbed to government-cum-Bank pressure and agreed to disclose their true profits and reserves. Publication of the figures began in February 1970, meaning that for the first time there was a reasonable degree of certainty about how the banks were doing relative to each other. The NatWest was by then a reality, and the *Banker* asked its Chairman, Robarts, about the bank's 'long-term objectives in world banking'. 'Size is not of itself important,' he replied. 'This was something that the dinosaurs never saw. If, from the successful conduct of our business, that is, providing the right services to our customers, we can grow to be the largest bank in the world, then I should be glad, not of being biggest but because I should regard it as the hallmark of success.'[55] The seasoned Robarts may not have been bewitched, but in the new world of global commercial banking there were plenty of others who were.

Most sectors of the City were touched by the merger mania. 'I remain convinced that most of the non-Clearing Bank financial units in this country – taking into account the much reduced purchasing power of sterling – are too small and many of them will be in danger of being forced into undesirable partnerships in order to face, say, American competition,' Bolton wrote to Cromer in February 1968, after Barings had declined BOLSA's offer to take a 20 per cent stake in it. Just over a year later Cromer told O'Brien that the partners of Barings had decided to form 'a charitable trust' (the Baring Foundation) in order 'to protect them from disrupting estate duty changes and to ensure the continuation of the firm'. O'Brien's note added that 'although Barings are aware that a number of eyes have been cast on them their present view is that it will be better for them not to link up with any other accepting house'.

A merchant banker with size firmly in his mind and still very much on the merger trail was Hill Samuel's Kenneth Keith, knighted in June 1969 after a rather grudging endorsement from O'Brien. That summer he even had serious discussions with Siegmund Warburg about uniting their two iconoclastic firms. Perhaps inevitably, several questions proved intractable. Would it be called 'Warburg-Hill Samuel & Co' or 'Hill-Warburg-Samuel & Co'? When would Grunfeld (to put it mildly, not on the same wavelength as Keith) retire? How could Warburgs' far lower salaries be reconciled with Hill Samuel's? And where was the common ground between Warburg's insistence on *haute banque* financial specialisation and Keith's wish to operate as broadly across the waterfront as possible? Typically undeterred by the failure of this intriguing might-have-been, Keith was still telling O'Brien in September that in his view 'there were too many merchant banks', to which the Governor cooly replied, 'that may be but the last wave of amalgamations had only just about been digested' and 'we ought now to have a period of consolidation before much further was done'. Keith did not let go, and the following February informed the *FT* that, as far as the merchant banking sector was concerned, 'natural forces are likely to bring about more mergers in the course of time'.[56]

In another sector, jobbing, where those 'natural forces' had already been at work since the mid-1950s, there had recently been the most momentous merger of all, with the creation in April 1968 of Wedd Durlacher, bringing together one of the two leading gilt-edged jobbers (Wedd Jefferson) and the dominant jobber in industrial equities (Durlacher Oldham Mordaunt Godson).[57] It was a union that could only have happened after the retirement of 'The Emperor', Esmond Durlacher, and the dominant figure in the new combined firm was Dick Wilkins from the Wedds side. There was an obvious complementarity behind the marriage, but arguably it was a pity that Durlachers did not remain a separate entity and start to compete against Wedds and Akroyds in the gilt market.

Between the different sectors, the barriers were still largely intact, notwithstanding some erosion in recent years. In the same conversation in September 1969 that he warned Keith against a new, premature round of amalgamations in the merchant banking sector, O'Brien went to some lengths to explain why he did not want to see the removal of those barriers. Hill Samuel had recently been approached by National Westminster, and although Keith was not keen on that particular possibility, he was anxious to ascertain the Governor's current views on the general question of associations. 'While Hill Samuel was expanding fast,' he explained, 'they have no pressing need for more money, although prospectively they might have.' O'Brien then treated his visitor to a set-piece:

> My own views were not based only on tradition. I continued to feel that too close an association between individual merchant banks and particular clearing banks was not in the best interests of the City. The merchant banks had always had the lion's share of the banking brain power in the City and they had been able to hold this position, if not without difficulty in recent years, due to their ability to offer not only work of the highest calibre but very attractive rewards for it. The former to a substantial extent depended upon the merchant banks being free to offer their services to all comers and to compete with each other on that basis. This situation would not endure if merchant banks became affiliated to particular clearing banks, who would naturally expect that their business should be given preference. Secondly, the clearing banks not unnaturally had a very different kind of organisation from the merchant banks. This did not throw up the kind of people who could suitably have an influential voice in merchant banking business. If over-close association resulted in merchant banking personnel being turned into organisation men of the clearing bank type there would be no gain that

I could see to offset the undoubted loss to the City. I would always welcome clearing bank management being galvanised by merchant banking brain power but I suspected the influence would tend to be all the other way.

O'Brien added that 'it was no secret that the Samuel Montagu/Midland Bank link-up did not have my approval and I should not be prepared to be equally accommodating to any future moves of that kind'. That was unambiguous enough and Keith did not press the point. O'Brien's strong negative may also have had implications as far as National Westminster was concerned, for in autumn 1969 (having scaled down National Provincial's involvement in the Rothschild-run European bank, now renamed Rothschild Intercontinental Bank) it announced that it was going it alone by converting County Bank, an old subsidiary of District, into the group's merchant bank. 'Though NatWest is to be congratulated on embarking on the biggest attempt by a clearing bank to challenge the merchant banks on their own ground so far,' the *Banker* commented, 'one can't help wondering whether it is really going about it in the right way.'[58]

Continuing deep-seated suspicions about breaking down traditional barriers were epitomised by attitudes at the Stock Exchange. Martin Wilkinson (knighted in the same list as Keith) was a reasonably forward-looking chairman, but in 1968 he was unable to push through the admission to the Exchange of an American brokerage firm, Hallgarten & Co, which had had a London office since 1912. The committee responsible for admissions decided that it must continue to debar members of overseas stock exchanges, on the explicit grounds that it was necessary to protect those brokers who 'could suffer very severely from the competition of the financially more powerful American firms'. The following year Wilkinson tried in another way to open up the Exchange, with the Council seeking to end the rule that restricted membership to British subjects; again he failed, defeated by a membership fearful of the prospect of large, well-capitalised American firms breaking into a hitherto ring-fenced market in which British firms bought and sold British securities on behalf of British clients. Whether inside or outside the Council, the capacity distinction remained sacrosanct – and certainly there was no welcome for someone like Michael Nightingale, who after a spell in New York observing American financial techniques had recently established in London his own firm, M.J.H. Nightingale & Co, which between the mid-1960s and mid-1970s was the only firm simultaneously combining the functions of issuing house, broker and jobber, enabling him to establish a pioneering market for investment in small UK companies outside the stock market.[59]

In the late 1960s, however, the burning question facing the Stock Exchange was the by now perennial one of how to introduce more capital into the jobbing system and thereby maintain its effectiveness in an investment world of increasingly one-way, institution-dominated markets. In April 1969 the Council considered a report from a special committee chaired by David LeRoy-Lewis of Akroyds on whether the answer was to allow firms to become limited liability companies and thereby attract capital from outside financial institutions. The report, broadly supportive of the concept, offered a useful checklist of how, in the City at large, the barriers were *starting* to break down:

(a) The Clearing Banks taking interests in Hire Purchase Companies and lately New Issue business.
(b) Merchant Banks diversifying by taking interests in Commodity Brokers, etc.
(c) The formation by Merchant Banks and some Insurance Companies of Unit Trusts and the link between these Trusts and Life Assurance Funds.
(d) Discount Houses taking interests in Firms doing Foreign Exchange business and Municipal Short Term Loan business.
(e) Insurance Brokers combining with Ship Brokers, Travel Agencies, etc.
(f) Pressure by Merchant Banks to become associated in some way with the Stock Exchange.
(g) Application by an American Broker to join the Stock Exchange.

Accordingly, 'if the integration of City Institutions is extended, encouraged by many of the same factors as prevail in Industry, the Committee consider that it is problematical how long the Stock Exchange will be able in isolation to command the position of strength which it now does'. Not everyone agreed that limited liability should be allowed, and soon the brokers H. & R. Wagner fired off a hostile letter to the Council, arguing that smaller brokers would be squeezed out and that it would lead to unhelpful revelations about profits and suchlike:

> A moment when we have made large profits in the last two years must be a bad time to divulge, as it would put a heavy weapon in the hands of those who wish to see reduced charges and do not understand – and will deliberately avoid understanding in order to make the point – the uncertain nature of our business, the unusual nature of the Stock Exchange experience of the last two years and the very high gearing element in our profit ratio.
>
> Other City Institutions, etc, have lost this privileged position. We should not throw it away . . .
>
> It seems to us that the sole reason for, and advantage of, the present proposal is to ease the financing of some firms and for this, the whole Exchange is asked to make long term sacrifices and open the doors to take-overs and loss of freedom and eventual prostitution of business.
>
> The financing may well be a relatively short term problem. Surely a better answer can be found from within the Stock Exchange itself.

The Council reasonably felt that no such answer had been found during two decades of recurrent diagnosis of the decline of the jobbing system, and from that summer non-members were permitted to take an equity stake in member firms on a limited liability basis. The maximum level, however, was set at 10 per cent; and when, in his *FT* interview not long afterwards, Keith publicly raised the question, 'We pay a lot of commission to the Stock Exchange; do we want to become members?', such a possibility, presumably involving majority shareholdings in member firms, remained purely hypothetical.[60]

*

'The lack of confidence arising from devaluation of the pound,' the annual report of the credit department at Barings noted gloomily at the end of 1967, 'is bound to be detrimental to international trade as a whole and to London in particular as a centre for commodity trading and for international financing.' It was, in its own terms, a justified pessimism. The Basle Agreement of July 1968 confirmed that sterling's days as a reserve currency were numbered, while the following month John Cooper of Schroders told Cairncross that that merchant bank was now advising its clients to invoice in dollars. 'I well understand the concern felt by you and others in the City at the withdrawal of authority to extend sterling credit for third country trade,' O'Brien wrote that autumn to Cromer, after his predecessor had apparently lodged a complaint; but the present Governor was adamant that, in the context of 'our present reserve and balance of payments position', there was no alternative. 'I must admit to some surprise,' O'Brien added, 'that you consider that the London houses would not be competitive if the financing of this third country trade was switched to a Euro-dollar basis.' O'Brien could afford to be sanguine, for that same year the Committee on Invisible Exports (of which the former journalist William Clarke was Director-General) demonstrated not only that even before devaluation the City had been reducing its dependence on sterling and increasingly using Eurodollar financing, but that the shift had done nothing to impair the City's major contribution to Britain's invisible earnings. Put simply, the City's international functions – in insurance, in brokerage, in banking, in merchanting – did *not* depend fundamentally on the strength or otherwise of sterling. By 1970 only 20 per cent of international trade was denominated in sterling, compared to 50 per cent in the 1950s, yet as an international financial centre the City had almost immeasurably advanced.[61]

The late 1960s represented a time of increasingly chronic financial instability: British devaluation in November 1967, the gold drama in March 1968, an acute Franco-German financial crisis in November 1968, French devaluation in August 1969, German revaluation in October 1969, and throughout it all the Bretton Woods system struggling to stay intact, as the dollar started to buckle under the strain of paying for the Vietnam War and the Great Society. The pervasive instability both increased the volume and accelerated the pace of short-term capital flows all round the world, mainly taking the form of Eurodollars, and in varying degrees national governments began to feel that their economic sovereignty was under threat.[62] For those directing the flows it could be an exhilarating, if sometimes unnerving, experience. 'Stability, a product of the Pax Britannica, no longer exists and the world of the future will be the oyster of the risk-taker,' Bolton pronounced in June 1969 – suitably enough in the first issue of a magazine, *Euromoney*, devoted to tracking the activities of such risk-takers, at a time when the *FT*'s coverage of the Euromarkets was still threadbare. Just as earlier in the decade, London-based practitioners in the new markets continued to be helped by policy decisions elsewhere. Most important was President Johnson's final attempt, announced at the start of 1968, to reduce the US balance-of-payments deficit. The aim was specifically to encourage US multinationals to borrow overseas rather than at home, and it had an immediate impact in driving many leading corporations into the welcoming arms of the Eurobond market. Then, in France four months later, the events of May not only reduced international confidence in Paris as a place for doing business, but put the French foreign exchange reserves under such pressure that, through a series of restrictions, the internationally minded banks there lost much of their freedom of manoeuvre. In addition Switzerland, which had already passed up the opportunity for running the primary market in Eurobonds, now squandered the chance to dominate the secondary market, through the refusal of its authorities to exempt Eurobond trading from stamp tax. In consequence, around the end of the decade White Weld moved its centre of gravity from Zurich to London, where the firm's tax adviser helpfully discovered a nineteenth-century exemption that levied tax on office overheads, not trading turnover, in the case of revenues arising from transactions where both counter-parties were non-resident in the UK. The Inland Revenue's consent was necessary, and by a happy coincidence the tax consultant's father was a retired Revenue official who had been the supervisor of the official dealing with the case.[63]

It was an unmistakable sign that London was moving towards a dollar standard when in May 1968 the Bank of England allowed most of the discount houses (except those with foreign exchange broking subsidiaries) to deal as principals in bills of exchange in currencies other than sterling. As far as the Eurodollar market itself was concerned, growth continued to be phenomenal: having been around $1,000m in 1960, $3,000m in 1961 and $10,000m in 1965, its estimated size in 1968 was $25,000m and in 1970 no less than $46,000m. London branches of US banks were by the late 1960s the utterly dominant force in the market, sending huge quantities of Eurodollars to their head offices (as much as $3bn in three weeks in June 1969), as well as relending to companies (mainly US subsidiaries) and relending inter-bank for liquidity purposes. Overall, the *Banker* estimated in August 1969, 'it would seem reasonable to assume that at present some 80 per cent of the Euro-dollar pool has been borrowed through London'.

The City's new, so-called parallel money markets in sterling also continued their irresistible rise, above all the inter-bank market in sterling deposits, attaining a size by the end of 1969 of around £2,000m – well above the total assets of the traditional discount houses. Mainly used by non-clearing banks to adjust their liquidity from day to day, it remained a market for those with strong nerves, given the preponderance of very short-term deposits and the volatility of interest rates. There was also, starting in October 1968, a market in sterling certificates of deposit to complement the one in dollar CDs that had begun two years earlier. There was some disquiet before it began, mainly on the part of discount houses unhappy about financing CDs 'largely or entirely by direct unsecured borrowing from the Interbank Market', as they explained to the Bank of England; but by autumn 1969 the sterling CD market had grown to a size of some £400m, as measured by total value of certificates outstanding. The dollar CD market was also growing, and neither could have done so without other discount houses adopting a more positive attitude and in effect providing a secondary market. Allen, Harvey & Ross and Gerrards were among those houses, as at last the penny dropped that the new money markets were where much of the potential for future growth lay.[64]

The growth of the inter-bank market had a particular significance in City history because of the way in which it encouraged fringe (or so-called secondary) banks to use its resources in order to take on many profitable lending commitments that the clearing banks, because of the credit ceilings applied to them, were unable to do. By 1970 almost ninety of these largely non-deposit banks were competing aggressively for funds in the wholesale banking market with little supervision.[65] The well-informed academic observer Jack Revell noted as early as September 1968 that 'any attempt to control the operations of these secondary banks by the imposition of liquidity controls or by requiring deposits with the Bank of England' would be 'very difficult'. The people running these banks varied greatly. Burston and Texas Commerce Bank, for example, involved a substantial minority stake by an American bank, but still in charge was Neville Burston, who back in 1955, at the age of only twenty-six, had established his own merchant banking business, N. Burston & Co, the first new bank to be recognised by the Bank of England since the war. He was a well-connected and, with good reason, well-trusted figure, and the

Texan involvement pushed him particularly towards Eurodollar loans. By contrast, the barrister and judo expert Gerald Caplan, who in 1961 acquired the financial company London and County and rapidly expanded its banking services (in the form of London and County Securities), ran his boardroom in a way that would later be scathingly described by Department of Trade Inspectors as 'like the court of a medieval king'. London and County Securities was floated in May 1969 (brokers: Schaverien, Habermann, Simon & Co) and, despite the prevailing gloom in the stock market, received a warm reception.[66]

Percy ('Pat') Matthews, the kingpin at First National Finance Corporation, would like to have been thought of as nearer to Burston than Caplan. 'Like most men who amass a fortune in quick time, Pat Matthews was for some time regarded with suspicion in the banking world,' Parsons at the Bank informed the Treasury in October 1968 about this entirely self-made man (and President of Aston Villa FC), who had come to the City only in his mid-thirties. 'He now seems to have lived that down and he certainly enjoys the wholehearted support of Hambros who speak very highly of him.' His first fortune was made in hire purchase, while at First National, effectively his own creation, he launched in 1969 a £29m takeover bid for one of the main hire-purchase concerns, Bowmaker. The move aroused considerable hostility, especially once Bowmaker's Chairman claimed that Matthews was going back on his word by bidding; in the event, as one journalist nicely put it, 'Bowmaker flopped into the arms of a favoured suitor, the equally established City company, C.T. Bowring.' For Matthews, it was a salutary episode. 'Once I knew what the City was about,' he reflected, 'I wanted to be part of it, not outside. I don't like being a maverick.'[67]

Within the Euromarkets the late 1960s saw the filling of the gap between the short and long ends, represented respectively by the Eurodollar and Eurobond markets. The origins of the syndicated loan market, primarily for medium-term Eurocurrency (mainly Eurodollar) loans, are not well documented, but by 1969 it had taken off, raising that year some $300–400m.[68] The syndicated nature of the loans permitted much larger sums to be lent than would have been possible by banks acting on their own, and it was a technique that encouraged the fairly rapid growth of consortium banks, following the pioneering example of Midland and International Banks (MAIBL) in 1964. By the end of the decade there were a dozen or so of these multinational banks (or 'Euro-currency consortia' as they were sometimes called), mainly based in London.[69] The Euromarkets were also enhanced by the creation of the floating rate note (FRN) issue, encouraging greater seamlessness between the syndicated loan market and the bond market. According to some authorities, it made its début in May 1969 with a $14.7m Dreyfus

Offshore Trust issue lead-managed by Kuhn Loeb; but generally the invention is attributed to a young American banker, Evan Galbraith of Bankers Trust in London, who came up with the idea early in 1970 and, after unsuccessfully trying several other banks, received the enthusiastic support of Warburgs. Sir Siegmund himself found an appropriate borrower, the Italian electricity authority ENEL, and early that summer Warburgs, Bankers Trust and White Weld successfully lead-managed a $125m issue. It would become part of Euromarket apocrypha that Galbraith had had the brainwave while taking a bath at home in Pelham Crescent; but what was undeniable was that, although it took some time for FRNs to catch on widely, their ultimate importance in the market would be huge.[70]

In the Eurobond market proper there was no shortage of excitement in what were still essentially pioneering days – 1968 was a particularly momentous year, with issues totalling the equivalent of $3,130m, way above the previous record set in 1967 of $1,916m. Over half the money raised in 1968 was in the form of convertibles for industrial and financial companies, most of them US corporations (no fewer than seventy in the course of the year) in the wake of LBJ's renewed encouragement to look abroad for funds. The mechanism of the market almost seized up under the strain, as a log-jam of delayed, mishandled and even lost Eurobond deliveries built up in back offices; eventually Morgan Guaranty took a very necessary initiative by establishing in December a combined depository, clearing and settlement system, Euro-clear, based in Brussels. London would have been a more obvious venue, but indecision on the part of the clearing banks and Accepting Houses Committee meant that this lucrative opportunity was lost. There was plenty of work for Euro-clear in 1969, and that June, in *Euromoney*'s first issue, Nicholas Faith noted 'how well the market has survived the past few feverish months in the Eurocurrency markets', primarily the Eurodollar market. He went on:

> In part, this is because it [i.e. the Eurobond market] is such a pure, unregulated market. Like a healthy, growing child, it stuffs itself for some time with whatever goodies take its fancy, refuses to listen to warnings that it will get indigestion, gets it, lies low for a few months, then gets hungry again. And this rhythm is not affected by outside events like balance-of-payments crisis, or student noises . . .[71]

One of the heaviest buyers of almost all Eurobond issues during these bubble years of 1968–9 was Bernie Cornfeld's celebrated but soon-to-be-notorious ('Do you sincerely want to be rich?') Investors Overseas Services (IOS), not London-based but reputed by summer 1969 to be spending £1m on the furnishings alone of the large house it had recently acquired in the West End. One of the keenest City supporters of Cornfeld and his rackety empire of international mutual funds had been Hambros, but when it came to the holding company of IOS going public in September with a $110m issue, Hambros refused to underwrite, as equally wisely did Warburgs and Rothschilds. By the following spring IOS was in irretrievable trouble, but its fall and eventual demise did not significantly damage the Eurobond market.[72]

Within the market, the league table for 1968 and the first half of 1969, in terms of managers or co-managers of internationally syndicated issues, revealed a top three of Deutsche, White Weld and Warburgs, with Rothschilds lying in sixth position and no other London merchant bank in sight. In particular, *Euromoney* commented, 'Hill Samuel and Schroder Wagg, the two biggest new issue houses in the London market, are not present.' The top position enjoyed by Deutsche owed much to the deliberate policy at this time of the West German government of encouraging the export of capital through the issue to foreign borrowers of DM-denominated bonds, which meant that in 1969 such bonds were almost as numerous in the market as dollar-denominated ones.[73] Moreover, like other big German and Swiss banks, Deutsche had considerable placing power, something the London merchant banks lacked, and it was already becoming apparent that ultimately the contest in the Eurobond primary market lay between the continental behemoths on the one hand and the more dynamic American investment banks on the other.

From whatever provenance, however, there was no doubt that the lead managers, co-managers and underwriters enjoyed a social cachet denied to the traders in the still rather struggling Eurobond secondary market. 'I lunch with Paul Sherwood of Strauss Turnbull, Stanley Ross of Kidder Peabody Securities, Walter Imthurn of Weedon and Richard Weguelin of Eurotrading,' Ian Kerr wrote in a playful retrospective diary entry that nicely captured the flavour of the times – in this case June 1969 in the George and Vulture:

> We are all cock-a-hoop about the success of the first bond dealers' meeting held at the Great Eastern Hotel in April [resulting in the formation of the Association of International Bond Dealers]. Maybe some of these snooty gilt-edged types will take us seriously now. They never have before. If they mention Eurobonds it's to call us 'the Mickey Mouse market'. I can see that the gilt boys still think we are a bunch of cowboys when a Wedd partner wearing the customary old Etonian tie passes our table and slips a grilled tomato into Stanley's suit pocket. It is a new beige number which will not mingle well with tomato . . .

Ross himself, later described by Paul Ferris as 'a tall stylish man with a taste for dark glasses and champagne and money', had left Strauss Turnbull in 1967 and was in the process of building up, from scratch, the London-based Kidder Peabody Securities.[74] This he did with much relish and self-publicising, but also an undisputed integrity, and in the process started to give respectability as well as some muscle to the secondary market.

By the end of the 1960s the City had once more become a truly cosmopolitan centre of finance, as it had been before the catastrophe of 1914. The figures said almost everything: in 1960 there were 77 foreign banks (14 of them American) with branches in London; by 1970 there were 159 (of which 37 were American). It was an emblematic moment when, in 1968, Bankers Trust moved the head office of its international department from New York to London. That year no fewer than eight US banks (including City National Bank of Detroit, First Wisconsin National Bank and Mellon National Bank) opened branches or representative offices in the City, followed in 1969 by another eight (including Crocker-Citizens, the Detroit Bank & Trust Co and Franklin National). The list of names in the *Banker's* annual survey of 'Foreign Banks in London' did not, alas, include the Last National Bank of Boot Hill. 'The Moorgate Saga' began in *Euromoney's* first issue, featured Herbie as the bank's London representative and was the creation of Christopher Fildes, the financial journalist who over the next three decades would follow most closely the domestic habits of the City and its inhabitants:

DEAR MOM
    Well, here we are in our London office, in the heart of the historic city, and only the eighty-seventh American bank to arrive! Your son feels very proud. We have a glass front door, and a shingle, and an experienced foreign exchange dealer, and a little girl to work the PX. Also we have an address on Moorgate, which is so important. I can see Moorgate from the bathroom window, but our front door is round the corner in Hangmans Alley. It's still awful expensive. Tomorrow we have a party to launch ourselves, and then another for the press guys, and then – the world will beat a pathway to our door.

DEAR MOM
    We had the parties, and I think they went well, there seem to be no ice-boxes in this country, and some of the press guys drank the gin as though it was warm and said something about a meeting in the Plough. But the City executives were kind, and said 'Anything I can do for you, old boy?' and 'Boot Hill – good for tombstones, eh?', and stayed on quite late, and from the bathroom window I saw one of them jump out at a 76 bus and hold it up like the Wells Fargo stage . . .[75]

Among the American banks, the most sizeable operation was that undertaken by Citicorp (in other words First National City Bank of New York, or Citibank). Running the bank from New York was Walter Wriston, who in the early 1960s had pioneered negotiable CDs, was a passionate believer in the free mobility of capital and later coined the oft-quoted axiom, 'countries do not go bust'. By 1969 Citicorp employed almost 700 people in London, where on 27–8 May all thirty-five directors assembled for the first overseas board meeting in the bank's 156-year history. Citicorp was also, to the consternation of British clearers, starting to compete hard in the UK corporate loan market.[76] The next biggest US operation was that of Chase Manhattan (about 400 staff in London), followed by Morgan Guaranty (about 325), where the Eurodollar book was the responsibility of the very able Dennis Weatherstone, the son of a London Transport worker who would move to New York in 1971 and eventually become Chairman of J.P. Morgan – a rise, it was often remarked, that would not have been possible in the more class-conscious City.[77] As for White Weld, at the cutting-edge of the Eurobond market (both primary and secondary), the presiding force behind its European operations was still Bob Genillard, who at the inaugural meeting of the Association of International Bond Dealers took pride in how that market had 'offered a vivid demonstration of the capacity of the international private sector to organise, on a complex and multi-national basis, the raising of substantial amounts of capital, both for private and public needs'; he argued that it would be 'in the interests of governments to encourage a gradually increasing overlap of the Eurobond market with their national markets'. Railing against what he called 'financial nationalism', he concluded that 'surely the future of the Western world in an era of constantly growing economic inter-dependence and instant communications lies in accepting multi-national finance and the development of a truly European and Atlantic financial community'. Genillard was not just a visionary. 'He drove people hard,' Stanislas Yassukovich remembered, 'and maybe at times was a little insensitive to their own preoccupations or ambitions. But he certainly produced the results.' He did, and in 1969 he, Yassukovich and two other White Weld partners succeeded in buying out, from the New York parent firm, the European office network. Yassukovich himself had been running the London office since 1967 and was an energetic, articulate, clear-sighted banker who would emerge as one of the major City figures. He would also, unlike many of the American incomers, become fully immersed in the English way of life, with a partiality for hunting, fishing and polo.[78]

Inevitably, there was some indigenous hostility towards the 'Avenue of the Americas', as Moorgate was becoming dubbed. 'The behaviour of the American banks in the Euro-dollar market was causing considerable antagonism,' Bolton told Parsons over the telephone in February 1969. 'Rates had already reached 8½% and a number of worth-while propositions were being ruined as a result.' Later that year, in the *Banker*, 'a general manager of a leading clearing bank' itemised the objections to the American invasion: pushing up City rents, high enough even before; 'touting of business'; 'poaching of staff'; and 'syphoning away Euro-dollars', with the effect of artificially increasing Eurodollar rates. The anonymous British banker, however, was inclined to discount these grumbles. 'Over many years the market dominance of the Big Five clearing banks led to a complacency which has now been rudely shattered by this new development,' he argued in relation to the hard-sell approach that apparently came as second nature to the American bankers. 'The days of waiting for customers or potential customers to come to the bank for help are over: increasingly the need is seen to approach the customer, telling him what services are now available . . .' More generally, he could not deny that the American banks in London had been 'the source of many new ideas later adopted by British banks', and he cited their pioneering of 'personal loans, negotiable certificates of deposit, special savings accounts, and the introduction of lending rates geared to the cost of money rather than to Bank rate, as well as the concept of the roll-over loan'. In sum, 'it ill becomes the City, with its reputation for financial flexibility, to complain about competition'.[79]

The following year, in *Euromoney*, Daniel P. Davison (in charge of Morgan Guaranty's London office) put forward 'One American's View of the City'. Recalling that back in the mid-1950s his bank had been so unenthused by London's prospects that it had allowed its lease fronting on Lombard Street to lapse, he stressed that the City's subsequent revival was not solely the result of business being driven out of Wall Street and of its own fortuitous geography and language. 'The absence of local capital requirements', 'generous and flexible tax treatment', the Bank of England's 'minimal' regulation of non-sterling business, 'the pool of skilled bankers available for hire', Britain's 'political stability' – all had played their part. What would happen if the US eventually mastered its balance-of-payments problems and lifted the financial controls of the 1960s? Davison was broadly sanguine:

> London's sole eminence may be somewhat diminished by renewed competition from Wall Street but the City will have a future. For one thing, success has made London a banking bazaar unrivalled in history. The Moscow Narodny Bank, whether it is appropriate Bolshevik doctrine or not, sits almost cheek by jowl with the Bank of China, and rubs elbows with the capitalist banking institutions of the West. There are about three times the number of American commercial banks in the City as there are in New York, our principal financial centre . . . The City of London beats Baghdad as a bazaar by a country mile . . .

In short, the American friend concluded presciently with almost British-style understatement, 'it is too convenient a place to do business to be ignored'.[80]

*

For many years the fortunes of the Euromarkets barely impinged upon the collective consciousness of the Stock Exchange. 'What have been the main special factors in the 1969 collapse?' Rowe & Pitman's James D'Albiac asked in August that year after several months of tumbling equity prices. His answer rather suggested that, as a Labour Chancellor, Jenkins was in a no-win situation as far as the City was concerned: 'Pride of place must go to the Government – for its failure to operate a successful credit squeeze last year and its unprecedented success in 1969.' However, the rest of the year saw the market's decline being checked, and in his January 1970 assessment of prospects D'Albiac was positively optimistic: 'We're all bullish now because the worst of the squeeze is over; because the balance of payments, sterling and the gilt-edged market are all improving; because far from needing deflation there is room in the economy for reflation – which, with an Election in the offing, it will no doubt get . . .' He did, however, sound a salutary warning to the more speculative: 'We must forget Poseidon: most of us missed it, and it is dangerously late to try to repair the damage.'[81]

Poseidon, though, was not so easy to forget, for there had been few (if any) more memorable gambles on the post-war stock market.[82] The fun had begun the previous September when, exploring near Mount Windarra, Poseidon (an Australian mining company) discovered nickel. The news of the find reached the market on the 29th, causing Poseidon's share price to jump from 20s 9d to 59s 6d. Within days the shares had leaped even more sensationally to £11; after three feverish months they reached £94; and in February 1970 they hit their peak of £124. 'Very exciting times,' Geoffrey Lederman of Smith Bros, one of the jobbing firms that did particularly well out of the Poseidon boom, recalled. 'It was only a question of how much better they opened up in the morning. Every day it was £3 higher, £5 higher . . .' Nor, being an Australian boom, was the London action solely during daytime, for some jobbers even circulated the home telephone number of the dealer who would be available until the small hours. For one youngish private client broker, Nicholas Goodison, the boom in Poseidon and other similar Australian mining ventures left a particularly strong impression:

> There was a tremendous backlog of settlement, because a lot of these Australian companies carried out their registration in huts in the desert, and you couldn't get your transfer registered. So there was a tremendous backlog, and a huge financial liability, arising out of that backlog. People were buying and selling, and rebuying securities again and again, during the Stock Exchange [fortnightly] accounts, to defer paying for the shares. There were potential huge losses when the Australian market collapsed, because

buyers could not afford to pay for their stock when it was delivered, at the old price . . .[83]

Collapse the market did, and by the time the Poseidon mine eventually came into production, more than four years later, the price of nickel had slumped and Poseidon's shares were almost worthless.

Before, during and after the Poseidon boom the Bank of England found itself for the first time in its history the specific subject of a formal parliamentary investigation.[84] The Select Committee on Nationalised Industries, under the vigorous chairmanship of the left-wing Labour MP Ian Mikardo, had long been itching to scrutinise the Bank, but had been staved off by Callaghan. The change of chancellorship in November 1967 belatedly gave Mikardo his wish. 'I'm not against an inquiry because I've discovered that the Bank of England is a closed book to us all,' Jenkins observed to a colleague in February 1968. 'We don't know nearly enough of what's going on because they don't let us into their secrets.' The prospect of a potentially wide-ranging inquiry displeased O'Brien considerably, and for much of that year he fought a rearguard action. 'I still hoped that this cup might pass from me,' he told Jenkins in July about the possibility of having to give evidence himself. 'I would not be prepared to forgo the protection of the Bank Act 1946 nor would I be willing to answer questions on matters of policy, real or hypothetical. This would narrow the field of examination in a way likely to exasperate the Committee and result in trouble for us all.' In the face of this forecast-cum-threat, Jenkins stayed calm, saying simply, 'we had better cross that stile when we came to it'. Three months later O'Brien raised the stakes, telling the Treasury that 'if it were accepted that he had to appear before the Committee, the Chancellor might well rue the day'. Jenkins at last yielded, to the extent of ensuring that the Committee's brief should exclude all 'policy' matters and be essentially an inquiry into how the Bank operated as an institution. 'He said that he was proposing to take a firm stand against Mr Mikardo,' O'Brien noted at the start of 1969 after a reassuring conversation with Jenkins. 'This might lead to some trouble in the House and a short, although maybe acrimonious, debate; nevertheless he had little doubt that the Government would win the day.'[85] There were indeed backbench protests, but these were duly overridden, and in April the Select Committee (with a Tory MP, Colonel C.G. Lancaster, in the chair, but Mikardo almost ever-present) began questioning witnesses.

Between then and March 1970 O'Brien made no fewer than nine appearances, at one point revealing for the first time the Governor's annual salary (£25,000). From the outset he stressed the paramount need to retain the Bank's operational independence, especially if it was to be able to continue to give worthwhile advice to the government of the day.

'The Bank has a large foot always in the official government camp, but not the whole of its being,' he explained on the first of his long afternoons:

> As a corporate entity it is independent, self-governing, not under the control of any Minister. People sometimes think that because of this the Bank is an unwilling executant of government policy. This is entirely without foundation. The value of the Bank's independence as an entity is that it enables it to form an entirely independent view of matters coming within its sphere, a view influenced by the market conditions in which it lives and within which of course government departments do not live . . . It has then an aspect which is not wholly of government, but which is of course devoted to the execution of government policy when that policy has been decided and after it has contributed its own view to the formulation of that policy.

O'Brien later wrote that during the almost year-long proceedings Mikardo had been 'intelligent and perceptive besides being most courteous at all times', but to read the evidence is to receive a clear impression of the Poplar MP doing his best on several occasions to needle the Governor. There was a particularly tart exchange after O'Brien had sought to justify the Bank's non-publication of accounts on the grounds that this at times enabled it discreetly to ensure the stability of the banking system:

> It helps you to do good by stealth, in other words? – Yes, indeed.
>
> But does that not also have the corollary that it helps you to drop clangers by stealth, to make mistakes by stealth, or, to put it another way, this facility of doing good by stealth creates as a corollary a situation in which whatever mistakes and however large they may be the Bank makes, there is no way in which they are ever publicly revealed? – Yes, that is so, but dropping clangers is not a thing which the Bank goes in for.

Overall, though, the tone of the sessions was constructive rather than otherwise, and in October another Labour MP, Russell Kerr, engaged O'Brien in a particularly interesting moment of dialogue:

> You [i.e. the Bank] are a very influential body which, unquestionably, is impregnated with a particular philosophy – it does not happen to be my philosophy, but that is no skin off our noses or your nose. Do not you see certain dangers in a democratic sense, in that however wisely you exercise your power, you are a body of influence and, therefore, of power which is irresponsible in the political sense? – . . . Of course we are influenced by the ethos of central banking in general. We believe in the paramount importance of maintaining the value of money, whereas other people might believe that inflation is something which brings other benefits. We would recognise that, but I contend that you need people nowadays who believe in the importance of money and even though you may have different opinions, you should not object to the fact that there is a very influential body which has different opinions which are having their weight, because I think that counter-balance, democratically, is very good.

O'Brien was of course not the only witness, and others included Cyril Kleinwort on behalf of the Accepting Houses Committee. An unwise reference to the accepting houses' 'very close understanding of the position and the difficulties under which the Governor works' earned him the Mikardo treatment, though he did not buckle:

> It does not sound to me as though he is conscious of working under any difficulties. It was a very able, confident, self-assured gentleman that we have had before us on many occasions. I did not think that he was in a neurotic state worrying about his difficulties. Why are you worrying on his behalf when he ain't worrying on his own behalf? – Because there are many restrictions of which of course you are aware which are not in the interests of the banking world generally and it is the duty of the Bank to impose those restrictions. This is never a very popular pastime.[86]

The final, disappointingly bland witness was Jenkins, on 18 March 1970, but he would not have been disappointed that the early controversy about the inquiry had gently subsided.

It was only a few weeks earlier that one of his Cabinet colleagues, Benn, had been to Threadneedle Street to lunch with O'Brien:

> I have never been to the Bank of England before and one really did have to go through about five great iron gates as if one were entering a prison. We then went up to the most beautiful dining room. He is a nice man, very agreeable but totally out of touch because he has worked for the Bank all his life and doesn't understand the attacks on him from outside . . . He said the usual stupid things about trade unions and wished the shareholders would play a larger part in companies. He lives in a dream world. It occurred to me with a great sort of flash of lightning that this is what is wrong with the City: the people in it don't make any effort to broaden their interests.

There were no such Bennite illuminations in the Select Committee's eminently sober report that was published in late May. Essentially it recommended that the Bank should behave more like other nationalised industries, with the publication each year of a full set of accounts. This less-than-momentous proposal was duly implemented, presumably to the dismay of Bolton, who in a broadside against the Select Committee published in the *Banker* soon after the report declared that 'the positive mania for information reveals the desire to interfere and to direct operations in markets that take a life-time to understand'. It was, he went on, 'quite impossible to suggest that the efficiency of the Bank of England can be judged by a profit and loss account' – rather, 'it can only be judged by the respect with which the Bank is held by the public, both at home and abroad'; according to Bolton, 'on the whole it commands a very wide measure of respect in practically every country in the world'. In fact, 'the general type of men and women who become Members of Parliament appear to know little about the historical background of Britain nor the position of the Bank of England in the world with its awesome responsibilities'; and it was high time that those MPs 'realised the weakness of the financial system of the Western world' and allowed central bankers to go about their business of protecting that system without being distracted by the self-indulgent impertinence of 'relentless cross-examination'.[87]

The Select Committee's was not the only inquiry in town. 'Lord Cromer came in,' O'Brien noted in October 1968, not all that long after it had conclusively emerged that Lloyd's insurance market had made a thumping loss (£38m) in 1965:

> He said that he had been approached by Mr Hogg, presumably of Hogg Robinson & Capel-Cure, one of the chief Lloyd's insurance brokers, about a proposal that a committee should be formed to examine the whole Lloyd's set-up, which at the moment seemed to be in rather a bad way. Mr Hogg wanted Lord Cromer to become chairman of this committee. This idea did not particularly smile on Lord Cromer, who was nevertheless prepared to take on the work if it had the backing of the chairman of Lloyd's.

O'Brien promised to sound out Ralph Hiscox, Chairman of Lloyd's, and he did so the next day:

> He [Hiscox] said that Mr Hogg had badly beaten the gun. It was true that a committee of Lloyd's had been considering for some time the possibility of an independent enquiry into certain aspects of their affairs. It had now been decided that this enquiry should be undertaken by a small sub-committee of selected members of Lloyd's, headed by an independent chairman. They had first asked Lord Poole to undertake this job but he could not do so. Instead, he [i.e. Poole presumably] offered a number of other names: the first four were Lord Cromer, Lord Shawcross, Sir Giles Guthrie, and Sir Duncan Oppenheim. Mr Hiscox had been on the point of approaching Lord Cromer. I encouraged him to do so, saying that I felt Lord Cromer could be persuaded to take on this job, which I thought was well worth doing.[88]

Soon afterwards the announcement was made that Cromer would head an inquiry, and over the next year or so his committee examined the weaknesses in the market's capital base (and thus capacity) and made various recommendations that were largely accepted: most importantly, Names would have the minimum 'show of wealth' required of them reduced from £75,000 to £50,000 (£100,000 to £75,000 in the case of foreigners), with in addition a system of 'mini-Names' introduced, each requiring demonstrable wealth of only £37,500 for the privilege of participating in a smaller number of underwriting syndicates than full Names did.[89] These proposals meant that over the next decade the quantity as well as the profile of Names attracted to Lloyd's would change dramatically. Yet ironically there was in retrospect no great need to have lowered the barriers to market entry in this way, given that from 1969 Lloyd's was entering a seven-year period of considerable prosperity.

The fatefulness of the decision was compounded by the rejection by Lloyd's of Cromer's proposal that, for the first time, companies (that is, outside the market) should become eligible for membership of syndicates. Lloyd's also chose to ignore Cromer's typically emphatic insistence that the institution needed to get its own house in order – above all the arrogant, potentially corrupt way in which the Names were treated by many of the managing agents in charge of the syndicates. Cromer also warned against conflicts of interest facing brokers who were involved in managing agencies and urged that there be a more adequate fund to protect Names against future losses. These recommendations, about the internal running of Lloyd's, were *not* included in the bastardised version of his December 1969 report that eventually became public in April 1970 – and it was not only the great unwashed who were not allowed to read the eighty-page real thing, but even the Names themselves. Nevertheless, full version or no, there was one fact about which everyone – from City grandee downwards – was still ignorant: while Cromer's working party was deliberating, a dying American called Clarence Borel, who for many years had fitted asbestos insulation in buildings all over the country, had gone to a small-town lawyer in Beaumont, Texas, and asked for help.[90] Lloyd's of London had been reinsuring the liability insurance for American asbestos companies since the 1930s. It was quite a moment to start opening up the market.

On 30 April 1970, just over a fortnight after the 'publication' of Cromer's report and the day before his firm was involved in the first placing of a stock (Imperial Tobacco) with a decimal coupon, a pillar of the old City departed. Sir Antony Hornby marked his retirement as senior partner of Cazenove's with a final series of maxims and thoughts for future generations at 12 Tokenhouse Yard:

> Our business has really been built up on trust and confidence. We are known for being able to keep secrets *absolutely* and *never* taking advantage of information given in confidence . . .
>
> One cannot do all the business. Let us try and do most of the best.
>
> One must be generous as well as competitive. One cannot prosper at other people's expense. One's friends and even competitors must be allowed to prosper as well.
>
> Never ask for or think of commission when tackling a business. The main thing is the business should be worthwhile doing. Sometimes one gets overpaid, sometimes underpaid – generally the former. It is harder to say 'No' than 'Yes' and very important to learn how to do so. Cazenove's should be hard to get and not available to all-comers. We must be careful to retain the 'style' of Cazenove's and the type of business that we do . . .
>
> Naturally one cannot just freewheel along on 'trust' alone. It is very

necessary now to know the answers . . . I really think we are now pretty efficient without being professionally qualified. I would class us as high-class amateurs amongst whom are one or two who might play for England. . .

We all enjoy ourselves. One must be happy above all things. One spends all one's life more or less in the office. It must be FUN.

It was not perhaps such unalloyed fun by this time at Barings, the house to which for half a century Cazenove's had always felt the closest tug of loyalty. There, the new world was beginning to seem positively threatening. 'We are beginning to lose customers to other Banks,' a manager, Graham Gilchrist, noted in March 1970, adding that 'we are also aware that many of our customers are being actively canvassed by other Merchant Banks'. Two months later, in another memo, he asked a series of hard, barely palatable questions: 'Do we really look after our customers? Are we thinking up our share of the new ideas floating around? Are we using our assets in staff and capital to the best advantage? In other words do we know the best way to achieve our aims?'[91] The unspoken assumption was that the answer was a fourfold 'no', and in fact at about this time or shortly afterwards a new executive committee was established with the aim of creating a more structured organisation, in effect splitting the bank into various profit centres. Gilchrist's disenchantment, however, ran deep, and it was not long before he left Barings to go to Union Discount, where he would rise to become senior Managing Director.

It was a measure of the changing mood among the City's old guard that there was even some envy at Barings in spring 1970 when that most aggressive and 'new' of merchant banks, Hill Samuel, was the subject of a full-length profile in *Management Today*, a recently established magazine whose very title was unsympathetic to the ways of the old City. Somewhat perversely, however, the author (Tom Lester) seemed to want to have it both ways:

> Merchant bankers, long the City's princes, have trodden the path taken by Royalty everywhere in recent years. Divested of their former trappings, they are seen to be merely human after all; and the world is disappointed. Despite the professionalism and vigour which Hill Samuel, far more than most, has brought into the genteel world of merchant banking, its new identity somehow lacks the charisma of the old world. The princes of finance and commerce now belong to a profit-conscious service business . . . Hill Samuel's modern offices in Wood Street, near St Paul's, are as anonymous as a Labour Exchange – even though it still maintains its own butlers . . .

Lester, though, did not deny Hill Samuel's considerable achievements – assets increasing over four years from £234m to £440m – nor by how a series of acquisitions, including most recently the ship-broking group

Lamberts and the innovative pension and life-assurance brokers Noble Lowndes, it was becoming a 'financial conglomerate' rather than a traditional merchant bank. He was also impressed by the quality of its high-level recruits, including Sir Richard Powell, a former Permanent Secretary at the Board of Trade, who was now one of the key five people on the Hill Samuel board. *Primus inter pares*, of course, remained Kenneth Keith, who when charged by Lester with the fact that Hill Samuel's 'popularity in the City is not overwhelming' and that it had 'the reputation of being sharp-witted' typically replied, without unnecessary elaboration, that 'the people who are jealous are the people who are not doing too well'. As for Hill Samuel's plans for future expansion, he did not give away any secrets but simply observed that 'it's what the customer thinks that matters'.[92]

Keith himself, Lester noted, was by now 'indisputably Established'. The same did not apply to Jim Slater, *the* epitome of new business and new City. 'The essence of the formula is that earnings, cash and assets are balanced against each other, giving the conglomerate a healthy look,' the *Economist* observed in February 1969 about Slater Walker's well-publicised methods. Yet it was in the course of that year that Slater began to 'deconglomeratise' – in other words, selling off his various industrial subsidiaries. The watershed occurred in the summer, as Slater, having passed the initial graphological test, had (in his own subsequent words) 'a number of meetings' with Warburg 'to see if a sensible working arrangement could be evolved'. The initiative was Warburg's, and his idea was that his bank and Slater Walker would each take a significant stake in the other. 'The banking and financial services side would then be concentrated in Warburgs and Slater Walker would be responsible for the industrial and overseas interests,' Slater recalled, probably accurately. 'I did not like this concept very much, so did not pursue it with much enthusiasm. After a few weeks we mutually agreed to take it no further . . .'[93] Warburg may have had a financially promiscuous streak (it was at about this time that he was talking with Hill Samuel), but it was a sign of how far Slater Walker had come that he should be prepared even to consider some sort of union.

Towards the end of 1969 the inevitable happened and Slater Walker at last moved into the City, in the shape of Ralli House (later Petershill House) at St Paul's Churchyard. The timing of this symbolic move was appropriate. 'I aimed during the seventies to establish Slater Walker as an international investment bank,' Slater wrote in 1977:

> I felt then, and still do today, that there is a vacuum waiting to be filled in international banking. The joint stock banks in this country are not prepared to even consider participating in the equity of companies that approach them for finance. The merchant banks and ICFC frequently take

small equity stakes in private companies, but the scale of their participation is usually very limited.

Slater may have been jobbing backwards, cloaking his activities in a more noble design than was really the case at the time, but the argument itself was a strong one. Certainly, when interviewed on television by Trevor Philpot for BBC's *Chief Executive* programme, Slater did not pretend to any friendly altruism:

> You are in a sense a new breed of person in British industry, aren't you? Now, you don't deal with one thing other than money, really?
> That is in a sense our product.
> How do you mean?
> Well, we are concerned [slight laugh] with making money. That is what we are trying to do. I regard my prime job, if I can put it that way, as a responsibility to my shareholders to provide for them an increasing return per annum on their capital employed. And this to my mind is what it's all about.

Making money . . . 'We are really an investment company,' Slater told William Davis, probably in the winter of 1969–70. 'I think the term should be investment bankers – with a lot of substance to back us up.'[94] To those in the financial press and elsewhere who bought the Slater story, even making claims for him that he did not necessarily make for himself, it seemed that the man who had given a shot in the arm to complacent British industry was now going to do the same to the City.

Oliver Poole, who in the late 1960s and early 1970s ran Pearsons as well as Lazards, was enough of a believer to follow Warburg even further down the primrose path. Early in February 1970, according to Slater's account, he suggested that Pearsons and Slater Walker 'might get together'; and 'as Pearsons was a company in the upper realms of the establishment the idea had great appeal for me', indeed 'from our point of view the proposal was almost dream-like'. Slater's enthusiasm was, if anything, heightened as it became clear to him during talks that the Cowdray family, which owned Pearsons and thus most of Lazard Brothers, was looking for a successor to Poole. By early April, with the negotiations having gone swimmingly, the two sides were ready to announce and a hotel had been booked for the press conference – only for Poole, literally one day before the announcement, to tell Slater that Lazard Frères in Paris was hostile to the merger, on the grounds that it would affect the banking business of Lazards, and that as a result Pearsons was backing out of the deal. For Slater it was a bitter blow, and coincidentally a bearish stock market in the last few days of April gave the shares of Slater Walker Securities a hard time, wiping nearly £25m off the group's market value. Slater countered by stressing that henceforth Slater Walker would be concentrating on its banking, investment and insurance divisions – reassurance that convinced the *FT*'s 'Lex' column, which took the line at the start of May that 'the overall impression is that the SWS share price could soon start to benefit from the coherence of its image, as distinct from the disparate and speculative quality of the past'. That same issue of the *FT* reported Slater saying that 'it is intended eventually to make SWS an established force throughout the banking world'.[95] Few at this stage were inclined to discount the possibility; some even imagined there might emerge a latter-day Nathan Rothschild operating in the shadow of St Paul's.

His competitors were hardly likely to include the staid clearing banks, but even there an important element of the new City was embryonically starting to take shape. The background was not only their increasing dislike during the 1960s of the quantitative system of controls on their lending, but also the way in which in all sorts of circles (both inside and outside the City) the whole question of money was at last coming out of the post-Radcliffe shadows. 'Monetary policy suddenly became fashionable last autumn,' Samuel Brittan noted in February 1969, though some confusion prevailed. 'In particular the relative parts to be played by interest rates versus credit rationing, and control of the money supply versus directives on specific categories of lending, are in a state of considerable uncertainty. This indeed applies to the whole philosophy of economic management at the present time.'[96] Later that year Jenkins established a joint Treasury/Bank committee (chaired by the Treasury's Sir Douglas Allen) to examine monetary policy; and the Bank (increasingly disenchanted with having to impose quantitative controls on the grumbling banks) managed to persuade the committee that Bank rate rather than such controls should become the main instrument of monetary policy.[97] The bankers also kept up the pressure, with Robarts (in his capacity as Chairman of the CLCB) telling the *Banker* in April 1970 that arbitrary ceilings were unfairly eroding the clearers' market share and that the fairer approach would be for a bank's lending powers to be matched to its ability to attract deposits.[98] A brave new deregulated world was beckoning, but neither Bank nor bankers imagined that it could come into being without a change of government.

'He thought there would be an election in September which Labour would lose,' Cecil King noted at the start of 1970 after dining with Warburg. 'He thought Heath would be a worse P.M. than Wilson and that after an interval – round about 1972–3 – there would be a coalition under Wilson. He thought Powell resembled the German party that in the 'thirties was to the right of the Nazis.' Over the next few months the conventional City wisdom remained that Wilson would wait until the autumn. In the event, encouraged by favourable opinion polls, Wilson took the gamble of announcing on 18 May that the general election would be exactly one month later. During the campaign, in which Labour stayed steadily ahead in the opinion polls and the stock market was largely pessimistic in tone, there were two main 'City' moments. The first occurred in late May when Ian Mikardo used the publication of the Select Committee's report on the Bank of England to displace Colonel Lancaster and chair a press conference. 'He proceeded to say some pretty rough things about the Bank,' O'Brien later regretfully noted, 'not at all in keeping with his courteous behaviour during our long examination. Once again the vulgar political animal had won the day.' Soon afterwards, on 1 June, an old friend of the Labour government's appeared on *Panorama* in order to dispute Jenkins's claim that Britain now had one of the world's strongest balance-of-payments positions. 'There's no question that any government that comes into power is going to find a much more difficult financial situation than the new Government found in 1964,' Lord Cromer controversially declared. 'The very large debts which are still outstanding – there seems to be some idea abroad that they have been completely paid off. This is very far from the case.' As for the specific question of the current £500m surplus on the balance of payments: 'When you take a closer look at it, as bankers do, the figures are not so glamorous as they appear on the surface.' The next day, responding to Cromer's comments, Wilson understandably compared the current surplus with the £800m deficit he had inherited in October 1964. ' "I do not see," he said bitterly,' *The Times* reported, ' "how the most committed politician could describe that as a worsening of the situation." '[99]

Right up to and including Thursday the 18th, traumatic news from Leon notwithstanding, almost all the opinion polls continued over-whelmingly to point to a Labour victory. In a rare display of prescience, however, the stock market scented a more congenial outcome, and each day during election week the Index rose. Heath's unexpected triumph produced a piquant coda for Jenkins, who after losing office put out feelers, but (in his own words) got a 'singularly unforthcoming' response from the City in terms of actual job offers. 'It could not fail to cross my mind that as an ex-Chancellor who had, maybe by luck, acquired some reputation for stringent management of the economy and for success in turning round the balance of payments, I was being treated utterly differently from the way that an analogous Conservative politician would have been.'[100] The 1970s would give the City the chance to show just how tribal its attitudes to Labour could be.

PART FOUR

1970–86

London! Biggest money market in the world, did you know that? Ten thousand million pounds a day turnover – ten thousand million a day. And there's a thousand ways of making it, you know. It's just a question of picking the right one.

Michael Travis, in Lindsay Anderson's *O Lucky Man!* (1973)

CHAPTER FOURTEEN

Night Nurse

There's no such thing as the City. There is certainly nothing like the 'City opinion' which the BBC likes to talk about. There are simply a lot of people trying to make money, swarming round the streets crowded between Temple Bar and the Tower. Banks, insurance firms, stockbrokers, shipping companies, the discount houses, commodity traders, all of them with their place in the system. Overgrown village, rumour mill, with the atmosphere of a regimental mess and the sense of humour of an Edwardian boys' paper, full of private language, secret rituals and enough games to last a working lifetime.

The disaffected voice belonged to Thomas Kane, hero and narrator of David Jordan's accomplished financial thriller, *Nile Green*, published in 1973. Kane himself is a merchant banker, working for the thrusting Thorne Reinhard (probably loosely modelled on Hill Samuel and/or Warburgs), and at one point he finds himself in the famous restaurant in Queen Victoria Street where more than just fish is on offer:

> Sweetings is where the City man goes for lunch when he's nostalgic for his schooldays, so it's usually pretty crowded . . . Bread and butter, brown and thin and damp, a memory of cricket on the lawn before Evensong. Ginger beer and lemonade. Sherbet. Rice pudding, apple pie, jam roly-poly and treacle tart. You don't see many women eating there which I suppose isn't surprising; they haven't the tribal memories to nourish . . .
>
> Someone behind me was saying, 'Did you say you were going back into Gilts?' in the elaborately casual tone of voice in which one would ask about the weather, and answered, nasal and fluting as an oboe: 'I'm stuck with those bloody Australians and oils are looking poorly' . . . The most remarkable thing about the top-drawer City type is his voice . . . It's the pitch, rather than the volume, which cuts through a crowded room like a chain-saw across a valley.[1]

*

At the time the City's own conventional wisdom was rather more flattering to itself. 'We talked about the success of London as a financial centre in recent years,' Cecil King noted after lunching in June 1971 with Gordon Richardson of Schroders. 'He said it was remarkable and had drawn to London very numerous branches of foreign banks, all anxious to make money. The Jewish element in all this is surprisingly very low. The competition is very severe. Compared with twelve years ago, Gordon says, he has to keep his eye constantly on the ball – could not, for instance, possibly spare the time for a trip to New York by sea.' Everywhere there were symbols of this 'new', forward-looking, cut-and-thrust City. The old London Bridge, built in the 1820s, was demolished in 1968 (subsequently re-erected at Lake Havasu City, Arizona) and replaced by an unmemorable effort; two years later Rothschilds, the last surviving major partnership in British banking, became a limited liability company; not long afterwards the market men of Union Discount started carrying walkie-talkies on their 'money walks' around the City so that they could be in constant touch with the state of the money book at 39 Cornhill; in 1973 the nightly watch on the nation's gold reserves by the picquet from the Brigade of Guards was replaced by more mundane electronic surveillance at the Bank of England; and that same year, most poignantly of all, road widening at Bishopsgate compelled the demolition of Barings' homely, elegant Victorian premises, replaced by a twenty-storey tower block. Sartorial standards were also changing in these years – above all they saw the swift demise of the bowler hat, the stiff white collar and the compulsory white shirt – but what mattered more was the passing of old ways of doing business. Stockbrokers by the early 1970s less often did the daily round of the merchant banking parlours, but instead relied much more on the telephone to take orders. Desk-bound in their offices, less often visiting the investing institutions or going down to the market floor to talk to the jobbers, many brokers (certainly in the larger firms) now relied on a mixture of in-house analytical reports and the market price display service that the Stock Exchange had introduced in February 1970.[2] All in all there was, for good or ill, a perceptible decline in the old intimacy and the reliance on personal contact.

A quarter century or so later the big office blocks that went up in the 1970s (such as those in Lower Thames Street, replacing the old ware-houses) evoked little more affection than the blocks of the 1960s. Simon Bradley, in his 1997 update of Pevsner, was especially rude about the Barclays building that went up in 1972 on the corner of Gracechurch Street and Fenchurch Street – 'a chamfered square tower of some thirty storeys, small upright windows each in a projecting pre-cast frame: a consistent and remorseless display of concrete'. Very much in a class of its own was Richard Seifert's still-under-construction NatWest Tower, on which work began in 1970 but was not eventually completed until 1981. Destined to be fifty-two storeys high and Britain's tallest building (pre-Canary Wharf), it seemed at the outset the acme of commercial modernity. 'Its relatively shallow office floors, the inclusion of ped-ways, and the need for widespread clearance to build it all,' in Bradley's words, 'followed 1960s methods that were already obsolescent by completion . . .'[3] During the 1970s it was the increasingly visible symbol of NatWest's global aspirations; but neither the bankers nor (more understandably) the Colonel himself could imagine the big trading-floor world that would be beckoning by the early 1980s.

In a sense that same blind spot also applied to the new Stock Exchange, another emblem of modernity, where trading began in June 1973, seven months after the formal opening by the Queen. One stockbroker, Nicholas Goodison, vividly recalled how it seemed at the time:

> The new Market was a large cavernous concrete building, public gallery again looking down through plate glass over one side of it. It runs up three storeys, so it's a tall building, with a pseudo-concrete dome over the top, a lot of acoustic tiling. Facing the Public Gallery, there's a concrete wall with a map of the world on it, with little lights showing the main centres of activity. On the floor, you've got something new, you've got organised jobbers' pitches, instead of the old higgledy-piggledy jobbers' pitches round pillars and all over the place. You've got some hexagons, built specially for the purpose, and with room for jobbers to get to telephone terminals and computer terminals inside the hexagons, and there are seats around the outside of the hexagons, and their boards on white plastic behind them, which they can pull down and write on, so everyone can see them. They still sit on the seats with their jobbers' books, and they're still standing out from the seats with their jobbers' books, but these hexagons are organised like a honeycomb all over the floor, but with room between each one for people who wish to scurry to and fro, to get the prices. All the way around the walls of this very large space there are telephones: literally all the way round, and only about two feet apart, black telephones and grey telephones. The black telephones are outside lines, and the grey telephones are owned by the broking firms and go direct to their offices. There are a number of electronic displays of the currencies throughout the world, and company news coming up on flash screens, so it's a more technological-looking Exchange now, more orderly looking, much less sense of atmosphere. The wooden floor has gone, the floor is rubberised, not boards, so the noise is much less, and the waiters are not yelling out, because all the contact with firms is being done now by telephone. There's very little public bidding and offering going on by the jobbers too, so those of us who have been brought up in the old Market slightly regret this rather clinical new floor, but it is very efficient and the communications are very efficient, and as long as you get your dealing done efficiently, and the client's getting the best deal, that's what the main aim is . . .

Efficient, yes, but the romance had gone. Once, at quarter past three, there had been the welcome sound of the waiter's rattle, allowing smoking for the last part of the trading day; now the Council decreed that there was to be no smoking, on the grounds that 'the floor of the new Market is of rubber tiles' and 'considerable damage and disfigurement would be caused to the floor if lighted cigarettes were allowed to fall on it'.[4] Many of the older members had hung on until the ceremonial royal opening (an occasion for full evening dress, including white tie and medals), and their departure soon afterwards conclusively confirmed the end of the old, larger-than-life House, for so many years a world within a world.

To many, it seemed that a virtuous circle was already in place. Following the 1967 Companies Act, which had removed the legal maximum of twenty partners, firms were becoming ever larger; simultaneously there continued the inexorable rise of the institutional investor (owning almost half the equity market by 1975); and under pressure from these institutions (particularly the more aggressive fund managers), allied to the start of price-earnings ratios in the mid-1960s and the 'performance cult' that developed as a result of the 1967–8 bull market (together with the disclosure requirements in the 1967 Act), the major stockbroking firms inevitably found it much harder to get away with second-rate investment analysis and service. Even the most prestigious brokers felt the need to raise their game: when the energetic, business-getting Michael Richardson moved in 1969 from Panmure Gordon to Cazenove's, he caused some consternation with his habit of taking copious notes at meetings, but in time his example was followed elsewhere; while at Rowe & Pitman it was decreed in March 1970 that henceforth partners must be at their desks by 9.30 in the morning. The trend was similar in other sectors, such as law and accountancy. Slaughter and May took the pioneering step in the mid-1960s of appointing an administrative partner and then in 1968 moved out of Austin Friars to rather bleak and characterless, but functional, modern offices in Basinghall Street; Price Waterhouse adopted a more sophisticated management structure from 1966 and nine years later relocated to the new Southwark Towers by London Bridge Station, on the 'wrong' side of the river. Both firms were growing rapidly and felt few sentimental regrets about the price of progress, even if it meant leaving the City's historical core centred on the Bank of England.[5]

The City was also, undeniably, becoming more open and meritocratic. To give just a trio of almost random examples: Nigel Elwes (admittedly a nephew of the senior partner) arrived at Rowe & Pitman in 1968 as the firm's first trained accountant; over the next few years the corporate finance department of Morgan Grenfell began deliberately to recruit young, qualified people (preferably with a business-school background), with newcomers including Patrick Spens and Roger Seelig; and at the medium-sized stockbrokers Kitcat & Aitken, Nils Taube, of part-Estonian descent and one of the founders of the Society of Investment Analysts, completed the long journey from office boy to senior partner in 1975. There was also, at long last, some measure of expanded scope and incentive for women in the City. In June 1968 the Bank of England announced that it now accepted the principle of equal pay – to be implemented from July 1969 over a four-year period – but in the public mind the crux was the Stock Exchange. In May 1971 a fresh proposal to admit women was once again rejected, by 1,287 to 955, provoking considerable adverse publicity, including in Parliament. A year later the Council considered a letter from Mrs Muriel Wood (née Bailey), now a 'senior executive' at the brokers Sternberg, Flower & Co. She asked that her membership application be reconsidered, in view of the London Stock Exchange's coming federation with other British exchanges that already had women members, and she went on:

> You will have on record your confirmation that on any change in the attitude of the Stock Exchange to Women Members, my application would be given first preference. It has recently, I am aware, been necessary for applicants to have passed the requisite examination, but with my long connection in Stock Exchange business, extending from 1925, I trust that this requirement would be waived in my case.

Her timely letter provoked a 24–5 vote to consider applications for women members for the Stock Exchange year beginning March 1973; a notice was posted to that effect (giving the membership no further opportunity for a ballot); and the first women members were indeed elected that March and after a few weeks totalled more than a dozen. It was as well for the City as a whole, not just the Stock Exchange, that this retreat was made, for the square mile was coming under unprecedented daily scrutiny. 'The City, far more than the regions of government and bureaucracy, has been opened up in the last few years to the influences of the mass media from outside its walls, and linked up to the machinery of journalism and advertising,' Anthony Sampson observed in 1971. 'Business supplements, books on the City, the television money programme, and the huge publicity that surrounds take-over battles, have all thrown light on to the square mile. To some old firms the shock has been sudden, as if they discovered a two-way mirror in their bedroom . . .'[6] The rise of financial PR was the City's inevitable response, often provided by financial journalists opting for the softer, better-paid life.

In fact, the forces of conservatism were far from extinguished. These forces included a conservation movement, heartened by the City Corporation's decision in 1971 to designate eight Conservation Areas and then the following year to oppose the Bishop of London's proposal to make nine churches in the City redundant. The year 1973 saw the publication of *Goodbye London* by Christopher Booker and Candida Lycett Green, whose detailed chapter on the City's threatened buildings justified their assertion that 'the pace of redevelopment is now such that within twenty years only little, carefully protected pockets of older buildings are likely to remain'. In November that year, following an informal meeting of members, the Stock Exchange's Chairman, George Loveday, sent a striking letter to the new Lord Mayor, Sir Hugh Wontner. After noting that the City owed much of its character to 'the admixture of small businesses and establishments which cater for the City's working population', he drew attention to 'the fact that the demolition currently going forward in Angel Court and Copthall Court will involve the disappearance of two theatre ticket agencies, a small art gallery, a jeweller's, two barber's shops, a betting shop, several confectioners and tobacconists, two bars and a restaurant'. Accordingly, 'it is becoming increasingly difficult in the City to obtain lunch-time snacks and meals at reasonable prices'. As it happened, the property boom of the early 1970s was on the verge of collapse, and partly in that context, the City Corporation quietly abandoned its ambitious plans to construct a thirty-mile ped-way network above the City's streets. Was it too little, too late? *Save the City*, a campaigning book published in 1976, certainly thought so. The traditional character of the City, it argued, 'derives from a largely medieval street and spatial pattern, modified in the 19th century, to which nearly all development conformed up to 1940. Then came extensive war-damage, followed by a period of comprehensive redevelopment as well as rebuilding, during which much of this pattern was destroyed.' Accusing the City Corporation of a 'spasmodic and inconsistent' record in conservation, it claimed that the post-war standard of architectural design had been 'unworthy of the City's status and significance', a lack of distinction that was typified by the new Guildhall Square: 'bleak and open, uninterestingly paved, and partly surrounded by buildings which are partially surfaced and which can aptly be described as gimmicky'.[7]

Part of the City's unique character had, historically, been the Dickensian image of the clerk at the high, sloping desk. That image was now anachronistic, though development in office technology was slower in the 1970s than might have been expected. The conventional typewriter remained dominant as word processors came in only slowly; fax machines were relatively rare in Britain (largely because of their slowness and high transmission costs); and it was not until late in the decade that small computers, suitable for office life, began to appear in any numbers. Moreover, even in the new Stock Exchange, for all its more clinical atmosphere, the day-to-day method of dealing remained essentially unchanged, while it was not until 1979 that the more advanced settlement system known as TALISMAN (Transfer Accounting and Lodgement for Investors, Stock Management for jobbers) became fully operational. An innate suspicion of the march of new technology would die hard. 'In common with a lot of my friends and contemporaries,' one stockbroker confessed to his readers in November 1971, 'I have had at times grave fears about this computer era into which we are now well launched':

> Some of us have been, and will continue to be, supplanted by machines. We resent this for many reasons, but two seem to predominate. Firstly, no machine can be as good as we are, with our fine education, our superb training, our delicate sensibilities, and our devotion to duty. Secondly we would like to continue to eat. As one of those who have spent their lives on the sanded floor of the Stock Exchange arena, I reckoned for a long time that my colleagues and I would escape computerisation for many moons to come. After all, who wants to deal with a computer? But already there are computer systems set up on both sides of the Atlantic trying to get at our business, and although they would so far seem to have enjoyed very little success, who knows, perhaps their day may arrive. It is by no means imminent, though, and if it ever does happen, I feel that I shall long have been translated to a wider sphere of operations. Think on this, those of you who are ever tempted to feed your business into a computer, dealing done that way will never be fun. Dealing certainly ought to be, and I think that between human beings it usually is.

The sceptic was Paul Bazalgette, senior dealing partner of Phillips & Drew and author of a humorous column in the firm's monthly *Market Review*. Phillips & Drew was far more into the joys of computing than most firms, but Bazalgette's views undoubtedly chimed with those of the floor of the House. Some twenty floors up, the Stock Exchange Council was aware of technological developments elsewhere, notably the computer-based dealing system NASDAQ (National Association of Securities Dealers Automated Quotations) that came onstream in the US in 1971, but never seriously contemplated the end of the familiar, face-to-face trading floor.[8]

There was only one systematic sociological study of the City in the 1970s, by Richard Whitley of Manchester Business School, but its findings (largely based on 1971 data) revealed how little the characteristics of the City élite had changed. Over four-fifths of the directors in his sample had attended fee-paying schools, with Eton easily dominant; Oxbridge was by far the favoured place of higher education; and nearly half belonged to one or more of London's nine most prestigious West End clubs. The sample also produced plenty of overlapping directorships, perhaps inevitable granted that more than three-quarters of the 402 directors were also directors of other companies. There were also, of course, manifold kinship relationships, and in all Whitley felt able to conclude that 'by outlining and measuring degrees of connection and commonalities between members of the financial élite' he had 'indicated a certain homogeneity of background and closeness of connection which enables us to treat them as an élite'.

Away from rarefied sociology, it was difficult to deny that (whether in merchant banks, clearing banks, stockbroking firms or elsewhere) strong elements of the old two-class system still existed. Take the chairmen of the 'Big Four' in 1973. Sir Archie Forbes of Midland was a Scottish chartered accountant, but Sir John Thomson of Barclays had gone to Winchester and Magdalen College, Oxford, besides being a member of the Jockey Club and a Lord Lieutenant of Oxfordshire; John Prideaux of National Westminster had joined the family merchant bank of Arbuthnot Latham after leaving Eton, while Eric Faulkner of Lloyds had, after Bradfield and Corpus Christi, Cambridge, joined the private bank Glyn Mills. These were impeccable pedigrees, whereas their four chief general managers had each joined his bank when still in his teens, three of them from state school. At Barclays, where it was still unthinkable for someone outside the bank's founding families to become Chairman, a particularly able and ambitious General Manager was Deryk Vander Weyer; unfortunately, at the end of the 1960s he had blotted his copybook (perhaps fatefully) by lunching one day in 'the Chairman's Mess' (as the senior dining room in the Lombard Street head office was called) and being reprimanded by a board member for the crime of scooping Stilton from the middle. When, some years later, his son Martin decided after leaving Oxford to embark on a banking career, he found that there existed 'throughout Barclays' an attitude of 'suspicion towards all graduates', on the grounds that 'anyone that had idled away three years at university was likely to be undisciplined, ignorant of the real world and too brainy for his own good'. This deeply entrenched mind-set explains much about the clearing banks' tribulations during the last quarter of the century. At the merchant banks too, although there was a much readier acceptance of brain-power, there were still distinctly finite limits to meritocracy. Alastair Ross Goobey, a manifestly intelligent young man, was a graduate trainee at Kleinwort Benson in the early 1970s, but soon left on realising that, in his own words, 'the pyramid narrowed very rapidly'.[9]

Others also found the City of the 1970s a far-from-progressive milieu. 'I remember once going to the men's loos, on the 23rd floor, and standing next to Lord Ritchie of Dundee, who was a past Chairman,' Michael Jenkins has said about going to the Stock Exchange in 1971 as Technical Director, in order to install what would become TALISMAN. 'And it subsequently came back to me, he made a comment to somebody, "I don't expect to see staff in the Council Member's loos."' Haruku Fukuda, who joined Vickers da Costa in 1972 to write a fortnightly newsletter on the Japanese economy, was struck by how her new colleagues 'followed their intuition much more than reasoned argument' and were 'always going out for long lunches and coming back having had five brandies'. The long lunches (up to two and a half hours) also coloured the impressions of another foreigner, Charles McVeigh III, an American banker:

When I first came to the City in 1973, everyone broke at around twelve-thirty for lunch, which became a major part of the day, whereas Americans tend to eat early and quickly and never drank anything at all . . . People had at least one or two drinks before lunch, wine with the meal and thought nothing of having port and at least one cigar afterwards. Interestingly, no business was done over lunch which, again, was completely different from America. You would wait until the end when you might, over a glass of port or as the dessert was being served, turn the conversation to some business area of mutual interest. Before that, one was positioning oneself socially with one's counterpart . . .

A rather older but equally critical newcomer, having come to Kleinworts in the late 1960s as an established lawyer, was Martin Jacomb. 'What was a factor for at least a decade after I arrived in the City,' he recalled with surprising emphasis for such a quietly spoken man, 'was the difference between the old-fashioned people based on inheritance and family and tradition and the people who relied on brains and ability. As the years went by the former were made to look more and more ridiculous – the idea that you gave business to somebody because he was at school with you and all that kind of crap . . .'[10]

A rigid social structure, entrenched attitudes and assumptions, accustomed and congenial ways of doing business – large parts of the City were not so *very* different from the City of the immediate post-war era. Some of those attitudes were revealed with particular vividness in two of the great Stock Exchange questions of the day: advertising and women. In spring 1971, under some pressure from the Monopolies Commission, the Council proposed to allow members to advertise. The result was a flurry of agitated protest from a range of broking firms:

> *Fenn & Crosthwaite.* We consider it inevitable that the long-term result will be the emergence of one or more 'thundering herds' [a reference to Merrill Lynch in the US], automated and computerised and able to take on the mass processing of small client business. This trend might have the effect in a number of years of reducing severely the number of broking firms . . .
>
> *Cazenove & Co.* It seems to us that permission to advertise represents the end of stockbroking as a profession with restrained ethical standards.
>
> *Albert A. Bendon & Co.* We wonder in whose interest the proposal lies. Possibly the Jobbers in that it could lead to increased turnover; and conceivably a broker of the future operating on the Juggernaut lines of America.

That May the membership rejected the proposal, by an apparently decisive 1,392 votes to 780, but in November 1973 the Council, under renewed pressure from the Monopolies Commission and without calling another referendum, pushed through the change. 'It is well known,' the brokers Beardsley & Co vainly protested ahead of the motion's confirmation, 'that the bigger the label the worse the cigar, and many members would deeply regret seeing their profession, which enjoys a monopoly, permitted by law, handed over to the mercy of preying jackals and vultures masquerading in the clothes of twentieth-century advertising consultants.'[11]

On the question of the other sex, where again the popular will was eventually ignored, the veteran broker Graham Greenwell spoke for many in his celebrated (or infamous) June 1971 letter to *The Times*, asserting that the Stock Exchange was 'not an institution which exists to perform a public service'; instead it was essentially a 'private men's club' and, as such, was perfectly entitled to choose whom it did or did not elect to membership. Even after the citadel fell, the aliens were given a pretty rough ride. 'The girls all got given nicknames by the men,' Jane Partington, who went on to the floor as a blue button in 1975 while still in her teens, remembered:

> I was the Night Nurse, there was Sweaty Betty, Super Bum, the Grimsby Trawler, the Road Runner, Stop Me And Pick One. They were very cruel. Stop Me And Pick One was because she had acne. You had to have broad shoulders and a good sense of humour because you would be the butt of a lot of jokes. They would even suggest that you had changed your bra from one day to the next. If you were dressed in red from head to foot they'd call you Pillar-box all day and try to post letters. You'd think carefully about what you wore. They'd sit ripping up newspapers and sticking it all together and then creep up and clip it on to your skirt so you'd walk off and have a thirty-yard tail behind you . . .

Dress sense was indeed crucial, and it was like a red rag to the bull if a woman appeared on the floor in a trouser suit. Eventually the presence of women became more or less accepted – 'I must admit some of the girl dealers, the female dealers were OK,' one jobber, Geoffrey Green of Bisgoods, grudgingly conceded – but the floor stayed essentially a male domain for the rest of its life.[12]

In some quarters there was an almost obstinate pride in sticking to the old rituals. Top hats and as personal an approach as possible, including the daily round of visits to banks, remained the discount market's mode. At the Bank of England O'Brien did commission an investigation by the US management consultants McKinsey & Co, but in practice he was unwilling to implement most of its recommendations, with the result that the Bank's organisational structure remained more or less unchanged throughout the decade, with the Chief Cashier still wielding more power than executive directors. On the face of it there was more progress at the Stock Exchange, where an initiative by Nicholas Goodison led to a July 1973 report on long-term strategic planning and the appointment in 1974 of the Exchange's first Chief Executive. Even so, the individual, often backward-looking member was still king, despite having been circumvented on the advertising and women questions, and in the words of that institution's historian, 'the room for manoeuvre possessed by the Council of the Stock Exchange continued to be constrained by the ability of the membership to block new proposals if they conflicted with their wishes'.[13]

Relatively few in the City saw the need for change. After all, why, when there was a comfortable living to be made (as, for most of the 1970s, there was), should people have thought any differently? When Ian Fraser, on leaving the Takeover Panel in 1972, was persuaded by Oliver Poole to go to Lazards, he discovered that the principal block to giving a sharper edge to the firm were the so-called 'Four Colonels', namely Mark Norman, Kit Dawnay, Denny Marris and Daniel Meinertzhagen, who were the senior directors under Poole and each of whom had had a distinguished war career. Poole had billed them in advance as 'unhungry', and Fraser soon after his arrival agreed:

> Charming though the Four Colonels were, they were all useless for our purposes. Norman's chairmanships included Gallahers and Dawnay's Wiggins Teape. On the rare occasions when they were in their offices at 11 Old Broad Street they seemed to spend their time dictating letters to their (Lazards) secretaries about their outside companies or the management of their country estates. Meinertzhagen [whose brother Luke was now senior partner of Cazenove's] was memorably lazy and it was quite usual to find him sitting at his desk after lunch, asleep with a copy of *The Times* over his face. Marris went on endless travels to Persia, bought beautiful carpets and talked, talked, talked . . .

Early on Fraser suggested that, *à la* Warburgs, inward and outward mail should henceforth be copied, along with summarised notes of every office meeting, to be distributed that same evening. 'Shock and horror' were the reaction. 'Dawnay told me that his office correspondence was no concern of anybody but himself and he would refuse to comply if such an instruction was issued. Norman told me that I should realise that this was Lazards, who already had a position, not Warburgs, who were trying to make one. Meinertzhagen threatened passive resistance . . .' The idea was dropped. Presumably there was also resistance from the department that looked after private clients, a particularly privileged corner of Lazards. It was run by Anthony (later Lord) Tryon, a former page of honour to the Queen and a friend of Prince Charles. His nickname, derived from the way he would finish his sentences, was almost Trollopian: 'Lord Ummm'.[14]

Phillips & Drew, supreme exponents of the 'what' school of stockbroking, continued to find that the 'who' factor remained critical in what was still – at heart – a people industry. At the start of the 1970s its senior partner asked a senior figure in the discount market why his firm had hitherto failed to gain more than a very small share of the short end of the gilts market. He was told that the only way in which it could break through was to employ an Old Etonian. Accordingly the firm recruited from de Zoete's one such, Peter Harrison. He was also the nephew of the then Government broker, Sir Peter Daniell, so he came with a double qualification, to which he added a likeable character and a mention in despatches from Borneo. This piece of recruitment did the trick, while Harrison also made his mark by successfully complaining, soon after his arrival at Lee House, that whereas the partners were treated to soft paper in their lavatory, those below the salt had to make do with the harder, less yielding 'Bronco' variety.[15] Conversely, when some years later David Eastham emerged *faute de mieux* as senior partner of Sebags, he found it a miserable experience: his colleagues persisted in regarding him as fundamentally an actuary, still in many City circles a damning thing to be called.

Overall, in the City of the 1970s, there was a still a formidable culture of mutual favours, epitomised by the sub-underwriting process, in which corporate brokers doled out almost invariably lucrative chunks of sub-underwriting to investing institutions in implicit return for their business in the secondary market. There was also still an obdurate culture of secrecy and lack of accountability – a culture strongly deplored by the journalist Richard Spiegelberg in his well-informed, even-handed survey of the City published in 1973. 'Only to itself is the City in any real sense accountable,' he argued. 'Values are established essentially by the City, for the City, in the City.' He did not, despite greatly increased financial coverage in the press, see the answer to this lack of accountability as lying in the fourth estate. Instead, he contended that several factors blurred the relationship between the City and financial journalism: the ownership question (he pointed to Pearsons owning the *FT*, the *Investors Chronicle* and a major stake in the *Economist* on the one hand, Lazards on the other); the presence of City men like Sir Kenneth Keith and Evelyn de Rothschild on the boards of large newspaper publishing companies; the dependence of the City pages of the national papers on financial advertising; the prevalence of share-pushing in some City pages; and the fact that 'good news in the City is easier to come by than bad news'. There was also, as a further source of non-accountability, the huge shift of investment power to the big institutions (insurance companies, unit trusts, pension funds and investment trusts). In all, it was a formidable case, and at the end of his book Spiegelberg asked, 'What safeguards are there that this mammoth power is not abused? As members of a democratic society, have the British public not assigned to the City the privilege of immunity – an immunity which no other power structure in the country of any comparable size enjoys?'[16]

*

To outsiders the City still seemed, fairly or unfairly, a dull place populated mainly by dullards. Jonathan Raban, in his wonderful study of London, *Soft City*, published in 1974, said as much: 'In many areas of the city, of course, the hierarchy still holds good: the lawyer, the broker on the Stock Exchange, the gentleman-publisher, wear rigid uniforms which announce their adherence to a firm tradition which yet survives in a naughty fluid world. But for the young without a profession, without precedents, the clothes they wear register the city's immense and arbitrary range of choice. They announce simply that you have chosen, made your personal bid for a fantasy . . .'[17]

CHAPTER FIFTEEN

Go-go

'I believe that there is a premium on size; that merchant banks are still too small; and that their future lies overseas, where they have to compete with people who have the support of big resources,' Kenneth Keith told the press at the end of June 1970, less than a fortnight after the election of the Heath government. The context was the announcement of a proposed merger between Hill Samuel and Metropolitan Estates and Property Co (MEPC), Britain's second-biggest property company. Keith himself was to be Executive Chairman of Metropolitan Hill Samuel, which would have a market capitalisation of almost £200m. Immediate City reaction was mixed, but Keith himself was adamant that 'money today is a wonderful commodity, and I have a feeling that it will become even more valuable'. As it soon became clear that there was strong opposition to the deal from MEPC institutional shareholders, Keith continued to insist that the City had no alternative but to change 'out of all recognition' – though he did add that he was still hoping to retire eventually to his 2,000-acre Norfolk farm. Other merchant banks naturally did not relish the prospect of such a hugely capitalised competitor, while according to Anthony Sampson the large insurance companies with major stakes in MEPC 'took fright at the size and speculative aspects of the merger, and were wary of Keith's reputation as an aggressive and over-bearing boss'. There was also, however, a deep, instinctive and widespread dislike of the whole concept of financial supermarkets. James Scrimgeour, whose family firm resigned in protest as brokers to MEPC, warned in a letter to *The Times* that the City's 'separate and individual activities would be submerged in vast corporations generally controlled at the top by a diminishing number of "businesscrats"'. By the end of July the City establishment (and in particular merchant banks with no love of Hill Samuel) had engineered a rival bid for MEPC from Commercial Union. Although it failed, it had the intended effect of spiking Keith's guns, meaning that that restless figure would have to look elsewhere for a final mega-combine to round off his City career.[1]

Nevertheless, the wider debate about the appropriateness or otherwise of ending the City's traditional demarcation lines continued. 'Old boundaries are not sacred in themselves, of course, but not every change is desirable,' the *Banker* commented in August 1970 on the news that Rothschilds had bought a 10 per cent stake in Wedd Durlacher. 'The main justification of the jobber system is that jobbers are separate from both brokers and investors. Merchant banks are of course the biggest of investors and if they are going to have an interest in the dealing process one of the vital boundaries of the City may perhaps be breached.' The following year, in his annual statement as Chairman of Mercury Securities (the holding company of Warburgs), Siegmund Warburg formally put the case for the status quo:

> Specialisation has been the great strength of the City of London and has been one of the decisive factors in enabling the City to remain the financial centre of Western Europe. It seems to me no coincidence that none of the cities on the Continent, where 'universal banks' combine inter alia the functions of merchant banks and joint stock banks and where there are no merchant banks comparable to those in London, has succeeded in detracting from the outstanding position of the City of London. I therefore hope that the City of London will continue to derive its strength from specialisation combined with co-operation among the members of its financial community.

At about the same time David Montagu, who for several years had been vigorously propagating the idea of what he liked to call 'department-store banking', publicly disagreed: 'I have never believed that the clearing banks could not do the work of the merchant banks any more than that Egyptian pilots could not get ships through Suez'.[2] His family merchant bank had been one-third owned by Midland since 1967, and presumably he believed that if at some point there was full consummation, then under his overall guidance the joint-stock men could yet acquire the requisite footwork and turn of speed.

Despite (or perhaps because of) having once worked for Brown Shipley, the new Prime Minister, Edward Heath, had no great regard for the wisdom of the City, which he believed to be badly in need of modernisation. During his first autumn in power the stock market drifted at around 350, rattled by high wage demands, recurrent strikes and liquidity concerns in British industry. At the heart of Heath's economic strategy (to be implemented by Anthony Barber at No 11 after the untimely death of Iain Macleod in July) was the notion that tax cuts and other stimulants of growth would be enough to discourage organised labour from making inflationary pay claims. O'Brien, who had actively supported the prices and incomes policy of the last three years of the Labour government, was unconvinced, and at Mansion House in October he flatly declared that he did not 'see how we can expect to maintain a fully employed, fully informed and increasingly well-off democracy, in which the development of wages and prices is left entirely to the operation of market forces', in that 'the bodies on both sides of the bargaining tables, the unions and employers in both the public and private sectors, are too big and too powerful for such a process to yield us the result most likely to contribute to our general welfare and prosperity'. He added (presciently in terms of both this and the next Conservative government) that 'if we try to rely on the marketplace and on the strict operation of fiscal and monetary policies, we shall find, I think, that we can achieve price stability only at the cost of unemployment that might be on a very large scale indeed'. These sentiments were so out of kilter with the government's free-market philosophy at this stage that over the next few months there was some speculation about whether O'Brien's governorship, due to expire at the end of June 1971, would be renewed for a further term.[3] In the end, perhaps by default, it was decided that O'Brien should remain in Threadneedle Street for at least two further years.

Heath's view of the City was not improved by the Rolls-Royce débâcle.[4] By September 1970 that famous company, a prime symbol of British industrial virility, was privately warning that it faced severe financial problems; and over the next two months, through heated negotiations within the City and between government and City, arrangements were made to keep Rolls-Royce going. A syndicate of accepting houses (led by Lazards, which had long been Rolls-Royce's merchant bank) would continue to provide a revolving acceptance credit of £20m, while the immediate cash shortage of some £60m would be met by the company's bankers (Midland and Lloyds, £5m each, the Bank of England £8m) and the government (£42m). Heath himself, 'not unnaturally angry and impatient', in O'Brien's subsequent words, had via the Governor leaned heavily on the bankers (both merchant and clearing) to obtain even those commitments, taking the line that 'all those who had advised or provided finance to the company hitherto have done well out of it, should have known in good time how its financial affairs were deteriorating and should now stand by it'. After one particularly 'acrimonious' meeting, O'Brien recalled, Heath, 'perhaps more than half seriously, offered me a peerage if I could rid him of one clearing banker who, in his opinion, was being particularly unhelpful'. O'Brien received even less thanks from the bankers, particularly Oliver Poole of Lazards, and George Bolton reported to Cecil King in November that 'what remained to O'Brien of his prestige had vanished with his clumsy attempts to raise money for Rolls-Royce'.

The collapse of Rolls-Royce, in early February 1971, was a profound shock to most of the City, with Sampson noting that even 'shortly before . . . many brokers were recommending the company to their clients'. The word from the Bank of England to the Fed was that the stock market had been 'stunned' by the news that a receiver had been appointed, though there was some satisfaction that the government, despite its avowed intent not to rescue 'lame ducks', would nationalise the company and thus prevent it from extinction. In due course a new chairman was appointed: none other than Kenneth Keith. As the dust settled, the accepting houses were, to put it mildly, extremely angry to discover that government, Bank and clearing banks had *not* in the event coughed up the supposedly promised £60m the previous autumn, following an investigation by Cooper Brothers (under Henry Benson) that had thrown fundamental doubts on Rolls-Royce's financial viability, even with that injection. They contended, probably with some justice, that they had not known that government support for Rolls-Royce was contingent on a satisfactory report from the investigating accountants. Or, as Gerald Thompson of Kleinworts laconically put it, in a memo about the matter, 'Put not your trust in princes.'[5]

More generally, the real significance of the episode for the City was that it threw an uncomfortable spotlight on the quality of its advice to British industry. 'One must sympathise with Mr Heath's dismay that so many parties deeply involved financially in the company should have had so little insight into how its affairs were progressing,' O'Brien later wrote. 'My own impression was that all were in a large degree blinded by the unique and longstanding prestige of the name Rolls-Royce.' At the time there was much public criticism, and the *Banker* conceded that 'the serene claim that bankers need not "understand industry" except from a financial point of view now sounds a little hollow', granted that 'it was precisely because the City has devoted so little effort to the understanding of modern technology that it failed to notice where Rolls went astray'. The City, it added, had 'certainly preserved, after the decline of the sterling system, an efficient money and capital market such as no other country in Europe can boast of', but that achievement did not obviate 'an urgent need for serious thought to be given to the right role of the banker in the affairs of industry'. Sampson summarised the problem more journalistically: Rolls-Royce had traditionally been the 'special province of Lazards', and for years 'the engineers didn't worry about money, and the bankers didn't worry about engineering'.[6]

In fact, from the late 1960s there had been a growing tendency towards City intervention in the affairs of British companies, most notably when Keith in the winter of 1969–70 successfully led a revolt of major institutional shareholders against the existing management of Vickers. Press response to that démarche was far from favourable ('the managerial expertise of the City is not the same as that of the industrial executive suite, and consequently the City's judgement of managers is fallible,' Robert Heller argued), but Rolls-Royce was clearly ammunition for the interventionists. No one in the City had such interventionist instincts as Charles Villiers, who after the unceremonious demise of the IRC early in the Heath government did not return to Schroders but went instead to Guinness Mahon as Chairman. It was time, he told the *Investors Chronicle* in March 1971, that merchant banks concentrated less on raising capital for British industry and more on 'the reorganisation of existing businesses':

> If you solve the financial problem without touching the industrial and management problem you will come unstuck. Once you have solved the industrial and management problems the financial one will come much easier. This is a reversal in the way City opinion usually thinks and I've got a feeling that the merchant banks will have to recruit into their organisations people who have got industrial and management experience. Up to now they have been hesitant about this . . .

As for the reluctance of institutional investors to get involved in the management questions of companies in which they had large stakes – in particular, to intervene constructively if things were going wrong – Villiers was also critical: 'It is a flaw in the system. It's a gap in our defences which other countries in various ways have begun to deal with, and we could do with a strong lead here.' That lead was unlikely to come from the new President of the Institute of Bankers, Andrew Carnwath of Barings, who two months later told the Institute that 'the cobbler should stick to his last' and that 'the City and those who work in it are not trained in most of the techniques of industry'. O'Brien, however, was more responsive, and during 1971–2 he tried, in his own words, 'to persuade the great institutional investors to use their muscle as large shareholders to induce greater efficiency in the companies in which they were invested'. It was an uphill task:

> I envisaged a standing committee or panel of institutional shareholders, who would appoint a full-time Director General, with a small staff, responsible for seeing that, when suitable cases for treatment had been identified, appropriate and effective action was taken.
> These ideas were a good deal too much for the majority of the insurance companies and the pension funds. Sensing that the chief general managers of the former, working through the British Insurance Association, were the biggest stumbling block, I tried to go over their heads to the chairmen of the insurance companies, a large and representative gathering of whom I invited to meet me in the Court Room of the Bank. From some, such as Kenneth Usherwood of the Prudential and Paul Chambers of the Royal, I received strong support but more sat on the fence or were definitely hostile, like Bill de L'Isle of the Phoenix . . .

In the event, 'a very much less assertive plan of campaign was agreed upon', consisting of 'a liaison committee [known as the Institutional Shareholders' Committee] which could bring the institutional investors together for discussion and the consideration of possible action if this should seem to be appropriate in a particular case'. This 'wishy-washy formula' was, O'Brien conceded, 'a rebuff' to himself; while the financial writer John Plender, in his study some years later of the rise of the institutional investor, would frankly call the ISC 'an emasculated organisation'.[7] The institutions would continue to remain the sleeping giants of British corporate life.

The Governor's radicalism did not extend to encouraging the creation of 'universal' banks. In this he disappointed Heath, who according to O'Brien 'wanted the banks to be much more assertive as they are in Germany, where they invest heavily in industrial companies themselves, exercise long-term proxies on behalf of their customers whose investments they manage and place many of their officials on the supervisory boards of industrial companies'. However, O'Brien, mindful of the 1931 banking crisis on the Continent, much disliked the idea of large deposit banks investing heavily in equities and believed that 'the best use of economic resources is most likely to be achieved if a large and unfettered capital market is there to choose which activities it will support and to decide on the price at which it will do so.' Keith, interviewed in 1971 (not long after the British application to join the EEC had at last been accepted), agreed on behalf of the merchant banks:

> I doubt whether you will see us reaching anything like the proportions of bank equity stakes in industry that there are in some continental countries. On the contrary, I think there they are too high, and what we must hope for is a more rapid expansion of the national capital markets in these countries, with the institutions and private investors coming in in a much bigger way. The City of London has a tremendous opportunity ahead of it in helping to bring this about.

Nonetheless, despite this fairly routine reaffirmation of faith in the Anglo-Saxon, non-corporatist model, the fact was that since the mid-1960s the public image of merchant bankers had increasingly become one of dynamic, industry-moulding financial supermen. This image would have taken something of a battering if more people had known that one of the most prestigious merchant banks, Morgan Grenfell, had come close to catastrophe through its foolish involvement in the late 1960s and early 1970s in the financing of films. Probably most to blame was Lord Catto, son of the former Governor, who seems to have succumbed to the tinsel glamour – even to the extent of dining with the stars (presumably including Brigitte Bardot) of *Shalako* on location. Almost forty years after he had given a pessimistic prognosis for merchant banks after the war, Bolton in *Euromoney* in March 1971 still saw cause for gloom: fund management, he asserted, had become 'barely a profitable activity'; 'their role of financing British industry abroad has been progressively restricted by successive Governments and overseas investment has been reduced to a bare minimum'; there was 'the problem of foreign competition in the Eurocurrency markets, notably the activities of the New York investment houses'; and all in all, 'unless the private banks find it possible to spread their wings and actively engage in world-wide financial business with larger capital resources, their importance will tend to diminish'.[8]

'We see ourselves as somewhat between the go-go and the stuffy,' Michael Verey of Schroders remarked in 1972, and there is no doubt that in the early 1970s the City's real go-go merchants were not the members of the Accepting Houses Committee. When in August 1971 *Management Today* published its annual City Growth League (for which Slater Walker, mistakenly judged to be still essentially an industrial concern, was not eligible), the major gains were for newcomers like Pat Matthews's First National Finance (top of the league), Tiny Rowland's Lonrho, Tom Whyte's Triumph Investment Trust and Nigel Broackes's Trafalgar House. 'The pickings,' the magazine's editor Robert Heller reflected sanguinely, 'have gone to self-made, sharp-eyed men who have muscled in on institutional territory and have extended that terrain [for example, in property and insurance as well as lending] beyond the dreams of the lifetime career employees in the City's marble halls. That is a thought which should give the senior inhabitants of those halls pause for considerable thought.'[9]

First National, whose City head office was in 'a featureless building on Finsbury Pavement' and whose activities included issuing house operations, dealing in equities, hire purchase, second mortgages, industrial leasing, property development and estate management, was also the subject of an admiring profile: 'It is not overly constrained by habit or precedence. It behaves, in fact, very like an alert private investor; flexible, opportunist, always ready to switch from a dull stock into something more attractive, and to take its profit where it can.' In charge of First National's investment banking activities at this time was Terry Maher (the future founder of Pentos), who was attracted by Matthews's ambition and 'enormous charisma', but found his 'highly emotional and volatile personality' increasingly wearing. 'Nothing ever appeared to be settled and I found it difficult to make any firm plan; it seemed to me that he was a master at creating insecurity and that one piece of the jigsaw was always missing and that he was the only person who knew where it was . . .'[10] The characterisation applied more widely, for it was not the least of the weaknesses of these new concerns that each was dominated by a single, often unpredictable, powerful individual.

By summer 1971 the ultimately infamous 'Barber boom' was under way. The stock market had been largely in the doldrums since 1969, but Barber's tax-reforming budget at the end of March (including the abolition of short-term capital gains tax) set off, once its implications had sunk in, a sustained bull market. At this stage there would have been few City backers for Siegmund Warburg's view, expressed soon afterwards one lunchtime at Warburgs, that the Chancellor was 'very, very shallow'. Unemployment, however, continued to rise, prompting Barber on 19 July to introduce a mini-budget of explicitly reflationary measures, which he naively hoped would encourage voluntary pay restraint on the part of the unions. *This* was the real start of the Barber boom, and later that month King noted, after seeing the Governor, that 'in general terms it became clear that he [O'Brien] thought the latest Budget had no economic justification but was forced on the Government by political necessity'. In its next circular to clients Rowe & Pitman considered sounding a warning note, but decided against:

> Jargon calls it overheating. If the stimulus to consumer spending gathers too great a momentum, the pressure of demand might become excessive, imports would rise much more than exports, the sterling parity would come under suspicion. Such fears, in the light of experience, are justifiable. However, they concern a still quite distant horizon and, with a strong balance of payments for the present manifested both in the visible trade returns and a capital inflow, there is ample time for a favourable stock market cycle before overheating has to be reckoned with.[11]

Given that by the end of July the FT 30-Share Index had risen by over one-third since March, it was hardly surprising that there was a temptation to gather the rosebuds while one might. Moreover, O'Brien's protestations about the overly political nature of Barber's July measures were rather undercut by his failure to prevent (if, indeed, he even tried to do so) the September cut in Bank rate from 6 to 5 per cent. In his defence, though, one should add that he genuinely found repugnant, quite as much as Heath and Barber did, the prospect of unnecessarily high unemployment.

There were, besides Barber's own fiscal and monetary policies, two other key elements to the boom. One had already come into play (the recent implementation of the Crowther Committee's report on consumer credit, effectively abolishing official control over hire-purchase terms and greatly liberalising the law relating to consumer credit); the other was just about to: the new, also more liberal, framework for the banking system, known as Competition and Credit Control (CCC).[12] The principal architect of CCC was John Fforde, a future historian of the Bank of England, but then the Bank's Home Finance Director. A highly able economist who had joined the Bank as an economic adviser in 1957, he was not everyone's idea of a banker. 'He said there is nobody now at the Bank who is taken seriously in the City, and the Bank itself no longer speaks for the City or any part of it,' King noted in November 1970 after luncheon with a typically trenchant Bolton. 'He was particularly contemptuous of Fforde.' King himself subsequently described Fforde as 'a nice man, very intelligent and very shy'.

The hard thinking behind CCC seems to have taken place during the last two or three months of 1970, with Fforde getting a sympathetic hearing from O'Brien, and arguably the Bank had at this time three overriding wishes as far as money control was concerned. The Governor explained the first in his memoirs: 'The Bank was worrying about the bad effects on the banking system of the repeated and prolonged periods of harsh credit restraint which had been necessary ever since 1957. The quantitative restriction of advances imposed on the banking system proper turned good bankers into non-bankers, forced on grounds of public policy to turn away business they would dearly have liked to do.' It was, in short, an obnoxious way of running a monetary system, just as obnoxious to the Bank as to the clearing bankers, and both O'Brien and Fforde well knew that that would also be the view of the new pro-market, pro-competition government. The second desire was to create, on behalf of the clearing banks, a level playing field between them and their competitors (whether foreign, UK 'fringe', or whatever), after the best part of a decade during which the clearers had effectively had one hand tied behind their backs. Or, as O'Brien put it, 'at the centre, where the banks stood, we had frustration and decay with waning competition, while on the periphery, where we had no control, there was great, sometimes frenetic, activity'. The third aim related to that 'control' aspect, where the hope was that the creation of a single, indivisible market for credit would encourage the clearing banks (infinitely more trusted than their upstart rivals) to get into such critical, almost unregulated areas as the wholesale sterling market. Was there a fourth desire? 'What O'Brien also had in mind and in real execution was to kill off the secondaries,' Charles Gordon, who knew his way about the secondary banking scene, wrote some twenty years later. 'The Bank considered that once the primary banks had powers to compete freely for business, the secondaries would not get a look in.' Gordon cites as evidence the Bank's own, understated explanation to an official inquiry some years after the introduction of CCC: 'The expectation was that perhaps, not immediately, but in a short while, the fringe would contract to a level of comparative unimportance.'[13] One cannot be certain, but he is probably right.

By this time the 'primaries' – above all the 'Big Four' – broadly welcomed competition, including if necessary even between themselves. Midland had been profoundly shocked in February 1970 when the first disclosure of true profits had revealed how far it, as well as Lloyds, had fallen behind, while between Barclays and National Westminster there was now the keenest of rivalries, with both banks intent on growth. In

November 1970 the clearers formally set out to the Bank their point of view:

> The result of the almost continuous curb on the progress of the clearing banks has been that they have lost ground in relation to other institutions whose activities have been controlled more lately, less comprehensively, or not at all . . .
>
> While lending controls are applied to a range of institutions, only the clearing banks are also subject to the cash and liquidity ratio requirements, and to calls for special deposits. . .
>
> The disadvantages of the ceiling method of lending control, which is necessarily highly arbitrary and discourages competitive development, need no elaboration . . .

Later that month Midland's chairman, Sir Archibald Forbes, called on Jasper Hollom (O'Brien's deputy at the Bank) to try to establish the truth of press speculation that the 'Interest Cartel' was under examination. However, Hollom gave little away, even implying (perhaps somewhat disingenuously) that the talk emanated mainly from Whitehall. Indeed, all the evidence is that there was relatively little direct input from the clearing banks into the creation of CCC. In July 1973, in an internal paper on another matter, Midland's Stuart Graham reflected that 'we should seek to influence opinion and not wait until the official view is published to the world, as was the case with Competition and Credit Control'.[14] At the time, however, that did not prevent considerable agonising.

The process began in January 1971. O'Brien used a private dinner with Barber to explain what he had in mind and more or less succeeded in bringing the Chancellor and his Treasury advisers on board, though not without a period of some resistance on the part of some of the latter. The clearers were also asked once again to examine the cartel question. Midland's records indicate a lively internal debate. 'The banks can only lose by abandoning or amending existing inter-bank agreements without a quid pro quo from the Authorities,' an internal memo of 28 January argued. 'It must be a cornerstone of Clearing Bank policy that, as part of the framework for any material change in Clearing Bank practices, there will need to be a "deal" with the Authorities in respect of existing comparative controls (ceiling and liquidity), tax disabilities, etc., vis à vis competitors.' Len Mather, the bank's Chief General Manager and a much-respected, utterly pragmatic career clearing banker, was sceptical. 'Why abolish the Cartel?' he asked in a memo less than a fortnight later. 'Are we being pressurised by uninformed press comment or do we really need as a bank to garner more deposits by cut-throat competition? Our customers are content . . .' And: 'The existing cartel arrangement works well. Are the prospects of open competition sufficiently attractive to make it worthwhile to disturb it?' Graham, also in February, explained the background to the situation with a compelling eloquence:

> It is undeniably true that the influence of the clearing banks in financial affairs has suffered a serious decline over recent decades, and to a great extent this has been caused by a reluctance on the part of the clearing banks considerably to adapt their role and attitudes to encompass changing circumstances; the banks have tended to shelter behind the cosy complacency of the CLCB [Committee of London Clearing Bankers]; also, the banks have unhesitatingly co-operated with the monetary authorities to an extent which has become subservient . . .
>
> The attitude of the clearers over the years has given rise to imperfect market conditions and, as in any such situation, a 'black' market (respectably in the City called secondary, inter-bank, etc.) has developed. The clearing banks can, to a large extent, overcome this because of the weight of their deposits and the coverage of their branch network, but it would mean the abandoning of the interest rating agreement, and the bidding up for deposits. Thus, they would compete, not only among themselves but also with other financial intermediaries . . .

Graham concluded by asserting that, realistically, the clearers could only abandon the cartel if: 'a) the direct controls on advances were removed, and b) any liquidity/cash controls that the authorities wished to impose were applied without exception to all financial institutions in the market'.[15] Graham's broader arguments held sway, for realistically, in the political as well as financial climate of early 1971, no-change was no longer an option – whatever the common-sensical attractions of Mather's blunt perspective.

'I believe it should be possible to achieve more flexible but still effective arrangements, basically by operating on the banks' resources rather than by directly guiding their lending,' Barber declared in his budget speech, and almost seven weeks later, on 15 May, the Bank published a four-page consultative document on *Competition and Credit Control.* It proposed, as far as the clearing banks were concerned, the end of both quantitative ceilings on lending and the interest-rate cartel; while *all* banks would maintain the same minimum liquidity ratio, at 12½ per cent less than half of the prudential ratio that had previously been required from the clearers. In essence, the deal for the clearers was that in return for agreeing to the abandonment of their cosy, familiar cartel, they would be free to compete on level terms with the secondary banks and others. 'The habits of the last decade will die hard,' the *Banker* commented in a generally favourable response to the Bank's paper. 'But it is important for the City as well as its customers that they should be well and truly buried.' Over the next three months the clearing bankers signified their willingness to accept the thrust of the proposals, while managing to persuade the Bank that building societies and savings banks should not be protected from competition for deposits. At the end of the summer session, Heath addressed his party's

1922 Committee and explained the new policy. 'I looked around the room and wondered how many of the MPs present fully comprehended what he was talking about,' Edward du Cann (who was by now chairman of the merchant bank Keyser Ullmann as well as a prominent Tory politician) later recalled. 'I doubt whether more than half a dozen had the least idea.'[16]

The new arrangements came into effect on 16 September. 'What the Bank of England has done,' *The Times* observed, 'is to change the traffic lights from red to green at a time when the banks' progress along the road towards greater competition and efficiency was being halted unnecessarily. If the banks fail to accelerate from now on it will be their own fault.' Forecasts (and metaphors) were rife at this historic juncture, and in the October issue of *Packshaw's Town Crier* (the organ of the local authority and money brokers Packshaw & Associates), Christopher Fildes prefaced his predictions with a typically perceptive, idiosyncratic glance back at 'twenty-five years of trying to regulate the economy's steam-pressure by sitting on the safety-valve':

> There's something to be said for the view that this method, however unsound, has in fact made the engine more efficient. Each new attempt at direct control has prompted ingenuity to the creation of new instruments and new markets. Controls on clearing bank lending drew borrowers' attention to the charms of bill finance, and did more than anything to revive the discount market and the bill on London. When the authorities swept bill finance into their net, other fish could be seen swimming outside. Leasing, factoring, the use of the 'fringe' merchant banks and finance houses, inter-company lending; the rocketing growth of the Euro-currency markets and the profusion of American and other foreign banks in London – these have many causes, but one in common: they have all offered back doors to borrowers in whose face the front door has been shut . . .
>
> Now borrowers find the front door re-opened, and the question is: what will become of the back doors? Will they lapse into disuse? At first sight it might seem so – for who, it is said, would pay a finance house's or a factor's rate of interest when he could go to his bank? But as the banks widen their margins, partly by the increasing use of fixed-term personal loans, partly by pushing overdraft rates up, the attractions of the front door become less marked. And that door is not, in fact, as freely open as it may appear, or as the banks could wish. Locked and bolted for so long, it has become rusty, and creaks obstinately on its hinges. So the well-oiled back doors will not want for users yet awhile . . .[17]

*

The early 1970s represented a time of fundamental monetary change almost everywhere. Above all, these were the years that saw the collapse of the post-war Bretton Woods system of fixed exchange rates, which had tied the whole world to the US dollar, redeemable at the rate of $35 to one ounce of gold. The break-up, after years of increasing strain intensified by the impact of the Vietnam War on the American economy, began in summer 1971: such was the flight of international funds out of the dollar that in May both the Deutschmark and the Dutch guilder were floated; and in August the US left the gold standard. Shortly before Christmas the world's finance ministers tried to put together a new system of fixed exchange rates (the Smithsonian Agreement) but, even with an expanded leeway permitted for other currencies to fluctuate against the dollar, it soon became clear that worldwide fixed exchange rates were no longer appropriate for a world of rapid economic shocks. The world's first financial futures market, enabling the hedging of currency fluctuation risk, began in Chicago in May 1972; just over a month later its founder, Leo Melamed of the Chicago Mercantile Exchange, was in London trying to encourage participation in it. During his visit to the Bank of England he suggested (probably to Hollom, the Deputy Governor) that if the Bank really wanted to help the new market it would kindly float the pound. A strained smile greeted the wisecrack – and the next day, 23 June, the newspaper headlines announced that this was what the British authorities had indeed decided temporarily to do, though for different reasons. The trade balance had been deteriorating rapidly, and the probability of an imminent docks strike had led to such pressure on sterling that the government decided that floating was preferable to another ignominious forced devaluation. Some in the Bank saw it as the soft option, a political evasion of the financial discipline of a fixed exchange rate, but O'Brien was not among them.[18] In February 1973 the yen was floated, soon afterwards the dollar was further devalued and on 19 March the major central banks formally abandoned their commitment to maintaining their exchange rates within a predetermined band in relation to the dollar. The era of flexible exchange rates had conclusively arrived.

Would the end of Bretton Woods give New York a chance to claw back some of the considerable ground that since the late 1950s it had *de facto* given to London? At the end of February 1973, with the near-certainty of the US going shortly to dismantle its capital controls, Midland's Forbes asked O'Brien how he saw London's future as an international financial centre: 'The Governor replied that to the extent that the Euro-dollar market had thrived on the artificiality induced by e.g. the Interest Equalisation Tax, London would inevitably lose some business, but the market was well established and in any case bankers did not come to London only for Euro-dollar business but also to service multi-national companies.' The terminology may have been somewhat confused (the IET had given birth to the Eurobond market), but O'Brien's point was well made. The offshore (or 'Euro') markets, largely based in London, were indeed now 'well established'; and he might justifiably have added that, despite some occasional doubts about destabilising aspects of those markets, the Bank in the early 1970s remained as keen as it had been in the 1960s to keep them based in London, along with as broad a range as possible of foreign bankers and others. Its supervision of newcomers, moreover, continued to rely almost wholly on an informal, personal touch. When Gottfried Bruder and his boss from Frankfurt were preparing the ground for the reopening in 1973 of Commerzbank's London branch (closed in 1914), they went to see James (Jim) Keogh, Principal of the Discount Office. What permissions were required? What regulations did they have to comply with? None, Keogh told them. What, then, was necessary in order to become an authorised bank in London? 'Keogh looked at us,' Bruder recalled, 'and he said: "in London a bank is a bank if I consider it to be one".' Once up and running there was also the occasional, indispensable afternoon ceremony. 'You had to go round and have a cup of tea at the Bank of England, from time to time, and explain what you were doing,' Philippe Muûls of Banque Belge remembers from that era. 'It was very informal.'[19]

In the City as a whole, major elements may have been excessively inward-looking and/or somnolent, but fortunately there were enough pockets of innovation to enable it to keep reinventing itself. 'What amazes me,' John MacArthur, Corporate Finance Manager at Kleinworts, reflected in 1971, 'is that in spite of recent constrictions, of pretty Draconian exchange controls, we have been successful in developing new financial instruments. The achievement is that while, as a source of capital, London is dead, as a source of ideas it is very much alive . . .' Complementing that innovation was London's hugely advantageous position in terms of critical mass – a market share and expertise accumulated down the generations. 'There is much more to London than money, bill and bond markets,' Bolton pointed out in *Euromoney* in 1972:

> For example, few pay more than passing attention to such organizations as the Baltic Exchange, unique in its world role of freight rates, shipping charters and so on. Everyone has heard of Lloyd's but few realise that the world reinsurance market is dominated by Lloyd's and the composite insurance companies. The Plantation House, the London Metal Exchange and other commodity markets have a world role shared only with New York. Lloyd's Register of Shipping is an organisation playing a unique role in establishing codes of safety in shipbuilding and ship management and everything to do with the ocean-wide movement of ships. All these and many other activities continue to grow and ensure the future of the London market . . .

The warehouses may virtually have gone (the Booker/Lycett Green 1973 guide to threatened buildings included a photograph of 50–58 Upper Thames Street and Queen Hithe Dock, the last 'working' Thames-side wharf in the City), but there were still many diverse strands to that densely populous international hub.[20]

In at least two areas, the messy, rather chaotic end of fixed exchange rates did the City a favour. One was the gold market, where London managed to revitalise itself – and recover from the apparent knock-out blow of the March 1968 temporary closure – by making a virtue of no longer being that commodity's *physical* centre. Instead, London became the speculative centre for gold, the place where the keenest two-way price could always be found, much stimulated by the price volatility that ensued once gold was no longer pegged at $35. Younger traders, often with a background in foreign exchange dealing, were now attracted to the market, for in the frank words of one of them, 'the simple spot quotation for gold in the international sense means *loco* London and nowhere else'.[21] The other area that benefited, for obvious reasons, was foreign exchange dealing itself, particularly as one venerable London institution moved with impressive speed to exploit the implications of the end of fixed parities.[22] 'As a result,' a Reuters internal memo observed in February 1972, 'industrial and commercial entities are forced to devote far closer attention to foreign exchange and money market operations, and stand to gain or lose considerable sums of money on these transactions. Our proposed service should fill an information gap.'

The foreign exchange market had up to now relied upon telephones and telex for the latest quotations, but when Reuters started its computerised 'Monitor' service in June 1973, *International Insider* noted that 'the system enables subscribers to receive the latest foreign exchange and deposit rates on television terminals' – a significantly quicker way, in a world where seconds counted, of transmitting market information. It was, at first, slow going to persuade the City to utilise the new service. When, soon after its launch, Russell Taylor of the Italian International Bank (one of the new consortium banks) asked Midland's foreign managers what they thought of it, he received a mouthful:

> It's bad enough having people like you around, queering our pitch, but Reuters is the end. What's the point of having decent dealers, if a television screen gives all the world the buying and selling prices from every Tom, Dick and Harry of a bank that thinks it ought to be a forex [i.e. foreign exchange] dealer? We used to take a good point out of any deal we did with a continental bank, even Deutsche Bank, for God's sake, and now we are lucky to get a fraction of that . . .

At the outset few of the established banks believed that Monitor would work, but in the course of the mid-1970s it became clear that they were wrong; and in 1977 even the London Foreign Exchange Brokers Association, which had mistakenly (if understandably) seen it as a threat to its business, ordered the service. That service's full name was Reuter

Monitor Money Rates, for it included a full range of money as well as foreign exchange rates, and it was a development brilliantly in tune with the much more fluid, much more international post-Bretton Woods financial world. 'In the broadest sense,' *Harvard Business Review* remarked in relation to Monitor before the 1970s were out (by which time its range had broadened to include bonds, equities and commodities), 'we have for the first time a genuine international economy in which prices and money values are known in real time in every part of the globe.'[23]

The 1970s transformed not only Reuter's fortunes, but also Derek Tullett's. As a young man in the mid-1950s he had joined the foreign exchange brokers Savage & Heath, rising by the mid-1960s to become Managing Director. Against much well-meaning advice, he decided in 1971 – just as Bretton Woods was breaking up – to start his own firm:

> It was a very difficult thing to do because by that time there were already a number of well-established brokerage houses in London. Getting a share of the market meant offering services to banks that other dealers weren't. In those days most of the broking houses concentrated on the Eurodollar market, that's where the money was. So we decided there might be room for us if we emphasised the foreign-exchange side of the business, while also providing dealing tables for Eurodollars and Certificates of Deposit.[24]

Tullett & Riley began with just fifteen people, but would eventually (by the late 1980s) become, as Tullett & Tokyo, the dominant international money broker. That too was the ambition of John Barkshire, who in 1972 reluctantly broke with Cater Ryder. For five years there had been at times an uncomfortable marriage between that traditional discount house and the money brokers Marshalls, the latter's people with increasing international ambitions. Caters 'did not understand our hours of work, our sudden decisions to travel,' one of them recalled; another that 'they found their life-style disrupted', in that 'we were noisy eight o'clockers, not necessarily public school'. There were also 'difficult questions of what was "proper remuneration"', so that altogether 'it was an interesting clash between the establishment of the City and the new emerging market'.

Barkshire himself was impeccably public-school and had come up on the Cater Ryder side, but in a fast-changing world he was convinced that the future lay in providing a full and internationally available range of money-market services – a vision that the more staid spirits at Cater Ryder, including the charming but ineffectual Chairman Francis Hoare, were simply unable or unwilling to encompass. Barkshire's solution, inspiring some rumbles from those in the City who considered it bad form, was a management buy-out, as Mercantile House Holdings was formed (with Barkshire as Chairman) to acquire Cater Ryder's international money-broking operations.[25] Restless, ambitious, acutely conscious that the world of money was starting to be transformed more fundamentally than at any time during the century, Barkshire was determined on a course of expansion almost come what may.

In general, at the short end of the markets, the Eurocurrency (mainly Eurodollar) market continued to grow, though not as spectacularly as it had done in the late 1960s. The greater excitement was in medium-term lending, above all in syndicated Eurocurrency credits, described in July 1972 by the financial journalist William Low as 'probably the fastest growing sector of the international money and capital markets'. He estimated that the volume of such loans arranged in 1971 totalled between $8bn and $9.2bn – well above the 'more publicised' Eurobond market's roughly $3.6bn. In terms of how these medium-term loans were structured, he explained that 'the most popular technique is for a bank or group of banks to arrange a syndicate of lenders, the number of which can range from three to fifty spread throughout the world'. At the cutting-edge of the market remained Manufacturers Hanover (Manny Hanny), the London-based subsidiary of Manufacturers Hanover Trust, with Low noting that under the 'inspired leadership' of Minos A. Zombanakis it had 'not only emerged as one of the largest medium-term operations but also has gained the reputation of being one of the most imaginative'. Zombanakis's own recollection of an important coup for Manny Hanny gives the authentic flavour of an innovative pioneer at work, in the process helping to shape a market:

> We noticed a mass exodus of funds from Italy, a flight of capital. It was said that $2 billion to $3 billion had left the country. I know Italy very well. I visited the governor of the central bank Guido Carli, and we talked about this phenomenon in 1970. I said, 'If you are worried about this exodus of funds, why don't we try to recycle these funds back to Italy?' That was long before the recycling of petrodollars.
>
> He said, 'What do you mean?' I said, 'If you designate to me one of your good borrowers, I can take him to the market and raise a hell of a lot of money for him, by paying a spread above the cost of money for banks. Money has left Italy and exists as deposits in foreign banks: it can come back as foreign money if we allow them a 1% spread over the deposit rate.'
>
> I gave him a letter of undertaking. Our first operation was $200 million to $300 million for IMI [Istituto Mobiliare Italiano]. I considered IMI to be the best-run financial institution in Italy at that time, the best credit rating. So I said, 'I hereby undertake to raise $300 million for you' – which was then a hell of a lot of money.
>
> He gave me a mandate and I put together a syndicate of banks for a five-year $300 million credit. Sure enough, it was a stunning success.
>
> We created the agent bank to act for the account of the others. We created the reference banks – the ones quoting the rates – so the agent could determine the base rate on which Libor was going to be formed. We described the responsibilities of the agent bank, and what the borrower had

to do in terms of representations and warranties. And we wrote up the clauses that were applicable to the loan: the rights and responsibilities of the borrower and the lenders. That agreement became known in the market as the standard agreement, or the IMI agreement . . .

Another growing form of medium-term lending, though on a smaller scale, was in London dollar CDs (certificates of deposit). It was a sector dominated almost wholly by White Weld, which in September 1972 persuaded Sumitomo Bank to issue the first-ever CD ($15m) by a Japanese bank. A flurry of similar issues immediately followed, though the Industrial Bank of Japan decided to go to Rothschilds for its CD issue (which, in the event, flopped), because it objected to being only fifth in the queue for White Weld's services.[26] Reserve asset management was not yet much talked about, but White Weld was ahead of the game in spotting that CDs, floating rate notes and so on were potentially very attractive to central banks on account of their instant liquidity.

As for the long end, the Eurobond market, it enjoyed in 1972 and 1973 its two highest-volume years up to then, with issues worth $5,508m and $3,709m respectively. Nevertheless, there remained significant weakness in the secondary market, prompting Bill Low's often provocative weekly on the Eurobond market, *International Insider*, to ask in September 1973, 'Is the day of the market maker over?':

> Over the years, the number of self-styled 'market makers' (i.e. those traders who maintain a book in a wide range of issues) has shrunk almost as fast as the primary sector has expanded. The result, of course, is that investors are locked into many bonds and the situation is getting steadily worse. There are two main reasons for this lamentable state of affairs. First, Eurobond trading always has been a peripheral activity for the majority of banks and brokers involved in the Euromarket. This means that little capital has been invested in the secondary market even in the halcyon days of the late 1960s. Secondly, most of the new issue houses have reached the conclusion – perhaps wrongly – that it is not necessary to maintain a strong secondary operation to help sell new offerings. The situation is most acute in the dollar convertible market, where Strauss Turnbull, one of the pioneers of the Eurobond market, has ceased to be a market maker.

Moreover, the Eurobond market as a whole still had at this time a surprisingly comfortable feel to it – certainly as seen from a latter-day perspective. The astringent and cerebral Michael von Clemm, who joined the pace-setting White Weld in 1972, recalled with a colleague (Jack Hennessy) twelve years later what they clearly viewed as having been a somewhat cosy, undemanding milieu, with an inordinate emphasis on etiquette:

> *von Clemm:* For years and years in this market, and therefore in this firm, everything was sort of frightfully club-like . . . If we were lead manager we'd

sit around and talk for hours about whether this Austrian bank should be a major bracket underwriter if the other three were minor bracket underwriters. And then you'd probably talk to all the Austrian banks, and negotiate their bracket with them, and so on. It was very hand-crafted, one at a time; and there were 100 deals a year, and if you had a 4.6% market share, you had, I guess, 4.6 deals.

Hennessy: You had a week to make a decision.

von Clemm: Months! These things had lead times, and open pricing. You could relax and wait and see what happened at the end. You'd get all the co-managers in the room, all co-managers would put in their two bits. We even used to put our allotment sheets down, our proposed allotments as to which minor bracket underwriter would get 20 or 30 bonds.

Hennessy: Everyone would get around a table and look at the list and talk for hours . . .[27]

It is a salutary perspective, if perhaps tinged with a certain younger-generation triumphalism. The Eurobond market had come a long way since Autostrade in 1963, achieving permanent critical mass in London, but *the* great leap forward was yet to happen.

Principally attracted by the various offshore markets, foreign banks were continuing to arrive in the City, though at a slower rate than in the late 1960s. Among them, it was American banks that continued to make their presence felt most visibly. 'Enter the central banking hall of a large American bank on Moorgate,' Spiegelberg wrote in 1973, 'and you will find a large expanse of open-plan office, girl receptionists to direct you and heavy advertising of the bank's services. In a British clearing bank a few doors away, the walls are lined with marble, there is a great mahogany and glass divide between the customer and the bank officials, and the use of display is ascetic.' The comparative figures underscored the contrast. Whereas in 1960 the deposits of US banks in the UK represented only 5 per cent of UK clearing banks' deposits, by the time Spiegelberg was writing the US deposits exceeded those of the clearers – a fact attributable not only to dollar deposits, but to the failure of the clearers to get enough into the newer money markets. It was also reckoned by about this time that, with their more astutely tailored products and competitive prices, the big US commercial banks (led by Citibank) had achieved a 25 per cent penetration of the UK large corporate loan business.[28]

American banks were also often key players in the rapidly burgeoning, mainly London-based consortium movement, where the early 1970s saw two particularly notable newcomers. One was Orion Bank, established in 1970 by Chase Manhattan, Royal Bank of Canada, National Westminster and Westdeutsche Landesbank; the other, beginning three years later, was the European Banking Company (EBC), owned by the EBIC Group (which included Midland and had grown out of the old European Advisory Committee) and with Stanislas Yassukovich as Managing

Director. Most of the consortium banks concentrated on medium-term syndicated lending, but Orion and EBC were more genuinely investment banks, being active also as issuers in the Eurobond market. By the mid-1970s London was host to almost three dozen consortium banks, and appreciably more if one includes those that did not fit the Bank of England's definition.[29] Among those that got the nod from the Old Lady was the Italian International Bank (IIB), which at about the time it started in January 1972 was told by Keogh that it was all right for it to operate in the City provided that, whatever it did, it did not 'do it in the streets and frighten the horses'.[30]

There were also, in a distinct category of their own, the Japanese banks and large securities houses. 'The Japanese people,' Emperor Hirohito told an audience at Guildhall in 1971, 'have always looked up to the City of London . . . as the depository of financial and commercial expertise and observed, with wonder and respect, its indomitable spirit of freedom, strict code of gentlemanly conduct, and courage to make a startling departure from old practices as occasion arises.' Not surprisingly he received a standing ovation for these warm words. However, when the following year the Ministry of Finance at last allowed Japanese banks to lend to non-Japanese entities, this led not only to a much-increased Japanese presence in the City, but also to a flooding of the syndicated loan market in the form of lower-spread, long-maturity loans arranged by Japanese banks. American and European bankers condemned these tactics as unnecessarily aggressive, accusing the Japanese of 'rate cutting' and, an even more heinous offence, 'dollar dumping'. Those discomfited by the phenomenon – essentially a reflection of the huge gold and dollar reserves that Japan had accumulated on the back of its new-found manufacturing and trading muscle – found consolation in their own apparently greater mental agility. 'I used to spend hours at Nomura,' Peter Ogden, a Morgan Stanley director, recalled of the 1970s. 'They wanted to know how you innovated. "How do you innovate?" They had 20 to 30 PhD students working on it. They couldn't understand how we kept having ideas and they didn't have any.'[31]

For Britain's two largest banks, Barclays and National Westminster, 'international' meant ambitious pursuit of big-league status. At Barclays the great apostle of international growth was Anthony Tuke, son of 'The Iron Tuke' who had chaired Barclays during the 1950s; he himself became Chairman of Barclays International (formerly Barclays DCO) in 1971, before two years later becoming Chairman of Barclays itself. 'Anthony and I had a vision,' a close colleague, Julian Wathen, later remembered, 'that we should turn the bank into a proper international bank. We wanted to compete with Citibank and see them off. We didn't see why we should be buggered about by the Americans.' Unfortunately, Wathen felt compelled to add, this attractive vision had 'one weakness' – namely, 'we didn't have the right people'.[32] That arguably was also the fundamental flaw at NatWest, where the meritocratic recruitment, training and promotion of potential senior managers was similarly backward, quite unlike Citibank since the late 1950s. Some of those who worked at NatWest in the 1970s recalled the fundamental change of direction from early that decade:

> We had McKinsey consultants in here to advise us in 1970, and they said we were too small to survive in a global economy and that we could only maintain our leadership by creating a bigger, more viable bank. And that is what we did . . .
>
> In 1970, we were just a UK bank and we had only three people abroad, all in New York City. To make up for all those years [going back to the 1920s, when Barclays DCO began] when Barclays was a global bank before we were, we got involved in sovereign loans . . .
>
> The theory was that your large domestic deposit base would be the foundation for starting businesses overseas and above all in the USA . . .

At the time, perhaps understandably, the bank did not admit to having any qualms about its new strategy. 'We are delighted with the way international business is going – it is a major contributor to profits,' Alex Dibbs, about to become Chief Executive and on his way to open an office in San Francisco, declared in September 1972. 'We are setting out to offer our services right across the world.' Asked in the same interview about the possibility of encountering 'world competition' in the process, Dibbs replied that he was 'not dismayed' by the prospect. 'The City of London,' he added, 'has an unparalleled reputation. But we must beware of becoming smug.'[33]

On the London Stock Exchange in 1971, following a Monopolies Commission recommendation and amidst some controversy, the rule preventing foreigners from becoming members was finally abolished. Prior to confirmation, Phillips & Drew's Peter Swan (himself an Australian) protested in vain:

> Over the years we have built up and are improving our high standard of business conduct. For these reasons the City and the Stock Exchange receive a large amount of overseas business because people abroad like to deal with us and trust the way in which we operate and they realise the protections that are here for them. However, I am worried for the future of the Stock Exchange if the restriction is removed because whilst a foreigner may no doubt pass his examinations, he may come from a country which does not have the same standards that we have built up in the City. Also please do bear in mind that he will have two loyalties.

Over and above these anxieties, Swan also envisaged 'an influx of Americans channelling business away from recognised London firms'.

However, while individual membership was now opened up, there remained an absolute veto on the admission of foreign firms. It was a serious error. By 1972 as many as forty-seven North American brokerage firms had London offices and were dealing in UK securities as well as dollar stocks; the Stock Exchange's adamantine insistence on staying a closed marketplace simply meant that an increasing amount of international business was bypassing it. Not that the great majority of member firms, still very much UK-oriented, were unduly concerned – an order of priorities confirmed in these years by their retrogressive attitude towards the much-debated question of whether the relatively few London broking firms with a physical presence in overseas securities markets were to be allowed to deal as principals in those markets, where unlike London there was no sacrosanct separation of capacity between broker and jobber. 'Do we really want the standards of our Member Firms to drop to those prevailing elsewhere – say in the USA?' Wilfred Rantzen of the jobbers Smith Bros asked the Council in November 1971. 'Do we really think a Firm can maintain a double standard, one at home and one abroad?' The broker Somerset Gibbs, of Capel-Cure Carden & Co, frankly feared infection:

> I do not believe it is possible to enact effective Rules which could isolate the London Market from the effects of this 'liberalisation'. The dangers may seem remote but as the UK becomes more closely integrated with Europe it is inevitable that more and more UK stocks will become quoted in Europe and vice versa. When this happens London Brokers and Jobbers without European or American affiliates will be at a disadvantage compared with their competitors who are Members of overseas Exchanges. To compete, the London Market will be forced to accept discretionary commissions and dual capacity which will inevitably lead to the disintegration of the Jobbing system and a major upheaval in the structure of the Market and Broking firms. If this interpretation is correct, then the cost to the Stock Exchange of granting 'a licence to compete overseas' to some of its Members could be severe indeed.[34]

In the course of 1972 a temporary compromise was agreed by which London brokers were permitted to operate dual capacity in North America, but not in Europe. In the context of what was starting to become an increasingly globalised securities industry, it was – in retrospect – the beginning of the end for the old, ring-fenced order.

*

On the domestic front, the two years that followed the introduction of Competition and Credit Control would become infamous for the explosion of more or less uncontrolled lending.[35] 'The freedom that was imposed in [September] 1971 was a tremendous spur to the inter-bank market,' George Blunden, then Deputy Chief Cashier at the Bank of England, recalled:

> There were many competitors in the inter-bank market. Many institutions conceived the idea that you could always get your deposits in large wholesale numbers. It became a case of liability management. And with that great growth in liquidity in the banking system, they turned to property. And property prices always went up – at least they had always, since the war. Ultimately, in the early 1970s, there were these two great myths around: that you could always get wholesale deposits and that you couldn't go wrong with investing in property . . .

It was, in the unprecedently competitive environment, an extraordinary couple of years. 'Almost for the first time in the whole history of banking,' a senior clearing banker remembered, 'you found your lending business and then scurried round for deposits.' Between September 1971 and the end of 1973 total sterling bank advances to UK resident borrowers rose by no less than 148 per cent. Crucial to the future course of events, and helping to feed the frenzy, was the unfortunate fact that most of this lending was not for the benefit of manufacturing industry, but rather the property and financial sector. Of course the explosion of bank lending, and the Bank of England's accompanying loss of control over the money supply, would not have happened without the Heath government's ultimately reckless (however well-intentioned) pursuit of economic growth at all costs. Perhaps O'Brien, Governor until June 1973, should have been more forceful in his efforts to restrain the politicians; but as the Chancellor (Barber) was unable to check Heath, it hardly seems fair to blame the man in the Bank. O'Brien himself, moreover, was not helped by the still largely Keynesian assumptions that prevailed among most of his senior colleagues, as among the more thoughtful reaches of the City at large. It was not until June 1972 that Gordon Pepper at Greenwells began his arch-monetarist *Monetary Bulletin*, which does not appear to have influenced City opinion significantly until the following year. But where the Bank *was* justifiably vulnerable to criticism was in its failure to react quickly enough to the changed, post-CCC world. Hamish McRae, writing towards the end of 1973, best expressed the problem:

> One of the main gripes of the money market at present is that the Bank of England does not understand how it works. In the old days the Bank, through its dealings in bills and its contacts with the discount houses, had a pretty good idea of what was happening in the money market. Now the discount market is no longer the centre of the money market. The Bank does not deal in CDs or in interbank deposits . . . When the Bank wanted to find out about the CD market it had to hand round a circular questionnaire to the banks.[36]

The Bank had prided itself for so long on its almost tactile understanding of the markets that this was a serious development, with – as it turned out – momentous consequences.

During the winter of 1971–2, immediately after the implementation of CCC and against the background of rapidly rising unemployment, the government's drive for growth moved into a significantly higher gear. The markets responded gratefully, with the FT 30-Share Index closing 1971 at 476.5, up over one-third on the year. 'Rarely has the investment background seemed so cloudless, or investors so unanimous in the optimism of their expectations,' Rowe & Pitman's *Market Report* declared at the start of 1972. 'Is it, somehow, all too good to be true?' The Chancellor himself boasted in his New Year's Day message that 'no government has ever before taken so much action in the space of one year to expand demand' and that 'the economy is expanding at twice the rate of the average of the last six years'. The Chancellor may or may not have had his private doubts at this stage, but Heath's determination to continue to boost activity probably hardened the following evening when he held a dinner party at Chequers, with guests including Jacob Rothschild, Nigel Broackes of Trafalgar House and (sitting next to the Prime Minister) Jim Slater. Just over a fortnight later, on 20 January, there was a deeply embarrassing moment for the City as the Index went above 500 on the same day that, for the first time since 1947, the jobless total reached seven figures. The *FT*'s leader could not deny that the conjunction made 'an easy anti-capitalist debating point', but maintained that historically 'the behaviour of the Share Index is, if anything, an encouraging sign', in that 'every major downturn in the Index has heralded a rise in unemployment' and, usually, vice-versa. The industrial as well financial temperature was rising – the miners were on strike, with the young Arthur Scargill in charge of the new device of 'flying pickets' – and Clive Jenkins, General Secretary of the white-collar union ASTMS, gave a blunt warning to capitalism's citadel. 'The City of London is going to be entirely organised,' he declared that month. 'I am absolutely clear of that. There will be resistance, there will be emotional attitudes; but against the background of legislation [the recent Industrial Relations Act] and the emotional atmosphere of the country the City will be unionised from top to bottom.'[37]

Slater's presence at Chequers was a mark of how successfully Slater Walker had bounced back since the various disappointments of 1970, including the break-off of talks with Pearsons, disappointing results and a faltering share price. In June 1971 he was applauded by *Management Today* for having 'produced the most convincing proof so far in Britain that genuine business growth can be created by, in effect, dealing in companies and in their securities'; also that year, in his study of *The Strategy of Takeovers*, the financial journalist Anthony Vice noted that although 'many other groups have tried to imitate the Slater technique of buying companies, reshaping their assets, and emerging with substantial profit', the fact remained that 'none of Slater's imitators has experienced anything like the success on anything like his scale'. Anthony Sampson, in his 1971 version of *Anatomy of Britain*, cited Slater as 'the very paragon of the new Heath-type Tory – self-made, hard-working, unsentimental, competitive', and in November that year Slater's fellow-speakers at the Institute of Directors' annual conference (5,000 leading British business-men assembled in the Albert Hall) included not only the Chancellor but also Lord Goodman, Lee Kuan Yew, the Prime Minister of Singapore, and Dr Billy Graham. In his speech Slater called on the government to incentivise managers through share-option schemes – or, in Slater Walker jargon, 'giving the boys a piece of the action'. 'The Master', as he was sometimes called by the numerous small shareholders who packed Slater Walker's annual meetings and slavishly followed his investment advice, seemed to be everywhere. Slater's erstwhile partner, Peter Walker, was now a member of the Cabinet, and Kenneth Fleet dubbed this period of the Heath government as 'the Slater Walker government'.[38] Even O'Brien was infected, wanting to make Slater a director of the Bank of England until dissuaded by more cautious voices. In fact, most of the seeds of his eventual downfall had already been sown: the creation of a host of satellite companies, at home and abroad, too many of them run by unsupervised, second-rate people; the decision, subsequently described by Slater as 'a cardinal error', to get into commercial (as opposed to investment) banking; the lure of an expanding property portfolio; and, early in 1972, the £33m flotation of Slater Walker's Dual Trust, before long nicknamed the 'Dustbin' on account of being seen as a dumping ground for Slater Walker's holdings in its less successful satellites.[39] For the moment, though, none of this mattered: Slater remained a phenomenon of his age on an almost untouchable high.

Two well-respected journalists, both writing in the *Sunday Telegraph*, contributed their fill to the legend. 'Slater's magic wand' was the title of Patrick Hutber's column, as City editor, a fortnight before Christmas 1971. In the context of rapidly rising share prices for two of Slater Walker's property satellites, Sterling Land and Thomas Stevens, he asked:

> How far can Jim Slater create values? I sometimes imagine him standing in front of a complex glass apparatus, the sort of thing used in fifth form science. Through it goes a flow of cash, of propositions, of buying opportunities. He turns a tap underneath and outside one of a row of beakers comes capital appreciation . . .

Hutber was also entirely sanguine about the quality of the people running the satellites, commenting that Slater 'seems to have found, untapped, a whole new vein of talent, particularly from the post-war grammar schools'. Barely a month later Graham Turner contributed a laudatory two-part feature. Slater, he reported, 'can see nothing to stop the company growing from its present £185m market capitalisation to between £750m and £1,000m within 10 years, on the way to achieving his ultimate objective of becoming the biggest investment bank in the world'. Or, in Slater's own words, 'It's like a knife and butter, and we're the knife'. Slater himself, still only forty-two, believed he was hitting his peak: 'Now I know what I am, and Slater Walker knows what it is. Watch out.' Turner also described the weekly ritual of the Monday morning meeting at 30 St Paul's Churchyard:

> It is run – or rather driven – by Jim Slater himself.
> He brings a sense of tension, of high voltage, into the room. This rapidly transmits itself to the rest of the gathering and helps produce a curious feeling of corporate exhilaration as they rattle through a huge range of topics. You have a feeling that somewhere outside something is going very fast, and that it can't be left untended for too long.
> Slater himself constructs immensely complicated doodles, deftly picks up any weakness in argument or clarity and seals each brief debate with a who-does-what-by-when decision.
> His language is marked by a series of stock phrases which, to experienced colleagues, are signposts to his pleasure, or lack of it. 'Over-simplifying,' for example, means 'this is the point'. 'If I can put it like this,' means 'you haven't got my point.' 'The point I'm making' means 'you've missed the point again' and 'are you with me?' means 'will you *never* get the point?'

Just in case any of this alarmed his more nervous readers, Turner was adamant that Slater Walker's 'accounting procedures' were 'conservative', and he finished with another supremely confident piece of Slater self-publicising: 'We're like an amoeba, an amoeba with a great capacity for survival and self-improvement, and we're very difficult to beat.'[40]
What is one to make of this gifted, charming but uncharmable, somewhat neurotic, ultimately rather cold man? Nigel Broackes, who had known him since 1966, would describe Slater well after the fall:

> He fascinated the financial press, and believed his own press cuttings; finance to him was a game of chess [of which Slater was a devotee], and he claimed the role of knight grand master; shares in companies, and companies themselves, were pawns; his involvement was intellectual, not emotional, and much of the game was played with himself and the satellites which he created to join him. His machine thrived on press support, and the image became self-breeding as his powers of patronage grew with the scale of his ability to buy and sell shares, and with the volume of commissions earned by the stockbrokers who were chosen to carry out his business.

Undoubtedly there was an arrogant streak. He once, it was claimed (again after the fall), described the point at which adolescence gives way to maturity as that point when you stop thinking that you think, and start knowing that you know, that everyone else is as stupid as they first seemed to be. Nevertheless, his autobiography, *Return to Go*, gives – perhaps misleadingly – a rather different impression: of an unpretentious, family-centred, surprisingly straightforward man, capable of looking back on the most dramatic part of his career with irony and even humour. That account was written in the immediate wake of the fall, while years later Slater would concede on television that in his pomp he did start to believe in his own publicity: 'You begin to feel you're walking on water . . . but it's thin ice in fact.'[41]

Nevertheless, neither in his memoirs nor subsequently would he properly confront the charge made by Charles Raw, in his hostile, exhaustive study of Slater Walker published in 1977, that even though the Slater Walker of the early 1970s liked grandly to call itself an international investment bank, in reality it was a systematic, quite shameless insider-dealing operation. 'The satellites', Raw claimed, played a key role in this 'machine for generating stock market profits around the world':

> Slater Walker had erected a mammoth paper chain of companies in the UK, Australia, South Africa, Canada, Singapore and Hong Kong, each with its own stock market quotation; and this was matched by a string of investment vehicles, its dealing companies, unit trusts, investment trusts, life assurance companies. Shares were then churned around this complex, with the effect that the value of the investments once again lost contact with any growth in the underlying businesses, but was determined only by the malleable forces that rule share prices and the eagerness of investors to join any promotion bearing the Slater Walker imprimatur.[42]

Moreover, when the dust settled during the second half of the 1970s and Slater Walker passed into the history books, it was amazing how little of substance that meteoric company had achieved. All those noble and dis-interested sentiments about restructuring and modernising British industry had proved so much hot air.[43] Again, the apposite recollection comes from Broackes. One day in 1970 the two men were lunching in 'the windowless basement' of Slater's City offices. On reaching the coffee stage, Slater leaned back and said: 'Let's face it: none of us here are interested in management!'[44]

The early months of 1972 were Slater's apogee. On 15 March, against the background of industrial strife and a sluggish industrial economy despite rising bank lending, consumer demand and share prices, Cecil King lunched at Schroders with Gordon Richardson and his directors. 'They had no news,' he complained, 'and the main impression left in my mind was that they are entirely concerned with the day-to-day problems of their business. They do not seem to bother to be well-informed on the larger issues confronting the country.' Six days later Barber presented the arch-expansionist budget of the post-war period. All the evidence is that O'Brien was frozen out of the budget-making process, and in his memoirs the Governor's deliberately moderate tone failed to conceal a certain bitterness:

> Cuts in revenue taxes plus other budget measures [such as major concessions on depreciation in order to stimulate investment] raised the public sector borrowing requirement in 1972/3 to the then unprecedented level of £3,360m. In this and other ways the Government laid the foundations for the credit splurge in 1972/3 which failed in its good intentions, fuelled the property boom and led to a sharply increased rate of inflation through an entirely excessive growth in the money supply. Thus an entirely unexpected burden was placed on the new arrangements for credit control of a more competitive banking system which, after the long-standing quantitative controls, needed a much more sedate economy than this in which to settle down. As a result the new credit arrangements, which had been so praised when first announced in May 1971, were to some extent discredited, especially so, of course, in the eyes of those politicians who had fathered the highly imprudent expansion of the economy which had been the root cause of the trouble.

At the time, however, most City opinion seems to have given Barber's budget a warm response; certainly the *FT*, in an editorial called 'A Calculated Gamble', played down its obvious inflationary dangers. The market continued upwards in April, and on 4 May King had lunch at another merchant bank, this time Kleinworts, where its Chairman Gerald Thompson was his rather more reflective host. 'He is alarmed by the progress of inflation. This is all very well for merchant banks – they are coasting downhill with the wind behind them, but what about the economy and the country? The inflationary situation favours the City at the expense of industry – particularly heavy industry. As a result an undue proportion of our bright young men are being sucked into the Stock Exchange and similar financial institutions.'[45] There were few, if any, indications that the City at large, head down and doing extremely well for itself, shared Thompson's concern.

Three days earlier, on Monday, 1 May 1972, the Slater Walker share price (which in 1970 had been down to 138p) hit its all-time high of 412p. The following Sunday, interviewed by John Davis in the *Observer*, Slater reiterated his ambition for Slater Walker (whose market capitalisation was now £220m) to achieve a market capitalisation for the group of £1,000m by 1982 at the latest. This would require, he explained, an annual compound growth of 15 per cent, much of which would be achieved through overseas operations. Keen to show that he had learned from the lessons of history, Slater looked back on his problems at the start of the decade: 'Having had a sky-high price-earnings ratio of 40 and then hit a bear market, I don't want to chase my tail all the time . . . It was a struggle I can tell you.' It was a line that Davis bought in its entirety, as he ended his piece with a prediction and a final quote: 'When the next bear market arrives, Slater, at least, is not going to be caught napping. "I'm good and ready for it."' That same day, in the *Sunday Times*, the paper's financial editor, Graham Searjeant, took a notably different tack as he retrospectively examined 'Seven days in the life of Jim Slater' at the start of the year. Tracking the dealings that Slater Walker had made during that week in its satellite and client companies, he found that it had been actively selling shares in most of them, especially those companies that were to go into the about-to-be-launched Slater Walker Dual Trust, the so-called 'Dustbin'. After commenting on the implicit wider dangers to a genuinely free market, and warning investors against buying into the satellites and being left at the top, Searjeant came, with a certain pardonable nervousness, to the crux of his case:

> There are also dangers to Slater Walker – though with the market booming, the satellites booming, share dealing being particularly successful and the group obviously heading for bumper earnings I would not claim to be making a timely warning.
> The essential animal has changed much more even than its two-year switch from industrial break-up to investment banking would suggest. The Slater Walker we knew and loved was the raider who bought shares at below their asset worth, turned them into cash to buy more assets at gathering momentum. Increasingly now the investments are in shares valued at a premium over their assets, and the whole circus has become a machine that earns a lot of its profit by generating the premiums that boost its own apparent assets – a seething pyramid of escalating paper.

It was a memorable phrase that should have set alarm bells ringing, though Searjeant added that 'fortunately, the master shows no signs as yet of losing his strategic touch'.[46]

Later that month the $20m Slater Walker issue that White Weld offered to the Eurobond market was heavily oversubscribed, with underwriting names on the tombstone including Barings, Rothschilds and Schroders. Also in May, Slater approached NatWest's Chairman, Sir John Prideaux, with a view to acquiring half of its merchant bank, County Bank, in return for NatWest taking a half-share in at least some of his property companies. 'I believe he has become stable and is developing into a person of considerable importance and influence in the City' was how Prideaux recommended the deal to his executives, but led by Alex Dibbs they managed to head him off. During the summer there was also the renewed possibility of an association between Slater Walker and Warburgs, this time along the lines of a full merger. Again the initiative came from Warburgs, where Warburg himself may have been conscious of a potential vacuum after his almost septuagenarian generation departed, but Slater was more than willing to run with the ball. Negotiations, he recollected, 'reached quite an advanced stage'; but when he put the proposal to his directors, he 'found everyone very unresponsive' and did not press them. Privately he concluded that some of them had been fearful of being swallowed up by the higher-calibre team at Warburgs. None of this, though, impeded the Slater Walker 'circus' during the rest of 1972. One academic visitor to Petershill House, Derek Channon of Manchester Business School, found 'an enormous *esprit de corps*' in the spartanly furnished offices there: 'People working at Slater Walker really do believe they are part of one of the fastest moving groups in the country. The pace is quite tremendous. The group is young, alive, open to ideas and there is never a dull moment. Everything takes place at enormous speed.' Or, as Slater himself told Channon, 'What we have here is a sort of earthy meritocracy'.[47]

As it transpired, the 1971–2 bull market peaked at 543.6 on 19 May, nine days after Patrick Sergeant had observed to the many small investors who faithfully followed his *Daily Mail* column that 'cash is unfashionable but, before too long, you may be awfully glad you've got it'. In fact, even though prices had peaked, the market atmosphere remained distinctly bullish, with the Index still above 500 at the year-end. 'There is a natural instinct to linger longer in the good times,' John Littlewood has written, 'and this bull market had been as good a party as any could remember . . . At moments like this, a bull market almost enters into a conspiracy with itself, fuelled by excitement and greed.'[48] Not surprisingly there continued to be considerable takeover activity, as in 1971, and the early summer saw a resolution of the huge (£435m), fiercely contested bid by Maxwell Joseph's Grand Metropolitan for Watney Mann, the third-biggest British brewing group. The City's sympathies were wholly with the besieged brewers – for some weeks little stickers proclaiming 'Hands Off Our Watneys' were plastered all over the square mile, including 'the Drain' – and there was an enormous amount of buying in the market on both sides.[49] In an exceedingly tight finish, marked by an unsuccessful appeal to the Takeover Panel to appoint independent accountants to observe the counting of acceptances, what almost certainly tilted the balance towards Grand Met was the Prudential's decision to accept the offer. Massive media attention accompanied the closing stages in late June and early July, and Ladbrokes even opened a book on the outcome. It was the first time that a major brewer had been taken over by an 'outsider' and, as such, came as an enormous shock to established City assumptions.

Far less publicised, but almost simultaneous with the Grand Met bid, were the agonies undergone by the jobbing firm Smith Brothers as they attempted between April and July to break into the gilt-edged market – just at the time when prices there, no longer (under CCC) supported by the Government broker, were falling rapidly.[50] 'I'd done some home-work but I found it a little bit foreign,' the partner most closely involved, Geoffrey Lederman, conceded. 'I thought you could go in there and use the methods that one uses in the equity market. The big two [Wedd Durlacher and Akroyd & Smithers] had a look at everything first of all, and while you were waiting on the fringes the whole market was changing, so it was a rather difficult operation, certainly for us. We retired hurt after a fairly short period of time and lost about £380,000, which was a pretty considerable sum to us in those days . . .' George Birks, dealing in gilts on behalf of Phillips & Drew, put it more bluntly: 'For reasons best known to themselves they decided to be very aggressive when they started, and because of this and the fact that they didn't realise that some stocks reacted independently of other gilt-edged stocks, they were doing deals in stocks which had they had the experience they wouldn't have done.'[51] However, even a more measured approach might not have worked, given that the very mechanism of the gilt-edged market was struggling to cope with the implications of CCC (the immediate context for the third-biggest jobbing firm there, Francis & Praed, departing from the Stock Exchange scene later that summer) and given also that Wedds' Dick Wilkins was implacably opposed to any potentially threatening newcomer, certainly one with the hard-trading, upstart characteristics of Smiths.

For O'Brien and others at the Bank these were dog days. 'The Governor can get no answers from the Chancellor and finds it hard to meet Ted,' John Stevens told King towards the end of May. 'The Bank cannot reduce the supply of money without causing a setback to the business recovery.' A month later the essentially political decision to float sterling – one that had already been foreshadowed in Barber's budget-speech assertion that henceforth growth would have a higher priority than maintaining parity – meant that a greater premium was placed on getting monetary policy right than at any time since the 1950s. In theory this was good news for the Bank, but in reality its control over monetary policy had rarely been so weak in peacetime. 'It would be quite wrong,' Barber informed the Commons soon after floating, 'to restrict the rate of growth of the money supply in a way which would hinder the rate of economic growth at which we are aiming.' Unfortunately, in addition to fuelling inflation, far too much of that money was going into property speculation; and when in August, in the first old-style informal directive since the coming of CCC, O'Brien requested that the banks should 'as necessary make credit less readily available to property companies and for financial transactions', the effect was nugatory. 'Money out of control' was the title of the *Banker's* very critical editorial in September marking the unhappy first anniversary of CCC:

> The growth of the money stock, by any definition, has been excessive for many months past, exceeding an annual rate of 20 per cent . . . Moreover, for the past year or so the main factor in this monetary explosion has been the rise of bank lending at an annual rate of about 50 per cent. As the demand for bank credit for manufacturing and other industry has remained sluggish, an unduly large proportion has obviously gone to inflate the value of existing resources, such as houses, building land and shares . . . For some time now the City has come to assume that the Bank has meekly implemented the Treasury's growth policy against its better judgement. No other explanation fits the strange delay in calling for Special Deposits or otherwise restraining the wild splurge of bank lending . . .

It was true, the *Banker* conceded, that short-term interest rates had risen during the summer; but the fact remained that 'real interest rates, taking inflation into account, are still very low'. As for the argument, being advanced in some quarters to defend official policy, that 'increases in the money stock do not fuel inflation unless the economy is at full stretch', this – according to the *Banker* – was simply 'Keynesianism gone mad'.[52] For the moment, though, the City ranks of the incipient monetarist counter-revolution were more or less confined to the scribblers, not the practitioners. For many at the Bank, the Barber boom may indeed have been 'Keynesianism gone mad', but that did not mean that Keynesianism itself was suddenly no longer valid.[53]

The previous month, *Management Today*'s annual City Growth League had revealed Slater Walker on top, followed by Pat Matthews's First National Finance Corporation (whose Chairman was Viscount De L'Isle, a former Governor General of Australia, but capable of reading a balance sheet), with Tom Whyte's Triumph Investment Trust also in the top five. 'The pace is now being set,' Robert Heller commented, 'by men who are outside the City, either in their attitudes or in their activities: and the revolution in the thinking of City institutions, and in their attitude towards the management of their mostly vast assets, has often not gone far enough or fast enough. In consequence, some have failed to achieve the results which, as professional investors in industrial companies, City institutions are supposed to stimulate.' In short (as Heller placed himself uncompromisingly on the side of what Gerald Caplan, supremo of London and Counties Securities, liked to publicise as 'The Energy Generation'), 'People who live in glasshouses are in a weak position to start throwing stones.'[54]

The authoritative history of the secondary, or 'fringe', banks that flourished in the late 1960s and early 1970s has yet to be written, but it is clear that there were, broadly speaking, some shared characteristics: in lieu of their own deposits, a heavy reliance on the rapidly growing, wholesale inter-bank market, which in the words of Midland's historians 'represented a chain-letter mechanism', in that 'it transferred cash deposits from individuals and corporations into the primary banking system (via the clearers, leading accepting houses and foreign banks) to secondary banks'; an irresponsible approach to accounting, including pretending that capital gains on investments were earnings to be valued at a multiple of 20 or more; a fatal attraction to lending to property developers and others in that buoyant, get-rich-quick world; and, in most cases, a single dominant figure at their head.[55] CCC may have been intended to enable the clearers to kill off the secondaries, but in practice it had provided plenty of rope for both. A quick glance at some of the leading secondaries, in the hour of their most conspicuous flowering, suggests something of their range and appetite, though leaving to one side Slater Walker as a sort of super-secondary.

Triumph Investment Trust was the £200m vehicle (with interests in, among other things, banking, hire purchase, insurance and property) of Tom Whyte, a Hungarian-born financier who had served time in the plastics industry; an £8.7m cash injection from Sir Max Rayne's property company London Merchant Securities enabled Edward Bates and Sons to expand considerably during 1972–3, especially in banking, corporate finance, investment management and insurance; subsidiaries of the Burston Group (still run by Neville Burston, with a former Lord Mayor, Sir Bernard Waley-Cohen, as Deputy Chairman) included not only Burston and Texas Commerce Bank, but also Burston Finance, which sold itself as a provider of 'medium-term facilities for development of, and investment in, freehold and leasehold property'; and Cripps Warburg (known as C.W. Capital until the end of 1972) was the joint creation of Stafford Cripps's nephew and Siegmund Warburg's only son, building an apparently sound merchant banking business until they foolishly decided to jump on the property bandwagon.[56] Cedar Holdings, successfully brought to the market by Barclays and Cazenove's in January 1971, was a well-run West End-based business, largely specialising in second mortgages, with some strong institutional backers. Unfortunately an uncontrolled lending splurge soon ensued, as the quality of its business sharply declined, complete with much self-aggrandising advertising and publicity.[57] J.H. Vavasseur, from 1968 the vehicle of three thrusting young financiers in David Stark, Jeremy Pinckney and Gervase Thomas, was active in foreign exchange broking (through the acquisition of Harlow Meyer), banking (Vavasseur Trust), money management and property. Early in 1973 it paid the handsome price of £18.5m for Barclay Securities, the vehicle of John Bentley, who after being an early, smooth-talking Slater protégé had acquired fame in his own right as a ruthless asset-stripper (especially in the toy and film industries). Soon after that acquisition, Vavasseurs had a new Chairman in the person of the *FT*'s recently retired editor, Sir Gordon Newton, an improbable guinea-pig. 'This was an error of judgement, which I realised after I had been there for only a few weeks,' he recalled. 'There was nothing wrong with the people involved; they were youngish, enthusiastic, and honest. It was just that I felt out of place.'[58]

Still, Newton was lucky not to be at London and County, where from 1971 there was a *real* guinea-pig on the board, in the person of Jeremy Thorpe, leader of the Liberal Party. Caplan's creation was growing fast in the early 1970s, and its failure in 1971 to acquire the small merchant bank Leopold Joseph was compensated for the following year when it bought (from Christopher Selmes, another of that era's 'whizz-kids') the industrial-cum-financial conglomerate Drakes. Its asset base thus trebled, and notwithstanding its increasingly high exposure to property, the *FT*'s 'Lex' soon declared that the current climate looked propitious for its 'high risk/reward make-up'.[59] Pat Matthews was an altogether more conservative operator than Caplan, and in 1972 his First National was given full bank status by the DTI. 'I'd like,' he remarked soon afterwards, 'to build up a very interesting company that would be there for many years to come, a solidly based financial institution in the City of London which keeps it word and plays the game with a very straight bat.'[60] Finally, far more established in a City sense than any of the other secondaries, there was Keyser Ullmann & Co, the result of a merger in 1962 between Keyser & Co (which traditionally had had strong links with Samuel Montagu) and M. Ullmann. Its Chairman from 1970 was the Tory politician and former City man Edward du Cann, while two years later the Prudential acquired a 12 per cent stake. Soon, however, a reasonably orthodox banking business became vulnerable to the property cycle, as first Keysers bought Central and District Properties, and then acquired the secondary bank that had expanded perhaps more rapidly than any other through property loans, Jack Dellal's Dalton Barton. By 1973, it was generally agreed, Keysers was flying, especially once it had sold on Central and District at a £28m profit.[61]

The Bank of England would later be much criticised for failing to apply adequate supervision during this period of headlong growth.[62] The standard defence was that, under the 1967 Companies Act, responsibility for that supervision fell at least as much on the DTI and the Treasury; but inevitably the retrospective spotlight was on Threadneedle Street, in particular the Discount Office, where since 1967 Hilton Clarke's successor as principal had been Jim Keogh. At the time of the appointment the discount market would have preferred George Blunden, but was told firmly by O'Brien that it was the Governor's choice. Keogh was a mercurial Irishman who tended to divide opinion, both inside and outside the Bank. He would in due course become the Bank's scapegoat and, a decade and a half later, die in self-imposed exile. 'He was a man of strong presence,' Christopher Fildes recalled in a notable tribute, 'with curling grizzled hair and a limp from a war wound which gave him continual pain and sometimes shortened his temper – he could and did ruffle the City's smoother feathers.'[63] He also, no doubt partly because of the pain, drank heavily, and in general was not quite of the all-round calibre of his predecessor. In the early 1970s he was in a no-win situation: the DTI was continuing to hand out certificates to new fringe banks as if they were confetti; CCC and the Barber boom were in their fateful conjunction; and at the Bank itself, little or no notice was taken of Keogh's warnings (based on close contact with some of them, including London and County) that trouble was brewing. One day he even read out to a senior consortium banker the draft of a memo to O'Brien, strongly urging that action had to be taken before market forces punctured the bubble with potentially catastrophic consequences. The banker subsequently asked Keogh what response there had been to that memo, and was told that it was still gathering dust in the Governor's drawer.

Irrespective of that story – impossible yet to document – the latter part of O'Brien's governorship must have been deeply frustrating, not least during autumn 1972, as the finance-and-property boom continued almost unchecked and, in Middlemas's words, 'real interest rates fell to historically low levels': around 1.2 per cent by the end of the year. In accordance with CCC's provisions, Bank rate had been replaced in October by the Minimum Lending Rate (MLR), which was intended to be more market-responsive, following rates rather than leading them; in practice it merely compounded the ineffectiveness of monetary policy. Towards the end of the year O'Brien even observed (in a much-quoted remark) that there was no such thing as a monetary policy that would simultaneously stimulate expansion and control inflation, despite Barber's claim that the government had managed to square that circle. However, if there was a greater villain than government in the Bank's eyes, it was undoubtedly the trade unions. On 9 November, three days after Heath had executed his fateful U-turn by introducing a Statutory Prices and Pay Standstill, a Fed memo recorded the thoughts of the Bank's Norman Robson:

> With respect to the exchange market, sterling began to decline yesterday and declined earlier today as people considered the rejection by the TUC [of] talks on prices and wages during the period of freeze. In essence, the TUC has painted itself into an impossible situation by balking all overtures from the government and has to continue to make intransigent statements to satisfy union membership.
>
> On the other hand, looking ahead to phase II of the prices and wages

policy, there will be need of some co-operation from the unions, and as long as they continue to be unyielding there is little hope for long-term improvement in the wage situation.[64]

More parochially, the Bank at about this time let it be known that it would no longer object to 100 per cent outside ownership of accepting houses. The determining context may well have been not only imminent British membership of the EEC, but also the fact that, in the course of the year, the Brandt family had reluctantly agreed to a full-scale sell-out to National and Grindlays, the clearing bank (whose business was mainly in India and East Africa) that even before the Midland/Montagu tie-up in 1967 had taken a majority stake in William Brandt, one of the most low-key accepting houses, lacking a corporate finance arm. Even so, Brandt's had grown considerably between 1965 and 1972, including in insurance and Eurodollar lending; and Peter Brandt subsequently claimed that, against the background of a major culture clash between Brandt's (still in its own building in Fenchurch Street) as merchant bankers and Grindlays as commercial bankers, they had been assured by the Bank that it would save Brandt's from full integration with Grindlays by finding an alternative owner. However, when push came to shove, as Brandt's sought to resist pressure from Lord Aldington of Grindlays for integration, any such assurances proved worthless. Peter Brandt's somewhat cynical explanation was that O'Brien knew that Aldington, as a former Tory politician, was close to Heath and that, with his own future peerage in mind, he was not prepared to stand up to him.

Predictably, other unions were soon in the air after the Bank's change of stance. Almost immediately there occurred in December 1972 the merger between Guinness Mahon and Lewis and Peat, where the dominant figure was still Harry Kissin, very keen on running an even larger, more highly diversified conglomerate and, in any future power struggle at Guinness Peat, always likely to get the better of Guinness Mahon's former Chairman, the more gentlemanly banker Charles Villiers. Were the merchant banks as a whole now up for sale? According to David Montagu's private estimate, made soon after the Bank's announcement, they all were – with Rothschilds the only exception. Perhaps ironically, when Midland the following summer completely bought out his own outfit, Samuel Montagu, he was not offered a seat on the main Midland board, took this as a calculated snub and was soon recruited by the consortium bank Orion as Chairman and Chief Executive. He reputedly walked out of his family bank without so much as a backward glance, professing for ever after the deepest contempt for clearing banks.[65]

Another banker who could never have been mistaken for a clearer was

Oliver Poole of Lazards. The financial journalist Douglas Moffitt nicely described his style, in its way the apotheosis of the cult of the merchant banker: 'He plays his role of discreet unavailability with great application, timing his boardroom arrivals and departures with great precision, gliding discreetly in and out of clients' offices, emerging with Grand Designs, setting up concepts and contacts and leaving others to the minutiae.'[66] During much of the second half of 1972 Poole's grand design was that two of the companies that Lazards advised – the shipping company P&O and the house-building and construction group Bovis – should merge through an agreed bid.[67] Unfortunately for Poole, soon after that cosy arrangement was announced on 10 August it became clear that the deal was in trouble, as the financial press gave it the thumbs-down, dissident P&O directors raised their voices in opposition and Morgan Grenfell masterminded opposition from P&O's institutional shareholders. During a protracted, complicated battle, lasting to mid-November, both sides spent a small fortune on newspaper advertising and there was even a rash of posters in the City proclaiming the not exactly sparkling slogan 'Save P&O. Tell Bovis no'. Finally, P&O's Chairman, Ford Geddes, and his board, which included Poole, were forced to accept defeat. Moffitt describes a compelling scene:

> When he [Geddes] faced his mutinous shareholders for the third time in five weeks at 3 p.m. on the afternoon of Friday 17 November, he announced no figures, but said the proxy count showed a rejection of the bid by a substantial majority, and said that he had no doubt that if the proposal were carried to a poll, it would be defeated. The Hall of the Chartered Insurance Institute went wild with jubilation. Geddes said he would resign. Wild applause. Before the resolution was formally put, Lazards were crucified. A call was made from the floor for the resignation and the hall erupted and hissed with hatred at mere mention of their name. It was an unprecedented display of emotion. Poole announced his intention to resign, and that Lazards would waive its fee. He was rewarded by jeers. He left a shaken man . . .

Poole's reputation had already suffered from the Rolls-Royce fiasco the previous year, but this was a far more serious, personal blow. 'Lazard legend lost in P&O's pool of tears' was the headline in Monday's *Daily Telegraph*, with Kenneth Fleet expressing the hope that 'its sorry involvement with P&O will precipitate the thorough overhaul that Lazards of all the remaining barnacle-bottomed four-funnellers left in the City so manifestly needs'. Poole left Lazards the following summer, and a year later (as the result of a stroke) quitted business life altogether. Arguably there was a larger, twofold significance to the P&O/Bovis episode: within the City it shifted the balance of power away from the merchant banks and towards the institutional shareholders, who henceforth would have to be 'sold' a deal well in advance of it going public; and between the City and the outside world there could never be quite the same blithe assumption that the City knew what was best for industry. By the end of 1972, with the pep starting to go out of the bull market, the industrial, social and economic situation deteriorating and asset-stripping becoming the object of the deepest opprobrium, the golden days of the takeover were over – at least for the time being.

One industrialist about to be permanently disenchanted with the City was David Morrell, Chairman of Mitchells, one of Britain's largest construction companies. It was fundamentally a sound, even flourishing business, but disaster struck after it won the contract to build a huge power station off the Kariba Dam in Zambia and found itself deceived by false geological reports and starved of money. Amidst widespread shock, it went into receivership at the end of January 1973. Fourteen years later, in a powerful, well-documented account, Morrell revealed some of the forces that had destroyed his company – and, in the process, cast an incidental but revealing searchlight on the ways of the City. In particular, he demonstrated how two of his principal financial advisers, the merchant bank Samuel Montagu (to which he had been sent by his bankers Midland) and the accountants Cooper Brothers, had been fundamentally hobbled, in terms of doing their job properly on behalf of Mitchells, by conflicts of interest. As early as spring 1972 he was disconcerted to discover from David Montagu that the impending flotation of McAlpines was going to be handled by Samuel Montagu; McAlpines, which dominated the British construction industry and had especially intimate links with the Conservative Party, had long seen Mitchells as a particular thorn in its flesh, largely because of Morrell's long campaign against existing methods of placing and managing public-sector contracts that, in his view, encouraged corruption. Over the next nine months Morrell received only minimal, sometimes even positively unhelpful, support from his merchant bank, especially at the most critical moments. As for Coopers, from whom he received even less benefit, he later discovered that the firm was also playing an advisory role to the consulting engineers Gibbs and the Central African Power Corporation (CAPCO), who between them (according to Morrell's account) had been perpetrators of a major fraud on Mitchells. 'For those of us who live, or perish, outside the City establishment,' he commented, 'the concept of conflict of interest must remain an impenetrable mystery.' On the first day of the receivership, he sat in his office receiving a flood of sympathetic, bewildered messages from all manner of people. One quarter, however, was silent: 'Where were the faceless ones and the "Yours evers" from the City?'[68]

The City was not criticised at the time for its handling of the Mitchells situation, but there was a clear sense during the winter of 1972–3 of it starting to come under fairly sustained attack. On 13 November the Stock Exchange's Chairman, Sir Martin Wilkinson, sent a strong letter of complaint to Lord Hill, Chairman of the BBC, following a recent *Money at Work* programme on BBC2 that had marked the Queen's opening of the new building. The treatment, he wrote, 'was biased in the extreme and much of the time was given to tendentious and abusive criticism, largely unsupported by evidence', including allegations of market malpractice. Less than a fortnight later there was a heated debate in the Commons about recent trends in takeovers, with both sides of the House singling out the asset-stripping activities of John Bentley for special criticism. Then, in early January, the Labour Party's General Secretary, Ron Hayward, told the Fabians that the question of nationalising the banks and insurance companies was no longer 'whether' but 'how'.[69]

Inevitably, a particular focus of external criticism was insider dealing – a practice that was widely believed, with some reason, to be endemic in the City.[70] Early in February Wilkinson and Shawcross (still at the Takeover Panel) urged Peter Walker, as Secretary of State for Trade and Industry, to consider including legal sanctions against insider dealing in the government's proposed new Companies Act. Walker responded positively, but the headline in the *Daily Telegraph*, 'Days of the Insider are Numbered', was on the optimistic side: for various reasons it took another seven years for legislation to be enacted. On this and other matters the prevailing City culture was still firmly in favour of self-regulation, though an exception was the stockbroker Victor Sandelson who in April, some fourteen years after his critical essay on the City establishment, argued in the *Sunday Times* that self-regulation was no longer able to cope with 'the growing difficulty of keeping an ebullient and inventive City within the confines of legality and general ethics'. Noting that 'it is by now widely accepted that the [Takeover] Panel is only limping sadly behind events', and calling for a British version of the SEC, he deftly sketched the larger context:

> When the City community was small and was drawn from a homogeneous social background a fairly effective discipline was imposed by the imperative need to remain 'reputable' in the eyes of one's equals and, especially, of the Governor of the Bank of England. This informal discipline still retains some force. But as the City has expanded and drawn heavily on a much wider social reservoir of talent, the 'gentlemanly' standards have lost much of their former force . . .[71]

No doubt there was some truth in this analysis, essentially a variant on the Cobbold-imposing-Etonian-standards line. Yet historically it was precisely those with the very best connections – whether school, club, sporting or family – who had been most enabled to benefit from insider dealing. On the basis of that compelling logic, the City would become more fundamentally honest only when it became more fundamentally meritocratic, and not before.

For most members of the Stock Exchange Council, the issue that really agitated them by 1973 was the threat from an unexpected quarter to the Stock Exchange's monopoly position as London's sole securities market.[72] The long-term background, up to about 1971, was recalled by Michael Verey of Schroders:

> What we were finding was that the stockbrokers were really getting too big a cut off the joint, and we had a great effort through the Accepting Houses Committee going to the Stock Exchange Council and saying, 'Look here, something has got to be done about this'. The commissions on gilt-edged were absolutely ridiculous. Originally, you see, it had been you shared the commission 50/50 with the stockbrokers; then it was altered to a third, by the Stock Exchange, and then to a quarter. And really stockbrokers for taking no risk of any sort or kind were really being too well rewarded and we were getting crosser and crosser at the Accepting House Committee meetings and they refused to budge. I remember one of their most senior chaps saying, 'Of course what you want is to share in our profits', which was perfectly true but they were just doing too well. We were giving away huge sums for those days in commissions to stockbrokers, nearly all business we'd created . . . So the Accepting Houses, finally getting very cross, started to investigate what turned out to be ARIEL . . .

Verey's main associate in determining to mount a challenge was Christopher Taylor-Young of Hill Samuel, and in general it was the big merchant banks that drove the Accepting Houses Committee to take action. Colin Leach was recruited (originally seconded) from Schroders at the start of 1972 to be Managing Director of the new venture, which in the course of that year acquired the very suitable name of ARIEL (Automated Real-Time Investments Exchange) because the basic idea was that, along the lines of the Instinet system in the US, it would provide an automated order-matching system, at lower cost than the Stock Exchange. It is worth emphasising, however, that what drove the merchant banks to take this action was dissatisfaction not so much with the general level of commissions, but with the fact that the Stock Exchange would not make a special exception for them and thus enable them to deal cheaply and pass on wholesale deals at the full retail rate, thereby netting the difference. The Accepting Houses Committee, Wilkinson told his Council in January 1972, wished 'to be accorded special treatment for their Members alone', but he had informed its representatives that that was out of the question.[73] The merchant banks, in short, were not altruists.

Plans for a computerised share-trading system were formally announced in May 1972, and within three months the Stock Exchange reacted by substantially cutting its equity and gilt commissions for higher-value bargains, widely seen as a panic measure. In September, addressing a meeting of the Society of Investment Analysts (including, taking notes, Paul Bazalgette of Phillips & Drew), Leach 'commenced with a somewhat recondite quotation which was intended to prove the proposition that "The Securities Industry can operate from Anywhere" and was not tied to any one location'; explained that 'subscribers will have television sets at the terminals in their offices, will be able to feed dealing intentions into their sets, and will be able to communicate anonymously with other subscribers should a deal appear likely'; accepted that 'the important "face-to-face" factor will be missing and that their build-up will necessarily be slow'; and, expressing the hope that ARIEL would 'recruit as subscribers the leading 200 or so British institutions', he summarised its ultimate objective as being 'to provide an inexpensive efficient trading market which will transcend National boundaries'.[74]

ARIEL was due to go live in early 1974, and during the winter of 1972–3 the Stock Exchange's opposition to it hardened. In January a special committee reported that 'it cannot be right for the Council to allow either brokers or jobbers to join ARIEL', in that 'to do so would inevitably increase ARIEL's potential share of turnover and, thereby, increase its credibility and saleability to the institutional investor'; while the following month Wilkinson told ARIEL's Director-General, Charles Clay, that the Accepting Houses Committee 'must expect hard commercial competition from the Stock Exchange' and that 'room for co-operation with the present system was difficult to see'. Fitful negotiations continued between the Stock Exchange and the AHC (whose members were ARIEL's sole shareholders), and there was even an attempt by the Stock Exchange to take over ARIEL, which was conclusively rejected in September 1973 on the grounds that this would involve ARIEL 'ceasing to provide a dealing facility and becoming a Stock Exchange information service'. What was the Bank of England's attitude? There had been a revealing episode that April, when O'Brien told Wilkinson that ARIEL had requested the Bank to act as its clearing and escrow bank. Wilkinson's immediate reaction was to tell O'Brien that 'if the request were met it would appear that official support was being given to ARIEL, which the Council would think was unfortunate in the circumstances'. The following week O'Brien told the clearing bank chairmen of ARIEL's request, and added that 'he had, after much thought and with some hesitation, declined to act because it seemed right to stay on the sidelines'.[75] Neutrality, however, was not quite the Bank's position, for at some point thereafter, prior to ARIEL's launch, Blunden categorically told Clay that the Bank, because of its unwillingness to lose control of the gilt market, was reluctant to see gilts being traded on the new system. It was a steer that no accepting house of that era was likely to ignore.

ARIEL's protagonists may also have been discouraged by the darkening economic background. The thrust of the wages and prices freeze was obviously anti-inflationary, but during O'Brien's last six months as Governor a combination of rapidly rising world commodity prices and the money supply being out of control meant that inflation was still running uncomfortably high at some 9 per cent – almost unprecedented in the post-war period. Neither fiscal nor monetary policy was toughened appreciably during this first half of 1973, as Heath seemed to become increasingly obsessed by the twin priorities of getting unemployment down and ensuring that home-owners did not have to pay a double-figure mortgage rate. 'We must face the fact that it was being widely criticised,' the clearing bank chairmen were told at the end of February by a beleaguered O'Brien, in relation to CCC. 'A substantial part of our difficulties could be ascribed to inflationary expectations and we must all hope that Phase II would be successful, but the large public sector borrowing requirement would make it more difficult to control the money supply in the coming year.' Shortly afterwards there was a harbinger of future traumas when the Bank and the clearers mounted a secret operation to rescue the banking department of the Scottish Co-operative Wholesale Society, which had got itself in a mess dealing in forward sterling CDs. Such help, the Barclays board solemnly recorded in its minutes, did not commit Barclays 'to join in the rescue of other banks if they got into difficulties'.[76]

The markets, meanwhile, were increasingly convinced that the government could neither deliver real economic growth nor contain inflation. Prices started to crumble on Monday, 22 January 1973, partly in fright at the dividend controls involved in the recently announced Phase Two plans; but arguably the real moment that the bear market set in came three days later, when the headline 'Jim Slater says shares are still too high' appeared above Patrick Sergeant's City column in the *Daily Mail.* The two men had lunched the previous day at Slater Walker's offices, and the result was one of those rare articles that truly made the financial weather. 'Mr Jim Slater thinks our shares are between too high and much too high. He will be surprised if the FT Index [currently 478.2] is better than 425 by June 30 . . .' Sergeant also revealed that Slater Walker had been going liquid ever since the previous May, adding that 'as lunch went on, Jim and I concluded that the best investment was – CASH', notwithstanding the risk of inflation. Sergeant concluded his piece with his own assertion that Heath was now far down the 'Socialist' road of controls: 'It does seem that Capitalism is over the top – at least for some years.' Almost immediately there ensued a wave of selling, especially by small investors, and Slater found himself much criticised. Much of that criticism merely reflected the jittery City mood, not helped by renewed turmoil on the industrial relations front, and in February the monthly circular that Cazenove's sent to its private clients was positively hysterical in tone, referring at one point to how 'the general lack of respect for important values (ignored murders in Ulster, indiscipline and public exhibitions of filth) have all helped to numb our minds'. In a more humorous, less apocalyptic vein, Paul Bazalgette told his readers that he had recently been to Germany, where 'recommending to fund managers that the time is fast approaching when they should be looking at the British market is, in their eyes, somewhat akin to offering threadbare clothing from a jumble sale to richly caparisoned Princes . . . They do not actually retch at the mention of such things as the British economy, sterling or labour relations, but the disfavour on their finely chiselled features is plain for all to see.'[77]

On 8 February, O'Brien's sixty-fifth birthday, it was announced that he would retire as Governor at the end of June, to be succeeded by Gordon Richardson of Schroders. Middlemas has argued that it was O'Brien's own initiative that he should go, reflecting his dissatisfaction with being unable to persuade the government to accept a substantial rise in MLR, but that was certainly not King's understanding at the time. 'Leslie O'Brien was sacked,' he noted on 9 March after lunch with John Stevens, 'under rather harsh circumstances, as he was not felt to fit in sufficiently quickly with Ted's financial and commercial ideas. Gordon Richardson was appointed to succeed him by the PM.' And on 3 April, after lunch with Bolton: 'George confirmed that Leslie O'Brien was sacked, and not allowed to suggest his successor.' A few weeks after the announcement Bolton wrote a letter to Richardson that was more than just congratulatory:

> You have taken over the responsibilities of the Governor of the Bank at a time when few men would welcome the challenge and your position is all the more exposed because, in recent years, the Bank has lost a great deal of power and influence in the City – the reasons being many and varied. Leslie O'Brien did a most remarkable job in helping to restore some of the lost internal morale [i.e. as a result of Cromer's governorship] but he never had the experience or the imagination to build up around him a group of independent-minded men who could make an impact both on Whitehall and the outside world. The tendency has been to promote from within and import the ready-made academic mind.[78]

This may not have been a wholly fair analysis, but it was essentially true; and it was certainly timely, coming as it did just as the post-war corporatist-cum-Keynesian consensus – of which Richardson, like Heath, was very much a part – was about to face its most searching challenge.

During the spring, O'Brien's deputy, Jasper Hollom, made a speech to the Lombard Association in which he accepted that the current rate of annual increase (some 25 per cent) in the money supply was too high, but muffled the impact by pointing to the difficulty of accurately controlling

M3, the most common method of measuring money supply. This did nothing to lessen the sense of a central bank almost powerless to act, as world commodity prices went up by unnerving leaps and bounds, inflation continued to bite and the FT 30-Share Index declined to 450.3 by the end of June. Perhaps not surprisingly, Gordon Pepper's monthly monetary broadsides were now starting to attract attention and even exert some influence. 'Nobody can deny that Mr Pepper's regular bulletins to clients are an important factor in the formation of City opinion on monetary trends,' William Keegan, the *FT*'s distinctly non-monetarist economics correspondent, noted in early May. 'To quote one Bank of England official not so long ago: "Things are quiet at the moment. Gordon Pepper has the flu."' Still, rather more on the mind of the average City man was the thought that, although things were not at present all that brilliant, they would surely be far worse under another Labour government. By May the Shadow Cabinet was actively considering the question of nationalising the financial institutions. 'A Committee of Enquiry into the Stock Exchange would be the right thing to do,' Wilson told his colleagues. 'It is an amateurish casino and should be an investment market. We should try to see whether we could use the pension funds for public purposes.' Callaghan was unconvinced: 'We are aiming at the wrong targets. The City may be immoral but you can't control the banks.' The amanuensis was Tony Benn, and soon afterwards 'Banks prepare for takeover by the State' was the stark headline in the *Daily Telegraph*. 'The 1984 Wedgwood Benn Government may or may not nationalise the 25 leading manufacturing companies (plus the newspapers) but it will assuredly put a huge public oar into banking and insurance,' Kenneth Fleet predicted in pseudo-Orwellian vein. 'The rapidly concentrating banking industry will look especially tempting, since it will not be too difficult for gilded political tongues to argue that banking power is excessive and irresponsibly exercised, and probably the mass of the electorate won't care too much anyway provided they are assured their deposits are safe . . .'[79]

Fleet's reference to 'the rapidly concentrating banking industry' had a particular resonance in the light of the bombshell announcement some six weeks earlier. 'Slater Walker and Hill Samuel merge in £1,500m finance group' was the front-page headline in *The Times* on 27 April, with Ian Morison in the same paper billing the proposed merger as 'probably . . . the most fascinating City development since the war'. The headline figure referred to gross assets, while net assets would be more than £150m; either way, the proposed new company, to be known as Hill Samuel Group, would instantly become the City's largest merchant bank. For Slater and Keith, who were all smiles at the inevitable press conference, this was poised to be the culminating moment of their careers. Why did they want to do it? In his autobiography Slater explained how various health problems early in 1973, combined with the generally darkening financial outlook, had led him to decide that 'I no longer wanted to run a large public company'. During late March he was talking anyway with Hill Samuel, and 'the idea of getting together grew on Kenneth Keith, Bob Clark and myself, as all of us felt that to succeed in international investment banking it was vital to have a large asset base and that there was considerable scope for rationalising our banking, investment and insurance interests'. Or, as he elaborated, 'Hill Samuel had the professional banking expertise and name, and were members of the exclusive Accepting Houses Committee, whereas we had the assets, a fast-growing merchant banking business and a network of international companies.' Moreover, 'this time the Slater Walker board were enthusiastic about the concept and authorised me to finalise negotiations'.

All of this made perfectly respectable business sense, but did Slater also fear, as the market turned down, that Slater Walker's days were numbered unless, fairly quickly, he found a safe place to park it? Trying not to job backwards, one can only guess. What is clear, however, is that Keith, undeterred by his MEPC setback three years earlier, was still intent on hitching Hill Samuel to a bigger balance sheet. He also saw Slater himself as a talented, self-made man who by now had valuable European and international know-how, whereas Hill Samuel's growth had been very much UK-oriented. In addition, it made a significant difference from Keith's point of view that Slater was willing (despite Slater Walker's £113m net assets, as against Hill Samuel's £40m) to be no more than Deputy Chairman. 'It was generally understood between us,' Slater recalled, 'that Bob Clark would dominate the banking side of the new business, and that I would run everything else with Kenneth Keith having the final say when necessary.' Or, as Morison at the time put it nicely: 'Both men [i.e. Keith and Slater] have very special and rare financial talents; for the good of the new group it must be hoped that they prove complementary ones.'[80]

Immediate press reaction was generally warm. The *Daily Telegraph* welcomed the creation of 'a comprehensive international banking group' that would be 'capable of challenging the big American, Japanese and European banks'. The *FT*, playing up the Slater contribution, saw the union as peculiarly fitting: 'While Hill Samuel is leading towards a breakdown of tradition, Slater Walker has from the beginning carved out its own traditions. There have been success stories in the City before and will be again, but never has there been anything quite so big, so successful, and so singular as the growth of SWS . . .' Nevertheless, over the next few weeks the share price of both Slater Walker and Hill Samuel dropped appreciably, admittedly in a declining market, while from the start the deal was damagingly opposed in the *Sunday Times* by Graham Searjeant and his American colleague Lorana Sullivan. 'If you judge by appearances,' their article on 29 April began, 'Jim Slater did his worst ever deal last week. Why, the City was asking, was Slater, the man who aims to be the biggest investment banker in the world, suddenly being so self-effacing?' The implication was clear, if for the moment silent, and Searjeant and Sullivan merely urged the government to refer the proposed merger to the Monopolies Commission. For a time, despite or perhaps because of the ultimate decision resting with Peter Walker, that seemed a real possibility. However, various pledges that Keith solemnly gave to the DTI on 22 May – including that 'it is our intention to develop on the lines of a European Banque d'Affaires and our policy will be directed to the long-term improvement of profitability, with due regard to the interests of employees, rather than to the realisation of short-term gains' – averted that potentially awkward outcome. As for Slater, he gave an upbeat interview to *Fortune*, the American business magazine. 'You can only really have one name,' he remarked of the loss of the Slater Walker name. 'We aim to be an international investment bank, and theirs is clearly the better banking name. Also, the disappearance of my name depersonalises the company and that suits me.' There was, he added, a 'clear understanding' that in time he would succeed Keith as Chairman, 'subject to the decision of the then board' – a board on which he did not deny that there would be a Hill Samuel majority. That, he insisted, was irrelevant. 'We discovered,' he said of the talks leading up to the merger announcement, 'that we have a common philosophy and a common aim – to build a great international investment bank. I'm very proud of our name, and if we were going on as we were, we would have kept it. But I like change, and the new name makes the point that we are changing.' In sum, he concluded wryly, 'This merger gives the wheel another turn.'[81]

As it happened, much of the City's attention during May was focused on another larger-than-life figure: Tiny Rowland.[82] Almost two years previously, in September 1971, Warburgs had resigned as Lonrho's merchant bank in protest against Rowland overriding its advice, though by spring 1972 Rowland had managed to achieve a semi-rehabilitation in the City by accepting pressure from O'Brien that the Lonrho board be broadened to include the eminently respectable Sir Basil Smallpeice, a former Managing Director of BOAC and Chairman of Cunard. Rowland did not mend his ways, and eventually Smallpeice and seven colleagues (the 'Straight Eight') sought through a High Court action to have him removed as Chief Executive. The trial, which lasted from 8 to 14 May, failed to achieve that, but by throwing up many damaging allegations about Rowland's running of Lonrho as a corrupt personal fiefdom it did inspire Heath, in the Commons on the 15th, to condemn the revelations as 'an unpleasant and unacceptable face of capitalism' – a phrase that almost instantly became associated not just with Lonrho, but with all the other buccaneers who had done so well out of the finance and property boom of the early 1970s. By this time Heath was frustrated and thoroughly disenchanted with the City, and the feeling was somewhat mutual. 'Recently Ted addressed a party of bankers at No 10,' King had noted in early April on the basis of information from Bolton. 'Tuke, chairman-designate of Barclays Bank, told him [i.e. Bolton] Ted had lambasted them for not investing more in British industry. This went down very badly.'[83] As for Rowland, the judge's decision that the management of Lonrho was ultimately a matter for the shareholders gave him his escape. On the last day of May the ranks of Lonrho's small shareholders gathered at the Central Hall in Westminster and, in defiance of the wishes of the City institutions and much of the financial press, backed Rowland amidst noisy, exultant scenes. It was as if, in the age of corporatism, Rowland was a latter-day Barney Barnato or Whitaker Wright, a capitalist hero.

In early June attention returned to the Hill Samuel/Slater Walker situation, with the deal due to be completed on the 21st. In particular, on the basis of some ingenious, detailed investigations, the *Sunday Times* stepped up its hostile campaign – in effect arguing that, because the sums no longer added up, Slater Walker was refusing to make adequate reliable information available to Hill Samuel's shareholders. That was on Sunday the 3rd, and the next day there was a significant shift from the *Daily Telegraph*'s Kenneth Fleet, who in his piece about 'the 1984 Wedgwood Benn Government' warned that 'with size, the notion of nimble merchant banking minds goes out of the window'. He added that Hill Samuel's clients had already been voicing 'their apprehension of having their companies' affairs handled by a group incorporating the biggest and most successful wheeler-dealing business ever developed, to wit Slater Walker'. Fleet also made clear his view about which party really needed the marriage: 'I think Jim Slater, in his considerable wisdom, "sold" the merger with Hill Samuel and Sir Kenneth Keith, for his own passionate but perhaps less practical reasons, "bought" it.' Just over a week later, on the 13th, even Patrick Sergeant, historically an admirer of both men, started to make sceptical noises, warning (partly in the context of a recent tie-up between Warburgs and Paribas) that the creation of huge financial-service conglomerates was liable to produce in the end 'all the clumsiness, surliness and slowness of a dinosaur'. The *Sunday Times* reiterated its opposition on the 17th, and the next day Sergeant issued a *cri de coeur* in his *Daily Mail* column under the headline 'Jim Slater must stop this disastrous bid'. After stressing that, unlike some, he had nothing against Slater Walker as such, he made his central point: 'The observer, they say, sees most of the game. I have known Mr Slater and Sir Kenneth a long time. I like and admire them both. I feel strongly that they could not work together.'[84]

Did Sergeant know that the relationship had already reached breaking point? 'As we began to run into criticism, and our share prices continued to weaken, tempers began to wear a little thin,' Slater wrote tactfully but revealingly about the weeks after the original announcement. 'Sir Kenneth Keith is a tough and able man who has a strong physical presence; I knew that, whilst I had enjoyed meeting him for lunch and at an occasional City cocktail party, I would not enjoy working for him, as I also liked my own way most of the time.' The storm broke on Saturday the 16th, ironically the day after the sudden, early death of Keith's old adversary, Julian Melchett, which conceivably influenced Slater's state of mind, though surely not Keith's. 'Kenneth telephoned me at home while I was having breakfast . . . He complained that I had not kept them fully advised about placing a large number of Slater Walker's shares in Bowater, which we had agreed to liaise about . . . I did not like being taken to task over my breakfast and made this very clear to Kenneth. By the time the telephone conversation had ended so had our plans to merge . . .' The formal announcement was made on Tuesday the 19th, and for once the wording, with its reference to how discussions had revealed 'fundamental differences of work-style and personalities', did not mislead. Hill Samuel later claimed that it was only during those discussions that it had a chance to examine Slater Walker's figures, and found them wanting; but almost certainly Slater's account, with its emphasis on personality, gives the truer story. For both sides the abandonment of the merger was a serious blow. For Hill Samuel it was another débâcle uncomfortably soon after the MEPC episode, but for Slater Walker it was nothing less than an intimation of mortality. Andreas Whittam Smith in the *Investors Chronicle* offered the most penetrating analysis:

The Slater Walker concept is founded very largely on confidence: confidence that hard assets, shares or whole companies are worth more in Slater Walker's hands than the market would normally be prepared to pay for them. While this confidence endured it was largely self-fulfilling.

But in the course of the merger debate the concept has been searchingly questioned. What has emerged is that first, the climate of opinion in the UK has in any case moved against the present style of Slater Walker operations. Second, the opportunities for these operations in the UK are no longer so thick on the ground. Third, Far Eastern markets that might have provided the future scope for operations outmoded here have turned down . . .

In short, 'the master of takeovers has failed in the one takeover which would have lifted him into a new league'.[85]

One other resonant figure was also contributing to a remarkable few weeks of City history. Sir Denys Lowson, that free-spending, publicity-conscious Lord Mayor during Festival of Britain year, had continued to be somewhat tainted. 'Colonel Sir Rex Benson came in,' Cobbold had noted in January 1959. 'The English Speaking Union have to appoint a Chairman of their Branch's Committee. They have in mind Denys Lowson but have some reservations on possible repercussions in the City. I said they would have to make up their minds. He was a good speaker and active but I could only confirm that it might put some City hackles up.' By then, in the context of the Prevention of Fraud (Investments) Act of 1958, which at last made the management of unit trusts a less lax affair, Lowson's 'ethical deficiencies' were, according to his biographer, 'increasingly resented in the City'. Accordingly, 'Few men of ability or moral courage would now work for Lowson, who was increasingly surrounded by cyphers. He had a phenomenal memory for financial intricacies and controlled his interests autocratically.'[86]

Eventually, in January 1972, a major investigation by John Roberts for the *Investors Chronicle* brought into the public arena for the first time something of the range of Lowson's interests and how they interconnected. 'By espionage I penetrated the true ownership of myriad cross-shareholdings in nominee names,' Roberts recalled. 'In essence, Lowson controlled a score of investment companies and trusts, each of which held small stakes in all the others so that cumulatively control lay within the informal group. This had the effect in many cases of the freely tradable shares in any company being few so that its stock market price was sensitive to small buying and could be driven up, enhancing the reported asset value of all others in the group.' A few months later, at a Drayton Group luncheon at Tallow Chandlers' Hall, Roberts's editor, Whittam Smith, found himself sitting at the same table as Lowson, but happily not quite near enough to compel conversation. (Jim Slater sat almost opposite the veteran stockbroker Murrough O'Brien, reputedly the original for John Beaver in Evelyn Waugh's *A Handful of Dust.*) Then, at the start of June 1973, another Roberts investigation appeared in the *Investors Chronicle.* This was very specific, revealing that during summer 1972 Lowson had acquired shares for himself and his family from the National Group of Unit Trusts, which he controlled, for about 62p each, before a few months later selling them on (mainly to Tom Whyte's Triumph Investment Trust) for £8.67p each – giving him a handy net gain of some £5m. On 11 July, after a pause for reflection, Lowson issued a statement: 'Although I considered the terms of the acquisition to be fair and reasonable, I have now come to the conclusion that it would be wrong for me to retain the benefits of the sale and that it would be in accordance with the best tradition of the City of London, which I have served for some 45 years, for me to restore the position.'[87]

The game, however, was up, and soon the DTI initiated an

investigation. Its report, in July 1974, found Lowson guilty of 'grave mismanagement'; Lowson had no alternative but to resign from his positions of control; and in September 1975, just hours after receiving an indictment summons for fraud, he died in the London Clinic. The *City Press* had once avidly followed his twelve months in the Mansion House, but it was now compelled to admit that Sir Denys was leaving behind him 'a sadly tarnished reputation'.[88]

*

'It is almost platitudinous to say that there is movement afoot for the greater control of the City,' Midland's Stuart Graham reflected in July 1973. 'This undoubtedly includes the domestic banking system, and I think this movement transcends the bounds of the party political dogma and is most probably the brain-child of Whitehall.' By 'Whitehall', Graham no doubt had in mind the Inter-Bank Research Organisation's report, 'The future of London as an international financial centre', commissioned by Lord Rothschild's think tank. As with all reports, only a few sentences were widely quoted:

> It is a fact that many people in the country doubt if the City is making a good enough contribution to the economy as a whole. The City is not generally well regarded by industry, by educated and professional people, or by the populace at large. Even in the City itself sober people say privately that some of our financial institutions are sluggish and complacent and in certain cases overpaid.

Accordingly, 'a conceptual framework is needed within which freely competitive financial institutions largely in the private sector will be seen to be capable of meeting the economic and social needs of modern society'.[89] As for 'the party political dogma', later that summer the Labour Party published a Green Paper formally proposing nationalisation of the banking and insurance sectors.

By this time, of course, the City had a new headmaster in the person of Gordon Richardson, Governor from the start of July. For several months he kept a low profile, and that autumn Bolton rather cruelly told King that the new Governor 'had been angling for the job for ten years' and that 'he wants the prestige and the peerage, but knows nothing of central banking'. Whatever the truth of those charges, the fact remained that Richardson was undeniably a class act – and, in City terms, had been since the mid-1950s. Henry Benson, who after retiring from Coopers became an adviser to the Governor, rightly described Richardson as both 'a man of scrupulous integrity' and 'a perfectionist'. Furthermore:

> He has a very gentle demeanour, but there is an iron fist in the velvet glove. Once he's made up his mind on an issue of principle, nothing will change it. There are some disadvantages in this in the sense that because he's

a perfectionist he sometimes delayed decisions, some for a little too long, while he was making up his mind and satisfying himself that the decision was the right one. But once he'd made up his mind then that was that.

Richardson also had a stronger physical presence than any Governor since Montagu Norman. Win Bischoff, who started at Schroders in 1966, remembered his first impressions: 'Very handsome man; he seemed to me to be quite tall but he wasn't. I think his personality was such that he seemed to be quite tall. Very elegant; very imposing. A god.' Stephen Fay, in his insightful study of the Bank in the 1970s and 1980s, had the perfect title for his chapter on Richardson: 'Elegant Meritocrat'.[90] At a potentially critical moment in its fortunes, the City could not have done much better.

Irrespective of the specific fate of Keogh's memo, by the time that Richardson took office there were already rumblings about the secondary banks, whose share prices by now were a long way below their 1972 peaks. A particular concern was Caplan's self-publicising stewardship of London and County Securities, and a well-respected banker, Hill Samuel's Donald Bardsley, had already been persuaded by the Bank to move there as a stabilising influence. In August, *Management Today*'s annual City Growth League saw Heller singing a different tune. He found 'the mounting unease, unleashed by the Lonrho affair, about the way in which the City makes its money' entirely understandable, given not only the way in which ' "thing-making" ' was 'actually used as a term of near-contempt by some City whiz-kids who have performed their wizardry on industrial companies', but also the far greater financial rewards available in the City than in making things: 'Any bright young man in search of a fortune would be ill-advised, say, to enlist in the cause of ensuring British Leyland's survival and growth: he would do far better by helping some merchant bank to swing a few million pound deals . . .' Heller then turned on 'the newcomers' like Slater Walker and First National, 'with their wheeling, dealing, corporate manoeuvres and so on': 'The truth is that much of the City's most spectacular growth has been created out of thin air . . .' Fortunately, he added, 'the climate has perceptibly changed', and 'devices such as insider-dealing or warehousing of shares are plainly on the way out', with the result that 'it will not be so easy in future to put together financial conglomerates at such breath-taking pace and with such conviction'.[91]

Did all this mean that the secondaries, in the late summer and early autumn, were suddenly drawing in their horns? Almost certainly not, to judge by the striking testimony of Richard Langdon, a leading City accountant who was also on the board of First National:

> By 1973 the game seemed to be coming to an end. There were signs of developers over-extending themselves. The writing was on the wall. But you

had created a high earnings capacity in the secondary banks and if you said you were going to put your balance sheet right by going for cash, it was withdrawing from the race, going into port. People said you couldn't do this . . . They said 'We can only go forward; we can't go back'. People who have known success don't believe in less success. If some advised going slow, people argued that you had to stay with it . . .

Nor did the more cautious clearing banks necessarily find it so easy to end the profitable lending binge, much of it to the secondaries, of the previous two years. Graham's July 1973 memo was suggestive:

> Given the market environment [i.e. CCC] in which we have to work, the Inter-Bank Market is essential. It is the only speedy and efficient market in which the large volume of volatile short-term funds with which we deal can be channelled into profitable use . . . There are inevitably the 'whiz-kids'. But, provided we deal only with first class names, pay due regard to volume in one hand, and watch market developments closely we should come to no harm.

Or, as Midland's monthly *Review* put it more generally in August, 'the banking system does not appear to be taking on any additional risk, since inter-bank borrowing and lending must net out'. At least, unlike Barclays and NatWest, Midland *was* trying to confine itself to 'first class names'.[92]

Heath's continuing deep reluctance to apply the monetary brakes did not help. Admittedly there were two sharp interest-rate rises late in July (largely because of the sterling crisis), and in September Richardson felt able to issue a reasonably tough new letter to the clearers about 'further restraint on lending for property development and financial transactions'; but the underlying economic policy reality was that Heath, Walker and a few other ministers still hoped against hope that, in the words of Heath's biographer, 'the Government was on the brink of achieving its break-through, despite the commodity price explosion, the alarming trade balance and the sinking pound'. After all, as late as September the *Economist* still felt able to state, with its usual impervious confidence, that 'Britain is two-thirds of the way to an economic miracle'.[93] Moreover, even though turnover remained (as it had been for several months) depressingly low, the Stock Exchange that month mounted a mini-rally on its new floor, with the Index gaining almost 7½ per cent, up to 429.4 by the end. On 6 October, however, Egypt invaded Israel and, in the City of London as in the whole Western world, all bets were off.

Two leading figures at Lloyd's had something marginally more parochial on their minds during that crisp early October. That institution had one of its periodic golf outings on Thursday the 4th, and paired on the Walton Heath course were Ralph Rokeby-Johnson and Roger ('Orator') Bradley. Small talk dried up after three holes, as each wondered whether the other would broach the unmentionable subject. At last, as they waited on the fourth tee, Bradley popped the question: 'What can you tell me?' Rokeby-Johnson's reply, eventually to become immortal, was given as a stage whisper: 'What I can tell you is that asbestos is going to change the wealth of nations. It will bankrupt Lloyd's of London and there is nothing we can do to stop it.'[94]

CHAPTER SIXTEEN

Very Sick

'Whatever the efficient market theory may say about all the news being discounted in the market at any given point, there can be no argument about the fact that if in October 1973 all the news was known, its significance was not appreciated for some days.'[1] George Blakey's point in his history of the post-war stock market is surely right. Above all, the news on the 17th that not only were the producer states going to cut back oil production by 5 per cent a month, but that the crude prices demanded by the Gulf States were going rise by at least 70 per cent, had remarkably little impact over the next three weeks. The FT 30-Share Index closed on Friday, 9 November at 430.3, almost exactly the level it had been at the start of October.

Moreover, despite a major dose of Governor's gloom in Richardson's first Mansion House speech, the brakes remained off, as banking advances during October rose by £850m and MLR even came down by a quarter-point, to 11.25. Still, it did not take a genius to detect that, globally speaking, the balance of economic power was shifting; and at this stage the main talking-point in the City's parlours seems to have been Morgan Grenfell's rapid, controversial exploitation of that shift. As the news leaked out that Morgans was organising a huge $200m loan to the Emirate of Abu Dhabi, there was a storm of protest from the merchant banks with Israeli allegiances and a general disbelief in Morgans' protestations that the loan was for peaceful purposes. The loan had been secretly negotiated by Morgan Grenfell's Chairman and Chief Executive, Sir John Stevens, and it may well have been the strain of the controversy that caused him to die suddenly on 27 October. He had been a dynamic influence, all the more notable given his central banking background, and his death effectively meant that Morgan Grenfell would put on hold until the 1980s any ambitions of rivalling Warburgs as the City's 'powerhouse' merchant bank.[2]

Wall Street was in a jittery state from the end of October, when the Arabs began talking about cutting oil supplies by 20 per cent or more, and on 9 November it had a particularly sharp fall. The impact of that, coupled with the miners' rejection of the Coal Board's latest offer, led to the London market losing almost 2 per cent on Monday the 12th. The next day it was hit by a veritable triple whammy: appalling trade figures for October, the start at long last of a serious credit squeeze (MLR being raised to 13 per cent) and the government's declaration, to counter the impact of the miners' already implemented overtime ban, of a national state of emergency. That day the Index lost 4 per cent, down to 405.5; and despite the fillip next day of a royal wedding, the slide continued almost unabated, with the Index down to 365 at the end of November. 'While retaining a basic belief that the Stock Market moves in a more or less regular cyclical pattern,' Rowe & Pitman told its clients at the start of December, 'we find it difficult to escape the conclusion that the events of the last three months will have far-reaching consequences. The era of cheap energy appears over despite the continuing flow of North Sea Oil discoveries. The terms of trade for most developed countries have been substantially worsened.' Pointedly, its *Market Report* added that 'what makes the oil situation an ideal cause for market panic is that its effects are essentially unquantifiable', granted that 'decisions about crude supplies are clearly political rather than economic and therefore there is no real basis for saying that the guess of any one investor is more or less valid than that of another'. Consequently, 'all this forms a basis for rumour and speculation rather than reasoned argument'.[3]

Less than five months after the stock market's successful, record-breaking £117m offer for sale by J. Sainsbury, the atmosphere was infinitely less propitious as Robert Fleming on Monday, 3 December completed arrangements for a much smaller (£1.7m) offer for sale on behalf of an excellent Scottish concern, Alginate Industries, which was engaged in the mysterious but profitable business of transforming brown seaweed into alginates. Headlines on that day's *FT* front page included 'Bid to avert all-out coal strike', 'Tight situation in power industry' and 'Fighting flares in Golan Heights', not to mention 'Sunday drivers left stranded'. Consequently, despite the intrinsic attractions of the company's prospects, the sub-underwriters were left with just under 90 per cent and dealings opened at way below the issue price. Was the City losing its head? That was certainly what the *Daily Mail* claimed in a dramatic front-page story on the 7th, while Hamish McRae argued in *Euromoney* that the City's black assumptions about the future of the British economy were essentially a 'Pavlovian reaction' to the trade figures and accompanying credit-restraint package of 13 November, reminiscent of previous juddering 'stops' after periods of 'go'. By contrast, he added, British industry was 'far more optimistic about growth and export prospects', and 'the fact that the City and industry should interpret the government's intentions so differently is a good yardstick of how little the two understand each other, not to mention the unhealthy contempt each has for the other's judgement'.[4]

The notion of a City-led panic is rather confirmed by a snatch from James Lees-Milne's diary. 'Sachie [Sir Sacheverell Sitwell] full of gloomy forebodings,' he noted on 12 December. 'Influential City friends warned him that "we" had only three months to clear out of England. Another told him to hoard his cartridges, for there would be shooting within that time.' The following evening, on television, Heath announced the start of the three-day week, and by the close of trading on Friday the 14th the Index languished at 305.9, representing a fall of 29 per cent since 9 November – five weeks of, in Littlewood's apt words, a 'bear market within a bear market'.[5]

These weeks had also seen the start – though most people did not yet realise it – of what would become known as the secondary banking crisis.[6] 'Thorpe's battered bank' was the headline in the *Guardian* on 27 November, after it had become known that Donald Bardsley, only recently recruited to London and County Securities (L&C), had resigned.[7] It emerged that there had been a 'clash in operating style' between him and Caplan, and L&C's share price plummeted. During the week a whisper also spread that L&C was in deep trouble, including a run on its deposits. All autumn an increasingly perturbed Bardsley had kept Keogh at the Bank posted about the deteriorating situation; and by late on Thursday the 29th Keogh was in effect being asked by L&C and its principal backers, Keyser Ullmann, Eagle Star and United Drapery Stores (UDS), to organise a rescue. Keogh at once sought out Alex Dibbs (National Westminster being L&C's principal clearing bank); and on the Friday, as urgent discussions took place at 41 Lothbury, L&C's share price hit a low of 40p (having at one point in 1973 been 303p), before dealings were suspended. How did Keogh and Dibbs decide to play it? The answer – somewhat remarkably as it would come to seem – was to look to *another* secondary bank to sort out the situation. That bank was First National Finance (FNFC). Pat Matthews was present at the Friday deliberations, apparently at Keogh's invitation, and it is unclear whether the idea came from him or from Keogh-cum-Dibbs. Either way, the hoped-for solution was that Keysers, Eagle Star and UDS would put up £20–25m, that NatWest would provide banking support and that FNFC would be offered 30 per cent of the equity of L&C at 5p per share by Caplan and would assume management responsibility.

However, over the weekend, as the financial press emphasised the possible serious consequences of L&C (including its twenty-three retail branches) going to the wall, a thorough inquiry on behalf of NatWest, Keysers and FNFC revealed that L&C was effectively insolvent and that therefore the equity was lost. By Monday the 3rd, with Keysers, Eagle Star and UDS almost certainly now wavering, the question was whether Matthews would do his stuff and prove that FNFC was indeed a serious, to-be-respected member of the City of London financial community. Hambros, his own principal backers, apparently advised him to stay out; but on Monday evening, after successfully insisting that FNFC would put up £5m front money only if a) Keysers, Eagle Star and UDS each did the same, and b) NatWest committed itself to £40m banking support, he agreed to become L&C's saviour. Most of L&C's old board quickly departed the scene, including Caplan and Thorpe, with Caplan being succeeded (on the Bank's nod) by Richard Langdon, senior partner of Spicer & Pegler and also a director of FNFC. The L&C problem was solved, at least temporarily, with little general sense that it was merely the tip of a much larger iceberg. Keogh, however, felt otherwise, and by mid-December he had set up what came to be called the Fringe Banks Standing Committee, comprising representatives of the Bank of England, the four leading clearers and Williams & Glyn's. By the never-to-be-forgotten 19th, it was already on its fourth meeting.[8]

Two days previously, on Monday the 17th, Barber presented an emergency mini-budget. In order to meet what he called 'our gravest situation since the end of the war', he made large public expenditure cuts, added 10 per cent on surtax, restored hire-purchase controls, announced that he would be introducing a development gains tax aimed at curbing property speculators, and – just over two years after the introduction of CCC – introduced the so-called 'corset'. Later that week, Midland's Forbes explained to his board that last aspect:

> The Chairman reported on recent restrictive measures which had been introduced by the Bank of England, principally to counter the growth in the money supply and the use of arbitrage operations in the inter-bank market. He explained that the banks had been offered the alternative of 'ceilings' on advances (similar to those imposed on previous occasions) or a limitation of the banks' ability to increase their deposits. The banks had chosen the latter method as giving them slightly more manoeuvrability.

For the secondary banks, the combination of immediate credit controls and the prospect of an early assault on the property sector – sending property shares into freefall, even as the market as a whole slightly recovered – was little short of lethal. 'The Government had set in motion the events which had led to the availability of credit on a huge scale; now it was reversing its policies at the very moment when the market which it had so casually fuelled (I will not say deliberately) had clearly over-reached itself,' Edward du Cann later wrote with unmistakable bitterness. 'The emergency budget hit the banking and property worlds just at the very moment when signs of serious crisis in both were becoming apparent. That budget was an act of unimaginable folly . . .'[9]

On Wednesday the 19th, probably in the morning, the Fringe Banks Standing Committee met. In Keogh's absence, it was chaired by his deputy, Rodney Galpin, who at an early stage mentioned 'the critical position of Cedar' (that is, Cedar Holdings). Then:

> On Cornhill Consolidated [described by the historian of the secondary banking crisis as 'a sizeable unquoted financial business with extensive share links'] Mr Wild [NatWest's Sidney Wild] said that National Westminster were not prepared to give further help. It was, he said, National Westminster's judgement that Cornhill did not warrant further banking support and had become an incurable case. National Westminster had £½m at risk ... The Group did not dissent from Mr Wild's view that the Company did not merit support ...
>
> The Group discussed the position of FNF [i.e. First National]. Mr Wild reiterated his comments on the quality of their business and asked for further support. The Group agreed to renew their overnight money (including the Bank of England's £5m) to provide overnight assistance totalling £23m (with Lloyds and Midland increasing their contribution to £5m each)... National Westminster would pick up the balance. Mr Wild thanked the Group.

Finally, after these specific cases had been considered and Barclays had mentioned 'one possible invalid' in the form of Western Trust and Savings (chaired by Harry Sporborg), came the fateful moment:

> Mr Wild suggested that a support fund should be set up as a means of providing the potentially large amounts of assistance which could be needed for joint rescue operations. He thought it might be no exaggeration to speak of a total of well over £1,000m. Mr Wild suggested a fund amounting initially to 1% of eligible liabilities with contributions coming from a wider grouping than just the clearing banks.

As far as one can tell from the record, initial discussion did not dissent from Wild's basic idea, the genesis of what would become known as the 'Lifeboat'; but it seems to have been agreed – perhaps with Bank of England prompting – that 'it would be difficult to widen the list of contributors beyond the London Clearing Banks without publicity, which should be avoided if possible as it might only exacerbate an already dangerous situation'.[10]

In at least three ways it had been a suggestive, important meeting. First, it was clear that First National, barely a fortnight after being entrusted with the care of London and County, was in serious difficulties itself. Second, it is most unlikely that Wild would have put up the idea of a 'support fund' without the say-so of his Chief General Manager, Alex Dibbs, who must have been keenly conscious that NatWest was in a more exposed position than any of the other clearers, should the secondary banks start to fall like ninepins. Dibbs himself was close to Keogh, and it is plausible that the concept of an overall support operation was essentially their joint initiative. Third, such an interpretation throws some doubt on the conventional historical wisdom that it was specifically the Cedar situation that precipitated the 'Lifeboat'. Undoubtedly it contributed, but the fact was that Cedar came under the umbrella of Barclays, not NatWest. For Dibbs, 'that big, burly figure of restless energy and fearlessness' (as Fildes called him), the value of the crisis in Cedar's affairs was that it helped to show that NatWest was not the only clearer with much to lose if traditional banking notions of moral hazard were applied too rigidly.[11]

The rest of the day was dominated by the question of Cedar Holdings, though in the afternoon Richardson had a secret meeting with the chairmen of the clearing banks in which he mentioned the possibility of a more general support operation.[12] As for Cedar, discussions about how to prevent an immediate collapse, as depositors stampeded for their money, had already begun at the Bank that morning and would not end until the small hours of the 20th.[13] Much turned on the attitude of Cedar's four main institutional backers (Phoenix and the pension funds of the electricity supply industry, the National Coal Board and Unilever). Hugh Jenkins, Investment Manager of the NCB pension fund, recalled something of the atmosphere during those seventeen hours of meetings and enforced companionship:

> We [i.e. the institutions] first saw the Governor. Jasper Hollom [Deputy Governor] was very much in evidence. Both acted magnificently. They knew the nature of the problem and their *sang froid* was remarkable. They were cool but very firm. Kenneth Cork [the City's celebrated insolvency expert] was a very central adviser. I can remember that huge room [the Court Room] full of people – and the other conference room that runs off it. We went from one room to another, moving about in small groups. We really got down to brass tacks at about seven in the evening. There were consultations and reconsiderations. The dialogue was going on between the institutions in a position to rescue Cedar, and Barclays Bank, plus merchant banks, lawyers and Kenneth Cork. By the evening the board of Cedar had been brought in . . .

Inevitably, there were some memorable moments: the stand-off between Hollom and Unilever's Cob Stenham, with Hollom successfully warning of the domino effect if Cedar went; the tactless serving of ham sandwiches to Cedar's mainly Jewish directors, as they waited downstairs for several hours to be brought in to the discussions; the human as well as financial qualities of Cork, who persuaded those largely confused, almost shell-shocked men that they had no alternative but to accept the institutions' conditions, in effect stripping Cedar of its property assets and closing its doors for new lending business. One of those eventually released into Threadneedle Street at about 3 a.m. was Timothy Bevan, Barclays' Deputy Chairman. 'My grandfather was a banker, my father was a banker, I'm a banker,' he observed with some haughtiness to Cork as he left the building. 'But in their day when anyone went bust they did it during working hours.'[14]

In all it was a £72m support package, but the public announcement a few hours later that Barclays and Cedar's institutional shareholders had, between them, made arrangements 'designed to ensure that the depositors and the account holders can be repaid as their monies become due' – an announcement made simultaneously with the suspension of Cedar's shares – had the very reverse of a calming effect. Suddenly, as it sunk in that a substantial concern like Cedar Holdings had in effect been brought low by a flight of deposits, it seemed as if the whole of the secondary banking sector was in jeopardy. The City rumour-mill got going with a vengeance, and by lunchtime the share price of many secondaries had plummeted by as much as one-third. Meanwhile, back at the Bank, the Fringe Banks Standing Committee was that morning having its fifth meeting, chaired by Keogh. Its tone was somewhat irascible: a Bank of England paper, based on Wild's suggestions, merely produced 'a long and totally inconclusive discussion'; while when Wild asserted that First National now needed £50m and asked for £10m from each of the Big Four and £5m from Williams & Glyn's and the Bank, he was informed that Midland would not go beyond £6m and that Lloyds at this stage was not willing to commit beyond £5m. The next morning, Friday the 21st, Forbes reported to Midland's board that the Bank of England 'had in mind the establishment of some form of "rescue fund"' and that he, his fellow-chairmen and the various chief general managers were to attend a meeting at the Bank of England that afternoon. There followed a lengthy discussion about 'the extent to which the Bank [i.e. Midland] should willingly agree to participate in rescue operations':

> While the Board recognised the importance of maintaining confidence in the banking institutions of the City, it was firm in its view that the Bank must have regard to its primary duty of assisting its own customers in the liquidity difficulties with which many of them would be faced in the difficult business conditions that lay ahead. The Board took the view that, while the Bank should be ready to join in helping in specific (and selective) cases, it should not willingly enter in advance into any general commitment, and that, to the extent that it might be necessary under pressure from the authorities to do so, it should seek substantial guarantees against loss.[15]

Granted that Midland had been so much more circumspect than either NatWest or Barclays in lending to the fringe banks, this unwillingness to write a blank cheque was hardly surprising.

At the meeting that afternoon, followed by another just two days after Christmas, Richardson deployed all his formidable powers of persuasion to achieve broad acceptance for the principle of a joint support operation. Soon afterwards Forbes updated his board:

The banks had accepted the view of the Governor that it was in the interests of all the City institutions that steps should be taken to prevent a possible chain reaction. They had, on the other hand, urged forcefully (as the Directors had at the last meeting of the Board) that the banks must be able to meet the very heavy demands for assistance which their own customers were bound to make if the three-day working week continued.

The Governor, Forbes added, had agreed to this, and that 'no attempt would be made to use the arrangements simply to postpone the liquidation of companies which were clearly not viable'. Moreover, the clearing bankers 'had urged strongly the necessity of the Bank of England itself participating substantially in the operation, and the Governor had agreed that the Bank [i.e. of England] should do so to the extent of ten per cent'. Forbes's report did not mention what seems to have been the case, that he himself had (at the meeting on the 21st) argued strongly against the whole concept of a general operation, as opposed to individual rescues, before agreeing to bow to the majority opinion. Notwithstanding the initial role of Dibbs, the chief general managers seem to have been less comfortable than the chairmen with the notion of a general rescue operation, and it would be a reasonable guess that Forbes's ultimate willingness to give way to Richardson's wishes did not cause unalloyed joy among his top management. However, presumably everyone at Midland (and indeed the other clearers) took comfort from Richardson's assurance, also reported by Forbes, that in terms of the *future* activities of the fringe banks, 'the whole system of licensing concerns of this description would be re-examined'.[16]

Richardson himself, some five years later, showed no misgivings when for the first time he publicly justified the Bank's decision to launch the Lifeboat:

> We had to support some institutions which did not themselves deserve support on their merits, and, indeed, institutions which fell outside the Bank's established range of supervisory responsibilities. But I felt, as I saw the tide coming in, that it was necessary to take the Bank beyond the banking system proper, for which it was responsible, into those deposit-taking institutions, because collapse there was capable of letting the wave come on to the institutions themselves; and the fact that very rapidly we had to extend our support to a wider circle, which included some reputable banking institutions, showed that our instinct that we were on very treacherous ground was sound . . . I have absolutely no hesitation in saying that, faced with the same circumstances again – regrettable though they were – I would take the same strategic decision and would act in the same way . . .[17]

Crisis management had long been a Bank of England speciality, and if there was one benign ghost that hovered over the Old Lady during that gloomy Christmas, it was surely that of William Lidderdale, Governor during the 1890 Barings crisis and architect of the original lifeboat. The

1973 version, under Hollom's calm, firm chairmanship, held its first meeting on 28 December and for the next year was in almost continuous session.

Despite the news on Christmas Eve of another steep rise in the price of crude oil – up from $5 a barrel to $11.50, four times what it had been at the start of the Arab-Israeli War – there was a sneaking feeling in the City at the start of 1974 that, at least as far as Britain was concerned, perhaps the worst was almost over. Maybe the TUC's Len Murray would be able to persuade Heath that the miners should be looked upon as an 'exceptional case', not bound by Phase Three; maybe Barber's recent fiscal as well as monetary tightening had been well enough judged to give the economy a soft, rather than hard, landing. 'Although it might appear impossible to recommend investment in either equities or Gilt edged,' Rowe & Pitman commented, 'we believe that we are very near the lows of both markets for the current cycles. It may seem difficult to exaggerate our medium-term problems but the advent of North Sea Oil will undoubtedly cause a major improvement in our real income by the early 1980s. With this in prospect it would be wrong for fund managers to lose all faith in equity investment.' For three weeks the Index stayed fairly stable at around 330, until it became clear that miners and government were on an irreconcilable collision course. On 24 January the NUM executive voted for a national coal-strike ballot, and by the 28th the Index had fallen to 301.7 – a fall of 44.5 per cent since the May 1972 peak of 543.6, which meant that this was *already* the most bearish post-war bear market. On 5 February it was announced that a full-scale strike would start on the 10th, and on the 6th an indignant *FT* laid into the NUM:

> Do the miners realise the implications of this appeal for the uncushioned operation of supply and demand? Do they recognise that what they take for themselves will be at the expense of others and that their manner of taking it is likely to lead, one way or another, to the growth of unemployment for their fellow-workers? . . . The heart of the present matter, ironical as it may seem, is that the Conservative Government is rightly unwilling to let the miners bring back unfettered 'free enterprise' into the running of the economy.[18]

It was, as they might have observed in points north, a piquant viewpoint from EC4. Next day, the 7th, Heath called a 'Who runs Britain?' election, to be held on the last day of the month.

The February issue of the *Banker* went to press as Heath was still pondering whether or not to make his gamble. 'The City is miserable,' it declared in a notably eloquent editorial:

> The market is poised to relapse to its three-year low. The banking system is under strain from the need to rescue some of its lesser brethren, and from the financial drain suffered by many companies as a result of the three-day

week. The 'bureaucrats of Brussels' still seem to want to harmonise the City's old easy-going ways out of existence. Peter Walker is still a Secretary of State. The Arabs are still making economic forecasting into a nonsense game. TV programmes continue to tilt their lances against the Square Mile. Books go on being published which say that the City doesn't do its job properly – or not as well as the smart boys across the Channel, or the Atlantic. And then there is the Labour Party threatening to pull the dear old place apart. The City has been kicked in its pocket, and in its pride, and you could not really blame it if it just decided to pack its bag and go somewhere where the sky is blue, the natives friendly and where a man's money is his own. Just possibly, that is what may happen. Messrs Wilson, Benn *et al* would then find themselves barking at an empty fortress.

Who would guess from this that the City is probably Britain's biggest exporter? To people in the City itself, the Labour Party and many other critics appear strictly mad. What on earth can be the national interest in destroying or sniping at one of the few really efficient and competitive sectors of its economy? Is there a single manufacturing industry in Britain that can hold a candle to the City in terms of international respect, earning power and future prospects? At a time when the world is crying out for services of all kind, and when Britain is perhaps more comfortably placed than any other major country to supply them, what is the point of the cavilling on TV, the cheap sneers by industrialists about making money rather than earning it, the invidious glances across the Channel as if they always order things better there? Why don't the industrialists first go and make their aluminium sheets better up there in Birmingham or wherever they live and then come and criticise us? Go and make £600 millions in *net* exports, year in year out, and then come and advise us how to try harder . . .

With that off its chest, the *Banker* acknowledged that 'by far the most common and influential class of criticism' was 'the pure emotional assertion that the City is no more than a band of robbers, who contribute little to the country whilst making fortunes for themselves', and that: 'This is probably what most people in Britain believe, either half-heartedly or completely. Indeed, how many City commuters can be sure that the wives they leave behind each morning do not often secretly think so themselves?'[19] Self-awareness had never been the City's strong suit, not least on the part of City husbands, but there was now an unprecedented sense of being under siege from alien forces in society at large.

Meanwhile, head down and eschewing publicity, Hollom's 'Control Committee' was pumping significant sums of money into the secondary banking sector during January and February. Importantly, the Bank of England was not willing to allow potentially threatened secondary banks to make their own, autonomous arrangements for financial support. Keyser Ullmann's du Cann, who had already tried and failed to get Keysers into the safe port of the Accepting Houses Committee ('They do not like some of your colleagues,' O'Brien had told him), remained unable to persuade the Bank otherwise, despite his well-grounded argument that any financial institution known to have been supported by the Lifeboat would inevitably lose much standing. The Lifeboat's specific actions were, of course, intended to be secret, but du Cann correctly assumed that such were the numbers involved in those arrangements that details would inevitably emerge. Between the Bank and the clearing banks, and among the clearers, there developed some real tensions as the operation started to unfold. By 14 January at least twenty-one 'patient companies' were under review and at least £210m had been lent, and the clearers told Richardson and Hollom that 'they wished to set some limit on their obligations under the scheme and to establish tighter controls over investigations, risk sharing and the disbursement of funds'. Well over half those funds disbursed had gone to First National, and they additionally expressed 'concern that the company was being allowed too much latitude to take on, and to advertise for, new business rather than devoting its energies to reducing the size of its book'. By the 25th the amount so far loaned was up to £310m (of which £150m had gone to First National); and when the clearers were told by Richardson that another £40m or £50m to FNFC 'would be sufficient to regenerate deposits and revive confidence', the banks agreed to go on supporting the Matthews outfit strictly on the twofold basis that they had participation in its management until their level of support had been 'substantially reduced' and that 'until it had reached some degree of financial stability, the Company [i.e. FNFC] should not be permitted to make take-over bids or expand into other fields'.[20]

By this time the broad outlines of the support operation were starting to enter the public domain, and the *Investors Chronicle* estimated that the cost was likely to be 'over the much-banded-about figure of £1,000m' – in fact, nearer to £1,200m. It added that the clearing banks were becoming 'increasingly uneasy about the extent to which they are being asked to commit themselves', that 'all of them agree that the 10 per cent involvement of the Bank of England in the operation so far is simply not good enough', and that 'they are also beginning to feel that perhaps the rescue net has been cast rather too wide, involving them in commitments beyond the dictates of commercial prudence'. Soon afterwards, on 29 January, the term 'Lifeboat' entered the City vocabulary with Margaret Reid's article in the *FT* headlined 'How the "Bankers Lifeboat" came to the rescue'. In it she quoted a top clearing banker – anonymous, but in fact Midland's Len Mather – as jocularly referring to the new combined operation as 'The National Joint Stock Bankers' Lifeboat Institution'. One of Mather's colleagues at Poultry, Stuart Graham, was a particularly critical joint-stock banker, especially in mid-February when the clearing banks were asked for a further £40–50m to enable a gradual run-down of

London and County. Not only that, but L&C's new Chairman, Richard Langdon, was now proposing fully to offload the bank to FNFC. In a memo on the 11th, Graham vented his feelings:

I favour forced liquidation [i.e. of L&C] at once – a view at present supported by Barclays and, to some extent, by Lloyds, but NOT by National Westminster or, more importantly, by the Bank of England. I do not think this action would give a 'bad press'; to some extent the City is expecting it, and the sooner we have a failure on the books the better our control over the other 'patients' – there is too much complacency about the rescue operation seeping into commercial language. As an aside, too, why should we add to our support to enable FNFC to grow fatter? . . .

Whilst we should not contemplate our own competitive position in regard to the rescue or support operation, it is somewhat galling to recall (1) that FNFC's acquisition of L&C will give it 22 outlets in various stores throughout the country, and (2) that FNFC's first railway station venture began this week at Liverpool Street Station.

Graham added that, should Hollom's wishes prevail upon the Lifeboat Committee as a whole, then it was important to insist that the run-down was as speedy as possible. In the event there seems to have been a compromise, with the Bank announcing that it and FNFC would assume joint and equal ownership of L&C's banking business.[21]

Transcending the secondary banking crisis, a couple of vignettes capture the underlying City mood in February 1974. 'Last night we dined at Westwood Manor with the Denys Suttons,' Lees-Milne noted on Sunday the 17th. 'The Tony Powells and Roger Manners the other guests. Lord Roger is a stockbroker. He says the City has come to a standstill. It expects a complete economic collapse any day, when we shall be in the same condition as Germany was in 1923. We must expect chaos, the £ to be worth 1 penny, if we are lucky, and the oil sheiks buying up our industries.' The other scene was recalled by Fildes a year or so later: 'The merchant banker topped up his claret glass and contemplated the political scene. It displeased him. What, he was asked, would he suggest if the Conservative Party were a company coming to his bank as a client? His eyes glinted for a moment. "Sack the chairman," he said. "It's always the right thing to do."' Even so, in a bitterly contested election campaign, during which Wilson promised to end the 'anarchy' in the City, there was not only a broad wish on the City's part that Heath would prevail, but also every expectation. Opinion polls were hopeful, and on the 28th, amid evening-paper placards that London was set to 'hammer' Labour, the Index closed at 337.8. The realisation overnight that Labour was going to win more seats than the Tories, though probably with no overall majority, caused the market next day to plunge by twenty-four points – at the time its biggest-ever one-day fall. Wilson became Prime Minister on 4 March, with the *FT* more in hope than expectation calling on him to 'find the resources within himself' to move beyond party considerations and 'promote a national effort to solve the economic crisis'.[22]

*

'Almost all members of the Labour Party regard the City as their implacable enemy,' the political journalist Nora Beloff had noted towards the end of 1973:

> There is a dominant feeling that the financial institutions, particularly the four great clearing banks and the insurance companies, wield excessive, because irresponsible, power over the national economy. Most Labour voters and all party activists would attribute to the City a major part of the blame for Britain's poor economic performance since the end of the war; and many, including Harold Wilson in his book recording his Prime Ministership, affirm that the financiers – at home and abroad – deliberately engineered the series of crises which destroyed the last Labour government.
>
> Agreeing, however, that something needs to be done to make the City more responsible to the public interest and less likely to torpedo a future Labour government, the party remains sharply divided on appropriate remedial action . . .

She was right. In his autumn speech to the Labour Party conference, Wilson had made a three-pronged attack on the City: calling for investment to be directed to productive, non-speculative purposes, through the establishment of a 'state-owned merchant bank', somewhat along the lines of the old IRC; arguing that there should be 'a high-level inquiry' into the Stock Exchange, which he called a 'casino' and accused of 'not channelling the tides of investment, so much as exaggerating the sloshing to and fro of the bilgewater of capitalism'; and castigating speculative futures dealings in the commodity markets. He did not, however, say anything about making the nationalisation of banks into official party policy – despite the wishes of his party's left wing – and a few months later such a commitment remained absent from the party's manifesto. Nevertheless, if that was some comfort to the City, the fact remained that anti-City animus was far from spent on the Labour Left; while the ensconcement of Michael Foot at Employment and Tony Benn at Industry was, as Littlewood puts it, 'received with foreboding, as these areas straddled the boundaries between the public and private sectors'.[23]

What of Denis Healey, the new Chancellor? He would never attain Benn's bogey-like qualities, but he had reputedly promised to squeeze the wealthy until 'the pips squeak' and the City's initial attitude towards him was at best guarded. He himself later claimed that his relations with the City 'were always relatively good' and that he 'never had much problem with the markets except when the Bank of England encouraged the City to play silly buggers'. Certainly, there were strains in the Healey-Richardson relationship: Healey was unfavourably struck by how the Bank still tried to uphold 'the cabbalistic secrecy' of the Norman era, 'seeing itself as the guardian of mysteries which no ordinary mortal should be allowed to understand'; Richardson was, according to Healey (almost certainly correctly), 'upset' by the Chancellor's insistence on making his 'own personal contacts with the financial institutions in the City', thereby subverting the Bank's traditional prerogative as sole intermediary between City and Treasury. Even so, Healey recognised Richardson as 'a highly intelligent and cultured' man, while Richardson in due course came to respect Healey as a capable, ultimately pragmatic operator, and initially each perhaps recognised that the other was learning on the job.[24] Each may also have acknowledged that the other had his own unreconstructed backwoodsmen to contend with.

'The City is pleased and prices are up – as is the pound,' King noted the day after Wilson had formed his new administration. 'It is presumably relief that we now have a Government, even if it is only a Labour one.' Whatever relief there was dissipated quickly, with first the massively inflationary pay settlement awarded to the miners and then growing apprehension about Healey's first budget, due on 26 March. Phillips & Drew's Paul Bazalgette, writing ahead of that event, invoked a humorous stoicism: 'Stand steady on the tumbril, me hearties, as it rolls on steadily towards the Tower or Tyburn tree. What's money if they leave you with your life – a choice traditionally accorded by the highwayman to his victim . . .' Healey's budget amply fulfilled such masochistic expectations, as the top rate of income tax was increased from 75 per cent to 83 per cent, and to 98 per cent on investment income. The index, 297.6 at the start of the 26th, closed the month at 267.4. Gloom was further compounded at the start of April with the hammering of Chapman & Rowe, a medium-sized broking firm. 'They were gambling and of course they couldn't pay for the stuff,' a jobber, Brian Carpenter, remembered. 'They had various stocks. They had enormous positions. They used to turn them over, old and new, and you watched it and you watched it and you watched it . . .'[25]

In fact, once the immediate impact of Healey's budget had worn off, there was briefly a mood that perhaps the new government was not as bad as all that. On 19 April, with the Index clambering above 300, the *Investors Chronicle* published a survey of City opinion suggesting that the worst of the bear market was over. 'We hope April 1 was the bottom, we know it can't be far away,' David Fuller at Chart Analysis said – though he added that he still saw 'very little evidence of a sustained rise in equities in the medium term'. The Index ended April at a respectable 297.9, prompting Rowe & Pitman's May circular to begin with the assertion that 'the burgeoning bull market is displaying greater strength than even the bulls had expected or dared to hope'. However, this expression of confidence was accompanied by the warning that 'its health over the coming months could prove fragile', especially if any of the factors behind the recent upturn (including the government's 'social contract' with the unions) took 'a turn for the worse'. Anyone who did believe that this semi-honeymoon between City and Labour was going to last was presumably not present at Williams & Glyn's at the end of April, when the Secretary of State for Industry dined with a handful of City luminaries, including the Earl of Airlie (Schroders) and Dundas Hamilton (Deputy Chairman of the Stock Exchange) as well as the Deputy Governor, Sir Jasper Hollom. Benn's diary recorded a dialogue of the deaf. 'How do we fit in to the planning agreements?' his host, Richard Lloyd, asked him:

> Well, the problem is, we are not getting investment, we haven't solved industrial relations and we haven't solved the problems of regional imbalance. We have to cooperate a bit more directly. I don't know much about the City and you will have to tell me what you can do.
> We must restore confidence.
> What is the political price of restoring confidence?
> Well, you have got to have better dividend distribution, otherwise equities will collapse.

'They were,' Benn added later in his diary, 'talking about workers' participation and involvement and getting workers to buy shares, and all that Tory crap. The guys were mainly hereditary bankers who sent their kids away to public school and they had no fight, never been through the fire . . .'[26]

One of the more stabilising influences that spring was the general City perception that, thanks to the Lifeboat operation, the worst of the secondary banking crisis was over. However, on 17 May – the last day for some time that the Index closed above 300 – it was reported that the large property company Stern Holdings, run by the Hungarian-born Willie Stern, was in cash difficulties. Other property companies, which had similarly expanded spectacularly during the Barber boom on the back of profligate bank lending, were also in trouble, and as early as 24 April there had been an anxious discussion between Richardson and the clearers. The Governor's view was that 'it was not a question of saving property companies for their own sake but of the possible consequences of their failure for the integrity of the banking system'; to which 'Sir John Prideaux said that he thought the clearing banks would prefer to see their commitments in the support group [i.e. Lifeboat] extended rather than become involved in supporting property companies, and this sentiment was echoed by the other Chairmen'. Stern was the big one, for by May the sobering fact was that, as a result of various recent attempts to prop it up, as well as loans going back to the palmy days, it owed banks and other lenders almost £160m. NatWest's exposure was just over £30m, while Keyser Ullmann was owed just over £20m. In a category all on its own was the ill-managed, ill-advised Crown Agents, with a staggering £40m lent to the Stern group. 'Something nasty is about to happen', the *FT*'s 'Lex' could not help but fear on 25 May, eight days after the Stern revelation, and by this time rumours of financial institutions in trouble were rife all over the City.[27]

In this increasingly febrile atmosphere, an extraordinary amount of attention was focused on the Annual General Meeting of Slater Walker, due to be held at the Connaught Rooms on 30 May. By the closing months of 1973, against the backdrop of the oil shock and accompanying sharp down-swing in general business confidence, Slater was (in his own retrospective words) aware that, given Slater Walker's 'very considerable borrowing', it was certain that 'the effect of any fall in stock and property markets would be very exaggerated for us'. He spent the first five months of 1974 building up a cash pile (some £50m) by selling as many assets as he could – including Slater Walker's remaining stake in Crittall-Hope Engineering, two industrial life-assurance companies, and the satellites in the US, Australia and South Africa – with the result that by May questions were beginning to be asked. 'Why has Slater Walker divested itself of so much equity all over the world in recent months?' the *Daily Telegraph* wondered. 'Unless Mr Slater gives an acceptable reason at the company's annual meeting next week, what started out as eyebrow-raised interest in Slater Walker's tactics could turn into genuine apprehension.' A few days later Patrick Hutber pursued the theme:

> Is he gathering in cash, they ask, for fear that property failures will set the fringe bank scene alight once more? Or does he foresee a horrendous economic or stock market crash? And so stockbrokers, with insufficient business to occupy their minds, shudder to each other. That is why the heat is on him to speak at Thursday's Slater Walker meeting, thus ensuring further publicity. Knowing him, and remembering the violently hostile reaction to his prediction of a market fall last year, I should think he will be reluctant to say very much. But silence from him, or gloom, will knock the market just as much as optimism could set it temporarily alight. He is paying the price for those happy years of headlines.

Slater was indeed mindful of all the criticism he had received after his bearish lunch with Patrick Sergeant; but though at the packed meeting, complete with overflow room, he refrained from committing himself to any specific forecast (as opposed to alternative hypotheses), he did utter a couple of much-quoted sentences: 'Many people in recent months have found you cannot always turn property into cash, you cannot always turn large lines of shares into cash, you cannot always turn pictures into cash. Cash you can always turn into other things.'[28]

Among those who took Slater's words to heart was Prince Rupert zu Loewenstein. 'Rupert, a merchant banker, advises against having any stocks and shares,' Lees-Milne noted a week and a half later. 'Don't invest in shares. Only have cash.' For Slater himself, with all his instincts telling him that the larger financial crisis was still far from over, the maddening thing must have been of what limited benefit those predictive powers were. 'Unfortunately a lot of our liabilities, property in particular, were difficult to get out of,' he recalled with some exasperation even a quarter of a century later. 'And although I could see it [i.e. the market crash] and I was selling off companies left right and centre, in the end I was stuck, for want of a better word . . .' If only, he must have reflected at the time, that merger with Hill Samuel – or other, earlier would-be marriages – had gone through. 'The older established banking companies usually have substantial hidden resources, a wider-spread loan portfolio and are strengthened by being members of the "club",' he reflected in his autobiography. 'By this I mean that there is an unspoken understanding that if in trouble members will help each other.'[29] Slater Walker had come close – very close – to joining that inner club, but for one reason or another had never managed it, and by this time it was too late.

Another of the City's clubs, the Stock Exchange, was now under the chairmanship of George Loveday, a stop-gap choice in 1973. One colleague recalled him as 'not necessarily the brightest of men', but another was kinder: 'George was delighted to get the job. He was a very bluff character, born in Argentina of tea-planting stock. Extraordinary man: never read his papers. He chaired meetings blind . . .' He also responded 'with great aplomb' to the market collapse of 1974, even though his own firm was going through a difficult time. That year also saw the extraordinarily belated appointment of the Stock Exchange's first Chief Executive, Robert Fell, and the going 'live' (in February) of the alternative dealing system, ARIEL. 'Challenging the Stock Exchange monopoly' was the *FT*'s headline, with one disgruntled leading institutional investment manager being quoted concerning the high cost of dealing on the Stock Exchange: 'There are very few professions which so successfully protect their inefficient members. Even the most inefficient stockbroker has been getting jam on one side of his bread if not both.'[30]

Nevertheless, the dice were loaded from the start against ARIEL effectively challenging the monopoly. The Stock Exchange not only prevented jobbers from participating, but also leaned on Extel to ensure that ARIEL did not have direct access to up-to-the-minute Stock Exchange prices and news; as for the Bank of England, it remained adamant in its refusal to allow ARIEL's request that gilts be put on the system – a particularly cruel refusal, given that there was about to be an explosion of gilts dealing in the context of rapidly increasing government debt. 'As usual it is not anxious to see rows in the City,' ARIEL's Managing Director, Colin Leach, mildly commented in an interview later in 1974, and there is little doubt that Richardson saw ARIEL as unacceptably divisive. Leach himself had reportedly complained right at the outset of ARIEL's life that he was struggling against 'the most savage opposition the City has seen for years', and the hyperbole was understandable. By late 1974 his system had, at best, gained about 2 per cent of institutional business; by August 1976 it was estimated that that share was down to about 1 per cent; and that was still roughly the market share by autumn 1978, as ARIEL prepared to wind up after four and a half years of fairly thankless struggle. By a satisfying irony, however, even as ARIEL was trying unavailingly to establish itself as a significant force, the Stock Exchange was informed in September 1974 by the Board of Trade that it was likely to be required to register its rules and regulations with the Office of Fair Trading, in order to establish whether they were competitive and operated in the public interest.[31] A long, slow fuse had been lit.

The Euromarkets were not exempt from the City's *annus horribilis*. There, an additional cause of nervousness was the Nixon administration's decision in late January to zero-rate the Interest Equalisation Tax, which in effect presaged the reopening of the New York foreign bond market. Other US capital controls were abolished or relaxed, and although adamant that 'the Euromarkets will not disappear', *International Insider* conceded in early February that 'there may be a contraction in certain sectors, notably the Eurobond market'. The magazine was right: there was some contraction, but the Euromarkets did *not* disappear – reflecting as much as anything the depth of the American banks' London roots since the late 1960s. There was, admittedly, a nasty moment in March when Healey's budget proposed to apply British income tax on up to 90 per cent of the earnings of foreigners residing in Britain; but after many protests, and even some American banks threatening to pull out, the clause in question was omitted from the final Finance Bill. One Euromarkets-oriented firm very much in London for the long run was Credit Suisse White Weld (as White Weld was renamed in the spring after an injection of capital from Credit Suisse, hitherto only a minor, passive shareholder). By contrast, it seems to have been at about the same time (though the exact chronology is uncertain) that Rothschilds took the decision no longer to compete for the lead management position in Eurobond issues. 'In retrospect the view we took in early 1974 was pessimistic,' the firm's John Loudon conceded three years later. 'Warburgs and Credit Suisse White Weld did the right thing by sticking it out.' Evelyn de Rothschild added: 'At the time we were very pessimistic for the prospects of the Eurobond market. The Arab boycott [i.e. of Jewish financial houses] and the collapse of the world capital markets combined to make things look dismal.' They did indeed, but another Jewish house, Warburgs, decided to tough it out. The merchant bank that had founded the Eurobond market was now the last one in the game.[32]

Not that it was a very enticing game during 1974, as the volume of Eurobond issues slumped almost as dramatically as new issues on the Stock Exchange. Grasping the big picture, the May issue of the 'Bond Letter' circulated by Barings sought to explain 'the virtual disappearance of primary and secondary market activity' in the international capital markets:

> For almost ten months now our markets have been exposed to spiralling rates [i.e. of interest] and severe foreign exchange fluctuations; hence, not surprisingly, almost every investment sector has been subjected to mass withdrawal of funds. Inflation, running at unprecedented levels, shows little sign of being brought under control. Further it is doubtful whether the necessary deflationary moves will be politically acceptable to Western Governments given the attendant risks of high unemployment . . .

May was a month of heightened fears in the Euromarkets as elsewhere, and on the 20th, in *International Insider*, William Low poured scorn on the current apocalyptic mood in the international financial community, citing in particular the unfounded rumours that the Swiss banking community was intending to withdraw from the London Eurodollar market. 'If some Swiss banks really believe that their London Eurodollar holdings might be frozen,' he pointed out, 'then they are ignoring reality. Eurocurrency business in London is handled on an external account basis and even during the dark days of the Second World War the British authorities refrained from blocking external accounts.' Nine days later (on the eve of Slater's 'cash is king' speech) there was a revealing discussion between Richardson and the clearers:

> Mr Biggs [Norman Biggs of Williams & Glyn's] drew attention to the indefinable and fragile nature of confidence – one could satisfy all kinds of ratio controls and still not inspire confidence. Agreeing, the Governor said that there had recently been a lot of wild talk about the survival of the euro-dollar market. Personally, he felt that if hard times were to come, and this was by no means certain, the market would contract as people drew in their horns; but he did not expect a breakdown. If oil money flows proved too much of a strain then special arrangements, including bilateral deals, would no doubt be made.

Confidence returned to neither the Eurodollar nor the Eurobond market during June. 'Unparalleled marking-down of bond prices, especially concentrated on UK names, led to falls of as much as six points in one day with two point spreads widely quoted' was how Barings described the situation in the latter market towards the end of that month. 'Many professionals finally declined to quote dealing prices for most UK issues, and the phrase "basis only" rang in many ears.' Barings accepted that 'traders cannot be condemned for being reluctant to lose money', but the fact was that 'if the present contraction continues, investor confidence in the Eurobond Market as a whole may suffer lasting damage'. In short, 'Where does the Secondary Market go from here?'[33]

The latest self-protective spasm in the Eurobond market probably owed much to the dramatic circumstances following the collapse on 26 June of a medium-sized German private bank, I.D. Herstatt.[34] Heavy, unsuccessful speculation in the foreign exchange forward market had led to the Bundesbank having little alternative but to pull the plug. Unfortunately, the decision to close it at 3.30 p.m. local time ignored the fact that the New York banks, which were settling many of the foreign exchange transactions, were still open. Consequently, with Herstatt's foreign exchange deals for that day still not settled, Chase Manhattan in New York (Herstatt's international clearing agent and facing potential claims against it of up to $1bn) stopped all payments into the Clearing House Interbank Payments System, the computer-based clearing system that had been established four years earlier to handle international money transfers. There was a serious danger that the system would be brought down, and at this juncture (late on Friday the 28th) it was fortunate that the clearing house's Chairman was Citibank's Walter Wriston. He insisted that the system stay open during the weekend and, overcoming opposition from British banks, allowed banks to recall payment orders. Confidence was restored by the end of the weekend, and as Wriston typically put it, 'the important thing is that we solved the problem without recourse to the government'. Even so, the ripples caused by Herstatt's failure were far from over. 'They are particularly nervous about the banks,' King noted after lunching on the Monday at Warburgs with Grunfeld and Roll. 'They think the policy of floating exchanges is not working well, and is encouraging irresponsible gambling. When Herstatt, the Cologne bank, closed, it appeared that the Chase Manhattan lost $30 million, and the main Seattle Bank $22 million. The trouble is that no one knows how far out these losses extend.' Herstatt also, it transpired, owed major sums to, among others, Hill Samuel, Citibank and Manny Hanny.[35]

During the first half of July the mood of the international banking community was fragile in the extreme. 'Only now is the enormity of the international financial crisis becoming apparent, and as each week passes more banks are forced to disclose their difficulties,' *International Insider* noted on the 15th. 'The next few weeks will prove crucial as to whether the banking system will survive or collapse on an unprecedented scale.' Nevertheless, the magazine also commented that the recent monthly Basle meeting of central bankers (with Richardson to the fore) had apparently confirmed that, if necessary, central banks would bale out commercial banks; and a week later it quoted a London banker: '10 days ago, I thought the whole structure would collapse. Now, I think the worst may be over.' Even though the Euromarkets suffered for several more months from the after-shock of Herstatt, the worst was indeed over. Moreover, the particular nettle that Richardson had grasped at Basle, and would grasp again there in September with persuasive effect vis-à-vis his fellow-central bankers, was the notion of what he called 'parental responsibility' – in other words, in the context of the increasing internationalisation of banking, 'the principle . . . that the parent and therefore its central bank should have responsibility for the branches and subsidiaries'. As far as the City was concerned, this of course particularly affected the consortium banks, and the upshot that autumn was that the Bank of England required shareholder banks to provide written guarantees ('comfort letters') for these joint ventures. In several cases, merchant banks (with small balance sheets and natural concerns about liability) sold out their stakes in consortium banks, often to US regional banks wanting an international presence and entry into the Euromarkets. Moreover, the very fact of shareholders having to provide letters of support could not but raise fundamental questions about the value and rationale of consortium banks. Although 1976 would see the peak in terms of numbers of consortium banks, this was arguably the beginning of the end of a distinctive phenomenon.[36]

The Bank of England also still had the secondary banking crisis on its mind. After the Stern property empire had fallen apart in May, the crux was how, in Reid's words, 'to ease the worst stresses in the property field', in the knowledge that 'a widespread collapse of property companies and the resounding crash from the unloading of their assets on to the market by liquidators would have wrecked the already tottering property market, with further dire consequences, too, for the fringe banks'. The Bank was again immensely fortunate to be able to call on Kenneth Cork, who by June was starting to build what became known as 'Cork's dam', heavily reliant on his persuasive powers over creditors and particularly crucial in blunting the impact of the Stern collapse. 'It was the only scheme of its kind ever produced,' he later reflected. 'The idea was that if you had £200m of property to dispose of in those conditions, you can sell £1m if £199m is held off the market . . . The mortgagees never gave up their right of sale, all we had the right to do was to say that, if the price was wrong, they should wait a month or two.' Nevertheless, for all Cork's virtuoso skills, there was a deep crisis in the property sector, and inevitably those secondary banks that had lent heavily found the confidence of their depositors draining away by the day. 'What it amounted to was really buying time so that the property market could recover' was how John

Quinton of Barclays described the Lifeboat operation by this stage, and he remembered Hollom saying at one point to the clearing bankers on the Lifeboat Committee: ' "Unless we save this bank, then the ripples will hit some of you people round this table". The temperature dropped about 10 degrees and we all said "Yes".'[37]

The institution in question may have been any one of four pre-occupying Hollom and the clearers during the late summer and early autumn: First National, Keyser Ullmann, United Dominions Trust and Edward Bates and Sons. FNFC was still making profits, but its heavy exposure to the property sector had rendered it increasingly vulnerable to market rumours, as its share price collapsed. 'I have never heard such rubbish,' Matthews declared hotly but unavailingly to the press. 'We certainly have no liquidity crisis.' It was, in practice, ever more reliant on heavy borrowings from the Lifeboat.[38] As for Keysers, there had been other serious misjudgements in addition to the huge property loans; and in July, once two of its more prominent figures had left, it was permitted to scramble into the Lifeboat. Bolton now told King that 'the secondary banks should have been allowed to go to the wall', but the previous autumn he had been just as certain that Keysers was 'the up and coming merchant bank'.[39] UDT, the third of the four major cases, was the largest finance house in the country and was also in serious trouble by July. To the alarm of the clearers, it was soon the Lifeboat's most avaricious passenger, notwithstanding the Bank's success in persuading its two largest shareholders, the Prudential and Eagle Star, to pump some £30m into it – news of which caused the Pru's share price to fall by 10 per cent in one day at the end of July.[40] Finally, there was Edward Bates, which in September became the last passenger to board the Lifeboat, given succour because of heavy debts in the Eurodollar market that, unless repaid, threatened to jeopardise that market's international reputation. Embarrassingly, as far as the Bank was concerned, only the previous December, with the secondary banking crisis already under way, it had licensed Edward Bates to deal in foreign currency.[41]

By the time of that embarrassment the Discount Office – aptly described by Moran as 'the symbol of the Bank's old way of gathering information through the informal City grapevine' – had been closed down, in July, and replaced by a new Banking Supervision Division, under George Blunden and much more heavily staffed. The scapegoat, undeniably, was Keogh, who after a brief spell as an adviser (presumably not much-consulted) to the Governor took early retirement. That was a personal tragedy, but the larger significance was that, again to quote Moran, 'the Bank was publicly discarding the long-established notion that supervision could be conducted as a by-product of intervention in the money markets'; this 'renunciation in turn destroyed the belief that it could be practised by a small number of people using chiefly their personal knowledge to form judgements about who could be trusted in the banking community'.[42] Put another way, the time-honoured virtues of trust and informality were not wholly jettisoned (Blunden himself was someone imbued with the Bank's very best traditions), but it was now accepted that they were no longer enough.

This historic shift very much had Richardson's stamp on it, but what he and Hollom could not contain that summer was the mounting alarm of the clearing banks about the rapidly growing size – actual and above all potential – of the Lifeboat operation. In practice, not all the banks were equally hawkish. When Tuke of Barclays and Faulkner of Lloyds told Richardson, around 15 August, that there must be an overall limit of exposure for the clearing banks, the figures that they individually mentioned were £2,000m and £1,500m respectively. However, when Prideaux of NatWest and Graham of Midland went to see Hollom on the 19th, Prideaux 'at once stated that he was not prepared to speak to these figures at this meeting'. He then 'stressed the growing concern of the banks at the distortion of the balance sheets that was being caused by the size of the rescue operation' and stated that 'he did not think that the Support Group would hold together on an "ad infinitum" basis'. In response, Hollom 'took the line that certain names in the Market, to wit, United Dominions Trust and Keyser Ullmann, would have to be supported', but added that 'he was perfectly amenable to receiving from the clearing banks their ideas as to the quantification of their total exposure'. Presumably he sensed that on the principle of the cap there was by now a united front on the part of the clearers. Two days later Prideaux, Tuke and Graham returned, with Prideaux quickly coming to the nub: 'Having regard to the present level of commitment at about £1,000m, and with the actual borrowing at around £900m, the banks thought that an overall limit of £1,200m should be established for Group Support. This figure represented about half of their banks' shareholders' funds, and was twice the amount of the sum originally envisaged.' To this proposition, Hollom 'did not demur'.[43] He could only hope that he would not have to look to his unsympathetic political masters for public money over and above the agreed figure.

All this had been against the background of a deepening 'blue' in the City at large. 'The reactions of Jack Jones [of the Transport Workers] and his friends to the modest NIESR suggestions about indexed wages were predictable but revealing,' Sir Peter Tennant of Barclays Bank International wrote to Bolton on 19 June. 'Perhaps they will have to drive us all into self-destruction before they understand what inflation means, or is it possible that they are following Lenin's dictum about destroying the currency in order to destroy capitalism?' That very day the FT 30-Share

Index was 53 per cent down on what it had been twenty-five months earlier, thereby exceeding the London market's historic fall between 1929 and 1932. It ended June at 255.1 (having started the month at 276.3), and on 3 July there was a further blow to any hopes that the Labour government might bring inflation under control when Foot ruled out a formal wage freeze, pinning his hopes instead on voluntary wage restraint. Next day the NUM rejected all forms of incomes policy. Healey's mini-budget later than month did not lighten the mood, and on the 31st the Index closed at 236.4, a fifteen-year low. That same day, while the government published its plans to nationalise the shipbuilding industry, the recently established Stock Exchange Liaison Committee (a mixture of various Stock Exchange representatives and figures from other parts of the City) was asked by Loveday in the chair to consider 'the present position of the City'. In a wholly inconclusive discussion, one of those present 'expressed the view that the City should get together more closely and not always be seen to be on the defensive', another that 'it would be important to avoid confrontation in any programme of propaganda on behalf of the City'. However, 'it was agreed that there was merit in keeping the question under review'.[44]

The second full week of August saw pessimism more rife than at any time so far in the year. Sterling was under pressure; the July trade deficit was £478m; the Triumph Investment Trust was rightly feared to be in trouble, despite Lifeboat help; Court Line, Britain's second-largest tour operator, collapsed; it was being alleged that some named composite insurance companies were in difficulties; and, perhaps most damagingly of all, Benn's White Paper, 'The Regeneration of British Industry', anticipated not only planning agreements with leading companies, but also the establishment of a National Enterprise Board. The Index began the week at 237.3 and finished it at 210.3. The tone of the Sunday press was epitomised by the *Sunday Telegraph*'s headline, 'Shares Plummet into the Unknown', and on Monday the 19th the Index dipped briefly below 200 – an event that, according to Littlewood, 'had a devastating psychological effect', as 'a paralysing pessimism took hold of a significant number of stock market practitioners, fund managers and company directors'.

On the 21st, the TUC General Secretary, Len Murray, launched a fierce attack on the City. 'People inside the City of London', he insisted, were 'doing the country no service', in that 'whether for selfish reasons or through an inability to understand the nature of economic development' they were 'spreading alarm and despondency'. He demanded that those people 'go out and see a factory working and see how irrelevant a small parcel of shares changing hands on the Stock Exchange is to industrial life'. For several days afterwards the invective flew: Dundas Hamilton on behalf of the Stock Exchange offered to provide a teach-in for trade union leaders; one of those leaders, Clive Jenkins, said that the Stock Exchange ought to be closed; and George Hutchinson, a political commentator on *The Times*, argued that the City, with its 'whining and wailing', was 'in danger of becoming a national millstone'. The following Sunday, in the *Observer*, the economist Alan Day (an old *bête noire* of the Bank of England) declared that 'at its most fundamental level the Stock Exchange crash marks the realisation of doubts . . . whether anything like our kind of mixed economy can survive'; noted that, should large-scale bankruptcies occur, then 'the enthusiastic Mr Benn and his allies are there quietly eager to pick up the pieces'; and asserted that 'there are highly responsible men on the Left who in private are prepared quietly to accept that we are in a pre-revolutionary situation'. Even the usually sober Rowe & Pitman *Market Report* succumbed to fears of apocalypse soon, declaring that 'a spectre of recession coupled with hyperinflation, sterling crisis, labour unrest and severe supply shortages is indeed truly horrific'.[45]

These were strange days, and on 4 September, writing to a sympathetic spirit in the person of Enoch Powell, George Bolton elaborated on how 'fear of a total collapse of the system is an all-pervading emotion':

> The sorry state of the stock market; the creation of a clearing banks' monopoly as smaller banks find business impossible; the collapse of the property markets; the cessation of investment in industry; the overwhelming consumer demand which plays such a large part in ensuring an adverse balance of payments, all contribute to the loss of creditability [*sic*] of the British Government at home and abroad.
>
> One consequence is the dangerous talk about dictatorship, which grows in appeal as Ministers assume that speeches about the evil of inflation are the equivalent of action. The power and influence of our system of representative government is daily eroded as continuous inflation damages the foundations of our social and political fabric. The time is near when someone like yourself, uncontaminated by the soft options gladly adopted by all recent Governments, should defend our constitution and clear the electorate's mind about the wretched alternatives.[46]

In his way one of the intellectual godfathers of the New Right, at last about to come into its own a decade and a half after Thorneycroft's resignation, Bolton was in the end – for all his grandstanding prose and his willingness to pursue sometimes elusive visions – a City man, which by definition meant operating within the existing order of things.

Bolton was writing the day after the fifth Stock Exchange hammering of the year, the brokers Tustain & L'Estrange. One of its eight partners was John Bridges, who perhaps took comfort from the knowledge that his wife Hermione (who had a baby the evening before the hammering) was one of the few women to have passed the Stock Exchange's membership exam. 'I can't deal – but my wife can,' he remarked wryly later in the week. Soon afterwards an analysis of the fortnightly account ending 30 August revealed that, out of the total value of purchases and sales of £1,510m, only £308m was in equities – traditionally, for almost all small and medium-sized broking firms, their very lifeblood. In addition to the handful of hammerings, some mergers between firms had already taken place and many more were actively in hand. Inevitably a process of widespread redundancies had also begun. 'If business does not improve for six months the survivors may not only be slim,' the *Sunday Telegraph* forecast. 'They may be downright thin.' Immediate events did not suggest an early revival. Amidst news that wages had doubled since the start of the year, Richardson on 4 September remarked wistfully to the clearing bank chairmen that 'what was needed was a break in inflationary expectations'; while on the 16th, as the government stepped in to support Ferranti, the Bank expressed serious concern about the state of corporate liquidity.[47] Two days later Wilson announced (to no great surprise) that the second general election of the year would be held on 10 October.

The following week, as a jaundiced electorate tried to summon up democratic enthusiasm, Commercial Union astonished the City with the announcement of a £62m rights issue.[48] This proved that the London capital market could still function, and as such would be credited with putting some much-needed heart into the City; but as 'Lex' pointed out, in the context of the yield basis being 17 per cent, 'if CU had not been able to get itself underwritten on those terms then that really would have been the end of the line for the primary market'. On 27 September, with the Index down to 181.6, the *Investors Chronicle* carried a relatively reassuring interview with Healey, who stated that 'the private sector is likely to be responsible for the greater part of our economic activity for as far ahead as I can see'. Asked whether the City had failed British industry, his answer was circumspect:

> In the last few years far too much money went from the City into unproductive fields, particularly property and the money markets. But that, I think, can be attributed to the policy of Competition and Credit Control combined with excessive expansion in the money supply at a time when the economy was overheating. I wouldn't care to take a final view of the performance of the City.

Healey did add, however, that 'the reaction of the City to events in the economy bears very little relation to the real strength of British industry'. Most opinion polls pointed to a Labour win with an adequate working majority; but at least, from the City's point of view, Healey was promising to take reflationary measures in his first post-election budget in order to tackle the problem of corporate liquidity, while the TUC had given its backing to the 'Social Contract', which in theory would help to reduce inflationary pressures. Moreover, to judge by a poll of just under 200 reasonably senior City people that appeared a week before the real polling day, the City was inclined to doubt the national opinion polls, with a majority expecting a Conservative/Liberal coalition to be the next government. As for personal voting intentions, the breakdown was predictable. Conservative: 73 per cent; Liberal: 18 per cent; not voting or undecided: 9 per cent; Labour: 0 per cent.[49]

On election day itself the Index closed at 195.4, but then lost 4½ points on the Friday as it became clear that Labour had won an overall majority, though of only three. The City, the *Investors Chronicle* commented in a cogent post-election editorial the following week, 'should ponder the fact of its political isolation and take steps to re-integrate itself into the community'. Could it really hope to reach out to the voter in Battersea quoted in Rowe & Pitman's latest circular? 'I'm not an ignorant git,' this candid figure had reputedly told a canvasser from the City during the campaign. 'I read the *Daily Express*. "Millions wiped off share values" – and we all know where they've gone, don't we? I expect you beggars have got it stashed abroad by now.'[50]

One of the City's earliest concerns, once Labour had been given its fresh mandate, was how to respond to an idea recently floated by Harold Lever, the member of the government most closely attuned to financial matters.[51] Interviewed by the *Sunday Times* on 15 September, he spoke of establishing 'a medium-term credit bank' in order to supplement the efforts of the commercial banks and ensure that industry did not suffer from the near-collapse of the capital market. As to how this would be done, the key passage ran:

> The situation requires that we don't spend years creating an entirely new mechanism. Existing skills must be tapped. The medium-term credit bank should say to the commercial banks, and perhaps other investment institutions of unquestioned credit: 'Look, you can have this money provided we get the appropriate certificate that you have passed it on in the form we require [later in the interview he spoke of trying to produce "a certain regional bias"]. You have in return a reward for your responsibility and risk taking . . .' To this extent the Government would be acting as a wholesaler of money, not a retailer.

Shortly afterwards Healey endorsed the idea, though there was no mention of it in Labour's manifesto. From the outset the City was hostile to the notion of a new, state bank, however worthy its objectives; and soon, especially following a letter from Morgan Grenfell's Philip Chappell in *The Times*, a view emerged among bankers that the most suitable vehicle for meeting Labour's aspirations in this field was Finance for Industry (FFI), created the previous year through the merger of ICFC and FCI, those twin pillars of the 1945 Labour/City settlement.[52]

On 20 October, a week and half after the election, Lever told Radio 4's *The World This Weekend* that the government was now seriously intending to establish a national investment bank in order to channel, through the commercial banking system, up to £1bn to industry. Seeking to allay the fears of City and industry, he insisted that this was not 'nationalisation by the back door'. Three days later Richardson and the clearers discussed the whole question. The Governor's line was that 'even if the action taken in the Budget [due on 12 November] was favourable and adequate in the longer run there would still be a massive interim financing problem'; that 'the private sector should make every effort to meet the need'; and that this was 'an excellent opportunity for FFI to establish itself as an important institution doing a vital job'. Whereupon:

> Discussion of the Governor's ideas for FFI was often entwined with comments on the Lever plan for an industrial investment bank. From these it was clear that all the Chairmen were opposed to the idea of acting as agents for Government finance to their customers . . .
>
> On FFI the central problem was funding. The Chairmen expressed sympathy with the Governor's aims but felt that their balance sheets would not support advances of £1,000m to FFI which might be locked up for 5 to 10 years. They had for some time been emphasising the likely strain on their balance sheets and it was hardly consistent to agree suddenly to find a large amount of medium-term money. It was also suggested that the problem would turn out to be too large for the private sector and that the most helpful approach might be to look for ways of combining private and public finance . . .

As they always did in these situations, the clearers also wondered whether the insurance companies and pension funds might make a contribution. Richardson and the clearers met again on 6 November, with the Governor unyielding on one fundamental point:

> His present aim was to demonstrate that up to £1,000m of funds could be found for British industry from the private sector, if the demand for such funds was forthcoming, since he believed that such a demonstration would have a most valuable effect. Partial reliance on public sector financing of the exercise would much diminish its impact, as well as having implications for the control of the operations.

His words had an effect. Two days later Midland's board agreed to participate – on the grounds that 'this step was much in the interest of preserving the whole concept of private enterprise' – and Healey duly announced the £1bn fund in his budget. The clearing banks would provide £300,000, with most of the rest coming from the 'institutions', in other words insurance companies and pension funds. Not all that institutional support was enthusiastically given, and Standard Life may not have been alone in adamantly refusing the Bank of England's request to contribute.[53] Still, the larger point held: like Norman between the wars,

Richardson had managed to keep the government out of the finance/ industry relationship.

This achievement, though, was far from banishing the underlying question that haunted the City during the autumn of 1974: would free markets ever flourish again? 'The Stock Market is very sick and we must appeal for help,' was George Loveday's plaintive cry at the Lord Mayor's Banquet soon after Wilson's fourth election victory in ten years. Rowe & Pitman's circular for November upped the rhetoric: 'This bear market is the financial equivalent of the Great War. Lamps going out, end of an era, casualties numbered in millions, does the country know what's *happening*, will it ever end?' Healey's budget on the 12th was in retrospect a turning-point in terms of ending the liquidity crisis in British industry, with its price-code relaxation and tax relief on stock appreciation; but at the time attention focused much more on how the public-sector borrowing requirement for 1974–5, which in March had been estimated at £2.7bn, was now estimated at £6.3bn. Consequently the Index, 194.3 on the eve of the budget, fell still further to 171.3 by the 27th. The next day Wilson attacked the 'weevils at work' in the Stock Exchange, but that week's real drama was reserved for Friday the 29th.[54] 'Bank of England denies NatWest rescue move' was the headline in the *Evening Standard*, causing Prideaux to issue a statement flatly denying the truth of any rumours questioning NatWest's financial position. These rumours had been caused by the considerable extent of NatWest's loans to secondary banks and the property sector, by speculation that the construction of Seifert's huge new 'tower' was one commitment too many and by the bank's expensive links with the crisis-hit Italian financier Michele Sindona. Prideaux himself later claimed that the episode was essentially a newspaper affair, but rumours about NatWest's lack of liquidity were circulating quite independently in the Stock Exchange.[55] Inevitably the very thought of one of the big banks being in trouble sent a collective shudder through the square mile. That particular fear quickly subsided, but over the next fortnight came a flow of bad news – a reputable forecast of 25 per cent as the inflation rate in 1975, the government agreeing to take a £50m stake in British Leyland in order to keep it going, the NUM seeking pay rises of up to 90 per cent. Thursday, 12 December was no exception, with news of a record trade deficit in November of £534m, and the Index closed that day at 150.0, a figure satisfying only for its roundness.

NatWest's *mauvais quart d'heure* reflected the blackness of the clouds that still hovered over the finance and property sectors, notwithstanding Richardson's recent achievement in persuading the government to lift the freeze on commercial rents. By this time the Lifeboat was not far short of reaching its £1,200m 'limit', and Midland's Stuart Graham continued to offer a particularly critical perspective on its operations. He himself had become during the summer one of the two Chief General Managers at Midland (which earlier in the year had, through Samuel Montagu, acquired the Drayton Group), with Malcolm Wilcox as the other one. Graham was to be primarily responsible for domestic banking and Wilcox for international. On 21 November, in the context of the absence of any repayments to the clearing banks from Triumph Investment Trust (now in severe difficulties and looking hopefully to the Lifeboat for further, urgent support), Graham sent Forbes a trenchant note:

> Are the clearing banks to be the sole losers in the Rescue Operation (apart, of course, from the 10% participation of the Bank of England), when action is dictated by environmental market conditions or political considerations? . . .
>
> Under the present system of support the clearing banks buy out all depositors, no matter who they are or how much they have deposited. In effect this means that in many cases we let other banks, finance houses, etc. off the hook, but in doing so we support the 'small' depositor . . .
>
> I think the whole Support Operation needs to be reconsidered. The initial idea that the operation was merely to provide a recycling of monies pending the restoration of public confidence in the supported companies has, I think, disappeared (if indeed it ever existed), and we are, perhaps, faced with the need to disband the bulk of such companies, leaving a small rump. I realise that in saying this it is contrary to the thinking of the Bank of England, but I think that, in great measure, the present predicament stems from the failure of the Bank of England properly to control the growth of the Banking Sector in recent years.

Triumph went into receivership, but that did not deter Graham from reiterating soon afterwards his general point, that 'if the companies [i.e. the fringe banks as a whole] are to be kept in existence, our lending, i.e. £1,200m, becomes of medium/long term – made available to keep competitors in being'. His suggestion was that the clearers should only support a 'competitor' organisation if it had a chairman and/or managing director recruited from a clearing bank.[56]

One institution that, for all its problems, stayed out of the Lifeboat was Slater Walker. There, 'retrenchment' (very much Slater's favourite word in this period) continued to be the order of the day, prompting 'Lex' to assert in October that there was 'no reason to be concerned' about the group's financial state. Slater himself remained the subject of considerable attention – for example, 'Mr Bearbull' in the *Investors Chronicle* in early November noted that 'the best "dealing" mind in the City' was now 'buying double options in commodities on the grounds that the only certainty nowadays is volatility'. Soon afterwards, interviewed by the *Banker*, he described Slater Walker's current policy as 'very much one of waiting and seeing' and expressed the view that North America was possibly 'the last bastion of capitalism'. Slater was also in the news that autumn when a member of the Shadow Cabinet, 'outed' for having stockpiled a huge quantity of tinned goods, said that she had got the idea from him. Apparently what Margaret Thatcher had in mind were Slater's widely publicised remarks at a brokers' lunch earlier in the year: asked in a light-hearted way what one needed in order to cope with all contingencies in the present situation, his answer had been an ample supply of tins of baked beans, a bicycle, krugerrands and a shot-gun.[57] It was, in retrospect, a tantalising moment of interaction between one era that was effectively over and another that was yet to start.

'After 1974,' Slater justly wrote three years later, 'most people who were active in the financial world would look at things very differently for the rest of their lives.' Or, as 'Lex' put it at the time, 'although we could foresee the general pattern of 1974, we had no real inkling of the scale of the crisis'. Davina Walter, granddaughter of a former partner, joined Cazenove's that year:

> Business was incredibly slack, everyone thought the market was going to disappear into a black hole, so there was no turnover and we were twiddling our thumbs. In the final quarter, the partners paid our bonus out of their own pockets and Cazenove's were the only stockbroking firm not to lay anybody off. I went round in a slight pink cloud, not realising quite how bad things were. The seriousness of the situation was brought home to me when I saw Coleman Street cordoned off because someone had jumped out of the window, committing suicide. I felt so sick at that. There were quite a few suicides . . .

From an older, more inside perspective, Kenneth Hill of Mullens remembered 1974 as 'a very sad and a very worrying time' in which 'everybody was looking over their shoulders'. One example of this corrosive anxiety stuck in his mind: 'There were certain broking firms whose cheques weren't accepted, which was a thing which was unknown before. They had to present bankers' drafts to people, one or two of them, which was very much against the spirit of the City, because our words were our bond.' For Graham Ferguson of Wedd Durlacher, it would become the never-to-be-forgotten year: '1974, I must admit I panicked. I thought it was the end of the capitalist system, I really did.' Another jobber, Brian Winterflood of Bisgood Bishop, seriously wondered whether or not to renew his season ticket to the City:

> Some days were interminably long. You couldn't believe that you weren't dealing. There were very few bargains and obviously we didn't want positions. It was tough, it really was tough. It was so tough that I actually started up a little business outside. I used to go up to the Caledonian Market and deal in bric-à-brac and things like that. We bought a little shop, my wife and myself, in the New King's Road and we turned that into a little antique shop. I remember very well getting up before

coming to the City and going to Portobello at 5 in the morning and going around to buy stock in the evening. I remember going down to Vallence Road, a road that totters used, behind Petticoat Lane. We used to go down there at 5 o'clock on a Sunday morning and you'd start at one end of this road and it was pitch dark and you'd have torches, and you'd be buying all your bits and pieces and take them back to your car. I remember very well that we'd been buying tables and chairs and so forth, and coming the other way as dawn broke was this guy Patrick Quirk, and he was selling carpet squares. He literally was selling carpet squares and he was making a living that way. He was still on the Stock Exchange but things were grim, you just had to supplement your income . . .

Nevertheless, it would perhaps be wrong to assume that the City of 1974 suddenly became the austerity City of 1947. When Sir Murray Fox, a chartered surveyor, became Lord Mayor in November, his first action was to send a message to the country by reducing the number of courses served at dinners in the Mansion House and Guildhall. Even so, at his opening banquet, the Prime Minister, the Archbishop of Canterbury and six High Court judges still sat down to soup followed by fish, roast beef with jacket potatoes and a pudding. At Pember & Boyle the worrying news came through that another broking firm, Grieveson Grant, had closed down its kitchen. 'There was a lengthy partners' debate about what they should do in order to cut back and save money,' Jeremy Wormell recalled. 'In the end it was decided that they would go from having four vegetables to three vegetables.'[58]

Pember & Boyle could probably afford to be relatively relaxed about the great question of the day, in that it specialised in gilts, where turnover held up far better than it did in equities. Indeed, a partner in one of the major gilt-broking firms (perhaps Pember & Boyle) told Nils Taube of Kitcat & Aitken that his firm had made more money in the bear market of 1974 than in the previous year. It is a reminder that there were winners as well as losers during this traumatic time. For example, although the great majority of brokers were equity-oriented and suffered accordingly, the jobbing fraternity was not too badly scathed. Valentine Powell of Pinchins, jobbing mainly in industrial shares, recalled the bear market of the mid-1970s as being 'extremely profitable for the jobbers':

It's a technicality of the business that if you sold a bear it meant you required very little capital to run your book with, because you were never buying stock, you were always selling stock to buy it back later. So provided you could borrow the stock and deliver it to your buyers, you never had a need for an overdraft; so we were short of stock and it was going the right way in market terms, we had a considerable balance at the bank in credit, so we were winning in both ways. And I think that in terms of relative advantage at that moment in time we had it over the brokers hand over fist . . .

In fact, the number of jobbing firms did contract (from nineteen in March 1974 to sixteen a year later), but the real decline was in broking firms (166 to 124 over the same period), mainly through mergers. Individual membership likewise declined (3,545 to 3,119); while in terms of the number of staff employed by London member-firms of the Stock Exchange, the best estimate is that there was a reduction of almost one-third between December 1973 (14,149) and December 1974 (9,717). Inexorably, a Stock Exchange world was dawning of bigger but fewer firms, substantial capital requirements and generally more stringent supervision by the authorities.[59]

Much the same trend would apply to the City at large, where among the bigger battalions there was much smug talk, coming out of 1974, of 'a flight to quality' – though arguably, in some instances, it was a case of size and/or social connection masking quality. Famously, Lord Poole was asked by Lord Cowdray how Lazards had succeeded in not being affected by the fall of the new financiers. 'Quite simple,' Poole answered. 'I only lent money to people who had been at Eton.' However, for one member of the Lifeboat Committee, the real lesson of 1974 was to be found in four lines of Kipling:

> Then the Gods of the Market trembled, and their smooth-tongued wizards withdrew,
> And the hearts of the meanest were humbled, and began to believe it was true
> That all is not Gold that Glitters, and Two and Two make four,
> And the Gods of the Copybook Headings limped up to explain it once more.[60]

*

The endgame of the second of the City's two great peacetime bear markets of the century began on Monday, 16 December with a meeting at the Prudential that would acquire an almost mythic quality.[61] Apparently on his own initiative, without any pushing from the Bank of England, one of the Pru's joint investment managers, Edward Hatchett, decided it was time that the investment institutions stopped sitting on their piles of cash and instead put some money into the equity market with a view to encouraging a recovery in prices. Accordingly the investment managers of the other leading insurance companies were invited to a lunch at Holborn Bars. Some declined to participate in the plan, but the almost immediate outcome was that four companies (Prudential, Legal & General, Commercial Union and Sun Alliance) between them went on a £20m buying spree. Despite this, however, the equity market remained for the time being in the doldrums, closing on Christmas Eve at 158.8, as the jobbers held on to their short, profitable bear positions. On the floor there was still a surprising amount of festive spirit: £120 was raised for charity through active trading in a thousand badges inscribed 'I am a weevil. Harold hates me.' And a particularly extrovert member, Eric 'Ginger' Baker, donned his Eighth Army khaki shorts and pith helmet and gave his annual rendition of 'Oh, for the wings of a dove', followed by some singing (mainly carols), before – as usual – a couple of men in white coats came to take him away. Meanwhile, it was rumoured that those firms that were offering their staff a choice of Christmas present – a partnership or a turkey – had run out of turkeys. Fortunately for what remained of the market's health, the more important news did not get out that the Bank of England was having to draw on its own reserves in order to avert the collapse of several major financial institutions. Details are still sketchy, but presumably the Lifeboat's agreed £1,200m had been used up. An appeal for help went out to the leading insurance companies, and though some toed the line, Standard Life again gave Richardson an uncompromising refusal.[62] Prudently run, never part of the City inner circle and with its head office still in Edinburgh, it saw no reason why its policy holders and pension clients should pay for an act of *noblesse oblige*.

On New Year's Eve, the day after Aston Martin went into liquidation, the Index closed at 161.4, having been 344.0 at the start of 1974. That evening it was announced that Burmah Oil, one of the three great oil companies, was going to have to be rescued by the Bank of England on behalf of the British government, as a result of serious mismanagement as well as wider economic circumstances. The sense of shock, not only in the City, was huge. 'I couldn't believe it,' Winterflood recalled, 'it was like Rolls-Royce again, and I thought, "My God, if they go bust we really are going to topple over the top". I sold all my shares . . .' Presumably he did so on Thursday, 2 January, when the Stock Exchange reopened and the Index dropped by 6.7 per cent, down to 150.6. Perhaps Winterflood had not had a chance to read Paul Bazalgette's just-published column in Phillips & Drew's *Market Review*. Noting that 1975 was 'the year of the Rabbit in the Chinese calendar' and that 'never in my Asian life have I ever known the turn of the year to be overlaid with such unvarying gloom in all quarters', he nevertheless refused to be dismayed:

A unanimous consensus, whether in the City or elsewhere, is nearly always wrong. Remember when the FT Index was over 500? 750 was a dead cert. then, and the go-go boys (all gone-gone now) said 1,000. I have just a tiny little feeling growing in me somewhere that the most redeeming feature of the present situation is that everyone is agreed that stark and unmitigated disaster lies ahead. We have very nearly discounted all these perils in our minds, our daily lives, and even possibly in share prices. If we haven't, well it can be only a matter of time before President McGahey is occupying that stately mansion at the end of the Mall, and quite a lot of you chaps are immured in the London Lubianka . . .

The following Saturday, the 4th, Peter Wilmot-Sitwell of Rowe & Pitman (which had just taken over the medium-sized brokers Read, Hurst-Brown) was shooting at Sandringham. He was asked by the Queen Mother, who had long had a connection with Rowe & Pitman, how the firm was faring in these difficult times. In reply, he said little more than that the general situation was 'worrying'. The next day, after church, the Queen Mother announced that she had prayed for an improvement in the market.[63]

There was no divine intervention on Monday the 6th, as against a background of rumours about liquidity problems at Bowater there was yet another downward movement in the Index, to 146.0, amounting to a 73 per cent fall in just over two and a half years. It was the lowest point since 3 May 1954, the week that Roger Bannister broke the four-minute mile. 'Is the UK turning into another Italy?' was *International Insider*'s headline on the 6th, about Britain's current inability, in either the private or public sector, to borrow on the international capital markets. And the magazine quoted a London-based foreign banker: 'Put crudely, the UK is now a second-rate credit and is fast turning into a borrower to be classed alongside an undeveloped country.'[64] It all seemed a long time since the optimistic exploits of the New Elizabethans.

CHAPTER SEVENTEEN

Conditionality

'To have been involved in the London stock market of January 1975 is an experience none of us will forget,' Rowe & Pitman's James D'Albiac wrote at the start of February:

> Few will remember it pleasurably. Following the Burmah Oil crisis there was a consensus of pessimism that surely equalled anything in market history. But within days the market was roaring upwards in a crescendo of buying. Despite what they may now claim, most investors were wrong-footed by this sudden change and remained imprisoned by the seemingly irrefutable logic of their gloom. Many, alas, are still locked in this unfortunate state . . .

The bare facts of this rally were that the FT 30-Share Index, having closed on the 6th at 146.0, reached 236.9 by the 31st. Friday the 24th, with its phenomenal 10.1 per cent rise of almost twenty points, was particularly a day to remember. It was, Littlewood recalls, 'the last day of the fortnightly Stock Exchange account, when speculators who had disbelievingly sold the market short were forced to close, in competition with jobbers and professionals who were desperately short of stock, while equally desperate institutions were panicking into the market before it was too late and running headlong into unit trusts, bearing liquidity problems compounded by money pouring in from the public.' That vortex of trading produced a turnover of £138m (monthly turnover during much of 1974 had averaged less than £850m), only to be surpassed by turnover the following Monday of £162m. Inevitably there was a strong streak of irrationality in the market's sensational bounce-back, in that much of the economic news remained gloomy; nevertheless, there was truth in D'Albiac's argument, which he had been propounding since Healey's budget in November, that 'this Labour government – duly moving to the right, the longer it stays in office – is in the process of coming to recognise the necessity for high profits and healthy share prices for the attainment of its humanitarian and social policies'. The bull market continued to roar away during February, with the Index reaching 301.8, more than double what it had been in early January. 'At the end of it all,' Littlewood writes of these eight weeks, 'feeling in the City was one of overwhelming relief. The patient had returned to good health after months in delirium.

Portfolios had survived. The Stock Exchange did have a future after all. Commissions and fees were rolling in again. Normal service had been resumed.'[1]

The City's mood during 1975 was also helped by the gradual receding of the secondary banking crisis.[2] The Lifeboat peaked at £1,285m in March (the Bank of England having to meet the excess above the agreed £1,200m limit), before slowly but surely that figure came down. Some of the fringe concerns were allowed to collapse. Triumph Investment Trust had already done so in November 1974, without inflicting any huge damage on the stability of the banking system as a whole, and it was followed by Burston Finance in February and London and County Securities in March. Three former directors of the latter were subsequently the subject of criminal proceedings, but L&C's top man, Gerald Caplan, stayed put in California, reputedly finding a role as Treasurer of Jews for Jesus. In the case of concerns allowed to go to the wall, it seems to have been the Bank of England that alone took responsibility for repaying the remaining outside depositors, involving (according to Reid) 'costs totalling many millions of pounds'. Naturally the Bank's preference was to see concerns (if there was a core viability) taken over by a larger group, reconstructed, put under new management, or some combination of the three. Vavasseur, for instance, was unbundled and gradually sold off in parts, including its very successful 'First Investors' unit trust business to Henderson Administration. Barclays acquired Mercantile Credit, while Cedar Holdings was reconstructed into a scaled-down business with a new Chairman, Simon Coorsh from Great Universal Stores, before eventually in 1979 being taken over by Lloyds and Scottish, the finance house controlled by Lloyds and the Royal Bank of Scotland.

FNFC was, predictably, a tougher nut to crack. Were the clearing banks going to continue to provide it with 'a bottomless purse', Midland's Graham asked in March 1975, as its fortunes continued to deteriorate, and shortly before the sale of part of the business to Chase Manhattan fell through because of a Fed veto. First National's figures got worse during the summer, and by August Graham was arguing that 'the capital has been effectively lost', 'the management have not succeeded' and 'drastic action is now needed, as it is axiomatic that further good money should not be put in to save the bad'. In short, in contrast to what he called the 'kid gloves' approach of the Bank of England, he wanted liquidation, which would have 'the over-riding advantage of crystallising the position and preventing further trading losses'.[3] In the event, the company during 1976 came under almost entirely new management, with Matthews himself making a suitably dignified exit.

Elsewhere, the most successful of the new brooms were those at United Dominions Trust (with Len Mather, formerly of Midland, as Chairman) and Keyser Ullmann (where Derek Wilde of Barclays succeeded du Cann as Chairman in March 1975, later joined by the Bank of England's experienced Roy Fenton as Chief Executive). The case of Edward Bates, the last one into the Lifeboat, was rather different. It was a complicated story, involving Arab interests, Greek shipping markets and the Gulf States' sterling balances, before in the course of 1976, with no immediate help available from the clearers, the Bank of England felt it had no alternative but to take the hit (of some £30m), though Barclays was involved in a subsequent reconstruction. Finally, well down the pecking order in terms of importance but with a special City piquancy, there was Cripps Warburg – taken over in February 1975 by Williams & Glyn's for a nominal price, apparently a rather grubby £1 note. George Warburg's personal reputation remained intact (soon afterwards he was being actively considered for a senior position in Finance for Industry), but predictably his father took it hard, forbidding any discussion at Warburgs of the matter.[4]

The City being the City, with its profound aversion to economic theories, there was also precious little discussion during 1975 about how, following the previous year's stagflationary trauma, the post-war Keynesian consensus was entering its death throes. There was, for example, only limited appreciation of the significance of the new leadership of the Conservative Party. 'The choice is very finely balanced,' the *FT* declared in February, when, after Heath had stood down, the choice lay between William Whitelaw and Margaret Thatcher; though after Thatcher won, the paper expressed some enthusiasm for her, should she manage to develop 'a practical and non-doctrinaire programme for reducing State control and enlarging the area of individual choice'. In the following month's *Euromoney* Fildes insisted that the City was shedding no tears for Heath – who had alienated 'his natural allies in the financial community . . . by his shift of policy away from market economics and towards the corporate state' – but argued that although the new leader's instincts were 'cleanly and unambiguously Conservative', the City would not be happy with the party, 'its natural ally', until 'it looks, first, a serious element in the political scene, and, second – and more difficult – a potential government'. For at least two years, moreover, there was little natural rapport between Thatcher and the City. 'Audiences of bankers or stockbrokers found her lectures on economics to be both simplistic and inflexible,' Middlemas has noted. 'It was as if, having mastered the brief, she could not progress further.'[5] And though she had firm supporters in the City (including John Baring at Barings and Michael Richardson at Cazenove's), the undeniable fact was that she was in opposition, with little prospect of immediate power; and the City had always preferred to deal with the practical realities of the here and now.

That meant the Labour government, where, prefigured to some extent by Healey's more business-friendly budget in November 1974, the plates were starting to shift. Above all, in January 1975, Healey's crucial speech to his Leeds East constituents ditched the time-honoured 'Phillips curve' by arguing that inflation caused unemployment and therefore the prime task of economic policy must be to keep it down. In the same speech he insisted that public expenditure must come under the straitjacket of cash limits, provoking Anthony Crosland's immortal remark, in relation to local authority spending, 'the party's over'. None of this, however, meant that the government was now embracing Friedmanite monetarism. In the same month as Healey's speech, Wilson held a City-oriented dinner at No 10 with a guest list supplied by Richardson. Among those present was the City's arch-monetarist, Gordon Pepper:

> After the meal the Prime Minister asked his guests to express their concerns. The response was silence. He tried again and the same thing happened. The Governor then tried and there was again silence. He then mentioned some of the subjects he thought were causing concern in the City and looked at me. I was easily the youngest and most junior in the room. I gulped and decided to speak up about monetary growth, the PSBR and public expenditure, whereupon all hell broke loose as far as I was concerned. Harold Wilson appeared to be allergic to having a monetary economist at his dinner table and I was lambasted . . .

Richardson himself would soon be engaged in overseeing – and ultimately adjudicating – a protracted intellectual exercise among the Bank's economists, with Christopher Dow leading the Keynesians and Charles Goodhart the monetarists.[6] Conscious of how the 1972–3 credit explosion had damaged the Bank's reputation, and in a sense taking to heart Bolton's advice at the time of his appointment, Richardson was determined to raise the Bank's game in the key area of shaping monetary policy.

As Governor, after the ordeal by fire of his first year and a half, Richardson was cutting an increasingly confident figure. 'Everyone now admits that you are the best government that we can hope to have at the moment,' he remarked in March 1975 to Edmund Dell, the Paymaster General, who was in effect Healey's deputy. 'Why are you doing so many silly things? The NEB will do no good at all . . .' That spring, the almost all-pervasive preoccupation was the spectre of Weimar-style 'hyper-inflation'. By April, when cash limits on public spending were adopted, the UK's consumer price index was increasing at an annual rate of 21.7 per cent, by far the highest rate of inflation among the industrial countries. Practically every week there was evidence that the much-vaunted Social Contract was in smithereens: on the 3rd the power workers accepted a 31 per cent pay deal, on the 14th civil servants accepted 32 per cent, four days later doctors accepted 35 per cent and on the 30th seamen declined 30 per cent. 'Awareness of the threat to their savings is spreading amongst all sorts of people, far away from the prudent money managers of the Square Mile or Charlotte Square [in Edinburgh],' Rowe & Pitman noted at the start of May; equally, outside as well as inside the City, everyone knew that it was politically impossible for the Wilson government to tackle wage inflation effectively until after the referendum on British membership of the EEC, due on 5 June.[7]

The City, as far as one can tell, was almost unanimously in favour of a 'Yes' vote. Two months ahead of voting the clearing banks had agreed to contribute £200,000 to the 'Britain in Europe' campaign; soon after-wards, after senior partners of Stock Exchange firms had been approached by the campaign for funds, the Council sent them an encouraging letter stating that in its view 'the withdrawal of the United Kingdom from the EEC would be disastrous both for the Nation and, in particular, the City of London', with an accompanying statement referring to 'the growing internationalisation of Stock Exchange business'. On referendum day itself, the Bank of England's Derrick Byatt discussed with the Fed over the telephone the unlikely eventuality of a 'No' vote. With the Fed promising help, 'Byatt indicated that, in that event, the Bank of England would strongly advise against closing the foreign exchange markets', adding that 'they [i.e. the Bank] would hope that a clear no vote would not be a reason for shutting down the market in a floating-rate environment'. Within hours it was clear that the British people had taken the *FT*'s advice and decided against committing 'a gratuitous act of irresponsible folly'.[8]

The referendum result has been plausibly identified as a key political moment of the mid-1970s, when the left wing of the Labour Party lost not only over the EEC issue, but also in terms of 'the right to claim that their political and economic wishes should dictate the political agenda, on the grounds that they alone spoke for the working class'. The symbolism was palpable as, within days, Wilson replaced Benn at Industry with the appreciably more moderate Eric Varley. 'He is very close to Harold and he told me what had happened,' Benn (who had been moved to Energy) noted after a conversation with Varley. '"I think Harold entered into some commitments with the City or somebody, and he has to get rid of you."' The next day, the 10th, the monthly investment circular by the brokers Simon & Coates exuded a sense of relief, declaring that after the referendum 'at least the worst fears of a siege economy can be put at rest' and that 'the Chancellor has two or three months' grace in which to work out his counter-inflationary policy'. Also plopping on institutional and other desks was the latest *Monetary Bulletin* from Pepper at Greenwells. 'The conventional demand stimulus cures for a recession are boosts to public expenditure, cuts in taxation and easier monetary policy,' he observed, in the context of rising unemployment. 'But all these remedies increase the money supply which would then fuel a further acceleration in inflation in due course.' So instead:

> The best policy is an all-out attack on inflation. If the secular trend of accelerating inflation can be broken, balance sheets can become pro-gressively stronger and many other problems will disappear. In particular, accelerating inflation is now the basic cause of rising unemployment. Interventionist policies can only preserve employment in the public sector and the largest companies in the private sector . . .[9]

It was an analysis with which Healey now broadly concurred. With the Left now weakened, the question was whether he could sell it to the rest of the Cabinet and the unions.

In managing to do so, he was considerably helped by sterling's acute difficulties during much of June. On the eve of the referendum the value of sterling against the dollar was 24.7 per cent less than it had been at the time of the Smithsonian parities created in December 1971; but by the 12th, after three days of heavy selling, the 'Smithsonian depreciation' was 26.2 per cent. 'Galloping devaluation' was the title of Padraic Fallon's *Euromoney* article charting the slide, in which he took the line that 'while wage inflation reigns unchecked, the pound must go on falling, and the balance of payments will be denied the opportunity to climb into healthy surplus'. That, he added, 'is why the chairman of one of the largest US banks, asked at the International Monetary Conference in Amsterdam what is the greatest source of international concern, laconically replied: "Britain".' In late June, after a brief pause, the currency slide continued – especially after the railwaymen successfully negotiated, in one of the classic Downing Street beer-and-sandwiches sessions, a 30 per cent settlement, news of which immediately knocked fifteen points off the stock market. Sterling's worst day was the 30th, with depreciation reaching 28.9 per cent, amidst reasonably well-grounded rumours that the Bank was deliberately allowing a nose-dive so that Richardson could put pressure on Wilson to back Healey in his campaign to persuade the unions to accept an incomes policy.[10]

If this was the tactic, it succeeded, and on 11 July an anti-inflation White Paper announced (with the broad consent of the unions) that wage rises were to be limited for the next year to £6 a week, with no rises for anyone earning over £8,500. Rowe & Pitman hailed the announcement as 'a watershed', showing that 'all sectors of the community' had 'grown aware that the mad merry-go-round threatened to whirl us off to disaster'. Praising Healey's 'stiffening' determination to win the battle against inflation – and declaring that 'behind him, the mood and will of the people is also stiffening' – D'Albiac even hazarded that the moment could mark 'the beginning of the end of the long period of growing union power' and 'of class fighting class at the expense of the community'. Undoubtedly there was huge relief in the City; but so soon after Heath's already infamous U-turn, there was also an underlying sympathy with the *FT*'s line that an 'incomes policy can be no more than a temporary expedient, inevitably accompanied by many disadvantages, and that the proper tools for regulating the economy in all but abnormal times are fiscal and monetary policy'.[11] In other words, 1940s-type solutions were no longer appropriate in the more open, 'floating' world after Bretton Woods.

In the next few weeks, the incomes policy more or less held, but international financial attention turned by the autumn to the rapidly growing public-sector borrowing requirement, with the Treasury's latest forecast running at £12bn, compared with £9bn in the spring. On 13 October, in a piece on the pound (now worth barely $2) that was bearish in the short term but bullish in the medium, *International Insider* offered a prediction: that in due course the Labour government would 'go to the IMF and sign a letter of intent which, by its stringent terms, will ensure competent economic management until 1980, when North Sea oil will come fully on-stream'. Three days later, at the Mansion House bankers' dinner, Healey's speech provoked what Richardson soon afterwards described to the clearers as 'a sharp reaction', reflecting 'disappointment that the expected announcement of measures to contain the growth of public expenditure had not been forthcoming'. Richardson's own Mansion House speech (he once described it to a colleague as 'the most important thing that the Governor does in the course of the year') had two key sentences: 'There is much debate over the appropriate role of monetary policy in the present circumstances. For my part I do not doubt that it has an important and powerful influence on the economy – though the force and timing of its impact may be difficult to predict.'[12] The language was typically guarded, but it was clear that the Keynesians were losing the battle for Richardson's soul.

Far removed from such recondite matters, the *FT*'s main front-page headline on Saturday, 25 October packed a punch: 'Jim Slater "retires from City"'.[13] With little appetite for the long-haul prospect of rebuilding the slimmed-down Slater Walker in a largely hostile environment, Slater had spent much of 1975 trying to find a buyer, preferably for the whole company. Tiny Rowland was one possibility, Adnan Khashoggi another, and Slater's close friend (and substantial shareholder in Slater Walker) James Goldsmith a third. But by now, in addition to the problems going back to the stock market and property crash, there was an increasingly dark shadow hanging over Slater Walker – the so-called 'Spydar's web'. Spydar Securities was Slater Walker's Far Eastern equivalent of Tokengate – essentially, a way of ensuring that Slater Walker executives involved in operations in the Far East received a slice of the action. By the autumn Spydar's affairs were under close scrutiny from the Singapore government, accompanied by much adverse publicity in *Private Eye* and the *Far Eastern Economic Review*. Moreover, each week there were rumours in the City that extracts were going to appear in the *Sunday Times* from Charles Raw's forthcoming investigative book on Slater Walker, its publication hitherto delayed by Slater's lawyers. Then on Monday, 20 October, Patrick Sergeant's column in the *Daily Mail* appeared, written from Singapore and emphatically taking the line that Spydar had become an albatross around Slater Walker's neck. At noon Slater went to see Blunden at the Bank of England and recommended that Goldsmith (with whom he had dined the previous Wednesday) should take over the running of the company. He then rang Goldsmith in Paris to tell him he was resigning, and Goldsmith arrived in London next day, seeing Richardson before going to Slater Walker to begin reshaping it.

Peter Parker (in his capacity as Chairman of the Rockware Group, in which Slater Walker had a stake) went to see Slater at St Paul's Churchyard a couple of days before the news broke and found him 'unusually unfocused'. Agreeing without demur to Parker's proposal, Slater 'scribbled numbers on a small sheet of paper as we talked'; as Parker got up, he saw that 'the scribbles were simply strings of noughts'. By Friday afternoon, even though no announcement had been made, Slater Walker's share price was collapsing completely. According to a subsequent Stock Exchange inquiry that found no evidence of suspicious dealing, a plethora of rumours was flying around the market – that 'Mr Slater was very ill and had been admitted to a Harley Street clinic', that 'Mr Slater had been seen in the City which was unusual for a Friday', that Slater Walker was 'having trouble in the property market' and that Goldsmith 'was trying to dispose of his shareholding'. Eventually, at 6.45 that evening, the news came through on the Extel tape. 'I find that my wish to retire from the City and the interests of Slater Walker Securities are now identical,' Slater's statement declared, adding that 'I am pleased to be handing over the chairmanship of Slater Walker Securities to Mr James Goldsmith, as a man of proven ability with a long record of success in the companies in which he is interested'. It was, the *Daily Telegraph* next day said, 'the end of one of the most remarkable stories in the City's long history – the rise of builder's son Mr Jim Slater and his creation of possibly the most remarkable investment machine ever seen'.[14]

Slater Walker itself, propped up by the Bank of England, staggered on for two years under Goldsmith, before in 1977 a major reconstruction saw the Bank of England (at considerable, much-criticised expense) taking over the banking arm, while other parts of the business were reconstituted under the name of Britannia Arrow Holdings. As for Slater, after surviving

various legal challenges, doing some well-timed property deals to help
restore his personal finances and writing some children's books as well as
his autobiography, he became during the 1980s an almost invisible man,
before re-emerging in 1992 with a best-selling and characteristically
incisive investment manual, *The Zulu Principle*. Like Clarence Hatry, the
financier who hit the rocks in 1929, he was resilient in adversity; also like
Hatry, Slater would never be forgiven by the City establishment, for sins
both real and imaginary.

A fortnight after Slater's departure Britain applied to the IMF for a
$2bn loan. During the rest of the year the economic news was poor, but
the stock market (ending the year with the Index on 374.8) went into 1976
in a surprisingly upbeat mood, encouraged partly by the IMF approving
the loan. 'How things can change in just a month!' Rowe & Pitman
declared in mid-January, soon after the Index reached 400:

> It seems an age since the worries of 1975: the yield gap, the Government's
> funding requirement and its consequences for inflation, the disastrous
> competition for available savings that any economic recovery would bring.
> Wall Street was labouring: the US revival seemed endlessly postponable.
> But now! Now the Government's borrowing requirement will be less
> than once feared and the reduced amount may already have been largely
> funded – three months before the end of the fiscal year. Interest rates are
> falling fast. The rise in gilts has been matched by the rise in equities, yet the
> yield gap has dropped by almost a point . . . Wall Street had blasted through
> its 1975 peak and breached 900 on the Dow amidst growing optimism for
> economic prospects in 1976 . . .

Optimism was also nourished by a significant event in the Eurobond
market, with the first dollar-denominated issue by a British nationalised
industry for two years. Overcoming much initial scepticism, particularly
on the part of continental investors, Warburgs succeeded in tapping the
market for a $60m, five-year deal for British Gas. The Bank of England
projected it as a 'showcase' issue, demonstrating that a major UK entity
could borrow on the finest terms (the coupon was a respectable 9 per
cent), but perhaps it was not *such* an achievement. 'In the argot of the
drug-addict,' *International Insider* commented shortly afterwards, 'the
international bond market is experiencing a "super-high": new issues keep
pouring out of the pipeline but investor enthusiasm shows no sign of
waning.' Consequently, 'in the market's current state of euphoria
borrowers – even if they are British – can do little wrong'.[15]

By this time, after the enforced inactivity of 1974 when it had raised
only $1.9bn, the Eurobond market was indeed rejuvenescent against a
background of falling interest rates, having raised $8.3bn in 1975 and now
starting to raise almost $15.2bn during 1976. In the secondary market these
were halcyon days for Stanley Ross, running Kidder Peabody's highly

profitable London operation and each week writing a gossipy, opinionated letter on 'The Week in Eurobonds'. He also wrote occasionally for *Euromoney,* and an October 1975 piece ('What a wonderful year for the Eurobond secondary market') conveys the authentic Ross flavour:

> The big question I am frequently asked is can the secondary market cope with the volume of issues flooding out from the primary? My answer is quite simple – don't worry about the secondary market. It takes care of itself by making prices *at which business can be done* regardless of the incidental wishes of New Issue managers who may or may not have any syndicate power up their sleeves to dictate initial price levels. Indeed I think that from this very question it is evident that there are a great number of people who still simply do not understand the true nature of the secondary market. It does not *have* to cope with anything at all *unless it wants to.* Except for the (very) few houses that maintain secondary markets as a service to their own primary market function, the majority of secondary sector operators have – as I have said so many times before – no responsibility whatsoever to anyone; thus realistic after issue prices *simply will not be made in paper that is unplaced or is unpopular.* The economic reality of the trading market-place soon unseats the cosmetic myth of overpriced and unwanted issues. That in short is how the market copes. It's as simple as that – to coin a phrase – *the primary market proposes, the secondary market disposes . . .*[16]

More generally, both the Eurobond market and the medium-term syndicated loans market were changing character in two distinct ways: first, the increasing dominance of the sovereign borrower over the corporate borrower; and second, the way in which both markets, but particularly that for syndicated loans, were becoming a prime vehicle for recycling oil money (often called petrodollars) to non-oil-producing countries. As a concomitant of this second trend, there was the controversial subject of the Arab boycott. Rothschilds, for example, found itself by early 1975 starting to be excluded from underwriting groups, and the same almost certainly applied to Warburgs. There, with the firm for a time rapidly sliding down the Eurobond lead-manager rankings as well as losing underwriting business, the response was uncompromising, led by Siegmund Warburg himself, even though he was theoretically in retirement in Switzerland. In his uniquely full interview some years later, Cary Reich asked him about it:

> **Your firm was faced with virtual extinction in the Euromarket because of the Arab boycott. Yet you managed to stand up to the boycott much better than other blacklisted houses. How were you able to do that?**
> I think we were just tougher. I mean, I would ring up my friends in the important European banks and say, 'I hear you seem to be giving in to this blackmail of the Arabs. I think that is very unfair to us and it's wrong in itself. Shall I interpret that as meaning you sympathise with anti-semitism?

, And don't kid yourself, we can – in the end – place just as well as those Arabs.'

In other words, you personally interceded and asked people why they were boycotting you?

And *how* I did. I certainly did not hesitate to use all the arguments, even some pretty, how shall I say, almost offensive arguments.

Do you think those appeals helped you to overcome the boycott?

I wouldn't say entirely, but to a large extent they did.

Did you ever figure out why you were on the blacklist, but Kuhn Loeb, for instance, wasn't?

It boiled down to the difference between the US state department and the British foreign office. I mean, this is not a question of slight nuances or shades of difference. It simply amounts to the fact that the state department backed up the American firms while the British foreign office didn't do the same for the British ones.

That was the difference?

Nothing else.

By 1976 the worst of the Arab boycott seems to have been over, perhaps because of a decisive intervention by the Bank of England early that year. The context was a large UK Electricity Council issue, which was being lead-managed by Orion Bank, relied heavily on Arab money and sought to exclude Rothschilds and Warburgs from the underwriting group. Those two houses complained bitterly to Richardson, who summoned Orion's William de Gelsey and told him to halt the issue. The latter protested that it was too late, to which Richardson countered, 'I think that you will find that it is not too late'. Orion had no alternative but to change the arrangements rapidly, with lenders found elsewhere and Rothschilds and Warburgs reinstated.[17] It was, in its way, a classic City episode.

For once, instinctive sympathies were probably with the Jews. Kenneth Hill of Mullens recalled how during this period, when 'the Arab world got interested in buying stock in the gilt-edged market', visiting Arabs were sometimes given a tour of the Stock Exchange floor. 'One or two of the high-spirited crowd were slightly rude and flippant to the visitors. I can remember saying to people, "I don't think I should do that if I were you. They are visitors, they are our guests, so for heaven's sake behave yourselves."'

Some twenty-two floors up in the Stock Exchange, the mid-1970s were years of change. George Loveday, after two years as Chairman, was succeeded in June 1975 by Michael Marriott, who came from the brokers Williams de Broe and, unlike most Council members, had a good understanding of the international market. Sadly, he soon suffered a heart attack at a public function, never came back to the Stock Exchange and died in December that year. His successor was elected early in January 1976, with the choice lying between: David LeRoy-Lewis, an unusually cerebral jobber at Akroyd & Smithers; Dundas Hamilton, a well-respected broker from Fielding, Newson-Smith, who in the late 1960s had written an excellent book called *Stockbroking Today*, and a much younger man, Nicholas Goodison, of the largely private client brokers Quilter Goodison. On the grounds that the Council, shaken by Marriott's death, would not be 'in the mood' for such 'a long-term chairman' as Goodison, and that Hamilton would lose votes on account of 'his occasionally outspoken views', *The Times* expected LeRoy-Lewis to get the job, though wondered about the appropriateness of a jobber as chairman, not only in terms of relating directly to the investing public but also at a time when 'changing patterns in the process of trading are likely to come under increasing debate'. In part reputedly because of behind-the-scenes activity by Dick Wilkins of Wedd Durlacher (the great rivals of Akroyds), Goodison was elected.[18]

'Central casting could never have supplied this angular ambitious aesthete as a typical stockbroker,' Fildes aptly wrote when Goodison retired from the position twelve years later. Undoubtedly, Goodison came in as a reformer, having been largely responsible for the shake-up in the Stock Exchange's management that led to the appointment in 1974 of its first Chief Executive. A memo from that year suggests how, even before becoming Chairman, he saw the need for fundamental change if the venerable institution was going to prosper in a rapidly shifting environment. 'We only stand a good chance of London remaining the central securities market in Europe if we encourage the financial power of our Member Firms,' he argued, adding that 'we cannot do this by placing artificial restrictions on their expansion'. That meant that 'opposition to dual capacity' was 'out of date', in that with dual capacity already accepted in the arbitrage and Eurodollar markets, the trend was inexorably in that direction. Moreover, 'in view of the international pressure to get nearer to the market-maker and to reduce dealing expenses the trend is likely to accelerate'. In short, 'We could be looking at a fundamental trend towards large organisations which are capable of dealing with all aspects of the securities business'.[19] Set against the Stock Exchange's deep attachment to the principle of separation of capacity, this was quasi-revolutionary stuff. Inevitably, it would be an uphill struggle for a reforming chairman (viewed by some as rather a cold fish) to take along with him what was still, in many ways, a deeply conservative club.

The Stock Exchange, though, was not at the centre of the tumultuous events of 1976, which began in March with a fraught episode in the long-running saga of sterling and the foreign exchange markets.[20] 'Bankers canvassed by *II* are still wary about sterling, although they acknowledge its relative recovery, even if in absolute terms of the weighted depreciation it is at its historic low,' *International Insider* noted on Monday the 1st. 'In prospect, they see it recovering gradually from current levels, with no further declines anticipated if the economy continues to recover, with the prime indicators the visible trade balance and the rate of domestic inflation.' Unbeknown, however, to those bankers, the Treasury had come to the view that, with cash limits and incomes policy both more or less satisfactorily in place, a carefully calibrated devaluation-by-stealth of sterling was now needed, from just over $2 to perhaps $1.90, in order to make British exports more competitive. An interest-rate cut was the Treasury's chosen means, and it was decided that MLR would be reduced on Friday the 5th by a quarter-point, to 9 per cent. At the Bank, according to Stephen Fay's account, Richardson 'disliked the whole concept of manipulating the currency', while Kit McMahon, as the Bank's Overseas Director, 'warned the Treasury that the market was unstable and might not behave as civil servants and ministers thought it ought to'.[21] Presumably backed by Healey, the Treasury insisted that its plan be executed.

Before this could occur, the entirely unscheduled drama on the afternoon of Thursday the 4th took place, as the pound fell sharply, at one point to a record low of $2.0125. There had been, *The Times* reported next morning, a 'sudden wave of selling . . . thought to have largely emanated from London', with currency dealers describing the sudden movement as 'inexplicable'. Before long, the precise circumstances of those few hours had become a matter of vexed, even bitter controversy. An early version was provided in a *Times* leader the following Tuesday:

> What appears to have happened is that the foreign exchange market misconstrued some heavy selling of pounds by the Bank of England – at the time the market did not know who was selling – as evidence either of hostile selling by another sterling area central bank or as a cunning attempt by the Treasury to drive the pound down in order to encourage export-led reflation. All the Bank of England, who may have been rather ham-fisted, were trying to do was to prevent a sharp rise in the price of a pound which, for some reason, it feared.

The *FT* was also critical, while according to *International Insider*, on the basis of its banker contacts, 'the Bank was supplying Sterling to the market as the Dollar was weak in order to top up the reserves'; unfortunately, 'it missed a turn in the market and was seen selling Sterling in a falling market', which 'was then followed by a dealer-inspired panic, and in currently thin markets Sterling's domino fell after the French Franc'. Barings, in its mid-March report on the foreign exchange and gold markets, stressed the international dimension:

> By Thursday the 4th it had become clear that MLR was again going to be allowed to fall. This, combined with the fact that the market believed the Bank of England to be selling sterling on Thursday afternoon when the

effective depreciation widened to 30.3%, created the expectant atmosphere of an exchange crisis. This atmosphere was already heavily charged by the previous speculative activity against the French franc, the depreciation of the lira and the devaluation of the peseta: moreover the psychologically significant $2 figure, which had been maintained for much longer than most of the market had expected, looked suddenly vulnerable. The rumours of a sizeable selling order from Nigeria (known to have been a substantial and previously firm holder of sterling) touched off the fuse . . .

In the event, the Bank took most of the stick, accused by the Treasury of having sold sterling in a falling market and thus of unnecessarily precipitating a sterling crisis. Such was also the view of Healey, who in his memoirs accused the Bank of having 'failed dismally' to 'outwit' the financial markets.[22] The Bank's defence was that it had started selling on the 4th as it became known that large buying orders from commercial banks were pushing the currency up, which it knew would displease the Treasury. Few, however, were prepared to listen.

The following days compounded the Bank's discomfort. On the 5th, despite Richardson's fears and apparently on Healey's instructions (notwithstanding his subsequent blame-shifting), MLR was duly cut, and the pound ended the day below $2 for the first time in its history, at $1.9820. 'Everything the authorities are doing seems designed to weaken the pound in the most dramatic way,' an opposition spokesman, Norman Lamont, commented. 'Today there was a mystifying cut in the minimum lending rate which can only weaken the pound further.' From Monday to Wednesday came unavailing efforts to halt the slide. On the afternoon of the 10th, a phone conversation sought to put the Fed in the picture:

> Byatt [Derrick Byatt, an adviser in the cashier's department] said the Bank of England had done everything it could to steady, to interrupt and to create a sense of hesitation in the decline of sterling's rate today. But no matter what the Bank of England did, it was not believed in the market . . . By the end of the day it had sold a total of $225 million . . . Today has been a record in every respect. The drop in the rate is the largest ever, to $1.92 . . .
>
> There continues to be talk in the market about Nigeria, especially after yesterday's confirmation that the country has undergone a program of [sterling] reserve diversification. The comment about the Nigerian announcement that appears in Sam Brittan's column in today's *Financial Times* reflects considerable consultation with the Bank of England. In essence they say that, yes, Nigeria has diversified but all that was done in the past.

In fact, the pound finished the day three cents down at $1.9127. The Treasury had got its devaluation, but certainly not by stealth, and certainly at the cost of international confidence in sterling – and, arguably, in the Bank of England. 'With the pound experiencing yet another of its swift devaluations,' Simon & Coates began its weekly investment circular on the 16th, after the immediate crisis had died down, 'Britain must surely now have run out of foreign volunteers to put surplus funds into sterling.'[23]

That same day Wilson surprised the world, not least the City, by announcing his resignation. 'Early scenes on the London trading floor were described as pandemonium,' *The Times* reported of the Stock Exchange, 'as dealers tried to assess the implications'; while in the City at large, there was widespread agreement that Wilson's decision was 'extraordinary', given the recent 'intense currency turmoil'. Looking ahead to the incomes policy's next stage, the paper's financial editor added that 'many people quite reasonably take the view that Mr Wilson is the only person capable of repeating something like the £6 a week agreement'. In the *FT* there was no warm tribute – 'we remarked many years ago that the Prime Minister's characteristic weakness is to mistake activity for action' – and few in the City, certainly those with memories going back to the Bank rate leak of 1957, would have been disappointed by its absence.[24] Yet one final phase lay ahead in Wilson's relationship with the square mile – a phase in which, by an ironic twist, he would do his least favourite place a surprising favour.

*

Before the mid-1970s surprisingly seldom was the City explicitly accused of bearing a prime responsibility for British industrial decline.[25] Occasionally an industrialist went public with a criticism – soon after the Pilkington flotation in 1970, for example, Lord Pilkington asserted that his company would never have been able to develop its crucial float-glass process if it had been under short-term stock-market pressures – but few, even on the Left, were inclined to cast the City as the villain of the piece.[26] Three main developments changed that: the comparisons, as Britain prepared to enter the EEC, between the closeness of bank/industry relations on the Continent (especially Germany) and the more detached relations in Britain; the way in which, during the Barber boom, all the City's money seemed to go to property, not industry; and the 1974 corporate liquidity crisis, which as the capital market dried up inevitably put the City under the spotlight. The politics of that autumn's hurried decision to expand the role of FFI accurately reflected the new terrain on which the City was fighting – a terrain made tougher by the fact of a Labour government, but which would have been uncomfortable even if Heath (who bitterly blamed the City for having failed to channel funds to industry rather than property) had been re-elected.

The debate, conducted with increasing bitterness, really got going in the winter of 1974–5. Over a century and a half after the economist-jobber David Ricardo had noted the Stock Exchange's addiction to the immediate, the CBI's Lucien Wigdor developed the theme at an *FT* seminar in November:

> Few companies can operate efficiently if the management is concerned to see that the actual profit declared each year should show at least a modest improvement on the previous year. Ideally companies should be in a position to opt – if necessary – for short-term downturns in profitability or cash flow, if this is due to major investment or restructuring designed to accelerate growth and profits in the medium and long term. And yet managements – because of the market's preoccupation with the short term – can be inhibited by their share valuations. The market does not readily accept deliberate short-term policies to utilise cash flow for longer-term benefits.

A few weeks later the City's bogeyman, Benn, cited the property boom of the early 1970s and asked the City to rethink its approach to investment decisions: 'What does it really profit a fund if it puts the money into something advantageous in the short term but contributes in that process to a denial of investment that British industry needs, so that the whole fund operates in a country which is going downhill?' Perhaps because he was talking to the *Investors Chronicle*, Benn was careful not to attach personal blame: 'I have never taken the view that what is wrong is that there are a lot of villains about who have in some personal and special way failed the nation.' He did add, however, that 'what you cannot do is to lecture people, from the comfort of a well-paid job, on their need to make sacrifices'. In late January 1975, at an Institute of Public Relations (IPR) dinner at Mansion House, the Stock Exchange's Dundas Hamilton rose to the City's defence:

> There is no question that today there is a body of opinion that rejects the principles on which the financial markets – indeed the whole of commercial life – have hitherto operated. These politicians have found their own allies, curiously enough, among those whom the financial community have often regarded as their chief clients.
>
> We have been widely blamed by industrialists as well as by politicians and economists because industry has not been able to find money in the market on the terms it would like and not on the terms that the market dictates.
>
> Lord Stokes [of British Leyland] has commented bitterly on the market rating of his company. Lord Kearton [of Courtaulds] has criticised the market because his share price falls if he announces a Rights Issue. Sir Fred Catherwood says that if the market does not support industrial investment it is an open invitation for the Government to do the job.
>
> What all these critics ignore is that the financial services industry in all its aspects, whether it be life assurance, unit trusts, pension funds, savings banks, and even the Stock Exchange, came into being to provide a service to investors. That is its origin and that is still its central purpose.
>
> If they fail in this service then pension funds will lose contributors, banks lose their depositors, unit trusts cease to attract new monthly investment

plans, and they will all cease to provide a potential source of industrial capital.

At the same dinner the IPR's James Derriman offered a salutary outsider's perspective. 'In some ways,' he argued, 'the City is victim of its own pre-eminence. It is equated with capitalism, and any schoolboy is aware that "two-faced" is nowadays a legitimate description of that system.'[27]

From late February 1975 the Stock Exchange's faltering credentials as a mechanism for raising industrial capital were boosted by a series of rights issues on the back of the improved secondary market. £1,200m was raised between then and the end of the year, shared among 166 companies – admittedly not all of them industrial, in that Royal Insurance, Midland Bank, Prudential Assurance and Sun Alliance made the four biggest rights issues. But in April the TUC's General Secretary, Len Murray, had no compunction about publicly dismissing the Stock Exchange as a 'relic of the 19th century', no longer relevant to the needs of British industry. 'We have been appalled in recent months,' he told the Royal Commission on the Distribution of Income and Wealth, 'when Stock Exchange movements have indicated a loss of confidence in British industry, and the consequences have been felt by the people we represent.' That could be dismissed as rhetoric, but later that month Benn set the cat among the pigeons by formally proposing not only the establishment of a National Enterprise Board, but also that pension and insurance funds should in future be compelled to channel into it and other public enterprises 'minimum proportions of their new funds'. That this was not easy-to-refute wild talk was shown in early May by the publication of a National Economic Development Office paper, which in essence argued for the same policy (that is, getting savings institutions to do more to finance industrial investment) but on a more voluntary, consensual basis.[28]

The immediate upshot was that the National Economic Development Council (Neddy) agreed on the 7th to set up a committee to keep the problems of the finance for industrial investment under permanent review. This compromise, time-buying move, which apparently had Richardson's full support, was described by the *FT* as 'an almost comically British outcome of the threats and warnings which have been heard on the subject in the last two weeks', but was nonetheless welcome. Lord De L'Isle, writing from Penshurst Place near Tonbridge, expressed something of the City's true feelings in a letter that appeared in the *FT* on the day of that compromise:

> A Government-directed plan to force investment upon industry in order to 're-industrialise' our economy, probably combined with import controls and the direction of the people's savings into selected industries, will increase the hunger of our raw material deficient economy for imports,

damage our export prospects and injure our ability to increase our invisible earnings through ever more stringent controls on overseas investment . . .

No hope for us in the Japanese-style industrial expansion. We lack the will to work, industrial discipline, the impetus to save and the encouragement of profits.

In our situation, 're-industrialisation' on *dirigiste* lines must be recognised as a design to hold down living standards, if not to lower them, within an increasingly centralised and political economy, for political ends.[29]

De L'Isle himself would remain Chairman of Phoenix Assurance for another three years, but he was about to make a less-than-voluntary departure from First National.

In late May the *Investors Chronicle* surveyed the attitudes of a cross-section of industrialists and institutional investors. It found that 'surprisingly few' of the former claimed ever to have been denied capital for a viable investment project, while the latter had 'one main recipe for increasing the investment flow in industry: let industry earn the profits to attract it'. The survey added that the institutional investors 'strongly resent any suggestion that they should be directed where to place their funds, possibly at uncommercial rates', but that they were 'surprisingly uninterested in supervising the way in which their very considerable funds are used, once they have been invested in company securities'. Over the next fortnight the magazine published various responses to its inquiry. 'When the basic co-ordinates on which businessmen and investors rest their decisions are swept away by inflation and political turmoil, no amount of governmentally inspired gimmickry will put the situation right,' declared Ronald Grierson, the former Warburgs and IRC man who had recently parachuted into the stockbrokers Panmure Gordon as senior partner. As for the notion that institutions had a duty to the companies in which they invested, he was scornful: 'This seems to me at variance with the whole concept of portfolio investment. The investor does as much as can be expected of him when he ventures his money in return for a piece of paper of doubtful intrinsic value representing a contingent share in the equity of a joint-stock enterprise.' On the same question, the Prudential's Ron Artus insisted that 'the core of the problem has lain not in the fringe of cases where institutions might have acted more effectively as catalysts to bring about improvements in managerial competence, but in the fact that the vast bulk of well-managed industry has chosen, because of its assessment of the risk-reward ratio, not to invest on a scale to match the international competition'. Clive Jenkins, the most articulate trade unionist of his generation, would have none of it:

The failure of our financial institutions to invest in domestic manufacturing industry is well documented: City leaders invariably reply that the potential rate of return did not justify any more investment. This ignores the fact that our history of continuous under-investment has created an out-dated capital stock that is often simply unable to produce adequate rates of return ... The short-term outlook of City decision-making is incompatible with the needs of restructuring our economy for stable long-term growth ... Ill-equipped to comprehend the intricacies of manufacturing investment given its production orientation and extended timescale, the City shows a wariness to lend to industry and a proclivity for those areas the City does understand – the property and short-term money markets ... I am *for* targeting and planning of investment flows – and public criticism of those directors of investment who fail to conform to nationally worthwhile and agreed criteria. The present situation is thoroughly bad and bellows for reform.

In short, Jenkins wanted nothing less than 'direct intervention by Government', presumably in order to implement the TUC's recent demand that it have 50 per cent representation on the boards of pension funds.[30]

On 9 June, the Monday after the EEC referendum, there appeared a report in *The Times* about new Labour plans – under the auspices of Benn, as Chairman of the party's Home Policy Committee – to nationalise the clearing banks. City reaction was instant. 'Nobody in their right minds think that the Arabs and others are going to leave money here to go into Banks to be directed by Mr Benn from the National Enterprise Board and the like,' Sir Kenneth Keith told *The World at One* that lunchtime, adding that nationalisation of the banks 'would be the end of the City of London as we know it today'. Bravely the interviewer pressed: 'Shouldn't, as Mr Benn suggests, the Banks play a more responsible role in investment and shouldn't their vast funds be directed into industry to regenerate industry?' The reply was pure Keith: 'I think this is a most frightful piece of nonsense. I am not aware of any really sensible profitable industrial endeavour which has been held back for lack of money.' Three days later, in a written parliamentary reply, Dell let it be known that the government had no plans to nationalise any of the main clearing banks.[31]

Following Benn's replacement at Industry by Varley, it was to him that later in June the recently formed City Capital Markets Committee, chaired by Ian Fraser of Lazards, sent a major set-piece defence of the City as a capital market. Its basic stance was unyielding:

> By and large, where UK companies have invested inadequately, it has been that they have not felt able, albeit for a variety of reasons, to do so, not that they could not raise the necessary funds ... It is no part of the function of institutional investors or of merchant banks and stockbrokers on behalf of private clients to promote investments which are not 'worthwhile' ...

As far as investment decisions generally were concerned, this City group emphasised how 'the discipline of market forces, where alternative suppliers are available', was far superior to 'the test of a single credit agency or monopoly investment body against which there is no appeal, and which is capable of gigantic errors of judgement'. There followed a full-frontal attack on the post-war consensus, though not without a glancing blow at the defence-of-sterling priority:

> Since 1945, British companies and businesses of all kinds have been forced to operate in an environment in which the risk of the endeavour has been, or has appeared to be, disproportionate to its rewards. The Governments of our Continental-European and Japanese competitors used their Marshall Plan funds mainly to re-equip their industries; we used ours in large part to finance, directly and indirectly, consumption. Our fiscal policies have been mainly directed towards social equality or towards consumerism; theirs have been mainly directed towards promoting investment. Our economic policies have been aimed at the preservation of jobs and the maintenance of sterling; theirs at the creation of national wealth at the expense sometimes of a certain rough justice . . .[32]

It must have been a minor disappointment to Fraser, who almost certainly penned this grand remonstrance, that the recipient was not Benn.

For the City's critics there was useful grist to the mill in the 'Coats Paton Affair', which made quite a few headlines between late May and mid-July. It began when Coats Paton, the large Glasgow-based textile manufacturer, announced that it was not going to pay its final dividend, giving as its main reason the way in which inflation had caused a huge rise in working capital requirements and thereby eaten up the group's entire cash flow. Peter Moody, the Pru's Joint Investment Manager, immediately said that an 'impossible situation' would develop if other companies followed this example, while the financial editor of *The Times* described the action as 'an emotional and extravagant gesture'. The stock market did not need to put its condemnation into words, as Coats Paton shares slumped 6½p on the day of the announcement, to 48½p, despite better-than-expected profit figures. 'The grim example of Coats' share price will be enough to deter other companies from following a similar course,' observed 'Lex', adding that 'the group has plainly underestimated the importance of dividends to a good number of its shareholders'. That was undoubtedly true – corporate liquidity difficulties or no – and soon afterwards the stakes were raised when the Investment Protection Committee of the Association of Unit Trust Managers, chaired by David Hopkinson of M&G, recommended its members to vote against the adoption of the 1974 report and accounts at the group's annual meeting in Glasgow on 11 July. Later in June the equivalent committee of the pension funds similarly recommended non-adoption; and though in the end, at a lengthy meeting, the report and accounts were adopted – with most of the institutional shareholders backing off from confrontation and the private shareholders strongly backing the board – sufficient wrath had been demonstrated to make the Glaswegian act of defiance almost certainly a one-off.[33]

However, if that was poor publicity for the City, then was the reconstituted, re-equipped Finance for Industry, with £1bn at its disposal, doing its bit to convince doubters? 'It is important for the reputation of the City that we remain in business as there is still a steady demand for our help,' Lord Seebohm, FFI's Chairman, wrote in May to NatWest's Prideaux – but the giveaway was 'still', reflecting the fact that the liquidity crisis was now easing. By January 1976 the sober reality was that, for all the early talk about FFI as a 'Santa with £1 Billion', it had since November 1974 advanced no more than £100m, with a further £104m committed.[34] The City was able to argue it both ways: that this fairly limited call upon FFI's resources demonstrated that the demand for medium-term finance was being almost wholly satisfied by the clearing banks; but that the very existence of this additional arm of lending showed the flexibility of its institutional response to a potential problem.

The City was far from off the hook, though. In his Mansion House speech in October 1975 Healey did not hold back from criticising the City's role in financing industry, citing a critical comparative study, *Company Finance in Europe*, recently published by the Institute of Chartered Accountants. A few days later Richardson told the clearers about a proposed new institution that he intended to call Equity Finance for Industry: 'It was the Governor's opinion that it was right that the institutions should be seen to respond to the alleged need for the City to provide this additional investment capability, even if the need did not exist (his personal view was that there was such a need) . . .' The background to this initiative was Richardson's appointment some six months earlier of the distinguished, recently retired accountant Sir Henry Benson to be his adviser on questions of industrial finance. Benson himself recalled his thinking:

> One of the things that seemed to me clear when I went to the Bank was that there was going to be a shortage of equity capital, because of inflation and the demand for money and the recession. And the idea was conceived of setting up Equity Capital for Industry [as it eventually became called] which would provide equity capital, which is what companies need in the recession period, and that the people who would be behind it would be the great bulk of the City institutions. Well, this was mooted. The Governor hesitated for a long time and he consulted a number of people. But eventually approved it . . .

Equally protracted discussions ensued and were still in progress by December when, at the second World Banking Conference, Ian Fraser addressed the London audience on the question 'Has the City failed the nation?' In public, as in private, he did not encourage faint hearts:

The City must be innovative. It has already produced FFI and it is now working on the new Equity Fund. It must continue to respond to change. I don't believe that its record of innovation is as bad as the critics allege – Eurobonds, Euroloans, project finance, commodity financing and a host of others. If it were as bad as is suggested would London be the financial magnet that it is? Is Britain the navel of the world in academic economics or in progressive socialism? I think not . . .

Confidence is the key. Without confidence there is no investment *by* companies; without investment *by* companies there is no call for investment *in* companies. The accusations by people like Samuels, Groves and Goddard [the three authors, at least two of them from the University of Birmingham, of the critical study cited by Healey] that the City has failed the nation by not seeing to it that more investment takes place is totally inaccurate and incorrect. It is based on a pathetic lack of understanding of the rationale and process of raising funds for industry and of the deployment of funds raised by industry. Let us hear no more of it. I am at a loss to understand how the Institute of Chartered Accountants can have lent its imprint to such a work.[35]

Temperamentally a hairy rather than a smooth man, Fraser was never entirely at ease in the City establishment, but as Robert Maxwell well knew, he was a formidable opponent.

During the early months of 1976 Richardson and Benson did not find it at all easy to get Equity Capital for Industry (ECI) under way. The proposed new institution had already, the Governor conceded to the clearers in late January, 'generated much controversy', and he added that 'there was no point in proceeding . . . unless people considered it had a useful role to play and would be successful, and he did not wish to bring any pressure to bear for its formation'. At the same meeting Midland's Lord McFadzean stated that his bank's view was 'firmly that the banks should not participate, either directly or indirectly, in providing equity for the Fund'. This new Bank of England baby was, the *Banker* correctly noted soon afterwards, 'causing the City far more heart-searching than the enlargement of FFI' – partly because it was going to involve a large number of parties, and partly because it was seen by the City as a potential 'rescue operation', in providing funds for companies otherwise unable to get them in the regular financial markets. Richardson talked again to the clearers in early March:

> The Governor mentioned that he had asked Sir Robert Clark of Hill Samuel, Mr Mackworth-Young of Morgan Grenfell and Mr Meinertzhagen of Lazards to look at the possibility of drafting a prospectus as he felt this would take some of the sharpness out of the conflict and, perhaps, overcome some of the difficulties by reconciling the differing views within each of the Houses mentioned. They all have close relationships with the Insurance Companies and it was hoped they would engage in a degree of canvassing in favour of ECI.

Another set of minutes referred to 'the conflict between those advocating a secondary role for ECI and those not wanting it'. Finally, in early summer, ECI was launched, but predictably it proved (in Plender's phrase) 'an emasculated organisation'. Benson regretfully explained why:

> Unfortunately the institutions said that ECI should only provide money if the existing machinery of the City couldn't provide it. Well, of course this was a hopeless proviso, because it virtually meant that it could scarcely get off the ground . . . I don't know whether the institutions who provided the capital felt that they might have been deprived of business because the company they were putting their money into would take business from them. Anyhow, it had a very difficult start. There was a certain amount of criticism of it having been formed. And the start was slow and rather unsatisfactory . . .

Some 350 financial institutions backed ECI, but with that key proviso in force for several years it struggled to make a significant impact, perhaps also reflecting a certain residual indifference on the part of now dominant institutional investors towards the problems of small and medium-sized companies.[36]

Almost simultaneous with ECI's difficult birth pangs, a familiar threat to the City (first seriously mooted in the 1930s) was once more gathering momentum. On 7 September 1976 the Labour Party's long-awaited report on 'Banking and Finance' called for the four major clearing banks and seven top insurance companies to be nationalised, as well as an unnamed merchant bank. The purpose would be to ensure that more of their assets were directed into loans for long-term industrial development. The *Daily Telegraph* no doubt summed up City reaction to these 'vicious proposals' when it declared that 'our savings are to be removed from the care of the prudent men to whom we have entrusted them and squandered on lame ducks by a pack of politicians who, on the evidence of the policy document, cannot even write proper English, whose boasted "experience of industry" is in fact either disastrous or nil, and whose record in picking industrial winners could be bettered by a blind drunkard with a pin'. Anticipating these proposals, the Committee of London Clearing Bankers had already commissioned a Mori poll on public attitudes to nationalisation, and four days after the report the *Economist* revealed that only 14 per cent were in favour, with even Labour voters viewing such a move as a vote-loser. A fortnight or so later, on the eve of the Labour Party conference at Blackpool, Callaghan – Wilson's successor – told his National Executive Committee: 'I should make my position quite clear. I will not be able to recommend the inclusion of this proposal in the next election manifesto. It would be an electoral albatross.' However, Callaghan successfully took much of the heat out of the situation by announcing that he would be setting up a committee to review the functioning of the financial institutions, especially in relation to British industry.[37] Subsequently, on 7 October, it was further announced that the Chairman would be Sir Harold Wilson.

'If you set out to invent a financial system whose job was to provide £20 billion to re-equip a nation's industry, you would not come up with the City of London' was the opening sentence of the *Economist's* survey of 'The Unchanging City', published two days later and written mainly by John Plender. He did not deny that short-termism was a real problem – 'companies investing in plant that will not show a return for 5 years are often rated on expectations about profits up to only 18 months or 2 years ahead' – but was inclined to blame not the stock market, but an ever-increasing post-war inflation, which meant that 'the calculation of returns on portfolio investment is hazardous'. In terms of City culpability, he pointed instead to the fact that 'there are too few people in the clearing bank system able to make specialist assessments of the investment projects' and that 'the institutions share that lack of specialisation', in that 'their main response when a company is running into trouble is limited to selling the shares'. By contrast, as far as bank lending as such was concerned, 'industrialists, who are the ones who are supposed to have suffered from the so-called medium-term lending gap, often have not heard of it'. Rather, the main thrust of Plender's analysis was on shortcomings in City *attitudes*:

> The City ethos is such that large numbers of talented people are duplicating each other's efforts in research and investment management to pick short-term winners in the stock market . . . The institutions cannot think long-term because they are involved in a competitive short-term race. They are tied to industry whether they like it or not, but cannot quite bring themselves to admit it . . . Money men in the City find it almost impossible to admit that there might be a gap in the services they offer. There is also a curious kind of financial orthodoxy in the City. The same men who are happy to back an over-geared property enterprise or secondary bank are quite capable of asking how they can conceivably be expected to put an investment like ECI into a high-income fund or a growth fund . . .

Arguably the City/industry gulf was still almost as deep as it had been between the wars. Then, Norman had sincerely tried, with the help of Bruce Gardner, to do something about it; now, it was Richardson abetted by Benson, the latter in charge of a new Industrial Finance Unit at the Bank, from where he did his best to persuade clearing banks, large shareholders and others to engage in what would later be called 'corporate workouts' – in effect providing emergency support to sound concerns facing liquidity difficulties. Essentially Benson's role was that of constructively knocking heads together, without committing any of the Bank's funds, and in so doing he made a significant contribution to the well-being of British industry.[38] However, it was work done almost entirely by stealth, and the gulf persisted, with mutually damaging perceptions on both sides.

Something – but not enough – of this surfaced in the Wilson Committee, formally set up in January 1977 'to Review the Function of Financial Institutions'. Its members included Cork and Prideaux on behalf of the City, Murray and Jenkins on behalf of the unions, and Professor Ralf Dahrendorf. Perhaps significantly, almost all its fifty-five meetings were held in Guildhall (not, as originally intended, Whitehall), while Cork took it upon himself to arrange plenty of informal, prejudice-eroding lunches between Wilson and leading City figures. With Wilson promising to conduct 'the most thoroughgoing probe there has ever been into the workings of the City', the first two years were devoted to gathering evidence. The great majority of it was dull, self-justifying and massively predictable, but Cork recalled one entertaining exchange between Jenkins and Richardson that did not make the official evidence. The subject was how the Bank advised the government on matters of financial policy:

> Where do you get advice?
> From my senior management, who then consult discount houses and clearing banks, if appropriate. My role as I see it is to represent the City's views to the Government and the Treasury.
> Did you not consult the trade unions?
> No, I did not do that.
> Surely you should invite the views of the trade unions on such matters?
> No. That is for the political people to do.
> How so?
> Let me ask you a question, Mr Jenkins. Do you consult management before you call a strike?

That, according to Cork, left the Welshman unusually 'short of words'.[39]

Most of the evidence came down in favour of the City, including that of a working party on the financing of North Sea oil, which found no shortage of either funds or innovation on the part of the financial institutions. Inevitably, much hinged on whether the industrialists were prepared to bare their teeth – and on the whole, mindful of not wishing to be seen as bowing to the unions, they were not. The CBI Working Party was led by Sir Arthur Knight of Courtaulds, who in his written evidence insisted that 'a reasonably competitive and diverse capital market exists in the UK' and that 'any shortfall in investment in this country must be blamed on the social and political background against which both investors and managers have to work'. In his oral evidence, in October 1977, he positively extolled the City:

> The actual cash that people have needed to support their investment

plans has by and large been available through the channels which exist. There are no problems on the small firms side . . . There is a recognition that in the last 10 or 12 years the arrival in London of the American banks has provided a competitive spur to which the commercial banks here have responded . . . The Stock Exchange, as an instrument, is regarded by the industrialists as highly effective, the envy of people in European countries who do not have such a highly developed Stock Exchange; it has enabled companies to raise large sums at moments of their choosing.

If Knight had a criticism, it was of the institutional investor: 'In terms of understanding what we are up to in our strategies and our commercial policies I would not have, in my experience, said that I have seen a lot of that.' Three months later, the Committee received a report from Coopers & Lybrand, based on interviews with forty-eight medium-sized companies:

> Views on merchant banking advice were mixed. Some were satisfied although we gained the impression generally that the advice was often not very important to them; as one company put it: 'we look to our financial advisers for comfort on decisions we have already taken'. Others were critical, saying that advice tended to lack imagination, that the merchant banks tended to 'sit on the fence' and that they did not get up and about enough to understand the practical affairs of industry . . . Overall, we received the impression that the 'City' was thought not to understand – or take enough trouble to understand – the real problems of industry. But most companies did not think this mattered much and was perhaps inevitable; in any event it did not seem generally to inhibit the raising of funds which was 'the City's real job' . . .[40]

In December 1978, in the *New Statesman*, Christopher Hird accurately predicted that the Wilson Committee's eventual report would be 'a mouse' – 'a big, fat, well-fed, stuffed-with-statistics mouse, but a mouse nonetheless'. It was to be another eighteen months before that report was published, by which time the political landscape had changed so utterly as to render it an almost complete irrelevance. It did make some specific criticisms about the City, and pointed to the huge, increasing, largely unaccountable power of the pension funds, but its main burden was that industrial investment had *not* been inhibited by any shortage of external finance. Even more forcefully repudiated, not surprisingly, was any notion of nationalising the banks.[41] The City/industry debate was still alive, but that moment had passed.

*

Back in 1976, despite the reassuring figure of Callaghan at No 10, the first nine months of the post-Wilson era proved a bumpy ride for politicians and markets alike.[42] Callaghan became Prime Minister on 5 April, the day before Healey delivered a budget in which he made most of his tax cuts conditional on achieving a 3 per cent incomes policy with the unions and perturbed the markets by announcing a projected PSBR for 1976–7 of £12bn. Nevertheless, talking to the clearers on the 7th, Richardson drew comfort from the passage in the speech affirming Healey's determination not to allow the money supply to get out of hand. At that same meeting Tuke of Barclays asked him for his views 'on the likely movement in the value of Sterling', again under renewed pressure, though less seriously than a month earlier:

> The Governor pointed out that the £ had had a lot to contend with during the last week; the retirement of the Prime Minster had puzzled overseas investors, who tended to be somewhat suspiciously searching for unfavourable reasons; the high level of support for Mr Foot in the election; the Paper [advocating import quotas] by the Cambridge Economic Policy Group (which the Bank did not consider to be very plausible); the Leyland strikes, which gave the appearance that we were bent on National self-destruction; the publication of reserve figures indicating the cost of supporting Sterling – all these factors had had an adverse influence on the pound.

The following week Callaghan had his first official meeting with the Chancellor: 'I was astonished when I saw D.H. He said that Bank had spent $2bn in supporting sterling since 1 Jan 1976.' Callaghan also saw the Governor:

> When I met Gordon Richardson it was uncannily like stepping back 12 years and listening to a record of one of my talks with Lord Cromer when he was Governor. The decline in the sterling rate was a direct response to unparalleled uncertainty and loss of confidence. The US was taking a gloomy view of sterling's future and industrialists were saying that all that appeared to be happening was that a bankrupt nation was selling off its stock. The Government's borrowing requirement was too high and in due course would crowd out investment by the private sector . . .

For the moment Callaghan would try to shrug this off as 'Governor's Gloom', but in truth the foreign exchange markets had been thoroughly rattled by sterling's débâcle in early March. The mid-April report by Barings nicely conveyed how they were operating on the edge of – and sometimes even beyond the edge of – reason:

> The reasons for the resumption of selling of sterling may, in the words of HM Treasury, have 'no economic justification': unfortunately currencies are not judged solely on the basis of purely economic criteria . . . They are also judged in relation to confidence and political capacity, judgement and popular willingness to take and accept those actions generally seen to be the minimum necessary to translate a bad situation into an acceptable one. It is on this general political and popular basis that sterling has been found wanting.

Overseas opinion regards the narrowness of the result of the parliamentary Labour Party's ballot and the subsequent Cabinet appointments as indicating such left-wing strength as would inhibit the taking of such measures as the reduction of public expenditure. The reaction of most TUC leaders to the Chancellor's 3 per cent pay rise norm against tax reliefs proposal has been one of such strident rejection as to confirm such opinion in the belief that the British people do not wish to get themselves out of the mess they are in, or that if they do, they are not going to be given the chance. And the troubles of British Leyland compound the mess . . .

On any objective count, only six out of the twenty-three members of the new Cabinet could be counted as 'left-wing'; but as ever, perception was all.[43]

'Concern is growing among leading bankers both in London and other centres that the Bank of England is not performing to its own high standards,' *International Insider* reported on 3 May. 'One method suggested by a European banker would be for the Bank of England to take advantage of the vacancy at the head of its foreign exchange department to bring in someone of recognised ability from outside the Bank.' In the event, Ted Bradshaw's successor as the Bank's chief forex trader was his previous number two, J.F. Tigar. On 5 May, Healey announced that a pay deal for the next year had been struck with the unions; but at almost 5 per cent it was significantly above expectations (Paul Neild, Phillips & Drew's high-profile economist, had forecast a 4 per cent pay norm), and over the next few weeks sterling had several bad days. There was also increasing concern about the prospective PSBR situation, with Gordon Pepper's strong criticism of its size ('completely inappropriate now that the economy has started to recover') and inevitable inflationary consequences receiving widespread publicity. Moreover, known to the Bank but almost certainly unbeknown to the government, the daily gilt-edged market reports of Pepper's firm, Greenwells, were being sent via the US Embassy in London straight through to William Simon, the US Treasury Secretary, at Simon's specific request.[44] He himself had made his fortune as a bond dealer, and almost certainly Pepper's stark insistence at this stage that there was no alternative to major public expenditure cuts played a part in shaping his perceptions.

On the foreign exchange markets, sterling continued to fall during the last days of May, even though MLR had been raised 1 per cent on the 21st, to 11½ per cent; as the stockbrokers Simon & Coates put it on the 25th, 'only a brave man would predict where and when sterling will eventually come to rest'. By 3 June, notwithstanding a 'don't panic' broadcast from Healey, sterling had fallen to a new low of barely $1.70, and at Bill Low's regular Thursday lunch for bankers the conversation was dominated by the troubles of the native currency. 'International operators,' he wrote almost immediately afterwards, 'all agree that sterling is undervalued on fundamentals but are unwilling to invest in markets which are hostage to the UK Government's borrowing requirements and its volatile Parliamentary behaviour.' And:

> International bankers spoken to by *II* over the past week place a large part of the blame for sterling's demise on the lacklustre performance of the Bank of England over the last six months both in the domestic and international markets. At the same time they have sympathy for the Bank which, after many times crying wolf, is truly in a Sterling crisis. There is little the Bank can do. A minimum lending rate of 15% by the end of the month is predicted by one leading Sterling banker with the added comment that this would be little help as the pound is beyond the support that hot money flows would give. He added that if the current run on Sterling helped to finally remove Sterling's reserve role – and switching into Swiss Francs is evidence of this – then some good would come as an end result.[45]

These assessments appeared in *International Insider*'s next issue, on Monday the 7th – by which point the plot had moved rapidly on.

On Friday the 4th the Dutch central banker Dr Jelle Zijlstra, also President of the Bank for International Settlements, proposed an international stand-by credit to support the pound. With the British government's blessing, this was duly arranged by the Bank of England, with a total of $5.3bn to come from the central banks of Germany, Japan, Canada, France and Switzerland, the BIS and the Federal Reserve and the US Treasury. There is some evidence that, even at this stage, Richardson was unhappy and would have preferred the government to go to the IMF, which from his point of view would have had the huge advantage of making the loan explicitly conditional on major public expenditure cuts. In any case, it seems to have been Richardson who played a key role in getting Edwin Yeo of the US Treasury to fly to London on Saturday the 5th and tell Healey to his face that there were no circumstances in which the stand-by credit would be extended beyond six months. In other words, the stand-by could be renewed once (after three months), but if it had not been repaid by early December, then the government would have no alternative but to go to the IMF if it wanted further assistance. On Monday the 7th, as Healey announced the stand-by credit (and the miners approved the new pay policy), sterling rose four cents, to just over $1.75. The pound was temporarily saved, but over the previous few feverish days both the Bank and the Treasury had told the Cabinet that it would not stay saved unless the PSBR was brought down from £12bn to £10bn. 'Though the Prime Minister may hold firm against public expenditure cuts,' Simon & Coates observed on the 8th, 'they are undoubtedly what the exchange market wants to see for next year at least. An exchange crisis helped the government carry the day with the unions and it could still provide the excuse for a round of cuts.'[46]

During the rest of June the Callaghan government was almost drowned by advice. The BIS urged Britain to set money-supply targets; the Ford administration wanted Britain to change her domestic economic policies; while closer to home Richardson not only privately pressed the case for going to the IMF, but also made an important speech in Brighton to the Chartered Institute of Public Finance and Accountancy:

> Incomes policy has proved valuable, but it would be foolish if we placed all our reliance on it. No one should, and I certainly do not, underestimate the continuing and direct relevance of prudent management of demand in the economy, including prudent monetary policy . . . There may be a case for expressing the rate of expenditure as envisaged by government in terms not of the increase of real output, but of the growth of money national income.

Early July at the latest also saw the start of a 'gilts strike', as the cash-heavy institutions declined to buy gilts and held out for higher interest rates, which they believed would come with what they saw as the government's inevitable recourse to the IMF. It was a tactic based on economic calculation rather than political prejudice, and over the next two or so months the Government broker, Tommy Gore Browne, came under increasing pressure to jettison his traditional operations in the secondary market and instead try to encourage gilt sales by public auction.[47]

Ultimately, though, the crux was whether the government had the willingness and/or capacity to deliver cuts of a size that would persuade the markets to take the heat off sterling. Healey wanted cuts of £2bn, Richardson presumably wanted more, but in the end (after seven acrimonious Cabinet meetings) the package announced on 22 July comprised cuts of just under £1bn. Healey's speech also made market-friendly noises about controlling the money supply, though without announcing any monetary targets as such. It was not enough. Immediate reaction from overseas was sceptical, with the pound (having recovered somewhat since early June) falling slightly, to just over $1.78; and, describing the package as 'a little disappointing', Neild of Phillips & Drew asserted that the government was 'being optimistic in hoping not to have to go to the International Monetary Fund before the end of the year'. Or, as Simon & Coates put it on the 27th (by which time the Index at just over 370 was almost fifty points off what it had been three months earlier), 'Markets have not been impressed by the Chancellor's package . . . The cuts continued the long British tradition of delaying necessary actions and then taking them in several half-hearted bites, ostensibly so as not to antagonise public opinion.'[48]

Perhaps the markets would have been more impressed if they had had a greater sense of history. In February 2000, on the occasion of the Labour

Party's centenary, one commentator (the political historian Brian Brivati) argued that the party had really 'passed away' on Wednesday, 21 July 1976, when by accepting the £1bn package of public expenditure cuts the Cabinet had 'abandoned Labour's historic mission to alter the nature of the capitalist economy' and, under pressure from the international financial markets, *de facto* 'conceded the argument that the market economy was a better way of allocating the economic cake than any form of state intervention or planning'. The cuts, according to Brivati, 'marked the intellectual and political defeat of both Croslandite revisionism and Footite fundamentalism', leaving the party's leadership with nowhere to go but to 'preach the positive virtues of surrender to the market' – which had *not* been the case in the financial crises, from 1931 on, of previous Labour governments. Henceforth, with faith in economic management now shattered, 'unemployment was a price to be paid for control of inflation and increased productivity'.[49]

For their part, though, the markets merely scented weakness and wanted more blood. After sterling had held fairly steady at about $1.77 during August, it managed to stay at that rate in early September only because of heavy (some $400m) Bank of England support. Then on the 8th, the day after Labour's proposals to nationalise the banks, came the news of an impending seamen's strike, with its echoes of the summer 1966 sterling crisis that had so fatefully knocked Wilson's government off course. The next day, as sterling lost almost three cents, the government instructed the Bank to spend no more money on propping up the pound, with Callaghan still hoping to repay the stand-by loan; and on the 10th, in order to try to get gilt sales moving again, Healey raised MLR to an unprecedented 13 per cent. Over the next fortnight, despite the interest rate rise, sterling headed in only one direction – $1.753 on Friday the 10th, $1.735 on the 17th and $1.706 on the 24th. By then the seamen's dispute had been settled, though hardly in accord with the incomes policy. On the afternoon of the 24th, the Bank of England's Roger Barnes unavailingly complained over the phone to the Fed about the irrationality of forex dealers:

> The market seems to be falling into the trap of reacting with excessive pessimism to developments in Britain. For example, the market ignored the major feature of the deal between the seamen and the TUC – that the TUC had put together a united front to persuade the seamen not to strike – and had focused only on the small adverse effect of some changes in fringe benefits.[50]

By this time Healey had told the Cabinet that another sterling crisis was on the way and that there was no alternative but to make an imminent application to the IMF.

On Monday the 27th, as the Labour Party conference at Blackpool began by passing a resolution against public expenditure cuts and by pledging its support to any local councils that refused to implement them, sterling lost three cents, falling to $1.68, apparently despite the Bank spending £100m in an attempt to hold the line at $1.70. 'The present weakness of sterling is partly political, engendered by the Labour party conference, the proposals to nationalise banks and insurance companies and the persistent advocacy of radical economic measures by the left,' Simon & Coates commented in their weekly investment circular on Tuesday the 28th. 'Britain is currently in the classic banking situation where deposits are being steadily withdrawn because of uncertainty over the extent of the ultimate support, regardless of the return being paid.' That morning, as sterling plunged even more sharply and prices began to collapse on the Stock Exchange, Healey and Richardson drove to Heathrow, from where the former was due to fly to Hong Kong for a gathering of Commonwealth finance ministers, before going on to the IMF meeting at Manila. At the airport Richardson persuaded Healey that it would be too risky for the Chancellor to be out of contact with the markets for as much as seventeen hours; consequently – in what was widely seen as an ignominious turn of events – they returned to London. At the end of a day marked also by Callaghan's Blackpool speech that explicitly repudiated Keynesianism ('We used to think that you could just spend your way out of a recession . . . I tell you in all candour that that option no longer exists. . .'), sterling was at $1.637.

On the 29th, almost simultaneously with the news that Ford workers were intending to strike, Healey announced the government's $3.9bn application to the IMF – at the time, the largest-ever application to that body. Sterling rallied three cents on the day, but share prices lost further ground, with the Index closing at 330.4, almost twenty points down on the week so far. After accusing the government of having 'created the effect of a Nero, fiddling away with great political artistry while the town burns', the *FT*'s strongly worded leader on Thursday morning declared that there were only two possible courses of action. One was 'to tighten the money supply more effectively – a process which, as the experience of Germany has recently shown, may well reduce unemployment by bringing down inflationary expectations'. The other was 'to cut public expenditure still further, especially in those areas which absorb large amounts of relatively unproductive manpower'. As for the strong union opposition this would involve, 'conventional ideas of what is politically feasible will now have to be revised'. That day at Blackpool there were, in the eyes of the City – and of international financial opinion more generally – two signal events: the conference's decision, despite Callaghan's warnings that he would never accept such a policy, to vote in favour of nationalising the banks and insurance companies; and the loud booing during Healey's five-minute speech, as he rejected all talk of a siege economy and spoke of the necessity of doing 'things we do not like as well as things we do like'.[51] By the end of a long week, sterling was at $1.669, while the Index closed at 317.5.

Callaghan later accused the markets of having behaved that week 'with all the restraint of a screaming crowd of schoolgirls at a rock concert', but had they really been so irrational? Barings, in its end-September report on the foreign exchange market, was at pains to argue not:

> The apparent spectacle of the policies of the Chancellor being rejected so vociferously at the Labour Party conference caused a further break in confidence since doubts were clearly aroused over the ability of the Government even to maintain, let alone sharpen up, their policies for the long period seen to be necessary to change the underlying weaknesses in the UK economy. Exchange dealers are often criticised for taking only the short view – and indeed they often necessarily do – but, in this instance, the medium and long views disturbed them equally.[52]

The report might have added that sterling's greater stability towards the end of the week was equally rational, after the announcement of the application to the IMF. For this to succeed, the markets knew, the British government would have to accept that wonderful thing, 'conditionality'. Put another way, the July package was now seen to be only a down-payment.

October proved a nervous, confusing month, pending the arrival in London of the IMF negotiating team. On the 7th, taking Richardson's advice that it was the only way to (in Healey's retrospective words) 'sell enough gilts to get money under control', the Chancellor raised MLR to a politically disastrous 15 per cent, after overcoming serious initial resistance from Callaghan, who was mistrustful of both Bank and Treasury. Soon afterwards a Labour backbencher, Jeff Rooker, introduced the Prohibition of Speculation Bill, targeted at both currency and commodity speculation, and accused the Bank of England of being guilty of 'treasonable mismanagement of the money markets'. There was no realistic possibility of the bill passing into law, but according to *International Insider*, 'international bankers regard it as firm evidence of the determination of certain sections of the present British government to squeeze the financial community until the proverbial pips squeak.' It added that 'several international banks with London operations are seriously considering reducing operations in the UK if the hostile climate does not improve'.

At the Mansion House on the 21st there was a well-orchestrated display of unanimity between Chancellor and Governor – Healey setting monetary targets, Richardson warmly supporting him in so doing – but three days later the *Sunday Times* changed the atmosphere by claiming that it was the IMF's intention to set sterling at $1.50. The next day, Monday the 25th, sterling fell by no fewer than seven cents, to $1.55; and on *Panorama*, Callaghan declared that if only the old problem of the sterling balances could be resolved, and the pound thereby cease to be a reserve currency, that would be more helpful to Britain than an IMF loan. By Wednesday the Index was down to 265.3 (having been over 300 barely a week earlier), while on Thursday sterling hit a new low of $1.53. 'Viewed from London,' observed Barings' end-October report, 'foreign exchange markets would seem to have reached in recent days that sort of crisis point when rumours of every kind abound and news items with little immediate relevance to the realities of the market-place nevertheless provoke extraordinary reactions in rates. Turmoil is everywhere, discussion is confusion and exchange rates move over wider and wider ranges as if capable of being blown almost in all directions at once.'[53] On 1 November the IMF mission (headed by a former Bank of England man, Alan Whittome) arrived in London, and the final phase of a protracted crisis began. Over the next six weeks, during the negotiations between IMF and government and then within government, the pound remained fairly stable, mainly between $1.62 and $1.67, nudging upwards as it became clear that a package of cuts was going to be agreed.

Meanwhile, following Callaghan's initiative, steps were being taken to bring to an end sterling's long role as a reserve currency and the means of international finance. In November the Bank of England issued Notice EC68, prohibiting the use of sterling as a finance medium for non-UK-related (that is, third-country) trade; and two months later an agreement was reached that enabled sterling to be run down as a reserve currency, with protective swap facilities in case it came under pressure in the interim. Would the demise of sterling's international role handicap London as an international financial centre? On 10 November, in an important letter to *The Times*, William Clarke argued on behalf of the Committee on Invisible Exports that it would not. The City, he emphasised, had since the 1960s been progressively 'moving from a sterling standard towards a Eurocurrency standard'. Accordingly, the City would 'lose little from a running down of Britain's reserve currency role, provided that currency convertibility were maintained', and would 'gain immeasurably from any moves designed to bring greater stability to the pound itself, especially if the major element of uncertainty produced by the existence of large and volatile sterling balances were removed or substantially reduced'.[54]

The City's main attention, though, was on the conditions of the IMF loan, and eventually on 15 December Healey announced the new package of cuts to the Commons. In essence, government spending was to be cut by £1bn in 1977–8 and £1.5bn in 1978–9. Press comment was generally critical, but the markets responded just about enthusiastically enough, with the pound closing the year worth $1.70 and the Index on 354.7. 'Investors' emotions are fickle,' Rowe & Pitman warned in the immediate aftermath of Healey's statement. 'We must remind ourselves, in any post-package euphoria, that the nation's problems are not going to be solved by any single package, and reflect on all the packages, measures, budgets and mini-budgets with which we have been almost permanently preoccupied for years now, but particularly since this Government took office . . .'[55]

In the end, the key figure, on which everything had hinged, turned out to have been wrong. The true PSBR in 1976–7 was £8.5bn, *not* £10.5bn as forecast by the Treasury. Had all the trauma been unnecessary? The answer is surely not, in that whatever the validity or otherwise of the £10.5bn forecast, what had mattered was the perception of the markets – that the Labour government could only be relied upon to pursue sound economic policies if it made *another* sacrifice, to supplement the one in July that the markets had immediately viewed as inadequate. The cuts, in short, were symbolic sacrifices to market nostrums of 'good' economic behaviour. For those attached to the economic sovereignty of the nation state there was now an uncomfortable awareness that, after the break-up of Bretton Woods, things had changed. For Britain's central bank, charged with the day-to-day running of Britain's currency, that was not necessarily good news; against that, the government was now committed to monetary targets, and in the dawning world of monetarism it would be perverse not to assume that the Bank of England would exercise an increasing influence over economic policy-making as a whole. Further-more, despite the occasional grumbles of international bankers, there was no reason to think that the events of 1976 had damaged London as an international financial centre. The Eurobond market, above all, had flourished as never before, with huge issues including $300m for the EEC, $125m for Hydro Quebec and $100m apiece for Denmark and Norway. There was one particularly emblematic moment. Morgan Stanley had hitherto based its European operations in Paris, but when it came to starting a trading capability in the secondary Eurobond market, it decided to site it in London.[56] The domestic problems of a medium-sized economy were, in short, no longer of critical relevance to the quite different concerns of a by now well-established offshore financial centre.

*

The very act of the Labour government reluctantly swallowing the IMF medicine seemed to transform the British economy during 1977. The government now had credibility in the financial markets, as demonstrated by the $1.5bn UK loan successfully raised in the Euromarkets early in the year; the medium-term prospect of North Sea oil transforming the British balance of payments was widely touted; sterling was stable at around $1.70; and interest rates fell rapidly, down to 5 per cent by October. Equities responded enthusiastically, with the Index starting the year at 354.7 (already well up on the dog days of the previous autumn) and in mid-September hitting a new high of 549.2. Simultaneously, there were even more remarkable gains in gilts. Soon afterwards in his monthly column Bazalgette pondered on 'the strange and sudden turn in Britain's fortunes':

> A year ago we were indeed in what Bunyon termed the Slough of Despond, or as another chap put it, the sedge was withered from the lake and no birds sang. There were other sick men in Europe, but we were indeed considered to be the sickest, an irredeemable set of idle, wasteful no-good villains for whom there was no possible way of climbing back to respectability . . . What do we find a bare year later? The £ so strong against the $ that it has to be held down by sheer brute strength. Balance of payments well in surplus, the gold and dollar reserves so large that we are fast running out of vaults in which to store them. Hot money fighting its way into the country through every crack and crevice, and a gilt-edged market which makes the rubber booms of my youth appear tame and tepid by comparison . . .[57]

Things then on the whole quietened down, with the Index ending 1977 on 485.4, while at the start of September 1978 it stood at 498.5.

But if it was a broadly improving situation, that was far from meaning that the old antagonism towards Labour and its supporters had suddenly vanished. In 1977 Martin Gibbs, senior research partner at Phillips & Drew and a recognised authority on the problem of inflation accounting, was asked to write a report for the Transport and General Workers' Union, which was currently submitting a pay claim to Fords. His report (included in the union's formal submission) found that the claim by the company to have made only £5.6m 'seriously understates the real profits of the year since it ignores the effect of inflation on the company's net liabilities'. It was not, Gibbs recalled, a piece of work that endeared him to his 'more Conservative partners and their clients', who 'felt that, by helping a trade union so publicly, I had effectively gone over to the enemy side'. And in the Stock Exchange's Annual Report for the year ending June 1978, after recognising that inflation had come down in the past two and a half years, Goodison went on:

> We want Britain's economy to thrive. We want the Government to recognise the important place of business in the economy and of individual effort in bringing prosperity about. If businessmen are reduced to complaining about the lack of incentive and if the young go abroad because of our so-called 'progressive' system of taxation, where does the fault lie? Let the Government drop its anti-business prejudices and allow industry and individual effort to thrive.

Or, as Rowe & Pitman put it in September, after Callaghan had fatefully decided not to call an autumn election, 'the fact that markets (in money terms) are high and rising does not imply that the City approves of this Government, is pleased that it will be around for some months longer, or is unaware of bureaucratic waste, the squandering of North Sea revenues and the stifling of enterprise through excessive marginal taxation'.[58]

The conjunction of circumstances in 1977–8 was favourable to increasing the Bank of England's influence on policy-making, and Richardson did not let the opportunity slip. The battleground was the attempt of the Keynesians, led by Sir Douglas Wass, Permanent Secretary at the Treasury, to fight back against the monetarists. Early in 1977 Wass warned Callaghan that if over-precise monetary targets continued to be pursued, 'many of us believe that the transitional adverse effect on economic activity and employment would be both serious and prolonged'. However, as during the next six or eight months sterling recovered, inflation came down and unemployment only marginally increased, the monetarists found themselves with the higher cards to play. There was also a personal element. Richardson saw himself (unlike O'Brien) not as the Permanent Secretary's opposite number, but as the Chancellor's; and his dealings with Wass tended to be condescending, even though they were both old boys of Nottingham High School. Moreover, when Callaghan during 1977 established 'The Seminar', a group that met roughly every other month to look at the big fiscal and monetary picture (under his chairmanship but Lever's leadership), Richardson – despite his membership – simply refused to allow it 'to issue him with instructions', in the words of Bernard Donoughue, from the Policy Unit at No 10. Donoughue also recalled the Callaghan/Richardson relationship: 'These two men always treated one another with considerable respect; after one particularly sharp discussion, when the Governor was being at his most impressively and courteously obstinate, Mr Callaghan said to me: "He has to do his job. I either back him or sack him, and I am certainly not going to sack him."'[59]

That 'particularly sharp discussion' may have been when 'The Seminar' met on 20 October 1977 and complained about the damage being done to industry, especially exports, by the newly strong pound. Richardson, however, insisted that if monetary targets were to continue to be met, then sterling must be allowed to float upwards, and by the end of the month he had got his way. Soon after being reappointed for a second term, he followed up that victory by delivering in February 1978 the inaugural Mais lecture, 'Reflections on the conduct of monetary policy', in which he endorsed the phrase of Paul Volcker (soon to be his American counterpart) about the need for 'practical monetarism' and characteristically argued that 'formulating a line of practical policy and trying to stick to it, while yet remaining appropriately flexible amid the uncertainties of day-to-day affairs, feels very different from devising ideal solutions in the seclusion of a study'. So no doubt it did, but by this time the Bank's John Fforde, an unenthusiastic monetarist, had already done much to improve the quality of monetary data and their regular monitoring and assessment. Was there a hidden agenda behind Richardson's monetarism? Certainly he believed that Keynesianism and an acceptable rate of inflation were no longer compatible; but there was also a significant phrase in his Mais lecture, where he described monetary targets as representing 'a self-imposed constraint, or discipline, on the authorities'. Presumably 'the authorities' was code for the politicians, and behind them the inflationary demands of a mass electorate. Just over half a century after Montagu Norman had couched the virtues of a return to the gold standard in much the same way, another central banker was seeking to construct a supra-political monetary policy.[60]

The Labour government's relationship with the gilt-edged market, as mediated by the Bank and the Government broker, remained fraught with difficulties. After Healey's thirteenth budget, on 11 April 1978 – in which the 1978–9 PSBR was forecast at £8.5bn, the growth target for sterling M3 for that year was declared to be 8-12 per cent and MLR was raised by 1 per cent to 7½ per cent – Rowe & Pitman's gilt-edged report noted that 'confidence has taken a sharp knock, and there is a chance that we will again have an "investors' strike", with the authorities being forced to take more drastic action to enable them to fund'. This expectation was justified. MLR increased on 5 May to 8¾ per cent and a week later to 9 per cent, but soon afterwards Rowe & Pitman observed ominously that 'the post-Budget rise in yields appears to be petering out and the weight of accruing institutional liquidity is leaning on a technical market distinctly short of willing sellers'.[61] The whole question was about to go political.

When Benn went to see Callaghan on 23 May, they had a lengthy discussion about the timing of the election, the Scottish situation, the attitude of the TUC, and so on, before Callaghan went on:

'But I am worried about one other thing, and you must keep this absolutely to yourself. There is a lot of funny business going on between the City of London and the Government over the gilt-edged market. The City are not buying gilts in an effort to push up interest rates. What should I do?'

I replied, 'To an ex-Chancellor with your experience, there's nothing whatever I can say except that there might be a case for facing it out with them.'

'My experience with the City,' said Jim, 'is that if they've got you by the knackers they'll squeeze you – even though they know they will have to give way eventually and then you can knock them out cold. They could do a lot of damage' . . .

I told him I didn't think the City wanted us to be defeated, and Jim agreed that they were only really concerned with their own game.

Two days later the matter was discussed at Cabinet. 'What Jim was anxious not to do was precipitate an immediate Election,' noted Benn, 'and he expressed his concern about the rise in the money supply and the City's refusal to buy gilts. He thought it might be necessary to take some pre-emptive measures. Harold Lever said the City were torn because they didn't want us to win but they didn't want Thatcher to win either.' Within a fortnight, on 8 June, Healey had produced a monetarist package, in which MLR went up 1 per cent to 10 per cent and the banking 'corset' was reimposed. The gilt-edged market hailed it as a victory 'for the City', and in Rowe & Pitman's words, 'the immediate euphoric response to the package enabled the Government Broker to enjoy a concentrated spell of substantial funding sales'.[62]

At about the same time, in the hope of avoiding further damaging gilt strikes, Donoughue at the Policy Unit put forward some suggestions aimed at producing 'a more even flow of gilt sales':

> The Treasury was sympathetic but the Bank of England was at first extremely hostile. However, the Prime Minister followed our suggestion of setting up a working group to look into ways of improving the operation of the gilt market. The working party's interim report in the late summer favoured the early introduction of a new convertible stock. However, this (and the final report in November) rejected most of our long-term suggestions – index-linked gilts and tender selling – on the basis that the present system worked successfully and that the market would be upset if these arrangements were disturbed.

In short, Donoughue concluded, 'it was clear that the Bank considered its own mode of working both to be perfect and nobody else's business'. The Bank's argument, then as later, was that index-linked bonds would cast doubt on the government's determination to curb inflation; but as the *Economist* pointed out, 'the introduction of an index-linked bond could just as easily be interpreted to mean that the government expected inflation to come down, because it was no longer afraid of a spiralling money cost of debt servicing'.[63] Almost certainly Donoughue was right to detect an element of institutional conservatism.

Another significant Labour/City sub-plot in the 1970s concerned the question of regulation. After the manifest regulatory failure that had led to the secondary banking crisis, any government would have started to draft new banking legislation; but from the Bank of England's standpoint it was crucial – certainly in Richardson's eyes – that the Bank henceforth take supervisory responsibility for all banks. With that in mind he successfully insisted that the new legislation embody a two-tier system, in effect distinguishing between 'proper banks' and licensed deposit takers. The Banking Act received the royal assent in April 1979 and came into operation six months later.[64]

More contentious politically was the familiar question of whether the policing of the financial markets as a whole should continue to rely on self-regulation, or whether something along the lines of the US Securities and Exchange Commission should be introduced.[65] For two years, from 1974 to 1976, the Department of Trade deliberated. Predictably, in its March 1975 submission, the Stock Exchange whole-heartedly endorsed the speed and effectiveness of self-regulation by practitioners. 'The effectiveness of the existing system of self-regulation within the financial community,' it stated, 'rests largely on the good communications and close relationships between the various bodies concerned. Within the City, this is achieved through the Bank of England; but, between the financial community and the Government, communication is not so readily achieved.' Presumably there were few doubts, but just in case David LeRoy-Lewis and two other Council members visited Washington and New York later that year, mainly to look at the SEC in action. 'The legalistic approach would not be beneficial to the regulation of the securities market in the UK,' LeRoy-Lewis reported. 'It is not sufficiently flexible and can be used at times to frustrate legitimate and desirable activities, especially in the take-over field. Certainly it gives rise to uncertainties and a level of legal activity which few in this country would wish to see emulated here.' Eventually, largely on Edmund Dell's say-so, the decision was taken to stick with self-regulation, but to attempt to make it more ambitious. This led to the launching in spring 1978 of the Council for the Securities Industry – an almost entirely toothless body stuffed with representatives of City institutions. Later that year this new self-regulatory watchdog made its first major public statement, on the hotly debated question of insider dealing, but symptomatically confined itself to a résumé of the problems involved.[66]

In the public mind, insider dealing was now becoming *the* test issue of City ethics. The precipitate February 1974 election had aborted Walker's proposed legislation, but from 1976 there was a renewed movement (including from the City Company Law Committee) to revive the proposal that insider dealing should be made a criminal offence. Dissenters included Sir Antony Hornby. 'Only those stockbrokers who buy shares for their clients in companies about which they know nothing or which are likely to go down will keep out of prison,' he publicly complained in December 1977. 'Only the buyer of Premium Bonds – the pure gambler – will be safe and respectable. The rest of us must either use a pin or be condemned to uninspired uniformity.' The following July the government published a White Paper that sought to define what insider dealing was – essentially, dealing on the basis of information that was both privileged and significantly price-sensitive – but in the expectation of an autumn general election the City took little notice. All that changed once Callaghan had decided not to go to the country. First, in a speech in late September, Goodison announced that he and the Stock Exchange Council were having second thoughts about the desirability of a legal ban on insider dealing, arguing that a practitioner-based body like the Council for the Securities Industry would be better equipped to stamp out the practice, which anyway did not lend itself easily to legal definition; then, on 20 October, Dell announced that he did intend to legislate. Yet only weeks later, it was February 1974 revisited. This time what came to the City's rescue was not a snap general election, but Dell's decision to leave the government and take up a position at Guinness Peat.[67] Once again the issue found itself in the proverbial long grass.

The so-called 'Sarabex affair' graphically highlighted how far the City remained a cluster of largely self-regulating and more or less closed shops.[68] For years the ten or so foreign exchange broking firms that made up the Foreign Exchange and Currency Deposit Brokers' Association (FECDBA) had enjoyed a cushioned existence, in particular through the Bank of England's adamant opposition to brokers being taken over by banks and its insistence that banks were not permitted to deal directly with each other in London in foreign exchange. 'The basic objection to any link between a principal and a broker in these markets is the obvious risk of conflict of interest that must arise,' O'Brien had formally stated in March 1973. 'The Bank continues to believe that the independence of brokers from principals in the London markets makes a major contribution to the breadth and efficiency of those markets and thus to their effectiveness for worldwide business.' Moreover, the Bank insisted that members of the British Bankers Association (BBA) and other authorised banks in London solely used members of FECDBA to conduct their foreign exchange business.

Four and a half years after the 'O'Brien Letter', it emerged that Sarabex, a London-based foreign exchange and money broker dealing mainly for Middle Eastern banks, had filed a formal complaint to the EEC about the restrictive practices operating in London, above all the impossible-to-fulfil condition that one could not become a member of FECDBA unless one was *already* providing BBA banks with 'a full service'. The news provoked a mixed reaction from London's bankers. 'Truly, a Catch-22 situation,' commented one, although another was less sympathetic: 'Some of London's ways of doing business may seem odd or unreasonable, but there are good reasons why this is so. Any change forced upon us by an outside body like the EEC could easily do more harm than good.'

International Insider was inclined to take the latter view: 'The Sarabex Affair could be the prelude to a wide-ranging attack by the EEC against The City of London. For example, wonders one Brussels bureaucrat, could the London discount houses with all their privileges withstand close scrutiny?' In a public letter to the EEC in November 1977 the Bank strongly defended existing arrangements, mainly on the basis that they were necessary to preserve an effective and orderly market.[69] The Bank now looked for support from the clearing banks, the main users of the foreign exchange market, but was disappointed – the clearers having taken legal advice and been told that they were on a hiding (in the form of potentially huge fines) to nothing. The NatWest's Bill Batt, acting head of the foreign exchange sub-committee of the British Bankers Association, had a difficult meeting with the Bank of England's John Page. 'I had hoped the clearing banks would support the Bank of England,' the Chief Cashier remarked frostily. In 1978 the Bank had to retreat and Sarabex became a member, though by then it had new people in charge, including former clearing bankers.

The outcome of the Sarabex affair was suggestive of the pressures for change, and there was a sense by this time of the City finding it increasingly hard to cling on to the old ways. Three aspects illustrate the point. The first, trivial but symbolic, was the sharp decline of the traditional City lunch – whether in the form of three hours of lavish, distinctly alcoholic hospitality or the so-called 'mixed lunch', where guests were plucked from different backgrounds and everything was discussed *except* the host's business. Kleinwort Benson's Martin Jacomb observed in 1978 that 'the days when you could discuss the theatre or the opera or hunting and fishing over lunch are finished', adding that 'the present generation knows we're here to do business and not waste time with an artificial social conversation'.[70] Second, the events of the mid-1970s had given an increasing, seemingly impossible-to-resist importance to size. For example, the mixture of the vicious bear market and sharply raised taxation had thinned the ranks of private investors, so that by the end of 1975 individuals held only 37.5 per cent of listed UK equities, as measured by market value, in stark comparison to the 65.8 per cent at the end of 1957 or even the 47.4 per cent at the end of 1969. In corporate broking, a clearly identifiable 'Big Three' (Cazenove's, Hoare Govett and Rowe & Pitman) were now well ahead; while in accountancy there was the 'Big Eight' (Arthur Andersen, Arthur Young, Coopers & Lybrand, Deloitte's, Ernst & Whinney, Peat Marwick, Price Waterhouse and Touche Ross), with Price Waterhouse being fairly typical in the way its partners rose from 87 in 1975 to 161 in 1982.[71] The third aspect, much harder to quantify, was the general growth of a somewhat more international outlook – partly in the context of an increasingly integrated financial world after the demise of Bretton Woods, partly in response to the prevailing feeling that the British economy was no longer a basket in which it was safe to put all one's eggs. These were the years of a huge, almost indiscriminate rush of lending to the Third World; of increasing cross-border investment in Europe and the start of global custody as a flourishing international banking service, offering multi-currency asset safekeeping, settlement, trade accounting and portfolio reporting; and of the Saudi Arabian Monetary Agency, in which Flemings, Barings and Credit Suisse White Weld played a major role in determining how the Saudis used their sky-high cash mountain.[72] People did not yet talk in such terms, but a global market was already starting to take shape.

As far as the City specifically was concerned, there was, notwithstanding the post-1976 domestic upturn, an obvious irony. 'Practically every day a foreign banker working in London can pick up his morning paper and read another story that documents the disintegration of the British economy,' Cary Reich wrote in *Institutional Investor* in spring 1977:

> It might be an article on the strike crippling one of the UK's biggest companies, British Leyland. Or it might be a piece on all the jobs that could be lost because of New York's refusal to grant landing rights to the Concorde. Or it might be a story about the bleak prospects for the pound on the world's foreign exchange markets.
>
> Yet the chances are the banker simply sighs, folds the newspaper and gets on with his morning's business totally unaffected. The thought of leaving the battered island would rarely occur to him, and if it did, he would dismiss it in an instant. Because whatever the country's problems may be, the City of London remains the world's pre-eminent international financial center, and the banker simply must be part of it.

The figures cited by Reich confirmed that irreducible fact: the number of foreign banks and consortia in London, which had been 278 in 1975 before dipping to 270 in early 1976, now stood at 298. This is not to say that there were no grumbles, with the Post Office's inflexible, slow-moving control over telephones a particular grievance. 'The difficulties in London stem from getting a number of things done logistically,' Charles McVeigh of Salomons told Reich. 'You want to expand the trading room, or you just want to get the clock fixed – all the simple things you take for granted in New York – and they take a lot longer to do in London, and become rather a hassle.' But of the thirty prominent foreign bankers whom Reich interviewed, only one, John McDaniels, was willing to think aloud the unthinkable:

> 'It should be understood,' he says, 'that if there are too many inconveniences in the way of the kind of business we do, there is no pre-ordained reason why business has to be done in London.' Airplanes, telephones and telexes – the tools of the banker's trade – are available

anywhere, he explains, and 'if the tax bite gets too hard – well, you can unplug these telephones rather quickly,' he adds. While admitting that BTI, Bankers Trust's merchant banking arm, isn't considering such a drastic step – he half-jokingly refers to it as 'the nuclear threat' – McDaniels already sees some disadvantages in a London base, not the least of which is the fact that BTI has to hold nearly half of its shareholders' funds in sterling. As for the oft-cited advantages of London, McDaniels remarks that 'the City of London is grossly exaggerated in terms of its skills – the printers here are marginally better than the printers in Paris – in the English language' . . .

The overwhelming consensus, though, was with Staffan Gadd of the Scandinavian Bank: 'I really don't see any threat from any other financial center in Europe. You don't move a bank just for tax reasons. You can set it up in a tax haven like the Bahamas, but you really don't get the same standing you would in London.' Or, as Libra Bank's Thomas Gaffney put it, 'We have a choice of either being close to the money or close to the customers. We choose to be close to the money.'[73]

The bullet points fronting a survey of the City, published in *Euromoney* in January 1978, had their own eloquence. The City was earning a £1.7bn net surplus in foreign exchange annually; had doubled its foreign income in the past two years; had more foreign banks than any other financial centre; had more American banks than New York; operated the largest international insurance market in the world; had a larger stock-market turnover than Frankfurt, Paris, Amsterdam and Brussels combined; accounted for the largest share of the worldwide Eurocurrency market; accounted for two-thirds of the world's shipping freight market; and operated some of the world's largest commodity markets. In that survey William Clarke conceded that New York was gearing up for a new international challenge, after its fortuitous domestic retreat of the 1960s, but professed himself 'moderately optimistic' about London meeting not only that challenge, but also the one from more specialist centres on the Continent. Clarke's confidence rested on two principal foundations: that London's foreign business embraced 'a far wider spectrum of activities' than was the case anywhere else; and that 'the volume of London's *international* business dominates its total turnover in a way that only Zürich can emulate'.[74] At the tail-end of two decades of almost continuous national relative economic decline, this was a remarkable achievement, albeit one virtually unheralded outside the square mile.

There persisted a sense, however, in which there were still two quite distinct Cities – one centring on the still largely UK-oriented stock market, the other focusing mainly on the much more international Euromarkets. The former was far more the natural terrain of the City establishment, a fairly representative example of which was Luke Meinertzhagen, senior partner of Cazenove's, with UK company (barely yet known as 'corporate') finance his speciality. Each day he would lunch at the City Club in Old Broad Street, where as yet it was almost unheard of for a Euromarket man to be a member. In general, the traditional investment community remained suspicious of huge swaths of the developed world. 'In 1975 I raised £1.7m for an investment trust targeted at Japan,' Christopher Heath remembered twenty years later about a key moment in his career when he was still at the stockbrokers Henderson Crosthwaite. 'There was a lot of resistance to the idea. "They're just a nation of copycats," people would say, or "They behaved badly in the war". It was quite a struggle . . .' Or take the experience of Ross Jones, who joined Gerrard & National in 1977 straight from Ampleforth and by his third year was doing the morning round of visits to banks that had lent the firm money. 'It was very narrow in those days,' he recalled in 1992, 'we might just have known what American interest rates were doing but no one looked at sterling-deutschmarks or had any idea when the Bundesbank were meeting. London was still a little island . . .' The fact that Gerrards was a successful, enterprising outfit only reinforced the point. Perhaps the most telling indication of London's insularity was how long it took to follow Chicago's example and start a financial futures market of its own. It was five years before the International Commodities Clearing House belatedly set the ball rolling in 1977, and it took another five years before London's market opened for business. Ideally, it needed someone of vision in the commodity futures markets to have come forward at an earlier stage; or perhaps the Bank of England should have been more proactive. Either way, although it was an opportunity eventually grasped, it was also an opportunity missed for an unnecessarily long time.[75]

The fact was that by 1979 only about 8 per cent of the £97bn in invested assets of the four main groups of UK institutional investors – insurance companies, pension funds, investment trusts and unit trusts – were abroad. Nicholas Goodison accurately recalled the prevailing climate, from a Stock Exchange standpoint, during most of the second half of the 1970s:

> We still had exchange controls. We had a Labour government intent on controlling absolutely everything, and no freedom of capital movement. British people were not allowed to take capital abroad; British institutions weren't allowed to invest capital abroad. Companies weren't allowed to invest capital abroad except by special Treasury permission, based on returns they would make on their capital, and if you wanted to buy foreign securities, you had to pay a phoney price for the dollars, which was a much higher price than the real price. So we were an insulated market . . .

Admittedly in 1977–8 there were certain exchange control relaxations, but these were largely done in an EEC context and of a mainly symbolic nature. Abolition was quite another matter. 'It is highly improbable that any Labour government would contemplate removing exchange controls without intense EEC pressure to do so, as much for political as economic reasons,' a James Capel discussion paper accurately asserted in November 1978. 'The left wing of the Labour party and the trades union movement are both bitterly opposed to the export of UK capital, seeing this as the exporting of job opportunities which would otherwise be open to British workers.' Nor did the City itself beat the drum hard for abolition. '"Steady on", I was told,' was how Thatcher recollected the reaction of City figures to whom she had broached the idea when in opposition. 'Clearly, a world without exchange controls in which markets rather than governments determined the movement of capital left them distinctly uneasy. They might have to take risks.' The retrospective scorn was justified, for allied to the City's abiding conservatism was its complete inability to envisage how abolition might revolutionise the scope and profitability of its international business. Arguably, though, it was not quite as simple as that, for it also seems to have remained the case (although seldom written about) that, despite the apparent constraints of exchange control, the City was able, through a tacit system of Bank of England nods and winks, to evade or circumvent those constraints up to an adequately satisfactory if rather unambitious point. Altogether, in conjunction with the instinctive attachment in some quarters of the Bank of England to exchange control as a key source of authority and intelligence, it was hardly surprising that the City was, as usual, not pressing for fundamental change.[76]

In June 1977 a notable episode brought together the national and international capital markets.[77] This was the £564m sale – at the time, the world's largest-ever equity offering – of the British government's 17 per cent stake in British Petroleum. Largely on the initiative of BP's Finance Director Quentin (Q) Morris, abetted by Lord Garmoyle of Scrimgeours and Frederick Whitemore of Morgan Stanley, a two-tranche approach was adopted, with one of the tranches (representing 20 per cent of the shares) going to the US. After consulting Garmoyle and others, the Bank of England on behalf of the Treasury took the view that there should be no single lead manager for the UK tranche, but that it should be done on a consortium basis, rather as with steel denationalisation in the mid-1950s. The consortium was to comprise ten merchant banks and five stockbrokers, including the Government brokers Mullens. Who would co-ordinate its activities? Inasmuch as BP had a regular merchant bank, it was Lazards; but to Ian Fraser's undisguised anger, the Bank plumped for Warburgs and its rising star, David Scholey. There followed a huge amount of detailed preparations, run out of the basement of BP's Britannic House headquarters off Moorgate. Eventually, by the afternoon of Monday, 13 June, an underwriting price of 845p was settled upon. Only final government approval was needed. At this point Richardson was asked to go to 10 Downing Street, where he was told that some Cabinet members – no names mentioned, but almost certainly led by Benn – were objecting to the sale. Confronted by this development, Richardson rang the Government broker, Tommy Gore Browne, to ask him what the consequences would be of not going ahead. Gore Browne's uncompromising reply was that even a twenty-four-hour delay might well defer the launch for months. As a thunderstorm over London began to build up that evening, the City's key figures in the BP sale waited for another telephone call from Richardson. Finally, amidst much tension, he rang Gore Browne at 8.45 p.m. to tell him, on the government's authority, to proceed. The next day, the issue was underwritten by 782 institutions. It was the first day of Royal Ascot, and at least one of the brokers involved, Nigel Elwes of Rowe & Pitman, was compelled to come to the office in half-change and place a certain amount of stock before being released to the races.[78] Over the following week the offer was made to the public and was 4.7 times oversubscribed. The way had been pointed, albeit unintentionally on the government's part, to the financial potential of the privatising process. The City had shown its paces; and not only was Scholey's name made, but Warburgs was now widely recognised as London's premier merchant bank.

For the merchant banking sector as a whole, the BP deal was a welcome bit of honey during a generally difficult period. 'In less than half a decade,' the *Economist* starkly observed in March 1979, 'Britain's merchant banks have become the genteel poor of the international banking community', and it stressed the importance of this lack of financial muscle: 'Internationally, a banker who prefers procuring finance to providing it can easily find himself out of his depth. The accepting houses have run into German, Swiss, American and even British clearing bank heavy-weights who can put quantities of cash on the table when offering a financial package.' Some end-1977 balance sheet footings were cited: whereas Kleinworts (the biggest of the London accepting houses) had £1.4bn, the figures for Deutsche, Barclays, Morgan Guaranty and Union Bank of Switzerland were respectively £31.0bn, £22.1bn, £16.3bn and £14.8bn. Moreover, adjusting for inflation, the balance sheet footings of most of the main merchant banks had shrunk significantly over the past four years – Kleinworts and Schroders by 23 per cent each, Hambros and Barings by 32 per cent each and Hill Samuel by 46 per cent. All was not gloom – corporate finance work had picked up, acceptance credits were growing because they enabled the 'corset' constraining the clearers to be bypassed, institutional pension fund management was a fast-growing area – but overall it was a far cry from 'the glamour and share ratings the merchant banks enjoyed earlier in the decade'. Above all, the merchant banks were no longer major players on the international scene – exemplified by the fact that in the Eurobond market the only significant force was Warburgs, which despite its lack of distribution still had strong relationships with borrowers. Of course there were partial exceptions (Lazards, for example, in export finance, or Barings as joint adviser to the Saudi Arabian Monetary Agency), but the larger point held. Did these distinctive, if chameleon-like, City creatures have a future? 'If sterling weakens again in the 1980s, as so many merchant bankers expect,' the *Economist* concluded, 'there will be a rather odd look once again about a financial system in which so much highly educated Oxbridge talent devotes its considerable brainpower to finding ways of remaining competitive in a business which foreigners are far better equipped to carry out anyway.'[79]

Even Warburgs and Morgan Grenfell – reckoned by the *Economist* to have bucked the downward trend in recent years – had their problems. At Warburgs there was the continuing failure to establish a convincing presence in the US; while Warburg himself, constitutionally unable in his old age to accept the R-word, badly failed to appreciate the potential of the firm's investment management side – though he was not alone, in that when in 1979 he tried to sell it to first Flemings and then Lazards, he was unable to do so, even at a knock-down price.[80] At Morgan Grenfell there had been a major injection of capital in 1974 when the Lloyd's insurance broker Willis, Faber & Dumas had increased its stake to 22 per cent; but two years later the flotation of Willis Faber saw the 'Old Guard' making the huge personal gains that helped to sow the seeds for the eventual coup by the 'Young Turks' which would fatefully change the bank's very character.[81] Elsewhere, the picture was broadly one of marking time. Lazards was quietly stagnating under 'the Four Colonels', with Daniel Meinertzhagen right up to his retirement in 1979 insisting that there must be no 'touting for business' in the increasingly important corporate finance sphere; neither Hill Samuel, in Keith's semi-absence, nor Samuel Montagu was particularly flourishing; Kleinworts had a strong balance sheet and was making some progress, but was still not quite in the first division; and Barings, under the conservative leadership of John Baring, enjoyed a certain amount of growth, mainly abroad, but without any expectation (or perhaps any wish) of returning to the great days.[82]

The three most interesting stories were at Hambros, Rothschilds and Schroders. 'Hambros Bank, the subject of widespread rumour about its tanker finance operations, emphasises that it has suffered no loss of principal or interest on any shipping loan,' *International Insider* reported in June 1975. In fact, Hambros had very nearly been holed below the waterline by its ill-judged involvement with a fraudulent Norwegian shipowner, Hilmar Recksten. That involvement not only cost the bank some £75m, but also badly damaged its reputation in Scandinavia, for almost a century and a half the emotional core of its business. Indeed, but for the firm's fortunate stake in Weinberg's Hambro Life insurance business, it might not have survived.[83]

At New Court there was growing disharmony between the Rothschild cousins, Evelyn and Jacob. A personality clash masked genuine matters of substance: in particular, Jacob – the more cerebral of the two – reacted somewhat apocalyptically to the City's general mid-1970s' crisis and pushed hard the strategy of a union-as-strength merger with Warburgs, but was unable to persuade Evelyn. Senior people were being almost forced into rival camps, prompting Rodney Leach, one of the most gifted bankers of his generation, to leave Rothschilds in 1976 and go to Edmond Safra's Trade Development Bank. The following year the cousins talked to *Euromoney*. 'Investment banking in New York is a murderous business today,' Jacob declared. 'The whole business is demoralised, and it doesn't know where it's going.' Evelyn (who was by now Chairman) countered, 'We don't want to give you the impression that we have no plans for the States. We take the view – would you not say so, Jacob? – that the States provide the best long-term opportunities for merchant banking.' Having already retreated from the Eurobond market, as well as having sold its stake in Rothschild Intercontinental Bank to American Express (which renamed it Amex Bank), Rothschilds was approaching the end of the 1970s in a divided, directionless state.[84]

At Schroders (where the young Martin Vander Weyer worked in the late 1970s in the banking division, which was 'staffed by blue-chip Oxbridge public school types and smooth Chelsea-dwelling Europeans', permitted half an hour after lunch to be spent on *The Times* crossword and discouraged 'naked displays of keenness and ambition'), the key decision was reached in 1976. The two candidates for chairman were the elegant fifteenth Earl of Airlie and James Wolfensohn, a dynamic, intellectually outstanding Australian. Wolfensohn was supported by the Schroder family and the bank's foreign directors, but Airlie, the safer choice, came through. 'I was going to change things significantly,' Wolfensohn (who soon afterwards moved to Salomons) recalled. 'I was going to change the structure, make it more goal-oriented, more aggressive. That would have upset the apple cart.' Wolfensohn would also have given the firm a more international character, perhaps sought to make it a force in the Eurobond market. Instead, the decision to plump for the Scottish earl revealed with rare clarity (as Vander Weyer's experience did) just how alive gentlemanly capitalism was in the upper reaches of the City. Wolfensohn himself offered the ultimate epitaph: 'They were scared that I would do these terrible things, like getting them into distribution . . . I had a different perception. I knew the merchant banks were vulnerable . . .'[85]

But were they vulnerable to the clearers? 'It's obvious that size is going to count in the end,' Hill Samuel's Sir Robert Clark pessimistically observed in 1977. 'There's a great deal you can do with brains, but you can't stay out in front with them. And clearly, if they set about it the right way, all the big banks can get as much talent as the merchant banks have.' The belief that brawn (in the shape of capital) and brains could successfully complement each other was particularly strong at this time, for example prompting Lord Camoys (formerly Tom Stonor, and one of the more capitalist gentlemanly capitalists) to throw in his lot with Barclays Merchant Bank (BMB), formed in 1975. BMB was certainly not a member of the Accepting Houses Committee or even the IHA, but reputedly its name went through on the nod at the Bank of England because the Governor was on holiday. There was little initial sign, though, that the merchant banks' dominant position in corporate finance was going to be seriously threatened by the clearers. 'Personalities matter,' a BMB man remarked in July 1977, 'and it will be years before people think of County Bank [NatWest's subsidiary] or BMB before Schroders or Warburgs.'[86]

The far bigger – and far more expensive – thrust of the clearers was in the international sphere. Barclays and NatWest having led the way, Midland by 1975 was anxious to catch up. That November the board considered a paper by Malcolm Wilcox and, after discussion, 'approved the strategy, objectives and ambitions, to date and for the future'. Namely: 'That Midland should aim to be, and be recognised as, a major international bank; this implied the consolidation of existing assets, and further investment over a period of years – both in money and personnel – to attain a requisite spread of business and improvement in earnings.' The immediate background seems to have been that Wilcox had commissioned a report from Stanford Research Institute, showing not only that Citibank was now biting into Midland's UK business, but that 60 per cent of Citibank's profits came from non-US sources. For the time being the bank refrained from making a major overseas acquisition, but it compensated by a heavy involvement in the syndicated loan market, mainly in South America. Lloyds was also increasingly minded to follow the conventional wisdom and pursue non-UK growth. When it was announced in September 1976 that Sir Jeremy Morse, formerly of the Bank of England, would become its next Chairman, he was quoted as saying that 'the next stage would be to develop the business prospects latent in the international operations'.[87]

By August 1977 the editor of the *Banker*, Robin Pringle, did not consider that the Big Four had got all that far in their ambition to stake a claim to an international presence. He conceded that NatWest was now going 'all out' for multinational corporations, that the clearers had 'built up a respectable position in the medium-term syndicated loan market' and that they had 'held on to their share in the Eurocurrency deposit market in London'; against that, their lack of placing power and expertise meant that they were not yet within 'the élite group' in the Euromarkets, especially the bond markets, while their impact on project financing had been disappointing. 'In short, they have not yet managed to combine the speed and flexibility of top-class merchant banking with the muscle of large commercial banks'. Undeterred, the clearers pressed on, with NatWest and Barclays each making a badly overpriced acquisition in 1978, respectively of National Bank of North America ($432m) and American Credit Corporation of Charlotte, North Carolina ($191m). Reassuring words about the acquisition of NBNA, essentially a consumer finance company, came from George Cathles, head of NatWest's strategic investment and international business: 'A bank like NatWest has to expand abroad. Any fool could have decided its overall strategy . . . We will be in the US for a hundred years.'[88]

NatWest's Chairman by this time was a classic gentlemanly capitalist, Robin Leigh-Pemberton, but he and the other clearing bank chairmen were seeing much of their traditional power significantly eroded. Lord Armstrong of Sanderstead, a former Permanent Secretary of the Treasury, succeeded Forbes at Midland in 1975, and with Tuke of Barclays, Faulkner of Lloyds and Prideaux of NatWest (as well as Sir Seymour Egerton of Coutts and Sir John Hogg of Williams & Glyn's) was present at what may have been something of a watershed encounter with Richardson in June 1976, certainly to judge by Midland's internal memo:

> The informal meeting appears to have been a somewhat disturbing affair with the Governor adopting from the start a peremptory attitude . . . The Chairmen appear to have parted in some disarray and certainly they seemed to be of the view that further informal meetings of this nature could not continue. The Chairmen are naturally unable to deal with the technical matters now being raised by the Bank of England without advance notice. It may be perhaps that the Chief Executive Officers might be invited to attend to support them.

It may have been a year or two later that Armstrong reputedly questioned his chief general managers about whether it was sensible for Midland to be committing itself so heavily to Third World loans. The reply, polite enough, was to the effect that it was none of his business.[89]

By the time *International Insider* noted in February 1979 that NatWest was 'emerging as an aggressive lead manager of syndicated loans', the syndicated loan market was in the process of growing rapidly, largely on the back of petrodollars. In 1977 there had been 460 loans totalling

$34,859m, in 1978 the respective figures were 1,019 and $81,763m, and in 1979 they would be 1,077 and $101,612m. It was notable that by 1979 as much as $43,833m was going to non-OPEC LDCs (less-developed countries), compared with $34,213m to OECD countries. 'I am frankly nervous about the level of international indebtedness of the developing countries,' Stanislas Yassukovich remarked as early as 1976. 'Far too many are now almost wholly dependent on their ability to renew Eurocurrency loans.' Most of these borrowers were indeed sovereign borrowers, or state/quasi-state entities, and the following year First Chicago's William Curran confessed that he had started 'backing away from balance-of-payments loans and from sovereign risks', on the grounds that 'a hundred per cent of your business is with governments and at the end of the day you have no relationships to speak of, at least not the lasting relationships you build with corporations'. However, notwithstanding Zaire's default in 1976 and Turkey's in 1977, the underlying reality was that there was no shortage of hungry borrowers, and for the most part the syndicated loan market was more than happy to oblige them. In 1978 the top five lead managers were Citicorp, Chase Manhattan, Manufacturers Hanover, Morgan Guaranty and Bank of America, with Lloyds Bank International (incorporating the old BOLSA) in tenth place. The only consortium bank in the top twenty was Orion Bank in fifteenth place, and it was becoming apparent that competition between the shareholders and their consortium banks was likely to spell the eventual end of the whole consortium banking movement. 'It is obviously my job and the job of my share-holders' senior representatives seconded here to get together and dodge these bullets before they strike home,' Orion's David Montagu had told *Euromoney* in 1976, with ultimately misplaced confidence. 'So far this has been extremely well handled. It has never caused what you might call a Gettysburg issue. On the rare occasions when we find ourselves in the same swing door for the same piece of business we make very sure that we get out of the swing door first . . .'[90]

The Eurobond market had already had its sharp upward swing before pausing for breath. 'Phrases like "fantastic", "incredible" and "unbeliev-able" are being freely used in the international bond market to describe the enormous flow of new issues,' *International Insider* noted in April 1977; more soberly, interviewed five months later, Rodney Leach referred to how 'the Eurobond market, after an unprecedented slump [i.e. in 1974], has for two years enjoyed an unprecedented boom'. Even allowing for inflation, the trend was striking, with a total of $8,316m being raised in 1975, $15,165m in 1976 and $18,087m in 1977, before in 1978 the mixture of rising interest rates and a weak dollar saw the total slipping to $12,253m. During that spurt, it was generally reckoned that the top three lead managers were Deutsche Bank (not yet running its Eurobond operation out of London), Credit Suisse White Weld and Warburgs. Some sensed that the Eurobond market, more than a decade after the pioneering Autostrade issue, was assuming a less intimate, perhaps less ethical character. 'The days of friendly co-operation and friendship changed dramatically in the mid-seventies when it became an ugly business and one or two people were very keen to make a name for themselves,' John Craven, who had moved in 1973 from Warburgs to White Weld, recalled. 'That's when unpleasant practices came in – in terms of paying investors under the table in order to take bonds and even a little bit of improper entertainment of guests in flats in London – and it undermined the whole spirit of the thing. It became big business and far more people got drawn in. The whole ethos changed.'[91]

Certainly it was becoming an increasingly competitive market, and in that respect a key figure was the Managing Director of UBS (Securities), which was quickly moving up the league table.[92] 'Armin Mattle will not need to crack his whip on this occasion,' an unnamed banker remarked in April 1976, in the context of the assured success of a UBS convertible. The somewhat sardonic reference was to Mattle's much-disliked, quasi-heretical insistence that all underwriters in syndicates run by UBS must either sell or take all the bonds to which they had committed themselves – as opposed to the more relaxed custom by which certain long-standing underwriters, above all London merchant banks, were permitted to return to the lead manager those portions of their allotments that they had been unable to unload. Mattle himself had only arrived in London in late 1974, and naturally the City squealed, even lodging protests right to the top of UBS in Zurich; but neither Mattle nor his superiors relented, and within a couple of years it had become standard practice for underwriters to take the stick. Mattle was a resolute figure in other ways. *International Insider* in January 1977 described him in action:

> Deal of the month, possibly the year, is Union Bank of Switzerland's bold – some would say foolhardy – $200 million placement on behalf of Mobil Oil International Financial Corp . . . Invitations were sent to just 20 banks . . . Most of the deal was placed in Switzerland, although not exclusively . . . When first announced, the deal aroused general astonishment in the international market where the terms were regarded as way out of line with prevailing market conditions . . . Some [bankers] claim UBS pitched the deal at these levels simply to win the client from Morgan Stanley. The last word goes to UBS's Armin Mattle who told *II*: 'It was great fun'.

Mattle may have had a somewhat brusque manner ('I do not engage in social chit-chat in order to keep nice relations, because I am busy at the critical time of an issue – which is precisely when everyone calls me,' he remarked a few months later), but he was the first Swiss big hitter in a market that in theory they should have dominated.[93]

Credit Suisse White Weld (CSWW) undoubtedly benefited from its Swiss connection, especially in terms of placing power, but essentially its character was Anglo-American, with key figures there in the mid- to late 1970s including Michael von Clemm and David Potter, as well as Craven.[94] An instinctive, energetic deal-maker, Craven led from the front, and CSWW remained in these years a Euromarket powerhouse, typified by its lead role in April 1977 for the first Eurodollar floating-rate certificate of deposit, a $10m issue for the Dai-Ichi Kangyo Bank – like other Japanese banks in the City, not yet permitted by their own authorities to tap the bond market by way of floating-rate issues. Occasionally even CSWW came unstuck, as was the case a few months later. 'In a subdued bond market,' *International Insider* noted on 26 September in its summary of the previous week, 'the highlight was the jumbo offering [on 20 September] by Citibank's affiliate, Citicorp Overseas Finance. Both the size of the issue ($300 million) and the tight terms (6¾% for 3 years and 7% for 4 years) aroused considerable interest. Market reaction is mixed, but the majority opinion appears to be that the deal will succeed.' In a sense it did, in that by Wednesday the 28th the book had been fully covered, with none of the 187 underwriters dropping out. The market, however, was already in a wobbly mood, against a background of alarming US money supply figures, and it was unfortunate that on the 29th the US Treasury forecast a huge US trade deficit for the year, sending the dollar sharply southwards. First-day trading in the Citicorp issue began the next day in a wave of selling, as the price for both tranches plummeted. 'The stuff just came out of the walls,' one underwriter later said, while according to a dealer, 'Those guys at Credit Suisse White Weld got a mouthful on the first morning.' That day, and over the weekend, CSWW was widely accused of having not only priced the issue too tightly, but also given way to the borrower's demands. The episode gave Mattle the opportunity for a typically expansive quote – 'I never comment on my competitors' failures' – but did no serious long-term damage to CSWW's reputation. Such had been the market's panicky mood that, as one underwriter put it, 'even if the Citicorp pricing had been a little more generous the price would still have gone to hell in a handbasket'. In mid-1978, as the result of a complicated series of transactions, Credit Suisse White Weld became Credit Suisse First Boston. The deal was done behind the back of Craven, who had apparently wanted CSWW to link up with the New York investment bank Dillon Read and may have had the ambition of transforming the White Weld operation into a frontline British merchant bank. He returned to Warburgs later that year, leaving von Clemm in charge at CSFB, amidst some uncertainty about its future.[95]

By now there was a new, very much all-American competitor, at this stage mainly in the secondary market, in the form of Salomon Brothers. After a low-profile arrival in London in 1968, and from 1973 playing itself in by trading Eurodollar CDs, it was only from March 1976 that the London subsidiary of the aggressive Wall Street bank began trading Eurobonds, making an immediate impact. 'Not only did it deal in bigger sizes than the market was used to – its quotes usually were good for at least $250,000 – but its spreads, often a half point or better, were tighter than anyone had ever seen,' noted an admiring profile ('Salomon: The spectacular debut of an international upstart') less than two years later. In a day-to-day sense, the two key figures behind the 1 Moorgate story were Eddie Aronson, the partner in charge of Salomon's international department, who laid the London foundations, and the younger, more suave Charles McVeigh III, who arrived in 1975 and was soon running the London operation, staffed at a senior level almost entirely by compatriots. 'From the point of view of the Brits,' he recalled, 'the Americans were setting a frightening standard in the City in terms of the hours we were keeping':

> We would come into the office at seven, which was a good hour or two before most of our English counterparts. We were using London very much as the base of our European business and the Continent was always an hour ahead. If you wanted to be on the phone by 8.15, you had to assimilate a lot of financial data that had come in from New York the night before and from the *Financial Times* to be able to be succinct and convincing. We would get on the telephone with clients using relative value financial data that we'd developed ourselves and start to build investment cases for selling one bond and buying another. Our method of valuation was considered pretty high-tech stuff in those days, even though most of it was manual. The office was buzzing from 8 o'clock with people on the phone, in any number of different languages . . . My management style in London was based on being completely integrated with my colleagues in New York, and their trust in what we were doing was a by-product of the amount of co-ordination and sharing of information that we did. There was a period in my life when I went to New York literally every single week . . .

Rival firms characterised the hectic trading room at 1 Moorgate as 'the London zoo', a miniature version of Salomon's already legendary 11,000-square-foot trading floor ('The Room') in New York, but as McVeigh observed in 1977, 'If people spoke in hushed voices and worked at a modest pace around here, a lot of the enthusiasm that is created by the environment would be gone.' Yet Salomons was also prepared to play an older game. Wolfensohn may have lost out to an aristocrat at Schroders, but one of the first things he did on joining Salomons in 1977 was to use his connections to organise a Salomon-sponsored gala concert at the Royal Opera House to mark the Queen's Jubilee, attended by a stellar audience.[96]

In the more traditionally British world of the Stock Exchange, by painful contrast with the cosmopolitan Euromarkets, irresistible pressures for change were starting to build. Above all this applied to the jobbing system, which by 1979 was down to just fourteen firms (a handful of them distinctly large), compared with a hundred firms less than twenty years earlier.[97] The system had three main problems: shortage of capital, disguised to some extent during the bear markets of the mid-1970s; the difficulties posed by dominant institutional investors all taking the same view at the same time; and the increasing bypassing of the jobbers' services, partly by brokers executing 'put-through' deals, where they effectively acted as the jobbers, and partly by the creation in New York of American Depository Receipts (ADRs) in UK equity shares, thereby making it as easy to trade in, say, ICI shares in New York as it was in London. Perhaps inevitably the jobbers turned defensively in upon themselves. The gilt-edged market had long been more or less a stitch-up between Wedds and Akroyds, while from about 1975 there was an informal jobbers' committee to monitor the so-called price spread agreements in the main equity shares. It was not quite a cartel – the irrepressibly competitive instincts of Smith Brothers prevented that – but it was heading that way. 'Many brokers are against the existence of price spread agreements amongst the jobbers, some very strongly so,' John Robertson, the Stock Exchange's Deputy Chairman, reported in early 1978 after visiting some ninety member firms. 'There is a general feeing that the small investor is being penalised by not being able to find a close price across the market and that this is proving a deterrent to business of the more speculative nature.'[98]

The jobbing system was not the only subject of Robertson's soundings: 'Considerable concern was expressed as to the encroachment of the Office of Fair Trading into our affairs. Almost universally firms are horrified at the thought of negotiating commissions.' Three years earlier, in the 'May Day' revolution of 1975, Wall Street had abandoned its fixed scale of brokers' commissions, but the bloodbath that this had led to encouraged few London brokers to wish to follow suit. Users of the Stock Exchange, especially the big institutional investors, felt particularly aggrieved about the high, inflexible commissions obtaining in gilts, producing (in the context of the explosion of government debt) inordinate, unjustified rewards for the ten or so broking firms favoured by Wedds and Akroyds. 'The gilt brokers should take a lot of blame,' Geoffrey Lederman of Smiths argued with some bitterness a decade later, after everything had changed. 'They had a glory run for several years and were coining it hand over fist and resisted very, very strongly any moves to reduce commissions, and this, I think, got up one or two noses, maybe politically as well.' Or, as M&G's David Hopkinson, a not unsympathetic outsider, would put it at about the same time, the Stock Exchange had 'built their own Pooh trap to fall into in that they were so slow in adjusting their commission scales'.[99]

The Office of Fair Trading (OFT) was starting to loom large over the Capel Court psyche – put to the back of the mind for weeks at a time, but never quite forgotten. In 1976 Roy Hattersley, as Secretary of State for Prices and Consumer Protection, issued the Restrictive Trade Practices (Services) Order, formally extending the Fair Trading Act to the service sector. The following April the Stock Exchange's rule book was registered with the OFT, which under its Director-General Gordon Borrie – like his Stock Exchange counterpart, Goodison, a determined, intelligent, angular figure – spent the next year and a bit considering it. At an early stage Goodison tried to see if he could get a reforming head of steam behind him that might blunt, or head off, the OFT's attentions. 'Clearly we must continue our efforts to cement relations with the users of our markets,' he told the Council in June 1977, reporting on a fact-finding trip to the US, 'but we must also convince both them and Government that we can continue to give them the biggest, fairest, most competitive and least restrictive market possible. The Office of Fair Trading should never have to comment adversely on our practices.' Accordingly, in terms of commissions, 'We appear already to have reached something like US negotiated rates. Do we have anything to fear from unfixing rates, providing we maintain an obligation to establish a price in the central market? Do our customers want us to unfix rates?' Goodison also raised the question of whether the markets should be made more competitive by asking outside houses to set up jobbing firms.[100]

Three months later the Stock Exchange's committee on commissions and dealings responded predictably to Goodison's suggestions, including the unfixing of rates:

> If the experience of America is anything to go by, history would suggest the possibility of the breakdown of the single capacity concept to which we are wed. It would indicate the rise of the bulk dealer and increasing competition between the larger firms at the expense of the smaller . . .
> The Committee believe that a minimum commission scale is the accepted principle in most Stock Exchanges throughout the world and we should fight to maintain it.

As for Goodison's other notion:

> The Committee believe that by inviting outside houses to join the Stock Exchange there is a danger that we will be inviting not only a change in the fabric of its membership, but also a change in the fundamental structure of the Stock Exchange. Their ideas of adhering to the rules will in all probability be different from ours and, insofar as they would join as a jobber with great influence over a huge amount of investment business, there is more than a probability that their views will prevail. The Committee

consider the encroachment of outside Institutions into the Stock Exchange
system as yet another step towards the breakdown of single capacity . . .

That unyielding response ended any chance of an early deal, and in June
1978 Lady Olive Wood, who headed the OFT's team on the case, sent a
circular letter to representatives of the Stock Exchange's main users
itemising seventeen practices enshrined in the rule book that the OFT
regarded as restrictive. Almost half involved single capacity and fixed
minimum rates of commission, while other frowned-upon practices
included so-called 'club rules', by which the Stock Exchange controlled its
membership. 'The Stock Exchange prepares to defend its rule book' was
the *FT*'s headline in October, with a reluctant Stock Exchange due
shortly to get together with the OFT to decide the programme of the
investigation.[101]

However, what was not really on the OFT's agenda was the whole
question of the Stock Exchange's (and therefore the City's) *international*
competitiveness. Nor, it has to be said, was it on the agenda of most
members. 'The majority of Firms did not claim to be deeply involved in
overseas securities,' Robertson's January 1978 report noted. 'The brokers
who are more active in overseas securities, in the main wish to see a
retention of the separation of capacities because they find that it works
quite satisfactorily . . . However, about five Firms would like to see a dual
capacity system in overseas securities because they feel that only in this
way will Member Firms be able to compete effectively with outside houses
and overseas markets.' Presumably it was this handful of firms that had
been disappointed a few years earlier, in 1974–5, when the compromise
solution of creating a type of member called an 'international dealer' –
permitted to operate as both broker and jobber, but only in non-sterling
securities – was abandoned under popular pressure. Not surprisingly,
there was even less enthusiasm for opening up the Stock Exchange as a
marketplace in which anyone could compete. By 1979 there were more
than fifty foreign broking houses in the City (over half of them American),
but none was a member firm of the Stock Exchange; instead, they were
doing business in their own markets that logically should have been done
in London.[102] Of course there were still exchange controls, but the Stock
Exchange's failure to grasp the international nettle owed at least as much
to conservatism, snobbery and fear. The largely sorry tale of options
(traditionally associated with out-and-out speculation, but with the
collapse of Bretton Woods a potentially valuable way of *limiting* risk)
revealed as much.[103]

By spring 1975, following the huge success over the previous two years
of the new Chicago Board Options Exchange, there was a move afoot for
the London Stock Exchange to establish an options exchange for Europe.

That July, however, Dundas Hamilton prefaced a report on the subject by warning that the Bank of England was concerned about possible ramifications:

> There is no doubt that any move by The Stock Exchange which could damage its reputation in the eyes of the present Government, or which could cause a set-back to the improved relations between the Government and the City of London, might well be the spark which caused the formation of a SEC. It seems to the members of the Committee that we must balance the advantages of a European Options Market in London against the possibility of this hastening the establishment of the SEC. In our view, the continuation of self-regulation over our traditional business is more important than securing a European Options Market in London.

Accordingly, the preferred option was 'a joint venture in some other European centre' – in other words, 'if we cannot, for political reasons, have the whole cake in London, let us at least have half overseas'. By the end of the year, with the threat of an SEC lifted, Hamilton's committee was pressing for London to start a bespoke traded options market; and in January 1976 it was told by Goodison that 'he had been able to obtain the approval of the Governor of the Bank of England, subject to the observation that The Stock Exchange must make its own political judgement on the question of whether setting up a traded options exchange might hurt its status'.

Unfortunately, the Stock Exchange could not bring itself to create an options market open to non-members as well as members, even though it recognised that that was the only way such a market could properly succeed; and by the end of 1976 it was in effect decided to sell the pass to Amsterdam, where the European Options Exchange (EOE) was due to open in spring the following year. Once the EOE was up and running, naturally the Stock Exchange rethought the matter, becoming anxious that a cash market for UK securities might grow up in Amsterdam on the back of the options. Eventually this led to the start, in April 1978 amidst strictly muted enthusiasm, of London's own Traded Options Market. Three months earlier Robertson had noted 'considerable apathy amongst the majority' of member firms, adding that 'generally speaking ignorance on this subject is widespread'; now Rowe & Pitman emphasised to its clients 'the apparently unfavourable tax treatment of options for net funds and private clients' and stated that 'the traded options market should only be used by those who fully understand the investment implications of their dealings'. A notable enthusiast for options was the jobber David Steen (of Pinchin Denny), who in November, seven months after opening, reflected that despite the problems concerning tax treatment of traded options, 'some 20 or so brokers contrive to execute a reasonable volume of business'. However, 'The remainder make only occasional use of the Market or are conspicuous by their absence. There is still a great deal of ignorance about the function and use of traded options and, until it is dissipated, it will inevitably engender a lack of confidence in the future viability of the Market.'[104] He did not need to add that London had had the chance to take the lead in options outside the US, but had muffed it.

One of Goodison's initiatives had been to establish a committee of senior partners, and in December 1977 one of its members, Ralph Vickers of Vickers da Costa, sent its Chairman a remarkable – and persuasive – indictment of the Stock Exchange. 'The present system,' he declared bluntly, 'is failing investors, both big and small; it is failing the companies that have, or ought to have, their shares quoted on the Stock Exchange; and it is failing Members . . .' In terms of the domestic market, he argued that it was 'almost incredible, by historical precedents, that a long bull market should produce only a handful of new flotations', and he went on, 'Ariel may have proved to be a paper tiger, but Merrill Lynch and Nomura are man-eaters, and there is plenty of other competition. Ariel may in fact have done The Stock Exchange more harm by failing than it would have done by succeeding, if its failure gives Members the illusory feeling that they are in an impregnable position.' Then, befitting his own history as a pioneer in Japanese securities, Vickers turned to his big theme:

> In international markets the position is worse. It is sad that while the banks, the insurers, the commodity brokers, even the bond dealers, have built up and extended the City's position in recent years, The Stock Exchange has allowed its formerly flourishing business in foreign shares to wither away. The excuses are many but threadbare . . . Each decline in the international business of Members is held to confirm the view that the business was not there in the first place, and therefore that it was correct to decide to do nothing to develop it; meanwhile more and more foreign brokers open offices in London in order to transact this supposedly non-existent business . . . London has a long history as an international stock market, and it still has the skills and contacts to recover the position; it must be given the freedom it needs in order to compete, or it will both deny its own vocation and weaken the City as a whole.

Vickers's solution was twofold: negotiated commissions generally and dual capacity to be permitted in international business. In passing, he noted that Lloyd's, operating dual capacity, 'has since the war been conspicuously better than The Stock Exchange at attracting domestic capital, at expanding international business, and at generating political goodwill'. In sum, he called for an end to 'internecine squabbling' and the Stock Exchange's 'established but discredited policy of allowing itself to be overtaken by events'.[105]

There was an unconscious piquancy in Vickers's comparison between the Stock Exchange and Lloyd's, for that latter institution was about to enter the stormiest, most troubled phase of its long history.[106] The troubles would come as a rude shock to many members of the British upper-middle class who, since the Cromer relaxations of 1969, had flocked to become external members (or Names) of Lloyd's. In 1970 there had been fewer than 5,000 external members, but by 1979 there were almost 14,000. With the market enjoying some excellent years, in particularly stark contrast to the stock market in the mid-1970s, the attractions were obvious; and if they were not, members' agents – engaged in an increasingly systematic recruitment campaign – did not hesitate to point out the tax advantages of becoming a Name. It was subsequently claimed that, in the years immediately after the 1973 Walton Heath golf-course conversation, knowledge about the scale of looming asbestos claims became widespread among Lloyd's insiders and that there was a conscious policy of recruiting as many new Names as possible to help the market meet the threat.[107]

However, the unfavourable headlines that from the late 1970s started to undermine the reputation of Lloyd's were not about asbestos. Instead, there was first an embarrassing row in 1977 as two brokers disputed a claim following a fire on board an Italian ship, the *Savonita*. On one side was a small broking firm, Pearson Webb Springbett, whose Chairman, Malcolm Pearson, awkwardly insisted that the claim was fraudulent; on the other was a much bigger broking outfit, Willis Faber, which warned that the London market would lose much Italian business if the claim was not settled. Questions were raised in the Commons (with Jonathan Aitken championing Pearson), but the eventual inquiry initiated by Lloyd's came down heavily on the side of Willis Faber. Its findings were not made public until December 1978, at which point the press gave Lloyd's a roasting. The *Economist* called the report 'a shoddy document that smacks heavily of kangaroo justice', while according to the *Sunday Telegraph*, 'Lloyd's has succeeded in making itself appear both incompetent and somewhat cowardly'.[108] To compound matters, following the *Savonita* affair, it emerged during the winter of 1978–9 that the 114 unfortunate members of the Sasse syndicate – run by Tim Sasse, a high-profile underwriter – faced losses of well over $20m on fire and computer leasing insurance in North America. Crucially it was becoming clear that these losses owed much to negligent underwriting.

Nevertheless, it was the *Savonita* rather than the Sasse affair that led in early 1979 to the establishment of an inquiry (headed by Sir Henry Fisher, a former High Court judge) into self-regulation in the Lloyd's market. 'Hal' Fisher was very much Gordon Richardson's choice (one lawyer trusting another), and indeed the inquiry itself may have been imposed by Richardson upon a reluctant Lloyd's chairman, Ian Findlay, who apparently found it hard to accept that there had been an erosion of commercial morality. 'I cannot really believe,' he was quoted as saying, 'the time has come when Lloyd's, as a society of underwriters and as an insurance market, needs a governing body equipped with, and ready to use, ever more draconian powers in the maintenance of law and order.' In short, 'if it really came to the point where one expected good faith, honesty and decency to be the exception rather than the rule, then one might well wonder whether it was worth carrying on at all'.[109]

*

'In the UK we now appear to be faced with either an inflationary explosion, or a fiscal and monetary squeeze that will check the inflation that causes severe damage to employment, investment and profits,' began the first Rowe & Pitman *Market Report* of 1979. 'Yet the market soldiers on with quiet insouciance, cheerfully absorbing each apparent body blow as if this onset of industrial civil war was taking place in Ruritania.' Over the next few weeks, as the 'winter of discontent' deepened, the stock market stayed calm, with the FT 30-Share Index never falling below 450. 'Perhaps,' as Rowe & Pitman surmised in January, 'investors are beginning to glimpse in the tribulations of the Labour Government an improvement in Conservative prospects in this Election year.' On 17 January (exactly a week after Callaghan had returned from Guadeloupe saying 'I see no chaos') a veteran City figure, never shy of painting the big picture, spoke to the Institute of Bankers:

> The Welfare State was born and is now foundering. The result of the success of the Keynesian school has been continuous inflation which until quite recently has been regarded as an incurable disease to be restrained by controls and abnormally high rates of interest. The symptoms are unemployment, rising prices, social unrest and demands for higher wages ...
> I can think of only one European country that has real possibilities of growth, and the name may surprise you. It is Great Britain. We are not a poor country but a very wealthy one, and in spite of being misgoverned for 30 years still command authority in all the international service industries. We are the only European industrialised country with surplus coal and oil resources. If we could throw away the stranglehold of the economists' demand management, substitute stable money and extinguish the disease of Socialism, we could become a proud people once more.[110]

Still going strong three years before his death, George Bolton had made his name as a man of the markets – and, unlike many in the City during the Keynesian heyday, had never lost faith in their curative qualities.

The Stock Exchange Council had little immediate interest in those sunlit uplands, for on 9 February, despite Goodison's best efforts and some supportive pressure from the Bank of England, Hattersley formally referred the Stock Exchange's rule book to the Restrictive Practices Court. 'A round table discussion had been expected,' Goodison explained later that month, 'but had not materialised despite repeated requests.' All hopes were now pinned on a change of government. Meanwhile, on Thursday, 22 February the last great City set-piece of the Labour era took place. This was the so-called 'Battle of Watling Street', as brokers, banks and other investors failed, amid scenes of pandemonium at the Bank of England's office there, to lodge applications for heavily oversubscribed new £1.3bn tap stocks. Mark Nickerson of Pinchin Denny, which had only recently started trading in gilts, recalled the episode from a jobber's perspective:

> A number of brokers' messengers failed to get their application forms for a tap into the Bank of England in time because the lifts had broken down. As our messengers had put in our application forms early we were unaware of what had happened, so a quietish morning suddenly became an absolute frenzy. We'd only been going about a year and a half and suddenly we were losing stock everywhere, and this was brokers covering themselves and their clients for having been left out of the auction. Of course the price went up very dramatically and I think we lost about £700,000 that day, without for most of the day realising what on earth had hit us. But we'd applied for a large amount of the stock, so we got everything back next morning – we had over 10 million and it opened at 6 or 7 premium. But it was a very uncomfortable day. There's nothing more disconcerting for a jobber than when the market is going against you and you don't know why – something's happened and you can't really fathom out what set everybody off . . .

Stockbrokers had to pay out compensation to aggrieved clients (mainly institutions) of at least £1m, while the Bank of England was widely criticised for allowing a thoroughly undignified situation in which City messengers, individual investors and others were all in a huge, unruly queue in Watling Street, trying by fair means or foul to get to the reception counters before the shutters came down at 10 a.m. However, there was apparently no question of the Bank of England paying compensation; as Littlewood remarks, 'the character of the City at the time was encapsulated in a comment by "Lex" on 16 March that "in a more litigious country the Bank would no doubt already be facing challenges in the courts"'.[111]

During March, as the feeling grew that Callaghan could not avoid a spring election, the stock market – confident of a Conservative victory – boomed. On the evening of the 28th the government lost a no-confidence vote, and by the end of the next day, when an election was called for 3 May, the Index stood at 540.8. The Tory manifesto, unveiled on 11 April, promised to switch the emphasis from direct to indirect taxation, cut back public expenditure, give an overarching priority to monetary policy and curb the power of the trade unions. 'The one hesitation in the City about the Tory manifesto,' noted Leith McGrandle, City editor of the *Evening Standard*, 'is not that the City doesn't like what it reads or hears but still can't believe that it would be possible to carry it all out. But, as Mrs T. might say, faint hearts never won elections.' He added that the City had 'written off' Callaghan's chances, and for most of the campaign that remained the case. Nevertheless, on Tuesday, 1 May there was a last-minute wobble. 'Anybody's Race? Jim Sniffs Hope' was the *Standard*'s headline, with one new opinion poll giving Labour a 1 per cent lead. The Index closed more than 14 points down, at 537.0, and McGrandle remarked that 'many in the City are astonished at the way the Conservatives have let Labour cast serious doubts on their tax-cutting proposals'. But two days later, on polling day, the mood was once more bullish. 'Shares vote for Maggie!' was now the *Standard*'s headline, as what it called 'a buying bonanza' saw the Index closing on 553.5, its all-time high.[112]

The Tories duly won, with an overall majority of forty-three, and on Friday the 4th the Index rose to a new high of 558.6. Paul Bazalgette, by now senior partner of Phillips & Drew, was carefully apolitical in his post-election contribution to the firm's *Market Review*, although he did have an eye on the aesthetics of the situation: 'Perhaps it is only because I am an ageing connoisseur of mature blondes that I advance the opinion that Prime Minister Margaret is a distinct improvement in female haute couture on the mid-Oriental and far-Oriental ladies who have preceded her to the wicket.' He also hoped that Mrs Thatcher would take the lead in a related matter:

> Heaven knows that recent female fashions, particularly in length of hemline, have been decidedly unacceptable, and it is my hope that all this will now change for the better. Let me remind you that when hemlines rise, so traditionally does the Stock Market. It is not the prime function of this column to tender investment advice, but you may feel inclined on this to get in, or if already in, to stay in.[113]

CHAPTER EIGHTEEN

Whistles of Incredulity

Thatcherism and the City would eventually prove to be a love story (of sorts), but in 1979 itself the City's deep relief that the 'natural party of government' was no longer in government was soon outweighed by the realisation that neither British nor global economic problems had disappeared overnight. From its high of 558.6 when Thatcher took power, the FT 30-Share Index dropped to 473.4 by the end of June and then for several months drifted rather aimlessly. For much of that time MLR was at a discouraging 14 per cent; during the summer there came the second oil shock as OPEC raised oil prices by an average of 15 per cent (though Britain itself was increasingly well cushioned by North Sea oil); and in October there was the first indication that zealous monetarism would lead to a deep manufacturing recession as Singer, maker of the renowned sewing machines, announced the closure of its Clydebank plant, with the loss of 3,000 jobs. There were also mixed feelings about Sir Geoffrey Howe's first budget, delivered on 12 June. Standard rate of tax down 3 per cent to 30 per cent, top rate down from 83 per cent to 60 per cent, public expenditure cut, dividend controls to end – all this was, broadly speaking, music to the City's ears, but there was also scepticism about whether Thatcherite economics could really reverse the economy's long-term decline. 'The new Government has embarked upon a high-risk economic strategy in an attempt to reverse this decline,' argued Phillips & Drew's influential economist, Paul Neild, in his budget commentary. 'We hope it succeeds. However, accelerating prices combined with a deteriorating world background are likely to seriously undermine, if not totally engulf, policies aimed at maintaining firm monetary control through either a transfer of resources from the public to the private sector or a shift in the burden of taxation from direct to indirect.' In short, 'experience suggests that the ability of the Government to dictate events is at the longest short-lived'.

So at the time it seemed, and so indeed in a sense it was. Yet in retrospect it has become ever clearer that, for good or ill, 1979 was *the* watershed. An encounter that summer, as related by David Thomas, could hardly have been more emblematic:

Pip Greenwell became more and more restless as his chauffeur inched his way through the traffic. They had left the City behind and swept through what seemed to Greenwell's monied eye the wastelands of Hackney. Yet as they pushed further north out of the centre of London, they had suddenly ploughed into a dense line of cars.

Greenwell was on his way to meet a man called Alan Sugar, who was thinking of selling some shares in his audio company, Amstrad. It was not likely to be the largest business deal ever handled by the senior partner of W. Greenwell, one of the City's most prosperous stockbrokers. But Greenwell, a product of Winchester, was a gentleman of the old school. He was punctual to a fault and, at this rate, he reckoned they would never reach Tottenham on time. He told his chauffeur to get a move on.

The stockbroker was much relieved when the car finally turned into the road housing Amstrad's headquarters, even though the sight which greeted him was not one to lift the spirit. Squashed between a railway line and a patch of derelict ground, Garman Road was completely made over to nondescript medium-sized factories and warehouses. Their proprietors were clearly too busy to worry about a lick of paint or any other decoration.

Matters did not improve when Greenwell was ushered through a hallway strewn with cardboard boxes into Alan Sugar's presence. At 32, Sugar seemed too young to be running a company which was thinking of going public. As if to underline his youth, the Amstrad chairman had parked the knot of his tie a couple of inches below the unbuttoned collar of his shirt. He was sporting a stubbly beard at a time when a clean-shaven face was part of the City's uniform.

This stocky, bearded youth appeared none too welcoming, as he stood there tense and with a scowl on his face. Greenwell wondered whether Sugar shared his distaste for being late, and thought it politic to ask forgiveness for this sin. 'I'm so terribly sorry we're late, but the fucking traffic was awful.'

The swear-word sounded odd when uttered in Greenwell's cultured voice. There was a moment of silence as it hung in the air between the stockbroker and the entrepreneur. Then the tension flowed out of Sugar's body and he broke into a grin. 'Thank God someone in the City speaks my sort of language,' he said as he stepped forward to shake Greenwell's hand.[1]

*

Stanley Ross, definitely born on Sugar's side of the tracks, had left Kidder Peabody Securities in early 1978 and later that year started his own operation, Ross & Partners, in the Eurobond secondary market. The following spring there was the first sighting of the distinctly Thatcherite development with which his name would always be associated.[2] 'Bond dealers have been detecting a significant growth in the practice known as "grey market dealing", where a market occurs in a new issue before the final price has been fixed,' *International Insider* noted in March 1979. 'Most dealers believe this kind of trading is healthy, but it is causing growing bitterness in some issuing houses. Attempts have been made to bring pressure to bear to prevent it, on the ground that it makes the job of an issue manager more difficult.' Amid 'suggestions that lead managers are having to allow for discounts equal to part or all of selling group concessions when they price their issues', the magazine quoted an unnamed dealer, quite possibly Ross: 'It is not the dealer who quotes a price who is to blame. The market will always price in accordance with supply and demand.' By early May the word was that the Association of International Bond Dealers (AIBD), under Yassukovich's chairmanship, wanted to kill off the grey market, on the grounds that it violated normal commercial trading practice. Interviewed soon afterwards, Ross was asked if he accepted that an active pre-market made dealings between underwriters and their clients more difficult:

> One can indeed understand the chagrin of the syndicate members whose clients can now see on the world's television screens the real prices at which bonds change hands in the first few days of the life of an issue. For many years there has been a problem of discontinuity of prices between the primary market and the secondary. All we seek to do is to iron out the credibility gap between suggested terms and the real world of the trading price.

Quite simply, Ross wanted the AIBD to 'recognise the potency of the market forces at work'. When it met in London at the end of the month he carried the day, with the board's proposed veto of the grey market being unceremoniously thrown out. A few weeks later CSFB's von Clemm exacted some revenge when a Credit Suisse $100m convertible allowed him to apply a bear squeeze on the grey market; but it was not long before Ross's innovation had become a healthy, permanent part of Eurobond life. 'We made the managers realise,' he recalled five years later, 'that if issues weren't realistically priced, they wouldn't be able to get away with it on the old-boy network, on the basis of "You support my issue, old chap, and I'll support yours next time" . . .' Even von Clemm came to acknowledge that Ross had done more than anyone to increase the efficiency of the Eurobond market. And Ross himself had a last word: 'I changed the way the new-issue market functions. Nobody loves me for that. But I don't really look for love and affection. I only look to make a turn.'[3]

During the last summer and autumn of the 1970s, there were other pointers suggesting that the 1980s would be a very different decade. At the International Monetary Conference in London that June, Citibank's Walter Wriston spoke invigoratingly of the irresistible rise of the world's financial markets and saw no reason why that rise should be halted:

> National borders are no longer defensible against the invasion of knowledge, ideas or financial data. The Eurocurrency markets are a perfect example. No one designed them, no one authorised them, and no one controlled them. They were fathered by controls, raised by technology and today they are refugees, if you will, from national attempts to allocate credit

and capital for reasons which have little or nothing to do with finance and economics . . .

It was not just physical boundaries that were poised to lose their relevance, but also boundaries within the financial sector. There was a clear harbinger in September, when a DM60m issue by Roylease, a subsidiary of the Royal Bank of Canada, was the first bond issue to be directly linked to a currency swap – a trail-blazer for future currency swaps and in effect a marriage of the foreign exchange and capital markets. The deal was structured by Philip Hubbard of Orion Bank, where only a few weeks later David Montagu's enforced resignation proved to be the signal sending the consortium banking movement into steep decline, as the individual shareholders sought to pursue their own ambitions. One of Orion's shareholders was NatWest, whose Chairman Robin Leigh-Pemberton reputedly insisted that Montagu's successor, an American banker called Jefferson Cunningham III, could not keep Montagu's Rolls-Royce; according to one of the participants in the drama, he did not mind a British chairman of Orion being driven around in one, but he did draw the line at an American.[4]

Breaking down the guild system was also implicitly on the agenda, with serious consideration by this time about starting London's own financial futures market. The Bank of England's Pen Kent, in a not ill-disposed exploratory survey in September, envisaged 'a physical dealing ring where the commodity and banking community would be prepared to mix their cultures', though he was unsure whether in practice that could be achieved. Kent's main concern was regulatory, but there was also the larger, commercial question of how great the demand would be for financial futures (or derivatives, as they would become called). John Barkshire, fresh from the successful flotation of Mercantile House during the summer, presented a study of 'Financial Futures' to the Mercantile board at the start of October in which he predicted that, within a few years, they would be achieving a higher turnover than that in the cash markets:

> The principal reason for this is that futures enable investment managers in banks, financial institutions and industry to hedge, or reduce, their exposure in the markets. In the 1960s and early 1970s the desire of investment managers was to maximise their profit and many did this successfully but the last decade has seen a dramatic increase in the volatility of the money markets and attendant rates and this has resulted in some spectacular losses, often by corporations whose main business did not lie in the securities industry. It was assumed that provided research was done thoroughly it was possible to forecast the future with reasonable accuracy and make investment decisions based on a long-term view: events have proved this to be incorrect and costly. Investment managers are therefore looking for ways of minimising risks . . .

An uncertain world became even more uncertain five days later, with the so-called 'Saturday Night Massacre' of 6 October, as the Fed announced that in order to curb inflation and bolster the dollar it would henceforth focus on the growth of the money supply rather than short-term interest rates – in effect, letting the market decide where interest rates went. The immediate upshot was a collapse in stock and bond prices, given added resonance by the realisation that Salomons, one of the lead underwriters in a recently flopped IBM issue, had managed to offset its heavy losses from unloading that issue by hedging in the Chicago financial futures market.[5] It was a signal lesson to investors, in the UK as elsewhere, and – some six years after the conclusive breaking-up of Bretton Woods – the importance of hedging, in the face of potentially devastating interest rate risk, started to be more widely appreciated.

For the City specifically, the day for the history books was Tuesday, 23 October 1979. The Trade Secretary, John Nott, told MPs that he did not intend to stop the referral of the Stock Exchange's rule book to the Restrictive Practices Court. This was, an aggrieved Goodison immediately claimed, a 'purely political' decision – and in that a newly elected Tory government did not wish to be seen bending over backwards to help its friends in the City, this was no doubt true. More importantly, though, Thatcher and her like-minded ministers (including Nott) saw vested City interests like the Stock Exchange as part of the British problem, not its solution, and positively relished the opportunity to shake them up.[6] That same day another parliamentary announcement was even more momentous in its implications.[7] 'Cheers and whistles of incredulity', according to one parliamentary report, greeted Howe's succinct statement abolishing UK exchange controls. There was no less incredulity outside Westminster. 'The City could hardly believe it,' the 'Lex' column began next day. 'After 40 years – longer than the working lifetimes of most people in banking and the stock market – exchange controls have gone.' One wisely anonymous clearing banker entered City folklore. 'I am sure we have planned for this,' he sought to reassure the public, 'but I have yet to find the man who did it.' The bewilderment was understandable, for few – including even at the Bank of England – had expected such a fundamental move so soon after the election. As usual Tony Benn took the intellectual high ground. 'International capitalism,' he recorded in his diary, 'has defeated democracy.'[8] It is not yet clear that he was wrong.

CHAPTER NINETEEN

A High-handed Deal

'Thank you so much for your resolute support for the Government's policies,' Margaret Thatcher's Parliamentary Private Secretary, Ian Gow, wrote in October 1980 to the Chairman of the Stock Exchange, Nicholas Goodison. He added that he was showing the text of Goodison's recent Mansion House speech to the Prime Minister, who had herself earlier in the month declared that the lady was not for turning. Shortly before Christmas, with recession deepening every day and the clamour growing for a 'U-turn', Siegmund Warburg wrote to Peter Spira (who was no longer at Warburgs):

> I have often felt in the course of this year a temptation to speak out publicly in favour of the courageous and positive elements in the policy of the Thatcher Government. Moreover I am shocked by the completely negative and destructive comments which emanate from various leading people in the City and in British industry who, instead of giving every possible help and backing to the Government, indulge in almost treacherous criticism rather than putting forward constructive suggestions . . .
>
> I am convinced that Mrs Thatcher has shown outstanding valour and fortitude in making it clear that after successive Conservative and Labour governments had encouraged the country to live far beyond its means this reckless course of self-indulgence is long overdue for a radical change. I think in starting this new chapter in Britain's post-war history that the Government has done great things in the fiscal and taxation field as well as in several other parts of the economic scene . . .[1]

Warburg's letter raises the larger question of whether City sentiment as a whole was supportive of Thatcherite economics during these early, highly controversial years of the Thatcher era. Broadly, as far as one can tell, it was – though no doubt at times for want of any plausible alternative. In retrospect, it was Howe's obstinate, unrelenting budget of March 1981 – raising the tax burden in the middle of a recession – that made it definitively clear that there would be no going back to the Keynesian economics of demand management. 'The strategy's last chance' was the title of the *FT*'s leader, declaring that 'praise is due for the courage to be "deflationary" at such a time, and by such unpopular means'. Within a week or two of the budget, no fewer than 364 academic economists had signed a letter arguing that 'there is no basis in economic theory or supporting evidence for the Government's belief that by deflating demand they will bring inflation permanently under control', that 'present policies will deepen the depression, erode the industrial base of our economy and threaten its social and political stability' and that 'the time has come to reject monetarist policies'. Market man's response to the 364 was encapsulated by Bazalgette's next contribution to Phillips & Drew's *Market Review*:

> I can't quite put my finger on it, but somehow they don't seem to have brought off whatever it was they were trying to achieve. Rather like the Charge of the Light Brigade, they meant well but have ended up as slightly humorous subjects. They formed up in their cloistered courts, mounted on a motley collection of nags, clutching a variety of largely obsolete weapons, blunderbusses, spears and lances, and then weren't quite sure where they were going. At least that's the impression they leave on me. One fancies that they will be visited with winks and nudges when they appear at academic sherry parties for some time to come. Devotees of other disciplines than their own will greet them with kindly smiles, designed to put them at their ease, but nevertheless indicating that they have been caught out in some foolish prank.
>
> Let us wave them farewell, poor fellows, with a song I would like to convert for their use. I haven't had time to compose the verses yet, but let us give them a rousing rendering of the chorus,

'. . . wi' Tom Balogh, Nicky Kaldor, Robert Neild,
Bryan Hopkin, Alec Cairncross, Frankie Hahn,
Old Uncle Wynne Godley and all –
Old Uncle Wynne Godley and all.'[2]

Joblessness, of course, was something that happened elsewhere: nine months later, in January 1982, unemployment reached three million, more than double what it had been when Thatcher came to power. In April 1982, however, inflation at last came down to single figures; that summer there were some real signs of economic recovery, as well as feats of derring-do in distant islands; in August there began in Wall Street what would be the greatest bull market of the century; and two months later the Index (414.2 at the end of 1979, 474.5 at the end of 1980, 530.4 at the end of 1981) at last crossed 600, a long fourteen years after reaching 500. Inflation, the all-pervasive phenomenon of those years, now seemed a monster slain, and in May 1983 the Index went through 700, partly on the back of justified confidence in a Tory election win the following month. In fact, the Index itself was so industry-based that it had become a somewhat blunt recorder of market mood, and a truer reflection of the new bullishness was the All Share Index, which on polling day, 9 June, stood at 442.8, up 58 per cent (compared with the ever less adequate 30-Share Index's 29.4 per cent) on 3 May 1979.[3]

Viewpoint, at this most polarised of moments in post-war British politics and society, was all. 'The bewilderment of the proverbial Birmingham manufacturer at the behaviour of the London stock market is a well-documented social phenomenon,' observed 'Lex' in April. James D'Albiac, in his first *Market Report* for Rowe & Pitman after Thatcher's landslide victory, almost admitted as much: 'It is a time when the "good news" that might appeal to headline writers in the popular press – "booming Britain! Surge in output brings hope to the unemployed" – would be bad news for our bull market.' It was a bull market, he believed, that still had a long way to run. 'Thatcherism, of one sort or another, appears,' he declared, 'to be the dominant economic philosophy in the world today: the British people have just re-elected a Government which is likely to pursue with the greatest vigour the logic of that philosophy.'[4] For almost everyone in the City, it was a prospect that pleased.

*

Had Warburg had the Governor of the Bank of England in mind as one of those 'treacherous' critics in December 1980? Certainly, government/Bank relations in the early 1980s were as bad as at any time since the days of Cromer, and this time round Labour was not even in power.[5] Howe subsequently wrote how he had come 'to rely a good deal' on Gordon Richardson's 'impressively measured wisdom', but there would be no such encomium in Thatcher's memoirs. Those privileged to watch the two of them in uncomfortable action together – the 'canine' politician, the 'feline' central banker – were struck by the hopelessness of the personal chemistry, at least after the initial, quasi-honeymoon phase. She found him patronising and vain, as well as frustratingly unwilling to take a strong, readily comprehensible line, quite apart from his being tainted as a survivor of the old corporatist order; he found her strident, impatient and almost wholly unwilling to accept that practicalities, not ideology, should determine the workings of monetary policy. Thatcher's instinctive prejudice against the received wisdom of Richardson and the Bank was fully shared by the financially very literate Nigel Lawson, Financial Secretary to the Treasury until September 1981. It was he who did much to create, by spring 1980, the Medium Term Financial Strategy as the centrepiece of macro-economic policy, including by far the most specific targets yet for monetary growth; according to Lawson, he did so against the 'deep-seated' opposition of the Bank, which 'wanted to retain complete and unfettered discretion over monetary policy'.[6]

As it happened, money supply appeared to go almost completely out of control during the summer, largely as a result of the enforced abandonment (following the abolition of exchange controls) of the so-called 'Corset' that restricted bank lending. Thatcher, however, personally blamed the Bank, and during a memorably stormy meeting in early September upbraided John Fforde and Eddie George, in the unfortunate absence of both Richardson and his deputy Kit McMahon (the latter still an unrepentant Keynesian). Richardson himself was much concerned about the damage that extraordinarily high interest rates were doing to British industry – with him and Benson continuing to act as 'honest brokers' to keep sound businesses afloat – and in November the Bank did win one battle by helping to engineer a 2 per cent reduction in MLR, to 14 per cent. But Thatcher, according to Middlemas's account, 'neither accepted the reasoning nor forgave the author [i.e. Richardson] and called the Bank "lender of first resort"'; again according to Middlemas, she ensured that the Bank's 'subsequent political occlusion' lasted for most of the rest of the decade. Such a reading perhaps exaggerates the degree to which the Bank was out of the loop during the 1980s, but it was striking that prior to Howe's epochal March 1981 budget, and contrary to custom, no formal advice was tendered by the Governor as to what its contents should be – an omission for which Howe was apparently not offered an explanation.[7]

Two aspects of that budget had a specific City interest. One was the introduction of index-linked gilts, still as strongly opposed by Richardson as they had been during the Callaghan government. He regarded them, in Lawson's words, 'as redolent of a banana republic and not far short of the end of civilisation as we knew it'. Others in the Bank and the gilt-edged market shared that attitude, but elsewhere in the City the push for a more flexible approach to government funding was led by David Scholey, who in tandem with Fredy Fisher (a former *FT* editor, now at Warburgs) drafted a succinct, one-page note that did much to assuage Thatcher's instinctive qualms about seeming to sanction inflation itself. The other aspect (popular or notorious according to taste) was Howe's 'one-off' £400m levy on the clearing banks. This 'windfall tax', as it was called, had as its justification their massive profits made on the back of high interest rates – profits all the more unpalatable to public opinion in the prevailing deep recession. The Chairman of the Committee of London Clearing Bankers, Jeremy Morse of Lloyds, was offered a choice between such a tax or the banks agreeing to finance part of the government's long-standing fixed-rate export credit scheme; he chose the former as the lesser evil, apparently without consulting his fellow-chairmen, who might have plumped differently. Either way there would have been bruised feelings. 'It was a direct attack,' one banker recalled. 'I remember we felt very hardly about it. We weren't absolutely sure of the reason, except a certain animus, I think, against the banks.' He was correct. It was not just that the Thatcher government had particular grievances against the banks – the provocative profits, the substantial wage rises, the failure to restrain lending after the Corset's removal – but also that they were viewed by the Prime Minister and those who thought like her as overfed, slow-moving relics of the now discredited paternalist consensus. The February after the levy, she dined at 54 Lombard Street, home of Barclays. 'She brushed aside small talk,' Deryk Vander Weyer's son wrote, 'and harangued the assembled company in the style to which the nation had by then become accustomed. The Barclays men present found her view of their business – and the need for it to play a more dynamic role in the economy – unfounded in any significant understanding of banking priorities. My father, nevertheless, found the experience "sexy" – I recall that he admired her figure . . .'[8]

Curiously, it was a clearing banker who – for the first time – was chosen to succeed Richardson as Governor after the expiry of his second term in June 1983.[9] Richardson himself, now in his mid-sixties, would have been happy to go on, but that was never a realistic possibility. Nor was the candidature of his deputy, Kit McMahon. In the City there was some talk of Scholey, but the most favoured runner was Morse – a classic banker in the Wykehamist mould, with much international experience, but seldom a man hot for certainties, not least in the field of monetary policy. The entirely non-City candidate was Philip Haddon Cave, the Financial Secretary of the Hong Kong administration, though as so often in this ritual dance it is impossible to know how serious a possibility he was. The name finally announced just before Christmas 1982 came as a complete surprise to almost everyone, whether inside or outside the City. It was NatWest's Chairman, Robin Leigh-Pemberton, as much a Kentish country gentleman as a professional banker. 'The failure to choose a successor with greater experience and standing both in international and domestic banking circles is a cause for concern,' the *FT* observed in a typically understated way, and right from the start the Governor-Elect was widely viewed – fairly or unfairly – as little more than Thatcher's puppet.[10] As so often during this Manichaean decade, she was taking her revenge, this time on the Old Lady.

She may also have been irked by a perceived reluctance on the Bank's part to get fully behind the early, pioneering phase of privatisation – so important in defining her government's character.[11] The process began in February 1981 with the £150m offer for sale of British Aerospace, a flotation managed by Kleinwort Benson in conjunction with an apprehensive Bank of England. Nor were all Kleinworts' co-underwriters much more bullish, with Schroders and Morgan Grenfell, for example, being reluctant participants, with little or no faith in privatisation as such. The issue, however, was three and a half times oversubscribed, and that autumn Kleinworts was again to the fore in the £224m privatisation of Cable and Wireless. The government had recently had to postpone its plans to privatise British Airways and much hinged on this Cable and Wireless issue, which was then a record for the size of the offer of shares in a previously unlisted company. The equity market at the time was thin and jobbers generally nervous, but the outcome was wholly gratifying to those concerned. 'Rush for Cable & Wireless Shares' was the *FT*'s headline at the end of October, and it quoted a harassed official at NatWest (receiving bankers to the sale): 'Some people can't read instructions. We've got cheques here attached to forms with matches, hairpins and industrial staples. We asked for pins.'[12] Popular capitalism, it seemed, was starting to return to the City scene.

The following year saw a piquantly contrasting pair of issues. In February 1982 the government sold Amersham International, a subsidiary of the United Kingdom Atomic Energy Authority. Rothschilds advised the government, Morgan Grenfell advised the company and Cazenove's was sole broker to the offer. In advance of the prospectus, 'Lex' stressed how tricky it would be to price: 'The problem is that there is a limit to the rating at which an issue can be underwritten, but there is no telling how the market will value a share like this. However glamorous Amersham's activities in diagnostic products, research chemicals and radiation sources may be, the profit record is not especially exciting.' In the event, the fifty million ordinary shares were offered at 142p each – subsequently viewed (including by Lawson) as a case of serious underpricing. 'This has all the making of a lively issue,' was how 'Lex' laconically put it. He was certainly right: the issue was oversubscribed 23.6 times and, amidst the scrimmage on the Stock Exchange floor, the shares opened at a premium of 48p. It was a field day for the stags and the Labour opposition called the sale 'a scandal'. Richard Lambert in the *FT* offered a judicious retrospective. After noting that the financial advisers had distanced themselves from the government's clearly mistaken decision to make an offer for sale rather than a tender, apparently reached on the grounds that a tender would have disadvantaged the small investors, he went on: 'What the bankers badly underestimated [i.e. in terms of the pricing] was the current rage in the stock market for anything with a technological tag. Stockbrokers who would not know a radioisotope if one landed on their nose started to talk knowledgeably about Amersham's glittering prospects. The Amersham bandwagon began to roll . . .' Justifiably observing that the issue had 'left a lot of red faces in its trail', Lambert looked ahead with some misgivings to the next privatisation offering, the oil exploration and production interests of the British National Oil Corporation, due in the autumn: 'It would be a terrible irony if as a reaction to Amersham, the Government insisted on a tender offer for Britoil – and then had a flop on its hands.'[13]

The Britoil issue duly took place in November, with Warburgs and Rothschilds as financial advisers. It was indeed (as Lawson insisted, overriding the objections of Rothschilds) a tender offer – the biggest ever made in the UK, being a tender of 51 per cent of Britoil shares (with a minimum tender price of 215p) that would raise at least £548m. The tender option was correctly seen as an attempt by government to prevent stagging and, even more importantly, not to be accused of underpricing a national asset. 'Lex' expressed the view of the square mile: 'The exercise is being conducted at a price and on terms which will stretch the goodwill between Whitehall and the City. The prospectus groans with devices designed to prevent unscrupulous investors from making a fast buck.' But, after noting that 'the full muscle' of the City had been applied in order to get the issue underwritten – and thereby showing that the underwriting system worked – he added, 'There is virtually no danger that Britoil will flop.' The following week was selling week, and by then the equity market had the jitters and, thanks to Sheikh Yamani, the prospects for the oil price were fading. The result was an almost entirely negative reaction on the part of the institutions, which made it plain that they disliked tender offers; the shares opened at a 20 per cent discount; and the sub-underwriters were left with 73 per cent. Inevitably an inquest followed. 'In opting for a tender method the government ignored the views of its City advisers,' declared 'Lex'; the *FT* itself summed up the whole sorry year by wistfully remarking that 'if history could be rewritten, it would have been the Amersham issue which would have been mounted on a tender basis rather than Britoil'.[14] The City did not quite feel pawns in a larger game, but there were certain shades of 1953 and steel denationalisation. Relatively few people, moreover, had yet grasped privatisation's potential, not least as a goldmine for the City itself.

*

Some things, it seemed, never changed. Royal Insurance had developed an empty site at 1 Cornhill into a prestigious banking hall and was looking by 1980 to let it to a tenant. The only serious offer came from Bank of Credit and Commerce International (BCCI), a rapidly growing concern, mainly servicing Muslim and Third World clients, registered in Luxembourg but with London as its international operating headquarters. Just across the road, the Bank of England heard what was afoot and told Royal's Chairman, Daniel Meinertzhagen, that the new tenants were unacceptable. Royal, accordingly, decided to convert the site into its own head office.[15]

Even so, BCCI was still free to pursue its nefarious activities; and as Peter Cooke, head of banking supervision at the Bank of England, frankly conceded, the explosion of international banking over the previous two decades conclusively meant that 'this is no longer a cozy club in a village called the City of London where everyone knows each other'. He was speaking in the light of the fundamental changes introduced in October 1979: the implementation of the Banking Act, which for the first time put the Bank's supervision within a statutory framework, and the abolition of exchange controls, which inevitably reduced its flexibility and informal authority. Cooke himself still hoped to get the best of both worlds. 'When we judge the reputation and standing of an institution relative to giving it our "seal of Good Housekeeping", we like to think we have the opportunity to get the views of those within the marketplace to help us make a decision,' he told *Institutional Investor* in March 1980. 'And a banker who doesn't play according to the market's rules – which are essentially our own – will lose, because the market will reject him.' The magazine also quoted a London-based French banker, still apparently happy to play by the old rules: 'If the Governor invites you to tea and casually mentions that he thinks credits to the textile industry are rather high, you rush home and cut your credits to the textile industry.'[16]

Certainly, even after the Banking Act, Richardson remained not averse to raising his eyebrows. The classic episode concerned the fruitless struggle for control over the Royal Bank of Scotland (RBS).[17] In March 1981, with Richardson's blessing, Standard Chartered (the not terribly dynamic London-based overseas bank) made a £334m bid for RBS (including the English branches of Williams & Glyn's). It soon emerged that Standard Chartered's great rival, the Hongkong and Shanghai Banking Corporation (HSBC), was not willing to let this pass without a contest, and its aggressive Chairman, Michael Sandberg, pitched up in London to tell Richardson of his intention to make the Royal Bank into his own bank's 'flagship in Europe'. The style of the two men was chalk and cheese, and Richardson informed him that any counter-bid would be 'unwelcome'. Sandberg was neither abashed nor deterred, and on 6 April HSBC announced a £498m bid. The Bank of England, not informed in advance, let it be known that it 'strongly disapproved'. Standard Chartered then raised its own offer, and at the start of May both bids were referred by government to the Monopolies Commission. Over the ensuing months Richardson waged a relentless campaign to ensure that Sandberg did not get his way. HSBC's willingness 'to go ahead with the bid in face of opposition from the Governor of the Bank suggested that the HSBC would not always be prepared to accept the Bank's customary authority and therefore would not necessarily provide the kind of cooperation the Bank expected from clearing banks' was how the Commission's eventual report summarised his arguments. 'If the Bank's authority was not fully accepted by the clearing banks, other more dirigiste, less flexible, and in the Bank's view less effective methods of dealing with the banking community would have to be introduced and the existing, well-tried and well-respected system would be compromised.'[18] As it happened, largely for quite different reasons, at the start of 1982 the Commission rejected both bids. For Richardson it was half a triumph, but no more than half.

In the wider field of investor protection, external faith in traditional methods of self-regulation was eroding quite rapidly, as the City was beset by a series of minor, but cumulatively important, scandals. In January 1980 the Stock Exchange took action (expulsion of one partner, with three others suspended) against the private client broking firm Hedderwick, Stirling, Grumbar & Co, where there had been systematic fraud in the gilts department. The punishments were announced on 5 February, and a week later, Tuesday the 12th, the Stock Exchange was again in the spotlight as Rowe & Pitman, on behalf of De Beers, executed a bold, highly controversial 'dawn raid', buying 16.5 million Consolidated Goldfields shares by 9.55 a.m. It was neither the first nor the last dawn raid, but there was much press criticism that not all shareholders were being treated equally. 'We are not doing anything unfair,' Rowe & Pitman's Alan Hurst-Brown insisted. 'We are dealing in the market place, and shareholders should be prepared to accept the rigours of the market. Aunty Fanny would not lose out if she did the sensible thing and gave her stockbroker discretion . . .'[19] Not long afterwards, in June 1980, there was perhaps some consolation for that mythical lady when – at long last – insider dealing became a criminal offence, though few were holding their breath that any such criminals would be put behind bars.

There were also at this time various scandals in the lightly regulated field of commodity dealing (described by a judge as 'a jungle suitable for hunting for large and experienced animals but one in which a small animal is at very serious risk' – in short, 'a most perilous state of affairs which merits attention by Parliament'); while in July 1981 the Manchester stockbroking firm Halliday Simpson wound itself up, with its share deals being investigated by the Stock Exchange. That particular scandal, involving irregular book-keeping, directly impinged upon a well-known City figure, Sir Trevor Dawson, popularly known as the 'galloping major'. After Harrow and the Army, he had gone in the mid-1960s to the merchant bank Arbuthnot Latham as a fund manager, and was now aged fifty, held some thirty directorships and was popular in racing and shooting circles. He was, however, suspected of having benefited improperly from a connection with Halliday Simpson, and in September 1981 he resigned from Arbuthnots. The following year the Stock Exchange's inquiry into the Manchester firm confirmed his apparent guilt, and in March 1983 he drank a glass of champagne in his Eaton Square flat before suffocating himself in a blue plastic bag. The deed was done just before midnight on the 14th, when one of the four policies on his life was due to expire. 'I have got no other choice,' he wrote to his estranged wife, 'if you and Michael [their 26-year-old spastic son] are to have any freedom.' Happily, all things considered, the insurers paid up.[20]

It was in the same month as the Halliday Simpson scandal broke that the Trade Secretary, John Biffen, asked Professor Jim Gower, author of *The Principles of Modern Company Law*, to undertake an inquiry into investor protection. Although in his late sixties, and a stranger to the City and its inhabitants, Gower accepted the commission and set about his task with huge energy. As early as October 1981 Goodison was telling Biffen that the Stock Exchange was 'apprehensive that the Gower Review was taking a wider brief than was originally intended and was developing into yet another statutory investigation of the Stock Exchange'. Three months later Gower published a discussion document, *Review of Investor Protection*, in which he castigated the shortcomings of the City's existing system of regulation in terms of 'complication, uncertainty, irrationality, failure to treat like alike, inflexibility, excessive control in some areas and too little (or none) in others, the creation of an élite and a fringe, lax enforcement, delays, overconcentration on honesty rather than competence, undue diversity of regulations and regulators, and failure to achieve a proper balance between Governmental regulation and self-regulation'.[21] It was quite a charge-sheet. The eventual Gower report was still some way off, but it was already clear that City regulation – or, more precisely, self-regulation – would never be the same again after this tough-minded one-man commission.

Few people were more committed to the tradition of self-regulation than the combative Peter Green, Chairman of Lloyd's from January 1980. He conceded, though, that the old disciplines were no longer so easy to enforce. 'If something was going on, it used to be sufficient for the chairman to say, "Look here, this has got to stop," and the chap would stand, cap in hand, and do as he was told,' he observed soon after taking office. 'Today if a headmaster tells a schoolboy to do something, he'll turn around and ask, "Why should I?" It's a little bit like that here.' Green was not, however, unduly concerned about the recent rash of scandals that had afflicted Lloyd's. The increasingly publicised question of conflict of interest between brokers and underwriters brought forth the assertion at one press conference that 'you don't have to practise incest even if you live with your mother and she's the only other person there'; at another press conference he even expostulated that he could not understand why reporters were so interested every time 'somebody at Lloyd's sneezes or picks his nose'.[22] In May 1980 the Fisher report was submitted. In effect it backed continuing self-regulation, calling for a new Lloyd's Act that would give enhanced disciplinary powers to a newly created governing Council, the majority of whose members would be internal. It also recommended that, on the grounds of inherent conflicts of interest, brokers should be compelled into divestment of their underwriting syndicates (also known as managing agencies). It was not a recommendation that enthused Green, but he publicly conceded that there was no alternative.

Over the next two years, as the Fisher report was transformed into the new Lloyd's Act, much went on at Lloyd's itself, usually behind closed doors.[23] There was, for one thing, the Christopher Moran saga. An aggressive, self-made broker, with a penchant for the high life, he had made his fortune while still young by successfully floating his own broking concern. In 1980, having been criticised in the *Daily Telegraph* over his involvement in a chain of complex reinsurance deals, he took the paper to court but lost the libel action; late in 1981, however, he was acquitted at the Old Bailey of insurance fraud. That verdict did not satisfy the authorities at Lloyd's, where he was found guilty of discreditable conduct in relation to a syndicate that he controlled, leading to his expulsion in October 1982. It seems to have been in early 1981 that Moran spilled the beans to Green about the Oakeley Vaughan members' agency, whose Chairman was the extrovert Charles St George – a familiar figure on the racecourse, but never pretending to know much about insurance – and whose syndicates included such Names as Lester Piggott and Henry Cooper. It transpired that Oakeley Vaughan was guilty of massive, dangerous overwriting. In September 1981 three directors were suspended for two years; St George received no more than a private reprimand, after persuading Green that no notice should posted in the Room; and it was not until 1988, when overtrading forced Oakeley Vaughan into liquidation, that its financially suffering Names began to learn the truth.[24]

That theme of belated knowledge applied in spades to anyone outside the market who was involved, wittingly or otherwise, in asbestos. In two distinct ways the first half of 1982 was the key. First, it is claimed, Green successfully persuaded his Committee not to divulge to anyone the findings of a recent, secret Bank of England inquiry into Lloyd's. According to someone who saw the relevant letter from the Bank to Green, summarising the inquiry's findings, it 'warned of enormous losses, resulting from asbestos claims which were about to engulf the Lloyd's market and of the disastrous effect they could have, not only on Lloyd's itself, but on those banks who had provided Lloyd's guarantees or lent money to Lloyd's syndicates'. Second, it is also claimed, Green equally successfully masterminded a cover-up of Lloyd's books in order to ensure that Parliament did not get wind of the rapidly gathering asbestos crisis *before* it passed the Lloyd's bill giving it immunity from civil suit. 'Why should a body that has been negligent be protected from its own negligence?' one Tory lawyer pertinently asked the Commons during a debate on the bill. Ironically, and perhaps influenced by the trade union analogy, the view from the opposition benches, as expressed by Michael Meacher, was that to withhold immunity 'would expose the Corporation of Lloyd's in a manner which would severely restrict the effectiveness of its supervisory and regulatory powers'.[25] Peter Green (knighted in June 1982) could not have put it better himself.

Meacher had, to be fair, as chairman of the committee scrutinising the Lloyd's bill, waged a doughty fight to ensure that the eventual Act would include compulsory divestment, overcoming Green's preference for a more voluntary approach. The bill received the Royal Assent in July 1982, and within a few weeks Lloyd's was facing two intensely embarrassing scandals. The first concerned the insurance group Alexander Howden (whose chairman was Kenneth Grob) and the phenomenally successful, legend-in-his-own-lifetime marine underwriter Ian Posgate, known in the market as 'Goldfinger' and regarded with respect and awe, rather than affection.[26] In the context of a takeover of Howden by the US-based Alexander & Alexander, it emerged that there was a serious shortfall in – and had been a serious misuse of – Howden assets. All this was in the public domain by September 1982. Two months later, at the start of November, the second scandal broke when Lloyd's announced that Peter Dixon, Chairman of PCW Underwriting Agencies Ltd (a subsidiary of Minet Holdings), had voluntarily suspended himself from all duties with the agencies, pending enquiries following information from Alexander Howden. Also heavily implicated was Peter Cameron-Webb, until recently Chairman of PCW. Sir Peter Miller (Green's eventual successor) recalled the atmosphere that memorable autumn:

> It was a hell of shock to us, because Lloyd's had bumbled along for years with immense success, really very profitable, one year's loss since the War, not bad for an institution in the risk business. We had always assumed that our great leading underwriters, of which Cameron-Webb was undoubtedly one, and our top brokers, of which Grob was undoubtedly one, were men of personal honesty, it never occurred to us that they were anything else; but the scam that was practised on Lloyd's, it's not the first time that that sort of scam had happened, was so easy because there were no regulations to stop them doing it. Everything was hidden . . .
>
> They owned syndicates. They said, 'Syndicate, you will reinsure risks' that, surprise, surprise, didn't bring any claims, and the reinsurance premium found their way through the broker's office into a Bermudan office, into so-called Panamanian insurance companies, Gibraltar in Cameron-Webb's case, Switzerland probably in both cases, and they made off with the money. . .

In the Howden case, Miller believed that the two architects of the scheme were Ronald Comery and Jack Carpenter, that Grob 'went along with it' and that Posgate 'was drawn in later on'; in the PCW case, he believed Dixon to be the 'éminence grise', with Cameron-Webb being led along 'by monetary greed and high rates of taxation'; and that by 1982 both scams had been worked for some four to five years, Howden's 'probably a little longer'. The figures were huge – Cameron-Webb and Dixon, for example, allegedly syphoned off £40m from syndicates – but Posgate for one would never concede that he had done anything fundamentally wrong. 'In business I believe in dog-eat-dog, the survival of the fittest, not protection of the weakest,' he told a journalist in 1982. 'It's human nature to get greedier and greedier and greedier.'[27]

That crop of scandals did not alter Gordon Richardson's essential belief in the virtues of self-regulation, whether at Lloyd's or elsewhere; but at the Bank there was a growing feeling that not only was Lloyd's badly under-managed, but that it needed more independent input. Shortly before Christmas Richardson asked Ian Hay Davison, formerly with Arthur Andersen, to go to Lloyd's as its first Chief Executive. With some reluctance, Davison eventually agreed: 'Above all I admired Gordon Richardson and he asked me: I would not have accepted for anyone else.' He started in February 1983, with a brief to clean up the place (including the tax-evasion aspect) and initiate a new rule book. By the time he arrived there was an increasing realisation that the framers of the new Lloyd's Act had, following Fisher, placed too much reliance on divestment (separating brokers and underwriters), while overlooking, in Davison's words, 'the much more serious abuses of conflicts of interest involved where agents put their own interests improperly ahead of their duties to their Names'. On television some thirteen years later Davison spelled out a particularly prevalent abuse:

> One of the things I discovered when I went to Lloyd's is that the underwriting agents all had their syndicates, and the Names were on the syndicates, but they all ran little syndicates on the side, called baby syndicates, to which only a few favoured friends belonged, and on the baby syndicate was put the most attractive business, and effectively they were diverting profits from the outside investors, the Names, to the pockets of the insiders, the members of the baby syndicate. This was quite clearly improper. I would have said that every single member of the Committee of Lloyd's was a member of a baby syndicate . . .

On the same programme, *Naked City*, Posgate took the line that there had been nothing uniquely venal about the Lloyd's of the early 1980s:

> The City has made its money out of conflict of interest, but it must be remembered that until recently conflict of interest was not a crime, and therefore there were many stockbrokers who bought shares and made their profits out of dealing in shares that were about to be taken over. It was always rumoured that there were certain merchant banks that before reporting the purchase or sale of a company allowed half an hour for the partners to make their purchases. Baby syndicates were no different . . .[28]

On which side of that rather deep divide was Peter Green? His initial

13 Lombard Street, 1957

14 ABOVE *Sir Siegmund Warburg*
15 RIGHT *Sir George Bolton*

16 ABOVE *Lord Cromer, 1961*
(on left, Pitt the Younger)
17 LEFT *Leslie O'Brien: outside
the Bank of England, 1966*

18 RIGHT *London Wall*
(Route 11), c 1966

Barings 1973, shortly before the
demolition of the old 8 Bishopsgate

19 *The Acceptance World*
20 *George Franklin, head messenger*
21 *Using comptometers to update the*
clients' ledgers

22 General
office

23 *Jim Slater and Sir Kenneth Keith, 26 April 1973*

24 *One of the first women allowed on the Stock Exchange floor, 10 March 1973*

Royal Exchange, 30 September 1982: the start of LIFFE

25 Gordon Richardson and John Barkshire (in the background, Mansion House and Mappin & Webb)
26 First minute of trading

27 *The City on the cusp of Americanisation, 11 June 1985: Broad Street Station (left) shortly to be pulled down, the Broadgate development under way*

public reaction to the breaking of the Howden affair had been to say that it was not the concern of Lloyd's; a few months later, having felt unable to resist the Bank's wish to parachute in Davison, he reputedly nicknamed the newcomer 'the Wyatt Earp of Lime Street' and cracked jokes about 'making Hay while the sun shines'. Davison himself did not doubt that although Green had no alternative but to accept his presence, 'to many of the traditional members of the Committee the presence of a chief executive was a standing slight upon Lloyd's', and they simply wanted Lloyd's 'to be master once more in its own house'. Green was tacitly on their side, but his days as Chairman were numbered. By summer 1983 he was under a twofold cloud: that the explanation for his insufficiently thorough investigation of Cameron-Webb was that the latter had once been employed by Green's father; and that he had, unbeknown to the 1,000 Names for whom he acted, placed reinsurance on their behalf with a Cayman-registered company in which he had a significant interest, a move designed not only directly to benefit himself but to enable his firm to cheat the Inland Revenue on a large scale. In September, 'tired and shell-shocked' according to a friend, Green resigned. Eventually a disciplinary tribunal would find that over a five-year period he had failed to ensure that the reinsurance arrangements were fair to his Names. For this 'discreditable conduct' he was fined £50,000. 'I may have been sailing a bit too close to the wind,' Green later observed. 'I thought I was trying to do my Names a lot of good but, you know, you learn by your mistakes.' At his memorial service in 1996 there was an adequate sprinkling of the great and the good (including the headmaster of his old school, Harrow), but none of the obituarists dissented from Godfrey Hodgson's verdict on this 'genial and essentially well-intentioned man' that 'his fall from grace was evidence that few, if any, of the insiders in the Lloyd's market succeeded in escaping the cosy insider deals and double standards bred by an atmosphere of privilege and secrecy'.[29]

*

Within ten days, the *Financial Times* was groaning with ads from fund managers, investment services, gold futures dealers, diamond merchants, money brokers and the Basle Stock Exchange, all offering to shepherd the unschooled Englishman into a brave new world without exchange controls. Over the next six weeks, bankers and brokers took even more specific steps to cash in on what appeared to be a bonanza. While Bankers Trust was setting up what it rather solemnly called a 'special task force' to study the new situation, First Chicago was quickest off the mark with a November 9 conference on new options in foreign-exchange management. Salomon Brothers took over the Berkeley Hotel Minima Theatre and flew in two New York partners to describe investment opportunities in non-sterling markets to 50 UK-based institutions . . .

In fact, as David Cudaback went on to explain in an early analysis of the impact of Howe's October 1979 abolition of exchange controls, it seemed for a time, partly in the context of the continuing high pound and high UK interest rates, that abolition was going to be one of the great non-events. 'We had expected that things would happen much more quickly, and that there would be more enquiries about gold, more currency accounts opened than has actually been the case,' Michael Mayo, Treasurer at Barclays Bank International, told Cudaback in early 1980. 'It's very difficult to make money overseas if one's own currency is strong,' John Manser, Investment Director for Save & Prosper (Britain's largest unit trust group), added. 'International investment is not that easy anyway, and major currencies now move 7 per cent against each other overnight – which, in my youth, was tantamount to revolution and the overthrow of a government. It's a frightening market and I wonder if anyone really has the courage to cope with it anymore.' Soon, though, international diversification of UK investment portfolios was fully under way. The figures for net investment by UK institutions in ordinary shares tell the story:

	UK securities	Overseas securities
1978	£1.924bn	£459m
1979	£1.990bn	£625m
1980	£2.501bn	£2.244bn
1981	£2.400bn	£2.458bn
1982	£2.472bn	£2.917bn[30]

More generally, with the UK financial system no longer insulated from external financial flows, abolition led to a much higher degree of integration between the UK and other financial markets. For some twenty years there had been the 'two Cities' – in Roberts's words, 'the free-wheeling, unregulated, international City of the Eurocurrency markets, and the sterling-based, cartelised, domestic City, whose bastion was the Stock Exchange'.[31] Now, with transactions across the markets possible in any currency, there was no longer any economic logic for that divide. The great question, though, was how well the natives would fare when the City once again became a seamless whole.

One prominent tribe did not enter the momentous decade with plaudits ringing in its ears. 'Something is seriously wrong with Britain's retail banking system,' the *FT*'s Michael Lafferty declared in May 1980. 'It is dominated by a handful of institutions known as the clearing banks whose profitability is the envy of commercial banks all over the world, yet its UK management is wholly in-bred and often less than sparkling. It is a system badly in need of a shake-up.' Which was the best way forward for these large, slow-moving, much-criticised organisations? Crucially, there was still a prevailing obsession with size for its own sake, as measured by total assets. This obsession took a blow – unfortunately, for most of the Big Four, not a fatal one – with the Latin American debt crisis, which burst upon the international banking world in August 1982 when Mexico suspended debt payments. The central bankers soon got involved, with Richardson playing a leading role at the critical IMF meeting in Toronto in early September, and eventually more than thirty countries were covered by rescheduling agreements.[32] In the immediate wake of the crisis, 'securitisation' (by which multinationals converted bank loans into tradable bonds) became the name of the game, thereby permanently reducing the profitability of wholesale banking. However, among the Big Four, only Lloyds – badly hit by the debt crisis – would have the sense and the absence of corporate grandiloquence to make a virtue out of grasping the retail nettle.

Barclays was still the top clearer throughout the first half of the decade, increasingly threatened by the more aggressive NatWest. Chairman at Barclays from 1981 was Timothy Bevan, from one of the bank's founding families – an advantage denied to the other main candidate, the more dynamic Deryk Vander Weyer, thereafter always known as the best chairman Barclays never had: according to a close colleague, the much-respected Sir Brian Pearse, 'they just didn't have the balls to make him chairman, and the whole bank resented it'. Unabashed, Bevan ran Barclays along distinctly Etonian lines (much swearing and loss of temper, occasional bursts of warmth), with scant regard for his board. 'Unbelievably Dickensian, and distinctly divided into aristocrats and peasants' was how one observer described it. 'Nobody ever challenged the aristocrats.'[33] Moreover, although there had been a Bevan in Lombard Street since 1767, there was little sign that this one possessed a coherent, let alone convincing, overall vision of where his bank was heading.

How different was it at 41 Lothbury and the NatWest Tower, formally opened by the Queen in June 1981? 'In London bankers' eyes,' noted *Euromoney* the following month in a profile of NatWest, 'it's a bank that can afford to give loans the quaint name of *advances*, to have a promotional ladder and a salary scale system that appear to be modelled on the British civil service, and to have a tradition where senior staff are called "Sir".' The article, though, was entitled 'The Puzzling International Approach of NatWest', and its thrust was that as yet the bank had failed to devise a plausible strategy for its increasingly important international business. It had massively overpaid for the National Bank of North America; more recently it had sold its Orion holding to a fellow-member of the consortium, Royal Bank of Canada, at a knock-down price; most senior people in the international division were from a strictly domestic banking background; and 'to those who do not know the bank well, the structure of National Westminster's international operations makes the

Roman Empire look like an easy management challenge'. There was one aspect that the profile did not touch upon. In April 1981 Robert Maxwell took over the near-bankrupt British Printing Corporation (BPC) and, through ruthless rationalisation, returned it to profit. BPC owed £17m to NatWest, money that the bank had not expected to get back; so when it did, it was not surprising that NatWest proved a loyal backer of Maxwell's subsequent ventures. Others also facilitated Maxwell's rehabilitation in the City – his biographer, Tom Bower, mentions for example Sir Robert Clark of Hill Samuel and the flamboyant stockbroker Jonny Bevan of Grieveson Grant – but nothing helped more than to have in his corner the utterly respectable, loan-friendly, morally neutral clearing bank.[34]

Midland began the 1980s having still failed, to Malcolm Wilcox's infinite frustration, to make a major overseas acquisition. The eyes of this sharp, pedantic, fiercely ambitious man were firmly set on following the example of the other clearers and buying a major American bank – a desire given added urgency early in 1980 when Congress began to take action aimed at curbing foreign bank acquisitions. Perhaps drawn together by their shared surname, Wilcox had for several years been on good terms with Thomas ('Atomic Tommy') Wilcox, Chairman of the California-based Crocker Bank, which he had been trying – including through an expansive loan policy – to build into the Citicorp of the West Coast. By summer 1980 the two Wilcoxes reached agreement: Midland would pay $595m for a 51 per cent stake, to be followed by a further $225m over three years; the deal was to be called not a takeover, but 'an alliance'; Midland was to grant Crocker 'maximum operational autonomy' for five years, unless its investment was found to be in 'jeopardy'; Midland, despite its majority shareholding, would have only three places on Crocker's board, with precisely nil representation in Tommy Wilcox's management team; and Crocker would determine the pace of Midland's phased investment.[35] It was manifestly a bad deal for Midland, which had not even managed to inspect Crocker's loans book, but the financial press greeted the announcement warmly and the main concern of Midland's institutional shareholders was Crocker's proximity to the San Andreas faultline. For Tommy Wilcox, wanting to end his banking career with a bang, it was the dream combination of a huge injection of capital with minimal strings attached. Symptomatically, when Midland asked to have its own representative office in the new, thirty-eight-storey skyscraper that Crocker was building in San Francisco, its request was rejected.

Over the next year and a quarter, as the US regulatory authorities went about their cumbersome business of sanctioning the deal, Crocker let rip with an explosion of loans, including a fair number to Latin America. 'The message was, "Leverage Midland's capital" and leverage we did, long before it came in,' one Crocker executive recalled. By the time the deal finally went through, in October 1981, the Chief Executive at Midland was Geoffrey Taylor, a capable Yorkshireman who was badly undermined in his relationship with the cocksure Tom Wilcox by his dislike of confrontation and unpalatable decisions. 'Getting information out of them was like trying to draw teeth,' Taylor recollected of his dealings with Wilcox and his circle. Nor was the mood at Poultry helped, to put it mildly, by the August 1982 debt crisis, which saw Midland about twice as exposed to Latin America as the other clearers. By early 1983, with Midland's investment in Crocker amounting to some $820m, there was increasing concern about its almost complete lack of input into Crocker's activities. By this time Tom Wilcox had nominally retired, but he was now chairman of Crocker's executive committee and had a successor, John Place, willing to do his bidding. In March, responding to Midland's anxieties, Place and his management team came to London to make a presentation to Taylor and 150 of his colleagues. They did so in the board room at the top of the Lutyens head office:

> It was [David Lascelles would write] a brilliant performance, with coloured slides and diagrams, glowing growth forecasts – and a new image for Crocker based on a lighthouse, the guiding light in rocky waters. It dazzled most of those present with its slickness. But there were also people in that audience who were beginning to view Crocker with a more jaundiced eye. They had seen the huge growth in loans; they had noted that Crocker was lending on terms that were forbidden in Midland; they had found that their budgets were being trimmed to finance a flashy investment on the far side of the world which brought them no benefits, no new business and no enhanced standing in the market. 'The US art of presentation . . . Bullshit baffles brains,' muttered one of them. A sense of foreboding began to build up in Midland through the summer of 1983 . . .[36]

So it did, but no one in Poultry yet had any real idea just how catastrophic the decision three years earlier had been.

For the merchant banks, which tended to find the troubles of the clearers a source of amusement, the early 1980s were generally a difficult time. Antony Gibbs, once a great name, was completely taken over in 1980 by the Hongkong and Shanghai Bank, which had had a 40 per cent stake since 1974, compelling it reluctantly to give up its membership of the Accepting Houses Committee; that same year Keyser Ullmann was sold for £43m to Charterhouse Japhet, which according to du Cann 'got a bargain'; not long afterwards Arbuthnot Latham had the first of its four changes of ownership during the decade, being sold to Dow Financial Services; and at Guinness Mahon there was almost constant upheaval, eventually leading to Harry Kissin (ennobled in 1974) leading a management buy-out of the commodities division and re-establishing it as Lewis and Peat Holdings.[37] Elsewhere there were two big blow-ups – one much publicised, the other kept largely quiet. The first was at Rothschilds, where Jacob left but his cousin Evelyn stayed. The rift had a strong personal element – with a far-from-helpful role being played by Jacob's father, Victor – but the two men also saw the future of Rothschilds very differently: Jacob, believing that soon the City's merchant banks would be facing a sustained challenge from the financially stronger US investment banks, argued that survival depended on bringing in outside capital, while Evelyn was obstinately unwilling to surrender family control. Such was Jacob's star quality that the widespread assumption was that his departure would permanently consign Rothschilds to the second division. Evelyn, however, made a strong start by recruiting in 1981 the corporate financier Michael Richardson from Cazenove's. The *Observer* justifiably called it 'a merchant banking master stroke', adding hyperbolically that 'Richardson is that rare City individual – a man of considerable ability, vision, charm and, above all, superb connections'. None more superb than that with the current occupant of No 10, and in due course (though not only for that reason) Rothschilds would be rivalled only by Kleinworts as *the* privatisation powerhouse.[38]

The other bust-up was at Hill Samuel.[39] There, in 1980, the board discovered that its non-executive Chairman, one Lord Keith, had more or less off his own bat tried to engineer a takeover by Merrill Lynch – on the grounds, not dissimilar to those of Jacob Rothschild, that in the coming world Hill Samuel no longer had the muscle to go it alone, and that to be halfway big, but with big aspirations, would be fatal. However, the board rejected the Merrill Lynch bid as too low; Keith, thirty-four years after arriving at Philip Hill, was compelled to step down (though remaining Chairman of Philip Hill Investment Trust); and soon there was a new Chief Executive, the aggressive Christopher Castleman, charged with reviving the glory days.

This was also a new era for Warburgs, after Siegmund Warburg died on 18 October 1982. His last months had been unhappy, presiding over the unravelling of Warburgs' latest attempt to achieve an effective American presence. 'He wants to reign, by sweetness and persuasion, but totally,' reflected one of those involved. Nevertheless, the tributes paid at his death were unanimous in acclaiming that no man had done more to restore London's fortunes as an international financial centre. He was, like Nathan Rothschild and Ernest Cassel before him, an undisputed giant of City history. How would Warburgs fare without him? Peter Stormonth Darling remembered the founder's own sense of foreboding:

> Some while before he died, and on more than one occasion, Siegmund told me with conviction, and I am sure others too, that within five years of his death Warburgs would break several of his most cherished rules. We would, he said, change the name of the quoted company, Mercury

Securities, to incorporate the Warburg name; we would produce glossy annual reports in place of the plain off-white ones we traditionally used (he actually used the word 'glazed'); we would have brochures with photographs of members of the firm, as all our competitors had; we would advertise; we would grow too big and have too many people; and worst of all, we would join the City establishment and inherit its complacency.

David Scholey was, again in Stormonth Darling's words, 'the reigning successor to Siegmund, with Henry Grunfeld and Eric Roll as his counsellors'. He was the son of Dudley Scholey, who had made his City career at Guinness Mahon, and since 1981 he had been a non-executive director of the Bank of England. Altogether he was a pragmatic, industrious, intelligent Englishman, with an attractive personality and the ability to motivate, but with little taste for iconoclasm, let alone intellectual abstractions. It was a challenging inheritance, not least because Warburgs was acknowledged as pre-eminent. In 1983, when Thomas Tilling found itself faced by a hostile bid from BTR, it unceremoniously dumped its traditional financial adviser, Schroders. The finance director explained: 'When you're fighting for your life, you need the best.'[40]

The BTR/Tilling contest was the first of the blockbuster takeover battles that did so much to define the City of the mid-1980s.[41] The battle opened with a dawn raid on 5 April and was eventually won on 8 June, the eve of the general election, and in several ways BTR's successful £600m bid set the trends for the future. It featured a dominant individual, in BTR's Owen Green; an aggressive tone embodied in widespread press advertising; unprecedentedly large offers financed through the equity market; and a hard sell to the institutions, involving flip charts and slide shows, though this was temporarily defeated by round plugs in a visit to the Pru. The contest also confirmed the arrival of Morgan Grenfell as a hot competitive force in the takeover field. From December 1979 the kingpin there, completely changing the character of the bank, was Christopher Reeves, formerly with Hill Samuel and much influenced by the example of Keith.[42] According to Dominic Hobson, who worked at Morgan Grenfell during the 1980s, the underlying approach of Reeves and his circle of 'public school bully boys' rested on loose management, rewards in share options as well as salaries and bonuses, and pursuit of profit that in turn would drive the bank's share price higher. Nowhere at 23 Great Winchester Street was this clearer than in the corporate finance department, where from 1979 there was a systematic policy of targeting companies that could potentially be persuaded into launching a takeover bid. Until 1982 (when he went to Henry Ansbacher) its driving force was Patrick Spens; thereafter the two stars were George Magan (who sold the idea to Green of an attack on Tilling and induced him to leave BTR's regular financial adviser, Hill Samuel) and Roger Seelig. Magan was perhaps the more attractive, less self-aggrandising figure, but they shared a ruthlessness in the conduct of takeover battles – in Magan's telling phrase, 'using every inch of the playing surface'.[43] They would also, without compunction, change the goal posts.

There had, however, always been more to merchant banking than headline-capturing takeovers. It was a significant as well as symbolic moment when in 1981 the Bank of England determined that it would no longer be solely the prerogative of members of the Accepting Houses Committee to have their bills rediscounted by the Bank at its 'finest rate'. Two or three years later Chips Keswick, Deputy Chairman of Hambros, looked back with engaging frankness on this wonderful perk: 'We all lived like fat cats on it for donkey's years. It was one of those gloriously English institutions which grew from power and privilege. I'm all in favour of monopolies. It was amazing it lasted until 1981.' Keswick was speaking to Paul Ferris, whose survey of the world's merchant and investment bankers, *Gentlemen of Fortune*, was written on the cusp of 'the City revolution' and published in 1984, almost a quarter of a century after his pioneering study of the square mile. 'Power has moved on; the international banker's language is English but his currency is the dollar,' he observed on page one. 'The City has done well, all things considered. But legends of banking parlours with coal fires, occupied by partnerships of rich gentlemen in a London at the centre of the world, are a drag on the market now. Who cares any more?' To prove his point, he gave some 1983 post-tax profit figures. Nomura Securities: $292m. Merrill Lynch: $230m. Kleinwort Benson ('the largest of London's merchant banks'): $32m. N.M. Rothschild & Sons: $3.6m.[44]

At about the same time an analysis by the stockbrokers Laing & Cruickshank helped to explain this striking discrepancy:

> Despite their venerable antecedents, the merchant banks have remained small. It is not widely appreciated that many houses only emerged in a corporate or quoted form in the last 20 years. Originally partnerships, they have preserved many of those characteristics such as an aversion to risk, the maintenance of secrecy, and the desire in many instances to retain control. Even now, 25% of the assets are in unquoted hands, and a further 24%, though quoted, are still firmly in family control. Their unwillingness to raise outside capital and the desire to keep control, have kept their capital base and their banking business small. Indeed smallness was for many years cultivated as a virtue on the grounds that it signalled flexibility, speed and quality of service. . .

So perhaps it did, but now, Laing & Cruickshank emphasised, lack of size was a rapidly increasing disadvantage. This particularly applied to their banking business, for the majority of houses the most important single source of profits, but by the early 1980s an increasingly competitive field – with not just the clearers muscling in but also the foreign banks, which by 1983 accounted for 17 per cent of all sterling lending and one-third of all corporate sterling lending. 'These developments make the long-run algebra for banking profits of the accepting houses rather unexciting,' Laing & Cruickshank noted. 'Because they are small prudence requires that they cannot afford to be as highly geared or as fully lent as their big competitors.'[45]

In their incisive overview, *The Square Mile* (1985), John Plender and Paul Wallace developed the larger theme, as they sought to explain why the merchant banks were in such a vulnerable position by 1983. In essence, their analysis was threefold: first, that they had missed out on international opportunities (above all the Eurobond market) through being overly oriented since the 1950s on safe, profitable activities relating to the UK economy, especially corporate finance and pension fund management; second, they had been too slow off the mark in seeing how, in an increasingly global market, 'the American way of designing capital issues, making the capital available to the borrower and distributing the resulting bonds or securities to investors, would become the international norm' – a slowness no doubt tied to the fact that 'they lacked the capital to take hundreds of millions of dollars' worth of bonds on to their books even if they wanted to'; and third, more generally, there was the psychological legacy of the mid-1970s British economic and financial crisis, putting the entrepreneurial spirit on hold.[46] These financial supermen were, in short, facing their greatest challenge.

The discount houses almost did not live to see the City revolution. During 1980 the high political priority being given to monetary control, together with the abolition of the 'Corset', meant that there were those, including some senior clearing bankers, who wondered whether the discount market had any significant role left to play. The London Discount Market Association's Chairman was Richard Petherbridge of Union Discount, where he had learned his craft under Trinder. That autumn he submitted to Richardson a series of papers from the discount houses setting out the case for their continued existence as intermediaries in the money market between the Bank and the clearers. Largely because the Bank knew that the discount houses would do its bidding, whereas for several years there had been disturbing signs of independence on the part of the clearers, the Bank agreed not to phase out the discount market. 'It is still as vital and integral a part of the banking scene as ever it was,' Blunden observed. 'To see it just as dark-suited men in top hats out on routine money rounds is totally misleading. Its role is much more demanding and important than that. Oh yes, it is very much alive.' The following year, in September 1981, one of the market's more venerable names, Smith St Aubyn, took a nasty cold shower when it mistakenly assumed that interest rates were on their way down and so built up its gilts portfolio. This faulty judgement cost it over £5m, and the house survived only through emergency help from its shareholders. The episode was kept quiet for several months, but became public in January 1982, as Tony Rudd, writing in the *Spectator*, argued that it was symptomatic of larger difficulties facing the money market:

> The problem arises when markets become very volatile. Then the delicate mechanism which allows the relatively modestly capitalised group of discount houses to balance the vast pyramid of short-term debt in the market can be thrown off its pivot. The operators who have been accustomed to dealing in a thirty-second or a sixty-fourth of a point suddenly find that they are having to cope with a move, up or down, of a whole point or more in a single afternoon. The strains are becoming enormous.
>
> Nothing is going to damp down this volatility short of a return to the orderly international markets the world was accustomed to before the Bretton Woods system broke down . . . The prospect for a return to that orderliness is remote at present. The only answer therefore in the markets is for the introduction of methods by which the growing risks can be effectively offset . . .[47]

Happily, Rudd saw comfort on the horizon, in the shape of London's new financial futures market, due to start operating later that year.

It had in fact been a long, quite difficult pregnancy for the City's newest exchange. 'Financial Futures in London?' was the title of the report published by the International Commodities Clearing House back in November 1979, asserting that London was suited to establish a successful market in financial futures, granted the existence of a wide array of standardised debt instruments, the Bank of England's central control over any would-be City market and the extensive international use of London's markets as a whole. Soon afterwards the visionary, formidably energetic and superb networker John Barkshire – who was at the start of trying to turn his own creation, Mercantile House, into (in the words of its historian, George Bull) 'one of the world's select, multinational, multi-service institutions' – came forward to set up a working party to investigate further the possibilities. Comprising generally sympathetic representatives from most of the elements likely to make up the market, it presented in July 1980 a feasibility study to the Bank of England. Stressing how a financial futures market would be able to minimise risk in an era of volatility in both exchange rates and interest rates, it gave autumn 1981 as the provisional date for the market's opening. The working party also engaged in some preliminary discussions with the Stock Exchange, which after thinking about it decided against pursuing a dominant degree of involvement – a possibility that few of the working party would have welcomed, but might well have been unable to resist.

During autumn 1980, while the Bank's deliberative wheels ground slowly, Barkshire and his colleagues organised a series of seminars and private presentations, attended by more than 2,000 City people. Barkshire recalled their reaction:

> To say that we had a majority in favour of what we were proposing would be an exaggeration. But there were very, very few who were against it, very few. There were the minority who were utterly opposed to it. It was new, it came from America, it knocked down the City barriers, it potentially threatened their closed shop, were generally the reasons that they were against it, which they would have put together under the heading of saying that this wasn't good for the City of London and anyway it wouldn't last. So, there was some very strong opposition, but it was very much in the minority.

Two important elements of the City were, for the most part, particularly unenthusiastic. One was the discount market. Gerrard & National's Brian Williamson, who was on the working party, remembered this particular presentation, in the basement of Union Discount, as a painful meeting in which most of the leading figures in the discount market, their 'top hats metaphorically on their heads', simply failed to grasp the underlying concepts. The other main negative attitudes came from the Stock Exchange's membership: most stockbrokers, still protected by minimum commission, found the likely commission rates unattractively low; there was the larger question of the new market's probable incompatibility with single capacity, which the Stock Exchange looked likely to have to defend before the Restrictive Practices Court; and, living a generally sheltered life, the natural tendency of many, if not most, firms was not to exercise the grey matter unnecessarily. In February 1981, at last, the Bank of England revealed that it had no objection in principle. 'I believe that the establishment of a financial futures market will be one of the most important things to happen in the City of London for a very long time,' Barkshire bullishly told the press soon afterwards. Not everyone was convinced, but in his own mind – one that took few prisoners – he was certain.

For a hundred and one reasons it was not actually until 30 September 1982 that the London International Financial Futures Exchange (LIFFE, pronounced 'life') began for real. During the year and a half of preparation, the single most important theme was that it was going to be a thoroughly eclectic market, transcending both nationality and traditional City divisions. By the eve of opening there were some 261 members in possession of the 373 available seats, with just under a hundred of the members being overseas-based. UK commodity brokers held 97 seats, followed by overseas banks (63), UK banks (55) and Stock Exchange firms

(35). As yet, there was little systematic attempt to make the market attractive to individual, Chicago-style operators, the so-called 'locals'; notwithstanding their liquidity-providing potential, they were too associated with speculation, and Barkshire at this stage was much concerned to stress the market's more respectable, 'hedging' characteristics. By a mixture of imagination and good fortune, the site for the new market was none other than the Royal Exchange – intensely historic and resonant in its associations, but for the past century hardly used for active trading. In 1979, with the roof unsafe, it had to be closed to the public; and almost the only activity left was the selling of charity Christmas cards, leaving the pigeons undisturbed for the rest of the year. The venue put LIFFE right at the heart of the City.

There was never any doubt that it would be an open outcry market, but it was a conscious decision to base it physically on the Chicago model of futures markets rather than on, say, the cocoa or coffee markets in London. This model had three prime characteristics: pits (not rings), with steep steps; open, low booths (not boxes that allowed private conversation); and a big display board. The Chicago model also dictated that the traders would wear coloured jackets, never before seen in the City. Each member chose something different, and almost the only one rejected by LIFFE was a Union Jack design, the worry being that it would be seen on television as selling the pound down the river. How much business would the jackets be doing? 'It is no coincidence that Chicagoans invented these instruments and so far have been the only ones to make them work well,' the *Economist* pessimistically observed. 'New Yorkers, by contrast, and possibly Londoners are temperamentally inclined to view the futures markets as an investment medium or a safety net, rather than a casino. If they all want to hedge and none to speculate, a financial futures market is on a one-way ticket to the mortuary.' The *FT*'s 'Lex' was particularly worried about the lack of interest – even understanding – shown to date by the market's potential end-users. 'Hands up who knows what a fill or kill contract is?' it asked any corporate treasurer who might be reading. The most non-committal assessment came from Gordon Richardson. 'The design of successful futures markets is notoriously difficult,' he told the Court a fortnight before opening, 'and no one has any real idea whether LIFFE will be a roaring success or just fade quietly into the background.'

On the first morning Richardson himself cut the tape, a bell was rung that had been a doorbell of the Royal Exchange after its rebuilding in the 1840s, and the multicoloured throng got down to business with undisguised enthusiasm. The next day the *FT* described 'the gum-chewing lady trader with a voice like a klaxon making her presence felt in the currency pit among her vividly dressed colleagues'; the *Daily Telegraph* spotted someone on the floor with the motto 'LIFFE is the pits' on his T-shirt; *The Times* wrote of how 'they came in orange, red and blue jackets, trying for attention and recognition in and around the pit at London's newest, biggest and most complicated commodity market'; the *Daily Mail* stressed the pandemonium of several hundred traders at work ('"Nine for two," shrilled a Cockney voice. "Nine bid for two." Every arm around seemed to fly towards the ceiling, accompanied by a deafening unanimous cry of "Yes!"'); and the *Daily Express* quoted a twenty-one-year-old dealer, Julian Rogers-Coltman (presumably not with a Cockney inflection): 'I know it looks hectic but it works. It is certainly a young man's game. In fact, it is an ideal opportunity for a young man without commitments to make money provided he's ready to work hard.' Laudable sentiments no doubt, but the new market's overall progress during the first six months was steady rather than spectacular, with most days fewer than 5,000 contracts being traded. In April 1983 the *Economist* declared without equivocation that LIFFE 'has been a flop' and 'is doing little more business now than when it opened its doors'. It blamed the uncertain tax situation (particularly as it related to institutions using the market) rather than the exchange itself, but the accompanying photograph of the trading floor was captioned 'the funny-jacket brigade'.

Things picked up somewhat during the early summer, helped by the election campaign giving a stimulus to the long gilt contract, and by the end of the first year daily trading volumes were running at almost 7,000. Even so, there was far from universal acceptance of the benefits conferred by the new market. A conference on financial futures on the eve of the first anniversary featured some well-publicised and distinctly damaging remarks by R.C. Wheway, Deputy Chief General Manager of the Halifax Building Society. Describing himself as 'only a potential user, and very much as a sceptic at that', he stressed that he thought 'most other building societies feel the same as we do' and that in his opinion 'an investment in a LIFFE contract by a building society would be illegal and immoral'. There were also doubts closer to home. Many firms had become members in the first place only for largely defensive reasons, and during the first year probably over half the membership stayed almost entirely passive. Moreover, quite a number of those who were active were struggling to make a profit, let alone decent money. Mike Stiller, floor manager for Tullett & Riley, recalled the 'big pain barrier' that most broking companies were having to go through at this time and, indeed, for some years to come; and Clara Furse, on the financial futures desk at Phillips & Drew, remembered one early day when she carried out a seventy-lot order for a client in gilts and as a result 'was an absolute star'. Overall, in terms of commitment to the market matched by resources, the contribution of the American banks was critical. 'It's difficult to imagine how different

LIFFE might be if Salomon Brothers hadn't committed itself so much at the beginning,' Williamson told *Euromoney*, and other committed American members included Citifutures and Continental Illinois. Williamson himself was emerging as Barkshire's likely successor as Chairman and had the enviable capacity of seeing a glass as half full rather than half empty. 'The Exchange reached its millionth contract target two months early,' he telexed an Australian well-wisher in October 1983, 'but fortunately has not been so successful as to cause envy and resentment in the City.'[48]

Williamson's point about the American contribution had a larger resonance. Not all the seventy-eight American banks in London in 1983 were starting to flex their muscles, but some were certainly doing so, including Goldman Sachs. When Peter Spira decided in 1982 to leave Sotheby's and return to the City, but not to his old firm Warburgs, he approached Goldmans among others. After a two-day grilling by the New York partnership he received and accepted a handsome offer – news that prompted an old friend who was chairman of a London merchant bank to write 'that I was out of my mind if I thought that Goldman Sachs would survive in London for more than an extremely short period'. Spira started at Goldmans (then based in Queen Victoria Street by Blackfriars Bridge) in January 1983; though far from finding it a sympathetic environment, he was immediately struck by the creative, business-getting zeal, reminding him of the formative, hungry years at Warburgs. Much of this competitive creativity was targeted at the British-cum-European corporate sector:

> One of the advantages that Goldman Sachs had over a lot of UK houses was that they had a whole raft of American products to offer European companies, ways of raising money in the States . . . Commercial paper in those days [i.e. the early 1980s] was very much an American product; that was a way of raising money short-term, and it could be cheaper than just raising from the bank, and Goldman Sachs were the leading house in commercial paper . . . We caused a tremendous amount of angst at the British merchant banks. They all hated us, because we actually produced brighter ideas, and were more dynamic than a lot of the British merchant banks . . .

By this time the American banks were making significant inroads in other areas, including energy finance, commodity finance and accepting. As for bank lending, by spring 1983 the Americans had by far the biggest share (44.2 per cent) of the foreign banks' lending to the UK market and accounted for 12.4 per cent of all bank lending in the UK.[49] In short, the American banks were like runners approaching the starting line before a race: creeping up, creeping up and just waiting for the gun to be fired.

One bank, fairly typically, tried to jump the gun. John Gutfreund, the already legendary Chairman of Salomons, came over from Wall Street late in 1982, not long after Warburg had died, and went to see David Scholey and a few of his colleagues at 30 Gresham Street. 'It was,' Stormonth Darling recalled, 'a pleasant enough meeting in which Gutfreund, puzzled perhaps that David responded to his approach with more politeness than enthusiasm, told us that we would all make much more money if Warburgs became part of Salomon – or, as he put it, would we "prefer to be country gentlemen?"' However, Stormonth Darling continued, 'Warburgs was not for sale. It would march to its own tune, without Siegmund's inspiration, in the expectation that it could compete on a global basis with firms such as Salomon Brothers, Goldman Sachs and Morgan Stanley, and without being acquired by any of them.'[50] Gutfreund and his wife Susan may have been (as Stormonth Darling noted) the inspiration for the Wall Street society couple in Tom Wolfe's *Bonfire of the Vanities*; but perhaps the ultimate vanity, more forgivable in the case of Warburgs than most, was the British assumption that the natives could take on the American invaders and somehow punch above their weight.

In one contest, of course, the natives had already more or less lost: the Euromarkets. There, the trend in the early 1980s was for the syndicated loan market to rise before falling back as a result of the international debt crisis, whereas the Eurobond market enjoyed notable growth, with issues up from $18.8bn in 1980 (itself a record) to $47.9bn by 1982, and then remaining at about that level the following year. The league tables for 1983 showed only one UK bank (NatWest, at no 4) in the top five lead managers for syndicated loans, with one other (Lloyds, at no 19) in the top twenty; while in terms of Eurobond lead managers that year, only Warburgs (at no 3) was in the top twenty, with Credit Suisse First Boston (CSFB) and Deutsche Bank taking the top two places by a country mile from the rest.[51]

The early 1980s was a time of almost ceaseless innovation in the Eurobond and closely related markets, as against a background of falling interest rates worldwide the competition for business became ever more intense.[52] Salomons, for example, pioneered at the turn of the decade so-called 'wedding warrant bonds', a complicated mechanism enabling borrowers to benefit as and when interest rates came down. There was also, as fashioned by CSFB for Pepsico in June 1981, the first publicly syndicated zero-coupon bond issue, a device that for a few years attracted many borrowers for tax-avoidance reasons. Then there was the increasingly fashionable floating-rate note market, where not only were 'flip flop', 'mini-max' and many other weird and wonderful floaters created, but maturities started lengthening, eventually into perpetuity. Nothing, though, attracted more attention than the coming of the so-called 'bought deal', beginning in April 1980 when CSFB bought outright from General Motors Acceptance Corporation $100m of GMAC bonds. Unlike previous fixed-price transactions in the market, the borrower was permitted no influence on how or when CSFB decided to place the large amount of paper that it now had on its books. The upside for CSFB (and others who followed its example) was the total control over distribution that a bought deal gave; the downside was the potential huge loss if market sentiment suddenly turned and no one wanted to buy the paper. By the mid-decade the bought deal was increasingly commonplace, usually following a telephone auction, and it made placing power – traditionally the Achilles heel of Warburgs – ever more crucial.

Finally, not always well understood but of huge importance in shaping the City of the 1980s, there was the world of 'swaps'. Margaret Reid, in her judicious 1988 overview of how the City changed at that time, is helpful:

> Created from virtually nothing since 1982, the swaps market can be considered a by-product of exchange control freedom, coupled with market imperfections which can never be ironed out. What is involved is the exchange of interest or currency payment obligations between two parties
> . . . The importance of these arrangements is that a company can, in effect, use a swap as a stepping-stone from the type of loan and currency it can most easily raise itself to any other in which it would rather be. Put another way, parties can 'redistribute risk' . . .
> Already the swaps system has made its own major contribution towards converting the various separate financial markets of the globe into a more linked-up world-wide market in which the borrower can choose the kind of currency or interest rate risks it prefers to shoulder, and on the best terms
> . . . In fact swaps have done more to knit up world markets with each other than almost any other single trend.[53]

Swaps were essentially an American creation, doing much to quicken capital flows and stimulate the emergence of a genuinely global market across the whole range of international securities, whether bonds, equities or derivatives; in which market the City had – unless it badly muffed the opportunity – a pivotal role to play.

Two remarkable, not entirely lovable men were largely responsible for CSFB's equally remarkable degree of dominance. 'A former Harvard Business School professor and Citibank executive, whose somewhat haughty manner puts off some people but who is recognised as one of the more aggressive, imaginative thinkers in the market,' *Institutional Investor* had written back in 1976 about Michael von Clemm, who became Chairman in late 1978. His faults – arrogance, impatience, lack of warmth – did not melt away, but as the same magazine aptly pointed out in its review of the first two years of the new regime, 'for the first time in his life von Clemm can act the part of the imposing man of high finance and not seem to be putting on airs'. More importantly, he also had the international vision – and was relentless in his pursuit of business from all quarters of the globe – at precisely the time that capital markets were becoming supremely international. In about 1983 Paul Ferris interviewed him in CSFB's London offices at 22 Bishopsgate, occupying quite a modern seven-storey block adjoining Credit Suisse. There he found 'a tall saturnine American with sunken eyes in a bony face', with undeniably 'something intimidating about him'. The interviewee did not confine himself to answering the questions. 'Do you know why our market is cheaper than the US [foreign bond] dollar market in New York?' he rhetorically asked Ferris, and went on:

> It's because we are selling the bonds to little people in small amounts, and these people will buy them at less favourable yields in order to get what they want. In the US debt market, I think anyone will tell you that 85 to 90% of the business is accounted for by between one and two hundred decision makers . . . We are selling to a retail, over-the-counter market that is totally diffused worldwide . . . We're on a completely different game, and to say that ours is a market of institutional investors is a total perversion and corruption of words . . .[54]

Von Clemm himself, though, did not do the selling, whether to the institutions or the retail market. 'We're not doing anything without turning to Hans and asking what's the feel of the market, what do you want me to emphasise, what should I stay away from, what's the blue plate special today,' he freely admitted in December 1980, some ten months after the arrival at CSFB of Hans-Joerg Rudloff. Born in Hamburg, this indispensable man had been educated at Berne and trained at Credit Suisse before spending twelve years with Kidder Peabody's European operation, dividing his time between Geneva and London. '*Fingerspitzengefühl* is what German-speaking bankers call the delicate touch when it comes to syndicating a Eurobond issue,' *Euromoney* observed at the time of his high-profile move to CSFB. 'Hans-Joerg Rudloff is known to possess that quality to an uncanny degree, making it his business to remember which clients might need a particular grade of paper, but never selling too hard.' At CSFB he rapidly made his mark, in human as well as business terms, and among other things became renowned for his increasing disdain for cosy, old-style relationship banking. 'When borrowers make financial firms bid against each other for their business,' he publicly noted, 'they can no longer expect advice from those financial firms.' Like von Clemm he had a reputation for ruthlessness. 'Everyone was pressuring me: the borrower said Rudloff had to be in on the deal, but most of the syndicate members threatened to pull out if CSFB were in,' a former syndicate chief at a big American house recalled of a particularly sharp episode during the mid-1980s. 'I remember Rudloff calling me up and saying, "I do not know who you are. But when I have finished with you, you will never work in London again."'[55] It was hardly the style of

Revelstoke or Bicester; it was not even the style of Warburg or Keith; but the world, in every sense, was changing.

*

'There has not yet been a good account of the Big Bang,' Sir Nicholas Goodison reflected in October 1996, almost ten years to the day after that celebrated event:

> The real cause I think was the abolition of exchange controls in 1979, because that completely freed international capital markets as far as London was concerned. It made it possible for far more attention to be paid to overseas markets by domestic investors. It forced member firms of the Stock Exchange to think more constructively about overseas markets than they ever had before. It freed capital movement, and it really was not possible after 1979 for the Stock Exchange restrictions to remain in force if you think about it historically. Other markets abroad, other practitioners abroad, were going to operate under freer rules, different rules. So change was inevitable from 1979 onwards . . .[56]

How inevitable, though, did it seem at the time? In late November 1979, at the same meeting of the Stock Exchange Liaison Committee at which Goodison regretfully reported that 'his approaches to Government had failed for political reasons' and that therefore the Stock Exchange rule book was still going to be referred to the Restrictive Practices Court, he touched on 'the question of allowing Members to compete with foreign brokers in overseas dealings'. The Stock Exchange Council, he explained, 'had the choice of leaving things as they are, a limited form of access by jobbers to non-Members, or more general greater freedoms from the constraints of single capacity'. He did not express an opinion, but added that 'the problems had been brought sharply into focus by the abolition of Exchange Control'.[57]

It was the most piquant of situations. At precisely the same time that the logic of the abolition of exchange controls compelled the London Stock Exchange to return to its pre-1914 roots and reorientate itself internationally, it found itself almost completely hobbled by having the well-intentioned but inappropriate Office of Fair Trading (OFT) on its back, with the eventual court case not expected to be heard before 1983 at the earliest. In another retrospective account, Goodison identified the two fundamental difficulties that, as a result, the Stock Exchange Council experienced during the early 1980s:

> Any reform that we were wanting to consider, to establish London as a more significant force on the world scene, had to go through a process of secret debate. We were unable to have a public debate because many of the debates and discussions we would have on individual rules might have been

considered as evidence in the Court, had it been public. And that was a ridiculous position to be in.

A very large number of people, both inside and outside the Stock Exchange, but particularly inside, thought that the rule that separated the broker and the jobber, the so-called 'single capacity' rule, was absolutely crucial to the quality of the Market, and to the protection of investors. It was an article of faith . . . It was very difficult even to discuss it, and it was being discussed in the context of overseas securities, particularly because in markets overseas different methods of dealing existed . . . If you wanted to compete [i.e. in overseas securities], you had to deal in the manner in which large overseas houses dealt, or you wouldn't compete with them, they would cut you to ribbons on prices, and they would do all the business . . . I don't know how many debates I held in the Stock Exchange Council, trying to get changes of rule to dealings in overseas securities during that period, most of which ended up with very little progress, because sooner or later somebody would stand up and argue passionately that if we changed things in overseas securities, that would imply we had to change in domestic securities, because wasn't ICI, wasn't BP an international stock? So there would be infection and the single capacity rule would change domestically and the Court case [i.e. the Stock Exchange's case] would be destroyed and the Market would have to change . . .

It was not, in other words, *just* the court case that held back liberalisation (or deregulation) of the Stock Exchange. Indeed, it could be argued that the long-impending court case enabled the forces of conservatism to hide behind it and try to ignore the inexorable implications of the abolition of exchange control. Inevitably there was a strong element of self-interest, in particular on the part of (again in Goodison's words) 'the smaller brokers who looked after purely domestic investors and who were clearly going to be very damaged by greater freedom', but also on the part of 'the dealers in the British government bond market, the gilt-edged securities, who had a very happy little cartel'. More generally there was obvious self-interest at work in the strong upholding of separation of capacity, but there was also a genuine belief that such separation protected the investor. It was a belief that was, in Goodison's phrase, 'deeply embedded in the Stock Exchange ethos'; and for all his own reforming, liberalising instincts – which were considerable – one that Goodison to an extent perhaps shared, however much his notably analytical mind told him that rapidly changing circumstances were rendering separation redundant.[58]

In June 1980 there was support for the Stock Exchange from a no longer influential quarter. The report of the Wilson Committee generally gave the City a far cleaner bill of health than might have been anticipated in the mid-1970s; and although it accepted that the existing Stock Exchange system required 'substantial change', it argued for removing the Stock Exchange from the debilitating threat of the court case and instead asking the Council for the Securities Industry to undertake an inquiry. In the face of a mute government response, Wilson himself wrote to Thatcher in October asking her to lift the case against the Stock Exchange, on the grounds that 'almost everything they do as a financial institution has now got to be transacted under the eyes of solicitors and barristers'. In her uncompromising reply Thatcher insisted that 'so far no arguments have been advanced to justify the substantial erosion of the principles of competition – supported by both main parties since the war – that the exemption of a body very much in the public eye would cause'. With no great instinctive warmth towards the City and troubled relations with the Bank of England, the government was happy enough to let the judicial procedure take its protracted course. It was probably at some point in 1980 that Goodison took tea with Gordon Borrie, recently reappointed as Director General at the OFT, and tried to persuade him to drop the case. Quite apart from the way in which it was inhibiting long-term decision-making, Goodison and his colleagues felt real concern that court-enforced change could lead to chaos, granted that the government was planning to allow only nine months for that change to be implemented. Borrie, however, was immovable, taking the line that as an independent statutory official his overriding duty was to get on with what Parliament required him to do. That was also his line through the early 1980s when any minister raised the possibility with him of stopping the case. 'My greatest mistake lay in being reluctant to promote a deal with the Stock Exchange on abolishing the market's restrictive practices,' he subsequently conceded with admirable honesty. 'I insisted on pursuing the matter through the courts.'[59]

In November 1980 the Stock Exchange *did* manage to take a successful initiative when it opened the Unlisted Securities Market (USM). Designed to raise money for companies too small, risky or new to be accorded a full quotation, it began with eleven companies (mainly from the oil exploration and technology sectors) and in time became a symbol of the Thatcherite enterprise culture. In 1992, by which time the heyday of the USM and that culture had become a memory, Hamish McRae recalled the inner history of the market's origins:

> The USM was started in the first place, not because the Stock Exchange, in its entrepreneurial wisdom, suddenly spotted a new business opportunity, but because its restrictive practices, and in particular the charges it made for seeking a listing, were driving companies outside the Exchange altogether. Small companies seeking funds from investors were going to 'over-the-counter' issuers [exemplified by M.J.H. Nightingale & Co] who were not members, and would do the job cheaper. They would then make a market in the shares themselves . . . The Exchange did not want to cut its charges on full listings, and to be fair, felt it did not want to weaken the implicit seal of approval that listing gave. So it created the USM as a way round its own rules; a way of protecting its *de facto* monopoly of issuing and trading in UK shares . . .[60]

Whatever its parenthood, the USM was at least a cherished baby, unlike the Stock Exchange's perennially struggling traded options market. 'There was,' John K. Hughes of the small broking firm Seligmann, Rayner & Co told the Options Committee in February 1980, citing the view expressed to him by a financial journalist, 'far more interest in traded options by the general public than there was amongst the majority of stockbrokers in promoting it.' Hughes added that in his own view 'the main reason for this is that brokers, as yet, are not prepared, unless they can help it, to get involved with what, in my opinion, is still a complicated system'. Almost a year later an internal report indicated that volume was improving (up from 413 contracts per day in December 1978 to 790 in December 1980) and that five major jobbing firms were more or less breaking even in their options dealings and were still broadly committed to the market. Nevertheless, there was continuing widespread broking indifference – even hostility – and as a result 'the jobbers' dealers on the floor of the market are frustrated, angry and demoralised'. Calling on a major promotional campaign from the Stock Exchange itself, the report added that the Council 'is widely believed to be half hearted in its approach to Traded Options'. This report made little or no difference, and in May 1983 a further assessment described turnover as 'still disappointing' and noted that the market was 'still operating at a loss'.[61]

Elsewhere in the Stock Exchange one episode in these years had a particular resonance. It occurred in early 1981, in the wake of the compromise introduction the previous June of a designated dealer system in overseas securities, an attempt to allow a carefully restricted measure of dual capacity without 'infecting' the single-capacity shibboleth in domestic securities. In its typically aggressive way, Smith Bros decided to transfer its trading in gold shares (including Kaffirs) from the floor of the House to its new dealing room. Reaction was strong:

> We are horrified, but not in the least surprised [L. Messel & Co protested] . . . As long as Smith Bros wish to be treated as fellow Members of the Stock Exchange, we believe their primary responsibility is to the broking Members rather than the outside international dealers who owe no allegiance to the Stock Exchange . . . We would be very surprised if, were this matter put to a vote of Members, the majority felt that they would be better served by faceless and preoccupied dealers at the end of telephones rather than by real Jobbers on the floor.

Michael Boyd-Carpenter of Carr Sebag & Co (a firm on the way out, as Sebags' precipitate, post-1960s, fall from grace gathered speed) agreed:

> Having all jobbers dealing in a particular security within close distance of each other allows a broker quickly and accurately to establish the market

'touch'. Such a facility is part and parcel of 'dealing to best advantage' . . . Without wishing to cast doubt on the integrity of anyone concerned, human nature is such that a flashing light on a direct line from say Goldman Sachs might prove to be a powerful incentive to ignore a signal on an outside line.[62]

Soon afterwards, bowing to Council pressure, Smiths agreed to undertake this business on the floor. Briefly, the waves were turned back.

In March 1981 the Stock Exchange submitted its statement of case (comprising 238 pages) to the Restrictive Practices Court. Unsurprisingly, it defended the existing rule book and in particular made much of the contention that if minimum commission was abolished it would almost certainly prove impossible to uphold single capacity. This was the so-called 'link' argument, largely formulated by David LeRoy-Lewis. It took the OFT a full year to reply, and in May 1982 the Stock Exchange's Restrictive Practices Case Committee (chaired by Peter Wills of Sheppards & Chase) expressed disappointment:

> The most striking feature of the OFT's Answer is the vigour with which it assails separation of capacity . . . The need for separation of capacity is denied; it is denied that there is effective competition between jobbers; and that separation of capacity is necessary in order to avoid conflicts of interest . . . It is not admitted that minimum commissions support separate capacity . . .

Wills's committee wondered therefore whether the best bet might not be 'to abandon the minimum commission structure, in whole or in part, and to abandon certain restrictions in the hope that we could win the case, or perhaps might secure exemption from the Court process on the strength of that major change in policy'. However:

> In the opinion of the Committee this is not really an option. First, if minimum commissions were abandoned we do not believe that commercial pressures would allow strict separation of capacity to be maintained even if the Director General [i.e. Borrie] felt able to permit it to continue. Second . . . we do not believe that the Director would give up his proceedings on the grounds that the remaining agreement between Stock Exchange Members (with minimum commissions abandoned) was of negligible anti-competitive effect. Third, it is uncertain that the Council could carry the Membership with it in such a course.

Instead, the recommendation to Council was that, while continuing to fight the case, it should 'undertake another political initiative to seek to have The Stock Exchange removed from the Court process'. By September 1982 the case was fixed to be heard in January 1984, and in a letter to his members Goodison reiterated the unsuitability of a court of law as a forum to examine the practices of a securities market. 'Efforts have been made,' he went on, 'to convince the Government of this and to persuade them that the examination should take place in a more appropriate forum. For the moment, however, Government does not appear to be willing to act . . .'[63]

From his particular standpoint Goodison recalled the experience of the early 1980s as being 'like Kafka wandering down the corridors with those doors', in that 'you didn't know what was behind the doors if you opened them, and it was very difficult to achieve progress'. Even so, within the Council as a whole, 'we were getting closer and closer to agreeing that change was necessary'. One change that was agreed – not directly relevant to the court case but of enormous latent implications – concerned outside ownership of member firms. The 10 per cent maximum permitted from the late 1960s had done little to alleviate undercapitalisation, a problem that was becoming ever more serious with the increasing institutional dominance of the market. This particularly affected jobbers, but in January 1982 a Council debate on the question saw fourteen out of twenty-seven in favour of raising the maximum external stake to 29.9 per cent for both jobbing and broking firms. Significantly, eight of the others were in favour of a maximum as high as 49 per cent. The 29.9 per cent ruling duly came into force, without much press attention, and in June 1982 the leading corporate brokers Hoare Govett announced that one of the big Californian banks, Security Pacific, was taking the new maximum stake. 'There were pound signs bouncing up and down behind the eyeballs' was how Roger Nightingale, an economist at Hoare's, recalled the reaction there to the news that Security Pacific was willing to pay £8m.[64] Later that year, in November, Rothschild Investment Trust (Jacob Rothschild's vehicle) took a 29.9 per cent stake in a medium-sized broking firm, Kitcat & Aitken. Other outsiders, meanwhile, continued to bide their time.

Assuming that the case did eventually get to be heard by the Restrictive Practices Court, there seem to have been few who expected the Stock Exchange to win the day. One who did was Ian Fraser of Lazards, particularly after his friend Mr Justice Lincoln had ruled in September 1982 that it would not be sufficient for the OFT simply to attack the Stock Exchange rule book, but that it must also formulate a viable alternative constitution. On the whole, though, expectations ran the other way, especially once it emerged that the Prudential would, if required, give evidence for the OFT. One in three at best was how a senior official at the Stock Exchange rated its chances by autumn 1982, and he gloomily quoted Yeats about things falling apart and the centre no longer holding. He was part of an increasingly embattled institution. Gilt commissions remained indefensibly high, while a proposed increase in equity commissions, purportedly in order to raise the capital base of member firms, received a

ferocious response in February 1982 from the National Association of
Pension Funds:

> We find it difficult to understand why brokers should seek a commission
> increase at a time when the economy is going through a tough time. Most
> if not all other companies in the private sector are suffering at the moment
> and the Stock Exchange seems to wish to see an increase in commission in
> order to obtain some recession-proofing. We question this. It would be a lot
> easier to reconcile this approach if we had clear-cut evidence that stock-
> broking firms had done the maximum to economise and rationalise . . .
>
> The *a priori* assumption is made [in the Stock Exchange's discussion
> paper] that users of the Stock Exchange are entirely happy with the present
> fixed commission structure and services provided. This assumption is made
> without the support of any scientifically based market research . . .
>
> The Stock Exchange has referred to the need to separate principal/agent
> roles. However, this separatism is under attack in overseas markets, whilst
> the development of the Financial Futures market will in our view make this
> separatism even more hazy. Is the Stock Exchange convinced that it can
> retain control over the development of dual capacity? . . .

The reference to LIFFE was pertinent, for there the order of the day was
to be dual capacity, and the Stock Exchange allowed member firms to
become members of the new market only on the basis that jobbers stuck
to being principals and brokers to being agents. LIFFE was also to be run
on a negotiated commissions basis, which again challenged traditional
practices in Capel Court. In September 1982, shortly before LIFFE swung
into action, a strongly worded article by Maggie Urry in the *Investors
Chronicle* had a prophetic ring:

> If single capacity and minimum commissions do not obtain in the futures
> market how long can they survive in the cash market? Dual capacity will
> creep from LIFFE from the backdoor into the Stock Exchange, and it will
> bring negotiated commissions with it . . . The Stock Exchange Council has
> only itself to blame. It has set its face against the winds of change which have
> been blowing through the City in recent years, and its features have frozen.
> It nearly killed its own traded options market by failing to spend enough on
> publicity. It could have been more involved in LIFFE if it hadn't adopted
> an 'ignore it and it might go away' attitude. It could have brought gilt
> futures under its own jurisdiction if it had been more flexible and forward-
> looking . . .

The title of this piece was bluntness itself: 'LIFFE spells death for Stock
Exchange sacred cows'.[65]

Nor, in terms of getting a head of steam behind it to fight the OFT, was
the Stock Exchange's cause helped by a growing perception that most of
its stockbroking firms had reacted sluggishly to the new opportunities for
trading in international securities.[66] There were some notable exceptions
– James Capel, for example, got heavily into the Japanese market after

1979, while in the same market Christopher Heath of Henderson Crosthwaite made in 1982 the lucrative, eventually legendary discovery of warrants – but even a progressive firm like Phillips & Drew was still significantly underperforming on the international side.[67] In October 1983 a revealing report by the Stock Exchange's Planning Committee gave six reasons why 'the market in overseas securities' had been 'substantially untapped by member firms', as opposed to 'London-based, non-member American broking houses':

i.   The natural markets in foreign currency securities no longer reside in the UK and our jobbing system fails to see enough of this business to make competitive prices in volume;

ii. unlike the UK domestic market, the international market is characterised by double capacity and negotiated commissions, which are reflected in 'net' prices which are often perceived by clients as being cheaper;

iii. in addition to not being able to match the dealing services of overseas competitors, most member firms find it difficult to compete on information and research;

iv. the imposition of rules by the Council in an effort to protect investors and our domestic system sometimes handicaps members as against their foreign competitors, who are operating in an essentially unregulated manner;

v.   the competitive advantages unique to the jobbing system in the UK domestic market are largely irrelevant in the overseas securities market;

vi. the capital base of many of our firms is simply not large enough.[68]

Was there also an attitude problem? The report was too tactful to suggest so, but it was surely intrinsic to such a lamentable failure.

It was against this background – the increasingly manifest need for change, but change being approached in the wrong way – that Richardson at last moved centre stage. Having since 1979 intermittently tried to persuade the government to find an alternative to the court case, he stepped up his campaign from 1982, as David Walker became an executive director and assumed responsibility for the City's markets. '"He abhors a vacuum," says a colleague, who has watched Walker involve himself in virtually all the City's recent preoccupations,' Stephen Fay noted some years later. 'He strides unstoppably through the corridors near his office like a ship under full sail ... Richardson spotted him in the Treasury, where he was unlike most civil servants, and when he came [in 1977] to the Bank it was clear that he was unlike most central bankers. He lacks their patience and prudence, and they call him Walker the Talker.' Increasingly concerned about the tardiness and impracticality of the judicial route, and about the damaging effects on London of Stock Exchange weakness, he commissioned the Bank's Andrew Treadgold to produce what became known in November 1982 as the 'Blue Skies' plan.

Based to a significant extent on fact-finding visits to New York, this envisaged an open, deregulated Stock Exchange, including an automated market-making system along the lines of NASDAQ. By early 1983 the Bank as a whole, including the gilts division under Eddie George, was fully behind a negotiated, out-of-court settlement. By this time Walker was also inviting himself to a series of informal lunches with senior figures at Stock Exchange firms. 'I rather deliberately gave the practitioners the full force of my vision,' he recollected. 'There was certainly some shock and horror that a director of the Bank would even suggest abandoning fixed commissions and single capacity. Initially they found the idea offensive. But by the end of March 1983, I noticed some willingness to entertain the notion of change.'[69] There was, no doubt, some difference at this stage between Walker's 'vision' and the Bank's (perhaps even Walker's) policy position, particularly on the capacity question. Certainly there was little appetite yet for thoroughgoing change in the gilt-edged market. It was, moreover, less than a year since the 1982 Lloyd's Act had emphasised the *virtues* of single capacity. In all probability it will not be before 2014, when the relevant papers become available, that one can really be sure what the Bank was up to – and how radical its vision was – during the winter of 1982–3.

The political dimension is part of that historical obscurity. What is clear, though, is that Lord Cockfield, who became Trade Secretary in April 1982 and had a personal background in industry, was unlike either of his two predecessors (Nott and Biffen), in that he began seriously to question the sense of continuing with the court case. In this, he may well have been influenced by Richardson, perhaps helped by the fact that the two men had enjoyed a positive business relationship when Cockfield was at Boots and Richardson at Schroders. A further influence was probably Jim Gower, who reputedly condemned the judicial approach as 'dotty'. In any event, Cockfield and Richardson had various conversations with Howe at No 11 about the problem, probably during the first four months of 1983. Howe himself may not have been entirely receptive. After all, he was not only a lawyer, but as a DTI minister in the Heath government had been largely responsible for the 1973 Fair Trading Act, which had extended restrictive practices legislation to services.[70] As for Thatcher, it is unclear whether she expressed a view prior to the June 1983 general election. Either way, by that summer time was running out if the plug *was* to be pulled on the court case – unless Parliament did so by October 1983, it would become unstoppable.

Immediately after the Tory victory on 9 June and the obligatory Cabinet reshuffle, Goodison sent a handwritten letter to Cockfield's successor, Cecil Parkinson. He asked him to lift the court case, warned that in the event of an adverse judgement he would not be able to guarantee the 'integrity' of the market and pointed out that in effect a decision had to be reached by the end of July, when Parliament was due to rise. Parkinson's instinctive response was positive. Back in autumn 1979 he had unsuccessfully advised Nott to lift the case; and for personal as well as political reasons he was attracted to the idea of leading the charge for reform:

> My own enthusiasm for making the changes was, I must admit, based on the fact that I had never been an admirer of the Stock Exchange. I audited [in a previous incarnation as a chartered accountant, between the mid-1950s and early 1970s] firms of both jobbers and brokers, and it seemed to me a very autocratic organisation which had more in common with a gentleman's club than a central securities market, and I felt it would become as redundant as the Manchester Stock Exchange unless we really opened it up to the big players . . .

Whether in fact Parkinson was quite so visionary in June 1983 it is impossible yet to know; but soon after receiving Goodison's letter he discussed the matter with the new Chancellor, Nigel Lawson, who as a former financial journalist understood the City far more intimately than Howe had. 'Cecil told me he favoured a deal in which the Stock Exchange would be exempted by law from the ambit of the Restrictive Practices Act in return for an undertaking that it would reform itself. I told him I agreed, provided the reform was genuine.' Lawson's own perception (again described retrospectively) was that largely as the result of 'woeful' undercapitalisation, 'while the City of London remained one of the world leaders – if not *the* world leader – across a whole range of financial markets, such as the foreign exchange market, in the securities market it was in danger of becoming a backwater'.[71]

Parkinson, in the midst of trying to sort out his tangled private life, badly needed Lawson's strong support, and together they managed to persuade Thatcher and William Whitelaw that although the immediate party politics of letting the Stock Exchange off the OFT hook were undeniably awkward, the potential gains were unignorable. A fortnight or so after the election, at a meeting at No 11, Lawson and Parkinson told Richardson (who was due to retire at the end of the month), and on the 29th Parkinson broke the news to a deeply unhappy Borrie. Then, on Friday, 1 July, Parkinson put the notion of a deal to an entirely receptive Goodison. 'I had been working on this for three years,' Goodison recalled, 'but I still think he was surprised that I agreed so quickly – for he was new to the process.' There followed two to three weeks of detailed, secret negotiations between Goodison and the government, with few ministers in the know and no role for Borrie. On Tuesday the 19th there was a leak in the *Guardian* that an out-of-court settlement was on the cards, requiring Thatcher to tell the Commons that afternoon that, although the case was still before the court, that 'does not preclude the Stock Exchange Council from making proposals to settle the matter'.[72] The leak also led to the hasty convening of an emergency Council meeting.

At that meeting, beginning at 11.30 on the morning of Thursday the 21st, Goodison started by saying that, because of the parliamentary timetable, he would have to make a definitive response to the government by Monday, on behalf of the Stock Exchange Council as a whole. He then outlined the previously secret discussions:

> It was repeatedly made very clear that the Cabinet was finely poised as to whether to do anything at all. Some high-level Ministers wanted instant abolition of MCs [minimum commissions]. This Government does not like price agreements. Most Ministers were anyway convinced that MCs would go as a result of the Court case. Ministers were protective about SC [single capacity]. They thought it strange to enforce SC on Lloyd's while dissolving SC at the Exchange. They had a genuine belief that SC has great value from the point of view of the structure of the market and for investor protection ... On Membership, Government did not seem to be clear what they wanted.

In short, Goodison told the Council, the dismantling of minimum commissions was the necessary price to get the Stock Exchange off the hook, though 'he knew that being asked to give MCs up would be a bitter pill for many'. However, 'He had persuaded Government that MCs should only be dismantled over a phased period. He had also insisted on a monitoring procedure so that Government could be aware of any dangerous effects of the dismantling of MC.' He went on:

> The Council had to make a choice of risks. If we continued with the Case there was the risk that MCs would be shot down and perhaps that SC and MR [membership rules] would also be shot down. The barriers to membership were an important part of the OFT's case. The OFT could not see the logic of there being securities houses outside the membership of The Stock Exchange that might be inside ... With the second choice, exemption by Government, the risks would be smaller in number but still very great. We would have the certainty of MCs abolished by the end of 1986. Many Council Members were convinced by the Link argument and they would feel that the abolition of MCs must inevitably endanger SC. There would be risks to MR too. We would be navigating in uncharted waters. There was a risk in letting HMG become the ultimate controller of our destinies. Politicians tended to be uncertain people.

Goodison then looked at the positive aspects of the choice, perhaps inevitably in a rather one-sided way:

> The advantage of staying before the Court was that we would get more time at the cost of confusion and uncertainty. The advantages of exemption were that we would get certainty, we would know where we were, even if we

were worried about the future. There would be an enormous release of resources in the Council and the Executive. Change would be controlled. The Bank would be deeply involved in the process of surveillance. The greatest advantage would be exemption from the attentions of the Court and the OFT . . .

Goodison also read out a statement from the new Governor, in which Leigh-Pemberton welcomed the proposed deal, emphasised the Bank's commitment to monitoring the process of abolishing minimum commissions and said that it would seek to ensure 'the observance of separate capacity as prescribed by legislation'. Lunch was looming, but there was just time for the Government broker, Nigel Althaus (who in 1982 had moved from Pember & Boyle to join Mullens after the sudden death of the previous incumbent), to make a statement. This included the important, reassuring assertion that 'if a conflict looked like emerging between the elimination of MCs and the stated objectives, including in particular the separation of capacity, I am sure that the Bank would be extremely sensitive to it and would seek to ensure that appropriate action was taken'.

Thursday afternoon, with a sense of history in the making, was devoted to discussion:

> Mr Stormonth Darling [Robin Stormonth Darling of Laing & Cruickshank] said that part of a stockbroker's business was the weighing up of risk reward ratios. They ought to be able to take the decision in this light. It was a choice of which was the lesser of two evils . . . The Government were driving a hard bargain . . . He thought that to accept the package was the best way to go in that it removed uncertainty and at least we would still have major control in the industry . . .
>
> Mr Nissen [George Nissen of Pember & Boyle] said that brokers were being forced to give up the only fixed point in a changing world (MCs). What were they giving it up for – monitoring and legislative backing for SC? He did not think it was possible to freeze SC by edict . . . He thought that we should accept the package now, and the time we gained might give us a chance to rethink . . .
>
> Mr Mitford-Slade [Patrick Mitford-Slade of Cazenove's] said that the best possible result we could get out of the Court would be much the same as the package now contained . . .
>
> Mr Edwards [Tim Edwards of Grieveson Grant] thought the package was the better commercial bargain. It offered us still 2½ years of controlled changes, it took us out of the OFT's grasp and it enabled self-regulation to continue . . .
>
> Mr Hugh Smith [Andrew Hugh Smith of Capel-Cure Myers] said that on first impressions he thought it an astonishingly favourable deal, far better than we could have achieved in Court . . .
>
> Hon N. Assheton [Nicholas Assheton of Montagu Loebl Stanley & Co] said that he did not care for what was a high-handed deal and he did not

think that legislation would make SC work. Nevertheless, the package let us get off the hook without loss of face . . .

Mr Elwes [Nigel Elwes of Rowe & Pitman] said that if we rejected the package we would be jeopardising future support by the Bank . . .

Mr Ross Russell [Graham Ross Russell of Laurence, Prust & Co] said he envied the certainty with which some Council Members had declared for the package. On a balance of probabilities he opted for controlled change via the package as against the cold shower of the Case. However he expected lots of unpleasantness ahead . . .

Mr Lawson [Richard Lawson of Greenwells] thought it terrible that Council Members had not been able to talk to their partners and felt there must be time for proper reflection. He asked that the debate could be continued the next day.

This request was agreed, and on Friday morning the discussion continued at 11.30:

Mr Lawson doubted that SC could survive for long once MCs had gone . . . After reflection however he would vote for the package whilst taking strong exception to the constraints put on the Council by the Government. To decide the future of the securities industry in two days without consulting members and users was intolerable . . .

Mr Stevens [Peter Stevens of Laurie Milbank & Co] said that it was the inner thoughts of the Bank of England which counted. The Bank was in a difficult political situation, but he had noted the Government Broker's statement and hoped that he read into it the determination of the Bank that the single capacity system should be maintained as the prime priority . . . He felt that the Council had been blackmailed and he had always been taught that one should stand up to blackmailers because they always came back for more. However, in these particular circumstances, he thought there was no alternative but to submit to the package as proposed . . .

The Government Broker said that the monitoring process would take full account of the dangers to SC. The Bank did not want the cavalry to arrive when the scalps were already hanging in the wigwams . . .

Mr Steen [David Steen of Pinchin Denny] was disturbed at the lack of awareness of the need for change shown in some speeches. Emotive phrases about blackmail did not help. SC had not been invented by God in the first week of creation . . . We should not be ashamed to ask for protection. Who owned what would be crucial to developments in the securities industry. Was the Government prepared to see a large slice of the industry in the hands of the foreigners? We would have to get down to discussion with the authorities . . .

Mr Kingsley [John Kingsley of Dunkley Marshall] said that he was a yes man. The Chairman congratulated him on the shortest speech.

Following this discussion there was a vote on the resolution to accept the package on offer. It had four elements: the Stock Exchange would dismantle the minimum commission system by the end of 1986; an appeal tribunal would be established, 'to review and if appropriate over-rule the

Council's decision to reject an applicant for Membership'; the Stock Exchange's present Appeals Committee would henceforth have a majority of people who were not Stock Exchange members of the Council; and, in liaison with the Bank of England, lay members would be brought on to the Council. The resolution was passed unanimously.[73]

'Doing the City a favour' was the headline in the *Economist* about news of the accord, and on Tuesday the 26th *The Times* took much the same, critical line. It was an unpromising background for Parkinson's attempt to sell the deal to the Cabinet that morning. 'Willy [Whitelaw] suddenly tossed a spanner in the works saying, "Are we doing the right thing?",' he recalled, 'and we had quite a lot of rumbling.' But eventually, after the Cabinet had insisted on an *ad hoc* sub-committee redrafting the statement later that day, Parkinson was able to announce the deal to the Commons on the afternoon of the 27th, expressing the wish that single capacity would be 'preserved for the time being in its present form'. The Labour reaction was predictable, with accusations that the Tories were 'selling out to and looking after its City friends'. The next day even the *Daily Telegraph*, on its City pages, did not disagree: 'Sir Gordon Borrie . . . has every reason to resent the way that a government committed to free markets and untrammelled competition has systematically abandoned its own guardian of competition policy.' Many senior partners of member firms, with only limited faith in the strategic capabilities of the Council, were also wondering whether all was necessarily for the best, and on the 29th some of them had the opportunity of questioning Goodison about the agreement. Most firms, according to Phillips & Drew's Bryce Cottrell, 'still seemed in a state of shock' and 'pretty worried', with almost all those present (including Goodison) being 'dubious if single capacity would be workable with negotiated commissions'. The next day Goodison was reported in *The Times* as conceding that the abolition of minimum commissions 'may prove incompatible with the present system of separate capacity'. And he added, 'We are entering uncharted waters.'[74]

During August, with everyone away on holiday, the main development was that the *FT* (which had been on strike for much of the summer) gave the deal its blessing. Towards the end of the month, however, various people wrote to Goodison about the question of lay membership of the Council, and some touched on the wider aspects of the agreement. 'In conclusion, I would congratulate you on removing this sword of Damocles' were the succinct words of Timothy Bevan on behalf of the Committee of London Clearing Bankers, while R.P.St G. Cazalet wrote as Deputy Chairman of the Association of Investment Trust Companies: 'I must conclude with how delighted I am for you and your colleagues that at long last you have managed to remove the case from the courts. I know how relieved you will be . . .' Another institutional investor, David

Hopkinson, Chairman of M&G, was altogether less inclined to offer his congratulations:

> As you know, we have always felt that gilt edged commissions were too high and possibly some equity commissions. In addition, we have felt that there should be some outside input in the Stock Exchange at Council or policy level. These aims seem to be more than met by the proposals and indeed, there seems an acute danger that the baby will be thrown out with the bath water because we do not wish to have a weakening of all the other Stock Exchange controls. Our position has not changed for one moment that if negotiated commissions means a jettisoning of single capacity, we would rather not have negotiated commissions . . .
>
> I cannot see how the small investor is going to benefit at all from the Government proposals and indeed, nobody seems to have given much thought to what happens when large financial conglomerates like Merrill Lynch start using their petty cash in order to force out of business all but the largest British firms of brokers. In addition, is it really desirable to encourage large financial conglomerates in this country with the banks, merchant banks, finance houses and stockbrokers all teaming up to exercise power which must be achieved at the expense of the smaller institutions and the smaller men?[75]

The thundering herd's petty cash . . . It is impossible to be sure to what extent the architects of the July 1983 deal had been conscious of how fundamentally it would change the character of the traditional, sterling-oriented, 'domestic' City, but it was not long before everyone was aware that the Yanks – and the banks – were in town.

CHAPTER TWENTY

Top Dollar

Jacob Rothschild was the first, rather chilling prophet of the new world. 'The rules by which London has so successfully played the game are being rewritten by our international competitors,' he declared at a London conference on 24 October 1983, before outlining 'a nightmarishly complicated scenario' in which financial conglomerates offering the widest possible range of services to the widest possible range of clients in the widest possible range of countries would become all-dominant. Barely two months before the start of 1984, his predictions sounded Orwellian: 'As the process of deregulation continues, the two broad types of giant institutions, the worldwide financial service company, and the international commercial bank with a global trading competence, may themselves converge to form the ultimate, all-powerful, many-headed financial conglomerate.' He declined, moreover, to make any sanguine noises about the City's ability to compete in this bracing environment. For too long, he argued, it had been inward-looking and risk-averse; its banks (even the clearers) were undercapitalised in comparison to its foreign competitors; as for its protected brokers and jobbers, Rothschild merely noted that Salomons had made more money in 1982 ($500m) than the member firms of the London Stock Exchange put together. The challenge, in short, was enormous, but it could not be ducked: 'We can expect the emergence of a number of financial conglomerates with interests straddling disciplines which have been traditionally distinct. I believe it is important that one or two concerns in the UK show themselves willing to jump in with both feet, and to play an active part in the redefinition of the financial sectors' competitive boundaries.'[1]

For all Rothschild's big-picture certainties, the prevailing mood in the City that autumn was one of confusion mingled with apprehension. Certainly there was no sense of either government or Bank of England magisterially unveiling a blueprint for the future. Parkinson fell to scandal in early October, Lawson was new as Chancellor (albeit supremely self-confident) and Leigh-Pemberton was not only new, but was viewed by the City and wider world as a weak Governor with a somewhat semi-detached attitude. Alan Clark may have found him (at a Neddy meeting) 'unexpectedly good, crisp and clear', but arguably the key word was the first one. Still, as Leigh-Pemberton justifiably observed at the Mansion House on 20 October, the circumstances were such that a blueprint was hardly possible:

> Individual firms need to make plans and dispositions in an environment that is already changing rapidly, quite apart from the changes – in particular the dismantling of minimum commissions – that will follow from the present agreement . . . But it has to be recognised that competitive pressures will do much to determine what sort of trading structure is needed for a flourishing Stock Exchange. We are of course giving all this close attention. It would make no sense, however, for the government or the Bank now to lay down rules which made the securities market less able to evolve and adapt to such pressure. That would be a sure way to make the central market in the Stock Exchange lose business, much no doubt to overseas competitors.[2]

How exactly the Stock Exchange evolved in the wake of the July agreement would, in short, largely be down to the practitioners themselves.

That, presumably, was the view of the Bank's David Walker, who between September and November had individual meetings with more than forty senior partners. 'Think the unthinkable, think radical' was one participant's recollection of Walker's message, and there is little doubt that he was strongly pushing the line that, in their own interests as well as those of London as an international financial centre, the City's indigenous broking and jobbing firms needed large injections of capital.[3] Walker may well also have done some specific marriage broking. What he did not do – could not do – was lay down the precise market structure within which those firms would eventually be operating. Apart from anything else, his colleague Eddie George, responsible for the gilts market, still saw single capacity as a desirable given. Nevertheless, the broader message was clear enough: that most conservative of institutions, the Bank of England, was now decisively in favour of change, particularly if it took the form of larger units in the securities industry. Granted that there was a general expectation that the 29.9 per cent maximum on outside ownership of Stock Exchange firms would be only temporary, how much did the question of the nationality of the prospective new owners figure at this stage in the Bank's thinking? Had it already conceived the idea of 'national champions' to fight the almost inevitable foreign invasion?

The Bank's 'immediate concern', Barry Riley speculated in November, 'is that there might be a sudden rush of mergers and link-ups, triggered by somebody's decision to take the first move . . . With the ending of the threat from the Restrictive Practices Court, there could now be a domino effect. There are a great many potential players, but there are not many aces in the pack for them to play with.' Of course, he added, 'all the potential bidders have the option of trying to poach analysts, dealers or salesmen – whether as individuals or teams – rather than paying large amounts of goodwill for whole firms'.[4] Granted that this was the 'chance of a lifetime', as the saying went, to break into London's hitherto ring-fenced securities industry, and that there were indeed appreciably more potential new entrants to this market than there were high-scoring existing broking and jobbing firms, it cannot have been easy to stand back and form a rational view as to whether it was wise to take the plunge, let alone at what price to take it. There would subsequently be much criticism of banks for having behaved in a herd-like, essentially irrational fashion. But arguably, even with the imminent disappearance of the old commissions cartel, it was not acquisition that was the faulty policy, but rather the way in which those acquisitions were managed, from the point of purchase onwards.

Warburgs, characteristically, had given the problem more thought than almost anyone else. Back in 1978 – when Warburgs was still failing to make an impact on the distribution side of the Eurobond market and American firms like Salomons were making serious inroads into London securities trading, with their block trades being crossed in New York – the bank had commissioned its resident guru, Andrew Smithers, to set out his long-term views. Correctly predicting that the commission cartel would finally crash, he recommended that Warburgs take an interest in a jobber, with Akroyd & Smithers (the most profitable firm on the Stock Exchange since the early 1970s) being the obvious possibility, quite apart from the family connection. In the early 1980s Warburg himself was broadly in favour, despite his long-standing hatred of stock exchanges, whether in New York or London, not to mention his perennial worries about Warburgs becoming over-large. The notion of Warburgs becoming an integrated bank appealed – in other words, getting into the securities and distribution business, the continental tradition of investment banking. After Warburg's death in October 1982 a particular weight attached to the views of Henry Grunfeld. He would recollect that crucial to the decision-making process was the observation of the New York experience since the end of fixed commissions in 1975, with the more ambitious houses flourishing. As for the younger generation, David Scholey perhaps relished the human as well as organisational challenge of welding together an integrated operation, while a rising figure, Simon (Lord) Garmoyle, was at ease in the securities world, having come from Scrimgeours. Among other merchant banks, Kleinwort Benson came down fairly early in favour of acquiring a broker, apparently motivated by the fear that if it did not possess a distribution capability in equities, then its increasingly flourishing corporate finance business would be vulnerable to those rivals that did. There was some internal dissent, but not as much as at Morgan Grenfell, where opinions were fatefully riven, leading to a policy of dither and prevarication. There seems to have been no such indecisiveness at Schroders, as Win Bischoff (becoming by 1983 the dominant figure at 120 Cheapside) recalled some ten years later:

> We looked very hard at what our strategy should be. At that stage we were really still quite a small bank in terms of financial resources; we were still very much exposed to Latin American debt; we had a geared balance sheet, i.e. we had debt in our balance sheet; our profitability was adequate but not superior; and our reputation was such that it would have been very difficult for us, even if we had wanted to, I think, to buy one of the major Stock Exchange firms . . .[5]

Among the clearers there was a similar policy, though for different reasons, at Lloyds, which now had a notably focused Chief Executive in the person of Brian Pitman. The key recollection comes from an anonymous member of the board:

> We had multiple, woolly objectives in 1983, and some of us felt they were *too* woolly. We had a big philosophical debate over two board meetings and switched from having multiple objectives to a single objective. Not everybody on the board agreed, but that was where we ended. Our single objective was creating shareholder value. We looked at the best performers in the world as models and found two in particular that stood out: GE [General Electric] and Coca-Cola. We then set a goal of doubling our shareholder value every three years . . .

The approach of Lloyds' three main rivals was rather different. Midland had talked to Greenwells even before the Parkinson/Goodison agreement, though by the autumn negotiations were in temporary abeyance; National Westminster was keen to add securities muscle to its relatively flourishing merchant banking arm, County Bank, though preferably without paying a king's ransom. And at Barclays it was big bucks time. Lord (Tom) Camoys, as the ambitious Chief Executive of Barclays Merchant Bank, was frustrated by its lack of progress, but still believed strongly that the marriage of capital and brains was the American-style way forward. Within weeks he had persuaded Barclays' Chairman, Timothy Bevan, that this was a unique opportunity for the bank to establish a presence in the world's capital markets and that no expense must be spared. 'We decided that we would go for the high ground as quickly as possible, because we knew by then that others were coming in,' Camoys recalled. 'There was Warburgs and there were the Americans and the competition was fierce.'[6]

How would the jobbers and brokers play the unique situation that was unfolding? No one knew for sure, but Riley in his November overview offered two predictions. One, that 'after a hugely profitable year in the London equity market the individuals and the firms no doubt have a highly inflated idea of what they are worth', was spot-on. The other would prove less accurate. 'If a big broker became associated with a merchant bank, would it be in danger of losing its business with other merchant banks?' he reasoned. 'Nobody likes trading with a direct competitor, which is a good reason for thinking that, whatever happens to the stock market's structure in the next few years, a good many sturdy independent firms are going to remain.' To be fair to Riley, at the time he was writing several significant firms envisaged such sturdiness applying to themselves. They included not only Cazenove's, which at a fairly early stage in the piece politely but firmly rejected an overture from Barclays, but also Phillips & Drew and the medium-sized brokers Simon & Coates. At Rowe & Pitman, where for several years there had been divisive debate about whether or not to seek an injection of outside capital, an interview that Nicholas Verey gave to the *Wall Street Journal* in late September reflected continuing mixed emotions:

> Whether we'll have to change our spots in the future, I don't know. It doesn't appear as if we'll be a boutique, a market maker or financial engineers. It's not as if we're dinosaurs. We'll try to respond to our clients' needs ... Ten or fifteen years ago, we assumed our independence ad infinitum. But everyone realises times are changing. If someone offered us a good price, we'd have to consider it pretty seriously ...[7]

It was probably soon afterwards that Rowe & Pitman decided that complete independence was no longer a sustainable option; and, like other firms that – for whatever mixture of reasons – had reached the same conclusion, it had to decide which suitor to favour. Considerations were not always mercenary. Brian Peppiatt later spoke revealingly of the thinking at Akroyd & Smithers:

> We knew we would have to go in with someone, because we couldn't see ourselves surviving on our own, because we always felt our middle management was pretty weak. We just really took two basic decisions. One was that we couldn't see ourselves going in with a clearing bank, because we couldn't see ourselves knuckling down to the clearing bank's mentality, whatever that might be, but it was completely different from ours, which was very entrepreneurial; and we couldn't see ourselves also going in with a foreign firm. Of course in those days I don't think we'd particularly ever considered the Japanese because they weren't enough on the world market, but when you thought of that you thought immediately about an American firm, and nothing against the Americans, but I don't think we ever saw ourselves fitting at all happily in there. So we always thought probably the merchant bank route was the route for us ...

In general, however, there were strict limits to such 'cultural' and other non-financial criteria. The most authoritative testimony on this matter came from the former White Weld man John Craven, whose corporate finance boutique, Phoenix Securities, had an advisory role in about two-thirds of the major mergers and acquisitions. 'When acting for brokers or jobbers,' he recalled, 'we always tried to get the partners to focus on longer-term issues such as the strengths and weaknesses of the banks they would join. I am bound to say it was not always possible to convince them to think of anything other than top dollar.'[8]

*

'RIT and Northern in £400m merger with Charterhouse' was the *FT*'s headline on 4 November, heralding the creation of a new entity to be called Charterhouse J. Rothschild and chaired by Jacob Rothschild. 'There is no blood on the carpet,' John Hyde, Chief Executive of Charterhouse (which included the merchant bank Charterhouse Japhet), confidently announced. 'It will be a super group at the end of the day.' Rothschild himself was now, according to Richard Lambert, 'going for the big time'; and more generally Lambert saw the move as what 'may turn out to be the first in a whole series of realignments among City firms'. Three days later it was announced that America's largest bank, Citicorp, was spending £20m on a 29.9 per cent stake in the brokers Vickers da Costa, as well as 80 per cent of its Far Eastern operations, which were the main attraction. 'The high price extracted by Vickers for the effective loss of its independence may strengthen the bargaining position of all those other brokers who are burning the midnight oil in talks with outsiders' was the not unduly cynical comment of 'Lex', who noted a multiple on average earnings over the past three years 'of no less than 15½'. This distinctly favourable arithmetic was a personal triumph for the firm's somewhat improbable Chairman since 1981, Sir Kenneth Berrill, the former head of the Think Tank. 'We were looking for a partner,' he explained. 'We talked to a number of people. We felt we had to make some move, given the rapid changes taking place in the London market.' He also anticipated an imminent rush of other such moves: 'I think there are genuine deals out there and not just an enormous amount of talk. It is not just the media which are pushing people into talking. The logic of events is pushing people into talking.'[9]

Then, on Monday the 14th, came the big one. In Lex's words, 'after a couple of warm-up fixtures over the last fortnight, the first City deal between two domestic first division players has now been unveiled'. This was the news that Warburgs was to buy a 29.9 per cent stake in Akroyd & Smithers, at an estimated £41m. Given that Warburgs was intent on buying into one of the two big jobbers, why Akroyds rather than Wedds? The answer was essentially a matter of style: whereas the Akroyds approach was measured and relatively cerebral, the tradition at Wedds owed much to the dominant influence until recently of Dick Wilkins and was one of taking big positions and relying on flair rather than science.

636

Wedds may or may not have been disappointed by Warburgs' choice – 'We are taking our time,' the firm stated after the news, adding that 'everyone else seems to be rushing into these things' – but the third-biggest jobber, Smith Brothers, possibly were, on the basis of similar origins (Jewish) meaning similar business attitudes. How good a deal was it for Warburgs? Noting that Warburgs was presenting it 'as a way of grafting on a much bigger capacity for international secondary market making', Riley in the *FT* was somewhat sceptical, arguing that 'inevitably its rivals are going to question whether Akroyd really adds up to the right kind of strategic acquisition, when its domestic activities are so much greater than its international market links'. Perhaps, he speculated, just as important a reason for Warburgs' willingness to spend so much on this minority stake lay in 'the defence of its own domestic market position' – in that Warburgs and the rest of the British merchant banks 'are anxious that, before too many years have passed, the American banks will make an attempt to cut through the traditional structures and fat underwriting margins of the domestic new issue market'. He also speculated that there had been some external pressure behind the union:

> The Bank of England has seen two broking firms – Hoare Govett and now Vickers da Costa – become linked to US banks, and there has been a fear that large sections of the London stock market would fall prey to the huge resources of the big American financial groups. The Bank has made no secret of its willingness to encourage the formation of strong British-owned securities market groupings to stave off the threat of American domination. Several broking firms with firm offers on the table from US banks are said to have been discouraged by the Bank from accepting.

Or, as Alex Murray nicely put it in the *Sunday Telegraph*, 'there is little doubt that the Bank smiled on the talks'.[10]

Of course, other business did not stop just because the City was engaged in a fundamental restructuring. Two major stories that autumn involved foreign concerns: Allianz and Crocker. Allianz Versicherung was Germany's largest insurance company, seeking with the help of Morgan Grenfell to gain majority control over a major British insurance company, Eagle Star. The City's natural instincts against such an attempt – British insurance companies, like British banks, were traditionally viewed as somehow immune to foreign takeover – were fortified by Morgan Grenfell's distinctly questionable tactics on behalf of Allianz, which by early November was competing against the tobacco giant, BAT Industries. Censured by the Takeover Panel, these tactics included a partial bid (the first in a hostile takeover bid since the infamous Gallaher episode in 1968) and a deliberately stalling approach (later disingenuously blamed on communications difficulties with a foreign client) that made it almost impossible for BAT to buy stock in the market. Eventually, in late December, BAT did win, but paid such a huge price (£968m) that Allianz made a £163m profit on its stake, enabling Morgan Grenfell's George Magan to claim a tactical victory. The whole episode had shown Morgan Grenfell's determination to push the conduct of contested takeovers into new terrain, but Magan was unabashed by criticism, claiming that 'we were all along alert not to let valour get the better of discretion'.[11] As for Crocker National Bank, it was now that the full scale of Midland's catastrophic misjudgement began to be known.[12] During the autumn routine examination of Crocker's accounts by American banking regulators revealed that Crocker's books were 'littered with loans to borrowers who had gone bankrupt, whose collateral had fallen with the collapsing California real estate market, or had simply disappeared'. The picture was little better with Crocker's Latin American loans, most of which were non-performing. Crocker was ordered to allocate $107m to its loan loss reserve, wiping out its earnings for the year. The sense of shock at Midland when the news came through was acute, and there was no alternative but to announce on 15 December that the Crocker situation would wipe no less than £75m off Midland's profits for 1983. The bank was in a hole, with little idea how to prevent it becoming ever deeper.

The day after Midland's reluctant revelations, another Stock Exchange deal was announced, as Rothschilds paid £6.5m for a 29.9 per cent stake in Smith Brothers. 'Gold card for Smith Bros' was Lex's headline, the column emphasising the smooth fit between Rothschilds' 'historic position at the centre of the London bullion market' and Smiths' 'particular expertise in the market for gold mining shares'. The idea was to set up an international dealing company, with Smiths owning 51 per cent and Rothschilds 49 per cent. 'The international dealing side is the attractive bit of the deal,' Michael Richardson of Rothschilds commented. 'But until the Stock Exchange approves the international dealing rules we will not know whether we are playing cricket or baseball.' Tony Lewis spoke for Smiths: 'It is a long-term deal. Quite substantial companies are now being set up, and we want to take our rightful place in international trading.'[13]

This was the last deal to be announced in 1983, but there was no let-up in the pace of secret meetings, amidst a swirl of rumours and counter-rumours. On 28 December a leader in the *FT* tried to apply some sober realism. Arguing strongly that 'there is a risk of going too far in the vogue for financial supermarkets', it made four major points: first, that 'in terms of style, structure and corporate culture, a clearing bank has very little in common with, say, a jobber'; second, that the appropriate price of entry into the Stock Exchange was very difficult to judge, not least given 'the maturity of the bull market and the fact that commission income is about to be slashed in some classes of business'; third, that the experience of Wall Street in recent years showed that 'the investment banking business is becoming increasingly "transactional" in nature', with company treasurers for example using different firms for different services, thereby rendering redundant the much-trumpeted idea of 'one-stop shopping'; and fourth, another lesson from Wall Street, 'the huge increase in the capital base of the US investment banks in recent years has not primarily been the result of mergers', but rather the key had been 'the large profits that they have made out of heavy trading activities in a bull market'. In sum, the *FT* contended, for 'the majority' of City firms 'organic growth is likely to be a more satisfactory course than indiscriminate merger activity'.[14]

There may or may not have been a pause for reflection, but on the second Monday of 1984 it was announced that the Anglo-American industrial and mining group Charter Consolidated was taking a 29.9 per cent stake in Rowe & Pitman, and that Rowe & Pitman was forming a joint company with Akroyds & Smithers to develop their existing international equity business, in the context of the liberalisation of the Stock Exchange's rules on international dealing, due to be implemented shortly. Justly describing this simultaneous announcement as Rowe & Pitman's 'each-way bet', 'Lex' equally correctly observed that it begged as many questions as it answered. Why Charter? Why not Morgan Grenfell, as most of the City had long anticipated in view of the deep family and personal connections between the two firms? It may have been that Morgan Grenfell, despite those connections, had put Cazenove's at the top of its shopping list for brokers and still had hopes in that direction; in any case, it had become clear to Rowe & Pitman that Morgan Grenfell had little intention of paying the right sort of price, perhaps because it lacked the resources. By contrast, Charter (one of Rowe & Pitman's biggest clients) offered the attractive combination of a major injection of capital (£16.2m) while still allowing the firm complete freedom, in particular to be able to act for all the merchant banks. What, however, about the implications of the new joint venture (known as ROWAK) with Akroyds, granted that that jobbing firm was now effectively under the Warburgs' umbrella? Rowe & Pitman's John Littlewood later maintained that this pioneering tie-up between broker and jobber 'in effect cast the die for the eventual link between Rowe & Pitman and S.G. Warburg' – but that was not necessarily how it seemed to many of Littlewood's partners, perhaps reluctant to think through the implications. 'We want to retain maximum flexibility,' Peter Wilmot-Sitwell, the senior partner, observed at the time of the double announcement. 'We don't know where we will be in five or ten years' time. This will give us the time to see where our market is going.'[15]

The much-awaited publication of Professor Jim Gower's *Review of Investor Protection* occurred on 18 January, three weeks after its author's seventieth birthday.[16] Since his discussion document almost exactly two years earlier (much criticised by the City), the Parkinson/Goodison agreement and everything that had begun to flow from it had significantly changed the regulatory climate, especially in terms of the conflicts of interest inherent in the creation of financial conglomerates. The previous autumn, during the generally lethargic Commons debates on the bill to exempt the Stock Exchange from proceedings under the Restrictive Trade Practices Act, two well-informed Tory backbenchers – Peter Tapsell, a partner in James Capel, and Nicholas Budgen – had highlighted the likely end to investor protection provided by single capacity and had called for an appropriate regulatory structure. In his actual report Gower envisaged a cluster of self-regulating bodies operating within a statutory framework and controlled by a single supervisory body, preferably a strengthened Council for the Securities Industry. 'Unless my proposals are implemented essentially on the lines proposed,' the report solemnly concluded, 'further serious scandals undermining public and international confidence are, in my view, inevitable.' Mindful of the rapidly changing background, and perhaps beguiled by the concept of continuing 'self-regulation' notwithstanding the proposed statutory framework, the City this time gave Gower a reasonably cordial response. Pleased that most people there seemed to accept his basic framework for regulation, Gower typically added 'so long, of course, as it does not apply to them'.[17] He was well aware that there was many a slip between recommendations and legislation.

Five days after his report attention was temporarily diverted from the unfolding City revolution by the news from the Eurobond market that three high-ranking executives at CSFB, accompanied by seven of their deputies, had left to join Merrill Lynch. There was considerable speculation about the causes of this mass defection, but most were agreed that the increasingly powerful position at CSFB enjoyed by Hans-Joerg Rudloff was integral to the story. Soon afterwards CSFB's big three – the American Chief Executive Jack Hennessy, the Chairman Michael von Clemm and Rudloff as Deputy Chairman – gave an extensive interview to Padraic Fallon of *Euromoney*. For Rudloff in particular it was an opportunity for some self-justification:

> People had been working for years to get a mandate from a client. Before the 'eighties that was the biggest thing in the world, so you executed it. Now we are still working for years sometimes to get a mandate, but it might happen, for example, that a firm cannot execute that mandate because the risk is too big. It's a total change of mentality, and it's very distressing, or frustrating, for someone who has been travelling to get that mandate, and

then to be told that unfortunately, on these terms, at the present time, the firm cannot undertake that risk . . . The theory changed from getting a mandate through your personal relationships, for services you offered the client. You now had to get a mandate *at a price*, which someone else had been fixing. That was a totally new experience for the old type of investment banker. And that doesn't go without any change in mentality. It does create frictions. Some people adapt [to] it very easily. Some don't . . .

I'm known as having very strong opinions. And I have very strong opinions about the market. That market is my life. Other people show up in that market for two years, and go back to other markets, or get rotated into it. Their identification with this market is not the same as mine. I have spent all my professional life in the market. That's where the strong opinion comes from . . .

The message of the interview as a whole was that CSFB intended to stay top dog. 'If you want to know one of the reasons why CSFB is number one so many years out of the total number of years that there's been a market, and so many years in a row recently, it's because when the US corporates became tremendously active, we had a big share of that business, and when they became inactive we had a big share of the government business, or the Canadian provinces, or the Asian business,' von Clemm grandstanded at one point. 'We have a global clientele. Who says we don't have roots? We have roots all over the goddamned place.' He did not mention that he himself, at the time of the mass exodus, had been on the point of resigning in order to move to another bank, but now felt that he had to stay. 'What are *your* intentions?' Fallon pointedly asked him. 'I'm waiting for a better offer. If you want an example of a better offer, if I was offered the job of president, I would take it.' 'Of the United States?' 'No. Of Harvard University.'[18]

On the same day as the turmoil at CSFB, a report was presented to the Stock Exchange's Markets Committee that surveyed how members saw the best way ahead in terms of dismantling commissions. 'Nearly all the major London firms that have replied,' it emerged, 'have come out strongly in favour of the Big Bang' – an early sighting of that celebrated tag. There were apparently several reasons for this preferred option: it would keep control in the matter of negotiating commissions in the hands of individual member firms; it was a solution that applied *equally* to all firms; and it would keep down computer costs. The survey also found that most City associations (including the Accepting Houses Committee, the Unit Trust Association and the Committee of London Clearing Bankers) were similarly minded. A fortnight later, on 7 February, there was a virtually unanimous vote by the Stock Exchange Council that the 'Big Bang' approach be adopted for the dismantling of the minimum commission structure, not earlier than autumn 1985. At the same meeting Patrick Mitford-Slade reported on the growing City conviction that retention of single capacity was no longer feasible. He explained why:

First, there was the growing internationalisation of the securities markets and the inevitable competition from overseas houses; second and more important, both the Government and the Bank of England had adopted a 'laissez faire' attitude. Neither body had been of any help in attempting to preserve single capacity but seemed to be driving the City inexorably towards financial conglomeration, in order to balance the power of the foreigner, and consequently towards opening up the securities markets, which would inevitably lead to dual capacity trading . . .

Some Members of the Council would think that single capacity should be retained, as some might say that it had been promised to the Membership. However, it had never been the Council's policy to retain single capacity under any circumstances . . .

No irrevocable decision was yet taken on this emotionally charged question, but the following week the Stock Exchange did announce that the new rules to liberalise dealing in overseas securities would take effect on 9 April, in effect permitting member firms to set up international dealing subsidiaries (IDs) to trade in overseas securities on a negotiated commission basis.[19]

There was one other change for market practitioners to digest. Monday, 13 February saw the start of the Financial Times-Stock Exchange 100-Share Index, an index formed of the shares of the 100 companies with the largest capitalisation and providing a more serious measure of portfolio performance than the FT 30-Share Index. Next day 'Lex' declared that 'the new FTSE Index – "footsy" to its friends – answers an obvious need for a market measurement which is both comprehensive and up-to-the-minute'. By the end of the week the spelling had changed; and though the older index did not immediately disappear from the headlines, in due course the neatly named 'Footsie' became the dominant measure of market sentiment and indeed a household name.[20] On Friday the 17th there were two significant announcements: first, that John Barkshire's Mercantile House was acquiring the City's oldest discount house, Alexanders; and second, that National Westminster was taking the maximum permissible stake in the fifth-largest jobbing firm, Bisgood Bishop. Barkshire was a man in a hurry. 'We don't believe there is time to build one's own structure,' he explained, as well as confirming that he had talked to the number one discount house, Gerrard & National, but had not made any offer. Instead, he professed himself happy that this move would be Mercantile's first step to becoming a 'major player' in the London securities market – the rationale being that Alexanders would add capital and market-making skills to Mercantile's trading capacity and overseas strengths, although it would still be necessary to acquire a stockbroking firm. 'If we can put all of that together we will have an excellent base from which to develop,' Barkshire concluded.[21] In recent years Mercantile had acquired the money brokers Charles Fulton & Co and the New York financial services group Oppenheimer (the latter for £90m), but this was the start of a whole new stage in his ambitious game.

As for the other announcement, NatWest said little, but Bisgoods' Chairman Ed Puxley rather grandiosely described the move as 'one step of our master plan to turn ourselves into an investment banking style operation' and added that the link would 'give us big muscle and a name worldwide'. NatWest was the first clearer publicly to make a move, and one of Puxley's senior colleagues, Brian Winterflood, would recall the strategy outlined to him soon afterwards by Charles Villiers, by autumn 1984 the Chairman and Chief Executive of NatWest's County Bank (and no relation to the Charles Villiers of IRC fame): 'His philosophy was that they would buy small, they would build on, and when the blood flowed in the streets, as inevitably it would because of what was going on, that we would pick up the pieces and that we would be one of the players of the future.' Apparently County had been allocated £300m by NatWest to build up an integrated investment bank that achieved 'minimum critical mass' before the blood – preferably other people's – started to flow. Surveying both deals, 'Lex' was unconvinced by the latest, rather expensive acquisition on the part of Barkshire's 'aspiring multi-services group', but was more positive about NatWest's surprise move. After all, there were only five significant jobbers, two had already gone (Akroyds to Warburgs and Smiths to Rothschilds) and it was not unreasonable that NatWest had 'taken the chance while it still can to add a jobbing arm, for a down payment equivalent to the cost of an hour or two's delay on the bank's next big loan repayment from Latin America'.[22]

With events moving fast, an article in the March *Institutional Investor* entitled 'Why the City will never be the same' performed a useful service by gathering together an array of City opinions. Win Bischoff of Schroders saw the pace of change on the Stock Exchange quickening if anything: 'There is a widely held suspicion that the restrictive practices are a house of cards – once some go, all will eventually go.' One anonymous stockbroker blamed malevolent forces: 'A small circle of merchant bankers persuaded the government that their interest in going into market making and stockbroking was consistent with the national interest. But that's open to question.' Another broker was more succinct: 'The government does not know what it's doing.' From a different vantage-point Kevin Pakenham, a fund manager with Foreign & Colonial, preferred to accentuate the positive: 'Deregulation is by definition experimental. No one knows what will come of it. But I think it will sweep away a lot of dead wood and force people to think clearly about what businesses they're in.'

Could the British come out ahead of the game? Timothy Jones of Akroyd & Smithers believed so: 'We don't see ourselves overtaking the Americans. But we do see ourselves holding our own in the European segment of a 24-hour-a-day world stock market.' Of course, from a strictly national point of view, much was likely to depend on how open-handed the authorities would be to the prospective foreign invasion. In the same article Parkinson's successor at the DTI, Norman Tebbit, made some distinctly welcoming noises: 'I don't have those chauvinist hang-ups that some people on the political left do, so I regard it as not unnatural that foreign institutions should take an interest in our stock exchange . . .'[23]

That was also, in effect, the message coming from the Bank of England. Nevertheless, in a speech in Edinburgh on 6 March explicitly addressing the question, Leigh-Pemberton did acknowledge that there was a balance to be struck:

> Recognition of the benefits that foreign participation can bring does not of course imply indifference to where control of major participants in our markets lies, and we would not contemplate with equanimity a Stock Exchange in which British-owned member firms played a clearly subordinate role, any more than we would like to see Lloyds or any other City market dominated by overseas interests. If this is to be avoided, and yet the door to foreign participation – and the vigour and fresh experience that it brings – is to be open, it will be necessary for British firms to be substantially strengthened so that they can compete on an even-handed basis. We have already seen a number of promising moves in this direction, and the Bank, for its part, will continue positively to encourage the development of a British securities trading capacity better able to compete in world markets.

'I have little doubt,' he added, 'that we have in this country the wits and skills to take on the keenest competition that the rest of the world can offer on a fair basis, but that wit and skill needs to be supported with adequate financial muscle.'[24]

As if by magic, it emerged the following Monday that not only was Midland's merchant banking subsidiary Samuel Montagu buying into Greenwells, but that Barclays was planning to acquire both a broker (de Zoete & Bevan) and a jobber (Wedd Durlacher), in the first three-way link.[25] Midland, despite Crocker, was still expansion-minded, though after earlier negotiations with Greenwells had faltered its own preference had been to spend less money on a smaller broking firm, Simon & Coates. It was only after *those* negotiations had run into trouble that, to its consternation, it found itself having to bless or wreck advanced negotiations between Montagu's Chief Executive, Staffan Gadd, and Greenwells. After some hesitation Midland gave its blessing and paid up. The other, notably ambitious union also owed something to happenstance. In the course of the previous autumn de Zoete's and Wedds had effectively thrown in their lot together, in the sense that they were for sale as a broker/jobber duo. The advice from Craven at Phoenix Securities was that they should steer clear of an American purchaser, and once Morgan Grenfell had dropped out of the running the effective choice lay between Kleinworts and Barclays. Not surprisingly, the clearing bank proved to have the deeper pockets, with Kleinworts' non-executive directors being particularly concerned about wagering 'too big a bite' of the merchant bank's capital. De Zoete's was happy enough with the Barclays option, its partners knowing that they would carry more clout with Barclays Merchant Bank than with the more formidable Kleinworts, but at Wedds there were serious misgivings, largely because some of the main partners felt instinctively happier with the people at Kleinworts, where Martin Jacomb had been among those pushing hardest for an alliance. Against that, decisively, Barclays offered not only more money upfront, but seemingly limitless financial backing in the future.

The eventual purchase price was something like £42m for de Zoete's and £100m (or possibly even more) for Wedds. The latter in particular was a lot of money for goodwill – admittedly of a top-flight jobber – while it is unlikely that de Zoete's (a top-of-the-second-division player) would have been at the head of Barclays' shopping list six months earlier. Nor, more generally, had much strategic thought gone into this major double acquisition. Even the house history of BZW (as the new investment banking entity would be known) concedes that Barclays had made the purchases 'with relatively little consideration of where it might lead the company'. Instead, driven in part by worries about the growing trend away from bank lending and towards securitisation (that is, tradable financial instruments), Barclays simply decided to take a punt, especially before the supply of jobbers ran out. Naturally, that was not the impression given at the time. 'We have put a lot of thought into this,' the bank's Andrew Buxton declared when the deal was announced, 'and we know where we are going.' Was there another dimension? The day after Midland and Barclays had shown their hands, the *FT* quoted one of the bankers saying about his deal, 'I have no doubt that I am doing my patriotic duty'.[26] Certainly, the Bank of England would have been gratified by both announcements; but it was Barclays' triple alliance that demonstrated that there was going to be at least one all-British, all-singing, all-dancing competitor in the new, cosmopolitan world.

On Tuesday, 13 March, Sir Gordon Borrie's fifty-third birthday, the Restrictive Practices (Stock Exchange) Act 1984 became law: the Stock Exchange was officially off the hook. That same day, as the FT 30-Share Index (which had been climbing almost continuously since the Tory election win the previous summer) hit a new high of 865.0, Lawson in his first budget gave share prices a major stimulus by introducing radical tax reforms, halving stamp duty and abolishing the national insurance surcharge. The mood in the City was buoyant, but it was not necessarily the most helpful background for making rational decisions about long-term involvement in the London securities market. Exactly a week later the Stock Exchange Council again discussed what structure that market should have once minimum commissions ended. Mitford-Slade 'said that the Floor of the House might become obsolete although many Market Makers [as jobbers were increasingly being referred to] would still want to make use of it at first, at least until information systems were bedded down'; George Birks, who had made his mark on the floor dealing in gilts for Phillips & Drew, commented that 'although he would be very sorry to see the system change, he strongly believed that the future lay in telephone and electronic dealings'; and the Council as a whole 'agreed that the relaxation of the 29.9% (up to 100%) figure was inevitable'. On the 22nd another tie-up was announced – Hambros buying a stake in the medium-sized stockbrokers and Eurobond market specialists Strauss Turnbull, with the two setting up a joint international dealing business with Société Générale – and the next day NatWest's Chief Executive, Philip Wilkinson, expressed his confidence that by the autumn the Stock Exchange would have lifted the 29.9 per cent maximum to 49.9 per cent, with 100 per cent outside ownership being permitted by 1985 or 1986.[27]

'Many people suppose that the last place in which revolutionary change was possible would be the City of London,' Andreas Whittam Smith reflected in the *Daily Telegraph* on Saturday the 24th. 'Yet that is a fair description of what is happening to the structure of the stock market. Almost every day new alliances are announced which would have been inconceivable a few years ago.' After summarising the mixture of institutional and international pressures at work, he looked further ahead:

> If an international market in Stock Exchange securities is gradually being created, it would be both desirable and perfectly logical that it should centre itself on London. The time zone is ideal and the City has every financial facility unlike, say, Paris, Frankfurt, Zurich or Amsterdam. Moreover, the world's leading investment banks are already camped out in force in the Square Mile to participate in the Euro-currency markets.
>
> This last observation, however, is a matter of foreboding for the cosseted firms of the London Stock Exchange. For some of the American firms in London, like Merrill Lynch, Salomon Brothers, and Goldman Sachs, are many times larger and better capitalised. They also trade in a way which has been forbidden to London Stock Exchange members, that is they act both as principals and agents, making markets and dealing directly with clients . . .
>
> These foreign firms in London, therefore, would be strong competitors in the British stock market. This is why the member firms of the London

Stock Exchange are rapidly making defensive alliances. Only a few of them – Cazenove is one – have the self-confidence to resist takeover offers from banks, whether British or foreign . . .[28]

It was a salutary perspective. Fear of infinitely better-resourced foreign invaders was clearly not the only reason why so many broking and jobbing firms were now starting to surrender their independence, but during these anxious months it can only have blunted whatever desire they still had to chart their own destiny.

'Not at that price,' Bill Mackworth-Young had replied when, after the Barclays announcement, he had been asked whether he wished Morgan Grenfell had bought Wedds. Whatever the commercial logic of that remark, the awkward fact was that, with Wedds now removed from the shop window, the only jobbing firm of any size still left unattached was the fourth-largest, Pinchin Denny. After some uncomfortable nego-tiations – during which, according to one account, the Morgan Grenfell people 'did not hide their disdain for the jobbers, some of whom would not have looked out of place in a street market' – an overall price of £21m was agreed, more than twice what Morgans had originally offered. The announcement of an initial 29.9 per cent stake was made on 9 April, with Mackworth-Young insisting that 'Pinchin was my first choice' and his colleague Christopher Reeves declaring with typical *chutzpah* that 'ours is not a defensive move but rather aggressive'.[29] All five jobbers were now lassoed, three by merchant banks and two by clearers, and attention inevitably turned to the significant stockbrokers not yet accounted for.

On 12 April the Stock Exchange published an important thirty-four-page discussion paper, which became known as 'The Green Book'. Safe in the knowledge that the Bank of England now accepted that there was no alternative to dual capacity, even in the gilt-edged market, it declared unequivocally at the outset the Council's view that, once negotiated commissions were introduced, 'single capacity cannot last'. The rest of the paper discussed the appropriate market structure and membership arrangements in view of that assumption. In terms of structure, there were two main proposals: first, that in the light of 'experienced and well-capitalised financial houses [i.e. non-members]' having 'said that they would like to deal direct with the Bank of England and make markets in gilt-edged stocks', and the Bank having 'made it clear that in principle it does not feel it can ignore these applications', there should be developed 'a new market system for gilt-edged securities on the lines of the market for Treasury Bonds in the USA', to be 'introduced at the time that fixed commission scales for gilt-edged securities are dismantled'; and second, in terms of equities, that 'the compatibility of a competing market-maker system with floor dealing in the long term is questionable', although in the short term, in the immediate period after the introduction of such a system, the Council envisaged the possibility of former jobbers preferring 'to maintain their market-making operation on the floor during market hours', while 'on the other hand new market-makers might wish to deal from their offices over the telephone'. As for membership, the expectation was that 'a change to enable up to 100% to be owned by a single non-member would take place at the time the dealing system changed and commissions became negotiable', while 'at the same time outside owners would be permitted to set up new Firms'.[30]

Launching the document, and no doubt aware that many smaller member firms had become increasingly uneasy about the way in which events had unfolded since his agreement with the government, Goodison insisted that these were urgent matters: 'We have not got time to pause if we are to achieve the deadline agreed with the Government.' As it happened, one of the earliest responses came from 10 Downing Street. 'It is very gratifying to see how far the debate has progressed since the Stock Exchange case was removed from the Restrictive Practices Court,' Thatcher wrote to Goodison on the 17th. 'I welcome the radical nature of the proposals which are being put forward. It is vital that the City adapts to changing circumstances and maintains its competitive position in world financial markets.'[31]

*

Up to this very day I have never, and I've discussed this obviously for many hours, I have never seen the connection between the abolition of the minimum commission and the abolition of single capacity. I've never understood the connection. It was one of these academic arguments that was raised at the time and it became the popular argument, therefore all of a sudden we found ourselves having to be dual capacity. But I could never see the necessity to. It happened in America. The specialist systems carried on in the States just the same despite negotiated commissions. But for some reason, Goodison, who I have a profound disrespect for in most things, because I think he was an academician – is that right? – and not a businessman, tossed up all these theoretical arguments but they were not practical arguments . . .

Such were the typically blunt views, expressed in 1990, of the jobber Tony Lewis of Smith Brothers. In practice, though, it was mainly the smaller brokers whom Goodison had to try to persuade in the mid-1980s that all was for the best. On the last day of April 1984, speaking to members on the floor of the Stock Exchange, he was, according to one member, 'received in stony silence' as he tried to convince them that the growing internationalisation of markets meant that there was no alternative to admitting outsiders. His arguments included the threat that, if members did not accept outsiders, the Bank of England might even take away the gilt-edged market from the Stock Exchange altogether. During May a movement of malcontent small- to medium-sized broking firms gathered steam, led by Seymour Pierce & Co's Jeremy Lewis. 'The view is that the measures are being steam-rollered through against the wishes of the membership,' he told the *FT*, while Alfred Harvey of the tiny firm of E.J. Collins & Co (and a member since 1955) added, 'I object to outsiders being able to come in and take advantage of the privileges that I have had to work hard for.' The proposed changes were, as Barry Riley put it in June, 'driving a wedge through the stock market community'. However, as he also noted, it was not so much the small firms with mainly private clients who were likely to be the losers, but rather 'the medium-sized firms which have earned a living out of the lower end of the institutional market' and 'have nothing to gain from the global market place, but have a lot to lose if they have to forgo the shelter of the fixed commission scale when competing for domestic security business'.[32] Backed by many of the instinctively change-resistant small firms, these medium-sized operators could hardly hope to halt the City revolution in its tracks, but what they could – and did – do was make life far from easy for those responsible for the constitutional aspect of that revolution.

Further notable unions were announced in mid-May: Barings' acquisition of Henderson Crosthwaite (Far East) with a view to renaming it Baring Far East Securities; and Mercantile House's purchase of not only the discount house Jessel, Toynbee & Gillett for £23.8m (in order to combine it with Alexanders, involving major redundancies at both), but also the maximum permitted stake in the stockbrokers Laing & Cruickshank for £7.5m. 'We have acquired the major bricks in constructing our securities house,' Mercantile's John Barkshire declared, though Lex's rather sour comment the next morning was that Barkshire 'has always aroused mixed feelings in the City but never can opinions of him have polarised as they did yesterday'. The column added that, although paying big prices, Mercantile 'has yet to show how all the pieces in the Meccano set will bolt together'.[33]

The deal struck by Barings seemed smaller beer, involving as it did a Japanese broking operation run by Christopher Heath with a staff of less than two dozen. Barings had originally wanted to stay out of the marriage market altogether, especially once it knew that Cazenove's was not for sale; but it was keen to achieve better distribution of its Japanese Eurobonds and shares, and at £5.8m for a 75 per cent stake the price was reasonably modest. The remaining stake, potentially immensely profitable, was at Heath's insistence kept by him and his partners. 'What happens if you make £10 million, and we pay out £2.5 million?' John Dare, in charge of Barings' Japanese business, reputedly asked him at an advanced stage in the negotiations. 'Won't your people just take the money and go home?' Heath's reply encapsulated how wide the culture gap was between the cautious banking tradition (apart from the 1890 lapse) at 8 Bishopsgate and the restless, high-octane ethos of modern securities trading that Barings was now embracing: 'You don't understand these guys. In our world, somebody who gets £1 million just wants to make £2 million. These are people who make money, and spend it.' And, tellingly, he explained how he would judge a would-be recruit on his lifestyle as much as anything: 'If he spends money on parties and racehorses, I say "fine" because he will want more. I want a guy who lives well, and is hungry.'[34]

The behavioural chasm between Heath's team and the more staid merchant bankers would eventually have profound regulatory conse- quences, but presumably Leigh-Pemberton had no such thoughts in mind when, on 23 May in the unpromising setting of the Stock Exchange Northern Unit Conference in Liverpool, he touched on the regulatory implications of the emerging City dispensation:

> Dangers become evident the moment one postulates the formation of financial groups which, in one manifestation or another, will be able to act as issuing house, market maker, investment manager and broker . . . I am quite clear in my own mind that, if Stock Exchange members are to be allowed to be both principals and investment managers within the same firm, the most convincing of Chinese walls must be erected between the two functions. Professor Gower, as you may know, is apt to say that there are often grapevines trailing over Chinese walls . . . If necessary, arrangements will have to be instituted to make sure that both sides of the wall are policed.

The Governor also touched on the comments on the Gower Report sent to the DTI: 'There is a general, although certainly not universal, belief in the advantage of significant practitioner involvement in the regulatory process, with favour widely found for channelling this through some structure of self-regulatory groupings.' In the light of this, he had decided to form an advisory group of senior City figures who would have Jacomb of Kleinworts as their Chairman and would in addition comprise Goodison, Barkshire, Brian Corby of Prudential, Hopkinson, Mackworth-Young, Morse, Scholey, Mark Weinberg of Hambro Life and Richard Westmacott of Hoare Govett.[35]

Over the next few months this genuinely distinguished body formu- lated a strong, practitioner-based case for the overall supervisory body being not so much a public agency or commission, but rather a private body with powers delegated to it by government and its members jointly appointed by the Bank of England and the DTI, not just the DTI.[36] By October, following representations along these lines by the Bank, the government had somewhat reluctantly agreed to establish, ahead of legis- lation, such a body – to be responsible for supervising the financial markets and to be called the Securities and Investments Board (SIB).

(There would also be a parallel regulatory body, the Marketing of Investments Board [MIB], to cover investment services such as life assurance and unit trusts, a hiving-off that probably owed much to the urgings of Weinberg.) The *FT* rightly noted that 'the proposed halfway house will be more acceptable to the City than a full statutory commission', but the *Economist* was worried that SIB had all the signs of a cosy stitch-up – indeed, would turn into 'yet another City club'. With a White Paper expected by the end of the year (in the event delayed by the Brighton bomb), the magazine frankly described as 'poor' the prospects for the creation of 'an effective hybrid agency largely created and run by the City to supervise more specialised bodies (the Stock Exchange, commodities dealers, etc), but which carries out stated public policy on investor protection and competition'. And it added that that agency could only hope to succeed if its chairman was 'a knowledgeable outsider, ready to make enemies'.[37]

During the month after Leigh-Pemberton's speech, two more of the main merchant banks decided to put their money on stockbroking nags: Hill Samuel bought into Wood Mackenzie (£5.98m for a 29.9 per cent stake), while Kleinwort Benson took an initial 5 per cent stake in Grieveson Grant on the basis of eventually paying £44m for complete control. Grieveson Grant was a decent enough outfit, but Kleinworts' Chairman Michael Hawkes unwisely let slip that he would have preferred to have bought James Capel, which unfortunately was too expensive.[38] Hill Samuel's decision to acquire a stockbroker was apparently much influenced by the assumption that whatever Warburgs did must be right. The corporate finance people were particularly keen, and John Chiene – the man almost single-handedly behind Wood Mackenzie's transformation from a small Edinburgh firm into a major London broking and research house – was undeniably an impressive, articulate figure, with some very able people working for him. Given the post-war history of the way in which Philip Hill had transmuted into Hill Samuel, it would have been hard to imagine it staying out of the City scramble. At Lazards, by contrast, all the instincts were otherwise, especially as the three Lazard houses (Paris and New York as well as London) were by now starting to come appreciably closer together. The forty or so London directors had already gathered at Leeds Castle in Kent for two and a half days of brainstorming, a decisive occasion recalled by the then Chairman, Ian Fraser:

> It was a critical weekend for the London firm because we all knew that the cost of failure and the reward of success were both likely to be high. There were many issues in the debate but the most important was the question: 'Should we or should we not join the crowd, buy ourselves a broker (probably at a steep price), seek to become an integrated securities house and

treble our size, or should we remain small, specialist, risk-averse and wait for the fashion to wash over and disappear?' We decided on the latter course – unanimously . . .³⁹

A decade or so later it would seem an obvious decision (the prudent avoidance of combining financial risk with strategic risk), but it was not so at the time; and in the event Lazards stuck to its guns, despite a series of hopeful approaches from Stock Exchange firms, and was the *only* significant merchant bank in the mid-1980s that completely refused to enter the securities business.

Lazards accordingly was more detached than most when in mid-July the Stock Exchange Council formally gave its blessing to the creation of an electronic marketplace to be known as SEAQ (Stock Exchange Automated Quotations). The idea was that competing market makers would use SEAQ in order to maintain at all times a continuous market, and the Council spoke confidently of 'a system which would take advantage of methods of communication that would enable members, wherever they were located, to see the prices made by market makers and to be able to deal with them on the floor and by the telephone'. The expectation was that, for the foreseeable future, trading on the floor would co-exist with telephone trading in dealing rooms, but in both cases reliant on the prices displayed on SEAQ screens. Significantly it was a system (largely modelled on the pioneering automated quotations system of the American NASDAQ market) that allowed members to continue acting in a single capacity, as agency brokers, if they chose to do so. Soon, inevitably, there was speculation that electronic trading would completely supersede floor trading. 'The inescapable fact is that it is now an international securities industry,' Peter Holloway of Wedd Durlacher told *Euromoney* a few weeks after the Stock Exchange's announcement. 'If we want to participate, we have to be able to offer a market-making capacity 24 hours a day.' However, Paul Killik of Quilter Goodison was among those who insisted that face-to-face dealing would at least see out the 1980s. 'The brokers,' he assured a journalist, 'will fight to keep the human element in trading; after all, you cannot look a screen in the eye, can you?'⁴⁰ Whatever the technological dynamics of the situation, let alone the cost implications, a twin-track strategy it would be, as London's securities industry began to prepare for the new world.

One of those firms was the medium-sized brokers Fielding, Newson-Smith, which on 20 July was bought into by National Westminster and thereby linked up with County Bank and the jobbers Bisgood Bishop. Its senior partner, Dundas Hamilton, recalled how two American banks, one European bank and one merchant bank had all been interested in Fieldings, but that after meeting County's Villiers at a cocktail party, NatWest came through strongest. It was partly the money, he explained, partly NatWest's international presence and partly the fact that 'they were very nice people and we thought very well managed'. NatWest itself (which had been in serious talks with Phillips & Drew, but had been unwilling to put a sufficiently high valuation on that firm's fund management business) was vulnerable to the charge that in Bisgoods and Fieldings it had plumped for two second-rankers; but as Christopher Fildes recollected, 'its people explained at the time that they saw no point in paying a premium for skills that were already obsolescent'.[41]

The following week there were two almost simultaneous announcements: that Grindlays (owners of Australia's profitable ANZ Bank) had moved for the brokers Capel-Cure Myers, with an attractive private client network; and that the American financial conglomerate Shearson Lehman-American Express had done the same for Jock Hunter's old firm, L. Messel & Co. At that firm, the debate about which offer to accept had become so impossible to resolve that the senior partner, David Lloyd, finally put the entire partnership in a room at the Great Eastern Hotel and insisted that no one left until an irrevocable decision had been reached. 'James Capel shanghaied and then there were seven' was the neat headline for a Kenneth Fleet piece in *The Times* on 7 August, on the back of news that talks between the Hongkong and Shanghai Bank and London's leading broker in the secondary market, James Capel, were at an advanced stage. That, according to Fleet, left only seven significant London brokers with their fates still undecided. Three of them, like Capel, were leading firms: 'Cazenove, whose future inspires the same kind of fascinated curiosity with which Europe watched the later careers of Louis XVI and Marie Antoinette; Phillips & Drew, whose old cloth-cap professionalism has now been polished to a high and much envied sheen; and Scrimgeour Kemp-Gee, whose rise to stardom is one of the stock market's better stories.' The other four, all stronger in gilts than equities, were Mullens, Nivisons, Laurie Milbank and Pember & Boyle.[42]

Fleet's list did not include Rowe & Pitman, presumably on the assumption that because of the mutual link with Akroyd & Smithers, it was already destined for the Warburgs camp. This was confirmed on 14 August, with the news that Mercury Securities (parent of S.G. Warburg & Co) was taking the maximum permissible stake in Rowe & Pitman. Perhaps the union had been inevitable since January, but at one point Peter Stormonth Darling had wondered aloud whether Phillips & Drew might not be a preferable alternative, being formidable in fund management as well as more powerful in the secondary market, not to mention much closer in ethos to the traditional Warburg disdain for upper-class English amateurism. He was told, however, that 'they were "not our kind of people", and were not in the same class as Rowe & Pitman'. Warburgs' inexorable drift into the City establishment was confirmed by the simultaneous news that it would also, with the encouragement of the Bank of England, be acquiring Mullens, which in the newly structured gilt-edged market would no longer be providing the Government broker. Warburgs, Akroyd & Smithers, Rowe & Pitman, Mullens: it made, on paper at least, a formidable alliance. Of course, the question on many people's lips was what Sir Siegmund would have made of this plan to create an across-the-waterfront US-style investment bank. 'The boldness of the concept would have earned his respect,' John Makinson reflected soon afterwards in the *FT.* 'Warburg, after all, owes its present position in the City to a succession of imaginative leaps . . .' Mindful also that the keeper of the flame, Henry Grunfeld, still attended the office daily, Makinson was inclined to hedge his bets: 'The links are bound to wreak fundamental changes within Warburgs. But the bank is unlikely to lose its distinctive personality overnight.'[43] For those with a taste for symbolism, Warburgs' recent move from Gresham Street to King William Street just north of London Bridge also lent itself to ambivalence: the new premises were undeniably bigger, better appointed and thus character-sapping; but by a satisfying twist it was in King William Street that Warburgs (and before it the New Trading Co) had originally set up shop.

The announcements continued to come. Later in August it emerged that Schroders was setting up its own stockbroking firm, with the unwieldy name Helbert Wagg & Co, Anderson Bryce Villiers, led largely by three former members of Panmure Gordon; and by early September not only had the tie-up between the Hongkong and Shanghai Bank and James Capel been confirmed, but it was revealed that Citicorp was acquiring a second stockbroking firm, Scrimgeour Kemp-Gee. The decision by Scrimgeours to go with Citicorp (rather than NatWest) seems to have been a rare case of a stockbroking partnership not selling itself to the highest bidder, but instead to the one it believed would have the resolve and financial clout not to retire from the fray when the inevitable price war broke out after the ending of minimum commissions. Nevertheless, at a sale price of some £50m for a partnership of barely fifty people, it was not *such* a sacrifice. Meanwhile, still concerned about the larger picture, especially as it affected small investors, David Hopkinson of M&G had sent Goodison a public letter at the end of August expressing his concerns about the headlong pace of change. Goodison replied on 6 September:

> You want to prevent the market from falling 'into the control of too few houses'. I assume that you must be referring particularly to the market in domestic securities. I told Cecil Parkinson in 1983 that there was a risk of this happening if fixed minimum commissions were abolished. We all know that this is one of the dilemmas of competition policy. Cut-throat price competition can lead to a few dominant suppliers. I hope in our case that it

will not happen. I hope that the big battalions will behave responsibly. But our domestic markets are relatively small, the commercial banks are relatively large, and the fear remains.[44]

So it did, and the latest Citicorp initiative would hardly have allayed Hopkinson's anxieties.

Later in September the publication of Laing & Cruickshank's annual report on accepting houses provided a moment for informed, somewhat sceptical stocktaking. Noting that there had been 'a sharp setback in merchant bank share prices in recent months' and that 'whatever their trading prospects, events have been completely dominated by their wholesale entry into the securities industry', the report went on:

> The market sees dangers and uncertainty ahead in a number of areas:
> * Merchant banks have bought brokers probably close to the peak in their highly cyclical earnings, and certainly ahead of structural changes which will depress profitability. They have also bought jobbers whose profits will suffer from reduced dealing spreads as the number of market makers rises, and the practice of principal trading spreads.
> * There is concern that merchant banks and brokers do not have the skills required for market making and principal trading. It is widely accepted that dual capacity trading will inevitably emerge from the Stock Exchange reforms, but this does not mean that novices endowed with capital will make profits.
> * There will be problems in merging the different cultural backgrounds of the merchant banks who are risk averse, with traders who are risk takers.

David Lascelles, in the *FT*'s survey of UK banking, was also cautious, observing that 'now that the euphoria has died down a bit', the banks would need to do the hard bit of having 'to work out how to pull together the securities operations they have assembled in greater haste than they may have wished'. However, he did see the creation of these big new financial groups as 'part of the much-desired evolution towards a service economy, and evidence that Britain can manage change even though this year's other big business news story, the miners' strike, suggests the opposite'. Indeed, he added piquantly, 'nothing could contrast more with the frustration and despair of the coalmen than the sense of opportunity coursing through the City'.[45]

The miners' strike also cast an indirect shadow over the Johnson Matthey affair.[46] By Tuesday, 25 September the Bank of England realised – rather late in the day, most observers subsequently reckoned – that Johnson Matthey Bankers (JMB), part of the Johnson Matthey Group, was insolvent, largely as the result of a rash overexpansion of its loans book. That in itself might or might not have caused a crisis, but the additional problem was that JMB was one of the five London banks authorised to deal in the London gold market. The others were Rothschilds, Kleinworts, Midland and Standard Chartered, the last three being the owners respectively of Sharps Pixley, Samuel Montagu and Mocatta & Goldsmid. By the end of the week, with rumours starting to circulate, the Bank of England was looking for a new owner for JMB, with the main hope being that the Bank of Nova Scotia would put in a bid. Leigh-Pemberton had been away in Washington at the IMF annual meeting, and it was his deputy, Kit McMahon, who for most of a very long weekend was left to take the strain. As early as the Saturday morning both Evelyn de Rothschild and Michael Hawkes (of Kleinworts) made it clear to him that there was a serious danger to the London gold market, and possibly even the London inter-bank market, if JMB was allowed to go. By Sunday afternoon the Canadians had pulled out of negotiations, having failed to receive indemnification against potential lawsuits, and the situation really started to become critical. Representatives of all possible interested parties, including London's clearing banks, were summoned for early that evening, for a series of conferences between McMahon and particular groups. At one point Hawkes mischievously decided to leave the room he had been assigned and have a quiet snoop around:

> In one room there were the Johnson Matthey bankers' books, and I spent a glorious two hours going through them. There wasn't a single name I'd ever heard of, and the amounts – £60 million to one name, £30 million to another – were absolutely staggering. We spent ages hanging around, lobbying every Bank of England man we could find and urging that Johnson Matthey must be rescued. Otherwise the gold market would go forthwith to Switzerland, and the malaise in the gold market might spread to other members of the market, perhaps even to the Midland Bank . . . Till 10.30 at night all this seemed of no avail, and I came to the conclusion that the Bank of England had decided to let Johnson Matthey go . . .

By then, however, McMahon had decided that there *was* systemic risk, and that whatever the implicit weakening of moral hazard there was no alternative to a rescue of JMB. Leigh-Pemberton was present by midnight, following a weekend in Kent; and in the small hours he talked to the clearers and sought to organise a 'Lifeboat' along the lines of the secondary banking rescue of 1973–4, apparently expecting it to be as relatively straightforward as it had been then. To his consternation they refused, apparently on the grounds that three years earlier Richardson had failed to fight their corner at the time of the windfall tax. Their attitude was an eloquent indication of the Bank's diminished authority. Some rather imprecise promises of help were eventually given, but it would be down to the Bank itself to take over JMB, though inevitably with no certainty about what the financial liability might be. The Chancellor, Nigel Lawson, was belatedly put in the picture at 7.30 a.m., and before the markets opened it was known that the Bank had taken responsibility. 'These arrangements enabled Johnson Matthey Bankers to trade normally and meet all its commitments,' stated the deliberately low-key announcement, and for the moment that seemed the end of the matter.[47]

Unfortunately for the Bank, the unholy alliance of Dennis Skinner and David Owen had other intentions. On 23 October Skinner, motivated by the hypocrisy of public funds for unprofitable banks but not for unprofitable mines, asked Lawson in the Commons if public money had been employed in the JMB rescue; Owen, in a letter to Lawson, not only pursued that tack, but argued that the danger to the gold market had been seriously overestimated and that the Bank's decision to take over JMB was mistaken, especially as 'such treatment has not been accorded to a number of other and much larger industrial and commercial companies which have also collapsed in recent years'. Lawson, already irked by being left in the dark in late September, dead-batted as best he could, but over the next few weeks Owen continued his campaign, amidst gathering talk of an establishment cover-up. Finally, on 17 December, Lawson sought to take the political heat out of the situation by announcing to the Commons that he was setting up an inquiry into the system of banking supervision. By a cruel stroke for the Bank, he was asked by the Labour backbencher Robert Sheldon (seventeen years after his costly question to Callaghan) what exactly the Bank's liability was. Wrongly believing that the Bank's only significant liability with regard to JMB was its half-share of a £150m indemnity, and not having been told that on 22 November the Bank had transferred to it £100m of liquid (sterling) reserves as working capital, Lawson gave a reply that inadvertently misled the House. When that emerged he understandably (if mistakenly) 'felt badly let down, as I made clear when I learned about it'.[48] In the West End as in the East End, the reputation of the Bank – and its still relatively new Governor – was at an alarmingly low ebb.

Preying on McMahon's mind when he had decided that JMB must be saved, in order to avert a domino effect, was the knowledge of Midland's seriously weakened state as a result of the Crocker imbroglio. Early in the year, as the huge losses continued to mount up, Midland had revoked Crocker's autonomy and sent in its own troubleshooters to try and get a grip on Crocker's dreadful loan book. It also hired a respected but (from Midland's point of view) overly ambitious Californian banker, Frank Cahouet, to take day-to-day control. 'Can Midland clean up the mess at Crocker?' *Institutional Investor* asked in July, and it quoted Cahouet's confident answer: 'Can Midland save Crocker? No. Crocker has to save Crocker. And Crocker *can* save Crocker.' That was not, however, the view of the US regulators, where attitudes to Crocker were hardening as a result of the near-collapse in May of Chicago's biggest bank, Continental

Illinois. By early December the regulators were telling Midland – and an apprehensive Bank of England – that there was no alternative to at least another $300m in bad loan provisions. Over an increasingly desperate few weeks the money was found to enable Midland to invest $250m more and arrange a $125m standby loan in case there was a run on Crocker. The apocalyptic mood was graphically caught when Midland's Finance Director, Michael Julien, saw in the Christmas issue of the *Investors Chronicle* a spoof account of Leigh-Pemberton having his turkey ruined by a flunkey announcing that another bank had collapsed. Julien rushed to show it to his Chief Executive, Geoffrey Taylor, reputedly crying, 'They know!'[49]

By now, after three final busy months in 1984, almost all the Stock Exchange marriages had been arranged. In mid-October, having failed to clinch a deal with either Rowe & Pitman or Phillips & Drew, Morgan Grenfell settled for the much cheaper (£10m) Pember & Boyle – an eminently respectable if rather unexciting firm, which unfortunately specialised in gilts at a time when equities offered by far the better money-making prospect. Mackworth-Young died a few days later, and Morgan Grenfell's chances of making a real go of it in the securities business further receded. Then, in early November, 'Swiss role for P&D' was Lex's witty way of greeting the news that Phillips & Drew had plighted itself to Union Bank of Switzerland (UBS). 'We weren't the highest bidders,' UBS told the *Wall Street Journal.* 'It was a combination of price and concept that made the difference.'[50] Later in the month Chase Manhattan simultaneously got its hands on two brokers (Laurie Milbank and Simon & Coates), and just before Christmas tie-ups were announced between North Carolina National Bank and Panmure Gordon, and Banque Bruxelles Lambert and Williams de Broë Hill Chaplin. A few more unions would be announced in 1985, but the main wave was over.

'Some of the purchases were calmly calculated, some derived from instinctive opportunism, but many were little more than a panic move to avoid being left out,' John Littlewood subsequently reflected. 'All too often, a rash temptation to buy a barely understood business was met by an equally rash temptation to sell out to a little-known buyer or an ill-defined future.' On the basis of known figures and some informed guesswork, he estimated that (once the initial stakes, mainly 29.9 per cent, had been raised in due course to 100 per cent, as almost invariably they were) a total of some £450m was paid for the nine leading brokers that sold out, another £400m for twenty-two broking firms that were more medium-sized and £300m for the five leading jobbers – coming to a grand total of some £1,150m for thirty-six firms. It was not a cheap exercise, and a notable feature was that a high proportion of the leading American banks and investment houses, including Bankers Trust, CSFB, Drexel

Burnham Lambert, Goldman Sachs, Morgan Guaranty, Morgan Stanley and Salomons, saw little advantage in buying at the top of the market and instead opted for organic growth. The same applied to Merrill Lynch, apart from its eventual acquisition in 1985 of a small gilts dealer; and it, like most of the others, already had a significant London presence. Moreover, some asked themselves, what exactly would they be buying? At one point Bank of America came close to acquiring Phillips & Drew – until, the story goes, a leading figure at the bank declared that he was damned if he was going to pay out a small fortune on 'assets that go up and down the elevator'. Admittedly there was usually a 'golden handcuffs' mechanism, but with money burning a hole in their pockets the natural desire of many of those assets was to be making the downward ride. There were also the haunting words of Brian Pitman, as he crisply explained in December 1984 why Lloyds was not going into the international securities business: 'It's unrealistic to believe you can be the best in every financial market and in every financial product.'[51]

For those who were taking the gamble (whether for aggressive or defensive reasons), there was perhaps comfort in the two words 'British Telecom'.[52] The Conservative government's decision to privatise just over 50 per cent of British Telecommunications, originally announced in March 1982, had huge City implications, in that it involved an equity issue of almost £4bn – the biggest that any stock market, let alone the London capital market, had ever seen – and moved the privatisation process into an altogether higher gear. In due course the mandate went to Kleinwort Benson, where the key figure was Jacomb, abetted by James (Lord) Rockley and David Clementi. Initially, there was far from universal confidence or indeed enthusiasm in the City. At a dinner party attended by Lawson but mainly comprising 'captains of industry and pillars of leading City merchant banks', the Chancellor was struck by how, with the notable exception of Jacomb, 'each and every one of them roundly declared that the privatisation was impossible: the capital market simply was not large enough to absorb it'. The government too had its moments of doubt, wanting to do the sale in more than one tranche, before bowing to Jacomb's insistence on a single tranche.[53] Partly because it could not be assumed that the institutions alone would bite off such a large issue, and partly because of the political attraction of spreading the virtues of popular capitalism, the government was determined to reach out to private investors and – beyond them – the general, more or less City-ignorant, public as a whole.

Could it be done? In his *Spectator* column in August 1984 Fildes expressed scepticism that the City would be able to sell BT to the mass of potential individual shareholders, lacking as it did 'road show' techniques, appetite, and so on. That autumn, however, a massive and – in City terms

– wholly unprecedented television advertising campaign, together with an equally systematic PR campaign to reach the tabloids, created a high degree of general awareness, helped no doubt by the generally bullish tendencies of the market, which was recovering strongly after a nasty dip in the summer. On 12 November, just over a fortnight after the release of the 'pathfinder' prospectus (itself an innovation), Arthur H. Poole was moved to write to the Stock Exchange. After outlining how, as 'an East End boy with nothing but an elementary school background', he had become an office boy with Bourke Schiff & Co in 1922 before eventually building up quite a clientele of private investors, finally with Henry J. Garratt & Co, he went on:

> You will never have a better opportunity than you have at this moment to attract the small investor, than the forthcoming Brit Telecom issue. I have been approached by so many people who have never invested before, as to whether they should apply for shares, and how they go about it. With other de-nationalised offers in the pipeline, and with the advent of thousands of would-be Clients, you have a real chance to recapture the long lost small investor . . .[54]

The formal offer for sale, or 'Impact Day' as it was called, occurred four days later, on 16 November: 3,012 million shares were to be sold at 130p each, raising £3,916m; 47 per cent of the issue was to be allocated to the UK investing institutions, 39 per cent to the British public and 14 per cent to overseas investors.

It was soon clear that the issue was a palpable hit, being no fewer than five times oversubscribed. When dealings began in the Stock Exchange on 3 December the shares were at an almost 100 per cent premium, and not surprisingly there were some hectic scenes on the floor, which when Poole watched them on television may have reminded him of nothing so much as the frenzied rubber boom of July 1925. Everyone was a winner, it seemed, in this most visible of triumphs for 'the market'; it was also, in retrospect, the episode that signalled that the Thatcher era was moving towards its high tide. Yet for the City itself, although profiting hugely, there was a disquieting aspect, as over the next few weeks much of the market in BT shares shifted (under Morgan Stanley's auspices) to New York, where Americans were eager to sell to British institutions.[55] It was the clearest possible indication that the market in leading equities was becoming global – and that, within that market, there would be no room for London to hide.

*

The mid-1980s would have been memorable even without the small matter of a local revolution. Febrile, driven by greed, pushing back the boundaries of acceptable behaviour, this was a brief, intense phase that in some ways was a rerun of the late 1920s, this time with added attitude. In each case, satisfyingly for the moralists, there was the same dénouement.

Unlike the bubble of the late 1920s, that of the mid-1980s had a strongly innovative element, especially in the Euromarkets, and left a far-reaching legacy. 'Many of the financial innovations in these markets,' Dimitri Vittas noted in the *Banker* in May 1985, 'have been linked with one or other of the big American institutions such as Citibank, Morgan Guaranty, Salomon Brothers or Merrill Lynch':

> Such innovations include the development of medium-term floating rate rollover credits, medium-term floating rate notes, perpetual floating rate notes and drop block bonds. More recently, revolving underwriting facilities (or note issuance facilities) and the related short-term Euronotes as well as transferable loan facilities have become prominent in the Eurocurrency markets. Two other innovations where American institutions have played a leading role and which are of an international character even though they may make use of domestic markets are interest rate swaps and currency swaps . . .
>
> European and Japanese institutions have been able to adopt, and quite often improvise, new instruments and techniques with considerable speed and flexibility. Their response to the American challenge has been swift and effective. Thus, the recent introduction of currency options, future rate agreements, flipflop perpetual notes, mismatch and minimax medium-term variable rate notes as well as of multiple component facilities, note tender panels and swap tender panels owes often as much to the inventiveness and ingenuity of British and other non-American institutions as to the large US names . . .

At about the same time the *FT*'s Euromarkets correspondent, Peter Montagnon, developed the theme:

> Nowadays commercial banks concentrate less and less on actually making loans. Instead, they are using their resources to generate fee income, for example by underpinning the sale by their customers of debt securities or Euronotes direct to end-investors or by arranging mutually advantageous exchanges of debt – or swaps – between one or more separate borrowers . . .
>
> The new-style banking has led to an explosion of business in the note issuance market where banks underwrite the continuous sale by their clients of short-term securities or Euronotes to investors, thereby providing a guarantee to the borrower that funds will be available over the medium term. Total note facilities outstanding are now generally estimated at some $40 bn, with most having been arranged since the start of 1984. Business is also booming in the debt exchange or 'swap' market. Salomon Brothers reckons that $80 bn worth of swaps were arranged world-wide last year . . .

Two months later, in July, Montagnon returned to the complicated, computer-driven world of swaps:

> A quiet but profound revolution has occurred in the $100bn-a-year

international bond market. Almost imperceptibly to all but the most specialist insiders the market has gone global. The rigid demarcations that once separated, say, the eurodollar bond market from its counterparts in West Germany and Japan have been broken down. Now, more than ever, practitioners are used to the idea of talking in terms of one market place, covering effectively almost the whole of the industrialised world . . .

Suddenly, borrowers are no longer restricted only to that particular market which offers the currency and type of debt they require. Instead they can pick and choose, launching issues in markets where they will get the best receptions or where funds are most readily available and then switching the debt into another currency, or from fixed to floating rate, or vice versa . . .[56]

It was inevitable that, sooner or later, central bankers would deliver some warning words. In September 1985, addressing an audience of bankers in Lausanne, Kit McMahon duly did so, arguing that international banking and 'financial activity more generally' had embarked in the past two to three years on changes that were 'probably as far-reaching as any in its long history'. He cautioned that 'we already know of cases where not even those in daily contact with the new instruments have grasped fully what it is that they are taking on'; accordingly, he did not expect 'the honeymoon period' of these new instruments to be of long duration.[57] Unfortunately (or not), the trend was irreversible. The barriers, whether national or functional, between the world's capital and money markets were coming down; nation states were increasingly engaged in competitive deregulation, with exchange controls, tax barriers and impediments to foreign access or the use of new instruments all being liberalised or removed at a bewildering pace; and in fine, there beckoned the delights of a global, seamless market in all things financial.[58]

The relevant Euromarket figures for 1985 literally spoke volumes: $231bn was issued in loans and Euronotes (compared with $102bn in 1983); $133bn was issued in Eurobonds ($48bn in 1983); $16bn was issued in Eurocommercial paper (less than $0.5bn in 1983); and almost $3.7bn was issued in the practically new field of Euroequities (more than twice the 1983 figure). For 1986 the relevant figures in these four categories were $217bn, $180bn, $6.1bn and $11.5bn – in three out of four cases a large jump upwards. In the Eurobond market itself, CSFB stayed on top of the keenly watched lead-management league table for both years. Von Clemm left in 1986 to assume responsibility for the worldwide capital market operations of Merrill Lynch, but Rudloff stayed, becoming an increasingly legendary (as well as powerful) figure. One of CSFB's traditional main rivals, Deutsche, had a more chequered time. That bank's decision early in 1985 to move its Eurobond business to London was rightly heralded as a significant mark of confidence in the City's future; but its three managing directors quarrelled about almost everything, including the colour of the wallpaper, and there were rows about whether the newly recruited head of trading, Stanley Ross, should be given a parking space and an office commensurate in size and status to theirs. Reputedly, the eventual word from Frankfurt was yes to the office, no to the parking space. The story symbolised Frankfurt's reluctance to let go, and the hamstrung consequence was that Deutsche that year, having almost invariably been in the top three, slipped to fifth place. In 1986, however, Deutsche bounced back to third, its reputation much helped by the successful $1bn issue for Canada in February, the first fixed-rate 'jumbo'. Big, tightly priced and very liquid, it was recalled by Paul Richards of Merrill Lynch as 'a terrific deal', being 'the first real benchmark bond, the first real treasury surrogate'.[59]

However, the most striking shift in the Eurobond league tables was the arrival, big time, of the Japanese houses. Nomura had been bubbling under for some years, but the breakthrough came in 1986 when it was second only to CSFB; while Daiwa, only once before in the top ten, took fifth position, ahead of Morgan Stanley, Salomons, Paribas and Merrill Lynch. Moreover, Nikko was tenth, Yamaichi twelfth and Industrial Bank of Japan seventeenth (two places ahead of Warburgs). The *FT*'s Clare Pearson reckoned that this rise owed something to the American investment banks 'paying relatively less attention to the Eurobond market as they carve out a share of the rapidly growing Euro-equity market', but she also noted the 'dogged determination' of the Japanese houses. 'There was always something cryptic in their methods,' Michael Lewis (who worked at Salomons in London from late 1985) recalled. 'The phone would ring at your desk and on the other end of the line would be Mr Yamamoto, whom you had seen off the previous night in a drunken haze, asking: "How now Rong Bond?" This was the Japanese way of asking for the price of 30-year US government bonds. "Ninety-six bid," you'd say. "I buy $100 million," he'd say, then hang up. A friend for life.'[60]

By now, the Eurobond secondary market was no longer the poor relation. Each year its turnover set a new record: roughly $1 trillion in 1983, more than $1.5 trillion in 1984 and approaching $2 trillion in 1985. In May 1985 *Institutional Investor*'s David Schutt described the scene at 107 Cheapside in the dealing room of Kidder Peabody Securities, with 'its bank of seven clocks':

> The Eurobond market's time is never quite its own these days. Starting with San Francisco at the far left on Kidder's wall, proceeding through New York, across the Atlantic to London and continental Europe, and then moving on to Kuwait before ending, roughly twenty feet away, in Tokyo the clocks suggest that each financial center claims its own portion of the London day. Tokyo is the morning, New York the early afternoon, and activity from other centers waxes and wanes throughout the day. The global

landscape has been compressed into a few thousand square feet of Kidder dealing room, where the world's events are reflected to the thirty-secondth by the bids and offers on video display terminals. Certainly, if the vaunted global marketplace is occurring anywhere, it's happening right now in London . . .

The Eurobond secondary market, Schutt went on, was becoming a different animal:

> The legendary maverick trader, the loner who made markets in good times and bad with the help of a handful of faithful employees, is today more likely to be working for a large foreign-owned bank or securities firm where he co-ordinates the activities of scores of traders. The Swiss investor, once the mainstay of the market, is rapidly losing his place to a variety of institutional investors, most notably the Japanese. Interest rate volatility, previously considered a peculiarly American aberration, is now a fact of life in the Eurobond market, bringing with it new risks and opportunities . . .

Who traded in this secondary market? A year later the same magazine's trader directory listed 147 leading firms, more than half of which were London-based. They included (to give an almost random selection) Bank of America International (1 Watling Street), Bank of Tokyo International (20/24 Moorgate), Dean Witter Capital Markets International (56 Leadenhall Street), Deutsche Bank Capital Markets (150 Leadenhall Street), First Interstate Capital Markets (162 Queen Victoria Street), Mitsubishi Finance International (1 King Street), Paine Webber International Trading (1 Finsbury Avenue) and Svenska International (17 Devonshire Square). The directory also listed many of the trading specialisations, typified by the fourteen relevant departments at Bache Securities (UK) at 9 Devonshire Square: US$ straights; Floating-rate notes; Zero coupons; Sinking funds; CDs; Warrants, DM bonds; Sf & C$ bonds; ECU & yen bonds; Eurosterling bonds; US domestic corporates, Yankee bonds; US governments; Supranationals; New issues; Interest rate swaps.[61] It would all have meant very, very little to a time traveller from the City of the 1950s.

'You just can't talk about the Eurobond secondary market anymore – you have to be more specific than that,' Morgan Stanley International's Managing Director, Archibald Cox Jr, told Schutt for his 1985 profile of that market. And, 'by way of illustration', Cox pointed to 'the clusters of convertible, foreign exchange, gold, silver, US Treasury and equity desks that fill Morgan's trading room to overflowing'. Some of those sectors clearly fell outside the Eurobond market, and the one with the highest profile by the mid-decade was foreign exchange dealing. Its recent growth, not only in London but undoubtedly led by London, had been phenomenal: in 1979 the average daily global foreign-exchange turnover was some $75bn; by 1984 that turnover had roughly doubled. In both years London's market share was about one-third, well ahead of its nearest rivals, New York, Zurich and Frankfurt. By late 1985 London's daily turnover ($25bn in 1979, $49bn in 1984) was up to an astonishing $90bn. The overwhelming majority of this forex activity was done between fifty or so of the largest banks in London, with only a small proportion (almost certainly less than 5 per cent) backed by a fundamental transaction on the part of a company, a government or a central bank.[62]

As the world's financial boundaries conclusively dissolved, and national governments began to quail before what Denis Healey in June 1985 memorably called 'an atomic cloud' of footloose and speculative capital flows, attempts by finance ministers to stabilise exchange rates often had a Canute-like quality. Lawson's approach was typically robust, having no compunction about risking Leigh-Pemberton's wrath by ringing up the Bank of England's foreign-exchange dealing room and telling them what to do. As for Thatcher, her free-market principles did not extend quite as far as admiring what one magazine article nicely called 'the biggest floating crap game in town'. 'Those whose eyes are glued to the screens and ears to the telephones of the world's exchanges have missed the point,' she angrily declared in February 1985 during a period of particularly intense currency turbulence, with sterling under the cosh.[63] The trauma of the pound almost dipping below the dollar early that year inevitably had the effect of moving up the agenda the question of whether Britain should join the European Monetary System (whose operating arm was the Exchange Rate Mechanism), which had begun in March 1979. Despite Lawson, the Treasury and the Bank forming an increasingly powerful alliance in the course of the year, Thatcher's opposition remained steadfast.[64] In her bones, she knew that the market could not be bucked.

*

Two important bits of unfinished business, neither redounding to the City's credit, were resolved in the course of 1985–6: Johnson Matthey and Crocker. In June 1985, almost nine months after JMB's collapse, Lawson published the findings of the joint Treasury-Bank committee that he had set up the previous December. Its proposals included ending the 1979 Banking Act's two-tier system of recognised banks and licensed deposit-takers; its replacement with a single authorisation to take deposits, thereby giving the Bank of England broader powers over all banks; regular dialogue between the Bank and the banks' auditors (JMB's auditors, Arthur Young, were about to be sued by the now Bank-owned JMB); 25 per cent of a bank's capital as maximum exposure to a single or related borrowers; and the Bank's much-criticised supervision staff not only to be increased, but to be given commercial banking experience. Lawson himself, in his accompanying statement to the Commons, did not deny the Bank's culpability: 'On this occasion the Bank did not act as promptly as it should have, and to some extent fell down on the job.' These were carefully measured words, but two days later the *FT*'s David Lascelles let himself go:

> For sheer drama, it is a tale of banking incompetence on a scale that defies belief: a small bank manages to lose £248m, more than half its loan book of £400m, and forces the Bank of England to mount one of the most elaborate rescue operations ever seen in the UK because it happens to be a vital cog in the delicate machinery of the international gold market . . .
>
> But for the history books, the big story will be the turning point that JMB represents in the evolution of banking supervision in the UK: the changes it has set in motion well may mark the end of the gentlemanly codes by which the Bank of England and the City have abided for decades, founded on trust and frankness.
>
> Instead, the teeming ranks of the 600 banks now crammed into London will be kept in line with more form-filling, closer scrutiny by accountants, more frequent meetings with a beefed-up team of Bank supervisors, and a string of new regulations that will be devised in the coming months.
>
> 'A sad day, but necessary,' was how a senior banker viewed the scene yesterday . . .

Inevitably, as in 1974 after the secondary banking crisis, there was a scapegoat at the Bank – this time the associate director for banking supervision, Peter Cooke. In fact, the Bank was perhaps fortunate to retain responsibility for banking supervision at all. Thatcher would have been more than happy to take it away, but was dissuaded by Lawson, largely on the grounds that, in his subsequent words, 'it was the unfettered responsibility for banking supervision that, as I saw it, largely gave the Bank its authority in the eyes of the City and thus more widely'. The Bank did have to pay a price, in the eventual establishment of a Board of Banking Supervision; but in practice this did not significantly undermine the Bank's supervisory authority, which was formally renewed in the 1987 Banking Act.[65]

Shortly before it emerged in September 1985 that Cooke was to be (in Stephen Fay's phrase) 'moved downwards and sideways', it was announced that the Deputy Governor, Kit McMahon, was to leave the Bank. His surprise successor, returning from semi-retirement, was George Blunden, a tough, thick-skinned operator to whom the new executive director in charge of supervision, Rodney Galpin, would report. As for McMahon, never a Tory favourite and inevitably tainted by the JMB episode, his new role would be the distinctly challenging one of Chairman and Chief Executive of Midland Bank. During 1985 and into the next year that battered institution gradually managed to extricate itself from the Crocker disaster, finally selling the Californian bank to Wells Fargo in May 1986. Overall, the Crocker venture had almost certainly cost it at least

£1bn, reducing it to a position, by the time it got rid of Crocker, where technically it was probably bankrupt. 'Clearly we are going to be, by the look of it, the smallest of the four clearing banks,' Geoffrey Taylor remarked on the eve of his departure as Chief Executive in September 1986, half a century after Midland had gloried in being the world's biggest bank.[66]

In his Lausanne speech just before the news broke that he was leaving the Bank of England, McMahon had mentioned futures as one of the areas that needed particularly careful watching by the financial authorities. He may well have had financial futures partly in mind, but in fact LIFFE – against a background of mainly steady rather than spectacular growth in the mid-1980s – was a notably well-run market, where there were no major scandals. Instead, within weeks of McMahon's speech it was a débâcle on the London Metal Exchange (LME) that seriously affected the reputation of London's futures markets, in a sense unfairly, given that the LME was really more of a forward cash market than a proper futures market.[67] Moreover, the particular market involved – the tin market – had for over a quarter of a century been operating on behalf of an international cartel, the International Tin Council (ITC), whose membership comprised twenty-two producer and consumer nations. This again was quite unlike a genuine futures market, such as the Chicago Board of Trade, driven by freely competing market forces. Indeed, the whole character of the LME in Plantation House had a clubbiness, even an exclusivity, quite unlike the great American models. Writing after the tin crisis had broken, H.J. Maidenberg explained how it had been 'too good a deal to give up':

> To better understand how good a deal it was, you have to visit the LME and observe how private deals are made in its silver, copper, aluminium, lead, zinc, nickel and tin 'rings'. Each morning and afternoon groups of about two dozen men and women enter the circle, sit on leather banquettes and for five minutes trade metal in quiet conversational tones. After their time is up, another group does the same until the cycle ends . . .[68]

The tin crisis broke in October 1985 when – against the background of a sharp drop in demand for tin, as well as the emergence of non-ITC countries (such as Brazil) as major tin exporters – the ITC's buffer-stock Manager, Pieter de Koning, announced that, with prices falling sharply, it could no longer afford to add to its buffer stocks. Moreover, the ITC owed the tin market, effectively the brokers and banks, some £500m (possibly more) and apparently had little or no intention of paying. Faced with this shocking situation, the LME decided on the 24th to suspend the tin market for an indefinite period. The winter saw protracted, slow-moving, complicated negotiations, before finally in March 1986 a so-called 'ringout' solution was achieved, by which the tin market reopened with an artificial price being set and all open contracts being settled at that price. Much litigation still lay ahead for ring-dealing members, but at least there was a functioning tin market once more. The LME itself would never be the same again: as the *FT* put it with needless circumspection, 'the days of the traders' club where a gentleman's nod is his bond are probably over'.[69]

So they were too at Lloyd's, after the traumatic revelations in 1982 of systematic malpractice. How endemic was the corruption? Ian Hay Davison found out after being brought in as Chief Executive in early 1983 at the instigation of the Bank of England. 'When I joined Lloyd's,' he famously observed, 'I had announced my determination to pick out the rotten apples. I then thought that to exclude the wrongdoers would solve the problem. But it was not as simple as that. Many of the apples were to some extent tacky, and the barrel itself appeared . . . to be infected.' Inevitably Davison encountered considerable resistance, though it would have helped if this undoubtedly intelligent, articulate man had been somewhat more emollient and generally better at dealing with people. Green's successor as Chairman from November 1983 was Peter Miller, who recalled with dismay Davison's inability to grasp that Lloyd's was 'a great market institution, marked by the bloody-minded independence of each individual underwriter, of each individual broker'. Miller was determined not to cede any more of the Chairman's traditional powers than he could get away with, and he frankly viewed Davison as somebody out to further his own career, as opposed to the cause of Lloyd's. 'My God, when the bullets fly, I don't see Ian's head above the parapet,' he would quote with apparent approbation the words to him of one of his deputy chairmen. Eventually, in November 1985, Davison announced his resignation. He had achieved some things (including taking action against baby syndicates, ensuring the public disclosure of syndicate accounts and ending the scandalous practice of offshore reinsurance with companies covertly run by Lloyd's underwriters), but crucially, as Tony Levene commented in the *Sunday Times* at the time of his resignation, he had 'failed to change Lloyd's belief in its own rectitude'. Almost as damagingly, he had failed to persuade the Director of Public Prosecutions to charge any of the sixty or so underwriters and brokers found guilty by Lloyd's of malpractice, particularly in relation to offshore reinsurance.[70]

By the time Davison quit, Lloyd's was coming under renewed external pressure, following the news in May 1985 that the underwriting Names in the Minet syndicates, already suffering badly as a result of the PCW scandal revealed in November 1982, were also liable for trading losses of no less than £130m incurred between 1979 and 1982. Miller unequivocally ruled out a Lifeboat operation for these Names, and in July the Labour spokesman on Trade and Industry, Bryan Gould, almost equally unequivocally warned that a future Labour government would end self-regulation at Lloyd's. In the coming months Gould also made much of the fact that one in eight Tory MPs was a Name; but despite the obvious political risks, the government decided – partly as the result of heavy lobbying by those MPs who were Names – to exempt Lloyd's from the Financial Services Bill that was going through Parliament in late 1985. Instead, the government appointed yet another committee, to be chaired by the eminent lawyer Sir Patrick Neill, to examine the 1982 Lloyd's Act from the point of view of investor protection. 'There are few commercial pressures on Lloyd's to force it to reform,' John Moore reflected pessimistically in the *FT* in November of that year. 'Business still flows to the market in large volumes, helped by the involvement in the market of the world's largest insurance brokers.' However, he concluded, 'unless Lloyd's succeeds in establishing order, the image of the whole of London's financial community could be seriously damaged'.[71]

The same was true in spades about the takeover fever that gripped the City in the mid-1980s. The indispensable background was an almost continuously sustained bull market, itself reinforced by the boom in takeovers, especially from autumn 1985. Ending 1984 at 952.3 (up 23 per cent on the year), the FT 30-Share Index crossed the thousand mark on 18 January 1985 and ended the year on 1131.4. On the eve of Big Bang in October 1986, the Index stood at 1251.6. (The new FTSE 100-Share Index, calculated to have started in 1984 at 1000, stood at 1232.2 at the end of 1984, 1412.6 at the end of 1985 and 1577.1 on the eve of Big Bang.) Rapidly rising share prices were naturally accompanied by rapidly rising equity turnover on the Stock Exchange, up from £56bn in 1983 and £73bn in 1984 to £105bn in 1985 and £181bn in 1986. As for takeover bids (of course not all of them successful), one measurement is the value of acquisitions of quoted UK companies in these years: £2.3bn in 1983, £5.5bn in 1984, £6.4bn in 1985 and £16.6bn in 1986. 'Rarely has the London Stock Market buzzed with so much takeover speculation,' the *FT* declared as early as January 1985, warning that 'it is not a healthy phenomenon'.[72] At that point, though, no one could have imagined quite what lay ahead.

Early on during these two hectic years occurred a takeover bid that vitally concerned an old City favourite.[73] One way and another the battle for control over Harrods had been going on since 1977, when Tiny Rowland acquired a significant stake in its owners, House of Fraser, and seemed to be destined for the chairmanship. During the tangled manoeuvring of the next four years, Rowland faced concerted City opposition, led by Warburgs and Cazenove's. 'Your world is the Square Mile and my world is the real world – that's your problem,' Rowland at one point reputedly told his stockbroker, the Hon Mervyn Greenway of Capel-Cure Myers, while pointing at a globe in Lonrho's Cheapside offices. 'In fact,' Rowland's biographer Tom Bower justly remarks, 'the "problem" was Rowland's confusion. The battle for the House of Fraser was within the Square Mile, not in Rowland's "real" world. When he declared war against Warburgs and the City to buy House of Fraser cheap, he ought of necessity to have set aside his "real world" of African shenanigans, personality play-offs, Third World motor car franchises and fought by the rules of the Square Mile.'[74] Nor was Rowland's cause helped by the fact that none of the prestigious merchant banks was willing to act on his behalf. Eventually, in 1981, the City establishment managed to get Rowland's £230m bid referred to the Monopolies Commission, which after taking its time came up with a fairly unconvincing set of reasons why Rowland was an unsuitable owner. Its report, however, was enough to enable the government to halt the bid.

Three years later there was a new would-be owner of Harrods: Mohamed Al Fayed. In August 1984, after Lazards had resigned, he and his brothers hitched up with a new merchant bank, Kleinwort Benson; and in November Rowland sold Lonrho's 29.9 per cent stake in House of Fraser to the Al Fayeds, apparently unaware of the Egyptian family's Knightsbridge ambitions. The dénouement came in March 1985. On Monday the 4th it was announced that the Al Fayeds had launched a £615m bid; that same day, when asked about the family's financial standing, Kleinworts gave the assurance that 'they are collectors of centres of excellence'.[75] Three days later the ban on Rowland bidding for House of Fraser was lifted, but it was too late for him to prevent a dawn raid, accompanied by well-targeted buying in the market, winning the day for the Al Fayeds on the 11th. With minimum press support (apart from his own paper, the *Observer*), Rowland subsequently waged a long, bitter campaign against the Al Fayeds and their City advisers, culminating in the 1988 publication, *A Hero from Zero: the Story of Kleinwort Benson and Mohamed Fayed*. By then a DTI report on the takeover of Harrods had been completed, but it was not published until March 1990. Finding that the Al Fayed brothers had repeatedly lied to their City advisers, the regulatory bodies and the press during the takeover, it blamed Kleinworts for having failed to undertake 'adequate independent verification or inquiry' before issuing false public statements that the Al Fayeds had more than adequate funds of their own to finance the offer. The implication was clear: Kleinworts, despite having little or no idea where the money for the bid came from, had been happy to assure the world (including the regulatory authorities) about the Al Fayeds' financial credibility in return for pocketing a sizeable fee. The episode had not, the press belatedly agreed, been the City's finest hour.[76]

In 1985 itself the City's attention soon turned to other bids, which came thick and fast throughout the rest of the year.[77] Four stood out, including two bitterly contested (including aggressive newspaper advertising) hostile bids – both ultimately successful – that summer: Burton Group's £553m bid for Debenhams and Guinness's £356m bid for the largest independent Scotch whisky company, Arthur Bell & Son. 'These two bids,' in Littlewood's judicious words, 'brought out into the open the subject of "warehousing", "concert parties" and other stratagems for obtaining friendly support to help the success of a bid . . . The problem with so-called friendly parties concerns any inducements or guarantees against loss made to obtain support.'[78] Warburgs was in the corner for Burtons, while Morgan Grenfell acted for Guinness – even though Bells had been one of its corporate clients since the early 1960s (formally until February 1983 and informally thereafter). 'I am appalled,' Bells' local MP, Bill Walker, declared in early July, when the Takeover Panel decided there was no conflict of interest on the part of the merchant bank.[79] The third bid came in October as Elders IXL, the Australian 'beer-to-sheep-dip' conglomerate, bid a staggering £1.8bn for the British food-and-drink giant Allied Lyons, despite being little more than a quarter of its size. Although traditionally serviced by Barings, the target company called on Warburgs to help save its life. This it did, with the help of a reference to the Monopolies Commission on the back of the exceptionally high leveraged aspect to the bid.[80] The final bid, launched in November, was the second attempt in less than a year by Scottish & Newcastle Breweries to gain control of the Cumberland brewers Matthew Brown. Morgan Grenfell led the attack, but came unstuck the following month when the Takeover Panel, belatedly baring its teeth, ruled that it had been illegitimate first to claim a ninety-minute extension of the bid deadline on the basis of a purported anomaly in the rules and then to use that extra time to get its client's holding of Matthew Brown shares above the 50 per cent mark.[81]

The panel's 'swift and fair ruling over the Matthew Brown affair could not have come at a more opportune moment', Kenneth Fleet noted in *The Times*, adding that 'many people in the City are worried about the image of arrogance and lack of care that has been growing in recent months'. Fleet was no friend of Labour's Bryan Gould, who had recently warned that 'the current climate of feverish speculation, bids and counter bids and general uncertainty is doing nobody much good', but he was compelled to concede that 'takeover games' were 'now being played harder than ever, with too much violence on the pitch'.[82] Gould's warning came on 12 December – ten days after Argyll Group and Imperial Group had made £1,860m and £1,220m bids for, respectively, Distillers and United Biscuits.

'It is a tough business. By their nature, they are very contentious. I do not think we have behaved improperly.' This defence in March 1985 by Morgan Grenfell's chief executive, Christopher Reeves, of his bank's

conduct in recent takeover battles (including the fierce, brilliantly successful campaign waged the previous autumn on behalf of Dixons against
Currys) was apparently justified by results. 'Morgan Grenfell has carved a
reputation for itself in the 1980s as the merchant bank to use in a takeover
battle,' noted the *Evening Standard*'s Anthony Hilton in April 1985, as he
presented the results of the latest league table compiled by the recently
established magazine *Acquisitions Monthly*. The figures showed that
Morgan Grenfell had been involved in more than one-third of all the bids
launched in the first quarter. It stayed on top for the rest of the year, with
the figures for 1985 as a whole showing that it acted as a financial adviser
in thirty-two takeovers with an aggregate value of £3.14bn. Next in the
table (ranked by value of takeovers) came Warburgs, Kleinworts and
Schroders. Inevitably Morgans started to be the subject of profiles, mainly
admiring in tone and highlighting the contribution of its two corporate
finance 'stars', George Magan and Roger Seelig. Gregory Miller's
December 1985 piece in *Institutional Investor* on 'Britain's M&A upstart'
had a memorable opening paragraph:

> The head of corporate finance at one of London's oldest and most
> distinguished merchant banks had spent an hour detailing the faults, real
> and imagined, of his chief rival: the client poaching, the bending of rules,
> the ruthless negotiating, the headline grabbing and, perhaps most unBritish
> (and least forgivable), the star system. Yet, in a moment of candour, he
> paused. 'Let's be frank,' he said. 'There's an element of sour grapes in all this.
> They've done – pardon my French – bloody well. And that grates my butt.'

The rest of the article made much of Morgans' tactical innovation
(including the practice, very lucrative to the bank, of cash-alternative
underwritings in the course of a bid); contrasted the two stars ('Seelig, 40,
is regarded as the most Americanised of the Morgan Grenfell crew, with
all the brashness of a New York investment banker', whereas 'Magan, also
40, is quiet, reserved, but intense'); conceded that their stardom was in
part the result of brilliant financial PR; and quoted Seelig's observation
that those who had lost out in the M&A wars 'may be just *reading* the
rules', whereas 'we *changed* most of the rules'. The arrogance was
undeniable, and later that month Stephen Aris, in a *Sunday Times*
overview entitled 'The City's Knights Ride Out', quoted the head of
corporate finance, the more reserved Graham Walsh, on Morgans'
startling rise: 'It's very much a business where success breeds success. Your
only real advertisement is the volume of business you can handle.'[83]
Morgans, in short, was on a roll, and the possibility of voluntarily
slackening the pace was inconceivable.

Not least in the context of two titanic, chronologically parallel takeover
battles. The initial bid on 2 December 1985 by Imperial for United
Biscuits (UB) was on an agreed basis and essentially a proposed reverse

takeover: Imperial, the by now rather dozy tobacco-to-potato-chips combine, was looking to acquire the greater management dynamism of UB, led by Sir Hector Laing. Four days later this friendly arrangement was put in jeopardy as Lord Hanson's Hanson Trust unveiled a £1,900m bid for Imperial itself.[84] Events moved up a gear in February 1986 when the latest occupant at the DTI, Paul Channon, controversially decided to refer the Imperial bid – but not the Hanson bid – to the Monopolies Commission. On the 17th Hanson bid £2,320m for Imperial and it seemed in the bag – only for it to be announced later that day that the Imperial bid for UB was now being turned round, with UB bidding £2,560m for Imperial, an offer recommended by Imperial's board. It was an audacious move, largely engineered by UB's merchant bank, the ubiquitous Morgan Grenfell. Over the next few weeks Morgans found itself in trouble not only with the Stock Exchange but also with the Bank of England, for having spent £360m – about twice the bank's net worth – in order to buy 14.9 per cent of Imperial. Ultimately, however, it was Imperial's institutional shareholders who determined the outcome. Although Laing was talking a high-class game of future synergies and so on, Hanson had delivered for them in the past; and in the words of a fund manager in early April, acknowledging Hanson's unrivalled record in making assets sweat, 'I will probably accept the Hanson paper because I cannot afford to miss out on short-term performance of shares'. With the two bids roughly equal at £2.5bn each (Hanson's share price having gone up since mid-February), this attitude cost Laing dear, with UB conceding defeat on 11 April. 'As far as Great Britain Ltd was concerned and building a food industry that would have a major part to play in China and Brazil and other developing countries, I was sorry the shareholders took the view that they did,' he reflected some years later. 'What I do criticise is the City taking a short-term view. I find it galling that they seem to keep looking for jam today.'[85] It was a cry that was increasingly to be heard over the next few years, but without doing much to disturb the City's resolutely myopic criteria.

The other, simultaneous takeover battle, in which questions of industrial logic rarely raised their head, was for the Scotch whisky company Distillers, in its way as non-entrepreneurial and ripe for takeover as Imperial.[86] This bid would eventually lead to the Guinness scandal, one of the great *causes célèbres* of modern City history, culminating in two high-profile trials in the early 1990s. The account that follows relies heavily on the DTI's report into the share-support operation on which the outcome largely turned. There are three necessary points to make. First, what went on in the bid was almost certainly not unique in the City of the mid-1980s – we just happen to know retrospectively a lot more about this particular bid. Second, little if anything was widely known at the time about the share-support operation, with disclosure – despite the rules of the Takeover Code – being very much not the name of the game. And third, for all our retrospective knowledge there is still quite a lot that we do not know and perhaps never will.

For several weeks before and after Christmas 1985 it seemed that the supermarket group Argyll, whose main financial adviser was Samuel Montagu, was going to have a clear run at Distillers. On Monday, 20 January 1986, however, Guinness (which had kept in place the same team that won the battle for Bells, with Morgan Grenfell and Cazenove's at its heart) launched a £2,190m counter-bid. It came with the agreement of Distillers, whose board the previous day had been persuaded by Kleinworts that, with continuing independence no longer a realistic possibility, this was the less bad option. On the morning of the bid Morgan Grenfell and Cazenove's completed the underwriting of £1.5bn of new Guinness shares in less than three hours, thereby doubling the company's share capital at a stroke. This striking achievement directly reflected the high reputation that Ernest Saunders, Chief Executive of Guinness, currently enjoyed among the City institutions. In the Argyll camp, where Saunders's counterpart was James Gulliver, there was considerable bitterness when it emerged a few days after the rival bid that Guinness, as advised by Morgan Grenfell, had insisted on Distillers footing Guinness's underwriting bill. This was a so-called 'poison pill', designed to make the acquisition of Distillers less attractive to Argyll. 'This is absolutely disgraceful,' Rupert Faure Walker of Samuel Montagu told the press on Friday the 24th. 'It means that the Distillers board have slipped £14m of shareholders' money into Guinness's sticky fingers simply to frustrate Argyll.'[87]

He would have been still more upset had he known what had been going on that week behind some very closed doors. It was crucial to the Guinness strategy that its share price kept above the underwritten price, and between the 20th and 23rd Jacob Rothschild's J. Rothschild Holdings (JRH, which no longer included Charterhouse) bought one million Guinness shares as a result of discussions between David Mayhew of Cazenove's and Nils Taube, JRH's investment director. 'The view taken by JRH,' the DTI report stated, 'was that if the Guinness bid were successful, earnings per share could rise significantly once new management had settled in with a corresponding increase in the share price. In addition, JRH regarded it as part of what Lord Rothschild [i.e. Jacob Rothschild] called its "foreign policy" to be helpful to Cazenove, and Morgan Grenfell, with a view to profitable co-operation in the future.'[88]

At about the same time a rather different sort of stockbroker from Mayhew was also enlisting support in the Guinness cause. This was Anthony Parnes, who had been a member of the Stock Exchange since

1968, was less than affectionately known in the market as 'The Animal' and was now a half-commission man at Laing & Cruickshank. The previous summer he had got involved in the battle for Bells because one of his clients, the well-connected Sir Jack Lyons, was a confidant of Saunders. The *de facto* Finance Director at Guinness, Olivier Roux, recalled the unsentimental education in takeover battles that he received during the Bells bid:

> Parnes told me that the City worked on the flowing and ebbing sentiments and whims which were largely dictated by the share price. It seemed to me a short-term view based on emotion at the expense of long-term fundamentals and careful analysis . . . I learned from Parnes that market tactics were a natural and entirely accepted and necessary part of contested bids. These tactics involved . . . organising supporters to purchase one's own company's shares to maintain price levels or to purchase offeree's shares in order to have them used to boost acceptances of the offer thereby helping the offerer to win. If supporters were involved it was the practice to make sure that any losses were covered through an informal agreement to that effect. He did imply, however, that one did run the risk of being reprimanded by the Takeover Panel if the supporters' dealings should have been disclosed but were not. He implied that this was a grey area and as most hostile bids involved these tactics and were therefore widespread there was no real cause for concern.[89]

One of Parnes's clients was the prominent businessman Gerald Ronson and, within a day or two of the bid for Distillers being launched, Parnes approached him (on Saunders's instigation) and got Ronson's agreement to support the Guinness share price, safe in the knowledge that Guinness would compensate him for any loss. On that undeniably attractive basis, Ronson authorised £10m for Parnes to play with, though over the coming weeks that pragmatic broker – one of whose clients in the early 1970s had been another Gerald, namely Caplan of London and County notoriety – was careful to ensure that the Ronson purchases of Guinness shares were made through a wide range of brokers, not just Laing & Cruickshank.

In fact, with the Guinness share price fairly quickly 'stabilising' after the bid and underwriting on 20 January, the powder was kept more or less dry over the next fortnight, though Ronson interests had bought some 1.4 million shares by 7 February. More visible was the ferocious PR battle. A series of aggressive advertisements appeared on the financial pages, and on 7 February, the day after Argyll raised its offer to £2,300m, Guinness issued a press release that went beyond parody: 'Scotch whisky does not need the theatrical posturing which we have seen from Argyll, which to date has included weak-kneed attempts to cast doubt on Guinness's record . . . Today the long-running Argyll farce sunk to new depths of ignorance.' That day, a Friday, saw the Guinness share price losing ground even though the market was rising; and, in the words of the DTI report, an 'extremely agitated and concerned' Saunders called a meeting of his financial advisers for the Sunday evening, at which he 'made his feelings known in strong terms' and 'blamed the brokers – perhaps unfairly – for a lack of vigilance'.[90] At this point only 2.8 million Guinness shares had been purchased by supporters and associates, but over the next four days (10–13 February) another 4.8 million shares were bought, including 1.5 million by Ronson interests. Having been down to 276p, below the underwriting price of 278p, at the close of trading on the Friday, the share price duly recovered, to 298p by Thursday the 13th.

The next day, however, came the major blow to the Guinness camp that its bid was to be referred to the Monopolies Commission. There was little sympathy from the press. The OFT's decision, Neil Collins wrote in the *Sunday Times* on the 16th, 'leaves Distillers wide open to Argyll, which should sweep to a well-deserved victory'. Declaring that Distillers had been 'trussed up' by Guinness 'in a disgraceful way', his parting shot was aimed at Seelig and his colleagues in Great Winchester Street: 'The Guinness experience should make the company's bankers, Morgan Grenfell, think twice before rushing round to underwrite a first bid which few thought would succeed. It earns fancy fees for the bank and the underwriters, but in the words of one banker, "It's just hurling clients' money away."'[91] Morgan Grenfell remained unperturbed; and partly on its advice – though perhaps owing at least as much to the American lawyer Thomas Ward, who was on the Guinness board – a remodelled, referral-avoiding £2.35bn bid by Guinness was unveiled on the 20th. Each side had now made two bids, but in market terms it was still the phoney war.

Over the next month the spotlight remained firmly on Morgans. By the end of February it had, under a perfectly legal indemnification agreement with Guinness, openly spent some £178m on Distillers shares (and, under a similar agreement with United Biscuits, even more on Imperial shares). The Bank of England was increasingly unhappy, and on the 28th issued a strongly worded notice requiring advance notice before the acquisition of such strategic stakes, and insisting that such stakes should not exceed 25 per cent of the bank's capital. 'Naming no names, the Bank has made it perfectly clear which organisation it takes to have been overstepping the mark,' was Lex's comment; but three days later the *FT*'s headline was 'Morgan Grenfell outflanks Bank', after it arranged for a consortium of three banks (including the British Linen Bank) to acquire, indemnified by Guinness, shares in Distillers up to the value of £111m. Morgan Grenfell were now officially the City's out-and-out bad boys. 'If you want to win your bid no matter what price you pay, then Morgans are the bank for you,' the veteran corporate financier John Gillum was quoted as saying on 6 March. 'But if you want a more reflective view, try somebody else.' There was also the old fear that disreputably conducted takeover battles were going to spell the end for self-regulatory policing, mainly by the Takeover Panel, and lead to something much more legalistic. 'The usually urbane voice of the merchant banker quivered with anger,' a feature ('Bulls shake the china shop') by Martin Dickson in the *FT* on the 12th began. ' "The time has come," he said, "to shoot a few of these blighters on the quarter-deck – and I mean shoot, not a gentle little tap on the knuckles." '[92]

Behind the scenes, meanwhile, the share support operation was quietly extended. By the end of February some 11.8 million Guinness shares had been acquired by supporters, and a new member of the 'fan club' was on the verge of being signed up. 'Rik' Riklis, head of the American corporation Schenley Industries, which among other things distributed for Distillers in the US, was in London on the 28th, a Friday, and that afternoon was taken by Ward to meet Saunders at Guinness's head office in Portman Square. The meeting went well, and Riklis recalled the immediate aftermath:

> I told him [Ward] that I was very impressed with Guinness and with Mr Saunders and I told him that we would like to show our support of the 'white knight' and the choice by the management, and we would like to buy some shares in Guinness if there are blocks available. He told me . . . he would put me in touch with their brokers and a man by the name of Mayhew [David Mayhew of Cazenove's] was going to call me at the hotel later in the evening. I did not quite catch up with Mayhew that evening, it was a weekend and I think he left for the country, but eventually I did before Monday, on a Sunday or something, I caught up with him and I told Mayhew . . . 'We are interested in buying some blocks of Guinness' and I authorised him to look for the blocks for us . . .

It was hardly a spontaneous, unsolicited offer on Riklis's part. Mayhew recalled that on the 27th, at the regular evening meeting at Portman Square between Guinness and its financial advisers, Schenley's name was raised as a possible purchaser of Guinness shares. He had asked whether Schenley was 'free to purchase' – in other words, not requiring public disclosure as a party acting in concert with Guinness – and had been assured by both Seelig and Ward that that was not a problem.[93] Mayhew subsequently insisted that, for his part, he was unaware until almost the end of the year of Schenley's role as a Distillers' distributor. In any event, on 3 March Schenley began to buy Guinness shares, at this stage through Cazenove's, totalling over 2.8 million shares by the 18th. At that point the big question was whether the latest Guinness bid was going to be referred to the Monopolies Commission.

Four things happened on Friday the 21st. The DTI announced that there would be no referral; Argyll made its final offer (£2,500m); key supporters piled into the market to buy Guinness shares, with Schenley purchasing two million and the Ronson interests one million, thereby pushing up the share price from 299p to 311p; and as a result, by the end of Stock Exchange trading that day, there was nothing to choose between the Guinness and Argyll paper offers. It had been a pivotal day. A key recollection, tinged with bitterness, came from Samuel Montagu's Faure Walker:

> It was from that morning onwards that suddenly this massive buying of Guinness shares started. The Guinness share price really took off with massive buying from every direction. That pulled the Distillers price up and it went beyond the level at which we could buy them so we couldn't get them. I think we only got a million or so . . . From this moment onwards we saw this massive buying of Guinness shares and we found it very hard to accept that it was traditional investment buying.[94]

By the end of 3 April the Guinness share price was 341p, with the bid's secret supporters having bought over 12.3 million shares since 21 March. Schenley (which from late March sought still greater secrecy by routing its orders via the London office of Drexels) topped the list with 4.75 million shares, followed by Ronson interests (2.7 million) and J. Rothschild Holdings (2.4 million). A new fan, brought to the party by Parnes, was Ephraim Margulies, Chairman of the S&W Berisford commodity trading empire. According to the DTI report, he not only 'arranged for Mr Parnes to receive support from a Berisford subsidiary in the US, Berisford Capital Corporation', but 'in addition, the good offices of the Margulies family provided Mr Parnes with support in the form of purchases by a Swiss private bank, subsequently attributed to a Panamanian registered corporation by the name of CIFCO'.[95] Between them, they bought 1.8 million Guinness shares during this phase.

Meanwhile, during these ten or so days after the latest Argyll bid, the key decision was being taken as to whether or not Guinness should increase its own offer. The DTI report again:

> The matter was hotly debated. Mr Saunders was keen to raise the Guinness offer: he wished to be certain of victory and disliked being in the position of offering the lower cash alternative. Cazenove and Morgan Grenfell were strongly opposed to an increase: they thought it would be well-nigh impossible to sub-underwrite an increased cash alternative, and they feared that an increased paper offer would weaken the share price with a consequent reduction in the value of the offer.

Helped by the surging share price, which meant that the Guinness paper offer enjoyed an edge over Argyll's, the financial advisers eventually won the argument. The Guinness offer, it was announced on Wednesday, 3 April, would not be increased. Whereupon:

> Mr Saunders indicated to those around him that efforts in support of the

Guinness share price should be redoubled. Mr Roux recalls Mr Seelig telling him that he would try to obtain support but that, if he did, 'you can't let me down'. According to Mr Roux, Mr Seelig indicated that if he got supporters to come in most of them would expect to be covered against loss, and it would be on that basis that their support could be obtained. It is highly likely that Mr Seelig had a similar conversation with Mr Saunders; in any event Mr Roux is confident that he himself would have reported the substance of his conversation with Mr Seelig to Mr Saunders. There is no direct evidence that Mr Seelig then received clearance to recruit supporters on the basis he had described but there is little doubt that without such clearance Mr Seelig would not have entered into the arrangements he did . . .[96]

As so often in takeover battles, going back at least to the Aluminium War, it would be the marketplace that determined who took the spoils; but, in this case, it would hardly be a fair marketplace.

The final fortnight was played out amidst high tension, with the stakes being particularly steep for Morgan Grenfell, as it saw Imperial being snatched away by Hanson. It could not, to put it mildly, afford another high-profile defeat. Almost everything hinged on the share price, especially as a major plank of the Guinness strategy was to publish almost daily a prominent advertisement in the financial press revealing how the gap was widening between the value of the Guinness offer and the current market value of a Distillers share. The Guinness share price climbed to 355p by 14 April, before subsiding somewhat as various holders (presumably not including members of the fan club) decided to take a profit. Mayhew recalled the distinctive atmosphere of this fortnight:

> They used to publish these advertisements and . . . whether it was one penny one way and one penny another way . . . was regarded as being of great [moment]. For that purpose I used to advise both Seelig and Roux of what the closing price looked like. Sometimes they would take the view that they knew where people would buy shares and support that price, at other times they did not. The price was sometimes changed and sometimes unchanged . . . I would guess it would . . . be between 2.30 and 3.00. I would ordinarily say 'it looks as if the closing price is going to be such-and-such' . . .[97]

Not surprisingly, the share-support operation now reached new levels. A little under 27 million Guinness shares had been bought by supporters up to 3 April; in the fortnight thereafter, more than 50 million were bought. Accounting for almost one-sixth of the entire Guinness share capital, this final spurt, at its most intense in the week beginning Monday the 15th, was undeniably a phenomenal operation.

Between 4 and 18 April six supporters bought especially heavily: Bank Leu (14.4 million shares); Ivan Boesky (12.2 million); Schenley (10 million); J. Rothschild Holdings (3.7 million); Berisford Capital

Corporation (2.4 million); and Henry Ansbacher clients (2.15 million). These six included three new names, of whom two (the figures reveal) were vitally important. Bank Leu was a large Swiss bank, brought into the Guinness net largely by Ward, though it helped that Saunders had once been a colleague at Nestlé of its chairman, Dr Artur Furer. Fortified by an advantageous agreement with Guinness, it bought its shares (through half a dozen different brokers, as arranged by Parnes) between the 15th and the 18th. 'None of these purchases,' the DTI report noted, 'nor the agreement by Guinness to repurchase the shares from the purchaser at original cost plus interest and costs, was disclosed under Rule 8 of the City Code.'[98] Boesky, the big-money New York arbitrageur, also came via Ward and was also amply recompensed. The involvement of the merchant bank Ansbachers, medium-sized and never part of the City establishment, was attributable to one of its managing directors, Lord Spens (formerly with Morgan Grenfell), agreeing to find clients to buy shares in the knowledge that any losses would be met. 'It is unlikely that anyone within Guinness or its advisers had a complete overview of every tentacle of the support operation,' the DTI report commented.[99] Certainly it would have been fun to be a fly on the wall if all the supporters had been put together in the same room.

Before the Guinness camp could claim victory, however, there was a final twist. On Thursday the 17th, one day before the bid closed, Warburg Investment Management decided to auction its block of some 10.6 million Distillers shares. Potentially, both bidders knew, this could tip the scales either way. The Guinness camp already had its permitted maximum of Distillers shares and therefore urgently needed to locate a friendly buyer who would not, at least purportedly, be in concert with Guinness. Again, Ward did the trick, coming up with Pipetec, a sub-subsidiary of Bank Leu. Outbidding Argyll, Mayhew bought the 10.6 million shares for Pipetec – in practice merely a convenient vehicle for Bank Leu, already indemnified by Guinness. Unsurprisingly upset, Faure Walker almost at once requested the Takeover Panel to ascertain whether the buyer (whose identity he did not know) was in a concert arrangement with Guinness. Later that day Roux sent the panel a letter approved by Ward, Seelig and Mayhew: 'We have spoken to Cazenove's and can confirm that the purchaser is not a subsidiary or associated company of Guinness, that such shares were not bought for our account and that we have made no financial arrangements with the purchaser with respect to such shares . . .'[100] Eleven years later the DTI report asserted: 'We regard it as most improbable that Mr Mayhew knew of the arrangement between Guinness and Bank Leu', in that 'Guinness had no positive reason to tell him and every reason to seek to avoid the risk of Mr Mayhew refusing to purchase the shares without proper disclosures being made, which would have negated its purpose'.[101] In any case, the battle was effectively over, and at lunchtime on 18 April the announcement was made by Morgan Grenfell that, with Guinness speaking for 50.74 per cent of Distillers, the bid had become unconditional. Apparently it only remained for 'Deadly Earnest' to book the celebration party in the Savoy.

It would be another eight months before the words 'Guinness' and 'scandal' became inseparable bedfellows, but in mid-July there were loud rumblings in the City and elsewhere as Saunders brazenly refused to adhere to various pledges (including one over the chairmanship of Guinness) that he had made during the battle for Distillers. Leigh-Pemberton gave him a semi-public dressing down; Wood Mackenzie, the company's joint brokers, resigned; and Cazenove's said that, although not resigning, it would not act for the company. Morgan Grenfell, by contrast, stood foursquare behind its man.[102] Moreover, the mood by now was just beginning to turn against aggressive takeover bids, especially with the surprising failure early in July of Dixons' £1.8bn bid for Woolworths.[103] Even so, with the market still broadly bullish, there persisted a confident assumption among the City's corporate financiers that the 'mega-bids' (as they were starting to be called) would keep on coming. Inevitably, the confidence was most evident at Morgan Grenfell, which in the wake of the controversy surrounding the Distillers battle – even without public knowledge of the share-price support operation – remained seemingly impervious to criticism. 'Some say we got round the rules,' Reeves told the *FT* in June in an interview that would become infamous. 'I think we innovated. Clients want to deal with people with original ideas, so new rules have to be created. We must not believe that rules are written in tablets of stone.' Seelig meanwhile was reflecting (to the financial journalist Ivan Fallon) on how, despite what he saw as the over-bureaucratic Takeover Panel, he still firmly believed in self-regulation:

> We get very frustrated when we don't think the rules are rational. I don't think we're incapable of following the general principles. I think there is still – and this is a bit medieval if you like – but there's still a tremendous degree of chivalry and the code of war under which we practitioners can operate. After all, I've got to live with these people for the next ten years. I can't actually play that badly . . . I fear that by maintaining statutes and turning it into a legislative thing it will actually worsen it, because once you do that then it will really be like income tax, I mean you'll stick to the letter of the text and not feel obligated to do anything more, whereas the general principles were really much more effective because they were expressing a spirit . . .[104]

*

By spring 1985 it was certain the 'Big Bang' would be in autumn 1986 (with Monday, 27 October as the date eventually set). There ensued some eighteen months of fairly frantic preparations in order to get ready for a new, largely unknown world. As everyday business was at a high pitch as the bull market roared on, there was precious little time for nostalgia or valedictory sentiments. The City was hurtling into the future.

That future might, or might not, include something that could legitimately be described as 'self-regulation'. Early in 1985, shortly before the unveiling of the White Paper on investor protection, Riley described the challenge facing the government – and, more particularly, Tebbit at the DTI – as being how 'to persuade the City that it will still be operating a system of self-regulation [defined by Riley elsewhere as 'the supervision of practitioners by regulators drawn from within their own ranks'] while, at the same time, reassuring Parliament and the public at large that he is strengthening statutory responsibility for the protection of investors'. The White Paper itself, published on 29 January, duly sought to strike a compromise, proposing self-regulatory organisations (SROs) under two regulatory bodies, the Securities and Investments Board (SIB) and the Marketing of Investments Board (MIB), which would have to satisfy statutory requirements and whose powers would be delegated to them by the Secretary of State. The chairman and members of these two boards would be chosen by the Secretary of State and the Governor of the Bank of England. The proposal that SIB was to be a private-sector body, as opposed to an independent statutory agency, undoubtedly represented a victory for the City lobby during 1984, though the *FT* argued that the latter approach would have created a body 'better equipped to handle the powerful financial conglomerates which are emerging in an increasingly international market place'. In the *Daily Telegraph* Whittam Smith's concern was that practitioners authorised to carry on investment business would henceforth 'have to abide by conduct-of-business rules that would include safeguards against abuses arising from conflicts of interest, protection of clients' assets, compensation, a duty to give "adequate and reasonable" advice having regard to a client's circumstances, disclosure of terms of business to customers, the keeping of proper records and arrangements to ensure the orderly conduct of business'. Consequently, he warned, 'the only means of securing compliance with the new rules may be by creating a great bureaucratic system of form-filling and inspection worthy of the old Austro-Hungarian empire'. A few weeks later Sir Kenneth Berrill was appointed as SIB's full-time Chairman. In June his hand was strengthened by the publication of the report on Johnson Matthey. 'The lessons cannot be confined to banking alone,' the *FT* insisted. 'The City of London is embarking upon a far-reaching revolution in the securities markets and elsewhere, and it is clear that a far

more determined and professional approach to regulation is required . . .
Taken together with the cloud over Lloyd's, the collapse of Johnson
Matthey Bankers is a serious blow to the City's claims to be regulated on
its own terms.' Or, as the *Banker* succinctly accepted, 'The City can no
longer be run as a "club".'[105]

During the second half of 1985, as the Financial Services Bill was being
drawn up, the defenders of old-style, nod-and-a-wink self-regulation felt
increasingly beleaguered. Evidence of fraud at Johnson Matthey, lack of
legal action against serious malpractice at Lloyd's, the DTI's pitiful record
of prosecution since insider trading had become a criminal offence five
years earlier, stories about illegal multiple-share applications for the
British Telecom issue, the imbroglio in the London tin market –
cumulatively, all these developments meant that the tide of opinion was
flowing against the City.[106] Berrill responded by talking increasingly
tough. The notion that SIB would have 'less power or fewer teeth' than
the US Securities and Exchange Commission was, he told a London
seminar in October, quite wrong. 'We do not intend to be a hostage of the
self-regulatory organisations,' he went on. 'The self-regulatory
organisations depend on the Securities and Investments Board for their
recognition and we'll have to demonstrate that they meet the criteria to do
so. There is every reason to make the maximum use of self-regulatory
organisations, but the tail cannot be allowed to wag the dog.'

By November, just weeks away from the Financial Services Bill (with
Michael Howard being the minister largely responsible), the atmosphere
was hotting up. On the 4th there was a hostile *Panorama* programme
about fraud in the City, prompting Goodison to complain to the BBC
Chairman, Stuart Young, about 'the prejudiced and naive manner in
which the programme was constructed', with no attempt 'to give a
balanced view about the intense effort which goes into regulation'. And a
fortnight later the Liberal leader, David Steel, wrote to Thatcher urging
her to act, lest the City sink into a 'slough of scandal', and wanting to see
evidence of 'a new determination to see that millionaires in the City are
subject to the same standards as ordinary law-abiding people'. For one of
Thatcher's former ministers, Sir John Nott, now Chairman and Chief
Executive of Lazards, the only realistic solution was to go the whole hog
and introduce an entirely statutory system of regulation. He told a
symposium in late November that while self-regulation within a statutory
framework 'may be the most effective method of controlling markets',
nevertheless it would 'founder politically in the next bear market', with
Parliament (and presumably public opinion) being unable to distinguish
between fraud and bankruptcy. 'When firms go bust, Parliament will cry
foul,' he predicted. 'When firms bearing excessive overheads and taking
new risks in the new environment go into liquidation and lose depositors'

or small shareholders' money, a wholly statutory system will be irresistible.' He added, characteristically, 'I do not like the prospect of City experts being parliamentary scapegoats for failures in the system'.[107]

Predictably, the Financial Services Bill, published on 19 December and controversially exempting Lloyd's, took little or no notice of his warnings. It was broadly along the lines of the White Paper, though envisaging only one board, SIB, which would oversee seven (subsequently five) SROs. The City was broadly welcoming, but as ever the devil lay in the detail; and in February 1986 SIB published its draft rules to deal with conflicts of interest in most types of broking, dealing and fund management groups. 'For even the most sympathetic and conformist investment firm,' the *FT* commented, 'this SIB rule-book will give a chilling impression of the sheer bureaucratic cost of the new regulatory regime. Customer agreement letters will have to spell out information under 14 different headings, and will have to be renewed each year. Comprehensive information on every transaction will have to be recorded and kept for at least three years . . .' Michael Prest, writing in *The Times*, was tempted to see the whole exercise as a massive deception: 'The SIB rules are comprehensive, and we are promised many more; and they are rules, not mere guidelines . . . By constructing the elaborate apparatus of SROs, the Government has skilfully disguised the true extent of the central direction. Orwell would have understood.' Indeed, he reckoned, 'anybody who fondly believed that London was not about to receive a Securities and Exchange Commission should think again'. Nor was Berrill himself, by now getting fully into his stride, apparently inclined to allay such fears. 'The SIB and the SEC in reality stand very close to each other in terms of their powers and duties,' he was quoted as stating that summer. It was beginning to dawn on some City heavyweights that perhaps this was the worst of both worlds: an American-style, legalistic system, yet one with an apparent core of 'self-regulation' that would enable politicians to blame the City when the next round of scandals took place. In Riley's apt retrospective words, 'the SIB turned out to be a statutory wolf dressed in self-regulatory sheep's clothing'.[108] Arguably, too many of the City's leading practitioners, including some of the members of the Jacomb committee of 1984, had taken their collective eye off the ball at the crucial moment.

Not without difficulty, the 'constitutional' implications of the fundamental restructuring of the securities industry continued to be worked out. In June 1985 the Stock Exchange membership was asked to vote on two proposals: that outside ownership of member firms should be permitted up to 100 per cent; and that corporate membership should replace individual membership. 'Central to the changes is the imperative need to attract business into The Stock Exchange,' Goodison had urged in his March letter to members setting out the proposed changes. 'It is no good maintaining or putting up barriers, especially in a country where there is no monopoly of business in securities.' In the event, Goodison got the first proposal through easily enough (coming into effect on 1 March 1986), but narrowly failed to obtain the requisite 75 per cent majority on the second change, largely as the result of opposition on the part of small broking firms. Within hours of the voting, however, it was clear that the implications would have been much more serious if the split vote had been the other way round. 'The mood around Throgmorton Street was that the rebels had secured a hollow victory,' Fleet reported. 'As the day wore on, that opinion came to be shared by directors of the banks and other groups who can now buy stock market firms. They realise that they can exercise all the rights of the membership through their newly-acquired employees.' That assessment was correct, though eventually, soon after Big Bang, individual voting rights were surrendered – for a consideration of £10,000 per member.[109] Given that over the years the backwoodsmen had been such a drag on progress, perhaps it was cheap at the price.

More challenging for the Stock Exchange, and springing directly out of the new regulatory dispensation, was the question of its relationship with the Eurobond market, full of echoes of past prickliness and missed opportunities going back to the mid-1960s. As recently as September 1984, soon after one of the Stock Exchange's member firms, Kemp Mitchell, had in effect been closed down by the Council because of alleged irregularities in Eurobond deals, Goodison had attacked the Eurobond market for not having 'the reputation for honesty that it should have'. He had even gone on to add, 'I have looked at Eurobond secondary market dealings and I don't like what I see.' Despite the Kemp Mitchell case, the White Paper in January 1985 virtually ignored the Eurobond market, but in the ensuing months Berrill did start to focus some attention on it, demanding that by the autumn it decide what sort of self-regulating organisation it intended to form or join. By late summer Ian Steers, running the London end of the Canadian investment bank Wood Gundy, was emerging as the spokesman of this famously free-wheeling, unregulated market. 'Between 70% and 80% of the market's turnover is done in London,' he told the *Wall Street Journal,* 'and the government has suddenly realised it has Europe's most dynamic financial market in its own back yard. The chief problem is designing a flexible mechanism to regulate this vast marketplace. There aren't any easy answers, because this market is 99.9% professional, and its dealings aren't part of the traditional financial markets here.' One of the market's veterans, Stanislas Yassukovich (by now Chairman of Merrill Lynch Europe), offered a wry perspective: 'The Eurobond market has created a lovely mystique about itself, and we tend to believe our own propaganda that we are somehow separate from everybody else.' Should it team up with the Stock

Exchange, which in the new dispensation was likely to be a 'recognised investment exchange'? Steers's instinctive preference was 'to manufacture our own suit of clothes'; for his part, Goodison would only say in August that 'the Eurobond market adds a totally different dimension because one's got to grapple to find out where it is and who's doing it and how they are doing it'.[110]

In mid-October matters suddenly became acrimonious. On Wednesday the 16th members of the two main Eurobond associations, the Association of International Bond Dealers and the International Primary Market Association, decided to join forces and form their own SRO. 'We want to be self-regulated by people who understand our business,' Steers told the press. He was openly dismissive about Stock Exchange claims that a self-regulatory organisation for international securities dealers would lead to a fragmentation of the central market in securities in the UK: 'I do not know what fragmentation means. Anyone who knows anything about the market knows that 90 per cent of the business [i.e. in front-line internationally traded stocks] has been done outside the Stock Exchange for a very long time. There is huge American and Japanese business and the biggest market in ICI is in New York. The Stock Exchange is talking in old-fashioned terms.' 'Lex' on the 17th emphatically agreed:

> The London Stock Exchange may believe that it can only win its uneven match against the Rest of the World XI if it is allowed to set the rules; little else can explain the Exchange's determination that the game should be cricket when everyone else wants to play baseball . . .
>
> The Stock Exchange has always taken a haughty view of the Eurobond market and it is unlikely that either the AIBD or IPMA can be persuaded at this stage that the Exchange loves them after all. The Exchange's concern is of course not with Eurobonds but with international equities. But to distinguish, as it does, so clearly between the two again suggests that the point has been missed. Not only is London experiencing a convergence between equity and debt instruments with the growing popularity of warrants and other whistles; the likelihood must be that, for wholesale customers, it is the Euromarket and not the London Stock Exchange which will provide the trading model . . .
>
> Over the past twenty years London has developed as the leading market in international debt in spite of the Stock Exchange. If London has the opportunity to establish the same pivotal role in equities, it should not be inhibited by the Stock Exchange . . .

The pressure was on Goodison, who that evening at the bankers' dinner at the Mansion House made remarks that were interpreted as representing continued opposition to the autonomous initiative of the international securities dealers, though he denied that he was seeking a monopoly for the Stock Exchange in the City. On the Saturday in the *FT*, Riley accused him of having adopted a 'heavily patronising' tone and caustically noted that 'the trouble is that Sir Nicholas is not dealing with grubby fringe firms craving respectability, but with the cream of the world's major securities houses', such as Merrill Lynch, Goldman Sachs, CSFB and Deutsche Bank.[111]

By the end of the month Goodison had backed down, to the extent of suggesting a joint market in international securities, to be established by the Stock Exchange in co-operation with the new self-regulatory organisation being set up by the international houses, the International Securities Regulatory Organisation (ISRO). Long, difficult, delicate negotiations still lay ahead, but eventually in September 1986 the so-called 'Treaty of Throgmorton Street' was signed. The Stock Exchange would now officially be called the International Stock Exchange, with Goodison as Chairman and Yassukovich as his deputy. From Goodison's perspective the crucial immediate point was that the Stock Exchange would not lose the rapidly growing market in international equities, which ISRO had plausibly threatened to try to take entirely under its own wing. The agreement also ensured that the Stock Exchange would become – as Goodison had long wanted – a genuinely international, open marketplace. 'All the world's players are here,' he told the *FT*. 'We could take business away from New York.' The agreement was, he added, 'the culmination of everything that has happened in the past few years'.[112]

Who, though, would call the shots in the future? The traditional member firms of the Stock Exchange, or ISRO's 180 or so member firms, the great majority of them foreign banks and securities firms? In the light of the fact that a giant like Merrill Lynch or Nomura could afford to buy *all* the member firms of the old Stock Exchange, the question was perhaps not too difficult. The big international houses were indeed now stakeholders in the London Stock Exchange, but they were unlikely to be passive stakeholders.

The episode had accurately reflected the growing importance of not only the international equity market as such, but also London's role within it.[113] One of the pioneers, predictably, was CSFB, which in summer 1985 really put the market on the map by helping Nestlé to raise the equivalent of $425m from three Euro-equity issues, underwritten by a syndicate of banks from seven countries and then sold direct to investors. According to 'Lex' in early August that year, 'the new buzzword in the international securities market is "Euroequity" – that inelegantly-named instrument which, we are told, threatens to make domestic stock exchanges redundant for top-class stocks and to usher in the era of 24-hour, global equity markets'. Investors, the column explained, were 'fast shedding their national prejudices in favour of international diversification', especially in the context of both the dollar and worldwide interest rates falling. Moreover, 'helped by the technology that brings world prices and research to their screens, US and Japanese fund managers, who might never have looked beyond their own markets five years ago, are now widening their investment horizons'.[114]

The Stock Exchange's response during the second half of 1985 was to develop an international version of its real-time market information service, Stock Exchange Automated Quotations (SEAQ), which was due to become operational with Big Bang in October 1986. This version, called SEAQ International, did not have to wait that long, on account of the liberalisation that already applied to dealing in overseas securities, and by late autumn more than two dozen international dealers were displaying prices on the system. Market makers contributing quotations included such non-members as Goldman Sachs, Merrill Lynch and Salomons, each of which had promised to join when allowed to do so. There was therefore a clear motive for ensuring that their allegiance to ISRO did not undermine that commitment. In April 1986 an 'electronic bridge', involving the exchange of real-time prices through a satellite link, was established between SEAQ International in London and NASDAQ in the US, the latter third only to the New York and Tokyo stock exchanges as the world's largest stock market. It was, proclaimed NASDAQ's David Hunter, 'the beginning of the global network for 24-hour equity trading . . . the start of a true world equity market'. By the time of the agreement in September between the Stock Exchange and ISRO, few disputed the assumption that, within that market, London was likely to dominate the European time zone. 'International firms have been investing vast amounts of capital in new equity trading desks in London to deal in the shares of the 500 or so companies which are viewed as truly international stocks,' Richard Lambert and Alexander Nicoll noted in the *FT*.[115] With most of the big international investment banks having made a sustained commitment for more than twenty years to London as *the* centre of the Eurobond market, it was always likely that they would do the same in relation to the supra-national equity equivalent that was rapidly starting to take shape.

Another, more domestic market attracting much anticipatory attention was that in British government debt, which was about to change fundamentally after two centuries of remarkable continuity. 'The smashing of the charmed circle of gilt jobbers with their cosy relationship with the Bank of England via the Government Broker is eagerly awaited,' the *Investors Chronicle* reported as early as July 1984. '"The market has been overbroked and underjobbed for a long time," complains Michael Hughes of de Zoete & Bevan. The jobbers themselves are putting a brave face on losing their exclusive niche. One jobber described the current system as "too introspective" . . .' These jobbers had essentially been the partners of Wedds and Akroyds, and over the next few months the Bank of England drew up the criteria that would help determine who would become primary dealers in the new, US-style gilt-edged market. 'Many people believe that primary dealership is the key to survival in the City revolution,' David Lascelles observed in October. 'Without it, brokers, jobbers and discount houses would be pushed to the sidelines and possibly into oblivion so the scramble for business is likely to be fierce.' And he quoted an anonymous American banker to the effect that his bank was prepared to lose money for several years in order to survive as a primary dealer, on the grounds that 'we see this as a way of getting into a new market, rather than immediately making a profit'.

Finally, in June 1985, the Bank published a list of the twenty-nine firms with which it would be prepared to deal in the new gilts market. It would have been thirty-one, but two prospective market makers pulled out at the last minute – Schroders and Drexel Burnham Lambert. The total capital commitment was estimated at over £600m (some four to five times bigger than the £100–150m currently being deployed in the market), and the *Economist*'s best guess was that there would be 'stabbing room only'. Those lined up for the widely expected bloodbath included major American banks like Bank of America, Bankers Trust, Chase Manhattan, Citicorp, Goldman Sachs and Merrill Lynch, as well as most of the main British merchant and clearing banks. Gordon Pepper's view was typically brusque: 'Given the degree of competition, anyone who's assuming that money can be made from the market in the first two years is indulging in wishful thinking.' Over the next year that remained the conventional wisdom, prompting Bank of America in March 1986 to withdraw as a primary dealer and then Union Discount to do the same four months later, despite having spent £0.25m on computer equipment for its gilts operation.[116] That left twenty-seven, each presumably believing that come October it could defy the harsh economic logic of an overjobbed market in an era of declining government debt.

Union Discount's experience was a salutary reminder of the money that, ahead of Big Bang, was starting to be poured into the seemingly bottomless pit of new technology. 'Open markets mean more competition, more volume, more complexity, above all more risk; technology offers tools to help. But selecting the right tools takes time, money and a clear view of the future. All are in short supply. Can British firms – and British markets – wire up and plug in to meet foreign rivals on equal terms? Or will they lose a chance in a lifetime to leapfrog the competition . . .' This introduction to the *Economist*'s July 1985 survey of technology and the City caught the increasingly febrile mood. The survey quoted a couple of British practitioners. 'You have got to have a rough idea of where you're heading or you can't buy the next bit of kit' (Robert Taylor of Morgan Grenfell). 'You've got to spend what it takes, otherwise you're dead in the water' (Richard Westmacott of Hoare Govett). But the survey's author, Merril Stevenson, also raised a fundamental question: 'Many of the dealer-support and banking systems now on the market or being developed offer some help in risk control. They all seem to fall short of what is wanted. Are British bosses, risk-averse by tradition, in danger of expecting too much from their systems and too little from themselves?' And she quoted one of the City's American heavyweights, Jack Hennessy of CSFB: 'If you've never gone to the casino, you don't know how to manage risk. It's embedded experience, betting the bank every day. The technology makes it all possible, but it's the people who make it happen.'[117]

Over the next year it proved increasingly difficult to stand back objectively from the race to avoid technological obsolescence, but in November 1985 the Stock Exchange's George Hayter did warn member firms against 'spending such enormous sums of money in preparation for the change' without thinking hard about the fixed overheads that they were 'building up for themselves in the months and years to follow, overheads which may make it more difficult for them to adapt, as they may need to, in response to changing business conditions or to a revised perception of their most successful business strategy in the new City'. Of course, much of this spending was now being underwritten by their new owners, and over the next six or so months a series of huge, high-tech, almost space-age dealing rooms were proudly unveiled by the outfits, such as Kleinworts and BZW, that intended to be among the big players. But if these had an obvious if pricy allure (some £18m worth of technology in BZW's case alone), the same did not apply to the back office, where a survey conducted by Coopers & Lybrand about three months before Big Bang found that, in the *Banker*'s summarising words, 'much of settlement will be done manually for the foreseeable future, management control of dealing exposure is, with few exceptions, lacking and support systems have yet to catch up to the sophistication of what the dealer has at hand'. The back office, though, had never been a favourite City subject, and what preoccupied decision-makers more was whether or not trading would continue on the Stock Exchange floor after Big Bang. In his November 1985 remarks, Hayter divulged that the Stock Exchange was proposing to minimise spending in developing the trading floor 'because it seems likely that its useful life for trading equities and gilts may be limited' and that 'we are therefore encouraging market makers and others to think in terms of a three-year life for the trading floor'. In fact, partly under pressure from member firms anxious to be able to play it both ways, the Stock Exchange did spend a significant amount of money ensuring that jobbers who chose to stay on the floor would not be short of screens, terminals and all the rest. Although there was a general consensus that there would be an immediate, ultimately irresistible shift away from face-to-face trading, by September 1986 as many as twenty-eight prospective market makers had signed up for a pitch, with Smith New Court making particularly trenchant noises about keeping at least four dozen dealers on the floor. Sentiment perhaps played a part, but there was also an understandable fear of telephone lines becoming completely jammed.[118]

In this final year before Big Bang there was significant restructuring at two of the City's oldest merchant banks. In November 1985 Barings announced a major capital reorganisation, involving the establishment of a holding company that would enable the banking side of the business to have greater freedom. The underlying purpose, Sir John Baring insisted, was that control did not pass to outsiders; and it was reiterated that Barings' approach to the City revolution would remain highly selective, with the only acquisitions being the Far Eastern part of the brokers Henderson Crosthwaite and a small jobbing firm, Wilson & Watford. Interviewed some months later, the Managing Director in charge of capital market activities, Andrew Tuckey, made a positive virtue out of the decision not to look for outside capital: 'We decided to put ourselves under one fundamental constraint. We wanted to maintain total independence. The best of Barings has come in the past from its independence, and we did not want to lose that.'[119] Further along Bishopsgate, at Hambros, there was less dynastic harmony, with the news in January 1986 that Jocelyn Hambro and his three sons (Rupert, Chairman of the bank since 1983, Richard and James) would all be leaving to form their own specialist corporate finance firm, eventually called J.O. Hambro. Hambros had increasingly been giving the appearance of fighting shy of the City revolution, with Rupert having asked publicly, 'Are the banks that are going into the new markets really big enough to compete with the likes of Nomura Securities and Merrill Lynch?' Granted that Hambros could not afford (with shareholders' funds of less than £200m) to compete in the big league, he now saw a happier future for himself as part of a boutique. This was, Fildes reflected, 'a turning point: the end of the power-base of a mighty City dynasty, and a blow, by implication, to the dynasties and principalities that survive'. The news came, he added, 'just as another great dynasty, the financial Smiths, itself linked to the Hambros by successive marriages, is bowing out of the money market', with Smith St Aubyn in due course being sold to a rival house, King & Shaxson.[120]

The financial Smiths had also played a significant part in the history of Morgan Grenfell, which by early 1986 – partly because of the decision to become an integrated house, partly because of the increasingly deep pockets required in the conduct of takeover battles – was in urgent need of more capital. For a time it seemed that a solution had been found through a union with Exco, built up by John Gunn in the first half of the 1980s as the world's largest money-broking operation; but late in February the Bank of England, with little love for Morgan Grenfell at that particular point in the Imperial and Distillers sagas, refused to give its blessing. The need did not go away, and that summer Morgans raised $200m through a perpetual floating-rate note issue on the Eurobond market and another £155m by floating one-fifth of itself. 'We're not going to win this war with one battle, it's going to take, like everything we have done has taken, a measured period of time,' Reeves predicted reassuringly not long afterwards. 'So we're being pretty measured in our approach.' And he went on, 'I think our philosophy is really very simple. We want to be a major force in each of the areas we have chosen, and we want to maintain our drive.'[121]

Morgan Grenfell was one of a handful of merchant banks faced by the challenge of attempting to build an integrated house and reconcile very different cultures. Not all succeeded. 'What I can't understand,' one stockbroker remarked to a journalist friend soon after being taken over by a merchant bank, 'is that they pay all this money for us and then treat us like dirt.'[122] That bank may well have been Morgan Grenfell, where an unstable mixture of hubris, lack of management and conflicting cultures characterised its preparations for Big Bang. The jobbing firm it had acquired, Pinchin Denny, was openly bad-mouthed by Morgan Grenfell people, while according to Hugh Sebag-Montefiore's account, 'morale was little better' at its brokers, Pember & Boyle. 'Partners who had once earned six-figure salaries became little more than £50,000-a-year sales clerks, though they were at least regarded as of the same class as the bank's directors.' From autumn 1985 the two men in charge of the new securities operation were John Holmes and Geoffrey Collier, who together started recruiting – on expansive salaries – salesmen and analysts who would add an aggressive edge. 'There are gentlemen and there are players,' Collier told one. 'We're not gentlemen.' One way and another it was not a formula for a happy ship.[123]

Things were somewhat better at Kleinworts, though there was still a large cultural divide between it and Grieveson Grant, the stockbroking firm it had acquired. The latter's partners were amazed by internal memos being sent to them in meticulously inscribed, pristine envelopes. 'We never used a new envelope inside the office,' one recalled. 'Anyway, we hardly ever wrote to each other – we talked!' In August 1986 the *Economist* asserted that of the British merchant banks, only Kleinworts and Warburgs were 'seriously in the running to join the super league of global investment banks centred on London, New York and Tokyo', and by general consent Warburgs was making the better fist of shaping into a cohesive whole the various component parts, Rowe & Pitman, Akroyd &

Smithers and Mullens, as well as Warburgs itself.[124] The achievement owed much to Scholey, who in a tactful but determined way managed to inculcate much of the formidable Warburg culture into brokers and jobbers who had known a very different world. Some may still have felt that Warburg's vision had been betrayed, but there was probably no integrated house that entered the new world with its morale as high.

Most observers reckoned that the only integrated British operation likely to match Warburgs was BZW – in other words, the combination of Barclays Merchant Bank, de Zoete & Bevan and Wedd Durlacher. From July 1985 it had a manifestly high-class chairman in Martin Jacomb, who had been passed over for the chairmanship of Kleinworts and then been further disenchanted by its failure to buy Wedds. Within weeks he faced a crisis, as Charles Hue Williams, the most senior figure at Wedds to have opposed the deal with Barclays, took himself and seven colleagues to none other than Kleinworts. 'It was quite simply a clash of cultures,' an anonymous City source told the *Sunday Times*. 'Career bankers find the prospect of young dealers earning several times their own salaries hard to stomach.' Yet when Colin Leach (of ARIEL fame) had made such a prediction to a Barclays main-board director at the time of the bank's purchase of de Zoete's and Wedds, he had been 'laughed out of court'. Martin Vander Weyer was an observant participant. '"We're trying to get used to you bankers and all your memos," Nick Durlacher said to me the first time I met him. He pronounced the last "mee-moes", as though he had never come across it before.' However, because 'the senior Wedds men were old-style City gents' and 'never as assertive as de Zoete's in the preparatory phase of BZW', the more serious rift was elsewhere. 'Bankers thought of brokers as unreliable, smooth-talking lightweights; brokers thought of bankers as stuffed-shirt dullards, more interested in the trappings of office than in maximising the bottom line.' Accordingly, Vander Weyer of BMB – despised by de Zoete's equally for its inferior corporate-client list and its huge offices with walnut-veneered desks – encountered 'a phalanx of cocksure partners, good at their business but determined not to be moulded into a corporate BZW ethos and largely blind to the idea of inter-departmental co-operation within a diversified financial conglomerate'.[125]

Ebbgate House, near London Bridge, was where these diverse elements attempted to bed down during the year before Big Bang. 'It was,' according to Vander Weyer, 'a building of no architectural merit whatever, a late-1970s speculative development which happened to have a central atrium big enough for BZW's equities trading floor. It had inadequate lifts, peculiarly ugly public areas and no interesting artwork.' Things were no better in Drapers Gardens, the pioneering Seifert building where NatWest's County Bank was attempting to integrate with the brokers Fielding Newson-Smith and the jobbers Bisgood Bishop. Tall and thin, leading to very poor internal communications, the building was entirely the wrong shape for an integrated investment bank. Right from the start, the internal dynamics did not work, with both Fieldings and, particularly, Bisgoods finding County's management excessively bureaucratic. 'Where it seemed to go wrong,' Brian Winterflood of Bisgoods recalled, 'was that there were endless meetings, and that tends to be the order of the day, that the culture of these sorts of organisations is that people need to be seen to be doing things . . .'[126] There was perhaps a larger point. The 'real' City – merchant bankers, stockbrokers, jobbers, money-market men – had never quite accepted clearing bankers as part of *their* village, and the fact that they were now waving large cheque books did not suddenly make them welcome.

Had London's broking and jobbing firms really imagined that they could take the money and somehow remain masters of their own destiny? One firm – the only major broker or jobber to remain independent – had no such illusions. 'We do not believe it right to sell the goodwill of the firm to a big brother,' John Kemp-Welch, joint senior partner of Cazenove's, declared in March 1985, at the firm's quinquennial office party (held at the Hilton, the firm having outgrown the Savoy). 'I can assure you that there has been no lack of opportunity to do so and that opportunity still remains today. In many ways it might have been a safer choice, a softer option, a less demanding, less challenging position to take. But we do not see Cazenove's becoming part of the securities division of some large bank only to lose our identity a few years hence . . .' No doubt it was true that the partners of Cazenove's were wealthier than most, but there was also a more cohesive culture, a stronger sense of the achievement of past generations in building up the firm's reputation and, above all, a profound dislike of the thought of being subordinate to 'a big brother'. Moreover, as Kemp-Welch added, there was a sound business argument for the independent route: 'I believe that securities markets will continue to expand as the mobility of capital increases, and that the services of a strong and independent firm of integrity which has market judgement and market capability of the highest order will be in great demand.'

There remained the question of how to implement this fundamental decision. The most critical area was capital, which Cazenove's would clearly need more of if it was to operate successfully in the new marketplace. The solution arrived at in the course of 1985–6 was that of raising fixed capital through a fifteen-year £32m variable-rate loan, carrying a return linked to the firm's profits, though with no equity stake as such. This capital was to be provided by twelve leading institutions, of which all but one were life insurance companies. They would have no say in the running of the firm. This arrangement (together with the creation of an institutional underwriting syndicate to enable the firm to compete in American-style bought deals) was unveiled in September 1986, six and a half weeks before Big Bang. 'We are distinct from our competitors, which will be advantageous,' Kemp-Welch told the *FT*. 'It gives continuity to clients at a time when great change is taking place and when, we believe, personal relationships will become of increasing importance within the new City.' Fildes was unstinting in his praise: 'Today, in their town house in Tokenhouse Yard, brick without, mahogany within, Cazenove look in one sense what they are, a firm of the old school – well-heeled, well-connected, well turned out. They are rated unique in their knowledge and command of the markets – showing companies how to use them, judging what the markets will take, making certain that they take it.' Of the firm's just-announced strategy, he went on: 'Cazenove have put their competitors to shame. There was nothing in the Big Bang reforms which required the major firms to forfeit their independence, often to foreign owners. They could have taken Cazenove's course.'[127]

*

During these final weeks leading up to the long-awaited 27 October 1986 there were two particularly illuminating episodes. 'The Yanks Muscle in on the City: Wall Street's finest are bringing their risky ways to London's markets' was the proud headline in the *New York Times* on 28 September, as it related how, when Robert Maxwell had 'unloaded a huge portfolio ten days ago, he did not take the usual route of asking British brokers to peddle the stocks bit by bit', but instead 'he invited three foreign investment houses to bid on the whole package, finally selling it to Goldman Sachs International, the London arm of the American investment house, for nearly $300 million'. As Goldman Sachs speedily sold on the shares before their prices fell, there was apparently 'awe' among London's 'cosy world of stockbrokers and floor traders' that Goldman Sachs 'would risk millions in losses for a profit that at best would be a thin one'. What was the motive? Goldmans itself was tight-lipped about the transaction, but according to the paper, 'the talk of the financial community is about the extraordinary risks that American investment houses are beginning to take as they aggressively try not only to gain a foothold in Britain's securities markets, but to dominate those markets as quickly as possible'.[128] The other episode, a few days later, involved another foreign bank and the much-touted Euro-equity market. This was the $2.1bn placing by Deutsche Bank Capital Markets in London of shares in Fiat that were being sold by Libya. Deutsche itself came somewhat unstuck, as a fall in the Fiat price in Milan brought down the price in London and left Deutsche having to take a significant portion of the shares onto its own books; nevertheless, in the *FT*'s words, 'the global nature of the placing', done from London but involving finance houses in at least six countries, 'highlighted the rapid development of a global market in the shares of the world's biggest companies'.[129]

For most practitioners, however, what really concerned them was whether the humdrum mechanics were going to work, come the great day. On Saturday, 18 October – two days after Leigh-Pemberton in his Mansion House speech had called on 'all market participants to exercise a degree of restraint' in the post-Big Bang world – there was a full-scale dress rehearsal for the new screen-quoted prices system, SEAQ. It did not go brilliantly. 'London Market's Big Bang Test Run is Fraught with Trading Glitches' was the *Wall Street Journal*'s snappy headline, while according to the *Guardian*, ' "Mickey Mouse" systems get blamed for Big Bang problems'. The Stock Exchange pronounced itself satisfied, but there were many complaints from individual member firms about how long it took for new prices to appear on dealing screens, about dealers refusing to answer the telephone and about telephone lines between brokers and market makers getting jammed. The gilts market dress rehearsal went rather better, though it was hindered by a fire at the Central Gilts Office in the Bank of England. Not surprisingly the sense of nervousness increased about this shift to a new way of dealing. 'Right up to the end of October,' Goodison recollected, 'I had market makers clamouring for space on the trading floor. I had American firms ringing me up saying, "We simply haven't got enough space on the trading floor. We must have it." All the market makers seemed to believe that the trading floor would survive . . .'[130]

Partly because of its arresting tag, Big Bang attracted an enormous amount of media attention, even before it happened. Accompanying that attention was a tendency, perhaps inevitable, to assume that it was a truly momentous event. However, one of the City's most acute minds, Tim Congdon, Chief Economist at Messels, argued otherwise in a compelling piece in the *Spectator* a week before the off. 'The importance of the Big Bang has been exaggerated,' he stated bluntly, and went on:

> It is a sideshow to, indeed almost a by-product of, a much Bigger Bang which has transformed international finance over the last 25 years. This Bigger Bang bears about the same relation to the Big Bang as the construction of Canary Wharf to the refurbishment of the Royal Exchange. One totally overshadows and dwarfs the other. Whereas the Bigger Bang is a new departure in the pattern of international financial activity, the Big Bang merely alters the way in which a long-established business is conducted; and whereas the Bigger Bang has affected the availability and form of finance to industries and governments around the world, the Big Bang's immediate relevance is mainly to the British corporate sector and the British Government. More fundamentally still, the Bigger Bang is – on all the relevant criteria – a multiple of the size of the Big Bang.

What did Congdon mean by 'the Bigger Bang'? In essence, 'the rapid growth of offshore (or Euro-) financial transactions and the tendency for the City of London to capture the lion's share of the associated business'. After noting that Eurocurrency deposits stood by March 1986 at almost $3,500bn, he made some intensely revealing comparisons:

> Last year the turnover in the Eurobond market was between $1,500bn and $2,000bn, while that on the Stock Exchange was, at $600bn, less than half as much . . . In 1985 the total amount of money raised on international markets was $256.5bn, according to figures prepared by the OECD. About 80 per cent of this was raised by the issue of securities, with the remainder accounted for by bank loans. So the flow of new securities coming on to the market was over $200bn a year, equivalent to about $800m each working day. By contrast, the London Stock Exchange raised just over $8bn in 1985, equivalent to a little more than $30m each working day.

Accordingly, 'an extraordinary situation has arisen where the Euromarket, which has no physical embodiment in an exchange building or even a widely recognised set of rules and regulations, is the largest source of capital in the world'. Even so, although 'in some senses the business belongs to no country, since it involves intercontinental flows of funds and cross-frontier communications', the fact was that 'most of the significant work is completed in large financial centres' – and 'of these, London is clearly dominant'. Therefore, 'in effect London has become host to the greatest and most rapidly growing capital market in the world'. *That*, according to Congdon, was 'the Bigger Bang', especially involving as it did major spin-off effects on London's foreign exchange dealing, money broking and fund management industry. He then turned to another conventional nostrum:

> The Big Bang is said to be necessary to improve the City's international competitiveness. The comment is extraordinary after a 25-year period in which London's world financial role has been transformed beyond all recognition. In 1960 its prime international function was to act as the clearing-house of the sterling area, which is now virtually defunct. Today it is the hub of a new and vast international capital market without rival anywhere. It is surely preposterous to describe the City as 'uncompetitive'. It would be more accurate to say that the London Stock Exchange has lost ground relative to the Eurobond market and that a change in rules is necessary to enable the Exchange to see business on more even terms. This is the sense in which the Big Bang is a by-product of the Bigger Bang.[131]

Congdon was surely right. The Stock Exchange in the mid-1980s was at last, after twenty semi-wasted years, seeking to reintegrate itself into the international market – a market that had now more or less returned to the seamless capital flows that had characterised the pre-1914 world. The real heroes of the story remained Bolton, Warburg and the other

Euromarket pioneers of the late 1950s and early 1960s.

Still, if one had spent the best part of a working lifetime on the floor of the Stock Exchange, the end of minimum commissions and single capacity, together with the move to largely screen and telephone dealing, did undeniably represent *quite* a big bang . . . Friday the 24th was the last day of the old world. It came complete with japes: a grey (or green, according to another account) pantomime horse, with kickable rear-end supplied by a clerk; pinstriped traders being sprayed all over by aerosol cans of multicoloured 'Silly String'; the appearance of a Spitting Image puppet of the Chancellor of the Exchequer; and at the end, as 3.30 approached, choruses of 'Auld Lang Syne' to a background of popping champagne corks. 'A little horseplay before the big race' was the headline next day in one paper, and that was about right.[132] It was time, at last, to get real.

CHAPTER TWENTY-ONE

Best Shampoo

The financial services revolution of the 1980s was accompanied, perhaps inevitably, by a revolution in the City's physical appearance and indeed whole way of life. Curiously, however, the single building that came to symbolise the new City had nothing at all to do with Big Bang and in fact had been conceived while Callaghan was still at No 10. It was in 1978 that Richard Rogers, fresh from building the Pompidou Centre in Paris, won the commission to build a new home for Lloyd's. He did so not with a specific design, but with what he called 'a design strategy', one that he insisted would not only be sympathetic to the surrounding 'intricate mesh of narrow streets', but responsive to an unknown future:

> The days of the fortress and the glass box are over. Both are inflexible straitjackets for their users, suppressing self-expression and technologically indefensible for different reasons. We propose a free and open-ended framework where the ever-changing performance is the dynamic expression of the architecture of the building . . . A place where ever-changing activities overlap in flexible well-serviced spaces, the café, the restaurant, the pub, the tailor, the bank, the meeting rooms, the underwriting Room, the food market, the sports room, the corner shop, the offices, each playing its role, growing or shrinking depending on demand.

The new Lloyd's was completed in 1986, and from the start its strikingly 'inside-out' design attracted enormous, mainly positive attention. 'The most consistently innovative building the City has seen since Soane's Bank of England, breaking absolutely with its usual preference for architectural safe investments,' Simon Bradley hailed it in his 1997 update of Pevsner:

> The services are not enclosed, but all piled up and clipped on, like the pipes and capsules of an oil-rig. The rationale, that services require replacement faster than the frame, is less convincing than the magnificent bravura with which the most unlikely units are marshalled into line: windowless round-ended staircases and stacks of portholed toilet pods all of stainless steel; ranks of external lifts like crystalline prisms; and six trim blue cranes on top. Pipes and ducts hurtle up the towers and snake out everywhere along the core . . .

Rogers had, in sum, given the City 'its first twentieth-century building that can truly be called famous, in the way that St Paul's or the Tower are famous'. It was not of course to everyone's taste. 'Poor old Lloyd's,' one underwriter observed in April 1986, gesturing at miscellaneous pipes and tubes. 'After three hundred years . . . We started off in a coffee-house and finished up in a coffee percolator.'[1] That may well have been the general feeling among underwriters and brokers; but for an increasingly embattled institution, the building was a helpfully potent symbol that it could change with the times.

Another, equally modernist design failed to happen in the 1980s, by when it already had a long history. 'Rudoph Palumbo's companies have been quietly amassing this block bit by bit over the years and now have control,' Oliver Marriott noted in 1967 about the in effect triangular island site bounded by Queen Victoria Street, Poultry and Bucklersbury. 'He plans to destroy the existing buildings [mainly Victorian offices] and promote a thin tower block on one corner of the site [the corner where the Mappin & Webb building stood, with its endearing Franco-Flemish tower], with an underground shopping concourse and an open square for pedestrians.' Although the architect of the proposed eighteen-storey, 290-foot building was one of the great figures of modernism, Mies van der Rohe, the opposition to it proved too strong and during the increasingly conservationist 1970s the whole scheme was more or less put in mothballs. When it surfaced again in the early 1980s it still faced opposition from the City Corporation, while the launch of a public inquiry in 1984 was the cue for the Prince of Wales to condemn the tower as 'yet another giant glass stump, better suited to downtown Chicago than the City of London'. Planning permission was formally refused in 1985, at which point Rudolph Palumbo's son, Peter, accepted that he was going to have to come up with a new design. 'Save London From Palumbo' had been Gavin Stamp's rallying cry in the *Spectator* while the battle was still on, but son (like father) knew the virtues of the long game.[2]

Stamp was writing in May 1985, and in the course of attacking Palumbo's scheme he also expressed indignation at the way in which the City Corporation's *mildly* conservationist Draft Local Plan, published the previous November, had been travestied by its opponents 'as an attempt to fossilise the City as a museum'. The undeniable fact, however, was that the draft plan had almost entirely failed to take account of the momentous changes of 1983–4, and within months of its publication the Corporation was coming under pressure to produce something more sensitive to the probable future needs of key financial practitioners – above all, the perceived need for vast, open-plan, high-tech trading floors where all the different arms of the new securities conglomerates could be housed under one roof. Such trading floors were not compatible with narrow Victorian frontages. As early as January 1985 a poll by Savills of 251 City occupiers revealed that more than two-thirds of respondents expected to be looking for large, open-plan areas, with nearly half feeling that floor sizes of over 10,000 square feet were 'most suited to their needs'.[3] Citicorp, the world's largest bank, was inevitably among those searching for such premises, even if they were not in the very centre of the City, and that summer its move to the northern edge of the Thames was effectively confirmed when the City Corporation gave its first consent to a new dealing floor – in the form of a conversion of the old Billingsgate fish market. For the moment, however, the November 1984 draft plan – affecting two-thirds of the square mile – was still on the table.

The final nail in its coffin was the entirely unexpected emergence of a new, rival development. Some years later the *FT*'s Vanessa Houlder provided an authoritative account of the remarkable turn of events:

> In February 1985, Dr Michael von Clemm went to the Isle of Dogs, a watery wasteland two miles east of the Bank of England, to look for a packaging plant for the Roux Brothers' restaurant chain [of which he had been a long-time backer, for gastronomic as much as business motives]. An enterprise zone had been set up [in 1981] in the area to attract development. From the barge where he was eating lunch, von Clemm spotted a disused banana warehouse. Forgetting the Roux Brothers, von Clemm started to toy with the idea of converting the warehouse into a back office for Credit Suisse First Boston.
>
> After several more visits he consulted Ware Travelstead, a US developer who advised First Boston on its real estate investments. Ware Travelstead turned von Clemm's idea on its head. He knew that the bank had wasted five years in trying, unsuccessfully, to obtain a new front office location in the City of London. The real question, he insisted, was: 'Can we consider Canary Wharf on the Isle of Dogs as a front office location?'
>
> The question was breathtaking in its audacity, suggesting a 180-degree reversal of London's pattern of development. For generations, any institution with wealth or influence has gravitated towards the west of London, while the east has been associated with poverty, dockyards and sweatshops . . .[4]

By that summer a financial consortium comprising CSFB, Morgan Stanley and First Boston Real Estate had been assembled, as had a development team under Travelstead, and soon afterwards the full plans were revealed. The Canary Wharf scheme would comprise 71 acres, feature Europe's three tallest towers and provide 8.5 million square feet of office and dealing space. It was intended to be operational by the end of the decade and would be the largest real-estate development in western Europe. Opinion was sharply divided as to its chances of success, but there was no disputing that Canary Wharf represented a direct challenge to the City planners.

The pressure was further increased in February 1986 when Salomons

announced that it was leaving the City for new premises near Victoria
Station, where it intended to establish the largest trading floor outside the
square mile. The following month saw the publication of the
Corporation's revised local plan, which allowed for the theoretical
creation of an extra 20 million square feet of office space in the square
mile.[5] Over the next year or so the official thinking became increasingly
clear: to preserve the historical 'core' at the very centre of the City; while
on its 'fringes' to encourage as much as possible appropriate reusage, such
as the Broadgate development on the site of the old Broad Street Station
or the Japanese securities giant Nomura's move to the former Post Office
headquarters in St Martin's le Grand – or even wholly new, improvised
usage, such as the construction of Alban Gate over London Wall or St
Paul's Vista over Upper Thames Street. Soon it seemed impossible to walk
any distance in the City without being aware of a skyline of cranes and the
dust and din (let alone the danger) of building works in progress. The man
most closely identified with this rapid and ambitious redevelopment of
much of the City was Michael Cassidy, Chairman of the Corporation's
Planning Committee for three years from 1986.[6] A finance-minded lawyer
who had just completed an MBA thesis on the Big Bang, he was intensely
aware of the potential threat to the City's critical mass – and international
credibility – if it failed to meet the spatial demands of the large new
international players, above all the Americans. Not everyone appreciated
this drastic liberalisation, or Cassidy's penchant for the limelight, but the
vision was both right and timely at a testing moment in City history.

One development above all encapsulated the new, aggressive,
'American' mood.[7] This was Broadgate, the brainchild of two genuinely
visionary developers, albeit very different characters, Stuart Lipton and
Godfrey Bradman. Although One Finsbury Avenue had already been
built (one of the City's pioneer atrium blocks along American lines, and
in due course occupied by Warburgs), the crucial breakthrough in terms
of the development as a whole was the demolition in 1985 of Broad Street
Station, to which generations of City men had travelled in the North
London Line's pre-1914 heyday. In July 1986 the Prime Minister, dressed
in blue but not disdaining a white hard hat, topped out the development's
first two phases, amidst much talk of this being the City's largest building
project since the Great Fire more than three centuries earlier. In addition
to Warburgs, tenants already included Shearson Lehman/American
Express, Security Pacific, Lloyds Merchant Bank and Union Bank of
Switzerland. For lovers of the Victorian City, of which Broad Street
Station was emblematic, there was an obvious sadness – though the considerable compensation was that the development (with its imaginative
sculpture, circular amphitheatre and skating rink, as well as shops and
restaurants) was of an altogether higher order than, say, the miserably

unimaginative blocks that went up on London Wall in the 1960s. Broadgate quickly came to symbolise an international financial centre that was assuming an increasingly cosmopolitan character. It was merely a geographical coincidence that that centre happened to be situated on what was still in many ways a tight little, right little island.

*

One day in 1980, engaged in some research at the Trump Street offices of the private client brokers Heseltine Moss, I listened to a broker on the phone. In his thirties, obviously public-school and obviously a hearty, he used three phrases that seemed so evocative of a certain City type that I jotted them down: 'Absolutely bloody livid . . . Pretty batey . . . Righty righty.' Spiritually he was surely a Sloane. 'The City is magic money – the only kind Rangers like,' declared *The Official Sloane Ranger Handbook* two years later. 'Brass without muck. You never have to see the industry ("widget factories") and commerce ("selling brushes") that make the money. There's something about the way the City works – the oldness, the public-schoolness, the merchant bank "word-is-my-bond" code of honour – that makes it all seem like an ancient profession, not business at all . . .'[8] In the event, the Sloanes would do pretty well out of the 1980s – but increasingly the money was no longer 'magic', as the City irrevocably abandoned its pretence that it was not a place of business. It had been becoming steadily more open and meritocratic since the 1960s, but that process was hugely intensified in the 1980s. Even the Bank of England, traditionally the great City bastion of paternalism, overmanning and jobs for life, changed fundamentally as a result of internal reforms in 1980. To outsiders it may have seemed a reassuring point of continuity in a decade of almost ceaseless upheaval, but in truth it was – at last – no longer Norman's Bank.[9]

Who were the City's new self-made men? Three who attracted considerable attention – each born between the late 1940s and early 1950s, each a somewhat larger-than-life figure – were Tom Wilmot, Terry Ramsden and John Hutchinson. Wilmot, the son of a Welsh carpenter who managed to become an RAF officer, had had a rough, peripatetic childhood and had the reputation for being a tough, abrasive operator. 'Tom's different,' a City acquaintance of his explained to a journalist in 1986. 'He's overweight, he smokes, he uses bad language. People want carefully manicured nails around here.' By this time his firm, Harvard Securities, was easily the biggest market maker in the rapidly growing – but essentially unofficial and unregulated – over-the-counter (OTC) market. 'The London Stock Exchange reviles him, brokers loathe him, and even his fellow OTC market makers resent him – all of which seems to bother Wilmot not one iota,' a profile that year asserted. And it quoted a grudgingly admiring rival: 'The clammy embrace of the establishment is something he has shunned. Not only that, but he has tried to find a way of stamping on their feet at the same time.' The Harvard approach was proactive – with no nonsense about waiting for phones to ring – and by this time it had more than 100,000 clients. 'We look at the retail side as a machine that needs feeding' was how Wilmot put it, likening the selling of stock (£2.5m worth in ten days being a typical target) to the selling of hamburgers; and, to prove he meant business, he was reputedly not averse to turning the fire extinguisher on any telephone salesman who needed sobering up after too long at the pub at lunchtime. 'Some people took it badly,' one former dealer recalled. 'They just didn't have a sense of humour.'[10]

Ramsden, a self-publicising deal-maker with a streetwise face and shoulder-length hair, was if anything even more of an outsider. A postman's son from Enfield, he had entered the City as a sixteen-year-old stock clerk and by 1986, eighteen years later, was estimated to be worth some £100m. One of the most prodigious punters in turf history, he owned seventy racing horses, a house in the country, a private jet, a helicopter and a stretch Mercedes limo that not only had the usual accoutrements of bar, television, telephone and telex, but even a fax machine. 'I know as much as anybody in London about how the Japanese financial system works,' he boasted that year, and it was indeed true that his particular forte was the Japanese warrant market, enabling him to build up (often undetected) a significant position in major Japanese companies – 'and then,' according to a less-than-admiring profile, 'to spring a bid . . . by what his critics say looks suspiciously like greenmail'. Ramsden himself shrugged off the ethical implications: 'Mr Nakasone [the Japanese Prime Minister] said he wants to liberalise the market. We are helping him liberalise his market.' They were cool words, but in his case nemesis was not very far away.[11]

'Hutch', the third of the trio to be featured in *Institutional Investor* in 1986, was not such a rank outsider, having become head of gilt trading at Wedd Durlacher in 1980 before moving five years later to Merrill Lynch, but nevertheless he had the reputation of being a self-made (grammar school, non-university background) and aggressive operator who declined to play by the traditional gentlemanly rules of the gilt-edged market. In the words of one broker, 'the old, established public-school people didn't appreciate this brash whiz kid'. Many in the market were convinced that trading losses lay behind his departure from Wedds, but Hutchinson himself adamantly denied this. All were agreed, however, that Hutchinson and Merrills, viewed by many in the City as an excessively competitive 'price gouger', would suit each other well. Hutchinson dismissed that kind of talk: 'What they're actually saying is, "We're very afraid of the US houses."' Anyway, he added, 'What the hell are they talking about me for?' It was a fair question, to which the short answer was that, quite apart from his influence in the market, the City was starting to attract unprecedented attention, press coverage of financial matters was rapidly expanding and, perhaps inevitably, there was developing a cult of the personality. 'John Hutchinson: The bad boy of gilts' the profile was headed – and in a way reassuringly so, for the City had always thrived as a people business, though never before in such a heavily publicised way.[12]

'We find the barrow-boy type is best at this game,' the head of the dealing department of one of the top commodity brokers told the *Sunday Telegraph Magazine* in October 1984. The 'game' was futures, in which 'we have our graduates from Oxford, Cambridge and Exeter to talk to clients and write reports, but the best dealer we ever had came straight from Dagenham at the age of 15'. The futures market where the emblematic meritocrats of the decade really came through was at LIFFE, populated as it was by Thatcher's stormtroopers. The media, it seemed at times, could not get enough of them. 'Life at LIFFE is fast and furious,' Michael Cockerell reported on BBC1 in March 1986:

> The dealers wear bright blazers in primary colours or broad stripes. They shout out their deals, wave their hands and hit their heads in a complex series of signals, looking like Technicolour tic-tac men gone slightly berserk. Almost all the dealers are young men in their twenties and early thirties. They come from working-class homes in the East End or the suburbs of London and work on commission or incentive payments. They earn from £15,000 up to £200,000 a year for a handful of the very top traders. These earnings represent the new power of the shop floor in the City . . .

Soon afterwards ITV's *First Tuesday* programme went behind 'the sedate columns of London's Royal Exchange', as the *TV Times* put it, and enabled the viewer to 'follow Mick, Bob and Nigel as they hurl themselves into a billion-pound maelstrom', in which 'frenzied atmosphere they are all too aware of their own futures and that they are working on borrowed time'. At one point Mick was asked exactly what a financial future was. Eventually, after a long silence, he gave up the struggle: 'You'll have to cut this. There's a good answer but I don't know it.'[13]

The conceptually challenged Mick may or may not have been a local – one of that bold band, not entirely encouraged by the market's 'authorities' despite the liquidity they gave, who traded entirely on their own account. Arguably, two stood out. One, profiled by the *FT* on LIFFE's first birthday, was Alan Dickinson, who at the start of 1983 had left his commodity trading job, withdrawn his savings, borrowed from the bank and taken out a second mortgage in order to become 'the first self-financed individual' to buy a seat on the exchange. 'It's a risky business,' he said, 'and you have to be prepared to take some nasty knocks, but with guts and determination and a bit of luck you can make a go of it. It's the only place in the City where you can set up your own operations without too much capital.' He reckoned to buy and sell a couple of times a minute, and some years later described himself as 'a very reactionary trader, a gut sort of trader'. He had learned by then rarely to run a position into a government announcement: 'I see no point in working day after day – scalping the market, jobbing it, trading it – and then going in and rolling some dice over a figure that could cost you two or three weeks' hard work . . . The main thing to do is not to lose all your ammo in one go.' Or, as the market saying went – provenance unknown – about the abiding danger of gradually amassing profits but then losing them all in one disastrous trading session: 'Feed like a pigeon and shit like an elephant.'[14]

Dickinson, probably the first trader on LIFFE to become a millionaire, was in his early thirties when he forged his reputation there, but the other dominant, self-made local was appreciably younger, born as recently as 1960. This was David Kyte, a north Londoner who worked for other firms before becoming a sole trader in January 1985 because, he claimed, 'I didn't want to have to laugh at other people's jokes.' His philosophy was simple. 'I trade anything that moves,' he informed *Euromoney* the following year, while not long afterwards he elaborated to the *Sunday Times Magazine*: 'If I lose £10,000 now, there's plenty more where that came from. If I make £10,000 it's not going to make such a great advance on my equity. I don't think of it as money any more. It's just points. If I'm up it gives me more to play with, that's it.' Tall and loud-voiced, but cool-headed, Kyte took to the high-adrenaline life of a local like a fish to water. 'There weren't a great deal of women on the floor,' he recollected. 'It was like a soccer dressing room for eight hours of the day. I loved it . . .'[15]

How thoroughgoing was the new meritocratic order of the 1980s? Obviously it varied from market to market, but undoubtedly there was some substance behind Derek Tullett's 1985 assertion that 'ability takes priority now – it's not who you know but what you know that matters'. Even at Cazenove's, where the same family names had appeared on the partners' list from generation to generation, nine of the thirteen new partners made between 1980 and 1986 had come to the firm unconnected, in other words without any particular partnership prospects – a far higher proportion than would have been conceivable in earlier times, and certainly before 1970 when the 'self-made' partner was a rarity. Yet overall it would be naive to imagine that the time-honoured virtues of class and connection suddenly no longer mattered. One of the most astute observers of the social scene, Nicholas Coleridge, said as much in his seminal *Spectator* article of March 1986 on 'The New Young Rich', an article partly prompted by the disconcerting news that a twenty-eight-year-old stockbroker friend had recently told him he expected to make £127,000 that year. Explicitly contradicting two recent Sunday colour-magazine articles, he stressed that most of these young men were *not* nouveau riche, but 'traditional upper-middle-class pinstripes'.[16] More-over, he might have reflected, whereas the conventional journalistic wisdom was that accent-wise it was now Uxbridge not Oxbridge that carried the clout, the fact was that the City, with its mixture of high financial rewards and ever more sophisticated financial instruments, was increasingly attracting highly qualified graduates with no previous connection to it.

The very top jobs in the City remained the preserve of the traditional ruling class. Leigh-Pemberton at the Bank of England, Goodison at the Stock Exchange, Scholey at Warburgs, Jacomb at BZW, not to mention Baring at Barings and Rothschild at Rothschilds – three of them were old Etonians, while the other three had slummed it at Harrow, Marlborough and Wellington. As for the familial aspect, there was a nice moment in 1984 when George ('Gowi') Mallinckrodt succeeded Airlie as Chairman of Schroders, his candidature presumably not hindered by being Bruno Schroder's brother-in-law. 'Even in a revolution,' Fildes commented, 'some things do not change.' Still, there was a new *Zeitgeist*, and shortly before Big Bang the Barclays board was widely praised when it chose John Quinton – *not* a member of one of the traditional ruling families – to succeed Bevan as Chairman. No doubt it helped the meritocratic cause that only a few weeks earlier Barclays had undergone the traumatic experience of being overtaken by NatWest as the largest British bank. 'To win the full support of the ruling clan,' a source close to the bank told the press, 'he must come up with a strategy that puts Barclays back on top in London.'[17]

There were (as Kyte recalled) relatively few women on the floor in LIFFE's early years. In December 1991, after that market's final day of trading in the Royal Exchange, a commemorative photograph was taken of the sixty people still trading who had traded back on the first day in September 1982. Only one (Gloria Hall) was a woman. Even so, by September 1983 LIFFE had in various capacities about 150 women on its floor, though outnumbered 4:1 by the men; as Neeta Brambhatt, dealing on the floor for Citifutures, told that month's *Cosmopolitan*, to succeed as a female trader 'you've got to be shrewd, forceful, precise – and above all daring'. Thick-skinned, she might have added, for the dealing culture both on the LIFFE floor and in the City's new dealing rooms was aggressively male and, indeed, outright sexist. Nicknames for female traders included 'Boiler' and 'Slapper', while Nancy Goldstone, an American who came to London in 1985 to set up a trading desk for currency options, never forgot her first day in a British dealing room: 'I was walking through and it was there on the wall right in front of me, a picture of a naked woman. I just stopped dead.' Nevertheless, opportunities were opening up, and later that year *Cosmopolitan* was optimistic enough to run a feature called 'Bang Go The City Girls', taking the line that the mixture of rapid expansion and internationalisation was at last making the City wide open to women. There was still of course a long, long way to go. At Cazenove's, for example, the concept of a woman in the partners' room remained more or less unthinkable; and in May 1985 it was computed that, among the City's top ten law firms, only twenty-seven out of a total of 608 partners were women. Things were only marginally different in the much less traditional, more international world of Eurobond trading. On the basis of *Institutional Investor's* directory a year later of the leading firms in the Eurobond secondary market (and counting only those both London-based and with obviously gender-denoting first names), out of 434 leading traders, 387 were men.[18]

One of the forty-seven exceptions was Valerie Thompson, who by May 1986 was head of secondary trading at Salomons. Hers had been a career wonderfully characteristic of the new City. She came from Dagenham, her father ran a greengrocer's shop, and after leaving school in 1971 at the age of fifteen she had started on the switchboard of the stockbrokers Hichens, Harrison & Co. By the mid-1970s she was a telex operator at Salomons, and by 1978 she was a Deutschmark trader on the dealing floor. 'I didn't know the first thing about the basis of economics,' she recalled fifteen years later. 'I never looked at the *Financial Times* – I couldn't even read the *Daily Mirror*. But I learned it. I learned it and I made money.' In 1980 she was briefly sent to New York in order to take an American exam, and soon afterwards came the real lift-off:

> When I got back to London – Salomon had just moved to Angel Court – the guy who traded Floating Rate Notes was just leaving for New York. I said, 'Who's going to trade the FRNs?' And he said, 'There's a delay in the guy coming to take over so I'll guess you'll pick it up.' It threw me in at the deep end and I knew nothing about it. It was the worst two weeks of my life. By twelve o'clock that first day I couldn't get out of the chair because I was totally soaked in sweat. I was dripping, my skirt and everything. Dealing in FRNs changed my life because I had all the other major houses – our competitors – ringing me up. I'm sure they were saying to one another, 'God, they've got some daft cow at Salomon that's never done this before. Ring her up and see.' It was as if they were the big boys who understood the rules of the game. I had to stand up and be counted. I was given a hard time but I managed not to lose money.
>
> When the guy arrived from America to take over, I handed the FRNs back and carried on with Deutschmarks and Euros and guilders – which I was much more comfortable with – but my appetite was whetted and towards the end of 1980 I began to become a specialist in the FRN market

and later took over responsibility for it. It was a period of tremendous growth – when I first got involved in FRNs there was a total of ten or fifteen billion dollars' worth of debt outstanding and maybe a hundred issues and by 1986 there was a total of about a hundred and fifty billion dollars and many more issuers including a lot of governments and banks worldwide.

I used to get up early but I wouldn't get to work until eight at the earliest. I've always worked better at the end of the day. Before I went to bed I would ring Tokyo and find out what had gone on in the Far East and I would ring New York. You'd trade in the night. You'd do it in your sleep. When you know the market inside out, you can do it with confidence. You just have to ask the right questions. If you don't ask, no one's going to volunteer stuff. I never minded the calls in the night . . .

I took trading very seriously. If there was a chance to do a trade and make the investor happy and the salesman happy, I'd be doing it. I guess my desire to make people happy was balanced out because I could also get my anger out. Emotionally, it was the best thing for me because all my pent-up anger against men and life that came from my childhood, I could express in trading with the other houses; I could kill the other houses, decimate them, wipe them out. I would swear more than most of the guys because it was a way of expressing something I felt deeply about. It was healthy stuff for me . . .

Or, as she put it more mildly in 1986 – interviewed by the *Observer* for a piece about the City's new traders that referred to her six-bedroom, four-bathroom house in Essex – 'what you learn is that lack of education needn't be an obstacle'.[19]

Thompson was well aware that her progress would almost certainly have been much slower if she had stayed with a British firm. 'Salomon were very good to me,' she emphasised. 'They knew I was a bit of a different animal. I wasn't a graduate who had gone through the programme with certain expectations. They didn't look on me as if I were a freak and they were forgiving and accommodating. As long as the results were there, they left you free to apply yourself in the way you felt comfortable.' Salomons itself was a rapidly expanding operation, and during the year or so before Big Bang perhaps the most prevailing sense in the City was of the American banks moving into the very centre of the picture, either through acquisition or ambitious organic growth. Whereas the response of the European banks to the City revolution was relatively muted, and the Japanese banks may well have been unofficially discouraged from making acquisitions (at a time when there was considerable controversy about the refusal of the Tokyo Stock Exchange to open up to foreigners), the Americans had few such inhibitions, even when their presence was less than warmly welcomed. 'They do things differently,' Unigate's corporate treasurer, Daniel Hodson, observed in September 1986. 'A man's word is his bond; let's hope things stay the same.' At about the same time the London managing director of one of the American banks conceded that some of the criticism of his compatriots was becoming nothing less than 'vitriolic'. That adjective applied to the strictures of a well-established commodity broker, Dick Oxley, who shortly afterwards opened up to a Sunday paper:

> The main people to benefit from the Big Bang are powerful New York houses who have now got their foot into the City. They've been kept at bay for all this time and rightly so, because much of big business in the States is controversial and the worst changes in the City have come from copying American methods. Standards have been lowered, and there is more greed and less foresight. Many think the will to win is synonymous with efficiency. But most of it is just ineffectual blather. Why, for instance, has it become obligatory to shout on the telephone?[20]

Two very different cultures were in play, and it was hardly surprising that they did not always mesh easily. Stanislas Yassukovich's father was, as a veteran banker, employed by Bankers Trust in the 1980s in an advisory role, and one day he accompanied one of that bank's thrusting young men to the Bank of England. Bankers Trust had recently acquired an old Greek bank, Rodocanachi, and was planning to rebrand it as Rodo International. The purpose of the visit was to get the Bank's blessing for the acquisition. The meeting went well, but right at the end the Bank man mentioned, seemingly as a casual, throwaway remark, that it would be a shame to change the name. As they walked along Threadneedle Street Yassukovich told his colleague that *that* had been the real burden of the meeting, but the younger American insisted that it had been merely small talk. Accordingly the new name stayed as Rodo International – and the Bank, unhappy with this, made life very difficult for it.

Generally it cannot have been a very comfortable experience for the newcomers. 'When I first came to this city,' Stephen Berger of Lehmans recalled in the mid-1990s, 'it was clear to me that American banks were viewed as the lowest forms of life, we were off the social scale, beneath the social scale, and frankly pretty much untouchables.' Still, most of them tended to take a pretty dim view of the natives. The classic text was Michael Lewis's best-selling *Liar's Poker* of 1989. Much of it is about Wall Street, but Lewis (a well-educated American bond salesman born in 1960) came to work at Salomons' London office in December 1985 and was there for just over two years, during which time the staff increased from 150 to 900. He did not feel inclined to take any lessons from his new hosts, or indeed from his new colleagues: 'They were less interested in the latest financial gadget to come out of America, than in establishing relationships with customers. There is a genus of European, species English, to whom slick financial practice comes naturally. The word for them in the Euromarkets is "spivs". Oddly, we had no spivs. Our Europeans – especially our Englishmen – tended to be the refined products of the right schools.' Uprightness, however, came at a price: 'For them work was not an obsession, or even, it seemed, a concern. And the notion that a person should subordinate himself to a corporation, especially an American corporation, was, to them, laughable.' Lewis added that in New York Salomons' nickname for them was 'Monty Python's Flying Investment Bankers'. Early on, his unflattering assumptions about the natives were confirmed when he was asked to call on the senior partner of a stock-broking firm. 'Curious about old English money men', Lewis accepted the invitation and found 'a portly, middle-aged figure in an ill-fitted suit, scuffed black shoes, and the sort of sagging thin black socks I came to recognise as a symbol of Britain's long economic decline':

> We sat in his poorly lit office surrounded by more unfinished work than I've ever seen in one place and talked for an hour. More accurately, he talked for an hour about world events. I listened. Finally he tired and called a car to take us to lunch. But before leaving his office he paged through his copy of *The Times* with a sharp pencil in his hand and said, 'I must make a bet'. He dialled what I gathered to be his bookie and placed two bets of five pounds each on horses racing that day. As he put down the phone, he said, 'I view the bond market as an extension of horse racing, you know.' I didn't, of course, and I got the feeling I was supposed to be impressed . . .
>
> Anyway, we then took one of those two-hour lunches for which the London office was fairly renowned in New York. Again he talked. Again I listened, about how the bond market rally was overdone, about how absurdly diligent he felt American bankers were, and about how his small firm was going to cope with giants like Salomon invading the City of London. He disapproved of work days longer than eight hours because, he said, 'You then arrive at the office in the morning with the same thoughts you left with late the night before' . . .

The firm was apparently bought out soon afterwards, enabling Lewis's host to 'float the short distance to earth in a golden parachute'. For Lewis himself, the big moment came in August 1986 as he managed to unload $86m worth of unwanted Olympia & York bonds on an overtrusting French client:

> For two days messages of congratulations arrived from distant points in the Salomon Brothers' system . . . The sweetness of the moment dulled the pain of knowing I had just placed my most cherished customer in jeopardy. The most important call of all came. It was from the Human Piranha. 'I heard you sold a few bonds,' he said. I tried to sound calm about the whole thing. He didn't. He shouted into the phone, '*That* is fuckin' awesome. I mean *fuckin'* awesome. I *fuckin'* mean *fucking* awesome. You are one Big Swinging Dick, and don't ever let anybody tell you different.' It brought tears to my eyes to hear it . . .[21]

Lewis would get bored sooner rather than later with the trader's life and would walk away from Salomons in 1988, but the honour was imperishable.

During the two years before Big Bang the American influence did much to alter the City's way of life. 'I have to get in at 8.00 a.m. now – before the Americans arrived the working day started at 9.15,' Neville Wood of Messels (in the process of being taken over by Shearson Lehman) told *Futures World* in January 1985. 'I arrive before the tea lady now.' It was not just a case of American-style hours for their own, virtuous sake – these extended hours reflected, as Riley observed in June 1986, both 'the globalisation of the investment industry, making it possible to transact business in other time zones' and 'the growing amount of professional trading in the markets', in the sense that 'because the professionals are at their desks all day watching screens, they are ready at any time to trade anything that moves' – but undoubtedly there was a cultural element in the shift. Over the next few months there were some telling signs. The stockbrokers of Haslemere, unhappy about the 7.15 being their first train to Waterloo, managed to persuade British Rail to run one at 6.44; it was decided that rehearsals for the Lord Mayor's parade could no longer be held at 8 a.m., on account of there being too much traffic on the roads, and would have to be at 7 a.m.; while at the other end of the day it was claimed by one British broker that it was now impossible to get a taxi in the City at 8 p.m., because everyone else was also working late. It was almost certainly during these two years that the American breakfast – a strictly working affair – came in a big way to the City, but better documented were the changing habits at lunchtime. Although long, heavy, alcoholic lunches were not quite consigned to oblivion (there were still, for example, reassuring chops to be had at Simpson's in Cornhill), the trend was all the other way, towards sandwiches and spritzers. Four months before Big Bang an American journalist, Michael VerMeulen, caught the flavour exactly:

> Croissant Express, a fast-food place situated at the exact center of Leadenhall Market, is fifteen-deep in blue flannel. The customers queue like good Londoners. Behind the counter, three hyperactive Oriental women slapped together more of the most popular item – French liver pâté, Swiss cheese and British lettuce inside a baguette. If you want, you can buy an American soft drink to wash it down, or maybe a German beer? Talk about the globalization of markets!
>
> Sandwich bars are booming in the City. There's a McDonald's franchise above the Monument tube. It's easier to find a magenta Mohawk haircut than a silk top hat on Gracechurch Street . . .

Time had become the new master. It was, as the Secretary of the City Club in Old Broad Street eloquently complained to another American journalist soon afterwards, a sad day when his members no longer had the leisure to sit around over a drink or two.[22]

Did the material rewards make it all worthwhile? 'Top salaries in the City fair make one gasp, they are so large,' none other than Margaret Thatcher confessed to *Newsnight* just over a year before Big Bang. Back in year zero (1979) things had been rather different – at Morgan Grenfell, for example, a director's remuneration was about £40,000, which was tidy enough but hardly a source of stunned disbelief. However, the whole point of the Thatcher project was no longer to pursue egalitarian goals, while a further stimulus to City pay levels was the outlawing in 1980 of insider dealing, thereby cutting off (or certainly discouraging) what had traditionally been a lucrative source of revenue to those in the know. Over the years the whole question of how much those who were something in the City actually earned had received surprisingly little outside attention, but that began to change in 1982 following the headline-attracting news that the leading Lloyd's underwriter Ian Posgate had been paid over £320,000 in a single year. 'People in the City have a great deal of contact with markets and with money,' Philip Burnford of Hay Management Consultants perhaps superfluously told the *Observer*, confirming that average earnings there were well above those in industry. 'They have to be very aware of market focus and they tend to apply the same principles to themselves.'[23]

Most of the figures, nonetheless, were still far from startling, with a survey by Lloyd Incomes Research that year into the merchant and international banking sectors finding that neither corporate finance executives nor chief foreign exchange dealers were likely to earn above £50,000. Nor did the situation significantly change over the next year or two. In his autumn 1983 survey of the wider situation, following the Parkinson/Goodison agreement, Jacob Rothschild found that, on the basis of published figures, top people in the City were far less well paid than on Wall Street; for instance, most directors at Rothschilds only got somewhere around £100,000, whereas their counterparts at Salomons or Morgan Stanley were likely to be receiving at least five times as much. It was the same further down the ranks. 'At the crunch point, you simply say to yourself, "One has been in business since eighteen hundred and something. There have been bad times and good times. If it means I must have leaner expectations, so be it,"' a senior manager at an accepting house told Paul Ferris at about that time. 'Wall Street has much greater orientation to personal gain. London wants to be successful, too, but the rewards are more in respect. They don't necessarily come through the wallet.'[24] However, through a mixture of American influence and competitive gearing-up for Big Bang, together creating an aggressive, bonus-driven culture, such an attitude was about to become almost antediluvian.

An important moment was the highly publicised episode in July 1985 when Kleinworts poached eight people from the Wedd Durlacher arm of

BZW, with the jobbers receiving between them £1m to defect, and upwards of £2m for their first year's salaries. Soon afterwards, on the basis of information from headhunters, the *Economist* revealed the latest salaries (probably including bonuses, share options and suchlike): £250,000 or more for top gilts dealers; up to £300,000 for Eurobond dealers; £200,000 for experts in American equities; £250,000 for currency dealers; and £150,000 for swaps specialists. 'All these figures,' the magazine added to cheer up its readers outside the square mile, 'are still barely half what similar people command in New York.' As a point of further comparison, the Governor of the Bank of England was currently on some £85,000 a year. A gold rush had begun, and the following month a financial recruitment specialist observed that 'an unprecedented number of accountants, lawyers and MBAs are coming to us looking for an opening in financial services, on the back of what they read about City salaries in the newspapers'.[25] New terms were also entering City vocabulary. Not just 'golden hello' (the opposite of a golden handshake) and 'golden handcuffs' (deferred payments in order to lock people in), but also the so-called 'Marzipan Set', usually comprising young high-fliers below the icing (partnership level or the equivalent) but above the cake (those unfortunates without serious prospects). When Chase Manhattan acquired two stockbroking firms (Simon & Coates and Laurie Milbank), it was in order to keep the marzipan boys sweet that it reputedly went out and bought thirty-seven Porsches in a single day.

In March 1986, soon after Thatcher had again distanced herself from the phenomenon ('On salaries in the City, I am the first to say this does cause me great concern. I understand the resentment . . .'), Nicholas Coleridge sought to offer some numerical perspective:

> It is difficult to estimate the number of young investment bankers, stockbrokers, and commodity brokers earning £100,000 a year. Perhaps there are only a couple of thousand, but they are so mobile and noisy that they give the impression of being far more numerous. Most are aged between 26 and 34, and two years ago they were being paid £25,000, in some cases even less, until the opening up of the City markets precipitated an epidemic of headhunting and concomitant salaries.

A few days later Michael Cockerell's *This Week Next Week* television programme on City earnings found an articulate defender of the new set-up in Philip Manduca, a twenty-seven-year-old former public-school boy who in the past year had been paid over £200,000 for trading for Rouse Woodstock in financial futures, currencies and Eurobonds:

> One can earn quite considerable amounts if one is successful in any given year. One can also earn as little as £20,000, which is, although big nationwide, a very small amount for the City at the moment. A dealer is very much assessed on his performance . . . And if he can't perform to the highest

salaries that are being offered and taken in the City at the moment, he will be fired. We are based purely on client business. The more business we do, the more profitable we are and the more one gets a percentage of that . . .

The pressures are very high, and as a consequence I think the rewards have to be high as well. You can't really survive very long in this business at the front end, on the dealing desk. You won't die dealing, but the incentive will diminish in time. It is very wearing and a selfish occupation, meaning that you don't have a lot of time for other people, such as wives, children and so on. Hence the rewards are very much like those for a football player – they have to be high early on . . .

The pre-Big Bang scramble, meanwhile, was continuing unabated, and that same month there were reports of Morgan Grenfell Securities picking up a four-man team of analysts from Grieveson Grant for a total package ('golden hellos' and promised first-year salaries) of somewhere in the region of £1.5m. Carl West-Meads, a personnel consultant, put it aptly during the summer: 'People have lost touch with what a salary market is. It's now a recruitment-premium salary market, and greed is exponential.' Of course, in addition to these mainly young dealers, analysts and others commanding such a remarkable premium, there were the former partners of stockbroking and jobbing firms – estimated to be 500 or more – who had become millionaires overnight through selling their firms to outside owners. There were also the well-established City figures running the merchant banks, who saw no reason not to have a share of the honey, especially since in many cases their business had been booming anyway. For their work in 1986 the directors of Morgan Grenfell received an average of some £225,000 – a fivefold increase on 1979.[26] The City revolution, like Guinness, had been good for them.

In a tiny park just north of London Wall, a plaque records that on 3 July 1979 a silver lime was 'planted by Mr J.T. Brown of Phillips & Drew'. A mere six or seven years later such a plaque – with its implication of employee and firm indissolubly linked – would have been almost satirical. 'The City on $1,000 a day' was the title of a bitterly humorous 'Lex' column in August 1985, purportedly 'a brief guide to the City job market' for those 'salaried individuals – company chairmen, senior civil servants and the like – anxious to increase their earnings by taking a job in the City'. Interpreting the job advertisement was crucial:

> In City terms, extensive experience means roughly one year in a similar position. A unique career opportunity is only an opportunity. No City jobs are unique and hardly any offer a career. A reference to long-term commitment can safely be ignored. There is no such thing as a binding contract in the City . . .
>
> Once in the City, change jobs as often as you can – every six months is roughly the norm. The financial market's appetite for staff is inexhaustible and a change of firm automatically produces a higher salary. If you prefer to

stay where you are, at least threaten to resign. This generally has a miraculous effect . . .

Inevitably these were the years of the rise and rise of the City headhunters. 'We're looking for younger people, better educated people, computer skills, more aggression, more oomph,' Rupert White of David Sheppard and Partners told a Sunday colour magazine on the eve of Big Bang. 'I don't come cheap, and I'm expected to produce results – so I'm not recruiting people who've merely got the taste to buy the right sort of stripey suit. They've got to be able to make money – a lot of money – for the client.' He did not, though, express a view on whether there might be a downside to the rapid erosion of the ties that used to bind. Presumably, if pressed, he would have agreed with the head gilts trader quoted in *Liar's Poker*: 'You want loyalty, hire a cocker spaniel.'[27]

Two worlds were colliding, and it seemed very clear to observers which one the force was with. In his March 1986 television report Michael Cockerell related an almost palpably symbolic encounter between those two worlds:

> The LIFFE dealers enjoy showing off their new-found wealth. At Green's Champagne Bar in the Royal Exchange, the traders in their bright blazers delight in marching in with a wad of notes and ordering 'two bottles of your best shampoo, please'. Miles Maskell, the owner of Green's, said: 'You can see the social transformation in the City each morning in the bar. At 11 o'clock the old-fashioned City types come in, who have been having a drink at that time all their professional lives. But at 12.30 the LIFFE boys come in and the decibel level rises dramatically. All the old-fashioned types beat a hasty retreat . . .'

In many ways the cultural antecedents of this new world lay in the hard-working, meritocratic ethos that Siegmund Warburg and his firm brought to the City during the twenty years after the war. That background gave an ironic weight to the experience of one of Warburg's most able protégés, Peter Spira, when at the start of 1983 he returned to the City after eight years out of it. His new employer was Goldman Sachs. 'Not only had the whole City become far more competitive, and less honest and honourable, than it was when I left it, but the internal competition and pressures in the top firms such as Goldman Sachs had to be seen to be believed,' he related somewhat ruefully. 'I had not realised the standards of achievement that were going to be expected of me by my brilliant but ruthless new American colleagues.' He went on:

> The absence of friends, the hostility of former friends [including at Warburgs] who regarded Goldman, and therefore me, as an arch-enemy rather than just a dangerous competitor, the zoological working environment and the constant pressure to perform and generate fees proved to be quite a shock. I also found it rather demeaning, when one of 'my'

clients did a deal through an investment bank other than Goldman Sachs, to receive an immediate fax from some spotty pipsqueak in New York asking a) whether I had tried to get that mandate and, if so, could I please send copies of my 'calling' memoranda immediately, and b) if I had not, why not? I just felt too old and, frankly, too senior for that sort of thing but I had to admit that it was a very effective spur to effort . . .

In particular, Spira found it difficult to get accustomed to the 'cold calling' that was expected of him; but he buckled down, performed well enough and in due course left through his own choice. He reflected dispassionately on his five years:

> The occupants of our offices were a strange mixture, combining dynamically ruthless but bright Americans, a mixture of extremely clever Englishmen and other Europeans and a number of barrow-boys who, with their cockney accents and flash suits, were making fortunes as traders. This was a typical reflection of the Thatcher years when talent in any form was amply rewarded on the basis of merit and it was no bar to success that a young trader, when entertaining a client to lunch, might stick his half-masticated chewing-gum under the dining-room table.

In short, 'I met many agreeable and brilliant colleagues, and a few unattractive hoodlums but rarely a fool in sight'.[28] What would Spira's mentor have made of it? The ambition, the intensity, the ruthless breaking-down of complacent, entrenched City assumptions, practices and coteries – of all these aspects of the 1980s' sea-change he would surely have been broadly supportive. But Warburg had always believed that achieving the highest, least amateurish standards as a financial practitioner was compatible with being a whole man, taking a cultured interest in the wider world. *That* was the possibility that was lost in the 1980s, as a new breed of City man (and woman) emerged who simply did not have the time, and often neither the inclination nor the attributes, even to begin to achieve that holistic ideal.

*

'La "City", un îlot de prospérité dans un océan d'austérité' was the evocative headline in a French paper in November 1982, as part of a series on the state of Britain as it started to come out of the deep recession of the early 1980s. That same year Anthony Sampson observed how, during the two decades since his first *Anatomy*, 'the contrast between the City and the rest of Britain has become more extreme', in that 'bankers and dealers have become more international while industrialists and others have been bogged down in the country's economic constraints, and politicians have pursued their own national policies'. In other words, 'the square mile of the City has become like an offshore island in the heart of the nation'.

Emphatically this seasoned, perceptive commentator did not see this bifurcation as a good thing:

> The inhabitants of this extraordinary island – like those of other banking islands such as Hong Kong, Singapore or Manhattan – view the world very differently from those on the mainland. They can see across the whole globe, but they see it through money; they clearly perceive Britain's economic problems, but they see the British people in terms of balance sheets. They are constantly dealing with bits of British industry, restructuring companies, joining their boards, merging them or rationalising them. But they still remain aloof from the real industrial problems; and their business (as Jim Slater described it) is making money, not things.

British politics was becoming more polarised than at any time since the war, with Thatcher and Foot as the respective party leaders, and the following year the City found itself at the centre of a major, hostile protest for the first time since the Chartists in 1848. This was the 'Stop The City' movement, which held its first demonstration in September 1983 and another, bigger one the following March, remembered years later by an organiser, Dave Morris:

> There is music, graffiti, London Bridge is briefly blocked, a claimants' group burns UB40 cards, many banks are picketed, some are occupied and a couple have windows smashed, there is street theatre everywhere, police harass activists and make arrests, managing to prevent a mobile carnival stage reaching the centre – but they can't stop large gatherings. Thousands of workers stop work to watch from their windows and tens of thousands more read the leaflets . . .
>
> Afterwards, there are rumours of a £100m shortfall due to the disruption. We feel triumphant but the media attacks the events, and the police step up their threats. There are two further days of action in the City, but numbers are down, and the arrests are up . . .

Nevertheless, Morris would claim, 'due to Stop The City, the secrecy and supposed invulnerability of the City was punctured for all time'.[29]

It was just after a Stop The City demo (probably the first one) that Paul Ferris asked a merchant banker ('oiled hair, pink cheeks') about the notion of more money being put into a high-unemployment place like Liverpool. Shaking his head, he replied, 'Politicians hire buses and take businessmen around Merseyside. Well. Would you invest there? In a lot of bloody-minded Liverpudlians? People complain that the City doesn't invest in places like Liverpool. Why should I? It isn't efficient.' Sadly, this merchant banker preferred to stay anonymous, as did the ninety-eight City people (mainly stockbrokers, jobbers and merchant bankers) interviewed by the sociologist David Lazar in 1985. His pioneering study brought out both the intrinsic satisfaction that many of his interviewees found in their work ('I do genuinely feel quite proud that I've got something right for somebody,' one stockbroker told him) and the way in which they viewed financial markets as an exciting, demanding arena ('Every day is a new challenge, every day is different,' one very senior jobber stressed); but its peculiar interest lay in the way he showed how most of those working in the City of London still inhabited remarkably narrow – and intolerant – mental parameters:

> A market maker stated that he supported progressive income tax because those who could afford to bear the burden should do so. He continued (referring to his colleagues): 'I'd probably get killed if you tell them I said that . . . [Laugh]'. A fund manager, who is a strong egalitarian, said when interviewed that he had given up discussing politics with his colleagues because it was so unpleasant to do so. A foreign exchange broker, who had been a Labour party member and still described himself as a socialist, replied when asked whether he was still a member, 'How could I be and do this job?'

'What makes these examples even more telling,' Lazar added, 'is that none of these individuals is particularly left-wing. One voted Conservative in 1983 and the other two are mainstream Labour supporters.' Of his interviewees, he felt able to give an ideological classification to ninety-one of them: 7 per cent were neo-liberals (that is, out-and-out supporters of the wholly free, unconstrained market); 46 per cent had an outlook somewhere between neo-liberalism and what he called 'Traditional Conservatism'; and 33 per cent were more or less traditional Conservatives. Lazar offered a helpful perspective on these figures:

> When interviewees are classified by ideology, it is clear that they are, in all but a small minority of cases, heavily influenced by Neo-liberal ideology. When we take account of the fact that the Traditional Conservative ideal-type is associated with the acceptance of the bulk of the privatisation programme and a severely weakened progressive income taxation system, it is clear that only a small minority of interviewees defend the post-1945 settlement . . .
>
> Effectively, the City 'dissenter' is an individual who favours the social institutions of the post-War consensus, usually somewhat diluted. Although those who defend the post-1945 political settlement do question the principle of the absolute superiority of the market, the uncritical acceptance of the capitalist nature of the economy by such dissenters is striking . . .[30]

The City, in short, was not for turning – and in retrospect, the ascendancy of the market had only just begun.

At the time that Lazar conducted his interviews, the imminence of Big Bang, the conspicuous consumption by many of those benefiting from it and the rise of individual share ownership on the back of privatisation made the City seem at the social cutting-edge in a way that had rarely been the case before. The young fashion designer Georgina Godley observed the phenomenon from a particularly interesting vantage-point. 'In 1981 I set up Crolla,' she recalled eleven years later:

We were all about trying to break down class barriers and attacking the vocabulary of the Establishment. We took all the rules of Savile Row and the traditions of the eccentric Englishman, and reinterpreted them using fabrics from all over the world. It was a way of bringing a more open-minded, Blitz and New Romantics culture into the City and turning menswear on its head.

The early Eighties were the beginning of the yuppie era – not that we called them that at first – the kids of east or south London making it big in the City; and their greed made us hugely successful. We appeased the guilt about their ferocious ambition and gluttony by providing clothes from a more pop, more democratic culture. It was the rebirth of the dandy allied to the formal trappings of the City, and that combination was very indicative . . .

There is little hard evidence, though, of how Middle England viewed the City in the mid-1980s. 'The price of country houses along the main roads of London, particularly the M4 motorway into the West Country, went up 30 per cent in a year,' Adrian Hamilton noted in his 1986 account of *The Financial Revolution*. 'Flats in the centre of London shot up at the same pace. In the City a new class of privileged was created, limited in number but large in individual gain. The public looked on in amazement.' That June the television documentary on the traders at LIFFE produced a mixed response. 'It looked and sounded like a prep school bun-fight in Petticoat Lane,' David Bradbury in the *Sunday Mirror* thought, while to Nancy Banks-Smith in the *Guardian* 'the din was indescribable, the screen full of faces and fists', making the whole thing nothing so much as 'like being a dog biscuit in Battersea'. A provincial reviewer, John Ogdon, was more interesting:

I was quite prepared to hate the dealers, but in fact they took me by surprise, not least because although they all seemed to live in mansions, most of them looked and sounded like extras from *Minder*. 'Eh! Oi! Oi! Oi! Oi! Aht, aht' bawled one, as the buyers went into something resembling the feeding frenzy of sharks. There were millions being made and lost here, by boys in ridiculous-looking jackets, shouting and bawling in conditions of complete chaos. Through it all – although the programme gave no reason for me to think so – I could not keep from thinking that in all this bedlam and panic, deals were being struck which might mean that somewhere in the Third World another village was being condemned to starvation.[31]

It was seldom that that connection – even the possibility of such a connection – surfaced in the public prints.

Four months later, in October 1986, the arrival of Big Bang itself enabled, at least potentially, a moment of stocktaking. 'Ancient prejudices against finance are being stimulated by the growing belief that the City has become an unpatriotic casino which pays itself obscenely high salaries for dancing on the grave of British industry,' David Goodhart and Charles

Grant declared in the *New Statesman* on the Friday before the 27th. On that memorable Monday morning, even the *FT*, for all its intimate knowledge of how thoroughly internationalised the City had become in its everyday functions and role, saw the City as inextricably entwined in the domestic economy:

> Uncertainty and volatility in the international monetary system currently permit those who live off capital flows to earn above-average returns. But bankers cannot defy the laws of economic gravity by earning more than their customers for ever. Nor is there any correlation between a sophisticated financial system and a successful economy; if anything, hyper-active capital markets impose a short-term view on industry and inhibit real investment. In short, financial efficiency must not be allowed to become an end in itself.

Such was the City's generally exultant mood that this was in effect a significant piece of self-criticism by the City's own paper. Nevertheless, at this self-consciously historic moment, the most engaging – and in a way most perceptive – commentary came, surprisingly enough, from Jon Akass in the *Daily Express*:

> For most people, the City is an alien place. The humblest lift-operator in a Moscow department store will have some inkling of how Communism is supposed to work. They would have endured lessons at school. Hardly anyone in Britain knows how capitalism is supposed to work and we are especially befuddled when it comes to the City. The Big Bang might clear the air just slightly because there is a suspicion that the old City cherished its mysteries and the notion that it was some kind of secret society. It is harder to be mysterious in front of a computer screen. Everybody is beginning to understand computers.
>
> For the first time in my life, I get a distant sense of excitement as the high-fliers arrive in their Porsches and prepare to do battle. From all accounts, the conflict will be merciless. There will soon be a lively market in second-hard sports cars. And bespoke tailors will be sending their bills to skid-row.
>
> There will be winners and losers, which we can all understand. But we will still not understand why and how.[32]

POSTSCRIPT

1986-2000

I looked out of the window. The tall grey buildings of the City of London pointed silently upwards out of the listless heat of the streets below. I noticed a kestrel gliding around the upper reaches of the Mercantile Union Insurance building a hundred yards to the west. The great financial centre slumbered on. It was difficult to believe anything was happening out there.

Michael Ridpath, *Free to Trade* (1995)

CHAPTER TWENTY-TWO

Hong Kong West

Monday, 27 October 1986 – Big Bang – did not prove a brilliant advertisement for the new order. 'Seaq and ye shall not find' was Lex's witty headline the next day, after the Stock Exchange's new computerised price and dealing information system had to be suspended for over an hour. However, in the City's new dealing rooms most of the systems stood up well enough, in contrast to the semi-disastrous dress rehearsal nine days earlier, and at the end of the day there was a general mood of qualified relief. From the start the Stock Exchange floor was less populous, and over the next few weeks, as phone-and-screen trading became the norm, the numbers rapidly dwindled. By January 1987 even the trading floor's staunchest supporter, Smith New Court, reluctantly decided there was no point in retaining a presence. Soon afterwards it became the sole preserve of the Stock Exchange's traded options market. 'We've got a viewing gallery and nothing to see,' Stephen Raven (now of Warburg Securities) lamented.[1] That was true enough, though the melancholy sight of all the spanking-new – but now abandoned – telecommunications technology on the floor served as a reminder of the City's abiding reluctance to embrace change until it was virtually a *fait accompli*.

Market sentiment was still mainly bullish in the closing months of 1986, with the FT 30-Share Index going into 1987 on 1313.9, representing a gain of 15.5 per cent on the year. The climate was therefore congenial in early December for the biggest privatisation so far, the £5,430m 'Tell Sid' sell-off of British Gas, following what the *Economist* rightly called 'a persistent, numbing but nevertheless effective advertising campaign'. Unlike BT, the issue was not a roaring success (two times oversubscribed, as opposed to five), but it was a success. Was a culture of private share ownership being established? By September 1987 (following recent British Airways and Rolls-Royce privatisations) the *FT* was still sceptical, noting that 'the hard fact is that private investors' business is more costly for the brokers' and that 'as long as that is the case the City's response to calls for popular capitalism will be lukewarm'.[2]

Big Bang itself had hardly happened when the City – and especially Morgan Grenfell – found itself under a blacker cloud of scandal than anyone could remember. The curtain-raiser was on 10 November 1986, as

Geoffrey Collier, joint head of securities trading at Morgan Grenfell, resigned because of insider dealing (for which he was eventually given a suspended prison sentence): 'Big Bang scandal as whizkid quits: £300,000-a-year bank chief' was the *Standard*'s predictable headline. Yet this was nothing compared to the story that was about to break. In early December, following revelations by the now-disgraced American arbitrageur Ivan Boesky, the DTI began an investigation into an alleged share-support operation during the weeks leading up to the Guinness takeover of Distillers earlier that year. 'Neither I nor anyone at Morgan Grenfell knew of, or had any contact with, Schenley or with Boesky over any special arrangements or sweetheart/support deals,' Morgan Grenfell's Roger Seelig flatly insisted to the press. 'We were not party in any way to any improper deals with Boesky, Riklis or Schenley.' Shortly after Christmas it emerged that Henry Ansbacher's Managing Director, Lord Spens, had given details to DTI inspectors about the informal indemnification arrangements that had been made between Seelig and himself during the closing stages of the takeover battle. Seelig's resignation from Morgan Grenfell was announced on the 30th. 'I am extremely sad,' commented Spens. 'The man has been thrown to the wolves. I consider it inconceivable that he was acting on his own authority. Roger was always very professional and very cautious.'[3] The pressure was still on Morgan Grenfell, which on 13 January 1987 (the day before Ernest Saunders was dismissed at Guinness) announced an internal review. The press scented a whitewash, and within days the government – anxious about public opinion, with a general election in the offing – was telling the Bank of England to take some action. The Bank (through the intermediary of Lord O'Brien of Lothbury) obliged, and Morgan Grenfell's Chief Executive, Christopher Reeves, and its head of corporate finance, Graham Walsh, resigned on the 20th. It was a total humiliation.

The Bank also insisted that Spens must walk the plank, which he duly did on the 22nd. By about the same time hints of the roles of Gerald Ronson, Sir Jack Lyons and the City men Anthony Parnes and Ephraim Margulies were starting to emerge. Inevitably, attention now turned to Cazenove's, and in particular David Mayhew. 'King Caz's deafening silence' was a *Standard* headline as early as the 21st, while four days later the *Observer* reported the government's determination that the firm 'should not escape censure for its role in the Guinness share support operation, even if there is no direct evidence that the firm was involved in any of the illegal activities'. The stakes were further raised on the 28th when a Labour frontbencher, Robin Cook, explicitly named Cazenove's as accomplices in the Guinness scandal. However, a statement next day by Cazenove's declared that an inquiry by the solicitors Simmons & Simmons had found no evidence of wrongdoing; and over the coming weeks and months, Mayhew himself remained in place, with no evidence that the Bank tried to persuade the two joint senior partners, John Kemp-Welch and Anthony Forbes, otherwise. Soon the headlines moved elsewhere, but few imagined that the Guinness affair would quietly die away, certainly not once the arrests began. Between April and October 1987 there were five (Saunders, Parnes, Lyons, Ronson and Seelig), prompting the *FT*'s Richard Lambert to observe with a certain relish that 'not since the South Sea Bubble in the early eighteenth century had so many top British financiers faced so many serious charges arising from a single event'.[4]

In January 1987, with the scandal unfolding amidst almost daily revelations, the same paper's David Lascelles reported that 'the Guinness affair has plunged the City into a mood of gloom, anxiety and even, in some corners, despair'. He added that 'people with long memories say they cannot recall a time when the City's reputation has been so badly battered by scandal, or when the threat of political repercussions has loomed so large'. Predictably, even though it was barely two months since the Takeover Panel had rebuked Hill Samuel and Cazenove's for not dissimilar share buying during the early autumn battle to prevent the British engineering company AE being taken over by Turner & Newall, all the City's instincts were to close ranks and deny that Guinness had been anything more than a one-off operation. Over a decade later Spens spoke feelingly on television:

> I felt rather as though one had put one's head above the parapet and had it shot off. The failure by people to stand up and be counted was stunning. The City retreated into a shell and started to go into a denial mode and say, 'We never did this, we never had anything to do with any of these practices' – it was astonishing, because they all had been.
> *Everyone had been doing this?*
> Everyone, absolutely everyone . . .

Nor did the publication in February 1987 of the Neill Report on Lloyd's improve City morale, as it spelled out that institution's endemic conflicts of interest (including the baby syndicates aspect) and recommended that henceforth its Council should have a majority of outside members. 'The power of insiders to control the market in their own interest was thus finally eroded,' Adam Raphael noted some years later in his coruscating study of Lloyd's. 'It was the end of a shameful era at Lloyd's which, more than anything else, buried the myth that "utmost good faith" still held sway.' Altogether, with the Conservative Party Chairman, Norman Tebbit, having recently made an uncomfortable comparison – 'We cleaned up the trades union movement and we'll clean up the City too' – these were awkward times for the Bank's Governor, Robin Leigh-Pemberton. Interviewed in February, he accepted that standards were coming 'under greater strain', and that it was 'inevitable' that 'we are going to have to have more bodies, more rules, and more law'. Not surprisingly, his interviewers pushed him on whether the emerging dispensation, essentially of practitioner regulation within a statutory framework, could work 'if people aren't concerned about public censure and the old City club atmosphere no longer exists'. The Governor's reply would not have dismayed any of his predecessors: 'I think that people are still very sensitive to public censure and the vast majority are proud of their standards.'[5]

Undeterred by a sharp decline in the number of takeover bids, the bull market roared on, especially during March 1987, either side of Lawson's expansive, pre-election budget. The FTSE 100 (increasingly the benchmark of market sentiment) rose above 2000 shortly before Lawson announced his tax cuts – double the level at which it had started just over three years earlier. Four days after the budget Caryl Churchill's play, *Serious Money*, opened at the Royal Court. 'We wanted to show the energy, skill and wit of this world,' she explained shortly beforehand. 'I think we were all surprised by how attractive the City is. I deliberately wanted to make all the characters as bad as each other. They are villains, but they're likeable villains . . .' Quite a lot of the action took place on the floor of LIFFE, which had just achieved record volumes and which both she and the actors had visited. Written in verse, with satirical gusto and attack, one of the strands of Churchill's play featured a LIFFE dealer called Scilla Todd, daughter of a wealthy, conventional stockbroker. 'It's a cross between roulette and space invaders,' Scilla explains to her father, who is appalled by the barrow-boy company his daughter is keeping. Frances Cairncross praised Churchill for having 'deftly caught the feel of the trading floor at LIFFE' and its language, 'a mixture of obscenity and gambling'. She also reflected that 'everyone in the play is driven by greed, or fear, or both'. Nevertheless, the City in general, and LIFFE in particular, loved it – a cause of some embarrassment to Churchill and her director, Max Stafford-Clark. 'Tickets are the hottest property in the market,' Fildes noted at the start of June. 'LIFFE's member firms have taken to block-booking the theatre, and take their brightly jacketed dealers along on works outings.' Soon afterwards the play transferred to the West End. Paul Barker, former editor of *New Society*, paid tribute to Churchill's achievement:

> This bravura new world worships money and power and youth . . . If you walk around the City now, you see that it is rebuilding itself in every street as a symbol of financial verve, dynastic dynamism, the sky's the limit. Caryl Churchill catches that verve: the gambling fever that has turned City jobs into a drug that makes addicts of the brightest and best, as well as the barrow boys. There is a pornography of money. You find it on every business page

and in every magazine. Caryl Churchill may have succumbed slightly to the tacky appeal of the new City, too. Notoriously, you can't truly parody something without having seen its charm . . .

Was the old City any better? 'Churchill's thesis is that Daddy [i.e. Scilla's stockbroker father] is corrupt, too,' Barker added. 'He always was. The olde English tradition was to be an insider trader while pretending that the English were above cheating.'[6]

Summer 1987 was in retrospect the apogee of both Thatcherism and the mid-decade City boom. 'Five more glorious years,' the chorus called for at the end of *Serious Money*, and on 11 June the electorate obliged. That day many of LIFFE's traders sported stickers proclaiming 'We all say YES to Maggie', and Bruce Clark of Reuters listened to some of Thatcher's children:

> 'It's so capitalist down here, you can't get away from it,' said 19-year-old trader Nick Prentice. Like many of his colleagues, he is fearful of Labour's taxation plans eating away at the salary he hopes to be earning in a few years' time. 'If the Conservatives don't win, you won't see half the people down here,' said a 23-year-old English trader with an American bank. 'Why should people risk 100 per cent of their money and then pay most of their gains in tax?' 'LIFFE definitely typifies Thatcherism,' said 26-year-old Martin Frewer, one of the few traders to have been educated at one of Britain's élite private schools. 'In a good way, of course,' he hastens to add . . .

On 16 July the FTSE 100 peaked at 2443.4 (and the FT 30-Share Index at 1926.2). The next few weeks saw a faltering, followed by a strong recovery through into early October. Stock markets elsewhere were similarly buoyant. The retrospective confession by Rod Schwartz of Banque Paribas could have been made by many others in the City: 'I played a full part in the literature which attempted to justify why the good times would last for ever, always coming up with a different angle to support something that any reasonable person stepping on to the earth from Mars would say must end. But I fell into the same trap that everybody else did, because you want it to last for ever, don't you? . . .'[7]

In September there was a moment of pure, top-of-the-market froth as the high-profile advertising agency Saatchi & Saatchi sought to take over Midland Bank. Although acting under advice from David Clementi of Kleinworts, the brothers did not get very far. Midland's Sir Kit McMahon had not left the Bank of England to become part of a worldwide advertising agency and comfortably outmanoeuvred Maurice Saatchi, who had a less than comprehensive grasp of banking matters. It is unclear how neutral a role the Bank itself played in this episode, but soon afterwards Leigh-Pemberton emphasised that in future he did not wish to see non-banking firms even attempting to take over British banks, particularly clearing banks. By then the Saatchi brothers had tried and failed elsewhere, with an unsuccessful approach to Hill Samuel, which itself had recently had the galling experience of its proposed acquisition by Union Bank of Switzerland very publicly falling through. Hill Samuel, badly needing some extra capital in the new world, was not necessarily averse to a tie-up with Saatchis, but what irrevocably sunk the deal was the news leaking out in the press of the Midland episode, provoking intense criticism of the very idea of Saatchi & Saatchi going into banking and sharply affecting its share price. That left Hill Samuel still 'in play' (as the phrase now went), and by mid-October a deal had more or less been agreed with the cash-rich, sense-poor Trustee Savings Bank (TSB), which had floated on the stock market the previous year and was willing to pay not far short of £800m, some six or seven times book value. At least Hill Samuel was still in the game, whereas one of the visionaries of the City revolution, John Barkshire, was not. Having gone too far too fast during the previous two or three years, in July 1987 Barkshire had sold his overambitious securities group, Mercantile House, for £500m to another financial group, British & Commonwealth, headed by his keen rival John Gunn.[8] Over the next few weeks it started to be dismembered (with Laing & Cruickshank being sold on to Credit Lyonnais), but the process was far from complete by the time of the dramatic events of the second half of October.

They began on the morning of Friday, 16 October, as those living in the south-east of England woke up to a scene of devastation. Telephone lines were down, trees lay across roads, trains were not running. In the City, the north end of Bishopsgate was cordoned off; the bowling green at Finsbury Circus was crushed by a huge tree; and the ongoing demolition of Lee House in London Wall spontaneously proceeded apace. Many City workers abandoned the struggle to get in, with the result that the London clearing system was suspended, thereby halting all payments between Britain's banks; trading on the Stock Exchange barely functioned; and several other exchanges failed to open at all. The can-do exception was LIFFE, hailed by *The Times* as 'irrepressible'. Altogether it was a bad day for the City, made worse towards the end by the ominous news that Wall Street, which had been steadily on the slide since the 6th, was losing a further hundred points or more, representing a fall of almost 5 per cent. Over the weekend, therefore, it was natural that many felt some queasiness about the prospects for the coming week – but no one imagined the scale of what was about to happen. As Sir David Scholey of Warburgs memorably put it, the train that hit the buffers was travelling flat out and fully loaded.[9]

The Crash of '87 – the most sensational event in the world's financial markets for over half a century – took place on Monday the 19th and Tuesday the 20th.[10] 'I've never seen so much business in all my life,' Nigel

Briggs, an equity trader, recalled about the London market on the Monday morning. 'Thousands and thousands of bargains. Every phone ringing. People clamouring to sell. It was absolute bedlam . . .' The selling continued for the rest of the day – however low the prices were put – and by the end the FTSE 100 had sustained a record 249.6 fall. 'Panic Hits The City' was the *Standard*'s headline, if anything understated. There was far worse to come on this 'Black Monday', for on Wall Street the Dow Jones Index then fell by 508 points, or 22 per cent. 'If it wasn't a meltdown it was certainly as hot as I want it to be,' said John Phelan, Chairman of the New York Stock Exchange.[11] Tuesday began with a veritable rout in the Far East – the Nikkei Index in Tokyo dropping by 12 per cent, the Ordinary Index in Australia by 25 per cent and the Hang Seng in Hong Kong by 33 per cent – and in London the FTSE fell by another 250.7 points. Over the two days it had dropped from 2301.9 to 1801.6, representing a 23 per cent fall. However, eventually some stability returned as later that day the Dow Jones rose by 6 per cent. Wednesday saw a similar bounce-back in London, before further falls on Thursday and Friday. Although markets remained nervous for some time, with the FTSE down to 1573.5 by 10 November, the worst was over.

The dramatic Monday and Tuesday had many piquant aspects. TSB, for instance, was still bidding for Hill Samuel. 'We were morally, but not legally, bound to continue with our bid for Hill Samuel in the new market circumstances,' TSB's Deputy Chairman, Ian Fraser, ruefully recalled. 'We did continue with the bid and at the same market price and we received undiluted hell from the financial press and all the stock market commentators. Everyone thought we should have cancelled our bid, claiming *force majeure*, and started again at a lower price. We comforted ourselves with the conviction that, if we had done that, we would have been slated just as violently for breaking our word.' At BZW, one of the City's biggest trading houses, where a particularly bullish book in equities was being run, losses over the two days amounted to £75m, which at least had the effect of moving risk management systems up the agenda. There were also some big losses at LIFFE – 'I know one who's £130,000 adrift,' one trader told the *Standard* about another – but for the exchange as a whole the crash was good news, with huge volumes being traded and, at least as important, a continuous market being provided, unlike its Chicago rivals or even arguably the Stock Exchange. Fortunes were made, of course, as well as lost. 'The 1987 Crash was terrific for us, we made a lot of money because we were a fixed-interest house and not an equity house,' Ross Jones of Gerrard & National remembered fondly some years later:

> On the night of Black Monday there was a dinner at the Savoy Hotel, the Lord's Taverners' Annual Dinner, and we had a table. Roger Gibbs [Chairman of Gerrards] came in and said something like, 'Wall Street's

down seven hundred points.' We rubbed our hands and said, 'Terrific. Suits our book' . . . The next morning the money supply figures were really bad and the gilt market fell further. The equity markets were nervous and going down. A member of our board phoned up and said, 'For God's sake, buy everything you can. They're going to slash interest rates.' We bought everything we could get our hands on. Within an hour and a half the American bond market had gone up five points, the gilt market had gone up three points. It was very exciting.

Jones added an evocative tailpiece: 'I was driving back along the Embankment in the rush hour that night with a colleague – I had an XJS Convertible – and a German car came up alongside and wound down the window and shouted, "You yuppies, you are all finished. It serves you right." He thought it was the funniest thing. We just sat there roaring with laughter . . .'[12]

Meanwhile, it was not only at TSB that the exact meaning of the words 'force majeure' was coming under scrutiny.[13] The week before the crash had seen the government's largest privatisation issue to date – £7,250m of British Petroleum shares, the world's largest-yet equity offering – fully underwritten. As markets plunged, with BP going down in two days from 350p to 286p, way below the underwriting price of 330p, Lawson was soon under heavy pressure (particularly from North American underwriters) to pull the issue. He believed that this would be not only morally wrong, in that the generally well-remunerated underwriting system was supposed to protect against precisely something like a stock market slump, but that pulling would also damage London's reputation as a trustworthy international financial centre. At first he was supported by the Bank of England, in the person of Blunden; but over the next week or so, leading up to the 30th when dealing in the new shares was due to begin, it seems that the Bank was persuaded otherwise by the silky-tongued Michael Richardson of Rothschilds, who spoke for the underwriting group. On the 29th, just hours before Lawson was due to tell the Commons how he proposed to resolve this intensely invidious situation, he received the Bank's advice: its first preference was to pull the issue; if that was deemed impossible, its second preference was for Lawson to institute a buy-back arrangement that would save the underwriters roughly three-quarters of the £1,000m that they stood to lose. Thoroughly unimpressed, Lawson rejected both options and announced a far more robust compromise, by which the issue went ahead but with a much less generous buy-back (or 'floor') arrangement. He was strongly supported by Thatcher, who had become 'increasingly outraged that the Bank had given so little weight in its deliberations to the sanctity of contract and the reputation of the City of London'. Lawson's scheme proved a resounding success – so much so that in his memoirs he would even allege, fairly or unfairly, that in the immediate aftermath the Bank attempted to claim the kudos, something that he found a bit rich. As for Richardson, there was no doubt truth in his rather plaintive remark after it was all over: 'I was the nut in the nutcracker.'[14]

Had the crash itself vindicated London's new market structure? The Stock Exchange's own report, published the following February, argued strongly that it had, and Goodison took the line that if the old jobbing system had still been in operation on 19 and 20 October, it would have seized up under the weight of selling orders and precipitated a financial crisis. On the much-discussed question of the difficulties that investors had experienced in dealing because of the market makers' failure to answer their telephones, the belief that they had not wanted to be forced to deal in a plunging equity market was categorically dismissed as implausible; the alternative explanation was that if investors failed to get through to market makers, this was simply an inevitable result of the unprecedented volumes of trading. 'An exercise in self-congratulation rather than self-criticism,' was the view of Labour's spokesman on the City, Tony Blair, and the press on the whole agreed. One equity trader, Mike Smith, was frank enough on television almost a decade later, as he recalled the Monday morning: 'All the phones were flashing. We didn't answer them. No, bugger that . . . Because if you didn't do that, you'd end up up to your eyeballs long of stock you didn't want.'[15]

There was also much agitated discussion in the immediate aftermath of the crash as to whether, in the new world of electronic, globally seamless markets, it heralded an era of permanent financial instability. The long, reassuring view was taken by Henry Grunfeld, still at the age of eighty-three a daily presence at Warburgs. Speaking to the *FT* in November – in his first-ever press interview – he conceded there were some things that did worry him. They included the complexity of financial instruments, widely traded by people who did not understand them properly; the hunger for market share, in the context of 'too many people trying to do the same thing and not doing it very well'; and the fact that markets were increasingly dominated by a generation that had never lived through a prolonged bear market. However, he saw no likelihood of a repeat of the events of the late 1920s and early 1930s, on the grounds that 'the degree of co-operation between governments and central banks is totally different today – it just won't happen'. After noting, with implicit reference to Warburgs and its bigger rivals, that 'capital follows brains, but brains don't necessarily follow capital', he returned at the end to his overriding theme:

> I just don't believe governments won't stick together and keep control. I think we have learned our lesson. I look back over 65 years and conclude that things could have turned out very, very much worse. I retain my optimism

in this respect. In the end, common sense will prevail.[16]

*

Happily, the October 1987 crash did indeed prove less momentous than the Wall Street crash of October 1929. Nevertheless, it severely affected financial confidence – and abruptly halted the often mindless optimism, sometimes taking the form of an arrogant masters-of-the-universe syndrome, that had characterised much of the City during the mid-1980s. Equity turnover in the Stock Exchange in 1988 was down by one-third on the previous year, while in the late 1980s trading in gilts remained thin against the background of unprecedented (for modern times) budget surpluses and an absence of new gilt issues. 'Big Bang: Big Bust, Big Lessons' was a headline in March 1989 in *Business Week*, which estimated that 'the City's major players have lost a staggering $2 billion since Britain's ballyhooed Big Bang of 1986'. Eight months later *Institutional Investor* went one better, as it looked back on a year of redundancies, readjustments and much-reduced profits, and asked apocalyptically, 'Will the City ever recover?' The story quoted Duncan Duckett, Chairman of Marshall & Co: 'Imagine London like a village. It had a fish-and-chip shop and a couple of corner cafés. Then suddenly in come French restaurants, McDonalds, pasta joints and sushi bars. Hell, people can only eat three meals a day.' In October 1991 the much-respected economist Stephen Lewis estimated total City job losses during the five years since Big Bang at 60,000, of which 10,000 had been in the securities industry. That year, however, saw the end of loss-making at most securities firms; the following year the equity market responded powerfully to the double stimulus of another Conservative election victory and the enhanced prospects for growth following Britain's enforced departure from the ERM; and in 1993 there was jam all round, as the UK equity market rose by 20 per cent and turnover was up by almost 35 per cent.[17] The City, in short, *had* recovered.

There was also a larger, more global story. The fall of the Berlin Wall in 1989 symbolised capitalism's conclusive victory in the great twentieth-century battle. It was, apparently, the end of history. The worldwide recession of the early 1990s was an unpleasant shock so soon after that heady triumphalism, but the international capital markets – spearheads of the new order – emerged unscathed. In 1992 the volume of Eurobond new issues was $270bn (compared to $135bn in 1987 and $215bn in 1989), with London being the location for about two-thirds of those issues and roughly the same proportion, or even a little more, in terms of secondary market trading. The world's markets were becoming ever more seamless, and in 1992 it was estimated by Baring Securities that at any one time no less than $2.2 trillion was moving around the world's stock markets, with that total increasing by $50bn a year. In June 1994, in *Euromoney*, Padraic Fallon celebrated 'The age of economic reason', in which national governments lay powerless before information mobility and the free market. It was a world of 'borderless finance' that, he believed, the pioneers of the Euromarkets had done much to create, having since the 1960s started 'to push back the frontiers of the domestic financial systems', until in the 1980s 'an explosion of domestic financial deregulation followed as a direct result'. Consequently, he went on:

> Today, it is hard to tell where international ends and domestic begins, and it no longer matters. Foreign firms play an important part in nearly every bond market in the world, and nearly every bond market has been restructured as a direct result of the influence of international markets. Equity markets flourish everywhere, most of them with a new structure imported from overseas, and often with foreign firms as the most active members. Barriers to cross-border capital flows, such as foreign exchange controls and currency convertibility, have disappeared in every advanced country, and will blow away in others. And financial derivatives have turned the wholesale financial markets into a world of rocket scientists, and once-noisy dealing rooms into almost studious floors of mathematicians.
>
> We now live in a world that is changing so fast it is almost shaking. Changes in world financial markets match, or at times exceed, changes in the production of industrial goods and services. Each has been internationalised and advanced, at an almost unbelievable pace of change.
>
> Much of that has to do with the great advances in information availability. But much has also to do with the barriers to growth that the spread of the market economy has removed over the past quarter century.
>
> There is much more to come . . .

For Fallon, as for all those flourishing in this new world, the prospect did not dismay. 'Brooklyn-born traders know the prices of French government bonds to the nearest basis point; traders in Marunouchi study computer charts showing the spreads between Mexican and EIB yen bonds; Essex youths scream orders for German government bonds . . .'[18]

Inevitably the arrival of a global marketplace heightened competition between the leading international financial centres. From the point of view of London and its role in the European time zone, the key rival was Frankfurt, especially after June 1989 when the Bundesbank Chairman, Karl Otto Pöhl, publicly declared his dissatisfaction with the fact that 'a substantial portion of the trade in German shares and bonds is taking place in London'. There followed rapid modernisation and deregulation of Germany's financial markets, above all those centred in Frankfurt. By 1991, with the start of the single European market coming up fast, and the possibility of a single currency in the more distant offing, the press was awash with articles gauging London's chances of fending off the European competition. 'Already more than one in 10 Frankfurt jobs are in financial services,' Mark Milner noted in April in the *Guardian*. 'If the German city wins the chance to play host to the proposed European Central Bank [ECB], German ascendancy over the City markets appears inevitable.'[19]

Soon afterwards the City Corporation commissioned the London Business School to undertake a thorough study of the City's international competitiveness. The City Research Project's interim report, published in July 1992, found that foreign exchange trading, international bank lending and international insurance were the three activities that earned the City the most money; that London had the greatest concentration (620,000 people in 1989) of financial employment in the world; and that it had the greatest number of foreign banks of any financial centre. Overall, the tone of the report was optimistic but determinedly uncomplacent. When almost exactly a year later it emerged that the eventual ECB would be located by the River Main, there was general agreement that although this would be a considerable fillip to Frankfurt's aspirations, that city still had a mountain to climb, with London way ahead in (among other things) international banking, international equities, asset management and foreign exchange. 'You couldn't contemplate moving out of London and going to Frankfurt or Paris or Brussels,' Richard Roddey, head of the European operations of the large US bank NationsBank, commented. 'If you are in Europe you have to be in London first.' Accordingly, when recently his bank had expanded its European presence, 'it didn't cross anyone's mind to be headquartered anywhere but London'.[20]

On the ground, these were the years in which famous old City names began to pass into the history books, particularly amidst the chequered volumes and undeniable overcapacity that characterised the securities industry in the late 1980s and early 1990s. Messels, Wood Mackenzie, Greenwells, Fielding Newson-Smith, Pember & Boyle, Pinchin Denny, Simon & Coates, Laurie Milbank, Vickers da Costa, Scrimgeour Kemp-Gee, Kitcat & Aitken – all these firms, among others, were closed down, decimated or stripped of their identity by their new owners between 1987 and 1993. When Citicorp in January 1990 simultaneously shut down Scrimgeours and Vickers, two excellent firms that it had acquired some five years earlier, the *Daily Telegraph* described it, with pardonable bitterness, as 'a shockingly impressive achievement'. By this time the fish market at Billingsgate had been turned by Richard Rogers into Europe's largest trading room, but it was never used, leaving the American bank with (in Fildes's words) 'nothing but a huge loss and a lingering aroma'. Most of the brutal action – essentially an admission of how flawed their Big Bang strategy had been in both conception and, especially, implementation – was taken by foreign banks, though it was the sudden demise in December 1988 of Morgan Grenfell Securities (including Pember &

Boyle and Pinchin Denny) that attracted the biggest headlines. 'It was the most difficult management decision I ever had to make in my life,' John Craven, who had gone to run Morgan Grenfell the previous year in the aftermath of the Guinness affair, recalled. 'It involved about 770 jobs and about £45m write-offs. It also involved going back on a statement we had made in the prospectus when we went public in 1986, on the back of which we'd raised a lot of money from the institutions.' On the day itself there was high emotion as Craven explained that the securities business was losing a million pounds a week and requested people to stop dealing immediately. 'We had one or two young chaps bashing down computer screens. We had one joker who, before he left, dialled the weather announcement in Sydney, Australia, and left the phone hanging and we found it 24 hours later.'[21]

Approaching the fifth anniversary of Big Bang, in October 1991, it was estimated that so far the overall cost of the exercise – buying the goodwill of London securities firms, before recapitalising and re-equipping them, followed by heavy trading losses, especially after the 1987 crash – amounted to some £4bn. Barry Riley gave a threefold explanation as to why the 'blind optimism' of the mid-1980s had proved so misplaced: the end of the old commissions cartel; the payment of inflexibly high salaries, more appropriate to banking than to stockbroking, where profits were inherently volatile; and (also causing basic overheads to rise sharply) the inhabiting of far grander premises than the securities firms had traditionally been used to. Inevitably this 'immense collective misjudgement' shed an increasingly favourable light on the stubborn decision by Cazenove's to stay independent. 'It looks more and more as if, contrary to almost everybody's predictions, Cazenove, that most traditional of firms, is emerging as one of the two or three big winners in the post-Big Bang world,' the *Evening Standard* noted as early as 1989. Other assessments followed suit, and not long afterwards Ivan Fallon in the *Sunday Times* was writing appreciatively of 12 Tokenhouse Yard as 'a last bastion of the old City', with all its reassuring continuity: 'the same discreet entrance just behind Throgmorton Street, the same creaking lift to the partners' floor, and the same old-world courteousness . . .'[22]

Among the clearers, only Lloyds of the Big Four (after quickly pulling out of an unwise involvement in gilts market making) unambiguously flourished during the seven or eight years after Big Bang. At Midland, McMahon made a valiant but ultimately unsuccessful attempt to turn the bank round, before leaving the task in 1991 to a seasoned commercial banker, Brian Pearse, whom the Bank of England parachuted in from Barclays.[23] For several years there had been talks between Midland (where McMahon was acutely conscious of how seriously short of capital it was) and the Hongkong and Shanghai Banking Corporation, and in June 1992 these culminated when HSBC – overcoming a rival bid from Lloyds – acquired a controlling interest. At NatWest the great fly in the ointment was its investment banking arm, County NatWest, already losing money and with its management in increasing disarray even before the immensely damaging Blue Arrow scandal broke not long after the crash. 'Obviously like everyone else our entry into capital markets and all those sort of things has been extremely disappointing,' Lord Boardman (who as Chairman would shortly fall on his sword because of Blue Arrow) reflected in October 1988. 'But our philosophy is, and was and remains, that we are going to be a major player in the global market.' NatWest did indeed stay in the investment banking game, with County NatWest being rebranded (and in effect starting all over again) as NatWest Markets in 1992; but by the mid-1990s it was still producing as much pain as pleasure. An unimpressed observer was Sir Ian MacLaurin, who joined the main board as a non-executive director in 1990:

> The trouble with the establishment at NatWest [though MacLaurin exempted Lord (Robert) Alexander, who had succeeded Boardman] was that they thought they were fantastic, and they treated their own people and their customers accordingly. The contrast with Tesco was extraordinary. Where we maintained a dialogue with our own people and our customers as a matter of company policy, it seemed to me that the hierarchs at the NatWest had little time for either. The world was out there, somewhere, peopled by sundry debtors and creditors, but all safely distanced from the cloistered retreat of Lothbury . . .[24]

At Barclays, NatWest's main rival, the investment banking experience had been less traumatic but hardly – taken in the round – a great positive. 'By any normal test of performance,' the *FT* commented in April 1991 on BZW, 'its first four years seem a very expensive mistake for Barclays. Rather than a success, the best that can be said for it is that BZW has not been as big a failure as others.' Over the next few years BZW started to make some decent money, as the bank as a whole struggled to recover from the consequences of its disastrously ambitious property lending in the late 1980s. By the time Barclays turned in 1994 to the improbable figure of Martin Taylor – an intellectual who was about as far from the stereotypical clearing banker as it was possible to get – to become its Chief Executive, both it and NatWest had been surpassed by Lloyds as Britain's number one clearer.[25] There, even after Morse's chairmanship had ended in 1993, Pitman continued to drive through with almost brutal single-mindedness the all-important concept of shareholder value, in a quite remarkable display of both focus and continuity.

Among the merchant banks, two were no longer independent by the end of the 1980s. Hill Samuel, under TSB's munificent, overpassive ownership from late 1987, went on a badly misjudged lending spree in the late 1980s, with the result that by 1992 it had some £500m of bad loans on its balance sheet and posted losses that year of £241m. Its once enviable corporate finance franchise had been almost entirely dissipated, and Hill Samuel spent most of 1993 effectively up for sale – but with no takers. The other merchant bank to have lost its autonomy was Morgan Grenfell, perhaps inevitably so as a result of Guinness, but also owing something to Craven's deal-making instincts allied to an ability to think strategically. 'Somebody said this is a terrible defeat,' he remarked in November 1989 after Deutsche Bank had agreed to pay the very full price of £950m – itself testimony to the rebuilding at Morgans since the Guinness affair had laid low the previous regime. 'I think it's a tremendous achievement,' he understandably added. At one point BZW had been seriously interested, but several directors of Morgans had been adamantly opposed to the prospect of becoming in effect a subsidiary of a British clearing bank. As for the actual new owners, Hilmar Kopper of Deutsche was asked four years later why his bank had made the acquisition. 'Because it gave us access,' he replied, 'to something that we did not have, that we were unable to develop: a distinct merchant bank culture, a distinct London marketplace culture.' Over those four years the Deutsche/Morgans relationship had worked surprisingly well, with the merchant bank expanding successfully into emerging markets as well as using Deutsche's connections to become a major presence in European corporate finance. Still under Craven's leadership, it had had, in *Euromoney*'s apt words, 'the pleasure of being able to prove its critics wrong'.[26]

By the mid-1990s it was generally agreed that the better strategy had been the non-integrated, niche approach, and the two names usually cited were Schroders and Lazards. 'Big Bang gave us a huge opportunity,' David Verey of Lazards recalled in 1996 of the late 1980s, when the bank's Chairman and Chief Executive was the former Tory minister Sir John Nott. 'We were able to increase our market share by leaps and bounds, not because of our own brilliance, but because other people were diverted.' Kleinworts, by contrast, had gone down the integrated route, encountered problems and lost a lot of money, including a much-publicised £34m hit in 1990 through a misjudged block trade in Premier Consolidated Oilfield; by the early 1990s it was more or less a house under siege, before starting to recover somewhat from 1993, partly through its globally welcome expertise in privatisation.[27]

There was, all commentators gladly accepted, one glowing exception to the 'niche' generalisation: Warburgs, the national champion in invest-ment banking. 'It dominates the UK market,' noted *Euromoney* in its August 1994 survey of the merchant banking sector. 'It is the only merchant bank to emerge from Big Bang with a top-class securities operation: it is, for example, broker to more British companies than any firm apart from Cazenove. Its research team has ranked number one in each of the last four years in the Extel survey of fund managers. Mercury Asset Management [of which Warburgs owned 75 per cent, with 25 per cent having been floated in 1987] is the second-largest money manager in the UK. Mercury's profitability – £109.5m pre-tax – last year is a comforting base of revenue for the firm.' However, the magazine asked, 'is Warburg a world-class player able to compete with Goldman Sachs and Morgan Stanley?'[28] On that the jury was still out, and from 1991 some had wondered about the wisdom of Scholey's successor as Chief Executive being an aristocrat, the sixth Earl Cairns, the former stockbroker Viscount Garmoyle. Simon Cairns had a good mind and an attractive manner, but it still seemed strange – or rather, perhaps even worse in the new world, peculiarly English.

After Big Bang, few imagined that the glory days of the merchant banks would ever return. In 1988 there were two ritually symbolic moments: the end of the Accepting Houses Committee and Hambros' sale of its Bishopsgate home to a Japanese development company. Charles Hambro, talking to the *FT*, noted that it was only a few years previously that he had had to check whether Nomura was creditworthy, whereas now Japan's most powerful securities house – an increasingly potent force in the Eurobond market – had a market capitalisation of £30bn. 'Sometimes,' he added wryly, 'I wonder whether we have been so clever after all.' Certainly there was a widespread assumption that the Japanese, on the back of the booming Tokyo stock market, were about to become a well-nigh irresistible force. 'Now the City is on the brink of a new era where Japanese, not American, money is moving in,' the *Independent on Sunday*'s Peter Koenig asserted in February 1990. 'Japanese bankers will almost certainly prove as brutal, combative and relentless as the Americans.' Later that year Nomura apparently sealed its intentions by moving to the newly named Nomura House, the former General Post Office in St Martin's le Grand. The leading figures in the Japanese houses in the City seldom gave interviews to the press or sought publicity, but in February 1992 one executive director at the City branch of a Japanese bank did speak frankly (if anonymously) to the sociologist Junko Sakai:

> The City, now, only has its own tradition and past legacy. The City will survive, but British houses will not remain at all. Most of them are now being taken over or becoming weak. There are many English merchant banks, but now they are called 'museums' . . They are not innovative and not in the forefront of knowledge and skills needed at the frontier. The City is extremely valuable, but English houses are declining in the long run. In reality, there are American houses, Japanese and continental banks in the City . . .

That same month, though, the Tokyo market (which had already peaked at the end of 1989) crashed. This not only abruptly burst the Japanese economic bubble, but simultaneously caused a major reduction in the capital of Japanese banks and severely affected the appetite of Japanese companies to issue bonds in the international capital markets, a mainstay of Japanese securities houses in recent years. Even before then, there had been a sense that the Japanese were not making quite the impact that might have been expected, perhaps reflecting partly the way in which decision-making was still concentrated in Tokyo, partly the lack of Japanese innovation in such relatively new financial instruments as swaps and options. It may also have been the case that even in the new City personal contacts still mattered. 'We are cheap money suppliers, but we are not respected by Western bankers,' a Japanese bank manager complained to Sakai in April 1992, with specific reference to the difficulty of becoming the lead manager of syndicated loans.[29] International banking was supposed to have become entirely 'transactional' (as opposed to relationship-based), but the reality was rather more complicated.

The American invasion, by contrast, was relentless. 'There was never any sense that old English bankers were competing with us in any way,' Michael Lewis contemptuously recalled in 1996. 'It was much more, how much did we have to pay them to clear out of town and do something else with their lives . . .' Among the American investment banks with global aspirations – significantly enhanced by the development of a market in global bonds, beginning with the $1.5bn issue for World Bank in September 1989 – Morgan Stanley, Salomons and Merrill Lynch were establishing an increasingly important London presence; but the highest-profile impact was that of Goldman Sachs, which from late 1991 had its European headquarters in the *Daily Telegraph*'s old Fleet Street home. Soon afterwards the London office was earning as much as 25 per cent of the firm's total profits, in large part due to a handful of phenomenally successful proprietary traders. Their king was Larry Becerra, recruited shortly before the move to Fleet Street. 'While most Goldman Sachs employees commuted to work on overcrowded trains or through impassable City streets,' Lisa Endlich later wrote, 'Becerra, dressed in his signature cowboy boots and faded Levis, rode to work on his Harley-Davidson. With his deep voice, flat American accent and mane of thick graying hair, Becerra was hard to miss . . . Outspoken, ebullient, confident, even arrogant, he attracted everyone with the edge of danger that seemed to cling to him . . .' In his first nine months Becerra made $58m for the firm. Another proprietary trader was the less flamboyant Henry Bedford, who during the April 1992 general election took a position in gilt futures that would have cost Goldmans some $8m if Neil Kinnock had become Prime Minister, but in fact produced a profit of $12m or more. The phenomenally successful proprietary trading continued into 1993, amidst protracted turmoil in the European currencies, and it seemed that the very culture of Goldmans, traditionally risk-averse, had changed. Now the catchphrase on the trading floor was 'Be big and be real', and when one Goldmans floor trader on a futures exchange queried a buy order that had not stated the amount, Becerra's reply left nothing to the imagination: 'Buy them 'til your hands bleed.'[30]

That hapless trader may well have been on the floor at LIFFE, which by the early 1990s, especially after its move in December 1991 to more spacious premises at Cannon Bridge, was confirming its position as London's premier derivatives exchange and the third-largest in the world. The annual volume figures were graphic: in 1987 a total of 13.5m contracts were traded (itself a big rise on the 6.9m in 1986); in 1991 the total was 38.5m, rising in 1992 to 71.9m and in 1993 to 101.8m (against the helpful background of ERM chaos). LIFFE's core domestic contracts – long gilt and short sterling – continued to perform very respectably, occasionally sensationally, especially short sterling during sterling's travails in autumn 1992. The phenomenal overall growth, however, would not have been possible without the emergence of a spectacularly successful new and more international contract. This was the futures contract in German government bonds, known as the Bund contract, launched in September 1988 – amidst some internal resistance – largely through the visionary drive of the American woman, Kim Albright, in charge of product development at the exchange. Once Frankfurt's own derivatives exchange opened in January 1990, and started trading Bund futures that autumn, a fierce battle developed for dominance in the Bund contract. By early 1992 it was clear that LIFFE had won, establishing a market share of some 70 per cent that hardly fluctuated over the next few years. Meanwhile, in terms of the City pecking order, LIFFE's rise was confirmed by its takeover in March 1992 of the Stock Exchange's traded options market, a month after it had left the Stock Exchange floor. Indeed, LIFFE was even starting to be seen as the City's 'fourth pillar', the time-honoured first three being the Bank of England, the Stock Exchange and Lloyd's. And in April 1993 the Treasury recommended to the Stock Exchange that it look to LIFFE as a model organisation, non-bureaucratic and providing a highly efficient marketplace – only a decade after stockbrokers had called 'ice cream man' and 'two 99s please' to futures traders in their coloured jackets as they stepped outside the Royal Exchange.[31]

The Stock Exchange itself (which reverted to its 'proper' name in 1991) was not blessed by high-calibre leadership in the late 1980s and early 1990s.[32] Andrew Hugh Smith, Chairman from November 1988, lacked the vision of his predecessor, while his Chief Executive from November 1989, Peter Rawlins, had perhaps the vision but not the human qualities or the intellectual humility to bring together so many competing interests.

Not all was negative, though. The Stock Exchange under Rawlins started to become a leaner, fitter organisation; from October 1991 the Council was replaced by a board of directors that included some major City figures; while in terms of business itself, the Stock Exchange established an almost unassailable lead as Europe's leading international equity market, with the *FT* noting in April 1992 that 95 per cent of European stocks bought or sold outside their home markets were now changing hands in London. One appalling saga, however, did much to blight its reputation. Back in 1981 work had started on a computerised, paperless successor to the TALISMAN settlement system. It was to be called TAURUS, standing for Transfer and Automated Registration of Uncertified Stock, but work was suspended in 1984 before being resumed three years later. The endless delays that followed were far from solely the Stock Exchange's fault. Richard Waters, for instance, observed in the *FT* in October 1989 that 'vested interests (banks, big and small brokers, registrars and others) had each fought their corner for so long that few are prepared now to cede ground to allow the system to be built'. But inevitably the Stock Exchange took most of the flak, as the press reaction to the continual postponement of the launch date became increasingly merciless. '"New timetable for Taurus": the phrase must be preset in the London Stock Exchange's word-processors,' the *Economist* declared in October 1991; while the *Independent* wanted to rename the system Tortoise or Tortuous.

Eventually, in March 1993, the sorry saga ended as the Stock Exchange pulled the plug on the whole project, which one way and another had cost upwards of £400m. Rawlins resigned, and it was left to the Bank of England to step in and develop a paperless settlement system, known as CREST, which became operational in August 1996. 'The cancellation of TAURUS does not impair London's ability to provide the world's leading international securities market,' Hugh Smith defiantly declared soon after the March 1993 humiliation. 'Business flows to our markets because of their depth and liquidity, and the extraordinary strength and diversity of the firms which operate them.' This was true enough, but as Michie, the historian of the Stock Exchange, remarks, 'what this left out was the exact role to be played by the London Stock Exchange'.[33] By the mid-1990s, with the Stock Exchange having long lost its main supervisory functions, that was increasingly the question that people were asking.

The Stock Exchange's problems were mild, however, compared to those of Lloyd's.[34] From the late 1980s the market there was sustaining heavy losses: by 1990 and 1991 as much as £2bn each year. The main causes were catastrophes (notably the Piper Alpha oil rig disaster of 1988 and Hurricane Hugo the following year), a sharp rise in US pollution liabilities (especially relating to asbestos) and sheer incompetence on the part of the market's so-called professionals. Following the semi-cleansing of the Augean stables in the mid-1980s, it was undoubtedly a less corrupt market than it had been, but that did not prevent a revolt of the external, non-working Names as the losses mounted up. By 1988 there were as many as 32,000 Names, following a high-powered recruitment campaign through that avaricious decade that had often bordered on the mendacious, and over the next few years many of those in the most seriously affected syndicates became fiercely litigious. 'Out there, the revolt of the shires is in earnest,' the novelist Julian Barnes memorably wrote in the *New Yorker* in 1993. 'The Names have witnessed negligence, fraud, complacency, and sardonic uncaringness; they have discovered the realities of money, how it works, and how those who live off it work.' Names under the financial cosh by the mid-1990s included, according to *Time* magazine figures, Camilla Parker Bowles (estimated potential exposure of $561,000), Sir Edward Heath ($1.4m), Frances Shand Kydd ($1.3m), Jeffrey Archer ($2m) and Ronald Ferguson ($1m). By the end of 1994 the 20,000 litigating Names were still refusing to be bought off, despite a £900m offer by Lloyd's. There was meanwhile, by the end of 1992, a new team in place there, with David Rowland as Chairman and Peter Middleton as Chief Executive, grappling to ensure the institution's very survival. They published their first business plan in April 1993, and managed to introduce £800m in corporate capital, thereby beginning the process of reducing the market's reliance on individual Names. Nevertheless, as the journalist (and litigating Name) Adam Raphael observed soon afterwards in his admirably dispassionate account, *Ultimate Risk*, 'the biggest financial smash this century is a possibility that cannot be ruled out'.[35] Once the City's most arrogant institution, against fairly severe competition, Lloyd's now found itself in an astonishing plight.

There was still – in the public perception at least – a whiff of scandal about Lloyd's, though that was nothing unusual during these years after Big Bang. Another scandal whose endgame was laboriously being played out was that of Guinness.[36] By autumn 1987 five of those involved had been arrested; while Lord (Patrick) Spens, formerly of Ansbachers, and David Mayhew of Cazenove's were arrested in spring 1988. The first Guinness trial – involving Ernest Saunders, Gerald Ronson, Anthony Parnes and Sir Jack Lyons – took place during summer 1990 at Southwark Crown Court and lasted 107 days. On 27 August, Bank Holiday Monday, all four were found guilty, between them convicted on twenty-eight charges of conspiracy, theft and false accounting. Three of them received prison sentences, while Lyons eventually escaped jail on the grounds of ill health. 'The danger is that when men are hell-bent for victory, greed is in the saddle and ordinary commercial probity and respect for the law are thrust aside and the individual voice of conscience will not be heard,' Mr Justice Henry declared before passing sentence. Inevitably this outcome, following the revelations about the share-support operation that had come out during the trial, damaged the City's reputation, though as Riley tartly commented in the *FT*, 'the City has always tended to have a much more starry-eyed impression of its own honesty than has the public at large'. The fact was, though, that of the guilty quartet only Parnes – whose success fee, as agreed by Saunders, had been a tidy £3.35m – was a real City person. In the event, perhaps regrettably, there never was a real 'City' trial. The second Guinness trial, involving Spens and Seelig, got under way in autumn 1991, but had made pitifully slow progress by the following February when it collapsed, largely on account of the judge's concern about the mental strain on Seelig, who had insisted on conducting his own defence. 'The whole of my working life I gave to Morgans and I made a significant contribution to the house,' he told the *FT* on the eve of the trial's collapse. 'And it's a matter of deep feeling that not only were they not prepared to stand by me but they actually tried to make me a scapegoat.' A few weeks later the trial of Spens was also ended, again on health grounds. There was supposed to have been a third Guinness trial, of Seelig and Mayhew, but the prosecution decided not to proceed – apparently because, as Spens had forcibly pointed out during his trial, the secret indemnifying of purchases of shares in a bid situation had also been done in 1986 in the Turner & Newall/AE battle, when the Takeover Panel had ruled that such an arrangement *was* compatible with the Takeover Code.[37]

For those still interested, there ensued a long wait (over five years) before the eventual publication of the DTI report, painstakingly compiled by David Donaldson, QC and Ian Watt. 'Even at this remove in time, some in the City may experience shock at what they see, and perhaps recognise, in the mirror of this report,' they concluded, possibly optimistically. 'Though our sensibilities may have been numbed by long confrontation with the evidence, three features still shine disturbingly through . . . Firstly, the cynical disregard of laws and regulation; secondly, the cavalier misuse of company monies; thirdly, a contempt for truth and common honesty: all these in a part of the City which was thought respectable.'[38] Perhaps surprisingly, the Guinness affair was not yet over, for by September 2000 the European Court of Human Rights had found that the trial of the first four defendants – Saunders, Ronson, Parnes and Lyons – had been in breach of their human rights.

The Blue Arrow scandal also involved a share-support operation.[39] This was hatched by County NatWest and Phillips & Drew at the time of the huge, £435m placing of Blue Arrow shares in September 1987 that enabled its ambitious bid for a far larger employment agency, Manpower, to continue. That winter it emerged, largely through dint of probings by the *Economist*, that the two advisers in fact had a secret 13 per cent holding.

Events thereafter proceeded at a leisurely pace. Charles Villiers and Jonathan Cohen, the two top men at County NatWest, resigned in February 1988; ten months later the DTI at last launched an investigation; its report, published in July 1989, led to prominent heads rolling at NatWest; in February 1992, after a year-long trial, four of the advisers to the Blue Arrow rights issue were found guilty (perhaps significantly, by an almost entirely male, working-class jury) of conspiracy to defraud, but received only suspended custodial sentences; and later that year the Court of Appeal quashed the convictions. The scandal, therefore, hardly amounted to Guinness proportions, but it hugely damaged the already bruised reputations of both County NatWest and Phillips & Drew, with the latter being given an increasingly rough ride by its disenchanted new owners, UBS.

Blue Arrow heralded a rash of other financial scandals. The sequence began in July 1991 when the Bank of England, acting in concert with bank regulators in other countries, managed to get closed down the fraudulent, money-laundering Bank of Credit and Commerce International (BCCI), the creation of a charismatic Pakistani called Agha Hasan Abedi, which operated worldwide but had its headquarters at 100 Leadenhall Street. BCCI's collapse broke all records, with depositors and investors losing at least $5bn and maybe as much as $20bn, and the Bank of England was severely criticised for having been too complacent for too long. The Bank could justifiably retort that it did not have global supervisory responsibilities for BCCI, but the episode did not enhance either its own or the City's reputation.[40] The next scandal, by contrast, was unalloyed City – the resignation in October 1991 of Mark Blundell, the youthful, ambitious Chief Executive at the London Futures and Options Exchange (FOX), after it emerged that he had apparently indemnified brokers in order to encourage them to trade on some of the exchange's less popular property and commodities contracts, thereby artificially inflating the overall trading volumes. The sums involved were peanuts compared to the BCCI affair, but the temptation to which Blundell had seemingly succumbed accurately reflected the intense competition that now existed between rival exchanges.[41]

Blundell, however, was only a bit player in the pageant, quite unlike Robert Maxwell, whose sudden death in November 1991 – and the subsequent revelations of his theft of £400m or more from the pension funds for which he had a fiduciary responsibility – put the City uncomfortably in the spotlight.[42] As Tom Bower's exhaustive researches would make clear, such an eminent merchant banker as Sir Michael Richardson had been among those in Maxwell's corner during his last, financially increasingly troubled years; while no individual bank had done more to keep the great bully afloat than Goldman Sachs. 'I took it on faith that

Robert Maxwell was an honest person,' Eric Sheinberg of Goldmans subsequently said of the man who, when he hit the water, owed his various bankers no less than £2.8bn. 'Now he turned out to be a crook, I can't help it – I didn't know. Here's somebody who's supposedly one of the richest people in the world, a good client of Goldman Sachs, a good client of many other firms, a good client of many banks, running around with kings, queens and presidents . . .' No doubt there is some truth in that and similar retrospective self-justifications. Nevertheless, Lambert surely has it right. 'Maxwell generated enormous fees for those who undertook his wheeling and dealing,' he observed in the *FT*'s end-of-century gallery of financial rogues. 'To their lasting discredit, enough people were prepared to hold their nose and take their money.'[43]

The final major scandal of the early 1990s had no such individual villain. This was the emerging revelation that, since the government had relaxed the rules in 1988 in order to encourage people to buy personal pensions, there had been mis-selling of personal pensions by the life insurance companies on an appalling scale, involving faulty advice to more than two million people to leave their existing occupational pension schemes.[44] By the mid-1990s those companies had neither apologised nor provided anything remotely approaching adequate compensation. Fairly or unfairly, much of the adverse publicity was targeted at the Prudential: it seemed a long time since 'the Man from the Pru' had epitomised all that was most solid and reassuring in the British financial services industry.

The immediate impact of these scandals on City regulation was surprisingly muffled. 'More law on this subject would be disastrous,' the *Daily Telegraph* warned in August 1990 after the Guinness verdicts. 'We still have the legacy from the last time things were tightened up, in the form of the Financial Services Act. The risk-takers and innovators on whom successful financial centres depend could hardly stand another blow like the FSA . . . There is a simple way to ensure nothing like the Guinness affair recurs, and that is to drive the markets away.' Indeed, it was less than three years since the City had more or less risen up in arms against the notion of Sir Kenneth Berrill's chairmanship of the Securities and Investments Board (SIB) being renewed. 'The City strikes back' was the *FT*'s headline in February 1988 greeting the news that Berrill was to be replaced by the Bank of England's David Walker, with the implicit remit of initiating a more flexible, less bureaucratic regime. This he duly delivered, but his voluntary departure in May 1992 helped to occasion renewed debate about the effectiveness of the current compromise of practitioner regulation under a statutory framework. Soon afterwards, reviewing an account of the Barlow Clowes affair (involving a fraudulent bond-washing outfit run by Peter Clowes that had been shut down by SIB in 1988), the historian Kathleen Burk mulled more generally:

On the whole, scandal does not stalk the streets. On the whole, the City renders valuable service, not only to clients but to the country. But it can no longer be as self-regarding as it once was. A government which encourages a mass shareholding public is a government which has some responsibility to that public for ensuring that there is a level playing-field. On the other hand, the Government has encouraged mass participation partly because it will be profitable for its supporters to become involved: it must therefore take care that it does not, through over-regulation, drive this very business away . . . The question is, who will judge between baby and bathwater?

Who indeed? By this time, however, the occasional City professional was prepared to question publicly whether self-regulation in any recognisable form still had a future. 'The thing is broken,' Barry Bennett of Kleinwort Benson Securities declared in July 1992. 'The question is whether we should try and mend it or take it away and buy another model. I would like us to go to an SEC.'[45] Although that was not yet practical politics (significantly, Labour had shied away from such a policy in the run-up to the election earlier that year), few on either side of the debate imagined that the run of scandals was suddenly going to dry up.

Another familiar debate concerned the City and its alleged short-termism. 'For goodness sake don't allow the market – by which I mean the City – to guide the destiny of your company,' Sir Terence Conran explained in a 1989 book called *Advice from the Top*, while in the same collection Sir Hector Laing of United Biscuits was typically robust about the inexorable rise of the institutional investor, by now owning some four-fifths of the UK equity market: 'Fund managers are intent on doing their best for their funds and have no interest whatsoever in the businesses they invest in or the people who are producing the profits.' This argument had been fuelled in the late 1980s by three notable takeover battles, each creating a widespread feeling (extending well beyond the City) that there was something wrong about the outcome. Hillards, the Yorkshire super-market chain, fell to Tesco in 1987 amidst claims by the defeated board of institutional irresponsibility. The next year another part of the northern landscape, Rowntrees, failed to repel an invader, the Swiss food combine Nestlé; and again the air was heavy with recrimination. Finally, in autumn 1989 came the takeover of the Bristol-based Dickinson Robinson group, makers of Sellotape and Basildon Bond stationery. The successful predator was Pembridge Investments, the Bermuda-based vehicle of Roland Franklin, a veteran of the secondary banking crisis. 'It hardly reflects credit on the City,' commented 'Lex', adding that 'the speed with which shareholders deserted the group ought to re-open the old debate about short-termism among the institutions'. In fact, a hostile CBI report had already appeared in November 1988 about the financial institutions' focus on short-term profits and their lack of long-term commitment to

British manufacturing industry; while in March 1989 the Trade and Industry Secretary, Lord Young, forthrightly attacked the City for failing to back 'some of Britain's brightest ideas', claiming that too little finance was available from banks and venture capitalists for high-risk, high-tech projects.[46]

In June 1990 the DTI held a one-day conference on 'Innovation and short-termism', at which – with some bitterness in the air – the two sides mainly talked at each other. 'You have my word,' Anthony Thatcher of the Dowty Group told the City's representatives, 'that the majority of my fellow industrialists are building at the same time as squeezing. We are driving for real shareholder value, but in a timescale that will not match the demands of some three-monthly review fund managers, who see equities as merely trading counters.' From a more academic perspective, Professor John Kay sought to transcend the divide: 'The problem is that we are now in the grip of what is essentially a deal-driven culture among both management and large parts of the City of London, and each of these sustains the other. On the one hand we see fee-hungry advisers and, on the other, we see managers who find expansion by acquisition a great deal easier than expanding through selling in the marketplace.' As in the mid-1970s, when the City/industry debate had also been keen and sometimes acrimonious, there was a background of economic difficulty, and again the Bank of England did much constructive work behind the scenes. The so-called 'London Approach' (or 'London Rules') was essentially a series of attempts to persuade groups of often diverse creditors that it was in their own interests to keep companies afloat. Led by Pen Kent, the Bank was involved in more than a hundred such corporate workouts, including such companies as Eurotunnel, Dan Air and Brent Walker. 'Being voluntary,' Kent reflected, 'the London Approach can of course only be effective as long as it commands general support within the banking community.'[47] Kent did not say so, but perhaps even in the 1990s there was still some opportunity for moral suasion.

By this time an almost entirely new debate had arisen. Nigel Lawson may have been an exceptionally strong Chancellor vis-à-vis the Bank of England – typified by the way in which in late 1987 he rode roughshod over the Governor in implementing his policy of shadowing the Deutschmark – yet in November 1988 he sent Thatcher a memorandum proposing 'to give statutory independence to the Bank of England, charging it with the statutory duty to preserve the value of the currency, along the lines already in place and of proven effectiveness for the US Federal Reserve, the National Bank of Switzerland, and the Bundesbank'. He went on:

Such a move would enhance the market credibility of our anti-inflationary stance, both nationally and internationally. It would make it absolutely clear that the fight against inflation remains our top priority; it would do something to help de-politicise interest rate changes – though that can never be completely achieved; above all there would be the longer-term advantage that we would be seen to be locking a permanent anti-inflationary force into the system, as a counter-weight to the strong inflationary pressures which are always lurking.

It was not, Lawson stressed subsequently, that he had any 'illusion that the Bank of England possesses any superior wisdom'. Instead, the benefit lay in 'the logic of the institutional change itself', through which an independent central bank would necessarily enjoy a far greater degree of market credibility than a government ever could; and 'this extra market credibility is what would make the successful conduct of monetary policy less difficult'. Thatcher was appalled:

> My reaction was dismissive . . . I did not believe, as Nigel argued, that it would boost the credibility of the fight against inflation . . . In fact, as I minuted, 'It would be seen as an abdication by the Chancellor . . .' I added that 'it would be an admission of a failure of resolve on our part'. I also doubted whether we had people of the right calibre to run such an institution.[48]

Faced by Thatcher's insistence that the control of inflation was ultimately a political problem, not amenable to institutional solutions, Lawson was compelled to let his secret proposal rest.

Less than a year later, however, the genie was out of the bottle, as Lawson's resignation speech of October 1989 gave him the opportunity to launch the proposal publicly. Immediate City reaction, as represented by its economists, was positive. 'It is an excellent idea,' Giles Keating of CSFB told *Euroweek*. 'The only tragedy is that it was not considered a long time ago. The credibility of the anti-inflationary policy would be much greater. Also, the markets would be far more inclined to regard sterling as a hard currency.' Interestingly, he added that if the change ever happened, 'the regulatory powers of the Bank would probably have to be hived off and placed with a new body'. Stephen Bell of Morgan Grenfell was also in favour, but more narrowly, observing that 'the government is answerable to the electorate if it gets things wrong', whereas 'if the central bank gets it wrong, who are they answerable to?' Leigh-Pemberton himself implicitly addressed that concern in an interview the following summer. After stressing that *complete* independence from Parliament or the executive was not an option, he went on:

> The question is rather whether the central bank as a free-standing body should have some sort of statutory accountability for monetary policy. Is there something about the operation of monetary policy that makes it quite different from other elements of economic policy or indeed other elements

of government policy?. . . . I think there is. It's special to the extent to which a country, a democracy, the people at large would regard the need to preserve the value of their money and to pursue monetary stability as something which is not one of the variables of everyday political or electoral policy.[49]

Tellingly, the interview appeared in the first issue of a magazine called *Central Banking*. Quite apart from those mentioned by Lawson in his memo, the Reserve Bank of New Zealand had gone independent in 1989, and by the early 1990s the cult of the central banker – with Paul Volcker as the great inflation-slaying exemplar of the previous decade – was gathering momentum. 'By far the most persuasive case for central bank independence was the rise of stateless money and global financial market integration,' Steven Solomon has convincingly argued about this growing trend following the 1987 crash. 'Broadly put, in a landscape in which tears anywhere in the interwoven financial fabric or abrupt alteration in the direction or size of international capital flows could disrupt prosperity across borders, it served the enlightened self-interest of citizens and capitalists everywhere to pool their sovereignty through the upgraded independence of all central bankers.'[50] That, of course, was not quite Leigh-Pemberton's language, though he did claim that if there had been an independent Bank in 1987–8, it would have been able to act more quickly to dampen down the Lawson boom – a boom that, ironically, had done much to tarnish Lawson's reputation while simultaneously enhancing the case for taking monetary policy out of the hands of politicians.

It was Lawson's successor, John Major, who in October 1990 – the dying weeks of the Thatcher era – at last took Britain into the exchange rate mechanism (ERM) of the European monetary system. Less than two years later, on 16 September 1992 (Black Wednesday), it all unravelled horribly, as Britain was forced out amidst humiliating scenes for the Major government, which had effectively staked its credibility on the non-devaluation of sterling. Even by 8.30 a.m., when Major refused the request of his Chancellor, Norman Lamont, to put up interest rates, there was heavy selling of the pound, by both speculators (such as George Soros) and institutions (including banks and pension funds). If the pound was to be defended, that left no alternative to massively expensive intervention by the Bank of England. 'It was incredible,' Mark Clarke, a foreign exchange dealer at the Bank of America, recalled of the atmosphere that morning. 'Obviously you can hear what's going on in the market, and you can hear wave after wave of selling hitting the market, being met with resistance and support by the Bank of England. They were buying such a phenomenal amount of pounds . . .' The Bank's Deputy Governor, Eddie George, subsequently explained the thinking: 'We decided that as the

London market came in we would intervene, on a scale which would make it quite clear that we were intervening, and that's what we did.'

At eleven o'clock a belated rise in interest rates (from 10 per cent to 12 per cent) failed to do the trick, with the markets scenting blood; and by late morning, with the Bank spending Britain's currency reserves at the alarming rate of £2bn per hour, both George and Lamont reckoned that the game was up and that British membership of the ERM would have to be suspended immediately. Major, however, decided on a final throw of the dice, and at 2.15 p.m. interest rates went up to 15 per cent – prompting the cry in one dealing room, 'Anyone want to buy a house?' Again the move was viewed by the markets as a sign of weakness, not strength, and after sterling had staged a tiny, flickering rally the Bank was soon buying pounds again. 'That afternoon,' Soros recollected, 'it became a veritable avalanche of selling.' Kenneth Clarke, one of the ministers close to Major, graphically evoked the sense of impotence at the other end of town: 'We had no power. The markets and events had taken over. It became increasingly obvious as the day went on that we were merely flotsam and jetsam, being tossed about in what was happening . . .' At about four o'clock, by which time the Bank had spent no less then £15bn in support of sterling, it was agreed to let it go. From a dealer's perspective, Mark Clarke remembered that moment, a cardinal one in the relationship between the nation state and the financial markets:

> At four o'clock suddenly the Bank of England wasn't supporting pounds. Instead of a load of noise coming out of the voice brokers and everything and around the dealing room, everyone sat in stunned silence, for almost two seconds or three seconds, and all of a sudden it erupted, and sterling just free-fell. That sense of awe, that the markets could take on a central bank and actually win. I couldn't believe it . . .[51]

Three and a half hours later Lamont stood outside the Treasury and announced to the television cameras that UK membership had been suspended – a *de facto* devaluation.

It had been an extraordinary day. As it drew to an end, Mark Clarke candidly told *Channel 4 News* that his team had made £10m. That sounded a lot, but it would soon emerge that Soros had netted a staggering $1bn on his day's work. For those of a patriotic bent, it was not a day that did much for the City's image. The *Sunday Telegraph*'s Trevor Fishlock vividly described how the government's 'Black Wednesday' was 'Delirium Day' in the square mile:

> With the pound falling with each second it was a chaotic day on the currency trading floors, a day of shrieking, bellowing and swearing as dealers shouted into telephones and kept half an eye on screens which showed the pound's deteriorating cardiogram trace. Men with glistening faces and staring eyes leaped to their feet, punched buttons and shouted themselves

hoarse from 7 a.m. until late in the evening. Tens of millions of pounds passed through their fingers in moments. To an outsider the sheer energy and noise of an exchange floor, the rapid-fire jargon, the evident enthusiasm and passion, the animal aggression, combine in a dizzying, exciting and baffling spectacle. You soon learn that a man who shouts 'five quid' means £5 million.

At the London International Financial Futures Exchange, the institutional or wholesale market, dealers crammed the sweltering, paper-littered dealing pits, shouting their offers and bids at the tops of their voices, signalling in fast tic-tac semaphore. Their bright striped blazers made the exchange floor a teeming mass, like Henley gone berserk. On Wednesday the exchange traded a record 886,000 contracts worth £254 billion . . .

Fishlock might have added that the sweaty atmosphere at LIFFE had not been helped by the air conditioning having been set for a cool autumnal day. After it was all over, two exhausted traders talked to the *Daily Mirror*. 'I thought it was a hell of a day when the first rate rise came,' declared one. 'But when the second hit us, the place went mental. It's been selling all day. I've never seen anything like it.' 'Gazza' French said his bit over a pint of lager: 'Thank Christ that's over. I knew it was going to be a long day. But I never thought Lamont would freak like that.' And he added, 'Now, when it all turns to dust, we can make a bit of dosh.' The paper's headline was 'SOLD down the river', but no amount of moral indignation could alter the underlying lesson of the day that the balance of power had shifted irrevocably towards the markets.[52]

Following Black Wednesday, the government had the painful task of rebuilding its economic-cum-monetary policy almost from scratch; not surprisingly, having been given such a savaging by the markets, it decided to give an increasingly prominent role to the Bank, in the hope that it would act as a credibility-enhancing buffer.[53] Over the next year and a half there was a series of incremental changes: from October 1992 the Bank became responsible for monitoring how well the government was doing in pursuing its anti-inflation target; in September 1993 Lamont's successor, Kenneth Clarke, announced that the Bank's Inflation Report would no longer be shown to the Treasury ahead of publication; two months later he let it be known that the Governor, Eddie George (who had succeeded Leigh-Pemberton in July), was now responsible for the exact timing of interest rate changes; and from April 1994 the minutes were published of the monthly meetings between Clarke and George. With the worldwide bandwagon for independent central banks rolling ever faster, there were some who believed that independence would be the perfect birthday present to mark the Bank's tercentenary in July 1994.

But Major was unpersuadable. 'The very real concern that I have always faced,' he told the Commons in June 1993, 'is one that I believe is spread widely across the House: the need for accountability to Parliament for decisions on monetary policy matters.' Later that month an MP very much coming from elsewhere, Diane Abbott, questioned the Governor-elect as part of a Treasury and Civil Service Committee inquiry into the Bank's role:

> *You do take the point that one of the reasons people are slightly wary of the Bank of England, which has no democratic controls at all, is that you do lead relatively cloistered lives, you do earn these huge salaries and do not appear to be quite in touch with the effects of your policies on people who earn slightly less than a quarter of a million a year?*
>
> I would dispute a great deal of that with the greatest possible respect . . . Our contacts with industry and business are very strong at every level, from the Court down through our agencies, to our contacts here in London. We understand just as much as anybody else the impact that it has on people who lose their homes and lose their jobs. As a matter of fact I think many of us are affected in terms of our own families. So I rather resent the suggestion that simply because we work in the Bank we are not sensitive to the impacts of the policies that we pursue. I think the point about the policies is that there is no dispute about the ends . . . The debate is about the means and, frankly, it is a very stressful thing to have to do, but if you actually believe that stability is necessary to achieve on a sustainable basis improvements in wealth and welfare, then you cannot shrink from doing the things which are necessary to establish the basis for that stability.

Few leading figures in the City would have dissented from George's robust defence – that autumn an eminent committee chaired by Lord Roll (of Warburgs) came down firmly in favour of independence – but George's predecessor, by now Lord Kingsdown, spoke with commendable candour on BBC Radio in May 1994:

> I think most people in the street are pleased with the concept of price stability – the idea that we don't have to go on living forever in circumstances in which we assume that prices are going to go up. But of course if the price of that is that economic expansion is somewhat slowed and rates of unemployment either go up or don't fall as quickly as people would like, well, there is a tension there, and it's a very understandable one. And should there be some change in the status of the Bank of England, of course this would be the real challenge for the central bank under this new position – to read the mood of the country, to reconcile that with its commitment to monetary stability, and to make sure that the two can march side by side. And there would undeniably be times I think when the central bank would come under pressure. 'It's been too restrictive'. 'It doesn't know what life is like out there, sitting in that great white building in the middle of the City' . . .[54]

The looming question, in other words, was whether unelected central bankers would have adequate political skills in a new, potentially dangerous dispensation. It was not a prospect that either Norman or Cobbold, to name but two, would have relished.

Every day – whatever the current debate, whatever the latest scandal – the 'old' City was clearly more and more on the way out. Three small examples: when Martin Vander Weyer returned to London in late 1989 after several years in the Far East, he was struck by how the 'breed of part-of-the-family City messengers and butlers, many of them ex-servicemen, partially disabled or otherwise disadvantaged, had been rendered extinct by the arrival of cost-reducing contracted-out catering and security services'; the following autumn, not long after a messenger had been robbed in the street of £292m of bearer securities, the introduction of the Central Moneymarkets Office (CMO) – in effect the Bank of England's electronic trading system for the money market – meant that the daily, physical carrying of £30bn-worth of money-market instruments around the City's streets would gradually be phased out; and in 1994 a director of the Bank of England since the early 1980s remarked that people no longer stood up when the Governor entered the room. In 1999 John McLaren, a corporate financier at Barings and then Morgan Grenfell between 1981 and 1996, before (like others) starting to write financial thrillers, offered an inside perspective on how the pace of change had accelerated:

> When I arrived, the City was beginning to throw off its reputation as a haven for well-dressed gents of often modest intellectual means. Soon it was shaken up by the barrow boys, but that was nothing compared with the seismic shift of the Nineties, when the Americans arrived in force, armed not with chewing gum and nylons but with very sharp elbows and a mission to convert Brits to the ways of Wall Street. It worked. Pay rocketed, job security evaporated and evenings off became an endangered species.
>
> As pay in the City outstripped almost all other sectors, only the smarter bankers saw that they were just in the right place at the right time. The rest seemed to feel that if they were paid so much more than other people, they must *be* better. If their arrogance hadn't got up so many noses, it would have been funny . . .[55]

In the early to mid-1990s almost everyone talking to the *City Lives* oral history project at the National Sound Archive agreed that it was an almost entirely new world. 'The City is going back to raw capitalism,' Ross Jones of Gerrards asserted. 'We're losing structure. It's going to get nastier. I look at the people retiring and I find it distressing that the people coming up don't have the same values.' According to Nick Durlacher, Chairman of LIFFE, the legacy of the 1980s had been to sweep away traditional, hierarchical assumptions about age and seniority: 'In many cases firms got rid of experienced talent at around the age of fifty. That may be a good or a bad thing, but there was a certain innate discipline in the old hierarchical structure . . . An awful lot of the businesses were partnerships where the senior people had their own money on the line – that gave a certain urgency to management supervision.' The new world seemed to belong to the ambitious, thrusting young, and Davina Walter of Henderson Administration probably spoke for many: 'I would say all mid-forty-year-olds working in the City are worried about keeping their jobs. Firms have yet to tackle this. It is piling on more and more pressures on us all without seeing what effect it's having. People are having health problems. It's live by the sword, die by the sword.' Even a notably successful American had his regrets. 'We've bred a very mercenary type of young person who comes to make the most amount of money he can in as short a period of time as he can, who doesn't feel a great deal of loyalty to the organisation,' Charles McVeigh of Salomons observed. 'So there's a tremendous turnover today. It's a by-product of the business. It's sad when people don't try to balance the monetary reward with a sort of psychic reward of trying to build something in a business that goes beyond their own wealth.'[56]

Certainly the City felt *physically* a different place, full of new con-structions (often unoccupied or barely occupied) following the great building splurge of the mid-to-late 1980s. Some – like Minster Court and the new Barclays head office, both the responsibility of Gollins, Melvin, Ward & Partners – were striking rather than pleasing. 'The architects have rejected both the slick envelopes of the City's 1970s office towers and the rigorous glamour of the Lloyd's building, in favour of the shock tactics of instant recognisability,' Simon Bradley wrote of the giant Minster Court development – 'three outrageously arch office blocks grouped into one jagged pile', at the north end of Mincing Lane. The largest of the three blocks, each with 'rosy polished granite cladding in a bewildering variety of fins and angles, like Hanseatic Gothic done in stiff folded paper', housed the London Underwriting Centre, a recent rival to Lloyd's. There, rising from the centre of a giant atrium, there was, Bradley noted, 'a stack of paired escalators (the tallest in the world on completion in 1993), dizzyingly suspended on four clusters of rods'. Still, he preferred it to the 'vast and boastful' new Barclays at 54 Lombard Street, with its 'three bulgy grey-clad towers of varying heights' facing Gracechurch Street round the corner. For those less architecturally well versed, the new building (begun in 1986 and completed in 1994) said one thing: hubris. Unfortunately, when the first big IRA bomb went off, in April 1992, the new monsters survived; instead it signed the death warrant of the Baltic Exchange building in St Mary Axe, built in the early 1900s and recalled wistfully by Bradley as 'not inventive, but a very attractive, spacious ensemble, of great interest as the last survivor of the type in the City'.[57]

The second bomb came a year later, doing much damage in and around Bishopsgate, including ruining – shockingly, but to little general lament – the NatWest Tower. After the Japanese banks had written to the Home

Secretary, saying that they would have to look at alternative locations if the safety of their nationals could not be guaranteed, that bomb led to the so-called 'ring of steel', a security cordon around the City that significantly reduced traffic levels and made it a rather more pleasant environment. In the very heart of the City, at No 1 Poultry opposite the Bank of England, it was not the IRA but the House of Lords that was responsible for the sad demolition in summer 1994 of the Mappin & Webb site. On the basis of a new, less aggressively modern design by James Stirling, the property developer Lord (Peter) Palumbo had finally got his way – although he was not helped by the Prince of Wales having, not inaccurately, compared the new design to a '1930s wireless set'. Also by the mid-1990s Canary Wharf was definitely in business – so much so that by April 1995, when BZW announced that it would be moving 1,800 staff there, the City Corporation was seeking not only to relax planning rules on listed buildings, but to reach an accord with its rival by which they would not engage in cut-throat competition in the search for new tenants.[58]

Michael von Clemm, a pioneer of Canary Wharf, died in the same year (1996) as Matthew Harding, in his way an icon of the 1990s. The extrovert Vice-Chairman of Chelsea Football Club liked to describe himself as 'a genuine Chelsea fan who was lucky to get rich', but few knew much about how he had become Britain's eighty-ninth richest man with a personal fortune estimated at £170m. In fact, he had made most of his money in the reinsurance market, really taking off from the late 1980s when his company, Benfield Group, started managing the reinsurance portfolios of some large German concerns. 'He was a natural salesman,' an insurance journalist, Edward Ion, remembered. 'Even when he went to sleep he was selling.' Ion was often a lunchtime guest at Benfields. 'Matthew hated playing at the City lunch affair so we used to get school dinners prepared by an overawed girl. The whole purpose was to get totally pissed. You didn't get a glass of wine, you got your own bottle.' Harding himself was not quite a self-made man – his father, a cargo underwriter at Lloyd's, had introduced him to Ted Benfield back in the early 1970s – but the aura he created was one of contempt for the establishment, whether City or football.[59]

During the 1990s the age of deference was ending even faster in the City than in society at large, and the prevailing, trader-based culture was aggressive, macho and generally in-your-face. 'Brokers no longer talk about a "bull market", but a market that's "got the horn", and traders now talk about a "hard on" if they think a price is going up instead of down,' Fiona Lafferty reported in August 1994. She was writing in the context of Samantha Phillips successfully taking the insurance brokers Willis Corroon to an industrial tribunal for unfair dismissal and sexual discrimination, having been told to 'back down, bimbo' after she had spoken out in a meeting with ten fellow-brokers. Lafferty's article, headed 'It's a man's language in the City', provided a dictionary of new-style City-speak: 'brass' was replacing 'bimbo' as the popular put-down of women; 'she's well offered' referred to an unattractive girl nobody wanted to take out; to be 'legged over' was to lose money on a bad deal, while to 'get shagged' was to lose a lot of money on the markets; and 'a Michael Jackson' was the new, topical slang for a small order, in other words anything 'under 10'. The newly meritocratic and classless City was far from being a home to enlightened values. 'Stories of City anti-Semitism abound,' Suzanne Glass reported in the *Independent on Sunday* in June 1995, 'even among those in their twenties and thirties, and more often than not they are Holocaust-related.' And she quoted a Jewish friend who was working in a large international investment bank: 'Nowhere in the world have I experienced such awful anti-Semitic comment as in the City. A few weeks ago I was on a company outing. Someone made a Holocaust joke about there being 11 holes in gas chambers, so that the Jews could block 10 with their fingers and the 11th would let in the gas. I couldn't believe my ears, so I asked him to repeat it. He did and I told him it was offensive. He said: "What's the problem? There are no Jews here." '60

For many people, of course, the City was just a job – probably more demanding than most, certainly better paid than most, but still just a job, not a way of life. 'I have no feeling about the City,' one young female Japanese manager flatly told Sakai in 1992. 'The City is an inhuman place and just a function for money trading.' For others it was different. 'Ms A', who had spent most of her twenties in the City (starting with a Japanese securities house in 1983 before moving in turn to a British merchant bank, an American bank and another bank), spoke revealingly in the early 1990s to the *City Lives* project:

> A lot of us were affected by the image of the City in the early eighties and got sucked in. If you are very ambitious and good at what you do, you can still make a lot of money in the City but the price you have to pay is a tremendous amount of stress, probably a ragged social and home life, and for what in the end? In my case, it has given me enough money to retrain and be able to do something else. But for other people it may be different. If you're an ambitious person in the City you may not have other things you want to do, you may want to do it for its own sake and that's where it becomes dangerous. I came across enough people like that to know I didn't want to rub shoulders with them too much longer. It creates an imbalance in a person's life and in their outlook. These people had the potential to make a great deal more out of other sides of their personalities because, on the whole, they were incredibly bright. When they were at university they were the movers and groovers – they weren't the creeps – but because they met the challenge of the City and became so totally focused, the other elements of their capabilities just withered and died . . .61

That perhaps was the *real* crime of the 1980s. It took the brightest and best of a generation – and consumed them in a bonfire of the vanities.

*

Two or three years before Big Bang the chairman of an accepting house spoke to Paul Ferris about proprietary trading – trading by a merchant bank as a principal, rather than merely as an agent. He did not commend it:

> Certainly we all do a bit of trading of one sort or another, because we find ourselves at the centres of markets in every conceivable financial and material commodity. If as a result of our connections somebody finds that copper is strong and getting stronger, we might have a plunge and buy ourselves a few thousand tons, just to make a short profit. Or we might buy some gilt-edged or some American Treasurys. But it's bad-quality business. It's not repetitive. It depends on a fluke of judgement and timing, and you get it wrong once in three times . . . We ought to be getting our profits from our skills and client connections and creative work. They give rise to a more dependable stream of profits. Who was it said that a skilful dealer is a quick telephone and rising market? Some wit. What I'm saying is that it's too dependent on the market . . .[62]

As the remarkable events of 1994–5 unfolded, these words should have resonated loudly – had anyone remembered them.

Driven by record low dollar interest rates, together with a rapidly expanding range of the financial instruments that were now being called by the umbrella term 'derivatives', 1993 was a bonanza year in the world's financial markets, particularly for the big trading houses. 'It is thought that the City created at least 250 millionaires,' the *Daily Telegraph*'s Neil Collins noted afterwards, 'and the most *junior* partner at Goldman Sachs was paid a $5m bonus.' For the first time since the Crash, the good times were indubitably back. They seemed likely to roar on well into 1994, until on 4 February Alan Greenspan at the Fed threw the markets (above all the world bond markets) into first turmoil and then gloom by raising interest rates by a half per cent. As he sought to counter inflationary dangers, there were five more interest rate rises over the next ten months. For houses like Goldman Sachs or Salomons, the consequences were not far short of catastrophic: the latter's London office, for example, lost $400m through proprietary trading in the course of the year. In early October there were shock warnings from both Warburgs and Hambros of sharply reduced profits; and although later that month there was a fillip to the City (and specifically Morgan Grenfell) in Deutsche's announcement that it intended to make London, not Frankfurt, the hub of its international investment banking operations, the mood as Christmas approached was far from festive. 'Thousands of City workers could see their Christmas bonuses slashed to as little as £10,000 this year – less than 5 per cent of what many took home last year,' the *Guardian* reported on 5 December to a presumably distraught readership. It quoted a senior dealer at a leading stockbroker: 'The share market has been dreadful. There is so much uncertainty about interest rates, the economy and politics and no one is buying or selling.' A senior employee (but not a partner) at Goldmans was more phlegmatic: 'People get miserable when the business is down, but we have to be grown-up about it. The fact is, it has not been a good year.'[63]

Three days later the City was startled by the news – in a joint statement prompted by a leak, and ensuing market speculation – that Warburgs and Morgan Stanley were 'discussing the possibility of combining their businesses, which they believe are uniquely complementary'.[64] For Warburgs, the root causes of this announcement went back partly to its decision at the time of Big Bang to adopt the ambitious, integrated approach; partly to its rapid – and very costly – expansion of its US operations since 1992; and partly to a decision taken early in 1994 to become a much bigger trading presence on the fixed-interest side, where Warburgs had never shone despite its historical strength in the Eurobond primary market. By a cruel twist of fate, that decision (against the wishes of Grunfeld) to take a major plunge into proprietary bond trading was taken on the very day, 24 February, that the world's bond markets cracked. At this point such was Warburgs' sky-high reputation – an estimate fully shared by Warburgs itself – that no one could have imagined how rapidly the wheels would fall off. 'I don't think Warburgs will be defeated,' Win Bischoff of Schroders remarked in March 1994 of Warburgs' global aspirations. 'There are too many good people there.' Seven months later the City received a nasty surprise as Warburgs announced first-half, pre-tax profits of only £62.5m, well under half of the record £148m in the same period the previous year, and issued a profit warning. 'I was really astonished,' one banking analyst told the *FT*. 'I had not entertained that profits could be £100m lower.' Another analyst, Philip Gibbs, perceptively argued that if Warburgs had indeed taken a cold shower because of proprietary trading, perhaps it had had no alternative if it wanted to compete with the big US investment banks, granted that 'the gospel now' was that 'if you deal in secondary markets, you have a much better chance of getting primary market business'. Nevertheless, the disappointing profits were made more embarrassing by the fact that no less than £57m had been contributed by Mercury Asset Management (MAM), three-quarters owned by Warburgs but operating autonomously. 'For Warburg, used to being the City's most powerful British investment house, this is a severe embarrassment,' the *Sunday Times* commented, and that was probably an understatement.[65]

By then Warburgs was already talking to Morgan Stanley, probably the only major investment bank not to have taken a hammering that year. The two banks had traditionally had a close relationship, and by early October discussions about sharing back-office costs had developed into the possibility of a full-blooded merger. Over the next few weeks negotiations gathered momentum, with the top men on both sides believing that (in the words of a subsequent Harvard Business School case-study) 'the prospective union could create the investment bank of the future, a global powerhouse with complementary operations in Europe, the United States and Asia'. For Warburgs, of course, such a union would be a tacit admission that its solo attempt to become one of the world's top investment banks had failed. Nevertheless, particularly in its newly straitened circumstances, the deal had some very considerable attractions:

> A merger with Morgan Stanley would allow Warburg to achieve, at long last, the superior US distribution network that had eluded David Scholey [now Chairman of Warburgs, with Cairns as Chief Executive] and his predecessors for the past two decades. Morgan Stanley's US operations, with over 6,000 employees, dwarfed Warburg's rapidly assembled 600-employee subsidiary in New York . . . Combining its US operations with those of Morgan Stanley would allow Warburg to expand distribution and pare expenses in a single transaction.
> Additionally, Warburg had long been a poor performer in fixed-income markets. The firm had never been able to break into the upper ranks of global bond underwriters, while Morgan Stanley was perennially among the top ten . . . A combined S.G. Warburg-Morgan Stanley fixed-income shop would issue over \$30 billion in primary debt offerings annually, becoming one of only four bond underwriters in the world to reach that level.[66]

Cairns and Scholey were enthusiastic supporters of the deal, while the firm's two wise old men, Grunfeld and Roll, both gave it their blessing. By early December, with a public announcement due to be made on the 19th, the creation of Morgan Warburg seemed likely to become a reality, though it was ominous that not all the key components were yet on board. In particular, MAM wanted to know that it was still going to be in the driving seat as far as asset management was concerned, and had not received satisfaction concerning how its minority shareholders were to be treated; on the Morgan Stanley side there was intense anxiety on the part of the corporate finance people in London (working out of Canary Wharf), who knew that their business was unprofitable and that they would be absorbed into Warburgs. That was roughly the state of play by the morning of Thursday the 8th, when the two banks were in effect compelled by the Stock Exchange either to abandon the deal or to admit publicly to the merger negotiations. They chose the latter course, but henceforth the negotiations would be in an all-too-public glare.

'On the Richter scale of City events,' the *Independent* noted the next day, the announcement registered 'a full ten'. It even provoked Goldman Sachs to call a full partners' meeting to discuss the implications. Exploring the wider meaning of what was in practice a takeover bid for Warburgs, granted that Morgan Stanley's shareholders were going to own two-thirds of the combined group, one commentator, Hamish McRae, was struck that the announcement had coincided almost to the minute with confirmation that Dresdner Bank was going to follow Deutsche's example and move its international investment banking headquarters from Frankfurt to London. 'They are not doing this because they relish the idea of travelling on the Tube, or because the theatre is better,' he observed laconically. 'They are moving here because London is the world market-place, and if a bank wants to participate in that market, London is the place to be.' Nevertheless, he did not deny that the fate of Warburgs, as 'the largest independent, British-owned investment banking group', was 'unsettling'; or that 'it would make many in the City uncomfortable if almost all the main players were non-British'. He added that although it was 'perfectly possible that this deal will not go through', come what may 'it seems unlikely that Warburg will remain independent – once a company signals that it may merge with another it usually ends up with a change of ownership'.[67]

The leak may have come from the Warburgs side. In any event, after a few days of unrelaxing discussions Morgan Stanley called off the deal, issuing on the 15th a unilateral statement to that effect, explicitly blaming MAM for having insisted on unacceptable conditions. As an informal coda, Stephen Waters, co-Managing Director of Morgan Stanley Europe, even asserted that MAM had been 'the reason for us to do this deal' – a claim justifiably rejected by Scholey as 'a subjective and selective alibi'. Three and a half decades after doing much the same to its opponents in the Aluminium War, Warburgs had been shafted by 'Mack the Knife' (Morgan Stanley's John Mack) and his colleagues. Financially weakened, with much of its prestige gone almost overnight, Warburgs was now acutely vulnerable. 'Any suggestion that this puts the firm up for sale, puts it on the line, or hangs it out to dry, or whatever, is dealer-speak,' Scholey publicly insisted, but the reality was otherwise. The first six weeks of 1995 saw a quickfire sequence of events, all pointing in the same direction: Warburgs, almost unthinkably, pulling out of the Eurobond market; its co-heads of equity capital markets defecting to Morgan Grenfell; and, amid fresh profit warnings, the resignation of Cairns. Scholey became Chief Executive and began the task of trying to restore morale, but as the *Independent*'s Jeremy Warner wrote on 17 February of the Warburgs drama, 'in the space of little more than two months, its persona has been transformed from one of calm, focused, switched-on management and professionalism to that of an apparently aimless and demoralised organisation'.[68]

Just over a week later, on Saturday the 25th, the news broke to an astonished world that Barings – after an impeccable, blameless 105 years – was once again deep in trouble.[69] At this stage little more was publicly known than that a Barings trader operating from the Singapore futures exchange (SIMEX) had run up huge, fraudulent losses, probably of at least £400m. Instead, over a long weekend, it was very much behind closed doors – just as in 1890 – that the City collectively addressed the question of whether Barings could be saved. Significantly 'the City' still meant, in the eyes of the Bank of England, which convened the emergency meetings, only the British banks, with the American, European and Japanese banks all excluded. The deadline set for any rescue was 10 p.m. on the Sunday, before the Japanese market, on which most of Barings' positions were open, began trading again.

That Sunday, with most of the outside world confidently expecting a rescue, though unaware that the latest estimate of losses had risen to £650m, there were several acutely piquant moments at the Bank, where those thrashing out possible solutions were mainly a mixture of clearing bankers (including Buxton of Barclays and Goodison of TSB) and not unnaturally alarmed merchant bankers (including Scholey of Warburgs, Craven of Morgan Grenfell, and Bischoff and Mallinckrodt of Schroders). At one point Peter Norris of Barings, in a notably unapologetic presentation of his bank's financial position, elicited audible gasps by revealing that in two days' time Barings intended to pay bonuses for 1994 of no less than £84m, even though its pre-tax profit for that year (excluding the profits from Singapore that were now realised to be fictitious) was only £83m. Under questioning, it also emerged from Norris, again to collective astonishment, that as much as £800m had been transferred from London to support the requirement for margin in SIMEX – a staggering piece of information that instantly made nonsense of the claim by Barings' Chairman, Peter Baring, that his bank had been powerless to prevent the fraud.

Nevertheless, it was not a sudden distaste for Barings that caused the rescue talks to fail, but three specific factors. First, George as Governor took the view (unlike Lidderdale in 1890) that if, however regrettably, Barings went to the wall, there was unlikely to be any systemic threat to the banking system as a whole; therefore there was no justification for asking the government to sanction the use of public money to bale out the City's oldest but no longer most important merchant bank. Second, the Bank was unable to find a buyer for Barings, with neither Merrill Lynch nor the Sultan of Brunei coming through in the end. And third, although the other banks were willing, at a suitable rate of interest, to lend £640m to Barings, thereby enabling it to recapitalise itself under new management, no way could be found of putting a cap on further losses that might arise from the positions still open in the Far East. It did not help that the very word 'derivatives' had such a fear-inducing ring, following some spectacular trading débâcles in America the previous year, nor that so few of those around the table properly understood them. 'It is perhaps salient to observe,' one of those present noted immediately afterwards, 'that there was a glaring lack of knowledge about this type of business and the inherent risks among a representative cross-section of leading British bankers.'[70] It was thus announced shortly after 10 p.m. that there would be no rescue package and that Barings was to be placed in administration. Such a resonant name, such a sudden demise – it was perhaps the most memorable, sad, blood-quickening moment in the City's peacetime history.

'They all want to read about the bank that's gone phut' was how my newsagent explained to me next morning at seven-thirty the absence of any copies of the *FT*. The story dominated the day's papers, and as William Rees-Mogg vividly put it in *The Times*, 'For those of us who can remember the Second World War, the loss of Barings has something of the same impact as the sinking of the *Hood*. At one moment in time it is unthinkable; at the next it has happened.'

By this time the trader who had managed to run up such crippling losses had been identified as Nick Leeson. He was twenty-eight, and had grown up in a council house in Watford, where his family still lived. 'Nick has worked hard for what he's got, and he deserves it all,' a younger sister told the *Daily Mirror*. 'He wasn't one of those public-school types who had it all handed to him on a plate.' He had disappeared from Singapore the previous Thursday, and no one knew where he was. That Monday morning – a day, curiously, in which a financial adventurer from another era, Bernie Cornfeld, died almost unnoticed in a London hospital – two particularly striking *Evening Standard* placards appeared all over London: 'Manhunt As The Pound Dives' and 'Bank Crash Savages Markets'. In fact, although a 6.6 per cent fall in Tokyo's Nikkei Index had pushed Barings' losses on its contracts up to £880m, the FTSE 100 lost only 12.4 points (closing at 3,025.3) and the pound recovered much of the ground it had lost earlier in the day. This relative steadiness came as a huge relief to both Governor and Chancellor. George talked of the importance of keeping the concept of 'moral hazard' in the banking system, while though Clarke conceded to the Commons that 'this failure is of course a blow to the City of London', he emphasised that 'it appears to be a specific incident unique to Barings centred on one rogue trader in Singapore'.[71] The phrase would stick, as the image of the rogue trader who had brought down the mighty Barings became one of the most compelling of the era.

Tuesday the 28th at last saw the first photographs of Leeson – fresh-cheeked, slightly chubby-faced, smiling, balding, wearing his navy-and-gold trader's jacket. The *FT* carried an interview with Peter Baring, who claimed that Barings had been running a low-risk business until 'the fraud', and speculated that Leeson might have been in a systematic conspiracy with an unknown partner in order to bankrupt the bank.[72] Meanwhile the administrators, Ernst & Young, had begun negotiations with parties interested in buying different bits of Barings. During Tuesday and Wednesday, with Leeson still evading his pursuers, there was growing evidence that Barings had known at least something of what was going on but had failed to act, provoking widespread ridicule for Peter Baring's conspiracy theory. Leeson was held early on Thursday, 2 March at Frankfurt airport, where he had hoped to change to a London flight; and by that evening a buyer, the Dutch bank ING, had been found for the whole of Barings, priced at an attractive £1. The next day Leeson, wearing his iconic baseball cap and clutching a Tom Clancy thriller, was remanded in custody by a Frankfurt court. For all concerned, even at the periphery, it had been an unforgettable week. That Friday afternoon I took part in a television discussion on the Barings crash and its implications. The venue was the English Speaking Union in Mayfair's Charles Street, and we sat in a large, elegant room on the first floor – amazingly, the drawing-room of the first Lord Revelstoke's London home, where in November 1890 he had sweated out what would now for ever be known as the first Barings crisis.

Most commentators had a view. Rees-Mogg thundered on the Tuesday about 'the grotesque timidity' of the Bank of England, arguing that it had 'avoided risking at most a few hundred million pounds', whereas 'the credit of London, which has been put in jeopardy, may be an unquantifiable asset, but it must be measured in hundreds of billions of pounds of Britain's future earning power'. He concluded gravely, 'The Bank of England exists to protect British credit. In this instance, it has failed in its prime duty.' The same paper's Graham Searjeant and Anthony Harris took a similar line, as did its leader writer; but on Wednesday the *FT*'s John Plender, arguably unrivalled among financial journalists for his grasp of the big picture, persuasively countered the Bank's critics:

> It is, of course, a case of mistaken identity. A City whose good name has been so dreadfully traduced no longer exists. London's competitive advantage in international finance has little, if anything, to do with the older cohorts of the merchant banking fraternity who financed world trade in the 19th century. For the best part of two decades the powerhouse of financial innovation has been located largely in the foreign banking and securities community . . .

Moreover, he added, 'in the absence of a club, successful lifeboats are not easily launched'. By the end of the week there was widespread agreement that George had got it right. 'The external impact of the crisis has so far been successfully contained, vindicating the decision not to rescue Barings,' the *Independent* noted on Saturday, while the next day the *Sunday Telegraph*'s Bill Jamieson argued that 'if the impression got around that domestic banks could be counted on to be baled out by their central bank, that would suggest a playing field so tilted as to drive out every non-resident bank'. And, he asked rhetorically, 'where would the City be then?'[73]

By this stage the agenda had moved on to the question of how much Barings – and, indeed, the Bank – were to be blamed for not having acted earlier, before the situation became so critical. 'Fingering Leeson alone is like blaming a lance-corporal for the outcome of the First World War,' a senior banker declared. 'It is ridiculous.' The head of treasury at a large merchant bank, who could not get over how Barings had transferred more than £400m from London to Singapore in the final six weeks, without apparently any effective controls being in place, agreed: 'Even Colombian drug barons don't throw that sort of money around without a few signatures.' To Jeff Randall in the *Sunday Times* it was all crystal-clear:

> In layman's terms, Barings' top team chose to smash through red light after red light in a craven chase for 'easy' profits. Then, in the final moments, when it was clear the next stop was a brick wall, they scrambled desperately to find someone, anyone other than themselves to blame.
>
> Leeson, the oik from Watford, looked the perfect fall-guy . . .
>
> What has shocked me more than anything are the reports from insiders of the rush by Barings' top executives to secure their own bonuses. Three senior City figures have told me that the first goal of the Barings' toffs in talks with would-be saviours has been to clinch personal payments before saving the firm. Yuk!

Already there was quite a lot of sneaking admiration felt in the City for 'the man with lots of balls but no Barings', as a broker in a City bar on the Friday evening had told a journalist.[74] As for his former employers, an adage that apparently had been circulating in the City for some years seemed never truer: 'You can tell a Barings man anywhere, but you can't tell him much.'

Nick Leeson was never really 'a Barings man'. He had gone to Baring Securities in 1989 as a book-keeper, and was sent to Singapore three years later to run its new futures office. Although responsible for settlement, he would also, as he had long wanted, have a chance to trade – a blurring of traditionally distinct functions apparently justified by the smallness of the office. Just before he left he was asked by one of his Watford friends whether he would be making any money in Singapore. 'Shagloads of it,' he replied in best trader argot.[75] Unfortunately he proved from the start a more or less hopeless trader, but so dreaded being ignominiously recalled to London that he began to hide his losses in a secret account – the infamous error account no. 88888. Within three months, by October 1992, the secret losses amounted to £4.5m, and Leeson saw no alternative but to go on trading, hoping to get the money back. By summer 1993, against the background of favourable market conditions, he had almost retrieved the situation – only to go on trading, make new losses, again hide them in the secret account and again hope to trade out of them. By the end of the year he was sleeping badly and hiding losses of £25m.

Back in London there had been a palace revolution at Baring Securities. Christopher Heath, famous in the late 1980s as the UK's highest-paid man, seemed to lose his golden touch in the early 1990s, as the Japanese stock market plunged; and in March 1993 the Deputy Chairman of Barings, Andrew Tuckey, engineered Heath's resignation as Chairman of Baring Securities. Ironically, as it would turn out, their main policy disagreement was that Heath wanted the resources to enable him to engage in larger-scale proprietary trading, in both the cash and derivative markets of the Far East, whereas Tuckey was concerned that this would make the Baring group as a whole too exposed to the performance of the securities business. He also, as a merchant banker, wanted much tighter control over the securities arm.

In fact a mixture of benign markets in mid-1993 and healthy (but in reality fictitious) profits coming from Singapore meant that Baring Securities appeared to flourish in the post-Heath era, so much so that when in September 1993 Peter Baring paid a routine visit to Brian Quinn, the Bank of England's head of banking supervision, the note of their meeting recorded that, in relation to Baring Securities, 'the recovery in profitability had been amazing, leaving Barings to conclude that it was not actually very difficult to make money in the securities business'. Baring added that the securities operation had become 'the biggest contributor' to the profits of the group as a whole. A few weeks later Barings initiated a joint venture in derivatives with Abbey National. 'Derivatives need to be well controlled and understood,' Peter Baring declared at the launch, 'but we believe we do that here.' Certainly that competence was not questioned by Christopher Thompson, the Bank of England's supervisor with direct responsibility for Barings, for soon afterwards he gave it a so-called 'informal concession', in effect enabling it to use as much of its capital as it wished in sending margin payments to the Singapore office, where Leeson was claiming to be acting on behalf of an in fact non-existent client and, contrary to the belief of his superiors in London, had none of his futures offset. Thompson's action, or rather non-action, was 'staggering', Stephen Fay justly observes, being 'more in keeping with the way the Bank of England was run more than a generation ago, when there were no written rules and assent was given on a nod and a wink'.[76]

So it went on. Between January and July 1994 the proprietary trading being done by Leeson apparently produced profits for Baring Securities of £30m, although by the time an internal, London-authorised audit in late summer had failed to uncover anything amiss, Leeson's secret losses were over £100m. 'We don't want to dampen the dynamism of Baring Securities,' Tuckey assured *Euromoney* at about the same time, 'we just want to focus the dynamism better.' By the end of the year the fake profits (immortalised by Peter Baring's description of them as 'pleasantly surprising') had become ever-bigger; Baring Securities had gone on sending out the lethal financial bullets, amounting to some three-quarters of Barings' capital; Leeson's secret losses were in the order of £160–£200m; and video footage of the SIMEX floor showed him staring blankly ahead, completely out of it.[77]

After a Christmas break away, Leeson did not want to return to Singapore in the New Year, but his wife Lisa – completely ignorant of what he had been up to – persuaded him that it would be crazy to forsake the imminent prospect of a £450,000 bonus. On 17 January, a week after his return, the Kobe earthquake and its violent impact on the Japanese financial markets drove Leeson into a final, utterly reckless frenzy of speculation, during which he made almost all the wrong trading decisions possible. His real losses were as much as £144m in a day, his declared profits as much as £10m in a day, and Barings blindly went on sending the margin payments, even after it had on 24 January gone over its overdraft limit with Citibank. But if blindly, then not quite blithely, as the often surreal transcripts of telephone conversations at Baring Securities during the final puzzled, belatedly anxious weeks revealed. 'I think we kind of go along a stumbling path, where we look at one thing at a time, and I think the dynamics are more complicated than that,' said Mary Walz, the head of equity derivatives trading, at one point. She and Ron Baker, her boss, then tried to get a grip on Leeson's increasingly bizarre explanations of his trading. They found it impossible and Baker groaned, 'All this work just drives me nutty. I just want to retire.'[78] At last, from about 17 February, the people in London started to apprehend something of the enormity of what Leeson had been doing and the position they were in. The charming, amoral, chameleon-like trader did his bolt on Thursday the 23rd, and the next day Peter Baring went round to the Old Lady to break the awkward news.

A month later the ensuing smash was already passing into history. Leeson would spend the next four and a bit years in jail, mainly in Singapore. His autobiography, inevitably called *Rogue Trader*, was published in 1996 to mixed reviews. For Tom Bower, seldom a friend of those in high places, it made 'a good case' for the view that Leeson had been 'the victim of the stupidity and greed of his superiors'. But Bryan

Appleyard, noting that Leeson's victim image had already been 'shored up by a pathetically soft television interview with David Frost', called it a 'vile and mendacious' account, whose 'emotional and factual dishonesty glares at you from every page'. At his press conference at Heathrow Airport in July 1999, following his release, Leeson made an explicit apology: 'I did wrong. I am not proud of my activities as a trader with Barings Bank in Singapore. I was foolish and very much regret what happened. But I have done my time.' A few months later it emerged that he had been offered a job as a trader. 'You would have thought that was inconceivable, wouldn't you?' he observed to a journalist. At ING Barings, which was soon under almost entirely new management and later in 1995 moved from 8 Bishopsgate to 60 London Wall, Saemy Japhet's old haunt, there was little inclination to dwell on the immediate past. Nor was there at the Bank of England, which during the two years after the débâcle received much criticism for a major failure of banking supervision. The real losers, however, were the people – many of them elderly, living far from the City and investing their life savings – who late in 1994 had subscribed to a £100m perpetual loan at 9.25 per cent issued by Barings in order to raise funds to send its star trader. 'We do quite a lot in the village and the income from this investment was to allow us to carry on,' Edward Pease-Watkin, a retired headmaster living in Herefordshire, told the *Evening Standard* in July 1995. 'It will be a lot harder now . . . The money they paid out in bonuses would have repaid the bondholders but I think they see us as people who really don't matter very much.' Not long afterwards Fay offered a crushing verdict: 'Had there been any real gentlemen left at Barings, they would have donated their bonuses to the bondholders; but there weren't.'[79]

It had been a story without heroes, a story that killed off the last whiff of romance about the money machine. 'Much more than money was lost to London with Barings,' Fildes, a veteran observer of the City scene and broadly sympathetic to its activities and inhabitants, wrote in sorrow as well as anger a year afterwards. 'Credit was lost, honour was lost. Leeson, the agent of this downfall, was greedy, ignorant and panicky by turns, and crooked too. But his panic, ignorance and greed were no more than a symptom of Barings' own. The house had been betrayed by what was false within.'[80] Traditionally, before the 1980s, the City had been viewed as stuffy, boring and unimaginative, but essentially honest and competent. In many ways it was a place that had been given a cumulative benefit of the doubt by outsiders who neither knew much about it nor wanted to. The events of the 1980s had significantly altered those perceptions; and now, after February 1995, the last illusions had been stripped. Never again, it seemed reasonable to assume, would the City be able to claim the moral high ground.

In spring 1995 itself the Barings trauma – so hard on the heels of Warburgs' afflictions – gave a particularly sharp edge to the publication on 13 March of the final report, *The Competitive Position of London's Financial Services*, by the City Research Project. 'You get fraud, mishaps everywhere,' one of the main people behind it, the City Corporation's Michael Cassidy, insisted as it was launched. 'The real picture, however, is that London is very much a top centre in a highly competitive business.' Stanislas Yassukovich, also much involved, entirely agreed: 'Barings is historically tragic, but it was a minor player in a very complex City. The decline of a British firm is much less important than the fact that people the world over bring their business to be done in London.' The report itself gave estimates of London's market share in the main international financial activities. They included 64 per cent of global cross-exchange securities trading, 11 per cent of worldwide turnover in interest rate and currency futures and options, 15 per cent of world turnover in commodity futures and options, 27 per cent of worldwide net forex turnover, 35 per cent of worldwide activity in swaps, 65–75 per cent of international Eurobond issues, 75 per cent of secondary trading in Eurobonds, 81 per cent of international fund management (as measured by total assets managed in Europe on behalf of institutional foreign clients), 7.5 per cent of international insurance (world total premiums for non-life direct business and reinsurance) and 50 per cent of world shipbroking commissions. These were generally impressive, soberly researched figures, but less than a week later the City's public image took a further dent with tabloid disclosures about the Bank of England's Deputy Governor, Rupert Pennant-Rea, who had come from the *Economist* less than two years earlier. His mistress, a journalist called Mary Ellen Synon, revealed that he had had her smuggled into the Bank under an assumed name and that they had made love on the carpet of the Governor's dressing room. Pennant-Rea's resignation letter on 21 March invoked history – 'Montagu Norman once said that "the dogs bark, but the caravan moves on" . . .' – but quite what the great defender of the Bank's honour would have made of it rather beggared belief.[81]

The hypothetical thoughts of another dead Titan were even more on people's minds over the next couple of months. One of the conventional wisdoms to emerge from the Barings débâcle had been that the writing was on the wall for much of the British merchant banking sector. 'There will be room for niche players specialising in high-quality advice and innovation but all those middling firms with an essentially national franchise look to be in trouble,' John Jay had forecast in the *Sunday Telegraph* in early March. 'This is the message for Kleinwort Benson, for N.M. Rothschild, for Schroder Wagg and for Warburg. The HSBCs, NatWests, Barclays and Deutsche Banks are already trampling on their territory, as are US investment banks. The US commercial banks may not be far behind. . .' By April there were two main bidders for the badly weakened Warburgs: NatWest and Swiss Bank Corporation (SBC). The prize went to SBC, which in Marcel Ospel had a head of its international and finance arm who impressed in both style and ability, had the inestimable advantage (in the eyes of most senior people at Warburgs) of not being a British clearing bank, and, unlike NatWest, was willing to make an offer that allowed a separate future for Mercury Asset Management. The deal was clinched in early May, with SBC paying the knockdown price of £860m, little more than the book value of Warburgs' investment banking business. Within days the word from the Warburg camp was not only that it was all for the best, but that such an outcome had long been anticipated. 'The whole idea that Siegmund would be terribly upset is not true,' one director told the *FT*. 'He always envisaged a merger at some stage with a bigger group.' Grunfeld, moreover, issued the most positive of statements, in which he praised SBC as 'a very progressive international bank' sharing a common European culture with Warburgs and described the failure of the Morgan Stanley deal as 'a blessing in disguise'.[82]

In truth, though, it had been a spectacular fall – in which arrogance played a significant part. 'They tried to make me feel as if it were they who were doing me a favour, as if they knew better than me,' a former corporate client had complained some three months before the final act. 'I was paying the bills, for heaven's sake.' According to an American investment banker, speaking at about the same time, there had been 'a real attitude problem, a cosiness and smugness of mentality which is out of tune with the modern world'. In short, he added, Warburgs had 'become English and City establishment through and through'. The definitive history of the fall of Warburgs has yet to be written, but four years later MAM's Peter Stormonth Darling offered a stimulating discussion. He did not deny that certain objective 'business' factors had been involved. These included the failure in 1986 to buy the US investment bank Wertheim and thereby establish a strong US presence; the move into proprietary trading; the loss of its distinctively European character through the acquisition of three British securities firms; the absence of what he called 'an employee ownership mentality', an absence that inevitably drove up the cost structure; and, by the end, an inadequate system of controls over a firm that had grown too large. Nevertheless, for all the possible validity of these and other causes, Stormonth Darling argued that at root what had happened was that 'those in charge simply forgot to apply some of the rules, never defined as such, which Siegmund Warburg used to drum into our minds constantly and repetitively'. Rules relating to personal behaviour, to the conduct of the business, to questions of expansion – all these, he believed, had been allowed to go by the board. 'Warburgs' big mistake was its expansion in 1994,' he concluded, 'coming after an excellent and record-breaking year in 1993. Siegmund used to speak about "expansion euphoria" . . .'[83]

Only a matter of weeks later, in late June 1995, Kleinwort Benson also agreed to be taken over – in its case for £1bn (about twice book value), by Dresdner Bank. 'I think we will be able to realise our goals more clearly and with greater security as part of the Dresdner Bank group than if we had stayed independent,' Lord Rockley declared, without any apparent misgivings. 'The offer is the right course for our shareholders, our business and our employees.' Less than nine years after Lawson had asserted on the eve of Big Bang that 'I do not share the pessimism of those who fear that British players will account for a disproportionate share of the casualties', it seemed that the City was going through a second Big Bang. How much did it matter, though, that the British merchant banks were – in terms of ownership – going down like ninepins? Yassukovich, responding to the announcement about Kleinworts, insisted that it did not: 'What matters is maintaining the competitive advantages that attracted them [i.e. the new foreign owners] to the City. We should look at it as a compliment not as a problem. Wimbledon is still the world's greatest tennis event, yet when did we last have an English player in the top 10 seeds?' Over the ensuing years the 'Wimbledonisation' of the City would occupy many column inches; and early in its life, the concept was given a further shot in the arm when it became known at the end of July 1995 that Smith New Court was selling out to Merrill Lynch, chosen in preference to Commerzbank for a price of £526m. 'This isn't the end of the road,' Smith New Court's Chairman, Michael Marks, reputedly told his colleagues. 'It's a new beginning. We want to create a better business.'[84] The demise of 'the brothers' did not inspire any great outpouring of grief, but it was another nail in the British coffin.

Inevitably the counter-argument was by now being heard. 'It is all very well to talk of the global marketplace, and global businesses where national interests no longer play a commanding role,' the *Independent* asserted on learning that Smith New Court was in talks with potential buyers. 'But things are never quite so clear-cut. Every firm has its roots somewhere, and that is where the strategic decisions are taken. Those decisions cannot help but reflect the national interest to some degree. Should there be a big investment banking shakeout in the future, the City may rue the fact that those deciding which way to jump are sitting in Frankfurt, Zurich, Amsterdam and New York.' Unsurprisingly those and similar concerns cut little ice with the magazine of the international bond markets – those markets that over the past three decades had done so much to reshape the world's financial architecture. 'Nationality will become less and less important in defining the culture of investment banks,' *Euromoney* prophesied in its July editorial:

> Senior investment-banking staff flow from one nationality of firm to another with increasing ease. Noticeable in London recently has been the number of expatriate Americans, brought over by their US employers, who have moved to European firms. Multi-cultural combinations are far from rare . . . Nationality is of little relevance in this increasingly interconnected world. What does matter is the ability of countries or cities to provide competitive environments that attract businesses (of whatever nationality) and to increase their market share as a global centre. That really *does* benefit a country . . . By that account, London looks ever more attractive as a financial centre – even if its investment banks are mainly dismal second-raters or all disappear into foreign hands.[85]

The British merchant banks, after all, had had a pretty good run, despite being mainly undermanaged and often underperforming. At last, with almost shocking abruptness, their time was just about up – all mystique gone, victims of a world that no longer needed to choose between brains (or a socially acceptable substitute) and brawn.

*

The five years since summer 1995 are too recent to offer much in the way of historical perspective, but the broad picture was of the City flourishing, both in itself and as an international financial centre relative to others. 'The City of London: Why It's the Center of Global Finance' boomed a cover of *Business Week* in March 1998, replete with inevitable colour photograph of a trader on the floor of LIFFE. Trading in international equities, forex trading, cross-border loans – in these, as by other familiar yardsticks, London still led the way. However, the magazine's Stanley Reed argued, there were something more interesting going on:

> The charge is being led by US banks and investment houses [the so-called 'bulge bracket' firms], which are using their record profits on Wall Street to pave the way for aggressive expansion abroad. Followed closely by European institutions that see their future in investment banking, these financial giants are bringing a massive infusion of capital and technology . . .
>
> The City's reawakening is part of a seismic shift in European economic, social, and political attitudes. A new equity culture is developing across Eastern and Western Europe as citizens realise that their cash-strapped governments will no longer be able to provide for their retirements. That change will mean a surge in demand for mutual funds and other investments for City firms to create and manage. A new generation of profit-driven managers and activist shareholders, meanwhile, is demanding that European corporations improve their performance. To do so, corporations are searching for cheaper and more creative sources of financing. That

means huge new quantities of equity and debt for City firms to underwrite. . .

Just over a year later, some four months after the launch (without Britain) of the European single currency, a survey by *Institutional Investor* found no hard overall evidence of Frankfurt managing to claw back London's considerable lead in the European time zone: 'London's critical mass is vast, and its gravitational pull seems to be increasing as a result of the single currency, technology and globalisation. Barring unforeseen new developments, the City will continue to prosper – and be the envy of financial center wanna-bes the world over.'[86]

For most of these five years the markets were bullish (for example the FTSE 100, having been just over 3,000 at the start of 1995, was well over 5,000 at the start of 1998 and by the end of summer 2000 was in the 6,600 region), but there was a nasty blip in 1998 as Russia defaulted and then the giant American hedge fund Long Term Capital Management virtually collapsed. Nearer home, there were – for the historically minded – moments of resonant irony during the general election campaign of April 1997. 'We accept, and indeed embrace, the new global economy,' Tony Blair declared in a speech at the Corn Exchange. 'I accept the need for economic discipline and embrace the role of free enterprise in the economy. There will be no retreat from any of that.' On the eve of polling, with opinion polls correctly predicting a Labour landslide, share prices soared to new heights. It was a reflection of how much not only Labour, but also the City, had fundamentally changed in character. There were still pockets of atavism – Blair got a rough ride some months later when he paid a visit to the floor of LIFFE – but in every sense it was a long time since the days of A.T. Lee.[87]

On 6 May 1997, only five days after the election, the new Chancellor, Gordon Brown, surprised and pleased the City by announcing that he was handing over responsibility to the Bank of England to set the interest rates that would seek to ensure the meeting of the government's inflation target. The nine-member Monetary Policy Committee (MPC), charged with doing the business, was to comprise the Governor and two Deputy Governors (all appointed by the government), four members ('recognised experts', in Brown's phrase) appointed by the government from outside the Bank, and two Bank nominees. Press reaction was mainly positive, though the *Economist* did observe that 'much as the chancellor and Eddie George might deny it, the Bank will be engaged in the highly political task of choosing how many jobs to sacrifice in order to hit the inflation target quickly rather than slowly'. Significantly, from left field, the *Guardian*'s Will Hutton – who in *The State We're In* (1995) had declared bluntly that 'to pass the control of interest rates to a quasi-private organisation run as an extension of one wing of the Conservative Party would be a disaster' – was now distinctly relaxed. Looking ahead optimistically to 'a Bank of England that is more distant from the "gentlemanly capitalist" culture of the financial system than any we have so far experienced', he argued that such a Bank, as part of a modernised British state, would finally lay to rest the ghost of Montagu Norman.[88] It was an appropriate invocation of the great man's name, for the new Chancellor knew his Labour history probably better than anyone else in the Cabinet and was well aware of how the 1931 financial crisis had destroyed an earlier Labour government – not to mention, of course, all those problems with the City that had so bedevilled the subsequent administrations of Attlee, Wilson and Callaghan. Brown presumably believed in the economic arguments for removing monetary policy from the temptations of the electoral cycle; but almost certainly there was also a political motive at work, a motive that was essentially defensive, even buck-passing.

As it turned out, the new arrangements were soon under widespread attack, as during much of 1998 the inflation-busting MPC kept interest rates high, despite the evident damage inflicted on the British economy by a strong pound. The Bank was uncomfortably exposed to forceful, at times even vicious, attacks – from both sides of industry, from columnists and cartoonists, even from demonstrators gathered by the Duke of Wellington's statue outside the Royal Exchange. George came under particular fire in October when he gave the impression in an interview that job losses in the North were a price worth paying to curb inflation in the South. By spring 1999 the storm had abated, with one commentator, Gavyn Davies of Goldman Sachs, looking back in May on the economy's pleasantly soft landing and praising as crucial 'the professional skills of Eddie George and a committee dominated by genuine monetary policy experts, instead of the businessmen and trade unionists who could so easily have been appointed'.[89] There was also by this time, adding to the plaudits, an increasingly drawn contrast between the relative openness and accountability of the central bank in London and the opaqueness of its European counterpart in Frankfurt. Nevertheless, the pound remained high, the North–South divide continued to widen and, entering the new century, the notion that monetary policy did not involve political – in the broadest sense of the word – judgements seemed wishful thinking. The shame was that elected politicians were no longer ultimately responsible for making those judgements.

The granting to the Bank of quasi-independence over monetary policy in May 1997 had been accompanied by the transferring from the Bank to the Treasury of day-to-day management of the gilts market. That same month, exactly a fortnight later, the Bank's role was further narrowed when Brown announced that it was to lose its responsibility for banking supervision, as part of a new system of financial services regulation that would see not only the supervision of banks, securities firms and fund managers, but also the regulation of the financial markets, brought under a single roof. The announcement came as a profound shock to the Bank and in particular to George, who reputedly told the Chancellor that it had been 'an intolerable betrayal' of an earlier promise to consult him before deciding to restrict the Bank's supervisory role.[90] He contemplated resignation, while Brown contemplated not reappointing him for a second five-year term, but in the event both men stepped back. The thinking behind the new regulatory arrangements was fairly obvious: the Bank's reputation for banking supervision had suffered from the BCCI and Barings episodes; more generally, there had been a plethora of financial scandals during the decade since the Financial Services Act, most recently (in September 1996) a fund management scandal at Morgan Grenfell; even New Labour had little sympathy for the concept of practitioner self-regulation, albeit within a statutory framework; and the increasing complexity of financial markets and financial instruments made the continuing existence of nine separate regulatory bodies seem too inflexible and too liable to turf wars.

The new super-regulator, named in September 1997 as the Financial Services Authority (FSA), was to be run by Howard Davies, who had been Pennant-Rea's successor as Deputy Governor; and in due course he found himself at Canary Wharf with some 2,000 budding regulators under him. Initially there was widespread support for the broad sweep of the changes – 'not only is the present system hopelessly bureaucratic,' 'Lex' commented the day after Brown's announcement, 'but self-regulation was never a terribly credible basis for public confidence in the first place' – but as the eventual Financial Services and Markets Bill began to make its ponderous way through Parliament, opposition from both inside and outside the City started to build up. 'No person or body should ever act as prosecutor, judge and jury combined,' the *Daily Telegraph* declared in July 1999, while the following spring a right-wing think tank, the Centre for Policy Studies, branded the FSA as one of the most powerful and least accountable institutions created since the Second World War. The City itself lobbied hard, and by summer 2000 the FSA's draconian powers had been significantly diluted, though in many eyes there remained the problem of inadequate accountability. Moreover, the bill was of such labyrinthine complexity, involving well over a thousand amendments, that it was clear that it would not become law until 2001 at the earliest. More than a quarter of a century after the secondary banking crisis it was still a moot point whether all the ensuing regulatory legislation and heartache had rendered the City a fundamentally cleaner place – not least in the ever-vexed area of frequently perpetrated, infrequently prosecuted insider dealing, still the classic white-collar crime.[91]

The Bank of England was not the only 'pillar' to find itself, in City terms, a diminished force. That certainly applied to Lloyd's, even though under David Rowland's leadership it did survive its life-threatening crisis, at last in summer 1996 managing to buy off the great majority of the Names who were threatening to take legal action, largely on the grounds of alleged fraud. Shortly afterwards, in a packed Room, Rowland rang the Lutine bell an unprecedented three times. 'Mr Rowland told the sea of underwriters, brokers and guests who lined the shiny metal galleries and stationary escalators,' the *FT* reported, 'that the three rings of the bell symbolised the suffering of Names who have borne losses totalling more than £8bn, the implementation of the [£3.2bn] recovery plan, and the start of work to restore international competitiveness.' Integral to Rowland's strategy was that the underwriting capacity of Lloyd's should increasingly come from corporate capital rather than that of individual Names; and over the next few years that indeed became the case, so that by the new century corporate members accounted for more than four-fifths of the market's capacity.

That change, although perhaps inevitable, was not necessarily all gain. 'The old Lloyd's died in the process, leaving a skeleton to be fleshed out to form a new trader to compete in a global market' was how Graham Searjeant in May 1997 persuasively interpreted Rowland's achievement and its likely legacy. 'This will lose the cost advantage of unlimited liability and rely on marketing, City finance and the concentration of expertise among surviving underwriters and brokers. Like the Stock Exchange, it will be in London rather than of London, dominated by large international interests.' Indeed, the following year, not long before stepping down as Chief Executive, the plain-speaking Ron Sandler apparently conceded that the market share enjoyed by Lloyd's in the world insurance market had more or less collapsed, which in part he attributed to the new arrangements being a more expensive way of doing business. The corporate investors were also becoming deterred by market losses, and in September 2000 it was reported that one of the leading underwriters at Lloyd's, David Shipley, was launching a £150m syndicate that he intended to fund largely from individual, unlimited-liability Names (of whom there were about 3,500 left). He wanted, he said, to 'recreate the old entrepreneurial owner-operator culture' of Lloyd's.[92] After all that had happened, though, it seemed a little early for the wheel to turn full circle again.

The third pillar was the Stock Exchange, where John Kemp-Welch, having done much to steer Cazenove's through the Big Bang era and its immediate aftermath, was Chairman for almost six years from July 1994.

Increasingly the Stock Exchange was trying to turn itself into a freestanding business, as opposed to an institutional club, and by the end of Kemp-Welch's chairmanship the member firms had voted almost unanimously to demutualise. No longer a monopoly provider, the Stock Exchange was conscious that it would survive only if it provided an efficient marketplace, and in July 1996, after a thorough strategic review, it published a business plan outlining how it intended to 'deliver the highest-quality services at the most competitive prices'. It did so in the comforting knowledge that its new trading system, SEQUENCE, was on the verge of successful completion – a considerable technological achievement in marked contrast to the earlier TAURUS débâcle, Moreover, in Michie's words, 'with the introduction of SEQUENCE the Stock Exchange had at its disposal an electronic platform that would support either a continuance of a quote-driven market, with competing market makers, or an order-driven market, for the automatic execution of orders'.[93]

The very possibility of an order-driven market had already caused a certain stir. It was not a prospect that pleased the big market markers (such as BZW) when the Chief Executive, Michael Lawrence, pushed the concept increasingly hard during 1994–5. Moreoever, by autumn 1995, with SEQUENCE approaching completion, it was clear that order-driven trading would soon become a practical possibility. However, at the key board meeting at the end of November, the representatives of the leading member firms agreed to the establishment of a steering committee on the subject; and over the next nine or so months these firms came to accept that the days of a wholly quote-driven market were numbered. Lawrence himself resigned as Chief Executive in January 1996. The widespread assumption was that the big market makers had claimed his head as punishment for his championing of an order-driven system; but the reality was that, like his predecessor, an unfortunate, ill-disguised streak of intellectual arrogance had created too many enemies.

The new Chief Executive from August 1996 was Gavin Casey, under whom the new order-driven system, SETS (Stock Exchange Trading Service), able to handle 3,000 transactions a minute, was introduced fourteen months later. Would it deliver the goods? 'Cheaper, more transparent trading conditions are good news for the London market,' the 'Lex' column claimed. 'It will increase participation by those who previously kept their distance, such as US institutional investors, and quantitative and derivative style traders who require the greater automation which Sets provides.' There was, accordingly, the prospect of rising volumes, falling costs, and 'a virtuous spiral of liquidity'. The euphoria did not last long. By December SETS was accounting for only 40 per cent of trades in the stocks it covered, and the *Independent*'s Jeremy

Warner frankly called it 'a disaster', especially in terms of its ability to 'distort share prices and disadvantage small investors'. A few months later the consultants Tempest carried out a comprehensive survey of Britain's largest companies and leading institutional fund managers, leading to the unambiguous conclusion that 'on most criteria, the centralised dealing desks give Sets a massive thumbs-down'. Volatile pricing was undoubtedly a serious problem. However, after two years most of the teething difficulties had been ironed out, and Casey was able to claim in January 2000 that 53 per cent of trades by value were being executed automatically through the SETS system, rather than through firms acting as principals. Altogether, it was a hybrid system of trading that had evolved, but on the whole it worked well. There still awaited, however, a day of technological humiliation. On Wednesday, 5 April 2000 – the last day of the tax year – the Stock Exchange's computer systems crashed and trading in UK equities did not start until mid-afternoon. 'Third World nightmare on Old Broad Street' and 'The day London's Stock Exchange died' were the headlines in one broadsheet, but perhaps the most apposite comment came from the veteran market maker Brian Winterflood, now running Winterflood Securities: 'This is the IT world for you. You drop your calculator and the battery falls out and suddenly you haven't got a brain.'[94]

In spring 2000, however, neither that ignominy nor the unfolding demutualisation was the big story. Almost two years earlier, in July 1998, the London Stock Exchange and its German counterpart, the Frankfurt-based Deutsche Börse, had announced that they intended to develop a common trading platform for the stocks of leading British and German companies. 'The strategic alliance creates a near centre of gravity from which the whole EU economy will benefit' was how Deutsche Börse's Weiner Seifert justified what he called a 'pre-emptive move against the inefficient fragmentation' of the European markets. He also emphasised, as did Casey, that the two exchanges were now more interested in co-operation than competition. City reaction was favourable, not least from the Bank of England, and James Dewhurst of Charterhouse Tilney Securities graciously acknowledged that the London Stock Exchange 'has to be applauded for acting with a degree of foresight which has left many of us surprised'. During the next year and a half, however, progress towards the acknowledged goal of a pan-European marketplace proved signally sluggish – so much so that the *Economist* declared in September 1999 that 'an alliance between the London and Frankfurt stock exchanges is dead in all but name' – until by early 2000 both exchanges seem to have concluded that a halfway house between complete separation on the one hand and a full-scale merger on the other was impossible.[95]

They opted for the latter. The announcement of a proposed new merged exchange, preposterously enough to be called iX (short for 'international exchanges'), was made on 3 May, together with the further intention of iX and NASDAQ jointly forming a separate market for 'new economy' stocks. After some hard bargaining, it had been agreed that London would provide the Chairman in order to balance Seifert as Chief Executive; and that the market for big, 'blue-chip' companies would be based in London and the market for smaller, high-growth companies in Frankfurt, where the Neuer Markt had been extremely successful. Who ultimately would call the tune? 'The reality is that this deal marks the end of any serious German aspirations to topple London as Europe's financial centre,' asserted the *Evening Standard*'s Anthony Hilton; but the *Economist*, in flat contradiction, insisted that it was 'a Frankfurt takeover in all but name'. Over the next few weeks it became the received wisdom that the big American investment banks had been in large part behind the proposed deal, and among London's smaller member firms a considerable head of steam built up against it. 'Everyone is up in arms about the merger,' Winterflood told the press. 'We don't know the detail of what is going to Frankfurt. They could get the cream and we could get the dross.' To Fildes, a long-standing critic of the Stock Exchange's direction, the whole thing looked like 'the symptom of a cumulative loss of nerve', and his piece in early June ended scathingly: 'Put together by the cook for the cooks, this pie would be eaten in haste and repented at leisure. There is no need to swallow it. Better to wave it away.' By July the deal was manifestly in trouble, amidst a strong (arguably media-driven) feeling in the City that the benefits it would provide to London were mainly illusory; and its chances further receded at the end of August when the relatively unknown Swedish technology company and stock-exchange operator, OM, made a sensational offer (of just over £800m) for the London Stock Exchange – the first-ever hostile takeover bid for a stock exchange. The offer was instantly rejected as 'wholly inadequate', but the Stock Exchange itself was now indubitably in play. 'Other exchanges may now feel like taking a pot-shot at London,' the *Economist* speculated a few days later. 'Or, since the difference between exchanges and technology companies seems to be eroding so fast, perhaps a highly rated tech company. Sweden's Ericsson, perhaps? Now that would be fun.'[96] There were, in short, no certainties left.

The Stock Exchange's decline had been long and gradual; by contrast, that of LIFFE, the City's so-called 'fourth pillar', was sharp and precipitate. In June 1997, still expanding rapidly and appearing invincibly ahead of all its European competitors, the exchange celebrated its imminent fifteenth anniversary with a memorable, no-expense-spared thrash at Syon House, made doubly unforgettable by a full-scale thunderstorm in the small hours. Amidst the *son et lumière*, fireworks and fountains, the Chief Executive, Daniel Hodson, remarked that he hoped it was not all just hubris, which might attract the envy and subsequent wrath of the gods. The following month the members of LIFFE's board spent two days at a country-house hotel, Hanbury Manor, in order to determine the exchange's technology strategy. In essence the choice was whether to stick to open outcry trading on a physical floor or to throw the bulk of the exchange's resources behind electronic trading. The latter method was recognised as cheaper, being far less labour-intensive, but LIFFE had flourished so remarkably under the open outcry system that there was considerable emotional allegiance to it. The board was split down the middle, which in effect meant a policy of no change. 'Nobody could deny the City would be a duller place without the testosterone-fuelled antics of the barrow boys in stripy jackets,' the *Independent* commented. 'But Liffe's renewed commitment to the system of open outcry looks nothing more than a victory of vested interests over technological and commercial reality.'[97]

Three months later, on 22 October, the very day that Blair was jeered on the floor at Cannon Bridge, more Bund contracts were traded on the screens of Eurex (as the German financial futures exchange was now called, after its recent merger with its Swiss counterpart) than in the pits at LIFFE. The following winter, fighting against brilliantly executed (if arguably at times unscrupulous) pricing tactics and marketing incentives as well as the Frankfurt screens, the increasingly anachronistic pits at LIFFE decisively lost the all-important battle for the Bund. The atmosphere on the board became acrimonious, culminating in late March 1998 with the resignation of David Kyte, the local who had built up a major trading firm of his own. The belated decision to cut rates in order to compete with Frankfurt should, he was quoted as saying, have been made the previous December. He added, 'The fact that it wasn't is disgraceful. I'm quite happy to make decisions – I do it for a living. The big problem is that nobody on the board can, and as a result we're getting deeper and deeper into the mire.'[98] Eventually, in June 1998, both the board and the membership agreed to move to electronic trading and to demutualise; but by then the horse had bolted. Hodson, in many ways the victim of a governance structure and accompanying internecine warfare beyond his control, resigned the next month.

There seemed a very real chance that the exchange would fold, but under the leadership of Brian Williamson, who had been chairman before in happier times, it managed over the next two years both to survive and to an extent to reinvent itself, taking on technology partners in order to expand the use of its electronic trading system, Connect, to other markets. London's as well as LIFFE's future lay, Williamson insisted, not with exchanges (and all the institutional paraphernalia that accompanied them) but rather with markets. It was a crucial distinction. By late 1999 the pits themselves – once such a sweaty, larger-than-life, sometimes foul-mouthed hubbub – were almost completely deserted. A last word on the traders who had populated them went to Claire Davenport, whose firm had manufactured many of their famously colourful blazers: 'We will really miss them. They were great fun to deal with – a lot of the traders were like children.'[99]

Nothing was sacred during the second half of the 1990s. Even the discount market had, metaphorically speaking, to hand in its top hat. Early in 1997, as the Bank of England ended the privileged position of the discount houses by switching its daily open-market operations to a gilt repos system open to all-comers, Union (the former Union Discount) announced that it was winding down its positions prior to putting itself up for sale; and in December 1998 the last discount house returned its licence to the Bank.[100] Other reminders of the City's past were also heading for oblivion: Morgan Grenfell, Midland and James Capel were among the names that completely or virtually disappeared. It was a time, not only in Britain, of large-scale consolidation across the banking and financial sectors. Lloyds and TSB merged in 1996, in the process more or less dismembering Hill Samuel; during 1997–8 there were mergers or takeovers involving Abbey National and Cater Allen, Price Waterhouse and Coopers & Lybrand (creating PricewaterhouseCoopers), and General Accident and Commercial Union; and in March 1999 the Prudential paid £1.9bn for the fund-management group M&G. None of these developments made huge waves outside the City, but in September 1999 the shock news that one of Britain's smaller clearing banks, the Bank of Scotland, had launched a £21bn bid for one of the four big clearing banks, NatWest, was very much a national story. Two years earlier NatWest had pulled out of investment banking, badly bruised by a £90m derivatives fiasco, but had continued to struggle to convince analysts in the City and elsewhere that it had the requisite focus and management. The Royal Bank of Scotland also entered the bidding fray, and eventually in February 2000 it carried the day and could look forward to turning NatWest into a leaner, meaner machine. 'I think the weight of history was against us,' remarked NatWest's Chairman, Sir David Rowland.[101] The judgement, perhaps because he was not a clearing banker by profession, was spot-on. Ever since Competition and Credit Control had torn down the protective barriers and thrown it into the jungle, NatWest had, like most of the other clearers, simply got too much too wrong for too long.

Meanwhile, other British outfits continued to fall to foreign predators. Merrill Lynch bought Mercury Asset Management (MAM) in early 1998 for £3.2bn, which as many noted was a far more favourable deal for the seller than Warburgs had managed three years earlier; at about the same time Australian Mutual Provident paid £382m for another UK fund management group, Henderson (formerly Henderson Administration); and in August 1998 the last of the big British insurance brokers, Sedgwick, accepted a £1.25bn bid from Marsh & McLennan, the world's biggest insurance broker. The end of the road had also been reached for Hambros, whose banking side was sold to the French bank Société Générale in December 1997 and much of its remaining assets some five months later to Investec of South Africa. Unswayed by more than a century and a half of mainly proud history, one banking analyst could not have put it more cruelly as the cherry-picking of Hambros got under way. 'It will not be mourned. Why should it be? It is an anachronism and the people who run the bank have not developed it. They will be able to spend more time riding to hounds.'[102]

There was then a lull in 1999, before in January 2000 Schroders received a handsome £1.35bn for selling its investment banking business to Salomon Smith Barney, by now the investment banking arm of Citigroup. 'What happens in all industries that are global is that there is pressure to rationalise, merge and focus,' Sir Win Bischoff, Chairman of Schroders, explained. 'That is what we are doing, rationalising and merging the investment bank and focusing our investment management business.' There was little sense of drama as yet another British merchant bank bit the dust, and as one commentator asked, 'how long can it be before Robert Fleming, too, bows to the inevitable and sells out to the foreigners?' The answer was not long in coming. Barely two months later Robert Fleming (having the previous year turned down a £3.5bn offer from Commerzbank) fell to Chase Manhattan for some £4.5bn. 'Once Fleming goes,' the *Independent* observed as the news broke, 'that leaves only N.M. Rothschild and Cazenove flying the flag', though perhaps it should also have added Lazards. 'Given the City's key position at the heart of global capital markets, and the pre-eminence of its market professionals,' the paper added, 'this is an almost impressively feeble achievement. British firms have found themselves in a classic competitive squeeze, outgunned by the superior management skills and systems of their larger American peers.' One British banker, now working for an American bank, was rather kinder: 'It is rather unrealistic for anyone to have believed that British firms could compete with the Americans internationally when they have that huge captive capital market all sewn up between the top three.'[103]

The world indeed seemed to belong to Goldman Sachs, Morgan Stanley and Merrill Lynch. Even so, there was still plenty of business for others, and the continuing survival of Rothschilds as a significant independent force (despite a disappointing performance in asset management) had an obvious historical resonance. Sir Evelyn de Rothschild's 'crab-like caution' may have 'driven some employees to distraction', Peter

Oborne noted in the *Spectator* in April 2000, but the sorry example of Barings was alone enough to justify this obsessively careful management of risk. He had also, Oborne went on, cultivated loyalty, resisted the growth of an American-style bonus culture and successfully overseen the development of privatisation expertise as a globally attractive asset. 'Whatever the future may hold,' Oborne concluded with perhaps pardonable hyperbole, 'Evelyn de Rothschild is entitled to look his magnificent ancestors in the face.'[104]

For the City as a whole the moment that 'Wimbledonisation' really came home was in October 1997 when Barclays finally decided to abandon its expensive attempt to establish BZW as a major force in global investment banking.[105] BZW's equities and corporate finance operations were subsequently sold to CSFB for only £100m, in what was generally agreed to be a botched sale, providing the finest hour for neither Barclays' Chief Executive, Martin Taylor, nor the bank's financial advisers, Goldman Sachs. There would be many retrospective assessments of why BZW had failed to become a genuine national champion; but perhaps in the end, although there were deep-seated relationship problems between clearing and investment bankers, as well as flawed leadership by David Band between 1988 and 1996, the mundane truth was that the US 'bulge-bracket' investment banking cartel, far better placed to tap into the immensely profitable US domestic markets, did indeed represent unbeatable competition. BZW, after all, was a *reasonably* profitable operation over the years – but not, Barclays' institutional shareholders emphasised, in comparison to highly profitable UK retail banking, above all as practised by Lloyds. Such pragmatic logic cut little ice with two City commentators. 'What happened to vision and ambition?' asked Jeremy Warner, while Christopher Fildes was moved to write an obituary:

> I am sorry to announce the demise of the City of London. It is part of our history, it has been with us ever since the legendary days of King Lud and the giants Gog and Magog, but all good things come to an end. As from today, it is being relaunched as Hong Kong West.
>
> This decision has been the subject of much heart-searching, although it does no more than recognise what had been happening in and to the City for years. It became inevitable when, last week, Barclays abandoned its attempt to build a British investment bank that could compete with the world. BZW was the last aspirant and now there are none.
>
> Already, two out of every five people working in the former City are employed by companies in foreign ownership. Now these foreign owners must see their way clear. They can build up their stake to 51pc and declare their takeover bid unconditional . . .
>
> The apologists are standing by to tell us that ownership is not important. What matters is to have the business here, with all that it contributes to the British economy, and British exports, and all the places where the bankers

spend their bonuses. The money that goes home is just a residual.

Stanislas Yassukovich, who arrived with the new markets 30 years ago, is not so sure. The real threat, he says, is a lack of commitment. The new masters come and go on short postings, with barely time to buy a house in the Boltons and sell it again. They have no stake in the place and no reason to concern themselves with its cause or its values. It will be the poorer for that.

To me, the City's genius has always been to reinvent itself. So Hong Kong West is just its latest invention. It is the first, though, in which its players have conceded that they cannot keep up with the game and must live by providing a playground for others. That must limit their scope and put their future into pawn. For all the City's faults, I cannot think of Hong Kong West as an improvement on it. I shall miss it.[106]

Over the next three years the debate rumbled on, with no shortage of apologists for the economic blessings of a predominantly foreign-owned City. There was, however, an illuminating episode in March 2000 as Deutsche Bank, about to take over Dresdner Bank, apparently threatened to close down Dresdner's London investment banking arm, Dresdner Kleinwort Benson. In the end the takeover did not happen, largely because of the problem of what to do about Kleinworts, but that did not invalidate Andreas Whittam Smith's reading of the larger implications:

> The Square Mile has survived many crises in the past 300 years: the South Sea Bubble; the Napoleonic wars; the banking crises of the Victorian era; the First World War, which ended the supremacy of the pound sterling in world trade, and the severe restrictions on financial markets that lasted from 1940 until 1960. There is always a new threat on the horizon to replace the one most recently overcome.
>
> I confess, however, to a bit more unease than usual. For in effect we have given the keys of the City of London to its global competitors. They could, if they chose, on grounds of national rivalry rather than pure commercial calculation, set about dismantling it. The threat is there, even if distant and, in many people's opinions, improbable. It could be the stuff of night-mares . . .[107]

To which the obvious rebuttal was that, in the age of globalisation and economic interdependence, such crude economic nationalism was long dead, certainly on the part of sophisticated international investment bankers. It was in itself a plausible assumption. But then, there had been a similarly plausible assumption, a similarly great illusion, almost a hundred years earlier – an illusion destroyed for the next half-century and more by the guns of August 1914.

Of course, one much-touted, supra-national threat was the coming of the euro. As early as September 1996, more than two years ahead of the eventual launch, George insisted that whether Britain was in or out of a single currency, the City would thrive. 'The euro is just a bigger

Deutschmark,' he declared. 'We have seemed to do perfectly satisfactorily handling the mark, just as we have the dollar and yen. I am sure that the City will cope.' Few observers then or later believed that George himself was an enthusiast for British participation in economic and monetary union – the prospect of the Bank of England becoming a branch office of the European Central Bank was hardly likely to enchant a Threadneedle Street man – while generally in the late 1990s there developed no coherent, overall 'City view' about what British policy should be. What *did* emerge quite clearly, however, after January 1999 was that the City was, if anything, benefiting from being outside the euro zone. In November that year the outgoing Lord Mayor, Lord Levene, who some months earlier had been publicly warning against Britain staying out, conceded that so far London had 'done more than hold its own', as well as specifically asserting that Britain's membership of the euro was not the key factor in whether foreign banks and financial institutions continued to do business in London. The following month saw similar remarks from George, tempting Hamish McRae to argue that just as the City back in the 1960s had reinvented itself on an essentially offshore basis, so at the turn of the century it could do the same in relation to the distinctly onshore, heavy-of-foot euro. By April 2000 the bald fact was that the City was handling more international euro-denominated transactions than Paris and Frankfurt put together. Naturally, though, nothing stood still, and by summer 2000 if the City did have a justifiably serious concern about continuing British non-entry, then it was perhaps in relation to the probable rapid development of a genuinely integrated European capital market. Europe's 'corporate bond market is still just a quarter of the size of America's, so the potential is huge,' the *Evening Standard*'s Anthony Hilton noted in June. And he added, 'The game is going to get a lot tougher. The City may find that a two-goal lead is not enough.'[108]

Nevertheless, it was arguable that if the City genuinely did face a threat to its future, that threat came not so much from questions of ownership or currencies, as from more intangible, internal causes. This view was seldom articulated, but Yassukovich expressed it eloquently in the *Spectator* in September 1999:

> Complacency, loss of distinct corporate culture, fragmented leadership, excessive bureaucracy, poor service, lower ethical and quality standards, lack of collective motivation; all of these diseases sap the strength of the once-healthy enterprise, and even an apparently overwhelming competitive advantage collapses. In one form or another these illnesses are all evident in the City . . .

He elaborated. Electronic delivery of financial products and services was diminishing the importance of location; the decline in syndication of large transactions was turning investment banks into huge, 'transactionally self-sufficient' financial supermarkets with less and less need to share deals with close neighbours; and both these trends were contributing to 'the loss of a City style and standard of dealing', thereby diluting its 'brand image' and competitive advantage. Yassukovich was also concerned about increasingly inflexible, bureaucratic regulation; a lack of leadership from the Bank of England, suffering a loss of authority after the stripping of its supervisory function; and the way in which the spread of an unhealthy bonus culture had 'undermined corporate loyalty and diminished collective responsibility for standards'.[109] The analysis was brilliant, but ironically it was as if Yassukovich – who had played his full part in breaking up the club – was now calling for a return to club rules, or at least those that were not flagrantly uncompetitive. That this was almost certainly a vain hope was more obvious than whether, as a result, the City would ultimately perish from within.

*

In 1997 a middle-aged stockbroker remarked to me that when he came to the City in the late 1960s, people there felt rather sorry for those working in industry on large factory floors; but that now, as he and his colleagues sat behind row after row of screens on vast dealing floors, it was as if the positions had been reversed. Writing soon afterwards, Valerie Thompson (the former Salomons trader and syndicate manager, now running a consulting firm in the capital markets) attributed the 'severe deterioration' in the quality of working life in the City to 'sell-outs and mergers':

> The chance to earn even more does not motivate bosses in the same way as the risk of ending up with less. The money one plays with nowadays doesn't belong to partners with a vested interest in knowing more than their best traders. When it did they would turn up every day to supervise, inspect, guide, question, reprimand or fire, but also to praise, nurture and encourage, both back and front office staff. Investment banks are now simply a collection of employees. Their capital belongs to shareholders who can cause a riot at agms if performance is not up to scratch, and who shudder, along with the establishment, at the mere thought of another Barings-type collapse.
>
> This business now functions to please less informed shareholders, the FSA [Financial Services Authority], auditors, the politically correct, and lawyers . . .
>
> Today a trading floor is a soulless place and the life of a trader bleak at best. Many get up at the crack of dawn and endure an uncomfortable and lengthy journey to work during which any form of expression likely to cause offence is prohibited. They then spend 10-plus hours working in a blue-grey battery factory devoid of emotion, where just about anything north of breathing can lead to a lawsuit or the sack. On top of this they are required/ordered to make money while operating within limits/restrictions imposed in an attempt to prevent any sort of a loss . . . So, while not in favour, I am not surprised so many City workers are taking drugs . . .[110]

The late 1990s, in short, were not the mid-1980s, and the City was becoming a duller, blander, less flavoursome place. It was somehow apt that in summer 1998 the demise of tea auctions, a prime symbol of the traditional City, coincided almost exactly with the decision to abandon the pits at LIFFE, an equally prime symbol of the new City.

The sparkiness was also reduced by changing recruitment patterns, particularly post-Leeson. A leading trader, with some twelve years' experience, was asked in July 1996 what it took to be a foreign exchange dealer:

> When I started in money broking, the best traders were like East End barrow boys. They had gut instinct, a quick mind and a real flair for the market. The guys who succeed today need to have a first-class Oxbridge Honours degree, super dealing skills and an outstanding mathematical mind to understand highly complex markets and equipment – computers, screens, telecom lines and new information systems. Besides concentrating on all the movement in front of you, you've got to work closely with senior dealers, financial engineers, risk managers, analysts and position keepers who keep traders up to date with long and short positions . . .

Tara Ricks, of the City recruitment specialists Joslin Rowe, agreed: 'We handle a lot of foreign exchange and money market vacancies. But demand is changing. In the last three to five years, a first-class academic background has become increasingly important.' The trend dismayed Valerie Thompson, who not long afterwards argued in spirited fashion that 'the current preference for graduates over those less schooled could see the demise of an element that has contributed much to the wealth and character of the City':

> Markets and firms are governed by inconsistent ground rules, conflicting agendas, and intense power struggles, played out with cunning and deviousness. Who is better equipped to withstand such chaos and still make money, the graduate or the barrow boy who has overcome financial, emotional and academic deprivation and is more used to adversity? . . .
> I regret deeply that few firms now allow people to transfer from the back to the front office. Not allowing them to work their way up works against diversity, and financial health. The meritocracy for which the City was beginning to become renowned is now close to dead. Investment banks of tomorrow will be plagued by conformity, and populated with the mediocre, incapable of an original thought or money-making idea, to say nothing of courage.[111]

Courage . . . In a rigidly structured, morally flat, vision-free landscape, where the technicians reigned supreme (as Hans-Joerg Rudloff regretfully observed as we gazed at a sea of screens in Canary Wharf in October 1999), it was almost a shocking word.

Barrow boy or graduate, stockbroker from Surrey or foreigner on a two-year secondment to London, the prevailing culture was workaholic. 'The new City values have bred some hideously topsy-turvy thinking,' the banker-turned-novelist John McLaren reflected in November 1999:

> In March I talked to a young Englishman who works for a big American investment bank. Proudly he told me how three times his plans to go skiing had been cancelled, once when he was packing his bags, once in his Heathrow-bound taxi and once in the departure lounge itself. If this had happened to me, I'd have been homicidal, but for him it was something to boast about. He said it felt great to be needed so much. To be fair, his approach may have been key to survival in that bank. A month later one of his colleagues was called in to be fired. The executioner began: 'Michael, how many weekends have you worked this year? Need I say more?'

The long hours, the pressure to perform, the unpleasant working environment, the job insecurity – it was no wonder that many City workers found release in drink. A particular favourite by 1999 – for the young and young at heart – was Red Bull, the high-caffeine energy drink, mixed with vodka and ice. Damien McCrystal, diarist for *Sunday Business*, reported from the front line that autumn. After commending the Corney & Barrow (which had once been the Greenhouse) behind the Royal Exchange as 'one of the few pleasant places remaining', and noting that two of Walbrook's bars, Deacon's and the Slug & Lettuce, were 'characterised by booming music, neon lights and crowds spilling on to the streets' and were 'to be avoided at all costs', he pinpointed the most important change since the 1960s:

> When I first started drinking in the Square Mile, virtually all pubs were closed by 8 p.m. Now the City is a drinking destination after work. The modern bars stay open and the music blares until 11 p.m. and beyond. Streets which were once empty are crowded with traffic and pedestrians. The last train home to Essex from Liverpool Street is known as the Vomit Comet. It is not a pretty sight, though it is, in a way, reassuring to the traditionalists . . .[112]

It gave no pleasure even to traditionalists that occasionally the pressure – or perhaps the meaninglessness – got too much and the time-honoured, ultimate exit was taken. Amschel Rothschild was a gentle, insecure, attractive character who should have been an archaeologist or a farmer or something to do with the arts, but in his early thirties he bowed at last to family pressure and joined the family bank. Although not a natural, he worked hard and in 1993 became Executive Chairman of Rothschild Asset Management. The business, though, fared indifferently (certainly in comparison to rival asset-management operations like that of Schroders), and by summer 1996 he may well have felt under pressure to produce better results; he may also have been becoming increasingly anxious about the expectation that he would eventually succeed to the chairmanship of

N.M. Rothschild as a whole. On a Sunday night in July, staying at the Hotel Bristol in Paris, he hanged himself in his £500-a-night room. The cause of death was originally given as a heart attack, but the shocking truth emerged later in the week. 'I don't think he would ever have gone into the City if he hadn't been a Rothschild,' a colleague said after it had come out. Amschel was forty-one.[113]

For most in the City, certainly the young and ambitious, it was the prospect of the crock of gold that, more than anything, drove them on. Given the material rewards that were on offer, it could hardly have been otherwise. 'The million-pound City man is back,' the *Independent* reported in June 1996. 'After several years of modest earning levels – in Square Mile terms at least – hundreds of top investment bankers, analysts and dealers are again enjoying salaries and bonuses of at least £1m this year.' And it quoted a headhunter to the effect that by the end of the year there would be at least 1,000 dollar millionaires in the City, and probably many more. The following January the City's 'Superwoman', Nicola Horlick, mother of five children aged under ten, became a *cause célèbre* when she was suspended on full pay by Morgan Grenfell from her high-flying fund management job. Amidst considerable publicity it emerged that over the past year she had earned more than £1m, and in due course she published her autobiographical take on the big question, *Can You Have It All?* It was also in January 1997 that a trio of job advertisements in the *FT* caused something of a stir: one sought a head of sales of convertible bonds for a base pay package of up to £1m; the same package was on offer for a derivatives expert with a PhD to research markets for an investment fund; and the third spoke of 'unlimited' pay for a top derivatives trader. 'I do sometimes sit down and think: "Can this be right?"' one investment banking millionaire confessed at this time to the *FT* about the City windfall in general. 'My answer is that it is not wrong.'[114]

After Carol Galley, the so-called 'Ice Maiden' at Mercury Asset Management, had emerged in May 1997 as Britain's highest-paid woman with a package worth £5.5m, there was something of a pause until late 1999, when City bonuses again hit the headlines, partly on the back of the huge number of merger and acquisition deals. There were no definitive figures, but the probability was that up to 500 bankers and dealers each received £1m or more, with a handful picking up something over £3m. As the good times continued into 2000, so expectations continued to rise about what constituted a just wage. 'We are having problems with our young recruits, new graduates who traditionally work 60- or 70-hour weeks devising clever corporate deals,' a merchant banker with one of the most respected City firms confided in April to the journalist Kevin Rafferty. 'Now they won't do it unless we guarantee them packages worth £1 million over two or three years.' Rafferty himself, who had recently spent three years at the World Bank, could not refrain from offering a global perspective: 'A cool £1 million by the age of 26 or 27 – guaranteed – that's more than senior World Bank staff can dream of in a life's work. As for the peasants of Bangladesh, Bolivia, India, Ivory Coast, Zimbabwe, they'd be happy with work that would allow them enough money to afford to eat and provide a safe shelter to raise their children.'[115]

It was a point made in a more local context by Bill Kirkman of Willingham, Cambridgeshire. 'On 23 December you reported that 1,500 City bankers and brokers had each received a bonus of more than £500,000,' he wrote to the *Independent* at the end of 1996. 'The total budget of the primary school of whose governors I am chairman is less than £500,000. The school has some 340 pupils. We have got our national priorities obscenely wrong.' Certainly there was a widening discrepancy between the workers' republic in the square mile and the rest of the island. Back in 1968, according to the annual New Earnings Survey, the average gross salary for a full-time non-manual male in Britain had been £1,648 a year, whereas in the City it had been £1,966. By 1995 the respective figures were £23,052 and £40,986. In fact, in 1995 there was a brief moment when it seemed that the City might be put in the dock. Will Hutton, author of that year's best-selling treatise-cum-polemic, *The State We're In*, unambiguously identified the City as a key villain of the piece: unduly privileged because of its close links to political power; unwilling to provide British industry with the 'patient, committed, long-term finance' that it needed; and instead, as an essentially market-based set of institutions, always seeking to churn and 'restlessly searching for the highest return', whether at home or abroad. However, as with Hutton's big idea – 'stakeholding' – the moment came and went. New Labour was elected in May 1997 on an explicitly free-market, implicitly pro-City ticket, and thereafter did not betray the square mile's trust. It is true that in June 1999 the City had a day to remember, as the 'Carnival against Capitalism' turned into a six-hour riot on the part of several thousand protesters – a riot forcibly repelled by LIFFE traders, and during which David Barnett of Cazenove's deliberately wore a stiff collar in defiance of advice from police to keep a low profile – but what was significant was that the initial protest did not take place even remotely within the political mainstream.[116]

By the end of the 1990s the question of the specific culpability of the City – for the state of British industry, for the state of world poverty – seemed to be hardly on the agenda at all. Recalling that there had once been 'a long-running, ill-tempered and inconclusive debate over what was called the City-industry divide', Graham Searjeant observed in December 1999 that that debate had now been stilled. 'That is not because the issues were resolved to the satisfaction of all in some constructive, hand-shaking synthesis,' he added. 'Rather, he who pays the piper calls the tune, so the City's view prevailed; industry had to shut up and play it their way. Hated City disciplines are now management consultants' clichés, embroidered in board-room mission statements.' It was, in sum, a case of 'City cultural supremacy'.[117] Nor, he could have added, was it a supremacy solely exercised over industry: in all sorts of ways (short-term performance, shareholder value, league tables) and in all sorts of areas (education, the NHS and the BBC, to name but three), bottom-line City imperatives had been transplanted wholesale into British society. In an age of weak nation states, discredited systems of representative democracy and infinitely mobile, infinitely amoral international capital, the City had – almost by default – won the arguments and was calling the shots.

Was that all there was to look forward to in the twenty-first century? 'Money: A Valediction' was the optimistic title of the final chapter of James Buchan's 1997 inquiry into the meaning of money, *Frozen Desire*, and he ended with an inspiriting vision:

> One day, who knows, the human race might stir. My heroes and heroines wake from their sleep and rub their eyes. Honour pushes credit away with an indescribable grimace of disgust. Charity runs shrieking from the Charity Ball and virtue and solvency discuss a separation, which becomes permanent. Liberty puts down her shopping-bag and rests her bunioned feet. The owl of Minerva opens one eye, then the other, and extends her tattered wings for flight. And as these dreams dissolve, the Age of Money, which came after the Age of Faith, will itself draw, as all things under the sun, to an end.[118]

Notes

BB	Baring Brothers Archives (at ING Barings)
BoE	Bank of England Archives
Cairncross	Diary of Sir Alec Cairncross (at University of Glasgow Archives)
CL	Cathy Courtney and Paul Thompson, *City Lives* (1996)
DBB	David J. Jeremy (ed), *Dictionary of Business Biography* (1984–6)
FRBNY	Federal Reserve Bank of New York Archives
FT	*Financial Times*
HSBC	HSBC Group Archives
IHA	Records of Issuing Houses Association (Guildhall Library)
JS	Centre for Metropolitan History, 'The Jobbing System of the London Stock Exchange: An Oral History' (Collection held at British Library National Sound Archive)
Lloyds	Lloyds TSB Group Archives
Macmillan	Diary of Harold Macmillan (Bodleian Library, Oxford)
NLSC	National Life Story Collection (at British Library National Sound Archive)
PRO	Public Record Office
RBS	The Royal Bank of Scotland Group Archives
SE	Records of London Stock Exchange (at Guildhall Library up to 1954)

All references are published in London unless otherwise stated.

CHAPTER ONE

1. Rose Macaulay, *The World My Wilderness* (1950), pp 67, 71–2, 56.

2. Jehanne Wake, *Kleinwort Benson* (Oxford, 1997), pp 320–1; Richard Roberts, *Schroders* (1992), p 313; *Exco International News*, Nov 1990; London Trust Co records at University College London Archives, E 4/2.

3. The best guide is Ranald C. Michie, *The City of London* (Basingstoke, 1992), pp 18–19, 35–8, 44–8.

4. Michie, *City*, pp 18, 35–6.

5. P.J. Cain and A.G. Hopkins, *British Imperialism: Crisis and Deconstruction, 1914–1990* (Harlow, 1993), pp 265–81.

6. Denzil Sebag-Montefiore, *The Story of Joseph Sebag and Co* (1996), p 23.

7. The two fullest biographical treatments of Warburg are: Jacques Attali, *A Man of Influence* (1986); Ron Chernow, *The Warburgs* (1993).

8. *Institutional Investor*, March 1980, pp 50–2, 55, 193.

9. Attali, pp 168, 190.

10. *DBB*, Gordon A. Fletcher and Peter J. Lee, 'Arthur William Trinder', vol 5, pp 552–7; George and Pamela Cleaver, *The Union Discount* (1985), pp 83–90.

CHAPTER TWO

1. BB, 200861, 2 Nov 1945; Piercy Papers (LSE), 9/162, 24 Nov 1945; RBS, 7517, 31 Dec 1945; HSBC 28.491, 11 Feb 1946; James Lees-Milne, *Caves of Ice* (1984, pbk), p 92.

2. JS, no 10, p 2; Nicholas Davenport, *Memoirs of a City Radical* (1974), p 185; B.H.D. MacDermot, *Panmure Gordon & Co* (1976), p 58.

3. Jim Tomlinson, 'Attlee's inheritance and the financial system' in *Financial History Review* (1994), pp 154–5; Hugh Dalton, *High Tide and After* (1962), p 53; Davenport, pp 72, 149.

4. See Jim Tomlinson, 'The Attlee Government and the Balance of Payments, 1945–51' in *Twentieth Century British History* (1991), pp 59–60.

5. John Fforde, *The Bank of England and Public Policy, 1941–1958* (Cambridge, 1992), pp 73–87; L.S. Pressnell, *External Economic Policy Since the War, Volume I* (1986), pp 262–341; D.E. Moggridge, *Maynard Keynes* (1992), pp 796–820. *Fighting for Britain*, the final volume of Robert Skidelsky's biography of Keynes, appeared after I had completed my draft.

6. Moggridge, p 806; Pressnell, p 315.

7. Moggridge, p 811; *FT*, 14 Dec 1945; Moggridge, p 821; John Barnes and David Nicholson (eds), *The Empire at Bay* (1988), pp 1052–3.

8. Accounts of the Bank's nationalisation include: Fforde, pp 4–30; Elizabeth Hennessy, *A Domestic History of the Bank of England, 1930–1960* (Cambridge, 1992), pp 207–12; Ben Pimlott, *Hugh Dalton* (1985), pp 457–61; Susan Howson, *British Monetary Policy, 1945–51* (Oxford, 1993), pp 110–17.

9. BoE, G 15/7, 1 Aug 1945; Fforde, p 6; Ben Pimlott (ed), *The Political Diary of Hugh Dalton* (1986), p 362.

10. Philip Geddes, *Inside the Bank of England* (1987), p 37; BoE, G 18/2, 27 Feb 1946.

11. Marguerite Dupree (ed), *Lancashire and Whitehall* (Manchester, 1987), vol 2, p 378; *FT*, 11 Oct 1945; Fforde, p 30.

12. BoE, G 15/19; *Thomas Sivewright Catto, Baron Catto of Cairncatto: A Personal Memoir and a Biographical Note* (Edinburgh, 1961), p 92.

13. BB, 200884, 5 Jan 1947; *Banker*, June 1947, p 139; BoE, ADM 14/4, 12 Nov 1948.

14. Fforde, p 778.

15. Tomlinson, 'Attlee's inheritance', p 145.

16. In general on the early years of ICFC, see: John Kinross, *Fifty Years in the City* (1982), pp 125–31; Richard Coopey and Donald Clarke, *3i* (Oxford, 1995), pp 45–8, 54–5.

17. BoE, G 3/173, 5 July 1945.

18. BoE, G 3/173, 28 Nov 1944; IHA, Ms 29, 328, vol 1; BB, 200841.

19. SE, Mss 14, 600A, vol 1, 4–25 March 1946, vol 2, 17 March 1947, 24 March 1947.

20. SE, Ms 14,600A, vol 1, 27 May–22 July 1946.

21. W.T.C. King, *The Stock Exchange* (1947); *Banker*, July 1947, p 33.

22. On Dalton and cheap money, see: Dalton, pp 124–5, 160–7, 178–84, 230–1; Pimlott, pp 461–5; Fforde, pp 330–57; G.A. Fletcher, *The Discount Houses in London* (1976), pp 65–7; Howson, pp 121–52, 166–76, 193–9; Alec Cairncross, *Years of Recovery* (1985), pp 427–40.

23. Pimlott, p. 462; BB, 200861, 15 May 1946.

24. Dalton, pp 162–6.

25. *Economist*, 19 Oct 1946; David Kynaston, *The Financial Times* (1988), p 177; *Banker*, Nov 1946, pp 67–71.

26. Judy Slinn, *Clifford Chance* (Cambridge, 1993), p 135; Laurie Dennett, *Slaughter and*

May (Cambridge, 1989), p 215; BB, 200884, 13 Feb 1947, 5 March 1947; *Banker*, June 1957, p 380.

27. *Journal of the Institute of Bankers*, Jan 1947, pp 9–19; *Banker*, Feb 1947, pp 79–80; HSBC, 192.088, 1 May 1947.

28. *Banker*, April 1947, pp 1–2; Kynaston, *Financial Times*, p 177; Lees-Milne, p 189; Dalton, p 184; Fforde, p 359.

29. BB, Dep 22.XXIII, pp 21–6 give Sir Edward Reid's account.

30. RBS, 07465, 3 June 1946; *FT*, 9 May 1947, 27 Feb 1946; BoE, G 3/99, 26 June 1947; Adrienne Gleeson, *London Enriched* (1997), pp 35–41.

31. David Kynaston, *Cazenove & Co* (1991), pp 185–6; BoE, G 3/99, 23 April 1947; BB, 200853; Kynaston, *Cazenove*, pp 186–7.

32. Accounts of the convertibility crisis include: Fforde, pp 141–64; Pimlott, pp 480–94; P.L. Cottrell, 'The Bank of England in its International Setting, 1918–1972' in Richard Roberts and David Kynaston (eds), *The Bank of England* (Oxford, 1995), pp 115–21.

33. *FT*, 15 July 1947; Fforde, p 157; Kynaston, *Financial Times*, p 179; BB, 200884, 20 Aug 1947.

34. Ron Chernow, *The House of Morgan* (New York, 1990), p 473.

35. *Banker*, Sept 1947, pp 131–3; *The Private Diaries of Sydney Moseley* (1960), p. 457; SE, Mss 14,600A, vol 3, 27 Oct 1947–vol 4, 8 Dec 1947.

36. Pimlott, p 521; BB, 200884, 30 Nov 1947.

37. *Banker*, Feb 1948, pp 125, 76–7; BoE, G 3/2, 28 June 1950, G 3/3, 7 July 1950, 11 July 1950, G 3/107, 1 April 1952; Piercy Papers (LSE), 9/162, 17 Nov 1945.

38. Kynaston, *Financial Times*, p 180; Pimlott, pp 547, 570, 572; BB 200884, 30 Dec 1948; HSBC, 28.493, 12 May 1948.

39. John Kinross and Alan Butt-Philip, *ICFC, 1945–1961* (1985), pp 145–8; Coopey and Clarke, pp 59–60.

40. IHA, Ms, 29,328, vol 1, 5 Nov 1948, 9 Dec 1948, 3 Feb 1949; PRO, T 233/872, 21 Jan 1949; IHA, Ms 29,328, vol 1, 2 June 1949.

41. On credit policy in 1948–9, see: Fforde, pp 359–70; Howson, pp 223–38; Alec Cairncross, 'Prelude to Radcliffe' in *Rivista Di Storia Economica* (1987), pp 2–8.

42. Alec Cairncross (ed), *The Robert Hall Diaries, 1947–53* (1989), pp 38, 41; Howson, p 231.

43. BoE, G 3/100, 8 Dec 1948; Fforde, pp 367–8.

44. *Hall*, p 84.

45. Dalton, pp 287–8; Kinross and Butt-Philip, p 95; Keith Middlemas, *Power, Competition and the State: Volume 1* (Basingstoke, 1986), p 142; Fforde, pp 366–7; Howson, p 236.

46. *Hall*, p 66.

47. Biographical sketches of Cobbold include: Fforde, p 38; *DBB*, R.P.T. Davenport-Hines, 'Cameron Fromanteel Cobbold, 1st Lord Cobbold', vol 1, pp 707–10; Jasper Hollom, 'Lord Cobbold', *Independent*, 9 Nov 1987; *Dictionary of National Biography, 1986–1990* (Oxford, 1996), pp 79–80.

48. BoE, C 160/178.

49. Howson, pp 236–7; Fforde, pp 231–2; BoE, G 3/1, 2 May 1949.

50. BoE, G 3/100, 8–10 Dec 1948, G 1/514, 14 Feb 1953, Pimlott, p 557; *Banker*, April 1949, p xxi.

51. Leslie O'Brien, *A Life Worth Living* (1995), pp 204–6.

52. SE, Ms 14,600A, vol 5, 7 Feb 1949; JS, no 39, pp 1–2; SE, Ms 14,600A, vol 5, 21 March 1949; Ranald C. Michie, *The London Stock Exchange* (Oxford, 1999), pp 352–62; BoE, G 3/14, 18 March 1949.

53. *Banker*, March 1949, pp 161ff, April 1949, pp 29–33; *Fraser's Magazine*, Oct 1876.

54. SE, Ms 14,600A, vol 6, 4 April 1949, 11 April 1949; *DBB*, W.J. Reader, 'Sir John Bevan Braithwaite', vol 1, pp 430–2; Michie, *London Stock Exchange*, p 355. In general on

Ansbachers, see Anon (Richard Roberts), *Henry Ansbacher* (1994).

55. Kynaston, *Cazenove*, pp 195–6.

56. S.J. Diaper, 'The History of Kleinwort, Sons & Co in Merchant Banking, 1855–1961' (Nottingham PhD, 1983), p 279; Kynaston, *Cazenove*, pp 201–2; BoE, G 3/102, 2 Aug 1949, 1 Sept 1949.

57. Devaluation accounts and analyses include: Fforde, pp 276–304; Howson, pp 238–59; Cairncross, *Years of Recovery*, pp 176–90; Cottrell, 'The Bank of England', pp 121–4; *Contemporary Record* (Winter 1991), pp 483–506.

58. BoE, G 1/70, 21 June 1949, 23 June 1949.

59. BoE, G 1/70, 5 July 1949.

60. BoE, G 1/70, 3 Aug 1949; Cairncross, *Years of Recovery*, pp 176, 189; *Hall*, p 64.

61. BB, 200970, 12 Sept 1949; Fforde, p 300.

62. Kynaston, *Financial Times*, p 189; John Littlewood, *The Stock Market* (1998), p 38.

63. *Moseley*, p 473; *Banker*, Oct 1949, p 7, Nov 1949, p 69; *Political Diary*, p 460; Howson, p 254.

64. *Political Diary*, p 464; *City Press*, 13 Jan 1950.

65. SE, Ms 14,600A, vol 7, 19 Dec 1949; BoE, G 3/1, 19 Dec 1949, G 3/103, 6 Jan 1950, 11 Jan 1950; SE, Ms 14,600A, vol 7, 16 Jan 1950; *Banker*, April 1950, p 18.

66. Kynaston, *Financial Times*, p 229; Ron Chernow, *The Warburgs* (1993), p 609; BB, 200970, 17 March 1950; BoE, G 3/2, 10 March 1950.

67. SE, Ms 14,600A, vol 7, 13 Feb 1950, 20 Feb 1950, 27 Feb 1950.

68. *DBB*, 'Braithwaite', p 431; SE, Mss 14,600A, vol 8, 30 Oct 1950, vol 9, 21 May 1951, 2 July 1951, 27 Aug 1951.

69. SE, Ms 14,600A, vol 8, 8 Aug 1950. See also *The Times*, 24 Oct 1986.

70. Lloyds, S/1/5/b/9–10; BoE, G 3/106, 30 Oct 1951.

71. Kinross, *Fifty Years*, pp 114–15; SE, Ms 14,600, vol 142, 18 Dec 1944; BoE, G 3/173, 3 Aug 1945, 14 Aug 1945, G 3/1, 11 April 1949, 20 June 1949, 23 June 1949, 26 July 1949.

72. *City Press*, 8 Sept 1950, 3 Nov 1950, 6 Nov 1950, 18 Sept 1975; Edward du Cann, *Two Lives* (Upton-upon-Severn, 1995), p 45; *City Press*, 3 Nov 1950.

73. BoE, G 3/4, 5 Jan 1951; RBS, 07986, 11 Jan 1951.

74. Kinross and Butt-Philip, p 224; BoE, G 3/105, 9 March 1951; Kinross and Butt-Philip, pp 224–5.

75. For an analysis of why the clearing banks so mistrusted ICFC, see Coopey and Clarke, pp 73–4.

76. Fforde, pp 170–219, tells the story.

77. Fforde, pp 213, 181; *Institutional Investor*, March 1980, p 210.

78. Kynaston, *Financial Times*, p 230; Fforde, pp 304–12.

79. On monetary policy during the final year of the Labour government, see: Fforde, pp 380–94; Howson, pp 288–98.

80. BoE, G 1/71, 2 Jan 1951, 17 Jan 1951, 19 Jan 1951; Philip M. Williams (ed), *The Diary of Hugh Gaitskell, 1945–1956* (1983), p 227.

81. BoE, G 1/71, 29 May 1951; *Hall*, p 158; BoE, G 1/71, 3 July 1951.

82. BoE, G 1/71, 5 July 1951; Fforde, p 370.

83. Kynaston, *Financial Times*, pp 226–8; *DBB*, 'Braithwaite', p 431; Lionel Fraser, *All to the Good* (1963), pp 199–200.

84. Read, Hurst-Brown & Co., *Monthly Letter*, 4 Oct 1951; SE, Ms 14,600A, vol 9, 22 Oct 1951; BoE, G 1/71, 22 Oct 1951; Kynaston, *Financial Times*, p 211.

CHAPTER THREE

1. BoE, G 1/71, Nov. 1951 (Maguire), 22 Oct 1951.

2. On the Conservative reassertion of monetary policy, see: John Fforde, *The Bank of England and Public Policy, 1941–1958* (Cambridge, 1992), pp 398–412, 444–8; Susan Howson, *British Monetary Policy, 1945–51* (Oxford, 1993), pp 310–16, 318–21.

3. Lord Butler, *The Art of the Possible* (1971), p 160; BoE, G 3/107, 12 March 1952; *DBB*, Gordon A. Fletcher, 'Lawrence Henry Seccombe', vol 5, pp 104–5; BB, 201015, 14 May 1952.

4. Accounts of 'Robot' include: Howson, pp 316–18; Butler, pp 160–2; Fforde, pp 417–44, 448–73; Keith Middlemas, *Power, Competition and the State: Volume 1* (Basingstoke, 1986), pp 192–204; Stephen J. Procter, 'Floating Convertibility: The Emergence of the Robot Plan, 1951–52' in *Contemporary Record* (Summer 1993).

5. PRO, T 236/3240, 16 Feb 1952.

6. BoE, C 160/24, 20 Feb 1952; Donald MacDougall, *Don and Mandarin* (1987), p 88; PRO, T 236/3240, 25 Feb 1952; BoE, G 1/122, 18 March 1952 ('Note for Record'); Butler, p 162; BoE, G 15/19, C 160/24, 29 Feb 1952.

7. PRO, T 236/3242, 18 March 1952, 27 March 1952.

8. PRO, T 236/3243, 6 May 1952; Alec Cairncross (ed), *The Robert Hall Diaries, 1947–53* (1989), p 233.

9. MacDougall, pp 102–3.

10. Butler, pp 160–1; *FT*, 5 March 1992; *TLS*, 5 May 1995, p 14.

11. Ranald C. Michie, *The City of London* (Basingstoke, 1992), p 26.

12. For a helpful long-run perspective on the City in the 1950s, see Richard Roberts, 'The City of London as a financial centre in the era of the depression, the Second World War and post-war official controls' in Richard Roberts (ed), *Global Financial Centres* (Aldershot, 1994), pp 13–25.

13. Michie, *City*, pp 35–8, 54–5, 94, 164–9.

14. Lionel Fraser, *All to the Good* (1963), p. 200; David Kynaston, *Cazenove & Co*, (1991), p 205; BoE, G 3/114, 8 Dec 1955.

15. BoE, G 3/107, 2 Jan 1952, G 3/5, 19 June 1952; Richard Roberts, *Schroders* (1992), p 337.

16. Jacques Attali, *A Man of Influence* (1986), p 201; Ron Chernow, *The House of Morgan* (New York, 1990), p 515.

17. For overviews of the clearing banks and their policies in the 1950s, see: Duncan M. Ross, 'British Monetary Policy and the Banking System in the 1950s' in *Business and Economic History* (1992); Francesca Carnevali and Leslie Hannah, 'The Effects of Banking Cartels and Credit Rationing on U.K. Industrial Structure and Economic Performance since World War Two' in Michael D. Bordo and Richard Sylla, *Anglo-American Financial Systems* (Burr Ridge, Ill, 1995).

18. Anthony Sampson, *The Money Lenders* (1981), p 121; Alex Danchev, *Oliver Franks* (Oxford, 1993), p 154.

19. See A.R. Holmes and Edwin Green, *Midland* (1986), pp 213–21.

20. J.R. Winton, *Lloyds Bank, 1918–1969* (Oxford, 1982), pp 147–8.

21. BoE, G 1/71, 15 Nov 1951.

22. R.S. Sayers, *Gilletts in the London Money Market* (Oxford, 1968), pp 154–5; W.M. Scammell, *The London Discount Market* (1968), p 222.

23. NLSC, C 409/057 (Barkshire), pp 52–6.

24. NLSC, C 409/057, p 70.

25. G.A. Fletcher, *The Discount Houses in London* (1976), pp 170, 172; Richard Spiegelberg, *The City* (1973), pp 163–4.

26. For an overview of the Bank and the City during the 1950s, see Fforde, pp 749–60.

27. George and Pamela Cleaver, *The Union Discount* (1985), pp 85–6; BoE, G 3/110, 15 Sept 1953; *Daily Telegraph*, 18 Dec 1995.

28. BoE, G 3/113, 27 Jan 1955, G 3/116, 4 July 1956.

29. BoE, G 1/71, 21 Nov 1951, G 3/107, 27 June 1952, 30 June 1952; Elizabeth Hennessy, *A Domestic History of the Bank of England, 1930–1960* (Cambridge, 1992), pp 118–21; HSBC, Oral History Collection, S.W.P. Perry-Aldworth, p 63.

30. A.W. Tuke and R.J.H. Gillman, *Barclays Bank Limited, 1926–1969* (1972), p 114.

CHAPTER FOUR

1. Richard Roberts, *Schroders* (1992), p 335; RBS, 07553, 12 Sept 1952.

2. For the Standstill story, see: Roberts, *Schroders*, pp 320–3; Jehanne Wake, *Kleinwort Benson* (Oxford, 1997), pp 331–4.

3. BoE, G 3/103, 4 Jan 1950, G 3/9, 21 Feb 1956.

4. *Banker*, May 1952, pp 243–51; BoE, G 3/6, 30 July 1953.

5. Elizabeth Hennessy, *A Domestic History of the Bank of England, 1930–1960* (Cambridge, 1992), p 233; David Wainwright, *Government Broker* (1990), p 83.

6. John Fforde, *The Bank of England and Public Policy, 1941–1958* (Cambridge, 1992), pp 611–12, is helpful.

7. BoE, G 3/111, 25 Feb 1954; BB, 201054, 10 Dec 1953.

8 The authoritative account of this episode is Kathleen Burk, *The First Privatisation* (1988). See also: Fforde, pp 733–43; David Kynaston, *Cazenove & Co* (1991), pp 209–11.

9. BoE, G 3/4, 1 Nov 1951; Fforde, p 738.

10. Burk, *First Privatisation*, p 95.

11. Burk, *First Privatisation*, pp 130–1, 135.

12. BoE, G 3/6, 20 Nov 1953, G 3/7, 25 Feb 1954, G 3/111, 13 April 1954.

13. A helpful account is Richard Roberts, 'Regulatory Responses to the Rise of the Market for Corporate Control in Britain in the 1950s' in *Business History* (January 1992).

14. Charles Gordon, *The Two Tycoons* (1984), p 42; David Clutterbuck and Marion Devine, *Clore* (1987), p 69.

15. *FT*, 17 Feb 1953; Roberts, 'Regulatory Responses', p 187.

16. BoE, G 3/6, 24 April 1953, 23 June 1953, 21 Oct 1953.

17. PRO, PREM 11/656, 13 Nov 1953; BoE, G 3/110, 13 Nov 1953. The fullest account of the battle for the Savoy is still George Bull and Anthony Vice, *Bid for Power* (1958), pp 29–46.

18. BoE, G 3/110, 18 Dec 1953, 21 Dec 1953, G 3/111, 13 Jan 1954.

19. *Banker*, Jan 1954, p 18; BoE, G 1/72, 2 Dec 1953.

20. BoE, G 3/112, 1 Oct 1954, 7 Oct 1954, 2 Nov 1954.

21. RBS, 07986, 6 Jan 1954; John Kinross, *Fifty Years in the City* (1982), pp 153, 180.

22. BoE, G 3/113, 9 May 1955; *Banker*, June 1955, p 341.

23. PRO, PREM 11/655, 15 March 1954, fos 5–6. On the general question of sterling, the gold market and London as an international financial centre, see P.L. Cottrell, 'The Bank of England in its International Setting, 1918–1972' in Richard Roberts and David Kynaston (eds), *The Bank of England* (Oxford, 1995), pp 124–7.

24. BoE, G 3/111, 2 March 1954; Hennessy, p 248.

25. Cottrell, p 127.

26. *Banker*, May 1954, p 241; BoE, G 3/7, 28 Sept 1954, 12 Nov 1954; *FT*, 1 Jan 1955.

27. Accounts of the monetary policy dramas of 1955 include: Fforde, pp 630–53; Alec Cairncross, 'Prelude to Radcliffe' in *Rivista Di Storia Economica* (1987), pp 14–18.

28. Fforde, pp 631–2; PRO, T 230/384, 9 March 1955; BoE, G 3/8, 1 April 1955, 7 April 1955.

29. Cairncross, 'Prelude', p 14; BoE, G 1/73, 18–19 April 1955; Alec Cairncross (ed), *The Robert Hall Diaries, 1954–61* (1991), p 33.

30. *FT*, 21–2 April 1955; BoE, LDMA 1/9. 29 April 1955; Read, Hurst-Brown & Co, *Monthly Letter*, 12 May 1955.

31. *Hall*, pp 42–3.

32. PRO, T 230/384, 28 July 1955, 2 Aug 1955; BoE, G 1/73, 3 Aug 1955; PRO T 230/384, 9 Aug 1955.

33. Kinross, *Fifty Years*, p 152; BoE, G 3/114, 1 Nov 1955; RBS, 07986, 1 Nov 1955; BoE, G 1/73, 4 Nov 1955.

34. BoE, G 3/8, 4 Nov 1955, 10 Nov 1955.

35. BoE, G 1/73 (back of file); Macmillan, dep d. 26, 21 July 1956, fo 123.

36. BoE, G 3/115, 6 Jan 1956; Macmillan, dep d. 25, 12 Jan 1956, fos 11–12; *Hall*, pp 59–60.

37. *Banker*, Feb 1956, pp 71–4.

38. *Hall*, p 62; BoE, G 14/152, 16 Feb 1956, G 1/74, 17 Feb 1956.

39. Macmillan, dep d. 25, 24 Feb 1956, fo 69; Philip M. Williams (ed), *The Diary of Hugh Gaitskell, 1945–1956* (1983), p 460.

40. BoE, G 1/74, 23 March 1956, 26 March 1956; *Hall*, p 65.

41. Macmillan, dep d. 26, 4 May 1956, fo 24, 4 July 1956, fos 94–5, dep d. 27, 24 July 1956, fo 4; BoE, G 3/9, 23 July 1956.

42. Generally on the Bank of England and the Suez Crisis, see: Fforde, pp 549–64.

43. *FT*, 28 July 1956; Macmillan, dep d. 27, 3 Aug 1956, fos 21–2; JS, no 7, p 6; *FT*, 1 Nov 1956; BoE, LDMA 1/10, 2 Nov 1956.

44. *FT*, 15 Dec 1956; BoE, G 1/74, 20 Dec 1956.

45. PRO, T 171/478, 28 Dec 1956, 31 Dec 1956.

46. Richard Fry (ed), *A Banker's World* (1970), p 28.

CHAPTER FIVE

1. Alec Cairncross (ed), *The Robert Hall Diaries, 1954–61* (1991), p 94; BoE, G 3/5, 19 June 1952, 5 May 1955.

2. BoE, G 3/115. 25 June 1956, G 3/116, 23 Nov 1956; Richard Roberts, *Schroders* (1992), p 349.

3. BoE, G 3/8, 12 Aug 1955, G 3/116, 16 Oct 1956, G 3/9, 7 Nov 1956.

4. BoE, G 3/113, 4 Jan 1955, G 3/9, 28 Dec 1956.

5. Ron Chernow, *The Warburgs* (1993), p 646; Jacques Attali, *A Man of Influence* (1986), p 202; Jehanne Wake, *Kleinwort Benson* (Oxford, 1997), pp 365–6.

6. Chernow, p 647; SE, Council, 6 May 1957, 9 Aug 1957, 12 Aug 1957, Committee on Gilt Edged Dealings (Sub-Committees of a Non-Permanent Character, vol 21), 25 April–24 May 1957; BoE, G 3/117, 2 May 1957.

7. BoE, G 3/10, 31 Jan 1957. The setting up of Radcliffe is explored by E.H.H. Green, 'The Influence of the City over British Economic Policy, *c.* 1880–1960' in Youssef Cassis (ed), *Finance and Financiers in European History* (Cambridge, 1992), pp 205–7.

8. BoE, G 3/75, 13 May 1957; PRO, T 233/1407, 17 May 1957; *Hall*, p 116.

9. Committee on the Working of the Monetary System, *Minutes of Evidence* (1960), qq 753, 762.

10. *Hall*, p 121.

11. HSBC, 192.153, 30 July 1957.

12. BoE, G 1/75, 22 Aug 1957; Macmillan, dep d. 29, 24 Aug 1957, fo 129.

13. Accounts of the September 1957 Bank rate rise and the ensuing 'leak' saga include: 'The Bank Rate Tribunal Evidence: A Symposium' in *Manchester School* (Jan 1959), pp 1–51; Paul Ferris, *The City* (1960), pp 115–57; Harold Macmillan, *Riding the Storm* (1971), pp 415–30; Richard A. Chapman, *Decision Making* (1968) and 'Decision Making Revisited' in *Public Administration* (1990); John Fforde, *The Bank of England and Public Policy, 1941–1958* (Cambridge, 1992), pp 669–93, 700–3.

14. BoE, G 14/152, 3 Sept 1957, 5 Sept 1957.

15. *Hall*, pp 126–7; BoE, G 1/75, 5 Sept 1957, 9 Sept 1957.

16. BoE, G 1/75, 10–11 Sept 1957; *Hall*, p 127.

17. BoE, G 1/75, 15–16 Sept 1957.

18. BoE, G 14/152, 13–14 Sept 1957.

19. BoE, G 1/75, 17 Sept 1957; Macmillan, dep d. 29, 17 Sept 1957, fos 153–4. The deflationary implications are explored in Scott Newton and Dilwyn Porter, *Modernization Frustrated* (1988), pp 129–31.

20. SE, Council, 14 Oct 1957; JS, no 4, p 18, no 20, p 18; Macmillan, dep d. 30, 20 Sept 1957, fo 2.

21. David Kynaston, *The Financial Times* (1988), p 264; BB, 210086, 1 Oct 1957; BoE, G 14/152, 25 Oct 1957.

22. Fforde, p 688; PRO, T 233/1429, 24 Sept 1957; BoE, G 3/118, 25 Sept 1957; PRO, T 233/1429, 18–19 Oct 1957, BoE, G 3/10, 18 Oct 1957.

23. BoE, G 3/77, 18 Nov 1957, G 3/10, 19 Nov 1957; *Hall*, p 134.

24. *Proceedings of the Tribunal appointed to Inquire into allegations that information about the raising of Bank Rate was improperly discussed* (1958), pp 2 (Whitmore), 4 (Wedd & Owen), 54 (Keswick letter/cable), qq 4205–10, 4311, 4485–90 (Keswick), 7289–93, 7459 (Kindersley).

25. *Hall*, pp 134–5; BoE, C 160/29, 16 Dec 1957; *Tribunal*, qq 8948–9, 8970, 8995.

26. *Hall*, p 140; BoE, C 160/149, 20 Dec 1957; John Littlewood, *The Stock Market* (1998), p 98.

27. BoE, G 1/75, 27 Dec 1957.

28. BoE, G 3/78, 6 Jan 1958; Kynaston, *Financial Times*, pp 264–5.

29. A particularly stimulating discussion is Bill Schwarz, 'Conservatives and Corporatism' in *New Left Review* (Nov/Dec 1987), pp 115–20.

30. *FT*, 3 Jan 1989.

31. PRO, T 233/1202, 10 Jan 1958; *Report of the Tribunal appointed to Inquire into Allegations of Improper Disclosure of Information relating to the Raising of the Bank Rate* (1958), paras 115–16.

32. BoE, G 3/119, 22 Jan 1958; Judy Slinn, *Linklaters & Paines* (1987), pp 191–2; *Guardian*, 22 Feb 1990.

33. *Hansard*, 3 Feb 1958, cols 829 (Butler), 859–61 (Wilson), 925 (Grimond), 4 Feb 1958, cols 995 (Walker), 1087 (Lever/Lee).

34. Janet Morgan (ed), *The Backbench Diaries of Richard Crossman, 1951–64* (1981), pp 662–3; *Hall*, p 146; Tom Lupton and C. Shirley Wilson, 'The Social Background and Connections of "Top Decision Makers"' in *Manchester School* (Jan 1959), pp 30–51.

35. BoE, G 14/156, 17 Feb 1958, G 3/119, 27 March 1958, 7 May 1958; Fforde, pp 700–3.

36. Monetary System, *Minutes of Evidence*, qq 3461 (Trinder), 3815, 3825 (Robarts).

37. BoE, ADM 12/8, 22 Aug 1958, G 3/120, 3 Oct 1958; Monetary System, *Minutes of Evidence*, qq 10716, 10729; Cairncross, DC 106/10/2, 7 Oct 1958.

38. Monetary System, *Minutes of Evidence*, qq 12324 (Gaitskell), 12381 (Butler); Cairncross, DC 106/10/2, 18 Dec 1958.

39. The fullest scholarly account (including bringing out developments during the two years before 1957) is Catherine R. Schenk, 'The Origins of the Eurodollar Market in London: 1955–1963' in *Explorations in Economic History* (1998). See also Gary Burn, 'The State, the City and the Euromarkets' in *Review of International Political Economy* (Summer 1999), pp 229–35.

40. Richard Fry (ed), *A Banker's World* (1970), p 28; Paul Einzig, *The Euro-Dollar System* (1964), p 35; *Euromoney*, June 1984, p 64.

41. George G. Blakey, *The Post-War History of the London Stock Market* (Didcot, 1994 pbk edn), pp 41–2; David Kynaston, *Cazenove & Co* (1991), p 222.

42. An excellent account of the phenomenon is John Littlewood, *The Stock Market* (1998), pp 120–8.

43. W.J. Reader and David Kynaston, *Phillips & Drew* (1998), pp 62–3; Edward du Cann, *Two Lives* (Upton-upon-Severn, 1995), pp 60–5.

44. HSBC, 192.152, 1957/8.

45. SE, Ms 14,600A, vol 11, 11 May 1953; BoE, G 3/119, 12 May 1958, 23 May 1958; SE, Council, 13 Oct 1958.

46. Fforde, pp 670–1, 689–91; A.R. Holmes and Edwin Green, *Midland* (1986), p 226.

47. BoE, G 1/76, 27 June 1958.

48. BoE, G 3/11, 24 April 1958; Richard Spiegelberg, *The City* (1973), p 107; *FT*, 23 July 1958; Spiegelberg, p 106.

49. Holmes and Green, pp 222–30, cover his arrival and impact.

50. BoE, G 3/118, 4 Dec 1957.

51. Holmes and Green, pp 224–5; BoE, G 1/77, 16–17 Oct 1958, G 3/120, 24 Oct 1958.

52. Roberts, *Schroders*, p 343; Kynaston, *Cazenove*, pp 230–1.

53. BoE, G 3/119, 12 Feb 1958, 26 March 1958, G 3/11, 15 July 1958; John Kinross, *Fifty Years in the City* (1982), pp 154–5.

54. Fforde, pp 595–605.

55. Andrew Shonfield, *British Economic Policy Since the War* (1958), pp 153–9; BoE, G 3/119, 9 May 1958.

56. Max Karo, *City Milestones and Memories* (1962), pp 133–5; George and Pamela Cleaver, *The Union Discount* (1985), p 90, *DBB*, Gordon A. Fletcher and Peter J. Lee, 'Arthur William Trinder', vol 5, p 556.

57. IHA, Ms 29,328, vol 2, 13 March 1951, 15 March 1951, 12 June 1952, 15 Sept 1954, 14 Oct 1954, 16 Dec 1954; *The Times*, 16 Sept 1958, 24 Sept 1958, 16 Oct 1958, 21 Oct 1958, 28 Oct 1958.

CHAPTER SIX

1. BoE, G 3/118, 2 Oct 1957, G 3/11, 26 March 1958, ADM 13/2, 9 May 1958.

2. Accounts of the Aluminium War include: 'How Reynolds Brought Off Its British Coup' in *Fortune*, June 1959, pp 112–15, 230, 235–40; Paul Ferris, *The City* (1960), pp 87–90; Lionel Fraser, *All to the Good* (1963), pp 236–41; William Davis, *Merger Mania* (1970), pp 32–7; Jacques Attali, *A Man of Influence* (1986), pp 210–16; George David Smith, *From Monopoly to Competition* (Cambridge, 1988), pp 322–6; Richard Roberts, 'Regulatory Responses to the Rise of the Market for Corporate Control in Britain in the 1950s' in *Business History* (Jan 1992), pp 192–3; John Fforde, *The Bank of England and Public Policy, 1941–1958* (Cambridge, 1992), pp 743–9; Ron Chernow, *The Warburgs* (1993), pp 647–53.

3. *DBB*, Leonard Sainer, 'Sir Charles Clore', vol 1, p 699.

4. BoE, G 1/179, 26 Nov 1958.

5. Macmillan, dep d. 33, 2 Dec 1958, fo 114; BoE, G 1/179, 1–2 Dec 1958; PRO, CAB 129/95, C (58), 247, 3 Dec 1958; BoE, C 160/30, 2 Dec 1958, G 1/179, 9 Dec 1958.

6. *The Times*, 16 Dec 1958, 6 Dec 1958; *Economist*, 10 Jan 1959; *The Times*, 20 Dec 1958.

7. BoE, G 1/179, 15 Dec 1958, 19 Dec 1958.

8. David Kynaston, *Cazenove & Co* (1991), pp 235–6.

9. BoE, G 1/179, 22 Dec 1958; Macmillan, dep d. 34, 27 Dec 1958, fos 16–17.

10. BoE, C 160/130, 31 Dec 1958, G 1/179, 31 Dec 1958.

11. *Evening Standard*, 1 Jan 1959.

12. BoE, G 1/179, 1 Jan 1959.

13. BoE, G 1/179, 2 Jan 1959; Roberts, p 192; BoE, G 1/179, 2 Dec 1958.

14. *Evening Standard*, 2 Jan 1959; *Daily Express*, 5 Jan 1959; *The Times*, 5 Jan 1959; *FT*, 5 Jan 1959; *Church Times*, 9 Jan 1959.

15. Macmillan, dep d. 34, 5 Jan 1959, fo 27, 7 Jan 1959, fo 32.

16. *The Times*, 12 Jan 1959; *FT*, 13 Jan 1959; BoE, G 3/12, 13 Jan 1959; *The Times*, 21 Jan 1959, 20 Jan 1959.

17. BoE, G 15/19; Attali, p 214; *CL*, p 154; *Institutional Investor*, March 1980, pp 193–4.

18. Edmund de Rothschild, *A Gilt-Edged Life* (1998), pp 182–3; Macmillan, dep d. 34, 2 Jan 1959, fo 25.

CHAPTER SEVEN

1. Paul Vaughan, *Exciting Times in the Accounts Department* (1995), pp 3–4; A.D. Penley-Edwards, *From the Globe to London Bridge* (Lewes, 1998), p 263; Peter Walker, *Staying Power* (1991), p 56.

2. NLSC, C 409/026, p. 74; Paul Ferris, *The City* (1960), pp 191, 197–8; Anthony Sampson, *Anatomy of Britain* (1962), p 401.

3. NLSC, C 409/026, p 39; Ferris, p 195; NLSC, C 409/034, pp 101, 103.

4. BoE, G 3/128, 23 Oct 1962, G 3/126, 20 Sept 1961.

5. Anthony Brown, *Hazard Unlimited* (1984), p 84, Godfrey Hodgson, *Lloyd's of London* (1984), p 120; NLSC, C 409/015, p 100.

6. Ferris, p 120.

7. William M. Clarke, *The City's Invisible Earnings* (1958), p 33; Richard Roberts, *Schroders* (1992), pp 328–36; Ferris, chap 4.

8. BB, 202934, credit department reports for 1957, 1960–4; Roberts *Schroders*, p 442.

9. The best overall guide is Ranald C. Michie, *The City of London* (Basingstoke, 1992), chap 2.

10. Michie, *City*, pp 17–18; Charles Gordon, *The Two Tycoons* (1984), p 153.

11. Clarke, *Invisible Earnings*, pp 73–4; William M. Clarke, *The City in the World Economy* (1967 Pelican edn), pp 108–12; BoE, G 3/113, 25 April 1955.

12. Hugh Barty-King, *The Baltic Exchange* (1977), p 387, R.C. Michie, 'The International Trade in Food and the City of London since 1850' in *Journal of European Economic History* (Fall 1996), p 397; *City Press*, 10 July 1959; Graham L. Rees, *Britain's Commodity Markets* (1972), pp 330–9 (wool), 259–65 (cocoa), 292–4 (shellac), 282–5 (rubber); Anon, *Two Centuries of Lewis & Peat* (1975), pp 52–64, *The Times*, 12 Dec 1997.

13. Rees, pp 229–39 (sugar), 246–54 (coffee), 361–81 (LME); *Daily Telegraph*, 12 Dec 1998; J.G. Links, 'Arthur Frayling', *Independent*, 11 March 1993.

14. Records of Tribble, Pearson & Co (Guildhall Library), Mss 18,223, box 2, 5 Feb 1953, box 1, 16 March 1954, box 2, 11 Oct 1955, box 3, 7 Jan 1957, box 2, 3 Feb 1958, 6 May 1958, 13 May 1958.

15. *The Times*, 24 Aug 1945.

16. C.H. Holden and W.G. Holford, 'The New Plan for the City of London' (July 1946), p 6, *The City of London: A Record of Destruction and Survival* (1951), pp 44–6, 231, 256. See also Gordon E. Cherry and Leith Penny, *Holford* (1986), and Richard Trench, *London Before the Blitz* (1989), pp 184–5, for an enthusiastic evaluation of the Holden/Holford plan.

17. SE, Council, 23 May 1955; Leslie Thomas, *In My Wildest Dreams* (1984), p 276; NLSC, C 409/057, p 107.

18. *Director*, Oct 1987, p 118; JS, no 9, pp 4–5; Judy Slinn, *Ashurst Morris Crisp* (Cambridge, 1997), p 200.

19. Oliver Marriott, *The Property Boom* (1967), pp 74–7, Judy Slinn, *Clifford Chance* (Cambridge, 1993), pp 140–1; Elizabeth Hennessy, *A Domestic History of the Bank of England, 1930–1960* (Cambridge, 1992), pp 70–6; Marriott, pp 74–7, Ian Nairn, *Modern Buildings in London* (1964), p 1; Alastair Ross Goobey, *Bricks and Mortals* (1992), p 24, Corporation of London (Stuart J. Murphy), *Continuity and Change* (1984), p 72.

20. Nikolaus Pevsner, *The Buildings of England: London 1: The Cities of London and Westminster* (1957), pp 199, 256, 238, 103–5.

21. Judy Slinn, *Linklaters & Paines* (1987), p 212; *City Press*, 16 Jan 1959, 20 March 1959, 8 May 1959, 19 June 1959, 10 July 1959, 13 Nov 1959.

22. In general on the five tower blocks by Route 11, see: Marriott, pp 70–4; Simon Bradley and Nikolaus Pevsner, *The Buildings of England: London 1: The City of London* (1997), pp 540–5.

23. Pevsner (2nd ed, 1962), p 237; Nairn, *Modern Buildings*, p 5; Marriott, pp 27–32.

24. For additional details, see Bradley and Pevsner, pp 131–2.

25. SE, Council, 6 Sept 1965; Rachel Hartley, *No Mean City* (1967), p 109.

26. *Spectator*, 13 April 1956; Pevsner (1957), p 168; *The Times*, 7–9 March 1962; *City Press*, 2 Nov 1962.

27. Pevsner (1962), p 108; Bradley and Pevsner, p 283.

28. *The Times*, 21, 25–6 March 1964; *Daily Telegraph*, 23 March 1964.

29. Bradley and Pevsner, p 537; Marriott, pp 116–17, Bradley and Pevsner, p 606, *Continuity and Change*, p 79; Pevsner (3rd ed, 1973), pp 261–2, 115–16, *Continuity and Change*, p 83, Bradley and Pevsner, p 531.

30. SE, Council, 28 Aug 1961, 17 Dec 1962; Bradley and Pevsner, pp 134, 342.

31. Sampson, p 346; *The Times*, 30 April 1990; Alexandra Younger, 'Graham Needham', *Independent*, 20 Nov 1993; David Piper, *The Companion Guide to London* (1964), p 332; Geoffrey Fletcher, *Offbeat in the City of London* (1968), pp 5, 37–8.

32. Ian Nairn, *Nairn's London* (1966), p 17.

33. Michie, *City*, p 14; records of Phillips & Drew (Guildhall Library), Ministry of Transport to F.A.A. Menzler, 9 April 1962; Pennie Denton (ed), *Betjeman's London* (1988), p 113.

34. *Post Office London Directory, 1957: Streets and Residents*, p 797.

35. *CL*, pp 62–3, 92–3.

36. Eric Street, *The History of the National Mutual Life Assurance Society* (1980), p 55; Paul Thompson, 'The Pyrrhic Victory of Gentlemanly Capitalism' in *Journal of Contemporary History* (1997), p 428; David Kynaston, *Cazenove & Co* (1991), p 182; JS, no 40, p 8.

37. Street, pp 58–9; *CL*, pp 5–6; Steve Humphries and John Taylor, *The Making of Modern London, 1945–1985* (1986), p 54.

38. Peter Spira, *Ladders and Snakes* (1997), p 81.

39. M.C. Reed, *A History of James Capel & Co* (1975), p 93; R.S. Sayers, *Gilletts in the London Money Market* (Oxford, 1968), p 175; David Wainwright, *Government Broker* (1990), p 93; Jehanne Wake, *Kleinwort Benson* (Oxford, 1997), pp 361–3; BB, 201040.

40. Thompson, 'Pyrrhic Victory', p 303; *FT*, 29 April 1994; NLSC, C 409/015, p. 66.

41. David Kinsella, 'The London Money Market – as seen from Smith St Aubyn – 40 years ago'.

42. Wake, p 363; JS, no 19, p 2; W.J. Reader and David Kynaston, *Phillips & Drew* (1998), pp 133–5.

43. Michie, *City*, p 14; BoE, G 3/118, 10 Oct 1957; Rees, p 185; Laurie Dennett, *Slaughter and May* (Cambridge, 1989), p 230. In general, see John Orbell, 'The development of office technology' in Alison Turton (ed), *Managing Business Archives* (1991).

44. Slinn, *Linklaters*, p 208; Slinn, *Ashurst*, p 169; Allen, Harvey & Ross scrapbook (Cater Allen records); JS, no 19, pp 2–3, *CL*, p 205; Reader and Kynaston, pp 135–6.

45. JS, no 40, pp 10–11; Reader and Kynaston, pp 136–43.

46. Reed, p 93; Ronald Palin, *Rothschild Relish* (1970), p 185; Reader and Kynaston, p 130; *The Times* (Tim Congdon), 8 July 1996.

47. Slinn, *Ashurst*, pp 165, 172; Humphries and Taylor, pp 70–1; Laurie Dennett, *A Sense of Security: 150 Years of Prudential* (Cambridge, 1998), p 330; BoE, G 3/131, 30 Jan 1964.

48. Sayers, *Gilletts*, p 175; BoE, G 3/130, 12 Sept 1963; NLSC, C 409/037, p 53.

49. Kynaston, *Cazenove*, pp 239–40; HSBC, Oral History Collection, G. Philip Stubbs, pp 4, 83–4.

50. Mary Murry, "'The Final Stroke of Nine'" in Ian Norrie (ed), *The Book of the City* (1961), pp 134–7.

51. *The Old Lady*, Sept 1998, p 120.

52. Michael Burns, 'Reminiscences of a Stockbroker's Clerk, or Whatever Happened to Ross-Munro, Duff & Co?'

53. Records of Antony Gibbs & Sons (Guildhall Library), Ms 16,896, 20 Sept 1958, 22 Sept 1958.

54. *Midbank Chronicle*, August 1963, p 87.

CHAPTER EIGHT

1. BB, 201040, 21 Dec 1948; BoE, ADM 13/8, 29 Jan 1965; *CL*, p 167; SE, Council, 3 May 1960; Frances Partridge, *Hanging On* (1990), p 87; *Guardian*, 12 May 1994.

2. Ranald C. Michie, *The London Stock Exchange* (Oxford, 1999) gives the most detailed account of the Council in action over the years.

3. John Littlewood, *The Stock Market* (1998), pp 68, 133–5; SE, Ms 14,600A, vol 10, 22 Sept 1952.

4. SE, Ms 14,600A, vol 11, 26 Jan–23 March 1953.

5. *Stock Exchange Journal*, Summer 1958, pp 15–16; SE, Council, 30 Dec 1963.

6. Anthony Sampson, *Anatomy of Britain* (1962), p 351; SE, Council, 4 March 1963, 20 Nov 1967, 4 Dec 1967; Michie, pp 432–3.

7. Michie, p 440; W.J. Reader and David Kynaston, *Phillips & Drew* (1998), p 124; Michie, p 465.

8. SE, Council, 20 July 1964; Reader and Kynaston, pp 38, 101–2.

9. SE, Council, 28 Nov 1966–8 May 1967; Michie, pp 453–4.

10. The best guide to these questions is Littlewood, especially pp 99–102, 106–8, 121–3, 128.

11. David Kynaston, *Cazenove & Co* (1991), p 250. On Goobey, see a perceptive assessment by Jonathan Davis, *Independent*, 24 March 1999.

12. Sampson, p 351; SE, Committee on Commissions, 21 Jan 1964.

13. SE, Ms 14,600A, vol 12, 2 Nov 1953, 9 Nov 1953; SE, Council, 4 March 1963.

14. SE, Council, 17 Oct 1955, 27 June 1966.

15. SE, Council, 20 May 1957; BoE, G 3/119, 13 Feb 1958, G 3/11, 18 Feb 1958; SE, Council, 17 Dec 1962, 6 Sept 1965.

16. *CL*, pp 63–4; Michie, pp 384, 429–31; JS, no 13, p 10.

17. W.J. Reader, *A House in the City* (1979), pp 178–81; Hurford Janes, *de Zoete and Gorton* (1963); Elizabeth Hennessy, *Stockbrokers for 150 Years* (1978), p 43; *CL*, p 10; Andrew Lycett, *From Diamond Sculls to Golden Handcuffs* (1998), pp 112–13, Littlewood, p ix.

18. *CL*, pp 38, 76–7, 197. On Pember & Boyle generally, see JS, no 31, pp 2–8.

19. On Hunter, see: JS, no 4, p 49; Nicholas Davenport, *Memoirs of a City Radical* (1974), p 185; Nigel Broackes, *A Growing Concern* (1979), pp 138–9. On Gilmour, see: Denzil Sebag-Montefiore, *The Story of Joseph Sebag and Co* (1996), pp 16, 23; *The Times*, 15 Feb 1977.

20. *CL*, pp 6–7 (Michael Verey, Sir Martin Jacomb, Mr A.); *The Times*, 23 Nov 1973, 28 Nov 1973.

21. Nicholas Coleridge and Stephen Quinn (eds), *The Sixties in Queen* (1987), p 126; Lycett, pp 57–85; Richard Kingzett, 'Julian Martin Smith', *Independent*, 6 July 1991.

22. Sampson, p 351.

23. Kynaston, *Cazenove*, pp 178–243.

24. Lycett, pp 77–80; Kynaston, *Cazenove*, pp 248–9; *Independent*, 26 Oct 1996; Kynaston, *Cazenove*, p 249.

25. Reader and Kynaston, pp 45–67, 96–101, 119, 143–4. In general on the rise of investment analysis, see Littlewood, pp 123–8.

26. Littlewood, pp 271–3, offers a balanced discussion.

27. *Director*, Oct 1987, p 118; *CL*, p 78; *Stock Exchange Journal*, Nov 1957, p 46; JS, no 13, p 15; John Gapper and Nicholas Denton, *All That Glitters* (1996), p 65; Paul Thompson, 'The Pyrrhic Victory of Gentlemanly Capitalism' in *Journal of Contemporary History* (1997), p 434.

28. *FT*, 13 Sept 1966, 20 Sept 1966.

29. Michael Burns, 'Reminiscences of a Stockbroker's Clerk, or Whatever Happened to Ross-Munro, Duff & Co?'

30. Bernard Attard, 'The Jobbers of the London Stock Exchange: An Oral History' in *Oral History* (Spring 1994), pp 43–8. See also: Bernard Attard, 'Making a Market: The Jobbers of the London Stock Exchange, 1800–1986' in *Financial History Review* (2000).

31. JS, no 35, p 5; Kynaston, *Cazenove*, pp 250–1.

32. Sebag-Montefiore, p 29; JS, no 15, p 4, no 9, pp 10–13.

33. JS, no 2, pp 12, 15, 4–5; Sebag-Montefiore, pp 29–30; JS, no 16, pp 4, 14–15.

34. JS, no 16, pp 8–9; Anthony Rota, 'George Lazarus', *Independent*, 15 Jan 1997.

35. *CL*, p 162; *The Times*, 13 Feb 1989, 18 Feb 1989, *Daily Telegraph*, 13 Feb 1989; Phillips & Drew records (Guildhall Library), memo, 'Party for Durlachers', 7 April 1967; JS, no 4 (David LeRoy-Lewis), p 50, no 20 (Graham Ferguson), p 33, *CL*, p 10 (George Nissen); Reader and Kynaston, p 83; JS, no 21, p 12.

36. JS, no 41, pp 22–3, no 14, p 6, no 31, p 8; BoE, G 3/123. 27 Jan 1960; JS, no 14, p 9; Rod Stern, 'Humphrey Mackworth-Praed', *Independent*, 30 Sept 1995.

37. JS, no 18, p 5; *List of Members of The Stock Exchange, 1955–56* (1955); JS, no 34, p 8.

38. JS, no 24, pp 6–10, no 41, pp 4–5, no 6, pp 3, 17, 29.

39. *FT*, 1 Jan 1952, 8 Jan 1952; BoE, G 3/107, 6 May 1952.

40. SE, Ms 14,600A, vol 11, 24 Nov 1952, 1 Dec 1952, 16 March 1953, 30 March 1953.

41. *Stock Exchange Journal*, Oct 1955, pp 37–8.

42. SE, Sub-Committees of a Non-Permanent Character, vol 21, Special Committee on Members' Capital, 1 Feb–8 March 1957, vol 23, Committee on Rule 88, 16 July 1958.

43. Michie, pp 393–4; *FT*, 15 Jan 1988 (John Colegrave letter), 24 Sept 1965; SE, Council, 13 Aug 1962, 22 July 1963; *FT*, 24 Sept 1965.

44. SE, Council, 7 Feb 1966, 13 June 1966, 3 Oct 1966, Sub-Committees of a Non-Permanent Character, vol 27 (3), 4 Nov 1966.

45. Donald Cobbett, *Before the Big Bang* (Portsmouth, 1986), pp 91–2; JS, no 41, p 3, no 9, pp 19–20.

46. JS, no 9, pp 5–6; *FT*, 24 Dec 1988; JS, no 15, p 12, no 32, p 22; *The Times*, 28 Oct 1966; JS, no 15, p 12.

47. Anthony Thwaite (ed), *Selected Letters of Philip Larkin, 1940–1985* (1992), p 157.

48. JS, no 14 (Angus Ashton), pp 7, 26, no 34 (Norman Whetnall), pp 6–7, no 3 (Gerald Lederman), p 7, no 6 (Tony Jenkins), pp 11, 41–2, no 9 (Brian Winterflood), p 15.

49. JS, no 24, p 14, no 6, p 15, no 34, p 14.

50. See Attard, 'Making a Market', for a full and persuasive analysis.

51. JS, no 7, p 20, no 15, p 14, no 8, p 19, no 20, p 33, no 25, p 25.

52. *CL*, p 77; JS, no 1, pp 26–7, no 38, p 6.

53. JS, no 3, p 7; *Director*, Oct 1987, p 117; SE, Council, 12 Jan 1959, 29 June 1959, 20 July 1959; *CL*, p 79; SE, Ms 14,600A, vol 12, 29 March 1954.

54. Thompson, 'Pyrrhic Victory', p 433; JS, no 13, p 13, no 42, pp 4–5, no 6, p 14.

55. JS, no 1, appendix 2, no 24, p 19, no 19, pp 9–10; Attard, 'Making a Market', p 18; JS, no 13, p 14.

56. JS, no 42, p 5, no 24, pp 16–17, no 1, p 27.

57. JS, no 30, p 9, no 12, pp 20–1, no 6, pp 9–10, 21–4.

58. Sampson, pp 352–3.

CHAPTER NINE

1. Lord Citrine, *Two Careers* (1967), p 298; George Soros, *The Crisis of Global Capitalism* (1998), p 74; Alec Cairncross (ed), *The Robert Hall Diaries, 1954–61* (1991), p 210; *Independent*, 14 March 1992, 18 March 1992.

2. *Punch*, 21 Aug 1963.

3. *CL*, pp 164–5; BoE, G 3/119, 28 Feb 1958; Frank Pakenham, Earl of Longford, *Five Lives* (1964), p 55; Sir Kenneth Cork, *Cork on Cork* (1988), pp 253–4, Robert Bruce, 'Sir Kenneth Cork', *Independent*, 16 Oct 1991.

4. Andrew Shonfield, 'The Plaintive Treble', in Arthur Koestler (ed), *Suicide of a Nation?* (1963), p 80; BoE, ADM 12/9, 8 May 1962.

5. *The Times*, 10 Sept 1988; Victor Sandelson, 'The Confidence Trick' in Hugh Thomas (ed), *The Establishment* (1959), p 133; Edward Beddington-Behrens, *Look Back Look Forward* (1963), p 141; Paul Thompson, 'The Pyrrhic Victory of Gentlemanly Capitalism' in *Journal of Contemporary History* (1997), p 433; NLSC, C 409/011, p 75.

6. BoE, G 3/107, 3 April 1952, G 3/108, 14 July 1952; NLSC, C 409/024, p 45; Peter Baring, 'Lord Ashburton', *Independent*, 22 June 1991.

7. David Kynaston, *Cazenove & Co* (1991), p 274; *CL*, p 5.

8. BoE, G 3/99, 24 Jan 1947, G 3/109, 26 Jan 1953, G 3/124, 8 July 1960.

9. Andrew St George, *JOH* (1992), pp 33–4, 64.

10. *Spectator*, 8 Nov 1957; NLSC, C 409/011, p 80; Edmund de Rothschild, *A Gilt-Edged Life* (1998), p 138; David Wainwright, *Government Broker* (1990), p 91.

11. Barry Riley, 'The Long View', *FT*, 18 Nov 1989; *CL*, p 84; St George, p 36; Kynaston, *Cazenove*, p 221; records of Cazenove & Co.

12. *Daily Telegraph*, 21 Dec 1994, 11 June 1996, 17 April 1999, *The Times*, 19 April 1999; BB, 200970, 11 Oct 1949; Keith Middlemas, 'Lord Franks', *Independent*, 17 Oct 1992; Anthony Montague Browne, *Long Sunset* (1995), p 348; *Daily Telegraph*, 6 July 1995; BoE, C 160/141, 2 Jan 1957.

13. Longford, pp 21–2, 50, BoE, G 3/11, 27–8 Jan 1958.

14. Paul Ferris, *The City* (1960), p 196; Jonathan Mantle, *For Whom the Bell Tolls* (1992), pp 20–1, 28; Ferris, pp 195–6; Thompson, 'Pyrrhic Victory', p 432; *Sunday Telegraph Magazine*, 22 Nov 1998.

15. *The Times*, 30 July 1996, *Daily Telegraph*, 30 July 1996, Godfrey Hodgson, 'Sir Peter Green', *Independent*, 31 July 1996.

16. Ferris, pp 62–5; George and Pamela Cleaver, *The Union Discount* (1985), p 91.

17. *Spectator*, 10 Dec 1988.

18. BoE, G 3/9, 25 Jan 1956; HSBC, 192.151, 26 Feb 1958; NLSC, C 409/031, p 96.

19. Tom Lupton and C. Shirley Wilson, 'The Social Background and Connections of "Top Decision Makers"' in *Manchester School* (Jan 1959), pp 30–51; *City Press*, 22 May 1959.

20. Sandelson, 'The Confidence Trick', pp 130–1, 139, 144; Anthony Sampson, *Anatomy of Britain* (1962), p 347; NLSC, C 409/134, pp 46–7; *Independent on Sunday*, 4 Oct 1992.

21. *Who's Who, 1958*, p 2188; NLSC, C 409/057, p 64, *Independent*, 29 Aug 1992; Cleavers, *Union Discount*, pp 84, 89, 97.

22. Letter inside Guildhall Library copy of Anon, *The House of Brandt* (1956); *FT*, 24 Sept 1963, Charles Gordon, *The Two Tycoons* (1984), p 143, *Spectator*, 15 Feb 1986; Sandelson, p 146, Sampson, p 385; Cathy Courtney, 'Lord Swaythling', *Independent*, 13 July 1998.

23. *FT*, 1 July 1960, 26 Sept 1961; de Rothschild, pp 181–2, Richard Kellett, *The Merchant Banking Arena* (1967), pp 100–1; *Queen*, 2 Aug 1961. See also Kathleen Burk, *Morgan Grenfell, 1838–1988* (Oxford, 1989), pp 157, 189.

24. BoE, G 3/2, 7 March 1950, 3 April 1950; J.R. Winton, *Lloyds Bank, 1918–1969* (Oxford, 1982), pp 141–2; Lupton and Wilson, p 36; Sandelson, pp 145–6; Longford, p 44.

25. Sampson, p 372; Martin Vander Weyer, *Falling Eagle: The Decline of Barclays Bank* (2000), p 78. In general on Barclays, see also Margaret Ackrill and Leslie Hannah, *Barclays: The Business of Banking, 1690–1996* (Cambridge, 2001).

26. Thompson, 'Pyrrhic Victory', p 300; Richard Roberts, *Schroders* (1992), p 350; Oliver Stocken and others, 'Sir Philip Shelbourne', *Independent*, 6 May 1993; Sampson, p 468; Thompson, 'Pyrrhic Victory', p 300; *DBB*, Edgar Jones, 'Henry Alexander Benson, Lord Benson', vol 1, pp 287–9, *CL*, p 58, Brian Jenkins and others, 'Lord Benson', *Independent*, 13 March 1995.

27. *The Times*, 2 Aug 1956, Laurie Dennett, *A Sense of Security: 150 Years of Prudential* (Cambridge, 1998), pp 316–18, Sampson, pp 408–11.

28. *The Times*, 14 April 1994; Roberts, p 336, Adrienne Gleeson, *London Enriched* (1997), p 61; HSBC, 192.120; Kynaston, *Cazenove*, pp 167, 222, 244–5, 290, 300; *DBB*, Christine Shaw, 'William Lionel Fraser', vol 2, pp 417–22, W. Lionel Fraser, *All to the Good* (1963), pp 199, 203–4, 210.

29. *CL*, p 5; Courtney, 'Swaythling'.

30. Peter Spira, *Ladders and Snakes* (1997), pp 76–7; BB, 210097, 9 May 1961.

31. *Queen*, 2 Aug 1961; Sampson, p 387; BoE, G 3/123, 20 April 1960; Kellett, pp 33, 150–8.

32. HSBC, 192.160, 18 June 1962; Sampson, pp 394–7 (there are only twelve – not twenty-five – chapters in Ecclesiastes); Barry Riley, 'Not quite establishment', *FT*, 26 Oct 1991; Antony Hornby, 'Harold Charles Gilbert Drayton' in *Dictionary of National Biography, 1961–1970* (Oxford, 1981), pp 309–10. T. Jackson, *The Origin and History of the Drayton Group* (Croydon, 1991) provides the fullest account of Drayton's life and career.

33. IHA, Ms 29,333, file 80, 12 Dec 1945, 17 Dec 1945, 4 Nov 1946, 5 Jan 1948, 25 Feb 1948, 5 May 1948, 1 July 1948, 26 June 1950 (*FT*), 12 July 1950, 12 Oct 1950; *Daily Telegraph*, 17 Dec 1997; BoE, ADM 13/6, 23 April 1963; *FT*, 26 Oct 1991; John Fforde, *The Bank of England and Public Policy, 1941–1958* (Cambridge, 1992), p 750. For another sympathetic assessment by a Bank man, see Sir George Blunden's entry on Salomon in *Dictionary of National Biography, 1986–1990* (Oxford, 1996), pp 394–5.

34. BoE, G 3/125, 14 March 1961, 24 March 1961, 26 June 1961.

35. Norman Scarfe, 'Anthony Foord', *Independent*, 19 Nov 1997; JS, no 20, p 10, no 31, p 6; *FT*, 30 Oct 1987; *Independent* (Jeremy Warner), 30 Aug 1997.

36. *CL*, p 68.

37. Macmillan, dep d. 46, 20 July 1962; *DBB*, W.J. Reader, 'Sir John Bevan Braithwaite', vol 1, p 431; E.W. Swanton, *Sort of a Cricket Person* (1972), p 12; *List of Members of The Stock Exchange, 1955–56* (1955); Ferris, p 26.

38. *The Times*, 20 June 1997; *Queen*, 18 Aug 1960; *The Times*, 14 Sept 1961; BB, 210086, 21 Feb 1955; *The Times*, 26 March 1999.

39. De Rothschild, pp 157–80 (gardens), 220–1.

40. St George, pp 128–46, 158–9. See also Andrew St George, 'Jocelyn Hambro', *Independent*, 24 June 1994.

41. *Queen*, 2 Feb 1960; records of Phillips & Drew (Guildhall Library), 7 April 1967.

42. Ferris, pp 16–17; Hugh Thomas (ed), *The Establishment* (1959), pp 12–13; NLSC, C 409/133, p 33; Thompson, 'Pyrrhic Victory', p 296.

43. BoE, G 3/107, 5 May 1952; *Time & Tide*, 29 Jan 1970; Adam Raphael, *Ultimate Risk* (1995 Corgi edn), p 62; William M. Clarke, *The City's Invisible Earnings* (1958), p 7.

44. BoE, G 1/399, 8 April 1958, 6 May 1958, 6 June 1958, 28 Nov 1958.

45. HSBC, 192.155, 29 June 1959, 2–3 July 1959.

46. Sandelson, p 148.

CHAPTER TEN

1. *Banker*, April 1959, pp 225–30; *Economist*, 11 July 1959; Ranald C. Michie, *The London Stock Exchange* (Oxford, 1999), p 406.

2. Leslie O'Brien, *A Life Worth Living* (1995), p 41; Alec Cairncross (ed), *The Robert Hall Diaries, 1954–61* (1991), pp 118, 192; Cairncross, DC 106/10/2, 16 Jan 1959; Bot, G 3/82, 20 Jan 1959.

3. Cairncross, DC 106/10/2, 25 Jan 1959, 21 Feb 1959.

4. Macmillan, dep d. 34, 17 Feb 1959, fo 94; Keith Middlemas, *Power, Competition and the State: Volume I* (Basingstoke, 1986), p 384; *FT*, 7 April 1959; John Littlewood, *The Stock Market* (1998), pp 105–6.

5. BoE, G 3/12, 29 May 1959, 19 June 1959, 24 July 1959, 29 July 1959.

6. Accounts of the episode include: W. Lionel Fraser, *All to the Good* (1963), pp 248–51; David Clutterbuck and Marion Devine, *Clore* (1987), pp 81–4.

7. *The Times*, 26 May 1959; William Davis, *Merger Mania* (1970), p 22; BB, 210095, 23 June 1959.

8. In general about the takeovers controversy during 1959, see Richard Roberts, 'Regulatory Responses to the Rise of the Market for Corporate Control in Britain in the 1950s' in *Business History* (Jan 1992), pp 193–5.

9. BoE, G 3/12, 19 May 1959; Roberts, p 194; *FT*, 7 July 1959; BoE, C 40/971, 10 July 1959, 21 July 1959, 18 Aug 1959.

10. *Economist*, 15 Aug 1959; BoE, LDMA 1/11, 29 May 1959; records of Accepting Houses Committee (Guildhall Library), Ms 29,295, vol 6, 11 June 1959; BoE, G 3/122, 24 July 1959; *Economist*, 15 Aug 1959; *City Press*, 23 Oct 1959; Jehanne Wake, *Kleinwort Benson* (Oxford, 1997), p 347.

11. BoE, G 3/84, 6 Aug 1959.

12. Discussions of the Radcliffe Report include: Brian Griffiths, 'Two Monetary Inquiries in Great Britain' in *Journal of Money, Credit and Banking* (Feb 1974); G.A. Fletcher, *The Discount Houses in London* (1976), pp 77–9; Alec Cairncross, 'The Bank of England' in Gianni Toniolo (ed), *Central Banks' Independence in Historical Perspective* (Berlin, 1988), pp 63–5.

13. *Hall*, p 209; *Economist*, 22 Aug 1959; BoE, G 3/84, 17 Aug 1959.

14. *Banker*, Sept 1959, pp 543, 545–6.

15. Read, Hurst-Brown & Co, *Investment Letter*, 18 Sept 1959; BoE, LDMA 1/11, 25 Sept 1959; Roberts, p 195; BoE, C 40/971, 28 Sept 1959, LDMA 1/11, 2 Oct 1959.

16. *FT*, 8 Oct 1959; Miles Jebb (ed), *The Diaries of Cynthia Gladwyn* (1995), p 241.

17. Paul Ferris, *The City* (1960), p 29; Littlewood, p 107; BoE, LDMA 1/11, 23 Oct 1959; Read, Hurst-Brown & Co, *Investment Letter*, 18 Dec 1959.

18. BoE, G 3/12, 16 Oct 1959, C 40/971, 21 Oct 1959; Roberts, p 196; *FT*, 31 Oct 1959.

19. Elizabeth Hennessy, *A Domestic History of the Bank of England, 1930–1960* (Cambridge, 1992), pp 320–2; BoE, G 3/122, 21 Oct 1959; *Hall*, p 220; BoE, G 3/85, 27 Nov 1959.

20. *Hall*, pp 223–4; BB, 202934, credit department report for 1959.

21. For other discussions, see: Michael Moran, *The Politics of Banking* (Basingstoke, 1984), p 25; Robert Elgie and Helen Thompson, *The Politics of Central Banks* (1998), pp 57–8.

CHAPTER ELEVEN

1. BoE, G 3/12, 13 Nov 1959, G 3/13, 17 Feb 1960; Macmillan, dep c. 21/1, 17 Feb 1960.

2. BoE, G 3/123, 8 April 1960; Samuel Brittan, *The Treasury under the Tories* (1964), p 206.

3. Read, Hurst-Brown & Co, *Investment Letter*, 25 May 1960; Macmillan dep c. 21/1, 17 June 1960; BoE, LDMA 1/12, 23 June 1960, G 3/123, 24 June 1960.

4. David Kynaston, *The Financial Times* (1988), p 284; BoE, G 3/87, 24 June 1960, LDMA 1/12, 22 July 1960.

5. Brittan, p 206; Alec Cairncross (ed), *The Robert Hall Diaries, 1954–61* (1991), pp 242–3; BoE, G 3/87, 30 June 1960.

6. PRO, PREM 11/3756, 1 Aug 1960.

7. BoE, G 15/19; *Hall*, pp 222, 225, 243, 245–6, 250, 252; Keith Middlemas, 'Lord Franks', *Independent*, 17 Oct 1992; *Hall*, p 252.

8. BB, 200884, 15 April 1947; *FT*, 11 Nov 1960; BB, 210090, 12 Nov 1960; Stephen Fay, *The Collapse of Barings* (1996), p 13; *Banker*, Dec 1960, p 777.

9. Brittan, pp 215–18; *The Times*, 5 Jan 1961, 7 Jan 1961, 9 Jan 1961.

10. W. Lionel Fraser, *All to the Good* (1963), p 262; PRO, PREM 11/3285, 4 Jan 1961, 11 Jan 1961; Charles A. Coombs, *The Arena of Internationals Finance* (New York, 1976), pp 58, 36–7.

11. BoE, G 1/252, 6 June 1961, G 3/91, 7 June 1961, LDMA 1/12, 16 June 1961.

12. BoE, G 3/91, 22 June 1961, C 160/151, 10 Sept 1962.

13. *Tatler*, 19 July 1961; BoE, G 3/139, 6 March 1964; NLSC, C 409/007, p 73.

14. BoE, G 1/252, 7 July 1961.

15. D.R. Thorpe, *Selwyn Lloyd* (1989), p 317; Cairncross, DC 106/10/3, 13 July 1961; BoE, G 3/239, 13 July 1961, 18 July 1961; Macmillan, dep d. 42, 23 July 1961, fo 2v.

16. *FT*, 26 July 1961; *The Times*, 26 July 1961; BoE, G 1/252, 6 Sept 1961.

17. *The Times*, 26 July 1961.

18. *Economist*, 15 Aug 1959.

19. BoE, G 3/12, 22 Sept 1959, 3 Nov 1959, G 3/122, 6 Nov 1959; *FT*, 10 Feb 1960.

20. For the fullest accounts, see Richard Roberts, *Schroders* (1992), pp 413–14, 418–20; Jehanne Wake, *Kleinwort Benson* (Oxford, 1997), pp 345–7, 368–75.

21. BoE, G 3/123, 22 March 1960; Roberts, p 419; *CL*, p 62; BoE, G 3/123, 3–4 May 1960; *FT*, 20 May 1960.

22. Charles Gordon, *The Two Tycoons* (1984), p 143; Roberts, p 422; information from Colin Leach; Anthony Sampson, *Anatomy of Britain Today* (1965), p 443. For an overall assessment of Richardson's impact on Schroders, see Roberts, pp 422–5.

23. Wake, pp 366–7; BoE, G 3/121, 11 March 1959, G 3/124, 22 Sept 1960; *Daily Telegraph*, 18 Nov 1960; BoE, G 3/89, 18 Nov 1960; Alastair Ross Goobey, *Bricks and Mortals* (1992), pp 25–6.

24. Dominic Hobson, *The Pride of Lucifer* (1990), p 105; Kathleen Burk, *Morgan Grenfell, 1838–1988* (Oxford, 1989), p 215; Ron Chernow, *The House of Morgan* (New York, 1990), p 563.

25. Generally on Rothschilds in the early to mid-1960s, see Niall Ferguson, *The World's Banker: The History of the House of Rothschild* (1998), pp 1013–17.

26. *Queen*, 7 Dec 1960; Edmund de Rothschild, *A Gilt-Edged Life* (1998), p 182; Ferguson, p 1014.

27. Accounts of the ICI/Courtaulds battle include: William Davis, *Merger Mania* (1970), pp 38–50; D.C. Coleman, *Courtaulds, volume III* (Oxford, 1980), pp 201–37; John Orbell, 'The Biggest Bid Yet' in *Barings World News*, Christmas 1991; John Littlewood, *The Stock Market* (1998), pp 113–15.

28. *FT*, 19 Dec 1961; information from Sir Arthur Knight; BoE, G 1/148, 19 Dec 1961, 20 Feb 1962, 22 Feb 1962; Kynaston, *Financial Times*, p 316; BoE, G 3/94, 28 March 1962; Orbell, p 22; *Observer*, 1 April 1962; Brian Widlake, *In the City* (1986), p 106.

29. *FT*, 13 Nov 1961; Littlewood, p 130; records of Accepting Houses Committee (at Guildhall Library), Ms 29,310, file 21; Wake, p 347; David Caruth, *A Life of Three Strands* (1998), p 13.

30. Jacques Attali, *A Man of Influence* (1986), p 221; BoE, G 3/128, 8 Nov 1962, G 3/136, 30 May 1963.

31. BoE, G 3/124, 30 Nov 1960.

32. Ranald C. Michie, *The London Stock Exchange* (Oxford, 1999), pp 463–4; Hugo Vickers and James Wright, 'Ralph Vickers', *Independent*, 16 Sept 1992; HSBC, 192.161; BoE, G 3/128, 4 July 1962; Anthony Sampson, *Anatomy of Britain* (1962), p 391.

33. Generally on Bolton, see: Richard Fry (ed), *A Banker's World* (1970); *DBB*, R.P.T. Davenport-Hines, 'Sir George Lewis French Bolton', vol 1, pp 364–9, Bolton's papers are now lodged at the Bank of England Archives. He awaits a biographer.

34. PRO, PREM 11/3758, 19 Dec 1960; Fry, p 78.

35. On the Eurodollar market between 1959 and 1964, see (in addition to my chap 5 references to Einzig, Schenk and Burn) Stefano Battilossi, 'Banking with Multinationals: British Clearing Banks and the Euro-Market Challenge, 1958–74' in Stefano Battilossi and Youssef Cassis (eds), *European Banks and the American Challenge, 1950s–1970s* (Oxford, 2001).

36. *The Times*, 24 Oct 1960; Catherine R. Schenck, 'The Origins of the Eurodollar Market in London: 1955–1963' in *Explorations in Economic History* (1998), p 234; BoE, ADM 13/4, 14 April 1961, 20 April 1961; Gary Burn, 'The State, the City and the Euromarkets' in *Review of International Political Economy* (Summer 1999), p 239; *Banker*, June 1961, pp 395–404.

37. Paul Einzig, *The Euro-Dollar System* (1964), p 8; *Banker*, June 1961, p 400; Battilossi.

38. BoE, C 160/32, 4 Feb 1960, G 1/252, 7 July 1961; PRO, T 295/25, 22 Aug 1961, 4 Dec 1961.

39. PRO, T 295/9, 6 July 1962, 22 Oct 1962, 12 Nov 1962.

40. Bo Bramsen and Kathleen Wain, *The Hambros* (1979), p 435; *FT*, 22 May 1962; BoE, G 3/128, 22 Nov 1962, ADM 12/10, 28 Jan 1963, EID 10/22, 29 Jan 1963; Bramsen and Wain, p 435.

41. *The Times*, 1 Feb 1963; Cairncross, DC 106/10/3, 23 Jan 1963.

42. BoE, ADM 13/6, 30 April 1963; PRO T 295/10, 30 April 1963.

43. Cairncross, DC 106/10/3, 1 May 1963; PRO, T 295/10, 3 May 1963, T 295/11, 30 May 1963, 18 July 1963, T 295/12, 26 Nov 1963; Cairncross, DC 106/10/3, 6 Jan 1964.

44. Accounts of the origins and early years of the Eurobond market are to be found in: Ian Kerr, *A History of the Eurobond Market* (1984); Kathleen Burk (ed), 'Witness Seminar on the Origins and Early Development of the Eurobond Market' in *Contemporary European History* (1992); Peter Shearlock and William Ellington, *The Eurobond Diaries* (Brussels, 1994); Gary Burn, 'The State, the City and the Euromarkets' in *Review of International Political Economy* (Summer 1999).

45. Kerr, p 17; Shearlock and Ellington, pp 8–11.

46. Kerr, p 17; Attali, pp 223–4.

47. BoE, C 160/154, 6 June 1962, 11 July 1962, G 3/96, 23 July 1962.

48. Attali, p 224; BoE, C 160/173.

49. Ian Fraser, *The High Road to England* (Wilby, 1999), pp 259–62, provides the fullest account of the Autostrade issue. See also: Burk, 'Witness Seminar', p 69; Richard Roberts, 'Birthday of the bond that carried London to the top', *The Times*, 14 Jan 1993; Peter Spira, *Ladders and Snakes* (1997), pp 115–17.

50. BoE, C 40/1213, 30 Jan 1963, 11 Feb 1963.

51. Fraser, pp 260–1; SE, Council, 29 April 1963, 13 May 1963.

52. *The Times*, 14 May 1963; *Banker*, June 1963, p 377.

53. *FT*, 2 July 1963; *The Times*, 2 July 1963.

54. *Euromoney*, June 1984, p 65.

55. In general on White Weld, see: *Euromoney*, June 1989, special supplement, p 52; Burk, 'Witness Seminar', pp 72–3.

56. Burk, 'Witness Seminar', p 69; BoE, G 3/137, 8 July 1963; Ron Chernow, *The House of Morgan* (1990), p 540; *Wall Street Journal*, 22 July 1963; FRBNY, C 261 England, 23 July 1963.

57. BB, 210097, 19 July 1963; *The Times*, 20 July 1963; BoE, C 160/35, 27 July 1963, G 3/137, 14 Aug 1963.

58. BoE, G 3/130, 22 Aug 1963, ADM 13/6, 23 Aug 1963, 25 Sept 1963, G 3/138, 27 Nov 1963.

59. BoE, G 3/127, 6 June 1962; PRO, T 295/10, 18 April 1963, 22 April 1963. In general on the Japanese loan, see BB, 210101.

60. *The Times*, 6 Aug 1963, 16 Aug 1963; BoE, ADM 13/6, 23 Aug 1963; PRO, T 326/158, 16 Oct 1963; *FT*, 24 Oct 1963.

61. BoE, G 3/136, 20 June 1963; Schenk, p 236; BoE, EID 10/22, 9 Nov 1963; *FT*, 19 Nov 1963.

62. BoE, EID 10/22, 4–5 Dec 1963; Schenk, p 237; *FT*, 25 Sept 1964; BoE, C 20/5, 16 March 1964.

63. *Banker*, Feb 1964, p 76, April 1964, p 209; *Euromoney*, June 1989, special supplement.

64. BoE, G 3/139, 16 March 1964, ADM 13/7, 31 March 1964, G 3/140, 23 April 1964, G 3/130, 31 Dec 1963, G 3/131, 18 March 1964; *FT*, 12 Oct 1964; BoE, G 3/242, 14 Oct 1964.

65. For a helpful discussion, see Richard Sylla, 'US Banks and Europe: strategy and attitudes' in Battilossi and Cassis, *European Banks*.

66. Sir Fred Warner, *Japan and the City of London* (Oxford, 1988), p 16; *Banker*, June 1971, pp 631–3; Duncan M. Ross, 'Cooperation versus Competition: Consortia and Clubs in European Banking' in Battilossi and Cassis, *European Banks*.

67. *The Times*, 5 Feb 1963; BoE, ADM 13/6, 14 March 1963; *CL*, pp 94–5.

68. BoE, G 3/93, 27 Nov 1961, LDMA 1/13, 19 Jan 1962, 16 Feb 1962.

69. BoE, ADM 12/9, 8 May 1962; PRO, PREM 11/3765, 16 May 1962; BoE, G 3/127, 28 May 1962, 26 June 1962.

70. PRO, PREM 11/4769, 5 Dec 1961; BoE, G 3/93, 19 Dec 1961; *The Times*, 21 March 1962.

71. BoE, G 3/128, 6 July 1962; Michie, p 425; *Sunday Telegraph*, 6 Jan 1963.

72. *Guardian*, 12 Jan 1963; PRO, PREM 11/4196, 13 Jan 1963, 15 Jan 1963.

73. On the theme of the City's relative isolation by the 1960s, see Michael Moran, 'Power, Policy and the City of London' in Roger King (ed), *Capital and Politics* (1983), pp 54–7.

74. BoE, G 3/128, 25 Oct 1962, G 3/135, 15 Jan 1963, 31 Jan 1963, G 3/136, 11 April 1963.

75. HSBC, 192.163, 9 Oct 1963; IHA, Mss 29,328, vol 3, 21 Jan 1964, vol 4, undated memo (c March/April 1964).

76. Harold Macmillan, *At the End of the Day* (1973), p 381; Littlewood, p 116.

77. *FT*, 5 March 1992; Brittan, p 62; *FT*, 19 Jan 1963.

78. BoE, ADM 13/5, 25 Sept 1962, 5 Dec 1962; Milton Gilbert, *Quest for World Monetary Order* (New York, 1980), p 65.

79. PRO, PREM 11/4199, 3–7 Oct 1963, BoE, G 3/130, 2–7 Oct 1963; Cairncross, DC 106/10/3, 14 Dec 1963; BoE, LDMA 1/13, 1 Nov 1963; Cairncross, DC 106/10/3, 21 Nov 1963.

80. SE, Council, 2 Sept 1963; BoE, G 3/139, 20 Jan 1964; BB, 210085, 7 Feb 1964.

81. PRO, PREM 11/4772, 26 Feb 1964, Cairncross, DC 106/10/3, 3 March 1964; PRO, PREM 11/4771, 24 July 1964.

82. *Banker*, Oct 1964, p 619; Richard Kellett, *The Merchant Banking Arena* (1967), pp 62–3, Sir Kenneth Cork, *Cork on Cork* (1988), pp 60–9, Edgar Jones, *True and Fair: A History of Price Waterhouse* (1995), pp 276–7, Littlewood, p 125; *FT*, 18 May 1962; Paul Ferris, *The City* (1965 Pelican edn), pp 36–7; *Banker*, Oct 1964, p 619.

83. Littlewood, p 118.

84. PRO, PREM 11/4777, 1–2 Oct 1964.

85. BoE, LDMA 1/14, 9 Oct 1964, G 3/242, 15 Oct 1964; *FT*, 6 Oct 1964.

CHAPTER TWELVE

1. FRBNY, C 261 England, 19 Oct 1964; Barbara Castle, *The Castle Diaries, 1964–1970* (1984), p xiii; Michael Clarke, *Fallen Idols* (1981), pp 45–6; Stephen Fay, *Portrait of an Old Lady* (1987), p 100; David Kynaston, *The Financial Times* (1988), p 329. More generally on the widespread assumption (especially as fostered by the press) that strong pound = strong Britain, see David Blaazer, ' "Devalued and Dejected Britons": the Pound in Public Discourse in the Mid 1960s' in *History Workshop* (Spring 1999), pp 121–40. See also, for a useful outline of events (by Kathleen Burk) in the three years from autumn 1964 and a stimulating discussion, 'Symposium: 1967 Devaluation' in *Contemporary Record* (Winter 1988), pp 44–53.

2. BoE, LDMA 1/14, 23 Oct 1964, G 3/142, 22 Oct 1964; Milton Gilbert, *Quest for World Monetary Order* (New York, 1980), p 67; *FT*, 28 Oct 1964; BoE, G 1/253, 28 Oct 1964; BB, dep 32.6 (ii), 28 Oct 1964.

3. *The Times*, 4 Nov 1964; *FT*, 4 Nov 1964.

4. Cromer's approach, and the November 1964 sterling crisis generally, is given a penetrating treatment in Keith Middlemas, *Power, Competition and the State: Volume 2* (Basingstoke, 1990), pp 118–19.

5. *FT*, 12 Nov 1964; *Sunday Telegraph*, 15 Nov 1964; *FT*, 13 Nov 1964; BoE, G 1/260, 13 Nov 1964.

6. *FT*, 17 Nov 1964; Tony Benn, *Out of the Wilderness* (1987), p 188; *FT*, 17 Nov 1964; Benn, p 189.

7. PRO, PREM 13/261, 18 Nov 1964; Alec Cairncross, *The Wilson Years* (1997), p 16; Jacques Attali, *A Man of Influence* (1986), pp 241–2.

8. *FT*, 21 Nov 1964; Charles A. Coombs, *The Arena of International Finance* (New York, 1976), p 124; BoE, C 160/36, 20 Nov 1964, G 1/260, 20 Nov 1964.

9. Kenneth O. Morgan, *Callaghan* (Oxford, 1997), pp 215–16; PRO, PREM 13/237, 21 Nov 1964, PREM 13/261, 21 Nov 1964; Richard Crossman, *The Diaries of a Cabinet Minister, Volume One* (1975), pp 68–9.

10. PRO, PREM 13/261, 24 Nov 1964.

11. PRO, PREM 13/261, 24 Nov 1964; Harold Wilson, *The Labour Government, 1964–1970* (1971), p 36.

12. BoE, G 3/242, 25 Nov 1964; Cairncross, *Wilson Years*, p 18; Wilson, p 36; Cairncross, DC 106/10/3, 29 Nov 1964.

13. BoE, G 1/260, 1 Dec 1964; Cairncross, *Wilson Years*, p 22; BoE, OV 44/132, 10 Dec 1964, 14 Dec 1964.

14. PRO, PREM 13/237, 21 Dec 1964; FRBNY, 'Contingency Planning Silver/Gold Market 1964–1973' (microfilm – roll UN), 28 Dec 1964; PRO, PREM 13/237, 23 Dec 1964.

15. Kynaston, *Financial Times*, pp 323–4; *Sunday Telegraph*, 20 Dec 1964; *Sunday Times*, 20 Dec 1964.

16. *Economist*, 19 June 1965; Leslie O'Brien, *A Life Worth Living* (1995), p 57.

17. *Banker*, Dec 1964, p 760.

18. Morgan, pp 218–19; James Callaghan, *Time and Chance* (1987), p 153; NLSC, C 409/031, p 125; Lord Wigg, *George Wigg* (1972), p 310; Nicholas Davenport, *Memoirs of a City Radical* (1974), p 211; Wilson, pp 32–3; Castle, pp 6–7.

19. BoE, G 1/260, 9 Feb 1965; PRO, PREM 13/275, 15 Feb 1965.

20. PRO, PREM 13/275, 16 Feb 1965; *FT*, 17 Feb 1965; Cairncross, DC 106/10/3, 24 Feb 1965; Cairncross, *Wilson Years*, p 54.

21. BoE, G 3/144, 9 March 1965, G 1/260, 10 March 1965, LDMA 1/14, 26 March 1965.

22. Cairncross, *Wilson Years*, p 47; BoE, G 1/260, 31 March 1965, G 3/144, 1 April 1965.

23. BoE, LDMA 1/14, 9 April 1965; John Littlewood, *The Stock Market* (1998), pp 145–7; Callaghan, p 181; SE, Council, 17 May 1965, 24 May 1965.

24. *The Times*, 14 June 1965, 16 June 1965; T. Jackson, *The Origin and History of the Drayton Group* (Croydon, 1991), p 145; *The Cecil King Diary, 1965–1970* (1972), p 19; BoE, G 3/146, 16 July 1965, 1 July 1965.

25. BoE, OV 44/133, 22 July 1965, 26 July 1965; *King*, p 27.

26. BoE, OV 44/125, 5 Aug 1965.

27. Middlemas, pp 167–8, Callaghan, pp 189–90.

28. Morgan, p 226; BoE, G 3/146, 6 Aug 1965; *Banker*, Oct 1965, p 648.

29. BoE, LDMA 1/14, 26 Nov 1965; Rowe & Pitman, *Market Report*, Dec 1965; Littlewood, p 148; Kynaston, *Financial Times*, p 326; BoE, G 3/147, 15 Oct 1965; BB, 210091, 24 Feb 1966.

30. Cairncross, *Wilson Years*, p 99; *King*, p 46; BoE, LDMA 1/14, 17 Dec 1965; *King*, pp 47–8; Callaghan, p 195; Christopher Zinn, 'Whitefella's outback elder', *Guardian*, 4 Nov 1997; O'Brien, pp 60, 62.

31. In general on Warburg and the Labour government, see: Attali, pp 239–47; Ron Chernow, *The Warburgs* (1993), pp 681–2.

32. PRO, PREM 13/278, 18 May 1965; *The Times*, 21 Nov 1964, 20 Nov 1965; BoE, G 3/252, 7 March 1966, 22 March 1966.

33. Rowe & Pitman, *Market Report*, March 1966; PRO, PREM 13/851, 9 March 1966.

34. *King*, pp 60–1; Castle, pp 111–12; Cairncross, DC 106/10/3, 15 March 1966; *FT*, 15 March 1966.

35. *King*, p 67; Callaghan, p 195; O'Brien, p 62; BoE, G 15/650, 'Notes by Lord O'Brien', *c* 1987; *Daily Telegraph*, 26 April 1966; information from Christopher Fildes; Cairncross, *Wilson Years*, p 134. For a helpful (if perhaps too generous) assessment of O'Brien's character and career, see Keith Middlemas, 'Lord O'Brien of Lothbury', *Independent*, 27 Nov 1995.

36. Morgan, pp 239–40, Littlewood, pp 149–50; BoE, LDMA 1/15, 20 May 1966; *Banker*, June 1966, p 353; BoE, G 1/260, 15 June 1966.

37. *King*, pp 74–5.

38. Accounts of the July 1966 sterling crisis include: Alec Cairncross, *Managing the British Economy in the 1960s* (1996), pp 150–4; Morgan, pp 240–7.

39. PRO, PREM 13/853, 12 July 1966; *FT*, 15 July 1966.

40. BoE, OV 44/135, 15 July 1966; PRO, PREM 13/853, 15 July 1966; Wilson, p 251.

41. O'Brien, p 65; BoE, LDMA 1/15, 21 July 1966.

42. BB, 204489, 10 Sept 1966; BoE, C 160/173, 28 Oct 1966; *Spectator*, 18 Sept 1999.

43. *Bank of England Quarterly Bulletin*, Sept 1967, p 258; Rob Stones, 'Government-finance relations in Britain, 1964–7' in *Economy and Society* (Feb 1990), pp 44–6; BoE, G 3/253, 2 June 1966; William M. Clarke, *The City in the World Economy* (1967 Pelican edn), esp pp 240–1.

44. Peter Shearlock and William Ellington, *The Eurobond Diaries* (Brussels, 1994), pp 129–30; Carl-Ludwig Holtfrerich, *Frankfurt as a Financial Centre* (Munich, 1999), pp 269–70; Richard Kellett, *The Merchant Banking Arena* (1967), p 1.

45. Guides to the parallel markets include: Paul Einzig, *Parallel Money Markets. Volume One, The New Markets in London* (1971); G.A. Fletcher, *The Discount Houses in London* (1976), pp 166–72. Specifically on the further development of the Eurodollar market, see Stefano Battilossi, 'Banking with Multinationals' in Stefano Battilossi and Youssef Cassis (eds), *European Banks and the American Challenge, 1950s–1970s* (Oxford, 2001).

46. Kellett, p 70; J.E. Wadsworth (ed), *The Banks and the Monetary System in the UK, 1959–1971* (1973), p 165; *Economist*, 29 Feb 1964; *Banker*, June 1966, pp 354–5, June 1976, pp 607–9, *Euromoney*, June 1984, p 72.

47. *Euromoney*, Feb 1972, p 69; *Banker*, April 1967, p 301; Ian M. Kerr, *A History of the Eurobond Market* (1984), pp 23–5, Niall Ferguson, *The World's Banker: The History of the House of Rothschild* (1998), p 1016; Ian Fraser, *The High Road to England* (Wilby, 1999), pp 269–70.

48. Shearlock and Ellington, p 25; BoE, ADM 13/9, 23 March 1966; BB, 204489, 10 Sept 1966; *Statist*, 10 Feb 1967; *Banker*, April 1967, p 302.

49. Kathleen Burk (ed), 'Witness Seminar on the Origins and Early Development of the Eurobond Market' in *Contemporary European History* (1992), pp 74–5, 84, 81.

50. For the regulatory background in the 1960s, see Richard Roberts, 'How the City put its house in order', *FT*, 5 Nov 1989.

51. Richard Spiegelberg, *The City* (1973), pp 172–4; BoE, G 3/266, 7 July 1967; Jehanne Wake, *Kleinwort Benson* (Oxford, 1997), pp 392–3; *The Times*, 18 July 1967; BoE, G 3/266, 24 July 1967.

52. *Economist*, 11 Nov 1967. The fullest account of the GEC/AEI battle is Robert Jones and Oliver Marriott, *Anatomy of a Merger* (1970), pp 265–313.

53. BoE, G 3/265, 27 June 1967; Anthony Vice, *The Strategy of Takeovers* (Maidenhead, 1971), p 19; BB, 210082, 2 Oct 1967, 25 Oct 1967.

54. JS, no 15, p 20; SE, Council, 10–11 Jan 1966, 18 Jan 1966, 4 April 1966, 12 April 1966, 18 July 1966 (bond-washing); SE, Council, 17 July 1967; Ranald C. Michie, *The London Stock Exchange* (Oxford, 1999), pp 427–8.

55. SE, Sub-Committees of a Non-Permanent Character, vol 27 (1), Committee on Rule 88, 31 Aug 1965, 28 Sept 1965, 5 Oct 1965, 26 Oct 1965, 8 Nov 1965, 16 Dec 1965; Kerr, p 84; Michie, p 466. For an overall account of the Stock Exchange and Eurobonds, see Michie, pp 465–7.

56. Littlewood, p 266; Elizabeth Hennessy, *Stockbrokers for 150 Years: A History of Sheppards and Chase, 1827–1977* (1978), p 46; David Kynaston, *Cazenove & Co* (1991), p 244; Denzil Sebag-Montefiore, *The Story of Joseph Sebag and Co* (1996), pp 58–63.

57. Jonathan Aitken, *The Young Meteors* (1967), pp 291–4. On how stockbroking changed from the mid-1960s, see the discussion in Littlewood, chap 23.

58. Cairncross, *Wilson Years*, p 61; Fraser, p 274; Benn, p 467; BoE, G 3/266, 23 Oct 1967; *New York Times*, 26 Feb 1967.

59. BoE, ADM 35/6, 14 April 1965, 9 June 1965; *Banker*, Sept 1965, pp 612–17; *FT*, 5 April 1967.

60. For plentiful detail about life at Warburgs in the 1960s, see a trio of memoirs: Peter Spira, *Ladders and Snakes* (1997), chap 7; Fraser, chaps 15–16; Peter Stormonth Darling, *City Cinderella* (1999), chaps 1–7.

61. NLSC, C 409/134, p 63; Stormonth Darling, pp 51, 19; Paul Ferris, *Gentlemen of Fortune* (1984), p 199; Stormonth Darling, pp 63, 59; Fraser, pp 270–1.

62. Stormonth Darling, p 59.

63. Fraser, p 280; Spira, p 260. Also on Grunfeld, see *FT*, 14 June 1999.

64. Spira, p 146; Stormonth Darling, p 33; *FT*, 20 Oct 1982; Chernow, pp 670–2. BoE, ADM 13/7, 19 Nov 1964, suggests that rivalry between London and New York houses in the Eurobond market may also have played a part in the divorce from Kuhn Loeb.

65. Stormonth Darling, p 43; Spira, p 152; Stormonth Darling, pp 55, 250–1, 35–6; Spira, pp 259–60.

66. On the creation of Hill Samuel, see Kellett, pp 79–80, 140–58.

67. *The Times*, 12 Jan 1965; Sebag-Montefiore, p 42.

68. *Sunday Telegraph*, 3 April 1966; BoE, G 3/245, 11 March 1966.

69. BoE, G 3/263, 28 June 1966, G 3/264, 7–8 July 1966, 12 July 1966, 14–15 July 1966, 20 July 1966, 2 Aug 1966, 21 Sept 1966, 26 Sept 1966, G 3/265, 10 Jan 1967; *FT*, 19 Sept 1967; Sebag-Montefiore, p 42, Wake, p 381.

70. Kathleen Burk, *Morgan Grenfell, 1838–1988* (Oxford, 1989), pp 192–5; Ian Fraser, 'Lord Poole', *Independent*, 29 Jan 1993; Andrew St George, *JOH* (1992), pp 50–4, *Investors Chronicle*, 3 Feb 1967; *CL*, pp 102–3, Ferguson, pp 1013–17.

71. Richard Roberts, *Schroders* (1992), pp 442, 449–54; *FT*, 20 May 1965; BoE, G 3/134, 13 July 1965; *FT*, 16 Nov 1966, *Economist*, 19 Nov 1966; BB, 204489, 22 Feb 1967.

72. HSBC, Acc 346, file re Montagu Trust Ltd and Samuel Montagu & Co Ltd, 1964–70, 6 Dec 1966, 22 Jan 1967; A.R. Holmes and Edwin Green, *Midland* (1986), p 254; HSBC, 373/3, 7 July 1967, 22 Sept 1967; BoE, G 3/266, 19 Sept 1967.

73. Holmes and Green, p 239; *Banker*, Oct 1967, p 831; BoE, G 3/266, 12 Oct 1967.

74. IHA, Ms 29,328, vol 5, 17 Sept 1965; *Economist*, 7 Oct 1967; *FT*, 2 Oct 1967.

75. *Sunday Telegraph*, 21 June 1964; Cairncross, *Wilson Years*, p 180; Margaret Ackrill and Leslie Hannah, *Barclays* (Cambridge, 2001); BoE, G 3/263, 10 Jan 1966, LDMA 1/15, 4 March 1966. For a suggestive portrait of Barclays in the 1960s, see Charles Gordon, *The Cedar Story* (1993), pp 51–7.

76. Discussions of these considerations include: J.R. Winton, *Lloyds Bank, 1918–1969* (Oxford, 1982), pp 174–6; Margaret Reid, *The Secondary Banking Crisis, 1973–75* (1982), pp 28–9; Stones, pp 43–4 (including the O'Brien quotation); Ackrill and Hannah.

77. See Holmes and Green, p 244, for the background.

78. HSBC, Acc 346, file re disclosure, 1966, 10 Aug 1966; Cairncross, *Wilson Years*, p 161; HSBC, Acc 346, file re disclosure, 1966, 12 Oct 1966, 16 Nov 1966.

79. BoE, G 3/264, 20 Dec 1966, G 3/265, 6 April 1967; Ackrill and Hannah; Holmes and Green, p 234; BoE, G 3/261, 26 Oct 1967.

80. BoE, G 3/134, 16 Dec 1965, G 3/265, 20 March 1967; Winton, p 195, Spiegelberg, pp 111–12; BoE, G 3/265, 22 June 1967; RBS, Margaret Ackrill, 'The National Westminster Bank Group' (1988), Part One, p 13.

81. On the discount market in the 1960s and its response to the parallel markets, see: E.R. Shaw, *The London Money Market* (1975), esp pp 78–81, 219–22; Fletcher, esp pp 172–4, 247–8, 263; George and Pamela Cleaver, *The Union Discount* (1985), pp 96–7.

82. Shaw, pp 220, 81; *Banker*, Jan 1970, pp 34–5; *Euromoney*, Feb 1972, p 37.

83. BoE, LDMA 1/14, 17 Dec 1965.

84. *Spectator*, 13 June 1987.

85. David Kynaston, *LIFFE* (Cambridge, 1997), pp 20–1; NLSC, C 409/057, pp 99–105.

86. There have been two main accounts of Slater's career: Charles Raw, *Slater Walker* (1977); Jim Slater, *Return to Go* (1977).

87. *Sunday Telegraph*, 3 March 1963, 26 May 1963; Raw, pp 95–7.

88. Peter Walker, *Staying Power* (1991), p 67; Raw, pp 116–17.

89. *FT*, 31 Oct 1964; Slater, p 61; Raw, p 117; Slater, pp 62–3.

90. *The Times*, 4 Feb 1965; Raw, pp 124–5.

91. *Sunday Telegraph*, 7 Feb 1965; *Sunday Express*, 16 May 1965.

92. Raw, chaps 10–13; Nigel Broackes, *A Growing Concern* (1979), pp 229–30; *Observer*, 15 Jan 1967.

93. Raw, pp 191–2; *Sunday Times*, 27 Aug 1967; Aitken, p 186.

94. Aitken, pp 294–5; Godfrey Hodgson, *Lloyd's of London* (1984), pp 35, 113, Adam Raphael, *Ultimate Risk* (1995 Corgi edn), pp 75–6.

95. PRO, PREM 13/855, 3 Aug 1966; King, pp 82–3.

96. Rowe & Pitman, *Market Report*, Nov 1966; Littlewood, pp 154–5, *King*, p 99; Crossman, *Vol Two* (1976), pp 119, 123; BoE, LDMA 1/16, 14 April 1967; BB, 210089, 3 May 1967.

97. Cairncross, *Wilson Years*, p 213; Rowe & Pitman, *Market Report*, Aug 1967; *King*, p 137.

98. BoE, G 3/260, 9 Aug 1967; Cairncross, *Managing*, p 179; *King*, pp 141–2.

99. BoE, LDMA 1/16, 15 Sept 1967; Cairncross, *Wilson Years*, p 236.

100. 'Symposium: 1967 Devaluation' (Cairncross); Callaghan, p 218, Morgan, pp 268–9; Leslie O'Brien, *A Life Worth Living* (1995), p 72. In general on the November 1967 sterling crisis and devaluation, see: Cairncross, *Managing*, pp 184–91; Morgan, pp 268–77.

101. *The Times*, 8 Nov 1967, Morgan, pp 269–70; O'Brien, p 72; Callaghan, pp 220–1, Morgan, p 271.

102. Morgan, p 271; *King*, pp 155–6; Morgan, pp 272–3.

103. Cairncross, *Wilson Years*, p 248; PRO, PREM 13/1447, 17 Nov 1967.

104. FRBNY, C 261 England, 21 Nov 1967; *The Times*, 18 Nov 1967.

105. BoE, C 160/39, 19 Nov 1967; Morgan, p 274; *The Times*, 21 Nov 1967; Stormonth Darling, p 71.

106. *Daily Telegraph*, 22 Nov 1967; BoE, G 3/262, 30 Nov 1967; John Fforde, *The Bank of England and Public Policy, 1941–1958* (Cambridge, 1992), p 300.

CHAPTER THIRTEEN

1. BoE, LDMA 1/16, 15 Dec 1967; *The Cecil King Diary, 1965–1970* (1972), pp 163, 170; BoE, LDMA 1/16, 19 Jan 1968; *King*, p 181; BoE, LDMA 1/16, 8 March 1968; Alec Cairncross, *Managing the British Economy in the 1960s* (1996), p 204; *King*, p 181.

2. *King*, p 183; Timothy Green, *The New World of Gold* (1985 edn), p 130; PRO, PREM 13/2051, 15 March 1968.

3. Alec Cairncross, *The Wilson Years* (1997), p 289, PRO, PREM 13/2051, 17 March 1968; BoE, G 3/268, 29 Aug 1968.

4. BoE, G 3/287, 19 March 1968; Roy Jenkins, *A Life at the Centre* (1991), p 231; *FT*, 20 March 1968; BoE, LDMA 1/16, 22 March 1968; Cairncross, *Wilson Years*, p 292.

5. *King*, pp 189, 191; PRO, PREM 13/2017, 9 May 1968; *Daily Mirror*, 10 May 1968; Leslie O'Brien, *A Life Worth Living* (1995), pp 58–9.

6. *King*, pp 203–9; Andrew St George, *JOH* (1992), p 43; PRO, PREM 13/2025, 24 June 1968, 26 June 1968.

7. BoE, LDMA 1/16, 24 May 1968; J.R. Winton, *Lloyds Bank, 1918–1969* (Oxford, 1982), pp 175–6; HSBC, Acc 346, file re Competition and Credit Control, 24 May 1968, 27 May 1968, 29 May 1968, 373/3, 31 May 1968.

8. Cairncross, *Wilson Years*, p 305; BoE, LDMA 1/16, 31 May 1968.

9. On Basle and the sterling balances, see P.L. Cottrell, 'The Bank of England in its International Setting, 1918–1972' in Richard Roberts and David Kynaston, *The Bank of England* (Oxford, 1995), pp 136–7.

10. PRO, PREM 13/2053, 29 Aug 1968, 31 Aug 1968; O'Brien, pp 79–80.

11. *Banker*, Oct 1968, pp 871, 873.

12. Samuel Brittan, *Steering the Economy* (1971 Penguin edn), pp 397–402; *King*, pp 272, 288; Tony Benn, *Office Without Power* (1988), p 136; BoE, G 3/291, 30 Dec 1968.

13. BoE, G 3/291, 15 Nov 1968; Cairncross, *Managing*, pp 224–5; BoE, G 3/269, 9 Jan 1969; HSBC, Acc 346, file re Competition and Credit Control, 27 Jan 1969.

14. BoE, G 3/293, 1 April 1969; J.E. Wadsworth (ed), *The Banks and the Monetary System in the UK, 1959–1971* (1973), p 447; HSBC, 373/4, 30 May 1969, 19 Sept 1969.

15. BoE, G 3/267, 23 May 1968, G 3/268, 8–9 Oct 1968, 30 Oct 1968, G 3/270, 28 July 1969. The support for O'Brien from the clearers and accepting houses is reflected in: BoE, G 3/268, 2 Oct 1968 (Robarts), 1 Nov 1968 (Forbes), G 3/269, 28 Jan 1969 (Parsons note re Mackinnon), G 3/270, 5 Aug 1969 (Thomson).

16. *FT*, 1 July 1985; Sir Gordon Newton, *A Peer Without Equal* (1997), p 127.

17. *King*, p 210; William Davis, *Merger Mania* (Wilby, 1999), p 189.

18. For a City slant on BL's creation, see: Lewis Whyte, *One Increasing Purpose* (1984), pp 107–11, 128–9; Ian Fraser, *The High Road to England* (Wilby, 1999), pp 281–2.

19. BoE, G 3/260, 7 July 1967, 23 Oct 1967.

20. Davis, pp 132–9; *FT*, 25 June 1968. The standard work on the IRC is Douglas Hague and Geoffrey Wilkinson, *The IRC* (1983); for a more critical perspective, see Jim Tomlinson, *Government and the Enterprise since 1900* (1994), pp 267–71. On Villiers, see Nicholas Faith and Richard Roberts, 'Sir Charles Villiers', *Independent*, 24 Jan 1992.

21. Davis, pp 79–90; Robert Jones and Oliver Marriott, *Anatomy of a Merger* (1970), pp 289–313; John Littlewood, *The Stock Market* (1998), p 164.

22. Davis, pp 140–4; Richard Roberts, *Schroders* (1992), pp 433–4.

23. Davis, pp 139, 144–8.

24. Jim Slater, *Return to Go* (1977), p 79; *FT*, 8 May 1968.

25. *FT*, 7 Sept 1968; Charles Raw, *Slater Walker* (1977), pp 248–9, 232; Slater, p 93.

26. Richard Spiegelberg, *The City* (1973), pp 174–6; IHA, Ms 29,328, vol 6, 21 June 1968; Spiegelberg, p 177; BoE, G 3/267, 25 June 1968, LDMA 1/16, 26 July 1968.

27. Accounts of the Gallaher affair include: Dominic Hobson, *The Pride of Lucifer* (1990), pp 114–23; Ron Chernow, *The House of Morgan* (New York, 1990), pp 565–8; David Kynaston, *Cazenove & Co* (1991), pp 263–8, mainly based on Morgan Grenfell records, Box P. 983.

28. Kynaston, *Cazenove*, p 264.

29. Kynaston, *Cazenove*, p 264.

30. Kynaston, *Cazenove*, p 264; BoE, G 3/268, 17 July 1968; Kynaston, *Cazenove*, pp 264–5.

31. Kynaston, *Cazenove*, p 265; Hobson, p 118; Kynaston, *Cazenove*, p 265; Cairncross, DC 106/10/3, 21 July 1968.

32. *The Times*, 19 July 1968; BoE, G 3/268, 19 July 1968.

33. *The Times*, 20 July 1968; *Sunday Telegraph*, 21 July 1968; SE, Council, 22 July 1968. See also JS, no 22 (Davie), pp 28–9.

34. BoE, G 3/268, 24 July 1968; Kynaston, *Cazenove*, p 266.

35. Boe, G 3/268, 26 July 1968; *The Times*, 26 July 1968; *Sunday Telegraph*, 28 July 1968.

36. SE, Council, 29 July 1968, 5 Aug 1968, 9 Aug 1968, 12 Aug 1968; Kynaston, *Cazenove*, pp 266–7.

37. *FT*, 14 Aug 1968; O'Brien, pp 86–7; *Evening News*, 16 Aug 1968.

38. *Daily Telegraph*, 14 Aug 1968.

39. Accounts of the battle include: Davis, pp 194–202; Spiegelberg, pp 179–81; Tom Bower, *Maxwell: The Outsider* (1988), pp 125–35; Hobson, pp 183–4; Chernow, *Morgan*, pp 568–73; Littlewood, p 169.

40. Bower, *Maxwell*, pp 51, 62–3, 96; Ron Chernow, *The Warburgs* (1993), p 693, Fraser, p 294.

41. Bower, *Maxwell*, p 135; Rodney Leach, 'Sins of Cap'n Bob', *TLS*, 28 Feb 1992.

42. Davis, pp 115–16, Roberts, *Schroders*, p 435, Littlewood, p 171. See also Simon London, 'Sunset days at Trafalgar', *FT*, 18 Nov 1995.

43. Davis, pp 222–33, Roberts, *Schroders*, pp 434–5.

44. Tom Bower, *Tiny Rowland* (1994 Mandarin pbk), pp 58–65; BoE, ADM 13/6, 4 July 1963; Bower, *Rowland*, pp 100–2, 126–8.

45. BoE, G 3/268, c 11 Nov 1968, 2 Dec 1968, 4 Dec 1968, G 3/269, 7 Jan 1969; Spiegelberg, p 182; Fraser, pp 279–80, 286–7.

46. BoE, G 3/269, 18 Feb 1969, 25 Feb 1969; HSBC, 200/864, 5 March 1969; Fraser, pp 292–3; Spiegelberg, p 183.

47. This version of the Pergamon/Leasco story derives from: Davis, pp 202–8; Spiegelberg, pp 30–1, 183–9; Frank Welsh, *Uneasy City* (1986), pp 26–9; Bower, *Maxwell*, pp 136–207, 219–22 (the most detailed account); Leach; Roberts, *Schroders*, pp 437–8; Edgar Jones, *True and Fair : A History of Price Waterhouse* (1995), pp 278–80; Littlewood, p 169; Fraser, pp 204, 294–307. See also, for an evocative photograph of Maxwell in action, Judy Slinn, *Ashurst Morris Crisp* (Cambridge, 1997), p 177.

48. Anthony Sampson, *The New Anatomy of Britain* (1971), p 552.

49. On the creation of NatWest, see RBS, Margaret Ackrill, 'The National Westminster Bank Group: A Report on the Merger of the National Provincial and Westminster Banks' (1983). On the abortive Barclays/Lloyds merger, see: Winton, pp 194–200; Margaret Ackrill and Leslie Hannah, *Barclays* (Cambridge, 2001). On both episodes, see Davis, pp 117–27.

50. BoE, G 3/267, 23 Jan 1968, 26 Jan 1968; Ackrill, 'National Westminster', Part One, pp 23–4.

51. PRO, PREM 13/2248, 5 Feb 1968; *FT*, 9 Feb 1968; Davis, pp 120–1; *Banker*, March 1968, p 196; NLSC, C 409/001, p 60.

52. Davis, pp 122–5; *Guardian*, 18 July 1968; Cairncross, *Wilson Years*, p 312; Davis, pp 125–6; *FT*, 18 July 1968.

53. BoE, G 1/16, 12 July 1968, G 3/268, 10 July 1968; Lloyds, HO/Ch/Pea/2, 17 July 1968; PRO, PREM 13/2248, 22 July 1968; Ackrill and Hannah.

54. PRO, PREM 13/2248, 22 July 1968; Lloyds, HO/Ch/Pea/2, 26 July 1968; O'Brien, p 85.

55. *Banker*, Dec 1968, p 1152, March 1967, p 252; BoE, G 3/268, 5 Dec 1968; Spiegelberg, p 118; *Banker*, April 1970, p 360.

56. BB, 204489, 12 Feb 1968; BoE, G 3/269, 19 March 1969, 16 Jan 1969; Jacques Attali, *A Man of Influence* (1986), p 261, Fraser, p 324; BoE, G 3/270, 10 Sept 1969; *FT*, 18 Feb 1970.

57. JS, no 19, pp 15–16, no 20, pp 12–13, no 21, p 14.

58. BoE, G 3/270, 10 Sept 1969; Niall Ferguson, *The World's Banker* (1998), p 1019; *Banker*, Oct 1969, p 1122.

59. Nicholas Goodison, 'Sir Martin Wilkinson', *Independent*, 30 Jan 1990; Ranald C. Michie, *The London Stock Exchange* (Oxford, 1999), pp 469, 454–5; John Burton, 'Michael Nightingale', *Independent*, 8 Feb 1991.

60. Donald Cobbett, *Before the Big Bang* (Portsmouth, 1986), pp 111–12; Michie, pp 436–7, SE, Council, 14 April 1969, 27 May 1969; *FT*, 18 Feb 1970.

61. BB, 202955, credit department's report for 1967; Cairncross, *Wilson Years*, p 319; BoE, G 3/290, 31 Oct 1968; William Clarke, 'The City's movement towards a Eurocurrency standard', *The Times*, 10 Nov 1976; C.R. Schenk, 'International Financial Centres 1958–71: competitiveness and complementarity' in Stefano Battilossi and Youssef Cassis (eds), *European Banks and the American Challenge, 1950s–1970s* (Oxford, 2001).

62. Schenk, 'International Financial Centres'.

63. *Euromoney*, June 1969, p 12; Schenk, 'International Financial Centres'; Peter Shearlock and William Ellington, *The Eurobond Diaries* (Brussels, 1994), p 16, *Euromoney*, June 1999, pp 31, 34.

64. *Banker*, June 1968, p 483; G.A. Fletcher, *The Discount Houses in London* (1976), p 167; *Banker*, Aug 1969, pp 773–4; Fletcher, p 168; Hamish McRae, 'London's Shifting Money Markets', *Banker*, Jan 1970, pp 33–40; BoE, LDMA 1/16, 1 May 1968, 3 May 1968; Fletcher, p 169.

65. The growth of the secondary banks is covered in Margaret Reid, *The Secondary Banking Crisis, 1973–75* (1982), chap 4.

66. *Banker*, Sept 1968, p 804; Reid, p 37, *Daily Telegraph*, 24 Jan 2000; Reid, pp 37–8, 47, *FT*, 2 May 1969, 5 May 1969, Littlewood, p 168.

67. BoE, G 3/290, 3 Oct 1968; Spiegelberg, p 241. In general on Matthews and FNFC, see: Spiegelberg, pp 234–42; Reid, pp 36–7.

68. *Euromoney*, Oct 1972, p 65; *Euromoney*, June 1989, special supplement.

69. In general on the consortium banks, see: Mary Campbell, 'The Multinational Banking Framework', *Banker*, June 1971, pp 628–39; Richard Roberts and Christopher Arnander, 'Here today, gone tomorrow', *International Financing Review* (1999, 25th anniversary issue); Richard Roberts, *Take Your Partners: Orion, the Consortium Banks and the Transformation of the Euromarkets* (Basingstoke, 2001); Duncan M. Ross, 'Cooperation versus Competition: Consortia and Clubs in European Banking' in Battilossi and Cassis.

70. *Economist*, 11 April 1970, Ian M. Kerr, *A History of the Eurobond Market* (1984), pp 34–6, 38, Attali, pp 263–4, *Euromoney*, June 1989, special supplement, Peter Spira, *Ladders and Snakes* (1997), pp 162–4.

71. *Euromoney*, Feb 1971, pp 60–1; Shearlock and Ellington, p 27; *Euromoney*, June 1984, p 65, Shearlock and Ellington, pp 33–43; *Euromoney*, Feb 1971, p 60, June 1969, p 20.

72. The IOS story is told in detail in Charles Raw, Godfrey Hodgson and Bruce Page, *Do You Sincerely Want to Be Rich?* (1971). See also: Kerr, p 33; Attali, p 259; *Euromoney*, June 1989, special supplement, p 270; NLSC, C 409/100, pp 165–7; Anthony Montague Browne, *Long Sunset* (1995), pp 344–8; Andrew Lycett, *From Diamond Sculls to Golden Handcuffs: A History of Rowe & Pitman* (1998), pp 89–91.

73. *Euromoney*, Jan 1970, p 13, Oct 1970, p 20.

74. *Euromoney*, June 1989, special supplement, p 270; Paul Ferris, *Gentlemen of Fortune* (1984), p 224; *Institutional Investor*, May 1978, pp 43–56 (profile of Ross by Cary Reich).

75. *Euromoney*, Nov 1971, p 59; *Banker*, July 1969, p 619, Oct 1969, p 1085; *Euromoney*, June 1969, p 34.

76. *Banker*, June 1969, p 585, Oct 1969, p 1085, *Euromoney*, June 1994, p 59; David Rogers, *The Big Four British Banks* (Basingstoke, 1999), p 216.

77. *Banker*, Oct 1969, p 1085; *Euromoney*, June 1994, p 50.

78. *Euromoney*, June 1969, pp 29–30; *Institutional Investor*, Nov 1976, p 36; *FT*, 3 Nov 1988 (Craven letter); *The Times*, 24 Aug 1996.

79. BoE, G 3/269, 18 Feb 1969; *Banker*, Oct 1969, pp 1063–71.

80. *Euromoney*, Dec 1970, pp 13–15.

81. Rowe & Pitman, *Market Report*, Aug 1969, Jan 1970.

82. On Poseidon, see: James Long, *Inside the Stock Exchange* (Hove, 1978) p 66; Littlewood, pp 169–70.

83. JS, no 2, p 18; Denzil Sebag-Montefiore, *The Story of Joseph Sebag and Co* (1996), p 37; NLSC, C 408/009, p 147.

84. For overall accounts of the Select Committee, see: Spiegelberg, pp 139–43; O'Brien, pp 95–9.

85. Richard Crossman, *The Diaries of a Cabinet Minister, Volume Two* (1976), p 667; BoE, G 3/268, 10 July 1968, 9 Oct 1968, G 3/269, 3 Jan 1969.

86. Select Committee on Nationalised Industries: Bank of England, *First Report* (1969–70, vi), p 120; O'Brien, p 97; Select Committee, pp 184–5, 1033, 1399–1400.

87. Benn, pp 233–4; *Banker*, Aug 1970, pp 820–5.

88. BoE, G 3/268, 9–10 Oct 1968.

89. On the Cromer Report, see: Godfrey Hodgson, *Lloyd's of London* (1984), pp 113–14; Adam Raphael, *Ultimate Risk* (1995 Corgi pbk), pp 75–80. The report itself is at the Bank of England Information Centre.

90. *Time*, 21 Feb 2000 (David McClintick), *Independent*, 26 Feb 2000 (James Dalrymple).

91. Kynaston, *Cazenove*, pp 274–5; BB, 204980, 25 March 1970, 12 May 1970.

92. *Management Today*, May 1970, pp 110–18.

93. *Economist*, 1 Feb 1969; Raw, p 215, Anthony Vice, *The Strategy of Takeovers* (Maidenhead, 1971), pp 1–11; Slater, pp 167–8.

94. Slater, pp 119–20; *The Mayfair Set*, BBC2, 25 July 1999; Davis, p 217.

95. Slater, pp 122–4; *Economist*, 2 May 1970; *FT*, 1 May 1970.

96. *FT*, 1 Feb 1969.

97. On the joint committee, see: Michael Moran, *The Politics of Banking* (Basingstoke, 1984), pp 51–3; Keith Middlemas, *Power, Competition and the State: Volume 2* (Basingstoke, 1990), pp 306, 443; Robert Elgie and Helen Thompson, *The Politics of Central Banks* (1998), p 58.

98. *Banker*, April 1970, p 359.

99. *King*, p 307; O'Brien, p 97; *The Times*, 3–4 June 1970.

100. Littlewood, pp 173–4; Jenkins, p 308.

CHAPTER FOURTEEN

1. David Jordan, *Nile Green* (1973), pp 9, 91–3.

2. *The Cecil King Diary, 1970–1974* (1975), pp 119–20; Simon Bradley and Nikolaus Pevsner, *The Buildings of England: London 1: The City of London* (1997), pp 316–17; *The Times*, 23 Sept 1970; George and Pamela Cleaver, *The Union Discount* (1985), p 106; Stephen Fay, *Portrait of an Old Lady* (1987), p 20; Philip Ziegler, *The Sixth Great Power* (1988), p 362; John Littlewood, *The Stock Market* (1998), p 271; David Kynaston, *Cazenove & Co* (1991), p 276.

3. Bradley and Pevsner, pp 510, 575.

4. NLSC, C 408/009, pp 151–4; SE, Council, 8 May 1973.

5. Littlewood, pp 442, 159–63; Andrew Lycett, *From Diamond Sculls to Golden Handcuffs: A History of Rowe & Pitman* (1998), p 92; Laurie Dennett, *Slaughter and May* (Cambridge, 1989), pp 229–30, 236–40; Edgar Jones, *True and Fair: A History of Price Waterhouse* (1995), pp 257, 271–3.

6. Lycett, p 86; Dominic Hobson, *The Pride of Lucifer* (1990), pp 125–6; Jonathan Davis, *Money Makers* (1998), pp 66–9; BoE, G 3/288, 4 June 1968; Ranald C. Michie, *The London Stock Exchange* (Oxford, 1999), pp 483–4, SE, Council, 1 May 1972; Anthony Sampson, *The New Anatomy of Britain* (1971), p 473.

7. Christopher Booker and Candida Lycett Green, *Goodbye London* (1973), pp 115–32; SE, Council, 13 Nov 1973; Bradley and Pevsner, pp 131–2; David Lloyd (ed), *Save the City* (1976), pp xiii, 50.

8. John Orbell, 'The development of office technology' in Alison Turton (ed), *Managing Business Archives* (1991), pp 68, 65, 74, 81; Michie, p 511; Paul Bazalgette, *Musings of a Market Man* (1983), Nov 1971; Michie, pp 503–4, Adrian Hamilton, *The Financial Revolution* (1986), pp 42–3.

9. Richard Whitley, 'Commonalities and Connections among Directors of Large Financial Institutions' in *Sociological Review* (Nov 1973), pp 613–32; Richard Spiegelberg, *The City* (1973), pp 131–2; Martin Vander Weyer, *Falling Eagle: The Decline of Barclays Bank* (2000), pp 67, 111; *Independent*, 25 Jan 1993.

10. NLSC, C 409/048, p 59; *CL*, pp 121–2, 198–9, 163–4.

11. SE, Council, 29 March 1971, 5 April 1971; Michie, p 482; SE, Council, 6 Nov 1973.

12. *The Times*, 22 June 1971; *CL*, p 175; *Naked City*, BBC2, 23 Oct 1996, testimony of Susan Shaw; JS, no 13, p 18.

13. Spiegelberg, p 157, NLSC, C 409/071, pp 103–11; Elizabeth Hennessy, 'The Governors, Directors and Management of the Bank of England' in Richard Roberts and David Kynaston (eds), *The Bank of England* (Oxford, 1995), pp 207–9; Michie, pp 480–1.

14. Ian Fraser, *The High Road to England* (Wilby, 1999), pp 327–8; CL, p 127; *The Times*, 17 Nov 1997.

15. W.J. Reader and David Kynaston, *Phillips & Drew* (1998), pp 155, 158.

16. FT, 31 Oct 1987 (Riley); Spiegelberg, pp 21–4, 245.

17. Jonathan Raban, *Soft City* (1974), p 55.

CHAPTER FIFTEEN

1. *FT*, 1–2 July 1970, 4 July 1970; Anthony Sampson, *The New Anatomy of Britain* (1971), p 535; Richard Spiegelberg, *The City* (1973), pp 17–18.

2. *Banker*, Aug 1970, p 808; records of Accepting Houses Committee (Guildhall Library), Ms 29,310, file 41; *The Times*, 25 Feb 1970, *Management Today*, Aug 1971, p 77.

3. George G. Blakey, *The Post-War History of the London Stock Market* (Didcot, 1994 pbk edn), p 101; John Littlewood, *The Stock Market* (1998), p 176; Leslie O'Brien, *A Life Worth Living* (1995), p 105; *The Cecil King Diary, 1970–1974* (1975), pp 54, 67–8.

4. City-oriented accounts include: A.R. Holmes and Edwin Green, *Midland* (1986), pp 274–6; Kathleen Burk, *Morgan Grenfell, 1838–1988* (Oxford, 1989), pp 198–200.

5. HSBC, 373/4, 13 Nov 1970; O'Brien, pp 107–8; *King*, p 54; Sampson, p 478; FRBNY, C 261 England, 5 Feb 1971; HSBC, Acc 346, Rolls-Royce, 1970–3, inc Thompson memo, 16 Feb 1971.

6. O'Brien, p 107; *Banker*, March 1971, p 236; Sampson, p 579.

7. Harold Evans, *Vickers* (1978), pp 159–69; *Investors Chronicle*, 19 March 1971; *Journal of the Institute of Bankers*, June 1971, p 146; O'Brien, pp 110–11; John Plender, *That's the Way the Money Goes* (1982), p 65.

8. O'Brien, pp 111–12; *Banker*, Dec 1971, p 1571; Burk, pp 195–8, Dominic Hobson, *The Pride of Lucifer* (1990), pp 128–37; *Euromoney*, March 1971, pp 6–7.

9. *Management Today*, Oct 1972, p 29, Aug 1971, pp 68–9.

10. *Management Today*, Aug 1971, pp 70–3; Terry Maher, *Against My Better Judgement* (1994), pp 13–18.

11. Littlewood, pp 179–80; *King*, pp 106, 126; Rowe & Pitman, *Market Report*, Aug 1971.

12. Prior to Bank of England records becoming available, the authoritative account of the coming of CCC remains Michael Moran, *The Politics of Banking* (Basingstoke, 1984), pp 30–53. See also: Spiegelberg, pp 119–22, 151–2; G.A. Fletcher, *The Discount Houses in London* (1976), pp 201–17; Margaret Reid, *The Secondary Banking Crisis, 1973–75* (1982), pp 29–33; Keith Middlemas, *Power, Competition and the State: Volume 2* (Basingstoke, 1990), pp 289–90, 305–8; O'Brien, pp 114–17; Margaret Ackrill and Leslie Hannah, *Barclays* (Cambridge, 2001).

13. *King*, pp 54, 116; O'Brien, p 114; Charles Gordon, *The Cedar Story* (1993), p 146.

14. Holmes and Green, p 244; HSBC, Acc 346, file re Competition and Credit Control, 6 Nov 1970, 23 Nov 1970, Acc 141, no 13 (one of two, this one called 'Capital Structure'), July 1973.

15. Reid, pp 31–2; HSBC, Acc 346, file re CCC, 28 Jan 1971, 8 Feb 1971, Acc 141, no 8, Feb 1971.

16. *Banker*, April 1971, p 345, June 1971, pp 565–75; HSBC, 373/4, 21 May 1971, 25 June

1971, 23 July 1971, 6 Aug 1971; Edward du Cann, *Two Lives* (Upton-upon-Severn, 1995), p 130.

17. Spiegelberg, p 121; *Packshaw's Town Crier*, Oct 1971.

18. David Kynaston, *LIFFE* (Cambridge, 1997), p 9; Middlemas, p 334; O'Brien, p 124.

19. HSBC, Acc 346, file re Bank of England, 28 Feb 1973; Janet Kelly, *Bankers and Borders* (Cambridge, Mass, 1977), pp 59–60; Adrienne Gleeson, *London Enriched* (1997), pp 87–8.

20. *Management Today*, Aug 1971, p 77; *Euromoney*, Dec 1972, p 6; Christopher Booker and Candida Lycett Green, *Goodbye London* (1973), p 121.

21. Timothy Green, *The New World of Gold* (1985 edn), pp 132–4.

22. The full story is told in Donald Read, *The Power of News: The History of Reuters, 1849–1989* (Oxford, 1992), pp 301–7.

23. Read, p 303; *International Insider*, 25 May 1973; Russell Taylor, *Going for Broke* (1993), p 166; Read, p 307.

24. Jeffrey Robinson, *The Risk Takers – Five Years On* (1990), p 17.

25. George Bull, 'The History of Mercantile House' (*c* 1985), pp 83–7, NLSC, C 409/057, pp 115–18.

26. *Economist*, 23 Sept 1972; *Banker*, July 1972, pp 929–31; *Euromoney*, June 1989, special supplement, Aug 1977, pp 66, 69.

27. *Euromoney*, June 1989, special supplement; *International Insider*, 24 Sept 1973; *Euromoney*, March 1984, p 53.

28. Spiegelberg, pp 95–6; Kelly, p 136; David Rogers, *The Big Four British Banks* (Basingstoke, 1999), p 24.

29. Richard Roberts, *Take Your Partners: Orion, the Consortium Banks and the Transformation of the Euromarkets* (Basingstoke, 2001).

30. Taylor, p 139.

31. *The Times*, 2 Aug 1996; Junko Sakai, *Japanese Bankers in the City of London* (2000), pp 31–3; *International Insider*, 27 June 1977, 6 March 1978; *Euromoney*, June 1989, special supplement.

32. Martin Vander Weyer, *Falling Eagle: The Decline of Barclays Bank* (2000), pp 56–7. See also Rogers, pp 72–5, for his analysis of Barclays and international overreach.

33. Rogers, pp 128–9; *British Empires*, Channel 4, 9 Jan 2000; *Management Today*, Sept 1972, p 30.

34. SE, Council, 8 March 1971; Ranald C. Michie, *The London Stock Exchange* (Oxford 1999), pp 495–7; SE, Council, 29 Nov 1971, 14 Aug 1972.

35. Guides to the Barber boom and monetary explosion during the two years after September 1971 include: Reid, pp 58–80; Moran, pp 55–84; Middlemas, pp 341–8, 378–80.

36. Peter Kirwin (ed), *A Tribute to the Bank of England* (1994), p 90; Reid, pp 59–60; *Euromoney*, Dec 1973, p 63.

37. Rowe & Pitman, *Market Report*, Jan 1972; Littlewood, p 182; Jim Slater, *Return to Go* (1977), p 155, Reid, p 71; *FT*, 21 Jan 1972; *Euromoney*, Jan 1972, p 23.

38. *Management Today*, June 1971, p 68; Anthony Vice, *The Strategy of Takeovers* (Maidenhead, 1971), p 1; Sampson, p 501; Slater, pp 150–1, Charles Raw, *Slater Walker* (1977), p 305; Reid, p 71; Raw, p 305.

39. Slater, pp 128–9, 160; Raw, pp 315–16.

40. *Sunday Telegraph*, 12 Dec 1971, 23 Jan 1972, 30 Jan 1972.

41. Nigel Broackes, *A Growing Concern* (1979), p 211; *The Times*, 27 Oct 1975 (Hugh Stephenson); *The Mayfair Set*, BBC2, 25 July 1999.

42. Raw, p 307.

43. *The Times*, 27 Oct 1975 (Stephenson), *FT*, 13 Oct 1977 (Barry Riley).

44. Broackes, p 211.

45. *King*, p 186; O'Brien, p 123; *FT*, 22 March 1972; *King*, p 200.

46. Raw, p 305; *Observer*, 7 May 1972; *Sunday Times*, 7 May 1972.

47. Ian M. Kerr, *A History of the Eurobond Market* (1984), p 41; *Euromoney*, June 1972, p 21; RBS, Margaret Ackrill, 'The National Westminster Bank Group: A Report on the Merger of the National Provincial and Westminster Banks' (1983), Part Four, p 13; Slater, pp 168, 162.

48. *Daily Mail*, 10 May 1972; Littlewood, p 188.

49. Littlewood, pp 185–6; T. Jackson, *The Origin and History of the Drayton Group* (Croydon, 1991), pp 193–5.

50. For background to the foray by Smiths, see: *Economist*, 15 July 1972; Fletcher, pp 225–9.

51. JS, no 2, p 22, no 42, p 14.

52. *King*, p 206; William Keegan and Rupert Pennant-Rea, *Who Runs the Economy?* (1979), p 135; Reid, pp 74, 77; *Banker*, Sept 1972, pp 1131–3.

53. On Bank thinking during the early to mid-1970s, see: Keegan and Pennant-Rea, pp 100–1; Stephen Fay, *Portrait of an Old Lady* (1987), p 78.

54. *Management Today*, Aug 1972, pp 52–3; Gordon, p 195.

55. Discussions of the methods of the secondary banks include: Jack Revell, *The British Financial System* (1973), pp 239–55; Reid, pp 34–5, 42–4, 61–7; Holmes and Green, pp 264–5. For a notably critical contemporary analysis, see John Littlewood's contribution in *Investment Analyst*, June 1973.

56. Reid, pp 37–9.

57. Gordon, esp chap 8 about the declining quality of Cedar's business.

58. Reid, pp 37, 94–5, Blakey, pp 131, 148–9, Spiegelberg, pp 229–34, Raw, pp 170, 250–1, 322; Sir Gordon Newton, *A Peer Without Equal* (1997), p xi.

59. *New Statesman*, 6 July 1979; Reid, pp 37–8, Blakey, pp 122, 132.

60. Reid, pp 36–7, Blakey, pp 121, 131–2; Spiegelberg, pp 241–2.

61. Du Cann, pp 129–34, Reid, pp 39, 170–1, Gordon, pp 197–8, Blakey, pp 121–2, 132.

62. Reid, pp 48–52, offers a balanced overview of the supervisory relationship between the Bank and the secondaries.

63. BoE, LDMA 1/16, 3 Feb 1967; Gordon, pp 234–5; Kirwin, pp 162–3.

64. Middlemas, p 344; *Spectator*, 23 May 1987 (Jock Bruce-Gardyne); FRBNY, C 261, England, 9 Nov 1972.

65. Spiegelberg, p 80; NLSC, C 409/070, pp 147–64; *FT*, 8 Dec 1972, *The Times*, 12 Dec 1997; Taylor, p 205 (for an alternative version of why Montagu left, see the obituary of Lord Swaythling in *The Times*, 6 July 1998); Cathy Courtney, 'Lord Swaythling', *Independent*, 13 July 1998.

66. *Investors Review*, 8 March 1974.

67. From a City perspective, the most detailed account of the P&O/Bovis battle is Douglas Moffitt, 'The Hundred Incredible Days', *Investors Review*, 8 March 1974, 22 March 1974, 5 April 1974. See also: Karin Newman, *Financial Marketing and Communications* (Eastbourne, 1984), pp 96, 118; Burk, pp 218–23 (inc Fleet quotation from *Daily Telegraph*, 20 Nov 1972); Hobson, pp 124–5; A.B. Marshall, *Taking the Adventure* (Wilby, 1999), pp 71–132; Ian Fraser, *The High Road to England* (Wilby, 1999), pp 314–17.

68. David Morrell, *Indictment* (1987), esp Part Three.

69. SE, Council, 13 Nov 1972; *FT*, 25 Nov 1972; *The Times*, 10 Jan 1973.

70. Fraser, pp 314–16, discusses the insider dealing question during his three years (1969–72) at the Takeover Panel.

71. *The Times*, 3 Feb 1973, 7 Feb 1973; *Daily Telegraph*, 7 Feb 1973; *Sunday Times*, 29 April 1973.

72. Accounts of ARIEL include: Littlewood, pp 265–6; Michie, pp 504–6.

73. JS, no 37, pp 15–16; SE, Council, 10 Jan 1972.

74. Records of Phillips & Drew (at Guildhall Library), 19 Sept 1972.

75. SE, Council, 22 Jan 1973, 19 Feb 1973; FT, 20 Sept 1973, *Daily Telegraph*, 20 Sept 1973; SE, Council, 10 April 1973; HSBC, Acc 346, file re Bank of England, 18 April 1973.

76. HSBC, Acc 346, file re Bank of England, 28 Feb 1973, 13 March 1973; Reid, pp 79–80; Ackrill and Hannah.

77. Littlewood, p 193; Slater, pp 174–6, *Daily Mail*, 25 Jan 1973; *Investors Guardian*, 6 March 1973; Paul Bazalgette, *Musings of a Market Man* (1983), March 1973.

78. Middlemas, p 345; *King*, pp 271, 279; BoE, C 160, 7 March 1973. On the question of why O'Brien retired in 1973, he himself insisted in his memoirs (*A Life Worth Living*, p 134) that the decision was simply fulfilling the agreement he had reached with Barber prior to the start of his second term in 1971.

79. Middlemas, p 345; Gordon Pepper, *Inside Thatcher's Monetarist Revolution* (1998), p 17, quoting *FT*, 3 May 1973; Tony Benn, *Against the Tide* (1989), p 33; *Daily Telegraph*, 4 June 1973.

80. *The Times*, 27 April 1973; Slater, pp 176–9, 181; *The Times*, 27 April 1973.

81. *Daily Telegraph*, 27 April 1973; *FT*, 27 April 1973; *Sunday Times*, 29 April 1973; Slater, p 179; *Fortune*, June 1973, pp 202, 206.

82. Tom Bower, *Tiny Rowland* (1994 Mandarin edn), chaps 5–6.

83. Bower, p 252 (Heath); *King*, p 278.

84. *Sunday Times*, 3 June 1973; *Daily Telegraph*, 4 June 1973; *Daily Mail*, 13 June 1973; *Sunday Times*, 17 June 1973; *Daily Mail*, 18 June 1973.

85. Slater, p 181; *The Times*, 20 June 1973; *Investors Chronicle*, 22 June 1973.

86. BoE, G 3/12, 2 Jan 1959; R.P.T. Davenport-Hines, in the forthcoming *New Dictionary of National Biography*.

87. *Investors Chronicle*, 28 Jan 1972; John Roberts, *Megalomania, managers and mergers* (1987), p 135; Jackson, pp 188–9; *Investors Chronicle*, 1 June 1973; Littlewood, p 199.

88. Littlewood, p 199; Roberts, *Megalomania*, p 136; *City Press*, 18 Sept 1975.

89. HSBC, Acc 141, no 13 ('Capital Structure'), July 1973; *Investors Chronicle*, 8 June 1973.

90. *King*, p 318; NLSC, C 409/009, p 121, C 409/111, p 56; Fay, chap 4.

91. Reid, p 68; *The Times*, 21 May 1973, Gordon, pp 193–5; *Management Today*, Aug 1973, pp 81–7.

92. Reid, p 69; HSBC, Acc 141, no 13 ('Capital Structure'), July 1973; Holmes and Green, pp 263–4, 271.

93. Reid, p 79; John Campbell, *Edward Heath* (1993), p 530.

94. David McClintick, 'The Decline and Fall of Lloyd's of London', *Time*, 21 Feb 2000.

CHAPTER SIXTEEN

1. George G. Blakey, *The Post-War History of the London Stock Market* (Didcot, 1994 pbk edn), pp 142–3.

2. Keith Middlemas, *Power, Competition and the State: Volume 2* (Basingstoke, 1990), p 380; Ron Chernow, *The House of Morgan* (New York, 1990), pp 606–8.

3. John Littlewood, *The Stock Market* (1998), p 201; Rowe & Pitman, *Market Report*, Dec 1973.

4. David Kynaston, *Cazenove & Co* (1991), p 287, *FT*, 3 Dec 1973; *Daily Mail*, 7 Dec 1973; *Euromoney*, Dec 1973, p 63.

5. James Lees-Milne, *Ancient as the Hills* (1997), p 110; Littlewood, p 202.

6. The three fullest accounts of the secondary banking crisis and its outcome are to be found in: Margaret Reid, *The Secondary Banking Crisis, 1973–75* (1982); Michael Moran, *The Politics of Banking* (Basingstoke, 1984); Charles Gordon, *The Cedar Story* (1993). See also

Keith Middlemas, *Power, Competition and the State: Volume 3* (Basingstoke, 1991), pp 30–4.

7. Gordon, p 197. On the L&C crisis and its resolution, see: HSBC, Acc 141, no 27, Memorandum 'A', 12 Feb 1974; Reid, pp 82–4; Gordon, pp 196–9; Blakey, pp 146–7.

8. HSBC, Acc 141, no 19, 19 Dec 1973. It has not yet proved possible to locate the minutes of the first three meetings.

9. Littlewood, p 202; HSBC, 373/5, 21 Dec 1973; Edward du Cann, *Two Lives* (Upton-upon-Severn, 1995), pp 134–5.

10. HSBC, Acc 141, no 19, 19 Dec 1973; Reid, p 91 (Cornhill).

11. *Spectator*, 7 Dec 1985.

12. Reid, p 12.

13. Easily the most detailed account of the Cedar rescue is Gordon, pp 214–80. See also: Reid, pp 3–10; *FT*, 22 June 1993 (Barry Riley's review of Gordon).

14. Reid, p 10 (Jenkins); Gordon, p 279 (Bevan).

15. Reid, p 11; HSBC, Acc 141, no 19, 20 Dec 1973, 373/5, 21 Dec 1973.

16. HSBC, 373/6, 4 Jan 1974; Reid, pp 14–15; HSBC, 373/6, 4 Jan 1974.

17. Stephen Fay, *Portrait of an Old Lady* (1987), p 62.

18. Rowe & Pitman, *Market Report*, Jan 1974; Blakey, p 152; *FT*, 6 Feb 1974.

19. *Banker*, Feb 1974, pp 151–5.

20. Du Cann, pp 135–6; HSBC, Acc 141, nos 22–5, 8–28 Jan 1974.

21. *Investors Chronicle*, 25 Jan 1974; Reid, p 203; HSBC, Acc 141, no 26, 11 Feb 1974; Reid, p 92.

22. Lees-Milne, p 131; *Euromoney*, March 1975, p 67; *FT*, 13 Feb 1974, 4 March 1974.

23. *Banker*, Dec 1973, p 1433; HSBC, 200/766, 2 Oct 1973 (transcript of Wilson's speech); Littlewood, p 205.

24. *Independent on Sunday*, 5 April 1992; Denis Healey, *The Time of My Life* (1989), pp 374–5.

25. *The Cecil King Diary, 1970–1974* (1975), p 350; Paul Bazalgette, *Musings of a Market Man* (1983), April 1974; JS, no 41, p 20.

26. *Investors Chronicle*, 19 April 1974; Rowe & Pitman, *Market Report*, May 1974; Tony Benn, *Against the Tide* (1989), p 145.

27. HSBC, 74 (Management Committee boxes), 24 April 1974; Reid, p 106, RBS, Margaret Ackrill, 'The National Westminster Bank Group' (1983), Part Four, p 7; Blakey, p 157.

28. Jim Slater, *Return to Go* (1977), pp 189–96, Blakey, p 165.

29. Lees-Milne, p 161; *The Mayfair Set*, BBC2, 25 July 1999; Slater, p 198.

30. NLSC, C 409/008, p 149, C 408/009, pp 144–5; *FT*, 11 Feb 1974.

31. Ranald C. Michie, *The London Stock Exchange* (Oxford, 1999), p 506; *Banker*, Dec 1974, p 1525; *FT*, 29 Sept 1978; *Banker*, Dec 1974, p 1522; *FT*, 14 Aug 1976, 29 Sept 1978; Michie, p 483.

32. *International Insider*, 4 Feb 1974; Peter Shearlock and William Ellington, *The Eurobond Diaries* (Brussels, 1994), p 29; Janet Kelly, *Bankers and Borders* (Cambridge, Mass, 1977), pp 64–5; *Euromoney*, Oct 1977, pp 122–3.

33. BB, 202469, May 1974; *International Insider*, 20 May 1974; HSBC, 74 (MC boxes), 29 May 1974; BB, 202469, July 1974.

34. In general on the collapse of Herstatt and its consequences, see: Reid, pp 115–17; Shearlock and Ellington, p 136; Marjorie Deane and Robert Pringle, *The Central Banks* (1994), pp 153–6.

35. *Euromoney*, June 1994, p 59; King, p 371.

36. *International Insider*, 15 July 1974, 22 July 1974; Reid, p 117; *Euromoney*, Nov 1977, p 85 (Nicholas Faith); Richard Roberts, *Take Your Partners: Orion, the Consortium Banks and the Transformation of the Euromarkets* (Basingstoke, 2001), pp 78–9, 178–9.

37. Reid, pp 102–8, Sir Kenneth Cork, *Cork on Cork* (1988), pp 93–102; NLSC, C 409/001, pp 72, 74–5.

38. Reid, pp 120, 130, Gordon, p 293.
39. Reid, pp 170–6, du Cann, pp 136–9; *King*, pp 374, 318.
40. Reid, pp 120–1.
41. Reid, p 144, Fay, p 62.
42. Moran, pp 114–17. See also: Reid, pp 195–6; Middlemas, *Volume 3*, pp 124–5.
43. Reid, pp 121–2; HSBC, Acc 141, nos 35–6, 19 Aug 1974, 21 Aug 1974.
44. BoE, C 160, 19 June 1974; Littlewood, p 208; SE, Liaison Committee, 31 July 1974.
45. *Sunday Telegraph*, 18 Aug 1974; Littlewood, p 209; *Banker*, Oct 1974, pp 1187–90 (Murray/Hamilton/Jenkins/Hutchinson/Day); Rowe & Pitman, *Market Report*, Sept 1974.
46. BoE, C 160/164, 4 Sept 1974.
47. *Sunday Telegraph*, 8 Sept 1974; HSBC, 74 (MC boxes), 4 Sept 1974.
48. For a full account, see Elroy Dimson and Paul Marsh, *Cases in Corporate Finance* (Chichester, 1988), pp 191–200. See also: Kynaston, *Cazenove*, p 289; Jehanne Wake, *Kleinwort Benson* (Oxford, 1997), p 411; Littlewood, p 212.
49. *FT*, 25 Sept 1974; *Investors Chronicle*, 27 Sept 1974; *Investors Review*, 4 Oct 1974.
50. *Investors Chronicle*, 18 Oct 1974; Rowe & Pitman, *Market Report*, Oct 1974.
51. For another account of the 'Lever Bank', see Richard Coopey and Donald Clarke, *3i* (Oxford, 1995), pp 123–7.
52. *Sunday Times*, 15 Sept 1974; *The Times*, 22 Sept 1974.
53. *FT*, 21 Oct 1974; HSBC, 74 (MC boxes), 23 Oct 1974, 6 Nov 1974, 373/6, 8 Nov 1974, Acc 141, no 46, 28 July 1975; Michael Moss, *Standard Life, 1825–2000* (Edinburgh, 2000), pp 283–4.
54. *Investors Chronicle*, 25 Oct 1974; Rowe & Pitman, *Market Report*, Nov 1974; Littlewood, p 213; *FT*, 29 Nov 1974.
55. Reid, pp 123–5, JS, no 15 (Powell), p 13.
56. Middlemas, *Volume 3*, p 65; Russell Taylor, *Going for Broke* (1993), p 214; HSBC, Acc 141, nos 38–9, 21 Nov 1974, 25 Nov 1974.
57. *Investors Chronicle*, 22 Nov 1974; Blakey, p 166; *Investors Chronicle*, 1 Nov 1974; *Banker*, Dec 1974, pp 1515–19; *Slater*, p 204.
58. Slater, p 205; *FT*, 24 Dec 1974; *CL*, p 130; JS, no 36, p 22, no 20, p 26, no 9, pp 29–30; *The Times*, 11 Nov 1999; *CL*, p 198.
59. Jonathan Davis, *Money Makers* (1998), p 86; JS, no 15, p 22; SE, 1977 Annual Report; Michie, pp 514, 489–91.
60. Anthony Sampson, *The Changing Anatomy of Britain* (1982), p 313; Middlemas, *Volume 3*, p 36.
61. Accounts include: John Plender, *That's the Way the Money Goes* (1982), pp 53–5; Laurie Dennett, *A Sense of Security: 150 Years of Prudential* (Cambridge, 1998), pp 338, 418; Moss, p 284.
62. Littlewood, p 218; *The Times*, 18 Dec 1974; *FT*, 24 Dec 1988 (Heather Farmbrough); *Sunday Telegraph*, 30 Aug 1998 (Winterflood profile); Moss, p 284.
63. JS, no 9, p 29; Bazalgette, Jan 1975; Andrew Lycett, *From Diamond Sculls to Golden Handcuffs: A History of Rowe & Pitman* (1998), p 122.
64. Blakey, p 171, *FT*, 7 Jan 1975; Littlewood, p 218; *International Insider*, 6 Jan 1975.

CHAPTER SEVENTEEN

1. Rowe & Pitman, *Market Report*, Feb 1975; John Littlewood, *The Stock Market* (1998), pp 216, 221; Rowe & Pitman, *Market Report*, Feb 1975; Littlewood, p 223.
2. The most detailed account is Margaret Reid, *The Secondary Banking Crisis, 1973–75* (1982), chaps 10–12.

3. Reid, p 128; David Wainwright, *Henderson* (1985), pp 92–3; Reid, p 129; HSBC, Acc 141, no 43, 4 March 1975, no 48, 22 Aug 1975.

4. Brian Goldthorpe, 'Leonard Mather', *Independent*, 14 May 1991; *Investors Review*, 31 Oct 1975; Reid, pp 144–5; HSBC, 74 (Management Committee boxes), 2 June 1975, Ron Chernow, *The Warburgs* (1993), p 692.

5. *FT*, 11–12 Feb 1975; *Euromoney*, March 1975, p 67; Keith Middlemas, *Power, Competition and the State: Volume 3* (Basingstoke, 1991), p 206.

6. Kenneth O. Morgan, *The People's Peace* (Oxford, 1990), p 378; Gordon Pepper, *Inside Thatcher's Monetarist Revolution* (1998), p 21; Stephen Fay, *Portrait of an Old Lady* (1987), p 70.

7. Edmund Dell, *A Hard Pounding* (Oxford, 1991), p 135; Rowe & Pitman, *Market Report*, May 1975.

8. HSBC, 373/7, 4 April 1975; SE, Council, 29 April 1975; FRBNY, C 261 England, 9 June 1975; *FT*, 5 June 1975.

9. Kathleen Burk, 'Symposium: 1976 IMF Crisis' in *Contemporary Record* (Nov 1989), p 39; Tony Benn, *Against the Tide* (1989), p 390; HSBC, 200/554, 10 June 1975, 200/766, June 1975.

10. *Euromoney*, July 1975, p 107; Littlewood, p 226; Dell, pp 162–3, Barbara Castle, *The Castle Diaries, 1974–76* (1980), pp 434–5.

11. Rowe & Pitman, *Market Report*, July 1975; *FT*, 14 July 1975.

12. Edmund Dell, *The Chancellors* (1996), p 419; *International Insider*, 13 Oct 1975; HSBC, 74 (MC boxes), 22 Oct 1975; Fay, p 71.

13. *FT*, 25 Oct 1975. In general on the Slater Walker endgame, see: Charles Raw, *Slater Walker* (1977), chap 22; Jim Slater, *Return to Go* (1977), chaps 16–19; Reid, pp 138–43, 183–9.

14. *Daily Mail*, 20 Oct 1975; Peter Parker, *For Starters* (1989), p 175; SE, Council, 23 Dec 1975 (which has other details about the events of Slater's last week at Slater Walker); Slater, p 219; *Daily Telegraph*, 25 Oct 1975.

15. Rowe & Pitman, *Market Report*, Jan 1976; *Institutional Investor*, Dec 1976, p 45; *International Insider*, 19 Jan 1976.

16. *Euromoney*, June 1989, special supplement, Oct 1975, p 63.

17. *Institutional Investor*, March 1980, p 194; Richard Roberts, *Take Your Partners: Orion, the Consortium Banks and the Transformation of the Euromarkets* (Basingstoke, 2001), pp 106–7.

18. JS, no 36, pp 16–17, no 24 (Raven), p 29; *The Times*, 5 Jan 1976; *Daily Telegraph*, 13 Feb 1989.

19. *Spectator*, 12 March 1988; SE, Council, 12 Nov 1974.

20. Accounts of the March 1976 sterling crisis include: Fay, pp 73–6; Kathleen Burk and Alec Cairncross, *'Goodbye, Great Britain': The 1976 IMF Crisis* (1992), pp 21–33.

21. *International Insider*, 1 March 1976; Fay, p 74.

22. *The Times*, 5 March 1976, 9 March 1976; *FT*, 9 March 1976; *International Insider*, 15 March 1976; BB, 202445, mid-March 1976; Denis Healey, *The Time of My Life* (1989), p 427.

23. *The Times*, 6 March 1976; FRBNY, C 261 England, 15 March 1976; HSBC, 200/554, 16 March 1976.

24. *The Times*, 17 March 1976; David Kynaston, *The Financial Times* (1988), p 430.

25. From an extensive literature, discussions of City/industry relations (including during the 1970s) include: Yao-Su Hu, *National Attitudes and the Financing of Industry* (1975); Grahame Thompson, 'The relationship between the financial and industrial sector in the United Kingdom economy' in *Economy and Society* (1977); John C. Carrington and George T. Edwards, *Financing Industrial Investment* (1979); William M. Clarke, *Inside the City* (1979), chaps 3, 7; Sir Arthur Knight, 'Wilson Revisited: Industrialists and Financiers' (Policy Studies Institute, Discussion Paper No 5, 1982); Michael Lisle-Williams, 'The State,

Finance and Industry in Britain' in Andrew Cox (ed), *State, Finance and Industry* (Brighton, 1986); Scott Newton and Dilwyn Porter, *Modernization Frustrated* (1988), chaps 6–7; Ranald C. Michie, *The City of London* (Basingstoke, 1992), chap 4; Will Hutton, *The State We're In* (1995), esp chaps 5–6; Ranald C. Michie, *The London Stock Exchange* (Oxford, 1999), pp 531–9; Geoffrey Owen, *From Empire to Europe* (1999), chap 14.

26. *Economist*, 9 Oct 1976.

27. Hu, p 60; *Investors Chronicle*, 6 Dec 1974; *FT*, 28 Jan 1975.

28. *Daily Telegraph*, 21 Jan 1976; *FT*, 9 April 1975; *FT*, 23 April 1975, 6 May 1975.

29. *FT*, 8 May 1975, 7 May 1975.

30. *Investors Chronicle*, 30 May 1975, 6 June 1975, 13 June 1975; Middlemas, p 79.

31. *The Times*, 9 June 1975; HSBC, 200/766, *The World at One*, 9 June 1975; *The Times*, 13 June 1975.

32. SE, Council, 1 July 1975.

33. *The Times*, 30 May 1975; *FT*, 30–1 May 1975; *The Times*, 7 June 1975, 12 July 1975.

34. HSBC, 200/752, 12 May 1975; Richard Coopey and Donald Clarke, *3i* (Oxford, 1995), p 125; HSBC, 74 (MC boxes), 26 Jan 1976.

35. *FT*, 17 Oct 1975; HSBC, 74 (MC boxes), 22 Oct 1975; NLSC, C 409/009, p 129; *Banker*, Feb 1976, pp 195–6.

36. HSBC, 74 (MC boxes), 26 Jan 1976; *Banker*, Feb 1976, p 163; HSBC, 74 (MC boxes), 3 March 1976; John Plender, *That's the Way the Money Goes* (1982), p 66; NLSC, C 409/009, p 129; Sidney Pollard, *The Development of the British Economy, 1914–1980* (1983), p 385.

37. *Daily Telegraph*, 8–9 Sept 1976; *Economist*, 11 Sept 1976; *The Times*, 25 Sept 1976.

38. *Economist*, 9 Oct 1976; Midlemas, pp 34–5, 73, Sir David Walker, 'Lord Benson', *Independent*, 13 March 1995, Pen Kent, 'Corporate Workouts: A UK Perspective' in D. Masciandaro and F. Riolo (eds), *Crisi D'Impresa E Risanamento* (Milan, 1997), pp 300–2.

39. Sir Kenneth Cork, *Cork on Cork* (1988), pp 104–10.

40. Clarke, *Inside*, p 44; Committee to Review the Functioning of Financial Institutions, *Evidence on the Financing of Industry and Trade* (1977–8), vol 2, pp 49–60, *Research Report No 1: Survey of Investment Attitudes and Financing of Medium-Sized Companies* (1978), pp 31–2.

41. *New Statesman*, 8 Dec 1978; *FT*, 26 June 1980 ('Wilson gives broad approval for City').

42. Accounts of the sterling/IMF crisis between April and December 1976 include: Burk, 'Symposium'; Dell, *Hard Pounding*, pp 212–91; Burk and Cairncross; Dell, *Chancellors*, pp 422–38; Kenneth O. Morgan, *Callaghan* (Oxford, 1997), pp 528–54.

43. HSBC, 74 (MC boxes), 7 April 1976; Morgan, *Callaghan*, p 523; James Callaghan, *Time and Chance* (1987), p 415; BB, 202445, mid-April 1976; Morgan, *Callaghan*, p 480.

44. *International Insider*, 3 May 1976; *The Times*, 20 April 1976; Littlewood, p 229, Pepper, pp 142–3, Burk, 'Symposium', p 43.

45. HSBC, 200/554, 25 May 1976; *International Insider*, 7 June 1976.

46. Burk, 'Symposium', p 45; HSBC, 200/554, 8 June 1976.

47. Fay, p 79; Burk and Cairncross, pp 52–3, *The Times*, 10 Sept 1988 (Gore Browne obituary), Peter Kirwin (ed), *A Tribute to the Bank of England* (1994), p 159.

48. *The Times*, 23 July 1976; HSBC, 200/554, 27 July 1976.

49. *New Statesman*, 28 Feb 2000.

50. FRBNY, C 261 England, 30 Sept 1976.

51. HSBC, 200/554, 28 Sept 1976; NLSC, C 409/037 (Sir David Walker), pp 93–4; Morgan, *Callaghan*, p 535; *FT*, 30 Sept 1976; Healey, p 429.

52. Callaghan, p 428; BB, 202445, end-September 1976.

53. *Institutional Investor*, June 1987, p 68; *International Insider*, 18 Oct 1976; Morgan, *Callaghan*, p 542; BB, 202445, end-October 1976.

54. *Euromoney*, Aug 1977, p 78 (Peter Hambro); Morgan, *Callaghan*, p 553; *The Times*, 10 Nov 1976.

55. Rowe & Pitman, *Market Report*, Dec 1976.

56. *Euromoney*, Dec 1976, p 54, Jacques Attali, *A Man of Influence* (1986), pp 288–9; Kathleen Burk, 'The House of Morgan Redivivus?: The Abortive Morgan International 1972–73' in *Business History* (July 1991), pp 194–5.

57. Littlewood, pp 233–43; Paul Bazalgette, *Musings of a Market Man* (1983), Oct 1977.

58. W.J. Reader and David Kynaston, *Phillips & Drew* (1998), p 168; SE, 1978 Annual Report; Rowe & Pitman, *Market Report*, Sept 1978.

59. Middlemas, p 140; Fay, p 69: Morgan, *Callaghan*, pp 508–9, Middlemas, p 526; Bernard Donoughue, *Prime Minister* (1987), p 102.

60. William Keegan and Rupert Pennant-Rea, *Who Runs the Economy?* (1979), pp 103–4, Healey, p 435, Middlemas, pp 143–4; *Bank of England Quarterly Bulletin*, March 1978, p 33; *The Times*, 18 April 2000 (obituary of Fforde); Frank Longstreth, 'The City, Industry and the State' in Colin Crouch (ed), *State and Economy in Contemporary Capitalism* (1979), p 189. See also Fay, pp 79–82, for a helpful account of the Bank's conversion to 'practical monetarism'.

61. Rowe & Pitman, *Market Report*, April–May 1978.

62. Tony Benn, *Conflicts of Interest* (1990), pp 305–7; Rowe & Pitman, *Market Report*, June–July 1978.

63. Donoughue, pp 143–4; *Economist*, 15 July 1978.

64. The fairly complex story is told in: Michael Moran, *The Politics of Banking* (Basingstoke, 1984), pp 118–30; Fay, pp 86–97.

65. For the background, see *FT*, 9 March 1978 ('Policing the markets').

66. SE, 4 March 1975, 11 Nov 1975; *FT*, 9 March 1978, 12 Oct 1978.

67. Michael Clarke, *Fallen Idols* (1981), p 232; *FT*, 21 July 1978; *Economist*, 30 Sept 1978; *FT*, 20 Oct 1978; Clarke, *Fallen Idols*, p 202.

68. Hamish McRae and Frances Cairncross, *Capital City* (1985 edn), p 92.

69. Adrienne Gleeson, *London Enriched: The development of the foreign banking community in the City over five decades* (1997), p 160; *International Insider*, 5 Sept 1977, 12 Sept 1977, 26 Sept 1977; *FT*, 16 Nov 1977.

70. Cary Reich, 'The lunch game', *Institutional Investor*, March 1978, pp 39–54.

71. Reader and Kynaston, p 174; David Kynaston, *Cazenove & Co* (1991), p 297; Edgar Jones, *True and Fair: A History of Price Waterhouse* (1995), pp 275, 287–8.

72. *FT*, 20 Feb 1989 ('Global Custody' survey); *Euromoney*, June 1999, p 35.

73. *Institutional Investor*, May 1977, pp 45–72.

74. *Euromoney*, Jan 1978, pp 69–87.

75. *Euromoney*, Oct 1995, p 67; CL, p 144; McRae and Cairncross, pp 213–14, David Kynaston, *LIFFE* (Cambridge, 1997), pp 1–78.

76. *Institutional Investor*, March 1980, p 145; NLSC, C 408/009, p 166; David Kynaston, 'The Long Life and Slow Death of Exchange Controls' in *Journal of International Financial Markets* (May 2000), p 41; Margaret Thatcher, *The Downing Street Years* (1993), p 44; Kynaston, 'Long Life', p 38.

77. Accounts of the BP sale include: *Institutional Investor*, Dec 1977, pp 40–4; David Wainwright, *Government Broker* (1990), pp 102–3; Littlewood, pp 236–7.

78. Andrew Lycett, *From Diamond Sculls to Golden Handcuffs: A History of Rowe & Pitman* (1998), p 124.

79. *Economist*, 31 March 1979.

80. Cary Reich, 'Probing the Mystique of Warburgs', *Institutional Investor*, Feb 1977, pp 27–34, Peter Stormonth Darling, *City Cinderella* (1999), pp 111–12

81. Kathleen Burk, *Morgan Grenfell, 1838–1988* (Oxford, 1989), pp 253–4, Dominic Hobson, *The Pride of Lucifer* (1990), pp 154–7.

82. Ian Fraser, *The High Road to England* (Wilby, 1999), pp 343–4; *Institutional Investor*, Jan 1981, pp 110, 119; Jehanne Wake, *Kleinwort Benson* (Oxford, 1997), p 413; John Gapper

and Nicholas Denton, *All That Glitters: The Fall of Barings* (1996), pp 92–101.

83. *International Insider*, 16 June 1975; *New Statesman*, 17 Aug 1979, 21 Sept 1979, *Institutional Investor*, Aug 1983, p 115, Paul Ferris, *Gentlemen of Fortune* (1984), pp 48–50, *Euromoney*, June 1989, special supplement, Andrew St George, JOH (1992), pp 56–8.

84. Charles Meynell, 'The Rothschild dilemma', *Euromoney*, Oct 1977, pp 121–33. See also: Cary Reich, 'Inside the Rothschild feud', *Institutional Investor*, July 1980, pp 49–62; Niall Ferguson, *The World's Banker: The History of the House of Rothschild* (1998), p 1021.

85. Martin Vander Weyer, *Falling Eagle: The Decline of Barclays Bank* (2000), p 111; Richard Roberts, *Schroders* (1992), p 484, *Euromoney*, Sept 1995, pp 50–1; Ferris, p 146.

86. *Institutional Investor*, Feb 1977, p 33; *Spectator*, 27 July 1985; *Banker*, July 1977, p 64. Also on BMB, see Vander Weyer, pp 63–5.

87. HSBC, 373/7, 21 Nov 1975; Russell Taylor, *Going for Broke* (1993), pp 219–22; *The Times*, 21 Sept 1976.

88. *Banker*, Aug 1977, pp 113–17; *Economist*, 31 March 1979; *Euromoney*, July 1981, pp 141–7.

89. HSBC, 74 (MC boxes), 10 June 1976; Taylor, p 216.

90. *International Insider*, 19 Feb 1979; *Euromoney*, June 1989, special supplement; *Banker*, Aug 1976, p 919; *Institutional Investor*, May 1977, p 57; Stan Hurn, 'Defining moments', *International Financing Review* (25th anniversary issue, 1999), pp 56–9; *Euromoney*, June 1989, special supplement, May 1976, p 58.

91. *International Insider*, 25 April 1977, 19 Sept 1977; *Euromoney*, June 1989, special supplement; *International Insider*, 13 March 1978; *CL*, p 105.

92. On Mattle, see: Armin Mattle, 'What a Eurobond underwriting commitment means', *Euromoney*, Dec 1976, pp 66–8; *Institutional Investor*, May 1977, p 64; Peter Shearlock and William Ellington, *The Eurobond Diaries* (Brussels, 1994), p 55.

93. *International Insider*, 19 April 1976, 17 Jan 1977; *Institutional Investor*, May 1977, p 64.

94. See Cary Reich's profile of CSWW in *Institutional Investor*, Nov 1976, pp 31–6, 64, 93.

95. Ian M. Kerr, *A History of the Eurobond Market* (1984), p 48, *International Insider*, 2 May 1977, 26 Sept 1977; Padraic Fallon, 'How the Citicorp issue rocked the Euromarkets', *Euromoney*, Nov 1977, pp 12–19; *Euromoney*, March 1984, p 50, *Institutional Investor*, May 1985, p 72, *FT*, 3 Nov 1988 (Craven letter).

96. *Institutional Investor*, Jan 1978, p 39; *CL*, p 117; *Institutional Investor*, May 1977, p 47, Jan 1978, p 33.

97. Clarke, *Inside the City*, pp 78–9. On the increasing problems facing the jobbing system by the late 1970s, see: JS, no 8 (Michael Sargent), pp 13–16, no 14 (Angus Ashton), pp 22–4, no 24 (Stephen Raven), pp 33–5.

98. JS, no 9 (Brian Winterflood), p 32 (re Smiths); SE, Council, 16 Jan 1978.

99. SE, Council, 16 Jan 1978; Littlewood, pp 293, 319–20; JS, no 2, p 24, no 33, p 6.

100. SE, Council, 17 June 1977.

101. SE, Council, 11 Oct 1977; *FT*, 9 Oct 1978.

102. SE, Council, 16 Jan 1978; Michie, *London Stock Exchange*, p 499; Clarke, *Inside the City*, pp 85–8.

103. Michie, *London Stock Exchange*, pp 527–31.

104. SE, Council, 29 July 1975, Special Committee on Dealing in Options, 15 Jan 1976, Council, 16 Jan 1978; Rowe & Pitman, *Market Report*, April 1978; SE, Options Committee, 28 Nov 1978.

105. SE, Council (apprendixes), 16 May 1978.

106. On Lloyd's by the late 1970s, see: Godfrey Hodgson, *Lloyd's of London* (1984), chaps 4, 7, 9; Adam Raphael, *Ultimate Risk* (1995 Corgi edn), chap 4.

107. *Time*, 21 Feb 2000.

108. Hodgson, p 218.
109. NLSC, C 409/015 (Sir Peter Miller), pp 109–10; Raphael, pp 91–2.
110. Rowe & Pitman, *Market Report*, Jan 1979; BoE, C 160.
111. SE, Liaison Committee, 28 Feb 1979; JS, no 11, pp 24–5; Littlewood, pp 244–5.
112. *Evening Standard*, 11 April 1979, 1 May 1979, 3 May 1979.
113. Bazalgette, *Musings*, May 1979.

CHAPTER EIGHTEEN

1. John Littlewood, *The Stock Market* (1998), pp 287–90; W.J. Reader and David Kynaston, *Phillips & Drew* (1998), p 181; David Thomas, *The Amstrad Story* (1990), pp 1–2.
2. Accounts of the start of the grey market and the reaction to it include: Anon (Stanley Ross), 'Ali Baba and the bear trap', *Euromoney*, Sept 1979, pp 18–22; David Cudaback, 'The revolution in Eurobond pricing', *Institutional Investor*, Oct 1979, pp 46–56; Ian M. Kerr, *A History of the Eurobond Market* (1984), pp 88–9; Peter Shearlock and William Ellington, *The Eurobond Diaries* (Brussels, 1994), pp 57–64.
3. *International Insider*, 12 March 1979, 7 May 1979, 14 May 1979, 4 June 1979; Paul Ferris, *Gentlemen of Fortune* (1984), pp 225–6.
4. Anthony Sampson, *The Money Lenders* (1981), p 112; *Institutional Investor*, Dec 1979, pp 106–8, Shearlock and Ellington, p 100; *Euromoney*, June 1989, special supplement.
5. David Kynaston, *LIFFE* (Cambridge, 1997), pp 17–18.
6. *FT*, 24 Oct 1979; Keith Middlemas, 'The Party, Industry, and the City' in Anthony Seldon and Stuart Ball (eds), *The Conservative Century* (Oxford, 1994), pp 486–8.
7. The background to the abolition of exchange controls is discussed in: David Kynaston, 'The Long Life and Slow Death of Exchange Controls' in *Journal of International Financial Markets* (May 2000); Richard Roberts, 'Setting the City Free: The Impact of the UK Abolition of Exchange Controls' in *Journal of International Financial Markets* (Aug 2000).
8. *Daily Telegraph*, 24 Oct 1979; *FT*, 24–5 Oct 1979; Tony Benn, *Conflicts of Interest* (1990), p 549.

CHAPTER NINETEEN

1. SE, Council (appendixes), 4 Nov 1980; Peter Spira, *Ladders and Snakes* (1997), p 239.
2. *FT*, 11 March 1981; *The Times*, 30 March 1981; Paul Bazalgette, *Musings of a Market Man* (1983), April 1981.
3. John Littlewood, *The Stock Market* (1998), p 316.
4. *FT*, 2 April 1983; Rowe & Pitman, *Market Report*, June 1983.
5. On government/Bank relations in the early 1980s, see: William Keegan, *Mrs Thatcher's Economic Experiment* (1985 Penguin edn), chap 5; Stephen Fay, *Portrait of an Old Lady* (1987), chap 7; Keith Middlemas, *Power, Competition and the State: Volume 3* (Basingstoke, 1991), pp 243–59; Nigel Lawson, *The View from No 11* (1992), chaps 7–8; Robert Elgie and Helen Thompson, *The Politics of Central Banks* (1998), pp 61–3.
6. Geoffrey Howe, *Conflict of Loyalty* (1994), p 139; Lawson, p 71.
7. Keith Middlemas, 'The Party, Industry, and the City' in Anthony Seldon and Stuart Ball (eds), *The Conservative Century* (Oxford, 1994), pp 489–90; Howe, p 204.
8. Lawson, pp 114–17, Jock Bruce-Gardyne, *Ministers and Mandarins* (1986), pp 97–9;

Lawson, pp 92–4; Margaret Reid, *All-Change in the City* (Basingstoke, 1988), pp 154–5; Martin Vander Weyer, *Falling Eagle: The Decline of Barclays Bank* (2000), pp 80–1.

9. The succession process is discussed in Fay, pp 126–7.

10. *FT*, 29 Dec 1982.

11. Accounts of the early privatisations include: Lawson, chaps 18–19; Jehanne Wake, *Kleinwort Benson* (Oxford, 1997), pp 416–17; Littlewood, pp 361–5.

12. *FT*, 31 Oct 1981.

13. *FT*, 9 Feb 1982, 12 Feb 1982, 20 Feb 1982, 27 Feb 1982.

14. *FT*, 11 Nov 1982, 20 Nov 1982, 23 Nov 1982.

15. *Daily Telegraph*, 3 March 1993.

16. Institutional Investor, March 1980, pp 155–6.

17. Fay, pp 122–6, provides an excellent account. See also: Anthony Sampson, *The Changing Anatomy of Britain* (1982), pp 309–11; Reid, pp 216–18.

18. Fay, p 124.

19. SE, Council (appendixes), 22 Jan 1980; Littlewood, pp 300–1, Andrew Lycett, *From Diamond Sculls to Golden Handcuffs: A History of Rowe & Pitman* (1998), pp 126–31.

20. Reid, p 244; *The Times*, 18 July 1981, 18 Feb 1983, 24 March 1983, 22 April 1983.

21. *The Times*, 5 Jan 1998 (obituary of Gower); SE, Council (appendixes), 27 Oct 1981; Michael Moran, 'Power, Policy and the City of London' in Roger King (ed), *Capital and Politics* (1983), p 64.

22. Neil Osborn, 'What's ailing Lloyd's of London?', *Institutional Investor*, March 1980, pp 81–92.

23. On Lloyd's in the early 1980s, see: Godfrey Hodgson, *Lloyd's of London* (1984), pp 285–361; Adam Raphael, *Ultimate Risk* (1995 Corgi edn), pp 89–124. There is also much of interest in Hugh Cockerell, *Lloyd's of London* (1984).

24. Raphael, pp 89–91; *Daily Telegraph*, 29 May 1992 (obituary of St George), Raphael, pp 279–85.

25. *Time*, 21 Feb 2000; Hodgson, p 318.

26. On the Howden affair, see also: *FT*, 18 Aug 1989 (reporting the acquittals at Southwark Crown Court of Grob and Posgate); Jeffrey Robinson, *The Risk Takers – Five Years On* (1990), pp 239–55.

27. NLSC, C 409/015, pp 128–30; Raphael, p 104.

28. Ian Hay Davison, *Lloyd's* (1987), pp 6, 59; *Naked City*, BBC2, 6 Nov 1996.

29. *Spectator*, 1 Sept 1984; *Institutional Investor*, Nov 1984, p 127; Davison, pp 154–5; *Institutional Investor*, Nov 1984, p 127; *Daily Telegraph*, 30 July 1996; *The Times*, 19 Sept 1996; Godfrey Hodgson, 'Sir Peter Green', *Independent*, 31 July 1996.

30. David Cudaback, 'Assessing the abolition of exchange controls', *Institutional Investor*, March 1980, pp 141–52; SE, Council (appendixes), 18 Oct 1983.

31. Richard Roberts, 'Setting the City Free: The Impact of the UK Abolition of Exchange Controls' in *Journal of International Financial Markets* (Aug 2000), p 136. This is a valuable article about a subject that, granted its generally recognised importance, has received surprisingly little scholarly attention.

32. *FT*, 3 May 1980; David Rogers, *The Big Four British Banks* (Basingstoke, 1999), pp 32–3; Fay, pp 132–5, Reid, pp 140–6.

33. Vander Weyer, pp 81–8.

34. *Euromoney*, July 1981, pp 141–7; *Independent*, 17 June 1992 (Hamish McRae); Tom Bower, *Maxwell: The Outsider* (1988), chap 12.

35. For the most detailed account of Midland's involvement with Crocker, see *FT*, 25 Jan 1988, 27 Jan 1988, 29 Jan 1988 (David Lascelles). See also: *Institutional Investor*, Dec 1978, pp 164–8, July 1984, pp 53–7; Russell Taylor, *Going for Broke* (1993), pp 219–24; Rogers, pp 177–80.

36. *Institutional Investor*, July 1984, p 55; *FT*, 25 Jan 1988, 27 Jan 1988.

37. *Daily Mail*, 26 April 1980; Edward du Cann, *Two Lives* (Upton-upon-Severn, 1995),

p 142; *Independent*, 28 Feb 1989; *The Times*, 12 Dec 1997 (obituary of Kissin).

38. *Observer*, 29 March 1981; Dominic Lawson, 'The Privateers of Privatisation', *Spectator*, 15 Oct 1988. On the feud, see: *Institutional Investor*, July 1980, pp 49–62 (Cary Reich); *Spectator*, 8 April 2000 (Peter Oborne).

39. Neil Osborn, 'The outsiders move in', *Institutional Investor*, Jan 1981, pp 115–19.

40. Ron Chernow, *The Warburgs* (1993), pp 703–5; Peter Stormonth Darling, *City Cinderella* (1999), p 115; *Daily Telegraph*, 18 Jan 1993.

41. Accounts include: Karin Newman, *Financial Marketing and Communications* (Eastbourne, 1984), pp 102–11; Dominic Hobson, *The Pride of Lucifer* (1990), pp 178–82.

42. Descriptions of the new order at Morgan Grenfell include: Gregory Miller, 'Britain's M&A upstart', *Institutional Investor*, Dec 1985, pp 79–82; Hugh Sebag-Montefiore, 'Morgan Grenfell: The Insider Story', *Observer Magazine*, 30 July 1989; Hobson, chap 5; Ron Chernow, *The House of Morgan* (New York, 1990), pp 661–9.

43. Chernow, *Morgan*, p 668.

44. Paul Ferris, *Gentlemen of Fortune* (1984), pp 176, 1, 25–6. It is worth noting that the last two figures were for not fully disclosed profits.

45. Laing & Cruickshank, *Accepting Houses: Annual Report* (1984), pp 10–11.

46. John Plender and Paul Wallace, *The Square Mile* (1985), pp 67–76.

47. George and Pamela Cleaver, *The Union Discount* (1985), pp 111–12; *Spectator*, 16 Jan 1982.

48. David Kynaston, *LIFFE* (Cambridge, 1997), chaps 1–3.

49. Spira, pp 253–7; NLSC, C 409/046, pp 362–5; *Investors Chronicle*, 10 June 1983.

50. Stormonth Darling, p 120.

51. *Euromoney*, June 1989, special supplement.

52. For a fuller guide to the innovations summarised in this paragraph, see Peter Shearlock and William Ellington, *The Eurobond Diaries* (Brussels, 1994), pp 88–102. See also: *Euromoney*, Aug 1980, pp 13–21 (Nigel Adam on the bought deal); *Institutional Investor*, Dec 1981, p 98; Hobson, pp 237–9; *Euromoney*, June 1999, pp 82–4.

53. Reid, pp 11–12.

54. *Institutional Investor*, Nov 1976, p 36, Dec 1980, p 129; Ferris, pp 219–23.

55. *Institutional Investor*, Dec 1980, p 127; *Euromoney*, Feb 1980, p 23; *Institutional Investor*, March 1984, p 63; *Euromoney*, June 1989, special supplement.

56. Michael David Kandiah (ed), '"Big Bang": The October 1986 Stock Market Deregulation' in *Contemporary British History* (Spring 1999), p 104. Accounts of the lead-up to the 1983 Parkinson/Goodison agreement include: Reid, pp 23–50; Cecil Parkinson, *Right at the Centre* (1992), pp 242–9; Lawson, pp 398–400; Steven K. Vogel, *Freer Markets, More Rules* (Ithaca, 1996), pp 93–106; Littlewood, pp 318–22; Kandiah, pp 100–32; Ranald C. Michie, *The London Stock Exchange* (Oxford, 1999), pp 543–53.

57. SE, Liaison Committee, 29 Nov 1979.

58. NLSC, C 408/009, pp 176–8; Kandiah, p 105.

59. Reid, p 36; SE, Council (appendixes), 25 Nov 1980; NLSC, C 408/009, p 179, Kandiah, p 127; *Independent on Sunday*, 11 Feb 1990.

60. Michie, pp 571–3, Littlewood, p 304; *Independent*, 22 Dec 1992 (McRae), 8 Feb 1991 (obituary of Nightingale).

61. SE, Options Committee, 29 Feb 1980, Committee on Commissions, Dealings and Options, 12 Jan 1981, 23 May 1983.

62. SE, Committee on Commissions, Dealings and Options, 3 Feb 1981.

63. SE, Council (appendixes), 9 March 1981, 20 May 1982, 27 May 1982, Liaison Committee, 15 Sept 1982.

64. NLSC, C 408/009, p 178; Kandiah, p 107; SE, Council, 19 Jan 1982; Littlewood, p 324; *Money for Nothing: How the Big Bang Bubble Burst*, ITV, 25 Feb 1991.

65. Ian J. Fraser, 'Sir Anthony Lincoln', *Independent*, 14 Aug 1991; Reid, pp 42–3; SE, Council (appendixes), 16 March 1982; Kynaston, *LIFFE*, pp 54–5.

66. Plender and Wallace, pp 84–7.

67. *CL*, p 124; John Gapper and Nicholas Denton, *All That Glitters* (1996), pp 76–7; W.J. Reader and David Kynaston, *Phillips & Drew* (1998), pp 182–3.

68. SE, Council (Appendixes), 18 Oct 1983.

69. Fay, p 27; Vogel, pp 104–5.

70. Reid, pp 46–7, 26.

71. Vogel, p 106, NLSC, C 408/009, p 183; Kandiah, pp 111–12; Lawson, pp 398–400.

72. Reid, pp 47–8; Parkinson, p 246, Vogel, p 106; Reid, p 48.

73. SE, Council, 21–2 July 1983.

74. *Economist*, 23 July 1983; *The Times*, 26 July 1983; Kandiah, p 112; Reid, p 49; *Daily Telegraph*, 28 July 1983; Reader and Kynaston, p 187; *The Times*, 30 July 1983.

75. Michie, p 552; SE, Council (appendixes), 6 Sept 1983.

CHAPTER TWENTY

1. *FT*, 25 Oct 1983, 4 Nov 1983, John Plender and Paul Wallace, *The Square Mile* (1985), pp 53–7.

2. Alan Clark, *Diaries* (1993), p 34; *Banker*, Nov 1983, p 93.

3. Margaret Reid, *All-Change in the City* (Basingstoke, 1988), pp 52–3.

4. *Banker*, Nov 1983, pp 97–8.

5. Jehanne Wake, *Kleinwort Benson* (Oxford, 1997), pp 423–4; Dominic Hobson, *The Pride of Lucifer* (1990), pp 207–9; NLSC, C 409/111, p 136.

6. David Rogers, *The Big Four British Banks* (Basingstoke, 1999), p 46; Plender and Wallace, p 110; Reid, p 58; Andrew Lorenz, *BZW: The First Ten Years* (1996), pp 10–13. Also on the thinking at Barclays, see Martin Vander Weyer, *Falling Eagle: The Decline of Barclays Bank* (2000), pp 128–9.

7. *Banker*, Nov 1983, pp 98–100; Lorenz, p 13; W.J. Reader and David Kynaston, *Phillips & Drew* (1998), p 188; Plender and Wallace, p 109; Andrew Lycett, *From Diamond Sculls to Golden Handcuffs: A History of Rowe & Pitman* (1998), pp 117–19, 136, *Wall Street Journal*, 29 Sept 1983.

8. JS, no 7, p 19; *FT*, 25 Oct 1996.

9. *FT*, 4 Nov 1983, 8 Nov 1983, 12 Nov 1983.

10. *FT*, 15 Nov 1983; *Sunday Telegraph*, 20 Nov 1983.

11. *Institutional Investor*, Dec 1985, pp 81–2, Hobson, pp 184–8 (inc Magan quotation), John Littlewood, *The Stock Market* (1998), pp 340–1.

12. *FT*, 27 Jan 1988 (David Lascelles).

13. *FT*, 17 Dec 1983.

14. *FT*, 28 Dec 1983.

15. *FT*, 10 Jan 1984; Littlewood, pp 324–5; *FT*, 13 Jan 1984. See also: Lycett, pp 137–8; Hugh Sebag-Montefiore, 'Morgan Grenfell', *Observer Magazine*, 30 July 1989.

16. Helpful guides to the Gower Report and the general regulatory story of the 1980s include: Maximilian Hall, *The City Revolution* (Basingstoke, 1987), pp 68–103; Barry Riley, 'Plenty of rules, too few regulators', *FT*, 13 Feb 1988; Michael Moran, *The Politics of the Financial Services Revolution* (Basingstoke, 1991), pp 57–79; Steven K. Vogel, *Freer Markets, More Rules* (Ithaca, 1996), pp 108–17.

17. *FT*, 15 Nov 1983, 2 Dec 1983 (Peter Riddell), 19 Jan 1984; Alison Eadie, 'Protecting the investor', *Banking World*, March 1984, pp 15–17; *Daily Telegraph*, 4 Feb 1998 (obituary of Gower).

18. *Institutional Investor*, March 1984, pp 41–4; Padraic Fallon, 'The CSFB Interview', *Euromoney*, March 1984, pp 46–69. On von Clemm's decision to stay, see *Euromoney*, June 1989, special supplement.

19. SE, Markets Committee, 23 Jan 1984, Council, 7 Feb 1984; Hall, p 19.

20. Littlewood, pp 342–3, David Kynaston, *LIFFE* (Cambridge, 1997), pp 131–3.

21. *FT*, 18 Feb 1984. See also profiles of Barkshire (and his ambitions in the early to mid-1980s) in *Observer*, 11 Jan 1987, *Independent*, 18 July 1987.

22. *FT*, 18 Feb 1984; *Blood in the Streets* (Fulcrum Productions, c 1989), unshown television film on County NatWest; *FT*, 18 Feb 1984.

23. Peter Koenig, 'Why the City will never be the same', *Institutional Investor*, March 1984, pp 103–13.

24. *Bank of England Quarterly Bulletin*, March 1984, pp 40–5.

25. For the background to the two announcements, see: Plender and Wallace, p 110; Hobson, p 208; Lorenz, pp 13–22; Wake, p 424; Vander Weyer, pp 130–2; Margaret Ackrill and Leslie Hannah, *Barclays* (Cambridge, 2001).

26. Wake, p 424; Lorenz, p 19; *FT*, 13 March 1984.

27. Reid, p 49; Littlewood, p 342; SE, Council, 20 March 1984; *FT*, 23 March 1984; *Daily Telegraph*, 24 March 1984.

28. *Daily Telegraph*, 24 March 1984.

29. Hobson, p 211; *Observer Magazine*, 30 July 1989; *FT*, 10 April 1989.

30. SE, *The Stock Exchange – A Discussion Paper*, April 1984.

31. *FT*, 13 April 1984; SE, Council (appendixes), 17 April 1984.

32. JS, no 16, p 25; *FT*, 1 May 1984, 11 May 1984; *Banker*, June 1984, p 26.

33. *FT*, 15 May 1984.

34. John Gapper and Nicholas Denton, *All That Glitters: The Fall of Barings* (1996), pp 102–6.

35. Speech by Robin Leigh-Pemberton, 23 May 1984 (text at Bank of England Information Centre).

36. On Jacomb's committee, see: Plender and Wallace, p 157; Moran, p 72; Vogel, p 110.

37. Hall, pp 74–5, 131; *FT*, 11 Oct 1984; *Economist*, 13 Oct 1984.

38. Wake, p 425.

39. Ian Fraser, *The High Road to England* (Wilby, 1999), pp 355–6.

40. Ranald C. Michie, *The London Stock Exchange* (Oxford, 1999), pp 574–5; Hall, pp 30–1; *Euromoney*, Oct 1984, p 83; *Banker*, Nov 1984, p 88.

41. *Blood in the Streets*; Reader and Kynaston, p 189; *Daily Telegraph*, 20 Nov 1995.

42. *The Times*, 7 Aug 1984.

43. Peter Stormonth Darling, *City Cinderella* (1999), pp 125–6; *FT*, 18 Aug 1984.

44. Plender and Wallace, pp 131–2; SE, Council (appendixes), 31 Aug 1984, 6 Sept 1984.

45. Laing & Cruickshank, *Accepting Houses: 1984 Annual Report* (Sept 1984), p 2; *FT*, 24 Sept 1984.

46. Accounts include: Will Ollard and Nick Routledge, 'How the Bank of England Failed the JMB Test', *Euromoney*, Feb 1985, pp 49–56; Plender and Wallace, pp 238–41; Frank Welsh, *Uneasy City* (1986), pp 56–65; Stephen Fay, *Portrait of an Old Lady* (1987), pp 141–72; Reid, pp 224–33; Nigel Lawson, *The View from No 11* (1992), pp 403–6; Andrew St George, *JOH* (1992), pp 79–80.

47. Fay, pp 153 (Hawkes), 155.

48. Fay, pp 159–60 (Owen); Lawson, p 405.

49. Suzanna Andrews, 'Can Midland clean up the mess at Crocker?', *Institutional Investor*, July 1984, pp 53–7; *FT*, 27 Jan 1988 (David Lascelles).

50. Hobson, pp 214–18; Reader and Kynaston, pp 189–90, *Wall Street Journal*, 6 Nov 1984.

51. Littlewood, pp 330–2; *Euromoney*, Feb 1984, p 35, Dec 1984, p 73.

52. Accounts of the BT flotation include: *CL*, pp 74–6; Wake, pp 417–18; Littlewood, pp 365–70.

53. Lawson, p 222; Elroy Dimson and Paul Marsh, *Cases in Corporate Finance* (Chichester, 1988), p 222.

54. *Spectator*, 11 Aug 1984, 18 Aug 1984; SE, Markets Committee, 10 Dec 1984.

55. Plender and Wallace, pp 49–50.

56. *Banker*, May 1985, pp 47–53; *FT*, 9 May 1985, 9 July 1985.

57. *Wall Street Journal*, 18 Sept 1985.

58. For a helpful overview on the rapid global deregulation of the mid-1980s, see John Plender, 'Capital loosens its bonds', *FT*, 8 May 1986.

59. *Euromoney*, June 1989, special supplement; *Institutional Investor*, Oct 1986, p 11; *Euromoney*, June 1989, special supplement, June 1999, pp 66–8.

60. *Euromoney*, June 1989, special supplement; *FT*, 17 Oct 1986; Michael Lewis, *The Money Culture* (1991), p 183.

61. *Institutional Investor*, May 1985, p 123, May 1986, pp 149–64.

62. *Institutional Investor*, May 1985, p 124; Adrian Hamilton, *The Financial Revolution* (1986), p 59; Reid, p 111. For an overall picture of the London foreign exchange market by the mid-1980s, see: Hamilton, pp 59–60; Reid, pp 110–12.

63. Kynaston, *LIFFE*, p 114; Philip Stephens, *Politics and the Pound* (1996), pp 83–4; *Investors Chronicle*, 30 March 1984; Hamilton, p 50.

64. On the 1985 sterling crisis and its aftermath, see: Lawson, chaps 37–40; Michael J. Oliver, 'The Macroeconomic Policies of Mr Lawson' in *Contemporary British History* (Spring 1999), pp 172–4.

65. *FT*, 21–2 June 1985; Fay, pp 25, 172, *FT*, 26 Sept 1985; Lawson, pp 408–9, Fay, p 169.

66. Fay, p 172; *FT*, 26 Sept 1985, 29 Jan 1988; *Banker*, Sept 1986, p 68.

67. The fullest account of the tin crisis is Ralph Kestenbaum, *The Tin Men* (1991). See also: *Futures*, Feb 1986, pp 66–8; Hamilton, pp 150–2; *CL*, p 116.

68. *Futures*, Feb 1986, p 66.

69. *FT*, 10 March 1986.

70. *Time*, 21 Feb 2000; NLSC, C 409/015, pp 138, 146; *Sunday Times*, 17 Nov 1985; *Naked City*, BBC2, 6 Nov 1996. For a penetrating analysis of the Davison/Miller relationship, see John Moore, 'An A1 tussle over the club rulebook', *FT*, 20 Nov 1985.

71. Plender and Wallace, pp 167–8, 201–5; *FT*, 20 Nov 1985.

72. Littlewood, pp 355–6; *FT*, 28 Jan 1985.

73. Accounts of the battle for Harrods include: Ivan Fallon and James Strodes, *Takeovers* (1987), pp 30–72; Tom Bower, *Tiny Rowland* (1994 Mandarin edn), chaps 8–12; George G. Blakey, *The Post-War History of the London Stock Market* (Didcot, 1994 pbk edn), pp 259–61; Littlewood p 349.

74. Bower, p 383.

75. *FT*, 5 March 1985.

76. *FT*, 8 March 1990; William Rees-Mogg, 'Shame on all their houses', *Independent*, 12 March 1990.

77. For an overview of the bids of 1985, see *FT*, 31 Dec 1985 (Charles Batchelor).

78. Littlewood, pp 350–1.

79. *The Times*, 5 July 1985. On the Guinness/Bells contest, see: Lisa Wood, 'A battle of rare ferocity', *FT*, 21 Aug 1985; Peter Pugh, *Is Guinness Good For You?* (1987), pp 31–54; Hobson, pp 321–32; Ron Chernow, *The House of Morgan* (New York, 1990), pp 669–70.

80. Littlewood, p 352.

81. Hobson, pp 226–7.

82. *The Times*, 13 Dec 1985.

83. *FT*, 19 March 1985; *Evening Standard*, 23 April 1985; *FT*, 16 Jan 1986; *Institutional Investor*, Dec 1985, pp 79–82; *Sunday Times*, 29 Dec 1985.

84. The battle for Imperial is related in: Fallon and Strodes, pp 171–4, 186–92; Dimson and Marsh, pp 151–77; Hobson, pp 336–8; Littlewood, pp 352–3.

85. *Economist*, 8 March 1986; *Sunday Times*, 6 April 1986; Derek Ezra and David Oates, *Advice from the Top* (1989), pp 102–3.

86. Much has been written about the Guinness scandal. Accounts of the battle for Distillers include: Pugh, esp chaps 4–8; Fallon and Strodes, pp 171–241; Nick Kochan and Hugh Pym, *The Guinness Affair* (1987); Hobson, pp 338–60; Jonathan Guinness, *Requiem for a Family Business* (1997); Littlewood, pp 352–4.

87. *FT*, 25 Jan 1986.

88. Department of Trade and Industry, *Guinness PLC: Investigation under Sections 432 (2) and 442 of the Companies Act 1985: Report by David Donaldson QC and Ian Watt QC* (Nov 1997), p 68.

89. DTI, p 39.

90. *Institutional Investor*, April 1986, p 96; DTI, pp 59–60.

91. *Sunday Times*, 16 Feb 1986.

92. *FT*, 1 March 1986, 4 March 1986; *Financial Weekly*, 6 March 1986; *FT*, 12 March 1986.

93. DTI, pp 146–7.

94. Hobson, pp 355–6.

95. DTI, p 63.

96. DTI, pp 62–4.

97. DTI, p 64.

98. DTI, p 218.

99. DTI, p 66.

100. Hobson, p 359.

101. DTI, p 224.

102. Hobson, pp 360–4. See also Lionel Barber, 'Broken glass in the drinks cupboard', *FT*, 17 July 1986.

103. Fallon and Strodes, p 261.

104. *FT*, 18 June 1986; Fallon and Strodes, p 278.

105. *FT*, 7 Jan 1985; Hall, p 75; *FT*, 30 Jan 1985; *Daily Telegraph*, 2 Feb 1985; *FT*, 21 June 1985; *Banker*, July 1985, p 3.

106. Hall, p 79.

107. *FT*, 10 Oct 1985; SE, Liaison Committee, 5 Nov 1985; *FT*, 19 Nov 1985, 28 Nov 1985.

108. Hall, pp 76–8; *FT*, 20 Dec 1985, 27 Feb 1986; *The Times*, 4 March 1986; Moran, p 58; *FT*, 13 Feb 1988.

109. SE, Council (appendixes), 21 March 1985; *FT*, 7 June 1985; *The Times*, 7 June 1985; Michie, p 578.

110. *FT*, 7 Sept 1984; *Wall Street Journal*, 5 Aug 1985; *FT*, 12 Aug 1985.

111. *The Times*, 17 Oct 1985; *FT*, 17 Oct 1985, 19 Oct 1985.

112. *The Times*, 1 Nov 1985; *FT*, 20 Sept 1986.

113. For an overview of the Euro-equity market in 1985/6, see *Economist*, 29 Nov 1986.

114. *FT*, 5 Aug 1985.

115. *Banker*, Dec 1985, pp 83–4; *FT*, 23 April 1986, 20 Sept 1986.

116. *Investors Chronicle*, 6 July 1984; *FT*, 15 Oct 1984, 18 June 1985; *Economist*, 22 June 1985; *Banker*, July 1985, p 5; *Euromoney*, Sept 1985, p 58; *FT*, 27 Oct 1986.

117. *Economist*, 6 July 1985.

118. *FT*, 21 Nov 1985; *Banker*, June 1986, p 69, *The Times*, 14 Oct 1986; *Banker*, Sept 1986, p 95; *FT*, 21 Nov 1985, 22 Sept 1986, 29 Sept 1986.

119. Philip Ziegler, *The Sixth Great Power* (1988), pp 362–3; *FT*, 5 Nov 1985; *Euromoney*, April 1986, p 99.

120. *FT*, 15 Jan 1986, 1 Feb 1986; *Spectator*, 15 Feb 1986. See also St George, pp 86–91.

121. Hobson, pp 280–90; *Banker*, Nov 1986, p 27.

122. *Independent*, 15 Oct 1997 (Hamish McRae).

123. Hobson, pp 292–8; Sebag-Montefiore, pp 22–3.

124. Wake, p 426; *Economist*, 16 Aug 1986, 30 Aug 1986.

125. *Sunday Times*, 14 July 1985; *TLS*, 7 July 2000: Vander Weyer, pp 132–4.

126. Vander Weyer, p 135; *Blood in the Streets*.

127. David Kynaston, *Cazenove & Co* (1991), pp 313–18; *Spectator*, 13 Sept 1986.

128. *New York Times*, 28 Sept 1986.

129. *FT*, 27 Oct 1986. See also Peter Shearlock and William Ellington, *The Eurobond Diaries* (Brussels, 1994), pp 122–4.

130. *The Times*, 17 Oct 1986; *Wall Street Journal*, 20 Oct 1986, *Guardian*, 20 Oct 1986; *The Times*, 20 Oct 1986; NLSC, C 408/009, p 201.

131. *Spectator*, 18 Oct 1986.

132. *FT*, 25 Oct 1986; *Today*, 25 Oct 1986.

CHAPTER TWENTY-ONE

1. Godfrey Hodgson, *Lloyd's of London* (1984), pp 297–8; Simon Bradley and Nikolaus Pevsner, *The Buildings of England: London 1: The City of London* (1997), pp 313–14; *Spectator*, 26 April 1986.

2. Oliver Marriott, *The Property Boom* (1967), p 68; *Spectator*, 4 May 1985.

3. *Spectator*, 4 May 1985; *Banker*, July 1985, p 33.

4. *FT*, 11 Jan 1992.

5. *FT*, 11 Feb 1986, 11 March 1986.

6. Jon Ashworth, 'Planner who built his name on controversy', *The Times*, 31 Dec 1996.

7. On the Broadgate development, see: Alastair Ross Goobey, *Bricks and Mortals* (1992), pp 50–6, 70–5; Bradley and Pevsner, pp 434–8.

8. Ann Barr and Peter York, *The Official Sloane Ranger Handbook* (1982), p 11.

9. Stephen Fay, *Portrait of an Old Lady* (1987), pp 105–12, Elizabeth Hennessy, 'The Governors, Directors and Management of the Bank of England' in Richard Roberts and David Kynaston (eds), *The Bank of England* (Oxford, 1995), pp 210–11.

10. Claire Makin, 'Tom Wilmot's bid for respectability', *Institutional Investor*, Aug 1986, pp 97–100.

11. *Institutional Investor*, April 1986, pp 107–8. Also on Ramsden: Peter Shearlock and William Ellington, *The Eurobond Diaries* (Brussels, 1994), pp 109–10; *Jackpot*, BBC2, 24 Aug 2000.

12. *Institutional Investor*, June 1986, pp 77–8.

13. *Sunday Telegraph Magazine*, 28 Oct 1984; *Listener*, 20 March 1986; David Kynaston, *LIFFE* (Cambridge, 1997), pp 170–1.

14. *FT*, 1 Oct 1983; Kynaston, *LIFFE*, p 91.

15. Kynaston, *LIFFE*, p 120; *Euromoney*, April 1986, supplement, p 13; *Sunday Times Magazine*, 1 Nov 1987; *Guardian*, 22 Jan 2000.

16. *Sunday Times Magazine*, 14 April 1985; David Kynaston, *Cazenove & Co* (1991), p 301; *Spectator*, 15 March 1986.

17. *Spectator*, 30 June 1984; Martin Vander Weyer, *Falling Eagle: The Decline of Barclays Bank* (2000), pp 90–6; *Institutional Investor*, Oct 1986, p 13.

18. Kynaston, *LIFFE*, pp 247, 94–5; *South Wales Argus*, 11 Aug 1988; *Cosmopolitan*, Oct 1985, pp 153–6; *FT*, 16 May 1985; *Institutional Investor*, May 1986, pp 149–64.

19. *CL*, pp 133–6; *Observer*, 12 Jan 1986.

20. *CL*, p 136; *Management Today*, Sept 1986, p 55; *New York Times*, 28 Sept 1986; *Sunday Express Magazine*, 26 Oct 1986.

21. *Naked City*, BBC2, 23 Oct 1996; Michael Lewis, *Liar's Poker* (1989), pp 182–3, 201–2, 216–17.

22. *Futures World*, 17 Jan 1985; *FT*, 30 June 1986, 27 Oct 1986; *Euromoney*, June 1989, special supplement; *Sunday Express Magazine*, 26 Oct 1986; *Sunday Telegraph Magazine*,

5 Oct 1986; *Institutional Investor*, June 1986, p 71; *Time*, 25 Aug 1986.

23. *Listener*, 20 March 1986; Dominic Hobson, *The Pride of Lucifer* (1990), p 191; *Observer Magazine*, 5 Sept 1982.

24. *Observer Magazine*, 5 Sept 1982; Paul Ferris, *Gentlemen of Fortune* (1984), p 181.

25. *Economist*, 20 July 1985; *Wall Street Journal*, 13 Aug 1985.

26. *Listener*, 20 March 1986; *Spectator*, 15 March 1986; *Listener*, 20 March 1986; Hobson, p 266; *Institutional Investor*, June 1986, p 118; Margaret Reid, *All-Change in the City* (Basingstoke, 1988), p 69; Hobson, p 191.

27. *FT*, 7 Dec 1996, W.J. Reader and David Kynaston, *Phillips & Drew* (1998), pp 202–4; *FT*, 12 Aug 1985; *Sunday Express Magazine*, 26 Oct 1986; Lewis, p 242.

28. Listener, 20 March 1986; Peter Spira, *Ladders and Snakes* (1997), pp 258–9, 269–71, 281–2, 297.

29. *Nice-Matin*, 3 Nov 1982; Anthony Sampson, *The Changing Anatomy of Britain* (1982), pp 295–7; *Big Issue*, 7 June 1999.

30. Ferris, p 180; David Lazar, *Markets and Ideology in the City of London* (Basingstoke, 1990), pp 63, 75, 90, 110–11, 118.

31. *Independent*, 8 April 1992; Adrian Hamilton, *The Financial Revolution* (1986), p 144; *Sunday Mirror*, 8 June 1986; *Guardian*, 4 June 1986; *Wolverhampton Express and Star*, 4 June 1986.

32. *New Statesman*, 24 Oct 1986; *FT*, 27 Oct 1986; *Daily Express*, 27 Oct 1986.

CHAPTER TWENTY-TWO

1. *FT*, 28 Oct 1986; *Business Week*, 12 Jan 1987.

2. George G. Blakey, *The Post-War History of the London Stock Market* (Didcot, 1994 pbk edn), p 277; *Economist*, 29 Nov 1986; John Littlewood, *The Stock Market* (1998), pp 371–2; *FT*, 15 Sept 1987.

3. *Standard*, 10 Nov 1986; *Observer*, 7 Dec 1986; *FT*, 31 Dec 1986. For an account of how Guinness was becoming a 'scandal', see Dominic Hobson, *The Pride of Lucifer* (1990), chap 11.

4. *London Evening Standard*, 21 Jan 1987; *Observer*, 25 Jan 1987; *FT*, 17 Oct 1987.

5. *FT*, 16 Jan 1987; *The Mayfair Set*, BBC2, 1 Aug 1999; Adam Raphael, *Ultimate Risk* (1995 Corgi edn), pp 125–7; *The Times*, 21 Jan 1987; *Independent*, 11 Feb 1987.

6. *London Daily News*, 4 March 1987; Caryl Churchill, *Serious Money* (1987), p 49; *TLS*, 3 April 1987; *Daily Telegraph*, 1 June 1987; *London Evening Standard*, 28 April 1987.

7. David Kynaston, *LIFFE* (Cambridge, 1997), p 174; *Naked City*, BBC2, 30 Oct 1996.

8. Ivan Fallon, *The Brothers* (1988), pp 305–12; *FT*, 14 Oct 1987, Margaret Reid, *All-Change in the City* (Basingstoke, 1988), p 158; Fallon, pp 312–15; *Independent*, 18 July 1987.

9. *Sunday Telegraph*, 18 Oct 1987; *The Times*, 17 Oct 1987; Littlewood, p 380.

10. Accounts include: Peter Pugh, *The City Slicker's Handbook* (1988), pp 100–7; Blakey, pp 208–9; Littlewood, pp 379–84; Michael David Kandiah, 'The October 1987 Stock Market Crash' in *Contemporary British History* (Spring 1999), pp 133–65.

11. *Naked City*, BBC2, 6 Nov 1996; *London Evening Standard*, 19 Oct 1987; *FT*, 20 Oct 1987.

12. Ian Fraser. *The High Road to England* (Wilby, 1999), p 358; *Sunday Business*, 20 Oct 1996; *London Evening Standard*, 23 Oct 1987; Kynaston, *LIFFE*, p 177; CL, p 146.

13. Accounts of the BP flotation include: Nigel Lawson, *The View From No 11* (1992), pp 757–75; Littlewood, pp 384–5; Kandiah, pp 160–4.

14. Lawson, p 771; *Business*, Dec 1987, p 78.

15. *FT*, 11 Feb 1988; *Naked City*, BBC2, 6 Nov 1996.

16. *FT*, 23 Nov 1987.

17. Littlewood, p 394; Richard Roberts, 'The Bank of England and the City' in Richard Roberts and David Kynaston (eds), *The Bank of England* (Oxford, 1995), pp 169–70; *Business Week*, 6 March 1989; *Institutional Investor*, Nov 1989, pp 50–8; *The Times*, 28 Oct 1991; Littlewood, p 438, *The Times*, 28 May 1992, *Euromoney*, June 1994, 'The 1994 Guide to World Equity Markets', p 32.

18. *The Times*, 14 Jan 1993 (Richard Roberts); Peter Shearlock and William Ellington, *The Eurobond Diaries* (Brussels, 1994), pp 116–25; *Euromoney*, June 1994, pp 28–35.

19. Carl-Ludwig Holtfrerich, *Frankfurt as a Financial Centre* (Munich, 1999), p 270; *Guardian*, 19 April 1991.

20. *FT*, 8 July 1992, *Observer*, 12 July 1992; *Independent on Sunday*, 18 July 1993.

21. David Kynaston, *Cazenove & Co* (1991), p 322; *Daily Telegraph*, 20 Nov 1995; *CL*, pp 112–13.

22. *FT*, 31 Aug 1991; Kynaston, *Cazenove*, p 332.

23. David Rogers, *The Big Four British Banks* (Basingstoke, 1999), pp 181–7. For a less positive assessment of McMahon's stewardship, see Russell Taylor, *Going for Broke* (1993), pp 271–3.

24. NLSC, C 409/006, p 71; Ian MacLaurin, *Tiger by the Tail* (1999), p 119.

25. Rogers, p 89; Martin Vander Weyer, *Falling Eagle: The Decline of Barclays Bank* (2000), chap 9.

26. *Euromoney*, Aug 1994, p 44, John Gapper, 'A countdown to oblivion', *FT*, 5 Sept 1996; *Daily Telegraph*, 28 Nov 1989; *Euromoney*, Jan 1994, p 30, Aug 1994, pp 43–4.

27. *FT*, 25 Oct 1996; *Sunday Telegraph*, 12 Feb 1995.

28. *Euromoney*, Aug 1994, p 42.

29. *FT*, 25 June 1988; *Independent on Sunday*, 11 Feb 1990; Junko Sakai, *Japanese Bankers in the City of London* (2000), pp 48, 36. In general, see Sakai, chap 2, for a helpful discussion about the muted impact of the Japanese houses.

30. *Naked City*, BBC2, 23 Oct 1996; *Euromoney*, June 1999, p 68; Lisa Endlich, *Goldman Sachs* (1999), chap 5.

31. Kynaston, *LIFFE*, chaps 5–7; *Guardian*, 6 April 1993; *FT*, 19 Nov 1999.

32. On the Stock Exchange between the late 1980s and mid-1990s there is much in Ranald C. Michie, *The London Stock Exchange* (Oxford, 1999), chaps 12–13.

33. *FT*, 9 April 1992, 9 Oct 1989; *Economist*, 26 Oct 1991; *Independent*, 18 Oct 1991; Michie, pp 609–10.

34. For a detailed account of Lloyd's during the late 1980s and early 1990s, see Adam Raphael, *Ultimate Risk* (1995 Corgi edn), chaps 7–12. See also the review of Raphael in *TLS*, 20 May 1994 (J.H.C. Leach).

35. *Independent*, 28 April 1994 (Hamish McRae); *New Yorker*, 20 Sept 1993; *Time*, 21 Feb 2000, p 43; Raphael, p 372.

36. The fullest account is Jonathan Guinness, *Requiem for a Family Business* (1997).

37. *FT*, 29 Aug 1990, 1 Sept 1990; Department of Trade and Industry, *Guinness PLC: Investigation under Sections 432 (2) and 442 of the Companies Act 1985: Report by David Donaldson QC and Ian Watt QC* (Nov 1997), p 302 (Parnes fee); *FT*, 12 Feb 1992; Guinness, *Requiem*, pp 330–2.

38. DTI, p 309.

39. On Blue Arrow, see: Littlewood, pp 390–1, Rogers, pp 131–3. For the fascinating testimony of one of the defendants, see Martin Gibbs, *Anecdotal Evidence* (privately published, 1996), chaps 28–30, 33.

40. Richard Roberts, *Inside International Finance* (1998), pp 203–6; Robert Pringle, 'The Bank of England and Central Bank Co-operation' in Roberts and Kynaston, p 143.

41. *FT*, 10 Oct 1991; Nicholas Bray, 'outFOXed', *GQ*, June 1992, pp 70–3.

42. The key account is Tom Bower, *Maxwell: The Final Verdict* (1996), following on from his *Maxwell: The Outsider* (1988).

43. Endlich, p 142; *FT*, 1 Jan 2000.

44. *FT*, 25 June 1997; Roberts, *Inside*, p 207; Laurie Dennett, *A Sense of Security: 150 Years of Prudential* (Cambridge, 1998), pp 371–2; Michael Moss, *Standard Life, 1825–2000* (Edinburgh, 2000), pp 343–4.

45. *Daily Telegraph*, 29 Aug 1990; *FT*, 29 Feb 1988; *London Review of Books*, 9 July 1992; *Independent*, 27 July 1992.

46. Derek Ezra and David Oates, *Advice from the Top* (1989), pp 40, 106–7; Kynaston, *Cazenove*, p 330 (the three battles); *The Times*, 5 Nov 1988; *Guardian*, 9 March 1989.

47. DTI, 'Innovation & Short-Termism Conference', 25 June 1990, Proceedings, 9.4, 13.2; Pen Kent, 'Corporate Workouts: A UK Perspective' in D. Masciandaro and F. Riolo (eds), *Crisi D'Impresa E Risanamento* (Milan, 1997), p 308.

48. Lawson, pp 789–91, 1059–60, 868–9; Margaret Thatcher, *The Downing Street Years* (1993), p 706.

49. *Euroweek*, 3 Nov 1989; *Central Banking* (Summer 1990), p 11.

50. Steven Solomon, *The Confidence Game* (New York, 1995), pp 501–2. Solomon's book has much to say about the growing importance of central banks, as does Marjorie Deane and Robert Pringle, *The Central Banks* (1994). The latter's foreword by Paul Volcker, dated July 1994, notes (p viii) that 'central banking is at a pinnacle of influence and respect'.

51. The eye-witness quotations in this account of Black Wednesday derive from *Black Wednesday*, BBC1, 16 Sept 1997. The house-buying inquiry is from *The Major Years*, BBC1, 18 Oct 1999.

52. *Independent*, 18 Sept 1992; *Sunday Telegraph*, 20 Sept 1992; Kynaston, *LIFFE*, pp 257–9.

53. A good guide to the Bank's enhanced status between 1992 and 1994 is Robert Elgie and Helen Thompson, *The Politics of Central Banks* (1998), pp 76–86.

54. Elgie and Thompson, p 80; Treasury and Civil Service Committee, *The Role of the Bank of England: Volume II, Minutes of Evidence* (1993–4), q 114; *Analysis*, Radio 4, 26 May 1994.

55. Vander Weyer, p 75; *FT*, 2 Oct 1990; *Daily Telegraph*, 6 Nov 1999. For a further sense of how rapidly the mores of the City were changing by the early 1990s, see also D.J. Taylor, 'Why I can't take the City seriously', *New Statesman*, 8 Nov 1999.

56. CL, pp 156–9.

57. Simon Bradley and Nikolaus Pevsner, *The Buildings of England: London 1: The City of London* (1997), pp 558, 538, 593.

58. *Independent*, 22 June 1993, *The Times*, 31 Dec 1996; Mark Girouard, *Big Jim* (1998), pp 236–41; *Independent*, 22 April 1995, *Building*, 28 April 1995.

59. *Evening Standard*, 23 Oct 1996; Alyson Rudd, *Matthew Harding* (Edinburgh, 1997), pp 47–62.

60. *Evening Standard*, 4 Aug 1994; *Independent on Sunday*, 4 June 1995.

61. Sakai, p 48; CL, p 142.

62. Paul Ferris, *Gentlemen of Fortune* (1984), pp 189–90.

63. *Daily Telegraph*, 5 Oct 1994; Endlich, p 201; *Guardian*, 5 Dec 1994.

64. Harvard Business School, 'Morgan Stanley and S.G. Warburg: Investment Bank of the Future' (March 1997), Part B, p 2. In addition to the two-part Harvard Business School case-study, the principal accounts of what happened to Warburgs in 1994–5 are: Peter Lee, 'Warburg – the morning after', *Euromoney*, Jan 1995, pp 20–3; John Gapper, 'Year that killed the global dream', *FT*, 22 May 1995; Peter Stormonth Darling, *City Cinderella* (1999), chaps 25–6.

65. NLSC, C 409/111, p 140; *FT*, 4 Oct 1994; *Sunday Times*, 9 Oct 1994.

66. Harvard, Part A, pp 13–15.

67. *Independent*, 9 Dec 1994.

68. *FT*, 19 Dec 1994; *Independent*, 17 Feb 1995.

69. Four books about the Barings drama were published within two years: Judith Rawnsley, *Going for Broke* (1995); Stephen Fay, *The Collapse of Barings* (1996); Nick Leeson,

Rogue Trader (1996); John Gapper and Nicholas Denton, *All That Glitters* (1996). Fay, together with Gapper and Denton, are the main sources for this account.

70. Fay, p 216.

71. *The Times*, 27 Feb 1995; *Daily Mirror*, 27 Feb 1995; Fay, photo opp p 150; *FT*, 28 Feb 1995.

72. *FT*, 28 Feb 1995.

73. *The Times*, 28 Feb 1995, 1 March 1995; *FT*, 1 March 1995; *Independent*, 4 March 1995; *Sunday Telegraph*, 5 March 1995.

74. *Sunday Times*, 5 March 1995.

75. Fay, p 78.

76. Fay, pp 109–10, *Economist*, 4 March 1995 (Peter Baring quotations); Fay p 113.

77. *Euromoney*, Aug 1994, p 43; Rawnsley, p 135; *Inside Story Special*, BBC1, 12 June 1996.

78. Gapper and Denton, p 300.

79. *The Times*, 24 Feb 1996; *Independent*, 23 Feb 1996, 5 July 1999; *FT*, 4 Dec 1999; *Evening Standard*, 17 July 1995; Fay, pp 232–3.

80. *Daily Telegraph*, 24 Feb 1996.

81. *Independent*, 13 March 1995; London Business School, The City Research Project, *The Competitive Position of London's Financial Services: Final Report* (March 1995), Table 2.5; *FT*, 22 March 1995.

82. *Sunday Telegraph*, 5 March 1995; *FT*, 22 May 1995, 13 May 1995.

83. *Independent*, 17 Feb 1995; Stormonth Darling, pp 246–51.

84. *Sunday Times*, 2 July 1995; *Euromoney*, Sept 1995, p 74.

85. *Independent*, 14 July 1995; *Euromoney*, July 1995, p 5.

86. *Business Week*, 23 March 1998; *Institutional Investor*, May 1999, pp 32–40.

87. *Independent*, 8 April 1997; *Daily Mail*, 23 Oct 1997.

88. Treasury Committee, *First Report: Accountability of the Bank of England* (1997–8), Appendixes, pp 1–5; *Economist*, 10 May 1997; Will Hutton, *The State We're In* (1995), p 291; *Guardian*, 7 May 1997.

89. *Daily Telegraph*, 22 Oct 1998; *Independent*, 17 May 1999.

90. *The Times*, 11 Sept 2000.

91. *FT*, 21 May 1997; *Daily Telegraph*, 1 July 1999; *The Times*, 11 April 2000; Martin Dickson, 'City regulation farce threatens to turn into tragedy', *FT*, 1 April 2000; *FT*, 11 Sept 2000.

92. *FT*, 5 Sept 1996; Stephen Fay, *The Global Powerhouse* (Corporation of London, Jan 2000), p 19; *The Times*, 15 May 1997; *FT*, 17 April 1998; *Mail on Sunday*, 10 Sept 2000.

93. London Stock Exchange, *Marketplace to the World* (August 1996), p 1; Michie, p 614. On another significant development a year earlier, the launch of AIM (Alternative Investment Market), see Michie, pp 619–20.

94. *FT*, 20 Oct 1997; *Independent*, 13 Dec 1997; *Guardian*, 30 April 1998; *FT*, 18 Jan 2000; *Independent*, 6 April 2000; *Daily Telegraph*, 6 April 2000. In general on SETS, see Michie, pp 614–18.

95. *Daily Telegraph*, 8 July 1998; *FT*, 8 July 1998; *Economist*, 18 Sept 1999.

96. Elizabeth Hennessy, *Coffee House to Cyber Market: 200 Years of the London Stock Exchange* (2001), p 199: *Evening Standard*, 3 May 2000; *Economist*, 6 May 2000; *Sunday Times*, 21 May 2000; *Daily Telegraph*, 5 June 2000; *FT*, 30 Aug 2000; *Economist*, 2 Sept 2000.

97. *Independent*, 10 July 1997.

98. Dominic Hobson, 'Losing to Germany at Home', *Spectator*, 17 June 2000; *The Times*, 27 March 1998.

99. *FT*, 17 Aug 2000; *Spectator*, 30 Sept 2000 (Williamson); *FT*, 19 Nov 1999.

100. *Independent*, 26 Feb 1997; *FT*, 23 Dec 1998.

101. *FT*, 12 Feb 2000.

102. *Independent*, 4 Dec 1997.

103. *Independent*, 19 Jan 2000, 24 March 2000. On the whole theme of the mass surrender of the British investment banking houses during the decade and a half after Big Bang, see Philip Augar, *The Death of Gentlemanly Capitalism* (2000).

104. *Spectator*, 8 April 2000.

105. For a detailed account of the fall and sale of BZW, see Vander Weyer, pp 226–45.

106. *Independent*, 4 Oct 1997; Daily Telegraph, 6 Oct 1997.

107. *Independent*, 13 March 2000.

108. *The Times*, 17 Sept 1996; *Daily Telegraph*, 9 Nov 1999; *Independent*, 16 Dec 1999, 18 April 2000; *Evening Standard*, 30 June 2000.

109. *Spectator*, 18 Sept 1999.

110. *Financial News*, 18 May 1998.

111. *Evening Standard*, 15 July 1996; *London Financial News*, 6 Jan 1997.

112. *Daily Telegraph*, 6 Nov 1999; *Independent on Sunday*, 31 Oct 1999; *Spectator*, 18 Sept 1999.

113. *Evening Standard*, 11 July 1996. See also: James Fergusson, 'Amschel Rothschild', *Independent*, 11 July 1996; Martin Amis, *Experience* (2000), pp 223, 225–6.

114. *Independent*, 13 June 1996; *The Times*, 16 Jan 1997; *FT*, 29 Jan 1997, 31 Jan 1997, 1 Feb 1997.

115. *The Times*, 29 Nov 1999, *Independent*, 9 Dec 1999; *Tablet*, 6 May 2000.

116. *Independent*, 2 Jan 1997; *The Times*, 8 July 1996 (Tim Congdon); *Guardian*, 3 Jan 1995; *Daily Telegraph*, 19 June 1999, 18 Aug 1999. For a critical, historically informed perspective on the relationship between New Labour and the City, see Robin Ramsay, *Prawn Cocktail Party* (1998).

117. *The Times*, 16 Dec 1999.

118. James Buchan, *Frozen Desire* (1997), pp 281–2.

Acknowledgements

I am grateful to the following for allowing me to reproduce material, including copyright material: The Bank of England; The British Library National Sound Archive; James Buchan; Michael Burns; Cazenove & Co; The Centre for Metropolitan History; Curtis Brown Ltd (on behalf of Paul Ferris); Richard Davenport-Hines; Sir Edward du Cann; Valerie Eliot (T.S. Eliot, *Collected Plays, 1935–1958*, published by Faber & Faber); The Federal Reserve Bank of New York; Graham Ferguson; Sir Ian Fraser; University of Glasgow Archives and the Estate of Sir Alec Cairncross; HSBC Holdings; Hodder & Stoughton (on behalf of Michael Lewis); Joan Horner; ING Barings; David Kinsella; Lloyds TSB Group; The London Investment Banking Association; The London Stock Exchange; John Murray; Mark Nickerson; Brian Peppiatt; Peters, Fraser and Dunlop Group (on behalf of Anthony Sampson); Stephen Raven; The Royal Bank of Scotland Group; Sir Patrick Sergeant; Peter Spira; Peter Stormonth Darling; Taylor Joynson Garrett; Norman Whetnall.

The following kindly supplied illustrations: The Governor and Company of the Bank of England (3, 5, 16, 17); Cazenove & Co (11); Guildhall Library, Corporation of London (1, 12, 13, 27); ING Barings (19–22); N.M. Rothschild & Sons (endpapers); Schroders (9, 10); Linda Tanner (15). I am grateful for reproduction permissions from Tom Hustler Photography (5, 19–22, 25, 26) and Ian Clook (27).

Archivists, librarians, curators and fellow-historians gave me much help in all sorts of ways. They include: Melanie Aspey; Bernard Attard; Kath Begley (and her colleagues at the Bank of England Information Centre); John Booker; Joanne Bradley; Kathleen Burk; Gary Burn; Youssef Cassis; Cathy Courtney; Heather Creaton; Henry Gillett; Victor Gray; Edwin Green; Leslie Hannah; Elizabeth Hennessy; John Keyworth; Sara Kinsey; Rosemary Lazenby; Fiona Maccoll; Ranald Michie; Sarah Millard; John Orbell; Rob Perks; Dilwyn Porter; Richard Roberts; Duncan Ross; Junko Sakai; Catherine Schenk; Judy Slinn; Susan Snell; Paul Thompson; Jehanne Wake; Jane Waller; Philip Winterbottom. The staff at the Guildhall Library continue to maintain the highest standards, and I am very grateful to them. John Littlewood and James D'Albiac generously lent me their impressive runs of Read, Hurst-Brown and Rowe & Pitman investment letters. Those working at *International Insider* were kind enough to allow me to forage through back issues. A practitioner-turned-academic, Daniel Hodson, kindly made available to me his recent stimulating Gresham College lectures, 'Can the City Adapt?'

A book like this must depend heavily on many other books, but I would like to mention specifically three studies of aspects of the post-war City. They are *The Bank of England and Public Policy, 1941–1958* by John Fforde; *The Eurobond Diaries* by Peter Shearlock and William Ellington; and *The Stock Market: 50 Years of Capitalism at Work* by John Littlewood. Each is a pleasure to read, each contains a multitude of new insights as well as facts, and between them they have hugely enhanced my understanding of the subject.

But even with their help and that of other excellent studies, not to mention the often underestimated financial press, the writing of contemporary City history has its problems – some obvious, others less so. The thirty-year rule meant that the records at the Bank of England and the Public Record Office were not available to me from 1970; by compensation, I was very fortunate to be able to consult Midland Bank records (at HSBC Group Archives) up to the late 1970s, Barings records similarly, and the records of the London Stock Exchange up to the mid-1980s (where I was much helped by Ranald Michie's pioneering trail through some particularly dense thickets). Inevitably, though, I have been reliant to a significant extent on the testimony of people who worked in the City, particularly for the post-1970 years. Building on the interviews I conducted when writing the histories of the *Financial Times*, Cazenove's, LIFFE and Phillips & Drew, I had (and greatly enjoyed) a further series of conversations specifically for this book. Most took place during autumn 1999, but some were earlier and a few were later. Those who kindly gave me the benefit of their knowledge and experience included: Christopher Arnander; Gerald Ashfield; Julian Baring; Nicholas Baring; William Batt; Christopher Beauman; Sir George Blunden; Lord Camoys; Michael Cassidy; Sir Robert Clark; Anthony Coleby; Charles Corman; Harold Cowen; Sir John Craven; Christopher Fildes; Rodney Galpin; Sir Roger Gibbs; Sir Nicholas Goodison; Henry Grunfeld; Peter Hambro; Jimmy Herbert; Sir Jasper Hollom; Sir Martin Jacomb; Lord Keith of Castleacre; Sir John Kemp-Welch; Pen Kent; Colin Leach; Rodney Leach; John Littlewood; Sir Kit McMahon; John Melbourn; Sir Peter Middleton; Sir Harry Moore; Dolf Mootham; Sir Jeremy Morse; Sir John Nott; Robin Packshaw; David Potter; Lord Richardson of Duntisbourne; Sir Michael Richardson; Stanley Ross; Edmund de Rothschild; Hans-Joerg Rudloff; Sir David Scholey; Anthony Seligman; Jim Slater; Anthony Solomons; Robin Stormonth Darling; Valerie Thompson; Michael Todhunter; David Verey; Sir David Walker; Edward Walker-Arnott; Stanislas

Yassukovich. In order to achieve the maximum possible historical frankness in my account, I have treated their information and opinions almost entirely on a non-attributable basis. Some readers may enjoy trying to guess the sources for particular passages; but I would stress that the reponsibility for what is included in the book is mine alone.

There are other thanks to offer: to the Authors' Foundation for two timely grants; to my agent Deborah Rogers; to Amanda Howard for typing my tapes; to John Littlewood and Christopher Fildes for reading and commenting on my draft; to Neil Bradford for designing the illustrations; to John Flower for drawing the map; to Mandy Greenfield for copy-editing; to Jo North for proofreading; to Marie Lorimer for the index; and, most especially, to Jenny Uglow, my editor. I am also grateful to her colleagues at Chatto, including Alex Butler, Mary Gibson, Alison Samuel, Rowena Skelton-Wallace and Stuart Williams, as well as to Will Sulkin at Pimlico.

My final debts are more personal: to family and friends. It is over thirteen years since I signed a contract to write a (one-volume) history of the City, almost eleven years since I started work on the task. I know all too well how, without their support, the stone I have been pushing might have rolled downhill. To Lucy, to Laurie, George and Michael, to my mother, to my late father, to everyone else who has a place in my heart – thank you.

London, autumn 2000

Index

The City of London in 1970

Key to numbers:
1 Bank of England
2 Barbican development
3 Barings
4 Billingsgate Market
5 Cannon Street Station
6 College of Arms
7 Fenchurch Street Station
8 General Post Office
9 Guildhall
10 Lloyd's
11 London Bridge Station
12 Mansion House
13 Monument
14 Plantation House
15 Rothschilds
16 Royal Exchange
17 St Paul's Cathedral
18 Stock Exchange
19 Tower of London
20 Warburgs

Rothschilds